Volume 3

The Broadman Bible Commentary

EDITORIAL BOARD

General Editor
Clifton J. Allen

Old Testament Consulting Editors
John I Durham
Roy L. Honeycutt, Jr.

New Testament Consulting Editors
John William MacGorman
Frank Stagg

Associate Editors
William J. Fallis
Joseph F. Green

Editorial Consultant
Howard P. Colson

BROADMAN PRESS • Nashville, Tennessee

The Broadman Bible Commentary

Volume 3

---

1 Samuel–Nehemiah

© Copyright 1970 · BROADMAN PRESS
All rights reserved

4211–03
ISBN: 0–8054–1103–8

The Bible text in this publication is from the Revised Standard Version of the Bible, copyrighted 1946 and 1952 by the Division of Christian Education of the National Council of Churches, and used by permission.

Dewey Decimal classification: 220.7
Library of Congress catalog card number: 78-93918
Printed in the United States of America

Contents

1–2 Samuel *Ben F. Philbeck, Jr.*

   Introduction 1

   Commentary on the Text 13

1–2 Kings *M. Pierce Matheney, Jr., and Roy. L. Honeycutt, Jr.*

   Introduction 146

   Commentary on the Text 156

1–2 Chronicles *Clyde T. Francisco*

   Introduction 297

   Commentary on the Text 305

Ezra–Nehemiah *Emmett Willard Hamrick*

   Introduction 422

   Commentary on the Text 432

Preface

The Broadman Bible Commentary presents current biblical study within the context of strong faith in the authority, adequacy, and reliability of the Bible as the Word of God. It seeks to offer help and guidance to the Christian who is willing to undertake Bible study as a serious, rewarding pursuit. The publisher thus has defined the scope and purpose of the Commentary to produce a work suited to the Bible study needs of both ministers and laymen. The findings of biblical scholarship are presented so that readers without formal theological education can use them in their own Bible study. Footnotes and technical words are limited to essential information.

Writers have been carefully selected for their reverent Christian faith and their knowledge of Bible truth. Keeping in mind the needs of a general readership, the writers present special information about language and history where it helps to clarify the meaning of the text. They face Bible problems—not only in language but in doctrine and ethics—but avoid fine points that have little bearing on how we should understand and apply the Bible. They express their own views and convictions. At the same time, they present alternative views when such are advocated by other serious, well-informed students of the Bible. The views presented, therefore, cannot be regarded as the official position of the publisher.

Throughout the Commentary the treatment of the biblical text aims at a balanced combination of exegesis and exposition, admittedly recognizing that the nature of the various books and the space assigned will properly modify the application of this approach.

The general articles appearing in Volumes 1, 8, and 12 are designed to provide background material to enrich one's understanding of the nature of the Bible and the distinctive aspects of each Testament. Those in Volume 12 focus on the implications of biblical teaching in the areas of worship, ethical duty, and the world mission of the church.

The Commentary avoids current theological fads and changing theories. It concerns itself with the deep realities of God's dealings with men, his revelation in Christ, his eternal gospel, and his purpose for the redemption of the world. It seeks to relate the word of God in Scripture and in the living Word to the deep needs of persons and to mankind in God's world.

Through faithful interpretation of God's message in the Scriptures, therefore, the Commentary seeks to reflect the inseparable relation of truth to life, of meaning to experience. Its aim is to breathe the atmosphere of life-relatedness. It seeks to express the dynamic relation between redemptive truth and living persons. May it serve as a means whereby God's children hear with greater clarity what God the Father is saying to them.

1-2 Samuel

BEN F. PHILBECK, JR.

Introduction

The books of Samuel recount the story of Israel's development under the leadership of Samuel, Saul, and David. During this period Israel's government was transformed from a loose tribal confederation under Samuel into a robust Oriental monarchy in the later years of David's reign. Exact dates for this period are impossible to establish because of the lack of precise chronological information for Israel's leaders before the divided monarchy. Nevertheless, Samuel appears to have been a young man when Shiloh was destroyed about 1050 B.C. (cf. comment on 1 Sam. 6:10-18), and Solomon's accession is generally conceded to have occurred between 971 and 961. Thus, these materials deal with Israel's history for a hundred-year period prior to about 965 B.C.[1]

I. Name

The English title of the books appears to rest upon rabbinic tradition that Samuel was the author of Judges, Samuel, and Ruth (*Baba Bathra*, 14b). Although he may well have provided some material about David's reign (1 Chron. 29:29), the text itself is anonymous. In any case, he could hardly have written about incidents which occurred after his death (1 Sam. 25:1).

The books of Samuel are properly to be regarded not as independent treatises but as portions of a larger history dealing with Israel's background from the time of Moses until the fall of Jerusalem in 586 B.C. Since a work of such magnitude could not be handled conveniently on a single leather scroll, it was divided more or less arbitrarily into smaller segments: Deuteronomy, Joshua, Judges, Samuel, and Kings.

When the Old Testament was translated into Greek (Septuagint) sometime before the end of the second century B.C., Samuel and Kings were further divided into four books designated *The Kingdoms a, b, c,* and *d*. This division was transmitted to Christian editions of the text by Jerome's adoption of the system in his translation of the Old Testament into Latin in A.D. 390-405. Samuel remained undivided in Hebrew manuscripts, however, until 1448.[2]

II. Purpose

The narratives in Samuel may legitimately be considered Israel's history of the establishment and development of a united monarchy over Israel and Judah. We must remember, however, that the biblical record was written primarily for a people whose interest in the past was motivated by concerns which differ considerably from those of the modern reader. The ancient Hebrews studied history not just to satisfy their intellectual curiosity but to gain an

---

[1] For a survey of the problems involved in dating O. T. events, see S. J. DeVries, "Chronology of the Old Testament," *IDB* (New York: Abingdon, 1962), I, 580-599.

[2] Thus both "books" of Samuel are written on a single scroll in the text found in Cave IV of the Dead Sea materials (cf. comment later on the text).

insight into the nature of God's relationship to his people.

Many items of interest to the modern historian were passed over very lightly or were altogether ignored. Thus, virtually no information is given about the structure of Israel's government under the judges, but the people's request for a king was strongly condemned as a repudiation of God's personal leadership (1 Sam. 8:7-8; 10:19). Likewise, the loss of the ark and the story of its fortunes among the Philistines is recorded in considerable detail (1 Sam. 4-6); but the fall of Shiloh, the apparent center of Israel's government at this time, is not mentioned in the books of Samuel. The same contrast is encountered in reference to Saul's reign. No notice is taken of the devastating political pressures he must have faced, and yet his failure as Israel's first king was accounted for on purely religious grounds (1 Sam. 13:1-14; 15:1-23). Similar circumstances could also be cited in David's rise and reign.

The historical circumstances underlying the books of Samuel are to be taken seriously, however. By and large these materials seem to have been compiled by men who dealt conscientiously with the materials before them (cf. later comment on the *structure* of the books) and who sometimes had early records (2 Sam. 1:18) or archives to use (2 Sam. 8:1-14; cf. Hertzberg, pp. 289-290). Nevertheless, biblical records themselves demonstrate quite clearly that ample allowance is to be made for variations in historical details (2 Sam. 21:19-cf. 1 Chron. 20:5; 2 Sam. 24:1-cf. 1 Chron. 21:1; 2 Sam. 24:9-cf. 1 Chron. 21:5).

Modern historians are becoming increasingly aware that it is impossible to write an absolutely objective account of any past event. Every record reflects the author's interests, both in his selection of significant events and in his description of them. The Bible is a good case in point since its authors employed their understanding of Israel's past to convey their theological viewpoints.

The author's purpose in Samuel, therefore, was not to write an abstract record of isolated events in Israel's past. Instead, he was attempting to extract from past occurrences the principles upon which the Lord based his relationship to his people. Both the author and his readers saw God as the ultimate authority behind all human history. The Lord was always working for the supreme good of Israel, whether he acted in judgment or in redemption (1 Sam. 12:6-13). Even after Israel demanded the establishment of the monarchy, the nation would prosper if both people and king were responsive to God's leadership. Divine judgment, however, would fall upon the rebellious (1 Sam. 12:14-15; 2 Sam. 23:1-7). Thus, Saul was rejected for his lack of obedience (cf. comment on 1 Sam. 15:1-35) and was replaced by David.

In accord with these principles, Nathan anticipated David's successful establishment as king of Israel and an enduring line of his descendants upon the throne (2 Sam. 7). In these leaders under God's leadership lay Israel's hope for the future.

III. Text

Since 1937 most translations of the Old Testament have used printed Hebrew texts which were based ultimately on a manuscript completed by members of the ben Asher family in A.D. 1008. At the present time, this is the oldest available Hebrew manuscript of the whole Old Testament. Several generations of this remarkable family had labored to complete the work of a long line of Hebrew scholars, called Masoretes, who attempted to record an authoritative text as it was pronounced in their day.

Unfortunately, the Masoretic Text of the books of Samuel was poorly preserved and a number of passages are unintelligible as they now stand. In most cases, a reasonable reading can be reconstructed by consulting the Septuagint and, where they exist, parallel passages in Chronicles. Since these sources were apparently based on textual traditions which frequently differed significantly from those used by the Masoretes, considerable latitude must be allowed for variation in the details of disputed passages.

In 1952 portions of two Hebrew scrolls of Samuel were discovered in a cave near Khirbet Qumran on the northwestern coast of the Dead Sea. While a majority of the materials have been reduced to brittle fragments, the texts of Samuel have fared a bit better in the inhospitable cave environment. The older manuscript of Samuel consists of only a few scattered lines of Hebrew, but the other is represented by at least portions of 47 of 57 original columns. The writing is estimated to belong to a style current in the first century B.C., so that this scroll appears to be at least 1000 years older than any other text of Samuel previously available. It is most significant that the manuscript preserves a text which is closer to the Hebrew underlying the Septuagint and the books of Chronicles than to the traditional Masoretic Text. The testimony of these two sources, therefore, is more important in the interpretation of the message of Samuel than we have realized heretofore.[3]

IV. Authorship

According to Jewish tradition, Samuel was the primary author of Judges and the books that bear his name. Information about the period following his death (1 Sam. 25:1) was thought to have been supplied by the prophets Gad and Nathan (cf. 1 Chron. 29:29–30). The books themselves are anonymous, and the manner of presentation gives no suggestion of indebtedness to a specific individual.

Recent study, however, suggests that the books of Samuel have been compiled from a larger body of early traditions about Samuel, Saul, David, the ark, etc. The existence of such material paralleling biblical narratives is explicitly mentioned at least twice in Samuel. The rights and duties of the king, for example, were written in a book which was "laid . . . up before the Lord" (1 Sam. 10:25). Similarly, a copy of David's lament over the death of Saul and Jonathan was said to be written in the "Book of Jashar" (2 Sam. 1:18).

The presence of a number of dual portrayals of parallel incidents in Samuel also suggests that the present books are based on earlier materials and traditions. Thus Eli is twice warned of the approaching downfall of his "house" (1 Sam. 2:27–36; 3:11–14). One account of Isarel's request for a king is strongly antagonistic toward the monarchy (1 Sam. 7:1—8:22), while the other represents that institution as a means of God's deliverance of his people (the main part of chs. 9–11). Saul is twice publicly acclaimed king (10:17–24; 11:15) and is twice rejected by the Lord (13:14; 15:23). David first becomes Saul's personal musician and armor-bearer (16:14–23) and is then unknown to Saul and his general when he slays Goliath (17:1—18:2). David was twice betrayed by the Ziphites (23:19–28; 26:1–5) and twice spared Saul who was pursuing him (24:1–22; 26:6–25). A double account is even given of the manner in which Saul met his death (1 Sam. 31; 2 Sam. 1).

A few such examples could be explained as coincidence, since actual experience is complex and varied. The remarkable frequency of these doublets, however, suggests a conscious effort to conflate independent cycles of tradition.

These factors among others have led most students of the books of Samuel to conclude that the editor of these books was dependent on earlier materials which he used quite conscientiously. To a surprising degree, each passage retained its own identity, free from a heavy-handed alteration which would have brought about a simpler but less meaningful story.

V. Composition

Although it now appears reasonable to assume that Samuel is based upon earlier

---

[3] Cf. Frank M. Cross, Jr. *The Ancient Library of Qumran and Modern Biblical Studies* (Garden City, New York: Doubleday and Company, 1958), pp. 30–33.

independent traditions, the stages by which these materials reached their present form are by no means certain. For the past century and a half, debate has raged as to whether these variants represent connected sources or independent fragments.[4]

The first serious attempts to recover the materials underlying Samuel were drawn from literary-critical techniques developed in the study of the Pentateuch. Most early commentators recognized in the historical books the same sources which they had identified in the first five books of the Old Testament. They held that two parallel narratives, again labeled J and E as in the Pentateuch, had been interwoven to provide the basic core of information about Israel's transition from a tribal to a monarchic government. They likewise identified a number of subsequent recensions and additions which brought the text to its present form.

More recently source analysts have acknowledged the difficulty of demonstrating enough constants (similarities of style, theology, historical outlook, etc.) within each cycle of tradition to establish a continuity with Pentateuchal documents. Nevertheless, it seemed to them that the doublets in Samuel, in particular, could be connected to form two separate, meaningful narratives at least as far as 2 Samuel 8.

Other observers noted that traditions about certain themes tend to come in blocks or complexes of well-integrated material. This led them to conclude that over the years stories had gradually been collected about the ark (1 Sam. 4—6; 2 Sam. 6), the establishment of the monarchy (1 Sam. 8—12), or the struggle for succession to the throne of David (2 Sam. 9—20; 1 Kings 1—2). These and other narrative complexes were thought to have finally been brought together by an editor who used the earlier materials to carry out his own theological purposes.

Since, therefore, no consensus has yet developed as to an explanation of the composition of Samuel, dogmatic solutions to the problem should be avoided.

In recent years, particularly, a growing body of evidence has magnified the role of oral tradition in the formation of biblical documents. Thus, an overly precise division of sources, down to fragments of single verses, is increasingly difficult to maintain.

Likewise, no one should expect a detailed history about the processes by which the present text was formed. Such penetrating analyses must await considerable improvement in our literary and historical arts. Nevertheless some cautious observations and suggestions are in order.

1. *The Basic Corpus*

An intriguing hint as to the structure underlying Samuel is suggested by the unusual point at which the division into the books of Samuel and Kings is made. The bulk of David's reign is contained in Samuel, but his death is related in the book of Kings. The principles of separation here differ considerably from those of earlier Old Testament books.

Ideally a separate book seems to have been devoted to each of Israel's great leaders, institutions, or historical periods. Genesis deals with the patriarchal period; Exodus—Israel's departure from Egypt; Leviticus—the priesthood; Numbers—the wilderness. Deuteronomy is devoted to Moses, Joshua to the Conquest, and Judges to Israel's settlement in Canaan.[5]

No satisfactory explanation has yet been given as to why David's ministry is recorded in Samuel and his death in the book of Kings. Hertzberg simply says that the events of 1 Kings 1—2 have more relevance for Solomon than for David. Moreover, the conditions here are too striking to appear to be the result of oversight or

---

[4] For a more detailed study of the critical approach to Samuel, see Ernst Sellin, *Introduction to the Old Testament,* revised and rewritten by Georg Fohrer; trans. David E. Green (Nashville: Abingdon, 1965), pp. 215–217, 522–523.

[5] Use of the biblical sequence here does not necessarily imply that the books came into being in this order. Likewise no conclusions are drawn as to the order in which these books were reduced to writing.

chance. If the book division at the end of Samuel is deliberate, a simple working hypothesis may be advanced. In the books of Samuel the story of each hero begins with the decline of the preceding leader and ends with the waning of his own influence.

The inclusion of a summary of each man's ministry prior to his decline rather than at his death further illustrates the author's studied arrangement of the narrative cycles. Thus, Samuel's accomplishments are heralded (1 Sam. 7:12–17) just before the announcement of his old age and rejection (8:1–9). Saul's reign as king of Israel is acclaimed (14:47–52) before the reasons for his rejection are recounted (15:1–35).[6]

A discrepancy may be noted, however, in that the summary of David's reign (2 Sam. 8:15–18) is widely separated from any indication that his end is drawing near (2 Sam. 23:1; 1 Kings 1:1; 2:1). Absalom's and Sheba's attempts to seize David's throne (2 Sam. 13—20) may imply that his prestige is on the wane, but other incidents after chapter 9 portray David at the height of his power. Both his lenient treatment of Mephibosheth (9:1–13) and the account of his war against the Ammonites (10:1—11:1) portray a man who is confident of his authority. Even his sin with Bathsheba (11:2–12:23) brings trouble within his house rather than an end to his reign.

Thus, following the summary of David's reign (2 Sam. 8:15–18), the narrative deviates from the pattern which it has followed previously. Chapter 9, however, has been widely recognized as the beginning of another independent literary complex, called the Succession Narrative (cf. the next section of this introduction).

A valid objection can be raised that the removal of chapters 9 ff. still leaves the author's "plan" without the anticipated description of the hero's decline. The first two chapters of Kings would adequately serve that function, but they have been adjudged a part of the Succession Narrative. Scholars have long recognized, however, that 1 Kings 2 has undergone numerous modifications. A portion of its complexity may, therefore, result from the inclusion of elements from an original (now lost) story of David's old age. Hence, the structure of the books of Samuel down through 2 Samuel 8 is organized around the "rise and reign" of the three principal characters.

Even this basic corpus of Samuel, however, made use of earlier variant traditions which may have already been organized into sources. Our author's reverence for their content and the frequent recurrence of doublets does suggest that at least two lines of tradition about this period were already in circulation.

A number of smaller literary units may also be isolated, but, in the main, they have been well integrated into the flow of the story. The structure of Hannah's song (1 Sam. 2:1–10), for example, is probably drawn from the monarchic period (see comment on the text), but the hymn very aptly expresses her joy in her vindication before Peninnah. The earlier stories about the ark (1 Sam. 4—6) are also only loosely bound to their context, but they provide a backdrop for David's religious strategy (2 Sam. 6) and Nathan's promise of an enduring dynasty (2 Sam. 7).

Any date which might be attached to the completion of the Samuel "document" would be most speculative. At best it would have been in the monarchic period, and fairly far removed from the incidents involved. The entire corpus appears to have been well established before the Succession Narrative was added, since the basic structure of each literary complex has survived intact.

2. *The Succession Narrative*

Most Old Testament scholars agree that 2 Samuel 9—20 and 1 Kings 1—2 belong

---

[6] Saul's rejection because of his sacrifice at Gilgal is introduced earlier (1 Sam. 13:8–15). The passage is difficult to interpret in the light of other sacrificial practices of the day, however. The theological judgment pronounced upon Saul may be secondary (cf. comment on the text).

to a literary unit dealing with the struggle for accession to David's throne. These chapters, called the Succession Narrative, lack the doublets and repetitions which were characteristic of 1 Samuel.[7] Instead they display a coordinated style, consistent character portrayals, and a unified theme. The author may have drawn from earlier materials for his treatment of the Ammonite war (2 Sam. 10:1—11:1; 12:26–31), Nathan's parable (2 Sam. 12:1–15), and a final chapter on David's death and Solomon's early acts (1 Kings 2). These materials, however, have been integrated into the story and make their own contribution to the development of the narrative.

On the other hand, a body of material on a variety of subjects (2 Sam. 21—24) interrupts the accounts of the contest for Israel's throne. Nothing in these stories seems to demand this specific context. Certainly they contain nothing which would require the disruption of a continuous narrative. Yet any meaningful explanation of the composition of Samuel needs to justify their inclusion at this point.

Here again, the simplest answer to the problem seems to be the most reasonable. The miscellaneous materials were added to the end of the book of Samuel after separation from Kings and the addition of the Succession Narrative had already taken place.

In summary, those responsible for the division recognized the plan of the basic corpus of Samuel and included the account of David's old age with the beginning of Solomon's saga in Kings. Sometime after the separation between Samuel and Kings had taken place, the Succession Narrative was added, and it too was divided according to the plan previously followed.

At a still later time the miscellaneous materials of 2 Samuel 21—24 were included at the end of the book, thus further violating the literary integrity of the Succession Narrative. Conceivably, the editor may have added the Succession Narrative and the supplementary materials to the basic corpus of Samuel at the same time the books were divided. Such a sequence seems unlikely, however.

3. Deuteronomic Editing

Samuel stands as an important segment of Israel's story from her entry into the Promised Land until the downfall of the kingdom of Judah (Deuteronomy-Kings). In the other historical books, especially Judges[8] and Kings, the story is told according to an easily recognizable pattern (cf. 1 Kings 15:1–8). The editor's theological viewpoint is quite clear. The doctrine of divine retribution is rigorously applied, and Israel's fortunes are inevitably tied to her righteousness or sin. Since this philosophy thoroughly underlies the arrangement of the books Deuteronomy-Kings, it is widely assumed that a single editor (or group of editors) of this persuasion was responsible for compiling this entire version of Israel's history.

Within the books of Samuel, however, the marks of Deuteronomic editing are notably sparse. This is in contrast with Joshua, Judges, and Kings in which the Deuteronomic framework is so pronounced. Even those who recognize the editorial hand in Samuel lack agreement as to where it is to be found. The Deuteronomic view of history is most clearly expressed in Samuel's farewell address (1 Sam. 12) which is reminiscent of Moses' final speech (especially Deut. 28). Otherwise, possible evidences of a Deuteronomic influence are confined to a few chronological notes (1 Sam. 4:18; 13:1; 2 Sam. 2:10–11; 5:4–5).

The books of Samuel cannot be torn out

---

[7] The separate existence of the Succession Narrative was first suggested by L. Rost in 1926 (*Die Überlieferung von der Thronnachfolge Davids*). For a brief summary of his view see Bentzen, II, 92.

[8] Under the judges Israel's history is portrayed as a series of cycles of sin, judgment, repentance, and deliverance (Judg. 2:16–23). When in times of peace the nation would lapse into sin, God would punish the people by delivering them into the hand of a foreign oppressor. Thus under the Lord's judgment, Israel would repent, and a judge would be sent to deliver God's people. The nation would then have peace for twenty or forty years before the cycle was repeated.

of their context, however, and the Deuteronomic character of that context must be recognized. A solution to the problem must lie in the nature of the materials upon which the books are based. Apparently the two basic literary complexes (1 Sam. 1—2 Sam. 8; 2 Sam. 9—20 and 1 Kings 1—2) used by the editor had been accepted in a relatively fixed form long before they came into his hands. Thus the Deuteronomic editors, who freely gave form to the more fluid traditions underlying the other historical books, altered as little as possible when arranging the more stable literary structures in Samuel.

4. Conclusions

In light of the foregoing discussion a number of observations are in order.

(1) The editors who separated Samuel and Kings did so at an early stage in the development of the present books of Samuel. They are assumed to be representatives of the "Deuteronomic school" who gave form to the broad history of Israel in Deuteronomy through Kings. The impact of these editors is far less noticeable in Samuel than in Joshua, Judges, and Kings.

(2) The book of Samuel was originally composed of the major portions of 1 Samuel 1—2 Samuel 8 plus a section, now lost, describing the declining years of David. This 'basic corpus' of Samuel demonstrates a literary plan which presents the rise and reign of Israel's early leaders. The climax of each account comes with a summary of the hero's accomplishments inserted when he is at the peak of his career. When one great man begins to decline, the story of his successor is considered to have begun.

(3) The editors who separated the books of Samuel and Kings recognized the literary structure underlying the basic corpus of Samuel and made their division in accordance with it—i.e., Solomon's story begins with the decline of David (1 Kings 1—2).

(4) The Succession Narrative (2 Sam. 9—20 and 1 Kings 1—2) was probably added after the books were divided, and the structural integrity of the narrative was sacrificed to preserve the literary plan of the basic corpus of Samuel.

(5) At some still later time, a body of miscellaneous materials was inserted at the end of Samuel (chs. 21—24), thus further dividing the once-continuous Succession Narrative.

VI. Historical Situation

By the middle of the eleventh century B.C., the political situation had become such in the hill country of Palestine that Israel's existence was severely threatened. Strangely enough, her problems did not result from pressures generated by major world powers but from small, vigorous local states.

The Egyptians, who had claimed at least nominal control of Palestine since the time of Thutmosis III (1490–1435 B.C.), had fallen on hard times. Lavish building programs, internal dissension, ineffective leadership, and attacks from foreigners (e.g., the Sea Peoples ca. 1170 B.C.) increasingly limited Egypt's power abroad. As the Tanite dynasty took control of the government in 1065 B.C., law and order broke down within the homeland; and Egypt's hopes of reestablishing control over her Asian empire were destroyed.

Mesopotamian powers were likewise limited and no nation was able to exploit Egyptian weakness by extending its boundaries west and south into Palestine. Assyria did enjoy a brief resurgence under Tiglath-pileser I (1116–1078 B.C.), but his successors were unable to solidify his gains. After dominating the Mesopotamian valley and moving into upper Syria under his rule, Assyria lapsed into a decline which lasted until the ninth century.

Although free from domination by world empires, Palestine was still the site of a bitter power struggle. During the twelfth and eleventh centuries B.C., technological advances prompted the rise of a number of strong local states in that area. When the old Hittite monopoly on iron fabrication was broken, even small countries could afford good weapons. Development of limed cisterns for water storage opened lands once too dry to support a sedentary population. The domestication of camels about this same time also drew people toward the wilderness as desert trade routes now became feasible and highly profitable.

Even after the conquest and settlement of Canaan, Israel found little respite from frequent wars with hostile neighbors. To the east, Edom, Moab, and even Ammon had developed flourishing states as early as the thirteenth century B.C. Invaders from this quarter periodically troubled Israel under the judges (Judg. 3:12–30; 6:1—8:28; 11:1–40), and Saul first won public support for his budding monarchy by defending Jabeshgilead from Ammonite attack (1 Sam. 11:1 ff.). Farther to the north, Israel faced Damascus and the Aramean states which were soon to test David's mettle (2 Sam. 8:3–12). Less spectacular, but perhaps more threatening, were the remaining Canaanite strongholds like Jerusalem, Megiddo, Tanaach, and Accho.

Israel's most dangerous rivals during this period, however, were the Philistines. This group settled on the southwest coast of Canaan after failing in their attempts to enter Egypt in the time of Ramses III (1175–1144 B.C.). They brought from their Aegean homeland a military heritage which made them and their kinsmen the scourge of the eastern Mediterranean world. During the period of the judges, they made periodic advances against Israel with varying success (Judg. 3:31; 13:1—15:20).

Renewing their aggressive policies about the middle of the eleventh century B.C., the Philistines soon swept over Israel. Following their victory at Aphek in which the ark of the Lord was captured (1 Sam. 4 ff.), they destroyed Shiloh, Bethzur, Tell Beit Mirsim, Gibeah, and Bethshan. Although their advance was slowed for a time during Samuel's ministry (1 Sam. 7:7–14), they apparently were not completely displaced from the hill country. When Saul came to the throne, he found them still located in the heart of Israelite territory (1 Sam. 13:3).

Under such pressures, Israel's future was clouded, and the seams which held the fabric of state together were strained to the breaking point. The judges were rarely able to unite the entire nation; and unless a tribe was directly threatened by an aggressor, it was unlikely to muster troops to provide for common defense (Judg. 4—5). Israel appeared doomed for destruction.

VII. Religious Teachings

1. Faith in Crisis

Israel's political problems were complicated by a religious crisis of dire proportions. Under the judges, a common faith in Yahweh had been the major factor drawing Israel's disparate tribes together. The people cherished memories of the Exodus and Conquest in which they saw God's protective hand evidenced by repeated and ultimate victory. As the Israelites adopted the agricultural pursuits of a sedentary culture, however, their commitment to the Lord was challenged by counter claims of various fertility gods: e.g., Baal, Dagon, and Ashera. Then Israel was repeatedly humbled during the eleventh century by nations professing loyalty to these same gods.

Thus, two great theological issues emerged from Israel's troubled political scene. Philistine military successes suggested to some that the Lord lacked the ability to protect his people from the power of their neighbors' gods. To others it seemed that Israel's old tribal system of government under the judges had outlived its usefulness and that a king was needed to unite the people.

These questions are vigorously addressed throughout the books of Samuel. From beginning to end, the stories of Samuel, Saul, and David are told against the background of a conviction in Yahweh's lordship over history. God's hand is seen in the selection of Israel's leaders (1 Sam. 3:1–20; 9:15–16; 16:1), the protection which he afforded them (e.g., 25:26), and in their rejection when they rebelled against him (15:35—16:7). The idea that the Lord was less powerful than the Philistines' gods is specifically rejected in the stories of the ark (1 Sam. 4—6). Although God allowed his ark to be captured by the Philistines, he brought about its return by humiliating Dagon and by sending a plague upon the Philistines. Israel's reverses, therefore, were seen to be the result of the people's violation of the Lord's will rather than any indication of weakness on his part.

The books of Samuel also repudiate the idea that inherent weaknesses in Israel's political system were bringing about the nation's downfall. The failure of Philistine aggressive designs during Samuel's ministry was seen as an indication that the old tribal system would work when the people put away their wicked ways (1 Sam. 7:3–14). God could and would work through a monarchic system of government, but the popular clamor for a king indicated the people's lack of understanding of their real problem. Israel lacked unity not because the tribal system itself was deficient, but because of faults within the people themselves. Each tribe became overly concerned with its own self-interest and neglected the needs of the nation. Israel could be united and vigorous only when the people submitted themselves to the Lord's leadership and worked for the common good.

2. Divine Retribution

"Israel's God is the Lord of history and the father of justice, who rewards the good and punishes the wicked!" This great affirmation of faith, commonly called the doctrine of divine retribution, is basic to an understanding of the books of Samuel. This conviction in the Lord's supremacy and in his moral government of the universe underlies Samuel's entire message.

David's story stands out above the many examples which could be cited. Although by no means perfect, David is portrayed, particularly during his earlier years, as a man who was sensitive to manifestations of divine leadership. As long as he was properly humble before God, the Lord protected him from Saul's insane persecution, brought him safely through a Philistine exile, and eventually placed him on the throne of Israel. Under his guidance the nation became a dominant power in world affairs. Nevertheless, when David, motivated by his involvement with Bathsheba, arranged for Uriah's murder, devastating rebellions broke out to plague the king's last years on the throne. Thus, Israel's fortunes, whether good or bad, were understood to be the moral recompense for the actions of Israel's people and their leaders.

Such a view of the nature of pleasure and pain was a significant advance beyond the concepts held by Israel's neighbors. The Babylonians, for example, felt themselves at the mercy of capricious gods who would not hesitate to destroy mankind but for their need of human servants.[9] Lacking a concept of secondary or intermediate causes, the ancients saw behind every force of nature the presence of an inscrutable god.

The Israelites also attributed every action, even evil ones, to divine initiative (cf. Isa. 45:7). Hence, Saul's evil spirit came from the Lord (1 Sam. 16:14), and David's fateful census was taken as a result of Yahweh's instigation (2 Sam. 24:1). Nevertheless, these actions were understood to be in some way the result of the Lord's wrath or judgment on the sins of his people.

Some ancient Israelites, however, yearned for a better understanding of those situations in which the doctrine of divine retribution did not seem to apply. They noticed that while the wicked might *tend* to suffer, many corrupt persons appeared to continue enjoying the "fat of the land." Likewise, others recognized that

---

[9] Cf. the Gilgamesh Epic, Tablet XI, lines 175–185. D. Winton Thomas, ed., *Documents from Old Testament Times* (New York: Harper and Brothers, 1958), p. 23).

goodness was no assurance of peace and prosperity. Against the background of teaching in the books of Samuel, Hosea, Job, and the Suffering Servant in Isaiah (cf. especially Isa. 52:13—53:12) provide further insights into the nature of righteous suffering.

In the light of the New Testament's clearer promise of an eternal judgment, however, God's justice in the supervision of human history may be seen in a different and fuller perspective. Thus, while Jesus indicated that God's blessings (Matt. 5:45) and human misfortune (Luke 13:4–5) fall alike on all people, he also taught that the just and the unjust would be separated for reward and punishment in the judgment (Matt. 13:47–50).

While the doctrine of divine retribution has obviously been modified during the passage of time, its significant contribution to the development of Israel's faith has in no way been diminished. Properly understood, this fundamental premise of the books of Samuel is still appreciated as a reminder that we live in a moral universe governed by a God who is both merciful and just.

VIII. Unity Within Diversity

In any comprehensive approach to the study of Samuel, one is confronted with a wide diversity of theological and historical positions which defy easy harmonization. David, for example, appears to suggest that Saul's pursuit was driving him into foreign territory where he would be beyond the Lord's providence (1 Sam. 26:19). Yet, the stories of the ark (1 Sam. 4—6) clearly depict Israel's God demonstrating his authority over his own people (cf. comment on 1 Sam. 6:19–21) and foreigners alike (5:1—6:18).

Similarly, different views were held toward the establishment of a monarchy in Israel. Generally, 1 Samuel 8—12 portrays the people's request for a king as a repudiation of divine leadership (1 Sam. 8:7). Nevertheless, the Lord selected Saul to reign over Israel so that he might deliver the nation from the hands of the Philistines. Even more significantly, the major portion of the books of Samuel focuses on the selection of a ruler who would be a man after God's own heart (1 Sam. 13:14). Thus through many persons and events, the Lord worked in history to make David king and then promised to give him an enduring line upon Israel's throne (2 Sam. 7).

As irreconcilable as these positions seem to be, it is precisely in such diversity that the depth of Israel's unity and the maturity of her faith are revealed. The people of God existed and flourished, not because they were of one mind nor because they pursued common goals, but because the Lord was working among them to accomplish his purposes in history. In fact, the kingdom of Israel was never genuinely united politically. Even under Saul and David, intense sectional rivalries and tribal jealousies left the county seriously divided (cf. comment on 1 Sam. 4:12–18 and 1 Sam. 24:1–17). Yet the ideal of a united Israelite state is so thoroughly impressed on the Old Testament that "children of Abraham" have periodically returned from world exile in renewed efforts to realize the potential that the Lord had envisioned for his people.

Thus, the message of Samuel is rooted in the language of struggle and dissension— between a system of judges and a monarchy, between Samuel and Saul, between Saul and David, or between David and the rebels. The Lord was seen as the motivating force behind the movements in Israel's history, but he was understood to work in such a way that he left men free (cf. comment on 1 Sam. 8:19–22 and 2 Sam. 15:26). The route which history follows, therefore, is tortuously involved and supremely frustrating (cf. comment on 2 Sam. 3:16–21). As free men—both good and evil—struggled with one another, God was working to establish the Israelite monarchy, to provide a measure of security for its people, and to set forth its basic laws of succession (2 Sam. 7).

The author of Samuel, therefore, clearly understood that the true unity of God's people lay in their common faith in a living and reigning Lord. Within a fellowship which is ultimately ruled by God, there is ample room for disagreements over goals, methods, and even doctrine. In keeping with the theology embodied in the books of Samuel, we might even say that God works through such conflict to keep his people in the main-stream of his will. In any case, his power and grace are sufficient to carry his plans through to a successful conclusion. Man, therefore, is entrusted with a freedom of conscience and action to respond to his understanding of divine leadership. Thus, the truly humble in life are promised the Lord's guidance, and the haughty will eventually fall prey to their own pride (1 Sam. 12:14-15; 2 Sam. 22:28).

Outline

I. The rise and "reign" of Samuel (1:1—7:17)
 1. Birth and dedication of Samuel (1:1—2:10)
    (1) Samuel's family visits Shiloh (1:1-8)
    (2) Hannah makes a vow (1:9-18)
    (3) Hannah dedicates Samuel (1:19-28)
    (4) The Song of Hannah (2:1-10)
 2. House of Eli rejected (2:11-36)
    (1) Eli's sons sin in office (2:11-17)
    (2) Samuel's family prospers (2:18-21)
    (3) Eli's rebuke fails (2:22-26)
    (4) Judgment pronounced on Eli's house (2:27-36)
 3. Samuel begins his ministry (3:1—4:1a)
    (1) Samuel serves in the temple (3:1-9)
    (2) The Lord judges Eli's house (3:10-14)
    (3) Samuel shares God's message (3:15-18)
    (4) Samuel becomes a prophet (3:19—4:1a)
 4. History of the ark (4:1b—7:2)
    (1) The ark is captured (4:1b-22)
    (2) The ark troubles the Philistines (5:1-12)
    (3) The ark is returned to Israel (6:1—7:2)
 5. Samuel delivers the people (7:3-17)
    (1) Victory won at Mizpah (7:3-11)
    (2) Samuel's ministry summarized (7:12-17)

II. The rise and reign of Saul (8:1—14:52)
 1. Samuel's influence fades (8:1-22)
    (1) Samuel's sons pervert justice (8:1-3)
    (2) Israel asks for a king (8:4-9)
    (3) Ways of a king described (8:10-18)
    (4) Israel remains resolute (8:19-22)
 2. God selects Israel's king (9:1—10:27)
    (1) Saul qualifies for office (9:1-2)
    (2) Saul seeks lost asses (9:3-14)
    (3) Saul meets Samuel (9:15-27)
    (4) Samuel anoints Saul (10:1-16)
    (5) Saul publicly designated king (10:17-27)
 3. Saul wins public support (11:1-15)
    (1) Ammonites attack Jabeshgilead (11:1-4)
    (2) Saul defeats the Ammonites (11:5-11)
    (3) People proclaim Saul king (11:12-15)
 4. Samuel counsels the monarchy (12:1-25)
    (1) Samuel defends record (12:1-5)
    (2) Israel's rebellion recorded (12:6-18)
    (3) Samuel pledges prayers (12:19-25)
 5. Israel wins independence (13:1—14:52)
    (1) War of liberation begun (13:1-15a)
    (2) Conditions of war described (13:15b-23)
    (3) Israel wins victory (14:1-23)
    (4) Victory sweep halted (14:24-46)
    (5) Saul's reign summarized (14:47-52)

III. The rise and reign of David (1 Sam. 15:1—2 Sam. 8:18)
 1. Saul rejected as king (15:1-35)
    (1) Saul violates cherem (15:1-9)
    (2) Saul rejected as king (15:10-23)
    (3) Samuel leaves Saul (15:24-35)
 2. David anointed future king (16:1-13)
 3. David joins Saul's court (16:14—18:5)
    (1) David becomes Saul's armor-bearer (16:14-23)
    (2) David battles the giant (17:1—18:5)
 4. Saul seeks David's life (18:6—20:42)
    (1) Saul attempts murder (18:6-16)
    (2) Saul uses the Philistines (18:17-30)
    (3) Saul seeks assassins (19:1-7)
    (4) Saul renews violence (19:8-17)

(5) Samuel offers refuge (19:18–24)
(6) David and Jonathan part (20:1–42)
5. David becomes a fugitive (21:1—26:25)
   (1) Priests at Nob aid David (21:1–9)
   (2) David feigns madness (21:10–15)
   (3) David gathers an army (22:1–5)
   (4) Saul loses priestly support (22:6–23)
   (5) David rescues Keilah (23:1–14)
   (6) Friends extend covenant (23:15–18)
   (7) Ziphites betray David (23:19–29)
   (8) Saul delivered to David (24:1–22)
   (9) David marries Abigail (25:1–44)
   (10) Ziphites repeat treachery (26:1–25)
6. David joins the Philistines (1 Sam. 27:1—2 Sam. 1:27)
   (1) David becomes a vassal (27:1–12)
   (2) Saul consults a medium (28:1–14)
   (3) Saul's house condemned (28:15–25)
   (4) David excluded from war (29:1–11)
   (5) Amalekites attack Ziklag (30:1–30)
   (6) Israel defeated at Gilboa (1 Sam. 31:1—2 Sam. 1:27)
      a. Saul commits suicide (31:1–13)
      b. Youth claims Saul's murder (2 Sam. 1:1–16)
      c. David mourns Israel's loss (1:17–27)
7. David becomes king (2 Sam. 2:1—8:18)
   (1) David reigns over Judah (2:1—4:12)
   (2) David rules all Israel (5:1—8:18)
      a. Elders "elect" David king (5:1–5)
      b. David establishes court (5:6–16)
      c. David stops Philistines (5:17–25)
      d. Ark brought to Jerusalem (6:1–23)
      e. Nathan prophesies dynasty (7:1–17)
      f. David offers thanks (7:18–29)
      g. David's reign surveyed (8:1–18)
IV. The succession narrative (9:1—20:26)
   1. David spares a friend's son (9:1–13)
   2. David faces Syrians and Ammonites (10:1–19)
   3. Tragedy follows sin (11:1—12:31)
      (1) David succumbs to lust (11:1–13)
      (2) David has Uriah killed (11:14–27)
      (3) Nathan accuses David (12:1–15a)
      (4) David loses a son (12:15b–25)
      (5) David defeats Ammonites (12:26–31)
   4. Amnon degrades Tamar (13:1–22)
   5. Absalom avenges his sister (13:23–39)
   6. Absalom returns to court (14:1–33)
      (1) Joab tests David (14:1–20)
      (2) Absalom returns to Jerusalem (14:21–33)
   7. Absalom usurps the throne (15:1—18:33)
      (1) Absalom becomes king (15:1–12)
      (2) David flees Jerusalem (15:13–37)
      (3) Saul's family opposes David (16:1–14)
      (4) Absalom enters Jerusalem (16:15–23)
      (5) Hushai stalls for time (17:1–14)
      (6) David escapes to Mahanaim (17:15–29)
      (7) Absalom killed in battle (18:1–18)
      (8) Absalom's death reported (18:19–33)
   8. David resumes his throne (19:1–40)
      (1) Israel recalls David (19:1–15)
      (2) David returns to Jerusalem (19:16–40)
   9. Sheba leads Israelite revolt (19:41—20:26)
      (1) Jealousy prompts war (19:41—20:2)
      (2) David's men pursue Sheba (20:3–22)
      (3) David's leaders listed (20:23–26)
V. Appendixes (21:1—24:25)
   1. Gibeonites execute Saul's sons (21:1–14)
   2. Philistines renew war (21:15–22)
   3. Song of David gives thanks (22:1–51)
   4. David's last words (23:1–7)
   5. David's "mighty men" listed (23:8–39)
   6. David takes a census (24:1–17)
   7. David builds an altar (24:18–25)

Selected Bibliography

BALY, DENIS. *The Geography of the Bible.* New York: Harper and Row, 1957.

BENTZEN, AAGE. *Introduction to the Old Testament.* 2 vols. Copenhagen: G.E.C. Gad, 1957.

BLACK, MATTHEW and H. H. ROWLEY (eds.). *Peake's Commentary on the Bible.* London:

Thomas Nelson and Sons, Ltd., 1962.
BRIGHT, JOHN. *A History of Israel.* Philadelphia: The Westminster Press, 1959.
BUTTRICK, GEORGE ARTHUR, et al. (eds.). *The Interpreter's Dictionary of the Bible.* 4 vols. New York: Abingdon Press, 1962.
CAIRD, GEORGE B. "The First and Second Books of Samuel: Introduction and Exegesis," *The Interpreter's Bible,* II, 855–1176. New York: Abingdon Press, 1953.
DRIVER, S. R. *Notes on the Hebrew Text and the Topography of the Books of Samuel.* Oxford: Oxford University Press, 1913.
HERTZBERG, HANS WILHELM. *I and II Samuel.* trans. J. S. BOWDEN. ("The Old Testament Library.") Philadelphia: The Westminster Press, 1964.

MCKANE, WILLIAM. *I and II Samuel.* ("Torch Bible Commentaries.") London: SCM Press, Ltd., 1963.
RUST, ERIC C. *Judges, Ruth and Samuel.* ("The Laymen's Bible Commentary.") Richmond: John Knox Press, 1961.
SMITH, HENRY PRESERVED. *A Critical and Exegetical Commentary on the Books of Samuel.* ("The International Critical Commentary.") Edinburgh: T. and T. Clark, 1899.
DE VAUX, ROLAND. *Ancient Israel.* trans. JOHN MCHUGH. New York: McGraw-Hill Book Co., 1961.
WRIGHT, GEORGE ERNEST and FLOYD VIVIAN FILSON (eds.). *The Westminster Historical Atlas to the Bible.* Revised ed. Philadelphia: The Westminster Press, 1956.

Commentary on the Text

I. The Rise and Reign of Samuel (1:1—7:17)

1. Birth and Dedication of Samuel (1:1—2:11)

(1) Samuel's Family Visits Shiloh (1:1–8)

¹ There was a certain man of Ramathaimzophim of the hill country of Ephraim, whose name was Elkanah the son of Jeroham, son of Elihu, son of Tohu, son of Zuph, an Ephraimite. ² He had two wives; the name of the one was Hannah, and the name of the other Peninnah. And Peninnah had children, but Hannah had no children. ³ Now this man used to go up year by year from his city to worship and to sacrifice to the LORD of hosts at Shiloh, where the two sons of Eli, Hophni and Phinehas, were priests of the LORD. ⁴ On the day when Elkanah sacrificed, he would give portions to Peninnah his wife and to all her sons and daughters; ⁵ and, although he loved Hannah, he would give Hannah only one portion, because the LORD had closed her womb. ⁶ And her rival used to provoke her sorely, to irritate her, because the LORD had closed her womb. ⁷ So it went on year by year; as often as she went up to the house of the LORD, she used to provoke her. Therefore Hannah wept and would not eat. ⁸ And Elkanah, her husband, said to her, "Hannah, why do you weep? And why do you not eat? And why is your heart sad? Am I not more to you than ten sons?"

The story of Israel's shift from a loose tribal confederation to a centralized dynastic state properly begins with an account of the rise and rule of Samuel. He played vital roles as Israel's last major judge, one of her earliest prophets, and as a guide in the selection of her first two kings. Through his influence the faith and ideals which had called Israel into being were successfully transmitted to the new system of government.

Samuel's background is told simply, but with a poignancy that marks the work of a master storyteller. Members of his family and the pressures under which they lived emerge with remarkable clarity.

Elkanah's inclination and ability to take his family on an annual pilgrimage to Shiloh suggest that he was pious and also a man of some substance. As the husband of two wives, he attempted to treat each woman fairly, but he was inevitably caught between their jealousies for each other. Hannah (the modern name "Grace") felt inadequate because of her inability to bear children, and Peninnah ("Pearl") resented Elkanah's special consideration for her rival. Nevertheless, he reacted with graciousness and affection in the midst of the tensions which made life difficult.

Ramathaimzophim—elsewhere in Samuel known simply as Ramah, "the Height" (1:19). To distinguish this town from a number of others of the same name, a fuller identification was necessary. The sentence is grammatically difficult and probably should read, "there was a certain man of Ramathaim (the Twin Heights), a Zuphite of the hill country of Ephraim." Ramah, Samuel's ancestral home, later became the center of his itinerant judicial administration (7:15-17).

To worship and to sacrifice. The annual pilgrimage described here and the one in Judges 21:19 seem to reflect conditions prior to the establishment of the three great feasts which became normative for Israelite worship. These festivals, associated with spring planting, harvest of winter grain, and harvest of summer crops, later became known as the feasts of Unleavened Bread, Weeks, and Booths (1 Kings 9:25; Ex. 23:14-17; Deut. 16:16).

In the pre-monarchic period, sacrifices were of two main types: the more prevalent communion sacrifice in which the people ate a portion of the slain animal, and the burnt offering in which the entire sacrifice was consumed upon the altar. The worship at Shiloh was of the former type, normally a joyous occasion in which good relations were established between God and his worshipers.

And her rival reflects a common Semitic term for "rival-wife" or "fellow-wife." All intimate social contacts involve a measure of inner tension, but the practice of polygamy made family life in ancient Israel extremely complicated (cf. Sarah's struggle with Hagar, Gen. 16; Rachel's estrangement from Leah, Gen. 30:1-8).

(2) *Hannah Makes a Vow (1:9-18)*

⁹ After they had eaten and drunk in Shiloh, Hannah rose. Now Eli the priest was sitting on the seat beside the doorpost of the temple of the LORD. ¹⁰ She was deeply distressed and prayed to the LORD, and wept bitterly. ¹¹ And she vowed a vow and said, "O LORD of hosts, if thou wilt indeed look on the affliction of thy maidservant, and remember me, and not forget thy maidservant, but wilt give to thy maidservant a son, then I will give him to the LORD all the days of his life, and no razor shall touch his head."

¹² As she continued praying before the LORD, Eli observed her mouth. ¹³ Hannah was speaking in her heart; only her lips moved, and her voice was not heard; therefore Eli took her to be a drunken woman. ¹⁴ And Eli said to her, "How long will you be drunken? Put away your wine from you." ¹⁵ But Hannah answered, "No, my lord, I am a woman sorely troubled; I have drunk neither wine nor strong drink, but I have been pouring out my soul before the LORD. ¹⁶ Do not regard your maidservant as a base woman, for all along I have been speaking out of my great anxiety and vexation." ¹⁷ Then Eli answered, "Go in peace, and the God of Israel grant your petition which you have made to him." ¹⁸ And she said, "Let your maidservant find favor in your eyes." Then the woman went her way and ate, and her countenance was no longer sad.

Despairing of any foreseeable end to her barrenness, Hannah finally appealed to the Lord. In return for God's gift of a son, she promised to set him aside for lifelong service as a Nazirite (Num. 6:1-8). She was willing to forego the normal family obligations which a child owed his parents. In effect she was giving up a guarantee of care in her old age.[10] Since Elkanah had other sons by Peninnah, these parental prerogatives were largely Hannah's to give.

Impressed by Hannah's earnestness which he mistook for intoxication, Eli added his own blessing to the barren woman's prayer for a son. Hannah's respite from the frustrations which marred her observation of the religious festival was achieved, not through the granting of her request for a son, but through the personal fulfillment of having genuinely prayed. Filled with a spiritual peace previously lacking, she joyously returned to the feast. In due time she was given her first son (cf. 2:21).

The temple of the Lord. The Hebrew word for temple is a common Semitic term,

---

[10] See John Van Seters, "The Problem of Childlessness in Near Eastern Law and the Patriarchs of Israel," *Journal of Biblical Literature* LXXXVII (December, 1968), 403.

but it is used of an Israelite sanctuary only in 1:9 and 3:3, prior to the time of David and Solomon.

The exact nature of this structure is unknown. Reference to this temple as a house (1:24) contrasts sharply with the strong reaction against the construction of an abode for the Lord in 7:6. This variation is perhaps best explained by concluding that the latter comes from a different source which was not familiar with the nature of the sanctuary at Shiloh. In any case, the structure at Shiloh was destroyed by Philistines about 1050 B.C.[11]

(3) *Hannah Dedicates Samuel (1:19-28)*

19 They rose early in the morning and worshiped before the Lord; then they went back to their house at Ramah. And Elkanah knew Hannah his wife, and the Lord remembered her; 20 and in due time Hannah conceived and bore a son, and she called his name Samuel, for she said, "I have asked him of the Lord."
21 And the man Elkanah and all his house went up to offer to the Lord the yearly sacrifice, and to pay his vow. 22 But Hannah did not go up, for she said to her husband, "As soon as the child is weaned, I will bring him, that he may appear in the presence of the Lord, and abide there for ever." 23 Elkanah her husband said to her, "Do what seems best to you, wait until you have weaned him; only, may the Lord establish his word." So the woman remained and nursed her son, until she weaned him. 24 And when she had weaned him, she took him up with her, along with a three-year-old bull, an ephah of flour, and a skin of wine; and she brought him to the house of the Lord at Shiloh; and the child was young. 25 Then they slew the bull, and they brought the child to Eli. 26 And she said, "Oh, my lord! As you live, my lord, I am the woman who was standing here in your presence, praying to the Lord. 27 For this child I prayed; and the Lord has granted me my petition which I made to him. 28 Therefore I have lent him to the Lord; as long as he lives, he is lent to the Lord."

Hannah was keenly aware that she was indebted to God who granted her request for a son. Nevertheless, her confession, *I have asked him of the Lord,* is not easily associated with its present context. As it stands, the statement offers a better explanation of the name Saul (sha'ul).[12] The name Samuel in Hebrew is derived from terms meaning "the name of God."

Nothing has been said previously about a vow by Elkanah. This may reflect a previous commitment to participate in an annual pilgrimage to Shiloh (cf. 1:3), or it may indicate that he has voluntarily shared Hannah's willingness to dedicate her son to divine service (Hertzberg, p. 28).

Samuel was probably about three years old before he was taken to the *house of the Lord at Shiloh.* This was the customary age for weaning in the ancient world (2 Mac. 7:27).

Elkanah returned home, and the boy ministered to the Lord before Eli (2:11). Nothing is said about Hannah who may have remained temporarily to care for her young son and to perform other functions at the temple. On the other hand, she probably accompanied her husband back to Ramah as the Greek version indicates (cf. 2:19).

(4) *The Song of Hannah (2:1-10)*

1 And they worshiped the Lord there.
  Hannah also prayed and said,
  "My heart exults in the Lord;
    my strength is exalted in the Lord.
  My mouth derides my enemies,
    because I rejoice in thy salvation.
2 "There is none holy like the Lord,
    there is none besides thee;
    there is no rock like our God.
3 Talk no more so very proudly,
    let not arrogance come from your mouth;
  for the Lord is a God of knowledge,
    and by him actions are weighed.
4 The bows of the mighty are broken,
    but the feeble gird on strength.
5 Those who were full have hired themselves
    out for bread,
  but those who were hungry have ceased
    to hunger.

---

[11] The fall of Shiloh is not recorded in Samuel or Kings, but the ark was placed in Kiriath-jearim after its return from capture by the Philistines (2 Sam. 7:2; cf. Jer. 7:12,14; 26:6,9; Psalm 78:60). See Joseph Blenkinsopp, "Kiriath-Jearim and the Ark," *Journal of Biblical Literature,* LXXXVIII (1969), 143-156.

[12] The name Saul is based on the Hebrew verb "to ask." A word play on this root is found in 1:20,27,28; 2:20.

The barren has borne seven,
 but she who has many children is forlorn.
6 The LORD kills and brings to life;
 he brings down to Sheol and raises up.
7 The LORD makes poor and makes rich;
 he brings low, he also exalts.
8 He raises up the poor from the dust;
 he lifts the needy from the ash heap,
to make them sit with princes
 and inherit a seat of honor.
For the pillars of the earth are the LORD's,
 and on them he has set the world.

9 "He will guard the feet of his faithful ones;
 but the wicked shall be cut off in darkness;
for not by might shall a man prevail.
10 The adversaries of the LORD shall be broken to pieces;
 against them he will thunder in heaven.
The LORD will judge the ends of the earth;
 he will give strength to his king,
 and exalt the power of his anointed."

The reference to the king in Hannah's song (v. 10) clearly indicates that the psalm was not originally composed to serve its present function. The institution of the monarchy was still in the future, much later in Samuel's life; and his bitter opposition to the establishment of a kingship in Israel (8:10–18) would hardly seem justified if this were the Lord's prophetic endorsement of that new form of government. More probably, a later psalm has been placed into this context to summarize the attitude of a woman who has at last been vindicated.

Although the major thrust of the psalm is occupied with the praise of the Lord for his sovereignty over all creation, there is a marked stress on the psalmist's conviction that God moves in history, rewarding goodness and punishing evil. This belief in divine retribution, which is widespread though not universal in the Old Testament, finds classic expression in v. 9.

Hannah would have found peculiar comfort in the idea that the roles of the humble and the exalted will frequently be reversed when the Lord vindicates the righteous. Quite possibly the psalm was selected for use here because of its combination of the praise of the Lord and the words found in 2:5b:

"The barren has borne seven,
 but she who has many children is forlorn."

In biblical records, however, Hannah had only six children including Samuel (2:21).

Verse 6 has been taken as early evidence of a belief in the resurrection of the dead. While this interpretation is certainly possible, it is not required. In Hebrew the ideas contained in the first three verbs are presented more or less independently—not necessarily that God kills and then restores life, but that God is responsible for death as well as birth, for sickness (*he brings down to Sheol*) as well as for the restoration of health. In any case, such passages must have later prepared the way for a growing awareness of personal vitality beyond the grave.

2. *House of Eli Rejected (2:11–36)*

(1) *Eli's Sons Sin in Office (2:11–17)*

11 Then Elkanah went home to Ramah. And the boy ministered to the LORD, in the presence of Eli the priest.
12 Now the sons of Eli were worthless men; they had no regard for the LORD. 13 The custom of the priests with the people was that when any man offered sacrifice, the priest's servant would come, while the meat was boiling, with a three-pronged fork in his hand, 14 and he would thrust it into the pan, or kettle, or caldron, or pot; all that the fork brought up the priest would take for himself. So they did at Shiloh to all the Israelites who came there. 15 Moreover, before the fat was burned, the priest's servant would come and say to the man who was sacrificing, "Give meat for the priest to roast; for he will not accept boiled meat from you, but raw." 16 And if the man said to him, "Let them burn the fat first, and then take as much as you wish," he would say, "No, you must give it now; and if not, I will take it by force." 17 Thus the sin of the young men was very great in the sight of the LORD; for the men treated the offering of the LORD with contempt.

Samuel's rise to influence is paralleled by the tragic decline of Eli's house. Samuel must have reflected on the anguish that Hophni and Phinehas caused Eli when, later, his own sons also proved to be corrupt (8:1–3).

The first series of charges against Eli's

sons are related in that they all involve division of the sacrifices. The blood was poured out and the fat was burned as a sacrifice to the Lord. The priest was to be content with whatever he first speared in a cauldron of boiling meat. The remainder of the sacrifice was reserved to be eaten by the worshipers.

Apparently Eli's sons wanted assurance of better cuts of meats and a larger portion of the sacrifice. Their actions may reflect fairly widespread discontent with the method of determining the clerical share. In any case, the priestly share was at other times spelled out both as to size and quality (Deut. 18:3; Lev. 7:31–34).

Hophni and Phinehas, however resorted to physical violence. They were unwilling to trust the Lord to provide for their needs.

Worthless men. The KJV here has "sons of Belial" in that the Hebrew $beliyy'al$ was simply transliterated and then treated as a proper name. It is true that Belial was used in post-biblical literature as a synonym for Satan; but in the historical books, it is best to translate it as the RSV has done.

(2) *Samuel's Family Prospers* (2:18–21)

18 Samuel was ministering before the LORD, a boy girded with a linen ephod. 19 And his mother used to make for him a little robe and take it to him each year, when she went up with her husband to offer the yearly sacrifice. 20 Then Eli would bless Elkanah and his wife, and say, "The LORD give you children by this woman for the loan which she lent to the LORD"; so then they would return to their home. 21 And the LORD visited Hannah, and she conceived and bore three sons and two daughters. And the boy Samuel grew in the presence of the LORD.

The insertion of these brief verses describing God's blessings on Samuel's family demonstrates the author's mastery of the storyteller's art. The passage adds little to the progress of the narrative, but the account of Samuel's simple ministry before the Lord and of Hannah's good fortune serve as a perfect foil for the misfortunes which are about to befall Eli's house.

The nature of the ephod which young Samuel wore is not clearly understood. Obviously, in this context it is taken to be an article of priestly apparel (cf. 2:28) which perhaps a mother could make for her son (2:19). While it could be a simple garment made from linen (cf. 22:18; 2 Sam. 6:14), it could also be an elaborate affair made of costly materials (Ex. 28:4–28; 35:27, 39:1–21). On the other hand, an ephod could stand by itself in a place of worship (1 Sam. 21:9) or even become an object of worship itself (Judg. 8:27; 17:5; 18:14).

(3) *Eli's Rebuke Fails* (2:22–26)

22 Now Eli was very old, and he heard all that his sons were doing to all Israel, and how they lay with the women who served at the entrance to the tent of meeting. 23 And he said to them, "Why do you do such things? For I hear of your evil dealings from all the people. 24 No, my sons; it is no good report that I hear the people of the LORD spreading abroad. 25 If a man sins against a man, God will mediate for him; but if a man sins against the LORD, who can intercede for him?" But they would not listen to the voice of their father; for it was the will of the LORD to slay them.

26 Now the boy Samuel continued to grow both in stature and in favor with the LORD and with men.

Serious charges are again leveled against Eli's sons, this time that they have had immoral relations with the women who served at the entrance to the tent of meeting. While such actions may have been acceptable to the Canaanites who were accustomed to the presence of "sacred prostitutes" [13] in their temple worship, promiscuity represented a grave violation of Jewish moral conduct. Especially in those periods when the struggle with Baalism was keenest, sexual offenses ranked along with idol worship as a most serious

---

[13] Canaanite Baalism, in particular, represented a form of worship in which both male and female prostitutes had a regular place among the temple personnel. The Old Testament is replete with condemnations of such practices (cf. Deut. 23:17; 2 Kings 23:4–7; Jer. 2:23–24; Ezek. 23:35–45). See B. A. Brooks, "Fertility Cult Functionaries in the Old Testament," *Journal of Biblical Literature*, LX (1941), 227–253.

transgression against God's will. Eli himself warns that since they have sinned against God, they are left without an advocate who would plead their case in the divine presence.

Although Hophni and Phinehas had to accept responsibility for their sin, the underlying cause for their rebellion is traced back to God: *for it was the will of the Lord to slay them.* This verse and a number of other passages in the Old Testament lay stress on God's sovereignty over history and on his use of men's actions to accomplish his own purposes. Thus the Lord hardened Pharaoh's heart that his own power might be demonstrated (Ex. 4:21). Even man's wrath is seen as accruing praise to God. (Psalm 76:10).

Nevertheless, in other times or perhaps in other circles, man was seen as a free agent who in most circumstances was able to determine his own destiny. He was still God's creature, but he was a free creature. Even if he had to reap the consequences of his rebellion, he could successfully resist God's desires (Gen. 3:1–25), since the Lord would permit for a time actions which were not in keeping with his will (Psalm 95:7–8). Second only to God, man was to subdue and rule the world around him (Psalm 8:5–9).

Biblical authors, therefore, lay stress first on God's omnipotence and then on man's freedom. Each concept is important in an adequate understanding of the other. Thus, although the stress is on Yahweh's control of history, man's freedom is acknowledged in that Eli's sons must accept the consequences for their actions.

(4) Judgment Pronounced on Eli's House (2:27–36)

27 And there came a man of God to Eli, and said to him, "Thus the LORD has said, 'I revealed myself to the house of your father when they were in Egypt subject to the house of Pharaoh. 28 And I chose him out of all the tribes of Israel to be my priest, to go up to my altar, to burn incense, to wear an ephod before me; and I gave to the house of your father all my offerings by fire from the people of Israel. 29 Why then look with greedy eye at my sacrifices and my offerings which I commanded, and honor your sons above me by fattening yourselves upon the choicest parts of every offering of my people Israel?' 30 Therefore the LORD the God of Israel declares: 'I promised that your house and the house of your father should go in and out before me for ever'; but now the LORD declares: 'Far be it from me; for those who honor me I will honor, and those who despise me shall be lightly esteemed. 31 Behold, the days are coming, when I will cut off your strength and the strength of your father's house, so that there will not be an old man in your house. 32 Then in distress you will look with envious eye on all the prosperity which shall be bestowed upon Israel; and there shall not be an old man in your house for ever. 33 The man of you whom I shall not cut off from my altar shall be spared to weep out his eyes and grieve his heart; and all the increase of your house shall die by the sword of men. 34 And this which shall befall your two sons, Hophni and Phinehas, shall be the sign to you: both of them shall die on the same day. 35 And I will raise up for myself a faithful priest, who shall do according to what is in my heart and in my mind; and I will build him a sure house, and he shall go in and out before my anointed for ever. 36 And every one who is left in your house shall come to implore him for a piece of silver or a loaf of bread, and shall say, "Put me, I pray you, in one of the priest's places, that I may eat a morsel of bread."'"

Only the broad outlines of the historical circumstances reflected in these important verses can be traced with any degree of certainty. It is apparent that a great upheaval in Israel's religious leadership accompanied the adoption of the monarchy.

In God's rejection of Eli's priestly house, the moral nature of his dealings with man become known. Divine promises and warnings do not operate mechanically so that they are applied irrespective of man's response. Instead, the Lord's actions are the outgrowth of his character and man's condition. The result is justice. In this particular case, Eli's house had, by it own actions, proved itself unworthy of continuing in its priestly office.

The relation of the present passage to its context suggests that Samuel was expected to be the faithful priest who would become the progenitor of an enduring priestly line.

He functioned as a judge, however, and was followed by his sons whose corruption prevented them from providing any enduring leadership in Israel (7:15-17).

A broader historical perspective may be assumed in which the judgment on Eli's house is seen climaxing in Solomon's expulsion of Abiathar from the priesthood of Jerusalem (1 Kings 2:27). Abiathar alone had survived the slaughter of the priests of Nob (22:11-23; cf. 2:33), only to support the wrong candidate for succession to the throne of David. When he was exiled to Anathoth, his place was taken by Zadok whose descendants served as the kings' counselors in Jerusalem.

During the Exile, Ezekiel anticipated that only the Zadokites would be allowed a priestly ministry in the restored Temple of Jerusalem. Ordinary Levites would be relegated to lesser positions of service (Ezek. 44:9-16). Apparently, therefore, Zadok was understood to be the *faithful priest* who was to become the progenitor of an eternal priesthood of the Lord (v. 35).

The idea expressed here that God sent punishment on the entire Levitic priesthood because of the sins of two of their number raises serious questions in the minds of many modern readers. The ancient Hebrews, however, had learned of the mutual influence which exists between an individual and the society of which he is a part. Not only is a community inevitably affected for good or ill by the actions of its members, it also in some way shares responsibility for their deeds. In any case, each individual bears ultimate responsibility for his own destiny (Deut. 24:16; Jer. 31:29-34; Ezek. 18:1-32). God's sovereignty is not arbitrary and mechanical. Although man is influenced by his environment, he may break the shackles of circumstance and provide a new influence on society instead.

3. Samuel Begins His Ministry (3:1—4:1a)

(1) Samuel Serves in the Temple (3:1-9)

¹ Now the boy Samuel was ministering to the Lord under Eli. And the word of the Lord was rare in those days; there was no frequent vision.
² At that time Eli, whose eyesight had begun to grow dim, so that he could not see, was lying down in his own place; ³ the lamp of God had not yet gone out, and Samuel was lying down within the temple of the Lord, where the ark of God was. ⁴ Then the Lord called, "Samuel! Samuel!" and he said, "Here I am!" ⁵ and ran to Eli, and said, "Here I am, for you called me." But he said, "I did not call; lie down again." So he went and lay down. ⁶ And the Lord called again, "Samuel!" And Samuel arose and went to Eli, and said, "Here I am, for you called me." But he said, "I did not call, my son; lie down again." ⁷ Now Samuel did not yet know the Lord, and the word of the Lord had not yet been revealed to him. ⁸ And the Lord called Samuel again the third time. And he arose and went to Eli, and said, "Here I am, for you called me." Then Eli perceived that the Lord was calling the boy. ⁹ Therefore Eli said to Samuel, "Go, lie down; and if he calls you, you shall say, 'Speak, Lord, for thy servant hears.'" So Samuel went and lay down in his place.

In stark contrast with Eli's infirmity and his sons' corruption, Samuel is portrayed as an upright youth who served as an attendant destined for a pivotal role as God's servant in a critical hour of Israel's history. Samuel's age at this point is unknown. He is called a boy (*na'ar*), which in biblical usage could refer to persons from infants (4:21) to adults (2 Chron. 13:7). The term may simply signify one who has not yet reached physical or mental maturity, or it may be used of a servant or personal attendant (1 Sam. 9:3).

National life had reached such a low ebb under the judges that many people must have wondered why the Lord's hand was no longer as vigorous in Israel's defense as it had been in the Conquest. At least a portion of the problem had to be attributed to the fact that there were too few men prepared to receive God's directions.

Although he had not reached the peak of his potential, Samuel was a more capable spokesman for God than a fully accredited, but decadent, priesthood.

Samuel's resting place in the temple by the ark of God suggests something other than an ordinary bed chamber. More probably we are to understand that the lad was serving in a priestly role, perhaps caring for the lamps which were kept burning all night before the holy place (Ex. 27.20-21; Lev. 24.1 f.). The source of Samuel's predawn summons went unrecognized either because of the boy's inexperience or because of the rarity of divine visitations.

When Eli finally recognized God's presence, he instructed Samuel as to the proper response to God's call. He was to indicate his willingness to listen. While Samuel was not actively seeking a divine manifestation, the larger context depicts one who was concerned over the Lord's leadership. God can speak through the "still small voice" to a man who is already searching for guidance, but the Lord is unlikely to overpower one who is insensitive to his direction.

There was no frequent vision. The text here is somewhat difficult, and the meaning is conjectural. We are probably to understand that *the word of the Lord was precious in those days* (cf. KJV) because the prophetic movement had not "burst forth" upon the people. Samuel is recognized in this context as a prophet (3:20) and later is associated with an ecstatic band at Ramah (19:18-24). This growing movement may well have helped preserve the essentials of Mosaic faith as Israel moved into a new phase of her national life.[14]

(2) The Lord Judges Eli's House (3:10-14)

¹⁰ And the Lord came and stood forth, calling as at other times, "Samuel! Samuel!" And Samuel said, "Speak, for thy servant hears." ¹¹ Then the Lord said to Samuel, "Behold, I am about to do a thing in Israel, at which the two ears of every one that hears it will tingle. ¹² On that day I will fulfil against Eli all that I have spoken concerning his house, from beginning to end. ¹³ And I tell him that I am about to punish his house for ever, for the iniquity which he knew, because his sons were blaspheming God, and he did not restrain them.

---

[14] See W. F. Albright, *Samuel and the Beginnings of the Prophetic Movement* (Cincinnati: Hebrew Union College Press, 1961).

¹⁴ Therefore I swear to the house of Eli that the iniquity of Eli's house shall not be expiated by sacrifice or offering for ever."

During the Lord's nocturnal appearance to Samuel, judgment on Eli's house is announced a second time (cf. 2:27-36). This time even the aged priest is implicated in his sons' sins. He had known of their wrongdoing and had taken no steps to curtail their activities.

The seriousness of their sin went beyond their own transgression. They had failed to provide the leadership which Israel so desperately needed. Presumably their punishment was in keeping with the former judgment pronounced upon them: they were to be permanently rejected as priests.

(3) Samuel Shares God's Message (3:15-18)

¹⁵ Samuel lay until morning; then he opened the doors of the house of the Lord. And Samuel was afraid to tell the vision to Eli. ¹⁶ But Eli called Samuel and said, "Samuel, my son." And he said, "Here I am." ¹⁷ And Eli said, "What was it that he told you? Do not hide it from me. May God do so to you and more also, if you hide anything from me of all that he told you." ¹⁸ So Samuel told him everything and hid nothing from him. And he said, "It is the Lord; let him do what seems good to him."

Samuel's reluctance to tell Eli of the Lord's rejection of his house is revealed in his attempt to return to a normal routine after his divine encounter. The fear which he experienced before his teacher was more a dread than terror or anxiety. Samuel had little to fear from the aged Eli, but his dread of a grim task is obvious. The true prophet of God takes no pleasure in delivering a message of doom and punishment.

May God do so to you and more also. This is a familiar oath pattern in the Old Testament (cf. Ruth 1:17; 1 Sam. 14:44; 1 Kings 2:23). Originally, it probably was preceded by a symbolic act such as the slaughter of an animal (Jer. 34:18) or by a dreaded curse (cf. Judg. 17:2). The speaker called for a similar fate to befall the one against whom the curse was directed. The formula is abbreviated here, but Eli's sentiments were vividly clear to Samuel.

Eli's calm acceptance of the fate pronounced against his house is characteristic of the fatalism exhibited by many Near Eastern people. All of life, even suffering and evil, is seen as the result of God's control over the world (cf. Job 9:13–24). By his response, Eli was simply recognizing his creatureliness alongside God's unrestrained autonomy.

(4) Samuel Becomes a Prophet (3:19—4:1a)

¹⁹ And Samuel grew, and the LORD was with him and let none of his words fall to the ground. ²⁰ And all Israel from Dan to Beersheba knew that Samuel was established as a prophet of the LORD. ²¹ And the LORD appeared again at Shiloh, for the LORD revealed himself to Samuel at Shiloh by the word of the LORD.
¹ And the word of Samuel came to all Israel.

As Samuel matured, his reputation as God's spokesman spread throughout the land. The only criteria by which a prophet could be evaluated hinged on the divine fulfillment of his messages. Many men could say, "Thus saith the Lord," but only those whose words were upheld by the events of life would be adjudged true prophets. The crucible of history provides a test both for the God who speaks (Isa. 41:26) and the man who speaks for him (Jer. 14:13–16).

Since the people recognized that God was speaking through Samuel's word, Shiloh again became an important sanctuary in Israel. God's presence in worship was not assured by impressive ceremony, a prestigious history, or even by the possession of holy objects such as the ark. True worship was dependent on man's willingness to open his life to divine control. Samuel's responsiveness to God's leadership opened a new prophetic era for Israel.

4. History of the Ark (4:1b—7:2)

(1) The Ark Is Captured (4:1b–22)

a. The Ark Brought to Aphek (4:1b–4)

Now Israel went out to battle against the Philistines; they encamped at Ebenezer, and the Philistines encamped at Aphek. ² The Philistines drew up in line against Israel, and when the battle spread, Israel was defeated by the Philistines, who slew about four thousand men on the field of battle. ³ And when the troops came to the camp, the elders of Israel said, "Why has the LORD put us to rout today before the Philistines? Let us bring the ark of the covenant of the LORD here from Shiloh, that he may come among us and save us from the power of our enemies." ⁴ So the people sent to Shiloh, and brought from there the ark of the covenant of the LORD of hosts, who is enthroned on the cherubim; and the two sons of Eli, Hophni and Phinehas, were there with the ark of the covenant of God.

This chapter introduces a section relating stories about the ark of the Lord in which Samuel is rarely mentioned (1 Sam. 4—6; 2 Sam. 6). Presumably these chapters were once circulated independently and are introduced here as important background material. The significance of the ark in this period is attested by the fact that nearly a third of all Old Testament references to it are found in the books of Samuel.

In ancient times the ark was associated with Israel's wilderness wanderings (Num. 10:33) and with the wars of conquest (Josh. 6). The term "Lord of hosts" or "Lord of the armies" reflects memories of God's past intervention in Israel's behalf.

When Israelite forces were put to flight by the Philistines in the crucial battle at Aphek, defeat was attributed, not to God's judgment upon the sins of his people, but to his physical absence from the field of combat (cf. also Num. 14:43–44).

Little distinction seems to have been made between the ark and the Lord himself. When the ark left camp in the wilderness, Moses said, "Arise, O Lord, and let thy enemies be scattered; and let them that hate thee flee before thee" (Num. 10:35). Similarly when it returned, he said, "Return, O Lord, to the ten thousand thousands of Israel" (v. 36). In Samuel's day, the ark was probably regarded as the Lord's throne, but it was still closely associated with his holiness and power.

The Philistines, first mentioned here in the books of Samuel, settled on the southwest coast of Canaan after an unsuccessful attack on Egypt about 1175 B.C. The military heritage and superior weapons of these people gave them a significant advantage over their loosely organized neighbors. Samson's battles (Judg. 13—15) and the Danite migration (Judg. 18) attest to the seriousness and duration of the Philistine threat to Israel's security.

b. The Ark Lost in Battle (4:5-11)

5 When the ark of the covenant of the LORD came into the camp, all Israel gave a mighty shout, so that the earth resounded. 6 And when the Philistines heard the noise of the shouting, they said, "What does this great shouting in the camp of the Hebrews mean?" And when they learned that the ark of the LORD had come to the camp, 7 the Philistines were afraid; for they said, "A god has come into the camp." And they said, "Woe to us! For nothing like this has happened before. 8 Woe to us! Who can deliver us from the power of these mighty gods? These are the gods who smote the Egyptians with every sort of plague in the wilderness. 9 Take courage, and acquit yourselves like men, O Philistines, lest you become slaves to the Hebrews as they have been to you; acquit yourselves like men and fight."

10 So the Philistines fought, and Israel was defeated, and they fled, every man to his home; and there was a very great slaughter, for there fell of Israel thirty thousand foot soldiers. 11 And the ark of God was captured; and the two sons of Eli, Hophni and Phinehas, were slain.

When Hophni and Phinehas brought the ark into the camp, the people gave a mighty shout which carried terror to the Philistines. This war cry has been associated with the formula which was recited when the ark entered or left camp (Num. 10:35-36). Such a brief incantation, however, is hardly long or impassioned enough to explain the despair which seized the enemy. More probably a wild outburst of frantic rejoicing accompanied the arrival of a sacred object which held out hope for an easy victory.

The Philistines were dismayed at the news from their enemies' camp. They recognized the lift that the ark would give to Israel's dispirited troops, for they had heard of the Lord's prowess against the Egyptians. Nevertheless they resolved to display the full measure of their manhood lest they themselves become slaves.

In a second battle, Israel was again defeated, but this time at an even more awesome price. The army was routed and worse still, the ark itself fell into enemy hands.

c. News of Disaster Kills Eli (4:12-18)

12 A man of Benjamin ran from the battle line, and came to Shiloh the same day, with his clothes rent and with earth upon his head. 13 When he arrived, Eli was sitting upon his seat by the road watching, for his heart trembled for the ark of God. And when the man came into the city and told the news, all the city cried out. 14 When Eli heard the sound of the outcry, he said, "What is this uproar?" Then the man hastened and came and told Eli. 15 Now Eli was ninety-eight years old and his eyes were set, so that he could not see. 16 And the man said to Eli, "I am he who has come from the battle; I fled from the battle today." And he said, "How did it go, my son?" 17 He who brought the tidings answered and said, "Israel has fled before the Philistines, and there has also been a great slaughter among the people; your two sons also, Hophni and Phinehas, are dead, and the ark of God has been captured." 18 When he mentioned the ark of God, Eli fell over backward from his seat by the side of the gate; and his neck was broken and he died, for he was an old man, and heavy. He had judged Israel forty years.

Although the text of v. 13 is somewhat confused, the general situation is clear. Eli, aged and blind, sat beside a city thoroughfare anxiously awaiting word from the battlefront. A Benjaminite runner, bearing obvious signs of mourning, doggedly paced over thirty miles to bring news of the disaster to Shiloh. A cry of despair trailed the courier's route until he came to the elderly priest.

Eli's whole world was bound up in the outcome of the battle. His two sons were in the thick of the fighting, sons for whom he maintained a father's love in spite of their persistent wrongdoing. His country's hopes for the future hinged on the fate of the thousands of young men who risked their lives there. Eli's primary concern, however, was for the safety of the ark of God. When he learned of its capture by the Philistines, he fell over dead, his neck broken.

For some of Israel's leaders the ark was mainly a religious object with psychological or magical powers to be exploited. For Eli, it represented a way of life. His entire career had been devoted to the service of the Lord whose earthly abode with men was symbolized by the presence of the ark. Its loss to a pagan people was more than the old man could stand.

The popular theology of the day also recognized the loss of the ark as a serious matter. The ark may well have been the focal point of Israel's entire political structure at this time. Martin Noth was the first to recognize a parallel between Israel's government under the judges and the amphictyonic leagues of the much later Aegean civilizations. Amphictyonies were systems held together by common worship at a central shrine (in Israel's case, the ark). Each clan or tribe supported rites at the sanctuary one month each year, or two months in a six-member league. Aside from these cultic duties and the necessity of providing troops for mutual defense, each tribe was completely autonomous. The judges arose largely during political distress and met with varying degrees of success in briefly uniting Israel. This system would obviously attach great importance to the ark and the chief priest who attended it. Israel on one day lost both.

This interpretation of Israel's premonarchic tribal structure has much to recommend it but should not be pressed too far. Materials about the period of the judges are too broad to allow a precise reconstruction of Israel's government at this time (see John Bright, pp. 142–160).

Most of the common people probably looked upon Israel's defeat at Aphek, and especially the capture of the ark, as a defeat of Israel's God. Many ancients believed that each nation had its own god who guided the fortunes of his people (cf. Judg. 11:24 and 1 Kings 11:33). Thus some feared that the Lord lacked power to defend his people or even his own personal throne among men.

The author of these verses, however, sees the defeat at Aphek as the result of God's judgment on the corruption in Eli's priestly line. Subsequent events (chs. 5—6) will show that the Lord has not become impotent but that his intervention in behalf of his people will require their submission to his leadership.

d. Birth of Ichabod (4:19–22)

19 Now his daughter-in-law, the wife of Phinehas, was with child, about to give birth. And when she heard the tidings that the ark of God was captured, and that her father-in-law and her husband were dead, she bowed and gave birth; for her pains came upon her. 20 And about the time of her death the women attending her said to her, "Fear not, for you have borne a son." But she did not answer or give heed. 21 And she named the child Ichabod, saying, "The glory has departed from Israel!" because the ark of God had been captured and because of her father-in-law and her husband. 22 And she said, "The glory has departed from Israel, for the ark of God has been captured."

The reaction of Eli's daughter-in-law to the grim news from Aphek must have been characteristic of all Israel's response. She grieved over the plight of her husband's priestly line, but her concern was for the larger disaster which had befallen the nation: *The glory has departed from Israel, for the ark of God has been captured.* Even the birth of a male heir, hastened by the shock of defeat, was insufficient to relieve her overwhelming gloom. She therefore named Phinehas' son Ichabod ("Where is the glory?" or "Inglorious"). Her death in childbirth is not specifically attributed to

God's judgment on his people, but it adds to the aura of despair which accompanied the disaster at Aphek.

(2) The Ark Troubles the Philistines (5:1–12)

a. Dagon Overthrown at Ashdod (5:1–5)

¹ When the Philistines captured the ark of God, they carried it from Ebenezer to Ashdod; ² then the Philistines took the ark of God and brought it into the house of Dagon and set it up beside Dagon. ³ And when the people of Ashdod rose early the next day, behold, Dagon had fallen face downward on the ground before the ark of the LORD. So they took Dagon and put him back in his place. ⁴ But when they rose early on the next morning, behold, Dagon had fallen face downward on the ground before the ark of the LORD, and the head of Dagon and both his hands were lying cut off upon the threshold; only the trunk of Dagon was left to him. ⁵ This is why the priests of Dagon and all who enter the house of Dagon do not tread on the threshold of Dagon in Ashdod to this day.

Having declared himself free of any physical dependence on Israel (cf. comment on 4:12–18), God quickly showed that the defeat at Aphek was not due to a lack of potency on his part. In two dramatic scenes the Lord demonstrated his superiority, first over the Philistine god and then over the warlike people themselves.

The modern reader's preoccupation with the techniques used in God's exercise of his dominion seriously obscures the major purpose of the biblical narrative. The ancient Israelites lacked our understanding of cause and effect and attributed all natural phenomena directly to God. He was the author of both good (Psalm 16:2) and evil (1 Sam. 16:14). His mighty works could be either very spectacular (Josh. 10:13) or quite ordinary (Isa. 8:18). The author of the present context was not concerned with how Dagon's image was overthrown but with the significance of the event itself. God was making his power known to all—whether the act was accomplished by his own hand, an earthquake, or by guerrilla raiders.

The Philistines at first attributed Dagon's prostration before the ark to mere chance. Only the accumulation of such "coincidences" convinced them that Israel's God might be responsible for their misfortunes.

The exact nature of the pagan custom involved in *do not tread on the threshold* is uncertain. The sanctity of the threshold among Israel's neighbors may have originated in the inclusion of the bodies of sacrificial victims in foundations of important buildings (1 Kings 16:34). If so, the severed head and hands of Dagon contain a specially grim irony. Nevertheless, in clear contradiction to Philistine theology, the Israelites provide (cf. v. 5) their own contemptuous answer as to why the priests of Dagon avoid contact with the threshold of his temple.

The practice of leaping over the threshold was clearly forbidden among Israelites (Zeph. 1:9). Nevertheless Ezekiel may imply that later Israelites, for decidedly different reasons, revered the threshold of the Temple in Jerusalem. A special offering was to be made there (46:2), and the sacred river flowing from the Temple was to originate at that point (47:1).[15]

b. Disease Devastates Philistia (5:6–12)

⁶ The hand of the LORD was heavy upon the people of Ashdod, and he terrified and afflicted them with tumors, both Ashdod and its territory. ⁷ And when the men of Ashdod saw how things were, they said, "The ark of the God of Israel must not remain with us; for his hand is heavy upon us and upon Dagon our god." ⁸ So they sent and gathered together all the lords of the Philistines, and said, "What shall we do with the ark of the God of Israel?" They answered, "Let the ark of the God of Israel be brought around to Gath." So they brought the ark of the God of Israel there. ⁹ But after they had brought it around, the hand of the LORD was against the city, causing a very great panic, and he afflicted the men of the city, both young and old, so that tumors broke out upon them. ¹⁰ So they sent the ark of God to Ekron. But when the ark of God came to Ekron, the people of Ekron cried out, "They have brought around to us the ark of the God of Israel to slay us and our people." ¹¹ They sent therefore

---

[15] The rather unusual term for threshold, *miphtan*, used in 1 Sam. 5:4–5, is found elsewhere in the Old Testament only in Ezek. 9:3; 10:4,18; 42:6; 47:1; Zeph. 1:9.

and gathered together all the lords of the Philistines, and said, "Send away the ark of the God of Israel, and let it return to its own place, that it may not slay us and our people." For there was a deathly panic throughout the whole city. The hand of God was very heavy there; 12 the men who did not die were stricken with tumors, and the cry of the city went up to heaven.

To many observers, the Philistine capture of the ark of the Lord (4:12–18) suggested an impotence on the part of Israel's God. The ancient author clearly shows that the defeat at Aphek represented God's judgment on national corruption, not a lack of divine power. First he proved his superiority over the Philistines' god (5:1–5), and then he demonstrated his control over their people.

The nature of the malady which afflicted the Philistines is uncertain. The word which is translated tumors (*'ophalim*), in the singular would be the same as the name Ophel (*'ophel*), which is used of a fortified hill or acropolis within a city (Neh. 3:26; cf. 2 Kings 5:24; Is. 32:14). Hence any bodily swelling or tumor could be indicated. The mention of mice in the next chapter (6:4 f.) suggests bubonic plague to the modern mind. This deadly pestilence is accompanied by discolored swelling of lymph glands, especially in the groin and armpits. No reference to mice is made in chapter 5, however.

On the other hand, the Masoretes who preserved the Hebrew text did not pronounce the word *'ophalim*. They ignored the written word and read *tehorim* instead. This term is used of rectal swellings which result from virulent types of dysentery. Hence, "hemorrhoids" would be a more suitable translation. In either case suffering and death could easily reach epidemic proportions since both dysentery and the plague are quite communicable.

When the plague struck Ashdod and environs, the men of the city began seeking an explanation of their misfortune. Strange circumstances surrounded the presence of the ark in the temple of Dagon, so the people tentatively concluded that Israel's God might be seeking vengeance upon them. Evidently they still hoped that the plague and their prized war trophy were unrelated. Otherwise they would hardly have been so eager to send the ark to other major Philistine cities. First in Gath and then in Ekron, death and suffering followed in its train.

(3) *The Ark Is Returned to Israel (6:1 —7:2)*

a. *Philistines Pay Reparations (6:1–9)*

¹ The ark of the Lord was in the country of the Philistines seven months. ² And the Philistines called for the priests and the diviners and said, "What shall we do with the ark of the Lord? Tell us with what we shall send it to its place." ³ They said, "If you send away the ark of the God of Israel, do not send it empty, but by all means return him a guilt offering. Then you will be healed, and it will be known to you why his hand does not turn away from you." ⁴ And they said, "What is the guilt offering that we shall return to him?" They answered, "Five golden tumors and five golden mice, according to the number of the lords of the Philistines; for the same plague was upon all of you and upon your lords. ⁵ So you must make images of your tumors and images of your mice that ravage the land, and give glory to the God of Israel; perhaps he will lighten his hand from off you and your gods and your land. ⁶ Why should you harden your hearts as the Egyptians and Pharaoh hardened their hearts? After he had made sport of them, did not they let the people go, and they departed? ⁷ Now then, take and prepare a new cart and two milch cows upon which there has never come a yoke, and yoke the cows to the cart, but take their calves home, away from them. ⁸ And take the ark of the Lord and place it on the cart, and put in a box at its side the figures of gold, which you are returning to him as a guilt offering. Then send it off, and let it go its way. ⁹ And watch; if it goes up on the way to its own land, to Bethshemesh, then it is he who has done us this great harm; but if not, then we shall know that it is not his hand that struck us, it happened to us by chance."

The text of chapter 6 is confused and the details of the story are difficult to reconstruct. At first the Philistine priests seem convinced that an offering will placate Israel's God: *Then you will be healed, and it will be known to you why his hand does not turn away from you.* Later, however, they are uncertain: *give glory to the God of Israel; perhaps he will lighten his hand from off you and your gods and your land.* The number of golden mice also varies. Verse 4 indicates that there are to be five of them, but v. 18 implies that there will be considerably more. Ancient Greek and Aramaic translations also offer readings which differ significantly from the Masoretic Text.

While the circumstances surrounding the return of the ark from the Philistines may be uncertain, the theological impact of the account is quite plain. The Lord who had punished Israel by allowing the nation to be defeated in battle now had also humbled the Philistine conquerors. He accomplished the return of his ark from an enemy land and stood ready to defend his privacy against inquisitive Israelites (6:19).

After seven long months of frustrating devastation, the Philistines were anxious to return the ark to *its place,* but they felt that they must follow proper protocol. The Philistine priests and diviners gave direction for the preparation of golden images of the plagues which had afflicted them.

The Philistine priests sound almost like practicing Yahwists, but their reference to Israel's Egyptian experience simply says, "Why wait until later? Let's see right now if God brought this upon us." To *give glory to the God of Israel* was to admit that he was responsible for the misfortunes which had befallen the land.

The Philistine's actions probably reflected a belief in sympathetic magic. The people hoped that somehow the images would help carry pestilence away from their troubled land. The value of their offering was designed to relieve them of responsibility for their guilt.

God's forgiveness however cannot be bought with the currency of empty ritual. Sacrifice apart from a transformed life invites God's judgment, not his grace (Isa. 1:11–17).

Without condoning this distorted view of religion, the ancient writer uses this experience to demonstrate afresh God's greatness. The Lord humiliated the Philistines' god, debilitated their people, and forced them to acknowledge publicly their subservience to him.

b. The Ark Back in Israel (6:10–18)

¹⁰ The men did so, and took two milch cows and yoked them to the cart, and shut up their calves at home. ¹¹ And they put the ark of the Lord on the cart, and the box with the golden mice and the images of their tumors. ¹² And the cows went straight in the direction of Bethshemesh along one highway, lowing as they went; they turned neither to the right nor to the left, and the lords of the Philistines went after them as far as the border of Bethshemesh. ¹³ Now the people of Bethshemesh were reaping their wheat harvest in the valley; and when they lifted up their eyes and saw the ark, they rejoiced to see it. ¹⁴ The cart came into the field of Joshua of Bethshemesh, and stopped there. A great stone was there; and they split up the wood of the cart and offered the cows as a burnt offering to the Lord. ¹⁵ And the Levites took down the ark of the Lord and the box that was beside it, in which were the golden figures, and set them upon the great stone; and the men of Bethshemesh offered burnt offerings and sacrificed sacrifices on that day to the Lord. ¹⁶ And when the five lords of the Philistines saw it, they returned that day to Ekron.

¹⁷ These are the golden tumors, which the Philistines returned as a guilt offering to the Lord: one for Ashdod, one for Gaza, one for Ashkelon, one for Gath, one for Ekron; ¹⁸ also the golden mice, according to the number of all the cities of the Philistines belonging to the five lords, both fortified cities and unwalled villages. The great stone, beside which they set down the ark of the Lord, is a witness to this day in the field of Joshua of Bethshemesh.

The Philistine diviners devised one last test of the Lord's involvement in the disasters which had befallen their country. Two cows, separated from their calves, were to be used to pull the ark on a cart built especially for that purpose. If the cows returned to their calves upon their release, the pestilence which had swept the land was to be considered a chance occurrence. If the cows moved on toward Bethshemesh, the nearest Israelite town, then the people would conclude that the Lord had afflicted them. Thus, God's involvement in human history was further attested when the calves were abandoned and the ark was borne toward home territory.

When the ark was returned to Israel, its first resting place was at Bethshemesh. The cart and the cows were used in a sacrifice to commemorate the event, and a large stone altar there served as a lasting testimony of the Lord's vindication of his honor. Nothing is said about returning the ark to Shiloh where it had been located before the battle of Aphek. Likewise, the Bible nowhere mentions the destruction of this strategic sanctuary although it is known to have fallen about this time. The author apparently had a more important purpose in mind. He was showing that although the ark had formerly been housed at Shiloh, it could legitimately be located anywhere in all Israel. In a real sense, therefore, the ark had already returned home.

c. Death Strikes Bethshemesh (6:19—7:2)

¹⁹ And he slew some of the men of Bethshemesh, because they looked into the ark of the Lord; he slew seventy men of them, and the people mourned because the Lord had made a great slaughter among the people. ²⁰ Then the men of Bethshemesh said, "Who is able to stand before the Lord, this holy God? And to whom shall he go up away from us?" ²¹ So they sent messengers to the inhabitants of Kiriathjearim, saying, "The Philistines have returned the ark of the Lord. Come down and take it up to you."
¹ And the men of Kiriathjearim came and took up the ark of the Lord, and brought it to the house of Abinadab on the hill; and they consecrated his son, Eleazar, to have charge of the ark of the Lord. ² From the day that the ark was lodged at Kiriathjearim, a long time passed, some twenty years, and all the house of Israel lamented after the Lord.

The history of the ark after it returned to Israel climaxes the theological argument which has been developed throughout chapters 4—6. As a consequence of the corruption of Eli's sons who attended the ark, the Lord allowed the ark to fall into enemy hands at Aphek. He then defended his honor and power by effecting the liberation of the ark from the Philistines. Now to make certain that his original lesson was not forgotten, the Lord rebuked his people for their failure to respect the divine transcendence.

The Israelites at Bethshemesh felt no danger imposed by the presence of the ark among them. Yahweh, after all, was their God and he had just exercised his power upon their enemies. They presumed that because they were Israelites, the Lord must be on their side. Their lack of fear of the ark soon emboldened them to satisfy their curiosity about the sacred relic. They felt that as God's chosen people, they were free of the rules of conduct which guide ordinary men. They were swiftly taught that, regardless of religious, biological, or national background, all men must subject themselves to divine control.

Presumably the plague which had devastated Philistia moved on into Israel and afflicted the Israelites as well. The sacrilegious treatment of the ark by the people of Bethshemesh provided a ready explanation of God's judgment, and the ark was moved on to Kiriathjearim.

At this point the theology lesson was complete, the story came to a standstill, and the ark spent twenty years in obscurity. It remained in Kiriathjearim under the care of Abinadab and his sons until it was brought to Jerusalem in honor in the time of David (2 Sam. 6; but cf. 1 Sam. 14:18).

5. Samuel Delivers the People (7:3–17)

(1) Victory Won at Mizpah (7:3–11)

³ Then Samuel said to all the house of Israel, "If you are returning to the Lord with all your heart, then put away the foreign gods and the Ashtaroth from among you, and direct your heart to the Lord, and serve him only, and he will deliver you out of the hand of the Philistines." ⁴ So Israel put away the Baals and the Ashtaroth, and they served the Lord only.
⁵ Then Samuel said, "Gather all Israel at Mizpah, and I will pray to the Lord for you." ⁶ So they gathered at Mizpah, and drew water and poured it out before the Lord, and fasted on that day, and said there, "We have sinned against the Lord." And Samuel judged the people of Israel at Mizpah. ⁷ Now when the Philistines heard that the people of Israel had gathered at Mizpah, the lords of the Philistines went up against Israel. And when the people of

Israel heard of it they were afraid of the Philistines. 8 And the people of Israel said to Samuel, "Do not cease to cry to the LORD our God for us, that he may save us from the hand of the Philistines." 9 So Samuel took a sucking lamb and offered it as a whole burnt offering to the LORD; and Samuel cried to the LORD for Israel, and the LORD answered him. 10 As Samuel was offering up the burnt offering, the Philistines drew near to attack Israel; but the LORD thundered with a mighty voice that day against the Philistines and threw them into confusion; and they were routed before Israel. 11 And the men of Israel went out of Mizpah and pursued the Philistines, and smote them, as far as below Bethcar.

After a rather lengthy digression dealing with the fortunes of the ark, the biblical author resumes the story of Samuel's career. In both sections there are important historical overtones, but neither account is primarily concerned with the strict narration of details. Under the influence of Eli and his corrupt sons, Israel had been weakened to the extent that her national existence was threatened by the expansion of Philistine power. Now under Samuel's leadership conditions tended to improve somewhat.

The account of the gathering at Mizpah provides a concise, almost stylized, view of the direction national affairs took now that a new prophetic era had been instituted in Israel (3:19–20). The central theme (v. 3) is a good example of an application of the doctrine of divine retribution (cf. Introduction): Religious purity will result in national prosperity. Under the influence of Samuel's distinguished career, Israel increasingly turned away from the Canaanite fertility cults and returned to a faith in God, thus gaining a temporary respite from Philistine aggression.

The worship of Baal and Ashtoreth was widespread among Israel's Canaanite neighbors. Both names are used in the plural here to refer to the several local varieties or manifestations of the principal male and female divinities in the Canaanite pantheon. Worship at their sanctuaries involved open practice of sexual rites which made them particularly abhorrent to proper Yahwists. These two terms, *the Baals and the Ashtoreth,* are frequently combined to designate the worship of all local pagan gods among Israel's neighbors (Judg. 2:13; 10:6; 1 Sam. 12:10).

The conditions underlying the assembly at Mizpah are not altogether clear. The whole campaign is related as a single incident although a considerable lapse of time seems likely (cf. v. 7).

We are probably to understand that Samuel was something of a military strategist as well as a prophet, priest, and judge. The author's stress, however, is not on this remarkable man but on God. The planning, work, and sacrifice of men were all forgotten in the face of the voice of God (thunder) which alone was given credit for the victory.

(2) Samuel's Ministry Summarized (7:12–17)

12 Then Samuel took a stone and set it up between Mizpah and Jeshanah, and called its name Ebenezer; for he said, "Hitherto the LORD has helped us." 13 So the Philistines were subdued and did not again enter the territory of Israel. And the hand of the LORD was against the Philistines all the days of Samuel. 14 The cities which the Philistines had taken from Israel were restored to Israel, from Ekron to Gath; and Israel rescued their territory from the hand of the Philistines. There was peace also between Israel and the Amorites.

15 Samuel judged Israel all the days of his life. 16 And he went on a circuit year by year to Bethel, Gilgal, and Mizpah; and he judged Israel in all these places. 17 Then he would come back to Ramah, for his home was there, and there also he administered justice to Israel. And he built there an altar to the LORD.

These verses mark the high point in Samuel's career, for the next chapter begins with the observation that he is old and his sons are perverting justice.[16] His role in the establishment of the monarchy and in the selection of Israel's first two kings was very important. Nevertheless, in the author's mind, that role belonged to another

[16] This summary marks the end of the "rise and rule" of Samuel (1 Sam. 1:1—7:17). The "rise and reign" of Saul follows (8:1—14:52). See Introduction V, 1.

segment of history. The period of the judges ended when the elders of the people said, "appoint for us a king" (8:5).

This summary of conditions under Samuel's judgeship, therefore, represents not only the author's estimate of Samuel, but also his understanding of Isreal's political system under the judges. First he records the erection of a memorial stone called Ebenezer at a site near Mizpah. Samuel explains that **Hitherto the Lord has helped us.** The stone itself plays no part in the symbolism. Samuel simply took a common place-name meaning "the stone of help" and through a play on words created a memorial embodying his confession of faith.

In this context, Ebenezer may refer to the preceding victory at Mizpah, but its inclusion at this particular point in history suggests a much broader application. The author is saying in effect that the system under the judges works when God's people remain true to him.

In broad sweeping terms the author next depicts a permanent Philistine withdrawal from Israelite territory and the return of the captured cities. These expressions apparently describe conditions by comparing them with other more troubled times, for when the war is resumed under Saul the Philistines have penetrated even more deeply into Israel's holdings (ch. 13). There is nothing inherently improbable, however, about a period of relative peace and prosperity during Samuel's early years. This peace comes in fulfillment of Samuel's earlier promise that the Lord would deliver his people from the Philistines if they would be loyal to him (7:3).

Thus at this point Israel had repented of her sins and had purged her worship of foreign gods. The Lord had responded faithfully by sending a noble judge, Samuel, and by delivering his people from their foreign oppressors. In apparent tranquility the period of the judges ends with Samuel administering justice as a circuit riding judge who serves as a spiritual guide to the people.

II. The Rise and Reign of Saul (8:1—14:52)

After the summary of Samuel's ministry in 7:12–17, attention is subsequently focused on Saul's rise to power (cf. Introduction V, 1). Samuel still has a role to play in the narrative, but he is no longer the center of the reader's attention. Before Saul's story can be told, however, some account must be given of the change in form of Israel's government.

This section of Samuel is clearly marked with ambivalent attitudes toward the establishment of the monarchy. The overall editorial outlook is abundantly clear. The essential soundness of Israel's tribal structure administered by a religio-political judge was stoutly defended (cf. 7:13). Limitations of the system are not totally ignored but are attributed to the people's failure to be faithful to the Lord who is, after all, the true head of Israel's government (cf. especially chs. 8 and 12).

On the other hand a contrary position, much more favorably disposed toward the monarchy (the major portion of chs. 9—11), is also found in this section. According to this view the Lord himself was providing a king to deliver Israel from the hand of the Philistines (9:15–16). He would work through the new system just as he had through the old (12:14–15).

The section as it now stands is so arranged that the anti-monarchic element is more pronounced. Nevertheless, the sentiment in support of an Israelite kingdom cannot be denied. Quite possibly both positions were independently maintained for a long period of time before they were eventually combined into their present form. The study of the processes underlying the composition of biblical texts is a legitimate branch of technical scholarship which should be recognized and encouraged. The major task facing the general reader, however, is that of interpreting the biblical record in its present form so that it may be seen as a meaningful guide for modern life.

Far from being a matter for concern, the

preservation of contradictory attitudes on social issues is an evidence of the vitality of biblical records. Under the leadership of either a judge or a king, there were political and religious values to be won or lost. God appears to have been using men who advocated both systems of government to guide his people through this difficult period. The resultant tensions helped preserve the values of both systems.

1. Samuel's Influence Fades (8:1–22)

(1) Samuel's Sons Pervert Justice (8:1–3)

¹ When Samuel became old, he made his sons judges over Israel. ² The name of his first-born son was Joel, and the name of his second, Abijah; they were judges in Beersheba. ³ Yet his sons did not walk in his ways, but turned aside after gain; they took bribes and perverted justice.

Although the author's convictions ran strongly against the monarchy, he clearly recognized many of the limitations of Israel's tribal structure under the judges. A basic problem in any system based on strong personalities revolves around the difficulty in providing for a smooth transmission of authority between administrations. First in the time of Abimelech (Judg. 9:6), then under Eli and now Samuel, an attempt was made to establish a dynastic system. Character and leadership ability, however, do not necessarily follow lines of blood relationship.

Emerging nations today encounter a similar difficulty in finding honest and reliable officials. Unfortunately not all people who are upstanding in private life are able to withstand the moral pressures of public trust. Corruption in high office will eventually undermine even the most stable government, and perversion of justice will alienate an otherwise loyal population. Israel's experience with Samuel's sons, therefore, provided grounds for a serious indictment of the whole tribal system administered by the judges.

As serious as these issues were, the demand for a king might have been postponed indefinitely had it not been precipitated by a military crisis of unprecedented proportions. In addition to the smoldering Philistine wars, Israel now faced an outbreak of hostilities with her trans-Jordan neighbors (12:12). Israel's very continued existence as a nation seemed to be at stake and no easy solutions were apparent.

(2) Israel Asks for a King (8:4–9)

⁴ Then all the elders of Israel gathered together and came to Samuel at Ramah, ⁵ and said to him, "Behold, you are old and your sons do not walk in your ways; now appoint for us a king to govern us like all the nations." ⁶ But the thing displeased Samuel when they said, "Give us a king to govern us." And Samuel prayed to the LORD. ⁷ And the LORD said to Samuel, "Hearken to the voice of the people in all that they say to you; for they have not rejected you, but they have rejected me from being king over them. ⁸ According to all the deeds which they have done to me, from the day I brought them up out of Egypt even to this day, forsaking me and serving other gods, so they are also doing to you. ⁹ Now then, hearken to their voice; only, you shall solemnly warn them, and show them the ways of the king who shall reign over them."

In view of the many limitations and problems within the tribal system, elders from each tribe gathered and asked Samuel's guidance in establishing a monarchy in Israel. Their desire to be *like all the nations* probably should be interpreted as something more than mere social conformity. A theocratic government embodying democratic principles does not always provide for efficient administration. They were willing to accept a totalitarian regime in order to gain enough centralized authority to meet quickly and effectively the demands of a changing society.

As serious as this problem was, the Israelites had other options open to them. They could have continued under God's leadership to search for improvements in the organization which embodied their personal and theological ideals. Instead, they turned to a new social structure which was based on values foreign to Israel's faith.

We should not conclude, however, that the Lord was unalterably opposed to the monarchy and irrevocably tied to the older system. A major strand of the present narrative (chs. 9—11) implied divine support of the Israelite kingship. Also once the monarchy was established, it soon became the accepted norm through which God dealt with his people (cf. Judg. 17:6; 18:1; 19:1; 21:25).

Israel's sin in requesting a king lay in the fact that her leaders externalized national weaknesses. They felt that a new system of government would solve their problems, while Israel's greatest limitations were due to spiritual attitudes. The people could have recovered a genuine unity of purpose and action by reexamining the foundation of their national existence—i.e., their commitment to the Lord. Instead, they sought to impose an artificial solidarity based upon force and external authority. Under such circumstances, the establishment of a monarchy promised ominous consequences.

(3) *Ways of a King Described* (8:10–18)

¹⁰ So Samuel told all the words of the LORD to the people who were asking a king from him. ¹¹ He said, "These will be the ways of the king who will reign over you: he will take your sons and appoint them to his chariots and to be his horsemen, and to run before his chariots; ¹² and he will appoint for himself commanders of thousands and commanders of fifties, and some to plow his ground and to reap his harvest, and to make his implements of war and the equipment of his chariots. ¹³ He will take your daughters to be perfumers and cooks and bakers. ¹⁴ He will take the best of your fields and vineyards and olive orchards and give them to his servants. ¹⁵ He will take the tenth of your grain and of your vineyards and give it to his officers and to his servants. ¹⁶ He will take your menservants and maidservants, and the best of your cattle and your asses, and put them to his work. ¹⁷ He will take the tenth of your flocks, and you shall be his slaves. ¹⁸ And in that day you will cry out because of your king, whom you have chosen for yourselves; but the LORD will not answer you in that day."

In Samuel's eyes the great danger in establishing a monarchy in Israel lay in the fact that the new political system would encourage the nation actually to become "like all the nations." His description of the *ways of the king* portrays a complete contradiction of the personal values embodied in the Yahwistic faith. People would lose their inividual freedom, and human dignity would be neglected. Young men would be conscripted to serve as laborers, soldiers, or craftsmen and young women for domestic service. Property would be expropriated. Israel might be saved, but the Israel of old would be lost forever.[17]

For all of Samuel's grim forecast, the king in Israel does not seem to have been given the free authoritarian hand which the monarch enjoyed in other Near Eastern nations. Yahwism, though beleaguered periodically by foreign cults, maintained a persistent stress on the dignity of man and on the value of human personality. Prophetic voices, emboldened by this heritage, dared to criticize the king and thus served as a check on his power (Mic. 3:1–4; Isa. 3:14–15).

A summary of the royal office from this perspective is reflected in Deuteronomy 17:14–20. The king was to be a native born Israelite, selected under divine guidance. He was to avoid all forms of ostentatious living, i.e., he should not accumulate cattle, goods, or wives. He was to follow divine regulation so that "his heart may not be lifted up above his brethren."

In actual practice, the character of Israel's kings varied widely. Not all would conform to the ominous royal portrait which Samuel painted, but the potential was always there. The new form of government embodied dangers against which Israel would constantly have to be on guard.

(4) *Israel Remains Resolute* (8:19–22)

¹⁹ But the people refused to listen to the voice of Samuel; and they said, "No! but we will have a king over us, ²⁰ that we also may be like all the nations, and that our king may govern us and go out before us and fight our battles." ²¹ And when Samuel had heard all the

---

[17] The conditions which Samuel describes are known to have existed among Israel's neighbors between the 18th and 13th centuries B.C. See I. Mendelsohn, "Samuel's Denunciation of Kingship in the Light of the Akkadian Documents from Ugarit," *Bulletin of the American Schools of Oriental Research*, 143 (October, 1956), pp. 17–22.

words of the people, he repeated them in the ears of the LORD. ²² And the LORD said to Samuel, "Hearken to their voice, and make them a king." Samuel then said to the men of Israel, "Go every man to his city."

Through the voice of his prophet Samuel, the Lord expressed his reluctance to grant a change in Israel's political structure. The prophet showed that the king's authoritarian efficiency, sought so eagerly by the elders, would in fact tend to undercut the basic principles of Yahwistic faith. Nevertheless, the people were free to make the choice, and they remained adamant that Israel should have a king.

This expression of man's ability to resist the divine will hardly seems in keeping with previous demonstrations of God's autonomy in human affairs (chs. 4—6). In Old Testament thought, however, the omnipotence of God and the freedom of man are maintained as a sublime paradox. Man is able to select his own courses of action, but he is not able to declare himself independent of the consequences of his actions. Thus Israel can have a king by continuing her demand for one, but then she will be without excuse. When the monarchy eventually bears the dread fruit predicted by the Lord's spokesman, Israel can expect no absolution from guilt. In the meantime, however, God will assist in the selection of a king.

2. God Selects Israel's King (9:1—10:27)

(1) Saul Qualifies for Office (9:1-2)

¹ There was a man of Benjamin whose name was Kish, the son of Abiel, son of Zeror, son of Becorath, son of Aphiah, a Benjaminite, a man of wealth; ² and he had a son whose name was Saul, a handsome young man. There was not a man among the people of Israel more handsome than he; from his shoulders upward he was taller than any of the people.

Saul's credentials as Israel's future king are concisely stated without apology or elaboration. Saul's natural qualifications for office were important because even his anointment by Samuel was not enough to make Saul king. Before he could assume the throne, he had to win public support from a seriously divided population.

A major problem facing Israel at this time was the division of the country along geographical and tribal lines. For more than a hundred years the northern and southern tribes had followed independent courses of action. The Song of Deborah in Judges 5, for example, portrays Israel as a corporate entity, facing a common foe, but only ten tribes are mentioned. Six are praised for responding to the call to arms and four are rebuked for their indifference, while Judah and Simeon are completely ignored. Apparently they were not considered a part of Israel's tribal league at this time. Since the poem is generally considered quite ancient and perhaps even contemporary with the events it describes (ca. 1150 B.C.), the importance of this testimony is apparent. The pursuit of narrow regional interests left Israel so seriously divided that it was really more like two nations than one.[18]

Saul's own tribal background equipped him for a mediating role in this sectional rivalry. Benjamin occupied a central position between the north and south so that the new king would not be too closely identified with either territory. Since the tribe was small, other interest groups would have little to fear or envy in Benjamin's growing influence.

On the other hand, ancient Israelites looked upon an outstanding family background as a prime qualification for leadership. A noble lineage was evidence of generations of proven ability and a long heritage of service and achievement. The prominence of Saul's family is attested by a genealogy which traces his ancestors back through five generations. His father is also called *a man of wealth* or a "mighty man of valor" (in Heb., *gibbor chayil*). Such persons probably constituted a natural landed

---

[18] The centrifugal forces which were undermining Israel's unity at this time were quite complex. For a more thorough treatment see Bright (pp. 154–160) or Martin Noth, *The History of Israel*, trans. P. R. Ackroyd (New York: Harper and Brothers Publishers, 1960), pp. 154–163.

nobility in the ancient world.[19] From his family, Saul received the social and spiritual nurture which brought him to the very threshold of greatness.

Probably equally important for Saul's initial successes was his commanding physical appearance. In a time when physical prowess and personal magnetism were deemed significant, Saul looked like a king. While his remarkable physique carried no assurance of success, it added substance to his threats of violence when decisive action was required in a military campaign against Ammon (11:7).

(2) *Saul Seeks Lost Asses (9:3–14)*

3 Now the asses of Kish, Saul's father, were lost. So Kish said to Saul his son, "Take one of the servants with you, and arise, go and look for the asses." 4 And they passed through the hill country of Ephraim and passed through the land of Shalishah, but they did not find them. And they passed through the land of Shaalim, but they were not there. Then they passed through the land of Benjamin, but did not find them.
5 When they came to the land of Zuph, Saul said to his servant who was with him, "Come, let us go back, lest my father cease to care about the asses and become anxious about us." 6 But he said to him, "Behold, there is a man of God in this city, and he is a man that is held in honor; all that he says comes true. Let us go there; perhaps he can tell us about the journey on which we have set out." 7 Then Saul said to his servant, "But if we go, what can we bring the man? For the bread in our sacks is gone, and there is no present to bring to the man of God. What have we?" 8 The servant answered Saul again, "Here, I have with me the fourth part of a shekel of silver, and I will give it to the man of God, to tell us our way." 9 (Formerly in Israel, when a man went to inquire of God, he said, "Come, let us go to the seer"; for he who is now called a prophet was formerly called a seer.) 10 And Saul said to his servant, "Well said; come, let us go." So they went to the city where the man of God was.
11 As they went up the hill to the city, they met young maidens coming out to draw water, and said to them, "Is the seer here?" 12 They answered, "He is; behold, he is just ahead of you. Make haste; he has come just now to the city, because the people have a sacrifice today on the high place. 13 As soon as you enter the city, you will find him, before he goes up to the high place to eat; for the people will not eat till he comes, since he must bless the sacrifice; afterward those eat who are invited. Now go up, for you will meet him immediately." 14 So they went up to the city. As they were entering the city, they saw Samuel coming out toward them on his way up to the high place.

The actual story of Saul's rise to power is divided into three shorter episodes: his selection by Samuel (9:3—10:16), his presentation to Israel (10:17–27), and his winning of popular support (11:1–15).

Saul came to Samuel's attention as he and a servant were searching for his father's lost asses. The route of their journey is obscure since the sites of Shalishah and Shaalim are unknown, but they concluded their search probably not more than twenty miles from home. After a long, fruitless effort, Saul's servant persuaded him to consult *the man of God* in the nearby town so that they might not have to return home empty-handed. Thus, Samuel was approached because of his reputation as a clairvoyant. Saul and his servant met Samuel on his way to supervise the sacrifices at the local high place. Worship at these local sanctuaries was later condemned because of its impurity (e.g., 2 Kings 23:18), but no stigma was attached to services there at this time.

This episode and subsequent passages in Samuel (chs. 10 and 19) are very important in the study of Old Testament prophecy. Although the term prophet is used as early as the patriarchal period (Gen. 20:7), little of a specific nature is known of the prophet's role or activities prior to Samuel's time. In the present context, Samuel appears primarily as a seer, but the reader is informed that a seer was also later called a prophet.

Unfortunately, an etymological study of the Hebrew words involved yields only very broad suggestions as to the early prophet's function. There are two words translated "seer" in the Old Testament: *ro'eh* used here, and *chozeh*. Both terms

---

[19] Saul's reference to his clan in 9:21 is an example of overstated modesty to heighten the reader's awareness of God's use of simple people to accomplish his will. This "lowly become great" motif is widespread in biblical literature (e.g., Judg. 6:15).

come from roots meaning "to see" so that a seer is one who sees or apprehends that which others fail to perceive.

The word "prophet" (*nabî*) is much more frequent in the Old Testament, occurring some 300 times. It is generally traced back to other Semitic roots meaning "to call" or "to announce," but the force of the Hebrew word is uncertain. It may mean "one who is called" or "one who announces." Even if the roots of all three terms could be analyzed exactly, however, their meanings still could have changed through centuries of varying usage.

Much more important for our purposes are the functions and activities of the prophet in the Old Testament. Samuel is portrayed as a clairvoyant (9:1–27), a concerned statesman (8:10–18), a kingmaker (10:1; 16:1), and as the leader of an ecstatic band of prophets (19:20). Such activities reflect the complex involvements of Israel's prophets.

Samuel's success in foretelling the future is in keeping with the legitimate role played by the predictive element in canonical prophecy. It was assumed that God would uphold the words of his spokesmen, and fulfillment in history was indicative of divine confirmation of the prophet's message. Samuel's status as a prophet, therefore, was evidenced by the fact that the Lord "let none of his words fall to the ground" (3:19; cf. 9:6; note also 1 Kings 22:28).

Accurate predictions were still important for the later "writing" prophets (cf. Lev. 28:9), but increasingly other verification of the prophet's message was sought. While no external tests of techniques could distinguish the true from the false prophet, in any era the latter would be betrayed by the inferior character of his life (Jer. 29:23) and message (Jer. 23:28). The moral and ethical messages of the great prophets of the eighth through the sixth centuries B.C. serve as the normative standard of prophetic insight in the Old Testament. We must remember, however, that Samuel stands at the beginning of Israel's prophetic movement and should be evaluated against his own and not a later background.

(3) *Saul Meets Samuel (9:15–27)*

¹⁵ Now the day before Saul came, the LORD had revealed to Samuel: ¹⁶ "Tomorrow about this time I will send to you a man from the land of Benjamin, and you shall anoint him to be prince over my people Israel. He shall save my people from the hand of the Philistines; for I have seen the affliction of my people, because their cry has come to me." ¹⁷ When Samuel saw Saul, the LORD told him, "Here is the man of whom I spoke to you! He it is who shall rule over my people." ¹⁸ Then Saul approached Samuel in the gate, and said, "Tell me where is the house of the seer?" ¹⁹ Samuel answered Saul, "I am the seer; go up before me to the high place, for today you shall eat with me, and in the morning I will let you go and will tell you all that is on your mind. ²⁰ As for your asses that were lost three days ago, do not set your mind on them, for they have been found. And for whom is all that is desirable in Israel? Is it not for you and for all your father's house?" ²¹ Saul answered, "Am I not a Benjaminite, from the least of the tribes of Israel? And is not my family the humblest of all the families of the tribe of Benjamin? Why then have you spoken to me in this way?"

²² Then Samuel took Saul and his servant and brought them into the hall and gave them a place at the head of those who had been invited, who were about thirty persons. ²³ And Samuel said to the cook, "Bring the portion I gave you, of which I said to you, 'Put it aside.'" ²⁴ So the cook took up the leg and the upper portion and set them before Saul; and Samuel said, "See, what was kept is set before you. Eat; because it was kept for you until the hour appointed, that you might eat with the guests."

So Saul ate with Samuel that day. ²⁵ And when they came down from the high place into the city, a bed was spread for Saul upon the roof, and he lay down to sleep. ²⁶ Then at the break of dawn Samuel called to Saul upon the roof, "Up, that I may send you on your way." So Saul arose, and both he and Samuel went out into the street.

²⁷ As they were going down to the outskirts of the city, Samuel said to Saul, "Tell the servant to pass on before us, and when he has passed on stop here yourself for a while, that I may make known to you the word of God."

This episode, unlike chapters 8 and 12, depicts the monarchy in a favorable light, and all characters appear charitably disposed toward the new institution. The Lord prepared Samuel for Saul's arrival by announcing in advance that the young man from Benjamin was to be Israel's future *prince* [20] (vv. 15–16). By his action God was providing leadership for his people that they might be delivered from their Philistine overlords. Saul acted with commendable modesty when Samuel informed him of his (future) ownership of Israel's wealth (v. 20*b*). Even Samuel appears free of hostility as he made Saul his honored guest in a special feast (vv. 22–24) and gave him the coolest place to sleep (vv. 25–26).

(4) *Samuel Anoints Saul (10:1–16)*

¹ Then Samuel took a vial of oil and poured it on his head, and kissed him and said, "Has not the LORD anointed you to be prince over his people Israel? And you shall reign over the people of the LORD and you will save them from the hand of their enemies round about. And this shall be the sign to you that the LORD has anointed you to be prince over his heritage. ² When you depart from me today you will meet two men by Rachel's tomb in the territory of Benjamin at Zelzah, and they will say to you, 'The asses which you went to seek are found, and now your father has ceased to care about the asses and is anxious about you, saying, "What shall I do about my son?"' ³ Then you shall go on from there further and come to the oak of Tabor; three men going up to God at Bethel will meet you there, one carrying three kids, another carrying three loaves of bread, and another carrying a skin of wine. ⁴ And they will greet you and give you two loaves of bread, which you shall accept from their hand. ⁵ After that you shall come to Gibeathelohim, where there is a garrison of the Philistines; and there, as you come to the city, you will meet a band of prophets coming down from the high place with harp, tambourine, flute, and lyre before them, prophesying. ⁶ Then the spirit of the LORD will come mightily upon you, and you shall prophesy with them and be turned into another man. ⁷ Now when these signs meet you, do whatever your hand finds to do, for God is with you. ⁸ And you shall go down before me to Gilgal; and behold, I am coming to you to offer burnt offerings and to sacrifice peace offerings. Seven days you shall wait, until I come to you and show you what you shall do."
⁹ When he turned his back to leave Samuel, God gave him another heart; and all these signs came to pass that day. ¹⁰ When they came to Gibeah, behold, a band of prophets met him; and the spirit of God came mightily upon him, and he prophesied among them. ¹¹ And when all who knew him before saw how he prophesied with the prophets, the people said to one another, "What has come over the son of Kish? Is Saul also among the prophets?" ¹² And a man of the place answered, "And who is their father?" Therefore it became a proverb, "Is Saul also among the prophets?" ¹³ When he had finished prophesying, he came to the high place.
¹⁴ Saul's uncle said to him and to his servant, "Where did you go?" And he said, "To seek the asses; and when we saw they were not to be found, we went to Samuel." ¹⁵ And Saul's uncle said, "Pray, tell me what Samuel said to you." ¹⁶ And Saul said to his uncle, "He told us plainly that the asses had been found." But about the matter of the kingdom, of which Samuel had spoken, he did not tell him anything.

As a sign of the Lord's selection, Samuel anointed Saul's head with oil. By this act, common in Israel and among her neighbors, either men or objects could be set apart for special religious functions. Thus, the stone at Bethel (Gen. 28:18), the ark (Ex. 30:26), priests (Ex. 28:41), prophets (1 Kings 19:16), as well as kings were consecrated for divine service.

Saul's anointment seems to represent outward recognition of a divinely appointed role rather than a sacramental act which conveyed special blessings to the new king. Indeed, Saul would later be rejected by God and would be afflicted with an evil spirit (16:14), but he would be recognized as "the Lord's anointed" until his death (2 Sam. 1:16). God's gift of a new heart does not necessarily imply a spiritual experience of the type found in the New Testament. Rather it denotes the strength of personality which was characteristic of a man of God.

To give Saul some external confirmation of the Lord's role in his selection, Samuel gave a threefold sign which could soon be

---

[20] The use of this term (*nagid*) is restricted primarily to Samuel, Kings, and the portions of Chronicles dependent on these two books. It is used mostly of the divinely appointed heir to a position of leadership. Its use reinforces the context's stress on the Lord's role in Saul's selection.

verified. First, Saul would encounter two travelers who would relate the recovery of his lost asses and his father's concern for him. Second, he and his servant would be given food for their homeward journey (cf. 9:7) by men going up to sacrifice at Bethel. And third, Saul would be overwhelmed by the spirit of the Lord when he encountered a band of prophets on his homeward journey.

Saul's contact with the prophets at Gibeathelohim makes an important contribution to the understanding of prophetism in early Israel. Although it would be unwise to conclude that all prophets functioned as a group, some bands of considerable size were common (19:20; 1 Kings 22:6; 2 Kings 4:43). Prophesying occurred with musical accompaniment (10:5; 2 Kings 3:15), and involuntary seizures were not considered unusual (19:18 ff.).

Such occurrences seem remarkably similar to practices among Canaanite prophets. In Elijah's time, for example, worshipers of Baal worked themselves into a frenzy, dancing, shouting, and even lacerating their bodies (1 Kings 18:26–29). While early Hebrew prophets may have shared some psychological manifestations with their heathen neighbors, such external similarities do not necessarily indicate internal likenesses. In marked contrast with the gross immorality and licentiousness of nearby pagan religions, Samuel stands in a long line of Hebrew prophets who steadfastly opposed such practices.

When Saul surrendered to the spirit of the Lord and began to prophesy (cf. vv. 6,16), his neighbors noted his behavior and began to ask, *Is Saul also among the prophets?* This saying was oft repeated and became a proverb with an implied social stigma. The people expressed amazement that Saul would risk the debasement of his family name and his high calling by participating in the prophets' eccentric behavior (cf. 19:24).

A local man countered with another question, *And who is their father?* Although the interpretation of this expression is uncertain, it is probably best understood as a positive assessment of the prophetic role. He is saying that Saul is not just one of the prophets; he is either their leader or patron as well.[21]

In spite of the dramatic fulfillment of Samuel's predicted signs, Saul kept his royal anointment secret even from his own family.

(5) *Saul Publicly Designated King (10:17–27)*

[17] Now Samuel called the people together to the Lord at Mizpah; [18] and he said to the people of Israel, "Thus says the Lord, the God of Israel, 'I brought up Israel out of Egypt, and I delivered you from the hand of the Egyptians and from the hand of all the kingdoms that were oppressing you.' [19] But you have this day rejected your God, who saves you from all your calamities and your distresses; and you have said, 'No! but set a king over us.' Now therefore present yourselves before the Lord by your tribes and by your thousands."
[20] Then Samuel brought all the tribes of Israel near, and the tribe of Benjamin was taken by lot. [21] He brought the tribe of Benjamin near by its families, and the family of the Matrites was taken by lot; finally he brought the family of the Matrites near man by man, and Saul the son of Kish was taken by lot. But when they sought him, he could not be found. [22] So they inquired again of the Lord, "Did the man come hither?" and the Lord said, "Behold, he has hidden himself among the baggage." [23] Then they ran and fetched him from there; and when he stood among the people, he was taller than any of the people from his shoulders upward. [24] And Samuel said to all the people, "Do you see him whom the Lord has chosen? There is none like him among all the people." And all the people shouted, "Long live the king!"
[25] Then Samuel told the people the rights and duties of the kingship; and he wrote them in a book and laid it up before the Lord. Then Samuel sent all the people away, each one to his home. [26] Saul also went to his home at Gibeah, and with him went men of valor whose hearts God had touched. [27] But some worthless fellows said, "How can this man save us?" And they despised him, and brought him no present. But he held his peace.

[21] The Hebrew word for 'father,' *'ab*, is frequently used as a term of respect and honor (2 Kings 2:12; 5:13; 6:21).

This passage resumes the story of the selection of Israel's king at the point where it was left in 8:22. Saul is portrayed as a superb example of Hebrew manhood, but his role as prince (*nagid*) goes unnoticed. Samuel mustered the people at Mizpah and supervised the casting of the lots as if Saul were unknown to him. Although Samuel as a seer could perhaps have anticipated Saul's choice by lot, the "search episodes" (9:1—10:16) make no effort to foreshadow his public selection, and this section takes no notice of Saul's anointment by Samuel.

As in chapter 8, the present passage as a whole indicates opposition to the establishment of the monarchy. The people's request for a king was again condemned as a rejection of the Lord's leadership. In spite of God's care during the exodus from Egypt and the conquest of Canaan, Israel refused to trust him during their current crisis. Nevertheless, the Lord continued to work in the best interests of his people as he guided in the selection of Saul of whom it could be said, *There is none like him among all the people.*

Wonder and awe at this demonstration of the divine will was heightened by the fact that at first Saul was not to be found among the people. Only after further inquiries of the Lord was he located in the baggage train. The divine lots were designed to give yes or no answers rather than vocal statements of fact such as that found in 10:22 (cf. 14:41–42). Nevertheless, a sequence of questions could easily have been devised which would have given the substance of that response.

Samuel persisted in his efforts to preserve some of the freedoms of the old tribal league as he codified the rights and duties of the kingship and enshrined them *before the Lord.* One such body of "constitutional safeguards" is reflected in Deuteronomy 17:14–20 (McKane, p. 79). Although these restraints were largely ineffective after Saul's reign, some members of Israel's society probably worked to keep the ancient ideals alive. Certainly within the Northern Kingdom the strength of the monarchy was continually limited by the political activities of the prophets.

From the very beginning of Saul's reign, the people of Israel were divided in their support of his rule. While all shouted, *Long live the king,* and some men *whose hearts God had touched* enthusiastically followed Saul all the way home, others asked, *How can this man save us?* They showed their contempt for the new ruler by withholding their gifts which were customary on such occasions.

The label *worthless fellows* attached to Saul's opponents reflects a favorable attitude toward the monarchy similar to that found in 9:1—10:16 and at variance with that in 10:17–25. Clearly the final author of the book of Samuel was dealing very conscientiously with the sources at his disposal whatever his own sentiments may have been.

3. Saul Wins Public Support (11:1–15)

(1) *Ammonites Attack Jabesh (11:1–4)*

¹ **Then Nahash the Ammonite went up and besieged Jabeshgilead; and all the men of Jabesh said to Nahash, "Make a treaty with us, and we will serve you." ² But Nahash the Ammonite said to them, "On this condition I will make a treaty with you, that I gouge out all your right eyes, and thus put disgrace upon all Israel." ³ The elders of Jabesh said to him, "Give us seven days respite that we may send messengers through all the territory of Israel. Then, if there is no one to save us, we will give ourselves up to you." ⁴ When the messengers came to Gibeah of Saul, they reported the matter in the ears of the people; and all the people wept aloud.**

Israel's dire straits at the end of the period of the judges is clearly demonstrated by the Ammonites' contempt for the people of Jabeshgilead. The Ammonites were a band of Semitic nomads whose territory lay in the highland plateau east of the Jordan River. Although distantly related to the Israelites (Gen. 19:38), they periodically raided their more settled neighbors and attempted to extend their holdings at Israelite expense (Judg. 11). The Ammonite attack on Jabeshgilead, a city on the Wadi Yabis probably not more than two or three miles from the Jordan, indicates the low ebb of Hebrew strength. Unable to envision any relief, the people of Jabesh offered to pay tribute and to become vassals of the Ammonites.

Nahash, king of Ammon, however, was bent on humiliating Israel as well as on taking her spoils. His conditions for surrender, calling for the mutilation of the entire captive population, were designed as a reproach on all Israelites for their inability to rescue one of their sister cities. Nahash's willingness to grant a seven-day armistice further demonstrates his assurance of ultimate victory. He was convinced that Israel was too weak to provide any effective relief for Jabesh, even if allowed time to do so.

(2) Saul Defeats the Ammonites (11:5–11)

5 Now Saul was coming from the field behind the oxen; and Saul said, "What ails the people, that they are weeping?" So they told him the tidings of the men of Jabesh. 6 And the spirit of God came mightily upon Saul when he heard these words, and his anger was greatly kindled. 7 He took a yoke of oxen, and cut them in pieces and sent them throughout all the territory of Israel by the hand of messengers, saying, "Whoever does not come out after Saul and Samuel, so shall it be done to his oxen!" Then the dread of the LORD fell upon the people, and they came out as one man. 8 When he mustered them at Bezek, the men of Israel were three hundred thousand, and the men of Judah thirty thousand. 9 And they said to the messengers who had come, "Thus shall you say to the men of Jabeshgilead: 'Tomorrow, by the time the sun is hot, you shall have deliverance.'" When the messengers came and told the men of Jabesh, they were glad. 10 Therefore the men of Jabesh said, "Tomorrow we will give ourselves up to you, and you may do to us whatever seems good to you." 11 And on the morrow Saul put the people in three companies; and they came into the midst of the camp in the morning watch, and cut down the Ammonites until the heat of the day; and those who survived were scattered, so that no two of them were left together.

The conditions described here make it rather clear that Saul had not yet made any effort to organize a formal government. The people of Jabesh still followed customs of the tribal league and sent messengers "through all the territory of Israel" (11:3). Saul was plowing in the field rather than attending to affairs of state, and the news from beyond Jordan was announced to the public before it was taken to the new king.

Saul's reaction was in keeping with the dynamic patterns established under the militaristic judges of the past. The spirit of God came mightily upon Saul (cf. Samson in Judg. 14:19), and he took immediate action to insure Israel's unity in this crisis. He slaughtered the oxen with which he had been plowing, dismembered their carcasses, and sent a portion to each tribe of Israel. Saul's violent actions gave added weight to the grim warning of the messengers: *"Whoever does not come out after Saul and Samuel, so shall it be done to his oxen"* (cf. Judg. 19:29). In the muster which followed, the separate enumeration of the men from Israel and Judah reveals the fragile nature of the unity imposed by the strength of Saul's personality. Nevertheless, one of the major shortcomings of the old tribal league had been remedied. The tribes were compelled to honor their commitment to send troops in time of military crisis.

Accounts of the battle are almost anticlimatic. Saul mustered a sizeable army [22] at Bezek, about 12 miles northeast of Shechem, and sent word to Jabeshgilead that relief would arrive the next day. After an overnight march of about 15 miles, Saul and his troops arrived at first light,[23] and

---

[22] The Hebrew word for "thousand" (*'eleph*) has a double meaning. In addition to its strict numerical significance, it can also refer to the subunit of a tribe from which the tribal muster was drawn (cf. Judg. 6:15). The ratio of about ten to one of Israel over Judah is roughly in keeping with other tribal enumerations. See G. E. Mendenhall, "The Census Lists of Numbers 1 and 26," *Journal of Biblical Literature*, LXXVII (1958), 52–66.

[23] Since the Hebrew day began at sunset, "on the morrow" refers to the evening of the day on which the message was sent. The night was divided into three sections: the head of the watches (Lam. 2:19), the middle watch (Judg. 7:19), and the morning watch (Caird, p. 940).

1 SAMUEL 12

the slaughter began. The Ammonites who were not killed were hopelessly scattered, and Israel's eastern flank was secure.

(3) People Proclaim Saul King (11:12–15)

12 Then the people said to Samuel, "Who is it that said, 'Shall Saul reign over us?' Bring the men, that we may put them to death." 13 But Saul said, "Not a man shall be put to death this day, for today the LORD has wrought deliverance in Israel." 14 Then Samuel said to the people, "Come, let us go to Gilgal and there renew the kingdom." 15 So all the people went to Gilgal, and there they made Saul king before the LORD in Gilgal. There they sacrificed peace offerings before the LORD, and there Saul and all the men of Israel rejoiced greatly.

Even with public (10:17–27) and private (9:1—10:16) manifestations of divine guidance in the establishment of the monarchy, Saul encountered stiff resistance (10:27). He chose to move slowly, therefore, and to await an opportunity to demonstrate the Lord's support of his cause (10:7). Saul's role in the decisive victory over Nahash won the support of a majority of the population. Soon the people were calling for the blood of those who still opposed the new government.

The stability of Saul's personality in the early years of his reign is clearly portrayed in his lenient treatment of those who had campaigned against him. Saul recognized that many of his adversaries fought him because they believed that their nation was rejecting the Lord's leadership in its request for a king. Loyalty from subjects such as these could not be forced, but it could be won. Saul struck right to the heart of the issue when he turned aside all personal acclaim with the simple words, *today the Lord has wrought deliverance in Israel.*

As the record now stands, Samuel's injunction for the people to go to Gilgal to *renew* the kingdom is not altogether clear. If the divine plan is just coming into complete fruition, then we would expect the kingdom to be established rather than renewed. On the other hand, opposition to the monarchy may have been so strong that Saul's early attempts to set up a government had met with defeat. Under these circumstances the kingdom would need to be renewed, but present records give no evidence of such a drastic rejection of Saul's leadership.

4. Samuel Counsels the Monarchy (12:1–25)

(1) Samuel Defends His Record (12:1–5)

1 And Samuel said to all Israel, "Behold, I have hearkened to your voice in all that you have said to me, and have made a king over you. 2 And now, behold, the king walks before you; and I am old and gray, and behold, my sons are with you; and I have walked before you from my youth until this day. 3 Here I am; testify against me before the LORD and before his anointed. Whose ox have I taken? Or whose ass have I taken? Or whom have I defrauded? Whom have I oppressed? Or from whose hand have I taken a bribe to blind my eyes with it? Testify against me and I will restore it to you." 4 They said, "You have not defrauded us or oppressed us or taken anything from any man's hand." 5 And he said to them, "The LORD is witness against you, and his anointed is witness this day, that you have not found anything in my hand." And they said, "He is witness."

This chapter is usually regarded as Samuel's farewell address to Israel, comparable in scope to that of Moses (especially Deut. 28 ff.) or Joshua (Josh. 24). If such is the case, however, the speech appears out of place in its present context. A summary of Samuel's ministry has been previously introduced (7:12–17) when he was at the height of his power before Saul began his rise to power (cf. Introduction, V, 1). On the other hand, Samuel's active ministry is not yet over, for he is yet to play a pivotal role in Saul's rejection and David's anointment before his death is recorded in 1 Samuel 25.

It appears likely, therefore, that Samuel's speech is to be construed as a major policy statement rather than as his farewell address. Up to this point, Saul's rise to power as king of Israel has been complicated by debate over the theological implications of a monarchic system within the Israelite state. Although both sides of the issue are reflected in the biblical record, the author's viewpoint has never been in question. He regarded the theocratic system under the old tribal league as Israel's legitimate political structure. The monarchy at best represented God's concession to the hardness of his people's hearts.

Nevertheless, after Saul's victory over the Ammonites, the monarchy became an established fact. Kings and dynasties could be changed, but the institution itself was no longer open to serious question. Samuel's speech, therefore, summarizes the theological principles upon which God will deal with his people under the new system of government.

Samuel began his address with a defense of his own ministry as a judge. The people agreed that as a jurist he was above reproach. He had not robbed anyone, taken bribes, or perverted justice. Even his sons, who previously were the source of considerable embarrassment for him (8:1–5), are noted here without reproach. By his defense Samuel sought to exonerate not only himself but also the whole theocratic system under the judges.

(2) Israel's Rebellion Recorded (12:6–18)

6 And Samuel said to the people, "The LORD is witness, who appointed Moses and Aaron and brought your fathers up out of the land of Egypt. 7 Now therefore stand still, that I may plead with you before the LORD concerning all the saving deeds of the LORD which he performed for you and for your fathers. 8 When Jacob went into Egypt and the Egyptians oppressed them, then your fathers cried to the LORD and the LORD sent Moses and Aaron, who brought forth your fathers out of Egypt, and made them dwell in this place. 9 But they forgot the LORD their God; and he sold them into the hand of Sisera, commander of the army of Jabin king of Hazor, and into the hand of the Philistines, and into the hand of the king of Moab; and they fought against them. 10 And they cried to the LORD, and said, 'We have sinned, because we have forsaken the LORD, and have served the Baals and the Ashtaroth; but now deliver us out of the hand of our enemies, and we will serve thee.' 11 And the LORD sent Jerubbaal and Barak, and Jephthah, and Samuel, and delivered you out of the hand of your enemies on every side; and you dwelt in safety. 12 And when you saw that Nahash the king of the Ammonites came against you, you said to me, 'No, but a king shall reign over us,' when the LORD your God was your king. 13 And now behold the king whom you have chosen, for whom you have asked; behold, the LORD has set a king over you. 14 If you will fear the LORD and serve him and hearken to his voice and not rebel against the commandment of the LORD, and if both you and the king who reigns over you will follow the LORD your God, it will be well; 15 but if you will not hearken to the voice of the LORD, but rebel against the commandment of the LORD, then the hand of the LORD will be against you and your king. 16 Now therefore stand still and see this great thing, which the LORD will do before your eyes. 17 Is it not wheat harvest today? I will call upon the LORD, that he may send thunder and rain; and you shall know and see that your wickedness is great, which you have done in the sight of the LORD, in asking for yourselves a king." 18 So Samuel called upon the LORD, and the LORD sent thunder and rain that day; and all the people greatly feared the LORD and Samuel.

Samuel had defended himself as an administrator of Israel's legal system, but he had made no claims as a military leader after the fashion of Gideon or Samson. This led Samuel to what was perhaps the most serious indictment of the old tribal league: it had been unable to unite the nation and, as a result, Israel was left at the mercy of her foes.

Such a charge against the provenance of God (cf. v. 12), however, was seen to be a misunderstanding of the principles upon which the Lord based his involvement in human history. Samuel recounted the highlights of Israelite history to demonstrate afresh God's plan for dealing with his people. In the same basic pattern as that encountered in Joshua and Judges, Samuel showed that Israel was delivered unto a foreign oppressor when the people sinned. When they repented, however, the Lord was faithful and soon sent his chosen deliverers: Jerubbabel, Barak, Jephthah, and even Samuel himself. Thus, the crisis precipitated by Nahash's attack on Jabesh-gilead should have prompted Israel to repent of her sins. Instead the people asked for a king. As further evidence that their actions constituted a rebellion against God's leadership, Samuel called for an unseasonable thunder storm in the harvest season. The people acknowledged their guilt and stood in awe of the Lord and of Samuel.

However wrong Israel may have been in asking for a king, the Lord granted them freedom to establish a monarchy. Through his prophet Samuel, he pledged to work through the new head of state as he had through the judges of old. If the people would respond to the Lord's leadership, all would be well. If not, then he would punish both the people and the king.

(3) Samuel Pledges Prayers (12:19-25)

19 And all the people said to Samuel, "Pray for your servants to the Lord your God, that we may not die; for we have added to all our sins this evil, to ask for ourselves a king." 20 And Samuel said to the people, "Fear not; you have done all this evil, yet do not turn aside from following the Lord, but serve the Lord with all your heart; 21 and do not turn aside after vain things which cannot profit or save, for they are vain. 22 For the Lord will not cast away his people, for his great name's sake, because it has pleased the Lord to make you a people for himself. 23 Moreover as for me, far be it from me that I should sin against the Lord by ceasing to pray for you; and I will instruct you in the good and the right way. 24 Only fear the Lord, and serve him faithfully with all your heart; for consider what great things he has done for you. 25 But if you still do wickedly, you shall be swept away, both you and your king."

The people of Israel feared that their independence in asking for a king would result in their final rejection by the Lord. Samuel assured them that only their own continued rebellion could separate them from God's care. Because of *his great name's sake*, i.e., simply because the Lord is who he is, he will not cast his people away arbitrarily. God freely chose to open himself for a special fellowship with Israel. The people could cut themselves off by pursuing *vain things which cannot profit or save*, but the way would ever be open for them to return unto the Lord.

Also, the people feared that Samuel would withdraw as their spiritual advisor since they had rejected his counsel about the kingship. He promised, however, to continue as their intercessor in prayer and as their guide in *the good and the right way*. A lesser man might have become bitter and thus brought about his own rejection as an instrument of God's grace.

5. Israel Wins Independence (13:1— 14:52)

(1) War of Liberation Begun (13:1-15a)

1 Saul was . . . years old when he began to reign; and he reigned . . . and two years over Israel. 2 Saul chose three thousand men of Israel; two thousand were with Saul in Michmash and the hill country of Bethel, and a thousand were with Jonathan in Gibeah of Benjamin; the rest of the people he sent home, every man to his tent. 3 Jonathan defeated the garrison of the Philistines which was at Geba; and the Philistines heard of it. And Saul blew the trumpet throughout all the land, saying, "Let the Hebrews hear." 4 And all Israel heard it said that Saul had defeated the garrison of the Philistines, and also that Israel had become odious to the Philistines. And the people were called out to join Saul at Gilgal.

5 And the Philistines mustered to fight with Israel, thirty thousand chariots, and six thousand horsemen, and troops like the sand on the seashore in multitude; they came up and encamped in Michmash, to the east of Bethaven. 6 When the men of Israel saw that they were in straits (for the people were hard pressed), the people hid themselves in caves and in holes and in rocks and in tombs and in cisterns, 7 or crossed the fords of the Jordan to the land of Gad and Gilead. Saul was still at Gilgal, and all the people followed him trembling.

8 He waited seven days, the time appointed by Samuel; but Samuel did not come to Gilgal, and the people were scattering from him. 9 So Saul said, "Bring the burnt offering here to me, and the peace offerings." And he offered the burnt offering. 10 As soon as he had finished offering the burnt offering, behold, Samuel came; and Saul went out to meet him and salute him. 11 Samuel said, "What have you done?" And Saul said, "When I saw that the people were scattering from me, and that you did not come within the days appointed, and that the Philistines had mustered at Michmash, 12 I said, 'Now the Philistines will come down upon me at Gilgal, and I have not entreated the favor of the Lord'; so I forced myself, and offered the burnt offering." 13 And Samuel said to Saul, "You have done foolishly; you have not kept the commandment of the Lord your God, which he commanded you; for now the Lord would have established your kingdom

over Israel for ever. **14 But now your kingdom shall not continue; the Lord has sought out a man after his own heart; and the Lord has appointed him to be prince over his people, because you have not kept what the Lord commanded you." 15 And Samuel arose, and went up from Gilgal to Gibeah of Benjamin.**

Many of the details of Israel's war of independence are vague and uncertain, but two facts stand out quite clearly. From the very beginning of Saul's proper reign over Israel, he faced two major conflicts: one against his Philistine overlords, and the other against Samuel, the man of God. The first would eventually cost Saul his life, and the latter would contribute even sooner to the loss of his mental stability. The details of these two struggles are no longer precisely known but their broad outlines can be discerned without difficulty.

Saul was . . . years old. This type of introductory formula, common in Kings, is used here in recognition of the fact that Saul's reign properly begins at this point. It is unusual, however, in that both the king's age and the length of his reign are missing from the Hebrew text. The number "two" does remain in regard to his reign but in such a form that it appears that another number has been omitted. The reference in Acts 13:21 to a 40-year reign of Saul reflects an early tradition, but it rests on no known Old Testament foundation.

Israel was in dire straits when Saul took office. The people were so hard pressed by the Philistines in the west that the trans-Jordan territories could be terrorized by the nomadic Ammonites (11:1–11). The Philistines controlled Palestine with local garrisons such as the one at Geba, less than seven miles north-northeast of Jerusalem, but they had complete freedom of movement throughout the country. The Philistines used Michmash as their own base shortly after it was used as an Israelite camp. Even more important was the Philistines' complete arms embargo on the territory occupied by Israel. Iron weapons had only recently come into use in the ancient Near East, and the Philistines maintained control of the secrets of blacksmithing (13:19 f.). Thus Saul's early battles were largely hit-and-run guerrilla raids carried out by poorly equipped civilian soldiers.

Israel's first victory in her war of independence was accomplished not by Saul but by Jonathan, who was only later identified as the king's son (13:16). As the commander of a thousand men, he overthrew the small garrison at Geba and by this act enraged the Philistines and enflamed the hearts of his countrymen for freedom. When an enormous army was sent to quell the insurrection, his troops dispersed to seek refuge in the rugged terrain nearby.

In the meantime, Saul was mustering a larger force at Gilgal. Confronted by the vastly superior Philistine army, his own position was extremely precarious. The morale of the civilian soldiers under his command was steadily deteriorating as reports of Philistine countermeasures came in. Desertions continually mounted, and even those troops which remained would be unwilling to engage in battle until the proper religious rites of preparation had been performed (Deut. 20:1–20; 23; cf. 1 Sam. 21:4–5). After waiting for Samuel the prescribed seven days (1 Sam. 10:8), Saul took matters into his own hands by offering the preparatory sacrifices. When Samuel finally arrived in camp, he indicated that Saul would be rejected as king for his presumptuous action.

Clearly serious conflicts existed between Samuel and Saul from the very earliest days of the monarchy, the actual reasons for their differences are not clear. Samuel simply said that Saul had *not kept the commandment of the Lord.* Saul's transgression has been customarily interpreted as a violation of the priestly role in offering sacrifice (Lev. 14:20). On the other hand, other non-Levites are known to have offered sacrifice without incurring divine wrath (Judg. 6:25–26; 1 Sam. 13:9; 1 Kings 18:30 f.).

Perhaps Saul had violated agreements made in his early contacts with Samuel. "Seven days you shall wait, until I come to you and show you what you shall do"

(10:8). Perhaps Samuel suspected the king of an undue willingness to dispense with divine counsel now that the throne was actually his. Quite possibly he feared that the combination of civil and religious authority would eventually lead to a situation in which religious practice would be considered as simply another affair of state. Whatever the motivating factors may have been, the author of this material was firmly convinced that the breach of fellowship between the king and his religious counselor occurred very early in Saul's reign.

(2) *Conditions of War Described (13:15b–23)*

And Saul numbered the people who were present with him, about six hundred men. 16 And Saul, and Jonathan his son, and the people who were present with them, stayed in Geba of Benjamin; but the Philistines encamped in Michmash. 17 And raiders came out of the camp of the Philistines in three companies; one company turned toward Ophrah, to the land of Shual, 18 another company turned toward Bethhoron, and another company turned toward the border that looks down upon the valley of Zeboim toward the wilderness.
19 Now there was no smith to be found throughout all the land of Israel; for the Philistines said, "Lest the Hebrews make themselves swords or spears"; 20 but every one of the Israelites went down to the Philistines to sharpen his plowshare, his mattock, his axe, or his sickle; 21 and the charge was a pim for the plowshares and for the mattocks, and a third of a shekel for sharpening the axes and for setting the goads. 22 So on the day of the battle there was neither sword nor spear found in the hand of any of the people with Saul and Jonathan; but Saul and Jonathan his son had them. 23 And the garrison of the Philistines went out to the pass of Michmash.

The grim conditions which faced the struggling Israelite monarchy are briefly summarized. Saul, with only 600 of his original 3,000 troops left, moved from Gilgal to Geba, a natural fortress just across from the Philistine outpost at Michmash. With their superior forces, the Philistines sent out raiding parties to devastate the territories from which the Israelite guerrillas needed to draw supplies. Saul was only able to keep his enemies from penetrating the country to the south where his greatest strength lay. Even there, however, his followers were at a distinct disadvantage because of the strict Philistine control over the manufacture of iron tools and weapons. The Israelites, however, were expert in the art of guerrilla warfare.

(3) *Israel Wins Victory (14:1–23)*

1 One day Jonathan the son of Saul said to the young man who bore his armor, "Come, let us go over to the Philistine garrison on yonder side." But he did not tell his father. 2 Saul was staying in the outskirts of Gibeah under the pomegranate tree which is at Migron; the people who were with him were about six hundred men, 3 and Ahijah the son of Ahitub, Ichabod's brother, son of Phinehas, son of Eli, the priest of the Lord in Shiloh, wearing an ephod. And the people did not know that Jonathan had gone. 4 In the pass, by which Jonathan sought to go over to the Philistine garrison, there was a rocky crag on the one side and a rocky crag on the other side; the name of the one was Bozez, and the name of the other Seneh. 5 The one crag rose on the north in front of Michmash, and the other on the south in front of Geba.
6 And Jonathan said to the young man who bore his armor, "Come, let us go over to the garrison of these uncircumcised; it may be that the Lord will work for us; for nothing can hinder the Lord from saving by many or by few." 7 And his armor-bearer said to him, "Do all that your mind inclines to; behold, I am with you, as is your mind so is mine." 8 Then said Jonathan, "Behold, we will cross over to the men, and we will show ourselves to them. 9 If they say to us, 'Wait until we come to you,' then we will stand still in our place, and we will not go up to them. 10 But if they say, 'Come up to us,' then we will go up; for the Lord has given them into our hand. And this shall be the sign to us." 11 So both of them showed themselves to the garrison of the Philistines; and the Philistines said, "Look, Hebrews are coming out of the holes where they have hid themselves." 12 And the men of the garrison hailed Jonathan and his armor-bearer, and said, "Come up to us, and we will show you a thing." And Jonathan said to his armor-bearer, "Come up after me; for the Lord has given them into the hand of Israel." 13 Then Jonathan climbed up on his hands and feet, and his armor-bearer after him. And they fell before Jonathan, and his armor-bearer killed them after him; 14 and that first slaughter, which Jonathan and his armor-bearer made, was of about twenty men within as it were half a furrow's length in an acre of land. 15 And there

was a panic in the camp, in the field, and among all the people; the garrison and even the raiders trembled; the earth quaked; and it became a very great panic. ¹⁶ **And the watchmen of Saul in Gibeah of Benjamin looked;** and behold, the multitude was surging hither and thither. ¹⁷ Then Saul said to the people who were with him, "Number and see who has gone from us." And when they had numbered, behold, Jonathan and his armor-bearer were not there. ¹⁸ And Saul said to Ahijah, "Bring hither the ark of God." For the ark of God went at that time with the people of Israel. ¹⁹ And while Saul was talking to the priest, the tumult in the camp of the Philistines increased more and more; and Saul said to the priest, "Withdraw your hand." ²⁰ Then Saul and all the people who were with him rallied and went into the battle; and behold, every man's sword was against his fellow, and there was very great confusion. ²¹ Now the **Hebrews who had been** with the Philistines before that time and who had gone up with them into the camp, even they also turned to be with the Israelites who were with Saul and Jonathan. ²² Likewise, when all the men of Israel who had hid themselves in the hill country of Ephraim heard that the Philistines were fleeing, they too followed hard after them in the battle. ²³ So the Lord delivered Israel that day; and the battle passed beyond Bethaven.

Guerrilla warfare today differs from that of the ancient Near East in one major respect. In the absence of explosives and other more recent armaments, small forces could successfully defend walled citadels on well-situated sites with relative ease. Thus a stalemate was reached with a Philistine garrison at Michmash, Jonathan with a small contingent at Geba, and Saul with about 600 Israelites at the nearby site of Migron. Michmash and Geba are located about two miles apart on opposite sides of a steep rocky ravine called Wadi Suweinit. The Philistines, again the stronger force, were able to establish an outpost out in the gorge itself (13:23).

Jonathan saw in this outpost a situation which could be turned to Israel's advantage. Its precipitous surroundings prevented its capture by a sizeable force, but its lack of fortification opened the possibility that it could be taken by surprise. Responding to a divine sign (v. 9–10), Jonathan was invited to advance by the Philistines who were deceived by his open approach and by the presence of only two men. After clambering up the face of the ridge, Jonathan and his armor-bearer fell upon the defenders so suddenly that the Philistines had no opportunity to exploit their numerical superiority within the confines of their hilltop camp. Soon twenty men were dead, and Israel had passed another milestone in her journey toward freedom.

Two special factors in this story are worthy of note at this point. First, Jonathan, not Saul, won the first two dramatic victories in Israel's war of liberation. This knowledge may well have provided a point of attack for those who opposed Saul's reign on other grounds. Second, in keeping with the theology of the old tribal league, Jonathan gave the Lord complete credit for his entire maneuver. As he remarked, *nothing can hinder the Lord from saving by many or by few*. The sudden flurry of activity caused by Jonathan's attack threw the entire Philistine force into confusion. Word of the rout eventually reached the raiders who were likewise staggered by this sudden reversal of Philistine fortunes. Truly this was a "world-shaking" turn of events.

While Jonathan's initial attack was still under way, watchmen in Saul's camp perceived the confusion of battle and brought the news to their leader. A quick survey of his troops revealed that thus far only Jonathan and his armor-bearer were involved in the skirmish. Saul now had to decide on the disposition of his major force in this encounter. At first he sought divine counsel on the matter. The Hebrew text notes the presence of the ark of God while early Greek translations refer to the ephod of Ahijah. Either is possible since both the ark (Judg. 20:27; cf. 1 Kings 2:26) and the ephod (1 Sam. 23:9–12; 30:7–8) were associated with the Urim and Thummim which were used to ascertain the will of the Lord (Ex. 28:30). In any case, Saul interrupted the priest whose hand was already extended in quest of the divine lot. The rising din of the fighting prompted

Saul on his own initiative to engage the Philistines with his entire force. The battle swiftly gained momentum, and soon even Philistine sympathizers and early deserters were drawn back into the Israelite cause.

(4) *Victory Sweep Halted* (14:24–46)

24 And the men of Israel were distressed that day; for Saul laid an oath on the people, saying, "Cursed be the man who eats food until it is evening and I am avenged on my enemies." So none of the people tasted food. 25 And all the people came into the forest; and there was honey on the ground. 26 And when the people entered the forest, behold, the honey was dropping, but no man put his hand to his mouth; for the people feared the oath. 27 But Jonathan had not heard his father charge the people with the oath; so he put forth the tip of the staff that was in his hand, and dipped it in the honeycomb, and put his hand to his mouth; and his eyes became bright. 28 Then one of the people said, "Your father strictly charged the people with an oath, saying, 'Cursed be the man who eats food this day.'" And the people were faint. 29 Then Jonathan said, "My father has troubled the land; see how my eyes have become bright, because I tasted a little of this honey. 30 How much better if the people had eaten freely today of the spoil of their enemies which they found; for now the slaughter among the Philistines has not been great."

31 They struck down the Philistines that day from Michmash to Aijalon. And the people were very faint; 32 the people flew upon the spoil, and took sheep and oxen and calves, and slew them on the ground; and the people ate them with the blood. 33 Then they told Saul, "Behold, the people are sinning against the LORD, by eating with the blood." And he said, "You have dealt treacherously; roll a great stone to me here." 34 And Saul said, "Disperse yourselves among the people, and say to them, 'Let every man bring his ox or his sheep, and slay them here, and eat; and do not sin against the LORD by eating with the blood.'" So every one of the people brought his ox with him that night, and slew them there. 35 And Saul built an altar to the LORD; it was the first altar that he built to the LORD.

36 Then Saul said, "Let us go down after the Philistines by night and despoil them until the morning light; let us not leave a man of them." And they said, "Do whatever seems good to you." But the priest said, "Let us draw near hither to God." 37 And Saul inquired of God, "Shall I go down after the Philistines? Wilt thou give them into the hand of Israel?" But he did not answer him that day. 38 And Saul said, "Come hither, all you leaders of the people; and know and see how this sin has arisen today. 39 For as the LORD lives who saves Israel, though it be in Jonathan my son, he shall surely die." But there was not a man among all the people that answered him. 40 Then he said to all Israel, "You shall be on one side, and I and Jonathan my son will be on the other side." And the people said to Saul, "Do what seems good to you." 41 Therefore Saul said, "O LORD God of Israel, why hast thou not answered thy servant this day? If this guilt is in me or in Jonathan my son, O LORD, God of Israel, give Urim; but if this guilt is in thy people Israel, give Thummim." And Jonathan and Saul were taken, but the people escaped. 42 Then Saul said, "Cast the lot between me and my son Jonathan." And Jonathan was taken.

43 Then Saul said to Jonathan, "Tell me what you have done." And Jonathan told him, "I tasted a little honey with the tip of the staff that was in my hand; here I am, I will die." 44 And Saul said, "God do so to me and more also; you shall surely die, Jonathan." 45 Then the people said to Saul, "Shall Jonathan die, who has wrought this great victory in Israel? Far from it! As the LORD lives, there shall not one hair of his head fall to the ground; for he has wrought with God this day." So the people ransomed Jonathan, that he did not die. 46 Then Saul went up from pursuing the Philistines; and the Philistines went to their own place.

As great as Israel's victory at Michmash was, it could have been greater had it not been for Saul's unwise oath. In his eagerness to pursue the Philistines, Saul pronounced a curse on anyone who paused before nightfall even long enough to eat. Exhausted as they were by the furious fighting, the people remained true to the king's instructons even when they found fresh honey in the woods through which they passed. Only Jonathan, who was unaware of his father's curse, refreshed himself with the rich food which nature had provided.

As darkness fell, however, the people fell upon the cattle they had taken as booty and ate the meat without waiting for the blood to be ritually drained from it. Thus they consumed the blood which was holy unto the Lord and should have been poured upon the side of the altar by a priest (Lev. 17:10-15; 1:5). When Saul learned of their violation of proper religious custom, he improvised an altar to avert further transgressions by his people.

When the people were refreshed, Saul was ready to resume pursuit of the Philistines until a priest suggested that the Lord should be consulted first. In what was obviously a long procedure, the Lord was entreated all day, but no answer was given. Now the momentum of attack was hopelessly lost, and Saul demanded all the more strongly to know who was at fault. Again the sacred lots were consulted and eventually Jonathan was selected. Under his father's questioning, Jonathan readily admitted that he had unknowingly transgressed his father's curse and declared himself ready to pay with his life. The innate fairness of the people prevailed, however, and no harm was allowed to come upon the one whose exploits had won the day for Israel. The king's son was ransomed, probably with an animal sacrifice, and the whole incident came to a close with both the Israelites and the Philistines going back to their places.

We should not be too upset if, as modern readers, we find our minds swarming with theological questions after reading this striking narrative. Indeed, it is precisely in experiences such as these that we find the historical crucibles in which the faith of the Old Testament was being refined. While the Israelites were not speculative philosophers, they did face up to the problems in their faith, and this incident provides a good example of their common sense approach to life.

The ancient author began with an accepted body of facts: Israel started the war of independence with a spectacular victory but was unable to sustain this initial drive. He then applied a valid religious insight: God involves himself in history and strengthens the arms of those whose causes are just. The writer is left with a theological problem, however. Why did not God, who had given the first victory, continue sweeping the Philistines away?

The standard answer and the most obvious one was that someone within the host of Israel had sinned and incurred the divine wrath (cf. Josh. 7). The biblical account makes it quite clear that in this particular case none of the principal characters is completely innocent. Saul had entered the battle at Michmash without completing his quest for divine counsel (14:19). Also, in the course of the fighting, he impetuously invoked a curse which deprived his men of the strength they needed to pursue the enemy. Likewise the people as a whole had incurred a ritual guilt by improperly disposing of the blood of animals they killed for food. Last and least, there was Jonathan who had inadvertently broken *his father's* oath by eating a bit of honey.

Now the ancient theologian is ready to pose his thorniest problem. What is to be done when the divine lot settles on the one whose offense appears the most innocuous, indeed who up to this point has been God's hero of the hour? In spite of a father's love for his son, Saul was prepared to execute Jonathan out of an awareness of divine obligation. The people, however, sensed that this solution would not adequately reflect the justice which is inherent in God's nature. Unconsciously, they relied more on their own innate spiritual perception than on any external means of understanding the divine will. They refused to allow any harm to come to their champion, Jonathan, and decided that he should be ransomed instead. This practice of substituting an animal for the life of a man is known elsewhere in the Old Testament, principally in the redemption of the firstborn (Ex. 13:13; 34:20; cf. 21:18,30). This course was apparently followed so that the judgment of the sacred lot would not be openly defied and yet the cause of justice would be served.

(5) Saul's Reign Summarized (14:47-52)

47 When Saul had taken the kingship over Israel, he fought against all his enemies on every side, against Moab, against the Ammonites, against Edom, against the kings of Zobah,

and against the Philistines; wherever he turned he put them to the worse. 48 And he did valiantly, and smote the Amalekites, and delivered Israel out of the hands of those who plundered them.

49 Now the sons of Saul were Jonathan, Ishvi, and Malchishua; and the names of his two daughters were these: the name of the first-born was Merab, and the name of the younger Michal; 50 and the name of Saul's wife was Ahinoam the daughter of Ahimaaz. And the name of the commander of his army was Abner the son of Ner, Saul's uncle; 51 Kish was the father of Saul, and Ner the father of Abner was the son of Abiel.

52 There was hard fighting against the Philistines all the days of Saul; and when Saul saw any strong man, or any valiant man, he attached him to himself.

This summary of Saul's reign is used by the biblical author to show that his story about Israel's first king has now reached its climax. Attention is about to be shifted to David, the next major character in the national drama (Introduction, V, 1). Stories about Saul will follow; but from this point on, his fortunes are declining while those of his successor are growing ever brighter.

Heretofore, Saul's major efforts have been expended in the attempt to secure a smooth transition from a tribal to a monarchic system of government in the midst of economic, political, and religious upheaval. Only the beginning of his own reign is recounted in any detail, but the establishment of the monarchy and the survival of the nation go hand in hand.

Indeed, Saul's whole reign is evaluated on the basis of his military accomplishments. Successful campaigns are listed against Ammon, Moab, and Edom, east of the Jordan, and against the Amalekites, in the far south. At least some contact with Aramean peoples is indicated by his battles against the *kings of Jobah*. The Philistines, however, continued to trouble Israel throughout Saul's days and were again in control of most of the land when he was killed in battle at Mount Gilboa.

Saul was also noted for his innovations in Israel's military organization. The old tribal league supported no standing army but utilized instead a militia drafted from its constituent members. Saul continued to depend largely on a conscripted army, but he pioneered in the development of a trained professional leadership. Thus, whenever he saw men of outstanding natural ability, *he attached* them *to himself*.

Even in these brief accounts of Saul's reign, we are able to see in him one of the great tragic figures of the Old Testament. His accomplishments were considerable, yet other men continually overshadowed him in the affections of his people (18:7). He was a man of natural piety (10:10; 14:44), yet he was eventually rejected by the Lord who had selected him as king. He was an important military figure, but David was greater. Whatever his shortcomings may have been, however, he helped prepare the nation to meet the years ahead.

III. The Rise and Reign of David (1 Sam. 15:1—2 Sam. 8:18)

1. Saul Rejected as King (15:1-35)

(1) Saul Violates Cherem (15:1-9)

1 And Samuel said to Saul, "The LORD sent me to anoint you king over his people Israel; now therefore hearken to the words of the LORD. 2 Thus says the LORD of hosts, 'I will punish what Amalek did to Israel in opposing them on the way, when they came up out of Egypt. 3 Now go and smite Amalek, and utterly destroy all that they have; do not spare them, but kill both man and woman, infant and suckling, ox and sheep, camel and ass.'"

4 So Saul summoned the people, and numbered them in Telaim, two hundred thousand men on foot, and ten thousand men of Judah. 5 And Saul came to the city of Amalek, and lay in wait in the valley. 6 And Saul said to the Kenites, "Go, depart, go down from among the Amalekites, lest I destroy you with them; for you showed kindness to all the people of Israel when they came up out of Egypt." So the Kenites departed from among the Amalekites. 7 And Saul defeated the Amalekites, from Havilah as far as Shur, which is east of Egypt. 8 And he took Agag the king of the Amalekites alive, and utterly destroyed all the people with the edge of the sword. 9 But Saul and the people spared Agag, and the best of the sheep and of the oxen and of the fatlings, and the lambs, and all that was good, and would not utterly destroy them; all that was despised and worthless they utterly destroyed.

According to the overall arrangement of the books of Samuel, this chapter dealing with Saul's rejection as king is actually part of the story of David's rise to power (Introduction, V, 1). As if for the first time (cf. 13:1–15), the reasons for Saul's rejection are recounted. In this chapter Saul is condemned for his failure to heed divine instruction.

Again the setting for the incident is in a war involving Israel. This time, however, the conflict is precipitated not by external pressures upon the Hebrew state but by a war of retaliation. The Lord called for the total annihilation of the Amalekites for their opposition to Israel during the Conquest (Ex. 17:8–16; Num. 14.45; Deut. 25:17–19). These people belonged to a loosely knit group of nomads in the southern wilderness who continually raided the Judean frontier.

This was "holy war" of the type properly associated with the old tribal league and practiced mainly during the conquest of Canaan. In such a war, the enemy and all his goods were placed under a ban (*cherem*), i.e., no booty was to be taken from the conquered foe. All people and animals were to be killed, and all property of value was to be burned as consecrated to the Lord (Josh. 6:17,21).

The total destruction of the enemy and his goods theoretically removed all personal profit motives, and those who participated in battle fought only for God's glory. Actually, however, many practical considerations might well remain. In Saul's battle against the Amalekites, for example, the association of the "holy war" concept with the old tribal league could have helped win support for Saul among those who still favored that political system. Likewise the people of Judah were drawn closer to Israel by Saul's help in subduing their troublesome neighbors to the south.

Saul's attack on **the city of Amalek** probably should not be considered a siege on one particular town. Since these people were nomads who had no walled cities such as were common elsewhere in Palestine, it seems more likely that the Israelites sent word for the Kenites to withdraw from Amalekite territory (v. 6) before they began a series of raids and ambushes on their enemies' camps (v. 5). Obviously not all the Amalekites were annihilated since David continued to battle them during his flight from Saul (30:1).

The biblical account is not so much concerned with the details of the campaign as with its conclusion: Saul failed to abide by the ban. He spared the king and the best of the cattle; and when his selectivity was noted, his motives immediately became suspect.

(2) *Saul Rejected as King (15:10–23)*

10 The word of the Lord came to Samuel: 11 "I repent that I have made Saul king; for he has turned back from following me, and has not performed my commandments." And Samuel was angry; and he cried to the Lord all night. 12 And Samuel rose early to meet Saul in the morning; and it was told Samuel, "Saul came to Carmel, and, behold he set up a monument for himself and turned, and passed on, and went down to Gilgal." 13 And Samuel came to Saul, and Saul said to him, "Blessed be you to the Lord; I have performed the commandment of the Lord." 14 And Samuel said, "What then is this bleating of the sheep in my ears, and the lowing of the oxen which I hear?" 15 Saul said, "They have brought them from the Amalekites; for the people spared the best of the sheep and of the oxen, to sacrifice to the Lord your God; and the rest we have utterly destroyed." 16 Then Samuel said to Saul, "Stop! I will tell you what the Lord said to me this night." And he said to him, "Say on."

17 And Samuel said, "Though you are little in your own eyes, are you not the head of the tribes of Israel? The Lord anointed you king over Israel. 18 And the Lord sent you on a mission, and said, 'Go, utterly destroy the sinners, the Amalekites, and fight against them until they are consumed.' 19 Why then did you not obey the voice of the Lord? Why did you swoop on the spoil, and do what was evil in the sight of the Lord?" 20 And Saul said to Samuel, "I have obeyed the voice of the Lord, I have gone on the mission on which the Lord sent me, I have brought Agag the king of Amalek, and I have utterly destroyed the Amalekites. 21 But the people took of the spoil, sheep and oxen, the best of the things devoted to destruction, to sacrifice to the Lord your

God in Gilgal." ²² And Samuel said,

"Has the LORD as great delight in burnt offerings and sacrifices,
 as in obeying the voice of the LORD?
Behold, to obey is better than sacrifice,
 and to hearken than the fat of rams.
²³ For rebellion is as the sin of divination,
 and stubbornness is as iniquity and idolatry.
Because you have rejected the word of the LORD,
 he has also rejected you from being king."

Saul seems to have been attempting to extract some personal benefits out of an expedition which was undertaken as a "holy war." While the Lord was due praise for winning Israel's battles (14:6), Saul erected a monument for himself at Carmel (just south of Hebron). He apparently also intended to make sport of Agag, the Amalekite king, or otherwise use him to demonstrate his own greatness. Even Saul's desire to sacrifice the choice animals at Gilgal may have had an ulterior motive. A regular sacrifice could be shared by the people (see comment on 1:1–8), whereas animals set apart under *cherem* could not.

To many modern readers Saul's punishment for his violation of the *cherem* in the battle against Amalek seems arbitrary and superficial. Samuel's beautiful psalm, however, highlights the key issue—obedience. Saul's alteration of the rules for the *cherem*, however, has already been shown to involve questionable judgments. Far more than blind conformity to cultic regulation is involved here. The rules for the *cherem* were no more inviolable than those for sacrifice. Saul was condemned because his judgments were at variance with God's will. In real life, decisions are inevitable, but man bears ultimate responsibility for perceiving the divine revelation. Saul was denied an enduring dynasty because of his rebellion against God's leadership.

The Lord's announcement of his rejection of Saul produced unusual reactions within Samuel. First he became angry, and then he cried to the Lord all night. Samuel's motives are not given, but presumably he was angry because the work in which he had invested so much of his life now seemed to be repudiated. His anger may also hide fear brought on by the apparent contradiction between these new developments and what he had understood as the Lord's will up to this time. Whatever the explanation of his anger, Samuel emerged from a night of anguished prayer ready to face Saul with the Lord's judgment.

The tragic side of Saul's personality again rises to the surface as he appears genuinely unaware of any wrong on his part in the Amalekite affair. He did not hesitate to welcome Samuel's presence on the journey to Gilgal. He claimed fulfillment of the Lord's command even after hearing Samuel's indictment. He may also have felt independent of responsibility in the people's actions. It is precisely this lack of ethical judgment, however, which most severely challenged his right to rule.

(3) *Samuel Leaves Saul (15:24–35)*

²⁴ And Saul said to Samuel, "I have sinned; for I have transgressed the commandment of the LORD and your words, because I feared the people and obeyed their voice. ²⁵ Now therefore, I pray, pardon my sin, and return with me, that I may worship the LORD." ²⁶ And Samuel said to Saul, "I will not return with you; for you have rejected the word of the LORD, and the LORD has rejected you from being king over Israel." ²⁷ As Samuel turned to go away, Saul laid hold upon the skirt of his robe, and it tore. ²⁸ And Samuel said to him, "The LORD has torn the kingdom of Israel from you this day, and has given it to a neighbor of yours, who is better than you. ²⁹ And also the Glory of Israel will not lie or repent; for he is not a man, that he should repent." ³⁰ Then he said, "I have sinned; yet honor me now before the elders of my people and before Israel, and return with me, that I may worship the LORD your God." ³¹ So Samuel turned back after Saul; and Saul worshiped the LORD.

³² Then Samuel said, "Bring here to me Agag the king of the Amalekites." And Agag came to him cheerfully. Agag said, "Surely the bitterness of death is past." ³³ And Samuel said, "As your sword has made women childless, so shall your mother be childless among women." And Samuel hewed Agag in pieces before the LORD in Gilgal.

³⁴ Then Samuel went to Ramah; and Saul went up to his house in Gibeah of Saul. ³⁵ And Samuel did not see Saul again until the day of his death, but Samuel grieved over Saul. And

the LORD repented that he had made Saul king over Israel.

Saul's personality problems which would later become apparent to all were already coming to the surface in the battle against Amalek. As his sense of inner security diminished, Saul became excessively concerned with public opinion. Even as king he was unwilling to resist the desires of the people. He was also anxious to maintain an appearance of accord with Samuel after his rejection by the Lord became final. Although these inner tensions are understandable in the light of his early struggle to establish the monarchy, they nevertheless severely impaired his ability to serve as Israel's king.

As an external sign of the Lord's rejection of Saul as king, Samuel performed two symbolic acts. The first has to do with the tearing of a robe as a sign that God had torn the kingdom from Saul's control. The RSV introduces a dramatic note in its rendering of v. 27: *As Samuel turned to go away, Saul laid hold upon the skirt of his robe, and it tore.* The Hebrew text, however, does not contain the name Saul, and it is Samuel who performs the act of prophetic symbolism.

Samuel's withdrawal from Saul, against his own personal inclinations, also symbolizes the Lord's withdrawal of support. Just as Saul's earnest entreaty won a temporary postponement of Samuel's departure, so God allowed Saul to continue to reign until his death; his heirs bore the brunt of his rejection.

The Glory of Israel represents the use of a description or an attribute of God as a substitute for the divine name. This practice was especially common in the later Old Testament period when Israelites took special precautions lest they violate the Third Commandment.

As the texts now stand, there is a direct contradiction between v. 29 and vv. 11,35*b*. The problem seems to be precipitated by the author's use of terms denoting human mental or emotional activity to refer to God. The question arose, Does God change his 'mind'? An ancient copyist may have included marginal comments containing such sentiments (cf. Num. 20.19) into the body of the text. On the other hand, a single author may have recognized in these conflicting statements a paradox of the divine nature. Either statement taken alone may lead to a misunderstanding of God's character. Together they represent an idea similar to that found in Psalm 103:8–9: God's patience is not without its limits. He does not turn a deaf ear to man's entreaties, but he is always true to his own character. Eventually, judgment is certain.

In today's language, we would not say bluntly that Saul had reached a point where God would no longer forgive him. However, his rebellion had developed so fully that his life would have to bear the fruits of the seeds he had planted. In spite of Saul's penitence, Samuel would do no more than postpone his final break with the king.

And Samuel did not see Saul again until the day of his death. This probably just means that Samuel withdrew from the official life in Saul's court since Saul apparently visited him in Naioth (19:24). The people of Israel knew by Samuel's withdrawal, however, that the king no longer enjoyed the prophet's confidence or support.

2. *David Anointed Future King (16:1–13)*

¹ The LORD said to Samuel, "How long will you grieve over Saul, seeing I have rejected him from being king over Israel? Fill your horn with oil, and go; I will send you to Jesse the Bethlehemite, for I have provided for myself a king among his sons." ² And Samuel said, "How can I go? If Saul hears it, he will kill me." And the LORD said, Take a heifer with you, and say, 'I have come to sacrifice to the LORD.' ³ And invite Jesse to the sacrifice, and I will show you what you shall do; and you shall anoint for me him whom I name to you." ⁴ Samuel did what the LORD commanded, and came to Bethlehem. The elders of the city came to meet him trembling, and said, "Do you come peaceably?" ⁵ And he said, "Peaceably; I have come to sacrifice to the LORD; consecrate yourselves, and come with me to the sacrifice." And he consecrated Jesse and his

1 SAMUEL 16

sons, and invited them to the sacrifice.

6 When they came, he looked on Eliab and thought, "Surely the LORD's anointed is before him." 7 But the LORD said to Samuel, "Do not look on his appearance or on the height of his stature, because I have rejected him; for the LORD sees not as man sees; man looks on the outward appearance, but the LORD looks on the heart." 8 Then Jesse called Abinadab, and made him pass before Samuel. And he said, "Neither has the LORD chosen this one." 9 Then Jesse made Shammah pass by. And he said, "Neither has the LORD chosen this one." 10 And Jesse made seven of his sons pass before Samuel. And Samuel said to Jesse, "The LORD has not chosen these." 11 And Samuel said to Jesse, "Are all your sons here?" And he said, "There remains yet the youngest, but behold, he is keeping the sheep." And Samuel said to Jesse, "Send and fetch him; for we will not sit down till he comes here." 12 And he sent, and brought him in. Now he was ruddy, and had beautiful eyes, and was handsome. And the LORD said, "Arise, anoint him; for this is he." 13 Then Samuel took the horn of oil, and anointed him in the midst of his brothers; and the Spirit of the LORD came mightily upon David from that day forward. And Samuel rose up, and went to Ramah.

Samuel's ambivalent attitude toward Saul is clearly demonstrated in this passage. Heretofore Samuel's reluctance to anoint Saul as king had been emphasized and only occasionally had hints been dropped of a friendship between the two men (10:1,24; 15:10). In the present context Samuel is moved both by affection and fear in his relationship with Saul.

The Lord interrupted Samuel's reflections on the king's fate and ordered the prophet to Bethlehem to anoint the ruler who would succeed Saul. Samuel's fear of incurring the royal wrath indicates what must have been the political realities of the day. The prophet's influence rested on his powers of persuasion, and the king's influence rested on his force of arms. To protect both the prophet and the newly designated prince (*nagid*) of Israel, Samuel was instructed to combine his quest for a king with a routine pilgrimage at Bethlehem.

Nothing in the story up to this point would explain the town elders' fearful attitude before Samuel. Possibly they were simply overawed by the visit of a person of national prominence to their village. The vehemence of their reaction, however, hints that more powerful issues were at stake. Perhaps, as Hertzberg (p. 137) suggests, the city fathers were afraid of becoming involved in the rift between Saul and Samuel. The later fate of the inhabitants of Nob (22:11–19) indicates that such a concern would not have been without foundation.

Samuel assured the elders that his intentions were peaceful and invited them to attend the sacrifice along with Jesse and his sons. We are told of the consecration of the participants in the ceremony, probably by a ceremonial of washing, but nothing more is said about the sacrifice itself. Plainly, the item of prime interest is the designation of the Lord's choice among Jesse's sons.

David's selection from among his brothers is reminiscent of Saul's choice by lot out of all the tribes of Israel (10:17–24). Eliab, Jesse's eldest son, made a favorable impression on Samuel but was not chosen by the Lord. Samuel's instructions not to consider the stature of the prospective candidates seems to indicate a repudiation of the qualifications for which Saul was chosen (10:23). God's concern now focused on the unseen qualities of character, leadership, and obedience. The drama of the moment was again heightened by the absence of the Lord's choice from the proceedings (cf. 10:22). When Jesse's youngest son David was brought from tending his father's sheep, Samuel was instructed to act, for this was to be the Lord's anointed.

With Samuel's anointment, **the Spirit of the Lord came mightily upon David from that day forward.** The external manifestations accompanying this occurrence varied considerably. Unlike Samson (Judg. 14:19) and Saul (1 Sam. 10:10–11; 19:23–24), David exhibited no violent forms of activity as an evidence of this experience. Apparently the presence of the *Spirit of the Lord* in David's life simply indicated that he was henceforth divinely equipped to perform in his role as king of Israel.

3. David Joins Saul's Court (16:14—18:5)

(1) David Becomes Saul's Armor-bearer (16:14–23)

¹⁴ Now the Spirit of the LORD departed from Saul, and an evil spirit from the LORD tormented him. ¹⁵ And Saul's servants said to him, "Behold now, an evil spirit from God is tormenting you. ¹⁶ Let our lord now command your servants, who are before you, to seek out a man who is skilful in playing the lyre; and when the evil spirit from God is upon you, he will play it, and you will be well." ¹⁷ So Saul said to his servants, "Provide for me a man who can play well, and bring him to me." ¹⁸ One of the young men answered, "Behold, I have seen a son of Jesse the Bethlehemite, who is skilful in playing, a man of valor, a man of war, prudent in speech, and a man of good presence; and the LORD is with him." ¹⁹ Therefore Saul sent messengers to Jesse, and said, "Send me David your son, who is with the sheep." ²⁰ And Jesse took an ass laden with bread, and a skin of wine and a kid, and sent them by David his son to Saul. ²¹ And David came to Saul, and entered his service. And Saul loved him greatly, and he became his armor-bearer. ²² And Saul sent to Jesse, saying, "Let David remain in my service, for he has found favor in my sight." ²³ And whenever the evil spirit from God was upon Saul, David took the lyre and played it with his hand; so Saul was refreshed, and was well, and the evil spirit departed from him.

The story of David's anointment is followed by two accounts of his admission to Saul's court. The first is associated with David's skill as a musician and the other with his victory over Goliath.

Following Saul's rejection as king, the *Spirit of the Lord* left him and *an evil spirit from the Lord* came upon him. Whereas God had blessed Saul's efforts in the earlier years of his reign, the king now found himself increasingly unable to function effectively. He became subject to seizures in which his normal personality was "set aside" and he appeared motivated by an "evil spirit." This evil spirit was associated with the Lord because the ancient writer could not conceive of any important event occurring apart from God's control (cf. Isa. 45:7, KJV). Only in later Old Testament thought were demonic powers introduced as the explanation of the origin of evil (1 Chron. 21.1, cf. 2 Sam. 24:1). In a similar vein, Christians are warned not to attribute man's temptation to God (James 1:13–15). Today we would say that Saul suffered from a mental or an emotional sickness.

Saul was convinced by members of his court to seek a musician whose skill in playing the lyre might soften the impact of the king's moody outbursts. David was recommended by one of Saul's younger servants as a good musician and as *a man of war*. He was *prudent in speech, and a man of good presence;* i.e., he was mature and settled, and the Lord was with him. When David came to court, he brought Saul a token gift of foodstuffs representing his ability to support himself. He came at the king's request, not out of economic necessity.

Under the influence of David's musical skill, Saul found at least temporary relief from the *evil spirit* which afflicted him, and he soon made the young man his armor-bearer. In this role David served as Saul's personal bodyguard, an office reserved for one who enjoyed the king's complete confidence. Thus David became a regular member of Saul's court.

(2) David Battles the Giant (17:1–18:5)

a. Goliath Issues a Challenge (17:1–11)

¹ Now the Philistines gathered their armies for battle; and they were gathered at Soco, which belongs to Judah, and encamped between Soco and Azekah, in Ephesdammim. ² And Saul and the men of Israel were gathered, and encamped in the valley of Elah, and drew up in line of battle against the Philistines. ³ And the Philistines stood on the mountain on the one side, and Israel stood on the mountain on the other side, with a valley between them. ⁴ And there came out from the camp of the Philistines a champion named Goliath, of Gath, whose height was six cubits and a span. ⁵ He had a helmet of bronze on his head, and he was armed with a coat of mail, and the weight of the coat was five thousand shekels of bronze.

1 SAMUEL 17

⁶ And he had greaves of bronze upon his legs, and a javelin of bronze slung between his shoulders. ⁷ And the shaft of his spear was like a weaver's beam, and his spear's head weighed six hundred shekels of iron; and his shield-bearer went before him. ⁸ He stood and shouted to the ranks of Israel, "Why have you come out to draw up for battle? Am I not a Philistine, and are you not servants of Saul? Choose a man for yourselves, and let him come down to me. ⁹ If he is able to fight with me and kill me, then we will be your servants; but if I prevail against him and kill him, then you shall be our servants and serve us." ¹⁰ And the Philistine said, "I defy the ranks of Israel this day; give me a man, that we may fight together." ¹¹ When Saul and all Israel heard these words of the Philistine, they were dismayed and greatly afraid.

A second account of David's introduction to Saul is found in the story of David's victory over Goliath. In this account David was a youth living at home caring for his father's sheep. He was present on the field of battle, not because he was Saul's armor-bearer but because he was bringing his brothers provisions from home. He was strong enough to kill bears or lions barehanded (17:34-37), but he was totally lacking in military experience (17:38-39). Until the time of his victory, he appeared to have been unknown to Saul (17:58); but through his newfound prominence he became a close friend with Jonathan, who immediately secured him a place in Saul's court (18:2).

The Vaticanus manuscript of the Septuagint preserves a considerably shorter version of the battle of Elah which removes many of the conflicts between chapters 16 and 17 (17:12-31 and 17:55—18:5 are omitted). The question remains as to whether this shorter reading or the longer Hebrew text is original. Generally it is easier to understand how a passage would be shortened in order to remove problems of agreement. It would be more difficult to explain why the story would be expanded in such a way that its inner cohesiveness was lost. Most students of the text, therefore, agree that the Hebrew version must be allowed to stand.

Since the two accounts cannot be successfully harmonized as they now stand, we presumably have independent versions of the manner in which Saul and David first happened to meet each other.

Now the Philistines gathered . . . at Socoh. Saul's strategic position in the battle at Socoh was considerably improved over that in his previous encounter with the Philistines. Rather than fighting at Michmash in the heart of his own territory (13:5), he was defending the valley of Elah, one of the major passes from the Philistine plain up into the highlands of Judah.

In a classic maneuver for ancient armies of approximately equal strength, the two forces had retired to defensive positions commanding opposite ridges of the same valley. Neither commander was willing to surrender the advantage of higher elevation to carry the battle to the enemy. In the stalemate which followed, the Philistines were gaining a psychological advantage through their gigantic warrior who daily challenged the Israelites to individual combat.

Goliath, of Gath, whose height was six cubits and a span. A cubit in ancient Israel was the distance from the elbow to the tip of the middle finger, an average of about 17 to 18 inches. A span was the distance between the fully extended thumb and little finger, about eight inches. Hence Goliath was about nine and a half feet tall. As had happened on other occasions in Israel's memory, the people's will to resist was being eroded by a man of epic proportions (Num. 13:32-33; Deut. 2:11,20; 3:11).

Some confusion is created by the use of the name Goliath in 2 Samuel 21:19 where a giant by that name from Gath, carrying a spear *like a weaver's beam,* was killed by a Bethlehemite called Elhanan. The similarities between this giant and David's victim have led some to conclude that the same episode underlies both accounts. They have hypothesized that David has been given credit for the exploits of one of his soldiers (21:22; cf. also 1:15—4:10). Others have suggested that Elhanan was David's given name, and David was the name he assumed upon ascending the throne. While these arguments are too complex to be rehearsed adequately in the limited space available here, we may observe that elsewhere biblical tradition closely associates David with a stunning victory over the Philistine giant in the battle for the valley of Elah (21:9; 22:10). A familiar name may have been secondarily added to the account of David's victory over *the Philistine* as he is regularly called (except for 17:4,23), but there are no compelling reasons for dissociating David from this spectacular victory.

b. David Visits His Brothers (17:12-23)

12 Now David was the son of an Ephrathite of Bethlehem in Judah, named Jesse, who had eight sons. In the days of Saul the man was already old and advanced in years. 13 The three eldest sons of Jesse had followed Saul to the battle; and the names of his three sons who went to the battle were Eliab the first-born, and next to him Abinadab, and the third Shammah. 14 David was the youngest; the three eldest followed Saul, 15 but David went back and forth from Saul to feed his father's sheep at Bethlehem. 16 For forty days the Philistine came forward and took his stand, morning and evening.
17 And Jesse said to David his son, "Take for your brothers an ephah of this parched grain, and these ten loaves, and carry them quickly to the camp to your brothers; 18 also take these ten cheeses to the commander of their thousand. See how your brothers fare, and bring some token from them."
19 Now Saul, and they, and all the men of Israel, were in the valley of Elah, fighting with the Philistines. 20 And David rose early in the morning, and left the sheep with a keeper, and took the provisions, and went, as Jesse had commanded him; and he came to the encampment as the host was going forth to the battle line, shouting the war cry. 21 And Israel and the Philistines drew up for battle, army against army. 22 And David left the things in charge of the keeper of the baggage, and ran to the ranks, and went and greeted his brothers. 23 As he talked with them, behold, the champion, the Philistine of Gath, Goliath by name, came up out of the ranks of the Philistines, and spoke the same words as before. And David heard him.

The biblical author now introduces David as if the reader were learning of him for the first time. He is again portrayed as the youngest of the eight sons of Jesse the Bethlehemite. The three oldest sons were serving in Saul's army at Elah while David *went back and forth from Saul to feed his father's sheep at Bethlehem.* This verse may attempt to reconcile the difference between chapters 16 and 17 by showing why David was not serving as Saul's armor-bearer. Even so, the reason why Saul appears unacquainted with David in 17:58 remains unanswered. Considered independently, however, the details of David's contest with Goliath and his introduction to Saul are fairly straightforward.

Jesse sent David to the Israelite war camp to take his three eldest sons supplementary provisions. An extra "gift" for their commanding officer was included as added insurance that the provisions would be allowed to reach their destination.

As a youth nearing manhood, David was eager to reach the field of battle. He left home very early, walked over 15 miles, and still arrived just as the Israelites were moving to their battle stations. Leaving his gifts with those guarding the base camp, David rushed into the ranks with just enough time to greet his brothers before the Philistine made his appearance.

c. David Accepts the Challenge (17:24-40)

24 All the men of Israel, when they saw the man, fled from him, and were much afraid. 25 And the men of Israel said, "Have you seen this man who has come up? Surely he has come up to defy Israel; and the man who kills him, the king will enrich with great riches, and will give him his daughter, and make his father's house free in Israel." 26 And David said to the men who stood by him, "What shall be done for the man who kills this Philistine, and takes away the reproach from Israel? For who is this uncircumcised Philistine, that he should defy the armies of the living God?" 27 And the people answered him in the same way, "So shall it be done to the man who kills him."
28 Now Eliab his eldest brother heard when he spoke to the men; and Eliab's anger was kindled against David, and he said, "Why have you come down? And with whom have you left those few sheep in the wilderness? I know your presumption, and the evil of your heart; for you

have come down to see the battle." ²⁹ And David said, "What have I done now? Was it not but a word?" ³⁰ And he turned away from him toward another, and spoke in the same way; and the people answered him again as before.

³¹ When the words which David spoke were heard, they repeated them before Saul; and he sent for him. ³² And David said to Saul, "Let no man's heart fail because of him; your servant will go and fight with this Philistine." ³³ And Saul said to David, "You are not able to go against this Philistine to fight with him; for you are but a youth, and he has been a man of war from his youth." ³⁴ But David said to Saul, "Your servant used to keep sheep for his father; and when there came a lion, or a bear, and took a lamb from the flock, ³⁵ I went after him and smote him and delivered it out of his mouth; and if he arose against me, I caught him by his beard, and smote him and killed him. ³⁶ Your servant has killed both lions and bears; and this uncircumcised Philistine shall be like one of them, seeing he has defied the armies of the living God." ³⁷ And David said, "The LORD who delivered me from the paw of the lion and from the paw of the bear, will deliver me from the hand of this Philistine." And Saul said to David, "Go, and the LORD be with you!" ³⁸ Then Saul clothed David with his armor; he put a helmet of bronze on his head, and clothed him with a coat of mail. ³⁹ And David girded his sword over his armor, and he tried in vain to go, for he was not used to them. Then David said to Saul, "I cannot go with these; for I am not used to them." And David put them off. ⁴⁰ Then he took his staff in his hand, and chose five smooth stones from the brook, and put them in his shepherd's bag or wallet; his sling was in his hand, and he drew near to the Philistine.

For over a month no major engagements had taken place. By now the giant's actions and the threat he posed for the morale of Israel were known to all. The troops were gossiping about the rewards offered as inducements for the one who would defeat Goliath. Again and again David entered into these discussions, not so much to hear a repetition of the rewards as to plant an idea: *"Who is this uncircumcised Philistine that he should defy the armies of the living God?"*

David's intention to inject himself into the very heart of the action was clearly perceived by his elder brother Eliab. He considered David presumptuous in that he was attempting to rise above his proper place in life. David feigned innocence, asking in effect, What harm does talking do?

Soon David's plans were realized when his words were reported to Saul and he was called before the king.[24] David's confident manner was apparently based on three factors. First, he was convinced of his physical ability to face the Philistine. As evidence of his prowess, David cited barehanded victories over wild animals encountered in his work. He may have lacked experience in the use of military weapons, but he was far from the untried boy envisioned by many modern readers.

A second and even more important motivating factor in David's confidence may be seen in his faith in the living God. He drew upon a backlog of personal experience for the assurance that the Lord would help him face the challenges of the future. Although David sometimes fell far short of the highest levels of ethical conduct, this strand of genuine personal piety seems to run throughout his life.

David's third reason for being confident of victory over the Philistine lay in the fact that he had a secret weapon—the sling. After putting aside the normal battle garb, he selected his ammunition from the bed of a stream, five stones, each about the size of a man's first. Barrages from this formidable weapon figured prominently in ancient military tactics (cf. Judg. 20:16), but David had the imagination, nerve, and skill to apply it successfully in individual combat as well.

d. David Defeats Goliath (17:41–54)

⁴¹ And the Philistine came on and drew near to David, with his shield-bearer in front of him. ⁴² And when the Philistine looked, and saw David, he disdained him; for he was but a youth, ruddy and comely in appearance. ⁴³ And the Philistine said to David, "Am I a dog, that you come to me with sticks?" And the Philis-

---

[24] The Vaticanus manuscript of the LXX omits the entire story of David's brothers and his journeys to Bethlehem (vv. 12–31). David was present on the battlefield, therefore, as Saul's armor-bearer. (See comment on 17:1–11.)

tine cursed David by his gods. ⁴⁴ The Philistine said to David, "Come to me, and I will give your flesh to the birds of the air and to the beasts of the field." ⁴⁵ Then David said to the Philistine, "You come to me with a sword and with a spear and with a javelin; but I come to you in the name of the LORD of hosts, the God of the armies of Israel, whom you have defied. ⁴⁶ This day the LORD will deliver you into my hand, and I will strike you down, and cut off your head; and I will give the dead bodies of the host of the Philistines this day to the birds of the air and to the wild beasts of the earth; that all the earth may know that there is a God in Israel, ⁴⁷ and that all this assembly may know that the LORD saves not with sword and spear; for the battle is the LORD'S and he will give you into our hand."

⁴⁸ When the Philistine arose and came and drew near to meet David, David ran quickly toward the battle line to meet the Philistine. ⁴⁹ And David put his hand in his bag and took out a stone, and slung it, and struck the Philistine on his forehead; the stone sank into his forehead, and he fell on his face to the ground.

⁵⁰ So David prevailed over the Philistine with a sling and with a stone, and struck the Philistine, and killed him; there was no sword in the hand of David. ⁵¹ Then David ran and stood over the Philistine, and took his sword and drew it out of its sheath, and killed him, and cut off his head with it. When the Philistines saw that their champion was dead, they fled. ⁵² And the men of Israel and Judah rose with a shout and pursued the Philistines as far as Gath and the gates of Ekron, so that the wounded Philistines fell on the way from Shaaraim as far as Gath and Ekron. ⁵³ And the Israelites came back from chasing the Philistines, and they plundered their camp. ⁵⁴ And David took the head of the Philistine and brought it to Jerusalem; but he put his armor in his tent.

David appeared before Goliath as a simple youth dressed and armed like a shepherd. His every move was calculated to feed the complacency of the giant and at the same time to heighten the theological impact of his impending victory. The action began with the exchange of verbal assaults. Goliath made light of David's boyish appearance and cursed him in the name of the Philistine gods. Accepting the giant's challenge, David summarized Israel's understanding of warfare. The battle was in the Lord's hands, and he would determine the outcome, not on the basis of military power, but according to his own will.

With the preliminaries over, the engagement moved swiftly to its climax. Before the combatants came within the range of conventional weapons, David used his sling and felled the giant in his tracks. Using Goliath's own sword, David beheaded his enemy, thus confirming the Israelite conviction that the Lord and not armaments determines the outcome of battle (cf. 14:6).

Unnerved by the unexpected defeat of their champion the Philistine soldiers fled their mountaintop defenses and thus became easy prey for the Israelite hosts. After pursuing the enemy for some ten to 15 miles, Saul's soldiers returned to enjoy the spoil of the Philistine camp.

David took the head of the Philistine . . . to Jerusalem. Jerusalem at this time was still controlled by the Jebusites who would have had no reason to celebrate an Israelite victory over the Philistines. Perhaps, as Hertzberg (p. 153) suggests, this reference reflects the existence of a famous relic of this battle in the city of Jerusalem long after it had been captured and made the capital of Israel. *He put his armor in his tent.* No such shelter had been mentioned or implied previously. Goliath's sword was obviously preserved, however, since it later came to light in the possession of the priests of Nob (1 Sam. 21:9).

e. Jonathan Befriends David (17:55—18:5)

⁵⁵ When Saul saw David go forth against the Philistine, he said to Abner, the commander of the army, "Abner, whose son is this youth?" And Abner said, "As your soul lives, O king, I cannot tell." ⁵⁶ And the king said, "Inquire whose son the stripling is." ⁵⁷ And as David returned from the slaughter of the Philistine, Abner took him, and brought him before Saul with the head of the Philistine in his hand. ⁵⁸ And Saul said to him, "Whose son are you, young man?" And David answered, "I am the son of your servant Jesse the Bethlehemite."

¹ When he had finished speaking to Saul, the soul of Jonathan was knit to the soul of David, and Jonathan loved him as his own soul. ² And Saul took him that day, and would not let him return to his father's house. ³ Then Jonathan

made a covenant with David, because he loved him as his own soul. ⁴ And Jonathan stripped himself of the robe that was upon him, and gave it to David, and his armor, and even his sword and his bow and his girdle. ⁵ And David went out and was successful wherever Saul sent him; so that Saul set him over the men of war. And this was good in the sight of all the people and also in the sight of Saul's servants.

Saul's questions about David's background are surprising only if the young warrior had already served as the royal armor-bearer (cf. 16:14—23). If, as seems likely, the story of David's victory over Goliath is an independent account of David's introduction to Saul, this question is to be expected. Since their previous meeting had been concerned mainly with preparations for battle, Saul now was learning about the background of his future son-in-law (cf. 17:25).

As a result of his victory over Goliath, David was immediately given a permanent place in Saul's court. From the very beginning, David received a surprisingly warm reception by members of the royal court, especially in view of the fact that he had risen so suddenly to prominence.

Jonathan, for example, took the initiative in what was to become his lifelong friendship with David. The covenant by which the two young men entered into a voluntary brotherhood with each other was established under his direction. The spirit of the entire covenant agreement is summed up in Jonathan's gift of his clothes and weapons to David. By this act all were informed that Jonathan loved David *as his own soul.* Just a short time later Jonathan was even willing to acknowledge that David, not he, would be the next king of Israel (23:17).

In his relationship with David, Jonathan is revealed as one of the choice characters in the Old Testament. He had nothing to gain, but he selflessly gave of himself for a friend. David's contribution to the friendship is not so well known, but something of his regard for Jonathan can be seen in his lament over the death of Saul and his son (2 Sam. 1:19—27).

The author concludes this section by summarizing David's life in Saul's court. He was successful in every task he undertook; he earned an important promotion in the army; and he won the friendship of the general population and of Saul's bureaucrats as well. Such a record was to prove too perfect for David's own good.

4. Saul Seeks David's Life (18:6—20:42)

(1) Saul Attempts Murder (18:6–16)

⁶ As they were coming home, when David returned from slaying the Philistine, the women came out of all the cities of Israel, singing and dancing, to meet King Saul, with timbrels, with songs of joy, and with instruments of music. ⁷ And the women sang to one another as they made merry,
"Saul has slain his thousands,
 and David his ten thousands."
⁸ And Saul was very angry, and this saying displeased him; he said, "They have ascribed to David ten thousands, and to me they have ascribed thousands; and what more can he have but the kingdom?" ⁹ And Saul eyed David from that day on.
¹⁰ And on the morrow an evil spirit from God rushed upon Saul, and he raved within his house, while David was playing the lyre, as he did day by day. Saul had his spear in his hand; ¹¹ and Saul cast the spear, for he thought, "I will pin David to the wall." But David evaded him twice.
¹² Saul was afraid of David, because the LORD was with him but had departed from Saul. ¹³ So Saul removed him from his presence, and made him a commander of a thousand; and he went out and came in before the people. ¹⁴ And David had success in all his undertakings; for the LORD was with him. ¹⁵ And when Saul saw that he had great success, he stood in awe of him. ¹⁶ But all Israel and Judah loved David; for he went out and came in before them.

As David's popularity reached its climax, Saul's fragile self-confidence could take no more. Suffering from the frustration of years of struggles with Samuel, with "worthless fellows" who opposed his rule (10:27), and with the Philistines; now Saul focused his hostilities on David, the favorite of the people, the anointed of the Lord.

Basically, Saul was jealous of the attention showered upon David. Saul's sense of insecurity could tolerate no competition for the affection of his people. On the other hand, Saul was beginning to suspect David of harboring political ambitions. While probably still unaware that David had previously been anointed by Samuel, Saul could see that the young man's popularity would eventually lead him to seek the throne. Finally, disturbing all of Saul's reasoning processes was the *evil spirit* which plagued him (cf. comment on 16:14–23). Saul's actions are increasingly portrayed as those of a demented personality. His confused emotional state is reflected in his rapid shift in attitudes toward David. He was successively moved by love (16:21), anger (18:8), fear (18:12), and awe (18:15).

The king finally resolved that David was to be killed, either by outright murder (vv. 10 f.), through battle with the Philistines (vv. 20 f.), or through the use of hired assassins (19:1 f.).

Saul's own attempts to murder David are associated with the evil spirit which periodically caused him to rave as a madman.[25] David was again serving as Saul's armor-bearer and musician when the king repeatedly tried to kill him with a spear (vv. 10–11; 19:9–10). When these attempts failed, Saul placed David in a military command. Rather than obscuring him from the public eye, however, this move only resulted in greater popularity.

(2) *Saul Uses the Philistines (18:17–30)*

17 Then Saul said to David, "Here is my elder daughter Merab; I will give her to you for a wife; only be valiant for me and fight the Lord's battles." For Saul thought, "Let not my hand be upon him, but let the hand of the Philistines be upon him." 18 And David said to Saul, "Who am I, and who are my kinsfolk, my father's family in Israel, that I should be son-in-law to the king?" 19 But at the time when Merab, Saul's daughter, should have been given to David, she was given to Adriel the Meholathite for a wife.

[25] The Hebrew word for "to rave" (*yitnabbe'*) in v. 10 is related to the word for "prophet" (*nabi'*). The verb is regularly translated "to prophesy," but its violent content is clearly marked in the present context. This passage bears further testimony to the ecstatic behavior of the early prophets.

20 Now Saul's daughter Michal loved David; and they told Saul, and the thing pleased him. 21 Saul thought, "Let me give her to him, that she may be a snare for him, and that the hand of the Philistines may be against him." Therefore Saul said to David a second time, "You shall now be my son-in-law." 22 And Saul commanded his servants, "Speak to David in private and say, 'Behold, the king has delight in you, and all his servants love you; now then become the king's son-in-law.'" 23 And Saul's servants spoke those words in the ears of David. And David said, "Does it seem to you a little thing to become the king's son-in-law, seeing that I am a poor man and of no repute?" 24 And the servants of Saul told him, "Thus and so did David speak." 25 Then Saul said, "Thus shall you say to David, 'The king desires no marriage present except a hundred foreskins of the Philistines, that he may be avenged of the king's enemies.'" Now Saul thought to make David fall by the hand of the Philistines. 26 And when his servants told David these words, it pleased David well to be the king's son-in-law. Before the time had expired, 27 David arose and went, along with his men, and killed two hundred of the Philistines; and David brought their foreskins, which were given in full number to the king, that he might become the king's son-in-law. And Saul gave him his daughter Michal for a wife. 28 But when Saul saw and knew that the Lord was with David, and that all Israel loved him, 29 Saul was still more afraid of David. So Saul was David's enemy continually.

30 Then the princes of the Philistines came out to battle, and as often as they came out David had more success than all the servants of Saul; so that his name was highly esteemed.

Saul's next scheme for arranging David's death involved hazardous combat against the Philistines. The king, fearing public reaction, hesitated to order David to expose himself to such danger. He, therefore, sought to trick David into voluntarily accepting the assignment.

Saul was publicly committed to offer a daughter in marriage to the man who defeated Goliath; however, custom demanded that the groom present the bride's family with a worthy gift as her purchase price. Saul first offered David the hand of his elder daughter Merab. Apparently David did not understand Saul's request that he *fight the Lord's battles* as a suggested marriage gift. In any case, he excused himself from the marriage on the basis of his humble origins; i.e., his family was too poor to pay a marriage price worthy of a princess.

A second opportunity to carry out Saul's "Philistine plan" occurred when his daughter Michal announced that she loved David. This time Saul would take no chances of being misunderstood. He sent messengers who assured David that the king would consider the marriage price well paid if his prospective son-in-law gave evidence of having killed 100 of the uncircumcised Philistines. Again Saul's plan collapsed when David was able to discharge his obligation safely, twice over, within the time period set by the king.[26] David became the king's son-in-law by his marriage to Michal, but Saul became more wary of him than ever before.

(3) Saul Seeks Assassins (19:1–7)

¹ And Saul spoke to Jonathan his son and to all his servants, that they should kill David. But Jonathan, Saul's son, delighted much in David. ² And Jonathan told David, "Saul my father seeks to kill you; therefore take heed to yourself in the morning, stay in a secret place and hide yourself; ³ and I will go out and stand beside my father in the field where you are, and I will speak to my father about you; and if I learn anything I will tell you." ⁴ And Jonathan spoke well of David to Saul his father, and said to him, "Let not the king sin against his servant David; because he has not sinned against you, and because his deeds have been of good service to you; ⁵ for he took his life in his hand and he slew the Philistine, and the LORD wrought a great victory for all Israel. You saw it, and rejoiced; why then will you sin against innocent blood by killing David without cause?" ⁶ And Saul hearkened to the voice of Jonathan; Saul swore, "As the LORD lives, he shall not be put to death." ⁷ And Jonathan called David, and Jonathan showed him all these things. And Jonathan brought David to Saul, and he was in his presence as before.

Thwarted in his two previous plans to do away with David, Saul now sought to convert his servants and his own son into assassins. By this action Jonathan was subjected to a painful test of loyalties. Had he kept secret Saul's intentions, his father would have been guilty of shedding innocent blood. Neither could Jonathan stand by while his friend's death was being instigated. In an effort to be true both to David and Saul, Jonathan tried to serve as a peacemaker.

The details of Jonathan's meeting with his father in the field are no longer known, but the broad outlines of his plan are clear. He had already informed David of his father's plot and warned him to stay hidden until his negotiations with the king were complete. Then in a private conference with his father, Jonathan defended David's innocence.

Let not the king sin against his servant. *Sin* in the Old Testament is not exclusively a theological term. It may be used, as it is here, of wrongs committed against another person. At the end of Jonathan's discourse, Saul vowed to end his plots against David; and a temporary peace was restored.

(4) Saul Renews the Violence (19:8–17)

⁸ And there was war again; and David went out and fought with the Philistines, and made a great slaughter among them, so that they fled before him. ⁹ Then an evil spirit from the LORD came upon Saul, as he sat in his house with his spear in his hand; and David was playing the lyre. ¹⁰ And Saul sought to pin David to the wall with the spear; but he eluded Saul, so that he struck the spear into the wall. And David fled, and escaped.

¹¹ That night Saul sent messengers to David's house to watch him, that he might kill him in the morning. But Michal, David's wife, told him, "If you do not save your life tonight, tomorrow you will be killed." ¹² So Michal let David down through the window; and he fled away and escaped. ¹³ Michal took an image and laid it on the bed and put a pillow of goats' hair at its head, and covered it with the clothes. ¹⁴ And when Saul sent messengers to take David, she said, "He is sick." ¹⁵ Then Saul sent the messengers to see David, saying, "Bring him up to me in the bed, that I may kill him." ¹⁶ And when the messengers came in, behold, the image was in the bed, with the pillow of goats' hair at its head. ¹⁷ Saul said to Michal, "Why have you deceived me thus,

---

[26] No time period is recorded in the present text. The phrase translated *a second time* in v. 21, however, actually reads "by two" (*bishtayim*) which doesn't fit well here. By adding one consonant, a more meaningful translation would be possible: *within two years* (*bishnatayim*).

and let my enemy go, so that he has escaped?" And Michal answered Saul, "He said to me, 'Let me go; why should I kill you?'"

Unfortunately, the brief but welcome period of peace which had been arranged through Jonathan's influence was not to last. Another skirmish in the war with the Philistines drew David back into the field, and again he came home in glory. As on previous occasions, an evil spirit prompted Saul to make yet another attempt on David's life. Dodging a spear, David fled to his own home, but messengers were sent to keep him from leaving the city. This time it was to be Saul's daughter who helped David escape.

Michal's support of her husband is not to be taken for granted. Marriages in important families were often arranged for political purposes in ancient Israel, and intrigue was commonplace. David's marriage to Michal was no exception. Saul had encouraged the union in an effort to have David killed by the Philistines. He later abrogated the marriage contract and gave Michal to another man, probably in an effort to keep David from claiming a legitimate tie to Israel's ruling house (25:44; 2 Sam. 3:15). Michal's devotion to her husband reflects honor upon her and adds weight to the indictment of Saul's unjust attacks upon David.

The ruse which Michal used in aiding David's escape was probably a bit more complicated than the English translations imply. The image used was the *teraphim*, a Hebrew term rendered variously in the Old Testament: household gods (Gen. 31:19 f.), *teraphim* (Judg. 17:5 f.; 2 Kings 23:24; Hos. 3:4), or idolatry (1 Sam. 15:23). Whatever use was made of the teraphim, they were ultimately rejected as a part of Israelite religious practice (1 Sam. 15:23; 2 Kings 23:24). In all probability Michal's use of these images conveyed theological overtones which are lost to modern readers.

(5) Samuel Offers Refuge (19:18-24)

18 Now David fled and escaped, and he came to Samuel at Ramah, and told him all that Saul had done to him. And he and Samuel went and dwelt at Naioth. 19 And it was told Saul, "Behold, David is at Naioth in Ramah." 20 Then Saul sent messengers to take David; and when they saw the company of the prophets prophesying, and Samuel standing as head over them, the Spirit of God came upon the messengers of Saul, and they also prophesied. 21 When it was told Saul, he sent other messengers, and they also prophesied. And Saul sent messengers again the third time, and they also prophesied. 22 Then he himself went to Ramah, and came to the great well that is in Secu; and he asked, "Where are Samuel and David?" And one said, "Behold, they are at Naioth in Ramah." 23 And he went from there to Naioth in Ramah; and the Spirit of God came upon him also, and as he went he prophesied, until he came to Naioth in Ramah. 24 And he too stripped off his clothes, and he too prophesied before Samuel, and lay naked all that day and all that night. Hence it is said, "Is Saul also among the prophets?"

After fleeing the royal court, David did not move toward Bethlehem as Saul would have expected but turned northward toward Ramah. Samuel was settled there as the presiding elder over a company of prophets. Naioth is not attested as a place name outside this context and may represent the proper name for the prophets' abode in or near Ramah. (See Driver, pp. 158-59, for a review of the possibilities). David sought shelter among this group while enjoying his first contact with Samuel since his anointment (16:13).

When Saul was notified that David was with Samuel in Ramah, he dispatched troops with orders to bring David back. Saul's plans were frustrated, however, when the soldiers fell under the influence of *the Spirit of God* and began "prophesying" among Samuel's band. Saul decided to capture David personally after his servants repeatedly had failed him, but he too was incapacitated by a "prophetic seizure." Apparently little distinction was made between the ecstatic trances which accompanied prophetic activity and the religious experience which gave them rise. The present context, at any rate, stresses the behavioral rather than the religious consequences of the prophet's influence. Thus Saul, upon reaching Naioth, disrobed and lay naked before Samuel an entire day.

In the light of this experience, the people again asked, *Is Saul also among the prophets?* In its previous context (10:10–12), the question implied that Saul brought reproach on himself and his family by associating with the undignified ecstatic prophets. In its present position, however, the proverb seems to question Saul's qualifications for membership in the prophetic band (McKane, p. 122). The prophets and their activities are too closely associated with Saul in tradition to be seriously challenged. On the other hand, Saul appropriated the external manifestations of spiritual activity without surrendering himself to the ethical demands encountered in a genuine fellowship with the living God. This is a devastating practice in any age.

(6) *David and Jonathan Part* (20:1–42)

a. *Friends Renew Covenant* (20:1–23)

¹ Then David fled from Naioth in Ramah, and came and said before Jonathan, "What have I done? What is my guilt? And what is my sin before your father, that he seeks my life?" ² And he said to him, "Far from it! You shall not die. Behold, my father does nothing either great or small without disclosing it to me; and why should my father hide this from me? It is not so." ³ But David replied, "Your father knows well that I have found favor in your eyes; and he thinks, 'Let not Jonathan know this, lest he be grieved.' But truly, as the Lord lives and as your soul lives, there is but a step between me and death." ⁴ Then said Jonathan to David, "Whatever you say, I will do for you." ⁵ David said to Jonathan, "Behold, tomorrow is the new moon, and I should not fail to sit at table with the king; but let me go, that I may hide myself in the field till the third day at evening. ⁶ If your father misses me at all, then say, 'David earnestly asked leave of me to run to Bethlehem his city; for there is a yearly sacrifice there for all the family.' ⁷ If he says, 'Good!' it will be well with your servant; but if he is angry, then know that evil is determined by him. ⁸ Therefore deal kindly with your servant, for you have brought your servant into a sacred covenant with you. But if there is guilt in me, slay me yourself; for why should you bring me to your father?" ⁹ And Jonathan said, "Far be it from you! If I knew that it was determined by my father that evil should come upon you, would I not tell you?" ¹⁰ Then said David to Jonathan, "Who will tell me if your father answers you roughly?" ¹¹ And Jonathan said to David, "Come, let us go out into the field." So they both went out into the field.

¹² And Jonathan said to David, "The Lord, the God of Israel, be witness! When I have sounded my father, about this time tomorrow, or the third day, behold, if he is well disposed toward David, shall I not then send and disclose it to you? ¹³ But should it please my father to do you harm, the Lord do so to Jonathan, and more also, if I do not disclose it to you, and send you away, that you may go in safety. May the Lord be with you, as he has been with my father. ¹⁴ If I am still alive, show me the loyal love of the Lord, that I may not die; ¹⁵ and do not cut off your loyalty from my house for ever. When the Lord cuts off every one of the enemies of David from the face of the earth, ¹⁶ let not the name of Jonathan be cut off from the house of David. And may the Lord take vengeance on David's enemies." ¹⁷ And Jonathan made David swear again by his love for him; for he loved him as he loved his own soul.

¹⁸ Then Jonathan said to him, "Tomorrow is the new moon; and you will be missed, because your seat will be empty. ¹⁹ And on the third day you will be greatly missed; then go to the place where you hid yourself when the matter was in hand, and remain beside yonder stone heap. ²⁰ And I will shoot three arrows to the side of it, as though I shot at a mark. ²¹ And behold, I will send the lad, saying, 'Go, find the arrows.' If I say to the lad, 'Look, the arrows are on this side of you, take them,' then you are to come, for, as the Lord lives, it is safe for you and there is no danger. ²² But if I say to the youth, 'Look, the arrows are beyond you,' then go; for the Lord has sent you away. ²³ And as for the matter of which you and I have spoken, behold, the Lord is between you and me for ever."

In light of the many attempts that had been made on David's life, one wonders that there was any question as to Saul's intentions. Jonathan, however, had only recently arranged a truce between his father and his friend (19:1–7), and Saul's subsequent actions were such that they were subject to varying interpretations. His latest attack on David with a spear was associated with the evil spirit which afflicted him only periodically and which was somewhat excused (19:8–10). Although David was convinced as to Saul's intentions in the incidents at his home and at Ramah, no overt attacks had been made. Jonathan, therefore, was justified in seeking further confirmation of his father's murderous designs.[27]

David proposed a test case involving the rites associated with the arrival of the new moon. Biblical regulations prescribe a sounding of the trumpet and special sacrifices for new moon observances (Num. 10:10; 28:11). Presumably, these were monthly celebrations since a lunar calendar was used. The fictitious sacrifice which David used as an alibi for his absence was to have been a family affair without any necessary connection with other new moon feasts.

The meal involved in the test was an intimate one involving only four major characters. David's absence could not be overlooked, but only Saul's angry rejection of David's alibi would be taken as an indication that the king was intent on killing him.

Both David and Jonathan were aware that the test they had arranged might precipitate a crisis which could seriously endanger their friendship. They felt a need to reaffirm their earlier covenant (18:3–4). Further, David sought assurance that Jonathan would warn him if Saul plotted against him. He knew that he could not continue to evade Saul's attacks without Jonathan's help.

Jonathan, on the other hand, was aware that if open conflict erupted between Saul and David, he could easily lose any claim to the throne. In such a case, he wished David well: *May the Lord be with you, as he has been with my father.* Jonathan asked that if he survived such a battle for the throne, the terms of their covenant be honored although they had fought on op-

[27] Other commentators take chs. 19 and 20 as parallel but divergent accounts of David's flight from Saul's court (McKane, p. 110). The two chapters may at one time have enjoyed independent circulation, but they have been more effectively united than many have been willing to admit. In their present form, the events in chapter 20 are more designed to reveal Saul's intentions to Jonathan than to David (cf. especially 20:1–4).

posite sides. He especially sought amnesty for his family.

The two friends renewed their pledges of loyalty to one another, arranged a secret ritual to warn David, and parted.

b. David Flees Saul's Court (20:24–42)

24 So David hid himself in the field; and when the new moon came, the king sat down to eat food. 25 The king sat upon his seat, as at other times, upon the seat by the wall; Jonathan sat opposite, and Abner sat by Saul's side, but David's place was empty. 26 Yet Saul did not say anything that day; for he thought, "Something has befallen him; he is not clean, surely he is not clean." 27 But on the second day, the morrow after the new moon, David's place was empty. And Saul said to Jonathan his son, "Why has not the son of Jesse come to the meal, either yesterday or today?" 28 Jonathan answered Saul, "David earnestly asked leave of me to go to Bethlehem; 29 he said, 'Let me go; for our family holds a sacrifice in the city, and my brother has commanded me to be there. So now, if I have found favor in your eyes, let me get away, and see my brothers.' For this reason he has not come to the king's table."

30 Then Saul's anger was kindled against Jonathan, and he said to him, "You son of a perverse, rebellious woman, do I not know that you have chosen the son of Jesse to your own shame, and to the shame of your mother's nakedness? 31 For as long as the son of Jesse lives upon the earth, neither you nor your kingdom shall be established. Therefore send and fetch him to me, for he shall surely die." 32 Then Jonathan answered Saul his father, "Why should he be put to death? What has he done?" 33 But Saul cast his spear at him to smite him; so Jonathan knew that his father was determined to put David to death. 34 And Jonathan rose from the table in fierce anger and ate no food the second day of the month, for he was grieved for David, because his father had disgraced him.

35 In the morning Jonathan went out into the field to the appointment with David, and with him a little lad. 36 And he said to his lad, "Run and find the arrows which I shoot." As the lad ran, he shot an arrow beyond him. 37 And when the lad came to the place of the arrow which Jonathan had shot, Jonathan called after the lad and said, "Is not the arrow beyond you?" 38 And Jonathan called after the lad, "Hurry, make haste, stay not." So Jonathan's lad gathered up the arrows, and came to his master. 39 But the lad knew nothing; only Jonathan and David knew the matter. 40 And Jonathan gave

his weapons to his lad, and said to him, "Go and carry them to the city." ⁴¹ And as soon as the lad had gone, David rose from beside the stone heap and fell on his face to the ground, and bowed three times; and they kissed one another, and wept with one another, until David recovered himself. ⁴² Then Jonathan said to David, "Go in peace, forasmuch as we have sworn both of us in the name of the Lord, saying, 'The Lord shall be between me and you, and between my descendants and your descendants, for ever.'" And he rose and departed; and Jonathan went into the city.

He is not clean. A number of incidents could render a man ceremonially unclean so that it would be improper for him to take part in a ritual celebration (Lev. 7:21; 11:24 f.; 15:16). Saul presumed that David was absent from the first day of the feast for one of these reasons.

Saul's anger was kindled against Jonathan. Saul violently rejected the rehearsed excuse for David's second day of absence and turned his wrath upon Jonathan. Saul had either discovered or had surmised the depth of his son's allegiance to David and felt that he was placing that friendship above the loyalty he owed his own family. The stream of abuse that was directed at Jonathan was only indirectly aimed at his mother. Saul exclaimed that Jonathan's preference for David stemmed from the fact that he had been an improper son from his very birth: *You have chosen the son of Jesse to your own shame, and to the shame of your mother's nakedness.*

Although Saul had again grievously misjudged Jonathan's basic loyalties (see comment on 19:1–7; 20:1–23), he thought that he was doing his son a favor. He could see that as long as David lived, Jonathan would never become king. Thus he rationalized away his own responsibilities for the compulsions which motivated his hatred for David.

Jonathan apparently did not really want to become king, certainly not if it meant going against David. Even after being warned of David's threat to his own rule, Jonathan replied quietly: *Why should he be put to death? What has he done?* Perhaps he sensed that God had already chosen David as Israel's next king, and he was prepared to accept that judgment. He possessed a quality totally lacking in his father. He was able to appreciate greatness in others without feeling inferior.

So Jonathan knew that his father was determined to put David to death. The next day Jonathan proceeded with the prearranged signal by which David would be informed of Saul's reaction to his absence. To make certain that there could be no misunderstanding, Jonathan added vocal instructions intended for David, but directed to his unsuspecting helper: *"Hurry, make haste, stay not."*

With the signal complete, the reader expects Jonathan to return to his father's court as David begins his exile. At this point, however, Jonathan sent his young helper back to the city with his weapons, and David stepped forth for an emotional leave-taking. The two friends had arranged their elaborate signal presumably because they considered it too dangerous for them to be seen together. When it became apparent that they were now traveling divergent paths, however, they could not part without saying farewell.

As the two friends prepared to pursue their separate, even conflicting destinies, they reflected on the covenant which united them. The Lord was to stand as mediator between their two families forever.

5. David Becomes a Fugitive (21:1—26:25)

(1) Priests at Nob Aid David (21:1–9)

¹ Then came David to Nob to Ahimelech the priest; and Ahimelech came to meet David trembling, and said to him, "Why are you alone, and no one with you?" ² And David said to Ahimelech the priest, "The king has charged me with a matter, and said to me, 'Let no one know anything of the matter about which I send you, and with which I have charged you.' I have made an appointment with the young men for such and such a place. ³ Now then, what have you at hand? Give me five loaves of bread, or whatever is here." ⁴ And the priest answered David, "I have no common bread at hand, but there is holy bread; if only the young men have kept themselves from women." ⁵ And David answered the priest, "Of a truth women

have been kept from us as always when I go on an expedition; the vessels of the young men are holy, even when it is a common journey; how much more today will their vessels be holy?" ⁶ So the priest gave him the holy bread; for there was no bread there but the bread of the Presence, which is removed from before the Lord, to be replaced by hot bread on the day it is taken away.

⁷ Now a certain man of the servants of Saul was there that day, detained before the Lord; his name was Doeg the Edomite, the chief of Saul's herdsmen.

⁸ And David said to Ahimelech, "And have you not here a spear or a sword at hand? For I have brought neither my sword nor my weapons with me, because the king's business required haste." ⁹ And the priest said, "The sword of Goliath the Philistine, whom you killed in the valley of Elah, behold, it is here wrapped in a cloth behind the ephod; if you will take that, take it, for there is none but that here." And David said, "There is none like that; give it to me."

After fleeing Saul's court, David stopped at Nob to seek provisions, arms, and divine counsel (22:10). Nob was presumably established by the priests who fled the Philistine destruction of Shiloh about the middle of the eleventh century B.C. In David's day it housed a sizable sanctuary staffed by some 85 priests (22:18). Located within sight of the city of Jerusalem, the town was on David's route south (Isa. 10:27–32; Neh. 11:31–32). Meeting David, Ahimelech, leader of the group at Nob, trembled with apprehension, much as the elders of Bethlehem had greeted Samuel (see comment on 16:1–13).

This episode adds another segment of the story of David's rise to power. The underlying theme or purpose here is much the same as in the preceding narratives about his life in court. The author will continue to demonstrate through David's "rags-to-riches" story that the Lord was working in history to bring him to Israel's throne.

David's pitiable condition before Ahimelech is a perfect picture of a humble beginning. He was utterly alone, having fled without food, armor, or retinue. When Ahimelech asked for an explanation of the conditions which were strange for so high an official of the king, David lied about a secret mission from Saul. Referring vaguely to a rendezvous with a small contingent of troops nearby, David secured enough food to carry him through a considerable journey.

Surely Ahimelech must have been even more suspicious about David's lack of arms, but at David's request he offered Goliath's sword. Thus he provided David with a weapon and a good "omen" as well. What a storyteller's delight! David did not even have a sword when he fled from Saul; and when he returned, he would have a whole army.

Nothing is said in this context about David's seeking divine counsel through Ahimelech, but it is prominently mentioned in the next chapter (22:10,13,15). Perhaps this feature of David's visit was omitted to heighten the reader's awareness of Ahimelech's innocence of any complicity with David's plans.

The vessels of the young men are holy. This is a euphemism referring to a soldier's sexual continence while on a military expedition. Warfare required ritual purity in ancient Israel, so sexual intercourse had to be avoided while on a campaign (Lev. 15:17). These young men, however, did not actually exist; they were a part of David's lie.

The author's skill in storytelling is illustrated in his reference to Doeg the Edomite. Although he plays no role in the present context, he is introduced in a single sentence which interrupts the flow of the story. The reader thus anticipates a more important role for him later on.

(2) David Feigns Madness (21:10–15)

¹⁰ And David rose and fled that day from Saul, and went to Achish the king of Gath. ¹¹ And the servants of Achish said to him, "Is not this David the king of the land? Did they not sing to one another of him in dances,
'Saul has slain his thousands,
  and David his ten thousands'?"
¹² And David took these words to heart, and was much afraid of Achish the king of Gath. ¹³ So he changed his behavior before them, and feigned himself mad in their hands, and made

marks on the doors of the gate, and let his spittle run down his beard. ¹⁴ Then said Achish to his servants, "Lo, you see the man is mad; why then have you brought him to me? ¹⁵ Do I lack madmen, that you have brought this fellow to play the madman in my presence? Shall this fellow come into my house?"

Many commentators regard the present account of David's visit with the king of Gath as a variant form of his experience as Achish's vassal (27:1–12). They point, for example, to the lack of wisdom in attempting to enlist as a Philistine soldier while armed with Goliath's sword. (Caird, p. 999; Rust, pp. 112–113.)

It is indeed strange that David would have planned on joining Achish's court without having anticipated some of the difficulties in doing so. There are some elements of the story, however, which may indicate that he was an unwilling guest of the Philistines. Thus they *speculate* as to his identity, he was *in their hands,* they *brought him* before the king, and he *escaped* to Adullam (22:1). This interpretation of his situation would be in accord with the superscription of Psalm 56: "A Miktam of David, when the Philistines seized him in Gath."

We may theorize, therefore, that David realized his danger as a lone fugitive anywhere in Israel. He had hoped to live inconspicuously among the Philistines in Gath, but suspicious soldiers seized him and brought him before Achish. When it appeared that his identity had been guessed, but before it could be proven, David feigned madness and escaped detection. Again he was saved by the care of the Lord and his own cunning. David's ruse—*feigned himself mad*—was well chosen since madmen were considered possessed by spirits (16:14).

Whatever its interpretation, David's experience before Achish serves in this context as a concrete evidence of his utter extremity. A theological question grips the mind of every reader: How will the Lord make a king out of his anointed? Israelites would later remember when he had to play the fool to save his life!

(3) *David Gathers an Army (22:1–5)*

¹ David departed from there and escaped to the cave of Adullam; and when his brothers and all his father's house heard it, they went down there to him. ² And every one who was in distress, and every one who was in debt, and every one who was discontented, gathered to him; and he became captain over them. And there were with him about four hundred men.

³ And David went from there to Mizpeh of Moab; and he said to the king of Moab, "Pray let my father and my mother stay with you, till I know what God will do for me." ⁴ And he left them with the king of Moab, and they stayed with him all the time that David was in the stronghold. ⁵ Then the prophet Gad said to David, "Do not remain in the stronghold; depart, and go into the land of Judah." So David departed, and went into the forest of Hereth.

David knew that he could not successfully elude Saul within Israelite territory, nor could he withstand his forces single-handedly. After failing in his attempt to escape quietly into Gath, he moved back to Adullam on the frontier between Israel and Philistia. Adullam is identified with the ruins *'aid-el-ma* about 12 miles southwest of Bethlehem and less than three miles off the valley of Elah, where David fought Goliath. There in a region of steep ravines and numerous caves, David began gathering an army.

In time David drew about 400 men from his own family and various malcontents from all Israel. In spite of its scruffy origins, this band was later to form the backbone of David's standing army, an innovation learned from the Philistines. But first he had to train, discipline, and support them while he evaded Saul.

While some members of David's family could gain protection from Saul by joining David's outlaws, his aging parents could not stand the pace. David, therefore, arranged refuge for them with the king of Moab (cf. Ruth 1:4; 4:18–22). Rabbinic tradition holds that the king of Moab betrayed David's trust and killed his parents. This would account for David's vicious treatment of the Moabites when he came to power (2 Sam. 8:2). The Bible, however, contains no other specific references to his parents.

Do not remain in the stronghold. Commentators have had difficulty in agreeing whether *the stronghold* refers to Mizpeh of Moab or to Adullam. Since subsequent references (2 Sam. 23:13; 1 Chron. 11:15) place the stronghold in a similar context with Adullam, Moab appears overruled. The terms *cave* and *stronghold* are not used interchangeably in the Old Testament, however, so it is perhaps best to consider the stronghold a proper name in this context referring to the general vicinity around Adullam in which David's outlaws found sanctuary (cf. also 2 Sam. 5:17).

The prophet Gad is mentioned in Samuel only here and in 2 Samuel 24, but he is otherwise known as one of the chroniclers of David's reign (1 Chron. 29:29). His advice that David should return to Judah seems strange since Adullam was at one time considered part of that tribe (Josh. 15:35). On the other hand, it had previously been a Canaanite town (Josh. 12:15); and as we have seen, Adullam was probably on the frontier between Judah and Philistia in David's day. Gad wanted David to be more closely allied with his own people at this time.

(4) Saul Loses Priestly Support (22:6-23)

⁶ Now Saul heard that David was discovered, and the men who were with him. Saul was sitting at Gibeah, under the tamarisk tree on the height, with his spear in his hand, and all his servants were standing about him. ⁷ And Saul said to his servants who stood about him, "Hear now, you Benjaminites; will the son of Jesse give every one of you fields and vineyards, will he make you all commanders of thousands and commanders of hundreds, ⁸ that all of you have conspired against me? No one discloses to me when my son makes a league with the son of Jesse, none of you is sorry for me or discloses to me that my son has stirred up my servant against me, to lie in wait, as at this day." ⁹ Then answered Doeg the Edomite, who stood by the servants of Saul, "I saw the son of Jesse coming to Nob, to Ahimelech the son of Ahitub, ¹⁰ and he inquired of the Lord for him, and gave him provisions, and gave him the sword of Goliath the Philistine."

¹¹ Then the king sent to summon Ahimelech the priest, the son of Ahitub, and all his father's house, the priests who were at Nob; and all of them came to the king. ¹² And Saul said, "Hear now, son of Ahitub." And he answered, "Here I am, my lord." ¹³ And Saul said to him, "Why have you conspired against me, you and the son of Jesse, in that you have given him bread and a sword, and have inquired of God for him, so that he has risen against me, to lie in wait, as at this day?" ¹⁴ Then Ahimelech answered the king, "And who among all your servants is so faithful as David, who is the king's son-in-law, and captain over your bodyguard, and honored in your house? ¹⁵ Is today the first time that I have inquired of God for him? No! Let not the king impute anything to his servant or to all the house of my father; for your servant has known nothing of all this, much or little." ¹⁶ And the king said, "You shall surely die, Ahimelech, you and all your father's house." ¹⁷ And the king said to the guard who stood about him, "Turn and kill the priests of the Lord; because their hand also is with David, and they knew that he fled, and did not disclose it to me." But the servants of the king would not put forth their hand to fall upon the priests of the Lord. ¹⁸ Then the king said to Doeg, "You turn and fall upon the priests." And Doeg the Edomite turned and fell upon the priests, and he killed on that day eighty-five persons who wore the linen ephod. ¹⁹ And Nob, the city of the priests, he put to the sword; both men and women, children and sucklings, oxen, asses and sheep, he put to the sword.

²⁰ But one of the sons of Ahimelech the son of Ahitub, named Abiathar, escaped and fled after David. ²¹ And Abiathar told David that Saul had killed the priests of the Lord. ²² And David said to Abiathar, "I knew on that day, when Doeg the Edomite was there, that he would surely tell Saul. I have occasioned the death of all the persons of your father's house. ²³ Stay with me, fear not; for he that seeks my life seeks your life; with me you shall be in safekeeping."

When Saul was informed that David was gathering troops and moving back into Israelite territory, his worst fears appeared confirmed. David seemed to be preparing for an all-out attack on his throne. Since David's rebels would be difficult to track down in the Judean wilderness, Saul decided to make an example of any who aided David's cause. A test case was provided when one of his servants, Doeg the Edomite, reported that Ahimelech, a priest at Nob, had given David counsel, provisions, and arms (cf. comment on 21:1–9).

Saul summoned all the priests of Nob to appear before him at Gibeah and charged them with having a major role in David's conspiracy to overthrow the kingdom.[28] Ahimelech admitted giving David aid but pleaded innocent of any subversive motives. He had been unaware of David's defection from Saul's court and had considered himself merely assisting one who was a loyal servant of the king.

Saul, however, was not moved by reason or justice but by a neurotic sense of persecution. Unable to get any native Israelites to take action against the *priests of the Lord,* Saul persuaded Doeg the Edomite to carry out his death sentence against them. Unsatisfied with the death of 85 men, Saul placed Nob under the ban and massacred every living inhabitant. Such was to be the fate of all who aided David and his rebels.

Saul's plan to make a gruesome example of the people backfired against him, however, for he had misjudged popular reaction to the murder of the priests. By his actions the king had alienated the religious community and had driven Abiathar, the sole surviving member of Eli's priestly line, into David's camp. Thus, David gained the friendship of those who continued to uphold religious institutions associated with the period of the judges. David could now claim endorsement both by the prophetic (16:13; 22:5) and the priestly establishments. Saul, on the other hand, had alienated himself from all religious support.

The phrase, *with his spear in his hand,* may mean that the spear was a scepter or a symbol of Saul's authority. On the other hand, the frequency with which it is mentioned may reflect Saul's growing distrust of those about him (18:10; 19:9; 20:33; 26:7). He felt that he had to provide his own protection and thus affected habits such as sitting with his back to a wall (20:25).

---

[28] Prophets and priests are known to have been active in such political maneuvers (2 Sam. 15:12; 16:23; 1 Kings 1:7). Some even initiated dynastic changes (1 Kings 11:26–40; 19:15–17).

Hear now, you Benjaminites. Saul reminded his fellow tribesmen that their jobs in court were dependent on his continuing rule. If David came to power, he would tend to favor Judeans as his advisers and officers.

I have occasioned the death. David acknowledged that his deception of Ahimelech had been responsible for the destruction of Nob. While he could not undo a previous wrong, David attempted to set matters right by offering protection to Abiathar. This friendship lasted as long as David lived.

(5) *David Rescues Keilah (23:1–14)*

¹ Now they told David, "Behold, the Philistines are fighting against Keilah, and are robbing the threshing floors." ² Therefore David inquired of the Lord, "Shall I go and attack these Philistines?" And the Lord said to David, "Go and attack the Philistines and save Keilah." ³ But David's men said to him, "Behold, we are afraid here in Judah; how much more then if we go to Keilah against the armies of the Philistines?" ⁴ Then David inquired of the Lord again. And the Lord answered him, "Arise, go down to Keilah; for I will give the Philistines into your hand." ⁵ And David and his men went to Keilah, and fought with the Philistines, and brought away their cattle, and made a great slaughter among them. So David delivered the inhabitants of Keilah.

⁶ When Abiathar the son of Ahimelech fled to David to Keilah, he came down with an ephod in his hand. ⁷ Now it was told Saul that David had come to Keilah. And Saul said, "God has given him into my hand; for he has shut himself in by entering a town that has gates and bars." ⁸ And Saul summoned all the people to war, to go down to Keilah, to besiege David and his men. ⁹ David knew that Saul was plotting evil against him; and he said to Abiathar the priest, "Bring the ephod here." ¹⁰ Then said David, "O Lord, the God of Israel, thy servant has surely heard that Saul seeks to come to Keilah, to destroy the city on my account. ¹¹ Will the men of Keilah surrender me into his hand? Will Saul come down, as thy servant has heard? O Lord, the God of Israel, I beseech thee, tell thy servant." And the Lord said, "He will come down." ¹² Then said David, "Will the men of Keilah surrender me and my men into the hand of Saul?" And the Lord said, "They will surrender you." ¹³ Then David and his men, who were about six hundred, arose and departed from Keilah,

and they went wherever they could go. When Saul was told that David had escaped from Keilah, he gave up the expedition. ¹⁴ And David remained in the strongholds in the wilderness, in the hill country of the Wilderness of Ziph. And Saul sought him every day, but God did not give him into his hand.

In keeping with the advice implied in the instructions of the prophet Gad (22:5), David hoped to gain support by proving himself a friend to the people of Judah. An opportunity was provided by a Philistine attack on Keilah, a walled frontier town of Judah about three miles below Adullam. The Philistine raid was aimed at plunder rather than permanent conquest, but the loss of a season's grain harvest would work a considerable hardship on the local peasants.

After twice seeking divine guidance and over the objections of his men, David moved to break the Philistine siege of Keilah. Although little is said about the battle itself, the Israelites probably began with a raid on the Philistine baggage train (cf. Hertzberg, p. 191). There David's men captured the enemy's beasts of burden and diverted attention from the main force which broke through and put the Philistines to flight. The siege was lifted, and David's men took up temporary quarters in the town.

Upon learning of the action of Keilah, Saul sensed an opportunity to catch David in a strategic blunder. Had David's rebels remained committed to the defense of even a well-fortified single site, they would have proved no match for the king's seasoned troops. David, however, recognized his tactical disadvantage and the danger which his continued presence brought upon the people of the city. Abandoning the town, he dispersed his men in the surrounding territory. David, therefore, resorted to his original guerrilla tactics and avoided pitched battles with Saul's superior forces.

David is again appealingly portrayed in this section. He is a skilled and daring leader of men, yet he modestly disclaims personal credit and recognizes the necessity of seeking divine leadership. In contrast with Saul's murderous attack on the inhabitants of Nob, David is understanding and considerate of the people of Keilah who would have surrendered him to Saul had they been called upon to do so. The impact of Saul's massacre of the priests of Nob is beginning to be seen. Saul directs his campaigns with considerable tactical insight only to have his plans frustrated by David's sensitivity to divine leadership.

The exact nature of the ephod is no longer known. It is usually described as an item of priestly wearing apparel (Ex. 28:28–29; 1 Sam. 2:18; 22:18; 2 Sam. 6:14), but it sometimes appears to be an image associated with a particular place of worship (Judg. 8:27; 1 Sam. 21:9). In the present context, however, the ephod is clearly associated with David's quest for divine leadership (23:6–12). Apparently, the priestly ephod served as a receptacle for the divine lot or the Urim and Thummin. Questions were carefully phrased by the priest, and the Lord responded by controlling the lot to give yes or no answers. The presence of Abiathar with the ephod in David's camp served as a visible reminder of God's leadership of David's cause.

(6) Friends Extend Covenant (23:15–18)

¹⁵ And David was afraid because Saul had come out to seek his life. David was in the Wilderness of Ziph at Horesh. ¹⁶ And Jonathan, Saul's son, rose, and went to David at Horesh, and strengthened his hand in God. ¹⁷ And he said to him, "Fear not; for the hand of Saul my father shall not find you; you shall be king over Israel, and I shall be next to you; Saul my father also knows this." ¹⁸ And the two of them made a covenant before the LORD; David remained at Horesh, and Jonathan went home.

Following his withdrawal from Keilah, David moved his men 15 to 20 miles farther southeast to the wilderness of Judah, east of Ziph and Maon. These towns, about three and one-half and eight and one-half miles south of Hebron respectively, lie along the western ridge of the arid slopes leading down to the Dead Sea. This territory provided David and his men with some pasturage and considerable protection, although Saul's steady pursuit (23:14) made continued concealment difficult.

Just as the growing pressures of David's outlaw existence were ready to erode his faith and his will to resist, Jonathan came forward, again seeking peace with his friend. The covenant which was concluded here in the wilderness of Ziph marks a decided advance beyond any previous pacts between the two men. This was in fact an offer to form a coalition government, with David at its head and Jonathan as second-in-command.

The biblical narrative gives no background leading up to David's and Jonathan's meeting, and no interpretation of its significance for Israel is noted. Nevertheless, we may speculate that the covenant of Ziph was the result of careful planning on the part of the two young men. They both understood that the deep cleavage which was developing within Israel was the result of Saul's irrational insecurity and fear which had driven David from the king's court. Likewise they could foresee that Saul's preoccupation with his search for David was reopening the way for a resurgence of Philistine power (cf. 23:1–14,27; 28:1—31:13). As matters now stood, neither David nor Jonathan could form a viable government without the other because each was backed by interest groups which were too powerful to be ignored.

A coalition, however, was still possible. Although David's patience and faith were drawn thin, he had not used his forces against Israel. Jonathan, for his part, was hopefully in a position to guarantee that Saul would be unable to capture his friend David. Together they would be able to restore peaceful rule to Israel. First, however, Saul had to be reckoned with.

From the very onset of Saul's illness, neither Jonathan nor David has been portrayed in actions which were detrimental to the king's best interests. Although they were convinced that the Lord was in the process of demonstrating his support of David's reign, there could be no thought of forcibly removing Saul from the throne. They would have to bide their time and wait for the Lord to deal with the reigning king according to his way and in his own time. *Saul my father also knows this* (see comment on 24:16–22).

(7) *Ziphites Betray David (23:19–29)*

19 Then the Ziphites went up to Saul at Gibeah, saying, "Does not David hide among us in the strongholds at Horesh, on the hill of Hachilah, which is south of Jeshimon? 20 Now come down, O king, according to all your heart's desire to come down; and our part shall be to surrender him into the king's hand." 21 And Saul said, "May you be blessed by the LORD; for you have had compassion on me. 22 Go, make yet more sure; know and see the place where his haunt is, and who has seen him there; for it is told me that he is very cunning. 23 See therefore, and take note of all the lurking places where he hides, and come back to me with sure information. Then I will go with you; and if he is in the land, I will search him out among all the thousands of Judah." 24 And they arose, and went to Ziph ahead of Saul.

Now David and his men were in the wilderness of Maon, in the Arabah to the south of Jeshimon. 25 And Saul and his men went to seek him. And David was told; therefore he went down to the rock which is in the wilderness of Maon. And when Saul heard that, he pursued after David in the wilderness of Maon. 26 Saul went on one side of the mountain, and David and his men on the other side of the mountain; and David was making haste to get away from Saul, as Saul and his men were closing in upon David and his men to capture them, 27 when a messenger came to Saul, saying, "Make haste and come; for the Philistines have made a raid upon the land." 28 So Saul returned from pursuing after David, and went against the Philistines; therefore that place was called the Rock of Escape. 29 And David went up from there, and dwelt in the strongholds of Engedi.

This is the first of two accounts of an attempt by the people of Ziph to deliver David into Saul's hands (cf. 26:1–25). In both contexts the treachery of the Ziphites immediately precedes an experience in which David demonstrates his reverence for Saul as the Lord's anointed after the king has been miraculously subjected to his power. Numerous other parallels also exist (cf. 23:19 and 26:1; 24:2 and 26:2; 24:16 and 26:17; 24:20 and 26:25; 24:22 and 26:25). The two accounts mutually support the general historical authenticity of the experience, but the specific circumstances surrounding the basic incident are difficult to ascertain.

David's and Jonathan's agreement to form a coalition government for Israel (cf. 23:15–18) still faced a basic problem: Saul remained on the throne and he continued in his pursuit of David. The Ziphites, well aware of Saul's power and vindictiveness, were prepared to *surrender* David as the people of Keilah had been before them (23:1–14). Learning that David's outlaws had been seen in the wilderness around Maon, Saul and his forces were scouting that area when news of a Philistine raid on Israel was brought to the king. Saul halted the search and withdrew to fight the Philistines without knowing that David was just beyond the next ridge. Undoubtedly later generations pointed to a specific mountain where David had so narrowly escaped capture by Saul: *therefore that place was called the Rock of Escape.*

Divine providence was again demonstrated in David's spectacular deliverance from almost certain capture by the king. The striking contrast between Saul's and David's personalities is seen by comparing this incident with the one which follows.

(8) Saul Delivered to David (24:1–22)

a. David Spares Saul (24:1–15)

¹ When Saul returned from following the Philistines, he was told, "Behold, David is in the wilderness of Engedi." ² Then Saul took three thousand chosen men out of all Israel, and went to seek David and his men in front of the Wildgoats' Rocks. ³ And he came to the sheepfolds by the way, where there was a cave; and Saul went in to relieve himself. Now David and his men were sitting in the innermost parts of the cave. ⁴ And the men of David said to him, "Here is the day of which the LORD said to you, 'Behold, I will give your enemy into your hand, and you shall do to him as it shall seem good to you.'" Then David arose and stealthily cut off the skirt of Saul's robe. ⁵ And afterward David's heart smote him, because he had cut off Saul's skirt. ⁶ He said to his men, "The LORD forbid that I should do this thing to my lord, the LORD's anointed, to put forth my hand against him, seeing he is the LORD's anointed." ⁷ So David persuaded his men with these words, and did not permit them to attack Saul. And Saul rose up and left the cave, and went upon his way.

⁸ Afterward David also arose, and went out of the cave, and called after Saul, "My lord the king!" And when Saul looked behind him, David bowed with his face to the earth, and did obeisance. ⁹ And David said to Saul, "Why do you listen to the words of men who say, 'Behold, David seeks your hurt'? ¹⁰ Lo, this day your eyes have seen how the LORD gave you today into my hand in the cave; and some bade me kill you, but I spared you. I said, 'I will not put forth my hand against my lord; for he is the LORD's anointed.' ¹¹ See, my father, see the skirt of your robe in my hand; for by the fact that I cut off the skirt of your robe, and did not kill you, you may know and see that there is no wrong or treason in my hands. I have not sinned against you, though you hunt my life to take it. ¹² May the LORD judge between me and you, may the LORD avenge me upon you; but my hand shall not be against you. ¹³ As the proverb of the ancients says, 'Out of the wicked comes forth wickedness'; but my hand shall not be against you. ¹⁴ After whom has the king of Israel come out? After whom do you pursue? After a dead dog! After a flea! ¹⁵ May the LORD therefore be judge, and give sentence between me and you, and see to it, and plead my cause, and deliver me from your hand."

Following his narrow escape in the wilderness of Ziph, David moved some 15 miles eastward into the wilderness of Judah to an area bordering on the Dead Sea. Life in this area is supported primarily by a hot spring named Engedi which emerges from the rocks nearly 400 feet above the Dead Sea. The surrounding territory except for the oasis adjacent to the spring is arid and rough, thus ideal for hiding fugitives.

The biblical narrative takes no notice of the outcome of Saul's expedition against the Philistines. Theirs may have been a swift nuisance raid or even a false alarm, for no battle is noted. Nevertheless, the king would not be deterred from his search for David. With 3000 crack troops he followed David to Engedi. Once again, however, the Lord intervened. This time to deliver Saul into David's hands.

David now had the power, seemingly a God-given opportunity, to remove the one last obstacle blocking his and Jonathan's plan to restore stability to Israel's government (23:15–18). The king could be killed or even captured, and the dissipation of Israel's energies, brought on by his persecution of a loyal subject, would be at an end. With Saul out of the way, a coalition government could be established, thus restoring reason and order to Israel's political structure.

David, however, was not anxious to assume personal control of matters under divine jurisdiction. Unlike Saul, he was willing to await the divinely appointed season (cf. 13:1–15) to carry out the Lord's command (cf. 15:1–23). David, therefore, restrained his men, who advised Saul's speedy execution, and cut off only the border of his robe instead.[29] If Saul was to be deposed as king of Israel, God would have to provide his own means for removing him from office. David would not lift up his hand against the Lord's anointed.

Nevertheless, the opportunity was to be fully exploited. Using the border of Saul's garment to prove that the king had actually been at his mercy, David rebuked Saul for his persistent willingness to believe him disloyal.

b. Saul Admits Injustice (24:16–22)

16 When David had finished speaking these words to Saul, Saul said, "Is this your voice, my son David?" And Saul lifted up his voice and wept. 17 He said to David, "You are more righteous than I; for you have repaid me good, whereas I have repaid you evil. 18 And you have declared this day how you have dealt well with me, in that you did not kill me when the LORD put me into your hands. 19 For if a man finds his enemy, will he let him go away safe? So may the LORD reward you with good for what you have done to me this day. 20 And now, behold, I know that you shall surely be king, and that the kingdom of Israel shall be established in your hand. 21 Swear to me therefore by the LORD that you will not cut off my descendants after me, and that you will not destroy my name out of my father's house." 22 And David swore this to Saul. Then Saul went home; but David and his men went up to the stronghold.

David proved his innocence of treasonable intentions by refusing to kill Saul in the cave at Engedi. The king, therefore, was forced to admit that his suspicions of David had been unjust all along and that he had been treating his subject unfairly. David had proved himself the better man by maintaining his composure in the face of serious provocation and by refusing to violate his integrity by returning evil for evil. In making this concession, Saul was acknowledging that he was no longer fit to rule. The administration of justice was a basic responsibility of the king, and his judgment had just been proven seriously deficient.

In the light of his confession of injustice, Saul acknowledged that David would rule in Israel; and he requested generous treatment of his family when David came to power. This passage is usually considered simply as an anticipatory statement of the role that David would eventually play in Israel (Hertzberg, p. 197; McKane, p. 147). As such, however, it is only very loosely tied to David's predicament at Engedi. Saul's concession apparently meant little to David in the way of encouragement, and it meant nothing to Saul if we are to judge by his actions.

On the other hand, Saul's statements outside the cave at Engedi are remarkably similar to those of Jonathan when he met with David in the wilderness of Ziph (23:15–18). There the two made a covenant to establish a coalition government with David at its head and Jonathan as second-in-command. It even appears that Jonathan's negotiations were made with his father's full knowledge and approval: "And

---

[29] McKane (pp. 148–9) suggests that by cutting off the king's robe, David was joining Samuel in rejecting Saul as the Lord's anointed (cf. 15:27). This would account for his contrition for his action (vv. 5–7) as he came to realize the enduring nature of God's blessing. Note the similarity of this act and that of Ahijah (1 Kings 11:26–40).

he [Jonathan] said to him, 'Fear not; for the hand of Saul my father shall not find you; you shall be king over Israel, and I shall be next to you; Saul my father also knows this' " (23:17).

It is true that Saul's actions subsequent to Jonathan's visit reflect no willingness on his part to step aside as king. Nevertheless, Saul may have encouraged this covenant and Jonathan's friendship with David to give his enemy a false sense of security. Jonathan would never have knowingly undertaken such a mission, but Saul appears capable of deceiving his own son in order to achieve his purposes (cf. 20:3).

If Saul actually had attempted to trick David with a false covenant, his plot with the Ziphites was all the more culpable. Likewise, God's frustration of his plans at the Rock of Escape (23:28) was even more appropriate, for Saul's treachery had come the full circle and the Lord had delivered him into David's hands at Engedi. God's powerful demonstration of support for David forced Saul to make an even less advantageous arrangement than the one which Jonathan had made with David at Ziph. This time Jonathan was not mentioned, but David reaffirmed his previous agreement to deal generously with Saul's (Jonathan's) family (20:42).

Saul may never have intended to keep this new agreement, and David certainly had every reason to be cautious. Even more suspicious of Saul's integrity than before, David went back to the stronghold when Saul went to Gibeah, hopefully to arrange for a transfer of power.

Unfortunately, nothing more is ever said about the outcome of Saul's recognition of David's right to rule (cf. comment on 24:16–22). It is interesting to note, however, that the nature of the biblical narrative changes somewhat at the end of chapter 24. The rapid development of David's rise to power pauses, and interesting sidelights on his outlaw existence are given: Samuel died (25:1); David acquired two wives (25:2–43) and lost another one (25:44). Only with a second version of the treachery of the Ziphites and of Saul's miraculous deliverance into David's hands (26:1–25) does the pace of the story resume. Then, sorely discouraged, David became a vassal of Achish king of Gath and awaited further changes in Israel. Perhaps, more deeply than we have realized, the new direction taken by the biblical narrative has been influenced by the death of Samuel (25:1; cf. 1 Chron. 29:29).

Is this your voice? These words fit better in 26:17 where darkness prevents Saul's easy recognition of David. In the present context Saul seems to be expressing amazement at David's graciousness: "Can you, David, really mean what you have said?"

I know. This term in Hebrew (*yada'ti*) may convey a broad variety of meanings in addition to its more common rendering reflected in the RSV. The translation "I confess" or "I acknowledge" would be more closely in accord with the interpretation in the comments above (cf. Jer. 3:13; 14:20; Psalm 51:3).

(9) *David Marries Abigail (25:1–44)*

This account of David's marriage to Abigail ranks as one of the literary masterpieces of the Old Testament. The author has combined sharp character portrayals, romance, intrigue, wisdom, and humor into one of the best examples of short story writing in ancient literature. It is not a simple story, however. What at first appears to be just a well-narrated account of one of David's more interesting marriages in reality tells of a subtle, but serious, moral crisis in David's life.

At Engedi David had refused to take God's administration of justice into his own hands. He had consequently treated Saul with utmost generosity in spite of the king's repeated attempts to take his life. In dealing with Nabal, however, David was ready to murder every male member of an entire family over an insult and needed food. Only God's timely intervention in the person of Nabal's beautiful wife restrained

a. David Sells Protection (25:1–17)

¹ Now Samuel died; and all Israel assembled and mourned for him, and they buried him in his house at Ramah.

Then David rose and went down to the wilderness of Paran. ² And there was a man in Maon, whose business was in Carmel. The man was very rich; he had three thousand sheep and a thousand goats. He was shearing his sheep in Carmel. ³ Now the name of the man was Nabal, and the name of his wife Abigail. The woman was of good understanding and beautiful, but the man was churlish and ill-behaved; he was a Calebite. ⁴ David heard in the wilderness that Nabal was shearing his sheep. ⁵ So David sent ten young men; and David said to the young men, "Go up to Carmel, and go to Nabal, and greet him in my name. ⁶ And thus you shall salute him: 'Peace be to you, and peace be to your house, and peace be to all that you have. ⁷ I hear that you have shearers; now your shepherds have been with us, and we did them no harm, and they missed nothing, all the time they were in Carmel. ⁸ Ask your young men, and they will tell you. Therefore let my young men find favor in your eyes; for we come on a feast day. Pray, give whatever you have at hand to your servants and to your son David.'"

⁹ When David's young men came, they said all this to Nabal in the name of David; and then they waited. ¹⁰ And Nabal answered David's servants, "Who is David? Who is the son of Jesse? There are many servants nowadays who are breaking away from their masters. ¹¹ Shall I take my bread and my water and my meat that I have killed for my shearers, and give it to men who come from I do not know where?" ¹² So David's young men turned away, and came back and told him all this. ¹³ And David said to his men, "Every man gird on his sword!" And every man of them girded on his sword; David also girded on his sword; and about four hundred men went up after David, while two hundred remained with the baggage.

¹⁴ But one of the young men told Abigail, Nabal's wife, "Behold, David sent messengers out of the wilderness to salute our master; and he railed at them. ¹⁵ Yet the men were very good to us, and we suffered no harm, and we did not miss anything when we were in the fields, as long as we went with them; ¹⁶ they were a wall to us both by night and by day, all the while we were with them keeping the sheep. ¹⁷ Now therefore know this and consider what you should do; for evil is determined against our master and against all his house, and he is so ill-natured that one cannot speak to him."

In a modern, well-ordered society, David's means of supporting his troops would be considered a form of illegal extortion. For restraining his own motley band (22:2) and warding off raids from passing bedouin (cf. 30:1 f.), David expected, and was prepared to collect, tribute from the local population.

While some property owners obviously objected to David's demands, his expectations do not appear to have been considered excessive by the standards of his own day. Apparently Nabal's own servants and even his wife felt that David was due some compensation for the protection he had afforded Nabal's shepherds in the wilderness. Moreover, David's men appeared for payment at the end of the shearing season when the property owner could normally be expected to give a feast and share his bounty with his neighbors (cf. 2 Sam. 13:23).

Although it is nowhere explicit, our author seems to imply that Nabal's rebuff to David is politically motivated. David is compared to a servant who has broken away from his master, a rebel whom Nabal was unwilling to support. David apparently encountered a considerable number of people who, like Nabal, the Ziphites, and the people of Keilah, remained loyal to Saul. Abigail, on the other hand, took provisions to David, not just because he was a powerful warlord, but because the Lord had appointed him prince (*nagid*) over Israel (25:30). The struggle for Israel's throne had become a bitterly contested issue which even divided many homes among God's people.

Now Samuel died (see comment on 24:16–22).

David now went **to the wilderness of Paran.** The Vaticanus manuscript of the Septuagint reads here **Maon,** and the rest of the present context assumes that locality. **Carmel** (Heb.: *garden-land*) refers to a village about seven miles south-southeast of Hebron and not the mountain promentory south of Accho (Josh. 15:55; 1 Sam. 15:12). The wilderness of Paran associated with Moses' time (Num. 13:26 cf. Deut. 1:1–22 was located near Kadeshbarnea and hence too far south to be the territory involved here.

Nabal was a Calebite. The author displays a rather low estimate of the Calebites who comprised a clan within the tribe of Judah. Note how the author associates Nabal's clan with his character (churlishness and ill-behavior) rather than with his home town.

They were a wall to us. Compare this figure of speech with Israel's experience at the Red Sea (Ex. 14:22).

b. Abigail Intercedes (25:18–31)

¹⁸ Then Abigail made haste, and took two hundred loaves, and two skins of wine, and five sheep ready dressed, and five measures of parched grain, and a hundred clusters of raisins, and two hundred cakes of figs, and laid them on asses. ¹⁹ And she said to her young men, "Go on before me; behold, I come after you." But she did not tell her husband Nabal. ²⁰ And as she rode on the ass, and came down under cover of the mountain, behold, David and his men came down toward her; and she met them. ²¹ Now David had said, "Surely in vain have I guarded all that this fellow has in the wilderness, so that nothing was missed of all that belonged to him; and he has returned me evil for good. ²² God do so to David and more also, if by morning I leave so much as one male of all who belong to him."

²³ When Abigail saw David, she made haste, and alighted from the ass, and fell before David on her face, and bowed to the ground. ²⁴ She fell at his feet and said, "Upon me alone, my lord, be the guilt; pray let your handmaid speak in your ears, and hear the words of your handmaid. ²⁵ Let not my lord regard this ill-natured fellow, Nabal; for as his name is, so is he; Nabal is his name, and folly is with him; but I your handmaid did not see the young men of my lord, whom you sent. ²⁶ Now then, my lord, as the LORD lives, and as your soul lives, seeing the LORD has restrained you from bloodguilt, and from taking vengeance with your own hand, now then let your enemies and those who seek to do evil to my lord be as Nabal. ²⁷ And now let this present which your servant has brought to my lord be given to the young men who follow my lord. ²⁸ Pray forgive the trespass of your handmaid; for the LORD will certainly make my lord a sure house, because my lord is fighting the battles of the LORD; and evil shall not be found in you so long as you live. ²⁹ If men rise up to pursue you and to seek your life, the life of my lord shall be bound in the bundle of the living in the care of the LORD your God; and the lives of your enemies he shall sling out as from the hollow of a sling. ³⁰ And when the LORD has done to my lord according to all the good that he has spoken concerning you, and has appointed you prince over Israel, ³¹ my lord shall have no cause of grief, or pangs of conscience, for having shed blood without cause or for my lord taking vengeance himself. And when the LORD has dealt well with my lord, then remember your handmaid."

David's role as the unofficial, and sometimes unwelcome, protector of life in the Judean desert seems to have been considered reasonably legitimate (cf. comment on 25:1–16). Nevertheless, we are not to conclude that David's plans for a violent redress of Nabal's insult are to be condoned. Such actions would be expected of a vicious brigand, but they were not worthy of God's chosen leader for his people. David had decided in the cave at Engedi that he would not raise up his hand against the lawful king of Israel. Now in Carmel he is led to see that he should not use his power to ride roughshod over his opponents among the common people either (25:26,33).

When Abigail learned of her husband's insulting rejection of David's request for tribute, she quickly assembled a gift of provisions and secretly went out to assuage David's wrath. Assuming full responsibility for the affront to David's pride, she begged him not to take vengeance into his own hands but to await the divine reckoning which was certain to come in good time. Her response was a wise one, indicating her awareness both of the political events that were rending Israel and of their theological significance as well.

Go on before me. Abigail sent her gift before her so that David might be well-disposed toward meeting her when she arrived (cf. Gen 32:13–21). The size of the gift seems fairly modest when compared to the number of David's men.

Abigail made a word play on Nabal's name: *for as his name is, so is he.* In Hebrew the root meaning is senseless or foolish. The word is especially used of one who lacks perception of ethical or moral values so that Abigail's pun is particularly fitting.

Now then, my lord, as the Lord lives. My lord stands for David, and *the Lord* represents God. This confusion does not exist in the Hebrew text where the consonants for God's proper name (*YHWH*) appear wherever the RSV has *the Lord.*

Bound in the bundle of the living is a figure of speech which appears to be based on the idea that a householder made a bundle of his most precious possessions so that he could protect them and give them his personal attention (Smith, p. 227). The ancients felt that *living* men in particular fell under God's direct supervision. Hence this statement represents Abigail's conviction that David would live a long, full life under God's personal care.

c. David Forgoes Vengeance (25:32-44)

32 And David said to Abigail, "Blessed be the Lord, the God of Israel, who sent you this day to meet me! 33 Blessed be your discretion, and blessed be you, who have kept me this day from bloodguilt and from avenging myself with my own hand! 34 For as surely as the Lord the God of Israel lives, who has restrained me from hurting you, unless you had made haste and come to meet me, truly by morning there had not been left to Nabal so much as one male." 35 Then David received from her hand what she had brought him; and he said to her, "Go up in peace to your house; see, I have hearkened to your voice, and I have granted your petition."
36 And Abigail came to Nabal; and, lo, he was holding a feast in his house, like the feast of a king. And Nabal's heart was merry within him, for he was very drunk; so she told him nothing at all until the morning light. 37 And in the morning, when the wine had gone out of Nabal, his wife told him these things, and his heart died within him, and he became as a stone. 38 And about ten days later the Lord smote Nabal; and he died.
39 When David heard that Nabal was dead, he said, "Blessed be the Lord who has avenged the insult I received at the hand of Nabal, and has kept back his servant from evil; the Lord has returned the evil-doing of Nabal upon his own head." Then David sent and wooed Abigail, to make her his wife. 40 And when the servants of David came to Abigail at Carmel, they said to her, "David has sent us to you to take you to him as his wife." 41 And she rose and bowed with her face to the ground, and said, "Behold, your handmaid is a servant to wash the feet of the servants of my lord." 42 And Abigail made haste and rose and mounted on an ass, and her five maidens attended her; she went after the messengers of David, and became his wife.
43 David also took Ahinoam of Jezreel; and both of them became his wives. 44 Saul had given Michal his daughter, David's wife, to Palti the son of Laish, who was of Gallim.

By diverting David from his retaliatory raid, Abigail had kept him from shedding innocent blood thereby bringing reproach upon his rule even before it began. Nevertheless, the author makes it clear that God is ultimately the chief actor in this drama. Abigail had served as the Lord's spokesman as he again protected and directed the life of his anointed prince.

Although the climax of the story had been reached, the denouement was no less interesting for the early reader. The ancient sense of fair play and ancient theology agreed in their demand that all wrongs must be set right before action came to an end. By declining to retaliate against Nabal, David allowed the responsibility for vengeance to reside with the Lord where it properly belonged.

Nabal's untimely death and his widow's subsequent marriage were understood as the divine vindication of David's innocence and propriety in the whole affair. David's honor had been defended by the Lord himself!

When Abigail told Nabal what had transpired, *his heart died within him.* The heart's role in the circulation of the blood was unknown to ancient peoples. In Hebrew psychology, the heart represented the center of man's inner being from which sprang his will, action, and reason. Nabal, therefore, was struck dumb and paralyzed. After lying in a coma for ten days, he suffered another attack and died.

David . . . wooed Abigail. David apparently had great respect for Abigail's wisdom as well as an appreciation for her beauty. On her part, Abigail was willing to serve as one of his most menial servants. Nothing is said of the material or moral support which this marriage provided for David, but it must have been considerable (Hertzberg, p. 205). The same could be said of his marriage to Ahinoam of Jezreel in Judah.

Saul had given Michal . . . to Palti. Saul may have justified his actions by arguing that David had spurned Michal and given her a bad name when he abandoned her in his flight from court (cf. Deut. 22:13-21; 24;1-4). On the other hand, Saul may have been moved by political motives. He may have been attempting to deny David any claim to a legitimate connection with Israel's royal family. Certainly this marriage had an unusual significance for David (2 Sam. 3:14-16).

(10) Ziphites Repeat Treachery (26:1-25)

a. David Penetrates Saul's Camp (26:1-12)

¹ Then the Ziphites came to Saul at Gibeah, saying, "Is not David hiding himself on the hill of Hachilah, which is on the east of Jeshimon?" ² So Saul arose and went down to the wilderness of Ziph, with three thousand chosen men of Israel, to seek David in the wilderness of Ziph. ³ And Saul encamped on the hill of Hachilah, which is beside the road on the east of Jeshimon. But David remained in the wilderness; and when he saw that Saul came after him into the wilderness, ⁴ David sent out spies, and learned of a certainty that Saul had come. ⁵ Then David rose and came to the place where Saul had encamped; and David saw the place where Saul lay, with Abner the son of Ner, the commander of his army; Saul was lying within the encampment, while the army was encamped around him.

⁶ Then David said to Ahimelech the Hittite, and to Joab's brother Abishai the son of Zeruiah, "Who will go down with me into the camp to Saul?" And Abishai said, "I will go down with you." ⁷ So David and Abishai went to the army by night; and there lay Saul sleeping within the encampment, with his spear stuck in the ground at his head; and Abner and the army lay around him. ⁸ Then said Abishai to David, "God has given your enemy into your hand this day; now therefore let me pin him to the earth with one stroke of the spear, and I will not strike him twice." ⁹ But David said to Abishai, "Do not destroy him; for who can put forth his hand against the Lord's anointed, and be guiltless?" ¹⁰ And David said, "As the Lord lives, the Lord will smite him; or his day shall come to die; or he shall go down into battle and perish. ¹¹ The Lord forbid that I should put forth my hand against the Lord's anointed; but take now the spear that is at his head, and the jar of water, and let us go." ¹² So David took the spear and the jar of water from Saul's head; and they went away. No man saw it, or knew it, nor did any awake; for they were all asleep, because a deep sleep from the Lord had fallen upon them.

The similarities between the contents of the present chapter and the events narrated in 23:19—24:22 are so striking that they cannot be ignored. A majority of commentators have concluded that the two passages are variant accounts of the same incident and that the author has included both in order to accomplish his own special purpose. On the other hand, many still insist that David was betrayed twice by the Ziphites, that Saul employed 3000 troops on both expeditions, that God miraculously delivered Saul into David's hands on both occasions, that each time Saul said, "Is this your voice, my son David," and that Saul confessed his injustices toward David at the conclusion.

The real question, however, is not whether these passages reflect a single or separate occurrences. It is far more important to discover why the biblical author chose to include two such similar incidents out of all the countless events that transpired between Saul and David. Of course we can never say with finality what went on in the minds of people who lived thousands of years ago. Nevertheless, we can note the outstanding differences between these two episodes and draw certain conclusions from our findings.

The forms of the stories involve differences of detail which are too numerous to list here, but by and large the same basic issues or theological interests are reflected in both passages. The present context, however, varies significantly from the first account of Ziphite treachery and subsequent events in four major aspects: it portrays David in a more daring role (vv. 4 f.); it tells of David's rebuke of Abner (vv. 15 f.); it reflects David's dread of leaving Israel (vv. 19 f.); and it gives a much more general view of Saul's blessing of David (v. 25). These differences will be discussed in greater detail in a consideration of specific verses.

The territory *on the east side of Jeshimon* is the area between the hill country of Judah and the Dead Sea. It is more frequently called the wilderness of Judah. Since Jeshimon was of indeterminate size, Hachilah could be considered to its east (v. 1) or south (23:19). Exact sites are unknown, but the area involved lay in a triangle between Hebron, Ziph, and Engedi.

Who will go down with me into the camp to Saul? Previous accounts of David's deliverance from Saul at the Rock of Escape (23:28) and in the cave at Engedi (24:1 f.) stressed divine instrumentality. David is pictured almost as a passive recipient of the Lord's grace and power. In the present context, however, David is portrayed as a daring warrior whose exploits and adventures are eagerly recounted. After luring Saul out into the wilderness, David personally scouted Saul's camp and spotted him sleeping in the midst of his entire army.

Again, as in the cave at Engedi, David refused to allow harm to come upon the Lord's anointed, preferring to leave Saul's destiny in the Lord's hands (cf. comment on 24:1–15, 16–22). The most he could do was to take Saul's spear and canteen as an evidence of his successful penetration of the king's camp.

As in the previous account, however, it is apparent that David was not working alone. The Lord had made the entire adventure possible by causing an unusually deep sleep to fall upon the king and all his men.

b. David Confronts Saul (26:13–25)

13 Then David went over to the other side, and stood afar off on the top of the mountain, with a great space between them; 14 and David called to the army, and to Abner the son of Ner, saying, "Will you not answer, Abner?" Then Abner answered, "Who are you that calls to the king?" 15 And David said to Abner, "Are you not a man? Who is like you in Israel? Why then have you not kept watch over your lord the king? For one of the people came in to destroy the king your lord. 16 This thing that you have done is not good. As the Lord lives, you deserve to die, because you have not kept watch over your lord, the Lord's anointed. And now see where the king's spear is, and the jar of water that was at his head."

17 Saul recognized David's voice, and said, "Is this your voice, my son David?" And David said, "It is my voice, my lord, O king." 18 And he said, "Why does my lord pursue after his servant? For what have I done? What guilt is on my hands? 19 Now therefore let my lord the king hear the words of his servant. If it is the Lord who has stirred you up against me, may he accept an offering; but if it is men, may they be cursed before the Lord, for they have driven me out this day that I should have no share in the heritage of the Lord, saying, 'Go, serve other gods.' 20 Now therefore, let not my blood fall to the earth away from the presence of the Lord; for the king of Israel has come out to seek my life, like one who hunts a partridge in the mountains."

21 Then Saul said, "I have done wrong; return, my son David, for I will no more do you harm, because my life was precious in your eyes this day; behold, I have played the fool, and have erred exceedingly." 22 And David made answer, "Here is the spear, O king! Let one of the young men come over and fetch it. 23 The Lord rewards every man for his righteousness and his faithfulness; for the Lord gave you into my hand today, and I would not put forth my hand against the Lord's anointed. 24 Behold, as your life was precious this day in my sight, so may my life be precious in the sight of the Lord, and may he deliver me out of all tribulation." 25 Then Saul said to David, "Blessed be you, my son David! You will do many things and will succeed in them." So David went his way, and Saul returned to his place.

The author heightens our awareness of the danger of David's adventure by noting how he puts a safe distance between himself and Saul's army before daring to awaken the king. Then, as if to prolong the drama, he addresses himself to Abner. The biting sarcasm of David's indictment of Abner is not directed as much toward the man himself as it is toward the futility of his task. Abner's loyalty to Saul is unquestionable. It was he who had introduced David to Saul (17:55-58) and he who sat in a honored position by the king's side at affairs of state (20:25). After Saul's death at Gilboa, it was Abner who attempted to establish Saul's son upon the throne of Israel (2 Sam. 2:8). David even seems to have had a genuine respect for his adversary of longstanding (2 Sam. 3:31-35). David's sarcastic rebuke of one with such impeccable credentials pointed out the futility of having even the best of men try to do a job when God is not in it. Abner had failed, not because he was a poor guard but because the Lord was working against him.

As David's conversation with Abner progressed, Saul recognized the familiar voice coming from the night and guessed David's identity. David immediately struck to the heart of the issue and asked Saul why he was pursuing him. If God was using Saul as an instrument of his wrath, David begged that forgiveness be granted speedily. If Saul's persecution were of human origin, however, David requested that a curse might fall on the men responsible. David recognized that he was being driven from Israel. In a plea addressed both to God and to Saul, David begged for some opportunity to be given so that he would not have to leave his own people. He was aware of all the dangers of exile: personal, political, and religious. He longed for another way, but he was being hunted like an animal and there seemed to be no other choice. The author has selected and arranged his materials with consummate skill to convey the dramatic significance of the momentous events that are taking place. As David faces in the next chapter his sojourn among the Philistines, this daring desert raid offers the author an opportunity to explore David's reluctance to take the decisive steps which are before him.

Go, serve other gods. In some stages of Old Testament thought, the people believed that the Lord could be worshiped only amongst his own people and in the territory occupied by them. Thus, Ruth's decision to stay with Naomi involved the acceptance of Naomi's God (Ruth 1:16; 2:12). Also when Naaman wanted to worship the Lord in his native land, he took Israelite soil upon which he might build an altar (2 Kings 5:17). David was reluctant to leave Israel because he felt that this would in some way separate him from his closest fellowship with God (cf. 22:5). Other Old Testament passages portray God's universal dominion (Judg. 5:19-23; 1 Sam. 6:1-9; Jer. 2:5-11), and David may even have known this side of God's nature in his mind. Nevertheless, David's emotions caused him to dread separating himself from his land, his people, and his God.

David used an interesting description of Saul's pursuit: *like one who hunts a partridge in the mountains.* This bird would not fly from danger unless abruptly startled, but it would run along the ground. Hunters would keep the bird moving until it was exhausted and then it could be captured with ease. This was exactly Saul's strategy in his pursuit of David.

You will do many things and will succeed in them. Saul's statements about David's future are much more guarded here than following their encounter at Engedi (24:20). In this context Saul's pronouncement is in the form of an enigmatic oracle that can be either hopeful or ominous depending on its interpretation. Saul simply said, "You will do many things and will succeed in them." Seen in a positive light, these words recognize David's ability and foresee a bright future for him. To the gullible and the naive, it sounded as if the king were again conceding victory to the rebels in the knowledge that David would ultimately triumph.

David, who knew Saul better, must have noted the things that were left unsaid.

Saul, for example, gave no indication that he sensed the loss of divine leadership or that he recognized God's power working through David's actions. Even more pointedly, he failed to associate David in any way with Israel's throne.

In short, David was informed that he was free to pursue his destiny in Israel only if he gave up all ideas of becoming king. Whatever hope was held out for a peaceful settlement of Israel's dynastic difficulties, after the experience at Engedi, had now been lost. With utter resolution David and Saul went their separate ways.

6. *David Joins the Philistines* (*1 Sam. 27:1 —2 Sam. 1:27*)

(1) *David Becomes a Vassal* (*27:1–12*)

¹ And David said in his heart, "I shall now perish one day by the hand of Saul; there is nothing better for me than that I should escape to the land of the Philistines; then Saul will despair of seeking me any longer within the borders of Israel, and I shall escape out of his hand." ² So David arose and went over, he and the six hundred men who were with him, to Achish the son of Maoch, king of Gath. ³ And David dwelt with Achish at Gath, he and his men, every man with his household, and David with his two wives, Ahinoam of Jezreel, and Abigail of Carmel, Nabal's widow. ⁴ And when it was told Saul that David had fled to Gath, he sought for him no more.
⁵ Then David said to Achish, "If I have found favor in your eyes, let a place be given me in one of the country towns, that I may dwell there; for why should your servant dwell in the royal city with you?" ⁶ So that day Achish gave him Ziklag; therefore Ziklag has belonged to the kings of Judah to this day. ⁷ And the number of the days that David dwelt in the country of the Philistines was a year and four months.
⁸ Now David and his men went up, and made raids upon the Geshurites, the Girzites, and the Amalekites; for these were the inhabitants of the land from of old, as far as Shur, to the land of Egypt. ⁹ And David smote the land, and left neither man nor woman alive, but took away the sheep, the oxen, the asses, the camels, and the garments, and came back to Achish. ¹⁰ When Achish asked, "Against whom have you made a raid today?" David would say, "Against the Negeb of Judah," or "Against the Negeb of the Jerahmeelites," or, "Against the Negeb of the Kenites." ¹¹ And David saved neither man nor woman alive, to bring tidings to Gath, thinking, "Lest they should tell about us, and say, 'So David has done.'" Such was his custom all the while he dwelt in the country of the Philistines. ¹² And Achish trusted David, thinking, "He has made himself utterly abhorred by his people Israel; therefore he shall be my servant always."

David left the wilderness of Ziph with a clearer understanding of his limited future in Israel. Even if Saul could be trusted to spare his life (26:21), the price of peace would be high. David would have to abandon his sense of divine mission to secure his personal safety. Since he was neither able to trust Saul nor willing to ignore his anointment as Israel's future king, Saul's persistent pursuit left David no alternative other than to leave Israelite territory.

David's life among the Philistines was also fraught with danger, however. On the one hand, there was always the possibility that Achish would uncover David's true goals and would take action against him. David's rather sizable personal army could have provided a measure of protection for him, but they would have had no hope of withstanding a concerted Philistine campaign.

On the other hand, David might cut himself off from his own people by associating with their Philistine foes. David's actions must have appeared treasonable at the time, and only later would his true motives have become known. Nevertheless, through a series of cunning ruses, David was able to convince Achish of his loyalty without raising his hand against his own people. The biblical narrative traces with apparent admiration David's skill in manipulating the Philistines, but throughout the whole there is an unspoken awareness that here again the Lord is manifesting his continuing care of Israel's future king.

David dwelt with Achish at Gath, he and his men. David had previously appeared before Achish alone (21:10–15). The conditions are so vastly different, however, that only the major characters are the same. The Philistines had now had time to learn that David was an outlaw from Saul's court. As the leader of 600 outcasts from Israelite society, David represented a powerful political tool which Achish hoped to use against his enemies. These men with their families probably represented a total group of about 2000 people. The problem of feeding this group would have helped persuade Achish to see that David's men were profitably employed.

Achish gave him Ziklag. Ziklag was a town about 16 miles south-southeast of Gath. Almost the same distance southwest of Hebron, the town was on the Israelite-Philistine frontier and hence in an ideal location for raids on Judah. We are not told how Achish came to be in possession of the town, but it is otherwise associated with the cities occupied by Judah (Josh. 15:31) or Simeon (Josh. 19:5). The reference to the *kings of Judah,* found only here in Samuel, reflects an editorial viewpoint after the division of the monarchy.

A year and four months refers to the total time David spent among the Philistines, not just his stay in Gath. This is such a short time, however, that it is not surprising that the other Philistine leaders refused to trust him or that Achish wanted the period to sound more impressive (29:3).

The Geshurites, the Girzites, and the Amalekites. The Amalekites were the remnants of Saul's slaughter among Israel's enemies in the wilderness south of Judah (cf. comment on 15:4–9). The Geshurites were a small nomadic group who wandered in northern Sinai east of Egypt (Josh. 13:2). The Girzites are otherwise unknown.

And David . . . left neither man nor woman alive. David's actions had nothing whatever to do with religious requirements for "holy war" (cf. comment on 15:1–3). He freely took spoil but killed all the people to keep word of his duplicity from filtering back to the Philistines. The biblical record does not censure David for his ruthless actions; so apparently he was excused in the mind of the biblical writer either on the grounds that these people were Israel's enemies or that as foreigners they were not due the consideration given Nabal (cf. 25:26).

David pretended to be raiding the Negeb (dry country) of the southern Israelite clans. The Jerahmeelites were eventually considered a part of Judah proper (1 Chron. 2:9), and the Kenites were traditionally friends of the Hebrew people (1 Sam. 15:6; 30:29). Both were nomadic groups whose territory can no longer be located with certainty.

(2) *Saul Consults a Medium (28:1–14)*

¹ In those days the Philistines gathered their forces for war, to fight against Israel. And Achish said to David, "Understand that you and your men are to go out with me in the army." ² David said to Achish, "Very well, you shall know what your servant can do." And Achish said to David, "Very well, I will make you my bodyguard for life."
³ Now Samuel had died, and all Israel had mourned for him and buried him in Ramah, his own city. And Saul had put the mediums and the wizards out of the land. ⁴ The Philistines assembled, and came and encamped at Shunem; and Saul gathered all Israel, and they encamped at Gilboa. ⁵ When Saul saw the army of the Philistines, he was afraid, and his heart trembled greatly. ⁶ And when Saul inquired of the Lord, the Lord did not answer him, either by dreams, or by Urim, or by prophets. ⁷ Then Saul said to his servants, "Seek out for me a woman who is a medium, that I may go to her and inquire of her." And his servants said to him, "Behold, there is a medium at Endor."
⁸ So Saul disguised himself and put on other garments, and went, he and two men with him; and they came to the woman by night. And he said, "Divine for me by a spirit, and bring up for me whomever I shall name to you." ⁹ The woman said to him, "Surely you know what Saul has done, how he has cut off the mediums and the wizards from the land. Why then are you laying a snare for my life to bring about my death?" ¹⁰ But Saul swore to her by the Lord, "As the Lord lives, no punishment shall come upon you for this thing." ¹¹ Then the woman said, "Whom shall I bring up for you?" He said, "Bring up Samuel for me." ¹² When the woman saw Samuel, she cried out with a loud voice; and the woman said to Saul, "Why

have you deceived me? You are Saul." ¹³ The king said to her, "Have no fear; what do you see?" And the woman said to Saul, "I see a god coming up out of the earth." ¹⁴ He said to her, "What is his appearance?" And she said, "An old man is coming up; and he is wrapped in a robe." And Saul knew that it was Samuel, and he bowed with his face to the ground, and did obeisance.

For some 16 months David had been able to avoid any hostile acts against his own people while he lived among the Philistines. During that time he had deceived Achish into thinking him completely loyal by pretending to carry out raids on Judah while he was actually attacking Israel's nomadic enemies in the far south. The opportunity for continuing such deception seemed to come to an end, however, as Achish informed David that he and his troops would be expected to fight for the Philistines in their forthcoming offensive against Israel. In this engagement, David would be unable to avoid having his actions directly observed by his Philistine overlords since Achish had appointed him his own chief bodyguard. As a means of heightening the suspense of his story, the author allows the reader to contemplate David's fate (resumed in 29:1—30:31) while he introduces an interesting account of Saul's final rejection by the Lord (28:3-25).

Saul is portrayed as a tragic figure whose life bore the marks of divine rejection. Badly alarmed by news of the Philistine mobilization, Saul earnestly sought instruction from the Lord, but he was denied guidance through the normal means of divine revelation. In utter desperation, he had a necromancer or spiritualistic medium located so that he could consult the ghost of Samuel who at one time had been his spiritual mentor.

The sad depths to which Saul had fallen are all too apparent in the story. Cut off from legitimate prophetic (15:35) and priestly (22:11-23) counsel, Saul turned to the necromancers and wizards who were prohibited by law (Lev. 19:31; 20:6) and whom he himself had purged from Israel earlier in his reign. The biblical account does not seem to have regarded the consultation of the dead as an impossibility or even as a hoax perpetrated by the "witch" of Endor. Instead, such practices were regarded as contaminating influences drawn from the religious customs of Israel's neighbors (Deut. 18:9-14). The pathetic picture of a rejected king is thus completed as Saul laid aside his royal robes for a humble disguise and sought one last desperate means to receive a favorable word from the Lord.

The Philistines . . . encamped at Shunem. In arranging his materials, the author apparently placed other values above chronological order. The events described here took place on the eve of the battle at Mount Gilboa (28:19) and would properly fit between chapters 30 and 31. The larger context traces the advance of the Philistines from Aphek, about ten miles northeast of Joppa (29:1), through the Valley of Jezreel (29:11; cf. 31:7) to Shunem, some six miles northwest of the spring at Mount Gilboa (28:4; cf. 29:1). Saul's journey to Endor, about eight miles north of his camp at Gilboa, therefore, was a rather daring escapade running through enemy lines.

When the woman saw Samuel, she cried out. No explanation is given as to why the medium recognized Saul only when she *saw* Samuel. Some Greek manuscripts read Saul rather than Samuel. Hence, when she saw (and recognized) Saul, she cried out. Apparently, only the woman saw Samuel's ghostly figure. Saul, however, seems to have heard Samuel's voice and to have conversed with him (28:15).

I see a god coming up out of the earth. The word god (*'elohim*) is a common noun. Used in the Old Testament it has a variety of meanings which include the God of Israel, idols, and spiritual beings of various types. Samuel is portrayed as a spirit, roused out of his slumber in Sheol where existence was seen as a state of weakness and forgetfulness (Psalm 88:4, 12).

(3) Saul's House Condemned (28:15-25)

15 Then Samuel said to Saul, "Why have you disturbed me by bringing me up?" Saul answered, "I am in great distress; for the Philistines are warring against me, and God has turned away from me and answers me no more, either by prophets or by dreams; therefore I have summoned you to tell me what I shall do." 16 And Samuel said, "Why then do you ask me, since the LORD has turned from you and become your enemy? 17 The LORD has done to you as he spoke by me; for the LORD has torn the kingdom out of your hand, and given it to your neighbor, David. 18 Because you did not obey the voice of the LORD, and did not carry out his fierce wrath against Amalek, therefore the LORD has done this thing to you this day. 19 Moreover the LORD will give Israel also with you into the hand of the Philistines; and tomorrow you and your sons shall be with me; the LORD will give the army of Israel also into the hand of the Philistines." 20 Then Saul fell at once full length upon the ground, filled with fear because of the words of Samuel; and there was no strength in him, for he had eaten nothing all day and all night. 21 And the woman came to Saul, and when she saw that he was terrified, she said to him, "Behold, your handmaid has hearkened to you; I have taken my life in my hand, and have hearkened to what you have said to me. 22 Now therefore, you also hearken to your handmaid; let me set a morsel of bread before you; and eat, that you may have strength when you go on your way." 23 He refused, and said, "I will not eat." But his servants, together with the woman, urged him; and he hearkened to their words. So he arose from the earth, and sat upon the bed. 24 Now the woman had a fatted calf in the house, and she quickly killed it, and she took flour, and kneaded it and baked unleavened bread of it, 25 and she put it before Saul and his servants; and they ate. Then they rose and went away that night.

Driven to the brink of hysteria by the growing menace of the Philistine war machine, Saul sought instructions from the disgruntled specter of his deceased prophetic advisor. Saul represented himself as a man who had earnestly attempted to learn the Lord's will through the normal means of revelation but who had been denied divine counsel. Samuel, however, had confronted him with the Lord's judgment, but Saul refused to admit that he had been rejected in favor of David as king of Israel.

Saul had at first attempted forcibly to alter the Lord's plans by killing David. Since that had failed, he was frantically searching for a favorable oracle which would give him some hope of victory in his forthcoming conflict with the Philistines. Alas, while God's judgment might be delayed (from 15:26 on), it could not be thwarted. Samuel announced even before the battle began that God's sentence on Saul was certain of completion. Saul was informed that in combat the next day, Israel's armies would be defeated and that he and his sons would join Samuel in Sheol. Shattered by the emotional impact of Samuel's dire pronouncements and weakened by a day-long fast, Saul sank to the floor in a faint.

The story of the woman's ministry to her fallen king is marked with a tenderness and sympathy which are characteristic of the author's underlying attitude toward Saul. Although Saul had stubbornly refused to acknowledge the Lord's selection of his successor, he had made an irreplaceable contribution to the history of his people. As Israel's first king, he had won a respect and love which even his later failures could not erase. Drawing strength from the meal prepared by the woman of Endor, Saul went out as a condemned man to meet his fate in battle the next day.

(3) David Excluded from War (29:1-11)

1 Now the Philistines gathered all their forces at Aphek; and the Israelites were encamped by the fountain which is in Jezreel. 2 As the lords of the Philistines were passing on by hundreds and by thousands, and David and his men were passing on in the rear with Achish, 3 the commanders of the Philistines said, "What are these Hebrews doing here?" And Achish said to the commanders of the Philistines, "Is not this David, the servant of Saul, king of Israel, who has been with me now for days and years, and since he deserted to me I have found no fault in him to this day." 4 But the commanders of the Philistines were angry with him; and the commanders of the Philistines said to him, "Send the man back, that he may return to the place to which you have assigned him; he shall not go down with us to

battle, lest in the battle he become an adversary to us. For how could this fellow reconcile himself to his lord? Would it not be with the heads of the men here? 5 Is not this David, of whom they sing to one another in dances,

'Saul has slain his thousands,
  and David his ten thousands'?"

6 Then Achish called David and said to him, "As the LORD lives, you have been honest, and to me it seems right that you should march out and in with me in the campaign; for I have found nothing wrong in you from the day of your coming to me to this day. Nevertheless the lords do not approve of you. 7 So go back now; and go peaceably, that you may not displease the lords of the Philistines." 8 And David said to Achish, "But what have I done? What have you found in your servant from the day I entered your service until now, that I may not go and fight against the enemies of my lord the king?" 9 And Achish made answer to David, "I know that you are as blameless in my sight as an angel of God; nevertheless the commanders of the Philistines have said, 'He shall not go up with us to the battle.' 10 Now then rise early in the morning with the servants of your lord who came with you; and start early in the morning, and depart as soon as you have light." 11 So David set out with his men early in the morning, to return to the land of the Philistines. But the Philistines went up to Jezreel.

Without overt moralizing, the author again used the arrangement of his narrative materials to call attention to Saul's and David's contrasting roles in the Lord's plans for Israel. With the outcome of the battle at Gilboa already known, the end of Saul's tragic story was in sight. David, on the other hand, was steadily being drawn toward the destiny which had been implicit in his anointment at the hands of Samuel (16:1-13).

Once again the Lord was working through the historical process to bring his will to pass. One government was being set aside and the way opened for another to come to power. Now at the end of a dangerous Philistine exile, David was about to be relieved of the necessity of going into battle against his own people, thus forfeiting his right to claim Israel's throne peacefully.

As the Philistine troops were passing in review at Aphek before beginning their march to Jezreel (see comment on 28:4), their leaders noted with alarm the presence of the Hebrews at the end of the column. Achish defended his decision to bring David and his men on the grounds that they had given him no reason to suspect their loyalty since David had first deserted to his cause some considerable time before. The lords of the Philistines, however, perhaps remembering the defection of Hebrew mercenaries in the battle at Geba (14:21), insisted on sending David back to Ziklag.

Achish relayed the orders of the Philistine commanders to David and, in the strongest possible terms, professed confidence in his vassal's loyalty. Although David probably was very reluctant to go to war against his own people, the role that he was playing required him to protest the decision to send him to the rear. Nevertheless, David and his men were prepared to leave for home at first light the next day.

Lest in battle he become an adversary to us. The term for adversary is the same as that underlying the name Satan. It is used here as a common noun in a context which sheds important light on other Old Testament occurrences (cf. Job 1 and 2; Zech. 3:1-2). The Philistines were afraid that David would use this as occasion to regain Saul's favor by turning against them (cf. 18:25-27).

So go back now; and go peaceably. Achish expected David to be disappointed at being refused permission to join in the battle against Israel, and probably many of his men were. Soldiers profited by taking spoils in battle, and now after a long march, David's troops were returning home empty-handed. On at least one other occasion, mercenaries are known to have raided towns of their erstwhile employers under similar circumstances (2 Chron. 25:9-13). Achish is encouraging David to avoid any such untoward incidents on the way home. The stress on spoil in the next chapter attests that booty was an important issue with David's men.

(5) Amalekites Attack Ziklag (30:1-30)

a. Nomad Raiders Sack Ziklag (30:1-15)

¹ Now when David and his men came to Ziklag on the third day, the Amalekites had made a raid upon the Negeb and upon Ziklag. They had overcome Ziklag, and burned it with fire, ² and taken captive the women and all who were in it, both small and great; they killed no one, but carried them off, and went their way. ³ And when David and his men came to the city, they found it burned with fire, and their wives and sons and daughters taken captive. ⁴ Then David and the people who were with him raised their voices and wept, until they had no more strength to weep. ⁵ David's two wives also had been taken captive, Ahinoam of Jezreel, and Abigail the widow of Nabal of Carmel. ⁶ And David was greatly distressed; for the people spoke of stoning him, because all the people were bitter in soul, each for his sons and daughters. But David strengthened himself in the Lord his God.

⁷ And David said to Abiathar the priest, the son of Ahimelech, "Bring me the ephod." So Abiathar brought the ephod to David. ⁸ And David inquired of the Lord, "Shall I pursue after this band? Shall I overtake them?" He answered him, "Pursue; for you shall surely overtake and shall surely rescue." ⁹ So David set out, and the six hundred men who were with him, and they came to the brook Besor, where those stayed who were left behind. ¹⁰ But David went on with the pursuit, he and four hundred men; two hundred stayed behind, who were too exhausted to cross the brook Besor.

¹¹ They found an Egyptian in the open country, and brought him to David; and they gave him bread and he ate, they gave him water to drink, ¹² and they gave him a piece of a cake of figs and two clusters of raisins. And when he had eaten, his spirit revived; for he had not eaten bread or drunk water for three days and three nights. ¹³ And David said to him, "To whom do you belong? And where are you from?" He said, "I am a young man of Egypt, servant to an Amalekite; and my master left me behind because I fell sick three days ago. ¹⁴ We had made a raid upon the Negeb of the Cherethites and upon that which belongs to Judah and upon the Negeb of Caleb; and we burned Ziklag with fire." ¹⁵ And David said to him, "Will you take me down to this band?" And he said, "Swear to me by God, that you will not kill me, or deliver me into the hands of my master, and I will take you down to this band."

After completing a journey of some 60 miles through the heart of Philistine territory, David and his men returned to Ziklag to find it abandoned and in ruins. Faced with the loss of wives, children, and property, David's men exhausted themselves mourning and then turned in wrath upon their leader. David had, in fact, been detected in a serious tactical error which, in addition to the immediate peril that it brought upon his life, could also jeopardize his role as the future king of Israel. By taking his full complement of troops to Aphek, he had left his home base defenseless against marauding bands of Amalekite raiders.

David's military lapse was not irretrievable, however, for the Lord was still working on his behalf. After receiving a favorable divine oracle that rescue was still possible, David and his men set out on a forced march to track down the desert raiders. At a time when speed was of the essence, David's men came upon a starving Egyptian who, as a former Amalekite slave, was ready to lead the Hebrews to the raiders' camp.

They killed no one, but carried them off. The Amalekites had stolen the people to sell as slaves. The fact that no one was killed in the attack suggests that David had left the town utterly without defenders. If he had intended to arrange to have his troops dismissed before the battle against Israel, it is difficult to understand why he would have taken his entire garrison, thus leaving Ziklag so seriously exposed. Perhaps, as McKane (p. 166) suggests, he had originally planned to use his troops to disrupt the Philistine attack. In such a case, he would need every man available to withstand Philistine retaliation.

But David strengthened himself in the Lord his God. Throughout the books of Samuel, David is portrayed as a man of genuine personal piety. Here in the midst of his own grief and despair, his fellowship with God provided the strength and stability that he needed to see that action was necessary if his people were to be saved.

Only in the strength of the Lord was he able to withstand the pressures imposed by his soldiers whose grief drove them to the brink of mutiny.

Two hundred stayed behind. With all of his troops fatigued by their strenuous march, David left the most exhausted to protect their surplus equipment and supplies. One wonders if this action was prompted by the lessons learned from the disaster at Ziklag.

I will take you down to this band. The discovery of the former Amalekite slave must have been understood as an evidence of divine guidance, for without him David's expedition had little hope of success. Even the slightest warning would have given the Amalekites an opportunity to use their hostages to the fullest advantage.

b. *David Routs Amalekites* (30:16–31)

16 And when he had taken him down, behold, they were spread abroad over all the land, eating and drinking and dancing, because of all the great spoil they had taken from the land of the Philistines and from the land of Judah. 17 And David smote them from twilight until the evening of the next day; and not a man of them escaped, except four hundred young men, who mounted camels and fled. 18 David recovered all that the Amalekites had taken; and David rescued his two wives. 19 Nothing was missing, whether small or great, sons or daughters, spoil or anything that had been taken; David brought back all. 20 David also captured all the flocks and herds; and the people drove those cattle before him, and said, "This is David's spoil."
21 Then David came to the two hundred men, who had been too exhausted to follow David, and who had been left at the brook Besor; and they went out to meet David and to meet the people who were with him; and when David drew near to the people he saluted them. 22 Then all the wicked and base fellows among the men who had gone with David said, "Because they did not go with us, we will not give them any of the spoil which we have recovered, except that each man may lead away his wife and children, and depart." 23 But David said, "You shall not do so, my brothers, with what the Lord has given us; he has preserved us and given into our hand the band that came against us. 24 Who would listen to you in this matter? For as his share is who goes down into the battle, so shall his share be who stays by the baggage; they shall share alike." 25 And from that day forward he made it a statute and an ordinance for Israel to this day.
26 When David came to Ziklag, he sent part of the spoil to his friends, the elders of Judah, saying, "Here is a present for you from the spoil of the enemies of the Lord"; 27 it was for those in Bethel, in Ramoth of the Negeb, in Jattir, 28 in Aroer, in Siphmoth, in Eshtemoa, 29 in Racal, in the cities of the Jerahmeelites, in the cities of the Kenites, 30 in Hormah, in Borashan, in Athach, 31 in Hebron, for all the places where David and his men had roamed.

Guided by the Amalekite slave who had been left for dead in the desert, David and his men came upon the group which had raided Ziklag as they celebrated over their plunder. After observing the situation carefully, the Israelites struck soon after dawn and continued mopping up remnants of the enemy throughout the day. David's vengeful rescue of his people was complete except for the Amalekite cavalrymen who were able to escape into the desert on their camels.

David's spoils were greater than his losses; for in addition to their own personal belongings, the Amalekites were carrying booty taken from wilderness communities belonging both to the Philistines and to the Israelites. David's men, who were probably still disgruntled over their unprofitable excursion to Aphek, began bickering over the distribution of their newfound wealth. The hardier soldiers who had taken part in the actual fighting wanted to exclude the stragglers who were charged with keeping the baggage train. David, however, remembering his own culpable failures at Ziklag, recognized that divine providence and not the force of Israelite arms had brought victory over the Amalekites. He, therefore, insisted that the goods be shared equally by all his troops wherever they had served.

Upon returning to Ziklag, David also sent a portion of his spoils to the elders of Judah for distribution in the areas where he and his men had roamed while fleeing from Saul. In addition to serving as partial payment for any inconveniences the people may have suffered at the hands of

David's men, these spoils also served as an important reminder that he had no part in the battle at Gilboa. He wanted no one to forget that when the Philistines attacked the Israelite forces in Jezreel to the north, he had been fighting *the enemies of the Lord* in the Negeb. Moreover, he was willing to share the fruits of his victory to prove it.

From twilight until the evening of the next day. The language is unusual here but not impossible. The word for twilight (*nesheph*) may refer to the half-light of dusk or dawn (Isa. 5:11; Jer. 13:16; cf. 2 Kings 7:5–12; Job 7:4). Since darkness would have allowed the Amalekites to escape, a single day of battle seems most likely. The phrase *of the next day* occurs only here in the Old Testament and is awkward in Hebrew. Suggested emendations for the phrase, which would associate David's slaughter among the Amalekites with the *cherem* concept (cf. comment on 15:1–3), are very unlikely, however. The RSV has captured the most probable interpretation.

The reference in v. 17 to *four hundred young men* designates the elite of the Amalekite forces. Except for the Lord's influence in support of his anointed, these men alone would have been sufficiently strong to inflict heavy losses on David's forces.

(6) Israel Defeated at Gilboa (1 Sam. 31:1—2 Sam. 1:27)

a. Saul Commits Suicide (31:1–13)

¹ Now the Philistines fought against Israel; and the men of Israel fled before the Philistines, and fell slain on Mount Gilboa. ² And the Philistines overtook Saul and his sons; and the Philistines slew Jonathan and Abinadab and Malchishua, the sons of Saul. ³ The battle pressed hard upon Saul, and the archers found him; and he was badly wounded by the archers. ⁴ Then Saul said to his armor-bearer, "Draw your sword, and thrust me through with it, lest these uncircumcised come and thrust me through, and make sport of me." But his armor-bearer would not; for he feared greatly. Therefore Saul took his own sword, and fell upon it. ⁵ And when his armor-bearer saw that Saul was dead, he also fell upon his sword, and died with him. ⁶ Thus Saul died, and his three sons, and his armor-bearer, and all his men, on the same day together. ⁷ And when the men of Israel who were on the other side of the valley and those beyond the Jordan saw that the men of Israel had fled and that Saul and his sons were dead, they forsook their cities and fled; and the Philistines came and dwelt in them.

⁸ On the morrow, when the Philistines came to strip the slain, they found Saul and his three sons fallen on Mount Gilboa. ⁹ And they cut off his head, and stripped off his armor, and sent messengers throughout the land of the Philistines, to carry the good news to their idols and to the people. ¹⁰ They put his armor in the temple of Ashtaroth; and they fastened his body to the wall of Bethshan. ¹¹ But when the inhabitants of Jabeshgilead heard what the Philistines had done to Saul, ¹² all the valiant men arose, and went all night, and took the body of Saul and the bodies of his sons from the wall of Bethshan; and they came to Jabesh and burnt them there. ¹³ And they took their bones and buried them under the tamarisk tree in Jabesh, and fasted seven days.

With the account of Saul's death and Israel's defeat at Gilboa, we arrive at the point toward which the biblical narratives have been working since Saul's rejection in chapter 15. After Saul's tragic encounter with Samuel's ghost or David's adventures at Aphek and Ziklag, this story seems almost anticlimactic. Nevertheless, it is told simply and with a considerable degree of sympathy and respect for Israel's rejected king.

The story begins late in the day as the Israelite battle lines commenced to crumble and as retreat turned into a rout. Saul, with the memory of his devastating experience at Endor the night before still fresh in his mind (28:3–25), watched three of his sons fall in battle before he himself was gravely wounded. Unafraid of death itself but dreading torture and humiliation such as Samson had known (Judg. 16:21–25), Saul sought death at the hands of his armor-bearer. When the young man, like David before him, refused to strike out against the Lord's anointed, Saul fell upon his own sword. Thus ended the first phase of Israel's experiment with a monarchy.

The death of Saul and his sons coupled

with the decimation of his troops at Gilboa had a disastrous effect on Israel. The Philistines were once again in control of the broad productive valleys of the north, and the Hebrews were restricted to the mountainous interior.

News of Israel's defeat spread rapidly as Philistine propagandists made the most of victory. Saul's armor was put on display in the temple of a Philistine goddess and his decapitated body was exposed along with the corpses of his sons on the walls of Bethshan. A measure of the respect that some Israelites retained for their fallen king is seen in the daring rescue of these bodies by the men of Jabeshgilead. Remembering Saul's rescue of their city at the beginning of his reign, they risked their lives to give the bodies of the king's house a proper burial.

Lest these uncircumcised come and thrust me through suggests that Saul does not appear to have feared death as much as life among the Philistines. The parallel account in 1 Chronicles 10:1–12, which omits *and thrust me through* from this verse, preserves the better reading (v. 4).

Saul took his own sword, and fell upon it. Suicide was both rare and abhorrent in Old Testament thought. Only three other examples are found in the entire Bible: 2 Samuel 17:23; 1 Kings 16:18; and Matthew 27:5 (Caird, p. 1039).

They forsook their cities and fled. Philistine penetration of the land east of Jordan is doubtful. Jabeshgilead, less than 20 miles away, was obviously still Israelite; and Ishbosheth based his Israelite kingdom in the trans-Jordan territory (2 Sam. 2:9). The reading in 1 Chronicles 10:7 is better, omitting *and those beyond the Jordan.*

On the morrow. The Israelites must have given a good account of themselves if the Philistines were not close enough to recognize and plunder the bodies of the king and his sons until the next day.

The words, *and burnt them there,* are perhaps best omitted with the reading of the parallel passage in 1 Chronicles 10:12. Burning of human bodies was normally an act of punishment or reproach in the Old Testament (Amos 2:1; Josh. 7:25; Lev. 20:14). Recent studies, however, indicate that the root normally translated "to burn" (*saraph*) may also mean "to anoint" as with burial spices (see Hertzberg, p. 233 fn).

It should be noted that 2 Samuel is really a continuation of 1 Samuel—hence the continuity of the outline (see the Introduction to both books).

b. Youth Claims Saul's Murder (1:1–16)

¹ After the death of Saul, when David had returned from the slaughter of the Amalekites, David remained two days in Ziklag; ² and on the third day, behold, a man came from Saul's camp, with his clothes rent and earth upon his head. And when he came to David, he fell to the ground and did obeisance. ³ David said to him, "Where do you come from?" And he said to him, "I have escaped from the camp of Israel." ⁴ And David said to him, "How did it go? Tell me." And he answered, "The people have fled from the battle, and many of the people also have fallen and are dead; and Saul and his son Jonathan are also dead." ⁵ Then David said to the young man who told him, "How do you know that Saul and his son Jonathan are dead?" ⁶ And the young man who told him said, "By chance I happened to be on Mount Gilboa; and there was Saul leaning upon his spear; and lo, the chariots and the horsemen were close upon him. ⁷ And when he looked behind him, he saw me, and called to me. And I answered, 'Here I am.' ⁸ And he said to me, 'Who are you?' I answered him, 'I am an Amalekite.' ⁹ And he said to me, 'Stand beside me and slay me; for anguish has seized me, and yet my life still lingers.' ¹⁰ So I stood beside him, and slew him, because I was sure that he could not live after he had fallen; and I took the crown which was on his head and the armlet which was on his arm, and I have brought them here to my lord."

¹¹ Then David took hold of his clothes, and rent them; and so did all the men who were with him; ¹² and they mourned and wept and fasted until evening for Saul and for Jonathan his son and for the people of the LORD and for the house of Israel, because they had fallen by the sword. ¹³ And David said to the young man who told him, "Where do you come from?" And he answered, "I am the son of a sojourner, an Amalekite." ¹⁴ David said to him, "How is it you were not afraid to put forth your hand to destroy the LORD's anointed?" ¹⁵ Then David called one of the young men and said, "Go, fall

upon him." And he smote him so that he died. ¹⁶ And David said to him, "Your blood be upon your head; for your own mouth has testified against you, saying, 'I have slain the LORD's anointed.'"

The present passage contains a second account of the death of Saul which is similar to the first in many respects yet differing at other crucial points. The major difference between the two is found in the role of the Amalekite messenger who brought David word of Saul's death. He told of a chance meeting with Israel's stricken king who asked to be quickly slain that he might avoid a lingering death. Upon carrying out Saul's request, the young man spoke of taking the king's crown and armlet, which he presented to David as substantiation for his story.

Although it is nowhere expressly stated that the Amalekite was lying, the arrangement of the two accounts suggests that the messenger observed the events at Gilboa roughly as they are described in the preceding chapter. After robbing Saul's dead body, he hastened to Ziklag with the story of his personal participation in the king's death in order to ingratiate himself with David. If such was the Amalekite's plan, however, he was fatally mistaken.

David, as a true Israelite, had persistently refused to raise his hand against the Lord's anointed. Only a foreigner like Doeg the Edomite (1 Sam. 22:18), or now this nameless Amalekite, would dare admit such a presumptuous act. Even though he had long been rejected as king, Saul was God's chosen person and God alone must judge. The Lord could smite him directly, cause him to die in battle, or let him die naturally, but no one man should take the life of God's chosen king (1 Sam. 26:10). David, therefore, called for his soldiers to execute the Amalekite for the guilt he had freely admitted with his own mouth.

Whatever may have happened on the side of Mount Gilboa, the biblical author uses this episode to make one fact quite clear: David had nothing whatever to do with Saul's death. He was busy far in the south when the king met his death in battle, and he was ready to kill anyone who so much as claimed to have raised his hand against the king.

David remained two days in Ziklag. Gilboa was some 85 air miles from Ziklag, far more by the route a runner would take. Such a journey must have consumed the better part of three days, especially for one already exhausted in battle. Presumably, David was returning from his battle with the Amalekites when Saul met his death.

They mourned and wept and fasted until evening. David's first emotion upon learning of Saul's death was that of grief. Although he must have been relieved to be free of Saul's persecution, and although the way was now clear for him to pursue his destiny as king of Israel, his grief appears genuine. His ties with Jonathan were strong, and his early association with Saul had been quite warm.

The delay introduced by the formal mourning which lasted until evening indicates that David's execution of the Amalekite was not an act of passion. It was his considered reaction to the violence done to the Lord's anointed.

c. David Mourns Israel's Loss (1:17-27)

¹⁷ And David lamented with this lamentation over Saul and Jonathan his son, ¹⁸ and he said it should be taught to the people of Judah; behold, it is written in the Book of Jashar. He said:
¹⁹ "Thy glory, O Israel, is slain upon thy high places!
How are the mighty fallen!
²⁰ Tell it not in Gath,
publish it not in the streets of Ashkelon;
lest the daughters of the Philistines rejoice,
lest the daughters of the uncircumcised exult.

²¹ "Ye mountains of Gilboa,
let there be no dew or rain upon you,
nor upsurging of the deep!
For there the shield of the mighty was defiled,
the shield of Saul, not anointed with oil.

²² "From the blood of the slain,
from the fat of the mighty,
the bow of Jonathan turned not back,

and the sword of Saul returned not empty.

23 "Saul and Jonathan, beloved and lovely!
In life and in death they were not divided;
they were swifter than eagles,
they were stronger than lions.

24 "Ye daughters of Israel, weep over Saul,
who clothed you daintily in scarlet,
who put ornaments of gold upon your apparel.

25 "How are the mighty fallen
in the midst of the battle!

"Jonathan lies slain upon thy high places.
26 I am distressed for you, my brother Jonathan;
very pleasant have you been to me;
your love to me was wonderful,
passing the love of women.

27 "How are the mighty fallen,
and the weapons of war perished!"

The whole tragedy of Saul's rejection and decline is caught up in David's elegy commemorating the death of the king and his son Jonathan. In spite of his erratic leadership against the Philistines and his unjust persecution of David, Saul still enjoyed a substantial measure of affection among his subjects. While the people perceived that the Spirit of the Lord had left him (1 Sam. 16:14), they took no pleasure in observing his progressive deterioration. Similarly, David had suffered much at Saul's hand, yet his sense of loss at the death of old friends was no less real.

David's elegy is probably best understood against the background of the elaborate funerary practices of the ancient Near East, in which public mourning figured so prominently (Jer. 16:4; 22:18; 1 Sam. 25:1). Professional mourners, mostly women, were widely employed (2 Chron. 35:25; Jer. 9:17; Amos 5:16; cf. 2 Sam. 1:24). Thus, in a real sense, this poetic dirge reflects both the personal and the national grief of Israel.

In the Old Testament, funeral laments employ a special rhythm in which the second part of the verse is shorter than the first. This pattern contrasts sharply with normal Hebrew poetic forms which depend heavily on symmetrical or parallel constructions. The resultant imbalance creates a haunting echo effect which is particularly well suited for conveying feelings of sadness and despair (cf. especially vv. 25–27).

The beauty and forcefulness of the language in David's lament attest his stature as a poet of genuine merit. Indeed, this work is properly recognized as the greatest elegy in the Hebrew language.

The heart of the entire poem is caught up in the lament proper: *How are the mighty fallen* (vv. 19, 25, 27): the nation has lost the finest examples of Israelite manhood. The poet's anguish is so intense that he cannot bear the thought of the Philistines' gloating over the importance of their victory. He even called for a perpetual curse to fall upon the battlefields where Saul and Jonathan lost their lives.

After giving voice to the enormity of Israel's sense of loss, David turned to eulogizing the deceased. United in death as in life, Saul and Jonathan had been capable warriors, attractive and strong. Saul was singled out for the prosperity that he brought to the nation; but for Jonathan, David could think of no higher compliment than to call him friend.

The Book of Jashar has special significance. Jashar means righteous. This is one of two canonical references to what seems to have been an ancient anthology of poems on themes of national interest (cf. Josh. 10:13).

The shield of Saul was *not anointed with oil.* The imagery here is difficult to recapture. It may lament the fact that after Gilboa, Saul's shield was abandoned and uncared for; i.e., the leather was no longer kept in condition by applying oil (cf. Isa. 21:5). On the other hand, the passage may suggest that Saul was not ritually prepared for battle (cf. comment on 1 Sam. 28:1–14).

In life and in death they were not divided. Attention is again called to the fact that, in spite of Jonathan's close friendship with David, he was never untrue to his father (cf. comment 1 Sam. 19:1-7; 20:24-42).

7. David Becomes King (2:1—8:18)

(1) David Reigns over Judah (2:1—4:12)

a. Rival Kingdoms Established (2:1-11)

¹ After this David inquired of the LORD, "Shall I go up into any of the cities of Judah?" And the LORD said to him, "Go up." David said, "To which shall I go up?" And he said, "To Hebron." ² So David went up there, and his two wives also, Ahinoam of Jezreel, and Abigail the widow of Nabal of Carmel. ³ And David brought up his men who were with him, every one with his household; and they dwelt in the towns of Hebron. ⁴ And the men of Judah came, and there they anointed David king over the house of Judah.
When they told David, "It was the men of Jabeshgilead who buried Saul," ⁵ David sent messengers to the men of Jabeshgilead, and said to them, "May you be blessed by the LORD, because you showed this loyalty to Saul your lord, and buried him! ⁶ Now may the LORD show steadfast love and faithfulness to you! And I will do good to you because you have done this thing. ⁷ Now therefore let your hands be strong, and be valiant; for Saul your lord is dead, and the house of Judah has anointed me king over them."
⁸ Now Abner the son of Ner, commander of Saul's army, had taken Ishbosheth the son of Saul, and brought him over to Mahanaim; ⁹ and he made him king over Gilead and the Ashurites and Jezreel and Ephraim and Benjamin and all Israel. ¹⁰ Ishbosheth, Saul's son, was forty years old when he began to reign over Israel, and he reigned two years. But the house of Judah followed David. ¹¹ And the time that David was king in Hebron over the house of Judah was seven years and six months.

With Saul's death and Israel's monstrous defeat at Gilboa, David faced a radically different political situation in Israel. Although the Hebrews still controlled many fortified towns which could not be captured without prolonged sieges, the Philistines were the dominant military power west of the Jordan. Since they did not follow up their victory in the Valley of Jezreel with other campaigns in the south, one suspects that they decided to attempt to weaken or control Israel through David, Achish's "vassal" (1 Sam. 27). They would learn in due time that David's true loyalties had always lain with his own people. In the meantime, David doubtlessly used the ensuing respite from war to solidify his position in Israel.

Among his own people, David again faced a nation seriously divided into political factions. In accord with a favorable response from the Lord, David moved with his private army from Ziklag to the cluster of small towns around Hebron. Acting independently of the northern tribes, the men of Judah established an autonomous southern kingdom and anointed David as its head. The remainder of Israel was nominally controlled by a government in exile located at Mahanaim, east of the Jordan. The titular ruler of the northern tribes was Saul's son, Ishbosheth, but the real power behind the throne resided with Abner, Saul's kinsman who was commander of Israel's armies.

The contrast between the two kingdoms contending for Israel's loyalties was quite pronounced. David came to power fresh from Philistine vassalage and supported by a non-Israelite type of military structure, his private army. Nevertheless, he had been anointed by Samuel and was currently endorsed by Abiathar, who traced his lineage back to Eli. David was elected king by representatives of the people and consecrated to his office at Hebron.

Ishbosheth, on the other hand, had little to recommend him other than the fact that he was Saul's son and was supported by Abner, who commanded what remained of the army after Gilboa. Although many Israelites may have followed Ishbosheth for sentimental reasons, he was without theological legitimacy, and the laws of primogeniture were not yet established in Israel. Nevertheless, David was again faced with deciding the kind of tactics which he would use in his rise to power as the king of all Israel.

The length of time involved in David's acquisition of authority over the northern tribes is not altogether clear. Ishbosheth is said to have reigned two years (2:10), but David is reputed to have reigned *in Hebron over the house of Judah* seven and one-half years (2:11). This is commonly explained by assuming that David moved his capital to Jerusalem seven and one-half years after coming to power in Hebron. Since David probably became king of all Israel soon after Ishbosheth's murder, he was more than just king over the house of Judah during the last five years or so of his residence at Hebron.[30]

The shrewdness and restraint with which David dealt with his Israelite opponents is reflected in his dealings with the people of Jabeshgilead, the staunchest of Saul's supporters. Upon learning of their daring expedition to Bethshan (1 Sam. 31:8–13), David immediately sent a message commending them for their courage and expressing his own affection for Saul. In closing, however, David reminded them that Saul was dead, and he was the duly elected king of Judah. Without maligning Saul's son or implying any threat of coercion, David clearly appealed for their support. While we are never told of the results of this appeal, such actions amply illustrate his conciliatory efforts.

b. *Civil War Erupts* (2:12–32)

12 Abner the son of Ner, and the servants of Ishbosheth the son of Saul, went out from Mahanaim to Gibeon. 13 And Joab the son of Zeruiah, and the servants of David, went out and met them at the pool of Gibeon; and they sat down, the one on the one side of the pool, and the other on the other side of the pool. 14 And Abner said to Joab, "Let the young men arise and play before us." And Joab said, "Let them arise." 15 Then they arose and passed over by number, twelve for Benjamin and Ishbosheth the son of Saul, and twelve of the servants of David. 16 And each caught his opponent by the head, and thrust his sword in his opponent's side; so they fell down together. Therefore that place was called Helkathhazzurim, which is at Gibeon. 17 And the battle was very fierce that day; and Abner and the men of Israel were beaten before the servants of David.

18 And the three sons of Zeruiah were there, Joab, Abishai, and Asahel. Now Asahel was as swift of foot as a wild gazelle; 19 and Asahel pursued Abner, and as he went he turned neither to the right hand nor to the left from following Abner. 20 Then Abner looked behind him and said, "Is it you, Asahel?" And he answered, "It is I." 21 Abner said to him, "Turn aside to your right hand or to your left, and seize one of the young men, and take his spoil." But Asahel would not turn aside from following him. 22 And Abner said again to Asahel, "Turn aside from following me; why should I smite you to the ground? How then could I lift up my face to your brother Joab?" 23 But he refused to turn aside; therefore Abner smote him in the belly with the butt of his spear, so that the spear came out at his back; and he fell there, and died where he was. And all who came to the place where Asahel had fallen and died, stood still.

24 But Joab and Abishai pursued Abner; and as the sun was going down they came to the hill of Ammah, which lies before Giah on the way to the wilderness of Gibeon. 25 And the Benjaminites gathered themselves together behind Abner, and became one band, and took their stand on the top of a hill. 26 Then Abner called to Joab, "Shall the sword devour for ever? Do you not know that the end will be bitter? How long will it be before you bid your people turn from the pursuit of their brethren?" 27 And Joab said, "As God lives, if you had not spoken, surely the men would have given up the pursuit of their brethren in the morning." 28 So Joab blew the trumpet; and all the men stopped, and pursued Israel no more, nor did they fight any more.

29 And Abner and his men went all that night through the Arabah; they crossed the Jordan, and marching the whole forenoon they came to Mahanaim. 30 Joab returned from the pursuit of Abner; and when he had gathered all the people together, there were missing of David's servants nineteen men besides Asahel. 31 But the servants of David had slain of Benjamin three hundred and sixty of Abner's men. 32 And they took up Asahel, and buried him in the tomb of his father, which was at Bethlehem. And Joab and his men marched all night, and the day broke upon them at Hebron.

Despite David's continuing efforts to maintain peaceful relations with Israel, hostilities soon flared into the open. Caught up in a civil war which neither side wanted and neither side could win, the two struggling kingdoms made an effort to reconcile

---

[30] Martin Noth, *The History of Israel*, trans. P. R. Ackroyd (New York: Harper and Brothers, 1960), p. 191.

their differences.

Delegations under the leadership of the military commanders of the two kingdoms met at Gibeon, six miles northwest of Jerusalem on the border between Israel and Judah. Although the conditions surrounding this meeting are not clearly stated, the distinguished credentials of the participants suggest that serious diplomatic negotiations were underway. The two groups sat facing each other on opposite sides of the *pool of Gibeon,* probably not more than 50 to 75 feet apart.

As a preliminary to the business session, Abner, the Israelite commander, suggested that young men from both sides entertain the group with a war game. The rules of the "game" are no longer known, but twelve young men from each side seem to have been engaged in mock combat. Either treachery or over-enthusiasm escalated the game into a fatal conflict. In the end, all 24 of the original combatants were killed, and Israel's forces suffered heavy casualties in the fighting which followed.

During the course of the ensuing battle, we learn the origin of the blood feud which developed between the families of the commanders of the opposing armies. As the Israelites were put to flight, Abner was being chased by Asahel, Joab's younger brother, who was an inexperienced warrior but an accomplished runner. Abner recognized his pursuer and vainly encouraged him to turn aside to find an opponent whose abilities would be more nearly in keeping with his own limited military experience. Recognizing that he could neither outdistance nor evade Asahel, Abner struck backward with his spear and killed his young opponent on the spot.

The Judeans continued to pursue the Israelites until Abner rallied his men on a hilltop, thus gaining a tactical advantage. In the shouted exchange which followed, additional insight is gained into the purpose of the original encounter. Abner implied that the civil war had been underway for sometime as he asked: *Shall the sword devour for ever? . . . How long will it be before you bid your people turn from the pursuit of their brethren?* He could foresee that a continuation of the bloodshed would be both devastating and useless. Joab replied that the warfare would have been over since that morning had it not been for Abner's ill-fated request for entertainment.

The phrase **in the morning** (*mehabboker*) is customarily interpreted as referring to the following morning. This is grammatically possible. But a more literal translation, "from the morning" or "since morning," seems more likely in this context. The Judeans halted their pursuit not because of Abner's request but because the Israelites had gained a superior strategic position. The ill-timed speech to which Joab referred occurred the morning of that very day. Had not Abner's request precipitated such carnage, a truce would have already been in effect. (But cf. McKane, p. 186, who holds that the fighting would have lasted all night if Abner had not called for an end to the battle.) Once the engagement had been broken off, the survivors of both armies began forced marches home presumably to inform their governments of the rupture of their negotiations.

c. David's Family Grows (3:1-5)

¹ There was a long war between the house of Saul and the house of David; and David grew stronger and stronger, while the house of Saul became weaker and weaker.
² And sons were born to David at Hebron: his first-born was Amnon, of Ahinoam of Jezreel; ³ and his second, Chileab, of Abigail the widow of Nabal of Carmel; and the third, Absalom the son of Maacah the daughter of Talmai king of Geshur; ⁴ and the fourth, Adonijah the son of Haggith; and the fifth, Shephatiah the son of Abital; ⁵ and the sixth, Ithream of Eglah, David's wife. These were born to David in Hebron.

In the long war following the incident at Gibeon, David's fortunes prospered while those of Saul's descendants continued to decline. David's growing political strength was paralleled by his growing family. Together they served as a reminder of the Lord's continuing support of his cause.

Six sons, so very important in ancient societies, were born in seven and one-half years, and this appears to be an incomplete list. No girls are mentioned, and only one child is named for each wife. Presumably these boys serve as representatives of God's bounty toward his servant David.

The list has its tragic side, however. Three of the boys, Amnon, Absalom, and Adonijah, play prominent but unhappy roles in the story of David's reign as king. The other three presumably died in infancy since they are not mentioned again.

The daughter of Talmai king of Geshur, Absalom's mother, was a princess of Geshur, a small Syrian state northeast of the Sea of Galilee. David may have arranged this marriage as a means of securing an ally to the rear of Ishbosheth's position at Mahanaim (Bright, p. 176).

Eglah, David's wife. The significance of the qualifying phrase is uncertain here since presumably all these women were David's wives. Perhaps David's name has replaced that of a former husband in an expression similar to that regarding Abigail in v. 3.

d. Abner Bargains with David (3:6–21)

6 While there was war between the house of Saul and the house of David, Abner was making himself strong in the house of Saul. 7 Now Saul had a concubine, whose name was Rizpah, the daughter of Aiah; and Ishbosheth said to Abner, "Why have you gone in to my father's concubine?" 8 Then Abner was very angry over the words of Ishbosheth, and said, "Am I a dog's head of Judah? This day I keep showing loyalty to the house of Saul your father, to his brothers, and to his friends, and have not given you into the hand of David; and yet you charge me today with a fault concerning a woman. 9 God do so to Abner, and more also, if I do not accomplish for David what the LORD has sworn to him, 10 to transfer the kingdom from the house of Saul, and set up the throne of David over Israel and over Judah, from Dan to Beersheba." 11 And Ishbosheth could not answer Abner another word, because he feared him.
12 And Abner sent messengers to David at Hebron, saying, "To whom does the land belong? Make your covenant with me, and behold, my hand shall be with you to bring over all Israel to you." 13 And he said, "Good; I will make a covenant with you; but one thing I require of you; that is, you shall not see my face, unless you first bring Michal, Saul's daughter, when you come to see my face." 14 Then David sent messengers to Ishbosheth Saul's son, saying, "Give me my wife Michal, whom I betrothed at the price of a hundred foreskins of the Philistines." 15 And Ishbosheth sent, and took her from her husband Paltiel the son of Laish. 16 But her husband went with her, weeping after her all the way to Bahurim. Then Abner said to him, "Go, return"; and he returned.
17 And Abner conferred with the elders of Israel, saying, "For some time past you have been seeking David as king over you. 18 Now then bring it about; for the LORD has promised David, saying, 'By the hand of my servant David I will save my people Israel from the hand of the Philistines, and from the hand of all their enemies.'" 19 Abner also spoke to Benjamin; and then Abner went to tell David at Hebron all that Israel and the whole house of Benjamin thought good to do.
20 When Abner came with twenty men to David at Hebron, David made a feast for Abner and the men who were with him. 21 And Abner said to David, "I will arise and go, and will gather all Israel to my lord the king, that they may make a covenant with you, and that you may reign over all that your heart desires." So David sent Abner away; and he went in peace.

The story of David's rise to power is at once both simple and complex. From a theological perspective, the ultimate outcome of the story has never been in doubt; David was destined by God to become king of all Israel (1 Sam. 16:1). Historically, however, the route by which David achieved that exalted office was tortuously involved and frustrating beyond measure. The present chapter tells of yet another abortive attempt to unite the kingdom under David by peaceful means (cf. comment on 1 Sam. 23:15–18; 2 Sam. 2:12–32).

The current attempt to reconcile the kingdoms of Israel and Judah stems out of a personal incident between Ishbosheth and Abner. Although Abner had always been the real source of power behind the throne of Israel, he seems to have made a genuine effort to keep Saul's government intact with Saul's own son as king. Nevertheless, as David's strength grew and Israelite influence waned, it became more and more apparent that the government at Mahanaim was a one-man affair. Finally, Ishbosheth confronted Abner with his suspicions that he was trying to become king in name as well as in deed.

The question of Ishbosheth in v. 7 is to the point:

Why have you gone in to my father's concubine: This was more than just a charge of flagrant immorality. The king's concubines were considered his personal property, and as such they became the possession of his successor. To claim a king's concubine, therefore was to claim the throne (cf. 2 Sam. 16:22; 1 Kings 2:22-23). It is uncertain whether Abner was guilty of the charge that Ishbosheth made against him. Some commentators, on the basis of textual support from recensions of one Greek version, contend that the words "and Abner took her" should be added to v. 7 (Hertzberg, p. 257). These words, however, are not found in the best texts, and they do not accord well with the remainder of the story. The RSV, therefore, has the better reading.

Abner, it seems, had never denied the possession of great power; but he was incensed that his constant generosity to Saul's family and friends had not established the fact that he had no desire to be king. Dismayed by the declining influence of his government in Israel and disappointed by having his motives misunderstood at home, Abner decided to throw his influence on the side of those who were working to reunite Israel under David's leadership.

Since he had made Ishbosheth king, an office which at this time commanded no real power, Abner did not need to hide his intentions. He openly consulted with the elders of Israel, some of whom had been supporting David all along, and won their support for his plans. Even the tribe of Benjamin, which had been most intimately involved with Saul's administration, recognized that Israel's hope for the future lay in reunification under David's leadership.

Abner immediately opened negotiations by sending emissaries to Hebron who proclaimed his authority over the northern kingdom and announced his willingness to negotiate with David. David, however, demanded that his wife Michal, Saul's daughter, be returned to him before any final agreements could be reached (cf. 1 Sam. 18:20-27). His motives were probably more practical than romantic in that his marriage to Michal provided him with a legitimate tie to Israel's first ruling house. In an effort to be certain that his terms were understood and that the king of Israel was a party to the negotiations, David sent messengers to Ishbosheth with his demands. Without power in his own right, Ishbosheth had no choice but to comply. Accompanied by the mourning of the husband to whom she had been given by her father, Michal went to be with David.

After these preliminary arrangements had been completed, Abner himself made a journey to Hebron to work out the details for the reunification of the kingdom. After having been cordially received and royally feted by his Judean hosts, Abner left to gather the elders of Israel who would formally request that David become their king (cf. 5:3).

e. Joab Slays Abner (3:22-39)

²² Just then the servants of David arrived with Joab from a raid, bringing much spoil with them. But Abner was not with David at Hebron, for he had sent him away, and he had gone in peace. ²³ When Joab and all the army that was with him came, it was told Joab, "Abner the son of Ner came to the king, and he has let him go, and he has gone in peace." ²⁴ Then Joab went to the king and said, "What have you done? Behold, Abner came to you; why is it that you have sent him away, so that he is gone? ²⁵ You know that Abner the son of Ner came to deceive you, and to know your going out and your coming in, and to know all that you are doing."
²⁶ When Joab came out from David's presence, he sent messengers after Abner, and they brought him back from the cistern of Sirah; but David did not know about it. ²⁷ And when Abner returned to Hebron, Joab took him aside

into the midst of the gate to speak with him privately, and there he smote him in the belly, so that he died, for the blood of Asahel his brother. 28 Afterward, when David heard of it, he said, "I and my kingdom are for ever guiltless before the LORD for the blood of Abner the son of Ner. 29 May it fall upon the head of Joab, and upon all his father's house; and may the house of Joab never be without one who has a discharge, or who is leprous, or who holds a spindle, or who is slain by the sword, or who lacks bread!" 30 So Joab and Abishai his brother slew Abner, because he had killed their brother Asahel in the battle at Gibeon.

31 Then David said to Joab and to all the people who were with him, "Rend your clothes, and gird on sackcloth, and mourn before Abner." And King David followed the bier. 32 They buried Abner at Hebron; and the king lifted up his voice and wept at the grave of Abner; and all the people wept. 33 And the king lamented for Abner, saying,

"Should Abner die as a fool dies?
34 Your hands were not bound,
  your feet were not fettered;
as one falls before the wicked
  you have fallen."

And all the people wept again over him. 35 Then all the people came to persuade David to eat bread while it was yet day; but David swore, saying, "God do so to me and more also, if I taste bread or anything else till the sun goes down!" 36 And all the people took notice of it, and it pleased them; as everything that the king did pleased all the people. 37 So all the people and all Israel understood that day that it had not been the king's will to slay Abner the son of Ner. 38 And the king said to his servants, "Do you not know that a prince and a great man has fallen this day in Israel? 39 And I am this day weak, though anointed king; these men the sons of Zeruiah are too hard for me. The LORD requite the evildoer according to his wickedness!"

Just as the peaceful reunification of Israel and Judah seemed assured of success, David's delicate negotiations with the northern kingdom were shattered by the willful intervention of his general and nephew, Joab. Either by David's design or by fortuitous circumstances, Joab had been away from Hebron when Abner arrived to discuss treaty arrangements. Abner had hardly left the city after completing his mission, however, when Joab, returning from a successful military expedition, learned of his visit to Hebron.

Motivated by a desire to avenge his brother's death (2:18–28) and a distrust of Abner's intentions, Joab reproached David for his failure to detain Abner, but to no avail. Joab, therefore, acted independently and sent messengers to bring Abner back to Hebron. Acting as if on official business, Joab met his opponent at the city gate and suddenly stabbed him without warning.

The gate of a fortified city was composed of a series of smaller chambers which could be closed off by heavy wooden doors and defended successively. Except in time of war these areas were used in the administration of justice and other civic functions (15:2). Presumably the assassination took place in one of these inner courts, in *the midst of the gate*.

Recognizing the seriousness of Joab's offense and the manner in which it would be received in Israel, David acted swiftly to dissociate himself from Abner's murder. The curse that David pronounced upon Joab's house (*who holds a spindle* points to men fit only for women's work) was particularly fitting, since Abner had been killed as a result of a blood feud designed to uphold Joab's family honor. Next, David arranged an elaborate state funeral for Abner and required Joab and his friends to attend dressed in sackcloth as mourners. David himself participated in the occasion, delivering both a lament over Abner's death and a tribute to his greatness in life. *Should Abner die as a fool dies?* lacks some of the warmth of David's lament over Saul and Jonathan (1:19–27). David decries Abner's death as the work of wicked men but suggests that it was due in part to Abner's own carelessness. Since he was not a prisoner, he should have been on guard against his enemy. Note that both Joab and Abishai are credited with Abner's death in v. 30.

The author made a valiant effort to demonstrate David's lack of complicity in this affair. He twice called attention to the fact that Abner's death was personally and not politically motivated and noted that even the people of Israel were convinced of David's innocence.

Nevertheless, David's inability to restrain Joab and his failure to take punitive measures against him seem unusual, to say the least. David had little to gain and much to lose by Abner's untimely death since Abner was already moving to unite the kingdom under David's rule. Therefore, it would seem that some factors other than personal involvement restrained David from taking action against Joab. David's decisions may have been influenced by the fact that Joab was the son of his sister Zeruiah, but political realities were probably the decisive factors behind his leniency. No doubt there were many in Judah who remembered the incident at Gibeon (2:12–32) and were, therefore, skeptical of Abner's peaceful intentions. In any case, David lamented his inability to take appropriate action and placed the whole matter before the Lord for true and final judgment.

f. Ishbosheth Murdered (4:1–12)

¹ When Ishbosheth, Saul's son, heard that Abner had died at Hebron, his courage failed, and all Israel was dismayed. ² Now Saul's son had two men who were captains of raiding bands; the name of the one was Baanah, and the name of the other Rechab, sons of Rimmon a man of Benjamin from Beeroth (for Beeroth also is reckoned to Benjamin; ³ the Beerothites fled to Gittaim, and have been sojourners there to this day).
⁴ Jonathan, the son of Saul, had a son who was crippled in his feet. He was five years old when the news about Saul and Jonathan came from Jezreel; and his nurse took him up, and fled; and, as she fled in her haste, he fell, and became lame. And his name was Mephibosheth.
⁵ Now the sons of Rimmon the Beerothite, Rechab and Baanah, set out, and about the heat of the day they came to the house of Ishbosheth, as he was taking his noonday rest. ⁶ And behold, the doorkeeper of the house had been cleaning wheat, but she grew drowsy and slept; so Rechab and Baanah his brother slipped in. ⁷ When they came into the house, as he lay on his bed in his bedchamber, they smote him, and slew him, and beheaded him. They took his head, and went by the way of the Arabah all night, ⁸ and brought the head of Ishbosheth to David at Hebron. And they said to the king, "Here is the head of Ishbosheth, the son of Saul, your enemy, who sought your life; the Lord has avenged my lord the king this day on Saul and on his offspring." ⁹ But David answered Rechab and Baanah his brother, the sons of Rimmon the Beerothite, "As the Lord lives, who has redeemed my life out of every adversity, ¹⁰ when one told me, 'Behold, Saul is dead,' and thought he was bringing good news, I seized him and slew him at Ziklag, which was the reward I gave him for his news. ¹¹ How much more, when wicked men have slain a righteous man in his own house upon his bed, shall I not now require his blood at your hand, and destroy you from the earth?" ¹² And David commanded his young men, and they killed them, and cut off their hands and feet, and hanged them beside the pool at Hebron. But they took the head of Ishbosheth, and buried it in the tomb of Abner at Hebron.

When news of Abner's assassination reached Israel's capital at Mahanaim, confusion gave way to chaos. Never a powerful leader in his own right, Ishbosheth had earlier watched his royal world crumble as first Abner and then the elders of Israel decided to seek a treaty by which David would become king of all Israel. In this period, the army, long the real source of authority in the northern kingdom, was controlled by Abner's dominant personality. Now that he was dead, the king's position became more precarious than ever as various groups began maneuvering to take advantage of the power vacuum which had developed within the northern kingdom.

Recognizing that the future of the entire nation now lay in David's hands, two ambitious army officers sought to win his favor by striking down his rival. The men, brothers from Beeroth in Benjamin, slipped into Ishbosheth's home during the midday siesta and killed the king in his bed. After beheading their victim, they marched all night through the Jordan valley to bring proof of their deed to David at Hebron.

The two conspirators presented their grim trophy to David and claimed that it was by their hands that the Lord had carried out vengeance on Saul's house. David, however, persisted in his belief that the

Lord was capable of carrying out his will without turning his people against one another (cf. 1 Sam. 26:10–11). After relating the fate of the Amalekite who claimed to have killed Saul, David had the assassins executed and their bodies mutilated and exposed. As the Benjaminites' corpses served as a public reminder of David's refusal to gain the throne of Israel by force, Ishbosheth's head was buried in Abner's tomb in Hebron.

The parenthetical note in vv. 2–3, *for Beeroth also . . . to this day,* has aroused much speculation as to its significance. At the time of the Conquest, Beeroth was one of four cities in a league headed by Gibeon (Josh. 9:17). Its site, as well as that of Gittaim, has not been positively identified. Some commentators suggest that the people of Beeroth fled because of severe persecution by Saul who suspected them of collaboration with the Philistines (Bright, p. 168; McKane, p. 197). Had this been the case, however, the presence of Baanah and Rechab as officers in Ishbosheth's army could hardly be explained. No completely satisfactory answer can be given on the basis of present information.

Verse 4, which interrupts the story of Ishbosheth's murder, serves to introduce *Mephibosheth* as a character of some importance in a forthcoming narrative (9:1–13). In a classic example of literary foreshadowing, the reader is led to anticipate his subsequent appearance and then, in the light of that experience, to reinterpret the first. Saul's house was coming to a sad state of affairs when only a crippled grandson remained to inherit his property.

(2) *David Rules All Israel (5:1—8:18)*

a. *Elders "Elect" David King (5:1–5)*

¹ Then all the tribes of Israel came to David at Hebron, and said, "Behold, we are your bone and flesh. ² In times past, when Saul was king over us, it was you that led out and brought in Israel; and the LORD said to you, 'You shall be shepherd of my people Israel, and you shall be prince over Israel.' " ³ So all the elders of Israel came to the king at Hebron; and King David made a covenant with them at Hebron before the LORD, and they anointed David king over Israel. ⁴ David was thirty years old when he began to reign, and he reigned forty years. ⁵ At Hebron he reigned over Judah seven years and six months; and at Jerusalem he reigned over all Israel and Judah thirty-three years.

The current which had so long been bearing David toward the throne of Israel was now too strong to be deterred by the deaths of Abner and Ishbosheth. In view of Israel's earlier resolution to "go with David" (3:17–19), his elevation to high office was in no way dependent on the assassination of the key leaders of the northern kingdom. Strong public reaction could have temporarily postponed the inevitable, but apparently David was able to convince the nation-at-large of his innocence in these murders. Actually, however, there were no other viable candidates for the office which he sought.

The account of David's assumption of the throne is starkly simple. The elders of Israel, as representatives of all the tribes, pledged David their loyalty in a covenant ceremony and anointed him king. They based their action on David's proven ability as a military leader under Saul and on their growing conviction that he was the Lord's chosen ruler for his people.

It is said that David *reigned forty years.* Since 40 years was frequently used as a convenient round number for a long period of indeterminate length, the figure may or may not be exact. On the basis of synchronisms with other known events noted in Josephus' works, the date of Solomon's accession is rather precisely computed to have occurred in 961 B.C.[31] David's reign, therefore, would extend from about 1000 to 961 B.C.

At Hebron he reigned. David's capture of Jerusalem is here associated with the beginning of his rule over Israel seven and one-half years after he became king over

---

[31] David Noel Freedman, "The Chronology of Israel and the Ancient Near East: Section A. Old Testament Chronology," *The Bible and the Ancient Near East,* ed., G. Ernest Wright (Garden City, New York: Doubleday, 1961), p. 209.

Judah at Hebron. This order, however, does not take into account Ishbosheth's reign of only two years over the northern kingdom (2:10). Since there are no indications of Israel's having waited five and one-half years after Ishbosheth's death before anointing David king, it is best to assume that David captured Jerusalem some five years after the kingdoms were united under his rule. Hence 5:6–10 would come after 5:17–25 in proper chronological sequence.

b. David Establishes Court (5:6–16)

⁶ And the king and his men went to Jerusalem against the Jebusites, the inhabitants of the land, who said to David, "You will not come in here, but the blind and the lame will ward you off"—thinking, "David cannot come in here." ⁷ Nevertheless David took the stronghold of Zion, that is, the city of David. ⁸ And David said on that day, "Whoever would smite the Jebusites, let him get up the water shaft to attack the lame and the blind, who are hated by David's soul." Therefore it is said, "The blind and the lame shall not come into the house." ⁹ And David dwelt in the stronghold, and called it the city of David. And David built the city round about from the Millo inward. ¹⁰ And David became greater and greater, for the LORD, the God of hosts, was with him.
¹¹ And Hiram king of Tyre sent messengers to David, and cedar trees, also carpenters and masons who built David a house. ¹² And David perceived that the LORD had established him king over Israel, and that he had exalted his kingdom for the sake of his people Israel.
¹³ And David took more concubines and wives from Jerusalem, after he came from Hebron; and more sons and daughters were born to David. ¹⁴ And these are the names of those who were born to him in Jerusalem: Shammua, Shobab, Nathan, Solomon, ¹⁵ Ibhar, Elishua, Nepheg, Japhia, ¹⁶ Elishama, Eliada, and Eliphelet.

The textual difficulties of these verses are too complex to rehearse here, but the general results of David's actions are readily apparent. About five years after he became king of all Israel (cf. note on v. 5), David moved his capital to Jerusalem, which he captured by the skill and daring of his own personal troops. This city provided him with an easily fortified base which bordered both on Israel and Judah but which as his own personal property was independent of loyalties to either one.

David's prosperity and the general well being of the kingdom during the early years of his reign are attested by his acquisition of a new capital, his rather pretentious building program, and his growing family.

The lame and the blind, who are hated by David's soul seems an unusually harsh and prejudicial view for a man of David's caliber. Recent commentators have offered a number of interpretations, none of which is completely successful in avoiding the problem. Apparently modern readers are not the first to have difficulty with the passage, however.

The parallel passage in 1 Chronicles 11:4–9, which otherwise follows the wording of Samuel almost verbatim, omits all reference to the lame and the blind. The last half of 2 Samuel 5:6 is omitted, and v. 8 is changed to read: "David said, 'Whoever shall smite the Jebusites first shall be chief and commander.' And Joab the son of Zeruiah went up first, so he became chief" (1 Chron. 11:6).

The Septuagint, however, reflects a text quite similar to that followed by the RSV with the exception of a small change in v. 8. Where the RSV reads *who are hated by David's soul*, the Greek version may be translated "and those who hate David's soul." This would require only a very slight alteration of the Hebrew text, but otherwise the difficulty remains.

c. David Stops Philistines (5:17–25)

¹⁷ When the Philistines heard that David had been anointed king over Israel, all the Philistines went up in search of David; but David heard of it and went down to the stronghold. ¹⁸ Now the Philistines had come and spread out in the valley of Rephaim. ¹⁹ And David inquired of the LORD, "Shall I go up against the Philistines? Wilt thou give them into my hand?" And the LORD said to David, "Go up; for I will certainly give the Philistines into your hand." ²⁰ And David came to Baal-perazim, and David defeated them there; and he said, "The LORD has broken through my

enemies before me, like a bursting flood." Therefore the name of that place is called Baalperazim. 21 And the Philistines left their idols there, and David and his men carried them away.

22 And the Philistines came up yet again, and spread out in the valley of Rephaim. 23 And when David inquired of the LORD, he said, "You shall not go up; go around to their rear, and come upon them opposite the balsam trees. 24 And when you hear the sound of marching in the tops of the balsam trees, then bestir yourself; for then the LORD has gone out before you to smite the army of the Philistines." 25 And David did as the LORD commanded him, and smote the Philistines from Geba to Gezer.

The Philistines had been willing, even anxious, for David to become king of Judah since any event which divided Israel could only work to their benefit. They probably also hoped that David, a former vassal of Achish, king of Gath, would be prone to favor his erstwhile overlords (cf. comment on 2:1–11). No doubt they noted with satisfaction the debilitating effects of Israel's civil war and the repeated frustration of efforts to reconcile the north and south.

When David emerged as the leader of a single state, the Philistines' policy changed, for now they would be opposed by a united people guided by a seasoned military leader of proven ability. Immediately they began mobilizing their armies for an expedition against the new king.

Lacking time to organize and train manpower drawn from all Israel, David had to rely mainly on his personal troops and Judean militia. With limited resources, he dared not commit his men to the defense of fortified sites where they could be isolated and reduced by the Philistines at their leisure (cf. his decision at Keilah: 1 Sam. 23:1–14). David, therefore, withdrew his forces to the stronghold in the wilderness around Adullam. From movable bases in that area, he was free to carry on the mobile guerrilla type war which he knew best.

Since David offered the Philistines no stationary target, they probably decided on a tactic designed to draw him out of the familiar territory where he gained his military start. By establishing a base in the valley of Rephaim southwest of Jerusalem, the Philistines could send raiding parties north or south to devastate Israelite territory until David came to the rescue.

Sensing the danger posed by the Philistine's position, David sought the Lord's counsel as to whether he should maintain his station in the south or go up to Rephaim. Assured of victory by the divine lot, David stealthily led his forces from the wilderness to take the initiative from the enemy. Bursting upon the Philistine host like floodwaters smashing through an earthen dam, the Israelites put their enemies to flight. In typical guerrilla form, David's men gathered the spoil, including the Philistine battle-gods, and faded into the countryside.

The Philistines regrouped their forces and returned to the same camp and probably the same strategy. Again David consulted the Lord, but this time was advised to avoid a frontal assault in favor of an attack from the rear. Using a balsam thicket for cover, David and his men circled into position and awaited a rustling in the treetops as the divine signal to advance. Again the Israelites were victorious, and the Philistines were dislodged from the mountains of south central Palestine.

The reference in v. 17, *and went down to the stronghold,* is not fully certain. In the present order of the text, *the stronghold* seems to refer to the citadel in Jerusalem. If, however, the capture of Jerusalem occurred considerably after the unification of the kingdom (cf. comment on 5:5), David had not yet taken Jerusalem when he defeated the Philistines in Rephaim. The stronghold mentioned here then refers to the wilderness around Adullam where David found protection when he first began raising a guerrilla army (cf. comment on 1 Sam. 22:5).

d. Ark Brought to Jerusalem (6:1–23)

1 David again gathered all the chosen men of Israel, thirty thousand. 2 And David arose

and went with all the people who were with him from Baalejudah, to bring up from there the ark of God, which is called by the name of the LORD of hosts who sits enthroned on the cherubim. ³ And they carried the ark of God upon a new cart, and brought it out of the house of Abinadab which was on the hill, and Uzzah and Ahio, the sons of Abinadab, were driving the new cart ⁴ with the ark of God; and Ahio went before the ark. ⁵ And David and all the house of Israel were making merry before the LORD with all their might, with songs and lyres and harps and tambourines and castanets and cymbals.

⁶ And when they came to the threshing floor of Nacon, Uzzah put out his hand to the ark of God and took hold of it, for the oxen stumbled. ⁷ And the anger of the LORD was kindled against Uzzah; and God smote him there because he put forth his hand to the ark; and he died there beside the ark of God. ⁸ And David was angry because the LORD had broken forth upon Uzzah; and that place is called Perezuzzah, to this day. ⁹ And David was afraid of the LORD that day; and he said, "How can the ark of the LORD come to me?" ¹⁰ So David was not willing to take the ark of the LORD into the city of David; but David took it aside to the house of Obededom the Gittite. ¹¹ And the ark of the LORD remained in the house of Obededom the Gittite three months; and the LORD blessed Obededom and all his household.

¹² And it was told King David, "The LORD has blessed the household of Obededom and all that belongs to him, because of the ark of God." So David went and brought up the ark of God from the house of Obededom to the city of David with rejoicing; ¹³ and when those who bore the ark of the LORD had gone six paces, he sacrificed an ox and a fatling. ¹⁴ And David danced before the LORD with all his might; and David was girded with a linen ephod. ¹⁵ So David and all the house of Israel brought up the ark of the LORD with shouting, and with the sound of the horn.

¹⁶ As the ark of the LORD came into the city of David, Michal the daughter of Saul looked out of the window, and saw King David leaping and dancing before the LORD; and she despised him in her heart. ¹⁷ And they brought in the ark of the LORD, and set it in its place, inside the tent which David had pitched for it; and David offered burnt offerings and peace offerings before the LORD. ¹⁸ And when David had finished offering the burnt offerings and the peace offerings, he blessed the people in the name of the LORD of hosts, ¹⁹ and distributed among all the people, the whole multitude of Israel, both men and women, to each a cake of bread, a portion of meat, and a cake of raisins. Then all the people departed, each to his house.

²⁰ And David returned to bless his household. But Michal the daughter of Saul came out to meet David, and said, "How the king of Israel honored himself today, uncovering himself today before the eyes of his servants' maids, as one of the vulgar fellows shamelessly uncovers himself!" ²¹ And David said to Michal, "It was before the LORD, who chose me above your father, and above all his house, to appoint me as prince over Israel, the people of the LORD—and I will make merry before the LORD. ²² I will make myself yet more contemptible than this, and I will be abased in your eyes; but by the maids of whom you have spoken, by them I shall be held in honor." ²³ And Michal the daughter of Saul had no child to the day of her death.

This chapter continues the summary of significant events associated with David's conquest of Jerusalem (5:1–16). The traditions themselves may have been originally preserved and circulated as a portion of a group of narratives dealing with the history of the ark (1 Sam. 4—6). Nevertheless, this incident in its present context is more than just an interesting episode about the ark. Indeed, the story yields both political and religious insights into David's early reign.

In Israelite thought, the ark symbolized the Lord's presence among his people, both on the march (Num. 10:33–36) and in battle (Josh. 6). From the ark, God dispensed wisdom and power to his people. Under the judges, the ark served as the focal point of Israel's religion and probably her tribal government as well (cf. comment on 1 Sam. 4:12–18). Nevertheless, the ark was virtually ignored following its return from capture by the Philistines (1 Sam. 7:1–2), and Saul apparently made no serious effort to restore it to a central position in Israel's life.

Saul came to power with the reluctant approval of the key leaders of this older system (1 Sam. 8—11), but his actions soon led to the alienation of both prophet (1 Sam. 13; 15) and priest (1 Sam. 22:11–19). During Saul's later years and throughout the reign of Ishbosheth, the tribal elders had little influence, as authority was increasingly centralized in the king and his court. Undoubtedly, these tensions poisoned the minds of many toward the monarchy itself.

David, however, was sensitive to these feelings and, wherever possible, worked within the framework drawn from an earlier generation. He had repeatedly avoided the use of raw power among his own people, even to accomplish what he believed to be God's will (cf. comment on 1 Sam. 24:6; 25:26). Apparently, David also had considerable respect for the tribal elders since only at their request did he assume the throne either in Judah (2 Sam. 2:4) or in Israel (5:1-3). Now we learn that David decided, with the approval of the elders (1 Chron. 13:2-4), to bring the ark to his new capital in Jerusalem.

After making elaborate preparations, David set out with an appropriate entourage to move the ark to its new home. The sudden death of Uzzah, an attendant who touched the ark, was taken as an omen of the Lord's wrath; and the procession was stopped immediately. David apparently took precautions lest some of the fury of the Lord should be attached to his family or the new capital city. For three months the ark was left with Obededom, a sojourner from Gath; and when it became apparent that he was being blessed not cursed, the journey was resumed.

The ark was brought the rest of the way into the city with full pomp and ceremony. When it had moved only six paces, a sacrifice was offered, celebrating an auspicious beginning of the journey. Dressed in a priestly linen ephod, David himself danced before the ark and guided it toward the tent which had been erected for its protection. Other sacrifices were completed, generous gifts of food were distributed among the people, and Israel had a day it would long remember.

Not all were pleased by the occasion, however. To Michal, Saul's daughter and David's wife, the public exposure and frenzied actions of a religious ecstatic seemed beneath the dignity of a king (cf. comment on 1 Sam. 10:1-16). How tragically, but typically, she failed to understand the obligations of high office. David understood more clearly, however, that his responsibilities were first to God and then to his people.

It may be noted that *Baalejudah* in v. 2 is not a place name but an expression meaning "rulers of Judah." It is so translated in the Septuagint. A place name, however, has apparently dropped out of the text. It was probably Kiriathjearim (1 Chron. 13:5-6) where the ark had been deposited in the care of Abinadab after its return from the Philistines (1 Sam. 7:1). Perhaps Kiriathjearim's earlier name Baalah was used, thus accounting for the confusion in the text. If the ark was still located in Kiriathjearim in David's day, the journey would not be long, for it lay only seven miles northwest of Jerusalem.

The Hebrew of vv. 6 and 7 is problematical and the details of this incident are unclear. The RSV draws heavily on the parallel passage in 1 Chronicles 13:6. Sudden death under such circumstances would be quite understandable, however, even within the natural order, i.e., through fright, exertion, etc.

e. Nathan Prophesies Dynasty (7:1-17)

¹ Now when the king dwelt in his house, and the LORD had given him rest from all his enemies round about, ² the king said to Nathan the prophet, "See now, I dwell in a house of cedar, but the ark of God dwells in a tent." ³ And Nathan said to the king, "Go, do all that is in your heart; for the LORD is with you."

⁴ But that same night the word of the LORD came to Nathan, ⁵ "Go and tell my servant David, 'Thus says the LORD: Would you build me a house to dwell in? ⁶ I have not dwelt in a house since the day I brought up the people of Israel from Egypt to this day, but I have been moving about in a tent for my dwelling. ⁷ In all places where I have moved with all the people of Israel, did I speak a word with any of the judges of Israel, whom I commanded to shepherd my people Israel, saying, "Why have you not built me a house of cedar?"' ⁸ Now therefore thus you shall say to my servant David, 'Thus says the LORD of hosts, I took you from the pasture, from following the sheep, that you should be prince over my people Israel; ⁹ and I have been with you wherever

you went, and have cut off all your enemies from before you; and I will make for you a great name, like the name of the great ones of the earth. 10 And I will appoint a place for my people Israel, and will plant them, that they may dwell in their own place, and be disturbed no more, and violent men shall afflict them no more, as formerly, 11 from the time that I appointed judges over my people Israel; and I will give you rest from all your enemies. Moreover the LORD declares to you that the LORD will make you a house. 12 When your days are fulfilled and you lie down with your fathers, I will raise up your offspring after you, who shall come forth from your body, and I will establish his kingdom. 13 He shall build a house for my name, and I will establish the throne of his kingdom for ever. 14 I will be his father, and he shall be my son. When he commits iniquity, I will chasten him with the rod of men, with the stripes of the sons of men; 15 but I will not take my steadfast love from him, as I took it from Saul, whom I put away from before you. 16 And your house and your kingdom shall be made sure for ever before me; your throne shall be established for ever.'" 17 In accordance with all these words, and in accordance with all this vision, Nathan spoke to David.

In this chapter we arrive at the theological crux of the books of Samuel. Indeed, the entire history of the southern kingdom and the emerging expectation of a Davidic messiah are indebted to the theological and political insights expressed here.

Nathan's prophecy is actually made up of two oracles which are drawn together by a play on the word *house*. The first oracle was an outgrowth of David's plan to build a house (temple) for the Lord. As a part of his efforts to focus Israel's religious and political life in Jerusalem, David proposed the construction of an elaborate temple to replace the tent which housed the ark.[32]

As David's powerful prophetic advisor, Nathan at first agreed (cf. v. 3) with the king's new plan. In a night of prayerful reflection, however, Nathan was led to see that David's greatest service for God was not the building of a temple but the successful resolution of Israel's problems of succession, hence the second oracle and the play on the word *house*. David would not build the Lord a house (temple), but the Lord would build David a *house* (dynasty).

The major thrust of Nathan's prophecy is found in the second oracle (vv. 8-16). It tells of God's continuing activity in support of David who was destined to be numbered among the world's most illustrious men. David's greatness would be achieved as God brought the three major provisions of Nathan's prophecy to pass. First, Israel would be granted peace to dwell securely in the land, free from foreign oppression. Second, when David died, he would be followed on the throne by an enduring line of his own descendants who would rule forever. Third, God promised to guide these future kings by sending adversity when they went astray. David's dynasty, however, would not be rejected as Saul had been for his transgressions.

Understandably, this view of the Davidic dynasty had profound implications for Israel's history and religion, especially after the southern kingdom became an independent state. Judah drew confidence from the fact that her rulers belonged to the house of David (cf. Psalm 78), and, in times of adversity, God's promises through Nathan's prophecy figured prominently in Temple liturgies (Psalm 89).

Nevertheless, the later kings of Judah proved to be such corrupting influences on the nation that hopes for a righteous ruler of David's caliber were increasingly projected into the future. These hopes were then transformed into an anticipation of a heavenly messiah when the monarchy failed altogether following Jerusalem's destruction by the Babylonians (Isa. 55; Ezek. 34).

While other biblical literature obviously draws on the concepts underlying Nathan's prophecy, a question remains as to the conditions under which an expectation of an enduring Davidic line arose.

Did Nathan's prophecy influence Judean dynastic practices, or is this passage a prophecy after the fact? Unfortunately,

---

[32] For a consideration of the motivating factors underlying David's plan, see R. E. Clements, *God and Temple* (Philadelphia: Fortress Press, 1965), pp. 40–62.

opinions vary widely. Some, such as H. P. Smith (p. 297) and R. H. Pfeiffer,[33] regard Nathan's prophecy as a creation of post-exilic theologians, placed on the lips of an earlier personality. Others, including Martin Noth[34] and H. W. Hertzberg (p. 283) consider the basic concepts underlying the material as products of the same historical context which the chapter describes. Against such a diversity of opinions, it would seem appropriate to attempt an analysis of the role Nathan's pronouncement (especially v. 16) would play in the political drama of David's united kingdom.

Under Israel's old tribal league, effective centralization of authority was almost nonexistent. In time of war the people were forced together under the leadership of the military judges, but the effectiveness of such unity varied with the seriousness of the external threat involved and the personal persuasiveness of each individual judge. With the renewal of aggressive policies among the Philistines, however, Israel's lack of a system to provide continuity of effective leadership at the national level proved a defect of near-fatal proportions. In an effort to correct this deficiency, Samuel, as the outstanding exponent of the old tribal leadership, assisted in the establishment of a more centralized government under the control of a king.

Saul's reign, however, had proved to be a fiasco. After an auspicious beginning both at home and in the field, Saul compounded the already serious divisive forces within Israel by his insane persecution of David. The nation was again crippled by conditions similar to those which had called the monarchy into being. Following Saul's death, the country's predicament was even more critical. With the kingdom divided, Israel was soon enveloped in a bitter civil war between David's supporters and the remnants of Saul's house. Only after repeated failures of peace negotiations, numerous assassinations, and finally the murder of Israel's king, was the kingdom finally reunited under David's leadership.

Against this background, it again became clear that the future of God's people would be seriously jeopardized unless the Israelites found a peaceful solution to their problems of succession. Thus, Nathan's prophecy was more than a simple statement of the conditions which would automatically follow in Israel. Rather, the prophet voiced the Lord's judgment in a *proposed solution* to Israel's dynastic difficulties. Henceforth, the legitimate king would be drawn from among David's descendants. There was no agreement yet as to which of his sons would occupy the throne (this problem is pursued in the Succession Narrative—2 Sam. 9–20; 1 Kings 1–2; cf. Introduction, V, 2); but at least a step was taken in the direction of reason and order.

Verses 5–7 have customarily been interpreted as a polemic against the dangers of an institutionalized religion. Nathan is understood to be prohibiting the construction of the Temple on the theological grounds that the Lord had not made his permanent abode in one house: *I have not dwelt in a house.* Rather, he had camped with his people in tents since leading them out of Egypt. The worship of the Lord, therefore, should not be confined to one particular building. Undoubtedly, these verses provided an important source of inspiration for the prophets who later spoke out about the abuses of the empty ritualism of worship in the Temple (Isa. 1:11–17; Jer. 7; Ezek. 8—9).

Commentators who have adopted this interpretation, however, have been embarrassed by v. 13 which speaks of David's son who would build a house for the name of the Lord. They have generally held that this verse, which seems to cut directly across the theology of vv. 5–7, is a later addition by a more recent scribe who knew of the existence of Solomon's Temple.

On the other hand, the entire passage

---

[33] Robert H. Pfeiffer, *Introduction to the Old Testament* (New York: Harper and Brothers, 1941), p. 371.

[34] *The Laws in the Pentateuch: Their Assumptions and Meaning* trans. D. R. Ap-Thomas (Philadelphia: Fortress Press, 1966), p. 16. This article originally appeared in German in 1940.

may be more naturally interpreted, not as prohibition, but as a postponement of the construction of a temple.³⁵ The Lord had always been content to live as his people had. Tents were perfectly adequate while Israel was on the march, and God had required no permanent abode. Then the Lord had selected David as prince over Israel and had strengthened his hands against the enemies of his people. When the people of Israel were firmly planted in their own place and when they knew peace, the Lord would create an enduring line for David's house on the throne of Israel. When his people were thus settled, then it would be proper for the Lord to be associated with a fixed "house."

f. David Offers Thanks (7:18-29)

¹⁸ Then King David went in and sat before the LORD, and said, "Who am I, O Lord GOD, and what is my house, that thou hast brought me thus far? ¹⁹ And yet this was a small thing in thy eyes, O Lord GOD; thou hast spoken also of thy servant's house for a great while to come, and hast shown me future generations, O Lord GOD! ²⁰ And what more can David say to thee? For thou knowest thy servant, O Lord God! ²¹ Because of thy promise, and according to thy own heart, thou hast wrought all this greatness, to make thy servant know it. ²² Therefore thou art great, O LORD God; for there is none like thee, and there is no God besides thee, according to all that we have heard with our ears. ²³ What other nation on earth is like thy people Israel, whom God went to redeem to be his people, making himself a name, and doing for them great and terrible things, by driving out before his people a nation and its gods? ²⁴ And thou didst establish for thyself thy people Israel to be thy people for ever; and thou, O LORD, didst become their God. ²⁵ And now, O LORD God, confirm for ever the word which thou hast spoken concerning thy servant and concerning his house, and do as thou hast spoken; ²⁶ and thy name will be magnified for ever, saying, 'The LORD of hosts is God over Israel,' and the house of thy servant David will be established before thee. ²⁷ For thou, O LORD of hosts, the God of Israel, hast made this revelation to thy servant, say-

---

³⁵ This passage, however, does not associate this postponement with any guilt connected to David's role as a great warrior (1 Chron. 22:8; 28:3). In Samuel, the Lord himself is credited with the defeat of David's enemies.

ing, 'I will build you a house'; therefore thy servant has found courage to pray this prayer to thee. ²⁸ And now, O Lord GOD, thou art God, and thy words are true, and thou hast promised this good thing to thy servant; ²⁹ now therefore may it please thee to bless the house of thy servant, that it may continue for ever before thee; for thou, O Lord GOD, hast spoken, and with they blessing shall the house of thy servant be blessed for ever."

David responded to God's promises through Nathan with a formal prayer of thanksgiving and commitment. The prayer resembles a hymn of praise in that while it deals with subjects related to man and his needs, its ultimate goal is the glorification of the Lord. David began his prayer by praising God for his many gracious acts in David's own life. It was not because of any goodness inherent in David but because of the graciousness of God's own heart that he took an insignificant shepherd and made him king.

Likewise, the very existence of the people Israel reflects glory on Isarel's God. The Lord reversed the customary order of affairs in which the nations of the world choose the god whom they serve. Instead, the Lord had called Israel into being and had repeatedly exerted himself in history on her behalf.

David concluded his prayer with an earnest appeal that the Lord would complete that which he had begun among his people. David promised that as long as Israel existed and as long as a member of his line sat upon the throne the name of the Lord would not go unpraised.

g. David's Reign Surveyed (8:1-18)

¹ After this David defeated the Philistines and subdued them, and David took Methegammah out of the hand of the Philistines.
² And he defeated Moab, and measured them with a line, making them lie down on the ground; two lines he measured to be put to death, and one full line to be spared. And the Moabites became servants to David and brought tribute.
³ David also defeated Hadadezer the son of Rehob, king of Zobah, as he went to restore his power at the river Euphrates. ⁴ And David took from him a thousand and seven hundred horsemen, and twenty thousand foot soldiers; and

David hamstrung all the chariot horses, but left enough for a hundred chariots. ⁵ And when the Syrians of Damascus came to help Hadadezer king of Zobah, David slew twenty-two thousand men of the Syrians. ⁶ Then David put garrisons in Aram of Damascus; and the Syrians became servants to David and brought tribute. And the LORD gave victory to David wherever he went. ⁷ And David took the shields of gold which were carried by the servants of Hadadezer, and brought them to Jerusalem. ⁸ And from Betah and from Berothai, cities of Hadadezer, King David took very much bronze.

⁹ When Toi king of Hamath heard that David had defeated the whole army of Hadadezer, ¹⁰ Toi sent his son Joram to King David, to greet him, and to congratulate him because he had fought against Hadadezer and defeated him; for Hadadezer had often been at war with Toi. And Joram brought with him articles of silver, of gold, and of bronze; ¹¹ these also King David dedicated to the LORD, together with the silver and gold which he dedicated from all the nations he subdued, ¹² from Edom, Moab, the Ammonites, the Philistines, Amalek, and from the spoil of Hadadezer the son of Rehob, king of Zobah.

¹³ And David won a name for himself. When he returned, he slew eighteen thousand Edomites in the Valley of Salt. ¹⁴ And he put garrisons in Edom; throughout all Edom he put garrisons, and all the Edomites became David's servants. And the LORD gave victory to David wherever he went.

¹⁵ So David reigned over all Israel; and David administered justice and equity to all his people. ¹⁶ And Joab the son of Zeruiah was over the army; and Jehoshaphat the son of Ahilud was recorder; ¹⁷ and Zadok the son of Ahitub and Ahimelech the son of Abiathar were priests; and Seraiah was secretary; ¹⁸ and Benaiah the son of Jehoiada was over the Cherethites and the Pelethites; and David's sons were priests.

This summary of the expanding Israelite empire and the burgeoning court in Jerusalem is used by the biblical author to indicate that his account of the rise and reign of David (1 Sam. 15:1—2 Sam. 8:18) has now reached its climax (cf. Introduction, V. 1). David's work is not yet over, but henceforth his role will be portrayed from a slightly different perspective. David's weaknesses (11:1–27; 13:21–22) are more readily acknowledged in the succeeding section, and attention turns to the determination of his successor.

Only representative engagements in David's wars with the Philistines have been selected for inclusion in the biblical record (5:17–25; 21:15–22; 23:9–17; and their parallel passages in 1 Chron.). These passages do not appear to be arranged in any chronological order, and the present reference to David's mastery over the Philistines simply states the final outcome of the struggle. The Philistines were never again a serious threat to Israel, and David was soon using Philistine mercenaries as he had earlier hired himself out to Achish, king of Gath. The site of Methegammah is unknown.

No explanation is given for David's extremely harsh treatment of the captured Moabites. He had at one time entrusted his parents to their keeping (cf. comment on 1 Sam. 22:1–5). Apparently such vicious tactics were not considered too uncommon in the ancient world since the author felt no necessity to justify David's actions. The omission of the grim consequences of this victory in 1 Chronicles 18:2, however, suggests that later generations considered this a blemish on the record of David's reign. This treatment of the Moabites in no way corresponds to the holy war concept of the *cherem* in which the total population and all their goods were to be destroyed (cf. comment on 1 Sam. 15:1–9).

David found an opportunity to extend his influence northward by exploiting the tensions that already existed between the kings of Zobah, Hamath, and Damascus. While Hadadezer, king of Zobah, was busy quelling a rebellion of his subjects near the Euphrates, David launched an expedition up the headwaters of the Jordan River between Mount Lebanon and Mount Hermon to attack him from the rear.[36] Since Hadadezer was unable to fight on two fronts simultaneously, David was able to raid almost at will. Spoil from the area

---

[36] This route seems likely, since otherwise David would have encountered the hostile Syrians of Damascus.

included gold, bronze, and enough warhorses for bragging purposes. Apparently, David felt that chariots were of little use in the mountainous fighting to which he was accustomed, since most of these animals were simply crippled and abandoned.

Existing political tensions in the area are reflected in the fact that, whereas the king of Hamath sent David a rich congratulatory gift for defeating Hadadezer, the people of Damascus sent an army to attack the Israelites. These troops were likewise unable to halt David's rampaging men, however. After a very successful campaign, David withdrew, leaving occasional garrisons around Damascus to represent his interests in what was still essentially enemy territory (cf. 10:6–19).[37]

After a victory over the Edomites in a campaign only vaguely remembered (cf. 1 Chron. 18:12; Ps. 60), David was left the major power between Mesopotamia and Egypt. He was in firm control of the land from the desert on the east to the Mediterranean on the west, from the Sea of Galilee in the north to the lower tip of the Dead Sea in the south. His outlying garrisons maintained marginal control over hostile tributaries, thus extending his influence from Kadesh on the Orontes River to the Gulf of Aqabah. Truly, *the Lord gave victory to David wherever he went.*

Although David was remembered as a king primarily for his military exploits, he also introduced a number of changes in the management of the kingdom. Even during the monarchy, the role of judge was of supreme importance; thus David supervised the administration of justice and undoubtedly heard the more important or difficult cases himself. Military authority was divided between Joab, commander of the militia, and Benaiah, leader of David's small standing army of professional soldiers. The distinctions between the roles of the scribe and the recorder are not known precisely, but both served as important advisors and officers of the king (cf. 2 Kings 18:18; Jer. 36:12 f.). Technical problems abound in the identification of the official priests of David's court and in the explanation of how David's sons (non-Levites) also functioned as priests. Nevertheless, we can see that David did not lack the religious support which prior narratives have shown to be so essential for any Israelite king.

Thus, David is portrayed at the height of his power as an eminently successful king. He had been able to transform his nation from a divided people subject to Philistine authority into an important world power. God's hand has been seen underlying the maze of historical episodes which had brought David to the pinnacle of success, and the author twice punctuates this summary with an observation of the Lord's role in David's victories (cf. vv. 6,14). From this point onward, the Lord will continue working in Israel's history, but David, as a declining monarch, will play an increasingly smaller role in that story.

IV. The Succession Narrative (9:1—20:26)

1. David Spares a Friend's Son (9:1–13)

¹ And David said, "Is there still any one left of the house of Saul, that I may show him kindness for Jonathan's sake?" ² Now there was a servant of the house of Saul whose name was Ziba, and they called him to David; and the king said to him, "Are you Ziba?" And he said, "Your servant is he." ³ And the king said, "Is there not still some one of the house of Saul, that I may show the kindness of God to him?" Ziba said to the king, "There is still a son of Jonathan; he is crippled in his feet." ⁴ The king said to him, "Where is he?" And Ziba said to the king, "He is in the house of Machir the son of Ammiel, at Lodebar." ⁵ Then King David sent and brought him from the house of Machir the son of Ammiel, at Lodebar. ⁶ And Mephibosheth the son of Jonathan, son of Saul, came to David, and fell on his face and did obeisance. And David said, "Mephibosheth!" And he answered, "Behold, your servant." ⁷ And David said to him, "Do not fear; for I will show you kindness for the sake of your father

---

[37] The Hebrew word translated "garrison" (*n*e*tsiv*) seems to have a connotation similar to the English term "post." Either can refer to a military establishment (cf. v. 14) or to a column or pillar (Gen. 19:26). David may, therefore, have erected monuments or bragging pillars rather than garrisons around Damascus.

Jonathan, and I will restore to you all the land of Saul your father; and you shall eat at my table always." ⁸ And he did obeisance, and said, "What is your servant, that you should look upon a dead dog such as I?"

⁹ Then the king called Ziba, Saul's servant, and said to him, "All that belonged to Saul and to all his house I have given to your master's son. ¹⁰ And you and your sons and your servants shall till the land for him, and shall bring in the produce, that your master's son may have bread to eat; but Mephibosheth your master's son shall always eat at my table." Now Ziba had fifteen sons and twenty servants. ¹¹ Then Ziba said to the king, "According to all that my lord the king commands his servant, so will your servant do." So Mephibosheth ate at David's table, like one of the king's sons. ¹² And Mephibosheth had a young son, whose name was Mica. And all who dwelt in Ziba's house became Mephibosheth's servants. ¹³ So Mephibosheth dwelt in Jerusalem; for he ate always at the king's table. Now he was lame in both his feet.

Up to this point, the stories about David have stressed his miraculous rise to power and his spectacular success in building an Israelite empire. With the survey of Israel's kingdom and court in chapter 8, however, the author has indicated that David's story has reached a turning point. Henceforth, attention will focus on the question posed by Nathan's prophecy in 7:1–17: Who will follow David on Israel's throne? This is the theme of the Succession Narrative (2 Sam. 9—20; 1 Kings 1—2).

The introduction of Jonathan's son Mephibosheth at the very beginning of this section spotlights the fact that Saul's descendants posed a substantial threat to the fulfillment of Nathan's prophecy. Under similar circumstances, it was customary for a ruler of a new dynasty to exterminate the entire house of his predecessor (2 Kings 10:8; 11:1) or even members of his own family if they were possible contenders for his throne (Judges 9:5; 2 Sam. 13:30).

As a matter of fact, Saul's sons were faring rather badly in Israel. Seven had already been surrendered to the inhabitants of Gibeon to assuage the blood guilt incurred by their father Saul (cf. comment on 21:1–9). By the time of the present episode, Saul's descendants were almost completely gone. At least some in Israel suspected David of arranging the timely disposal of his adversaries (16:7–8).

The biblical author, therefore, placed the story of David's relationship with Mephibosheth in a prominent position to demonstrate that David, as a man of character, remained true to his covenant with Jonathan (1 Sam. 29:42; cf. 24:21 f.). After considerable probing, Mephibosheth was located in Lo-debar, an unknown town somewhere near Mahanaim. The young man was understandably terrified by his sudden summons to appear before the king. Using a figure of speech which David himself had originated, Mephibosheth disclaimed all political ambitions saying, *"What is your servant, that you should look upon a dead dog such as I?"* (cf. 1 Sam. 24:14). We are probably to understand that he was genuinely innocent of any designs on the throne. Nevertheless, as long as he or his son lived, David was running a risk that someday Israel would once again turn to Saul's house for leadership (cf. 16:3; 19:24–30).

Therefore, while David was generous to Mephibosheth, he was cautious as well. He granted Mephibosheth princely status and gave him Saul's family estates, thus assuring him of an adequate income for life. David, however, required his ward's presence at the royal table where his every action could be observed. He even charged Ziba to act as steward of Saul's lands so that Mephibosheth would have no business reasons for being away from the king's court.

Thus, David again used discretion and generosity in carrying out his sense of divine vocation.

2. *David Faces Syrians and Ammonites (10:1–19)*

¹ After this the king of the Ammonites died, and Hanun his son reigned in his stead. ² And David said, "I will deal loyally with Hanun the son of Nahash, as his father dealt loyally with me." So David sent by his servants to console him concerning his father. And David's servants came into the land of the Ammonites.

³ But the princes of the Ammonites said to Hanun their lord, "Do you think, because David has sent comforters to you, that he is honoring your father? Has not David sent his servants to you to search the city, and to spy it out, and to overthrow it?" ⁴ So Hanun took David's servants, and shaved off half the beard of each, and cut off their garments in the middle, at their hips, and sent them away. ⁵ When it was told David, he sent to meet them, for the men were greatly ashamed. And the king said, "Remain at Jericho until your beards have grown, and then return."

⁶ When the Ammonites saw that they had become odious to David, the Ammonites sent and hired the Syrians of Bethrehob, and the Syrians of Zobah, twenty thousand foot soldiers, and the king of Maacah with a thousand men, and the men of Tob, twelve thousand men. ⁷ And when David heard of it, he sent Joab and all the host of the mighty men. ⁸ And the Ammonites came out and drew up in battle array at the entrance of the gate, and the Syrians of Zobah and of Rehob, and the men of Tob and Maacah, were by themselves in the open country.

⁹ When Joab saw that the battle was set against him both in front and in the rear, he chose some of the picked men of Israel, and arrayed them against the Syrians; ¹⁰ the rest of his men he put in the charge of Abishai his brother, and he arrayed them against the Ammonites. ¹¹ And he said, "If the Syrians are too strong for me, then you shall help me; but if the Ammonites are too strong for you, then I will come and help you. ¹² Be of good courage, and let us play the man for our people, and for the cities of our God; and may the Lord do what seems good to him." ¹³ So Joab and the people who were with him drew near to battle against the Syrians; and they fled before him. ¹⁴ And when the Ammonites saw that the Syrians fled, they likewise fled before Abishai, and entered the city. Then Joab returned from fighting against the Ammonites, and came to Jerusalem.

¹⁵ But when the Syrians saw that they had been defeated by Israel, they gathered themselves together. ¹⁶ And Hadadezer sent, and brought out the Syrians who were beyond the Euphrates; and they came to Helam, with Shobach the commander of the army of Hadadezer at their head. ¹⁷ And when it was told David, he gathered all Israel together, and crossed the Jordan, and came to Helam. And the Syrians arrayed themselves against David, and fought with him. ¹⁸ And the Syrians fled before Israel; and David slew of the Syrians the men of seven hundred chariots, and forty thousand horsemen, and wounded Shobach the commander of their army, so that he died there. ¹⁹ And when all the kings who were servants of Hadadezer saw that they had been defeated by Israel, they made peace with Israel, and became subject to them. So the Syrians feared to help the Ammonites any more.

While most of the accounts of David's foreign wars were recounted prior to or as a part of the summary of his reign (8:1–18), the present narratives about the Ammonite war are included here to provide a backdrop for the Bathsheba story. Although the war stories contain very few concrete chronological references, the present narrative seems to provide an explanation for the outbreak of hostilities both with the Ammonites and the Syrians. Indeed, Bright (pp. 181–182) considers David's war with Ammon his first in the building of Israel's empire. The action against Moab (8:2,13 f.), Edom (8:13–14; 1 Kings 11:15–18), and Syria (8:3–12) would then follow.

If the preceding order is correct, the growth of the empire is to be understood, not as the product of David's ambition, but as the result of divine protection in the face of international provocation. Certainly, in the Ammonite campaign, it was Hanun and not David who wanted war.

Although Israel and Ammon had been enemies during Saul's early days (1 Sam. 11:1–11), David had been able to reestablish—and he apparently intended to maintain—amicable relations with his neighbors to the east. At the death of the king of Ammon, he sent diplomatic envoys to convey his regrets and to reaffirm his peaceful intentions. Nevertheless, in acts calculated to humiliate David's officials and to cast ridicule on his government, Hanun the new king of Ammon sent Israel's delegation home in disgrace. Hanun would hardly have caused them such serious loss of face had he not been reasonably well assured of military support in the event of Israelite retaliation.

In any case, Hanun was well supplied with troops when David inevitably sought to redeem the dignity of his men (cf. David's reaction to Nabal's rebuff, 1 Sam.

25:21–22). When Joab approached with the choice soldiers of Israel's army, the Ammonites mustered outside the city gates inviting attack, while mercenaries from nearby Syrian states waited to strike the Israelites from the rear. Sensing his enemies' familiar entrapment tactics, Joab used some of his troops to fight the Syrians while the rest, under Abishai's command, engaged the Ammonites. When the Syrians gave way before Joab and his men, the Ammonites retreated within the city so that the engagement ended with Israel victorious but with Hanun safe.

Ammon's Syrian allies, no doubt alarmed by news of Joab's victory, regrouped their troops and began bringing in reinforcements from the distant corners of their holdings. Learning of this immense mobilization of enemy forces, David seized the initiative by crossing the Jordan and striking with the entire Israelite army. The Syrians again fled after suffering severe losses in lives and property. Henceforth, the Syrians refrained from dabbling in trans-Jordanian politics.

Shaved off half the beard (v. 4). In the ancient Near East, a full beard was considered a mark of masculinity and maturity. The beard was shaved normally only as a sign of mourning or of impending doom (Isa. 15:2; Jer. 41:5). David had his diplomats stay in Jericho until their beards grew out lest they be walking indictments of his power and prestige.

3. Tragedy Follows Sin (11:1—12:31)

(1) David Succumbs to Lust (11:1–13)

¹ In the spring of the year, the time when kings go forth to battle, David sent Joab, and his servants with him, and all Israel; and they ravaged the Ammonites, and besieged Rabbah. But David remained at Jerusalem.
² It happened, late one afternoon, when David arose from his couch and was walking upon the roof of the king's house, that he saw from the roof a woman bathing; and the woman was very beautiful. ³ And David sent and inquired about the woman. And one said, "Is not this Bathsheba, the daughter of Eliam, the wife of Uriah the Hittite?" ⁴ So David sent messengers, and took her; and she came to him, and he lay with her. (Now she was purifying herself from her uncleanness.) Then she returned to her house. ⁵ And the woman conceived; and she sent and told David, "I am with child."
⁶ So David sent word to Joab, "Send me Uriah the Hittite." And Joab sent Uriah to David. ⁷ When Uriah came to him, David asked how Joab was doing, and how the people fared, and how the war prospered. ⁸ Then David said to Uriah, "Go down to your house, and wash your feet." And Uriah went out of the king's house, and there followed him a present from the king. ⁹ But Uriah slept at the door of the king's house with all the servants of his lord, and did not go down to his house. ¹⁰ When they told David, "Uriah did not go down to his house," David said to Uriah, "Have you not come from a journey? Why did you not go down to your house?" ¹¹ Uriah said to David, "The ark and Israel and Judah dwell in booths; and my lord Joab and the servants of my lord are camping in the open field; shall I then go to my house, to eat and to drink, and to lie with my wife? As you live, and as your soul lives, I will not do this thing." ¹² Then David said to Uriah, "Remain here today also, and tomorrow I will let you depart." So Uriah remained in Jerusalem that day, and the next. ¹³ And David invited him, and he ate in his presence and drank, so that he made him drunk; and in the evening he went out to lie on his couch with the servants of his lord, but he did not go down to his house.

This story of David's sin with Bathsheba serves as a theological introduction to the body of the Succession Narrative. Our study up to this point has revealed a conviction on the part of the author that God exerted himself in the affairs of men, rewarding good and punishing evil. Israel's fortunes in particular were influenced by the spiritual condition of the people and especially by the moral stature of her leaders.

Thus, the nation prospered under Samuel's upright guidance (1 Sam. 7:13), but his corrupt sons contributed heavily to the failure of the old tribal league under the judges (1 Sam. 8:1–9). Similarly, Israel's armies met with considerable success during the early years of Saul's reign, but the Philistines regained the upper hand when he was rejected for resisting God's leadership (cf. comment on 1 Sam. 13:1–15;

15:10–23).

On the other hand, David as a man after God's own heart (1 Sam. 13:14) had met with unqualified success. He was not portrayed as a perfect man (1 Sam. 20:5–6; 21:1–5), but the Lord intervened repeatedly to protect him and to help him avoid serious moral transgression (1 Sam. 25:32–33). Under David's leadership, Israel was transformed from two struggling kingdoms, dominated by Philistine rule, into a major power in the eastern Mediterranean world.

As Isarel began having serious internal difficulties, however, the people sought a theological justification for the change of national fortunes. One ready answer was provided by David's flagrant moral transgressions in the Bathsheba affair. While this sordid episode undoubtedly compounded many national problems and precipitated others, David's lust for Uriah's wife was not the only cause for Israel's difficulties. The sectional rivalries which Saul had faced (cf. comment on 1 Sam. 9:1–2) had merely been glossed over when David became king of all Israel. They were thus awaiting only slight provocation to erupt again (20:1; 1 Kings 12:1–5). In addition, under David's leadership the country had embarked on a policy of international involvement, and work on the new capital in Jerusalem was developing along Phoenician lines (5:11). Plans were even under way to take the ark of the Lord out of its tent and place it in a temple comparable to the king's palace (7:1–7,13).

These problems were not overlooked, but the author focused attention on the crux of the issue. David's failures as leader of his people resulted not from the magnitude of the problems which he faced but because of moral and spiritual deficiencies within. Power did and still does tend to corrupt the powerful. What David had learned as a fugitive (1 Sam. 25:32–35), he had forgotten as king of Israel. His sin with Bathsheba was but the outward expression of his inward resistance to God's leadership.

The remainder of the Succession Narrative, therefore, will trace the theological fallout of this experience with special emphasis on the struggle for Israel's throne. The most grievous tragedies to befall David and the nation will be seen as fitting retribution for the wrongs that he committed against Uriah (12:10–12).

Armies took to the field *in the spring of the year*—normally between April and June after the spring rains had ended and after the peasants in the militia had completed work on their basic grain crops. After abandoning the attack the preceding fall, David resumed the siege of Rabbah, modern Amman, by sending a major force under Joab's command to pillage the land and to encamp around the city.

David's *walking upon the roof* was quite natural. The flat roofs of ancient houses were often used for choice sleeping and living areas (cf. 1 Sam. 9:25).

Bathsheba was the daughter of Eliam, a member of David's elite troops (23:34), and the granddaughter of Ahithophel, one of his advisors. Ahithophel later supported Absalom's rebellion (15:12,31), perhaps as a consequence of David's unwholesome relationship with Bathsheba.

So David sent messengers, and took her. Such an arrangement could not be kept secret in a city as small as Jerusalem was at the time. The biblical author takes no notice of Bathsheba's complicity in this affair, but under Jewish law she was equally guilty for her failure to cry out (Deut. 22:22–24). They were both subject to a death penalty.

Now she was purifying herself. See Leviticus 15:19–24. This was considered to be a woman's most fertile period.

When it became apparent that nature had trapped David and Bathsheba in their sin, David sought to hide his guilt. Uriah was recalled from the front and encouraged, in the guise of royal beneficence, to resume his role as a husband. **Wash your feet** is probably a euphemism for sexual intercourse; at least Uriah understood it as such. Either because he suspected the king's true motives or because he was unwilling to enjoy a privilege which his fellow soldiers could not share, Uriah refused to return home and quartered instead with the royal guard. When David's scheme to weaken Uriah's resolve with strong drink failed, he could see no way out of his dilemma other than to have Uriah killed.

(2) David Has Uriah Killed (11:14–27)

14 In the morning David wrote a letter to Joab, and sent it by the hand of Uriah. 15 In the letter he wrote, "Set Uriah in the forefront of the hardest fighting, and then draw back from him, that he may be struck down, and die." 16 And as Joab was besieging the city, he assigned Uriah to the place where he knew there were valiant men. 17 And the men of the city came out and fought with Joab; and some of the servants of David among the people fell. Uriah the Hittite was slain also. 18 Then Joab sent and told David all the news about the fighting; 19 and he instructed the messenger, "When you have finished telling all the news about the fighting to the king, 20 then, if the king's anger rises, and if he says to you, 'Why did you go so near the city to fight? Did you not know that they would shoot from the wall? 21 Who killed Abimelech the son of Jerubbesheth? Did not a woman cast an upper millstone upon him from the wall, so that he died at Thebez? Why did you go so near the wall?' then you shall say, 'Your servant Uriah the Hittite is dead also.' "

22 So the messenger went, and came and told David all that Joab had sent him to tell. 23 The messenger said to David, "The men gained an advantage over us, and came out against us in the field; but we drove them back to the entrance of the gate. 24 Then the archers shot at your servants from the wall; some of the king's servants are dead; and your servant Uriah the Hittite is dead also." 25 David said to the messenger, "Thus shall you say to Joab, 'Do not let this matter trouble you, for the sword devours now one and now another; strengthen your attack upon the city, and overthrow it.' And encourage him."

26 When the wife of Uriah heard that Uriah her husband was dead, she made lamentation for her husband. 27 And when the mourning was over, David sent and brought her to his house, and she became his wife, and bore him a son. But the thing that David had done displeased the LORD.

David had badly bungled efforts to conceal his adultery with Bathsheba, first by implicating servants in his folly and then by exhibiting an overly solicitous attitude toward a suspicious husband. His plan to dispose of Uriah was no less transparent. With utter ruthlessness, David called on Joab to order his troops to leave Uriah to face his doom alone in the midst of battle. Recognizing the disastrous effects that such open treachery would have on the morale of his troops, Joab showed an even greater disregard for human life as he kept the king's plan secret and ordered his men into battle. Using tactics that were certain to result in high casualties, Joab employed a contingent of his finest troops in a fruitless assault near the city wall (the enemy's water supply? cf. 12:27). The Ammonite capital remained secure for the time being, but Uriah, along with a goodly number of his companions, was dead.

Almost as if he were baiting the king's anger, Joab instructed his messenger to reserve news of Uriah's death until the end of his report. In any case, David's outburst of anger at Joab's violation of the most basic siege tactics was suddenly stilled when he learned that Bathsheba's husband was dead (see note on v. 23 below). The reader is left to wonder how many other times Joab was tempted to use his knowledge of this sordid affair as a tool to manipulate his commander-in-chief.

After a brief period of mourning for her husband, Bathsheba moved to the palace and bore David's son. Thus it appeared that David had successfully avoided paying the consequences for his sin. The matter was not closed, however, for while Uriah was dead, the issue was not. The measure of the Lord's displeasure was yet to be seen.

The Septuagint of v. 22 indicates that David responded as Joab had anticipated he would. This reading is probably preferred since in Hebrew the messenger's report to David in v. 23 begins with a word (*ki*) which frequently introduces an answer to a previous question. Thus David asked, *Why did you go so near the wall?* The messenger replied because **the men** *gained an advantage over us.* (Cf. McKane, p. 231.)

And when the mourning was over. The usual period of strict mourning was seven days (Gen. 50:10; 1 Sam. 31:13). Remarriage of a widow soon after the death of her husband was probably fairly common in the ancient Near East. Unless such a woman returned to her father's house or had children to support her, she was left without protection or property rights (Gen. 38:11; Num. 27:8–11).

(3) Nathan Accuses David (12:1–15a)

¹ And the Lord sent Nathan to David. He came to him, and said to him, "There were two men in a certain city, the one rich and the other poor. ² The rich man had very many flocks and herds; ³ but the poor man had nothing but one little ewe lamb, which he had bought. And he brought it up, and it grew up with him and with his children; it used to eat of his morsel, and drink from his cup, and lie in his bosom, and it was like a daughter to him. ⁴ Now there came a traveler to the rich man, and he was unwilling to take one of his own flock or herd to prepare for the wayfarer who had come to him, but he took the poor man's lamb, and prepared it for the man who had come to him." ⁵ Then David's anger was greatly kindled against the man; and he said to Nathan, "As the Lord lives, the man who has done this deserves to die; ⁶ and he shall restore the lamb fourfold, because he did this thing, and because he had no pity."
⁷ Nathan said to David, "You are the man. Thus says the Lord, the God of Israel, 'I anointed you king over Israel, and I delivered you out of the hand of Saul; ⁸ and I gave you your master's house, and your master's wives into your bosom, and gave you the house of Israel and of Judah; and if this were too little, I would add to you as much more. ⁹ Why have you despised the word of the Lord, to do what is evil in his sight? You have smitten Uriah the Hittite with the sword, and have taken his wife to be your wife, and have slain him with the sword of the Ammonites. ¹⁰ Now therefore the sword shall never depart from your house, because you have despised me, and have taken the wife of Uriah the Hittite to be your wife.' ¹¹ Thus says the Lord, 'Behold, I will raise up evil against you out of your own house; and I will take your wives before your eyes, and give them to your neighbor, and he shall lie with your wives in the sight of this sun. ¹² For you did it secretly; but I will do this thing before all Israel, and before the sun.' " ¹³ David said to Nathan, "I have sinned against the Lord." And Nathan said to David, "The Lord also has put away your sin; you shall not die. ¹⁴ Nevertheless, because by this deed you have utterly scorned the Lord, the child that is born to you shall die." ¹⁵ Then Nathan went to his house.

As a skilled spokesman for the Lord, Nathan recognized that a rebuke is useless unless it is heeded and that the most difficult subjects can often be approached obliquely. Nathan appealed to the highest qualities in David's character as he posed a test case before the nation's highest arbiter of justice. The story was a simple one, superbly told. Caught up and infuriated by the drama, David angrily pronounced judgment before he learned the identity of the defendant. All too soon, however, he heard Nathan's apt words, *You are the man.*

Both king and prophet based their judgments on the law of retaliation (Ex. 21:24; Lev. 24:20; Deut. 19:21) in which the punishment was precisely fashioned to fit the crime. Although David's emotions told him that the rich man deserved to die, he restricted himself to the fourfold repayment prescribed by law (Ex. 22:1). This is an excellent example of the humane intentions of the "eye-for-an-eye" philosophy in Old Testament law. Restrictions were needed to prohibit excessively harsh sentences, pronounced by emotionally aroused judges. David's sins may have merited capital punishment, but the rich man's theft of a single lamb, however prized, certainly did not.

Nathan's judgment on David was likewise aptly tailored to fit his transgression. As David had used the sword of the Ammonites to achieve his purpose against Uriah, so his own house (dynasty) would continually be smitten by violence (chs. 13—18). As David had taken another man's wife in secret, so his own wives would be degraded publicly (16:20–23). Nathan's next statement, however, appears to bend both logic and justice. One would expect the judgment to follow former lines. Since David had taken Uriah's life, he was expected to have to pay with his own. Nevertheless, this portion of his sentence was borne by Bathsheba's son. David would live, but the child born out of this illicit affair would have to die.

The phrase *deserves to die* captures the sense of the Hebrew idiom (the man who has done this is "a son of death"). This should not be interpreted as a royal sentence of death, however, since other Old Testament uses of the expression give no evidence of its execution (cf. especially 1 Sam. 26:16 and a related phrase in 1 Kings 2:26).

Thus says the Lord . . . I gave . . . your master's wives into your bosom. Women in the king's harem were considered his personal property, and as such they became the possession of his successor (cf. comment on 2:7).

The child that is born to you shall die. The idea that God punishes a child for the sin of its parents is modified in other Old Testament passages. The ancient Hebrews recognized that the consequences of man's sin are often passed on to his descendant (Ex. 20:5–6). They also learned, however, that each individual is punished for his own sin (Ezek. 18:1–4,20).

(4) David Loses a Son (12:15b–25)

And the LORD struck the child that Uriah's wife bore to David, and it became sick. ¹⁶ David therefore besought God for the child; and David fasted, and went in and lay all night upon the ground. ¹⁷ And the elders of his house stood beside him, to raise him from the ground; but he would not, nor did he eat food with them. ¹⁸ On the seventh day the child died. And the servants of David feared to tell him that the child was dead; for they said, "Behold, while the child was yet alive, we spoke to him, and he did not listen to us; how then can we say to him the child is dead? He may do himself some harm." ¹⁹ But when David saw that his servants were whispering together, David perceived that the child was dead; and David said to his servants, "Is the child dead?" They said, "He is dead." ²⁰ Then David arose from the earth, and washed, and anointed himself, and changed his clothes; and he went into the house of the LORD, and worshiped; he then went to his own house; and when he asked, they set food before him, and he ate. ²¹ Then his servants said to him, "What is this thing that you have done? You fasted and wept for the child while it was alive; but when the child died, you arose and ate food." ²² He said, "While the child was still alive, I fasted and wept; for I said, 'Who knows whether the LORD will be gracious to me, that the child may live?' ²³ But now he is dead; why should I fast? Can I bring him back again? I shall go to him, but he will not return to me."

²⁴ Then David comforted his wife, Bathsheba, and went in to her, and lay with her; and she bore a son, and he called his name Solomon. And the LORD loved him, ²⁵ and sent a message by Nathan the prophet; so he called his name Jedidiah, because of the LORD.

For at least the second time, David recognized that he had been responsible for the misfortune which fell upon others (cf. 1 Sam. 22:22). Although he sought in each case to ameliorate the suffering which he had caused, he was unable to halt the consequences of his deeds.

When his son by Bathsheba became ill, David expressed his grief and penitence by fasting and sleeping upon the ground. He earnestly prayed that the lad's life might be spared until all hope for a reprieve from Nathan's sentence was gone. When his servants announced the child's death, however, he washed himself, worshiped, and resumed the normal affairs of life. By his startling reversal of the usual order of mourning customs, David demonstrated that his actions were genuine, not the result of mere religious formality. His open practicality would have been eminently satisfying to the ancient Hebrews who often faced death and recognized that, whenever possible, life must go on.

The death of Bathsheba's son, however, called attention to political as well as religious reality. David's sin against Uriah was potentially serious enough to undermine the stability of Israel's monarchy. Nathan's promise that the Lord would not overthrow David's ruling line (7:14–16) was being put to the test.

Against this background, the birth of a second son to David and Bathsheba was of signal importance. Whereas the Lord had denied Michal offspring as a sign of his displeasure, he gave Bathsheba a son to show that he was still working to build David an enduring house for Israel's throne. Thus, David called his son Solomon (related to the Hebrew word for peace) in recognition of his renewed fellowship with the Lord, and Nathan called the boy Jedidiah (Beloved of the Lord) as a means of foreshadowing the child's role in Israel's future.

Who knows whether the Lord will be gracious to me. Death is man's natural end in life just as birth is his beginning. Seen from God's point of view, death itself need not be evil or unpleasant. David saw that the punishment involved fell upon him in the loss of his child.

"I shall go to him, but he will not return to me." This statement does not necessarily imply a developed belief in life after death among the ancient Hebrews. David is simply saying that in keeping with his mortal nature, he will eventually join his son in Sheol, the abode of the dead (cf. comment on 1 Sam. 28:1-14).

(5) *David Defeats the Ammonites (12:26-31)*

26 Now Joab fought against Rabbah of the Ammonites, and took the royal city. 27 And Joab sent messengers to David, and said, "I have fought against Rabbah; moreover, I have taken the city of waters. 28 Now, then, gather the rest of the people together, and encamp against the city, and take it; lest I take the city, and it be called by my name." 29 So David gathered all the people together and went to Rabbah, and fought against it and took it. 30 And he took the crown of their king from his head; the weight of it was a talent of gold, and in it was a precious stone; and it was placed on David's head. And he brought forth the spoil of the city, a very great amount. 31 And he brought forth the people who were in it, and set them to labor with saws and iron picks and iron axes, and made them toil at the brickkilns; and thus he did to all the cities of the Ammonites. Then David and all the people returned to Jerusalem.

After the biblical author brought his story of David and Bathsheba to a close, he then told of the successful conclusion of the Ammonite war. Since David's sin, unlike Achan's transgression (Josh. 7:1-26), was openly confessed and thoroughly expiated, it did not adversely affect the outcome of Israel's siege of Rabbah.

After Joab had gained control of Rabbah's water supply, making its surrender inevitable, he invited David to preside over the city's ultimate downfall. David mustered Israel's militia and arrived in time for his troops to share in the final struggle and in the plundering of the city. David himself received credit for the victory, and the crown of Ammon was added to those of Israel and Judah which he already wore (5:1-5).

The terminology *took the royal city* would normally suggest the entire capital city, but in v. 27, Joab claimed possession of only the *city of waters.* Some have suggested that v. 26 be emended to read *city of waters* with v. 27, but the two expressions may represent local terms for defensive positions within the city which successively fell to Israelite pressure. If such is the case, an especially bitter and protracted battle would be indicated. Note, for example, Josephus' account of the final struggle for the tower of Antonia during the battle of Jerusalem in A.D. 70 (*The Jewish War,* ch. 20).

The weight of the king's crown was a talent of gold. Although exact equivalents between ancient and modern systems of measurement are impossible to ascertain, a talent seems to have weighed in the neighborhood of 75 pounds. The immense size of the Ammonite crown suggests that it adorned an idol and that David used only a gem from it in his own crown. In such a case, the phrase *of their king* (*malkam*) should be read to indicate the name of an Ammonite deity Milcom (cf. 1 Kings 11:5).

David's treatment of the captured Ammonites is not clear. The RSV, making very minor revisions in an otherwise unintelligible text, portrays David using the people in various roles as slave laborers. The parallel passage in 1 Chronicles 20:3 (KJV), however, indicates that he tortured (sawed) them with agricultural implements. Although David has shown himself capable of such inhumane acts (8:2), the RSV has probably captured the better reading.

4. Amnon Degrades Tamar (13:1-22)

1 Now Absalom, David's son, had a beautiful sister, whose name was Tamar; and after a time Amnon, David's son, loved her. 2 And Amnon was so tormented that he made himself ill because of his sister Tamar; for she was a virgin, and it seemed impossible to Amnon to do anything to her. 3 But Amnon had a friend, whose name was Jonadab, the son of Shimeah, David's brother; and Jonadab was a very crafty man. 4 And he said to him, "O son of the king, why are you so haggard morning after morning? Will you not tell me?" Amnon said to him, "I love Tamar, my brother Absalom's sister." 5 Jonadab said to him, "Lie down on your bed, and pretend to be ill; and when your father comes to see you, say to him, 'Let my sister Tamar come and give me bread to eat, and prepare the food in my sight, that I may see it, and eat it from her hand.'" 6 So Amnon lay down, and pretended to be ill; and when the king came to see him, Amnon said to the king, "Pray let my sister Tamar come and make a couple of cakes in my sight, that I may eat from her hand."

7 Then David sent home to Tamar, saying, "Go to your brother Amnon's house, and prepare food for him." 8 So Tamar went to her brother Amnon's house, where he was lying down. And she took dough, and kneaded it, and made cakes in his sight, and baked the cakes. 9 And she took the pan and emptied it out before him, but he refused to eat. And Amnon said, "Send out every one from me." So every one went out from him. 10 Then Amnon said to Tamar, "Bring the food into the chamber, that I may eat from your hand." And Tamar took the cakes she had made, and brought them into the chamber to Amnon her brother. 11 But when she brought them near him to eat, he took hold of her, and said to her, "Come, lie with me, my sister." 12 She answered him, "No, my brother, do not force me; for such a thing is not done in Israel; do not do this wanton folly. 13 As for me, where could I carry my shame? And as for you, you would be as one of the wanton fools in Israel. Now therefore, I pray you, speak to the king; for he will not withhold me from you." 14 But he would not listen to her; and being stronger than she, he forced her, and lay with her.

15 Then Amnon hated her with very great hatred; so that the hatred with which he hated her was greater than the love with which he had loved her. And Amnon said to her, "Arise, be gone." 16 But she said to him, "No, my brother; for this wrong in sending me away is greater than the other which you did to me." But he would not listen to her. 17 He called the young man who served him and said, "Put this woman out of my presence, and bolt the door after her." 18 Now she was wearing a long robe with sleeves; for thus were the virgin daughters of the king clad of old. So his servant put her out, and bolted the door after her. 19 And Tamar put ashes on her head, and rent the long robe which she wore; and she laid her hand on her head, and went away, crying aloud as she went.

20 And her brother Absalom said to her, "Has Amnon your brother been with you? Now hold your peace, my sister; he is your brother; do not take this to heart." So Tamar dwelt, a desolate woman, in her brother Absalom's house. 21 When King David heard of all these things, he was very angry. 22 But Absalom spoke to Amnon neither good nor bad; for Absalom hated Amnon, because he had forced his sister Tamar.

Now that the author of the Succession Narrative has accounted for the approaching turmoil within David's house (cf. comment on 11:1-13), he turns to the basic question underlying his work: Who will succeed David on the throne? All that follows must be read against a background of political intrigue in which each of the major characters is to be viewed as a potential king of Israel. Of the 17 sons of David already mentioned (3:2-5; 5:14-15), only four are to figure prominently in the ensuing narratives: Amnon, Absalom, Adonijah, and Solomon. Each will be examined and rejected in turn until only God's own choice remains.

In a story tragically similar to David's affair with Bathsheba, the author depicts Amnon, Israel's crown prince, as a man of base character totally unredeemed by nobler qualities or mitigating circumstances. The cold premeditation with which he plotted his attack on Tamar was repugnant even in a society long acquainted with sexual excesses of every type (Gen. 19; Judg. 19:22-26; 21:16-24). While polygamy was still practiced and human frailty was tolerated (Gen. 38; Judg. 16; 2 Sam. 11; 1 Kings 11), the kingdom of Israel was not to be entrusted to one who would use raw power to pursue his goals irrespective of the rights of others. This, of course, was precisely the issue with which David had so often struggled in his utilization of power (1 Sam. 25; 2 Sam. 11). David, however, had been quick to confess guilt and to seek to make amends when confronted with his error. Amnon, on the other hand, arrogantly expelled Tamar after abusing her and stubbornly refused to honor the requirements of the law prescribed in such cases (Deut. 22:28–29). Even had he lived, Amnon was obviously unfit to rule over Israel since he could not adequately control himself.

Tamar's protest, *for such a thing is not done in Israel*, apparently assumed that Amnon's intentions were honorable, i.e., that he intended to marry her. She observed that marriages in which the groom captured his bride (cf. Judg. 21:16–24) were suitable only for the *wanton fools* or coarse rabble. Such an arrangement would reflect on the noble background of both the woman and the man. Amnon could properly arrange the marriage by asking her father (David) for permission which she was certain he would grant: *for he will not withhold me from you*. Only later did Tamar realize that Amnon had no intention of marrying her.

Apparently marriages between half brothers and sisters were not condemned in Israel at this time (cf. Abraham and Sarah; Gen. 20:12), but they were later expressly forbidden (Deut. 27:22; Lev. 18:9,11). Such consanguineous marriages were probably common among Israel's neighbors and were the rule rather than the exception within the Egyptian royal family.

This wrong in sending me away is greater than the other which you did to me. Amnon's gravest sin was in his failure to accept moral responsibility for his abuse of Tamar. Israelite law required a man who had seized and forced an unbetrothed virgin then to marry her (Deut. 22:28–29). When a man entered into the most intimate of all human contacts with a woman, he became morally obligated to provide for her personal well-being.

Now hold your peace, my sister; he is your brother. Absalom saw the futility of publicizing Tamar's unhappy estate. Since the offense did not cross family lines, a blood feud was not in order; but as an intrafamily dispute, the administration of justice was David's responsibility. Unfortunately, his indignation resulted in no constructive action, and the seed of discord planted here was allowed to grow to full flower in the lives of his two sons. Amnon doubtlessly continued in his selfish abuse of others, and Absalom was left for two years silently plotting his revenge.

5. Absalom Avenges His Sister (13:23–39)

23 After two full years Absalom had sheepshearers at Baalhazor, which is near Ephraim, and Absalom invited all the king's sons. 24 And Absalom came to the king, and said, "Behold, your servant has sheepshearers; pray let the king and his servants go with your servant." 25 But the king said to Absalom, "No, my son, let us not all go, lest we be burdensome to you." He pressed him, but he would not go but gave him his blessing. 26 Then Absalom said, "If not, pray let my brother Amnon go with us." And the king said to him, "Why should he go with you?" 27 But Absalom pressed him until he let Amnon and all the king's sons go with him. 28 Then Absalom commanded his servants, "Mark when Amnon's heart is merry with wine, and when I say to you, 'Strike Amnon,' then kill him. Fear not; have I not commanded you? Be courageous and be valiant." 29 So the servants of Absalom did to Amnon as Absalom had commanded. Then all the king's sons arose, and each mounted his mule and fled.

30 While they were on the way, tidings came to David, "Absalom has slain all the king's sons, and not one of them is left." 31 Then the king arose, and rent his garments, and lay on the earth; and all his servants who were standing by rent their garments. 32 But Jonadab the son of Shimeah, David's brother, said, "Let not my lord suppose that they have killed all the young men the king's sons, for Amnon alone is dead, for by the command of Absalom this has

been determined from the day he forced his sister Tamar. ³³ Now therefore let not my lord the king so take it to heart as to suppose that all the king's sons are dead; for Amnon alone is dead."

³⁴ But Absalom fled. And the young man who kept the watch lifted up his eyes, and looked, and behold, many people were coming from the Horonaim road by the side of the mountain. ³⁵ And Jonadab said to the king, "Behold, the king's sons have come; as your servant said, so it has come about." ³⁶ And as soon as he had finished speaking, behold, the king's sons came, and lifted up their voice and wept; and the king also and all his servants wept very bitterly.

³⁷ But Absalom fled, and went to Talmai the son of Ammihud, king of Geshur. And David mourned for his son day after day. ³⁸ So Absalom fled, and went to Geshur, and was there three years. ³⁹ And the spirit of the king longed to go forth to Absalom; for he was comforted about Amnon, seeing he was dead.

In the second half of the chapter, Absalom and David emerge as the principal actors—Absalom for what he did and David for what he did not do. When after two full years David had taken no steps to punish Amnon for his assault on Tamar, Absalom moved to take matters into his own hands. Thus, in seeking to administer justice within the family, Absalom is already assuming duties which properly belong to his father. Although the author attached no political motives to Absalom's premeditated murder of his elder brother, one can see here the same attitudes which emerge later in Absalom's attempts to seize the throne (2 Sam. 15—19).

The author however portrays Absalom's role in this whole narrative complex (chs. 13—19) with a great deal of sympathy and warmth. He can in no way condone Absalom's refusal to leave Tamar's revenge in the hands of the Lord (cf. 1 Sam. 25:33), but he is aware that David's failure to exert himself as father and king had created a vacuum of authority which begged to be filled. The story is told without overt editorializing, but the reader can easily sense the author's ambivalence in his treatment of the two major characters.

Absalom created an opportunity to retaliate against Amnon by organizing an elaborate party to which he invited David's entire court. The feast was to be held at the climax of the sheep shearing season on Absalom's farm at Baalhazor about 15 miles north of Jerusalem (cf. 1 Sam. 25:1–17). As Absalom had no doubt anticipated he would, David declined to attend but agreed to add his blessing to the occasion. Absalom, however, probably feigning an interest in developing a prestigious guest list, persisted until David finally agreed to send a personal representative in his place. (The Hebrew indicates that David *sent* [*wayyishlach*] Amnon with Absalom.) Crown Prince Amnon was to attend at the head of the whole body of the king's sons. At a prearranged signal, Absalom's servants murdered Amnon, and the rest of the king's sons fled.

The first report of Absalom's treachery indicated that all David's sons had been killed. *Absalom has slain all the king's sons.* The king's grief over the loss of his sons was compounded by the fear that Absalom's actions signalled an attack on the throne. Israel could soon be engaged in a civil war. But the fact that Absalom did not kill all the king's sons indicates that political motives were not primary in his murder of Amnon.

David's sorrow was only partly diminished when the true facts became known, for he still had lost two sons. Amnon had been murdered and Absalom had gone into an exile from which there could be no easy return. David's own emotions were also complicated by the realization that the two most likely candidates as the future king of Israel were no longer available. Whatever other difficulties he might have to face, David would always be concerned with a peaceful succession to the throne of Israel.

So Absalom fled, and went to Geshur. Absalom exiled himself in his mother's home state of Geshur, a small kingdom northeast of the Sea of Galilee. David soon felt inclined to invite Absalom to return but apparently could not feel justified in doing so. The text appears confused since

Absalom's flight is recorded three times, and vv. 37 and 38 seriously overlap.

6. Absalom Returns to Court (14:1–33)

(1) Joab Tests David (14:1–20)

¹ Now Joab the son of Zeruiah perceived that the king's heart went out to Absalom. ² And Joab sent to Tekoa, and fetched from there a wise woman, and said to her, "Pretend to be a mourner, and put on mourning garments; do not anoint yourself with oil, but behave like a woman who has been mourning many days for the dead; ³ and go to the king, and speak thus to him." So Joab put the words in her mouth.

⁴ When the woman of Tekoa came to the king, she fell on her face to the ground, and did obeisance, and said, "Help, O king." ⁵ And the king said to her, "What is your trouble?" She answered, "Alas, I am a widow; my husband is dead. ⁶ And your handmaid had two sons, and they quarreled with one another in the field; there was no one to part them, and one struck the other and killed him. ⁷ And now the whole family has risen against your handmaid, and they say, 'Give up the man who struck his brother, that we may kill him for the life of his brother whom he slew'; and so they would destroy the heir also. Thus they would quench my coal which is left, and leave to my husband neither name nor remnant upon the face of the earth."

⁸ Then the king said to the woman, "Go to your house, and I will give orders concerning you." ⁹ And the woman of Tekoa said to the king, "On me be the guilt, my lord the king, and on my father's house; let the king and his throne be guiltless." ¹⁰ The king said, "If any one says anything to you, bring him to me, and he shall never touch you again." ¹¹ Then she said, "Pray let the king invoke the LORD your God, that the avenger of blood slay no more, and my son be not destroyed." He said, "As the LORD lives, not one hair of your son shall fall to the ground."

¹² Then the woman said, "Pray let your handmaid speak a word to my lord the king." He said, "Speak." ¹³ And the woman said, "Why then have you planned such a thing against the people of God? For in giving this decision the king convicts himself, inasmuch as the king does not bring his banished one home again. ¹⁴ We must all die, we are like water spilt on the ground, which cannot be gathered up again; but God will not take away the life of him who devises means not to keep his banished one an outcast. ¹⁵ Now I have come to say this to my lord the king because the people have made me afraid; and your handmaid thought, 'I will speak to the king; it may be that the king will perform the request of his servant. ¹⁶ For the king will hear, and deliver his servant from the hand of the man who would destroy me and my son together from the heritage of God.' ¹⁷ And your handmaid thought, 'The word of my lord the king will set me at rest'; for my lord the king is like the angel of God to discern good and evil. The LORD your God be with you!"

¹⁸ Then the king answered the woman, "Do not hide from me anything I ask you." And the woman said, "Let my lord the king speak." ¹⁹ The king said, "Is the hand of Joab with you in all this?" The woman answered and said, "As surely as you live, my lord the king, one cannot turn to the right hand or to the left from anything that my lord the king has said. It was your servant Joab who bade me; it was he who put all these words in the mouth of your handmaid. ²⁰ In order to change the course of affairs your servant Joab did this. But my lord has wisdom like the wisdom of the angel of God to know all things that are on the earth."

David suffered a common misfortune in that he could deal with other men's sons more equitably than he could his own. Joab, therefore, sensing David's ambivalence toward Absalom, arranged to have a woman from Tekoa bring a "loaded" test case before the king.

Although this episode lacks the crispness of Nathan's parable (12:1–6), it is nonetheless artistically constructed in its own right. The woman of Tekoa laid aside the bearing and stature implied in her title *a wise woman* (*chᵉkamah*) and displayed the humble earthiness which one would expect of a woman from a small town in the Judean desert. Using language that was redundant, effusive, and repetitious in turn, she played her role so convincingly that David was caught up in her ruse.

Joab's story did not exactly parallel David's difficulties with Absalom, but it did involve some of the same basic principles. In each case, a just solution demanded that the requirements of the law of blood revenge (cf. Gen. 9:6) be modified in the light of special extenuating circumstances. In the story posed by Joab, David recognized that justice would not be served by executing the last surviving male in a family that otherwise faced extinction. He, therefore, ordered the clan to cancel the vendetta.

Thus, David was forced to acknowledge the complexity of Absalom's case. He was technically guilty of murder, but it seemed that David's own negligence was at least a contributing factor to the deed. In the final analysis, however, Israel's need for Absalom was the most eloquent argument for his return from exile. As long as he opposed Absalom's return, David was led to believe that he was arraigned *against the people of God.* Apparently, Joab and many of the people felt that Israel's future was in jeopardy unless Absalom returned as the crown prince. Finally convinced by the woman's eloquence and by the awareness that even Joab stood against him, David allowed Absalom to return home from Geshur.

On me be the guilt, my lord. This should probably be a simple declarative sentence. When David promised to give an order protecting the widow's son, she claimed to be afraid since the people would blame her and not the king. David promised her royal protection, but the woman persisted until he affirmed his judgment in an oath unto God. The "actress" from Tekoa was leading David on until he had no possible retreat.

(2) *Absalom Returns to Jerusalem (14:21–33)*

21 Then the king said to Joab, "Behold now, I grant this; go, bring back the young man Absalom." 22 And Joab fell on his face to the ground, and did obeisance, and blessed the king; and Joab said, "Today your servant knows that I have found favor in your sight, my lord the king, in that the king has granted the request of his servant." 23 So Joab arose and went to Geshur, and brought Absalom to Jerusalem. 24 And the king said, "Let him dwell apart in his own house; he is not to come into my presence." So Absalom dwelt apart in his own house, and did not come into the king's presence. 25 Now in all Israel there was no one so much to be praised for his beauty as Absalom; from the sole of his foot to the crown of his head there was no blemish in him. 26 And when he cut the hair of his head (for at the end of every year he used to cut it; when it was heavy on him, he cut it), he weighed the hair of his head, two hundred shekels by the king's weight. 27 There were born to Absalom three sons, and one daughter whose name was Tamar; she was a beautiful woman.

28 So Absalom dwelt two full years in Jerusalem, without coming into the king's presence. 29 Then Absalom sent for Joab, to send him to the king; but Joab would not come to him. And he sent a second time, but Joab would not come. 30 Then he said to his servants, "See, Joab's field is next to mine, and he has barley there; go and set it on fire." So Absalom's servants set the field on fire. 31 Then Joab arose and went to Absalom at his house, and said to him, "Why have your servants set my field on fire?" 32 Absalom answered Joab, "Behold, I sent word to you, 'Come here, that I may send you to the king, to ask, "Why have I come from Geshur? It would be better for me to be there still." Now therefore let me go into the presence of the king; and if there is guilt in me, let him kill me.'" 33 Then Joab went to the king, and told him; and he summoned Absalom. So he came to the king, and bowed himself on his face to the ground before the king; and the king kissed Absalom.

The author doesn't dwell on Joab's reasons for desiring Absalom's return from exile, but the tone of the preceding narrative suggests that he felt it was for the good of the country. Presumably, he was afraid that something might happen to David before a qualified heir to the throne had been designated. In such a case, the internal power struggle would leave Israel easy prey for her enemies. Joab apparently hoped that, upon Absalom's return, David would champion the cause of the one who so much looked and acted the part of Israel's future king.

Joab's hopes were not realized, however. Absalom was allowed to return to Jerusalem, but David refused to see him. For two years Absalom remained a virtual prisoner within his own home (cf. Hertzberg, p. 334), and the question over Israel's line of succession to the throne remained unresolved.

When Absalom could bear his growing isolation no longer, he resorted to arson to gain Joab's attention and demanded an audience with the king. An insight into Absalom's character is suggested by the fact that he could face exile or death, but he could not tolerate being ignored. His desperate gamble paid off, however, and he regained the king's favor.

Let him dwell apart in his own house. Few personal differences are resolved when the principals isolate themselves from each other. Communication is essential if reconciliation is to take place. It would seem that David should have punished Absalom severely or forgiven him completely. In any case, the middle ground was totally ineffective.

The comments in vv. 25–27 about Absalom's comeliness and family are introduced here to foreshadow the events which follow. Absalom is portrayed as a mature man with considerable public appeal and influence. He is, in fact, the man who will present David with his most severe challenge; a man who will successfully seize the throne only to lose his life in battle.

7. Absalom Usurps the Throne (15:1—18:33)

(1) Absalom Becomes King (15:1–12)

¹ After this Absalom got himself a chariot and horses, and fifty men to run before him. ² And Absalom used to rise early and stand beside the way of the gate; and when any man had a suit to come before the king for judgment, Absalom would call to him, and say, "From what city are you?" And when he said, "Your servant is of such and such a tribe in Israel," ³ Absalom would say to him, "See, your claims are good and right; but there is no man deputed by the king to hear you." ⁴ Absalom said moreover, "Oh that I were judge in the land! Then every man with a suit or cause might come to me, and I would give him justice." ⁵ And whenever a man came near to do obeisance to him, he would put out his hand, and take hold of him, and kiss him. ⁶ Thus Absalom did to all of Israel who came to the king for judgment; so Absalom stole the hearts of the men of Israel.

⁷ And at the end of four years Absalom said to the king, "Pray let me go and pay my vow, which I have vowed to the Lord, in Hebron. ⁸ For your servant vowed a vow while I dwelt at Geshur in Aram, saying, 'If the Lord will indeed bring me back to Jerusalem, then I will offer worship to the Lord.'" ⁹ The king said to him, "Go in peace." So he arose, and went to Hebron. ¹⁰ But Absalom sent secret messengers throughout all the tribes of Israel, saying, "As soon as you hear the sound of the trumpet, then say, 'Absalom is king at Hebron!'" ¹¹ With Absalom went two hundred men from Jerusalem who were invited guests, and they went in their simplicity, and knew nothing. ¹² And while Absalom was offering the sacrifices, he sent for Ahithophel the Gilonite, David's counselor, from his city Giloh. And the conspiracy grew strong, and the people with Absalom kept increasing.

After Absalom was returned to his normal place in the king's court, he became the focal point of a movement designed to undermine David's authority among his people. While the reader has been free to speculate as to Absalom's political ambitions up to this point, the author makes it clear that Absalom was now determined to become king of Israel. He and his conspirators met with a considerable degree of success largely because legitimate complaints could be lodged against David's government. People were traveling long distances to bring legal disputes before the king in Jerusalem, only to find that no one had been deputized to hear their cases. While difficulties in the administration of justice could be traced back to Moses' day (Ex. 18:13 f.), the demands of a growing government inevitably cut David off from the man in the street.

Absalom, however, capitalized on the king's remoteness by making an effort to appear in public as the common man's friend. He sympathized with those who were kept waiting for an audience in the king's court and protested publicly that he was not given an opportunity to serve the people. *O that I were judge* (lit., "O that he might appoint me judge") suggests that Absalom smarted under the fact that David refused to give him a key post in the government. He took the time to learn of the complainants' backgrounds and treated all comers, not as subjects, but as friends. The author of the Succession Narrative, however, pointed out the superficiality of Absalom's popular approach by noting that he also affected the accouterments of royalty. His chariot and 50-man bodyguard would certainly have been unnecessary except as an indication of his desire to become king. As a final commentary on his demagogic ways, the author says that Absalom *stole* (not won) *the hearts of the men of Israel.*

After four years of such activities, the conspiracy came to a head. Absalom first made arrangements to go to Hebron on the pretext that the pilgrimage was in fulfillment of a vow he made while in exile. No doubt he expected to gain support from those who remembered that he had been born there (3:3) and from those who were offended by David's transfer of the capital to Jerusalem (Hertzberg, p. 337). In any case, Hebron was the site of a venerable holy place at which David himself had first become king (cf. comment of 2:1–4). Secret arrangements were made to have Absalom acclaimed king by popular demonstrations throughout the country. These were timed to occur simultaneously upon his elevation to the throne at Hebron.

All went well and Absalom's conspiracy quickly gained momentum. Some innocently followed Absalom without fully understanding his ultimate goals or the issues that were involved. Others, such as Ahithophel, Bathsheba's grandfather, willingly gave their support because of long-standing grievances against David. Whatever their motives, so many people throughout Israel opposed David that his government was seriously imperilled.

(2) *David Flees Jerusalem (15:13–37)*

13 And a messenger came to David, saying, "The hearts of the men of Israel have gone after Absalom." 14 Then David said to all his servants who were with him at Jerusalem, "Arise, and let us flee; or else there will be no escape for us from Absalom; go in haste, lest he overtake us quickly, and bring down evil upon us, and smite the city with the edge of the sword." 15 And the king's servants said to the king, "Behold, your servants are ready to do whatever my lord the king decides." 16 So the king went forth, and all his household after him. And the king left ten concubines to keep the house. 17 And the king went forth, and all the people after him; and they halted at the last house. 18 And all his servants passed by him; and all the Cherethites, and all the Pelethites, and all the six hundred Gittites who had followed him from Gath, passed on before the king.
19 Then the king said to Ittai the Gittite, "Why do you also go with us? Go back, and stay with the king; for you are a foreigner, and also an exile from your home. 20 You came only yesterday, and shall I today make you wander about with us, seeing I go I know not where? Go back, and take your brethren with you; and may the LORD show steadfast love and faithfulness to you." 21 But Ittai answered the king, "As the LORD lives, and as my lord the king lives, wherever my lord the king shall be, whether for death or for life, there also will your servant be." 22 And David said to Ittai, "Go then, pass on." So Ittai the Gittite passed on, with all his men and all the little ones who were with him. 23 And all the country wept aloud as all the people passed by, and the king crossed the brook Kidron, and all the people passed on toward the wilderness.
24 And Abiathar came up, and lo, Zadok came also, with all the Levites, bearing the ark of the covenant of God; and they set down the ark of God, until the people had all passed out of the city. 25 Then the king said to Zadok, "Carry the ark of God back into the city. If I find favor in the eyes of the LORD, he will bring me back and let me see both it and his habitation; 26 but if he says, 'I have no pleasure in you,' behold, here I am, let him do to me what seems good to him." 27 The king also said to Zadok the priest, "Look, go back to the city in peace, you and Abiathar, with your two sons, Ahimaaz your son, and Jonathan the son of Abiathar. 28 See, I will wait at the fords of the wilderness, until word comes from you to inform me." 29 So Zadok and Abiathar carried the ark of God back to Jerusalem; and they remained there.
30 But David went up the ascent of the Mount of Olives, weeping as he went, barefoot and with his head covered; and all the people who were with him covered their heads, and they went up, weeping as they went. 31 And it was told David, "Ahithophel is among the conspirators with Absalom." And David said, "O LORD, I pray thee, turn the counsel of Ahithophel into foolishness."
32 When David came to the summit, where God was worshiped, behold, Hushai the Archite came to meet him with his coat rent and earth upon his head. 33 David said to him, "If you go on with me, you will be a burden to me. 34 But if you return to the city, and say to Absalom, 'I will be your servant. O king; as I

have been your father's servant in time past, so now I will be your servant,' then you will defeat for me the counsel of Ahithophel. 35 Are not Zadok and Abiathar the priests with you there? So whatever you hear from the king's house, tell it to Zadok and Abiathar the priests. 36 Behold, their two sons are with them there, Ahimaaz, Zadok's son, and Jonathan, Abiathar's son; and by them you shall send to me everything you hear." 37 So Hushai, David's friend, came into the city, just as Absalom was entering Jerusalem.

Upon learning of the success of Absalom's bold move at Hebron, David ordered the evacuation of his government and troops from Jerusalem. In view of Absalom's broad base of popular support, David could see that he was again faced with a superior tactical force. Once more he had to resort to guerrilla tactics (cf. comment on 1 Sam. 23:1-14; 2 Sam. 5:17-25). Had he remained in Jerusalem, no matter how strong its defenses, David's influence in Israel would have been neutralized, and hunger would have necessitated his eventual surrender. With a highly mobile force of professional soldiers, however, David was still a potent, even decisive, factor in Israelite politics.

The author presents a tense and moving scene as David hurriedly decided which of his followers would remain in Jerusalem and which would accompany him on his flight into the wilderness. His (civil) servants would go to keep his government intact; and his standing army, including all the Philistine mercenaries, would be an absolute necessity.

Others, however, remained behind. David left ten concubines facing an uncertain fate (16:20-23) to symbolize his continuing claim on the royal palace. Abiathar and Zadok, custodians of the ark, were willing to follow him, but David decided to leave them behind as spies. Their positions as priests in the institutionalized worship in Jerusalem gave them an excuse to remain and also provided them a measure of protection. Finally, David left Hushai, a trusted counselor and friend, to infiltrate Absalom's corps of advisors. Here, if he were able to gain Absalom's confidence, he could undermine the influence of Ahithophel, the most astute of all Absalom's strategists. At last, arrangements complete, David made his escape just before Absalom entered the city.

So the king went forth, and all his household after him. David was to establish a base camp at Mahanaim (17:24-29), where the families of his troops could dwell in comparative safety. Until they crossed the Jordan and established this camp, David's band was far from the mobile fighting force that he needed. During this crucial march, David was practically helpless because his hurried departure prohibited adequate preparation and organization to care for the families of those who accompanied him (15:16,22).

Let him do to me what seems good to him. David's religious philosophy was far removed from the fatalistic outlook which is so common in the Near East. Whereas a fatalist is passively resigned to whatever fate his deity consigns him, David was busily engaged in doing everything within his power to determine his own future. Nevertheless, he was convinced the Lord was in basic control of life, and his will would ultimately be enacted in human history.

David left Jerusalem, *weeping as he went.* The author vividly portrays David's reluctance to leave as he depicts him pausing at the last house in the city, beside the Kidron (vv. 23 f.), and on the Mount of Olives (vv. 30 f.). No doubt, David wept because this was considered his city, but most of all because he remembered that it was his son who was seeking his life (16:11; 17:3-4).

Turn the counsel of Ahithophel into foolishness. Ahithophel's advice was considered almost on a par with a divine oracle (16:23). He was well known to David and highly regarded by Absalom. David recognized that his greatest threat lay in Ahithophel's wisdom. For this reason Hushai's role as a spy was most important.

(3) Saul's Family Opposes David (16:1-14)

1 When David had passed a little beyond the summit, Ziba the servant of Mephibosheth met him, with a couple of asses saddled, bearing two hundred loaves of bread, a hundred bunches of raisins, a hundred of summer fruits, and a skin of wine. 2 And the king said to Ziba, "Why have you brought these?" Ziba answered, "The asses are for the king's household to ride on, the bread and summer fruit for the young men to eat, and the wine for those who faint in the wilderness to drink." 3 And the king said, "And where is your master's son?" Ziba said to the king, "Behold, he remains in Jerusalem; for he said, 'Today the house of Israel will give me back the kingdom of my father.'" 4 Then the king said to Ziba, "Behold, all that belonged to Mephibosheth is now yours." And Ziba said, "I do obeisance; let me ever find favor in your sight, my lord the king."

5 When King David came to Bahurim, there came out a man of the family of the house of Saul, whose name was Shimei, the son of Gera; and as he came he cursed continually. 6 And he threw stones at David, and at all the servants of King David; and all the people and all the mighty men were on his right hand and on his left. 7 And Shimei said as he cursed, "Begone, begone, you man of blood, you worthless fellow! 8 The LORD has avenged upon you all the blood of the house of Saul, in whose place you have reigned; and the LORD has given the kingdom into the hand of your son Absalom. See, your ruin is on you; for you are a man of blood."

9 Then Abishai the son of Zeruiah said to the king, "Why should this dead dog curse my lord the king? Let me go over and take off his head." 10 But the king said, "What have I to do with you, you sons of Zeruiah? If he is cursing because the LORD has said to him, 'Curse David,' who then shall say, 'Why have you done so?'" 11 And David said to Abishai and to all his servants, "Behold, my own son seeks my life; how much more now may this Benjaminite! Let him alone, and let him curse; for the LORD has bidden him. 12 It may be that the LORD will look upon my affliction, and that the LORD will repay me with good for this cursing of me today." 13 So David and his men went on the road, while Shimei went along on the hillside opposite him and cursed as he went, and threw stones at him and flung dust. 14 And the king, and all the people who were with him, arrived weary at the Jordan; and there he refreshed himself.

The attention devoted to the details of David's flight from Jerusalem attests the seriousness of Absalom's rebellion. Not only was David's personal hold on the throne being challenged, but regional and tribal rivalries were again threatening to destroy Israel's unity. While Absalom's coup d'etat represented neither a dynastic change nor a secessionist movement, it did offer Saul's followers an opportunity to reestablish an independent kingdom over the northern tribes. The nation was not split along sectional lines at this time, but the two following incidents show that powerful divisive pressures lurked just beneath the surface of Israelite politics.

David was scarcely out of sight of Jerusalem when he encountered Ziba, the steward over Saul's properties, bearing token support for David's cause and news of Mephibosheth's ambitions. Although Ziba's gifts were of modest proportions, they were nonetheless important. Guerrilla forces which lack adequate logistic support cannot exist without many such evidences of popular sympathy (17:27-29).

Mephibosheth could hardly anticipate that Absalom was coming to Jerusalem to invite him to become king of all Israel. Quite possibly, however, he may have hoped to use the confusion to establish a kingdom like that of Ishbosheth over the northern tribes (*the house of Israel*). On the other hand, Ziba may have slandered his master for personal gain. When David later returned to Jerusalem, he did not know whether to believe Ziba or Mephibosheth; so he divided Saul's property.

At Bahurim, a short distance east of Jerusalem, David encountered Shimei, a distant relative of Saul, who voiced the hostile feelings of many of his fellow tribesmen (cf. 20:1). Throwing stones and cursing, Shimei charged David with complicity in the violent deaths which had decimated Saul's house (cf. 1:10; 3:27; 4:8; 21:1-14). Abishai, brother of the fierce and bloody Joab, offered to take off Shimei's head for his impertinence. David, however, recognized that more was to be gained by lenience than by a harsh display of force. He, therefore, quietly endured the taunts of this Benjaminite and made his way on to the Jordan. When David returned to power, he must have enjoyed Shimei's abject apology (19:16–23), for he never truly forgave his offense. At the end of his life when some of the regional tensions had cooled somewhat, David instructed Solomon to seek an opportunity to avenge the insult at Bahurim (1 Kings 2:8–9).

(4) Absalom Enters Jerusalem (16:15–23)

¹⁵ Now Absalom and all the people, the men of Israel, came to Jerusalem, and Ahithophel with him. ¹⁶ And when Hushai the Archite, David's friend, came to Absalom, Hushai said to Absalom, "Long live the king! Long live the king!" ¹⁷ And Absalom said to Hushai, "Is this your loyalty to your friend? Why did you not go with your friend?" ¹⁸ And Hushai said to Absalom, "No; for whom the LORD and this people and all the men of Israel have chosen, his I will be, and with him I will remain. ¹⁹ And again, whom should I serve? Should it not be his son? As I have served your father, so I will serve you."
²⁰ Then Absalom said to Ahithophel, "Give your counsel; what shall we do?" ²¹ Ahithophel said to Absalom, "Go in to your father's concubines, whom he has left to keep the house; and all Israel will hear that you have made yourself odious to your father, and the hands of all who are with you will be strengthened." ²² So they pitched a tent for Absalom upon the roof; and Absalom went in to his father's concubines in the sight of all Israel. ²³ Now in those days the counsel which Ahithophel gave was as if one consulted the oracle of God; so was all the counsel of Ahithophel esteemed, both by David and by Absalom.

As Absalom arrived at Jerusalem, he learned that he had barely missed success in his plan to bottle up David in the city. David's narrow escape into the wilderness with the core of a respectable army presented Absalom's forces with a new tactical crisis, demanding an entirely different strategy. Clearly, ultimate victory could be won or lost on the strength of decisions reached in the first crucial hours after Absalom's arrival in Jerusalem.

Of the people who remained in the city, probably a majority appeared ready to assist the new regime. Absalom knew that many of these could not be trusted, but the remainder could offer invaluable goods and services to his cause. Hushai, David's counselor, was a good example of the dilemma posed by such persons. If he were sincere in his transfer of loyalty, no one could provide greater insight into David's plans and tactics. Clearly he would have to be watched, but his potential usefulness was too great for his offer of assistance to be rejected outright.

Although David had narrowly escaped being trapped in Jerusalem, Absalom's capture of Israel's capital city still represented a tremendous psychological victory for his supporters. As all eyes were still focused on the events connected with the fall of the city, Absalom sought a means by which he might extract the greatest propaganda benefits from his victory. At the suggestion of Ahithophel, another of David's former counselors, Absalom decided to proclaim himself king by publicly taking possession of his father's concubines (cf. comment on 3:7). In addition to its royal significance, this act was calculated to drive a personal wedge between father and son (Deut. 22:30). Apparently some of Absalom's followers wanted an assurance that their leader would not arrange a last-minute truce with David, thus leaving his fellow conspirators seriously compromised (McKane, p. 257). Perhaps Ahithophel also felt that Absalom's actions would serve as fitting retribution for David's treatment of Uriah and Bathsheba (cf. comment on 11:3).

(5) Hushai Stalls for Time (17:1–14)

¹ Moreover Ahithophel said to Absalom, "Let me choose twelve thousand men, and I will set out and pursue David tonight. ² I will come upon him while he is weary and discouraged, and throw him into a panic; and all the people who are with him will flee. I will strike down the king only, ³ and I will bring all the people back to you as a bride comes home to her husband. You seek the life of only one man,

and all the people will be at peace." ⁴ And the advice pleased Absalom and all the elders of Israel.

⁵ Then Absalom said, "Call Hushai the Archite also, and let us hear what he has to say." ⁶ And when Hushai came to Absalom, Absalom said to him, "Thus has Ahithophel spoken; shall we do as he advises? If not, you speak." ⁷ Then Hushai said to Absalom, "This time the counsel which Ahithophel has given is not good." ⁸ Hushai said moreover, "You know that your father and his men are mighty men, and that they are enraged, like a bear robbed of her cubs in the field. Besides, your father is expert in war; he will not spend the night with the people. ⁹ Behold, even now he has hidden himself in one of the pits, or in some other place. And when some of the people fall at the first attack, whoever hears it will say, 'There has been a slaughter among the people who follow Absalom.' ¹⁰ Then even the valiant man, whose heart is like the heart of a lion, will utterly melt with fear; for all Israel knows that your father is a mighty man, and that those who are with him are valiant men. ¹¹ But my counsel is that all Israel be gathered to you, from Dan to Beersheba, as the sand by the sea for multitude, and that you go to battle in person. ¹² So we shall come upon him in some place where he is to be found, and we shall light upon him as the dew falls on the ground; and of him and all the men with him not one will be left. ¹³ If he withdraws into a city, then all Israel will bring ropes to that city, and we shall drag it into the valley, until not even a pebble is to be found there." ¹⁴ And Absalom and all the men of Israel said, "The counsel of Hushai the Archite is better than the counsel of Ahithophel." For the LORD had ordained to defeat the good counsel of Ahithophel, so that the LORD might bring evil upon Absalom.

The basic decision facing Absalom and his advisors concerned the tactics to be used against David who was still just a few hours away from Jerusalem. Ahithophel favored an immediate attack, to be launched that very night, so that David could be stopped before he was able to ford the Jordan River. Ahithophel saw that once David was able to lose himself in the wilderness beyond Jordan, he would be able to prolong the struggle and fight the kind of war his troops knew best. If, however, his men could be trapped with their families and baggage before crossing the Jordan (15:16,22), Absalom's forces would have a decided advantage. Moreover, there was a distinct possibility that David himself might be killed, in which case all resistance would collapse.

Such an expedition was not to be undertaken lightly, however. David's men were professional soldiers; and, since they had voluntarily abandoned Jerusalem, the conditions of battle might be of their own choosing. A forced march during the night would be particularly hazardous, for such a maneuver almost invited an ambush.

Absalom, therefore, called on Hushai for an alternative proposal. Recognizing that David had not anticipated that Absalom's forces might immediately press their pursuit beyond Jerusalem (15:28; cf. 17:16), Hushai tried to stall the attack. Comparing David's soldiers with their families to bears robbed of their cubs, Hushai reminded Absalom of the strength of his opponent. He then discounted the possibility that the war would be won with a single blow, since David, a cunning desert fighter, would hardly be so naive as to sleep in the open with the main body of his troops. Finally, Hushai noted that even modest losses to Absalom's troops in this first battle might have disastrous effects on his followers in any prolonged conflict. In short he disapproved of Ahithophel's plan.

Instead Hushai recommended a power play which sounded good, but which actually represented the very tactics which David hoped his pursuers would follow. In contrast with David's mobile force of well-trained men, Hushai recommended a massive army of green conscripts drawn from all Israel. Instead of accepting Ahithophel's offer of mature leadership, Absalom himself should command the expedition. To draw Israel's leaders even farther away from David's true tactics, Hushai implied that, in face of such an overwhelming force, David would be likely to seek refuge in a city where he could be easily captured. Hushai had played his role as a spy quite well!

In spite of the fact that Hushai's advice ignored David's past history as a guerrilla leader, Israel's leaders accepted his plan.

This departure from wisdom and logic elicited a rare editorial comment from the ancient author. Such a decision was understandable only if *the Lord had ordained to defeat the good counsel of Ahithophel, so that the Lord might bring evil upon Absalom.*

(6) David Escapes to Mahanaim (17:15-29)

¹⁵ Then Hushai said to Zadok and Abiathar the priests, "Thus and so did Ahithophel counsel Absalom and the elders of Israel; and thus and so have I counseled. ¹⁶ Now therefore send quickly and tell David, 'Do not lodge tonight at the fords of the wilderness, but by all means pass over; lest the king and all the people who are with him be swallowed up.'" ¹⁷ Now Jonathan and Ahimaaz were waiting at Enrogel; a maidservant used to go and tell them, and they would go and tell King David; for they must not be seen entering the city. ¹⁸ But a lad saw them, and told Absalom; so both of them went away quickly, and came to the house of a man at Bahurim, who had a well in his courtyard; and they went down into it. ¹⁹ And the woman took and spread a covering over the well's mouth, and scattered grain upon it; and nothing was known of it. ²⁰ When Absalom's servants came to the woman at the house, they said, "Where are Ahimaaz and Jonathan?" And the woman said to them, "They have gone over the brook of water." And when they had sought and could not find them, they returned to Jerusalem.

²¹ After they had gone, the men came up out of the well, and went and told King David. They said to David, "Arise, and go quickly over the water; for thus and so has Ahithophel counseled against you." ²² Then David arose, and all the people who were with him, and they crossed the Jordan; by daybreak not one was left who had not crossed the Jordan.

²³ When Ahithophel saw that his counsel was not followed, he saddled his ass, and went off home to his own city. And he set his house in order, and hanged himself; and he died, and was buried in the tomb of his father.

²⁴ Then David came to Mahanaim. And Absalom crossed the Jordan with all the men of Israel. ²⁵ Now Absalom had set Amasa over the army instead of Joab. Amasa was the son of a man named Ithra the Ishmaelite, who had married Abigal the daughter of Nahash, sister of Zeruiah, Joab's mother. ²⁶ And Israel and Absalom encamped in the land of Gilead.

²⁷ When David came to Mahanaim, Shobi the son of Nahash from Rabbah of the Ammonites, and Machir the son of Ammiel from Lodebar, and Barzillai the Gileadite from Rogelim, ²⁸ brought beds, basins, and earthen vessels, wheat, barley, meal, parched grain, beans and lentils, ²⁹ honey and curds and sheep and cheese from the herd, for David and the people with him to eat; for they said, "The people are hungry and weary and thirsty in the wilderness."

At the end of his conference with Absalom, Hushai was still uncertain as to the rebel king's final battle plans. The elders of Israel seemed impressed with Hushai's proposals, but they could be attempting to deceive him in order to trap David. Just to be on the safe side, Hushai made arrangements to inform David of the entire debate over strategy and warned him to seek refuge in the trans-Jordan wilderness immediately.

David's line of communication with his spies in Jerusalem involved the priests Zadok and Abiathar and their sons, Ahimaaz and Jonathan. The younger men had hidden outside Jerusalem, probably because they had anticipated that all former members of David's court would be forbidden to leave the city. Zadok and Abiathar entrusted Hushai's message to a servant girl who regularly brought water from Enrogel, a spring about a quarter of a mile south of the city walls. The peril surrounding David's partisans in Jerusalem is suggested by the fact that the priests' sons were recognized at the spring and were able to escape pursuit only by hiding in the well of friends in Bahurim. The narrow margins by which David and his people escape danger serve to heighten the reader's awareness of divine participation in these events. God was working to deliver David and to defeat Absalom. Thus, David was able to shepherd his band to safety beyond Jordan.

When Ahithophel learned that Absalom was committed to the strategy proposed by Hushai, he was convinced that his own fate was sealed. He could see that the rebels had no hope of a military victory over David as long as they so seriously misinterpreted their enemy's tactics. Having no way to anticipate David's surprisingly lenient treatment of those who had unsuccessfully rebelled against him (19:13), Ahithophel set his affairs in order and killed himself.

When David and his men reached Mahanaim, they were pathetically unprepared either to live or to fight. The secrecy with which Absalom's conspiracy had been carried out and the suddenness of his attack on Jerusalem had left little time to prepare for a march through the wilderness. Fortunately, David's vassals beyond Jordan decided to remain loyal to him. They may have been seeking preferential treatment in the event that, as they expected, he emerged the victor in this struggle. On the other hand, they may have hoped to encourage another devastating Israelite civil war which would leave them free to pursue their own destinies. Whatever their motives, they provided the supplies which were essential if David's cause was to be kept alive.

Absalom, meanwhile, had not been idle. As David hurriedly gathered provisions (and perhaps additional troops?) from his allies, Absalom mustered an army from all Israel and placed it under the command of Amasa who was a cousin of Joab and another of David's nephews. Accompanied by his massive army, Absalom crossed the Jordan and encamped in Gilead in search of David and his men.

Then David came to Mahanaim. Although the site of Mahanaim is unknown today, it seems to have been a strongly fortified city in the highlands of Gilead. It had, of course, been the capital of the northern kingdom under the reign of Ishbosheth (2:8). It seems quite possible that in keeping with David's guerrilla tactics, many of his people were camped in the wilderness surrounding the city (17:29).

Shobi the son of Nahash. David had installed Shobi to rule Ammon after the fall of Rabbah (10:1—12:31). Machir, from Lo-debar in eastern Gilead, had earlier protected and cared for Mephibosheth. Perhaps he supported David for his lenient treatment of Jonathan's heir (9:4–13). Barzillai, an aged man of wealth, won David's enduring appreciation for the support which he supplied in this dark hour (cf. 19:31–39; 1 Kings 2:7).

(7) *Absalom Is Killed in Battle (18:1–18)*

¹ Then David mustered the men who were with him, and set over them commanders of thousands and commanders of hundreds. ² And David sent forth the army, one third under the command of Joab, one third under the command of Abishai the son of Zeruiah, Joab's brother, and one third under the command of Ittai the Gittite. And the king said to the men, "I myself will also go out with you." ³ But the men said, "You shall not go out. For if we flee, they will not care about us. If half of us die, they will not care about us. But you are worth ten thousand of us; therefore it is better that you send us help from the city." ⁴ The king said to them, "Whatever seems best to you I will do." So the king stood at the side of the gate, while all the army marched out by hundreds and by thousands. ⁵ And the king ordered Joab and Abishai and Ittai, "Deal gently for my sake with the young man Absalom." And all the people heard when the king gave orders to all the commanders about Absalom.

⁶ So the army went out into the field against Israel; and the battle was fought in the forest of Ephraim. ⁷ And the men of Israel were defeated there by the servants of David, and the slaughter there was great on that day, twenty thousand men. ⁸ The battle spread over the face of all the country; and the forest devoured more people that day than the sword.

⁹ And Absalom chanced to meet the servants of David. Absalom was riding upon his mule, and the mule went under the thick branches of a great oak, and his head caught fast in the oak, and he was left hanging between heaven and earth, while the mule that was under him went on. ¹⁰ And a certain man saw it, and told Joab, "Behold, I saw Absalom hanging in an oak." ¹¹ Joab said to the man who told him, "What, you saw him! Why then did you not strike him there to the ground? I would have been glad to give you ten pieces of silver and a girdle." ¹² But the man said to Joab, "Even if I felt in my hand the weight of a thousand pieces of silver, I would not put forth my hand against the king's son; for in our hearing the king commanded you and Abishai and Ittai, 'For my sake protect the young man Absalom.' ¹³ On the other hand, if I had dealt treacherously against his life (and there is nothing hidden from the king), then you yourself

would have stood aloof." ¹⁴ Joab said, "I will not waste time like this with you." And he took three darts in his hand, and thrust them into the heart of Absalom, while he was still alive in the oak. ¹⁵ And ten young men, Joab's armor-bearers, surrounded Absalom and struck him, and killed him.

¹⁶ Then Joab blew the trumpet, and the troops came back from pursuing Israel; for Joab restrained them. ¹⁷ And they took Absalom, and threw him into a great pit in the forest, and raised over him a very great heap of stones; and all Israel fled every one to his own home. ¹⁸ Now Absalom in his lifetime had taken and set up for himself the pillar which is in the King's Valley, for he said, "I have no son to keep my name in remembrance"; he called the pillar after his own name, and it is called Absalom's monument to this day.

David had not abandoned Jerusalem to be trapped behind the city walls of Mahanaim! He had chosen to fight in the nearby *forest of Ephraim* (actually east of the Jordan in Gilead) where the dense underbrush would separate and demoralize Absalom's green militia and give his own professional soldiers an enormous advantage. Knowing that large scale maneuvers would be impossible in such terrain, David divided his troops into three sections under the command of Joab, Abishai, and Ittai the Gittite, loyal veterans all. Remaining behind, David sent his men forth with final instructions to *deal gently . . . with the young man Absalom.*

The battle proper went about as David had expected. Both armies scattered abroad, and his own professionals inflicted severe casualties on Absalom's troops in hand-to-hand combat. Even more of the untrained Israelite recruits deserted into the woods than were wounded in battle (cf. the humorous figure of speech in v. 8).

Finally, the chance occurrence which Ahithophel had envisioned (17:2) actually came to pass; but Absalom, not David, was the victim. In a moment of distraction, Absalom had allowed himself to be trapped by a tree and, thus, rendered defenseless before David's men. Nevertheless, ordinary soldiers, remembering David's final instructions, could not even be bribed to strike down the helpless rebel king. Only when their fearless and brutal leader Joab had struck the first blow would any of David's men raise a hand against Absalom. Then all of Joab's bodyguard added thrusts so that no one man would have to bear the brunt of David's wrath alone. The body was then buried under a mound of rocks in the woods, and the battle was over.

But you are worth ten thousand of us. The Hebrew idea may be well rendered in an English idiom: We are "a dime a dozen." David, however, was irreplaceable since without him, resistance to Absalom would collapse.

Deal gently. David's instructions may have rested on more than parental concern. Throughout his career he was notably tolerant of native Israelites who opposed him politically (cf. comment on 2:1–32; 19:22). He faced a constant struggle to keep the north and south united. Joab, for example, was much more brutal than David desired (3:39).

Thrust them into the heart of Absalom. Only a man of great power could thus defy a direct order of the king. Joab commanded troops who were undoubtedly loyal to him personally. If Abner was the power behind Ishbosheth's throne (2:8–9), then Joab must have been an important power behind David's.

(8) *Absalom's Death Reported (18:19–33)*

¹⁹ Then said Ahimaaz the son of Zadok, "Let me run, and carry tidings to the king that the Lord has delivered him from the power of his enemies." ²⁰ And Joab said to him, "You are not to carry tidings today; you may carry tidings another day, but today you shall carry no tidings, because the king's son is dead." ²¹ Then Joab said to the Cushite, "Go, tell the king what you have seen." The Cushite bowed before Joab, and ran. ²² Then Ahimaaz the son of Zadok said again to Joab, "Come what may, let me also run after the Cushite." And Joab said, "Why will you run, my son, seeing that you will have no reward for the tidings?" ²³ "Come what may," he said, "I will run." So he said to him, "Run." Then Ahimaaz ran by the way of the plain, and outran the Cushite.

²⁴ Now David was sitting between the two

gates; and the watchman went up to the roof of the gate by the wall, and when he lifted up his eyes and looked, he saw a man running alone. 25 And the watchman called out and told the king. And the king said, "If he is alone, there are tidings in his mouth." And he came apace, and drew near. 26 And the watchman saw another man running; and the watchman called to the gate and said, "See, another man running alone!" The king said, "He also brings tidings." 27 And the watchman said, "I think the running of the foremost is like the running of Ahimaaz the son of Zadok." And the king said, "He is a good man, and comes with good tidings."

28 Then Ahimaaz cried out to the king, "All is well." And he bowed before the king with his face to the earth, and said, "Blessed be the LORD your God, who has delivered up the men who raised their hand against my lord the king." 29 And the king said, "Is it well with the young man Absalom?" Ahimaaz answered, "When Joab sent your servant, I saw a great tumult, but I do not know what it was." 30 And the king said, "Turn aside, and stand here." So he turned aside, and stood still.

31 And behold, the Cushite came; and the Cushite said, "Good tidings for my lord the king! For the LORD has delivered you this day from the power of all who rose up against you." 32 The king said to the Cushite, "Is it well with the young man Absalom?" And the Cushite answered, "May the enemies of my lord the king, and all who rise up against you for evil, be like that young man." 33 And the king was deeply moved, and went up to the chamber over the gate, and wept; and as he went, he said, "O my son Absalom, my son, my son Absalom! Would I had died instead of you, O Absalom, my son, my son!"

After reaching the climax of the battle in the forest of Ephraim, the author turns to an account of the means by which David learned of his son's death. The story is told artistically with full awareness of the drama and pathos of the moment. The aging king is portrayed still waiting anxiously just inside the city gate for any word from the front. Finally, a runner appeared in the distance and, soon, another! The first reported only that Absalom had been defeated in battle, but the second brought news of his death. Between the two they evidenced the agonizing ambivalence of David's men as the exultation of victory was stilled by their guilty knowledge of Absalom's death.

It is commendable that David was still deeply concerned for the well-being of a son who was seeking his life (16:11). David's grief, however, caused him to withdraw from life and to neglect the needs of men who had been truer sons than Absalom ever had. The lack of meaningful communication between father and son since the murder of Amnon probably complicated David's adjustment to the death of his son. He must have been aware that his failures as a father had contributed to his son's ignoble end in life. Very often, immoderate grief is born out of a repressed sense of guilt.

You are not to carry tidings today. The word *tidings* regularly refers to good news (yet cf. 1 Sam. 4:17 which is an exception). This clause is not a direct command; it is a simple declaration of fact: You are not a man of good news today. There could be no good news that day because the king's son was dead.

Go, tell the king what you have seen. Commentators have speculated that Joab sent the Cushite, an Ethopian, to keep Ahimaaz from being associated in David's mind with the bad news of Absalom's death (1:15–16; 3:10; cf. McKane, p. 266). This supposition, however, would leave unanswered the question as to why Joab eventually surrendered to Ahimaaz's insistent pleas. It seems more likely that Ahimaaz knew the general results of the battle (vv. 6–8) but was just then being informed of Absalom's fate. The Cushite was dispatched to carry the report because he did not know the details of Absalom's death.

I do not know what it was. Ahimaaz, however, had been told of Absalom's death. Either this statement is a deliberate lie or it was accepted that a messenger was expected to relate only his own experience. By mentioning the activity he had seen, Ahimaaz prepared David for the bad news which was to follow but disclaimed any firsthand knowledge of the matter. Thus, Ahimaaz appeared before the king innocent of complicity in Absalom's death.

8. David Resumes His Throne (19:1-40)

(1) Israel Recalls David (19:1-15)

¹ It was told Joab, "Behold, the king is weeping and mourning for Absalom." ² So the victory that day was turned into mourning for all the people; for the people heard that day, "The king is grieving for his son." ³ And the people stole into the city that day as people steal in who are ashamed when they flee in battle. ⁴ The king covered his face, and the king cried with a loud voice, "O my son Absalom, O Absalom, my son, my son!" ⁵ Then Joab came into the house to the king, and said, "You have today covered with shame the faces of all your servants, who have this day saved your life, and the lives of your sons and your daughters, and the lives of your wives and your concubines, ⁶ because you love those who hate you and hate those who love you. For you have made it clear today that commanders and servants are nothing to you; for today I perceive that if Absalom were alive and all of us were dead today, then you would be pleased. ⁷ Now therefore arise, go out and speak kindly to your servants; for I swear by the Lord, if you do not go, not a man will stay with you this night; and this will be worse for you than all the evil that has come upon you from your youth until now." ⁸ Then the king arose, and took his seat in the gate. And the people were all told, "Behold, the king is sitting in the gate"; and all the people came before the king.

Now Israel had fled every man to his own home. ⁹ And all the people were at strife throughout all the tribes of Israel, saying, "The king delivered us from the hand of our enemies, and saved us from the hand of the Philistines; and now he has fled out of the land from Absalom. ¹⁰ But Absalom, whom we anointed over us, is dead in battle. Now therefore why do you say nothing about bringing the king back?"

¹¹ And King David sent this message to Zadok and Abiathar the priests, "Say to the elders of Judah, 'Why should you be the last to bring the king back to his house, when the word of all Israel has come to the king? ¹² You are my kinsmen, you are my bone and my flesh; why then should you be the last to bring back the king?' ¹³ And say to Amasa, 'Are you not my bone and my flesh? God do so to me, and more also, if you are not commander of my army henceforth in place of Joab.'" ¹⁴ And he swayed the heart of all the men of Judah as one man; so that they sent word to the king, "Return, both you and all your servants." ¹⁵ So the king came back to the Jordan; and Judah came to Gilgal to meet the king and to bring the king over the Jordan.

Contrary to Joab's expectations, Absalom's murder caused a precipitous decline in the morale of David's troops. At the very time when swift and decisive measures were necessary to capitalize on the lack of leadership in Israel, David was immobilized by his own guilt-laden remorse over his son's death. Men who had risked their lives in battle were understandably disappointed to learn that their leader's concern was focused solely on the fate of one whom they had been led to regard as the enemy. Probably many others were afraid that David might be planning to punish those who were suspected of violating his order to spare Absalom. Thus, the longer David delayed making a public appearance, the more uncertain became the future of his cause.

In his confrontation with Joab, David was forced to recognize the grim facts of political reality. His policies were being challenged, and he was faced with wholesale desertion. To many, it seemed that his conciliatory attitude toward the enemy (16:11; 19:22) and his grief over the death of his rebellious son were born out of a lack of concern for his own supporters. David, therefore, laid aside all other interests and joined his people in the streets.

In view of the difficulty that David was having within his own party, it is surprising that he was able to regain the throne of a united Israel. After Absalom's murder, Ahithophel's suicide, and Amasa's disastrous defeat, however, neither Israel nor Judah possessed a leader who could gain enough support to guide the nation. Finally the common people of the northern kingdom prevailed upon their elders to ask David to return to the throne.

In an effort to reunite his former kingdom, David made a special appeal to the elders of Judah that they might follow the lead of their northern neighbors. In keeping with his long-standing policy toward fellow Israelites, David dealt very generously with those who were deeply implicated in the revolt against him (vv. 16–30). He even agreed to accept Amasa,

Absalom's general, in his own government as commander of the militia, provided he could muster such an army (20:4–5). Apparently, David was motivated mainly by political factors since Amasa was no closer kin to David than was Joab (cf. 8:16; 17:25). David used similar terms in claiming kinship to Amasa and to all the people of Judah (vv. 12–13).

David's motivations for making this change have been hotly debated and roundly criticized (McKane, pp. 271–272). It should be noted, however, that Joab retained the less prestigious, but the immediately more powerful, post as commander of David's standing army of foreign mercenaries (20:7). This was the army that had just defeated Israel's militia in the forest of Ephraim. Potentially, Amasa could have been in a position to wield great influence in David's government, but until he was dispatched to raise and train a conscript army, his role was largely honorary. As the matter turned out, he didn't live that long (20:10).

David may have chosen to ignore Joab's responsibility for Absalom's death to avoid dissention at this time. Joab's secret could hardly have been kept from him (18:13), but the biblical author reflects no interest on David's part to learn the details of Absalom's death. While David did not publicly castigate Joab for his disobedience, definite signs of tension between the king and his general became apparent (19:13). Undoubtedly, David intended to rebuke Joab as when Abishai was made supreme commander of the expedition against Sheba (20:6). Nevertheless, throughout the campaign, Joab remained the dominant personality. Although Absalom's death was not specifically mentioned as a cause, David eventually called on Solomon to avenge the innocent blood shed by Joab (1 Kings 2:5–6).

(2) *David Returns to Jerusalem* (19:16–40)

16 And Shimei the son of Gera, the Benjaminite, from Bahurim, made haste to come down with the men of Judah to meet King David; 17 and with him were a thousand men from Benjamin. And Ziba the servant of the house of Saul, with his fifteen sons and his twenty servants, rushed down to the Jordan before the king, 18 and they crossed the ford to bring over the king's household, and to do his pleasure. And Shimei the son of Gera fell down before the king, as he was about to cross the Jordan, 19 and said to the king, "Let not my lord hold me guilty or remember how your servant did wrong on the day my lord the king left Jerusalem; let not the king bear it in mind. 20 For your servant knows that I have sinned; therefore, behold, I have come this day, the first of all the house of Joseph to come down to meet my lord the king." 21 Abishai the son of Zeruiah answered, "Shall not Shimei be put to death for this, because he cursed the LORD's anointed?" 22 But David said, "What have I to do with you, you sons of Zeruiah, that you should this day be as an adversary to me? Shall anyone be put to death in Israel this day? For do I not know that I am this day king over Israel?" 23 And the king said to Shimei, "You shall not die." And the king gave him his oath.

24 And Mephibosheth the son of Saul came down to meet the king; he had neither dressed his feet, nor trimmed his beard, nor washed his clothes, from the day the king departed until the day he came back in safety. 25 And when he came from Jerusalem to meet the king, the king said to him, "Why did you not go with me, Mephibosheth?" 26 He answered, "My lord, O king, my servant deceived me; for your servant said to him, 'Saddle an ass for me, that I may ride upon it and go with the king.' For your servant is lame. 27 He has slandered your servant to my lord the king. But my lord the king is like the angel of God; do therefore what seems good to you. 28 For all my father's house were but men doomed to death before my lord the king; but you set your servant among those who eat at your table. What further right have I, then, to cry to the king?" 29 And the king said to him, "Why speak any more of your affairs? I have decided: you and Ziba shall divide the land." 30 And Mephibosheth said to the king, "Oh, let him take it all, since my lord the king has come safely home."

31 Now Barzillai the Gileadite had come down from Rogelim; and he went on with the king to the Jordan, to escort him over the Jordan. 32 Barzillai was a very aged man, eighty years old; and he had provided the king with food while he stayed at Mahanaim; for he was a very wealthy man. 33 And the king said to Barzillai, "Come over with me, and I will provide for you with me in Jerusalem." 34 But

Barzillai said to the king, "How many years have I still to live, that I should go up with the king to Jerusalem? 35 I am this day eighty years old; can I discern what is pleasant and what is not? Can your servant taste what he eats or what he drinks? Can I still listen to the voice of singing men and singing women? Why then should your servant be an added burden to my lord the king? 36 Your servant will go a little way over the Jordan with the king. Why should the king recompense me with such a reward? 37 Pray let your servant return, that I may die in my own city, near the grave of my father and my mother. But here is your servant Chimham; let him go over with my lord the king; and do for him whatever seems good to you." 38 And the king answered, "Chimham shall go over with me, and I will do for him whatever seems good to you; and all that you desire of me I will do for you." 39 Then all the people went over the Jordan, and the king went over; and the king kissed Barzillai and blessed him, and he returned to his own home. 40 The king went on to Gilgal, and Chimham went on with him; all the people of Judah, and also half the people of Israel, brought the king on his way.

Although David had received an invitation from both northern and southern tribes to return as king of Israel, the aftermath of Absalom's rebellion had demonstrated how extremely tenuous his hold on the Hebrew throne really was. Absalom had enjoyed widespread, though not universal, popular support, and Judah had been particularly reluctant to return David to power. David, therefore, used every possible opportunity to demonstrate his willingness to forgive past wrongs in order that he might gain support for his effort to hold the people of God together.

As David made his way back to Jerusalem, he was met at the Jordan by representatives from Israel and Judah who were to escort him back to the city. Several of these people who had figured prominently in his flight from the capital were present to make their peace with the returning king.

Shimei, who had cursed David so fluently as he passed through Bahurim, stood first in line among the Benjaminites to request the king's forgiveness for his earlier imprudence. In accord with his brother Joab's harsh and vindictive outlook, Abishai suggested that Shimei be executed for his abuse of the Lord's anointed king. David, however, rebuked the sons of Zeruiah and proclaimed an amnesty in honor of his return to the throne. Actually, David was no more forgiving than Abishai or Joab (cf. 1 Kings 2:8–9), but he believed that political necessity required a conciliatory approach, at least until the monarchy gained wider acceptance. The tensions which frequently erupted between David and Joab must ultimately be traced back to this basic controversy over the treatment to be given opponents of David's regime (cf. 3:28,39; 16:10; 19:13; 20:6; 1 Kings 2:5–6).

Also among those coming to meet David was Mephibosheth, Jonathan's son, who had previously been charged with an attempt to further his own political ambitions during David's flight from Absalom (16:1–4). Since David had no means for discriminating between Ziba's charge and Mephibosheth's countercharge (v. 26), he compromised and divided Saul's property between them. While he may have retained serious reservations about the propriety of Mephibosheth's actions in his absence, he continued to remain true to his covenant of friendship with Jonathan (1 Sam. 20:42; cf. 2 Sam. 21:7).

As David approached the Jordan on his return to Jerusalem, he was coming to the end of one of the darkest periods in his entire life. He had been deposed by a rebellious son who had gained the support of a goodly portion of the people of Israel. He had escaped from Jerusalem by the narrowest of margins only to arrive with his mercenary troops in the highlands beyond the Jordan without provisions. Understandably, David felt deeply indebted to his loyal subjects whose material support enabled him to regain the throne. The aged Barzillai stands as the representative of those whom David could never adequately repay and to whom he felt an enduring obligation. Barzillai's descendants, therefore, were ever to find a ready acceptance in Israel's royal court (1 Kings 2:7).

9. Sheba Leads Israelite Revolt (19:41—20:26)

(1) Jealousy Prompts War (19:41—20:2)

⁴¹ Then all the men of Israel came to the king, and said to the king, "Why have our brethren the men of Judah stolen you away, and brought the king and his household over the Jordan, and all David's men with him?" ⁴² All the men of Judah answered the men of Israel, "Because the king is near of kin to us. Why then are you angry over this matter? Have we eaten at all at the king's expense? Or has he given us any gift?" ⁴³ And the men of Israel answered the men of Judah, "We have ten shares in the king, and in David also we have more than you. Why then did you despise us? Were we not the first to speak of bringing back our king?" But the words of the men of Judah were fiercer than the words of the men of Israel.
¹ Now there happened to be there a worthless fellow, whose name was Sheba, the son of Bichri, a Benjaminite; and he blew the trumpet, and said,
"We have no portion in David,
 and we have no inheritance in the son of Jesse;
every man to his tents, O Israel!"
² So all the men of Israel withdrew from David, and followed Sheba the son of Bichri; but the men of Judah followed their king steadfastly from the Jordan to Jerusalem.

The fragile nature of the united kingdom at this juncture of Israel's history is revealed in the trivial grievances which were sufficient to precipitate renewed resistance to David's rule. In the festivities which accompanied David's return to Jerusalem, the men of Israel felt that the tribe of Judah had unfairly been given the more prominent role. Judah's tie of kinship was balanced against Israel's larger size and priority in calling for the king's return, and kinship won out.

This insignificant dispute over protocol undoubtedly would have passed without incident had it not been for the presence of a fiery Benjaminite who probably hoped to further his own royal ambitions at David's expense. Taking advantage of David's proclamation of an amnesty, Sheba the son of Bichri, renounced David's leadership and persuaded the Israelite contingent to withdraw from the procession to Jerusalem. The Judeans, however, probably accompanied by some individuals from the northern tribes (cf. Shimei the Benjaminite, 1 Kings 2:8), continued to escort David toward the capital city.

We have ten shares in the king. The ten northern tribes were theoretically opposed by Judah and Simeon in the south (cf. comment on 1 Sam. 9:1-2). In fact, however, Simeon was no longer functioning and Judah had grown to include all the territory south of Benjamin. The ideal twelve-tribe system was so firmly entrenched in the minds of the people that the larger number was retained even when the disappearance of one tribe was clearly recognized (1 Kings 11:29-32). It should be noted that this was long after the division of the tribe of Joseph to compensate for the disappearance of Levi as a secular tribe (Gen. 48:1-22; Num. 1:47-54; cf. Deut. 33:1-29).

(2) David's Men Pursue Sheba (20:3-22)

³ And David came to his house at Jerusalem; and the king took the ten concubines whom he had left to care for the house, and put them in a house under guard, and provided for them, but did not go in to them. So they were shut up until the day of their death, living as if in widowhood.
⁴ Then the king said to Amasa, "Call the men of Judah together to me within three days, and be here yourself." ⁵ So Amasa went to summon Judah; but he delayed beyond the set time which had been appointed him. ⁶ And David said to Abishai, "Now Sheba the son of Bichri will do us more harm than Absalom; take your lord's servants and pursue him, lest he get himself fortified cities, and cause us trouble." ⁷ And there went out after Abishai, Joab and the Cherethites and the Pelethites, and all the mighty men; they went out from Jerusalem to pursue Sheba the son of Bichri. ⁸ When they were at the great stone which is in Gibeon, Amasa came to meet them. Now Joab was wearing a soldier's garment, and over it was a girdle with a sword in its sheath fastened upon his loins, and as he went forward it fell out. ⁹ And Joab said to Amasa, "Is it well with

you, my brother?" And Joab took Amasa by the beard with his right hand to kiss him. 10 But Amasa did not observe the sword which was in Joab's hand: so Joab struck him with it in the body, and shed his bowels to the ground, without striking a second blow; and he died. Then Joab and Abishai his brother pursued Sheba the son of Bichri. 11 And one of Joab's men took his stand by Amasa, and said, "Whoever favors Joab, and whoever is for David, let him follow Joab." 12 And Amasa lay wallowing in his blood in the highway. And any one who came by, seeing him, stopped; and when the man saw that all the people stopped, he carried Amasa out of the highway into the field, and threw a garment over him. 13 When he was taken out of the highway, all the people went on after Joab to pursue Sheba the son of Bichri.
14 And Sheba passed through all the tribes of Israel to Abel of Bethmaacah; and all the Bichrites assembled, and followed him in. 15 And all the men who were with Joab came and besieged him in Abel of Bethmaacah; they cast up a mound against the city, and it stood against the rampart; and they were battering the wall, to throw it down. 16 Then a wise woman called from the city, "Hear! Hear! Tell Joab, 'Come here, that I may speak to you.'" 17 And he came near her; and the woman said, "Are you Joab?" He answered, "I am." Then she said to him, "Listen to the words of your maidservant." And he answered, "I am listening." 18 Then she said, "They were wont to say in old time, 'Let them but ask counsel at Abel'; and so they settled a matter. 19 I am one of those who are peaceable and faithful in Israel; you seek to destroy a city which is a mother in Israel; why will you swallow up the heritage of the LORD?" 20 Joab answered, "Far be it from me, far be it, that I should swallow up or destroy! 21 That is not true. But a man of the hill country of Ephraim, called Sheba the son of Bichri, has lifted up his hand against King David; give up him alone, and I will withdraw from the city." And the woman said to Joab, "Behold, his head shall be thrown to you over the wall." 22 Then the woman went to all the people in her wisdom. And they cut off the head of Sheba the son of Bichri, and threw it out to Joab. So he blew the trumpet, and they dispersed from the city, every man to his home. And Joab returned to Jerusalem to the king.

Upon his arrival in Jerusalem, David moved immediately to clarify the status of his concubines who had been publicly possessed by Absalom (16:20-22). David provided for their material needs since they still belonged to him, but he isolated them under guard because of their treatment by Absalom. David's actions implied no voluntary impropriety on the part of the women, but to have resumed a conjugal relationship with them could have been interpreted politically (cf. comment on 16:20-22). Since David denied all legitimacy to the interlude of Absalom's reign, he discharged his responsibilities toward his concubines but avoided further contact with them.

Although Sheba's flight with a thousand or so supporters (19:17 f.) posed no immediate military threat, David knew all too well that, given time, a rebel could gain enough support to be very troublesome. He, therefore, allotted Amasa, his former enemy, just three days to return with the Judean militia. When Amasa failed to return within the specified time, David felt that he could wait no longer. Stripping himself of all reserves and personal protection, David dispatched his loyal mercenary troops and professional soldiers to run Sheba down before he became established.

As David's troops went out in search of Sheba, David's position was a very precarious one. Not only was he facing an insurrection within the northern tribes, but he was also only able to exercise marginal control over his own forces. Following the collapse of Absalom's rebellion, David had reorganized his command. As a result of Joab's insubordination in the forest of Ephraim (18:9-15), David had sought to restrict his power and influence. Amasa had been placed over the militia (cf. comment on 19:13); and now in the campaign against Sheba, Abishai, Joab's brother, was given command of David's professional soldiers (vv. 6-7). Joab, though continually loyal to David, was too strong-willed to accept these moves without resistance.

The campaign against Sheba was hardly underway when Joab struck swiftly and treacherously to gain control of the expedition. As Amasa arrived at Gibeon, somewhat tardily bringing the militia from Judah, he was deceitfully murdered. As in the earlier instances of Abner and Absalom, Joab acted alone and with utter ruthlessness to eliminate his opponent. The untrained Judean militia, having little or no personal allegiance for their leader, hardly paused before joining forces with his assassin (vv. 11-13). Joab emerged as a military commander of such great strength that David was unable to take any further action against him. It was not until sometime after Solomon's accession to the throne that Joab was repaid for his excessive cruelty and brutality (1 Kings 2:31-32).

David's forces, united now under Joab's command, pressed on northward, keeping Sheba on the move until he sought refuge in Abel of Bethmaacah about five miles west of Dan. A disappointing response to his call to war may have forced Sheba to retreat all the way to Israel's frontier, or he may have hoped to gain support from neighboring Aramean states which had earlier opposed David (10:6-8; 13:37-39). In any case, he committed a grave tactical error which cost him his life (cf. comment on 1 Sam. 23:1-14 and 2 Sam. 15:13-23). Rather than hiding in the open country or leaving Israelite territory until he had sufficient strength to return in force, Sheba sought safety in a fortified city. Joab, therefore, laid siege to the city and began preparing to storm the walls.

When the hopelessness of Abel's predicament became apparent, a local woman noted for her wisdom negotiated an amnesty for the city in exchange for Sheba's life. When Sheba's head was unceremoniously dumped over the wall, the last serious external threat to David's throne was at an end.

Joab remained a potent factor to be reckoned with, but apparently he had no ambition to wear the crown personally. While David had many reasons to disapprove of his general's tactics, he never had cause to doubt his loyalty. As Joab returned to Jerusalem in control of all the military forces in Israel, he was the de facto ruler of the nation. Nevertheless, he remained true to David, who waited in the capital city without even the protection of his mercenary troops. No doubt Joab would have encountered considerable resistance within the army had he moved against David, but certainly no one ever had a better opportunity to seize control of Israel's government.

David had survived many serious crises, and the way was still open for a fulfillment of Nathan's prophecy (7:12-16), but the basic question remained unanswered. David had, as yet, made no move to designate his successor, and he would postpone that decision until the very end of his life (1 Kings 1-2).

Lest he get himself fortified cities and cause us trouble. Either David thought Sheba had more support than was actually the case or else he was using a stratagem to lure his enemy into a tactical error. David knew that a small force must avoid the temptation to hide behind city walls (cf. comment on 15:13-23), but apparently Sheba did not.

All the Bichrites assembled, and followed him in. As it stands, the Hebrew of this verse is filled with problems, but the RSV reading fits in well with the context. Rather than enjoying the support of all Israel, Sheba had enticed only his own family to follow him.

They were wont to say in old time. The nature of the old proverb about Abel is beyond recovery from the Hebrew text.

(3) *David's Leaders Listed (20:23-26)*

23 Now Joab was in command of all the army of Israel; and Benaiah the son of Jehoiada was in command of the Cherethites and the Pelethites; 24 and Adoram was in charge of the forced labor; and Jehoshaphat the son of Ahilud was the recorder; 25 and Sheva was secretary; and Zadok and Abiathar were priests; 26 and Ira the Jairite was also David's priest.

This list of officials in David's court is quite similar to that found in 8:15-18. The present tabulation serves as a commentary on the nature of the monarchy at the end of David's reign. Joab had regained his role as Israel's chief military leader in spite of his demotion following his murder of Absalom and his repeated differences with

David. Benaiah was still commander of the ever important professional soldiers who were the mainstay of David's power.

The only change of major consequence lay in the addition of Adoram as the overseer of a forced labor battalion. The use of slave labor on royal projects may have been initiated in an effort to exploit the services of foreigners captured in battle (12:31). Nevertheless, in time, Adoram (Adoniram in 1 Kings 5:13–14) would command 30,000 native Israelites who were drafted to serve on Solomon's building projects. Adoram became so identified with this detested facet of Israel's monarchy that he was stoned to death when the kingdom was divided under Rehoboam (1 Kings 12:18). The forced labor post had not grown to such proportions under David, but he introduced this significant departure from the democratic processes under Israel's old tribal structure.

V. Appendices (21:1—24:25)

1. Gibeonites Execute Saul's Sons (21:1-14)

¹ Now there was a famine in the days of David for three years, year after year; and David sought the face of the Lord. And the Lord said, "There is bloodguilt on Saul and on his house, because he put the Gibeonites to death." ² So the king called the Gibeonites. Now the Gibeonites were not of the people of Israel, but of the remnant of the Amorites; although the people of Israel had sworn to spare them, Saul had sought to slay them in his zeal for the people of Israel and Judah. ³ And David said to the Gibeonites, "What shall I do for you? And how shall I make expiation, that you may bless the heritage of the Lord?" ⁴ The Gibeonites said to him, "It is not a matter of silver or gold between us and Saul or his house; neither is it for us to put any man to death in Israel." And he said, "What do you say that I shall do for you?" ⁵ They said to the king, "The man who consumed us and planned to destroy us, so that we should have no place in all the territory of Israel, ⁶ let seven of his sons be given to us, so that we may hang them up before the Lord at Gibeon on the mountain of the Lord." And the king said, "I will give them."

⁷ But the king spared Mephibosheth, the son of Saul's son Jonathan, because of the oath of the Lord which was between them, between David and Jonathan the son of Saul. ⁸ The king took the two sons of Rizpah the daughter of Aiah, whom she bore to Saul, Armoni and Mephibosheth; and the five sons of Merab the daughter of Saul, whom she bore to Adriel the son of Barzillai the Meholathite; ⁹ and he gave them into the hands of the Gibeonites, and they hanged them on the mountain before the Lord, and the seven of them perished together. They were put to death in the first days of harvest, at the beginning of barley harvest.

¹⁰ Then Rizpah the daughter of Aiah took sackcloth, and spread it for herself on the rock, from the beginning of harvest until rain fell upon them from the heavens; and she did not allow the birds of the air to come upon them by day, or the beasts of the field by night. ¹¹ When David was told what Rizpah the daughter of Aiah, the concubine of Saul, had done, ¹² David went and took the bones of Saul and the bones of his son Jonathan from the men of Jabeshgilead, who had stolen them from the public square of Bethshan, where the Philistines had hanged them, on the day the Philistines killed Saul on Gilboa; ¹³ and he brought up from there the bones of Saul and the bones of his son Jonathan; and they gathered the bones of those who were hanged. ¹⁴ And they buried the bones of Saul and his son Jonathan in the land of Benjamin in Zela, in the tomb of Kish his father; and they did all that the king commanded. And after that God heeded supplications for the land.

This chapter introduces a series of materials not directly related to the theme of the preceding section (chs. 9—20) which was concerned with the succession to David's throne. The incidents which follow are in random order and the specific context of each must be determined individually. Some of the materials obviously go back as far as David's days as a fugitive (cf. 23:13 f.). The conclusion of the Succession Narrative is associated with the beginning of Solomon's reign (1 Kings 1—2) according to the principles discussed in the Introduction (V. 2).

The present account of the conflict between the Gibeonites and Saul's house is only tangentially related to the stories of David's dynastic difficulties. Although David seems to have been blamed by some for attacks on Saul's descendants (16:5–14), he is portrayed here in a rather favorable light. Had his involvement in the episode been politically motivated, he would hardly have bypassed Jonathan's son to attack the offspring of a concubine or the sons of one of Saul's daughters.

The Gibeonites' complaint grew out of Saul's attack on them in violation of their ancestor's covenant with Israel during the Conquest (vv. 2,5; cf. Josh. 9:15,19). He probably had suspected them and other foreign populations within Israel of collaborating with the Philistines. As members of a foreign minority within Israel, the Gibeonites had no rights to demand, and they were in no position to initiate a blood feud to protect their own. Saul, however, had broken a solemn covenant contracted under the Lord's aegis. In such cases, God's honor was understood to be involved in bringing the guilty party to justice. In keeping with the Hebrew understanding of corporate responsibility, Saul's whole family, indeed all Israel, shared the responsibility for his guilt (Josh. 7; cf. comment on 1 Sam. 2:27–36).

When David sought a divine explanation of a particularly severe famine which had afflicted the land, Saul's violation of Israel's covenant with the Gibeonites was remembered (cf. comment on 1 Sam. 5:6–12 and 2 Sam. 14:24–46). Although expiation of guilt by payment of redemption money was possible under some circumstances (Ex. 21:30), the Gibeonites refused to allow it in this case. In keeping with the law of retaliation (Ex. 21:14; Lev. 24:20), they demanded capital punishment of representative members of Saul's household. The Gibeonites probably exposed the corpses of Saul's descendants as a reminder that any who violated Israel's treaty with Gibeon would suffer a similar fate at the Lord's hand.

When the executions took place at the beginning of the barley harvest (about the middle of April), Rizpah, Saul's concubine and mother of two of the young men, began a vigil to protect the bodies from scavengers. Her heroic watch, which may have lasted until early autumn, undoubtedly captured the imagination and the sympathy of all Israel. In the limelight of public attention, David recognized an opportunity to disassociate himself from any responsibility for these deaths. He, therefore, brought Saul's and Jonathan's bones from Jabeshgilead for re-interment in Saul's family tomb. When the fall rains came on schedule, signifying a return of the Lord's favor, David gathered the young men's remains and gave them an honorable burial among their own people in Benjamin. The site of Zela is otherwise unknown.

2. *Philistines Renew War* (21:15–22)

15 The Philistines had war again with Israel, and David went down together with his servants, and they fought against the Philistines; and David grew weary. 16 And Ishbibenob, one of the descendants of the giants, whose spear weighed three hundred shekels of bronze, and who was girded with a new sword, thought to kill David. 17 But Abishai the son of Zeruiah came to his aid, and attacked the Philistine and killed him. Then David's men adjured him, "You shall no more go out with us to battle, lest you quench the lamp of Israel." 18 After this there was again war with the Philistines at Gob; then Sibbecai the Hushathite slew Saph, who was one of the descendants of the giants. 19 And there was again war with the Philistines at Gob; and Elhanan the son of Jaareoregim, the Bethlehemite, slew Goliath the Gittite, the shaft of whose spear was like a weaver's beam. 20 And there was again war at Gath, where there was a man of great stature, who had six fingers on each hand, and six toes on each foot, twenty-four in number; and he also was descended from the giants. 21 And when he taunted Israel, Jonathan the son of Shimei, David's brother, slew him. 22 These four were descended from the giants in Gath; and they fell by the hand of David and by the hand of his servants.

These brief notices of renewed war with the Philistines have obviously been brought together because of their common interest in Israelite victories over Philistine giants. Only one account devotes even meager attention to the circumstances surrounding the action, so that it is impossible to speak with any certainty as to the nature of the warfare involved. Many commentators associate these contests with the Philistine wars which followed David's reunification of Israel and Judah under one crown

(5:17 f.). There is nothing inherently improbable about a renewal of the Philistine conflict later in David's reign. As a matter of fact, the dissolution of central authority following Absalom's and Sheba's rebellions almost certainly invited aggressive attacks by Israel's neighbors. The limited interests and scope of the biblical narratives, however, do not allow us to reconstruct the details of this period of David's reign.

The first giant was killed by Abishai, who came to David's rescue as the latter grew weary in battle against the Philistines. David's men who became concerned for his safety and for Israel's future demanded that he cease accompanying his troops into battle (cf. 18:3). It is interesting to note that the author of Chronicles omitted this admission of human frailty on David's part while he included the next three stories of victories over the Philistine giants (1 Chron. 20:4–8).

The author of Chronicles, however, apparently sensed a problem in the account of the death of Goliath, a Gittite at the hands of Elhanan, a Bethlehemite (cf. comments on 1 Sam. 17:1–11). In any case, the passage in Chronicles affords no grounds for confusion with David's earlier exploits since the text differs considerably from the reading in Samuel: "and Elhanan the son of Jair slew Lahmi the brother of Goliath the Gittite, the shaft of whose spear was like a weaver's beam" (1 Chron. 20:5).

War with the Philistine at Gob. Gob is not otherwise attested in the Old Testament, and its location is no longer known. The account in Chronicles which is parallel to this locates the action at Gezer (1 Chron. 20:4).

Then Sibbecai the Hushathite slew Saph. Sibbecai was one of David's mighty men (1 Chron. 11:29; but cf. 2 Sam. 23:27). He commanded a division of 24,000 men in the portion of the militia which served during the eighth month of each year (1 Chron. 27:11). The Hushathites seem to have been from Judah near Bethlehem (1 Chron. 4:4).

3. Song of David Gives Thanks (22:1–51)

¹ And David spoke to the Lord the words of this song on the day when the Lord delivered him from the hand of all his enemies, and from the hand of Saul. ² He said,

"The Lord is my rock, and my fortress, and my deliverer,
³ my God, my rock, in whom I take refuge,
my shield and the horn of my salvation,
my stronghold and my refuge,
my savior; thou savest me from violence.
⁴ I call upon the Lord, who is worthy to be praised,
and I am saved from my enemies.

⁵ "For the waves of death encompassed me,
the torrents of perdition assailed me;
⁶ the cords of Sheol entangled me,
the snares of death confronted me.

⁷ "In my distress I called upon the Lord;
to my God I called.
From his temple he heard my voice,
and my cry came to his ears.

⁸ "Then the earth reeled and rocked;
the foundations of the heavens trembled
and quaked, because he was angry.
⁹ Smoke went up from his nostrils,
and devouring fire from his mouth;
glowing coals flamed forth from him.
¹⁰ He bowed the heavens, and came down;
thick darkness was under his feet.
¹¹ He rode on a cherub, and flew;
he was seen upon the wings of the wind.
¹² He made darkness around him
his canopy, thick clouds, a gathering of water.
¹³ Out of the brightness before him
coals of fire flamed forth.
¹⁴ The Lord thundered from heaven,
and the Most High uttered his voice.
¹⁵ And he sent out arrows, and scattered them;
lightning, and routed them.
¹⁶ Then the channels of the sea were seen,
the foundations of the world were laid bare,
at the rebuke of the Lord,
at the blast of the breath of his nostrils.

¹⁷ "He reached from on high, he took me,
he drew me out of many waters.
¹⁸ He delivered me from my strong enemy,
from those who hated me;
for they were too mighty for me.
¹⁹ They came upon me in the day of my calamity;
but the Lord was my stay.
²⁰ He brought me forth into a broad place;
he delivered me, because he delighted in me.

21 "The Lord rewarded me according to my righteousness;
  according to the cleanness of my hands he recompensed me.
22 For I have kept the ways of the Lord,
  and have not wickedly departed from my God.
23 For all his ordinances were before me,
  and from his statutes I did not turn aside.
24 I was blameless before him,
  and I kept myself from guilt.
25 Therefore the Lord has recompensed me according to my righteousness,
  according to my cleanness in his sight.

26 "With the loyal thou dost show thyself loyal;
  with the blameless man thou dost show thyself blameless;
27 with the pure thou dost show thyself pure,
  and with the crooked thou dost show thyself perverse.
28 Thou dost deliver a humble people,
  but thy eyes are upon the haughty to bring them down.
29 Yea, thou art my lamp, O Lord,
  and my God lightens my darkness.
30 Yea, by thee I can crush a troop,
  and by my God I can leap over a wall.
31 This God—his way is perfect;
  the promise of the Lord proves true;
  he is a shield for all those who take refuge in him.

32 "For who is God, but the Lord?
  And who is a rock, except our God?
33 This God is my strong refuge,
  and has made my way safe.
34 He made my feet like hinds' feet,
  and set me secure on the heights.
35 He trains my hands for war,
  so that my arms can bend a bow of bronze.
36 Thou hast given me the shield of thy salvation,
  and thy help made me great.
37 Thou didst give a wide place for my steps under me,
  and my feet did not slip;
38 I pursued my enemies and destroyed them,
  and did not turn back until they were consumed.
39 I consumed them; I thrust them through, so that they did not rise;
  they fell under my feet.
40 For thou didst gird me with strength for the battle;
  thou didst make my assailants sink under me.
41 Thou didst make my enemies turn their backs to me,
  those who hated me, and I destroyed them.
42 They looked, but there was none to save;
  they cried to the Lord, but he did not answer them.
43 I beat them fine as the dust of the earth,
  I crushed them and stamped them down like the mire of the streets.

44 "Thou didst deliver me from strife with the peoples;
  thou didst keep me as the head of the nations;
  people whom I had not known served me.
45 Foreigners came cringing to me;
  as soon as they heard of me, they obeyed me.
46 Foreigners lost heart,
  and came trembling out of their fastnesses.

47 "The Lord lives; and blessed be my rock,
  and exalted be my God, the rock of my salvation,
48 the God who gave me vengeance
  and brought down peoples under me,
49 who brought me out from my enemies;
  thou didst exalt me above my adversaries,
  thou didst deliver me from men of violence.

50 "For this I will extol thee, O Lord, among the nations,
  and sing praises to thy name.
51 Great triumphs he gives to his king,
  and shows steadfast love to his anointed,
  to David and his descendants for ever."

A slightly variant form of this poem is also found in the book of Psalms (ch. 18). A superscription in each instance associates the song with David, and there seem to be no overpowering internal arguments against such a connection.[38] Nevertheless, the scope of the psalm is too broad to allow a setting in any one period of David's life. Indeed, conditions from his entire career seem to have been used in the development of literary forms which served to express all men's feelings of thanksgiving and praise. A detailed analysis of the background and structure of the poem will be reserved for consideration in the volume dealing with the Psalter, but a few words about its role in the present narratives are in order at this point.

[38] Mitchell Dahood, *Psalms I* ("The Anchor Bible." [Garden City, N. Y.: Doubleday, 1965]), p. 104.

The song is explicitly designed to celebrate David's deliverance from Saul and other unnamed enemies. Indeed, the comparisons of the Lord to a rock (vv. 2,3,32,47), a fortress (v.2), a stronghold (v.3), and a refuge (v.33) suggest David's experiences as a fugitive from Saul's insane jealousy. Likewise David's pessimistic concern for his future just before his Philistine exile (1 Sam. 27:1) would accord well with the psalmist's extremity depicted in vv. 5–6.

On the other hand, the psalm seems also to deal with conditions drawn from a much later period of David's life. His successes in building an empire at the expense of his neighbors may be reflected in the cringing subservience which foreigners paid the psalmist (vv. 44–46). Similarly, David's victories in the various civil wars directed against him seem to be suggested here. Thus, he was delivered from strife with his own people (cf. the marg. reading of v. 44). His enemies appealed to the Lord, but he rejected their pleas (v. 42). The reference to David's escape from the enemies who were too strong for him (v. 18) is suggestive of his precarious position during Absalom's rebellion, but the conditions are too vague to assert a positive relationship.

Some verses within the poem, however, do not seem to fit the known conditions of David's life. The psalmist, for example, appears to regard the Lord's blessings and deliverance as the result of his own goodness (vv. 21–31). He claims to have clean hands (v. 21) and a conscience clear of transgressions against God's law (v. 23). Such statements would hardly seem appropriate for one who felt constrained to commit murder in order to cover his marital infidelity (ch. 11).

Taken at face value, these verses would not genuinely apply to any man, certainly not to David. They are the outgrowth, however, of a theology which held that Israel's righteous God always rewarded good and punished evil *in this world*. David's repeated deliverance, therefore, was taken as prima facie evidence that he had pleased God. To be sure, the psalmist's case is still overstated; but this may be the result of the ancient oriental's frequent indulgence in hyperbole. Actually the psalmist himself seems to be aware of the dangers of man's thinking of himself more highly than he ought to think (v. 28). The Lord, therefore, was seen as the deliverer of the humble who would yield to his leadership, but as a stern judge for the haughty who resisted his directions. Seen in this light, these verses may yet be taken as an outgrowth of David's experience, for he was notably willing to confess his guilt when he had been led to recognize it (1 Sam. 25:32; 2 Sam. 12:13).

The theme of the entire psalm is summarized in the two final verses in that the Lord is praised as the effective power behind all David's successes. Whether expressed or implied, an awareness of divine providence underlies the entire narrative from David's anointment at the hands of Samuel to his victory over Sheba and his followers. The psalmist speaks of the Lord's intervention on his behalf in terms of a divine theophany in which God appeared riding on a storm to disperse his foes (vv. 8–16). Such figurative language was common in the ancient world (cf. Isa. 19:1 and Psalm 104:3 ff.), but it did not exclude a more mundane view of military success. Nevertheless, while physical prowess and skill with arms were understood to play an important role in the outcome of battle, the Lord was recognized as the source of even these worldly arts (vv. 34–43). Thus God was working in history to fulfill his promise of an enduring line for David upon the throne of Israel (v. 51; cf. 7:1–29).

4. David's Last Words (23:1–7)

1 Now these are the last words of David:
The oracle of David, the son of Jesse,
   the oracle of the man who was raised on high,
   the anointed of the God of Jacob,
   the sweet psalmist of Israel:
2 "The Spirit of the LORD speaks by me,

2 SAMUEL 23

    his word is upon my tongue.
3 The God of Israel has spoken,
    the Rock of Israel has said to me:
When one rules justly over men,
    ruling in the fear of God,
4 he dawns on them like the morning light,
    like the sun shining forth upon a cloudless morning,
    like rain that makes grass to sprout from the earth.
5 Yea, does not my house stand so with God?
    For he has made with me an everlasting covenant,
    ordered in all things and secure.
For will he not cause to prosper
    all my help and my desire?
6 But godless men are all like thorns that are thrown away;
    for they cannot be taken with the hand;
7 but the man who touches them
    arms himself with iron and the shaft of a spear,
    and they are utterly consumed with fire."

This brief psalm is of paramount importance in the study of the ideal role of the king in ancient Israelite thought. The ideas expressed here are related to, but go beyond, those found in Samuel's farewell address (cf. especially 1 Sam. 12:14-15), and in Nathan's prophecy (2 Sam. 7:1-17). The placement of the song at the end of David's career appears to be patterned after the "blessings" or farewell addresses of Israel's earlier great leaders (Jacob, Gen. 49; Moses, Deut. 33; Samuel, 1 Sam. 12; cf. also the later work, *The Testaments of the Twelve Patriarchs*).[39]

In these verses, the sacral role of the king emerges quite clearly. He had been exalted and set apart by the Lord, and his pronouncements carried with them divine authority. When the king ruled according to God's leadership, he brought the whole nation into a right relationship with the Lord. He brought prosperity to his people just as the sun and the rain bring fertility to the soil. As God's own choice for the throne, David was promised an enduring line (cf. 7:11-14), whereas the usurper, though potentially dangerous, was certain of eventual destruction (cf. 1 Sam. 12:15).

[39] Aubrey R. Johnson, *Sacral Kingship in Ancient Israel*, 2d. ed. (Cardiff: University of Wales Press, 1967), pp. 16-19.

5. David's "Mighty Men" Listed (23:8-39)

8 These are the names of the mighty men whom David had: Joshebbasshebeth a Tahchemonite; he was chief of the three; he wielded his spear against eight hundred whom he slew at one time.
9 And next to him among the three mighty men was Eleazar the son of Dodo, son of Ahohi. He was with David when they defied the Philistines who were gathered there for battle, and the men of Israel withdrew. 10 He rose and struck down the Philistines until his hand was weary, and his hand cleaved to the sword; and the Lord wrought a great victory that day; and the men returned after him only to strip the slain.
11 And next to him was Shammah, the son of Agee the Hararite. The Philistines gathered together at Lehi, where there was a plot of ground full of lentils; and the men fled from the Philistines. 12 But he took his stand in the midst of the plot, and defended it, and slew the Philistines; and the Lord wrought a great victory.
13 And three of the thirty chief men went down, and came about harvest time to David at the cave of Adullam, when a band of Philistines was encamped in the valley of Rephaim. 14 David was then in the stronghold; and the garrison of the Philistines was then at Bethlehem. 15 And David said longingly, "O that someone would give me water to drink from the well of Bethlehem which is by the gate!" 16 Then the three mighty men broke through the camp of the Philistines, and drew water out of the well of Bethlehem which was by the gate, and took and brought it to David. But he would not drink of it; he poured it out to the Lord, 17 and said, "Far be it from me, O Lord, that I should do this. Shall I drink the blood of the men who went at the risk of their lives?" Therefore he would not drink it. These things did the three mighty men.
18 Now Abishai, the brother of Joab, the son of Zeruiah, was chief of the thirty. And he wielded his spear against three hundred men and slew them, and won a name beside the three. 19 He was the most renowned of the thirty, and became their commander; but he did not attain to the three.
20 And Benaiah the son of Jehoiada was a valiant man of Kabzeel, a doer of great deeds; he smote two ariels of Moab. He also went down and slew a lion in a pit on a day when snow had fallen. 21 And he slew an Egyptian, a handsome man. The Egyptian had a spear in his hand; but Benaiah went down to him with a staff, and snatched the spear out of the Egyptian's hand, and slew him with his own spear. 22 These things did Benaiah the son of

Jehoiada, and won a name beside the three mighty men. 23 He was renowned among the thirty, but he did not attain to the three. And David set him over his bodyguard.

24 Asahel the brother of Joab was one of the thirty; Elhanan the son of Dodo of Bethlehem, 25 Shammah of Harod, Elika of Harod, 26 Helez the Paltite, Ira the son of Ikkesh of Tekoa, 27 Abiezer, of Anathoth, Mebunnai the Hushathite, 28 Zalmon the Ahohite, Maharai of Netophah, 29 Heleb the son of Baanah of Netophah, Ittai the son of Ribai of Gibeah of the Benjaminites, 30 Benaiah of Pirathon, Hiddai of the brooks of Gaash, 31 Abialbon the Arbathite, Azmaveth of Bahurim, 32 Eliahba of Shaalbon, the sons of Jashen, Jonathan, 33 Shammah the Hararite, Ahiam the son of Sharar the Hararite, 34 Eliphelet the son of Ahasbai of Maacah, Eliam the son of Ahithophel of Gilo, 35 Hezro of Carmel, Paarai the Arbite, 36 Igal the son of Nathan of Zobah, Bani the Gadite, 37 Zelek the Ammonite, Naharai of Beeroth, the armorbearer of Joab the son of Zeruiah, 38 Ira the Ithrite, Gareb the Ithrite, 39 Uriah the Hittite: thirty-seven in all.

The inclusion of the exploits and the names of David's most important mercenary soldiers is in keeping with the importance of the role that the group played in David's reign. In the days of the judges and even under Saul's rule, Israelite power had been based primarily in the militia which was called together only in cases of emergency. The army was frequently under manned, since the central government lacked a means of enforcing a call to arms. Saul had begun gathering Israel's most promising warriors about him as a cadre of professional military leaders (1 Sam. 14:52), but it remained for David to make the most of this departure from ancient tribal practice.

David's first band of professional soldiers was not of the highest caliber (1 Sam. 22:2), but they provided him with a measure of protection against Saul's murderous pursuit. After Saul and Jonathan were killed in the battle at Mount Gilboa, David's private army was probably quite influential in Judah's decision to elect him king (2:1-4). Then, following his elevation to the throne over all Israel, David used his men to capture Jerusalem, his new capital city (5:6-10). The clearest demonstration of the importance of David's military innovations, however, came during the revolutions designed to unseat him from power. Had it not been for the unswerving loyalty of his foreign mercenary troops (15:13-23), David could hardly have survived Absalom's rebellion followed immediately by Sheba's revolt. By gaining a base of power committed wholly unto him personally, David brought the realization of Nathan's prophecy (2 Sam. 7:1-17) a step nearer fulfillment.

Outstanding achievement or merit among David's mercenary troops appears to have been rewarded by membership in one of two special orders of military recognition. The smaller, more elite group, called simply *the three*, was composed of men who had distinguished themselves by spectacular exploits against the enemy during Israel's Philistine campaigns (vv. 8-12). Members of this band are not listed with the larger body of *the thirty*, but Joshebbasshebeth (Jashobeam, cf. 1 Chron. 11:11; 27:2) elsewhere appears as the commander of a contingent of David's militia. Other men won similar renown (v. 22) or rose to higher rank (20:23), but no others attained the same degree of eminence that they had achieved.

The three men who risked their lives to bring David water from the well at Bethlehem were members of *the thirty* and hence distinguished from the men previously mentioned. The incident occurred during the Philistines' attack on David after he became king over all Israel (5:17-25). The main body of the Philistines were encamped in the valley of Rephaim near Jerusalem and a smaller garrison occupied Bethlehem. Three unidentified soldiers from David's army near Adullam brazenly infiltrated the Philistine lines and brought their commander the drink he had whimsically requested. Feeling that his men had hallowed the water by so seriously risking their lives, David poured it out as an offering unto the Lord (Lev. 17:11-13). This brief episode amply illustrates the intense loyalty which passed between David and his *mighty men*.

Membership in *the thirty* seems to have changed from time to time as replacements became necessary. Thus, Chronicles lists 16 men who are not found here (1 Chron. 11:41–47). The present list begins with Asahel, Joab's brother who was killed earlier by Abner (2:18–23), and the last man included was Uriah the Hittite, whom David had murdered. Although Joab is not mentioned as a member of the group, he is presumably to be included. He is more prominent than his two brothers, Abishai and Asahel, and certainly more so than his armor-bearer who also made the list (v. 37). Joab's omission probably accounts for the later observation that there were *thirty-seven in all* (v. 39) when only 36 names are given in the chapter (for a convenient survey of the names, cf. Driver, pp. 362–63). A comparison with the parallel passage in 1 Chronicles 11:10–41a reveals considerable variation in the enumeration, however, and dogmatism must be avoided.

6. David Takes a Census (24:1–17)

¹ Again the anger of the LORD was kindled against Israel, and he incited David against them, saying, "Go, number Israel and Judah." ² So the king said to Joab and the commanders of the army, who were with him, "Go through all the tribes of Israel, from Dan to Beersheba, and number the people, that I may know the number of the people." ³ But Joab said to the king, "May the LORD your God add to the people a hundred times as many as they are, while the eyes of my lord the king still see it; but why does my lord the king delight in this thing?" ⁴ But the king's word prevailed against Joab and the commanders of the army. So Joab and the commanders of the army went out from the presence of the king to number the people of Israel. ⁵ They crossed the Jordan, and began from Aroer, and from the city that is in the middle of the valley, toward Gad and on to Jazer. ⁶ Then they came to Gilead, and to Kadesh in the land of the Hittites; and they came to Dan, and from Dan they went around to Sidon, ⁷ and came to the fortress of Tyre and to all the cities of the Hivites and Canaanites; and they went out to the Negeb of Judah at Beersheba. ⁸ So when they had gone through all the land, they came to Jerusalem at the end of nine months and twenty days. ⁹ And Joab gave the sum of the numbering of the people to the king: in Israel there were eight hundred thousand valiant men who drew the sword, and the men of Judah were five hundred thousand.

¹⁰ But David's heart smote him after he had numbered the people. And David said to the LORD, "I have sinned greatly in what I have done. But now, O LORD, I pray thee, take away the iniquity of thy servant; for I have done very foolishly." ¹¹ And when David arose in the morning, the word of the LORD came to the prophet Gad, David's seer, saying, ¹² "Go and say to David, 'Thus says the LORD, Three things I offer you; choose one of them, that I may do it to you.'" ¹³ So Gad came to David and told him, and said to him, "Shall three years of famine come to you in your land? Or will you flee three months before your foes while they pursue you? Or shall there be three days' pestilence in your land? Now consider, and decide what answer I shall return to him who sent me." ¹⁴ Then David said to Gad, "I am in great distress; let us fall into the hand of the LORD, for his mercy is great; but let me not fall into the hand of man."

¹⁵ So the LORD sent a pestilence upon Israel from the morning until the appointed time; and there died of the people from Dan to Beersheba seventy thousand men. ¹⁶ And when the angel stretched forth his hand toward Jerusalem to destroy it, the LORD repented of the evil, and said to the angel who was working destruction among the people, "It is enough; now stay your hand." And the angel of the LORD was by the threshing floor of Araunah the Jebusite. ¹⁷ Then David spoke to the LORD when he saw the angel who was smiting the people, and said, "Lo, I have sinned, and I have done wickedly; but these sheep, what have they done? Let thy hand, I pray thee, be against me and against my father's house."

The last story about David in the prime of life involves three major incidents: a census (vv. 1–9); a plague (vv. 10–17); and the purchase of a site on which the Temple was to be built (vv. 18–25).

The entire episode seems to be based upon changes that David was initiating in Israel's military posture. Prior to the establishment of the monarchy, Israel had enjoyed a loosely knit government in which each tribe was virtually independent in all matters except those related to religion and war. During the period of the judges, Israel was drawn together primarily by her common worship and by the necessity of providing troops for mutual defense (cf.

comment on 1 Sam. 4:12–18). Even in times of national emergency, each tribe was responsible for mustering its own troops and frequently a tribe would refuse to commit its own militia for service in a distant section of the country (cf. Judg. 5). In the face of mounting external pressures, leaders within Israel felt constrained to seek a new form of government which would be better able to provide a standing deterrent to foreign aggression (cf. 1 Sam. 8:20; 12:12).

Since Saul had encountered pressures from almost all quarters opposing the very idea of an Israelite monarchy, his government retained the major features of the old tribal federation (cf. Bright, p. 169). David, on the other hand, had introduced new and sweeping reforms, particularly in regard to the nation's military structure. From the very beginning of his reign, David had depended heavily on his professional standing army (cf. comment on 23:8–39); and now apparently he was proposing a reorganization of the tribal militia as well.

While censuses for other purposes were permissible (Ex. 30:11 ff.; Num. 1:2 ff.; 26:1 ff.), the military interests inherent in David's enumeration (v. 9) suggest that he was contemplating levying a conscription quota on each of the tribes.[40] Even Joab could see that the people would violently resist such a draft and futilely urged David to forego such a plan (v. 3).

Unfortunately, David had not anticipated the strong religious reaction to his military registration. In view of the earlier intimate relationship between Israel's worship and war, the people regarded his move as an attack on the theological principles on which the nation had been established. When a serious plague struck Israel shortly after the census was complete, it was taken as a sign of the Lord's displeasure. Presumably, the Lord, who was angry with Israel for some unstated reason, had incited David to take the census that he might have an occasion to vent his wrath on his people.

While such a view was undoubtedly intended to exalt God as the ruler of all life and human history (cf. Isa. 45:7 in the KJV), it is not without theological difficulty. It is true that the entire universe is ultimately operated under God's authority and control, but later biblical thought makes it clear that the Lord seeks to lead man toward the good rather than the harmful. The author of the books of Chronicles seems to have grasped this fact, for his version of this verse indicates that Satan incited David to number the people (1 Chron. 21:1; cf. also Rom. 8:28; James 1:13).

Confronted with the public reaction to his census, David was ready to confess his error and guilt, even before any demonstration of divine displeasure was evident (v. 10 f.). He readily accepted full responsibility for his deeds and sought to shield his people from suffering (v. 17). In the face of imminent judgment, however, David preferred to cast himself and his people upon the divine mercy rather than to fall into the hands of a human foe.

Again the anger of the Lord. Apparently, the word *again* refers to the three-year famine in 21:1–14. No mention of the Lord's anger is found in the earlier context, however.

In Israel there were eight hundred thousand valiant men who drew the sword, and the men of Judah were five hundred thousand. The figures are unertain since the parallel passage in Chronicles calls for 1,100,000 men in Israel and 470,000 in Judah with no men from Levi or Benjamin (1 Chron. 21:5–6).

The Lord repented of the evil. The order appears disturbed here. Verse 16 implies that God had already stopped the plague short of Jerusalem, and yet the rest of the chapter takes no notice of this fact (cf. especially vv. 17,21,25). Perhaps this verse had been transposed from another location.

---

[40] George E. Mendenhall, "The Census Lists of Numbers 1 and 26," *Journal of Biblical Literature*, LXXVII (1958), 56.

7. David Builds an Altar (24:18–25)

¹⁸ And Gad came that day to David, and said to him, "Go up, rear an altar to the LORD on the threshing floor of Araunah the Jebusite." ¹⁹ So David went up at Gad's word, as the LORD commanded. ²⁰ And when Araunah looked down, he saw the king and his servants coming on toward him; and Araunah went forth, and did obeisance to the king with his face to the ground. ²¹ And Araunah said, "Why has my lord the king come to his servant?" David said, "To buy the threshing floor of you, in order to build an altar to the LORD, that the plague may be averted from the people." ²² Then Araunah said to David, "Let my lord the king take and offer up what seems good to him; here are the oxen for the burnt offering, and the threshing sledges and the yokes of the oxen for the wood. ²³ All this, O king, Araunah gives to the king." And Araunah said to the king, "The LORD your God accept you." ²⁴ But the king said to Araunah, "No, but I will buy it of you for a price; I will not offer burnt offerings to the LORD my God which cost me nothing." So David bought the threshing floor and the oxen for fifty shekels of silver. ²⁵ And David built there an altar to the LORD, and offered burnt offerings and peace offerings. So the LORD heeded supplications for the land, and the plague was averted from Israel.

The narrative about David's census leads naturally into the story of his purchase of the threshing floor of Araunah for a holy place. Since the account lacks specific details requiring a late period in David's reign, presumably, it was introduced at this point to provide a transitional link with Solomon's reign. The materials in chapters 20–24 do not deal with the central issue of their immediate context, i.e., the problem of finding the proper successor for David's throne (cf. Introduction). The present story which culminates in the purchase of the Temple site is, therefore, used to direct the reader's attention toward the one responsible for building Israel's central place of worship. Hence the parallel account in 1 Chronicles 21:1–27 moves on to tell of David's accumulation of materials to be used in Solomon's building campaign (22:1 f.).

When Araunah learned of David's need for his property, he was prepared to give the king not only his land but his animals for sacrifice and his tools for fuel as well. David, however, declined the Jebusite's generous offer because he had learned the nature of true sacrifice. Offerings unto the Lord are important, not because of what they do for God, but because of what they do for man. Through a true sacrifice, one recognizes afresh that all of his life and substance belong ultimately to God. In the act of giving, the worshiper dedicates not only his property but also his personality to the Lord of life.

1-2 Kings

M. PIERCE MATHENEY, JR., AND ROY L. HONEYCUTT, JR.

Introduction

I. The Name

The books of the Old Testament which we call 1 and 2 Kings were originally one book. They were printed as one book in the Hebrew Bible until the sixteenth century, A.D., and are, in the Hebrew order, the fourth book of the Former Prophets. The Hebrew title of this book means Kings. But in the Greek Septuagint translation, the one book was written on two scrolls and thus divided into two books. This division occurs at a most inappropriate place, splitting the account of the reign of Ahaziah, son of Ahab. The Septuagint similarly divided the book of Samuel; and it entitled the whole history First, Second, Third and Fourth Kingdoms (or Reigns). For the purposes of this commentary, we will recognize that the two books of Kings are one by using one Introduction [1] for both books.

1 and 2 Kings commonly are designated as historical books, and so they are. It is important that the modern reader understand the significance which the people of Israel attached to their history. He should know the sense in which "history," as the Bible understands this term, corresponds to modern concepts of history. The basic meaning of Old Testament history is that Israel, God's covenant people, saw history as "his-story." They believed that Yahweh was sovereign Lord of history, using men and nations to work out his redemptive purposes. On the other hand, the biblical historians were not as interested as the modern historian in facts for the sake of facts. If there is any such thing as "objective" history, the Old Testament writers always go beyond this to search for meaning. It is the peculiar blending of events and interpretations of these events through which God has spoken by holy men of his own choosing. This constitutes the revelation of God in history. One tenet of our faith in this Lord of history is that he inspired the telling, writing, and preservation of this great story of his judgment and redeeming love.

II. The Text

The Hebrew text of the books of Kings presents relatively few problems for the commentator. Recent discoveries, and the best scholarly research on the early versions, have tended to establish the reliability of the Masoretic Text in the large majority of cases (Montgomery-Gehman, p. 24, fn. 9). The sensational archaeological finds at Qumran, however, have reemphasized the value of the Septuagiant translation (Gray, pp. 46–48). Consequently, those readings from the Septuagint of the books of Kings which seem to be interesting for interpretation, or preferable to the Hebrew text, will be noted in the commentary on specific passages. A special situation with regard to the parallel passages of

---

[1] Prepared by M. Pierce Matheney, Jr., also the author of the commentary on the text of 1 Kings. Roy L. Honeycutt, Jr., is the author of the commentary on the text of 2 Kings.

Kings with portions of the books of Chronicles, Isaiah, and Jeremiah will have to be taken into account in the commentary on those particular sections. No further detailed discussion of this subject is required since the two most recent technical commentaries on Kings have ample and excellent discussions of the text (Montgomery-Gehman, pp. 3–24; Gray, pp. 43–55).

III. The Author(s)

The author or authors of the books of Kings are not known. The Jewish Talmud says that Jeremiah wrote them, but this is a late tradition with no evidence to commend it. There is no obstacle to a belief in the authority and inspiration of any biblical book in the simple recognition that its human author is unknown.

But there is a broader context to the books of Kings that allows one to make some statements about the author, whom we choose to call "the historian." He was a member of prophetic schools in Jerusalem which wholeheartedly supported the reform of Josiah. Since a portion of the present book of Deuteronomy was probably the law book which became the basis of that reform, it has become customary for scholars to refer to the Deuteronomic historian(s). Indeed the whole corpus of books called the Former Prophets—namely Joshua, Judges, Samuel, and Kings—are known as the Deuteronomic history. The chief storyteller with whom we are concerned is that historian who set the acts of Solomon and the annals of the divided kingdom in the light of God's controversy with his people. Technical Old Testament study has suggested that he lived and wrote during the era of Josiah's reform, ca. 621–609 B.C.

Then about 550 B.C., after the destruction of Jerusalem, an editor in the Babylonian exile wrote the conclusion of 2 Kings, from the death of Josiah to the release of Jehoiachin in Babylon (2 Kings 23:26—25:30). Perhaps, as some scholars view his work, this exilic editor revised certain portions of Kings to prepare his readers for the outcome (e.g., 1 Kings 9:6–9). However, since this Deuteronomic editor of Kings was in full sympathy with the work of the chief historian, this updating of the story by no means detracts from it, but rather serves to complete it.

The historian speaks primarily of God's judgment seen in the events of Israel's history. His theological viewpoint is that of the book of Deuteronomy (e.g., Deut. 28). God has chosen for himself a people. He has covenanted with this people, promising blessings upon those who obey his commandments. But he has warned against disobedience, which will result in destruction and exile. The story of the decline of the Hebrew kingdoms is told during Josiah's reform to encourage obedience. The bad example of north Israel, and the destruction which has already befallen that kingdom, is a special warning to Judah. The fall of Judah is added by the exilic editor to the story in order that the whole history may serve as a warning to exilic and postexilic generations that God will perform his prophetic word among the nations of men. The historian is particularly interested in the prophets and their warnings to various kings, vindicated in the outcome of events.

IV. The Sources

From this particularly theological viewpoint, the historian has made use of certain written sources. He cites three of these: (1) the book of the acts of Solomon (1 Kings 11:41); (2) the Book of the Chronicles of the kings of Israel (1 Kings 14:19); and (3) the Book of the Chronicles of the kings of Judah (1 Kings 14:29). The latter two are not to be confused with our biblical books of Chronicles. They were rather the official court annals of the divided kingdoms, or prophetic summaries of these. In addition to these, the historian also used other written or oral sources which are distinguishable as lying behind the present form of the books.

The first of these is the Court History (a document referred to by some commentators as the "Succession Narrative") of the succession to David's throne. The limits of this important eyewitness document are usually stated as 2 Samuel 9—20, and 1 Kings 1—2. Since the latter two chapters provided the introduction to the story of Solomon, they have been used in Kings, separated from the rest of this source by the appendix to the books of Samuel, 2 Samuel 21—24. The author of this succession history may have been Nathan the prophet (cf. 1 Chron. 29:29), or one of the other active participants in the events described.

A second additional source used by the historian of Kings was concerned with a more positive evaluation of the kingship of Ahab, the "Solomon of the North," than that which is found in the Elijah stories. This source is found in 1 Kings 20 and 22, now separated by the famous Naboth incident, but placed together by the Septuagint version of Kings.

A third, and most significant, additional source used to give the books of Kings some of their weightiest religious teaching is the cycle of prophetic stories from North Israel having to do with Elijah and his disciple-successor, Elisha. Elijah the Tishbite is the most important prophet between Samuel and Amos. The nucleus of what must once have been a larger biography is found in 1 Kings 17—19; 21; and 2 Kings 1—2. Intertwined with 1 Kings 19 and 2 Kings 2 is the beginning of the somewhat different but quite extensive story of Elisha. Whereas we may suppose Elisha himself preserved the story of his master, Elijah, perhaps Gehazi or others of the sons of the prophets have related the wondrous deeds of Elisha, the leader of these prophetic schools (cf. 2 Kings 8:1-6). The account of these deeds is preserved in 2 Kings 2—10 and 13, not all the stories of which regard Elisha as the central figure but all belonging to the period of his prophetic leadership.

Finally, a last additional source has to do with the canonical prophet, Isaiah, and his significant role in the Assyrian crisis during the reign of Hezekiah of Judah. This story is told in both 2 Kings 18—20 and in a slightly different form in Isaiah 36—39. This material was written about Isaiah, rather than by him, perhaps by one of his disciples, and is similar to other biographical material of his book, important to a reconstruction of his role as counselor to kings of Judah during the crises of their reigns. It is probably neither possible nor necessary to say which is the prior account of these events concerning Hezekiah, or whether both have drawn on common oral or written material. Most scholars seem to favor the view that the material common to the two books has been added to the book of Isaiah from 2 Kings.

There is a similar question about the portions of 2 Kings 25 found in Jeremiah 52, with the difference that the author of this account of the fall of Jerusalem was probably an eyewitness and participant in the events recorded. He it is who completed the account of the chief historian of Kings beyond the death of Josiah, writing during the Babylonian exile at least as late as the accession of Evil-Merodach, son and successor of Nebuchadnezzar, whose kind treatment of Jehoiachin is the final incident of the whole story. There may have been other special sources lying behind the books of Kings as we now have them, such as special priestly or Temple records, but the above-mentioned are the main sources used by the historian. Though he has without a doubt shaped them to his theological purposes, the historian has given a faithful account from the materials available to him of the story of the kingdom from Solomon to its downfall.

V. The Framework

It is the historian's unique use of the three written sources which he mentions by name that gives his account of the monarchy its distinctive flavor. The encompassing of roughly 400 years of events forced a principle of selectivity upon the historian in his use of these sources. He simply refers the readers to known and presumably available documents for the further details which could not be used to illustrate the lessons of his account. The obvious place to refer to these details, so tantalizing to the modern interpreter, was the formula material at the beginning and end of each king's narrative. The joining of David's death to the beginning of Solomon's consolidation of power occurs in typical phraseology in 1 Kings 2:10–12, with the last phrase repeated at the end of the chapter to indicate the end of the material derived from the Court History of the succession to David's throne. He names his chief source of Solomon's reign at the conclusion of his use of its material—see 1 Kings 11:41–43.

This formula language provides the beginning and end of the accounts of each king of the divided monarchy with monotonous regularity. The historian solved his primary problem of treating contemporaneous monarchs of North Israel and Judah, without fragmenting the story of each, in a logical way. He followed the pattern of telling the whole story of each king whose accession to the throne fell within the length of reign of his neighboring king, then alternating to bring the accounts of that neighboring kingdom up to date.

In the first example of this practice we can see how this would cause some unevenness. During the 22 years of Jeroboam's reign in Israel, Rehoboam, Abijam, and Asa all began their reigns in Judah. But the unusually long reign of Asa necessitated the inclusion of the historian's reference to the war with Baasha before the historian was able to tell how Jeroboam's son Nadab was murdered and his power usurped by this Baasha. One may notice the added reference to the civil war, appended to the concluding formula of Nadab's reign, to see how the historian remedied this unevenness (cf. 1 Kings 15:16,31–32). Then he proceeds to catch up the story of Israel by dealing with the accounts of all her kings whose reigns began during Asa's long tenure in Judah (cf. 1 Kings 15:25 ff.,33 ff.; 16:8 ff.,15 ff.,23 ff.,29 ff.). Consequently, six chapters of North Israelite history intervene between Asa and Jehoshaphat.

He is so committed to the use of these introductory and concluding formulas for the reigns of each king that he even provides them for Zimri, who ruled only seven days! (cf. 1 Kings 16:15,20). The formulas for Judah are more extensive than those for North Israel.

In the introductory material, the historian gave the following information concerning each king: (1) the date of his accession in terms of the year of reign of his neighboring king; (2) the length of his reign in years; (3) the judgment of the historian as to the quailty of his reign in regard to his fidelity to divine expectations. In addition, concerning the kings of Judah, the writer added between items (1) and (2) the age of the particular king and when he began his reign, and between items (2) and (3) the king's mother's name along with that of her father. The latter item is understandably included since, in Judah's polygamous court, the queen mother's identity was counted as vital information; and indeed her influence on the new king's religion was often significant.

For the concluding formulas, the historian (1) cited his written source, (2) sometimes added a terse, summary phrase characterizing the events of that king's reign, and (3) told of his death and the succession of his son to power, occasionally adding information which had been omitted from the beginning formula.

Incorporated within this elaborate and monotonous framework, the language of which so clearly reveals the theological tendencies of the historian, were those further items concerning the religion, building activities, or wars of each king which might serve his purpose. These derive from one of the written or oral sources at his disposal for the period down to the seventh century, at which time he told the dramatic story of good king Josiah and his reforms, events in which the historian was probably a participant as well as a contemporary. The editor who completed the historian's work in the Exile was careful to set the remaining events within a similar framework.

VI. The Chronology

The most technical subject for any detailed consideration of the books of Kings or of the history of the divided monarchy is the chronology. In Israel's earlier history, the difficulties with chronology involve a scarcity of dates as well as a certain lack of precision. But for the three and one-half centuries of the two kingdoms, there is a surprising abundance of data, purporting to be quite precise, all presumably based on official records available to the historian of Kings.

Until the past few decades, it had long been assumed by those who paid most attention to these matters that the system of lengths of reigns and the synchronisms of reigns within each kingdom to contemporary kings in the other were mutually contradictory, and that one or the other would have to be changed or discarded. In addition, both systems seemed too long in time when compared to newly recovered data from Egypt and Mesopotamia. But more recent scholarship in this science of ancient chronology has instead emphasized the reconciling of almost all the biblical data on the basis of clues gleaned partly from the ways in which those surrounding kingdoms counted their reigns. Especially the monumental work of Edwin R. Thiele [2] has provided a right methodology, which assumes that biblical data are accurate and explainable to those who have the patience to search for these clues.

Viewed in this way, the chronology of Kings proves to be amazingly accurate for its day, though most of the dates are still approximations within a few years' variance. Fortunately, through the interrelationships of this relative biblical chronology and the fixed Assyrian chronology, an absolute dating for the biblical events can be attempted. The Assyrian eponym list, a "man-of-the-year" and "event-of-the-year" type of catalog, has been given fixed dates by an eclipse of the sun calculated by astronomers to have occurred in May-June, 763 B.C., at Nineveh. The battle at Qarqar, in which both Ahab of Samaria and Benhadad of Damascus fought against Shalmaneser III of Assyria, is thus datable to 853 B.C. King Jehu of Israel is portrayed on the famous Black Obelisk as paying tribute to the same Shalmaneser in 841 B.C. Other kings, from Menahem to Manasseh, also are recorded as paying tribute; and the dates of these payments are important to the solving of the chronological problems of a very difficult period during the subjection and fall of Israel and the subjection of Judah to the military might of Assyria.

Another important aid to recovering an exact dating for the fall of Assyria and the last days of Judah is the recently discovered Babylonian chronicle. Sometimes it is possible now to date the season, even the month and day, of the events during the years 616 to 587 B.C. which mark the rise of the neo-Babylonian empire at the expense of both Assyria and Judah.[3]

The most important of Thiele's clues for reconciling the biblical data with the chronologies of these surrounding nations is the theory of a number of co-regencies. Some of these overlapping reigns are mentioned in the sources, particularly for Judah, where the practice was much more frequent in the established Davidic dynasty. The book of 1 Kings begins with the story that sets this pattern, as the ailing King David is forced by events to select his son Solomon as his co-regent and successor. Similarly, events also forced this pattern at the end of Judah's history, when Jehoiachin was taken into exile to Babylon. Although he had only reigned three months, both Judean and Babylonian evidence indicate that he continued to be regarded as the legitimate king, whereas his uncle Zedekiah ruled in Jerusalem as a kind of

---

[2] *The Mysterious Numbers of the Hebrew Kings* (rev. ed. Grand Rapids, Mich.: Wm. B. Eerdmans Publishing Co., 1965).

[3] Jack Finegan, *Handbook of Biblical Chronology* (Princeton University Press, 1964), pp. 308–328.

KINGS: INTRODUCTION

co-regent. The biblical records also tell how the leprosy of Azariah (Uzziah) caused him to make Jotham his son a co-regent for a decade at the end of his long reign. Thiele finds evidence for four other co-regencies in Judah, indicated on the chart of dates below by parentheses.

In contrast, there was only one co-regency in Israel; but the greater uncertainty of dynastic succession provided two instances of rival kingship. Tibni was rival to Omri for four years, and Pekah seems to have ruled in Gilead while Menahem and Pekahiah occupied the main kingdom in Samaria. Other clues which help to establish Thiele's system are the different ways of reckoning the new year at different historical periods in the two kingdoms and different ways of counting the accession year of a new king.

VII. Chronology for the Divided Kingdom [4]

Judah		Israel	
Rehoboam	931–913	Jeroboam	931–910
Abijam	913–911		
Asa	911–870	Nadab	910–909
		Baasha	909–886
		Elah	886–885
		Zimri	885
		Omri	885(881)–874
Jehoshaphat	873(870)–848	Ahab	874–853
Jehoram	853(848)–841	Ahaziah	853–852
Ahaziah	841	Joram	852–841
Athaliah	841–835	Jehu	841–814
Joash	835–796	Jehoahaz	814–798
Amaziah	796–767	Jehoash	798–782
Azariah	792(767)–740	Jeroboam II	793(782)–753
		Zechariah	753–752
		Shallum	752
		Mehahem	752–742
		Pekahiah	742–740
Jotham	750(740)–732	Pekah	752(740)–732
Ahaz	735(732)–715	Hoshea	732–722
		Fall of Samaria	721
Hezekiah	715–687		
Manasseh	697(687)–642		
Amon	642–640		
Josiah	640–609		
Jehoahaz	609		
Jehoiakim	609–598		
Jehoiachin	598–597		
Zedekiah	597–587		
Fall of Jerusalem	587		

VIII. The Theology

Certain themes occur over and over in the way that the historian structures his telling of the story of the kings. The underlying and central theme is the inevitable fulfillment of the prophetic judgment word of the Lord. This has to do with the basic covenant theology of the Mosaic faith that obedience to the Lord's commandments

---

[4] Thiele, op. cit., p. 205, with some minor variations based on my own research and that of Gray, pp. 55–74.

brings blessing and disobedience brings cursing or punishment (cf. Deut. 28). To this emphasis on covenant law is the added loyalty to an ideal of kingship associated with the name of David and with the dynastic oracle of Nathan spoken to David (2 Sam. 7). These two themes may be seen in the advice of the dying David to his son and successor, Solomon, in 1 Kings 2:2–4.

The promise to David, that there would never fail to be a descendant of his on the throne at Jerusalem, certainly did not absolve Solomon or any of his successors from the urgent necessity to obey the Lord in their conduct and with wholehearted allegiance. This conditional blessing is communicated to Solomon in a second vision like the one at Gibeon, according to 1 Kings 9:2–9. The division of the kingdom arose because Solomon failed to obey this warning (cf. 1 Kings 11).

This division of the kingdom brings into focus another very important theme of the historian—the absolute necessity for purity and centrality of worship. It was clear from the history of the tribal confederacy that, although there was the central sanctuary of the ark at Shiloh for the annual covenant renewal festival, as long as the local high places (formerly Canaanite shrines) were used in the worship of Yahweh, Israel's loyalties would be divided.

This explains the great emphasis on Solomon's building of the Jerusalem Temple, which the historian thinks of as the one place where the Lord will make his name to dwell (cf. Deut. 12:1–14). This, too, is fulfillment of the promise to David, who himself intended to build the Temple (2 Sam. 7). The story of the dedication of the Temple makes clear that it is above all a place for national prayer and repentance of sin in a time of trouble (1 Kings 8). Although historically the Temple began its life as little more than a royal chapel, situated next to the palace, by Josiah's time it had become a national sanctuary. By virtue of his reform, it is the only true place of worship.

From this point of view, the establishment by Jeroboam of a rival cult in Bethel and Dan, using the dangerous symbol of a golden calf in worship, is rank heresy. Even though God inspired him by the word of Ahijah the prophet to revolt against the oppressive measures of Solomon's monarchy, still the "sins of Jeroboam" became the curse that blighted every northern king and resulted finally in the downfall of Samaria. This is such an important lesson for the historian's own day that he preaches a long sermon when he comes to the downfall of Israel (cf. 2 Kings 17:7–18).

The other villain of the story, besides Jeroboam, was Manasseh, that King of Judah who reversed all the good reforms of Hezekiah, even bringing pagan cult objects into the Temple area itself. It was the sins of Manasseh that king Josiah had to undo; and after the first telling of the story in his era, the judgment of the exilic editor pinpointed these sins of Manasseh as the ultimate cause of destruction and exile (cf. 2 Kings 21:2–16; 24:3–4). This judgment on Manasseh shows that with the fall of Israel, the theme of cultic unity recedes before that of cultic purity. Ultimately, the historian tells his woeful tale of the decline and fall of the Hebrew kingdom to authenticate the high ideal of a pure and unified worship of the Lord, led by an ideal king like a "new David," good king Josiah.

The final verdict of the exilic editor seems to be that there is hope for restoration if the exiles will only learn the lessons of history and repent (cf. 1 Kings 8:46–53). He sees some inkling of hope in the recent release of Jehoiachin, through whom David's legitimate line is reckoned (2 Kings 25:27–30; cf. Ezek. 1:2; Jer. 22:24–30; Hag. 2:20–23; 1 Chron. 3:17,19). Only in an extended sense could this hope be called "messianic." [5] Yet the same prophetic theology in which the Lord entered into controversy with the present kings, ending in their rejection, is that

---

[5] Gerhard von Rad, *Old Testament Theology*, Vol. I, tr. D. M. G. Stalker (New York: Harper & Brothers Publishers, 1962), p. 344.

which turned Israel's hopes toward a future, ideal king of the restored Davidic line.

IX. The Context

The immediate Old Testament setting of the books of Kings was the work of the Deuteronomic historian, but their literary and theological context is broader than that. In the discussion of the sources, it has already been noted that portions of Kings bear a special relation to portions of the books of Chronicles, Isaiah, and Jeremiah. The historical period covered by the books of Kings is the very time most crucial to the growth of Israel's sacred literature. The epic sources of God's dealings with his people from the patriarchs to the Conquest, prefaced by the stories of creation and mankind's beginnings, were probably first collected and written down in the era of Solomon.

The Northern Kingdom had its own version of this national epic, as well as its own codification of divine law, both of which were written and preserved during these centuries. The literature of Israel's Temple worship begins to be collected with David and Solomon and grows throughout the period of the kingdoms. The formal wisdom movement begins with Solomon and continues throughout the period, as is indicated by the growth of the wisdom literature. Most important of all, the institution of Hebrew prophecy grows in relationship to that of monarchy, and the flowering of the great writing prophets is in direct relation to the decline and fall of the Hebrew kingdoms.

It is one of the axioms of modern Old Testament scholarship that the growth of these Old Testament traditions was vitally affected and shaped by the history and worship of the people who preserved them. So one cannot write a commentary on the books of Kings without speaking also of other laws, narratives, psalms, proverbs, and prophetic oracles which provide this broader literary and historical context. Especially, the political role of an Isaiah or Jeremiah is reflected in the stories about these prophets, as well as in their oracles, and reflects back upon a similar role played by Elijah. Then, also, the prophetic theology of history reflected in narratives of Kings finds confirmation in the oracles of the writing prophets, who proclaimed God's controversy with his people, resulting in judgment and destruction. One must continually be reminded that the interpretation of any particular portion of the Old Testament hinges on seeing it in relation to the whole.

X. The Relevance

The books of Kings continue to have importance and meaning for our lives today. When they were first written, the history was being retold during Josiah's reform, or in the Babylonian exile, to show God's people what he had done, was doing, and intended to do through the events interpreted as revelatory. The great optimism that Josiah's reform would restore the kingdom of David and bring in the kingdom of God, proved unwarranted, or at least premature. But even the defeat of exile, the ceasing of kingdom in the usual sense, proved ultimately to deepen and renew Israel's faith that Yahweh God was and is the true King. This faith shines through the telling and retelling of Israel's story.

For example, even when the Northern Kingdom has sunk to its most dangerous level of compromise with Canaanite Baal worship, Elijah is standing in the breach to lead the people to see and reaffirm that not Baal but Yahweh is God. The same prophet who is so strong in the public encounter with rival prophets is seized by fear and self-pity when threatened by their determined sponsor. Indeed, as James so aptly says, "Elijah was a man of like nature with ourselves" (5:17a). The same Lord who answered by fire on Mount Carmel was not in the fire-quake-wind of the storm at Mount Horeb. The same Lord whose angel comforted Elijah on his journey upbraided him with the demand of unfulfilled tasks and ongoing responsibilities. The "still small voice" of revelation drowned out the whinings of self-pity. It still speaks to those ready to listen today. God's remnant will survive the prophetic revolt against Jezebel's Baal (1 Kings 19:18). Neither the onslaughts of Sennacherib (2 Kings 19:30–31) nor the apparent death of the monarchy (2 Kings 24:12 ff.; 25:27 ff.) can ultimately thwart the rule of God among his people. This message of the King of kings lives today.

Outline of 1 Kings

I. The Solomonic kingdom (1 Kings 1:1—11:43)
  1. Succession to the Davidic throne (1:1—2:46)
    (1) Choice of Solomon (1:1–53)
    (2) Consolidation of power (2:1–46)
  2. Wisdom of Solomon (3:1—4:34)
    (1) Dream at Gibeon (3:1–15)
    (2) Judgment of the harlots (3:16–28)
    (3) Officials of Solomon (4:1–19)
    (4) Prosperity and extent of kingdom (4:20–28)
    (5) Reputation for wisdom literature (4:29–34)
  3. Temple of Solomon (5:1—7:51)
    (1) Treaty with Hiram, King of Tyre (5:1–18)
    (2) Time of Temple building (6:1–38)
    (3) Palace and other buildings (7:1–12)
    (4) Metalwork for the Temple (7:13–51)
  4. Dedication festival for the Temple (8:1—9:9)
    (1) Procession of the ark (8:1–11)
    (2) Blessing of the assembly (8:12–21)
    (3) Prayer of dedication (8:22–53)
    (4) Benediction (8:54–61)
    (5) Consecration sacrifices (8:62–66)
    (6) Divine promise and warning (9:1–9)
  5. Commercial enterprises of Solomon (9:10—10:29)
    (1) Sale of twenty cities (9:10–14)
    (2) Forced labor for building projects (9:15–22)
    (3) Red Sea fleet (9:23–28)
    (4) Visit of the queen of Sheba (10:1–13)
    (5) Wealth of Solomon (10:14–22)
    (6) Solomon in his glory (10:23–25)
    (7) Horse and chariot trade (10:26–29)
  6. Apostasy and punishment of Solomon (11:1–43)
    (1) Turning to gods of foreign wives (11:1–8)
    (2) Resulting division of kingdom (11:9–13)
    (3) First adversary, Hadad of Edom (11:14–22)
    (4) Second adversary, Rezon of Damascus (11:23–25)
    (5) Third adversary, Jeroboam of Ephraim (11:26–40)
    (6) Death of Solomon (11:41–43)
II. Beginning of the divided kingdom (12:1—16:34)
  1. The revolt of Jeroboam (12:1–33)
    (1) Assembly at Shechem (12:1–5)
    (2) Foolish policy of Rehoboam (12:6–15)
    (3) Successful rebellion (12:16–24)
    (4) Sins of Jeroboam (12:25–33)
  2. Prophetic judgment on Jeroboam (13:1—14:20)
    (1) Word of the Lord against Bethel (13:1–34)
    (2) Word of Ahijah from Shiloh (14:1–20)
  3. Reign of Rehoboam in Judah (14:21–31)
    (1) Sins of Rehoboam (14:21–24)
    (2) Invasion of Shishak of Egypt (14:25–28)
    (3) Death of Rehoboam (14:29–31)
  4. Reign of Abijam (15:1–8)
  5. Reign of Asa (15:9–24)
    (1) Partial reform by Asa (15:9–15)
    (2) Civil war with Baasha (15:16–22)
    (3) Death of Asa (15:23–24)
  6. Reign of Nadab in Israel (15:25–26)
  7. Revolt of Baasha in Israel (15:27–34)
  8. Doom of Baasha's dynasty (16:1–7)
  9. Revolt of Zimri (16:8–20)
  10. New dynasty of Omri (16:21–28)
  11. Beginning of Ahab's reign (16:29–34)
III. The prophetic revolt (1 Kings 17:1—22:53)
  1. Prophets and Ahab (17:1—22:40)
    (1) Elijah and the drought (17:1–24)
    (2) Contest at Mount Carmel (18:1–46)
    (3) Revelation at Mount Horeb (19:1–21)
    (4) Wars with Benhadad of Aram (20:1–43)
    (5) Vineyard of Naboth in Jezreel (21:1–29)
    (6) Last battle of Ahab (22:1–40)
  2. Reign of Jehoshaphat in Judah (22:41–50)
  3. Beginning of Ahaziah's reign in Israel (22:51–53)

Outline of 2 Kings [6]

Part One: Prophetic Revolution (2 Kings 1:1—13:25; cf. 1 Kings 17:1—2 Kings 13:25)

I. The last days of Elijah (1:1—2:25)
  1. Prophetic judgment upon Ahaziah's faithlessness (1:1–18)
  2. Elisha, Successor to Elijah: the translation of Elijah (2:1–25)
II. Elisha's establishment on the national political scene: his prophetic counsel in the Moabite war (3:1–27)
  1. The Deuteronomic appraisal of Jehoram (3:1–3)
  2. The Moabite war and Elisha's counsel (3:4–27)
III. Prophetic concern for human need: miracles by Elisha (4:1—6:7)
  1. Provision for the prophet's widow and family (4:1–7)
  2. The blessing of motherhood for the Shunammite woman (4:8–37)
  3. "Death in the Pot": The ruined pottage (4:38–41)
  4. The multiplication of the loaves (4:42–44)
  5. The healing of Naaman the Syrian (5:1–27)
  6. The floating axe head (6:1–7)
IV. Elisha and the Aramean wars (6:8—8:15)
  1. Elisha captures an Aramean raiding party (6:8–23)
  2. Deliverance of Samaria from seige (6:24—7:20)
  3. Further consideration for the Shunammite woman (8:1–6)
  4. Elisha's role in the Aramean coup (8:7–15)
V. The rebellion of Jehu and the purge of Baalism (8:16—10:36)
  1. Judah's involvement in the purge of Jehu: a Deuteronomic appraisal of Judean kingship (8:16–29)
  2. Elisha instigates the rebellion of Jehu (9:1–13)
  3. The assassinations that purged Israel of Baalism (9:14—10:27)
  4. An appraisal of Jehu's reign (10:28–36)
VI. Reformation in Judah under Joash (11:1—12:21)
  1. The usurpation of Athaliah and Joash's coronation (11:1–21)
  2. The repair of the Temple: an independent tradition (12:1–16)
  3. The fate of Joash (12:17–21)
VII. The trials of Israel and the death of Elisha (13:1–25)

[6] Prepared by Roy L. Honeycutt, Jr.

  1. Aramean advances under Hazael (13:1–13)
  2. Elisha's prophetic action and the reversal of Hazael (13:14–25)

Part Two: Decades of Bitterness and Defeat in Israel and Judah (14:1—17:41)

I. Sectional warfare between Judah and Israel (14:1–22)
  1. The occasion for the war (14:1–10)
  2. Judah's defeat by Israel (14:11–14)
  3. A summary of Amaziah's reign (14:15–22)
II. A Succession of Evil Kings (14:23—17:6)
  1. Jeroboam II of Israel (14:23–29)
  2. Azariah (Uzziah) of Judah (15:1–7)
  3. Turmoil in Israel (15:8–31)
  4. Two Judean kings (15:32—16:20)
  5. Hoshea, last king of Israel (17:1–6)
III. The fall and subsequent resettlement of Israel: a later appraisal (17:7–41)
  1. A Deuteronomic appraisal of the disintegration of the Northern Kingdom (17:7–23)
  2. A priestly view of the resettlement (17:24–41)

Part Three: Decades of Renewal and Eventual Destruction: The Kingdom of Judah Alone (18:1—25:30)

I. Prophetic renewal: Hezekiah and the Assyrian crisis (18:1—20:21)
  1. Hezekiah's reformation and independence (18:1–12)
  2. The Isaiah tradition (18:13—20:19)
  3. The Deuteronomic appraisal of Hezekiah (20:20–21)
II. Decades of faithlessness and apostasy (21:1–26)
  1. Manasseh (21:1–18)
  2. Amon (21:19–26)
III. Josiah and the religious reformation (22:1—23:30)
  1. Josiah (22:1–2; cf. 23:28–30)
  2. The inception of the reformation (22:3–20)
  3. Implementing the reform (23:1–25)
  4. The failure of the reformation and the last act of Josiah (23:26–30)
IV. The destruction of Jerusalem and the fall of Judah (23:31—25:30)
  1. Jehoahaz (23:31–35)
  2. Jehoiakim (23:36—24:7)
  3. Jehoiachin (24:8–17)
  4. Zedekiah (24:18—25:21)

5. The aftermath of Jerusalem's fall: two appendices (25:22–30)

Selected Bibliography

ALBRIGHT, W. F. *The Biblical Period from Abraham to Ezra*. New York: Harper & Row, 1963.

BRIGHT, JOHN. *A History of Israel*. Philadelphia: The Westminster Press, 1959.

BRUCE, F. F. *Israel and the Nations*. Grand Rapids: Wm. B. Eerdmans Publishing Co., 1963.

DENTAN, ROBERT C. *The First and Second Books of Kings; The First and Second Books of the Chronicles*. ("The Layman's Bible Commentary," Vol. 7.) Richmond: John Knox Press, 1964.

DE VAUX, ROLAND. *Ancient Israel: Its Life and Institutions*. New York: McGraw-Hill, 1961.

FOHRER, GEORG. *Introduction to the Old Testament*. Trans. David E. Green. Nashville: Abingdon Press, 1965.

GOTTWALD, NORMAN K. *All the Kingdoms of the Earth*. New York: Harper & Row, 1964.

GRAY, JOHN. *I and II Kings: A Commentary*. Philadelphia: The Westminster Press, 1963.

HEATON, E. W. *The Hebrew Kingdoms*. ("The New Clarendon Bible: Old Testament." Vol. III.) Oxford: Oxford University Press, 1968.

The Interpreter's Dictionary of the Bible. 4 Vol. Nashville: Abingdon Press, 1962.

MAUCHLINE, J. "I and II Kings," *Peake's Commentary on the Bible*. Ed. MATTHEW BLACK and H. H. ROWLEY. London: Thomas Nelson Ltd., 1962.

MONTGOMERY, JAMES A. and GEHMAN, HENRY SNYDER. *A Critical and Exegetical Commentary on the Books of Kings* in *The International Critical Commentary*. Edinburgh: T. & T. Clark, 1951.

NOTH, MARTIN. *The History of Israel*. New York: Harper & Brothers, 1960.

PRITCHARD, JAMES B., ed. *Ancient Near Eastern Texts Relating to the Old Testament*. Princeton: Princeton University Press, 1950.

ROBINSON, GORDON. *Historians of Israel (1) 1 and 2 Samuel, 1 and 2 Kings*. No. 5 in "Bible Guides." New York: Abingdon Press, 1962.

SNAITH, NORMAN H. "The First and Second Books of Kings: Introduction and Exegesis" *The Interpreter's Bible*, Vol. 3. New York: Abingdon Press, 1954.

THOMAS, D. WINTON, ed. *Documents from Old Testament Times*. London: Thomas Nelson and Sons, Ltd., 1958.

WEISER, ARTUR. *The Old Testament: Its Formation and Development*. Trans. DOROTHEA M. BARTON. New York: Association Press, 1961.

WESTERMANN, CLAUS. *Basic Forms of Prophetic Speech*. Trans. HUGH CLAYTON WHITE. London: Lutterworth Press, 1967.

WRIGHT, G. ERNEST. *Biblical Archaeology*. Philadelphia: Westminster Press, 1957.

Commentary on the Text

I. The Solomonic Kingdom (1 Kings 1:1—11:43)

Solomon was the third king of what is usually called the united monarchy. The reigns of Saul and David are narrated in the books of Samuel. The first half of 1 Kings is the story of the reign of Solomon. The historian introduces his main narrative of the "Acts of Solomon" (chs. 3—11) with an excerpt from another source telling how Solomon came to power.

1. Succession to the Davidic Throne (1:1—2:46)

Reference has already been made in the Introduction to the Court History from which the first two chapters of 1 Kings were taken to provide an introduction to the reign of Solomon. This vivid, eyewitness account of the tragedies that beset David's later years has as its theme the troubles surrounding the succession to David's throne.

(1) Choice of Solomon (1:1–53)

The climax of these troubles comes when David is old and sick, perhaps no longer virile, and therefore presumed to be on his deathbed. The oldest surviving son from David's many marriages, after the murder of Amnon and revolt of Absalom, was Adonijah. But Solomon was the son of his favorite wife, Bathsheba.

a. Old Age of David (1:1–4)

¹ Now King David was old and advanced in years; and although they covered him with clothes, he could not get warm. ² Therefore his servants said to him, "Let a young maiden be sought for my lord the king, and let her wait upon the king, and be his nurse; let her lie in your bosom, that my lord the king may be warm." ³ So they sought for a beautiful maiden throughout all the territory of Israel, and found Abishag the Shunammite, and brought her to the king. ⁴ The maiden was very beautiful; and she became the king's nurse and ministered to him; but the king knew her not.

The scene is set for Adonijah's unsuccessful coup by the first four verses of the chapter. David was about 70 years old (2:11; 2 Sam. 5:4–5), an advanced age in biblical times (Psalm 90:10). Though *they covered him with clothes, he could not get warm.* Since this did not improve the king's condition, his courtiers suggested that a virgin of marriageable age be brought as a concubine into David's harem. She would wait on the king and *be his nurse,* which indicated that she would fill the office of an attendant or perform the duty of service or companionship. *Lie in your bosom* was often used to refer to sexual intimacy, but here it is modified by the primary purpose of the suggested remedy, the supplying of vital body heat by physical contact.

Abishag was from Shunem (modern Solem) on the western slope of the hill of Moreh, northwest of Jezreel, in the territory of Issachar (Josh. 19:18).

But the king knew her not—that is, carnally. This poignant note is included to set the stage for the request of Adonijah, since he would not have dared to ask for one who had actually become David's concubine. It may also reflect the notion of surrounding nations that a people's welfare depended on the potency of their king and that a man could not remain as king if he became impotent (Snaith, pp. 19–20).

b. Ambitions of Adonijah (1:5–10)

⁵ Now Adonijah the son of Haggith exalted himself, saying, "I will be king"; and he prepared for himself chariots and horsemen, and fifty men to run before him. ⁶ His father had never at any time displeased him by asking, "Why have you done thus and so?" He was also a very handsome man; and he was born next after Absalom. ⁷ He conferred with Joab the son of Zeruiah and with Abiathar the priest; and they followed Adonijah and helped him. ⁸ But Zadok the priest, and Benaiah the son of Jehoiada, and Nathan the prophet, and Shimei, and Rei, and David's mighty men were not with Adonijah.

⁹ Adonijah sacrificed sheep, oxen, and fatlings by the Serpent's Stone, which is beside Enrogel, and he invited all his brothers, the king's sons, and all the royal officials of Judah, ¹⁰ but he did not invite Nathan the prophet or Benaiah or the mighty men or Solomon his brother.

Adonijah, David's fourth son, was next in the line of succession after Amnon and Absalom (2 Sam. 3:2–4). Following the bad example of his brother Absalom (2 Sam. 15:1), Adonijah tried to usurp his father's throne. The outrunners were both for safety and for show and evidently comprised a special group in the royal forces since Saul's day (1 Sam. 22:17; de Vaux, pp. 221–222).

David did not challenge his son's pretensions, just as earlier he allowed Absalom to get away with this kind of conduct and worse for four years (2 Sam. 15:7). The historian, in one of his rare moralisms, makes clear the sentimentally lenient, disastrous relationship David had to his sons. The wisdom literature is particularly aware of the father's duty to rebuke and discipline his sons (Prov. 13:24; 19:18; 22:6; 23:13 f.).

Besides David's senility and permissiveness, the historian also notes Adonijah's handsomeness (cf. 1 Sam. 16:12; 2 Sam. 14:25), also his position as the next-oldest surviving son, as giving strength to his bid for the throne. He had secured two able partisans from David's wilderness and Hebron period of leadership as supporters for his court intrigue. Joab was the leader of the tribal militia, a fierce but able general, loyal to David's and his own interests. Abiathar the priest, the last survivor of Eli's household, had been David's consultant during the early period.

The writer then lists the opposition party, the members of which ultimately thwarted Adonijah's claims. These were leaders who had become important in David's Jerusalem period of kingship. Zadok was not of the same priestly line as Abiathar (de Vaux, p. 373). Chronicles gives Zadok an Aaronite genealogy through Eleazar (1 Chron. 24:3), also attributing to him a ministry at the tabernacle at Gibeon (1 Chron. 16:39). Because Zadok is connected with the ark when he first appears in action as David's priest (2 Sam. 15:24-29), some have supposed that he was Uzzah's brother and that he had served before the ark at Kiriathjearim (1 Sam. 7:2; 2 Sam. 6:3-4, translating Ahio as "his brother"). The most popular theory of Zadok's pivotal importance for Israel's religion among modern scholars is that he was serving as priest-king in pre-Davidic, Jebusite Jerusalem.[7]

Benaiah, the son of Jehoida, was general of David's bodyguard of foreign mercenaries, the Cherethithes and Pelethites (2 Sam. 8:18), and also one of his renowned mighty men from his early outlaw band (2 Sam. 23:20-23). But the mastermind of the Solomonic party was Nathan the prophet, who along with Bathsheba succeeded in moving King David to decisive action.

Shimei and Rei are unknown, being given neither title nor pedigree. Shimei is certainly not that son of Gera who had cursed David on the day of his humiliating flight from Absalom (2 Sam. 16:5 ff.). Perhaps he was that other Shimei, mentioned later as Solomon's officer over Benjamin (1 Kings 4:18). Rei probably should be regarded as a title (de Vaux, p. 123).

As Absalom had done at Hebron (2 Sam. 15:12), so Adonijah uses a clan festival as an occasion for being acclaimed king (cf. 1:25). The location of the feast is identified with the modern "Job's Well, south of the junction of Kidron and Hinnom valleys (Wright, p. 126). Adonijah's guest list is included to demonstrate his awareness of the Solomon party at court. The historian notes that Solomon himself was the only one of Adonijah's half brothers uninvited to the feast.

c. Wise Counsel of Nathan (1:11-14)

[11] Then Nathan said to Bathsheba the mother of Solomon, "Have you not heard that Adonijah the son of Haggith has become king and David our lord does not know it? [12] Now therefore come, let me give you counsel, that you may save your own life and the life of your son Solomon. [13] Go in at once to King David, and say to him, 'Did you not, my lord the king, swear to your maidservant, saying, "Solomon your son shall reign after me, and he shall sit upon my throne"? Why then is Adonijah king?' [14] Then while you are still speaking with the king, I also will come in after you and confirm your words."

The succeeding paragraphs of the chapter reveal the literary style of the author of the Court History at its best. Using the device of verbal repetition well known from the oral epic narrative, he sets a series of scenes and dialogues into an urgent sequence that dramatically describes the precipitous, sometimes simultaneous events of that fateful day (Gray, p. 85). The news of Adonijah's attempted coup reaches Nathan who quickly moves to use the influence of David's favorite wife.

The role of Nathan, giving *counsel*, in what is frequently described as merely a court intrigue has surprised some who see his rebuke of David over the Bathsheba affair as a more proper prophetic stance. But in the early period both the priest Abiathar and the seer Gad had served as consultants to David (1 Sam. 22:5; 23:6,9; 2 Sam. 24:11,18). Nathan is here establishing that political role of prophecy in the Jerusalem tradition which Isaiah so well exemplifies two centuries later. His concern for the dynastic succession to David's throne flows properly out of the oracle delivered to David in connection with the Lord's refusal of his offer to build a temple

---

[7] This hypothesis, definitively set forth by H. H. Rowley, "Zadok and Nehushtan," *JBL*, LVIII (1939), pp. 113-141, has been used to explain the predominance of Canaanite influence on the symbolism and architecture of the Solomonic Temple and its cult.

(2 Sam. 7:11 ff.).

Did you not . . . swear—the content of such an oath had not been stated previously in the history and was presumably known only to Nathan, Bathsheba, and very few others. David's neglect in not making his choice public sooner is understandable, not only in terms of his own personality and relationship to his sons, but also in the threat that such a designation might have diminished his own authority in his waning years. A previous interest of Nathan in Solomon, as well as an incidental reference to David's choice of him as successor, may be seen in the special name, Jedidiah (Beloved of Yahweh), which Nathan by word of the Lord gave Solomon at his birth (2 Sam. 12:24–25).

d. Petition of Bathsheba (1:15–21)

15 So Bathsheba went to the king into his chamber (now the king was very old, and Abishag the Shunammite was ministering to the king). 16 Bathsheba bowed and did obeisance to the king, and the king said, "What do you desire?" 17 She said to him, "My lord, you swore to your maidservant by the LORD your God, saying, 'Solomon your son shall reign after me, and he shall sit upon my throne.' 18 And now, behold, Adonijah is king, although you, my lord the king, do not know it. 19 He has sacrificed oxen, fatlings, and sheep in abundance, and has invited all the sons of the king, Abiathar the priest, and Joab the commander of the army; but Solomon your servant he has not invited. 20 And now, my lord the king, the eyes of all Israel are upon you, to tell them who shall sit on the throne of my lord the king after him. 21 Otherwise it will come to pass, when my lord the king sleeps with his fathers, that I and my son Solomon will be counted offenders."

Following Nathan's wise counsel, the queen mother rushed into the king's bedchamber, unbidden by David. This presumptuous manner of entry violated court custom of the ancient Near East, while elsewhere in the scene this is scrupulously followed. Bathsheba improves Nathan's suggested approach (1:13) by changing the question into a statement of fact and adding that the oath was a sacred one. *Adonijah is king* is a statement of fact rather than a question, proved by the actions described next, which the king does not know.

The expression *all Israel* means the whole covenant community, including the tribes of Israel and Judah (2 Sam. 2:4; 5:1–5). Although the religious nation was one people, the political divisions between the two tribal groupings of Israel (North) and Judah (South), which originated early in their history, persisted despite the unifying genius of David's personal achievement and finally resulted in the division of the kingdoms at the death of Solomon (Heaton, pp. 1–2,6).

Bathsheba defines the king's responsibility to designate his successor, not to relinquish his power of kingship. This designation of a co-regent sets a pattern for succession in the Davidic dynasty in Judah which evidently supersedes the principle of primogeniture (Deut. 21:15–17, cf. de Vaux, p. 101).

Be counted offenders means, literally, "become sinners," in the political rather than religious sense. Doubtless Adonijah would have regarded both Bathsheba and Solomon as potentially dangerous rivals until some pretext were found to dispose of them. All who followed Nathan's initiative to stop Adonijah would be similarly accounted guilty of being found on the wrong side.

e. Confirming Speech of Nathan (1:22–27)

22 While she was still speaking with the king, Nathan the prophet came in. 23 And they told the king, "Here is Nathan the prophet." And when he came in before the king, he bowed before the king, with his face to the ground. 24 And Nathan said, "My lord the king, have you said, 'Adonijah shall reign after me, and he shall sit upon my throne'? 25 For he has gone down this day, and has sacrificed oxen, fatlings, and sheep in abundance, and has invited all the king's sons, Joab the commander of the army, and Abiathar the priest; and behold, they are eating and drinking before him, and saying, 'Long live King Adonijah!' 26 But me, your servant, and Zadok the priest, and Benaiah the son of Jehoiada, and your servant Solomon, he has not invited. 27 Has this thing been brought about by my lord the king and

you have not told your servants who should sit on the throne of my lord the king after him?"

The interruption of Bathsheba heightens the dramatic effect (cf. the messengers of Job's misfortunes, Job 1:16–18). By participating in the festival of acclamation, Adonijah's partisans were covenanting by sharing his meal, as well as giving the familiar word of acclamation. The entire list of the uninvited is given (cf. 1:8,10,19); and Nathan implies that, to judge from the public events, David must have designated Adonijah behind their backs.

f. Promise of David (1:28–31)

28 Then King David answered, "Call Bathsheba to me." So she came into the king's presence, and stood before the king. 29 And the king swore, saying, "As the LORD lives, who has redeemed my soul out of every adversity, 30 as I swore to you by the LORD, the God of Israel, saying, 'Solomon your son shall reign after me, and he shall sit upon my throne in my stead'; even so will I do this day." 31 Then Bathsheba bowed with her face to the ground, and did obeisance to the king, and said, "May my lord King David live for ever!"

David's response shows mental agility, if not full physical strength, as he is spurred to action by the double report. Having summoned Bathsheba, the king confirms his original oath of private designation with a second solemn oath of public, immediate action. It is a favorite oath of David (2 Sam. 4:9) on the life of Yahweh, and his ransoming of the king from every distress. The power of the spoken word and the theology of a living and saving God are emphasized by such oaths. Bathsheba responds in courtly language with a wish appropriate to a newly acclaimed king, or an old one. *Forever* refers here, as frequently in the Old Testament, to earthly life.

g. Anointing of Solomon (1:32–40)

32 King David said, "Call to me Zadok the priest, Nathan the prophet, and Benaiah the son of Jehoiada." So they came before the king. 33 And the king said to them, "Take with you the servants of your lord, and cause Solomon my son to ride on my own mule, and bring him down to Gihon; 34 and let Zadok the priest and Nathan the prophet there anoint him king over Israel; then blow the trumpet, and say, 'Long live King Solomon!' 35 You shall then come up after him, and he shall come and sit upon my throne; for he shall be king in my stead, and I have appointed him to be ruler over Israel and over Judah." 36 And Benaiah the son of Jehoiada answered the king, "Amen! May the LORD, the God of my lord the king, say so, 37 As the LORD has been with my lord the king, even so may he be with Solomon, and make his throne greater than the throne of my lord King David."

38 So Zadok the priest, Nathan the prophet, and Benaiah the son of Jehoiada, and the Cherethites and the Pelethites, went down and caused Solomon to ride on King David's mule, and brought him to Gihon. 39 There Zadok the priest took the horn of oil from the tent, and anointed Solomon. Then they blew the trumpet; and all the people said, "Long live King Solomon!" 40 And all the people went up after him, playing on pipes, and rejoicing with great joy, so that the earth was split by their noise.

True to his oath, David summons his three trusted advisers, listed above as the Solomon party, and orders the anointing of Solomon. This account is one of two detailed descriptions in Kings (cf. 2 Kings 11:12–20) of the coronation ritual in Judah (de Vaux, pp. 102–107). David commands a procession to the Gihon spring on the eastern slope of Ophel, the old Jebusite city, and its chief water supply from ancient times.

Ordinary folk still rode on asses (2:40). The horse had not yet been introduced as a riding animal in Israel. But since David had become king, the mule had taken on significance as the riding animal of royalty (cf. 2 Sam. 13:29; 18:9). Solomon's action in riding David's *own mule* was a sign to the people that he, rather than Adonijah, was the king's own designated successor. Zadok anointed Solomon (cf. v. 39), although the authority of prophetic designation was conferred by Nathan.

The prophets from Samuel (1 Sam. 10:1; 16:13) to Elisha (2 Kings 9:1–6) had a prominent part in designating and rejecting kings. Anointing was a sign not only for designation of the next king, but also for the indwelling Spirit of the Lord. Kingship had been by covenant agreement with the people, through tribal representatives (1 Sam. 10:24; 11:15), who frequently had a part in the anointing ceremony (2 Sam. 2:4; 5:3). But with the establishment of the dynasty, Solomon's anointing took on a different meaning as succession to power already recognized. In this departure from the old ways lay the seeds of division, when prophetic designation disagreed with dynastic principle (11:30–31; 12:15–20).

The next act of coronation was the sounding of the trumpet blast. Then came the acclamation, followed by the actual enthronement. *Sit upon my throne* means begin to reign as co-regent of the incumbent. *Ruler* designated the leader or prince of the tribal confederacy, whose leaders specifically refused the Canaanite title, "king," which properly belonged only to Yahweh (Judg. 8:22–23; 1 Sam. 8:4–9). Thus David presumed to pass along to Solomon the privileges of an office formerly conferred only by the elders of Israel and Judah. Benaiah gave the loyal response to the king's decree, and a devout wish for the prosperity of Solomon's kingship.

Cherethites and Pelethites (Cretans and Philistines) made up the mercenary guard over which Benaiah was commander. Their presence was the deciding power factor in the outcome (Bright, pp. 189–90). *The tent* refers to the tent which David had set up for the ark, north of the old city (2 Sam. 6:17), which became sanctuary for Adonijah and Joab (1:50; 2:28). The last verse emphasizes the joyous noise which alerted the Adonijah party some distance away down the Kidron valley.

h. Bad News for Adonijah (1:41–48)

⁴¹ Adonijah and all the guests who were with him heard it as they finished feasting. And when Joab heard the sound of the trumpet, he said, "What does this uproar in the city mean?" ⁴² While he was still speaking, behold, Jonathan the son of Abiathar the priest came; and Adonijah said, "Come in, for you are a worthy man and bring good news." ⁴³ Jonathan answered Adonijah, "No, for our lord King David has made Solomon king; ⁴⁴ and the king has sent with him Zadok the priest, Nathan the prophet, and Benaiah the son of Jehoiada, and the Cherethites and the Pelethites; and they have caused him to ride on the king's mule; ⁴⁵ and Zadok the priest and Nathan the prophet have anointed him king at Gihon; and they have gone up from their rejoicing, so that the city is in an uproar. This is the noise that you have heard. ⁴⁶ Solomon sits upon the royal throne. ⁴⁷ Moreover the king's servants came to congratulate our lord King David, saying, 'Your God make the name of Solomon more famous than yours, and make his throne greater than your throne.' And the king bowed himself upon the bed. ⁴⁸ And the king also said, 'Blessed be the LORD, the God of Israel, who has granted one of my offspring to sit on my throne this day, my own eyes seeing it.'"

The noise of Adonijah's feast was decreasing as that of the acclamation of Solomon kept growing louder. Ths trained ear of the old warrior, Joab, heard the trumpet blast from afar. This was accompanied by *uproar* or tumult and commotion (the Hebrew word could signify the sound of a beehive or a multitude; cf. Ex. 32:17–18).

Jonathan the son of Abiathar had served David well during Absalom's revolt as spy and runner-messenger (2 Sam. 15:27 ff.; 17:17 ff.). Adonijah calls him *a worthy man* and supposes he will *bring good news* (same word which describes prophetic proclamation in Isa. 40:9; 52:7; 61:1, the Greek translation of which, *euangelizō*, means "gospelize"). But the tidings were bad for Adonijah, who was still under the control of his father, King David, whose throne he sought to usurp.

The addition of further details completes the account of the coronation ritual, especially noting the homage paid by David's officials and leading citizens of Jerusalem. David thanks God for his faithfulness to the royal covenant prophecy (2 Sam. 7:12), and the great gift of a son as successor. *My own eyes seeing it* implies a peaceful succession as well as the personal satisfaction of David, who remembers the frustrations of King Saul over this matter as well as the bloody history of his own family.

i. Humbling of Adonijah (1:49–53)

⁴⁹ Then all the guests of Adonijah trembled, and rose, and each went his own way. ⁵⁰ And Adonijah feared Solomon; and he arose, and went, and caught hold of the horns of the altar. ⁵¹ And it was told Solomon, "Behold, Adonijah fears King Solomon; for, lo, he has laid hold of the horns of the altar, saying, 'Let King Solomon swear to me first that he will not slay his servant with the sword.'" ⁵² And Solomon said, "If he prove to be a worthy man, not one of his hairs shall fall to the earth; but if wickedness is found in him, he shall die." ⁵³ So King Solomon sent, and they brought him down from the altar. And he came and did obeisance to King Solomon; and Solomon said to him, "Go to your house."

The partisans of Adonijah knew that their complicity in the rebellion was discovered, leaving them terrified before the wrath of the new king. *Adonijah feared Solomon* because of what he had doubtless planned to do to Solomon, it being customary for usurpers to eliminate all rivals (15:28–29; 2 Kings 9—10). Adonijah fled to sacred ground for sanctuary and grasped the most sacred part of the altar, its horns. The custom of temporary asylum was known in other ancient Near Eastern countries. It is provided for in Israelite law only in the case of the manslaughterer (Ex. 21:12–14). This is related to the more permanent protection of the cities of refuge (Num. 35:9–34; Deut. 19:1–13). Word reached Solomon of Adonijah's action and his fearful insistence on an oath of clemency. The verbal oath was sacred and unretractable, once solemnly uttered. *Not one of his hairs shall fall to the earth* is a vivid oath of pardon, of popular and royal usage (1 Sam. 14:45; 2 Sam. 14:11). Solomon gave a conditional pardon depending on trustworthiness, and forbidding *wickedness*—political intrigue. *Go to your house* indicates a good behavior in the matter of forswearing all political ambition and activity. Adonijah was hardly under house arrest (2:13 ff.).

This marks the end of Adonijah's brief rebellion, with the story of his personal demise told in the next chapter. It is useless to speculate whether he would have made a better king than Solomon (Dentan, p. 21). He was spoiled and impetuous like his half brothers, Amnon and Absalom, whereas Solomon seems deliberate and circumspect in his administrative wisdom.

(2) Consolidation of Power (2:1–46)

The anointing of Solomon served to thwart temporarily the ambitions of Adonijah. But Solomon's throne power was not yet secure. As long as David lived, Solomon could only act as his co-regent and designated son. Hence, it was only after the death of David that he could act decisively to silence permanently all opposition to his kingship. In the case of two individual enemies, there was the further obligation to carry out the will of his dying father concerning the clearing of bloodguilt and curse from the dynasty.

a. Last Wishes of David (2:1–9)

¹ When David's time to die drew near, he charged Solomon his son, saying, ² "I am about to go the way of all the earth. Be strong, and show yourself a man, ³ and keep the charge of the LORD your God, walking in his ways and keeping his statutes, his commandments, his ordinances, and his testimonies, as it is written in the law of Moses, that you may prosper in all that you do and wherever you turn; ⁴ that the LORD may establish his word which he spoke concerning me, saying, 'If your sons take heed to their way, to walk before me in faithfulness with all their heart and with all their soul, there shall not fail you a man on the throne of Israel.'
⁵ "Moreover you know also what Joab the son of Zeruiah did to me, how he dealt with the two commanders of the armies of Israel, Abner the son of Ner, and Amasa the son of Jether, whom he murdered, avenging in time of peace blood which had been shed in war, and putting innocent blood upon the girdle about my loins, and upon the sandals on my feet. ⁶ Act therefore according to your wisdom, but do not let his gray head go down to Sheol in peace. ⁷ But deal loyally with the sons of Barzillai the Gileadite, and let them be among those who eat at your table; for with such loyalty they met me when I fled from Absalom your brother. ⁸ And there is also with you Shimei the son of Gera, the Benjaminite from Bahurim, who cursed me with a grievous curse on the day when I went to Mahanaim; but when he came down to meet me at the Jordan,

I swore to him by the Lord, saying, 'I will not put you to death with the sword.' ⁹ Now therefore hold him not guiltless, for you are a wise man; you will know what you ought to do to him, and you shall bring his gray head down with blood to Sheol."

In the Old Testament, a man's dying words were especially significant. *The way of all the earth* confirms that David shared the traditional Hebrew views of Sheol, the grave, with no clear evidence of belief in life after death. *Show yourself a man* is equivalent to "play the man" (cf. 1 Sam. 4:9). *The law of Moses* refers to the law for the king (cf. Deut. 17:18–20). This is a key passage for the judgment of the behavior of the other kings of the Davidic dynasty, as to whether they lived up to its ideal.

His word refers back to the dynastic oracle of Nathan (2 Sam. 7:11–16), but in terms emphasizing its conditional nature. *Faithfulness* emphasizes covenant truthfulness and fidelity, and therefore involves total commitment. The king must be a virtuous example for all God's people. The same qualifications are an abiding ideal for leadership in God's kingdom through the ages. The Old Testament does not gloss over the human characteristics of its heroes —hence David's charge to Solomon in vv. 5–9. David cites two instances of Joab's brutality, in which the men whom he murdered had an agreement with David and should have received safe conduct from his men. But both were potential rivals. So Joab was looking out for his own interests, which he interpreted as those of David.

But this charge by David to Solomon is not an expression of personal vengeance; it is rather the satisfaction of a primitive idea of the danger to the dynasty of unavenged innocent blood (cf. 2 Sam. 21:6–9). Some scholars have insisted that this is so unlike David's generosity that these verses must have been added by an editor to justify Solomon's treatment of Joab.⁸ That this explanation is unnecessary is proved by the inclusion of Shimei, who was no part of Adonijah's pretensions.

Act therefore according to your wisdom (cf. also v. 9) means practical political adroitness. The manner of one's death seemed to affect his existence in Sheol, so that a violent death would be undesirable, though in Joab's case appropriate. *Deal loyally with the sons of Barzillai*—a more acceptable charge according to our sensibilities is David's remembrance in "loyal love" of this Transjordanian chieftain (2 Sam. 17:27–29; 19:31–40).

The power of Shimei's curse was still active against the dynasty, according to the ancient belief in the efficacy of the solemnly uttered word. Even though David had forgiven Shimei (2 Sam. 19:23), evidently he felt that the technical terms of his oath would be nullified by his death. Behind these dreadful commands of David lies his concern that his successor should inherit a throne unencumbered by any old impediments.

b. Death of David (2:10–12)

¹⁰ Then David slept with his fathers, and was buried in the city of David. ¹¹ And the time that David reigned over Israel was forty years; he reigned seven years in Hebron, and thirty-three years in Jerusalem. ¹² So Solomon sat upon the throne of David his father; and his kingdom was firmly established.

Slept with his fathers is the regular expression in Kings for the death of the reigning king, including burial in the family tomb. David's tomb is thought to have been identified through recent excavations (de Vaux, p. 58). *The kingdom was firmly established* fits better in v. 46, where it provides the editorial notice of the end of the court history.

c. Foolish Request of Adonijah (2:13–18)

¹³ Then Adonijah the son of Haggith came to Bathsheba the mother of Solomon. And she said, "Do you come peaceably?" He said, "Peaceably." ¹⁴ Then he said, "I have something to say to you." She said, "Say on." ¹⁵ He said, "You know that the kingdom was mine, and that all Israel fully expected me to reign; however the kingdom has turned about and

---

⁸ Theodore H. Robinson, *A History of Israel* (Oxford: Clarendon Press, 1932), pp. 244–245.

become my brother's, for it was his from the Lord. 16 And now I have one request to make of you; do not refuse me." She said to him, "Say on." 17 And he said, "Pray ask King Solomon—he will not refuse you—to give me Abishag the Shunammite as my wife." 18 Bathsheba said, "Very well; I will speak for you to the king."

It is rather ironic that Adonijah thought he could use Bathsheba, who had helped Nathan to achieve the anointing of Solomon. The death of David provided the opportune time for Adonijah to make his next political move, if he intended to do so. According to the rule of primogeniture, Adonijah should not have been demoted in favor of a younger son (Deut. 21:15-17; cf. de Vaux, pp. 53, 100–101). But he expresses what the historian and his people believed, that Yahweh is the Lord of history and is the source of all events.

Give me Abishag was a foolish request, even if David's beautiful nurse had not become his concubine, since she was included in his harem. Perhaps the historian is attributing to Adonijah the same lust that proved Amnon's downfall and which so poignantly mirrored the sins of his father David.

d. Elimination of Adonijah (2:19-25)

19 So Bathsheba went to King Solomon, to speak to him on behalf of Adonijah. And the king rose to meet her, and bowed down to her; then he sat on his throne, and had a seat brought for the king's mother; and she sat on his right. 20 Then she said, "I have one small request to make of you; do not refuse me." And the king said to her, "Make your request, my mother; for I will not refuse you." 21 She said, "Let Abishag the Shunammite be given to Adonijah your brother as his wife." 22 King Solomon answered his mother, "And why do you ask Abishag the Shunammite for Adonijah? Ask for him the kingdom also; for he is my elder brother, and on his side are Abiathar the priest and Joab the son of Zeruiah." 23 Then King Solomon swore by the Lord, saying, "God do so to me and more also if this word does not cost Adonijah his life! 24 Now therefore as the Lord lives, who has established me, and placed me on the throne of David my father, and who has made me a house, as he promised, Adonijah shall be put to death this day." 25 So King Solomon sent Benaiah the son of Jehoiada; and he struck him down, and he died.

Though Bathsheba regarded the request as only a small favor, Solomon interpreted it as the sort of political "wickedness" that he had expressly forbidden when he released Adonijah to his house (1:52-53). The right of the father's harem was a significant right of succession (2 Sam. 3:7; 12:8; 16:21-22; cf. de Vaux, p. 116). Solomon had no political alternative other than to put this interpretation upon it. The mention of *Abiathar . . . Joab* shows the relative insecurity of the new king's position, and also serves as an agenda for the elimination of all opposition. *God do so to me* is an emphatic undesignated curse or symbolic gesture designed to authenticate the truth of the oath of which God is the guardian (*IDB*, III, pp. 575–577). *Benaiah . . . struck him down*—the first of a bloody trilogy of executions by the loyal strong man of Solomon's partisans.

e. Banishment of Abiathar (2:26-27)

26 And to Abiathar the priest the king said, "Go to Anathoth, to your estate; for you deserve death. But I will not at this time put you to death, because you bore the ark of the Lord God before David my father, and because you shared in all the affliction of my father." 27 So Solomon expelled Abiathar from being priest to the Lord, thus fulfilling the word of the Lord which he had spoken concerning the house of Eli in Shiloh.

Anathoth was a small village just north of Jerusalem, near Nob, the last sanctuary of the house of Eli. King Saul's slaughter of this whole priestly family for aiding the escaping David caused Abiathar to join David as his priest during his outlaw days (1 Sam. 21—22). *At this time* is an implied threat which puts Abiathar on his good behavior during his banishment. Some scholars propose a textual emendation of *ark* to "ephod" (cf. 1 Sam. 14:18; Montgomery, p. 100). But this is unnecessary for Abiathar had indeed borne the ark since its establishment in the Jerusalem tent-sanctuary of David (2 Sam. 15:24–29).

Solomon expelled Abiathar from the Jerusalem sanctuary. The king could hardly have prevented Abiathar from serving as priest of the local high place in Anathoth where there were still priests in Jeremiah's day (Jer. 1:1). The Deuteronomic history is bound together by a chain of prediction-fulfillments. The historian is referring to the prediction by the anonymous man of God to Eli (1 Sam. 2:27–36). The confirmation by subsequent event was one of the distinguishing marks of true prophecy (Deut. 18:21–22).

f. Blood Vengeance on Joab (2:28–35)

28 When the news came to Joab—for Joab had supported Adonijah although he had not supported Absalom—Joab fled to the tent of the LORD and caught hold of the horns of the altar. 29 And when it was told King Solomon, "Joab has fled to the tent of the LORD, and behold, he is beside the altar," Solomon sent Benaiah the son of Jehoiada, saying, "Go, strike him down." 30 So Benaiah came to the tent of the LORD, and said to him, "The king commands, 'Come forth.'" But he said, "No, I will die here." Then Benaiah brought the king word again, saying, "Thus said Joab, and thus he answered me." 31 The king replied to him, "Do as he has said, strike him down and bury him; and thus take away from me and from my father's house the guilt for the blood which Joab shed without cause. 32 The LORD will bring back his bloody deeds upon his own head, because, without the knowledge of my father David, he attacked and slew with the sword two men more righteous and better than himself, Abner the son of Ner, commander of the army of Israel, and Amasa the son of Jether, commander of the army of Judah. 33 So shall their blood come back upon the head of Joab and upon the head of his descendants for ever; but to David, and to his descendants, and to his house, and to his throne, there shall be peace from the LORD for evermore." 34 Then Benaiah the son of Jehoiada went up, and struck him down and killed him; and he was buried in his own house in the wilderness. 35 The king put Benaiah the son of Jehoiada over the army in place of Joab, and the king put Zadok the priest in the place of Abiathar.

Joab knew that he was next on Solomon's list. *Although he had not supported Absalom* indicates that the historian remembers Joab's loyalty to David during the most trying and crucial revolt of his favorite son. Joab's support of Adonijah was not intended as any disloyalty to David, whose legitimate successor was presumed to be his oldest surviving son. The claim of sanctuary which had availed for Adonijah (1:50 ff.) could not avail for Joab. The fearfulness of violating the altar and its potent horns by such an execution is shown by Benaiah's reluctance and the necessity for a second command. Joab's preference to die at the altar is honored by Solomon, and this second sentence of execution provides a speech of justification for carrying out his father's last wishes regarding Joab's *bloody deeds* (cf. vv. 5–6). The words *without cause . . . two men more righteous and better than himself* were not in the charge of David. This does not mask the political benefit to Solomon of getting rid of a dangerous old warrior.

The final irony of Joab's long service as chief strongman to David is that the same ruthlessness by which he put down all his rivals is the instrument by which his successor eliminates him. God's judgment on brutal violence is well expressed by Jesus' word in Gethsemane, "All who take the sword will perish by the sword" (Matt. 26:52).

g. Retribution on Shimei (2:36–46)

36 Then the king sent and summoned Shimei, and said to him, "Build yourself a house in Jerusalem, and dwell there, and do not go forth from there to any place whatever. 37 For on the day you go forth, and cross the brook Kidron, know for certain that you shall die; your blood shall be upon your own head." 38 And Shimei said to the king, "What you say is good; as my lord the king has said, so will your servant do." So Shimei dwelt in Jerusalem many days.

39 But it happened at the end of three years that two of Shimei's slaves ran away to Achish, son of Maacah, king of Gath. And when it was told Shimei, "Behold, your slaves are in Gath," 40 Shimei arose and saddled an ass, and went to Gath to Achish, to seek his slaves; Shimei went and brought his slaves from Gath. 41 And when Solomon was told that Shimei had gone from Jerusalem to Gath and returned, 42 the king sent and summoned Shimei, and said to him, "Did I not make you swear by the LORD, and solemnly admonish you, saying, 'Know for

certain that on the day you go forth and go to any place whatever, you shall die'? And you said to me, 'What you say is good; I obey.' ⁴³ Why then have you not kept your oath to the LORD and the commandment with which I charged you?" ⁴⁴ The king also said to Shimei, "You know in your own heart all the evil that you did to David my father; so the LORD will bring back your evil upon your own head. ⁴⁵ But King Solomon shall be blessed, and the throne of David shall be established before the LORD for ever." ⁴⁶ Then the king commanded Benaiah the son of Jehoiada; and he went out and struck him down, and he died.

So the kingdom was established in the hand of Solomon.

Shimei was a Benjaminite from Bahurim, wealthy enough to lead a thousand men to meet David when he begged amnesty for the terrible curse (2 Sam. 19:16 f.). The sole survivor of Saul's family is to stay in Jerusalem. *The brook Kidron* is in the valley just east of Jerusalem and would have to be crossed going to Benjaminite territory. Shimei readily accepted the conditions of amnesty. The extradition of runaway slaves was provided for in Babylonian law and was known throughout the Near East in the second millennium B.C. (Montgomery, p. 97). Personal negotiations were often necessary in such cases—which may account for Shimei's going to Gath for them. As the king's rebuke indicates, oath-breaking was a severe crime. *King Solomon shall be blessed* in being rid of the old curse, and any harmful effects of it. By discharging the last wishes of his father, Solomon claims again the dynastic promise. Shimei could have well afforded to let the two slaves go had he realized how scrupulously Solomon would guard the oath.

The kingdom was established. The Septuagint adds at this point a compendium or miscellany of matters about Solomon. With this note the historian concludes his use of the marvelous documentary source about the succession to the Davidic throne.

2. Wisdom of Solomon (3:1—4:34)

The next nine chapters of 1 Kings may be viewed as a unit in which the historian makes use of the "book of the Acts of Solomon" (cf. 11:41 f.). The style is episodic and anecdotal, and contains a variety of materials. The wisdom of Solomon is of two kinds. First, there is the administrative wisdom to govern God's people, for which he prays to God in his dream at Gibeon. Then there is a proverbial wisdom associated with Solomon's authorship of Wisdom Literature.

(1) Dream at Gibeon (3:1–15)

The historian authenticates the choice of Solomon to succeed David by telling the story of Solomon's prayer for wisdom, and the Lord's gracious answer granting his wish. But first the historian includes a chronological note about Solomon's early marriage to the daughter of Pharaoh. This serves the purpose of beginning the story of Solomon where it will end, with the story of his apostasy to the religions of his foreign wives.

a. Marriage Alliance with Pharaoh (3:1–2)

¹ Solomon made a marriage alliance with Pharaoh king of Egypt; he took Pharaoh's daughter, and brought her into the city of David, until he had finished building his own house and the house of the LORD and the wall around Jerusalem. ² The people were sacrificing at the high places, however, because no house had yet been built for the name of the LORD.

It was part of Solomon's foreign policy, by which he kept the peace and established trade relations with many nations, that he should take many foreign wives in marriage alliances. As the first of these, the daughter of Pharaoh became Solomon's queen, with her own special palace. This was a unique arrangement, since previous Pharaohs had refused to give their daughters in marriage to foreign kings. With this notice belong those further words about Pharaoh's daughter (9:16,24) where it is told that Solomon received the destroyed city of Gezer as a dowry.

b. Prayer of Solomon (3:3–9)

³ Solomon loved the LORD, walking in the statutes of David his father; only, he sacrificed and burnt incense at the high places. ⁴ And the

king went to Gibeon to sacrifice there, for that was the great high place; Solomon used to offer a thousand burnt offerings upon that altar. ⁵ At Gibeon the Lord appeared to Solomon in a dream by night; and God said, "Ask what I shall give you." ⁶ And Solomon said, "Thou hast shown great and steadfast love to thy servant David my father, because he walked before thee in faithfulness, in righteousness, and in uprightness of heart toward thee; and thou hast kept for him this great and steadfast love, and hast given him a son to sit on his throne this day. ⁷ And now, O Lord my God, thou hast made thy servant king in place of David my father, although I am but a little child; I do not know how to go out or come in. ⁸ And thy servant is in the midst of thy people whom thou hast chosen, a great people, that cannot be numbered or counted for multitude. ⁹ Give thy servant therefore an understanding mind to govern thy people, that I may discern between good and evil; for who is able to govern this thy great people?"

The historian introduces the prayer by giving a religious estimate of Solomon. *Solomon loved the Lord,* but a restriction has to be added—*only, he sacrificed . . . at the high places,* especially the great high place at Gibeon. Gibeon (modern el-Jib), some six miles northwest of Jerusalem, has been recently excavated by J. B. Pritchard (cf. *IDB,* II, 391–393). The tabernacle with its bronze altar of sacrifice was said to be there (1 Chron. 16:39).

Perhaps Solomon had gone to Gibeon, not only to sacrifice burnt offerings, but to inquire of the Lord. A very common method of divine communication was believed to be a significant dream (cf. 1 Sam. 28:6). Such a dream frequently occurred in a sanctuary (cf. Jacob, Gen. 28:11–16, and Samuel, 1 Sam. 3:3–9). This account has been compared to dream revelations to various Pharaohs of Egypt. In the Canaanite religious literature from Ras Shamra, both King Keret and the ancient worthy Daniel (cf. Ezek. 14:14,20; 28:3) have dream visions (Gray, p. 120).

Ask what I shall give you. The dream is here a means of direct revelation of a word of God, and not of symbols needing interpretation. This mysterious command by God turns out to be a testing of the young king's priorities. Solomon responds with the courtly language of humble subservience to God. He expresses inadequacy concerning the burdens of his new office and the everyday management of the affairs of state. The population had increased noticeably during the united monarchy (Albright, pp. 55–56). *An understanding mind to govern* is literally "a hearing heart to judge," and refers to that practical wisdom required of the king as court of appeal for difficult cases such as the one that follows. *Discern between good and evil* seems therefore to refer to legal decision here. This rather pious prayer must be balanced against the realistic account of how he failed to live up to its ideals (cf. 11:4,6).

c. Answer of the Lord (3:10–15)

¹⁰ It pleased the Lord that Solomon had asked this. ¹¹ And God said to him, "Because you have asked this, and have not asked for yourself long life or riches or the life of your enemies, but have asked for yourself understanding to discern what is right, ¹² behold, I now do according to your word. Behold, I give you a wise and discerning mind, so that none like you has been before you and none like you shall arise after you. ¹³ I give you also what you have not asked, both riches and honor, so that no other king shall compare with you, all your days. ¹⁴ And if you will walk in my ways, keeping my statutes and my commandments, as your father David walked, then I will lengthen your days."
¹⁵ And Solomon awoke, and behold, it was a dream. Then he came to Jerusalem, and stood before the ark of the covenant of the Lord, and offered up burnt offerings and peace offerings, and made a feast for all his servants.

The granting of Solomon's request for wisdom by God reminds one of the word of James (1:5). God congratulated the young king for his value judgments and for the unselfishness of his prayer. He might have made selfish or even vengeful requests, but he thought first of his responsibilities to God's people. Were one to evaluate the reign of Solomon purely from a human standpoint, his wealth might be attributed to his commercial genius. But the particular interpretation of Scripture is that his wisdom was a special gift of God, so that all which his administrative and practical wisdom earned is also a gift of God. The Davidic covenant was made conditional to each succeeding generation of the dynasty, the length of one's earthly reign depending upon his obedience to God. This scene serves to authenticate the leadership of Solomon over God's people, the dream revelation having taken the place of the charismatic leadership of earlier days.

(2) *Judgment of the Harlots* (3:16–28)

16 Then two harlots came to the king, and stood before him. 17 The one woman said, "Oh, my lord, this woman and I dwell in the same house; and I gave birth to a child while she was in the house. 18 Then on the third day after I was delivered, this woman also gave birth; and we were alone; there was no one else with us in the house, only we two were in the house. 19 And this woman's son died in the night, because she lay on it. 20 And she arose at midnight, and took my son from beside me, while your maidservant slept, and laid it in her bosom, and laid her dead son in my bosom. 21 When I rose in the morning to nurse my child, behold, it was dead; but when I looked at it closely in the morning, behold, it was not the child that I had borne." 22 But the other woman said, "No, the living child is mine, and the dead child is yours." The first said, "No, the dead child is yours, and the living child is mine." Thus they spoke before the king.

23 Then the king said, "The one says, 'This is my son that is alive, and your son is dead'; and the other says, 'No; but your son is dead, and my son is the living one.'" 24 And the king said, "Bring me a sword." So a sword was brought before the king. 25 And the king said, "Divide the living child in two, and give half to the one, and half to the other." 26 Then the woman whose son was alive said to the king, because her heart yearned for her son, "Oh, my lord, give her the living child, and by no means slay it." But the other said, "It shall be neither mine nor yours; divide it." 27 Then the king answered and said, "Give the living child to the first woman, and by no means slay it; she is its mother." 28 And all Israel heard of the judgment which the king had rendered; and they stood in awe of the king, because they perceived that the wisdom of God was in him, to render justice.

The Targum is embarrassed by the term *harlots* and reads "innkeepers." Prostitution was tolerated in Israelite society as a necessary evil, though fornication with harlots was regarded as unwise (Prov. 23:26–28). It of course stands condemned in the light of the whole tenor of biblical teaching. In the present case, the harlot is seen as one helpless before the law, with no one to plead her case. Therefore special appeal is made to the king. The plaintiff in the case tells a vivid story of a heartless crime, to which in the nature of the case there would have been no witnesses. Her major premise is that a mother will recognize her own child even in early infancy. The defendant merely disputes the truthfulness of the story.

The young king shows a divine wisdom beyond his years, a discernment and practical sagacity much admired in Israel. His stratagem for getting at the truth is a decisive, shocking proposal to kill the remaining child. The love of the real mother is a tender certainty upon which the king realizes he can depend. The sentence of judgment says nothing of the punishment of the other woman who had been guilty of such cruelty. The whole point of the story is not the case itself but the wisdom by which it was settled, *the wisdom of God.*

(3) *Officials of Solomon* (4:1–19)

These records are included from the annals to illustrate Solomon's administrative genius; they follow a tendency begun under David (cf. 2 Sam. 8:15–18; 20:23–26).

a. Court Officials (4:1–6)

1 King Solomon was king over all Israel, 2 and these were his high officials: Azariah the son of Zadok was the priest; 3 Elihoreph and Ahijah the sons of Shisha were secretaries; Jehoshaphat the son of Ahilud was recorder; 4 Benaiah the son of Jehoiada was in command of the army; Zadok and Abiathar were priests; 5 Azariah the son of Nathan was over the officers; Zabud the son of Nathan was priest and king's friend; 6 Ahishar was in charge of the palace; and Adoniram the son of Abda was in charge of the forced labor.

The **high officials** (lit., princes) were Solomon's cabinet or department heads. (1) Azariah, son of Zadok, was the priest and successor to his father. This indicates that the list refers to a time later in Solomon's administration (modifying v. 4b). (2) Elihoreph and Ahijah, sons of Shisha, were the secretaries, keepers of official documents. (3) Jehoshaphat, son of Ahilud, was recorder, who called matters to the king's attention (same as David's recorder). (4) Benaiah, son of Jehoida, was commander of Solomon's strong standing army. (5) Azariah, son of Nathan, was chief tax collector over the district officers mentioned in 4:7–19. (6) Zabud, son of Nathan, was the "king's friend," a royal counselor like his father. (7) Ahishar, in charge of the palace, was the royal chamberlain. The three officials—secretary, recorder, and chamberlain—were modeled after the organization of the Egyptian court (de Vaux, pp. 129–132). (8) Adoniram, in charge of the forced labor, has been identified with the Adoram mentioned late in David's reign, and again after Solomon's death (2 Sam. 20:24; 1 Kings 12:18).

b. Provincial Officials (4:7–19)

7 Solomon had twelve officers over all Israel, who provided food for the king and his household; each man had to make provision for one month in the year. 8 These were their names: Benhur, in the hill country of Ephraim; 9 Bendeker, in Makaz, Shaalbim, Bethshemesh, and Elonbethhanan; 10 Benhesed, in Arubboth (to him belonged Soco and all the land of Hepher); 11 Benabinadab, in all Naphathdor (he had Taphath the daughter of Solomon as his wife); 12 Baana the son of Ahilud, in Taanach, Megiddo, and all Bethshean which is beside Zarethan below Jezreel, and from Bethshean to Abelmeholah, as far as the other side of Jokmeam; 13 Bengeber, in Ramothgilead (he had the villages of Jair the son of Manasseh, which are in Gilead, and he had the region of Argob, which is in Bashan, sixty great cities with walls and bronze bars); 14 Ahinadab the son of Iddo, in Mahanaim; 15 Ahimaaz, in Naphtali (he had taken Basemath the daughter of Solomon as his wife); 16 Baana the son of Hushai, in Asher and Bealoth; 17 Jehoshaphat the son of Paruah, in Issachar; 18 Shimei the son of Ela, in Benjamin; 19 Geber the son of Uri, in the land of Gilead, the country of Sihon king of the Amorites and of Og king of Bashan. And there was one officer in the land of Judah.

This list also comes from later in Solomon's kingship since two of the district governors were sons-in-law to Solomon (4:11,15). The *twelve officers* does not reflect the twelve-tribe confederacy, but rather a practical measure to keep the large and elaborate court establishment in Jerusalem in provisions. According to the descriptions of these district boundaries, Solomon deliberately changed the old tribal boundaries to gain firmer control and, also, to balance the economic resources of the districts.[9]

The geographical ordering of the districts begins with the Ephraimite hill country. The next three districts lie to the west, one to the north, two on the east, three in Galilee, and two in the south. The Hebrew text of v. 19 does not have the name *Judah*, except as the first word of the next verse. There are twelve districts without Judah, and some have supposed that Solomon exempted Judah from the burden of taxation. It is likely that Judah had already been organized on a separate basis by David (de Vaux, pp. 133–135).

(4) Prosperity and Extent of the Kingdom (4:20–28)

20 Judah and Israel were as many as the sand by the sea; they ate and drank and were happy. 21 Solomon ruled over all the kingdoms from the Euphrates to the land of the Philistines and to the border of Egypt; they brought tribute and served Solomon all the days of his life.

22 Solomon's provision for one day was thirty cors of fine flour, and sixty cors of meal, 23 ten fat oxen, and twenty pasture-fed cattle, a hundred sheep, besides harts, gazelles, roebucks, and fatted fowl. 24 For he had dominion over all the region west of the Euphrates from Tiphsah to Gaza, over all the kings west of the Euphrates; and he had peace on all sides round about him. 25 And Judah and Israel dwelt in safety, from Dan even to Beersheba, every man under his vine and under his fig tree, all the days of Solomon. 26 Solomon also had forty thousand stalls of horses for his chariots, and twelve thousand horsemen. 27 And those officers supplied provisions for King Solomon, and for all who came to King Solomon's table, each one in his month; they let nothing be lacking. 28 Barley also and straw for the

---

[9] G. Ernest Wright, "The Provinces of Solomon," *Eretz-Israel*, Vol. 8 (1967), pp. 58–68.

horses and swift steeds they brought to the place where it was required, each according to his charge.

This miscellany includes statements of the kingdom's prosperity (vv. 20,25), of the extent of the empire (vv. 21,24), of the provisions for the court (vv. 22–23,27), and the chariot animals (vv. 26,28). Population growth, indicated by *as many as the sand by the sea,* was a sign of prosperity (cf. Gen. 22:17). An idealization of the peace and material prosperity of the Israelite farmer, each dwelling contentedly *under his vine and under his fig tree,* becomes a typical description of Hebrew everyday happiness (2 Kings 18:31; Mic. 4:4; Zech. 3:10).

The ideal extent of Solomon's empire is given twice: first in general terms in v. 21 and then in more precise terms in v. 24—*from Tiphsah to Gaza.* The military conquests of David had been consolidated through trade agreements by Solomon. Such a Syro-Palestinian empire was only possible when the greater empires of Egypt and Mesopotamia were weak. Tiphsah was a crossing place at the great western bend of the Euphrates river, the northeastern boundary of the Aramean kingdom of Hamath (2 Sam. 8:3–12). The southern extent was Gaza, the southernmost of three Philistine coastal cities which maintained a measure of independence. On the east, Edom, Moab, and Ammon were under Solomon's direct control. Phoenicia retained its independence through its trade agreements with Solomon (Bright, pp. 192–193, Plate V).

The daily provision for Solomon's elaborate court establishment illustrates what the district officers were responsible for providing each day of their particular month. If a "measure" equals 6.5 bushels, each district would be taxed about 5000 bushels of flour, 10,000 bushels of meal, 900 oxen, and 3,000 sheep, besides the deer and fowl. Assuming the district population was less than 100,000 persons, this was indeed a "heavy yoke" of taxation (12:4; cf. Albright, p. 56).

Part of Solomon's glory was his extensive force of horses and chariots. *Forty thousand* should be emended to read "four thousand" (cf. one LXX MS; 2 Chron. 9:25). This would fit quite well with the figure of 1400 chariots (10:26). *Twelve thousand horsemen* refers not to cavalry but to charioteers or their horses. The district officers also had to provide the grain and straw for the horses.

(5) *Reputation for Wisdom Literature (4:29–34)*

²⁹ And God gave Solomon wisdom and understanding beyond measure, and largeness of mind like the sand on the seashore, ³⁰ so that Solomon's wisdom surpassed the wisdom of all the people of the east, and all the wisdom of Egypt. ³¹ For he was wiser than all other men, wiser than Ethan the Ezrahite, and Heman, Calcol, and Darda, the sons of Mahol; and his fame was in all the nations round about. ³² He also uttered three thousand proverbs; and his songs were a thousand and five. ³³ He spoke of trees, from the cedar that is in Lebanon to the hyssop that grows out of the wall; he spoke also of beasts, and of birds, and of reptiles, and of fish. ³⁴ And men came from all peoples to hear the wisdom of Solomon, and from all the kings of the earth, who had heard of his wisdom.

The second meaning of the word wisdom in the traditions about Solomon is an international, cultural wisdom that became the basis for his reputation as the author and collector of wisdom literature. This wisdom is connected with his international diplomatic relationships, particularly with the king of Tyre, the queen of Sheba, and the Pharaoh, his father-in-law (Thomas, pp. 172–186).

This list of men, than whom Solomon was wiser, begins with *the people of the east,* which might mean Arabian, Babylonian, or Aramean peoples. *All other men* has been emended to read "all the Edomites," since the names given have been associated by some scholars with the sons of Esau (Gen. 36), the wise men of Edom noted in Obadiah 8, and the friends of Job. According to another interpretation of these names, they were Canaanite wise men of the musical guilds which David is reputed to have organized.[10] The poetry of the Canaanites recovered at Ras Shamra, ancient Ugarit, has made probable a connection of Hebrew and Canaanite wisdom.

This attempt to catalogue Solomon's wisdom literature production is a part of the same tendency that attributes all of Proverbs (1:1; but cf. 30:1; 31:1), Ecclesiastes, and Song of Solomon to Solomon. He has become in the collection of wisdom traditions an authority figure, similar to Moses for the law and David for the Psalms. A recent discovery from Cave 11, Qumran, the extensive Psalms scroll, contains a similar catalogue of the literary productions of David. He is credited with 3,600 psalms, and his songs for specified cultic occasions were 450.[11]

The subjects of Solomon's wisdom literature included comparisons from all the flora and fauna of the natural world (cf. Prov. 30:15 ff.). Comprehensive catalogues of the created order (cf. Psalm 104; Job 38) are known from Egyptian and Mesopotamian literature. Solomon has set the court life of Jerusalem in the sophisticated culture of the empires with which he maintained diplomatic and commercial arrangements. But all this "glory" was not without its price to the distinctiveness of Israel's covenant faith.

3. Temple of Solomon (5:1—7:51)

Solomon had a reputation not only as a wise man but also as a builder, particularly the builder of the Jerusalem Temple. The religious interest of the historian is revealed by the amount of material that he includes from the Temple archives. The preparation for building, the arrangement of the structure with decoration, furniture, and metal work comprise this section of the story.

---

[10] W. F. Albright, *Archaeology and the Religion of Israel* (Baltimore: The Johns Hopkins Press, 1956), pp. 126-129; cf. 1 Chron. 6:33,44; Psalms 88—89.
[11] J. A. Sanders, *The Psalms Scroll of Qumran Cave 11* (Oxford: At the Clarendon Press, 1965), pp. 91-93.

(1) Treaty with Hiram, King of Tyre (5:1-18)

a. Solomon's Purpose to Build (5:1-6)

¹ Now Hiram king of Tyre sent his servants to Solomon, when he heard that they had anointed him king in place of his father; for Hiram always loved David. ² And Solomon sent word to Hiram, ³ "You know that David my father could not build a house for the name of the Lord his God because of the warfare with which his enemies surrounded him, until the Lord put them under the soles of his feet. ⁴ But now the Lord my God has given me rest on every side; there is neither adversary nor misfortune. ⁵ And so I purpose to build a house for the name of the Lord my God, as the Lord said to David my father, 'Your son, whom I will set upon your throne in your place, shall build the house for my name.' ⁶ Now therefore command that cedars of Lebanon be cut for me; and my servants will join your servants, and I will pay you for your servants such wages as you set; for you know that there is no one among us who knows how to cut timber like the Sidonians."

Hiram sent his messengers to Solomon not long after he had succeeded David as king. This is the same Hiram who had built David's palace in Jerusalem. *Because of the warfare,* David had been too busy fighting his battles to build a temple. Two other reasons are given why David did not build a temple. Nathan's oracle indicated that the Lord preferred a tent sanctuary, rather than a Canaanite type of sanctuary (2 Sam. 7:4-7). Chronicles interprets that it was unfitting for a man of many bloody battles to build a sanctuary to the Lord (1 Chron. 22:8-9; 28:3). Rather, a man of peace (the meaning of the name Solomon) would be the appropriate builder of God's temple.

Solomon took advantage of the greetings of Hiram to do business with him. Solomon prized the skills of the Phoenicians as well as their building materials. After David had conquered the Philistines, whose sea power had monopolized the coast of Palestine for two centuries, the Phoenicians gained supremacy on the sea. Hiram was dependent on Solomon because Solomon controlled the land routes of trade with Arabia.

b. Hiram's Provisions of Timber (5:7-12)

⁷ When Hiram heard the words of Solomon, he rejoiced greatly, and said, "Blessed be the LORD this day, who has given to David a wise son to be over this great people." ⁸ And Hiram sent to Solomon, saying, "I have heard the message which you have sent to me; I am ready to do all you desire in the matter of cedar and cypress timber. ⁹ My servants shall bring it down to the sea from Lebanon; and I will make it into rafts to go by sea to the place you direct, and I will have them broken up there, and you shall receive it; and you shall meet my wishes by providing food for my household." ¹⁰ So Hiram supplied Solomon with all the timber of cedar and cypress that he desired, ¹¹ while Solomon gave Hiram twenty thousand cors of wheat as food for his household, and twenty thousand cors of beaten oil. Solomon gave this to Hiram year by year. ¹² And the LORD gave Solomon wisdom, as he promised him; and there was peace between Hiram and Solomon; and the two of them made a treaty.

Hiram agreed not only to supply the materials, but to supervise their shipment by rafts from Tyre down the coast (to Joppa, 2 Chron. 2:16). In return, Solomon had to supply food for Hiram's court, *twenty thousand cors of wheat,* about 130,000 bushels (cf. 4:22). *Beaten oil* was the finest handpressed olive oil. The huge amount may indicate that some of this produce was for trade (Gray, p. 146). This was a huge drain upon the economy of the kingdom under Solomon. *Made a treaty* is, literally, "cut a covenant." This Hebrew phrase refers to the religious ceremony of sharing a sacrificial meal together. This treaty continued to be of advantage to Solomon, for he obtained his metal worker from Tyre, and also the help of Hiram in building a fleet (9:26-28; 10:11,22). On the other hand, there was a religious danger in such covenants (Ex. 23:32; 34:12,15; Deut. 7:2; Judg. 2:2). Solomon sealed this alliance with an addition to his harem, for Sidonian women are listed among those foreign women whom he is said to have loved, and it is said that his heart was turned away after Ashtoreth, the goddess of the Sidonians (11:1,4-5).

c. Forced Labor for Lebanon (5:13-18)

¹³ King Solomon raised a levy of forced labor out of all Israel; and the levy numbered thirty thousand men. ¹⁴ And he sent them to Lebanon, ten thousand a month in relays; they would be a month in Lebanon and two months at home; Adoniram was in charge of the levy. ¹⁵ Solomon also had seventy thousand burden-bearers and eighty thousand hewers of stone in the hill country, ¹⁶ besides Solomon's three thousand three hundred chief officers who were over the work, who had charge of the people who carried on the work. ¹⁷ At the king's command, they quarried out great, costly stones in order to lay the foundation of the house with dressed stones. ¹⁸ So Solomon's builders and Hiram's builders and the men of Gebal did the hewing and prepared the timber and the stone to build the house.

This account of Solomon's forced labor appears to be contradicted by the idealistic statement of the historian in another section that Solomon did not enslave any Israelites in his forced labor (9:22). The 150,000 mentioned in v. 15 may have been a levy raised out of former Canaanite city-states that David had conquered (Noth, p. 211). For these the 3,300 overseers would have been an appropriate number, approximating one overseer to every 50 workers. The 30,000 were an emergency team for cutting timber in Lebanon, and served in relays of 10,000 per month.

Admittedly, this was quite an imposition upon free Israelite farmers who were already burdened down with a heavy court establishment and taxation. This too was a "heavy yoke" (12:4), for which Jeroboam and the northern tribes would exact a bitter repayment. But Solomon had begun a great undertaking, and this building task required the best materials and workmanship.

(2) Time of Temple Building (6:1-38)

This literary account, along with the slightly differing descriptions in Chronicles and Ezekiel (2 Chron. 3—4; Ezek. 40—43), is all that remains of Solomon's Temple. It was evidently drawn in its details from a Temple archive. The historian was interested in the Temple more than all the other buildings of the royal complex, and it was by no means the largest.

a. General Plans for the Structure (6:1–10)

¹ In the four hundred and eightieth year after the people of Israel came out of the land of Egypt, in the fourth year of Solomon's reign over Israel, in the month of Ziv, which is the second month, he began to build the house of the LORD. ² The house which King Solomon built for the LORD was sixty cubits long, twenty cubits wide, and thirty cubits high. ³ The vestibule in front of the nave of the house was twenty cubits long, equal to the width of the house, and ten cubits deep in front of the house. ⁴ And he made for the house windows with recessed frames. ⁵ He also built a structure against the wall of the house, running round the walls of the house, both the nave and the inner sanctuary; and he made side chambers all around. ⁶ The lowest story was five cubits broad, the middle one was six cubits broad, and the third was seven cubits broad; for around the outside of the house he made offsets on the wall in order that the supporting beams should not be inserted into the walls of the house.
⁷ When the house was built, it was with stone prepared at the quarry; so that neither hammer nor axe nor any tool of iron was heard in the temple, while it was being built.
⁸ The entrance for the lowest story was on the south side of the house; and one went up by stairs to the middle story, and from the middle story to the third. ⁹ So he built the house, and finished it; and he made the ceiling of the house of beams and planks of cedar. ¹⁰ He built the structure against the whole house, each story five cubits high, and it was joined to the house with timbers of cedar.

The writer emphasized the date for the beginning of the Temple building to show how rapidly Solomon began his most important task. *Four hundred and eightieth year,* as other evidence indicates, is a general priestly date for twelve generations of 40 years each (BBC, Vol. 1, p. 323).

The ground plan and general dimensions of the Temple are clear. The archaeological discoveries of this century have provided remarkable architectural and artistic evidence for the reconstruction of the details of Solomon's Temple.¹² *The House* is the general Semitic name for a temple which was simply conceived as a house for the deity. The Solomonic temple was not given a proper name as many of the ancient Near Eastern temples were. The house consisted of the two inner rooms of the sanctuary, with a third room, the vestibule or porch, in front. According to the standard cubit of approximately 18 inches (the measurement from a man's elbow to the tip of his middle finger), the general dimensions of the house were 90 feet long, 30 feet wide, and 45 feet high. The vestibule was the same height and width as the sanctuary, but only 15 feet in depth.

The windows were rather narrow slits in the upper part of the main structure, above the side chambers mentioned in this section. These side chambers surrounded three sides of the house proper and consisted of three stories of storehouses or treasuries. *The nave* was the main room, or holy place as it is later called, and was designated by a Hebrew word which could mean either temple or palace, emphasizing the royal theology of the kingship of Yahweh. *The inner sanctuary* was at the rear of the Temple, the very dwelling place of God, later called the holy of holies (lit., the holiest), a perfect cube of 30-foot dimensions. Verse 7 interrupts the description of the storehouses with a reverent editorial notice concerning the ritual silence of the building of the Temple.

b. Covenant of Divine Presence (6:11–13)

¹¹ Now the word of the LORD came to Solomon, ¹² "Concerning this house which you are building, if you will walk in my statutes and obey my ordinances and keep all my commandments and walk in them, then I will establish my word with you, which I spoke to David your father. ¹³ And I will dwell among the children of Israel, and will not forsake my people Israel."

This section disturbs the account of details of the building itself to deal with a

¹² Paul Leslie Garber, "A Reconstruction of Solomon's Temple," *Archaeological Discoveries in the Holy Land* (New York: Thomas Y. Crowell Company, 1967), pp. 100–111; cf. Wright, pp. 136–145.

matter of utmost theological significance. It is introduced by what is normally a prophetic speech formula, indicating that it is a Deuteronomic reminder of the dynastic covenant word of Nathan to David (2 Sam. 7). That covenant would be conditioned upon the obedience of each succeeding king on the Davidic throne (cf. 2:4; 3:14). Also, the promise of God's presence among his people would be conditioned upon their obedience.

c. Interior Plans (6:14–22)

14 So Solomon built the house, and finished it. 15 He lined the walls of the house on the inside with boards of cedar; from the floor of the house to the rafters of the ceiling, he covered them on the inside with wood; and he covered the floor of the house with boards of cypress. 16 He built twenty cubits of the rear of the house wth boards of cedar from the floor to the rafters, and he built this within as an inner sanctuary, as the most holy place. 17 The house, that is, the nave in front of the inner sanctuary, was forty cubits long. 18 The cedar within the house was carved in the form of gourds and open flowers; all was cedar, no stone was seen. 19 The inner sanctuary he prepared in the innermost part of the house, to set there the ark of the covenant of the Lord. 20 The inner sanctuary was twenty cubits long, twenty cubits wide, and twenty cubits high; and he overlaid it with pure gold. He also made an altar of cedar. 21 And Solomon overlaid the inside of the house with pure gold, and he drew chains of gold across, in front of the inner sanctuary, and overlaid it with gold. 22 And he overlaid the whole house with gold, until all the house was finished. Also the whole altar that belonged to the inner sanctuary he overlaid with gold.

The interior woodwork of the house itself was of cedar paneling and cypress flooring (cf. 5:8). Since the most holy place was a perfect cube, its height dimension was ten cubits smaller than the height of the house itself. The paneling of the holy place was carved with floral decorations. The innermost sanctuary, which was prepared for the ark, was ornately decorated with gold inlay. It was probably separated from the holy place by doors (de Vaux, pp. 313–314). In front of these was the incense altar, made of cedar and overlaid with gold.

d. Twin Cherubim (6:23–28)

23 In the inner sanctuary he made two cherubim of olivewood, each ten cubits high. 24 Five cubits was the length of one wing of the cherub, and five cubits the length of the other wing of the cherub; it was ten cubits from the tip of one wing to the tip of the other. 25 The other cherub also measured ten cubits; both cherubim had the same measure and the same form. 26 The height of one cherub was ten cubits, and so was that of the other cherub. 27 He put the cherubim in the innermost part of the house; and the wings of the cherubim were spread out so that a wing of one touched the one wall, and a wing of the other cherub touched the other wall; their other wings touched each other in the middle of the house. 28 And he overlaid the cherubim with gold.

One of the most interesting stories of the results of biblical archaeology is the recovery of the form or shape of the cherubim. Josephus (*Antiq.* VIII,3,3) says that "nobody can tell or even conjecture, what was the shape of these." As is now known from the Meggido ivories, a cherub was a guardian figure like the Egyptian sphinx (a human-headed, winged lion; cf. Heaton, p. 226). The guardian function of the cherub reminds one of the colossal winged bulls customarily placed at the entrance of Mesopotamian palaces and temples. Since Canaanite art uses the cherub as the arm rest of a throne chair, the primary purpose of the cherubim in Solomon's Temple must have been to serve as the throne of the invisible Yahweh. These awesome figures, 15 feet tall with a 15-foot wing spread, inspired the imagination of Ezekiel in his throne-chariot vision (Ezek. 1).

e. Art Work and Decoration (6:29–38)

29 He carved all the walls of the house round about with carved figures of cherubim and palm trees and open flowers, in the inner and outer rooms. 30 The floor of the house he overlaid with gold in the inner and outer rooms. 31 For the entrance to the inner sanctuary he made doors of olivewood; the lintel and the doorposts formed a pentagon. 32 He covered the two doors of olivewood with carvings of cherubim, palm trees, and open flowers; he overlaid them with gold, and spread gold upon the cherubim and upon the palm trees. 33 So also he made for the entrance to the

nave doorposts of olivewood, in the form of a square, 34 and two doors of cypress wood; the two leaves of the one door were folding, and the two leaves of the other door were folding. 35 On them he carved cherubim and palm trees and open flowers; and he overlaid them with gold evenly applied upon the carved work. 36 He built the inner court with three courses of hewn stone and one course of cedar beams.
37 In the fourth year the foundation of the house of the LORD was laid, in the month of Ziv. 38 And in the eleventh year, in the month of Bul, which is the eighth month, the house was finished in all its parts, and according to all its specifications. He was seven years in building it.

The motif of the cherubim guarding palm trees, probably thought of as a "tree of life," is well known from ancient Near Eastern art (cf. Gen. 3:24). *Pentagon* has been interpreted as allowing the doors of the holy of holies to swing wider than would normally be the case with a square doorpost (cf. v. 33). The inner court was built with *three courses of hewn stone and one course of cedar beams.* Archaeology has amply illustrated the particular kind of construction for walls that is described here. It seems to have been followed in the Solomonic buildings at Meggido, as it was in the temple of Tell Tainat, very similar to Solomon's Temple. Cyrus ordered the postexilic Temple to be built the same way (Ezra 6:4; de Vaux, p. 316). Thus Solomon completed his beautifully ornate yet comparatively small royal sanctuary, which took him only approximately half the time that he spent building his own palace nearby. This Temple was primarily for the use of the royal court in Jerusalem. However, its major purpose was the housing of the ark, which gave it a continuing national significance.

(3) Palace and Other Buildings (7:1–12)

North of the ancient city of David stretched the great court containing Solomon's administrative complex of palace buildings, and at the northernmost side the Temple court. Solomon's own private palace, along with that for his queen, formed a middle court just south of the Temple area. The present passage is quite brief, in relation to the description of the Temple in chapter 6 and when compared with the description of the bronze work for the Temple in the rest of this chapter.

a. Administrative Complex (7:1–8)

¹ Solomon was building his own house thirteen years, and he finished his entire house.
² He built the House of the Forest of Lebanon; its length was a hundred cubits, and its breadth fifty cubits, and its height thirty cubits, and it was built upon three rows of cedar pillars, with cedar beams upon the pillars. ³ And it was covered with cedar above the chambers that were upon the forty-five pillars, fifteen in each row. ⁴ There were window frames in three rows, and window opposite window in three tiers. ⁵ All the doorways and windows had square frames, and window was opposite window in three tiers.
⁶ And he made the Hall of Pillars; its length was fifty cubits, and its breadth thirty cubits; there was a porch in front with pillars, and a canopy before them.
⁷ And he made the Hall of the Throne where he was to pronounce judgment, even the Hall of Judgment; it was finished with cedar from floor to rafters.
⁸ His own house where he was to dwell, in the other court back of the hall, was of like workmanship. Solomon also made a house like this hall for Pharaoh's daughter whom he had taken in marriage.

The word *house* here refers to the entire complex of five buildings, so that, not surprisingly, it took Solomon 13 further years to finish his great building program for Jerusalem (cf. 9:10). First there was *the House of the Forest of Lebanon.* The most imposing building of the whole area was this large armory (cf. 10:17; Isa. 22:8), with the poetic name based on the use of much cedar in its interior construction. The writer gives enough particulars to indicate something of its magnificence.

Next there was *the Hall of Pillars,* proceeding northward within the complex. Because its length was 50 cubits, the same as the breadth of the preceding building, this building has sometimes been seen as a porch attached to the armory. Others interpret its significance as an entrance to the next building northward, *the Hall of the*

Throne . . . the Hall of Judgment. This was the place of public access to the king and was regarded as the supreme court of appeal for all the people. It was in this building that the great ivory throne described later (10:18–20) was placed for the king. Further north was Solomon's own palace in a separate court, to which was attached his queen's palace.

b. Masonry of the Court (7:9–12)

9 All these were made of costly stones, hewn according to measure, sawed with saws, back and front, even from the foundation to the coping, and from the court of the house of the Lord to the great court. 10 The foundation was of costly stones, huge stones, stones of eight and ten cubits. 11 And above were costly stones, hewn according to measurement, and cedar. 12 The great court had three courses of hewn stone round about, and a course of cedar beams; so had the inner court of the house of the Lord, and the vestibule of the house.

The description of the stonework and the foundation work for this extensive building project emphasizes the exactness of the masonry and the costliness of the work. It was probably during this latter part of Solomon's building program in Jerusalem that he extended its wall, built the Millo ("filling," perhaps a raised platform for his palace), and closed up the breach of David (9:15; 11:27).

(4) Metalwork for the Temple (7:13–51)

Most of this section has to do with the bronze metalwork made by a special Phoenician metalworker in the Jordan valley. This metalwork was intended for use in the Temple court, where the people gathered for worship. One important piece of the Temple furnishings that is missing from this account is the large bronze altar of burnt offering. It is included in the book of Chronicles between the making of the large bronze pillars and the making of the molten sea (2 Chron. 4:1). It is presumed later in the account in Kings (8:22,54,64; 9:25). Some interpreters have supposed that the shape of this altar is identical with the one pictured by Ezekiel, namely that of a Babylonian temple-tower of three stages (Ezek. 43:13–17; cf. Wright, p. 139, fig. 93); but Ezekiel's altar is more likely to have been the shape of the new altar provided by King Ahaz, modeled upon a Mesopotamian altar which he had seen at Damascus, and with which he replaced the Solomonic altar (2 Kings 16:10–16).

a. Hiram, the Tyrian Metalworker (7:13–14)

13 And King Solomon sent and brought Hiram from Tyre. 14 He was the son of a widow of the tribe of Naphtali, and his father was a man of Tyre, a worker in bronze; and he was full of wisdom, understanding, and skill, for making any work in bronze. He came to King Solomon, and did all his work.

This Hiram is not to be confused with King Hiram of Tyre, who sent this skilled craftsman to perform special duties for Solomon's Temple building (2 Chron. 2:13 f.). In Chronicles, he is said to be the son of a Danite woman. Here his mother is called *a widow of the tribe of Napthali.* In any case his father was a man of Tyre and a worker in bronze, who taught his trade to his son.

Wisdom, understanding, and skill were elements of craftsmanship and were regarded as a special gift of God, as in the priestly account of Bezalel (Ex. 31:2–5). These words then must be taken in their practical sense, which is likely the original meaning of the word wisdom in Hebrew usage. Some have supposed that Hiram the metalworker was also a kind of Phoenician architect, a specialist in Canaanite temple building. However, according to this account he was primarily a metalworker.

b. Pillars of Bronze (7:15–22)

15 He cast two pillars of bronze. Eighteen cubits was the height of one pillar, and a line of twelve cubits measured its circumference; it was hollow, and its thickness was four fingers; the second pillar was the same. 16 He also made two capitals of molten bronze, to set upon the tops of the pillars; the height of the one capital was five cubits, and the height of the other capital was five cubits. 17 Then he made two nets of checker work with wreaths of chain work for the capitals upon the tops of the pillars; a net for the one capital, and a net for

the other capital. ¹⁸ Likewise he made pomegranates; in two rows round about upon the one network, to cover the capital that was upon the top of the pillar; and he did the same with the other capital. ¹⁹ Now the capitals that were upon the tops of the pillars in the vestibule were of lily-work, four cubits. ²⁰ The capitals were upon the two pillars and also above the rounded projection which was beside the network; there were two hundred pomegranates, in two rows round about; and so with the other capital. ²¹ He set up the pillars at the vestibule of the temple; he set up the pillar on the south and called its name Jachin; and he set up the pillar on the north and called its name Boaz. ²² And upon the tops of the pillars was lily-work. Thus the work of the pillars was finished.

The most impressive monuments to Hiram's skill were these two magnificent bronze pillars. The column of each was 27 feet high and almost six feet in diameter. It was hollow with a thickness for the metal of about three inches. Surmounting the column was a capital in the shape of a bowl seven and one-half feet high, six feet of which was covered with a lily-work design decorated with ornate chains of pomegranates. These were free standing columns in front of the Temple (2 Chron. 3:17).

Many symbolic and cultic functions have been suggested for these bronze pillars, in addition to their obvious decorative value. Albright thinks they were gigantic incense stands, with fire perpetually burning in their bowl-shaped capitals.¹³ They may have been given some historical significance as representations of the pillar of fire by night and the pillar of cloud by day which signified Yahweh's leadership in the wilderness (cf. Isa. 4:5). Others have regarded them as stylized *maṣṣeboth*, like the stone pillars that flanked the entrances to Canaanite temples (de Vaux, p. 314).

The best clue to the meaning of the pillars of bronze is their names *Jachin* ("He shall establish"), and *Boaz* ("in the strength of"). These have been supposed to be the first words of inscriptions relating to the role of the Temple as a visible testimony to the stability of the Davidic dynasty. Thus Jachin may have meant: "He will establish the throne of David for ever"; and Boaz may have meant: "in the strength of Yahweh shall the king rejoice" (*IDB*, II, 780–781). Though other symbolism has been suggested in connection with cosmic phenomena, it is much more appropriate to seek for some historical meaning.

c. *Molten Sea* (7:23–26)

²³ Then he made the molten sea; it was round, ten cubits from brim to brim, and five cubits high, and a line of thirty cubits measured its circumference. ²⁴ Under its brim were gourds, for thirty cubits, compassing the sea round about; the gourds were in two rows, cast with it when it was cast. ²⁵ It stood upon twelve oxen, three facing north, three facing west, three facing south, and three facing east; the sea was set upon them, and all their hinder parts were inward. ²⁶ Its thickness was a handbreadth; and its brim was made like the brim of a cup, like the flower of a lily; it held two thousand baths.

No less remarkable than the bronze pillars was the molten sea. Its round bowl was 15 feet across and seven and one-half feet high. It also was cast out of thick bronze, ornately decorated. The bowl rested upon four pediments of three oxen each, facing the four directions. Much has been made of the cosmic symbolism of this huge basin, on the basis of its Hebrew name *yam* (sea; Wright, p. 140). In the Canaanite religious literature Yam is a chief enemy of Baal in the struggle for kingship (Thomas, p. 129). Chronicles notes that the sea served a practical function, for the washings of the priests (2 Chron. 4:6). However, its height seems prohibitive of this function. Surely its chief practical value was as a storage basin for water which would have been supplied by some siphon arrangement to the lavers of the ten stands.

d. *Bronze Stands and Lavers* (7:27–39)

²⁷ He also made the ten stands of bronze; each stand was four cubits long, four cubits wide, and three cubits high. ²⁸ This was the construction of the stands: they had panels, and the panels were set in the frames ²⁹ and on the panels that were set in the frames were

---

¹³ *Op. cit.*, pp. 144–148.

lions, oxen, and cherubim. Upon the frames, both above and below the lions and oxen, there were wreaths of beveled work. 30 Moreover each stand had four bronze wheels and axles of bronze; and at the four corners were supports for a laver. The supports were cast, with wreaths at the side of each. 31 Its opening was within a crown which projected upward one cubit; its opening was round, as a pedestal is made, a cubit and a half deep. At its opening there were carvings; and its panels were square, not round. 32 And the four wheels were underneath the panels; the axels of the wheels were of one piece with the stands; and the height of a wheel was a cubit and a half. 33 The wheels were made like a chariot wheel; their axles, their rims, their spokes, and their hubs, were all cast. 34 There were four supports at the four corners of each stand; the supports were of one piece with the stands. 35 And on the top of the stand there was a round band half a cubit high; and on the top of the stand its stays and its panels were of one piece with it. 36 And on the surfaces of its stays and on its panels, he carved cherubim, lions, and palm trees, according to the space of each, with wreaths round about. 37 After this manner he made the ten stands; all of them were cast alike, of the same measure and the same form. 38 And he made ten lavers of bronze; each laver held forty baths, each laver measured four cubits, and there was a laver for each of the ten stands. 39 And he set the stands, five on the south side of the house, and five on the north side of the house; and he set the sea on the southeast corner of the house.

The description of these ten stands and the lavers which fitted within them is a very technical and involved document. The stands were six feet square and four and one-half feet high, each containing a laver of some 200-gallon capacity, which would have made quite a heavy object. Since the stands were wheeled vehicles, presumably they were intended to be movable. The panels of the stands were certainly ornately decorated with animal figures. Chronicles assigns a cultic function to these stands with their lavers, the washing of the utensils for the burnt offerings (2 Chron. 4:6).

e. Casting of the Bronze (7:40-47)

40 Hiram also made the pots, the shovels, and the basins. So Hiram finished all the work that he did for King Solomon on the house of the Lord: 41 the two pillars, the two bowls of the capitals that were on the tops of the pillars, and the two networks to cover the two bowls of the capitals that were on the tops of the pillars; 42 and the four hundred pomegranates for the two networks, two rows of pomegranates for each network, to cover the two bowls of the capitals that were upon the pillars; 43 the ten stands, and the ten lavers upon the stands; 44 and the one sea, and the twelve oxen underneath the sea.

45 Now the pots, the shovels, and the basins, all these vessels in the house of the Lord, which Hiram made for King Solomon, were of burnished bronze. 46 In the plain of the Jordan the king cast them, in the clay ground between Succoth and Zarethan. 47 And Solomon left all the vessels unweighed, because there were so many of them; the weight of the bronze was not found out.

This section provides a kind of summary of all the bronze vessels and furnishings for the Temple. The larger of the Temple vessels were made of burnished bronze, whereas the smaller implements were of gold (7:50). *In the plain of the Jordan . . . between Succoth and Zarethan* was the nearest place to Jerusalem where the clay was proper for molding these mammoth works of bronze. Recent excavations at the site of ancient Succoth, *Tell Deir 'Alla,* reveal that it was a center of metallurgy in the kingdom (Gray, p. 185). The amount of bronze work described in this chapter certainly must have taxed the burgeoning metal industry, which Solomon had established south of the Dead Sea.

f. Temple Vessels (7:48-51)

48 So Solomon made all the vessels that were in the house of the Lord: the golden altar, the golden table for the bread of the Presence, 49 the lampstands of pure gold, five on the south side and five on the north, before the inner sanctuary; the flowers, the lamps, and the tongs, of gold; 50 the cups, snuffers, basins, dishes for incense, and firepans, of pure gold; and the sockets of gold, for the doors of the innermost part of the house, the most holy place, and for the doors of the nave of the temple.

51 Thus all the work that King Solomon did on the house of the Lord was finished. And Solomon brought in the things which David his father had dedicated, the silver, the gold, and

the vessels, and stored them in the treasuries of the house of the Lord.

The last section in the chapter is not closely related to what immediately precedes. The description of all the bronze furnishings of the Temple court seemed to call for some emphasis on the inner furnishings of the house. *The golden altar* is probably the incense altar referred to already in connection with the holy place (6:20,22). *The golden table for the bread of the Presence* was like the table in the tabernacle (Ex. 25:23–30; BBC, Vol. 1, pp. 433–434). The ritual of providing bread for the Lord's sanctuary had certainly been purged of any pagan notions of feeding the god, and the bread was rather an acknowledgment of the Lord's bounty in providing food for his people.

The ten lampstands, five on each side of the holy place, are certainly different from the seven-branched lampstand of the tabernacle and of Herod's temple (Ex. 25:31–40; BBC, Vol. 1, p. 434). Most of the small utensils listed have been illustrated from archaeological excavations (Wright, pp. 141–142). *The things which David his father had dedicated* is probably a reference to the booty and gifts won by David in his battles in the last phase of his Transjordan and Aramean campaigns (2 Sam. 8:9–12). This is the only note in Kings of a theme which was dear to the Chronicler, the plans and preparations by David for this Temple. Nevertheless, the Temple is Solomon's great achievement for the religious life of his people.

4. Dedication Festival for the Temple (8:1—9:9)

The religious significance of Solomon's Temple in the worship of Israel must have increased and changed through the centuries. Thus various levels of development appear in this account of its dedication. The story begins with a procession of the ark to its resting place in the most holy place, includes a long speech and prayer of Solomon, and concludes with an account of the festival. Added to the dedication story proper is a response of the Lord to Solomon's prayer.

(1) Procession of the Ark (8:1–11)

¹ Then Solomon assembled the elders of Israel and all the heads of the tribes, the leaders of the fathers' houses of the people of Israel, before King Solomon in Jerusalem, to bring up the ark of the covenant of the Lord out of the city of David, which is Zion. ² And all the men of Israel assembled to King Solomon at the feast in the month Ethanim, which is the seventh month. ³ And all the elders of Israel came, and the priests took up the ark. ⁴ And they brought up the ark of the Lord, the tent of meeting, and all the holy vessels that were in the tent; the priests and the Levites brought them up. ⁵ And King Solomon and all the congregation of Israel, who had assembled before him, were with him before the ark, sacrificing so many sheep and oxen that they could not be counted or numbered. ⁶ Then the priests brought the ark of the covenant of the Lord to its place, in the inner sanctuary of the house, in the most holy place, underneath the wings of the cherubim. ⁷ For the cherubim spread out their wings over the place of the ark, so that the cherubim made a covering above the ark and its poles. ⁸ And the poles were so long that the ends of the poles were seen from the holy place before the inner sanctuary; but they could not be seen from outside; and they are there to this day. ⁹ There was nothing in the ark except the two tables of stone which Moses put there at Horeb, where the Lord made a covenant with the people of Israel, when they came out of the land of Egypt. ¹⁰ And when the priests came out of the holy place, a cloud filled the house of the Lord, ¹¹ so that the priests could not stand to minister because of the cloud; for the glory of the Lord filled the house of the Lord.

The meaning of the Temple was centered in the presence of the ark. This ancient covenant shrine had been used in tribal migrations and warfare as a sign of God's presence with his people. When it was recovered by David, it had been brought up to the city of David with a solemn procession (2 Sam. 6).

The makeup of this covenant assembly belies the opinion that Solomon's Temple was merely a royal chapel with little national significance. *Zion* was originally the hill which David took from the Jebusites (2 Sam. 5:7), but later the name was applied to the Temple area northward. *The feast in the seventh month* was the Feast of Tabernacles, an ancient agricultural new year festival. This was perhaps an occasion for an annual celebration of the kingship of Yahweh (cf. Psalms 132; 24:7-10).

Two tables of stone are mentioned in accordance with the Deuteronomic view of the ark as a container of the Decalogue (cf. 8:21; Deut. 10:1-5). This explains its name, the ark of the covenant. As He had taken possession of the tabernacle, so Yahweh now manifests his presence in the Temple. *Cloud . . . glory* were originally associated with the Lord's appearance in the storm.

(2) *Blessing of the Assembly (8:12-21)*

12 Then Solomon said,
"The LORD has set the sun in the heavens,
but has said that he would dwell in thick darkness.
13 I have built thee an exalted house,
a place for thee to dwell in for ever."
14 Then the king faced about, and blessed all the assembly of Israel, while all the assembly of Israel stood. 15 And he said, "Blessed be the LORD, the God of Israel, who with his hand has fulfilled what he promised with his mouth to David my father, saying, 16 'Since the day that I brought my people Israel out of Egypt, I chose no city in all the tribes of Israel in which to build a house, that my name might be there; but I chose David to be over my people Israel.' 17 Now it was in the heart of David my father to build a house for the name of the LORD, the God of Israel. 18 But the LORD said to David my father, 'Whereas it was in your heart to build a house for my name, you did well that it was in your heart; 19 nevertheless you shall not build the house, but your son who shall be born to you shall build the house for my name.' 20 Now the LORD has fulfilled his promise which he made; for I have risen in the place of David my father, and sit on the throne of Israel, as the LORD promised, and I have built the house for the name of the LORD, the God of Israel. 21 And there I have provided a place for the ark, in which is the covenant of the LORD which he made with our fathers, when he brought them out of the land of Egypt."

The speech of Solomon begins with an ancient poetic fragment from the Book of Jashar (LXX has "Book of Songs," but cf. Josh. 10:13; 2 Sam. 1:18; Gray, pp. 195-196). Then Solomon turns and blesses the assembly with praise to the Lord for his fulfillment of the covenant promise to David regarding the Temple.

The Lord has set the sun in the heavens (based on the LXX) means that the Lord is the sovereign of creation (cf. Psalm 19:1-6). But on earth the Lord will *dwell* (tabernacle) *in thick darkness.* The darkness of the windowless inner sanctuary is identified with the dark storm cloud on Sinai (Ex. 20:18; cf. Psalm 18:10-11). The mystery of Israel's God, who is at once transcendent sovereign of creation and imminent Lord of worship, is here beautifully expressed. *Dwell* (sit) is a different word than in the preceding verse. Here it is boldly claimed that Yahweh actually lives in the Temple; whereas, according to the theology of the following prayer, Yahweh dwells in the heavens, and only his name is enshrined in the earthly sanctuary (8:27-30; cf. Wright, pp. 144-145). This development in Temple theology may be understood if later the earthly sanctuary is thought of as a microcosm of the true, heavenly abode of God (cf. Isa. 6:1-8).

The blessing is praise for the Lord's faithfulness to his promises to David. *I brought my people out of Egypt* (cf. v. 21) makes a strong connection here between the Sinai covenant and the Davidic covenant in the salvation-history. This summary of the Nathan oracle (2 Sam. 7) ignores the prior existence of a temple of Yahweh at Shiloh (1 Sam. 1:9; Jer. 7:14). Solomon rejoices in being the son of promise, the legitimate heir who inherited the throne power and sealed its permanency with the building of a dynastic Temple.

(3) *Prayer of Dedication (8:22-53)*

Solomon acts as covenant mediator in this dedication ceremony. Intercessory prayer is usually the function of the prophet as covenant mediator (cf. Ex. 32; 1 Sam. 7:5). Before the altar of the burnt offering the king stood as supplicant with raised hands, a typical attitude of prayer (cf. Isa. 1:15). Then he knelt (8:54; cf. 2

Chron. 6:13), publicly humiliating himself before the Lord as representative of the people. The content of the prayer claims the covenant promises, asks for a hearing of Temple intercessions, then adds a list of national disasters and emergencies for which prayer and penitence may be directed toward the God of heaven, who is Lord of the Temple.

a. Promise to David (8:22–26)

22 Then Solomon stood before the altar of the LORD in the presence of all the assembly of Israel, and spread forth his hands toward heaven; 23 and said, "O LORD, God of Israel, there is no God like thee, in heaven above or on earth beneath, keeping covenant and showing steadfast love to thy servants who walk before thee with all their heart; 24 who hast kept with thy servant David my father what thou didst declare to him; yea, thou didst speak with thy mouth, and with thy hand hast fulfilled it this day. 25 Now therefore, O LORD, God of Israel, keep with thy servant David my father what thou hast promised him, saying, 'There shall never fail you a man before me to sit upon the throne of Israel, if only your sons take heed to their way, to walk before me as you have walked before me.' 26 Now therefore, O God of Israel, let thy word be confirmed, which thou hast spoken to thy servant David my father.

The basis of all true prayer is the character of God: *There is no God like thee*. The practical monotheism of the Mosaic covenant is moving in the direction of an explicit monotheism (cf. 8:60; Deut. 4:35). The covenant relation is the gracious saving act of a loving God, keeping his promise to David. Promise in the Davidic covenant is unconditional to the dynasty, but to each holder of its throne it is conditioned on his obedience.

b. Divine Hearing of Temple Prayers (8:27–30)

27 "But will God indeed dwell on the earth? Behold, heaven and the highest heaven cannot contain thee; how much less this house which I have built! 28 Yet have regard to the prayer of thy servant and to his supplication, O LORD my God, hearkening to the cry and to the prayer which thy servant prays before thee this day; 29 that thy eyes may be open night and day toward this house, the place of which thou hast said, 'My name shall be there,' that thou mayest hearken to the prayer which thy servant offers toward this place. 30 And hearken thou to the supplication of thy servant and of thy people Israel, when they pray toward this place; yea, hear thou in heaven thy dwelling place; and when thou hearest, forgive.

There was strong skepticism from the beginning that a temple could ever "house" the God of heaven. This is similar to prophetic reactions against the people's superstitious trust in temple and cult, whenever these became dissociated from an obedient life (Isa. 1:10–17; Jer. 7:4 ff.). This prophetic reserve about the value of physical temples was stated again most forcefully at the time when Zerubbabel rebuilt the Temple after the Exile (Isa. 57:15; 66:1–2; cf. Acts 7:47–50). The vocabulary of *prayer* is rich here, the first word meaning prayer in general but sometimes applied specifically to intercession (cf. 19:4; Jer. 11:14). *Supplication* means to beg a favor on the basis of God's grace. *Cry* usually means a loud outcry of praise to Yahweh, but here it means an entreaty. The sanctuary is a house of prayer (cf. Isa. 56:7), toward which the prayers of the people should be symbolically directed, confident that the Lord, from his heavenly dwelling, hears the prayers of his worshipers.

c. Oath of the Temple (8:31–32)

31 "If a man sins against his neighbor and is made to take an oath, and comes and swears his oath before thine altar in this house, 32 then hear thou in heaven, and act, and judge thy servants, condemning the guilty by bringing his conduct upon his own head, and vindicating the righteous by rewarding him according to his righteousness.

The first of seven specific instances of the need for petition toward the sanctuary is the sacred oath of purgation. The sin against the neighbor is damage or injury the perpetrator of which is unknown, the guilt of the accused undetermined by any witnesses. God had by oath or ordeal rendered judgment directly in such cases from ancient times (Ex. 22:7–8; Num. 5:11–22). The power of such an oath is a self-curse, harmful to the guilty, harmless to the innocent. Punishment and reward were conceived by the Deuteronomists as being expressed in a material way in this life. Such poetic justice frequently happens in the Old Testament as well as in human experience generally.

d. Military Defeat (8:33-34)

33 "When thy people Israel are defeated before the enemy because they have sinned against thee, if they turn again to thee, and acknowledge thy name, and pray and make supplication to thee in this house; 34 then hear thou in heaven, and forgive the sin of thy people Israel, and bring them again to the land which thou gavest to their fathers.

This petition reminds one of the cycle in the Book of Judges: apostasy, defeat, repentance, deliverance. **Because they sinned against thee.** The Deuteronomic philosophy of history said that calamity is evidence of sin needing punishment. However, sin is only one of the possible reasons for suffering. Human experience did not always then (e.g., Job), and does not always now, fit into this neat, mechanical scheme of the Deuteronomists. The normal word for man's repentance is simply to *turn* to God. **Bring them again to the land** would normally presuppose exile (cf. 8:46-53; 9:6-9) and may belong to a later period. Yet military prisoners and slaves would result from any defeat in battle, so that the reference may be quite early.

e. Drought (8:35-36)

35 "When heaven is shut up and there is no rain because they have sinned against thee, if they pray toward this place, and acknowledge thy name, and turn from their sin, when thou dost afflict them, 36 then hear thou in heaven, and forgive the sin of thy servants, thy people Israel, when thou dost teach them the good way in which they should walk; and grant rain upon thy land, which thou hast given to thy people as an inheritance.

Rain was the gift of life in a relatively dry land, and was regarded rather literally as descending through the "windows of heaven" from God's storehouses, the waters above the firmament. God could also withhold rain as a sign of his displeasure (cf. Isa. 5:6). This meant literal starvation in a land where food was never too plentiful. Punishment of sin and forgiveness of the sinner are both designed by God to teach his people *the good way in which they should walk.*

f. Plagues of Various Sorts (8:37-40)

37 "If there is famine in the land, if there is pestilence or blight or mildew or locust or caterpillar; if their enemy besieges them in any of their cities; whatever plague, whatever sickness there is; 38 whatever prayer, whatever supplication is made by any man or by all thy people Israel, each knowing the affliction of his own heart and stretching out his hands toward this house; 39 then hear thou in heaven thy dwelling place, and forgive, and act, and render to each whose heart thou knowest, according to all his ways (for thou, thou only, knowest the hearts of all the children of men); 40 that they may fear thee all the days that they live in the land which thou gavest to our fathers.

Famine is better related to the preceding case of drought, but it could also be caused by pestilence, insect damage, or siege by the enemy. Joel is a magnificent example of ritual prayer, lamentation, and repentance in the case of a great locust plague. **Whatever prayer.** This category became a catch-all for national and individual needs. God knows the needs of those who pray to him, and depend on him for an answer (cf. Matt. 6:8; Rom. 8:26-27). True religion in the Old Testament is frequently defined as the "fear of the Lord," that is, reverent awe and not a slavish fear.

g. Prayer of the Foreigner (8:41-43)

41 "Likewise when a foreigner, who is not of thy people Israel, comes from a far country for thy name's sake 42 (for they shall hear of thy great name, and thy mighty hand, and of thy outstretched arm), when he comes and prays toward this house, 43 hear thou in heaven thy dwelling place, and do according to all for which the foreigner calls to thee; in order that all the peoples of the earth may know thy name and fear thee, as do thy people Israel, and that they may know that this house which I have built is called by thy name.

The *foreigner* was on a different basis in the law codes from the "resident alien, sojourner," who was better protected. The Deuteronomic code allowed some exploitation of foreigners (Deut. 14:21; 15:3; 23:20). Solomon was generous toward the worship of foreigners, although this became a problem in connection with his provision for the worship of his foreign wives (11:1-8). There is a genuine element of hospitality to strangers and proselytes in the Old Testament (Ruth; Isa. 2:2-4; 56:6-8; Zech. 8:20-23).

h. *Military Prayer from Afar (8:44-45)*

44 "If thy people go out to battle against their enemy, by whatever way thou shalt send them, and they pray to the LORD toward the city which thou hast chosen and the house which I have built for thy name, 45 then hear thou in heaven their prayer and their supplication, and maintain their cause.

This case is really preparatory to the one following. **By whatever way thou shalt send them** means the Lord was consulted through prophet or priest before battle. The extension of the power of Yahweh worship to the foreign territory is an interesting tendency of an aggressive monotheism. Prayer toward the Temple from afar was more strongly emphasized after the Exile and dispersion (cf. Dan. 6:10).

i. *Prayer of an Exiled People (8:46-53)*

46 "If they sin against thee—for there is no man who does not sin—and thou art angry with them, and dost give them to an enemy, so that they are carried away captive to the land of the enemy, far off or near; 47 yet if they lay it to heart in the land to which they have been carried captive, and repent, and make supplication to thee in the land of their captors, saying, 'We have sinned, and have acted perversely and wickedly'; 48 if they repent with all their mind and with all their heart in the land of their enemies, who carried them captive, and pray to thee toward their land, which thou gavest to their fathers, the city which thou hast chosen, and the house which I have built for thy name; 49 then hear thou in heaven thy dwelling place their prayer and their supplication, and maintain their cause 50 and forgive thy people who have sinned against thee, and all their transgressions which they have committed against thee; and grant them compassion in the sight of those who carried them captive, that they may have compassion on them 51 (for they are thy people, and thy heritage, which thou didst bring out of Egypt, from the midst of the iron furnace). 52 Let thy eyes be open to the supplication of thy servant, and to the supplication of thy people Israel, giving ear to them whenever they call to thee. 53 For thou didst separate them from among all the peoples of the earth, to be thy heritage, as thou didst declare through Moses, thy servant, when thou didst bring our fathers out of Egypt, O Lord GOD."

This section may have been added to Solomon's prayer by the exilic editor of Kings, and yet v. 48 implies that Solomon's Temple as still standing. The dispersion of the Northern Kingdom, according to the mass deportation policies of Assyria, later implemented against Judah by Sennacherib, provided the occasion for such a prayer as this. *There is no man who does not sin*. This truth is frequently stated in the Bible. Sin is the universal experience and condition of the human race. The rich vocabulary of sin in this prayer for repentance merits attention. *Sin* means "go astray, err, miss the mark or way." *Perversely* is the word from which iniquity is derived, and means "to twist, distort." **Wickedly** comes from a word meaning "be loose, disjointed, ill-regulated, abnormal." *Transgressions* is better translated "revolts, rebellions." These words are emphasized in the penintential Psalms (32, 51, 130), to which this prayer may be compared.

Repentance must be total, unconditional, wholehearted turning to God. In contrast with v. 34, there seems little hope among these exiles for early restoration to their homeland. Assyrian or Babylonian captivity must be indicated by this circumstance. *The iron furnace* is a very colorful metaphor of the Deuteronomic salvation-history (Deut. 4:20, cf. Jer. 11:4). These last verses referring rather forcefully to the doctrine of election provide a kind of concluding motive to the whole prayer, appealing to God's love for the people whom he has chosen.

(4) *Benediction (8:54-61)*

54 Now as Solomon finished offering all this prayer and supplication to the LORD, he arose

from before the altar of the LORD, where he had knelt with hands outstretched toward heaven; ⁵⁵ and he stood, and blessed all the assembly of Israel with a loud voice, saying, ⁵⁶ "Blessed be the LORD who has given rest to his people Israel, according to all that he promised; not one word has failed of all his good promise, which he uttered by Moses his servant. ⁵⁷ The LORD our God be with us, as he was with our fathers; may he not leave us or forsake us; ⁵⁸ that he may incline our hearts to him, to walk in all his ways, and to keep his commandments, his statutes, and his ordinances, which he commanded our fathers. ⁵⁹ Let these words of mine, wherewith I have made supplication before the LORD, be near to the LORD our God day and night, and may he maintain the cause of his servant, and the cause of his people Israel, as each day requires; ⁶⁰ that all the peoples of the earth may know that the LORD is God; there is no other. ⁶¹ Let your heart therefore be wholly true to the LORD our God, walking in his statutes and keeping his commandments, as at this day."

This blessing concludes the prayer as Solomon's previous blessing (8:12–21) had introduced it, with covenant language. Whereas the covenant promises referred to there were Davidic, these are Mosaic. *Rest* usually refers to the gift of the land, the conquest of which was only completed with David's wars, to which the Solomonic peace and Temple-building provided a fitting climax (cf. Deut. 12:10). *Not one word has failed.* Fulfillment of the divine promises is a strong binding theme within the Deuteronomic history and a strong motivation for retelling the mighty saving deeds of Yahweh. Solomon invokes the most precious promise of Scripture, *God be with us.* *Our fathers* refers to the patriarchs and to Moses and Joshua (Gen. 21:22; 26:3; 31:3; Ex. 3:12; Josh. 1:5).

That he may incline our hearts to him recognizes human dependence on divine grace. The talk about man turning to God in repentance is futile without this ministry of God in a man's heart, turning him into the way of obedience. *Be near* is the same word that is used in the presentation of sacrifice by worshiper and priest. Solomon beautifully captures the spiritual meaning of sacrifice with his emphasis on his own and his people's prayers which accompanied their sacrifices. *That all the peoples of the earth may know* means Israel was never vindicated purely for her own sake: the evidential value of the salvation-history was intended for the nations to recognize *that the Lord is God.* *Be wholly true* does not seem to fit the rest of the blessing, which is addressed to God. This closing exhortation may be a clue to the re-use of this prayer at an annual covenant-renewal festival. *As at this day* could refer to each successive occasion when the people renewed their covenant, reaffirming their faith in the promises of God.

(5) *Consecration Sacrifices (8:62–66)*

⁶² Then the king, and all Israel with him, offered sacrifice before the LORD. ⁶³ Solomon offered as peace offerings to the LORD twenty two thousand oxen and a hundred and twenty thousand sheep. So the king and all the people of Israel dedicated the house of the LORD. ⁶⁴ The same day the king consecrated the middle of the court that was before the house of the LORD; for there he offered the burnt offering and the cereal offering and the fat pieces of the peace offerings, because the bronze altar that was before the LORD was too small to receive the burnt offering and the cereal offering and the fat pieces of the peace offerings.
⁶⁵ So Solomon held the feast at that time, and all Israel with him, a great assembly, from the entrance of Hamath to the Brook of Egypt, before the LORD our God, seven days. ⁶⁶ On the eighth day he sent the people away; and they blessed the king, and went to their homes joyful and glad of heart for all the goodness that the LORD had shown to David his servant and to Israel his people.

This section resumes the description of events after v. 11 and thus provides the narrative framework for the great speech and prayer of Solomon. *A hundred and twenty thousand sheep* seems excessively large, even to feed a great assembly like this one, and is omitted by the Septuagint. If the *burnt offering and the cereal offering* refer to the regular daily offerings, then Solomon was consecrating the normal worship routine for the daily practice of the Temple cult hereafter (Snaith, pp. 88–89). Only *the peace offerings,* which were the animals shared with the worshipers, would have been so numerous that not all the fat portions could be accommodated on the regular altar. *The feast* is the Feast of Tabernacles, celebrated here according to the Deuteronomic pattern of a seven-day festival followed by dismissal on the eighth day (Deut. 16:13,15). People had assembled from the farthest borders of the land (cf. comment on 4:21). Now they could return joyfully to their homes, having witnessed one of the great covenant occasions in their life as a people of God.

(6) *Divine Promise and Warning (9:1–9)*

¹ When Solomon had finished building the house of the LORD and the king's house and all that Solomon desired to build, ² the LORD appeared to Solomon a second time, as he had appeared to him at Gibeon. ³ And the LORD said to him, "I have heard your prayer and your supplication, which you have made before me; I have consecrated this house which you have built, and put my name there for ever; my eyes and my heart will be there for all time. ⁴ And as for you, if you will walk before me, as David your father walked, with integrity of heart and uprightness, doing according to all that I have commanded you, and keeping my statutes and my ordinances, ⁵ then I will establish your royal throne over Israel for ever, as I promised David your father, saying, 'There shall not fail you a man upon the throne of Israel.' ⁶ But if you turn aside from following me, you or your children, and do not keep my commandments and my statutes which I have set before you, but go and serve other gods and worship them, ⁷ then I will cut off Israel from the land which I have given them; and the house which I have consecrated for my name I will cast out of my sight; and Israel will become a proverb and a byword among all peoples. ⁸ And this house will become a heap of ruins; every one passing by it will be astonished, and will hiss; and they will say, 'Why has the LORD done thus to this land and to this house?' ⁹ Then they will say, 'Because they forsook the LORD their God who brought their fathers out of the land of Egypt, and laid hold on other gods, and worshiped them and served them; therefore the LORD has brought all this evil upon them.'"

The dedication of the Temple is not complete without the Lord's response to Solomon's prayer. This second appearance of the Lord to Solomon provides both a promise and a warning. The promise is that the Lord will heed Solomon's prayer and accept this royal Temple as his own. This is tied in with the promise to David about his dynasty. But, as the historian has already made clear, this promise is conditioned on Solomon's obedience. The threat in vv. 6–9 of the destruction of the Temple may have come from the postexilic editor.

Verse 1 gives a summary of Solomon's building enterprises (see 9:10,19). It is hardly necessary to suppose that after the building and dedicating of the Temple, Solomon had to wait 13 years for the answer to his prayer. This second appearance is like the one at Gibeon, an answer to prayer, and perhaps a night vision (cf. 2 Chron. 7:12). *Consecrated* points to a divine act. Solomon could consecrate the court of the Temple (8:64), but only the Lord can truly consecrate man's worship. *Walk before me . . . with integrity of heart and uprightness* is covenant language (cf. Gen. 17:1). The ethical standards of Davidic kingship were so high that none of David's earthly successors could live up to them. The covenant promise in v. 5 leads in the direction of the messianic promises of Isaiah. Without such promise, seen by the Christian interpreter as fulfilled in the New Testament, the story of Kings would be one of tragic human failure.

The change of pronouns in v. 6 (*you*, plural) must either refer to the dynasty, *you or your children*, or it must be regarded as a warning to the people by an editorial hand. *Serve other gods* is the cardinal sin against the Mosaic covenant, apostasy coupled with idolatry. *I will cut off Israel* reminds one of the great lesson of the fall of Samaria (2 Kings 17:7–18). A *proverb and a byword* means here a taunt, a "sharp, cutting word." *This house will become a heap of ruins* reminds one of the prophetic prediction of Micah (3:12; cf. Jer. 26:18). Even if this section has a postexilic form, it contains a genuine preexilic threat. The passersby will question why Yahweh would do this to his own land and house. The answer is that his people have abandoned their covenant Lord. This dire threat was about to or had already come true.

5. Commercial Enterprises of Solomon (9:10—10:29)

Solomon is idealized in this section of miscellaneous notices as a wealthy merchant prince. His commercial enterprises included his Red Sea trade to Ophir, his caravan trade with south Arabia, and his horse and chariot trade. The riches of Solomon and also his international reputation are evidences to the historian of Solomon's wisdom.

(1) Sale of Twenty Cities (9:10-14)

10 At the end of twenty years, in which Solomon had built the two houses, the house of the Lord and the king's house, 11 and Hiram king of Tyre had supplied Solomon with cedar and cypress timber and gold, as much as he desired, King Solomon gave to Hiram twenty cities in the land of Galilee. 12 But when Hiram came from Tyre to see the cities which Solomon had given him, they did not please him. 13 Therefore he said, "What kind of cities are these which you have given me, my brother?" So they are called the land of Cabul to this day. 14 Hiram had sent to the king one hundred and twenty talents of gold.

In addition to the covenant which Solomon had with Hiram king of Tyre (5:10-12), Solomon had to arrange for a large amount of gold to finance his building and commercial enterprises. There were some border towns in western Galilee near Acco in the tribe of Asher which he was willing to barter to the Phoenician king. Hiram's displeasure with these cities is preserved in the popular etymology of the name *Cabul* (like nothing), worthless land (cf. Josh. 19:27). The amount of gold seems excessive. It has been estimated as being worth about one and one-half million dollars (Snaith, p. 93). It is the same amount brought to Solomon by the Queen of Sheba (10:10), but it is small compared to some other amounts mentioned (9:28; 10:14).

(2) Forced Labor for Building Projects (9:15-22)

15 And this is the account of the forced labor which King Solomon levied to build the house of the Lord and his own house and the Millo and the wall of Jerusalem and Hazor and Megiddo and Gezer 16 (Pharaoh king of Egypt had gone up and captured Gezer and burnt it with fire, and had slain the Canaanites who dwelt in the city, and had given it as dowry to his daughter, Solomon's wife; 17 so Solomon rebuilt Gezer) and Lower Bethhoron 18 and Baalath and Tamar in the wilderness, in the land of Judah, 19 and all the store-cities that Solomon had, and the cities for his chariots, and the cities for his horsemen, and whatever Solomon desired to build in Jerusalem, in Lebanon, and in all the land of his dominion. 20 All the people who were left of the Amorites, the Hittites, the Perizzites, the Hivites, and the Jebusites, who were not of the people of Israel —21 their descendants who were left after them in the land, whom the people of Israel were unable to destroy utterly—these Solomon made a forced levy of slaves, and so they are to this day. 22 But of the people of Israel Solomon made no slaves; they were the soldiers, they were his officials, his commanders, his captains, his chariot commanders and his horsemen.

The king's building projects at key cities around the country, as well as Jerusalem, required forced labor. There is archaeological confirmation of Solomonic walls and gateways at Hazor, Megiddo, and Gezer (Gray, pp. 227–228). These three fortresses guarded the great trunk road that connected Mesopotamia to Egypt diagonally through the land of Palestine. Megiddo had added importance as a store-city, district headquarters, and chariot city (Wright, pp. 130–132). Perhaps each of the provincial capitals was such a store-city.

The remnants of the Canaanites' city-states were impressed into state slavery; but the statement that Solomon did not use an Israelite corvée appears to be contradicted by other statements (5:13–18; 11:27–28). This abuse of the corvée was regarded as a "heavy yoke" by the people (12:4), to whom it seemed a violation of their covenant freedoms under the old tribal confederacy (Bruce, p. 37). Samuel's warning concerning the manner of king who would someday rule over Israel had been fulfilled by Solomon (1 Sam. 8:10–18).

(3) Red Sea Fleet (9:23-28)

23 These were the chief officers who were over Solomon's work: five hundred and fifty, who had charge of the people who carried on the work.
24 But Pharaoh's daughter went up from the city of David to her own house which Solomon had built for her; then he built the Millo.
25 Three times a year Solomon used to offer up burnt offerings and peace offerings upon the altar which he built to the LORD, burning incense before the LORD. So he finished the house.
26 King Solomon built a fleet of ships at Eziongeber, which is near Eloth on the shore of the Red Sea, in the land of Edom. 27 And Hiram sent with the fleet his servants, seamen who were familiar with the sea, together with the servants of Solomon; 28 and they went to Ophir, and brought from there gold, to the amount of four hundred and twenty talents; and they brought it to King Solomon.

The three notices with which the section begins are quite detached from their context. Verse 25 supplements the account of the king's festival sacrifices (8:62–64; cf. 3:3-4,15). *Three times a year* points to the three pilgrimage festivals—Unleavened Bread, Weeks, and Tabernacles (2 Chron. 8:12–16). *So he finished the house* seems to refer to the round of ritual which initiated the usage of the Temple and its environs. Hence v. 25 is intended to magnify the role of the king in the Jerusalem cult (Gray, pp. 235–236).

The main subject of this section is the exploitation by King Solomon of a very profitable sea trade along the coasts of the Red Sea. Since the Phoenicians had begun to conduct an ever increasing sea trade westward, Solomon turned to Hiram and his Phoenician seamen to build and sail his Red Sea fleet. At the head of the Gulf of Aqaba, Solomon built his new seaport of Eziongeber. The excavation of this ancient city has amply illustrated the Solomonic use of this port as a storage center for his metals industry.[14] The refined metals from mines in the Arabah were stored, and perhaps further refined, for shipment from the port city.

Various locations have been proposed for *Ophir*, the farthest and richest port of call for the fleet's trading journeys, such as India, Africa, and Arabia. The abundance of fine gold seems to indicate southeast Arabia. Almug wood, a variety of sandalwood, seems to favor the west coast of India (10:11–12). The ivory and two kinds of monkeys seem to indicate East Africa (10:22). The likeliest suggestion is that Solomon traded along the coasts of the Red Sea in southwest Arabia and northeast Africa. Through the middlemen of Sheba, he could thus have obtained all the products mentioned from these various places.

(4) Visit of the Queen of Sheba (10:1–13)

1 Now when the queen of Sheba heard of the fame of Solomon concerning the name of the LORD, she came to test him with hard questions. 2 She came to Jerusalem with a very great retinue, with camels bearing spices, and very much gold, and precious stones; and when she came to Solomon, she told him all that was on her mind. 3 And Solomon answered all her questions; there was nothing hidden from the king which he could not explain to her. 4 And when the queen of Sheba had seen all the wisdom of Solomon, the house that he had built, 5 the food of his table, the seating of his officials, and the attendance of his servants, their clothing, his cupbearers, and his burnt offerings which he offered at the house of the LORD, there was no more spirit in her.
6 And she said to the king, "The report was true which I heard in my own land of your affairs and of your wisdom, 7 but I did not believe the reports until I came and my own eyes had seen it; and, behold, the half was not told me; your wisdom and prosperity surpass the report which I heard. 8 Happy are your wives! Happy are these your servants, who continually stand before you and hear your wisdom! 9 Blessed be the LORD your God, who has delighted in you and set you on the throne of Israel! Because the LORD loved Israel for ever, he has made you king, that you may execute justice and righteousness." 10 Then she gave the king a hundred and twenty talents of gold, and a very great quantity of spices, and precious stones; never again came such an abundance of spices as these which the queen of Sheba gave to King Solomon.
11 Moreover the fleet of Hiram, which

---

[14] Nelson Glueck, "Ezion-Geber," *Biblical Archaeologist*, Vol. XXVIII, No. 3 (September, 1965), pp. 70–87; cf. Wright, pp. 132–136.

brought gold from Ophir, brought from Ophir a very great amount of almug wood and precious stones. ¹² And the king made of the almug wood supports for the house of the Lord, and for the king's house, lyres also and harps for the singers; no such almug wood has come or been seen, to this day.

¹³ And King Solomon gave to the queen of Sheba all that she desired, whatever she asked besides what was given her by the bounty of King Solomon. So she turned and went back to her own land, with her servants.

This story has been made famous by Jesus' reference to the reverence paid to Solomon's wisdom by the "queen of the south" (Matt. 12:42). Her remarkable journey was 1500 miles from southwest Arabia by camel caravan, and perhaps its chief purpose was the negotiation of a trade agreement for the control of the traffic in spices and other exotic goods. Whether Solomon's sea trade with the same area, mentioned by a parenthesis inserted in this account (10:11-12), would have forced the queen of Sheba and the kings of Arabia (10:15) to make such an agreement with Solomon is not specifically stated. The fame of Solomon was also in some sense the name or reputation of the Lord who had so materially blessed him. *Hard questions,* literally, "riddles," is a reference to the kind of wisdom literature attributed to Solomon (4:29-34). But Solomon's wisdom is also reflected in his buildings, his elaborate court establishment, and even in his worship. *No more spirit in her* means that she was literally deflated by such surpassing wealth.

The admiration of the writer and later Israel for Solomon shines through the pious speech of the queen of Sheba. Israel loved to recount such stories of praise for Israel and her God in mouths of foreigners. *Then she gave the king* tribute money such as was collected from other kings and merchants whose trade routes of necessity passed through Solomon's territory (10:15,24-25). *Abundance of spices,* the most precious commodity of the Sabean caravan trade which here makes its entrance upon the scene of history, was the famous frankincense and myrrh, immortalized in the narrative of Jesus' birth (Matt. 2:11; cf. *IDB*, IV, pp. 144-146).

(5) *Wealth of Solomon (10:14-22)*

¹⁴ Now the weight of gold that came to Solomon in one year was six hundred and sixty-six talents of gold, ¹⁵ besides that which came from the traders and from the traffic of the merchants, and from all the kings of Arabia and from the governors of the land. ¹⁶ King Solomon made two hundred large shields of beaten gold; six hundred shekels of gold went into each shield. ¹⁷ And he made three hundred shields of beaten gold; three minas of gold went into each shield; and the king put them in the House of the Forest of Lebanon. ¹⁸ The king also made a great ivory throne, and overlaid it with the finest gold. ¹⁹ The throne had six steps, and at the back of the throne was a calf's head, and on each side of the seat were arm rests and two lions standing beside the arm rests, ²⁰ while twelve lions stood there, one on each end of a step on the six steps. The like of it was never made in any kingdom. ²¹ All King Solomon's drinking vessels were of gold, and all the vessels of the House of the Forest of Lebanon were of pure gold; none were of silver, it was not considered as anything in the days of Solomon. ²² For the king had a fleet of ships of Tarshish at sea with the fleet of Hiram. Once every three years the fleet of ships of Tarshish used to come bringing gold, silver, ivory, apes, and peacocks.

The historian wishes to illustrate from the miscellaneous items in the annals of Solomon's kingdom concerning his magnificent wealth. *Six hundred and sixty-six talents of gold,* over $16 million (Snaith, p. 99), seems like an exaggeration, not even including the taxes from his caravan trade. The large oblong shields, of the type which protected a man's whole body, were four times as valuable as the smaller round shields. In the account which tells how Shishak, king of Egypt, plundered these treasures, we are told that their purpose was for use in ceremonial processions to the house of the Lord (14:25-28). The magnificent ivory throne, decorated with ivory inlay and gold leaf, was probably of Phoenician workmanship. Its seven levels and the calf and the lion decorations symbolized the perfection, power, and overlordship exercised by the king sitting in judgment.

The reference to golden drinking vessels is explained by another description of the wealthy sea trade. *Tarshish* is either Tartessus in Spain, or Nora in Sardinia, both of which were Phoenician trading colonies in the western Mediterranean. These ships were large oceangoing vessels which served to carry copper ingots for the Phoenician mining operations. *Peacocks* (as translated) is based on an analogy with a Sanskrit word, but a better analogy comes from an Egyptian word meaning baboons.

(6) Solomon in His Glory (10:23–25)

23 Thus King Solomon excelled all the kings of the earth in riches and in wisdom. 24 And the whole earth sought the presence of Solomon to hear his wisdom, which God had put into his mind. 25 Every one of them brought his present, articles of silver and gold, garments, myrrh, spices, horses, and mules, so much year by year.

Jesus put all of this splendor in a new perspective in his teaching against anxiety over material things, saying of the lilies of the field that "even Solomon in all his glory was not arrayed like one of these" (Matt. 6:29). God had abundantly fulfilled his promise, not only to give Solomon the wisdom that he requested, but also the riches and the honor which he had not requested.

(7) Horse and Chariot Trade (10:26–29)

26 And Solomon gathered together chariots and horsemen; he had fourteen hundred chariots and twelve thousand horsemen, whom he stationed in the chariot cities and with the king in Jerusalem. 27 And the king made silver as common in Jerusalem as stone, and he made cedar as plentiful as the sycamore of the Shephelah. 28 And Solomon's import of horses was from Egypt and Kue, and the king's traders received them from Kue at a price. 29 A chariot could be imported from Egypt for six hundred shekels of silver, and a horse for a hundred and fifty; and so through the king's traders they were exported to all the kings of the Hittites and the kings of Syria.

Solomon's administrative districts provided the supplies for his horses (4:26–28), district capitals, and store-cities. Solomon also provided cities for his chariots and horsemen (9:19). Through his large standing army, strategically stationed around the country, Solomon maintained peace in the possessions which he inherited from David his father. The statement about his material prosperity (cf. 2 Chron. 1:15; 9:27) may be inserted at this point to indicate that Solomon made money out of his trade in horses and chariots.

Egypt and Kue. Kue has now been identified as Cilicia in southeast Asia Minor, a famous horse breeding region. Some scholars believe that the word for Egypt, *mitsraim,* should be read instead *mutsri,* a region in Capadocia just north of Cilicia (Gray, p. 250). But Solomon's treaty with Egypt probably would indicate the reading Egypt is correct. Thus king Solomon served as a kind of middleman to provide the Arameans and Syro-Hittites with these expensive items. In the development of the Deuteronomic code, the passage on the law of the king contains a dark hint that Solomon may have sold some Israelites into slavery in Egypt in order to obtain his horses and chariots (Deut. 17:16–17).

With this climax of materialism, a new status quo has been achieved with a noticeable absence of prophetic advice, no prophet having been mentioned in the account since Nathan's participation in the anointing of Solomon. But a prophetic word against Solomon's apostasy to the gods of his foreign wives and a prophetically inspired rebellion by one of his forced-labor leaders was about to shake the status quo and tear the kingdom from his son.

6. Apostasy and Punishment of Solomon (11:1–43)

Up to this chapter, the historian has chosen to emphasize the good aspects of the reign of Solomon. There have been only hints of the oppressive taxation and forced labor. Other indications have been given of his opening up of the kingdom to foreign influences through diplomatic and trade relations sealed by intermarriage. The result is that the monarchy has evolved from the simple military leadership of the tribal confederacy under Saul to an Oriental despotism under Solomon.

(1) Turning to Gods of Foreign Wives (11:1-8)

¹ Now King Solomon loved many foreign women; the daughter of Pharaoh, and Moabite, Ammonite, Edomite, Sidonian, and Hittite women, ² from the nations concerning which the LORD had said to the people of Israel, "You shall not enter into marriage with them, neither shall they with you, for surely they will turn away your heart after their gods"; Solomon clung to these in love. ³ He had seven hundred wives, princesses, and three hundred concubines; and his wives turned away his heart. ⁴ For when Solomon was old his wives turned away his heart after other gods; and his heart was not wholly true to the LORD his God, as was the heart of David his father. ⁵ For Solomon went after Ashtoreth the goddess of the Sidonians, and after Milcom the abomination of the Ammonites. ⁶ So Solomon did what was evil in the sight of the LORD, and did not wholly follow the LORD, as David his father had done. ⁷ Then Solomon built a high place for Chemosh the abomination of Moab, and for Molech the abomination of the Ammonites, on the mountain east of Jerusalem. ⁸ And so he did for all his foreign wives, who burned incense and sacrificed to their gods.

Solomon's fabulously large harem was a sign of both his abundant wealth and the astuteness of his foreign policy. The king was thoughtful enough of his foreign wives to provide them opportunity for their own worship. But the judgment of the historian is that such broadminded tolerance had disastrous consequences upon the loyalty of the king to Yahweh. The danger of idolatry and apostasy was the basis for the Deuteronomic regulations against intermarriage covenants (Deut. 7:3-4; 17:17; Joshua 23:7 ff.).

Seven hundred wives seems exaggerated to most commentators (but cf. Snaith, p. 102). Comparative figures with other royal harems would seem to indicate a number of wives closer to 70, the number of wives usually being smaller than the number of concubines (de Vaux, pp. 115–116; cf. 2 Chron. 11:21; Song of Sol. 6:8). This passage has doubtless provided the basis for attributing the Song of Solomon to the authorship of Solomon (cf. *IDB*, IV, 420–426).

According to the historian, these politically expedient intermarriages began to have an insidious influence against pure Yahwism when the king built pagan sanctuaries on the Mount of Olives, which remained until Josiah's day (2 Kings 23:13). *Ashtoreth*, or Astarte, fertility goddess and consort of Baal, had been a stumbling block to the Israelites ever since the Conquest (Judg. 2:13), but she is not to be confused with the Canaanite mother-goddess, Asherah, also associated with Baal, and also a stumbling block to the Israelites (Judg. 3:7; 1 Kings 15:13; 18:19). *Milcom* or *Molech* was the bloodthirsty war god of the Ammonites, in whose worship child sacrifice was practiced (2 Kings 23:10), and is perhaps to be identified with *Chemosh*, a war god of neighboring Moab (2 Kings 3:27; Judg. 11:24).

(2) Resulting Division of Kingdom (11:9–13)

⁹ And the LORD was angry with Solomon, because his heart had turned away from the LORD, the God of Israel, who had appeared to him twice, ¹⁰ and had commanded him concerning this thing, that he should not go after other gods; but he did not keep what the LORD commanded. ¹¹ Therefore the LORD said to Solomon, "Since this has been your mind and you have not kept my covenant and my statutes which I have commanded you, I will surely tear the kingdom from you and will give it to your servant. ¹² Yet for the sake of David your father I will not do it in your days, but I will tear it out of the hand of your son. ¹³ However I will not tear away all the kingdom; but I will give one tribe to your son, for the sake of David my servant and for the sake of Jerusalem which I have chosen."

The prophetic theology of the Deuteronomic historian of kings is nowhere more clearly stated than in this adverse judgment against Solomon. *The Lord was angry* illustrates how the Old Testament attributes human emotions to God; but these emphasize the personal relationship of the Lord with his people.

The revelations to Solomon—*appeared*

to him twice—make his apostasy all the more horrible. Only the second of the two appearances mentions the warning stated in v. 10 (9:6–9).

I will surely tear the kingdom from you. Perhaps this word of judgment came from Ahijah the Shilonite (11:29), since the threefold use of the verb *tear* in this passage reminds one of the symbolic action of the prophet performed for Jeroboam (11:30–31). The word of judgment is mixed with grace, with the disaster delayed until the days of Solomon's son, and the tribe of Judah remaining loyal to the Davidic dynasty. Nevertheless, the bad example of Solomon and his apostasy to the gods of his foreign wives would be remembered five centuries later (Neh. 13:26).

(3) *First Adversary, Hadad of Edom (11:14–22)*

14 And the LORD raised up an adversary against Solomon, Hadad the Edomite; he was of the royal house in Edom. 15 For when David was in Edom, and Joab the commander of the army went up to bury the slain, he slew every male in Edom 16 (for Joab and all Israel remained there six months, until he had cut off every male in Edom); 17 but Hadad fled to Egypt, together with certain Edomites of his father's servants, Hadad being yet a little child. 18 They set out from Midian and came to Paran, and took men with them from Paran and came to Egypt, to Pharaoh king of Egypt, who gave him a house, and assigned him an allowance of food, and gave him land. 19 And Hadad found great favor in the sight of Pharaoh, so that he gave him in marriage the sister of his own wife, the sister of Tahpenes the queen. 20 And the sister of Tahpenes bore him Genubath his son, whom Tahpenes weaned in Pharaoh's house; and Genubath was in Pharaoh's house among the sons of Pharaoh. 21 But when Hadad heard in Egypt that David slept with his fathers and that Joab the commander of the army was dead, Hadad said to Pharaoh, "Let me depart, that I may go to my own country." 22 But Pharaoh said to him, "What have you lacked with me that you are now seeking to go to your own country?" And he said to him, "Only let me go."

Solomon had once described the peace of his realm to Hiram: "There is neither adversary nor misfortune" (5:4). One cannot tell from the present story how soon this situation changed. Two defections from the extent of David's empire are here recorded as divine punishments.

Hadad had survived David's Edomite campaign (2 Sam. 8:13–14) and an extended purge by Joab, and had fled by stages to Egypt. While he was still a small lad, he seems to have been hidden in the wilderness near Edom until a Pharoah arose who was not kindly disposed toward Solomon. According to v. 21, the deaths of David and Joab signalled the return of Hadad to Edom. But if he achieved any power there so early in Solomon's reign, it was only mischief (11:25), not sufficient to prevent the king's extensive metals industry, shipping or caravan trade through Edom.

(4) *Second Adversary, Rezon of Damascus (11:23–25)*

Much more significant for the next two centuries of Israel's history was the defection of Rezon. A former ally of Hadadezer of Zobah, who was head of the Aramean coalition defeated by David (2 Sam. 8:3–8; 10:6–8,15–18), Rezon had become leader of a band of outlaws in a manner very similar to David himself. David had garrisoned Damascus as an important outpost of his empire. Fairly early in Solomon's reign Rezon and his marauders seized Damascus. Though it is doubtful whether he was powerful enough to challenge Solomon's control of caravan trade in this region, his defection weakened Solomon's empire.

(5) *Third Adversary, Jeroboam of Ephraim (11:26–40)*

23 God also raised up as an adversary to him, Rezon the son of Eliada, who had fled from his master Hadadezer king of Zobah. 24 And he gathered men about him and became leader of a marauding band, after the slaughter by David; and they went to Damascus, and dwelt there, and made him king in Damascus. 25 He was an adversary of Israel all the days of Solomon, doing mischief as Hadad did; and he abhorred Israel, and reigned over Syria.

The attempted rebellion of Jeroboam happened in the latter years of Solomon's reign. The building of the Millo was connected with the end of his 20-year building period in Jerusalem (cf. Gray, p. 224). The dynasty had changed in Egypt, to which Jeroboam fled, with the accession of Shishak (ca. 940 B.C.). The Septuagint has a different version of the revolt of Jeroboam (Montgomery, pp. 251-254).

a. An Able Labor Leader (11:26-28)

26 Jeroboam the son of Nebat, an Ephraimite of Zeredah, a servant of Solomon, whose mother's name was Zeruah, a widow, also lifted up his hand against the king. 27 And this was the reason why he lifted up his hand against the king. Solomon built the Millo, and closed up the breach of the city of David his father. 28 The man Jeroboam was very able, and when Solomon saw that the young man was industrious he gave him charge over all the forced labor of the house of Joseph.

Evidently Jeroboam's father, Nebat, died early. Jeroboam's mother, Zeruah, is called a widow. *Zeredah* was a site in the hill country of Ephraim between Ramah and Shiloh, which Jeroboam is said in the Greek version to have fortified. This may supply the content of the lifting up of *his hand against the king.* The motive for rebellion is hinted at by the connection of Jeroboam's service to Solomon with the Ephraimite forced labor, the "heavy yoke" his fellow tribesmen were bearing for the king's ambitious building program (cf. 12:4). The course of events which follows serves only to demonstrate the king's judgment of Jeroboam's ability, even if the outcome was disastrous to his kingdom and that of his son.

b. Deed and Word of the Prophet Ahijah (11:29-39)

29 And at that time, when Jeroboam went out of Jerusalem, the prophet Ahijah the Shilonite found him on the road. Now Ahijah had clad himself with a new garment; and the two of them were alone in the open country. 30 Then Ahijah laid hold of the new garment that was on him, and tore it into twelve pieces. 31 And he said to Jeroboam, "Take for yourself ten pieces; for thus says the LORD, the God of Israel. 'Behold, I am about to tear the kingdom from the hand of Solomon, and will give you ten tribes 32 (but he shall have one tribe, for the sake of my servant David and for the sake of Jerusalem, the city which I have chosen out of all the tribes of Israel), 33 because he has forsaken me, and worshiped Ashtoreth the goddess of the Sidonians, Chemosh the god of Moab, and Milcom the god of the Ammonites, and has not walked in my ways, doing what is right in my sight and keeping my statutes and my ordinances, as David his father did. 34 Nevertheless I will not take the whole kingdom out of his hand; but I will make him ruler all the days of his life, for the sake of David my servant whom I chose, who kept my commandments and my statutes; 35 but I will take the kingdom out of his son's hand, and will give it to you, ten tribes. 36 Yet to his son I will give one tribe, that David my servant may always have a lamp before me in Jerusalem, the city where I have chosen to put my name. 37 And I will take you, and you shall reign over all that your soul desires, and you shall be king over Israel. 38 And if you will hearken to all that I command you, and will walk in my ways, and do what is right in my eyes by keeping my statutes and my commandments, as David my servant did, I will be with you, and will build you a sure house, as I built for David, and I will give Israel to you. 39 And I will for this afflict the descendants of David, but not for ever.'"

The succession of prophetic men is continuous from the time of Samuel. Now another figure appears in the role of kingmaker, like unto Samuel and Nathan: Ahijah the Shilonite. The political role of the prophet was directly connected to the covenant relation with Yahweh. If the reigning king had violated this covenant, the prophet did not hesitate to stir up a rebellion against him. That Ahijah was from the ancient central sanctuary of the tribal confederacy in Shiloh may be significant for his prophetic role.

Part of the uniqueness of this narrative is the symbolic act of Ahijah. This is the earliest full-fledged example of a feature of prophetic proclamation and implementation of the word of the Lord that becomes increasingly important, reaching its climax in Jeremiah and Ezekiel. The prophet's *garment* was frequently involved (1 Sam. 15:27-28; cf. 1 Kings 19:19; 2 Kings 2:8ff). The Hebrew word for *new garment* indicates a wrapper, an outer garment, and is a different term than the robe of Samuel, or the mantle of Elijah, which becomes the typical prophetic garment (cf. Zech. 13:4). The *twelve pieces* stand for the twelve tribes of Israel as a religious confederation, although the geographical and political realities have changed since the earlier period (cf. 4:7–19). *Ten tribes . . . one tribe* (LXX and Old Latin versions read two tribes for David in vv. 32,36). The number of southern tribes is confused, since the position of Benjamin as the border tribe is ambiguous and disputed. Bethel, now in Ephraim, constitutes the southern border of the ten tribes, so that Benjamin is counted with Judah at the time of the division (cf. 12:23).

The life of David and of his successor on the Davidic throne was the *lamp* of Israel (2 Sam. 21:17; Psalm 132:17). The ordinary word for lamp (*ner*) is here spelled (as in 1 Kings 15:4; 2 Kings 8:19) *nyr*, which might be translated "dominion." [15]

If you will hearken. Ahijah maintained the covenantal ideals of the old tribal confederacy, as Samuel had with Saul, making the continuance of Jeroboam's dynasty conditional on his obedience to Yahweh. Thus the kingship of the North developed differently from that in Judah, and prophecy played a more important political role.

c. Flight of Jeroboam to Egypt (11:40)

40 Solomon sought therefore to kill Jeroboam; but Jeroboam arose, and fled into Egypt, to Shishak king of Egypt, and was in Egypt until the death of Solomon.

Ahijah's oracle to Jeroboam stirred him to some act of rebellion, to which Solomon reacted as he had to the threat of Adonijah's party (2:13 ff.). For the first time in the Old Testament, the name of the Pharaoh is given, *Shishak,* the first Pharaoh of the new Libyan Dynasty. His support of Jeroboam was motivated by the revival of the Egyptian policy of military intervention in Palestine (14:25–28). The opportune time for rebellion was always the death of the powerful monarch, so Jeroboam remained *in Egypt until the death of Solomon.*

(6) Death of Solomon (11:41–43)

41 Now the rest of the acts of Solomon, and all that he did, and his wisdom, are they not written in the book of the acts of Solomon? **42** And the time that Solomon reigned in Jerusalem over all Israel was forty years. **43** And Solomon slept with his fathers, and was buried in the city of David his father; and Rehoboam his son reigned in his stead.

This brief evaluation of Solomon's administrative deeds emphasizes *his wisdom.* Despite the king's failures, he still made a positive contribution to God's kingdom. His great achievements were the building of the Jerusalem Temple and the authorship and collection of wisdom literature. Indeed, Solomon's kingship provided wealth and leisure for a surge of literary activity (cf. Noth, pp. 218–224).

II. Beginning of the Divided Kingdom (12:1—16:34)

The kingdom of David was a dual monarchy, governed from a tribally neutral capital, Jerusalem, which was the personal property of David and his successors. David made this dual monarchy a base for his Syro-Palestinian empire, which was commercially exploited by Solomon. David's kingship over the tribes of Israel, formerly loyal to Saul, was by covenant with the tribal elders (2 Sam. 5:3). But the accession of Solomon to David's throne was by court intrigue rather than tribal covenant, and Solomon proceeded to violate the freedoms of the old tribal confederacy by imposing heavy burdens of taxation and forced labor. The assembly at Shechem expressed the determination of the ten northern tribes either to change this Solomonic despotism or to rebel against it. The foolishness of Rehoboam precipitated the revolt of Jeroboam, with its disastrous consequences. Politically, the empire was lost, and a bitter civil war arose. Religiously, Jeroboam committed the North to a rival cult which provoked the wrath of the Lord

---

[15] Paul D. Hanson, "The Song of Heshbon and David's Nîr," *Harvard Theological Review,* Vol. 61, No. 3 (July, 1968), pp. 297–320.

against him and all his successors. The first two dynasties failed to achieve dynastic power or succession. The dynasty of Omri ended the civil war with Judah, but precipitated a prophetic revolt against Ahab and his sons. In Judah, Rehoboam and his successors were militarily weak and religiously unsatisfactory. The religious interest of the historian now shifted from the kings to the prophets.

1. The Revolt of Jeroboam (12:1–33)

Jeroboam has made his appearance as one of Solomon's adversaries (11:26–40). Rehoboam has succeeded Solomon in Jerusalem and Judah, but has not yet been confirmed as king of all Israel. This section deals not only with the split itself, but with those measures taken by Jeroboam to make the split permanent.

(1) Assembly at Shechem (12:1–5)

¹ Rehoboam went to Shechem, for all Israel had come to Shechem to make him king. ² And when Jeroboam the son of Nebat heard of it (for he was still in Egypt, whither he had fled from King Solomon), then Jeroboam returned from Egypt. ³ And they sent and called him; and Jeroboam and all the assembly of Israel came and said to Rehoboam, ⁴ "Your father made our yoke heavy. Now therefore lighten the hard service of your father and his heavy yoke upon us, and we will serve you." ⁵ He said to them, "Depart for three days, then come again to me." So the people went away.

The redress of legitimate tribal grievances had evidently long been neglected by Solomon. Even without the leadership of Jeroboam, there would have been trouble for an inexperienced young king trying to fill Solomon's place. How active a part Jeroboam took in the negotiations of the assembly with Rehoboam has been disputed. The Hebrew of v. 2 (cf. 12:20) and the Septuagint version of the revolt indicate that Jeroboam remained in Egypt. But 12:3,12 (cf. 2 Chron. 10:2) have him already on the scene assuming the leadership to which he is later formally elected.

Shechem was an ancient rallying place for the tribes, the scene of a periodic covenant renewal ceremony (Deut. 11:29–30; 27:11 ff.; 31:10 ff.; Josh. 8:30–35; 24:1–28,32). *We will serve you* was a commitment. There is no reason to doubt the good faith of the tribes who had indeed borne a *heavy yoke* of taxation and forced labor under Solomon.

(2) Foolish Policy of Rehoboam (12:6–15)

⁶ Then King Rehoboam took counsel with the old men, who had stood before Solomon his father while he was yet alive, saying, "How do you advise me to answer this people?" ⁷ And they said to him, "If you will be a servant to this people today and serve them, and speak good words to them when you answer them, then they will be your servants for ever." ⁸ But he forsook the counsel which the old men gave him, and took counsel with the young men who had grown up with him and stood before him. ⁹ And he said to them, "What do you advise that we answer this people who have said to me, 'Lighten the yoke that your father put upon us'?" ¹⁰ And the young men who had grown up with him said to him, "Thus shall you speak to this people who said to you, 'Your father made our yoke heavy, but do you lighten it for us'; thus shall you say to them, 'My little finger is thicker than my father's loins. ¹¹ And now, whereas my father laid upon you a heavy yoke, I will add to your yoke. My father chastised you with whips, but I will chastise you with scorpions.'"

¹² So Jeroboam and all the people came to Rehoboam the third day, as the king said, "Come to me again the third day." ¹³ And the king answered the people harshly, and forsaking the counsel which the old men had given him, ¹⁴ he spoke to them according to the counsel of the young men, saying, "My father made your yoke heavy, but I will add to your yoke; my father chastised you with whips, but I will chastise you with scorpions." ¹⁵ So the king did not hearken to the people; for it was a turn of affairs brought about by the LORD that he might fulfil his word, which the LORD spoke by Ahijah the Shilonite to Jeroboam the son of Nebat.

Like Solomon, Rehoboam had been born "to the purple" in Jerusalem. David spoiled his sons Amnon, Absalom, and Adonijah, who rejected wise counsel for foolish vanity. Evidently Solomon did no better with Rehoboam. *The old men* were Solomon's officials (4:1–6), who gave crafty advice still practiced by politicians at election time. *The young men* were also reared in the sumptuous court of Solomon and foolishly supposed there was no end to material prosperity based on cruel despotism. *Chastise* was an important word in the wisdom schools for the kind of discipline these young men lacked (Prov. 19:18; 29:17). *Turn of affairs* is a unique word for change of fortune, but not a fatalistic concept. To fulfill his prophetic word by Ahijah, the Lord would indeed turn things around (cf. 2:15; 1 Sam. 2:7).

(3) *Successful Rebellion* (*12:16–24*)

16 And when all Israel saw that the king did not hearken to them, the people answered the king,
"What portion have we in David?
We have no inheritance in the son of Jesse.
To your tents, O Israel!
Look now to your own house, David."
So Israel departed to their tents. 17 But Rehoboam reigned over the people of Israel who dwelt in the cities of Judah. 18 Then King Rehoboam sent Adoram, who was taskmaster over the forced labor, and all Israel stoned him to death with stones. And King Rehoboam made haste to mount his chariot, to flee to Jerusalem. 19 So Israel has been in rebellion against the house of David to this day. 20 And when all Israel heard that Jeroboam had returned, they sent and called him to the assembly and made him king over all Israel. There was none that followed the house of David, but the tribe of Judah only.

21 When Rehoboam came to Jerusalem, he assembled all the house of Judah, and the tribe of Benjamin, a hundred and eighty thousand chosen warriors, to fight against the house of Israel, to restore the kingdom to Rehoboam the son of Solomon. 22 But the word of God came to Shemaiah the man of God: 23 "Say to Rehoboam the son of Solomon, king of Judah, and to all the house of Judah and Benjamin, and to the rest of the people, 24 'Thus says the LORD, You shall not go up or fight against your kinsmen the people of Israel. Return every man to his home, for this thing is from me.'" So they hearkened to the word of the LORD, and went home again, according to the word of the LORD.

Israel raised the cry of Sheba's rebellion against David (2 Sam. 20:1), reminding the tribal representatives of previous trouble between the two groups. The prosaic comment, *departed to their tents,* understands those gathered to be dwelling like an army in the field near Shechem (Gray, p. 283). *The people of Israel* over whom Rehoboam continued to reign may refer to Benjamin, which was previously identified with the northern tribes, or perhaps to pious Israelites who defected to Judah (2 Chron. 11:16). *Adoram,* according to several versions, should read Adoniram, with whom this taskmaster is to be identified (1 Kings 4:6). If he is the same as David's head of forced labor, he has been serving about half a century (2 Sam. 20:24). Rehoboam showed a tasteless folly in sending an officer who would be such a forceful reminder of the reason for rebellion. The reply of the assembly was an effective deed of rebellion, that caused Rehoboam to flee for his life.

This division of the kingdom was a day of disaster, so remembered two centuries later (cf. Isa. 7:17). The Septuagint adds Benjamin to *Judah only,* to agree with vv. 21–24. Shemaiah is called *the man of God,* which is a synonym for prophet with the prophetic guilds (cf. 13:1). This is the only account we have of him in Kings, although the Septuagint's version of Jeroboam attributes to Shemaiah rather than Ahijah the symbolic tearing of the garment (11:29 ff.). Chronicles tells of his oracle to Rehoboam during the Shishak invasion (2 Chron. 12:5 f.), and some interpreters have supposed that the threat of that Egyptian intervention is the political motive for his forbidding the battle here. *Thus says the Lord* was the familiar prophetic speech formula, also used by Ahijah (11:31). *This thing is from me* is to be understood as declaring that God is the Lord of history, and causes even disastrous rebellion to be the means of accomplishing his purpose.

(4) *Sins of Jeroboam* (*12:25–33*)

25 Then Jeroboam built Shechem in the hill country of Ephraim, and dwelt there; and he went out from there and built Penuel. 26 And Jeroboam said in his heart, "Now the kingdom will turn back to the house of David; 27 if this people go up to offer sacrifices in the house of the LORD at Jerusalem, then the heart of this

people will turn again to their lord, to Rehoboam king of Judah, and they will kill me and return to Rehoboam king of Judah." ²⁸ So the king took counsel, and made two calves of gold. And he said to the people, "You have gone up to Jerusalem long enough. Behold your gods, O Israel, who brought you up out of the land of Egypt." ²⁹ And he set one in Bethel, and the other he put in Dan. ³⁰ And this thing became a sin, for the people went to the one at Bethel and to the other as far as Dan. ³¹ He also made houses on high places, and appointed priests from among all the people, who were not of the Levites. ³² And Jeroboam appointed a feast on the fifteenth day of the eighth month like the feast that was in Judah, and he offered sacrifices upon the altar; so he did in Bethel, sacrificing to the calves that he had made. And he placed in Bethel the priests of the high places that he had made. ³³ He went up to the altar which he had made in Bethel on the fifteenth day in the eighth month, in the month which he had devised of his own heart; and he ordained a feast for the people of Israel, and went up to the altar to burn incense.

Jeroboam set about immediately to consolidate his kingdom. He fortified the ancient tribal center of Shechem as his first capital, a fact confirmed by archaeology (Wright, p. 147). Later he fortified Penuel, across Jordan, perhaps at the time of Shishak's invasion. Just as David and Solomon had sought to make Jerusalem a religious center, so Jeroboam felt the necessity to establish religious centers in the north for political reasons. The Judean historian of Josiah's time was never able to forgive Jeroboam and his successors for this counter-cult, though a kingdom which was politically divided could hardly be expected to remain united religiously.

To the *two calves of gold* (young bulls) a covenant saying is addressed, which at once connects this new symbolism with the ancient story of Aaron and the golden calf (Ex. 32:4,8), where a virtually identical formula is used. The name, *gods*, could just as well be translated "God," except that it has here a plural verb, and in Exodus a plural pronoun. This is not to be interpreted as the gross idolatry which it later tended to become, but rather a new symbolism like the cherubim and ark of Solomon's Temple. But the bulls of Bethel and Dan, unlike the Jerusalem symbols, seem to have been in public view, and the inevitable association with Canaanite fertility worship justifies the judgment of the historian that *this thing became a sin.* By the time of Hosea, the worship of these calves is virtually a Baal worship, scorned and condemned as idolatry (Hos. 8:5–6; 10:5–6; 13:2).

Bethel was the "royal sanctuary" in Amos' day (Amos 7:13) and certainly was thus more important than Dan. It was a sacred place of the patriarchs, especially Jacob (Gen. 28:10–22; 35:1–15). The sanctuary at Dan claimed a priesthood descended from Moses, and was a pilgrimage shrine at the northern border of the kingdom (Judg. 18:30).

Further offenses of Jeroboam had to do with his maintenance of the local high places, appointment of non-Levitic priests, changing the harvest festival to the eighth month, and officiating at Bethel to inaugurate the worship there. All this is condemned from the viewpoint of the Deuteronomic historian and the Jerusalem priesthood. It was the beginning of a course that issued in gross idolatry and brought the righteous judgment of God.

2. Prophetic Judgment on Jeroboam (13:1—14:20)

The importance of the prophetic movement in Israel is emphasized by the fact that the same prophet who designated a man as king could also pronounce God's judgment against that king and all his potential successors. Ahijah the Shilonite serves this prophetic function of kingmaker and king-breaker for Jeroboam. The wickedness of Jeroboam's Bethel cult, from the viewpoint of the Jerusalem Temple, is also condemned by an anonymous man of God from Judah, whose mission against Bethel has reminded some of the similar task of Amos (7:10–15; cf. 3:14; 5:5; 9:1).

1 KINGS 13

(1) Word of the Lord Against Bethel (13:1–34)

Growing out of the same circles of prophetic tradition which preserved the narratives about Ahijah, Elijah, and Elisha are stories of anonymous prophets (18:4; 20:13,22,35–43; 22:6; cf. Judg. 6:8; 1 Sam. 2:27; 10:5). These are the "sons of the prophets," or members of prophetic guilds, later located at such centers as Bethel and Jericho (2 Kings 2:3 ff.; cf. Gibeah and Ramah in 1 Sam. 10:10; 19:18 ff.) and subject to a master such as Elisha (2 Kings 2:7,15; 4:1,38; 9:1). A very important lesson of discipleship in these prophetic schools was absolute obedience to the word of the Lord and the disciple's mission (2 Kings 4:29; cf. Luke 10:4). The oracles of and narratives about the great canonical prophets were likely preserved by such schools of disciples (Isa. 8:16; 50:4–5; Jer. 36:2,32).

a. Man of God from Judah (13:1–10)

¹ And behold, a man of God came out of Judah by the word of the Lord to Bethel. Jeroboam was standing by the altar to burn incense. ² And the man cried against the altar by the word of the Lord, and said, "O altar, altar, thus says the Lord: 'Behold, a son shall be born to the house of David, Josiah by name; and he shall sacrifice upon you the priests of the high places who burn incense upon you, and men's bones shall be burned upon you.'" ³ And he gave a sign the same day, saying, "This is the sign that the Lord has spoken: "Behold, the altar shall be torn down, and the ashes that are upon it shall be poured out.'" ⁴ And when the king heard the saying of the man of God, which he cried against the altar at Bethel, Jeroboam stretched out his hand from the altar, saying, "Lay hold of him." And his hand, which he stretched out against him, dried up, so that he could not draw it back to himself. ⁵ The altar also was torn down, and the ashes poured out from the altar, according to the sign which the man of God had given by the word of the Lord. ⁶ And the king said to the man of God, "Entreat now the favor of the Lord your God, and pray for me, that my hand may be restored to me." And the man of God entreated the Lord; and the king's hand was restored to him, and became as it was before. ⁷ And the king said to the man of God, "Come home with me, and refresh yourself, and I will give you a reward." ⁸ And the man of God said to the king, "If you give me half your house, I will not go in with you. And I will not eat bread or drink water in this place; ⁹ for so was it commanded me by the word of the Lord, saying, 'You shall neither eat bread, nor drink water, nor return by the way that you came.'" ¹⁰ So he went another way, and did not return by the way that he came to Bethel.

There are two indications that the story of the fulfillment of this remarkable prediction in the time of the historian has influenced the form of the narrative. One is the notice that Josiah is the name of the Davidic king who will desecrate the Bethel altar, which the great majority of scholars take to be a scribal gloss. The other is the use of the term "cities of Samaria" (13:32), meaning the province of Samaria. Samaria was not built or named until the beginning of Omri's reign (16:24), and did not become a province until the Assyrian invasion (ca. 734 B.C.). This use of the term Samaria is noticeable in the account of Josiah's reform, which erroneously states that the old Bethel prophet was from Samaria (2 Kings 23:17–19).

The connection of the story with the end of the previous chapter seems to indicate the occasion to be the dedication festival of the Bethel altar (cf. 8:2,22,62–66). *Sign* is an ominous portent or prediction, a sign of the prophet, confirming the genuineness of his prophetic word by a present happening. The king who gestures against the man of God, commanding his arrest, is marvelously smitten, and requests intercessory prayer from one who is so obviously a man of God. *Entreat now the favor* means, literally, "stroke the face," a conventional yet striking expression for smoothing the Lord's angry countenance through prayer.

The invitation of Jeroboam is probably not to permanent service at Shechem or Bethel, but rather to a feast in the banquet hall (cf. 1 Sam. 9:22). Just as Balaam, the Babylonian diviner, is pictured as a true prophet who refuses payment or reward (Num. 22:18; 24:13), so the man of god replies, *If you give me half your house, I will not go in with you.* The command not to eat or drink with anyone at Bethel has to do with refusing covenant relations with those associated with the condemned altar (cf. 1 Cor. 10:18). Returning by a different way seems to be one of those commands upon the obedience of which good prophetic discipleship depended (cf. 2 Kings 9:3), so it is immediately reported that the man of God obeyed.

b. Testing of Prophetic Obedience (13:11–19)

¹¹ Now there dwelt an old prophet in Bethel. And his sons came and told him all that the man of God had done that day in Bethel; the words also which he had spoken to the king, they told to their father. ¹² And their father said to them, "Which way did he go?" And his sons showed him the way which the man of God who came from Judah had gone. ¹³ And he said to his sons, "Saddle the ass for me." So they saddled the ass for him and he mounted it. ¹⁴ And he went after the man of God, and found him sitting under an oak; and he said to him, "Are you the man of God who came from Judah?" And he said, "I am." ¹⁵ Then he said to him, "Come home with me and eat bread." ¹⁶ And he said, "I may not return with you, or go in with you; neither will I eat bread nor drink water with you in this place; ¹⁷ for it was said to me by the word of the LORD, 'You shall neither eat bread nor drink water there, nor return by the way that you came.'" ¹⁸ And he said to him, "I also am a prophet as you are, and an angel spoke to me by the word of the LORD, saying, 'Bring him back with you into your house that he may eat bread and drink water.'" But he lied to him. ¹⁹ So he went back with him, and ate bread in his house, and drank water.

One of the severe problems of the history of prophecy is the phenomenon of "false" prophets. The incident of Micaiah's dispute with Ahab's 400 prophets is a clearer instance of the problem than the present story (22:5–28). Nevertheless the old prophet from Bethel is in some sense the rival of the man of God from Judah. There is no hint of a divine command to motivate his deceitfulness; rather the story seems to be retold as a warning of what might happen to the unwary prophetic disciple who does not obey his marching orders to the letter. *An angel spoke to me* is regarded by the story as an inferior medium of revelation to the direct command by the word of the Lord already quoted. *But he lied to him* is perhaps a deduction by the writer from the sequel. According to early Israel's theology of testing, such a deception could be attributed to divine inspiration (cf. the lying spirit in the mouth of Ahab's prophets, 22:22–23). Later such a temptation would be attributed to Satan (cf. 2 Sam. 24:1; 1 Chron. 21:1).

c. Punishment of Disobedience (13:20–25)

²⁰ And as they sat at the table, the word of the LORD came to the prophet who had brought him back; ²¹ and he cried to the man of God who came from Judah, "Thus says the LORD, 'Because you have disobeyed the word of the LORD, and have not kept the commandment which the LORD your God commanded you, ²² but have come back, and have eaten bread and drunk water in the place of which he said to you, "Eat no bread, and drink no water"; your body shall not come to the tomb of your fathers.'" ²³ And after he had eaten bread and drunk, he saddled the ass for the prophet whom he had brought back. ²⁴ And as he went away a lion met him on the road and killed him. And his body was thrown in the road, and the ass stood beside it; the lion also stood beside the body. ²⁵ And behold, men passed by, and saw the body thrown in the road, and the lion standing by the body. And they came and told it in the city where the old prophet dwelt.

Now that his ruse has proved successful the old prophet of Bethel receives a genuine judgment oracle about the impending death of the man of god. The *lion* is frequently associated in this kind of narrative with divine punishment (20:36; 2 Kings 17:25–26). The roaring of the lion became quite a significant judgment symbol for Amos (1:2; 3:4,8,12; 5:19). The peculiar behavior of the lion and the ass are regarded as a sign that they were under the Lord's control (cf. Num. 22:21–30).

d. Moral of a Strange Story (13:26–32)

²⁶ And when the prophet who had brought him back from the way heard of it, he said, "It

is the man of God, who disobeyed the word of the LORD; therefore the LORD has given him to the lion, which has torn him and slain him, according to the word which the LORD spoke to him." ²⁷ And he said to his sons, "Saddle the ass for me." And they saddled it. ²⁸ And he went and found his body thrown in the road, and the ass and the lion standing beside the body. The lion had not eaten the body or torn the ass. ²⁹ And the prophet took up the body of the man of God and laid it upon the ass, and brought it back to the city, to mourn and to bury him. ³⁰ And he laid the body in his own grave; and they mourned over him, saying, "Alas, my brother!" ³¹ And after he had buried him, he said to his sons, "When I die, bury me in the grave in which the man of God is buried; lay my bones beside his bones. ³² For the saying which he cried by the word of the LORD against the altar in Bethel, and against all the houses of the high places which are in the cities of Samaria, shall surely come to pass."

The fulfillment of the judgment word against the man of God seems to convince the old prophet of Bethel of the genuineness of the young man's mission and message. He then treats the body with great respect, burying it in his own tomb where he plans to be buried. This grave, marked by a monument, was the occasion for the preservation and retelling of this strange story, which was repeated to Josiah in the fulfillment of the Lord's judgment against Bethel 300 years later (2 Kings 23:15–20). It is too extreme to call this story a midrash or folk tale, and to judge it as wholly unhistorical (cf. Montgomery, p. 260, Dentan, pp. 51–52). The kernel of historicity in the condemnation of Bethel is the ancient oral tradition on the basis of which this edifying story of the testing of prophetic obedience was handed down by the guild of disciples.

e. *Continuing Wickedness of Jeroboam* (13:33–34)

³³ After this thing Jeroboam did not turn from his evil way, but made priests for the high places again from among all the people; any who would, he consecrated to be priests of the high places. ³⁴ And this thing became sin to the house of Jeroboam, so as to cut it off and to destroy it from the face of the earth.

With the verbal repetition from the section on the sins of Jeroboam, the historian indicates that the prophetic word has not won the king to repentance *from his evil way* (12:30–32). It was the illegitimate priesthood of Jeroboam's Bethel cult which particularly offended the Jerusalem historian here rather than the golden calves. For Jeroboam, the continuance in sin despite prophetic warnings meant the destruction of his *house,* his possibility for a dynasty.

(2) *Word of Ahijah from Shiloh* (14:1–20)

The prophet who designated Jeroboam (11:29–39) is now old and blind, but he still acted as a consultant (cf. 1 Sam. 9:5–9). The king demonstrates a fear of the prophetic party, a dread of the sort of unfavorable oracle which is actually given when he sends his wife in disguise. At least he did not consult a foreign deity as did Ahaziah in a similar matter of sickness (2 Kings 1:2–4).

a. *Inquiry Concerning a Sick Prince* (14:1–5a)

¹ At that time Abijah the son of Jeroboam fell sick. ² And Jeroboam said to his wife, "Arise, and disguise yourself, that it be not known that you are the wife of Jeroboam, and go to Shiloh; behold, Ahijah the prophet is there, who said of me that I should be king over this people. ³ Take with you ten loaves, some cakes, and a jar of honey, and go to him; he will tell you what shall happen to the child."
⁴ Jeroboam's wife did so; she arose, and went to Shiloh, and came to the house of Ahijah. Now Ahijah could not see, for his eyes were dim because of his age. ⁵ And the LORD said to Ahijah, "Behold, the wife of Jeroboam is coming to inquire of you concerning her son; for he is sick. Thus and thus shall you say to her."

Ahijah appears at the beginning and the end of Jeroboam's story, though there is no record of their continuing relations in the meantime. It is assumed in this oracle of condemnation that he shared the historian's reaction to the innovations of Jeroboam. He is said to live in Shiloh, though it cannot be determined whether there was a prophetic guild there. It was customary to bring the prophetic consultant a gift (cf. 1 Sam. 9:7–8; 2 Kings 5:15; 8:8), the modesty of the present hero being dictated by the disguise of the queen as an ordinary woman. It was forbidden in Hebrew law to trip a blind person or lead him astray (Lev. 19:14; Deut. 27:18). Esau complained of Jacob's deceit in disguising himself before blind Isaac (Gen. 27:35–36). But the prophet has had a warning word from the Lord, and already knows who she is and why she is there (cf. 1 Sam. 9:16–20).

b. Doom of Jeroboam's Dynasty (14:5b–16)

When she came, she pretended to be another woman. ⁶ But when Ahijah heard the sound of her feet, as she came in at the door, he said, "Come in, wife of Jeroboam; why do you pretend to be another? For I am charged with heavy tidings for you. ⁷ Go, tell Jeroboam, 'Thus says the Lord, the God of Israel: "Because I exalted you from among the people, and made you leader over my people Israel, ⁸ and tore the kingdom away from the house of David and gave it to you; and yet you have not been like my servant David, who kept my commandments, and followed me with all his heart, doing only that which was right in my eyes, ⁹ but you have done evil above all that were before you and have gone and made for yourself other gods, and molten images, provoking me to anger, and have cast me behind your back; ¹⁰ therefore behold, I will bring evil upon the house of Jeroboam, and will cut off from Jeroboam every male, both bond and free in Israel, and will utterly consume the house of Jeroboam, as a man burns up dung until it is all gone. ¹¹ Any one belonging to Jeroboam who dies in the city the dogs shall eat; and any one who dies in the open country the birds of the air shall eat; for the Lord has spoken it."' ¹² Arise therefore, go to your house. When your feet enter the city, the child shall die. ¹³ And all Israel shall mourn for him, and bury him; for he only of Jeroboam shall come to the grave, because in him there is found something pleasing to the Lord, the God of Israel, in the house of Jeroboam. ¹⁴ Moreover the Lord will raise up for himself a king over Israel, who shall cut off the house of Jeroboam today. And henceforth ¹⁵ the Lord will smite Israel, as a reed is shaken in the water, and root up Israel out of this good land which he gave to their fathers, and scatter them beyond the Euphrates, because they have made their Asherim, provoking the Lord to anger. ¹⁶ And he will give Israel up because of the sins of Jeroboam, which he sinned and which he made Israel to sin."

The prophet greets her with instant recognition, rebuke for her deception, and *heavy tidings*. The answer to the inquiry is postponed to vv. 12–13, for the prophet's chief word is to Jeroboam about the destiny of his dynasty. Much of the language of Ahijah's oracle becomes normative for denunciation by the prophets of Israelite dynasties (16:1–7; 21:19–24). *Tore* refers to Ahijah's symbolic act and its interpretation (11:30–31). The historian regards the promise to northern dynasties as conditioned on obedience, as measured by the Davidic ideal (cf. 11:38). *Other gods . . . molten images* is the historian's interpretation of the golden bulls in the light of what they had come to mean (12:28–30).

Dogs are scavengers in the ancient Near East, and not pets. *Birds* are the vultures and ravens. The meaning of the saying is that the offspring of Jeroboam will not receive burial in the family tomb, a very severe punishment. *Beyond the Euphrates* is an elaboration of the Ahijah oracle by later prophetic preaching in the eighth century B.C., when the Assyrian menace became a real threat of judgment.

c. Death of Jeroboam (14:17–20)

¹⁷ Then Jeroboam's wife arose, and departed, and came to Tirzah. And as she came to the threshold of the house, the child died. ¹⁸ And all Israel buried him and mourned for him, according to the word of the Lord, which he spoke by his servant Ahijah the prophet. ¹⁹ Now the rest of the acts of Jeroboam, how he warred and how he reigned, behold, they are written in the Book of the Chronicles of the Kings of Israel. ²⁰ And the time that Jeroboam reigned was twenty-two years; and he slept with his fathers, and Nadab his son reigned in his stead.

Quite incidentally the story notices that the house of the king, perhaps his new capital, is seven miles northeast of Shechem at Tirzah, which becomes the capital of Baasha's dynasty (15:33; 16:6). The site of

Tirzah was more easily fortified than that of Shechem, so that Jeroboam may have relocated there as early as the Shishak invasion (14:25–28). The historian chooses not to give the details of the civil war between the two kingdoms, that had been postponed by the invasion of Shishak. There are two notices of intermittent warfare between Rehoboam and Jeroboam (14:30; 15:6), and there is also a notice of war between Jeroboam and the next king of Judah, Abijam (15:7; cf. 2 Chron. 13). Though Jeroboam is dead, the historian will continue to notice the baleful influence of his "sins" for the next two centuries.

3. Reign of Rehoboam in Judah (14:21–31)

If Jeroboam was a bad king in the eyes of the historian, Rehoboam was not much better. It has already been told how his foolish Shechem policy helped disrupt the kingdom. Now it is concluded that he promoted the Canaanite cults of the high places, and had to pay a large tribute to Shishak out of the Temple treasury.

(1) Sins of Rehoboam (14:21–24)

²¹ Now Rehoboam the son of Solomon reigned in Judah. Rehoboam was forty-one years old when he began to reign, and he reigned seventeen years in Jerusalem, the city which the LORD had chosen out of all the tribes of Israel, to put his name there. His mother's name was Naamah the Ammonitess. ²² And Judah did what was evil in the sight of the LORD, and they provoked him to jealousy with their sins which they committed, more than all that their fathers had done. ²³ For they also built for themselves high places, and pillars, and Asherim on every high hill and under every green tree; ²⁴ and there were also male cult prostitutes in the land. They did according to all the abominations of the nations which the LORD drove out before the people of Israel.

This is the postponed introductory formula, containing Rehoboam's age at the beginning of his reign, *forty-one years old.* Perhaps Solomon had already begun his foreign marriages with the one to Naamah the Ammonitess before his accession to the throne—else the 40-year length of his reign was an approximation. The *seventeen years* of Rehoboam's reign is considered too long by those who date the schism at 922 B.C. But the date should probably be 931 B.C. (see the Introduction). The only thing good the historian can say about Rehoboam is that he reigned in Jerusalem, where the proper central sanctuary was located. But he followed Solomon's broadminded tolerance, especially of the Canaanite-type of high place. *Pillars* were symbols of the male deity, Baal. *Asherim* were wooden posts or stylized trees symbolizing the female mother-goddess Asherah (cf. 15:13), the consort of Baal.

As is now known from the Ras Shamra texts, these symbols were not just local deities, but the great gods and goddesses of the Canaanite pantheon. The Canaanite agricultural fertility worship used imitative magic to induce the fertility of crops, herds, and human families. Included were sexual rituals, using female and *male cult prostitutes,* men dedicated to a worship which proved a severe stumbling block to Israel. Indeed the history of Israel's faith is largely centered in this struggle of Mosaic Yahwism with Canaanite culture and religion.

(2) Invasion of Shishak of Egypt (14:25–28)

²⁵ In the fifth year of King Rehoboam, Shishak king of Egypt came up against Jerusalem; ²⁶ he took away the treasures of the house of the LORD and the treasures of the king's house; he took away everything. He also took away all the shields of gold which Solomon had made; ²⁷ and King Rehoboam made in their stead shields of bronze, and committed them to the hands of the officers of the guard, who kept the door of the king's house. ²⁸ And as often as the king went into the house of the LORD, the guard bore them and brought them back to the guardroom.

After the death of Solomon, Shishak began to prepare to invade Palestine, which he did in the fifth year (ca. 926 B.C.). First he had to achieve recognition by the priests of Thebes, on whose temple of Amun at Karnak he later inscribed the list of Palestinian cities which he plundered. Though the present account is only interested in what he did to Rehoboam and Jerusalem, most of the cities Shishak lists are in the north (cf. his victory stele at Megiddo, Wright, p. 148). Jeroboam learned the dangers of trusting in Egypt the hard way. It is not clear whether Jerusalem was taken, but indications in Chronicles (2 Chron. 12:1-12) are that the city was spared by the payment of a large tribute from the Temple treasuries. The *shields of gold* from Solomon's armory (10:16-17) were replaced with bronze shields. After the Shishak invasion, Rehoboam fortified a group of cities in the southern and western approaches to Judah as a line of defense against any further invasions (2 Chron. 11:5-12,23).

(3) *Death of Rehoboam (14:29-31)*

29 Now the rest of the acts of Rehoboam, and all that he did, are they not written in the Book of the Chronicles of the Kings of Judah? 30 And there was war between Rehoboam and Jeroboam continually. 31 And Rehoboam slept with his fathers and was buried with his fathers in the city of David. His mother's name was Naamah the Ammonitess. And Abijam his son reigned in his stead.

The standard formula language for the death of a king in the divided monarchy includes the notice about the civil war. *Abijam* is called Abijah in Chronicles, where there is a more detailed personal history of Rehoboam's family (2 Chron. 11:18-23).

4. *Reign of Abijam (15:1-8)*

1 Now in the eighteenth year of King Jeroboam the son of Nebat, Abijam began to reign over Judah. 2 He reigned for three years in Jerusalem. His mother's name was Maacah the daughter of Abishalom. 3 And he walked in all the sins which his father did before him; and his heart was not wholly true to the LORD his God, as the heart of David his father. 4 Nevertheless for David's sake the LORD his God gave him a lamp in Jerusalem, setting up his son after him, and establishing Jerusalem; 5 because David did what was right in the eyes of the LORD, and did not turn aside from anything that he commanded him all the days of his life, except in the matter of Uriah the Hittite. 6 Now there was war between Rehoboam and Jeroboam all the days of his life. 7 The rest of the acts of Abijam, and all that he did, are they not written in the Book of the Chronicles of the Kings of Judah? And there was war between Abijam and Jeroboam. 8 And Abijam slept with his fathers; and they buried him in the city of David. And Asa his son reigned in his stead.

The name of Abijam ("My father is Yam," a Canaanite sea-god) may provide a clue to his religion. He was not the oldest son of Rehoboam, but rather of his favorite wife, Maacah, the daughter of Absalom, for whose sake Abijam was appointed crown prince (2 Chron. 11:18-22). The religious apostasy only grew worse under Abijam, and it was only God's grace to the Davidic dynasty that allowed him to rule at all.

War between Abijam and Jeroboam. Chronicles draws on Judean sources of its own to describe a victory of Abijam against Jeroboam in this border warfare, in which Bethel and portions of southern Ephraim fell temporarily to Judah ("story of the prophet Iddo," 2 Chron. 13:22). This may be related to Abijam's league with Damascus, if he exploited the Aramean threat to the Northern Kingdom in the same manner as did Asa his son (15:19, cf. Bright, p. 215).

5. *Reign of Asa (15:9-24)*

Fortunately for Judah, her next Davidic king brought a marked improvement through religious reform. Asa ruled for a long time, and the account of his reign in Chronicles is greatly expanded by prophetic narratives. Asa's reign began with ten years of peace, during which he fortified some cities and built up an army. Then he had to repel a raid of an Egyptian force under Zerah the Ethiopian at Mareshah, driving them back as far as Gerar (2 Chron. 14). After Asa's religious reforms, he had more serious external troubles with Baasha, who had meanwhile usurped the throne of Israel. Unfortunately, Asa followed the shortsighted policy of relying on

Aramean intervention against North Israel (cf. 2 Chron. 16:7–10).

(1) Partial Reform by Asa (15:9–15)

9 In the twentieth year of Jeroboam king of Israel Asa began to reign over Judah, 10 and he reigned forty-one years in Jerusalem. His mother's name was Maacah the daughter of Abishalom. 11 And Asa did what was right in the eyes of the LORD, as David his father had done. 12 He put away the male cult prostitutes out of the land, and removed all the idols that his fathers had made. 13 He also removed Maacah his mother from being queen mother because she had an abominable image made for Asherah; and Asa cut down her image and burned it at the brook Kidron. 14 But the high places were not taken away. Nevertheless the heart of Asa was wholly true to the LORD all his days. 15 And he brought into the house of the LORD the votive gifts of his father and his own votive gifts, silver, and gold, and vessels.

In Chronicles, a covenant festival and reform inspired by the prophecy of Azariah in his fifteenth year resulted in the removal of the queen mother (2 Chron. 14:1–4; 15:1–19). *Twentieth year,* compared with Abijam's reign of three years, beginning with Jeroboam's eighteenth year (vv 15: 1–2), reveals the inclusive reckoning of Judah at this time by which Abijam's reign would have counted one full year and parts of two others. This same system of antedating was used in Israel at this time, as Nadab's two years' reckoning indicates (15:25,33). *Asa did what was right,* that is, in the judgment of the historian he restored cultic purity, though still not quite achieving cultic unity. He removed the features of the apostasy under Rehoboam and Abijam, including *idols* and one prominent idol worshiper, his grandmother Maacah. As queen mother during his early reign, she must have had a great influence (cf. 2 Kings 9:30 ff.; 11:1 ff.). She was a devotee of the Canaanite mother-goddess, Asherah (cf. 14:15,23). Her wooden *abominable image* Asa cut down and burned in Kidron valley between Jerusalem and the Mount of Olives. *Votive gifts* is a small note in Abijam's favor; perhaps these are spoils of battle (cf. 8:51; 2 Sam. 8:11–12).

(2) Civil War with Baasha (15:16–22)

16 And there was war between Asa and Baasha king of Israel all their days. 17 Baasha king of Israel went up against Judah, and built Ramah, that he might permit no one to go out or come in to Asa king of Judah. 18 Then Asa took all the silver and the gold that were left in the treasures of the house of the LORD and the treasures of the king's house, and gave them into the hands of his servants; and King Asa sent them to Benhadad the son of Tabrimmon, the son of Hezion, king of Syria, who dwelt in Damascus, saying, 19 "Let there be a league between me and you, as between my father and your father: behold, I am sending to you a present of silver and gold; go, break your league with Baasha king of Israel, that he may withdraw from me." 20 And Benhadad hearkened to King Asa, and sent the commanders of his armies against the cities of Israel, and conquered Ijon, Dan, Abelbethmaacah, and all Chinneroth, with all the land of Naphtali. 21 And when Baasha heard of it, he stopped building Ramah, and he dwelt in Tirzah. 22 Then King Asa made a proclamation to all Judah, none was exempt, and they carried away the stones of Ramah and its timber, with which Baasha had been building; and with them King Asa built Geba of Benjamin and Mizpah.

The historian is unavoidably ahead of his story in Israel as he tries to cover all the long reign of Asa in Judah. The Northern Kingdom was growing stronger, as is evidenced by Baasha's attempt to fortify Ramah, only five miles north of Jerusalem. This means Abijam's gains were only temporary, although in the border warfare in Benjamin and south Ephraim there may have been several changes of control (2 Chron. 13:19; 15:8).

Benhadad . . . King of Syria. The genealogy of this royal house of Damascus has been confirmed by the discovery of an Aramaic inscribed monument of this Benhadad to the god Melqart (Thomas, pp. 239–240). He is probably the father of the Benhadad whom Ahab fought (20:1,34). Hazael usurped the throne of Benhadad II at prophetic instigation, and was in turn succeeded by his son, Benhadad III (19:15; 2 Kings 8:7–15; 13:3,24–25). The ninth century B.C. is dominated by the relations between the divided kingdom and

Aramea (or, Syria). Hadad was their name for the storm god, Baal, whose manifestation as Rimmon ("Thunderer") was particularly revered (2 Kings 5:18).

A *league is a covenant,* like Solomon's treaty with Tyre (5:12), only this is more military than commercial (cf. 20:34). *My father and your father.* Abijam had relied on Tabrimmon at the time of his war with Jeroboam. *Break your league with Baasha* reveals how opportunistic the Arameans were in playing one kingdom against the other. Benhadad attacked Baasha from the north, conquering several cities of Naphtali and Dan in regions of Galilee and Mount Hermon. Baasha had to return to Tirzah, and Asa used his building materials from Ramah to fortify Mizpah and Geba further north on the ridge road to Bethel. If Mizpah is to be identified with modern Tell-en-Nasbeh, the archaeological excavations there provide impressive evidence of the walls of Asa and the period of incessant civil war in the Benjaminite territory (Wright, p. 150).

(3) Death of Asa (15:23-24)

23 Now the rest of all the acts of Asa, all his might, and all that he did, and the cities which he built, are they not written in the Book of the Chronicles of the Kings of Judah? But in his old age he was diseased in his feet. 24 And Asa slept with his fathers, and was buried with his fathers in the city of David his father; and Jehoshaphat his son reigned in his stead.

Eight kings and usurpers of North Israel from Jeroboam to Ahab came and went during the 41 years of Asa (ca. 911–870 B.C.), so that the historian must now turn his attention from Judah to Israel until he can begin again with Jehoshaphat (22:41 ff). Toward the end of his reign, he developed some kind of foot disease, perhaps necessitating a co-regency with his son Jehoshaphat (2 Chron. 16:12).

6. Reign of Nadab in Israel (15:25-26)

25 Nadab the son of Jeroboam began to reign over Israel in the second year of Asa king of Judah; and he reigned over Israel two years. 26 He did what was evil in the sight of the Lord, and walked in the way of his father and in his sin which he made Israel to sin.

During what little time he had, *two years,* Nadab followed the way of Jeroboam and reaped the sins of his father. The brevity of any attempted dynasty in Israel shows the comparative instability of the Northern Kingdom.

7. Revolt of Baasha (15:27-34)

27 Baasha the son of Ahijah, of the house of Issachar, conspired against him; and Baasha struck him down at Gibbethon, which belonged to the Philistines; for Nadab and all Israel were laying siege to Gibbethon. 28 So Baasha killed him in the third year of Asa king of Judah, and reigned in his stead. 29 And as soon as he was king, he killed all the house of Jeroboam; he left to the house of Jeroboam not one that breathed, until he had destroyed it, according to the word of the Lord which he spoke by his servant Ahijah the Shilonite; 30 it was for the sins of Jeroboam which he sinned and which he made Israel to sin, and because of the anger to which he provoked the Lord, the God of Israel.

31 Now the rest of the acts of Nadab, and all that he did, are they not written in the Book of the Chronicles of the Kings of Israel? 32 And there was war between Asa and Baasha king of Israel all their days.

33 In the third year of Asa king of Judah, Baasha the son of Ahijah began to reign over all Israel at Tirzah, and reigned twenty-four years. 34 He did what was evil in the sight of the Lord, and walked in the way of Jeroboam and in his sin which he made Israel to sin.

Nadab's army was laying siege to Gibbethon, an important Philistine fortress on the Ephraimite border west of Gezer, where Israel was still encamped when Omri became king (16:15-17). Presumably Baasha of Issachar was Nadab's army commander over the troops from his tribe, or his chief commander. Whether he conspired with the prophetic party is not stated, but his slaughter of Jeroboam's remaining heirs is interpreted as the fulfillment of Ahijah's judgment word (14:14). This may be the reason that the burial notices for Nadab and his brothers are omitted (cf. 14:10-11). *Tirzah* was certainly Baasha's capital, whether he or one of his predecessors built the citadel of the

1 KINGS 16

king's house which made it such a strong fortress (cf. 14:17; 16:18). The evil of Baasha is described in the traditional way, his own dynasty proving no better than that which it replaced (cf. 16:7).

8. Doom of Baasha's Dynasty (16:1-7)

¹ And the word of the LORD came to Jehu the son of Hanani against Baasha, saying, ² "Since I exalted you out of the dust and made you leader over my people Israel, and you have walked in the way of Jeroboam, and have made my people Israel to sin, provoking me to anger with their sins, ³ behold, I will utterly sweep away Baasha and his house, and I will make your house like the house of Jeroboam the son of Nebat. ⁴ Anyone belonging to Baasha who dies in the city the dogs shall eat; and anyone of his who dies in the field the birds of the air shall eat."

⁵ Now the rest of the acts of Baasha, and what he did, and his might, are they not written in the Book of the Chronicles of the Kings of Israel? ⁶ And Baasha slept with his fathers, and was buried at Tirzah; and Elah his son reigned in his stead. ⁷ Moreover the word of the LORD came by the prophet Jehu the son of Hanani against Baasha and his house, both because of all the evil that he did in the sight of the LORD, provoking him to anger with the work of his hands, in being like the house of Jeroboam, and also because he destroyed it.

The judgment word of the Lord is pronounced against Baasha and his dynasty by the prophet *Jehu the son of Hanani*, who belongs to a later time in Judah according to Chronicles (2 Chron. 19:2; 20:34). If the analogy of Ahijah's relation to the house of Jeroboam may be applied here, Jehu probably had a part in the rise of Baasha to this leadership. Baasha's *might* had to be strong to survive 24 years against the dreadful precedent of assassination which he had set, and which soon struck down his son. *Also because he destroyed it.* Is Baasha condemned for carrying out the purge against Jeroboam's dynasty? Although the Hebrew is very obscure, the context of the verse surely indicates Baasha was destroyed because he became like the very kings whom he replaced, provoking Yahweh to anger with idolatry (cf. 16:13).

9. Revolt of Zimri (16:8-20)

⁸ In the twenty-sixth year of Asa king of Judah, Elah the son of Baasha began to reign over Israel in Tirzah, and reigned two years. ⁹ But his servant Zimri, commander of half his chariots, conspired against him. When he was at Tirzah, drinking himself drunk in the house of Arza, who was over the household in Tirzah, ¹⁰ Zimri came in and struck him down and killed him, in the twenty-seventh year of Asa king of Judah, and reigned in his stead.

¹¹ When he began to reign, as soon as he had seated himself on his throne, he killed all the house of Baasha; he did not leave him a single male of his kinsmen or his friends. ¹² Thus Zimri destroyed all the house of Baasha, according to the word of the LORD, which he spoke against Baasha by Jehu the prophet, ¹³ for all the sins of Baasha and the sins of Elah his son which they sinned, and which they made Israel to sin, provoking the LORD God of Israel to anger with their idols. ¹⁴ Now the rest of the acts of Elah, and all that he did, are they not written in the Book of the Chronicles of the Kings of Israel?

¹⁵ In the twenty-seventh year of Asa king of Judah, Zimri reigned seven days in Tirzah. Now the troops were encamped against Gibbethon, which belonged to the Philistines, ¹⁶ and the troops who were encamped heard it said, "Zimri has conspired, and he has killed the king"; therefore all Israel made Omri, the commander of the army, king over Israel that day in the camp. ¹⁷ So Omri went up from Gibbethon, and all Israel with him, and they besieged Tirzah. ¹⁸ And when Zimri saw that the city was taken, he went into the citadel of the king's house, and burned the king's house over him with fire, and died, ¹⁹ because of his sins which he committed, doing evil in the sight of the LORD, walking in the way of Jeroboam, and for his sin which he committed, making Israel to sin. ²⁰ Now the rest of the acts of Zimri, and the conspiracy which he made, are they not written in the Book of the Chronicles of the Kings of Israel?

The strong Baasha was succeeded by a weak son, Elah, who was murdered by one of his military leaders in Tirzah. Zimri, the assassin, was not successful in his palace revolt because the general of the army, Omri, was made king and soon disposed of Zimri. There is no longer any pretense of prophetic designation or kingship by covenant.

Zimri is a professional soldier, perhaps not even an Israelite, since no father or tribe is listed for him. While his army was in the field at Gibbethon, Elah was *drinking himself drunk* (cf. 20:16) in the house of his royal chamberlain, Arza, who may have plotted the murder with Zimri. *His kinsmen or his friends* means anyone who would avenge his death, going beyond the prophetic judgment word about the elimination of male heirs. Zimri had good reason to fear reprisal for his dastardly deed for which his name became a byword (2 Kings 9:31). We have no details for the religious apostasies of the house of Baasha and must assume they were the same as the "sins of Jeroboam."

The seven-day reign of the usurper was chiefly significant for carrying out the massacre of Baasha's dynasty. He evidently had little support among the people even in Tirzah. Word of the conspiracy soon reached the army at Gibbethon where the tribal levies were again besieging the Philistine stronghold (cf. 15:27). The people immediately made their general, Omri, king and followed him in swift march to Tirzah. When Zimri saw his cause was lost, he took his own life by burning the palace stronghold, thus becoming one of the rare cases of suicide in the Old Testament (cf. Ahithophel, 2 Sam. 17:23).

10. New Dynasty of Omri (16:21-28)

21 Then the people of Israel were divided into two parts; half of the people followed Tibni the son of Ginath, to make him king, and half followed Omri. 22 But the people who followed Omri overcame the people who followed Tibni the son of Ginath; so Tibni died, and Omri became king. 23 In the thirty-first year of Asa king of Judah, Omri began to reign over Israel, and reigned for twelve years; six years he reigned in Tirzah. 24 He bought the hill of Samaria from Shemer for two talents of silver; and he fortified the hill, and called the name of the city which he built, Samaria, after the name of Shemer, the owner of the hill.
25 Omri did what was evil in the sight of the Lord, and did more evil than all who were before him. 26 For he walked in all the way of Jeroboam the son of Nebat, and in the sins which he made Israel to sin, provoking the Lord, the God of Israel, to anger by their idols. 27 Now the rest of the acts of Omri which he did, and the might that he showed, are they not written in the Book of the Chronicles of the Kings of Israel? 28 And Omri slept with his fathers, and was buried in Samaria; and Ahab his son reigned in his stead.

Omri did not gain the support of all the people for four more years (16:15,23), because Tibni, the son of Ginath, disputed his claim to the throne. Yet in his brief reign of 12 years, only the last eight of which can be counted for Omri as sole ruler, he founded the strongest dynasty yet to rule North Israel. It is a testimony to the religious bias of the historian that such a short section is given to such a talented king. We are dependent mostly upon extrabiblical sources for a more just estimate of his political, military, and economic activities.

Of the two contenders for the throne, Tibni is given a genealogy and Omri is not. Omri is sometimes supposed to have been a Canaanite mercenary in the service of Baasha and his son (Gray, p. 330). *Tibni died.* The fact that he held out four years against a soldier of Omri's ability shows that Tibni had considerable support. *Six years he reigned in Tirzah.* On the supposition that he controlled the fortress which he took from the hapless Zimri, this means he reigned a like period of six years in Samaria. Archaeologists have excavated both Tell-el-Farah (ancient Tirzah) and Samaria with results that strikingly confirm the biblical account.[16]

The strategic choice of his new capital at Samaria and his private ownership of the strongly fortified and centrally located hill has earned Omri the title, "David of the North." In the building of the fortifications and royal palace he used Phoenician workmanship, obtained by a commercial treaty with Tyre. The dire religious consequences of this alliance were the result of the intermarriage of Omri's son, Ahab, to Jezebel, the daughter of Ethbaal, the Sidonian king of Tyre (16:31). But the commercial aspects offset the growing influence of Da-

---

[16] Kathleen M. Kenyon, *Archaeology in the Holy Land* (New York: Frederick A. Praeger, Publisher, 1960), pp. 260-269.

mascus, whose king, Benhadad I, was strong enough to take some cities from Omri and attain some commercial concessions in the new city of Samaria (20:34).

The chief prophetic reaction to the religious syncretism of Omri and Ahab occurs in Ahab's reign (16:31–33). The only hint of this here is the statement that Omri *did more evil than all who were before him.*

The might that he showed. It is known from the Mesha inscription that Omri reconquered Moab for Israel (Thomas, pp. 195–198). In the minds of Assyrian kings who began their push westward during Omri's reign, the kingdom of Israel was the "house of Omri" for the next century and a half (Wright, pp. 151, 156). Most important of all, it was Omri and his son Ahab who reestablished peaceful relations with Judah after a half century of border warfare. And yet, as the prophetic narratives of Elijah and Elisha make clear, the infection of Israel's religion with Jezebel's Tyrian Baal cult was a disaster nullifying all of the strengths of Omri and Ahab.

11. Beginning of Ahab's Reign (16:29–34)

29 In the thirty-eighth year of Asa king of Judah, Ahab the son of Omri began to reign over Israel, and Ahab the son of Omri reigned over Israel in Samaria twenty-two years. 30 And Ahab the son of Omri did evil in the sight of the LORD more than all that were before him. 31 And as if it had been a light thing for him to walk in the sins of Jeroboam the son of Nebat, he took for wife Jezebel the daughter of Ethbaal king of the Sidonians, and went and served Baal, and worshiped him. 32 He erected an altar for Baal in the house of Baal, which he built in Samaria. 33 And Ahab made an Asherah. Ahab did more to provoke the LORD, the God of Israel, to anger than all the kings of Israel who were before him. 34 In his days Hiel of Bethel built Jericho; he laid its foundation at the cost of Abiram his first-born, and set up its gates at the cost of his youngest son Segub, according to the word of the LORD, which he spoke by Joshua the son of Nun.

If Omri may be referred to as "the David of the North," then Ahab is "the Solomon of the North." Especially significant to the historian is his provision for Jezebel of a sanctuary with altar, pillar, and Asherah to her god, Baal Melqart. This was the policy of Solomon for his foreign princesses, but Solomon never had a wife with the missionary zeal of Jezebel. She not only wanted her own worship in Samaria, but also tried to convert Israel to Baal Melqart.

This paragraph (vv. 29–34) gives the historian's regular introduction to Ahab's reign. The conclusion is postponed by a remarkable series of prophetic and annalistic narratives (22:39–40). Like a ghost out of the past, the last verse of this section recalls the present effect of an ancient curse (Josh. 6:26). Perhaps on Ahab's orders, since he may have had cause to fear a Moabite revolt, Jericho was fortified at this time. Perhaps accidental fatalities occurred which were interpreted as the fulfillment of the ancient word (Montgomery, p. 288). However, child sacrifice was practiced by the worshipers of Baal Melqart, so that these may be foundation sacrifices offered to protect the new construction from the effects of the curse. If so, it provided a specific example of the results of Ahab's apostasies.

III. The Prophetic Revolt (1 Kings 17:1 —2 Kings 13:25)

It should be observed that the historian's account of the prophetic revolt actually continues to 2 Kings 13:25.

The program of the prophetic revolt against the Omri dynasty is contained in the threefold commission to Elijah to anoint Hazael as king of Damascus, Jehu king of Israel, and Elisha as his prophetic successor (19:15–16). The last of these tasks Elijah does immediately, but it is Elisha who incites Hazael and sends one of his prophetic disciples to anoint Jehu (19:19–21; 2 Kings 8:7–15; 9:1–3). Jehu's bloody purge of Ahab's sons has its parallel in Judah in the revolt against Ahab's daughter, Athaliah.

1. Prophets and Ahab (17:1—22:53)

Two kinds of literature are combined in this section. The clash between Yahweh and the Tyrian Baal is told in stories which magnify the role of the prophet Elijah (chs. 17–19,21). The first three chapters are a unit about the great drought, the contest on Mount Carmel, and the flight of Elijah to Horeb. The ethical boldness of Elijah is revealed in the incident of Naboth's vineyard (ch. 21). Elijah does not appear in the other stories, in which Ahab is the chief character and appears in a much more favorable light (chs. 20, 22).

(1) Elijah and the Drought (17:1–24)

The most important leader of the true worship of Yahweh since Moses and Samuel was Elijah the Tishbite. He was an isolated figure, appearing suddenly to announce the drought. The first group of stories deals with the personal life of the prophet and his helpfulness to a widow of Zarephath who befriended him during his flight from Ahab. The prominence of the miraculous element in the stories of Elijah and Elisha has caused some scholars to assign them to the literary categories of saga and legend. However, it is noticeable that the miracles of the Old Testament cluster about the great historical crises, here the Aramean wars combined with the internal threat of an aggressive alien religion.

a. Provisions in Gilead (17:1–7)

¹ Now Elijah the Tishbite, of Tishbe in Gilead, said to Ahab, "As the LORD the God of Israel lives, before whom I stand, there shall be neither dew nor rain these years, except by my word." ² And the word of the LORD came to him, ³ "Depart from here and turn eastward, and hide yourself by the brook Cherith, that is east of the Jordan. ⁴ You shall drink from the brook, and I have commanded the ravens to feed you there." ⁵ So he went and did according to the word of the LORD; he went and dwelt by the brook Cherith that is east of the Jordan. ⁶ And the ravens brought him bread and meat in the morning, and bread and meat in the evening; and he drank from the brook. ⁷ And after a while the brook dried up, because there was no rain in the land.

The land of Palestine is totally dependent upon its rainfall (cf. Deut. 11:10–11). The prediction of drought by Elijah is a direct challenge to the Canaanite storm god Baal, by Yahweh, God of Israel, true Lord of creation. The first two stories are told to indicate how severe the drought had become in Phoenicia as well as Israel. As in the wilderness narratives, where God had provided food and drink for his people, so here in marvelous ways he provided for his prophet. Elijah's home was in Gilead on the Wadi Cherith, east of Jabeshgilead.

Before whom I stand. Here and in 18:15, Elijah defines his prophetic office as a ministering attendant in the Lord's presence, ever ready to serve as his messenger. *Ravens.* There is no need to try to rationalize the miracle story by changing the vowels in the Hebrew word and interpreting it as "steppe-dwellers." Its early usage is collective; the plural would indicate late usage. The miraculous element belongs in all these prophetic narratives as a testimony to Israel's faith in Yahweh's control over his created order (cf. 19:5–8). He who feeds the young ravens (Job 38:41) can use these unclean, voracious scavengers (Lev. 11:15; Prov. 30:17) to preserve his prophet for the coming crisis. *Bread* and *meat* remind one of the manna and quail (Ex. 16:8). In many ways Elijah is described as a new Moses.

b. Widow of Zarephath (17:8–16)

⁸ Then the word of the LORD came to him, ⁹ "Arise, go to Zarephath, which belongs to Sidon, and dwell there. Behold, I have commanded a widow there to feed you." ¹⁰ So he arose and went to Zarephath; and when he came to the gate of the city, behold, a widow was there gathering sticks; and he called to her and said, "Bring me a little water in a vessel, that I may drink." ¹¹ And as she was going to bring it, he called to her and said, "Bring me a morsel of bread in your hand." ¹² And she said, "As the LORD your God lives, I have nothing baked, only a handful of meal in a jar, and a little oil in a cruse; and now, I am gathering a couple of sticks, that I may go in and prepare it for myself and my son, that we may eat it, and die." ¹³ And Elijah said to her, "Fear not; go and do as you have said; but first make me a little cake of it and bring it to me, and

afterward make for yourself and your son. 14 For thus says the LORD the God of Israel, 'The jar of meal shall not be spent, and the cruse of oil shall not fail, until the day that the LORD sends rain upon the earth.' " 15 And she went and did as Elijah said; and she, and he, and her household ate for many days. 16 The jar of meal was not spent, neither did the cruse of oil fail, according to the word of the LORD which he spoke by Elijah.

The famine was severe in Phoenicia also, as Josephus (*Antiq.*, VIII, 13,2) tells of such a famine during Ethbaal's reign. Zarephath lay south of Sidon, on the Phoenician coast. Jesus noticed in his inaugural sermon how ironic it was that the prophet should have to flee his own country for the sinful Canaanite cities (Luke 4:25–26; cf. 10:13–14). The widow was one of the helpless classes in society for whom the Lord showed great concern (see Ex. 22:22; Isa. 1:17). This widow's generosity in sharing her last meal with the prophet was marvelously rewarded.

c. Reviving of Her Son (17:17–24)

17 After this the son of the woman, the mistress of the house, became ill; and his illness was so severe that no breath was left in him. 18 And she said to Elijah, "What have you against me, O man of God? You have come to me to bring my sin to remembrance, and to cause the death of my son!" 19 And he said to her, "Give me your son." And he took him from her bosom, and carried him up into the upper chamber, where he lodged, and laid him upon his own bed. 20 And he cried to the LORD, "O LORD my God, hast thou brought calamity even upon the widow with whom I sojourn, by slaying her son?" 21 Then he stretched himself upon the child three times, and cried to the LORD, "O LORD my God, let this child's soul come into him again." 22 And the LORD hearkened to the voice of Elijah; and the soul of the child came into him again, and he revived. 23 And Elijah took the child, and brought him down from the upper chamber into the house, and delivered him to his mother; and Elijah said, "See, your son lives." 24 And the woman said to Elijah, "Now I know that you are a man of God, and that the word of the LORD in your mouth is truth."

Seemingly unrelated to the provision of food during the famine, this story was told to illustrate that Elijah was indeed a man of God and a prophet of his true word (v. 24). Although it is not actually said that the boy died, such is presumed by the protest of the woman to Elijah and his indignant cry to the Lord. The potent actions of the prophet were intended by contact to pass the warmth of his flesh and the vitality of his breath into the inert body (2 Kings 4:34–35; cf. Acts 20:10). *Soul* would be better translated by "life." *Revived* is the same root word as *lives* in the next verse, referring to resuscitation of the physical life. Although there was no explicit doctrine of the resurrection of the dead in Israel until quite late in the Old Testament period (Dan. 12:2), such stories as this provide some hint of the divine power over death only fully revealed in the resurrection of Jesus Christ.

(2) Contest at Mount Carmel (18:1–46)

The bringing of the rain after the severe drought may be regarded as the proper clue to the interpretation of the sacrificial ordeal between the Baal prophets and Elijah. The scene of the dramatic contest is a promontory ridge which juts out into the Mediterranean Sea from the coast of Palestine. It is the first place to receive the autumn rains sweeping in from the west and southwest.

a. Severity of the Famine (18:1–6)

1 After many days the word of the LORD came to Elijah, in the third year, saying, "Go, show yourself to Ahab, and I will send rain upon the earth." 2 So Elijah went to show himself to Ahab. Now the famine was severe in Samaria. 3 And Ahab called Obadiah, who was over the household. (Now Obadiah revered the LORD greatly; 4 and when Jezebel cut off the prophets of the LORD, Obadiah took a hundred prophets and hid them by fifties in a cave, and fed them with bread and water.) 5 And Ahab said to Obadiah, "Go through the land to all the springs of water and to all the valleys; perhaps we may find grass and save the horses and mules alive, and not lose some of the animals." 6 So they divided the land between them to pass through it; Ahab went in one direction by himself, and Obadiah went in another direction by himself.

The search of Ahab and his chief official, Obadiah, for water and pasture for the royal animals is convincing evidence for the effect of the prolonged drought. The *third year* was expanded by later tradition to three and one-half years (Luke 4:25; James 5:17), but this was the third autumn since the abundant "former rains" had occurred. When Jezebel persecuted the prophets of Yahweh (cf. vv. 13,22; with the aid of the people, 19:10,14), Obadiah saved them. Evidently Ahab maintained nominal allegiance to Yahweh, despite his wife's innovations (cf. the names of their children). Ahab's concern for the animals betrays their importance in warfare (cf. 4:26,28).

b. Obadiah the Steward (18:7-16)

⁷ And as Obadiah was on the way, behold, Elijah met him, and Obadiah recognized him, and fell on his face, and said, "Is it you, my lord Elijah?" ⁸ And he answered him, "It is I. Go, tell your lord, 'Behold, Elijah is here.'" ⁹ And he said, "Wherein have I sinned, that you would give your servant into the hand of Ahab, to kill me? ¹⁰ As the LORD your God lives, there is no nation or kingdom whither my lord has not sent to seek you; and when they would say, 'He is not here,' he would take an oath of the kingdom or nation, that they had not found you. ¹¹ And now you say, 'Go, tell your lord, "Behold, Elijah is here."' ¹² And as soon as I have gone from you, the Spirit of the LORD will carry you whither I know not; and so, when I come and tell Ahab and he cannot find you, he will kill me, although I your servant have revered the LORD from my youth. ¹³ Has it not been told my lord what I did when Jezebel killed the prophets of the LORD, how I hid a hundred men of the LORD's prophets by fifties in a cave, and fed them with bread and water? ¹⁴ And now you say, 'Go, tell your lord, "Behold, Elijah is here"'; and he will kill me." ¹⁵ And Elijah said, "As the LORD of hosts lives, before whom I stand, I will surely show myself to him today." ¹⁶ So Obadiah went to meet Ahab, and told him; and Ahab went to meet Elijah.

Obadiah recognized Elijah perhaps by his hairy garment (2 Kings 1:8). Ahab had conducted an extensive search for the elusive prophet, so that Obadiah was fearful of raising any false hopes with him that Elijah would indeed appear. That Ahab's chamberlain should fear for his life is testimony that the monarchy of Israel had not much respect for ancient covenantal rights of its citizens. Although Obadiah regarded the movements of the prophet as quite unpredictable (cf. Ezek. 3:12,14), Elijah assured him with an oath that he would meet Ahab.

c. Challenge to Ahab (18:17-19)

¹⁷ When Ahab saw Elijah, Ahab said to him, "Is it you, you troubler of Israel?" ¹⁸ And he answered, "I have not troubled Israel; but you have, and your father's house, because you have forsaken the commandments of the LORD and followed the Baals. ¹⁹ Now therefore send and gather all Israel to me at Mount Carmel, and the four hundred and fifty prophets of Baal and the four hundred prophets of Asherah, who eat at Jezebel's table."

The king brings a rather serious charge against the prophet when he labels him *troubler of Israel*. But the prophet boldly turns the accusation back upon the king. Ahab and Omri have abandoned the Lord and gone after *the Baals,* local manifestations of the Canaanite storm and fertility god. Elijah orders a full covenant assembly at Mount Carmel, including Jezebel's imported prophets. The 400 prophets of Asherah are not mentioned again, so that they may not have accepted the challenge along with the Baal prophets.

d. Challenge to the People (18:20-24)

²⁰ So Ahab sent to all the people of Israel, and gathered the prophets together at Mount Carmel. ²¹ And Elijah came near to all the people, and said, "How long will you go limping with two different opinions? If the LORD is God, follow him; but if Baal, then follow him." And the people did not answer him a word. ²² Then Elijah said to the people, "I, even I only, am left a prophet of the LORD; but Baal's prophets are four hundred and fifty men. ²³ Let two bulls be given to us; and let them choose one bull for themselves, and cut it in pieces and lay it on the wood, but put no fire to it; and I will prepare the other bull and lay it on the wood, and put no fire to it. ²⁴ And you call on the name of your god and I will call on the name of the LORD; and the God who answers by fire, he is God." And all the people answered, "It is well spoken."

Like Joshua at another famous covenant assembly, Elijah appeals to the people to "choose this day whom you will serve" (Josh. 24:15). *Limping*. The Hebrew word is the same as that which describes the peculiar ritual dance of the Baal prophets (18:26). *Different opinions*— literally, hopping from one leg to another (Snaith, p. 154)—is a metaphor for halfhearted or double-minded indecision (Psalm 119:113). The prophet challenges impossible spiritual neutrality. The people refused to commit themselves pending the outcome of the contest.

Elijah does not count as prophets those whom Obadiah hid in the time of persecution (18:4,13), for he is the only one acting as a prophet, standing in the breach for Yahweh to challenge the prophets of Baal. *Answers by fire* probably means lightning (Job 1:16; Ex. 9:23–24; Psalm 18:12–14; 29:7; 148:8), although the element of fire is quite general in theophany language, especially connected with Sinai (Ex. 3:2; 19:16,18; 20:18; cf. 1 Kings 19:12). The element of fire became closely associated with Elijah himself (2 Kings 1:10 ff.).

e. Failure of Prophets of Baal (18:25–29)

25 Then Elijah said to the prophets of Baal, "Choose for yourselves one bull and prepare it first, for you are many; and call on the name of your god, but put no fire to it." 26 And they took the bull which was given them, and they prepared it, and called on the name of Baal from morning until noon, saying, "O Baal, answer us!" But there was no voice, and no one answered. And they limped about the altar which they had made. 27 And at noon Elijah mocked them, saying, "Cry aloud, for he is a god; either he is musing, or he has gone aside, or he is on a journey, or perhaps he is asleep and must be awakened." 28 And they cried aloud, and cut themselves after their custom with swords and lances, until the blood gushed out upon them. 29 And as midday passed, they raved on until the time of the offering of the oblation but there was **no voice; no one answered, no one heeded.**

The Baal prophets perform their ritual first, and it takes them all day. To call on the name of one's god may have overtones of magic or of prayer. The continuing repetition of the name may also serve to produce a state of ecstasy. *Voice* can mean "thunder" in the context of storm theophany of either Baal or Yahweh (Psalm 29; cf. Thomas, pp. 125, 128). The ritual dance in Baal worship was perhaps intended to induce ecstasy (Montgomery, pp. 301–302). The dance had a place in Israelite worship, and early prophecy as well (Ex. 15:20; 1 Sam. 10:5,10; 2 Sam. 6:5,16).

With bitter irony, at noontime Elijah mocked the Baal mythology, now known from the Ras Shamra texts, of the dying-rising god. During the drought, or dry season of the long Palestinian summer, they believed the god Mot (death) had killed Baal. Then they performed mourning rituals to bring him back to life by sympathetic magic. These were rain-making ceremonies for the producing of the vital autumn rains upon which the fertility of the year's crops vitally depended (Thomas, pp. 130–133).

Elijah was not merely enjoying a bit of sarcasm, but rather combatting false religion with every weapon at his disposal. That the god might be *asleep* was a concept known to Yahweh religion, but at least once it was specifically denied (Psalm 44:23–24; 121:3–4). *Awakened* was used as an anthropomorphic metaphor for Yahweh's saving activity (Psalm 35:23; 59:4–5; 78:65).

After Elijah's mocking speech, the Baal prophets became more frenzied. Their self-laceration *with swords and lances,* the climax of their ecstasy, was a piece of mimetic magic to bring rain or attract the sympathy of Baal (Gray, pp. 350–351). Self-wounding was perhaps known among Hebrew ecstatic prophets as well (cf. 20:35,37,41; Hos. 7:14–16; Zech. 13:6). *Raved on* is an intensive form of the Hebrew word meaning to prophesy, which means in Baal prophecy what it meant in Yahweh prophecy sometimes, "to rave like a madman" (cf. 2 Kings 9:11; Jer. 29:26). This classic description of Canaanite ecstatic prophetism thus provides some points of comparison with early Hebrew prophecy, but also a startling contrast with the later more exalted Hebrew prophetic expression.

f. Preparation of the Lord's Sacrifice (18:30-35)

30 Then Elijah said to all the people, "Come near to me"; and all the people came near to him. And he repaired the altar of the Lord that had been thrown down; 31 Elijah took twelve stones, according to the number of the tribes of the sons of Jacob, to whom the word of the Lord came, saying, "Israel shall be your name"; 32 and with the stones he built an altar in the name of the Lord. And he made a trench about the altar, as great as would contain two measures of seed. 33 And he put the wood in order, and cut the bull in pieces and laid it on the wood. And he said, "Fill four jars with water, and pour it on the burnt offering, and on the wood." 34 And he said, "Do it a second time"; and they did it a second time. And he said, "Do it a third time"; and they did it a third time. 35 And the water ran round about the altar, and filled the trench also with water.

Elijah's own calm behavior is a startling contrast to the futile raving of the ecstatics of Baal. The prophet here is serving as covenant mediator, a "prophet like unto Moses" (Ex. 32:15-35, BBC, Vol. 1, p. 453). *The altar of the Lord* which Elijah repaired marked an ancient sanctuary. *Twelve stones* bears historical reminiscences of Sinai (Ex. 24:4), and Gilgal (Josh. 4:4 ff.). Doubtless this is an example of the ritually correct altar of unhewn stones (Ex. 20:25; Deut. 27:5-6). *Four jars . . . a third time,* twelve in all, may be the same symbolism as the twelve stones.

What is the proper interpretation of such a ritual? The closest analogy of a ceremony of covenant mediation, presided over by Samuel in the time of the Philistine crisis, seems to interpret water-pouring as a symbol of repentance (1 Sam. 7:3-14). When Samuel offered a burnt offering and cried out to Yahweh, the answer which decided the battle in Israel's favor was a mighty thunder. In "holy war" Yahweh fought for his people with his weapons of the storm: hail, thunder, lightning, flashfloods (Josh. 10:11; Judg. 5:20-21; Hab. 3:3-15). The prophet Elijah may be assuring the people and his opponents that there are no tricks, making the miracle all the more miraculous. But the sequel seems to indicate an acted prayer for rain, related to the other symbolic acts of the prophets which were thought of as powerful initiators of that which they symbolized (cf. 11:30; 22:11; 2 Kings 13:14-19).

g. Answer by Fire (18:36-40)

36 And at the time of the offering of the oblation, Elijah the prophet came near and said, "O Lord, God of Abraham, Isaac, and Israel, let it be known this day that thou art God in Israel, and that I am thy servant, and that I have done all these things at thy word. 37 Answer me, O Lord, answer me, that this people may know that thou, O Lord, art God, and that thou hast turned their hearts back." 38 Then the fire of the Lord fell, and consumed the burnt offering, and the wood, and the stones, and the dust, and licked up the water that was in the trench. 39 And when all the people saw it, they fell on their faces; and they said, "The Lord, he is God; the Lord, he is God." 40 And Elijah said to them, "Seize the prophets of Baal; let not one of them escape." And they seized them; and Elijah brought them down to the brook Kishon, and killed them there.

The prayer of the prophet is a simple and dignified appeal to Yahweh, God of the fathers, with a threefold invocation of the divine name (cf. Num. 6:24-26). *Servant* is a title particularly appropriate to the function of the prophet as covenant mediator in intercessory prayer. *Turned their hearts back.* A similar ministry is attributed by late prophetic teaching to Elijah as the prophetic forerunner of the day of the Lord (Mal. 4:5-6). *Fire of the Lord fell.* The Hebrew verb distinguishes this divine fire from that which is sometimes said to spring miraculously from the sanctuary or altar itself and consume the sacrifice (Lev. 9:24; Judg. 6:21; cf. "fire from heaven" in 1 Chron. 21:26; 2 Chron. 7:1).

The interpretation that this fire theophany is lightning does not in any way nullify the miraculous element (notice it ate up everything in the vicinity!), since in the order of the account it must have fallen from a cloudless sky (18:41–45). This miracle falls in the category of the mighty acts of God in salvation-history. The immediate decision and confession of the people is testimony to the marvelous event. Vengeance upon the Baal prophets is to be compared with the Israelite "holy war" concept (1 Sam. 15:32–33; cf. 2 Kings 10:19 ff.), even though this act must be judged by the Christian interpreter in the full light of the teaching and spirit of Christ. (Dentan, p. 62).

h. End of the Drought (18:41–46)

⁴¹ And Elijah said to Ahab, "Go up, eat and drink; for there is a sound of the rushing of rain." ⁴² So Ahab went up to eat and to drink. And Elijah went up to the top of Carmel; and he bowed himself down upon the earth, and put his face between his knees. ⁴³ And he said to his servant, "Go up now, look toward the sea." And he went up and looked, and said, "There is nothing." And he said, "Go again seven times." ⁴⁴ And at the seventh time he said, "Behold, a little cloud like a man's hand is rising out of the sea." And he said, "Go up, say to Ahab, 'Prepare your chariot and go down, lest the rain stop you.' " ⁴⁵ And in a little while the heavens grew black with clouds and wind, and there was a great rain. And Ahab rode and went to Jezreel. ⁴⁶ And the hand of the LORD was on Elijah; and he girded up his loins and ran before Ahab to the entrance of Jezreel.

The lightning was forerunner of the much-needed rain. Notice that King Ahab was expected to eat the festival meal despite what had happened. To the prophet, there may have been hopes that Ahab has renewed his covenant with Yahweh also. This may be the significance of his willingness to return with him to Jezreel. *The top of Carmel* reaches a height of 470 feet and would provide Elijah an excellent vantage point toward the sea. But Elijah refuses to look for himself, being so occupied with his concentration in prayer.

Put his face between his knees. Some have interpreted the prophet's position as imitative of the shape of a cloud, but he is simply prostrated in prayer. *Seven times* is a significant number in symbolic actions. *Cloud* means "dark cloud, cloud-mass, rain-cloud," and it is said to be small at first because of its distance. Elijah's urgent warning to Ahab to cross the valley before the Kishon became impassable was speedily vindicated by a stormy downpour. *Hand of the Lord* is an expression for prophetic inspiration to ecstatic activity (cf. 2 Kings 3:15; Ezek. 1:3; 3:14,22; 37:1; 40:1), here a 17-mile run before Ahab's chariot.

(3) Revelation at Mount Horeb (19:1–21)

Elijah had won a great victory for the Lord at Mount Carmel, but he had also aroused the wrath of Jezebel. Fearfully, the prophet fled into the desert, discouraged and ready to die. He was strengthened for the long journey to Horeb (Sinai), where he had an experience like that of Moses (Ex. 33:18–23). He was reassured that there was more work to be done for the prophetic revolt against the foreign Baal worship. God had a faithful remnant which would survive the Jehu purge. Elijah then chose Elisha to be his successor.

a. Wrath of Jezebel (19:1–3)

¹ Ahab told Jezebel all that Elijah had done, and how he had slain all the prophets with the sword. ² Then Jezebel sent a messenger to Elijah, saying, "So may the gods do to me, and more also, if I do not make your life as the life of one of them by this time tomorrow." ³ Then he was afraid, and he arose and went for his life, and came to Beersheba, which belongs to Judah, and left his servant there.

If Elijah had any illusions about being accepted at the court of Jezreel, they were at once shattered by the messenger of the queen conveying her dread oath to kill him. He knew from her previous persecutions (18:4,13) that she meant what she said. The fear of Elijah is recorded again when Ahaziah tried to arrest him (2 Kings 1:15). Indeed, "Elijah was a man of like nature with ourselves" (James 5:17). Beersheba was at the southern border of Judah, later a pilgrimage sanctuary for Israel (Amos 5:5; 8:14). *His servant* was a "lad, personal attendant," the same who aided his vigil for the rain cloud (18:43). This word indicates the same position of service which Gehazi filled for Elisha (2 Kings 4:12,25).

b. Flight of Elijah to Horeb (19:4–8)

⁴ But he himself went a day's journey into the wilderness, and came and sat down under a broom tree; and he asked that he might die, saying, "It is enough; now, O LORD, take away my life; for I am no better than my fathers." ⁵ And he lay down and slept under a broom tree; and behold, an angel touched him, and said to him, "Arise and eat." ⁶ And he looked, and behold, there was at his head a cake baked on hot stones and a jar of water. And he ate and drank, and lay down again. ⁷ And the angel of the LORD came again a second time, and touched him, and said, "Arise and eat, else the journey will be too great for you." ⁸ And he arose, and ate and drank, and went in the strength of that food forty days and forty nights to Horeb the mount of God.

The prophet became quite hungry, thirsty, and tired from his wilderness journey, but was sustained by divine provision. *Broom tree* was not the juniper of Lebanon, a large tree, but a small shrub of the desert stream beds. Here he became so disheartened that he wanted to die. After he had slept, food and drink were ministered by the angel of the Lord to his weary prophet (cf. 17:3 ff.). In the strength of this marvelous food, he pressed southward on his long journey.

c. Voice of the Lord (19:9–12)

⁹ And there he came to a cave, and lodged there; and behold, the word of the LORD came to him, and he said to him, "What are you doing here, Elijah?" ¹⁰ He said, "I have been very jealous for the LORD, the God of hosts; for the people of Israel have forsaken thy covenant, thrown down thy altars, and slain thy prophets with the sword; and I, even I only, am left; and they seek my life, to take it away." ¹¹ And he said, "Go forth, and stand upon the mount before the LORD." And behold, the LORD passed by, and a great and strong wind rent the mountains, and broke in pieces the rocks before the LORD, but the LORD was not in the wind; and after the wind an earthquake, but the LORD was not in the earthquake; ¹² and after the earthquake a fire, but the LORD was not in the fire; and after the fire a still small voice.

God's question is something of a personal rebuke to the prophet who replies out of self-pity, complaining that all are faithless except himself. *Jealous* could as easily be translated "zealous," the same characteristic in Jehu resulting in fanatical slaughter of the Baal worshipers (19:17, cf. 2 Kings 10:16–17). The description of the apostasy and persecution has led some scholars to feel the Horeb experience logically precedes that on Mount Carmel, but this involves too arbitrary a rearrangement of the text. The Lord passed by the prophet to the accompaniment of his storm theophany, a mighty wind, an earthquake, the fire. But the Lord was not in the storm phenomena. The essence of his revelation to the man of his choosing is in *a still small voice,* a voice of low whisper, the sound of stillness after the storm (Psalm 107:29).

d. Prophetic Task (19:13–18)

¹³ And when Elijah heard it, he wrapped his face in his mantle and went out and stood at the entrance of the cave. And behold, there came a voice to him, and said, "What are you doing here, Elijah?" ¹⁴ He said, "I have been very jealous for the LORD, the God of hosts; for the people of Israel have forsaken thy covenant, thrown down thy altars, and slain thy prophets with the sword; and I, even I only, am left; and they seek my life, to take it away." ¹⁵ And the LORD said to him, "Go, return on your way to the wilderness of Damascus; and when you arrive, you shall anoint Hazael to be king over Syria; ¹⁶ and Jehu the son of Nimshi you shall anoint to be king over Israel; and Elisha the son of Shaphat of Abelmeholah you shall anoint to be prophet in your place. ¹⁷ And him who escapes from the sword of Hazael shall Jehu slay; and him who escapes from the sword of Jehu shall Elisha slay. ¹⁸ Yet I will leave seven thousand in Israel, all the knees that have not bowed to Baal, and every mouth that has not kissed him."

Fearing to look upon God's face, the prophet hides his own in his hairy mantle and hears once again the insistent question. This time the response to his complaint is a new task. No time for self-pity when there is work to be done! The command to anoint Elisha is somewhat strange, since only kings and priests were anointed (but cf. Isa. 61:1). In any case Elijah designated his successor by a symbolic investiture, rather than by anointing. *Abelmeholah* was a city in Gilead near Tishbe, Elijah's own home. The schematic nature of the passage is indicated in that Elisha does not slay anybody in the prophetic reform. *I will leave,* or "I have left," the form of the verb in the Hebrew indicating certainty that God will spare these in the purge. *Seven thousand* provides an early witness to the doctrine of a remnant, which became quite a significant part of later prophetic preaching (cf. Isa. 6:13; 10:20–23).

e. Call of Elisha (19:19–21)

19 So he departed from there, and found Elisha the son of Shaphat, who was plowing, with twelve yoke of oxen before him, and he was with the twelfth. Elijah passed by him and cast his mantle upon him. 20 And he left the oxen, and ran after Elijah, and said, "Let me kiss my father and my mother, and then I will follow you." And he said to him, "Go back again; for what have I done to you?" 21 And he returned from following him, and took the yoke of oxen, and slew them, and boiled their flesh with the yokes of the oxen, and gave it to the people, and they ate. Then he arose and went after Elijah, and ministered to him.

Only one of the three commanded tasks did Elijah perform immediately. Elisha is called as his successor, but has no further part in the story until Elijah's death scene (2 Kings 2). Elisha's father was a well-to-do farmer, owner of twelve yoke of oxen. Elijah performed a symbolic action with his famous mantle (cf. 2 Kings 1:8; 2:8,13–14), portraying the continuity of the prophetic office in this call to discipleship. Elisha is allowed to have a farewell feast with his parents and friends before assuming his service to his prophetic master (cf. Luke 9:61–62).

(4) Wars with Benhadad of Aram (20:1–43)

The prophets who advise Ahab in the conduct of his military affairs are chiefly concerned with the ordering of the "holy war" by which Yahweh will give Israel the victory. Both battles are defensive, the first in response to a siege of Samaria. Ahab's willingness to release Benhadad on covenant terms advantageous to Israel is condemned by a prophetic use of parable to cause the king to judge his own action. However this covenant has to be judged from the broader historical perspective of the coalition of Syro-Palestinian kings who banded together with Benhadad and Ahab to stop Shalmaneser III of Assyria at the battle of Qarqar.

a. Siege of Samaria (20:1–6)

1 Benhadad the king of Syria gathered all his army together; thirty-two kings were with him, and horses and chariots; and he went up and besieged Samaria, and fought against it. 2 And he sent messengers into the city to Ahab king of Israel, and said to him, "Thus says Benhadad: 3 'Your silver and your gold are mine; your fairest wives and children also are mine.'" 4 And the king of Israel answered, "As you say, my lord, O king, I am yours, and all that I have." 5 The messengers came again, and said, "Thus says Benhadad: 'I sent to you, saying, "Deliver to me your silver and your gold, your wives and your children"; 6 nevertheless I will send my servants to you tomorrow about this time, and they shall search your house and the houses of your servants, and lay hands on whatever pleases them, and take it away.'"

The stronghold which Omri had built and Ahab completed was such a strong defensive position that it took the Assyrian siege machines three years to capture it (2 Kings 17:5). *Thirty-two kings* were vassals of the Aramean kingdom of Damascus, soon to be replaced by military commanders as a result of the outcome of this battle (20:24). *Thus says Benhadad.* This is the regular speech-formula for royal messengers, the secular use of which helps the interpreter to define the role of the prophets as messengers of the Lord's royal council. The second demand is more humiliating than the first, for unlimited search and seizure of the palaces of Samaria would be unreasonable. Some scholars interpret Ahab's willingness to submit to the first demand as evidence that Israel is already a vassal of Damascus (cf. 20:34).

b. Challenge to Battle (20:7-12)

7 Then the king of Israel called all the elders of the land, and said, "Mark, now, and see how this man is seeking trouble; for he sent to me for my wives and my children, and for my silver and my gold, and I did not refuse him." 8 And all the elders and all the people said to him, "Do not heed or consent." 9 So he said to the messengers of Benhadad, "Tell my lord the king, 'All that you first demanded of your servant I will do; but this thing I cannot do.'" And the messengers departed and brought him word again. 10 Benhadad sent to him and said, "The gods do so to me, and more also, if the dust of Samaria shall suffice for handfuls for all the people who follow me." 11 And the king of Israel answered, "Tell him, 'Let not him that girds on his armor boast himself as he that puts it off.'" 12 When Benhadad heard this message as he was drinking with the kings in the booths, he said to his men, "Take your positions." And they took their positions against the city.

Ahab took counsel with the tribal elders of the districts (20:14), who had evidently sought refuge from the Aramean armies in the capital fortress. Ahab had tried to keep peace by conciliating Benhadad and offering to pay tribute, but even the elders agree that the demands are unreasonable. The pagans Benhadad and Jezebel used the same oath formula to swear by their gods as Israelites used to swear by their God (19:2; cf. 2:23). To Benhadad's threat to reduce Samaria to so many handfuls of dust, Ahab replies with a very pithy proverb of the "he who laughs last" variety.

c. Prophetic Battle Plan (20:13-15)

13 And behold, a prophet came near to Ahab king of Israel and said, "Thus says the LORD, Have you seen all this great multitude? Behold, I will give it into your hand this day; and you shall know that I am the LORD." 14 And Ahab said, "By whom?" He said, "Thus says the LORD, By the servants of the governors of the districts." Then he said, "Who shall begin the battle?" He answered, "You." 15 Then he mustered the servants of the governors of the districts, and they were two hundred and thirty-two; and after them he mustered all the people of Israel, seven thousand.

Not only the elders, but also anonymous prophets have advice for the king in a time of "holy war." Yahweh wants to give the Aramean hordes into the king's hand, as evidence of Yahweh's loyalty to his covenant people (cf. Ex. 6:7; Ezek. 6:7). Ahab accepts the promise and inquires concerning the Lord's battle plans. *Servants of the governors* were young professional soldiers in the service of the district commanders. This verse gives a rare glimpse of the administrative system of North Israel, perhaps organized by Omri (de Vaux, p. 137). *Begin the battle* may mean "clinching" the attack begun by the young guerrilla fighters, so that Ahab is to follow quickly with the 7000, rather than lead the 232 (Gray, p. 377).

d. First Victory (20:16-22)

16 And they went out at noon, while Benhadad was drinking himself drunk in the booths, he and the thirty-two kings who helped him. 17 The servants of the governors of the districts went out first. And Benhadad sent out scouts, and they reported to him, "Men are coming out from Samaria." 18 He said, "If they have come out for peace, take them alive; or if they have come out for war, take them alive." 19 So these went out of the city, the servants of the governors of the districts, and the army which followed them. 20 And each killed his man; the Syrians fled and Israel pursued them, but Benhadad king of Syria escaped on a horse with horsemen. 21 And the king of Israel went out, and captured the horses and chariots, and killed the Syrians with a great slaughter. 22 Then the prophet came near to the king of Israel, and said to him, "Come, strengthen yourself, and consider well what you have to do; for in the spring the king of Syria will come up against you."

Benhadad was so overconfident that he was carousing in the army booths. When the small troop emerged from the city, he was uncertain of their intent until they had begun hand-to-hand combat. Apparently at this juncture the vassal kings panicked. Though Israel pursued the fleeing Arameans quickly, Benhadad escaped to fight another day. The same prophet perhaps who had ordered the battle plans now warned Ahab that though he had won one battle, the war would be renewed.

e. New Plans in Aram (20:23-25)

23 And the servants of the king of Syria said to him, "Their gods are gods of the hills, and

so they were stronger than we; but let us fight against them in the plain, and surely we shall be stronger than they. 24 And do this: remove the kings, each from his post, and put commanders in their places; 25 and muster an army like the army that you have lost, horse for horse, and chariot for chariot; then we will fight against them in the plain, and surely we shall be stronger than they." And he hearkened to their voice, and did so.

The interpretation of this defeat by the counselors of Benhadad reveals an interesting theology of polytheism. In the eyes of Arameans, Israel's gods are mountain gods who specialize in mountain warfare. *The plain* refers to the tableland of Transjordan. The idea seems to be that the horses and chariots of Aram would be more effective and the greater number of troops more overwhelming on level land (cf. Josh. 11:4; 17:16; Judg. 1:19; 4:3). *Commanders* may mean governors, indicating a reorganization of the loose confederation of Aramean kings into an Aramean empire with Damascus as its capital.[17]

f. Second Victory at Aphek (20:26–30a)

26 In the spring Benhadad mustered the Syrians, and went up to Aphek, to fight against Israel. 27 And the people of Israel were mustered, and were provisioned, and went against them; the people of Israel encamped before them like two little flocks of goats, but the Syrians filled the country. 28 And a man of God came near and said to the king of Israel, "Thus says the LORD, 'Because the Syrians have said, "The LORD is a god of the hills but he is not a god of the valleys," therefore I will give all this great multitude into your hand, and you shall know that I am the LORD.' " 29 And they encamped opposite one another seven days. Then on the seventh day the battle was joined; and the people of Israel smote of the Syrians a hundred thousand foot soldiers in one day. 30 And the rest fled into the city of Aphek; and the wall fell upon twenty-seven thousand men that were left.

True to the warning of the prophet, *in the spring*, the time when kings mounted their campaigns (cf. 2 Sam. 11:1; 2 Chron. 36:10), Benhadad was back again, this time with an army that *filled the country*.

[17] Benjamin Mazar, "The Aramean Empire and Its Relations with Israel," *Biblical Archaeologist*, Vol. XXV, No. 4 (Dec., 1962), pp. 98–120.

Aphek is to be identified, not with the old Philistine marshaling point in the Plain of Sharon (1 Sam. 4:1; 29:1), but a site on the main road east of Lake Galilee between Israel and Damascus (Gray, p. 380). This assumes that Israel was once again in control of her Transjordan territories, so often the battleground between these opposing armies. Whether *a man of God* is the same anonymous prophet who advised Ahab before or the same member of the prophetic guilds who confronted him after the battle, is not specified. Yahweh will give Israel the victory in order to disprove the slander against his sovereignty of the whole earth. Though the number of Aramean casualties may be exaggerated (only 20,000 foot soldiers fought for Aram against the Assyrians at Qarqar), it was a great victory, including the razing of Aphek whither Benhadad fled.

g. Ahab's Covenant with Benhadad (20:30b–34)

Benhadad also fled, and entered an inner chamber in the city. 31 And his servants said to him, "Behold now, we have heard that the kings of the house of Israel are merciful kings; let us put sackcloth on our loins and ropes upon our heads, and go out to the king of Israel; perhaps he will spare your life." 32 So they girded sackcloth on their loins, and put ropes on their heads, and went to the king of Israel and said, "Your servant Benhadad says, 'Pray, let me live.' " And he said, "Does he still live? He is my brother." 33 Now the men were watching for an omen, and they quickly took it up from him and said, "Yes, your brother Benhadad." Then he said, "Go and bring him." Then Benhadad came forth to him; and he caused him to come up into the chariot. 34 And Benhadad said to him, "The cities which my father took from your father I will restore; and you may establish bazaars for yourself in Damascus, as my father did in Samaria." And Ahab said, "I will let you go on these terms." So he made a covenant with him and let him go.

What was politically expedient and militarily advantageous to the kings of Israel was not always religiously pleasing to their prophets. *Merciful* is the familiar term, *chesed*, meaning covenant loyalty. This reputation had perhaps been earned by Omri in previous relationships between the two nations. *Sackcloth* symbolizes ritual humiliation as in mourning. *My brother* is a covenant term indicating the desire of Ahab to end the vassal relationship and make a parity treaty with Benhadad. *Watching for an omen* means "observing the signs, practicing divination," so that they seized on Ahab's first favorable word as a sign that he would spare Benhadad.

Ahab graciously received Benhadad in his personal chariot, perhaps the one in which he died (22:35). *My father took from your father.* Unless the word "father" is loosely interpreted as predecessor, in which case the reference could be to Benhadad I and Baasha, this must refer to previous conquests over Omri. *Bazaars* is literally "streets" or special quarters for trading. Omri had been forced into a vassal treaty in which the commercial advantages in Samaria, his capital city, had belonged to Damascus. Now the advantage in trading passes to Ahab, who lets Benhadad go in exchange for these concessions. Like the similarly profitable covenant of intermarriage with Phoenicia, this treaty with Aram was condemned by the prophets.

h. Prophetic Parable Against Ahab (20:35–43)

35 And a certain man of the sons of the prophets said to his fellow at the command of the Lord, "Strike me, I pray." But the man refused to strike him. 36 Then he said to him, "Because you have not obeyed the voice of the Lord, behold, as soon as you have gone from me, a lion shall kill you." And as soon as he had departed from him, a lion met him and killed him. 37 Then he found another man, and said, "Strike me, I pray." And the man struck him, smiting and wounding him. 38 So the prophet departed, and waited for the king by the way, disguising himself with a bandage over his eyes. 39 And as the king passed, he cried to the king and said, "Your servant went out into the midst of the battle; and behold, a soldier turned and brought a man to me, and said, 'Keep this man; if by any means he be missing, your life shall be for his life, or else you shall pay a talent of silver.' 40 And as your servant was busy here and there, he was gone." The king of Israel said to him, "So shall your judgment be; you yourself have decided it."

41 Then he made haste to take the bandage away from his eyes; and the king of Israel recognized him as one of the prophets. 42 And he said to him, "Thus says the Lord, 'Because you have let go out of your hand the man whom I had devoted to destruction, therefore your life shall go for his life, and your people for his people.'" 43 And the king of Israel went to his house resentful and sullen, and came to Samaria.

The first of three prophetic condemnations of Ahab (Elijah, 21:21; Micaiah, 22:17) comes from an anonymous member of *the sons of the prophets*, the prophetic guild. It reminds one of the strange story of prophetic discipleship during Jeroboam's dynasty (especially the part about the lion, 13:24 ff.). It is not explained why this prophet wants someone to smite and wound him, unless this serves as part of his disguise before Ahab on the battlefield. *Bandage over his eyes* evidently means there was some distinguishing mark around the eyes of a member of the prophetic guild (cf. Montgomery, p. 325; Zech. 13:6), which Ahab easily recognized.

Just as Nathan induced David to judge his own case by the use of a parable or fictitious legal dispute, so this prophet pretends to be a soldier or spectator to the battle to whom was committed a prisoner. The high valuation placed on the captive's life would represent more than the price of a slave, and may indicate an intention to hold him for ransom. Ironically, Ahab replies, *So shall your judgment be; you yourself have decided it,* without his realizing it is his own case that hangs in the balance. Benhadad was not just Ahab's captive, a valuable prize of war, but the man of Yahweh's ban (devotion to destruction), and as such he belonged to the Lord. The condemnation centers upon the disobedience of the king to the prophetic ordering of the "holy war" (cf. 1 Sam. 15). *Your life shall go for his life* picks up a phrase from the parable (v. 39). That Ahab would forfeit his own life in battle against the same man whom he had released (22:31) is poetic justice. Ahab went away *resentful and sullen*. This statement is a transition to

(5) Vineyard of Naboth in Jezreel (21:1-29)

If the Mount Carmel encounter demonstrates the prophetic religion of Elijah as monotheism, the incident of Naboth's vineyard proves it to be ethical monotheism. Nowhere is there a plainer contrast between kingship as Israel understood it and kingship as it had become under Canaanite influence. Naboth's innocent blood cries out for an avenger. Elijah is Yahweh's man of the hour, confronting the king on the confiscated property.

a. Denial of Ahab's Request (21:1-4)

1 Now Naboth the Jezreelite had a vineyard in Jezreel, beside the palace of Ahab king of Samaria. 2 And after this Ahab said to Naboth, "Give me your vineyard, that I may have it for a vegetable garden, because it is near my house; and I will give you a better vineyard for it; or, if it seems good to you, I will give you its value in money." 3 But Naboth said to Ahab, "The LORD forbid that I should give you the inheritance of my fathers." 4 And Ahab went into his house vexed and sullen because of what Naboth the Jezreelite had said to him; for he had said, "I will not give you the inheritance of my fathers." And he lay down on his bed, and turned away his face, and would eat no food.

Jezreel was the site of the king's winter *palace*. The main palace was in Samaria, the capital of the Omri dynasty. Ahab's offer to Naboth for his vineyard seems like a perfectly legitimate business deal. But the property was not Naboth's to sell, for a man's inheritance was his father's and his son's as well as his, and it was inalienable by Israelite law (Num. 27:8-11). Ahab recognized the justness of Naboth's refusal, though he sulked peevishly around the palace at Samaria.

b. Scheme of Jezebel (21:5-10)

5 But Jezebel his wife came to him, and said to him, "Why is your spirit so vexed that you eat no food?" 6 And he said to her, "Because I spoke to Naboth the Jezreelite, and said to him, 'Give me your vineyard for money; or else, if it please you, I will give you another vineyard for it'; and he answered, 'I will not give you my vineyard.'" 7 And Jezebel his wife said to him, "Do you now govern Israel? Arise, and eat bread, and let your heart be cheerful; I will give you the vineyard of Naboth the Jezreelite."

8 So she wrote letters in Ahab's name and sealed them with his seal, and she sent the letters to the elders and the nobles who dwelt with Naboth in his city. 9 And she wrote in the letters, "Proclaim a fast, and set Naboth on high among the people; 10 and set two base fellows opposite him, and let them bring a charge against him, saying, 'You have cursed God and the king.' Then take him out, and stone him to death."

The queen, out of her own autocratic background, rebukes the king for accepting the Israelite limitations of covenant kingship. Jezebel proceeds to show Ahab how her father Ethbaal might have done it in Tyre. It is hard to believe she could have used Ahab's name and seal without his collusion in the matter. The *nobles* were "freeholders, landed citizenry," who formed with the elders a town council. *Fast* here is an indication of some corporate guilt bringing calamity unless it is purged from the community. *On high* means in the place of honor. They "set him up" for false accusation by honoring him. *Two base fellows* were "sons of Belial," that is, worthless men (cf. Prov. 19:28a). This technically fulfills the legal requirement of two (or three) witnesses in the assessing of the death penalty (Deut. 17:6; cf. Matt. 26:60). In the old Covenant Code, reviling the tribal leader (ruler, prince) was equivalent to cursing God (Ex. 22:28; cf. BBC, Vol. 1, p. 426). Stoning was the method of capital punishment, which best expressed the community involvement in the legal process (Lev. 24:10-23).

c. Judicial Murder of Naboth (21:11-14)

11 And the men of his city, the elders and the nobles who dwelt in his city, did as Jezebel had sent word to them. As it was written in the letters which she had sent to them, 12 they proclaimed a fast, and set Naboth on high among the people. 13 And the two base fel-

lows came in and sat opposite him; and the base fellows brought a charge against Naboth, in the presence of the people, saying, "Naboth cursed God and the king." So they took him outside the city, and stoned him to death with stones. ¹⁴ Then they sent to Jezebel, saying, "Naboth has been stoned; he is dead."

Jezebel's malicious commands were performed to the letter, a testimony to the power of the crown and its willingness to subvert the rights of its citizens. *Outside the city* avoided contamination (cf. Acts 7:58). The witnesses whose testimony condemned the man symbolically cast the first stones (cf. John 8:7).

d. Spoils of Injustice (21:15-16)

¹⁵ As soon as Jezebel heard that Naboth had been stoned and was dead, Jezebel said to Ahab, "Arise, take possession of the vineyard of Naboth the Jezreelite, which he refused to give you for money; for Naboth is not alive, but dead." ¹⁶ And as soon as Ahab heard that Naboth was dead, Ahab arose to go down to the vineyard of Naboth the Jezreelite, to take possession of it.

Either the property of slain criminals was forfeited to the crown, or this is an illegal confiscation of property by the king. Jehu noted, in the fulfillment of Elijah's doom oracle, that Naboth's sons were slain with him (2 Kings 9:26). This was the law of corporate responsibility, the sins of the fathers being visited upon the sons (cf. Ex. 20:5; Josh. 7:24). For Ahab and Jezebel, this ancient custom served to rid the property from any further legal claim.

e. Prophetic Confrontation (21:17-19)

¹⁷ Then the word of the LORD came to Elijah the Tishbite, saying, ¹⁸ "Arise, go down to meet Ahab king of Israel, who is in Samaria; behold, he is in the vineyard of Naboth, where he has gone to take possession. ¹⁹ And you shall say to him, 'Thus says the LORD, "Have you killed, and also taken possession?"' And you shall say to him, 'Thus says the LORD: "In the place where dogs licked up the blood of Naboth shall dogs lick your own blood."'"

In this second classic encounter between Elijah and Ahab (cf. 18:17-19), the prophet is commanded to catch the king red-handed. It is a most instructive story for the later emphasis of the writing prophets on social justice. In his rebuking of the king, Elijah stands in the prophetic tradition with Samuel, Nathan, and Ahijah. As usual the prophet appears with dramatic suddenness. *Have you killed*—the Hebrew verb from the Sixth Commandment here has its most severe meaning of premeditated murder (Ex. 20:13; cf. BBC, Vol. 1, p. 415). *Dogs* were prominent in prophetic doom oracles (21:23), here and in the conventional scavenger saying about the birds (21:24; cf. 14:11; 16:4).

f. Judgment Oracle by Elijah (21:20-24)

²⁰ Ahab said to Elijah, "Have you found me, O my enemy?" He answered, "I have found you, because you have sold yourself to do what is evil in the sight of the LORD. ²¹ Behold, I will bring evil upon you; I will utterly sweep you away, and will cut off from Ahab every male, bond or free, in Israel; ²² and I will make your house like the house of Jeroboam the son of Nebat, and like the house of Baasha the son of Ahijah, for the anger to which you have provoked me, and because you have made Israel to sin. ²³ And of Jezebel the LORD also said, 'The dogs shall eat Jezebel within the bounds of Jezreel.' ²⁴ Any one belonging to Ahab who dies in the city the dogs shall eat; and any one of his who dies in the open country the birds of the air shall eat."

Ahab's accusation of Elijah has advanced from "troubler of Israel" (18:17) to the more personal *my enemy.* Elijah has *found* Ahab, in the double sense of meeting him in a certain situation and also finding out or detecting his crime. *Sold yourself* is figurative of the slavery of sin (21:25; 2 Kings 17:17). The language of these verses is that of prophetic doom oracles against the dynasties of *Jeroboam* (14:10-11) and *Baasha* (16:3-4), which has replaced the more specific prediction of Ahab's death in the previous command of Yahweh. *And of Jezebel* really belongs with the personal word against Ahab (21:19). Jehu gives his own oral tradition of these oracles (2 Kings 9:26,36-37) in connection with their fulfillment.

g. Evils of Ahab (21:25-26)

²⁵ (There was none who sold himself to do what was evil in the sight of the LORD like

Ahab, whom Jezebel his wife incited. 26 He did very abominably in going after idols, as the Amorites had done, whom the Lord cast out before the people of Israel.)

The historian captures the opportunity for an editorial comment about the evil reign of Ahab (cf. 16:30–33), a judgment which is noticeably absent from the death formula (22:37–40). *Incited*—allured, instigated, seduced, enticed—is the verb used of the testing or tempting action which early Israel attributed to God (2 Sam. 24:1), whereas later theology blamed Satan (1 Chron. 21:1; cf. Job 2:3). The historian understands Jezebel to be Ahab's chief temptation, but does not thereby condone his yielding to her. The threat implied by the horrible example of the Amorites is that Israel also must be *cast out* for her idolatry.

h. Humiliation and Postponed Doom (21:27–29)

27 And when Ahab heard those words, he rent his clothes, and put sackcloth upon his flesh, and fasted and lay in sackcloth, and went about dejectedly. 28 And the word of the Lord came to Elijah the Tishbite, saying, 29 "Have you seen how Ahab has humbled himself before me? Because he has humbled himself before me, I will not bring the evil in his days; but in his son's days I will bring the evil upon his house."

There is no reason why the ritual humiliation of Ahab, symbolic of his repentance, should be regarded as insincere (cf. 2 Kings 20:1–5). It was not his own death, but the death of his dynasty, which was thereby temporarily averted. Those oracles predicting the personal fate of the king and queen (21:19,23) were both fulfilled (22:38; 2 Kings 9:35–37). *Dejectedly* is literally "softly, gently," not the pouting mood described previously (20:43; 21:4–5). *His son's days*. Two sons of Ahab ruled Israel, Ahaziah and Jehoram, but it was in the days of the latter that the prophetic purge was executed by Jehu (2 Kings 9:1—10:28). Once again, the Lord's punishment is tempered by his mercy (cf. 18:41–46). The story of Elijah is concluded in 2 Kings (1:2—2:18).

(6) Last Battle of Ahab (22:1–40)

After his decisive victories over Benhadad II, Ahab joined the coalition of kings against Assyria at the battle of Qarqar on an equal basis with Benhadad. Evidently, Benhadad had not kept his agreement to return all the cities (20:34), and Ramothgilead was still in Aramean hands. The main interest of the story lies in the contrast between the victory oracle of the institutional prophets and the prediction of Ahab's death by Micaiah, son of Imlah, otherwise unknown. This is the first formal encounter between the true and false prophets. The correct name for these victory prophets is "lying" prophets (22:22; cf. 13:18; Jer. 23:25–26). Micaiah insists on speaking the true word of Yahweh, even though it spells doom for the king. Though Ahab commands that Micaiah be held in prison, and tries to avoid his fate, he is later mortally wounded by one of the archers.

a. Alliance with Jehoshaphat (22:1–4)

1 For three years Syria and Israel continued without war. 2 But in the third year Jehoshaphat the king of Judah came down to the king of Israel. 3 And the king of Israel said to his servants, "Do you know that Ramoth-gilead belongs to us, and we keep quiet and do not take it out of the hand of the king of Syria?" 4 And he said to Jehoshaphat, "Will you go with me to battle at Ramoth-gilead?" And Jehoshaphat said to the king of Israel, "I am as you are, my people as your people, my horses as your horses."

Jehoshaphat is pictured in this narrative as ally or vassal of Ahab (later of Jehoram, 2 Kings 3; but cf. 1 Kings 22:49). This alliance was sealed by the marriage of Ahab's daughter, Athaliah, to Jehoshaphat's son, Jehoram (2 Kings 8:18,25–27). This involved severe consequences later for Judah (2 Kings 11). *Ramothgilead* was an important fortification, Solomon's district capital for Bashan (4:13), in Transjordan due east of Jezreel. As soon as Israel and Aramea stopped Shalmaneser III of Assyria, they resumed their border warfare. *My people . . . my horses*. Jehoshaphat's answer to Ahab may indicate that he has little choice in the matter (cf. 20:4).

b. Victory Word of War Prophets (22:5-12)

⁵ And Jehoshaphat said to the king of Israel, "Inquire first for the word of the LORD." ⁶ Then the king of Israel gathered the prophets together, about four hundred men, and said to them, "Shall I go to battle against Ramoth-gilead, or shall I forbear?" And they said, "Go up; for the Lord will give it into the hand of the king." ⁷ But Jehoshaphat said, "Is there not here another prophet of the LORD of whom we may inquire?" ⁸ And the king of Israel said to Jehoshaphat, "There is yet one man by whom we may inquire of the LORD, Micaiah the son of Imlah; but I hate him, for he never prophesies good concerning me, but evil." And Jehoshaphat said, "Let not the king say so." ⁹ Then the king of Israel summoned an officer and said, "Bring quickly Micaiah the son of Imlah." ¹⁰ Now the king of Israel and Jehoshaphat the king of Judah were sitting on their thrones, arrayed in their robes, at the threshing floor at the entrance of the gate of Samaria; and all the prophets were prophesying before them. ¹¹ And Zedekiah the son of Chenaanah made for himself horns of iron, and said, "Thus says the LORD, 'With these you shall push the Syrians until they are destroyed.'" ¹² And all the prophets prophesied so, and said, "Go up to Ramoth-gilead and triumph; the LORD will give it into the hand of the king."

True to the ideals of "holy war," Jehoshaphat wants to inquire of Yahweh before the battle (cf. 20:13-14,22,28). It is somewhat surprising to find 400 Yahweh prophets at Ahab's court, in the light of the previous persecutions by Jezebel (18:4; 19:10). In this different literary source, Elijah does not appear, but Micaiah serves a similar function as the lone prophet of doom. These court prophets say what the king wants to hear, yet the previous victory oracles to Ahab in his Aramean wars came true (20:13 ff.). In any case, Jehoshaphat is not impressed and calls for further inquiry. It would be interesting to know the previous encounters by which Micaiah earned his reputation as a prophet of doom.

The story portrays an impressive scene before the gate of Samaria with the kings on their thrones, dressed in their royal robes, *at the threshing floor,* a large level, open space suitable for this kind of *prophesying* (cf. 18:29). *Zedekiah,* the leader of the court prophets, has a good Yahweh name. Symbolic action could be used by false prophets as well as true (cf. Jer. 28); but without the genuine command of Yahweh, it has distinctly magical overtones. The horns are a symbol of power, not necessarily of Baal, and are appropriately related to the Joseph oracle in the Blessing of Moses (Deut. 33:17). *Push* means gore and describes the prophet's symbolic action with the horns (cf. 2 Kings 13:14-19). Both act and word were believed to convey real power to accomplish the victory being predicted.

c. Doom Oracle of Micaiah (22:13-18)

¹³ And the messenger who went to summon Micaiah said to him, "Behold, the words of the prophets with one accord are favorable to the king; let your word be like the word of one of them, and speak favorably." ¹⁴ But Micaiah said, "As the LORD lives, what the LORD says to me, that I will speak." ¹⁵ And when he had come to the king, the king said to him, "Micaiah, shall we go to Ramoth-gilead to battle, or shall we forbear?" And he answered him, "Go up and triumph; the LORD will give it into the hand of the king." ¹⁶ But the king said to him, "How many times shall I adjure you that you speak to me nothing but the truth in the name of the LORD?" ¹⁷ And he said, "I saw all Israel scattered upon the mountains, as sheep that have no shepherd; and the LORD said, 'These have no master; let each return to his home in peace.'" ¹⁸ And the king of Israel said to Jehoshaphat, "Did I not tell you that he would not prophesy good concerning me, but evil?"

The king's messenger has some politically expedient advice for Micaiah, that he should agree with the majority opinion and give in to the king's wishes. Micaiah objects with an oath to any human principle of control over his oracle. Yahweh himself is the only authority of the prophet's word. Once the prophet knows this word of the Lord, no human authority can keep him from delivering the message. Micaiah's first answer is in shocking agreement with the victory oracle of the court prophets. We might suppose he has yielded to pressure and conformity, except that his later explanation leads us to see that Micaiah wants Ahab to go to his doom. But Ahab detects the mocking irony of the uncharacteristic victory oracle in the mouth of Micaiah, and adjures him in the name of Yahweh to tell the true vision. The oracle of the scattered sheep and the interpretation are in poetic form in Hebrew. The image of the shepherd signifying the king was a common metaphor in biblical and ancient Near Eastern literature (cf. Ezek. 34).

d. Plan of Divine Council (22:19–23)

19 And Micaiah said, "Therefore hear the word of the LORD: I saw the LORD sitting on his throne, and all the host of heaven standing beside him on his right hand and on his left; 20 and the LORD said, 'Who will entice Ahab, that he may go up and fall at Ramoth-gilead?' And one said one thing, and another said another. 21 Then a spirit came forward and stood before the LORD, saying, 'I will entice him.' 22 And the LORD said to him, 'By what means?' And he said, 'I will go forth, and will be a lying spirit in the mouth of all his prophets.' And he said, 'You are to entice him, and you shall succeed; go forth and do so.' 23 Now therefore behold, the LORD has put a lying spirit in the mouth of all these your prophets; the LORD has spoken evil concerning you."

Micaiah hastens to add another vision to contradict King Ahab's comment ("I told you so") to Jehoshaphat. This scene of Yahweh as King and his heavenly host of messenger spirits and angelic advisers is the divine council, the prototype for prophetic call experiences (Isa. 6:1–8; 40:1–11), which authenticates their predictions (Amos 3:7), and distinguishes them from the lying prophets (Jer. 23:18,22). The call for volunteers reminds one of Isaiah's call experience (Isa. 6:8), but the mission in this case is to *entice* Ahab to his death (cf. Jer. 20:7; Deut. 13:1–5; Ezek. 14:9).

This is an ancient theology in which there are no secondary causes. *Lying spirit* should be compared with the "evil spirit from the Lord" which tormented King Saul after the Spirit of Yahweh had departed from him (1 Sam. 16:14). For preexilic Israel, things both good and evil were attributed in given instances to God. This simple monistic view of attributing all things to divine sovereignty became increasingly problematical to the faith of the Jews after the destruction of Jerusalem. Even when the doctrine of Satan developed, however, he is still pictured as a servant of God in the divine council (Job 1—2; Zech. 3). James flatly states that God tempts no one but is the author of all good things (1:13–17). The human limitations of Micaiah's belief that God inspired men to lie (cf. 13:18) are one evidence for progressive revelation. The New Testament views on the problem of evil (Luke 13:1–5; John 9:1–3) are certainly to be preferred for understanding and for faith.

e. True and False Prophecy (22:24–28)

24 Then Zedekiah the son of Chenaanah came near and struck Micaiah on the cheek, and said, "How did the Spirit of the LORD go from me to speak to you?" 25 And Micaiah said, "Behold, you shall see on that day when you go into an inner chamber to hide yourself." 26 And the king of Israel said, "Seize Micaiah, and take him back to Amon the governor of the city and to Joash the king's son; 27 and say, 'Thus says the king, "Put this fellow in prison, and feed him with scant fare of bread and water, until I come in peace." ' " 28 And Micaiah said, "If you return in peace, the LORD has not spoken by me." And he said, "Hear, all you peoples!"

Zedekiah's slap on the cheek is a deliberate insult (Job 16:10; Lam. 3:30; Psalm 3:7; Mic. 5:1; Isa. 50:6). Of two contending parties, only one could be possessed of *the Spirit of the Lord* (cf. 1 Sam. 16). Micaiah gives a private confirmation oracle to Zedekiah, in the nature of a curse (v. 25; cf. Amos 7:16–17; Jer. 28:15–17). Ahab's treatment of Micaiah reveals that Jezebel was not the only source of persecution. The threat of perpetual prison or perhaps death is in Ahab's word, *until I come in peace*. But Micaiah accepts the test of all true prophecy, namely that it will come to pass (Deut. 18:20–22; Jer. 28:9). *"Hear, all you peoples!"* Were there peoples assembled to witness this scene? These are the same words with which the canonical prophet Micah (1:2) begins his preaching, so they may be a gloss here, especially since the Septuagint omits the phrase (Gray, p. 807). But such an appeal to bystanders to witness a word later to be fulfilled is not inherently improbable.

f. Wounding of Disguised Ahab (22:29–36)

²⁹ So the king of Israel and Jehoshaphat the king of Judah went up to Ramoth-gilead. ³⁰ And the king of Israel said to Jehoshaphat, "I will disguise myself and go into battle, but you wear your robes." And the king of Israel disguised himself and went into battle. ³¹ Now the king of Syria had commanded the thirty-two captains of his chariots, "Fight with neither small nor great, but only with the king of Israel." ³² And when the captains of the chariots saw Jehoshaphat, they said, "It is surely the king of Israel." So they turned to fight against him; and Jehoshaphat cried out. ³³ And when the captains of the chariots saw that it was not the king of Israel, they turned back from pursuing him. ³⁴ But a certain man drew his bow at a venture, and struck the king of Israel between the scale armor and the breastplate; therefore he said to the driver of his chariot, "Turn about, and carry me out of the battle, for I am wounded." ³⁵ And the battle grew hot that day, and the king was propped up in his chariot facing the Syrians, until at evening he died; and the blood of the wound flowed into the bottom of the chariot. ³⁶ And about sunset a cry went through the army, "Every man to his city, and every man to his country!"

The story of Ahab's last battle does not give the king's motive in disguising himself for the battle. Perhaps he had advance word of Benhadad's plans to concentrate the battle against the person of the King (v. 31). Certainly, he was trying to avoid the outcome predicted by Micaiah, as well as the doom from Elijah (21:19), and the anonymous prophet (20:42). That Jehoshaphat would go in his (Ahab's, according to LXX) kingly robes, while Ahab went disguised as an ordinary soldier, must indicate his reluctant participation as a vassal to the king of Israel (cf. 2 Kings 3:11 ff.). When the chariot captains of Aramea concentrate on Jehoshaphat, only his cry of alarm saves him from Ahab's fate. Through divine intervention Ahab's ruse fails, and he receives a mortal wound from a random arrow. Heroically, Ahab remained with his troops throughout the day, as his life's blood flowed down into his chariot. At sunset, about the time he died, the cry went through the army calling off the attack (cf. 22:17).

g. Death of Ahab (22:37–40)

³⁷ So the king died, and was brought to Samaria; and they buried the king in Samaria. ³⁸ And they washed the chariot by the pool of Samaria, and the dogs licked up his blood, and the harlots washed themselves in it, according to the word of the LORD which he had spoken. ³⁹ Now the rest of the acts of Ahab, and all that he did, and the ivory house which he built, and all the cities that he built, are they not written in the Book of the Chronicles of the Kings of Israel? ⁴⁰ So Ahab slept with his fathers; and Ahaziah his son reigned in his stead.

Jezreel would have been closer than Samaria, but the king would have been taken to Omri's burial place at Samaria. The historian's summary regards the events at the pool of Samaria as an approximate fulfillment of the prediction of Elijah (21:19), though poetic justice would have been served had it happened in Jezreel where later his son Jehoram died (2 Kings 9:26). The reference, **harlots washed,** was not mentioned in Elijah's prediction. It implies a desecration of the king's blood. **The pool of Samaria** may be archaeologically identifiable, along with **the ivory house,** a magnificent palace full of ivory inlay furniture and other Phoenician decoration (Wright, p. 153–154; Heaton, pp. 79, 88). The architecture of Samaria set a pattern for wealthy north Israelites in the following century as did the acts of social injustice like that against Naboth, by which the wealth was gained (Amos 2:6; 3:15; 6:4; Mic. 6:16). **Slept with his fathers** elsewhere always means died peacefully, but here only refers to burial in the family tomb.

2. Reign of Jehoshaphat in Judah (22:41–50)

⁴¹ Jehoshaphat the son of Asa began to reign over Judah in the fourth year of Ahab king of Israel. ⁴² Jehoshaphat was thirty-five years old when he began to reign, and he reigned twenty-five years in Jerusalem. His mother's name was Azubah the daughter of Shilhi. ⁴³ He walked in all the way of Asa his father; he did not turn aside from it, doing what was right in the sight of the Lord; yet the high places were not taken away, and the people still sacrificed and burned incense on the high places. ⁴⁴ Jehoshaphat also made peace with the king of Israel.
⁴⁵ Now the rest of the acts of Jehoshaphat, and his might that he showed, and how he warred, are they not written in the Book of the Chronicles of the Kings of Judah? ⁴⁶ And the remnant of the male cult prostitutes who remained in the days of his father Asa, he exterminated from the land.
⁴⁷ There was no king in Edom; a deputy was king. ⁴⁸ Jehoshaphat made ships of Tarshish to go to Ophir for gold; but they did not go, for the ships were wrecked at Eziongeber. ⁴⁹ Then Ahaziah the son of Ahab said to Jehoshaphat, "Let my servants go with your servants in the ships," but Jehoshaphat was not willing. ⁵⁰ And Jehoshaphat slept with his fathers, and was buried with his fathers in the city of David his father; and Jehoram his son reigned in his stead.

For the time of the divided monarchy, the historian of Kings seems more interested in the kings and prophets of Israel, whereas Chronicles concentrates on Judah (for example, see account of the reign of Jehoshaphat, 2 Chron. 17—20).

Continuing the stability of rule achieved by the long reign of Asa his father, Jehoshaphat ruled for 25 years. Also, like his father before him, he achieved limited religious reform (cf. v. 46), and the historian's basic approval. His alliance with Ahab is not condemned here (but cf. 2 Chron. 19:1–3), but it certainly caused trouble later because of Athaliah's behavior in the Jezebel pattern.

Jehoshaphat was a strong king, militarily. He fought not only in alliance with Ahab but with Jehoram against neighboring nations (2 Kings 3). He had evidently reestablished control over Edom, since he tried to reestablish the sea trade of Solomon from Eziongeber. However, he was prevented from success by an unfortunate accident to the ships in port (cf. 9:26 ff.). He refused an offer from Ahaziah of Israel for a second attempt in partnership.

3. Beginning of Ahaziah's Reign in Israel (22:51–53)

⁵¹ Ahaziah the son of Ahab began to reign over Israel in Samaria in the seventeenth year of Jehoshaphat king of Judah, and he reigned two years over Israel. ⁵² He did what was evil in the sight of the Lord, and walked in the way of his father, and in the way of his mother, and in the way of Jeroboam the son of Nebat, who made Israel to sin. ⁵³ He served Baal and worshiped him, and provoked the Lord, the God of Israel, to anger in every way that his father had done.

The historian's formula language introducing the brief reign of Ahab's first son is separated from his concluding formula (2 Kings 1:17–18) by an incident in the ministry of Elijah. It is a similar pattern to the treatment of Ahab (16:29–34), and the religious judgment against him is the same.

As was noted in the Introduction, the Greek and English bibles make an arbitrary division at this point between 1 Kings and 2 Kings. However, the prophetic revolt against Phoenician Baalism had already made a significant beginning with Elijah, Micaiah, and their anonymous prophetic contemporaries.

2 Kings: Part One
Prophetic Revolution (1:1—13:25)

The whole of 1 Kings 17 through 2 Kings 13 is concerned primarily with the prophetic revolution epitomized in the activities of Elijah and Elisha. The editor of Kings retains a basic concern for the annals of the kings of Israel and Judah; the continued development of successive individual dynasties within both nations, as well as their dynastic and diplomatic interrelationships. But this is overshadowed by his theological concern for the prophetic revolution which both brought an end to the explosion of Baalism attendant to the activity of Jezebel and precipitated a purified worship of Yahweh.

It is not just the rise and fall of two nations that the writer(s) traces, but the fortunes of a religion, especially the manner in which apostasy and faithlessness inevitably pass beneath the keen edge of history's judgment. The smoldering cities of Samaria and Jerusalem, the wasted villages of both North and South, and the displaced populaces of both nations are haunting reminders to those who sow the wind that they may expect to reap the whirlwind (cf. Hos. 8:7).

I. The Last Days of Elijah (1:1—2:25)

The closing days of Elijah's life are occupied primarily with the faithlessness of king Ahaziah (1.1–18) and the choice of a prophetic successor in the person of Elisha (2:1–25).

1. Prophetic Judgment upon Ahaziah's Faithlessness (1:1–18)

Through successive crises of both personal and corporate dimensions, the temptation to turn to other media of revelation was a constant threat to Israel. It continues to threaten biblical religion with a legion of false options to biblical revelation.

(1) Historical Note Illustrating the Judgment Motif (1:1)

¹ After the death of Ahab, Moab rebelled against Israel.

Verse 1 introduces 2 Kings with a degree of abruptness inconsistent with the separate nature of the book in the English canon. This may be explained in part by the suggestion that 1 and 2 Kings are actually one book.

The observation that *Moab rebelled against Israel* after the death of Ahab is doubtless related to the fuller account of Moab's rebellion under Mesha which appears in 3:4 ff., and is equally at home in the context of 1 Kings 22:1 ff. Despite the tenuous relationship which the verse sustains to the present text, the redactor has deliberately left or inserted the verse at this juncture as a fitting commentary upon the faithlessness of Ahaziah.

(2) A Judgment Narrative on Ahaziah's Faithlessness in Seeking Revelation from Baal (1:2–16)

Seeking to determine the outcome of critical injury, Ahaziah sought the counsel of Baalzebub. Elijah condemns this and pronounces Ahaziah's fate for having departed from normative Israelite religion in such a time of crisis. When the king's armed forces seek to take Elijah they are consumed.

² Now Ahaziah fell through the lattice in his upper chamber in Samaria, and lay sick; so he sent messengers, telling them, "Go, inquire of Baalzebub, the god of Ekron, whether I shall recover from this sickness." ³ But the angel of the Lord said to Elijah the Tishbite, "Arise, go up to meet the messengers of the king of Samaria, and say to them, 'Is it because there is no God in Israel that you are going to inquire of Baalzebub, the god of Ekron?' ⁴ Now therefore thus says the Lord, 'You shall not come down from the bed to which you have gone, but you shall surely die.'" So Elijah went.

The occasion and declaration of Elijah's judgment word (vv. 2–4). Homes were often constructed with a lattice work surrounding the roof, the whole construction being known as the *upper chamber*. Apparently, the lattice work was open to permit the free flow of breezes, but so screened as to obstruct vision. Mention is made in the Old Testament of such construction on roof tops (Neh. 3:31; Jer. 22:14), and even above the gates to a city (2 Sam. 18:33).

Rather than consulting the will of Yahweh through normative means, Ahaziah sent *messengers* (*malek*, the same word as angel in the *angel of the Lord*) to *inquire* of Baalzebub concerning the possibility of his recovery. The verb *inquire* (*darash*, resort, seek) is used all but exclusively of resorting to a place with a religious objective (Amos 5:5; Deut. 12:5), of consulting Yahweh (Gen. 25:22; Ex. 18:15; 1 Sam. 9:9), or of consulting a heathen god or necromancer (Ezek. 14:10; 1 Sam. 28:7).

It may also be used of seeking deity through prayer and worship (Deut. 4:29; Hos. 10:12). The word became a technical term for seeking divine revelation.

Baalzebub means Lord of flies, but it is exceedingly questionable that the text should be translated "flies" or that *zebub* was original to the text. The Greek text of Kings accepted the Hebrew *zebub*, however, and interpreters have suggested that Baalzebub was a god who warded off plagues borne by flies; hence Lord of flies (*muian theon* in LXX).

The appearance of *zebul* with Baal is attested in the Ras Shamra literature as *Zbl-b'l*, Prince Baal. However, Baalzebul was a more cosmic than local deity. He was the chief contender with Yahweh in the times of Elijah and Elisha (cf. 1 Kgs. 18:20 ff.).

Better New Testament texts, including the Chester Beatty papyri, refer to Beelzebul rather than Beelzebub (cf. Matt. 10:25; 12:24; Mark 3:22; Luke 11:15 ff.; cf. KJV "Beelzebub"). Assuming that the text originally read Baalzebul, the alteration to Baalzebub was apparently a deliberate and forceful pun ridiculing Prince Baal as "Lord of Flies."

It is impossible to be more specific about the particular nature of the **angel of the Lord** than to suggest that Elijah was so impressed with the personal, dynamic quality of the word which came to him from the Lord that he spoke of it in individual terms. Few people today would press the literal concept of physical beings who travel from heaven to earth and back again. Nor is it especially helpful to suggest that the angel of the Lord may have been a prophetic person, an extension of the Lord's revelation in human form. Most likely, the concept of the angel of the Lord was a profound but nonliteral means of speaking of God's presence—a presence that ancient people probably conceived in literal, physical form, as some persons still do, but an understanding which is neither obligatory for the contemporary reader nor prerequisite to a proper grasp of the reality of God's presence for Elijah.

The truth of the experience is the same, regardless of one's explanation of the angel of the Lord. Elijah came to apprehend in an unmistakable, personal, and dynamic fashion the will of God concerning Ahaziah's appeal to Baalzebul. On the basis of a legitimate, divine conviction, the prophet issued his judgment word. As a consequence of an unfaithfulness which is implied although not stated in the passage of judgment, Ahaziah is to die.

⁵ The messengers returned to the king, and he said to them, "Why have you returned?" ⁶ And they said to him, "There came a man to meet us, and said to us, 'Go back to the king who sent you, and say to him, Thus says the LORD, Is it because there is no God in Israel that you are sending to inquire of Baalzebub, the god of Ekron? Therefore you shall not come down from the bed to which you have gone, but shall surely die.'" ⁷ He said to them, "What kind of man was he who came to meet you and told you these things?" ⁸ They answered him, "He wore a garment of haircloth, with a girdle of leather about his loins." And he said, "It is Elijah the Tishbite."

The reception of Elijah's judgment word (vv. 5–8). **Tishbite** is an adjective presupposing an area or village Tishbe. Although efforts have been made to equate Tishbe with Transjordan Listib, there is no evidence of an occupation at that site before Byzantine times, and no site can be located for a "Tishbe." Cohen associates Tishbite with *toshab*, a term used to designate outsiders who were granted rights of permanent settlement. He further argues that Elijah may well have been of Rechabite background, an assumption consonant with the Rechabite allegiance to the desert traditions (one of which must surely have been an extreme fidelity to Yahweh, God of Sinai). A Rechabite heritage would well suit aspects of Elijah's life and character, and, all things considered, Cohen's thesis is more promising than the location of a "Tishbe" east of the Jordan (cf. IDB).

The Hebrew text suggests only that Elijah was a *baʻal seʻar*; an owner, possessor (*baʻal*, lord) of hair. Hair (*seʻar*) may refer to that of animals as material (Gen. 25:25;

Zech. 13:4), but it is often used of human hair (Judg. 16:22; 2 Sam. 14:26), and especially of the long hair of a woman (Ezek. 16:7, Song of Sol. 4:1, 6:5). Zechariah spoke of prophets who "put on a hairy mantle" (Zech. 13:4), and the garb of John the Baptist was probably an imitation of Elijah (Matt. 3:4). While the RSV is probably correct in its translation, "a garment of haircloth," an equally strong argument could be made that Elijah had long hair, quite analogous to the Nazarite, although he is not known to have assumed Nazarite vows (one of which precluded cutting the hair).

⁹ Then the king sent to him a captain of fifty men with his fifty. He went up to Elijah, who was sitting on the top of a hill, and said to him, "O man of God, the king says, 'Come down.'" ¹⁰ But Elijah answered the captain of fifty, "If I am a man of God, let fire come down from heaven and consume you and your fifty." Then fire came down from heaven, and consumed him and his fifty.

¹¹ Again the king sent to him another captain of fifty men with his fifty. And he went up and said to him, "O man of God, this is the king's order, 'Come down quickly!'" ¹² But Elijah answered them, "If I am a man of God, let fire come down from heaven and consume you and your fifty." Then the fire of God came down from heaven and consumed him and his fifty.

¹³ Again the king sent the captain of a third fifty with his fifty. And the third captain of fifty went up, and came and fell on his knees before Elijah, and entreated him, "O man of God, I pray you, let my life, and the life of these fifty servants of yours, be precious in your sight. ¹⁴ Lo, fire came down from heaven, and consumed the two former captains of fifty men with their fifties; but now let my life be precious in your sight." ¹⁵ Then the angel of the LORD said to Elijah, "Go down with him; do not be afraid of him." So he arose and went down with him to the king, ¹⁶ and said to him, "Thus says the LORD, 'Because you have sent messengers to inquire of Baalzebub, the god of Ekron,—is it because there is no God in Israel to inquire of his word?—therefore you shall not come down from the bed to which you have gone, but you shall surely die.'"

The response to Elijah's word of judgment (vv. 9–16). The king's intention is not stated: whether the life of Elijah was endangered can only be implied, and it may well be that the king sought only to hear the judgment word directly from the mouth of the prophet. Or, the fate of those who sought to harm the prophet may have had a salutary effect upon the king. It is clear, however, that once Elijah went to the king his life was not endangered, and the prophet merely repeated the judgment word previously given.

The narrative is closely akin to the spirit of the Elisha narratives, and it is perhaps for this reason that when Kings was divided into two books (an artificial division) this narrative was placed together with the Elisha narratives. This narrative and those associated with Elisha have probably come to us through the hands of the sons of the prophets who treasured memories of the actions of Elijah and Elisha. In the process of oral transmission it seems likely that successive prophets transformed the original historical nucleus of various stories by the addition of materials somewhat akin to the character of stories associated with the saints at certain stages of Christian history.

An element of progression which deliberately heightens the tension of the account emerges in several aspects of the total narrative. For example, the command of the first captain, **O man of God, the king says, "Come down,"** gives way to the more authoritative, **O man of God, this is the king's order** (ko 'amar, a phrase drawn from prophetic terminology, and, in fact, previously used by Elijah), **"Come down quickly."** Again, in the first instance a fire from the heavens destroyed the captain and his group, but in the second instance it was the *fire of God* which came down. This deliberate heightening of the tension within the narrative is designed to serve as a framework in which the address of the third captain takes the form of an entreaty.

The narrative illustrates the divine protection of the prophet and the fact that his life can only be yielded voluntarily to the king. Such a story was doubtless used as a means of extolling the magnitude of Elijah among the sons of the prophets and other believers. Not even a king and his army could dictate to Elijah the prophet.

Few persons would defend the morality of calling down fire from heaven upon groups of fifty as in the present narrative. The New Testament certainly repudiates a comparable proposal on the part of James and John—whose proposal reflects the motif of the 2 Kings passage (Luke 9:54 f.; cf. Lev. 10:2; Rev. 11:5).

The judgment word (1:3 f., 6 ff., 16 ff.) doubtless became an ideal for countless members of prophetic schools as well as later prophets. Elijah became the paragon of prophets, as Moses was for law, David for psalms, and Solomon for wisdom. He faced the king on his own ground, declared the word of God, and rested with confidence in a protection that arose from outside himself.

(3) Deuteronomic Appraisal of Ahaziah (1:17–18)

17 So he died according to the word of the LORD which Elijah had spoken. Jehoram, his brother, became king in his stead in the second year of Jehoram the son of Jehoshaphat, king of Judah, because Ahaziah had no son. 18 Now the rest of the acts of Ahaziah which he did, are they not written in the Book of the Chronicles of the Kings of Israel?

The concluding summary on the reign of Ahaziah confirms the death of the king as a consequence of *the word of the Lord which Elijah had spoken.* No further moral or religious appraisal is necessary, since this has already been sufficiently dealt with previously in the present chapter. Especially, however, is further elaboration unnecessary since a full Deuteronomic appraisal of Ahaziah appears at the conclusion of 1 Kings.

2. Elisha, Successor to Elijah: the Translation of Elijah (2:1–25)

The problem of succession to a prophet so prominent as Elijah in the era prior to classical prophecy (eighth and seventh centuries) was of concern, not only to the prophet involved, but to the schools of the prophets as well (cf. 2:3,5,7).

(1) The Selection and Testing of Elijah's Successor (2:1–8)

1 Now when the LORD was about to take Elijah up to heaven by a whirlwind Elijah and Elisha were on their way from Gilgal. 2 And Elijah said to Elisha, "Tarry here, I pray you; for the LORD has sent me as far as Bethel." But Elisha said, "As the LORD lives, and as you yourself live, I will not leave you." So they went down to Bethel. 3 And the sons of the prophets who were in Bethel came out to Elisha, and said to him, "Do you know that today the LORD will take away your master from over you?" And he said, "Yes, I know it; hold your peace."
4 Elijah said to him, "Elisha, tarry here, I pray you; for the LORD has sent me to Jericho." But he said, "As the LORD lives, and as you yourself live, I will not leave you." So they came to Jericho. 5 The sons of the prophets who were at Jericho drew near to Elisha, and said to him, "Do you know that today the LORD will take away your master from over you?" And he answered, "Yes, I know it; hold your peace."
6 Then Elijah said to him, "Tarry here, I pray you; for the LORD has sent me to the Jordan." But he said, "As the LORD lives, and as you yourself live, I will not leave you." So the two of them went on. 7 Fifty men of the sons of the prophets also went, and stood at some distance from them, as they both were standing by the Jordan. 8 Then Elijah took his mantle, and rolled it up, and struck the water, and the water was parted to the one side and to the other, till the two of them could go over on dry ground.

The geographical focus of vv. 1–8 is the three centers associated with the schools of the prophets: Gilgal (although this is the Gilgal north of Bethel, not in the Jordan valley), Bethel, and Jericho.

In three successive scenes Elijah seeks to dissuade Elisha from following him, suggesting that he is going only so far as Bethel, Jericho, or Jordan. In each instance, however, Elisha professes his determination to accompany the prophet Elijah, using a formula which was probably an expression common to the culture of the day, *As the Lord lives, and as you yourself live, I will not leave you.* This threefold repetition suggests a deliberate effort on the part of the editor to suggest the faithfulness of Elisha to Elijah, marking him in the process as a loyal follower suitable as a successor to the prophet Elijah. Succession depends upon fidelity to the given responsibilities of one's ministry.

The ***whirlwind*** is often associated with the coming of Yahweh (cf. Isa. 29:6; Ezek. 1:4; 13:11,13; Zech. 9:14; Psalms 107:25; 148:8; Job 38:1; 40:6). It appears as subject in Isaiah 40:24; 41:16; Jeremiah 23:19; 30:23; and as object in Psalm 107:29. Snaith observes that only in Psalm 107:25 is $s^{e \cdot}arah$ used of an ordinary tempest.

The phrase ***sons of the prophets*** refers to men associated together in a guild or brotherhood. They lived a communal life, although they were not celibate. Apparently they were organized under a common leader who bore the title "father." They were ecstatic and susceptible to frenzied actions which often caused some to look askance at their conduct (cf. 1 Sam. 10:9 ff.; although these ecstatics were not specifically called sons of the prophets, they were in all probability their spiritual progenitors). While Elisha is closely associated with them, Elijah appears as a solitary who is not surrounded by them.

As fifty men from the sons of the prophets stood at a distance watching, Elijah parted the waters of the Jordan by smiting them with his mantle. The parallels are so clear that it is all but impossible to read this without recalling both the crossing of the Red Sea and the crossing of the Jordan. There are, in fact, many parallels between Moses and Elijah, and R. P. Carroll has not only proposed that Moses was the prototype of the prophetic office (as Deuteronomy suggests, Deut. 18:15–18) but has suggested the strong possibility of a line of succession which includes Elijah.[1] According to Carroll, especially does Elijah parallel Moses as an example of the "Mosaic prophet proclaiming the word of Yahweh to the people and mediating the covenant between Yahweh and his people."

[1] R. P. Carroll, "The Elijah-Elisha Sagas: Some remarks on Prophetic Succession in Ancient Israel," *Vetus Testamentum*, XIX, no. 4, 400 ff.

(2) The Promise of Succession (2:9–12a)

⁹ When they had crossed, Elijah said to Elisha, "Ask what I shall do for you, before I am taken from you." And Elisha said, "I pray you, let me inherit a double share of your spirit." ¹⁰ And he said, "You have asked a hard thing; yet, if you see me as I am being taken from you, it shall be so for you; but if you do not see me, it shall not be so." ¹¹ And as they still went on and talked, behold, a chariot of fire and horses of fire separated the two of them. And Elijah went up by a whirlwind into heaven. ¹² And Elisha saw it and he cried, "My father, my father! the chariots of Israel and its horsemen!" And he saw him no more.

The present chapter demonstrates no awareness of the prior selection of Elisha as Elijah's successor (cf. 1 Kings 19:19 ff.), and one may properly conclude that the two traditions existed independently of one another during the course of their development prior to incorporation in the present books of Kings. Elisha's request for a ***double share of your spirit*** does not reflect the ambition of a disciple who hopes to outstrip his master. He appeals to the Deuteronomic law that gave the eldest son a double portion of his father's goods (cf. Deut. 21:17). Elisha requests that he be acknowledged as Elijah's heir, inheriting the role traditionally associated with the firstborn.

An examination of Old Testament usages of ***spirit*** (*ruach*) reveals that vital energy is a common connotation. The spirit equipped successive generations with power, wisdom, courage, strength, and talent. Thus, Elisha sought the energizing power which characterized the ministry of Elijah, and one purpose of the numerous miracle stories associated with Elisha is the confirmation of that transfer of power.

The promise of prophetic succession rests on that potential to discern the hidden powers of God at work in the world, the insight necessary to perceive the presence of God which many, though having eyes, yet never see. ***If you see me as I am being taken from you, it shall be so for you.***

Later, as Elijah went up by a whirlwind, Elisha cried out, ***My father, my father! the chariots of Israel and its horsemen.***

This phrase probably originated in the Elisha cycle and is used in 6:17 and 13:14. Fire theophanies were often associated with the appearance of Yahweh, and the storm phenomenon probably is the background for the expression the "chariots of fire" (6:17). In turn, the present phrase *the chariots of Israel and its horsemen* probably became a way of describing the appearance of Yahweh (cf. 6:17; 13:14; Isa. 66:15).

The text does not say that Elijah was carried into heaven on the chariot, popular interpretations to the contrary. He was carried up *by a whirlwind into heaven,* a way of saying that God came for him.

The passages (2:10 ff.; 6:15 ff.) speak of the constant presence of unseeen spiritual powers at hand, but which are passed over, unseen, and unnoticed. The fact that it is not given to every man to perceive the *chariots of Israel and its horsemen* should encourage all the greater sensitivity to their presence and an increasing diligence to perceive realities available to those with eyes to see. True spiritual perception of the proper order is a rare gift, one to be cultivated and treasured.

(3) *Elisha Confirmed as Successor to Elijah (2:12b–25)*

Three specific areas of activity confirmed the succession of Elisha to the role of Elijah: (1) smiting the water by the inherited power of Elijah (vv. 12b–14), (2) the inability to find Elijah or his body, thereby confirming his translation (vv. 15–18), and (3) the cleansing of the waters of Jericho (vv. 19–22).

Then he took hold of his own clothes and rent them in two pieces. 13 And he took up the mantle of Elijah that had fallen from him, and went back and stood on the bank of the Jordan. 14 Then he took the mantle of Elijah that had fallen from him, and struck the water, saying, "Where is the LORD, the God of Elijah?" And when he had struck the water, the water was parted to the one side and to the other; and Elisha went over.

Yahweh's power mediated through Elisha (vv. 12b–14). The continuing mark of validation for the prophetic office is the power of Yahweh mediated through that office. Prophets without power can hardly lay legitimate claim to succession. When power is lacking, so is the prophetic function.

Rending one's garment(s) was a common expression of grief: *Then he took hold of his own clothes and rent them in two pieces.* It may well be, however, that Elisha's action was a type of symbolic action closely akin to that of Ahijah in the tearing of Jeroboam's garment to signify the division of the kingdom (1 Kings 11:29 ff.), or the action of Saul who tore Samuel's garment, albeit by accident, and which Samuel then interpreted as a sign of the passing of the kingdom from Saul to his successor (cf. 1 Sam. 27 ff.). Other expressions of grief being absent and in view of the symbolic action previously established in the tearing of a garment, the probability is that Elisha's action in tearing the garment in two pieces symbolizes his own succession to Elijah's role.

The question, *Where is the Lord, the God of Elijah?* is designed to test whether or not the Lord's power has in fact been transmitted to Elisha. The parting of the water, imitative of Elijah's previous action, confirms the fact that the Lord's power is, indeed, now mediated through Elisha, that he is the true successor to Elijah.

15 Now when the sons of the prophets who were at Jericho saw him over against them, they said, "The spirit of Elijah rests on Elisha." And they came to meet him, and bowed to the ground before him. 16 And they said to him, "Behold now, there are with your servants fifty strong men; pray, let them go, and seek your master; it may be that the Spirit of the LORD has caught him up and cast him upon some mountain or into some valley." And he said, "You shall not send." 17 But when they urged him till he was ashamed, he said, "Send." They sent therefore fifty men; and for three days they sought him but did not find him. 18 And they came back to him, while he tarried at Jericho, and he said to them, "Did I not say to you, Do not go?"

The search for Elijah, and the confirmation of his translation (vv. 15–18). The belief that Elijah had suffered an accident or otherwise been removed is normal. The whirlwind may well have been a "dust-devil, which might accompany the sirocco [a hot, desert wind storm] east of the Jordan. Fire suggests the sirocco, and the visible progress of an accompanying dust-storm might be compared to horses and chariots" (John Gray, p. 425). Specifically, the fifty suggest that the Spirit of the Lord may have *caught him up and cast him upon some mountain or into some valley.* That is, Elijah may have been possessed by the Spirit and in such an ecstatic state, or trance, may have fallen off some precipitous cliff.

As *The Jerusalem Bible* suggests, "The fruitless search merely establishes the fact that Elijah is no longer in this world: what has become of him is a mystery on which Elisha is not prepared to elaborate. The text does not say that Elijah did not die, though this conclusion was in fact drawn." Upon the basis of this tradition, however, Elijah was reckoned together with Enoch as having been translated to be with God. From thence he was expected to return (cf. Mal. 3:23; 4:5), and the New Testament places Moses and Elijah together in the transfiguration (Matt. 17:3 ff.), a relationship that should not be surprising, if one examines the many parallels between the two figures within the Old Testament.

[19] Now the men of the city said to Elisha, "Behold, the situation of this city is pleasant, as my lord sees; but the water is bad, and the land is unfruitful." [20] He said, "Bring me a new bowl, and put salt in it." So they brought it to him. [21] Then he went to the spring of water and threw salt in it, and said, "Thus says the Lord, I have made this water wholesome; henceforth neither death nor miscarriage shall come from it." [22] So the water has been wholesome to this day, according to the word which Elisha spoke.

[23] He went up from there to Bethel; and while he was going up on the way, some small boys came out of the city and jeered at him, saying, "Go up, you baldhead! Go up, you baldhead!" [24] And he turned around, and when he saw them, he cursed them in the name of the Lord. And two she-bears came out of the woods and tore forty-two of the boys. [25] From there he went on to Mount Carmel, and thence he returned to Samaria.

Two deeds of wonder which further confirm the succession of Elisha (vv. 19-25). The miraculous cleansing of the waters of Jericho and the death of the 42 boys who mocked the prophet are the first of numerous wonders which uniquely characterize the life of Elisha. The life of no other person in the Old Testament is attended by such a multiplicity of unique deeds. That behind these acts there are historical deeds performed by the prophet is doubtlessly correct. But that such deeds have undergone literary expansion by the sons of the prophet is also assumed to be correct. With the Elisha narratives one enters a world apart from most of the Old Testament and entirely removed from the great prophets of the classical era such as Amos, Hosea, Isaiah, or Micah. Yet, the stories still bear a positive witness, for they testify not only to the recognition of Elisha's succession within the schools of prophets, but testify as well to the esteem and regard with which Elisha was held by later generations. Thus, the value of the narratives rests not so much in the historicity of single events as in the witness which they bear to the judgment later generations passed upon Elisha's life.

Cleansing the waters of Jericho is reminiscent of Moses' action in cleansing the water at Marah (cf. Ex. 15:22 ff.). Gray suggests that the use of salt and a new dish indicate a rite of separation. Jericho had been under the ban since its destruction during the Conquest, and the action of Elisha, according to Gray, is a reflection of earlier rites whereby Jericho and its vital spring were brought from the realm of the ban for common occupation, "which had been forbidden under the sanction of the curse (Josh. 6x.17,26)" (p. 428).

Thus, the story of Elisha's cleansing of the spring is probably based upon an older ritual of separation whereby Jericho was made accessible to occupation. The story has been placed in a new context and given a new meaning by the redactor. It became one means of validating the succession of Elisha. His ability to perform wonders of cleansing identify him as a holy man, a man with the unique power of God operative through him. By such action the sons of the prophets gave evidence of the power which Elisha manifested in their midst.

The death of 42 *small boys* (specifically identified as small or little ones) is included at this juncture as a means of instilling respect for the successor to Elijah. Few interpreters would defend the morality of such a narrative and no interpreter would defend this as a pattern of moral action or as a reflection of divine judgment; it is best understood as a popular story which was used to instill respect for the prophetic office.

Stories such as the death of the 42 boys should be understood in light of the redactor's theological purpose, however, to say nothing of the cultural and social conditions of the time. Admittedly the death of the little boys is premoral, even from the Old Testament ethical standard, to say nothing of the New Testament. But the theological purpose of the redactor is of primary significance. Using a popular story which doubtless circulated in the ninth century B.C., he vividly demonstrated the awe and wonder associated with Elisha the prophet. Despite modern judgments of the morality of the story, the redactor is admirably successful in utilizing a popular narrative to illustrate a legitimate fact—the veneration of the prophetic office, to say nothing of Elisha himself.

II. Elisha's Establishment on the National Political Scene: His Prophetic Counsel in the Moabite War (3:1–27)

Having shown how Elisha was established as the legitimate successor to Elijah within prophetic circles, the redactor of 2 Kings now uses Elisha's counsel in the Moabite war as the means of illustrating the prophet's establishment on the national political scene.

1. The Deuteronomic Appraisal of Jehoram (3:1–3)

¹ In the eighteenth year of Jehoshaphat king of Judah, Jehoram the son of Ahab became king over Israel in Samaria, and he reigned twelve years. ² He did what was evil in the sight of the LORD, though not like his father and mother, for he put away the pillar of Baal which his father had made. ³ Nevertheless he clung to the sin of Jeroboam the son of Nebat, which he made Israel to sin; he did not depart from it.

Successive kings of Israel are judged by the Deuteronomic standard of the single sanctuary (cf. Deut. 12:1 ff.); and despite the outward measure of success which came to an Israelite king, no king of the North is ever commended. Each king is condemned for the *sin of Jeroboam the son of Nebat*, i.e., the scandalous offence of the sanctuaries at Dan and Bethel, but especially the golden calves which were the northern counterpart to the southern ark of the covenant (God was thought to have been enthroned above each).

Jehoram, son of Ahab and brother of Ahaziah, followed Ahaziah to the throne (Ahaziah had no son to succeed him). Although not fully commended, his condemnation by the Deuteronomic editor is less severe than that of other kings, being tempered by the fact that his evil was *not like his father and mother* (i.e., Ahab and Jezebel). Further, *he put away the pillar of Baal*, a cultic object used in the worship of Baal.

2. The Moabite War and Elisha's Counsel (3:4–27)

The conquest of Moab by Omri and the subsequent rebellion against the Omrides which was led by Mesha, king of Moab, is fully documented in one of the finer Palestinian literary parallels to the Old Testament. A brief excerpt follows: "As for Omri, king of Israel, he humbled Moab many years (lit., days), for Chemosh was angry at his land. And his son followed him and spoke (thus), but I have triumphed over him and over his house, while Israel hath perished for ever!" ("The Moabite Stone," *ANET*, ll. 5 ff.).

(1) The Coalition of Israel and Judah (3:4-8)

⁴ Now Mesha king of Moab was a sheep breeder; and he had to deliver annually to the king of Israel a hundred thousand lambs, and the wool of a hundred thousand rams. ⁵ But when Ahab died, the king of Moab rebelled against the king of Israel. ⁶ So King Jehoram marched out of Samaria at that time and mustered all Israel. ⁷ And he went and sent word to Jehoshaphat king of Judah, "The king of Moab has rebelled against me; will you go with me to battle against Moab?" And he said, "I will go; I am as you are, my people as your people, my horses as your horses." ⁸ Then he said, "By which way shall we march?" Jehoram answered, "By the way of the wilderness of Edom."

Because Mesha had fortified northern approaches to Moab, Jehoram needed the cooperation of Judah and Edom in order to attack from the south. The rebellion may well have begun during the reign of Ahaziah (cf. 1:1) and continued into the reign of Jehoram, for Ahaziah reigned for only two years.

(2) The Desperation of the Coalition (3:9-12)

⁹ So the king of Israel went with the king of Judah and the king of Edom. And when they had made a circuitous march of seven days, there was no water for the army or for the beasts which followed them. ¹⁰ Then the king of Israel said, "Alas! The Lord has called these three kings to give them into the hand of Moab." ¹¹ And Jehoshaphat said, "Is there no prophet of the Lord here, through whom we may inquire of the Lord?" Then one of the king of Israel's servants answered, "Elisha the son of Shaphat is here, who poured water on the hands of Elijah." ¹² And Jehoshaphat said, "The word of the Lord is with him." So the king of Israel and Jehoshaphat and the king of Edom went down to him.

Passing through Edom (cf. vv. 8*b*-9), the expedition made a *circuitous march* (KJV, "they fetched a compass," i.e., they traveled in circular fashion following each of the points of the compass in turn). In the process they apparently expended their water supply (v. 9). Reference to Elisha as the one *who poured water on the hands of Elijah* is a way of suggesting that Elisha was Elijah's servant. He poured the water when Elijah washed his hands.

(3) Prophetic Counsel and Its Confirmation (3:13-20)

¹³ And Elisha said to the king of Israel, "What have I to do with you? Go to the prophets of your father and the prophets of your mother." But the king of Israel said to him, "No; it is the Lord who has called these three kings to give them into the hand of Moab." ¹⁴ And Elisha said, "As the Lord of hosts lives, whom I serve, were it not that I have regard for Jehoshaphat the king of Judah, I would neither look at you, nor see you. ¹⁵ But now bring me a minstrel." And when the minstrel played, the power of the Lord came upon him. ¹⁶ And he said, "Thus says the Lord, 'I will make this dry stream-bed full of pools.' ¹⁷ For thus says the Lord, 'You shall not see wind or rain, but that stream-bed shall be filled with water, so that you shall drink, you, your cattle, and your beasts.' ¹⁸ This is a light thing in the sight of the Lord; he will also give the Moabites into your hand, ¹⁹ and you shall conquer every fortified city, and every choice city, and shall fell every good tree, and stop up all springs of water, and ruin every good piece of land with stones." ²⁰ The next morning, about the time of offering the sacrifice, behold, water came from the direction of Edom, till the country was filled with water.

Since Ahab and Jezebel had surrounded themselves with prophets of Baal, Elisha suggests that in the present moment of need the king should turn to those prophets (v. 13). The statement is closely akin to Jeremiah's sarcastic rebuttal: "But where are your gods that you made for yourself? Let them arise, if they can save you, in your time of trouble" (Jer. 2:27 f.). Jehoram's response specifies that a prophet of Yahweh is needed, as though Elisha has suggested the prophets of Baal. Jehoram answered, *No; it is the Lord who has called these three kings.* The narrative is deliberately and pointedly sarcastic in its attack upon the association of Ahab's dynasty with the prophets of Baal.

The necessity of a minstrel before Elisha gave the oracle (v. 15) suggests that the prophetic oracle at this stage in the development of prophecy may have been given during an ecstatic trance. This state of ecstasy could be excited or induced by the use of musical instruments, and such excitation was surely present among the forerunners of the sons of the prophets (cf. 1 Sam. 10:5 f.).

The cause of this abundance of water in Moab (v. 20) was a heavy rain in Edom which produced a flash flood much farther up the wadi. Hence, the prophecy was fulfilled quite precisely. Water in abundance was brought apart from the sight of wind or rain.

(4) Moabite Despair and the Withdrawal of Israel (3:21-27)

21 When all the Moabites heard that the kings had come up to fight against them, all who were able to put on armor, from the youngest to the oldest, were called out, and were drawn up at the frontier. 22 And when they rose early in the morning, and the sun shone upon the water, the Moabites saw the water opposite them as red as blood. 23 And they said, "This is blood; the kings have surely fought together, and slain one another. Now then, Moab, to the spoil!" 24 But when they came to the camp of Israel, the Israelites rose and attacked the Moabites, till they fled before them; and they went forward, slaughtering the Moabites as they went. 25 And they overthrew the cities, and on every good piece of land every man threw a stone, until it was covered; they stopped every spring of water, and felled all the good trees; till only its stones were left in Kirhareseth, and the slingers surrounded and conquered it. 26 When the king of Moab saw that the battle was going against him, he took with him seven hundred swordsmen to break through, opposite the king of Edom; but they could not. 27 Then he took his eldest son who was to reign in his stead, and offered him for a burnt offering upon the wall. And there came great wrath upon Israel; and they withdrew from him and returned to their own land.

The water which came down from the red sandstone hills of Edom shone in the morning sun like blood, and the Moabites assumed that there had been a great battle in which the opposing kings had slain one another. The word Edom *'edom* is closely related to the Hebrew word for red (*'adom*, to be red, or ruddy). There is also an interesting play on the word for blood, *dam*. The statement of the Moabites, *This is blood*, is suggestive of the manner in which the Old Testament may easily be misunderstood through an unduly literal interpretation; as, for example, the suggestion that the water literally turned to blood.

Child sacrifice was more common in Moab than in Israel, although there are illustrations of the practice in the Old Testament (cf. Judg. 11:30-31; 1 Kings 16:34; Mic. 6:7). It is probable that the scene of the king sacrificing his closest son, the one destined to succeed him as king, so moved and excited the Moabites that they fell upon the coalition and defeated it through their frenzied attack.

III. Prophetic Concern for Human Need: Miracles by Elisha (4:1—6:7)

Collected within this broader section are at least six wonder stories associated with Elisha. In the ancient world such miracle stories were established means of emphasizing the stature of a religious leader. The miracles associated with Elisha may be conveniently gathered around three categories. First, some of the narratives fall into the category of the popular story or biographical type represented in stories such as those in 2:1-18,19-20,23-24; 4:1-7, 38-41,42-44; 6:1-7; 13:20 f. Such traditions are characterized by a heightened emphasis upon the miraculous or unusual, quite comparable to acts of magic in other cultures.

Second, there is another circle of miracles which stands in much more direct relationship to historical narrative, actually developing in the area between historical narrative and saga. A historical nucleus rests at the core of each and has been elaborated on from within the prophetic community of later generations. Most nearly approximating legend and saga these accounts arose because of the veneration of the man of God within the circle of prophetic disciples. Illustrations are 4:8-37; 8:1-6; 5:1 ff.

Third, stories such as 3:4-27; 6:8-23; 6:24—7:20; 8:1-15; 9:1 ff.; 13:14-19 combine saga and history. As Artur Weiser suggests, "The roots of the traditions lying on the borderland between saga and history go back to historical traditions and seem to have arisen only when older historical narratives were combined with traditions of the prophets" (Weiser, p. 177).

Although the collection of such stories around a central figure such as Elisha ran the risk of developing a personal cult, Walther Eichrodt suggests that taken as a whole the miracle stories are concerned with human need and "the miracle stories [present] the man of God as the helper of the people, not as one who works miracles for effect or as demonstrations of power. . . . Behind the wonder-working *nabi'*, men can discern the directing and succouring hand of his God (cf. I Kings 17:16 ff.,24; II Kings 2:13 ff.; 7:1; 4:1 ff.)." [2]

1. Provision for the Prophet's Widow and Family (4:1–7)

¹ Now the wife of one of the sons of the prophets cried to Elisha, "Your servant my husband is dead; and you know that your servant feared the Lord, but the creditor has come to take my two children to be his slaves." ² And Elisha said to her, "What shall I do for you? Tell me; what have you in the house?" And she said, "Your maidservant has nothing in the house, except a jar of oil." ³ Then he said, "Go outside, borrow vessels of all your neighbors, empty vessels and not too few. ⁴ Then go in, and shut the door upon yourself and your sons, and pour into all these vessels; and when one is full, set it aside." ⁵ So she went from him and shut the door upon herself and her sons; and as she poured they brought the vessels to her. ⁶ When the vessels were full, she said to her son, "Bring me another vessel." And he said to her, "There is not another." Then the oil stopped flowing. ⁷ She came and told the man of God, and he said, "Go, sell the oil and pay your debts, and you and your sons can live on the rest."

The multiplication of oil for the needy widow is reminiscent of the earlier account of the widow of Zarephath who was delivered from famine by the action of Elijah (1 Kings 17:8 ff.). That the two children were at the point of being sold to settle family debts is altogether consonant with Old Testament practices (cf. Ex. 21:7; Lev. 25:39; Neh. 5:5). Thus, in the context of then current social customs the creditor was acting in an altogether acceptable manner.

Elisha's response suggests that the resolution of the widow's crisis was limited only by the degree of her faith. The amount of oil received was limited only by the number of vessels that she collected. Further, the filling of the vessels was carried out apart from the presence of Elisha: *She went from him and shut the door upon herself and her sons.* The action is that of God, not Elisha.

Willingness to spend one's self in meeting human need is a constant prerequisite to the prophetic brotherhood, and the measure of one's concern for others remains the measure of the degree to which one fulfills the prophetic calling.

2. The Blessing of Motherhood for the Shunammite Woman (4:8–37)

The birth and revival of the Shunammite woman's son is a double wonder ascribed to Elisha.

(1) The Birth of a Son to the Shunammite Woman (4:8–17)

⁸ One day Elisha went on to Shunem, where a wealthy woman lived, who urged him to eat some food. So whenever he passed that way, he would turn in there to eat food. ⁹ And she said to her husband, "Behold now, I perceive that this is a holy man of God, who is continually passing our way. ¹⁰ Let us make a small roof chamber with walls, and put there for him a bed, a table, a chair, and a lamp, so that whenever he comes to us, he can go in there." ¹¹ One day he came there, and he turned into the chamber and rested there. ¹² And he said to Gehazi his servant, "Call this Shunammite." When he had called her, she stood before him. ¹³ And he said to him, "Say now to her, See, you have taken all this trouble for us; what is to be done for you? Would you have a word spoken on your behalf to the king or to the commander of the army?" She answered, "I

---

[2] W. Eichrodt, *Theology of the Old Testament*, I, J. A. Baker, trans. (Philadelphia: The Westminster Press, 1961), 326.

dwell among my own people." ¹⁴ And he said, "What then is to be done for her?" Gehazi answered, "Well, she has no son, and her husband is old." ¹⁵ He said, "Call her." And when he had called her, she stood in the doorway. ¹⁶ And he said, "At this season, when the time comes round, you shall embrace a son." And she said, "No, my lord, O man of God; do not lie to your maidservant." ¹⁷ But the woman conceived, and she bore a son about that time the following spring, as Elisha had said to her.

The distinction between the holy and the common probably led to the belief that a holy man should be provided with a room separated from the others. It is around this theme of generosity to the prophet that the narrative revolves. While the narrative was not designed to exploit generosity manifested by the people, it was doubtless a paradigm on proper conduct toward prophetic persons.

Numerous children were a sign of divine blessing in the Old Testament, while their absence was interpreted as a curse, or, at best, a reproach from the Lord. The birth of a child to aged or barren parents is a common motif used to depict the unique action of God within the life of faith. The wonder birth narrative occurs of Abraham and Sarah in the narratives of the patriarchs (Gen. 18:1–15), of Manoah and his wife, parents of Samson (Judg. 13:2 ff.), and of Elkanah and Hannah, parents of Samuel (1 Sam. 1:3 ff.). Within the New Testament Elizabeth conceived John the Baptist at an advanced age (Luke 1:39 ff.), but the ultimate example of the miraculous birth narratives is that of Mary (Luke 1:26 ff.).

(2) *The Revival of the Child* (4:18–37)

¹⁸ When the child had grown, he went out one day to his father among the reapers. ¹⁹ And he said to his father, "Oh, my head, my head!" The father said to his servant, "Carry him to his mother." ²⁰ And when he had lifted him, and brought him to his mother, the child sat on her lap till noon, and then he died. ²¹ And she went up and laid him on the bed of the man of God, and shut the door upon him, and went out. ²² Then she called to her husband, and said, "Send me one of the servants and one of the asses, that I may quickly go to the man of God, and come back again." ²³ And he said, "Why will you go to him today? It is neither new moon nor sabbath." She said, "It will be well." ²⁴ Then she saddled the ass, and she said to her servant, "Urge the beast on; do not slacken the pace for me unless I tell you." ²⁵ So she set out, and came to the man of God at Mount Carmel.

Appeal to Elisha (vv. 18–25a). Since the malady which struck the boy occurred in the field during harvesttime and affected the child's head (vv. 18 f.), the assumption that he suffered a severe heat stroke is plausible. It is clearly stated that the child died, but it appears that his mother kept the child's death a secret. There is no record that she told anyone, merely requesting a servant and an ass for transportation. Also, her husband assumed that she was visiting the prophet on the same basis that persons normally consulted men on holy days. Note, for example, his reminder, *Why will you go to him today? It is neither new moon nor sabbath.*

The woman acts in the confidence that Elisha who made possible the child's birth can bring about his recovery. The urgency and anxiety of the woman are obvious in her exhortation (v. 24).

When the man of God saw her coming, he said to Gehazi his servant, "Look, yonder is the Shunammite; ²⁶ run at once to meet her, and say to her, Is it well with you? Is it well with your husband? Is it well with the child?" And she answered, "It is well." ²⁷ And when she came to the mountain to the man of God, she caught hold of his feet. And Gehazi came to thrust her away. But the man of God said, "Let her alone, for she is in bitter distress; and the Lord has hidden it from me, and has not told me." ²⁸ Then she said, "Did I ask my lord for a son? Did I not say, Do not deceive me?" ²⁹ He said to Gehazi, "Gird up your loins, and take my staff in your hand, and go. If you meet any one, do not salute him; and if any one salutes you, do not reply; and lay my staff upon the face of the child." ³⁰ Then the mother of the child said, "As the Lord lives, and as you yourself live, I will not leave you." So he arose and followed her. ³¹ Gehazi went on ahead and laid the staff upon the face of the child, but there was no sound or sign of life. Therefore he returned to meet him, and told him, "The child has not awaked."

The mission of Gehazi the servant (vv. 25b–31). Upon detecting the child's death (it is never directly mentioned) Elisha cautions Gehazi to maintain absolute silence while hastening to the woman's house with the staff in order to restore the youth. The command to silence arises out of the belief that silence was necessary in order for Gehazi to retain the power communicated through him by Elisha. Norman H. Snaith suggests that "many examples of this necessity of silence are given in books on primitive religion and customs. . . . There are also numerous allusions to the magic power of silence." (Snaith, p. 207.)

The staff was a medium of power in the plague narratives, and the use of Moses' rod by Aaron is paralleled by Gehazi's use of Elisha's staff. The tension of the narrative is heightened by the failure of the staff to restore the child. His restoration must await the personal prayer and power of the prophet Elisha. Such an emphasis is strangely analogous to the inability of Jesus' disciples to heal the child, and the manner in which only he could perform the healing wonder (cf. Matt. 17:14 ff.), a narrative which has certain elements of the Elijah tradition (cf. Matt. 17:1 ff).

32 When Elisha came into the house, he saw the child lying dead on his bed. 33 So he went in and shut the door upon the two of them, and prayed to the Lord. 34 Then he went up and lay upon the child, putting his mouth upon his mouth, his eyes upon his eyes, and his hands upon his hands; and as he stretched himself upon him, the flesh of the child became warm. 35 Then he got up again, and walked once to and fro in the house, and went up, and stretched himself upon him; the child sneezed seven times, and the child opened his eyes. 36 Then he summoned Gehazi and said, "Call this Shunammite." So he called her. And when she came to him, he said, "Take up your son." 37 She came and fell at his feet, bowing to the ground; then she took up her son and went out.

Elisha restores the child's life (vv. 32–37). Through the personal ministration of Elisha the life of the child is restored. The suggestion has been made that the child but appeared to be dead, and that this severe illness was later interpreted as death within the community of the prophets. This view does not do justice to the text. Efforts to explain Elisha's action or that of Elijah in 1 Kings 17 as a form of artificial respiration are far wide of the mark. One should hear the stories as they were intended, as a person living two and a half millennia ago, prior to the modern, scientific era. Whether one interprets the stories literally or as wonder stories in the category of saga and legend, the narrative suggests that Elisha did in fact restore the life of the child. That this is most likely a wonder story in the category of saga and legend is most probable; even so, that the story should be weakened by rationalistic explanations is to miss the point of the redactor's purpose.

The nature of the stories should not rob the modern reader of their significance for the faith community. They were legitimate media of revelation which declared that Elisha, the prophetic holy man, was uniquely endowed with power from God; that such power was used in humanitarian efforts; and that the community of faith treasured the accounts of his exploits and extolled his life for later generations.

3. Death in the Pot: the Ruined Pottage (4:38–41)

38 And Elisha came again to Gilgal when there was a famine in the land. And as the sons of the prophets were sitting before him, he said to his servant, "Set on the great pot, and boil pottage for the sons of the prophets." 39 One of them went out into the field to gather herbs, and found a wild vine and gathered from it his lap full of wild gourds, and came and cut them up into the pot of pottage, not knowing what they were. 40 And they poured out for the men to eat. But while they were eating of the pottage, they cried out, "O man of God, there is death in the pot!" And they could not eat it. 41 He said, "Then bring meal." And he threw it into the pot, and said, "Pour out for the men, that they may eat." And there was no harm in the pot.

The word *gourds* (*paqqu'oth*) occurs only in the present passage, and one is left without comparative usages as an aid in determining its connotation. Brown, Driver, and Briggs suggest, however, that it was a wild cucumber (*citrullus colocynthis*) with purgative properties.

Whether the meal had properties which counteracted the *paqquʻoth*, or whether Elisha's action was a kind of symbolic action whereby the power of the prophet was transferred to the pot in such manner as to bring about a reversal of the poisonous or purgative power of the gourds, may be debated. Again, however, undue emphasis upon such details may cause one to miss the redactor's purpose. Through this medium he illustrated once again the prophetic power of Elisha.

4. The Multiplication of the Loaves (4:42–44)

⁴² A man came from Baalshalishah, bringing the man of God bread of the first fruits, twenty loaves of barley, and fresh ears of grain in his sack. And Elisha said, "Give to the men, that they may eat." ⁴³ But his servant said, "How am I to set this before a hundred men?" So he repeated, "Give them to the men, that they may eat, for thus says the Lord, 'They shall eat and have some left.'" ⁴⁴ So he set it before them. And they ate, and had some left, according to the word of the Lord.

The multiplication of the loaves has its parallel in the New Testament feeding of the thousands (cf. Matt. 14:13–21; 15:32–39; Mark 6:30–34; 8:1–10; Luke 9:10–17), a parallel which suggests that an intensive investigation would likely show surprising but supportive continuity between the central motifs of Moses, Elijah, and Jesus.

Elisha receives the firstfruits as a holy man, just as the priest did at the sanctuary. The central motif of the passage is clear: Yahweh provides for the needs of his own, and the sacramental meal shared because of his power is satisfying (cf. Gray, p. 450 for the view that this was a sacramental meal). His resources are more than adequate for the needs of man, and a central function of the prophetic office is to bring about proper contact between divine power and human need.

5. The Healing of Naaman the Syrian (5:1–27)

Although Naaman and his healing constitute the central focus of this narrative, there are actually two distinct motifs within the chapter: Naaman's leprosy and its cure (vv. 1–19a) and the avarice of Gehazi (vv. 19b–27).

(1) The Exaltation of Prophecy in Israel (1–19a)

¹ Naaman, commander of the army of the king of Syria, was a great man with his master and in high favor, because by him the Lord had given victory to Syria. He was a mighty man of valor, but he was a leper. ² Now the Syrians on one of their raids had carried off a little maid from the land of Israel, and she waited on Naaman's wife. ³ She said to her mistress, "Would that my lord were with the prophet who is in Samaria! He would cure him of his leprosy." ⁴ So Naaman went in and told his lord, "Thus and so spoke the maiden from the land of Israel." ⁵ And the king of Syria said, "Go now, and I will send a letter to the king of Israel."

So he went, taking with him ten talents of silver, six thousand shekels of gold, and ten festal garments. ⁶ And he brought the letter to the king of Israel, which read, "When this letter reaches you, know that I have sent to you Naaman my servant, that you may cure him of his leprosy." ⁷ And when the king of Israel read the letter, he rent his clothes and said, "Am I God, to kill and to make alive, that this man sends word to me to cure a man of his leprosy? Only consider, and see how he is seeking a quarrel with me."

Hope springing from the union of two crises (vv. 1–7). Naaman, although he had achieved the full range of honors for which many men might seek, was a leper—a condition which cast a long shadow over all his accomplishments. Yet this crisis was intersected by a second, the presence of an Israelite slave girl in his household, a girl who had been taken captive by an Aramean raiding party. From such an intersection of crises came the suggestion that Naaman visit the prophet of Samaria, Elisha.

The Hebrew word for leprosy (*tsaraʻath*) is generic and covers a full range of skin diseases, and is even used for mold in houses (cf. Lev. 14:34 ff.). The Greek word *lepra* signified the appearance of rough, scaly patches on the skin, corresponding to psoriasis, a skin disease which assumes several different forms (cf. "Leprosy," IDB). Another Greek medical term, *elephantiasis,* describes a much more serious disease more comparable to modern leprosy. The Greek of the Old Testament employed *lepra* "to include psoriasis, leucodermia, ringworm, and the like, as well as true leprosy" (*Ibid.*). Hence, it is impossible from terminology alone to determine the specific nature of the malady which is described.

Leprosy was not only greatly feared because of the physical suffering involved, but because of the social rejection. Lepers were ritually unclean and thus isolated from holy things (a common OT view in the case of physical conditions which were not medically or scientifically understood; as, for example, menstruation and childbirth).

⁸ But when Elisha the man of God heard that the king of Israel had rent his clothes, he sent to the king, saying, "Why have you rent your clothes? Let him come now to me, that he may know that there is a prophet in Israel." ⁹ So Naaman came with his horses and chariots, and halted at the door of Elisha's house. ¹⁰ And Elisha sent a messenger to him, saying, "Go and wash in the Jordan seven times, and your flesh shall be restored, and you shall be clean." ¹¹ But Naaman was angry, and went away, saying, "Behold, I thought that he would surely come out to me, and stand, and call on the name of the Lord his God, and wave his hand over the place, and cure the leper. ¹² Are not Abana and Pharpar, the rivers of Damascus, better than all the waters of Israel? Could I not wash in them, and be clean?" So he turned and went away in a rage. ¹³ But his servants came near and said to him, "My father, if the prophet had commanded you to do some great thing, would you not have done it? How much rather, then, when he says to you, 'Wash, and be clean'?" ¹⁴ So he went down and dipped himself seven times in the Jordan, according to the word of the man of God; and his flesh was restored like the flesh of a little child, and he was clean.

Naaman's cure (*vv. 8–14*). Naaman's hostility in response to Elisha's actions sprang from at least three considerations. First, Elisha did not come out to Naaman, an act which Naaman resented, since socially the prophet would have been beneath Naaman's rank. Second, Elisha failed to execute the ritual actions and speak the words which Naaman felt to be ritually appropriate. Naaman, in effect, wanted to prescribe his own cure. Third, Naaman resented the command to dip in the Jordan. The Jordan was certainly less attractive than rivers of Damascus. George Adam Smith, for example, has a graphic description: "Mostly silent and black in spite of its speed, but now and then breaking into praise and whitening into foam, Jordan scours along, muddy between banks of mud, careless of beauty, careless of life" (Snaith, p. 211).

¹⁵ Then he returned to the man of God, he and all his company, and he came and stood before him; and he said, "Behold, I know that there is no God in all the earth but in Israel; so accept now a present from your servant." ¹⁶ But he said, "As the Lord lives, whom I serve, I will receive none." And he urged him to take it, but he refused. ¹⁷ Then Naaman said, "If not, I pray you, let there be given to your servant two mules' burden of earth; for henceforth your servant will not offer burnt offering or sacrifice to any god but the Lord. ¹⁸ In this matter may the Lord pardon your servant: when my master goes into the house of Rimmon to worship there, leaning on my arm, and I bow myself in the house of Rimmon, when I bow myself in the house of Rimmon, the Lord pardon your servant in this matter." ¹⁹ He said to him, "Go in peace."

Naaman's commitment to Yahweh (*vv. 15–19a*). In response to his healing Naaman vows that *There is no God in all the earth but in Israel,* an advanced theological concept for the day, one that had only begun to emerge with clarity in Israel. Naaman's offer of a *present* is probably genuine in spirit, but it also serves the literary purpose of highlighting the magnanimous conduct of Elisha while at the same time providing an appropriate backdrop against which the later avarice of Gehazi focused.

Naaman leaves Elisha with two requests.

His desire for dirt from Israel is closely linked to the common belief that gods were identified with the land itself—an attitude that continued even in Israel for an embarrassingly long period of time. There is a strong tradition that the synagogue in Neharda, Persia, was built of stone and earth brought from Jerusalem, and the empress Helena is said to have brought holy soil from Jerusalem to Rome (cf. James A. Montgomery and Henry S. Gehman, p. 377).

Naaman's second request dealt with the necessity of accompanying his master (apparently the king of Syria) when he worshiped Rimmon, or, better, Ramman, the god of storm and rain better known as Hadad. Elisha apparently grants both requests, for the text records that Elisha sent Naaman away with the traditional benediction, "Go in peace."

(2) *The Avarice of Gehazi* (vv. 19b–27)

But when Naaman had gone from him a short distance, 20 Gehazi, the servant of Elisha the man of God, said, "See, my master has spared this Naaman the Syrian, in not accepting from his hand what he brought. As the Lord lives, I will run after him, and get something from him." 21 So Gehazi followed Naaman. And when Naaman saw some one running after him, he alighted from the chariot to meet him, and said, "Is all well?" 22 And he said, "All is well. My master has sent me to say, 'There have just now come to me from the hill country of Ephraim two young men of the sons of the prophets; pray, give them a talent of silver and two festal garments.'" 23 And Naaman said, "Be pleased to accept two talents." And he urged him, and tied up two talents of silver in two bags, with two festal garments, and laid them upon two of his servants; and they carried them before Gehazi. 24 And when he came to the hill, he took them from their hand, and put them in the house; and he sent the men away, and they departed. 25 He went in, and stood before his master, and Elisha said to him, "Where have you been, Gehazi?" And he said, "Your servant went nowhere." 26 But he said to him, "Did I not go with you in spirit when the man turned from his chariot to meet you? Was it a time to accept money and garments, olive orchards and vineyards, sheep and oxen, menservants and maidservants? 27 Therefore the leprosy of Naaman shall cleave to you, and to your descendants for ever." So he went out from his presence a leper, as white as snow.

The exploitation of Naaman at the hands of Gehazi is intended both as an explanation of Gehazi's name ("avaricious"), and as a constant warning against the temptation of those associated with the prophetic office to exploit that ministry. Gehazi's deception is twofold. First, he lied to Naaman when he asked that Naaman give silver and garments for two sons of the prophets who had only recently come from the hill country. To the shame of all, a few continue to exploit unsuspecting persons on the pretext of giving aid to needy religious causes. Religious charlatans of the twentieth century are but little different from Gehazi. Second Gehazi lied to Elisha when the prophet asked, "Where have you been, Gehazi?"

The judgment pronounced upon Gehazi is strangely akin to the New Testament warning that one may gain the externals and lose the real values of life. (Matt. 16:26). The translation in *The Jerusalem Bible* is graphic and captures the spirit of the text well: "Now you have taken the money, you can buy gardens with it, and olive groves, sheep and oxen, male and female slaves. But Naaman's leprosy will cling to you and to your descendants for ever" (vv. 26 f.). This is a constant and haunting warning to those who would magnify the externals of life at the expense of spiritual realities, and especially does it sound a clarion warning to those within the prophetic office who abuse that office through either avarice or other forms of exploitation.

6. *The Floating Axe Head* (6:1–7)

1 Now the sons of the prophets said to Elisha, "See, the place where we dwell under your charge is too small for us. 2 Let us go to the Jordan and each of us get there a log, and let us make a place for us to dwell there." And he answered, "Go." 3 Then one of them said, "Be pleased to go with your servants." And he answered, "I will go." 4 So he went with them. And when they came to the Jordan, they cut down trees. 5 But as one was felling a log, his axe head fell into the water; and he cried out,

"Alas, my master! It was borrowed." ⁶ Then the man of God said, "Where did it fall?" When he showed him the place, he cut off a stick, and threw it in there, and made the iron float. ⁷ And he said, "Take it up." So he reached out his hand and took it.

The necessity for enlarging their place of dwelling suggests the progressive growth of the prophets under the leadership of Elisha. It is impossible to locate the site being vacated, but it may well have been the school near Jericho which was involved. Especially is this true since they visited Jordan to secure necessary beams for their new buildings. The Jordan Valley was often referred to as a luxuriant jungle (cf. Jer. 12:5; 49:19; 50:44; Zech. 11:3).

Gray suggests that the historical event or factual basis resting behind the miracle of the floating axe head "may be that Elisha with a long pole or stick probed about the spot indicated (an important point in the text) until he succeeded either in inserting the stick into the socket, or, having located the hard object on the muddy bottom, moved it until the man was able to recover it." (Gray, p. 460).

This proposed reconstruction is helpful not only for understanding this single event, but as an example of the manner in which historical events were elaborated across successive generations until the narrative becomes a combination of saga and legend, inextricably interwoven.

However, a primary weakness of rationalistic interpretations of Old Testament miracle stories is their failure to deal forthrightly with the theology and purpose of the final redactor. Admittedly, the original factual events may have developed as Gray suggests. But the fact remains that the theological purposes of the redactor are embodied only in the form that the narrative now possesses. Thus, whether one interprets the miracle stories literally or as cases of combined saga and legend used to glorify the prophet and express the high regard with which he was held in the prophetic circle, the miracle stories should be interpreted for what they are in present form, not what they were in original nucleus.

Interpreted as it now stands the miracle story illustrates the ancient principle of imitative magic or contactual magic. Through imitative magic the wood thrown upon the water floats, and the axe head, imitating the wood, also floats. Contactual magic caused objects once in contact to rejoin. Whatever one's attitude toward the historical antecedents of the story, the focus is the same: Elisha possessed such stupendous power that he caused a lost axe head to float.

IV. Elisha and the Aramean Wars (6:8—8:15)

The narratives on the Aramean wars reflect the continuing role of Elisha as a prophet of national prominence. The editor's purpose is to indicate the manner in which the prophetic renewal which began in Elijah continued in Elisha, while at the same time extolling the individual grandeur of Elisha. The popular wonder stories of previous chapters are not present in this section, and the narratives under consideration are best categorized as a combination of saga and legend. The veneration of the man of God within the circle of his disciples is of primary concern.

1. Elisha Captures an Aramean Raiding Party (6:8–23)

(1) Frustration of the King's Plans (6:8–14)

⁸ Once when the king of Syria was warring against Israel, he took counsel with his servants, saying, "At such and such a place shall be my camp." ⁹ But the man of God sent word to the king of Israel, "Beware that you do not pass this place, for the Syrians are going down there." ¹⁰ And the king of Israel sent to the place of which the man of God told him. Thus he used to warn him, so that he saved himself there more than once or twice.

¹¹ And the mind of the king of Syria was greatly troubled because of this thing; and he called his servants and said to them, "Will you not show me who of us is for the king of Israel?" ¹² And one of his servants said, "None, my lord, O king; but Elisha, the prophet who is

in Israel, tells the king of Israel the words that you speak in your bedchamber." 13 And he said, "Go and see where he is, that I may send and seize him." It was told him, "Behold, he is in Dothan." 14 So he sent there horses and chariots and a great army; and they came by night, and surrounded the city.

Elisha's considerable travel throughout the land, to say nothing of his contacts with many persons (some of whom, such as the Israelite maid of the Naaman narrative, may have been in Damascus, even serving in the Aramean court) is probably the historical nucleus of the ability of Elisha to tell the king of Israel about the Aramean attacks.

(2) *Blinding and Capture of the Aramean Soldiers (6:15–23)*

15 When the servant of the man of God rose early in the morning and went out, behold, an army with horses and chariots was round about the city. And the servant said, "Alas, my master! What shall we do?" 16 He said, "Fear not, for those who are with us are more than those who are with them." 17 Then Elisha prayed, and said, "O LORD, I pray thee, open his eyes that he may see." So the LORD opened the eyes of the young man, and he saw; and behold, the mountain was full of horses and chariots of fire round about Elisha. 18 And when the Syrians came down against him, Elisha prayed to the LORD, and said, "Strike this people, I pray thee, with blindness." So he struck them with blindness in accordance with the prayer of Elisha. 19 And Elisha said to them, "This is not the way, and this is not the city; follow me, and I will bring you to the man whom you seek." And he led them to Samaria.

20 As soon as they entered Samaria, Elisha said, "O LORD, open the eyes of these men, that they may see." So the LORD opened their eyes, and they saw; and lo, they were in the midst of Samaria. 21 When the king of Israel saw them he said to Elisha, "My father, shall I slay them? Shall I slay them?" 22 He answered, "You shall not slay them. Would you slay those whom you have taken captive with your sword and with your bow? Set bread and water before them, that they may eat and drink and go to their master." 23 So he prepared for them a great feast; and when they had eaten and drunk, he sent them away, and they went to their master. And the Syrians came no more on raids into the land of Israel.

The appearance of horses and chariots at Dothan, which was only 12 miles from Samaria, the capital, suggests that this was in all probability a raiding party as opposed to a full-scale army (cf. however, "a great army," v. 14). In response to the fear of his servant, Elisha assured him that *those who are with us are more than those who are with them.* Evidently Elisha has reference to the reality of unseen but actual spiritual forces available not only to the prophetic community, but equally to every man of faith.

The *horses and chariots of fire round about Elisha* symbolized the reality of the Lord of hosts, who is often associated with fire as a symbol of his presence. The motif is comparable to that of 2:10 ff., and the chariots of Israel and the horsemen which Elisha saw at the time of Elijah's translation. Both contexts speak of the reality of unseen spiritual powers available to men of perception and sensitivity.

Deliverance came for Elisha and his servant as the Lord, in response to Elisha's prayer, struck the Arameans blind. The word *blindness* is an intensive plural, and except for this verse occurs only in Genesis 19:11. The motif of miraculous blinding is identical in both sagas (6:18; Gen. 19:11).

The prophet is addressed as *father* by the king, who inquires concerning whether or not he should kill the captured warriors. There is textual evidence for inserting "not" in the phrase, *Would you slay those whom you have [not] taken with your sword and with your bow?*, a commendable emendation. Since it was the custom to put one's enemy to death in Israel (cf. 1 Sam. 15:33; 1 Kings 20:42), Elisha's appeal for the lives of the Arameans rested on the assumption that they had not been taken in battle.

2. *Deliverance of Samaria from Siege (6:24—7:20)*

(1) *Famine in the City (6:24–31)*

24 Afterward Benhadad king of Syria mustered his entire army, and went up, and besieged Samaria. 25 And there was a great famine in Samaria, as they besieged it, until an ass's head was sold for eighty shekels of silver,

and the fourth part of a kab of dove's dung for five shekels of silver. 26 Now as the king of Israel was passing by upon the wall, a woman cried out to him, saying, "Help, my lord, O king!" 27 And he said, "If the LORD will not help you, whence shall I help you? From the threshing floor, or from the wine press?" 28 And the king asked her, "What is your trouble?" She answered, "This woman said to me, 'Give your son, that we may eat him today, and we will eat my son tomorrow.' 29 So we boiled my son, and ate him. And on the next day I said to her, 'Give your son, that we may eat him'; but she has hidden her son." 30 When the king heard the words of the woman he rent his clothes—now he was passing by upon the wall —and the people looked, and behold, he had sackcloth beneath upon his body—31 and he said, "May God do so to me, and more also, if the head of Elisha the son of Shaphat remains on his shoulders today."

The desperate circumstances are reflected not only in exorbitant prices, but in the consumption of normally unclean foods and the practice of cannibalism. The ass was considered unclean. Various efforts have been made to explain the reference to *dove's dung*. Some contend that extreme times led men to eat actual excrement (Snaith). Others, however, suggest that the term is a popular name for some food such as roast chickpeas (Gray). *The Jerusalem Bible* corrects the text to read "wild onions." It is impossible to conclude with certainty anything beyond the fact that the food was abnormally expensive, and probably unpalatable.

The reference to cannibalism is shocking but not unknown during times of extremity in the Old Testament (cf. Deut. 28:56 ff.; Ezek. 5:10; Lam. 2:20; 4:10). One detects in the controversy between the two women a likely but grotesque parallel to the judgment Solomon gave between the two harlots who claimed the same child (cf. 1 Kings 3:16 ff.).

The king's displeasure with Elisha has no apparent foundation in fact and may well be the reflection of his own anxiety and frustration. It has been suggested that the famine was related to Elisha's prediction of 8:1 f., but this would not seem to be the case. The famine was apparently limited to Samaria, and this because of the siege. The Aramean army lived off the land, and following the siege there was no lack of supplies in the camp.

(2) *Elisha Predicts Relief* (6:32—7:2)

32 Elisha was sitting in his house, and the elders were sitting with him. Now the king had dispatched a man from his presence; but before the messenger arrived Elisha said to the elders, "Do you see how this murderer has sent to take off my head? Look, when the messenger comes, shut the door, and hold the door fast against him. Is not the sound of his master's feet behind him?" 33 And while he was still speaking with them, the king came down to him and said, "This trouble is from the LORD! Why should I wait for the LORD any longer?"
1 But Elisha said, "Hear the word of the LORD. thus says the LORD, Tomorrow about this time a measure of fine meal shall be sold for a shekel, and two measures of barley for a shekel, at the gate of Samaria." 2 Then the captain on whose hand the king leaned said to the man of God, "If the LORD himself should make windows in heaven, could this thing be?" But he said, "You shall see it with your own eyes, but you shall not eat of it."

Within a day, Elisha predicted, the siege would be lifted and in marked contrast with the inflated prices and the unpalatable food of the siege the finest food would be bought at the most reasonable price. The certainty of such an unbelievable assertion was grounded in the fact that the prediction was *the word of the Lord*.

(3) *The Abandonment of the Aramean Camp* (7:3-8)

3 Now there were four men who were lepers at the entrance to the gate; and they said to one another, "Why do we sit here till we die? 4 If we say, 'Let us enter the city,' the famine is in the city, and we shall die there; and if we sit here, we die also. So now come, let us go over to the camp of the Syrians; if they spare our lives we shall live, and if they kill us we shall but die." 5 So they arose at twilight to go to the camp of the Syrians; but when they came to the edge of the camp of the Syrians, behold, there was no one there. 6 For the Lord had made the army of the Syrians hear the sound of chariots, and of horses, the sound of a great army, so that they said to one another, "Behold, the king of Israel has hired against us the

kings of the Hittites and the kings of Egypt to come upon us." 7 So they fled away in the twilight and forsook their tents, their horses, and their asses, leaving the camp as it was, and fled for their lives. 8 And when these lepers came to the edge of the camp, they went into a tent, and ate and drank, and they carried off silver and gold and clothing, and went and hid them; then they came back, and entered another tent, and carried off things from it, and went and hid them.

The panic-stricken flight of the Arameans was probably precipitated by the rumor of an approaching army of undetermined origin. The disorder which characterized their flight suggests the belief that a catastrophe was imminent, and the fact that they fled in disarray toward the Jordan further suggests that the enemy was west of Jordan.

(4) *A Day of Good News (7:9–15)*

9 Then they said to one another, "We are not doing right. This day is a day of good news; if we are silent and wait until the morning light, punishment will overtake us; now therefore come, let us go and tell the king's household." 10 So they came and called to the gatekeepers of the city, and told them, "We came to the camp of the Syrians, and behold, there was no one to be seen or heard there, nothing but the horses tied, and the asses tied, and the tents as they were." 11 Then the gatekeepers called out, and it was told within the king's household. 12 And the king rose in the night, and said to his servants, "I will tell you what the Syrians have prepared against us. They know that we are hungry; therefore they have gone out of the camp to hide themselves in the open country, thinking, 'When they come out of the city, we shall take them alive and get into the city.'" 13 And one of his servants said, "Let some men take five of the remaining horses, seeing that those who are left here will fare like the whole multitude of Israel that have already perished; let us send and see." 14 So they took two mounted men, and the king sent them after the army of the Syrians, saying, "Go and see." 15 So they went after them as far as the Jordan; and, lo, all the way was littered with garments and equipment which the Syrians had thrown away in their haste. And the messengers returned, and told the king.

The sudden reminder of the four lepers has become a watchword for many lest they selfishly ignore others; *We are not doing right. This day is a day of good news.* The motif of God's deliverance of the city from the midst of crisis is a motif which appears elsewhere in the Old Testament (cf. 18:13 ff.).

(5) *A Day of Fulfillment (7:16–20)*

16 Then the people went out, and plundered the camp of the Syrians. So a measure of fine meal was sold for a shekel, and two measures of barley for a shekel, according to the word of the Lord. 17 Now the king had appointed the captain on whose hand he leaned to have charge of the gate; and the people trod upon him in the gate, so that he died, as the man of God had said when the king came down to him. 18 For when the man of God had said to the king, "Two measures of barley shall be sold for a shekel, and a measure of fine meal for a shekel, about this time tomorrow in the gate of Samaria," 19 the captain had answered the man of God, "If the Lord himself should make windows in heaven, could such a thing be?" And he had said, "You shall see it with your own eyes, but you shall not eat of it." 20 And so it happened to him, for the people trod upon him in the gate and he died.

Fine food was sold at a reasonable price in the city, and the captain who had ridiculed the idea of such a wonderful deed, even if the Lord himself acted and opened the windows of heaven (cf. 7:2), did live to see the fulfillment of that pledge but died without sharing its benefits.

3. *Further Consideration for the Shunammite Woman (8:1–6)*

1 Now Elisha had said to the woman whose son he had restored to life, "Arise, and depart with your household, and sojourn wherever you can; for the Lord has called for a famine, and it will come upon the land for seven years." 2 So the woman arose, and did according to the word of the man of God; she went with her household and sojourned in the land of the Philistines seven years. 3 And at the end of the seven years, when the woman returned from the land of the Philistines, she went forth to appeal to the king for her house and her land. 4 Now the king was talking with Gehazi the servant of the man of God, saying, "Tell me all the great things that Elisha has done." 5 And while he was telling the king how Elisha had restored the dead to life, behold, the woman whose son he had restored to life appealed to the king for her house and her land. And Gehazi said, "My lord, O king, here is the woman, and here is her son whom Elisha

restored to life." 6 And when the king asked the woman, she told him. So the king appointed an official for her, saying, "Restore all that was hers, together with all the produce of the fields from the day that she left the land until now."

During the absence of the widow, her husband had apparently died (cf. his advancing age at the time of Elisha's first acquaintance with the family, 4:14), and her land may have reverted to the king; or, the land may have passed to a near kinsman, as was possible in Old Testament times (cf. Ruth 4:1 ff.; also, on the seven-year reversion of property, Ex. 21:1; Deut. 15:1 ff.).

4. Elisha's Role in the Aramean Coup (8:7–15)

7 Now Elisha came to Damascus. Benhadad the king of Syria was sick; and when it was told him, "The man of God has come here," 8 the king said to Hazael, "Take a present with you and go to meet the man of God, and inquire of the LORD through him, saying, 'Shall I recover from this sickness?' " 9 So Hazael went to meet him, and took a present with him, all kinds of goods of Damascus, forty camel loads. When he came and stood before him, he said, "Your son Benhadad king of Syria has sent me to you, saying, 'Shall I recover from this sickness?' " 10 And Elisha said to him, "Go, say to him, 'You shall certainly recover'; but the LORD has shown me that he shall certainly die." 11 And he fixed his gaze and stared at him, until he was ashamed. And the man of God wept. 12 And Hazael said, "Why does my lord weep?" He answered, "Because I know the evil that you will do to the people of Israel; you will set on fire their fortresses, and you will slay their young men with the sword, and dash in pieces their little ones, and rip up their women with child." 13 And Hazael said, "What is your servant, who is but a dog, that he should do this great thing?" Elisha answered, "The LORD has shown me that you are to be king over Syria." 14 Then he departed from Elisha, and came to his master, who said to him, "What did Elisha say to you?" And he answered, "He told me that you would certainly recover." 15 But on the morrow he took the coverlet and dipped it in water and spread it over his face, till he died. And Hazael became king in his stead.

The account of Elisha's participation in the elevation of Hazael as king of Aram is not ony an illustration of the prophet's enlarging role within the political spectrum, but is a means of fulfilling the original commission given to Elijah that he anoint Hazael to be *king over Syria*, Jehu as king over Israel, and Elisha as "prophet in your place" (1 Kings 19:15 ff.). With the Aramean *coup* each of those commands except the anointing of Jehu has been fulfilled, although two were fulfilled through Elisha, not Elijah (1 Kings 19 is most likely an independent tradition).

Reference to Benhadad as the *son* of Elisha (v. 9) is a revealing term of respect analogous to that which existed in the schools of the prophets (wherein Elisha was known as father and the prophets as sons).

Elisha's statement, *You shall certainly recover*, refers to Benhadad's recovery from his sickness. The observation that *the Lord has shown me that he shall certainly die* has reference to the assassination of Benhadad.

Reference to Elisha as having *fixed his gaze* suggests the rigid facial expressions characteristic of a trance, which was itself associated with the giving of a prophetic oracle. At the time of the trance, Elisha began to weep, apparently because he envisioned what Hazael would do to Israel (cf. Amos 1:3 ff.).

Assyrian annals of this era corroborate the ascension of Hazael to the throne; "Hazael, son of a nobody, seized the throne" (Montgomery and Gehman, citing the Berlin inscription). "Son of a nobody" suggests that Hazael was a usurper, unrelated by blood kinship to the dynastic line of Benhadad.

V. The Rebellion of Jehu and the Purge of Baalism (8:16—10:36)

In keeping with the larger thematic motif of the prophetic revolution which extends from 1 Kings 17 through 2 Kings 13, the final redactor of Kings is concerned to illustrate the purge of Baalism in Israel. The Jehu rebellion, although of lesser importance from one perspective than the Elijah conflict with the prophets of Baal at

Carmel (cf. 1 Kings 18), is of crucial significance.

1. Judah's Involvement in the Purge of Jehu; a Deuteronomic Appraisal of Judean Kingship (8:16–29)

Thematically, the redactor includes the appraisals of Jehoram and Ahaziah at this juncture in 2 Kings because of their religious solidarity with the apostasy of the North.

(1) The Reign of Jehoram (8:16–24)

16 In the fifth year of Joram the son of Ahab, king of Israel, Jehoram the son of Jehoshaphat, king of Judah, began to reign. 17 He was thirty-two years old when he became king, and he reigned eight years in Jerusalem. 18 And he walked in the way of the kings of Israel, as the house of Ahab had done, for the daughter of Ahab was his wife. And he did what was evil in the sight of the LORD. 19 Yet the LORD would not destroy Judah, for the sake of David his servant, since he promised to give a lamp to him and to his sons for ever.
20 In his days Edom revolted from the rule of Judah, and set up a king of their own. 21 Then Joram passed over to Zair with all his chariots, and rose by night, and he and his chariot commanders smote the Edomites who had surrounded him; but his army fled home. 22 So Edom revolted from the rule of Judah to this day. Then Libnah revolted at the same time. 23 Now the rest of the acts of Joram, and all that he did, are they not written in the Book of the Chronicles of the Kings of Judah? 24 So Joram slept with his fathers, and was buried with his fathers in the city of David; and Ahaziah his son reigned in his stead.

Jehoram, son of Jehoshaphat, should not be confused with Joram (elsewhere called Jehoram, cf. 3:1 ff.) the son of Ahab. Joram (*yoram*) and Jehoram (*y^ehoram*) are variant spellings.

Jehoram married Athaliah of the Omride dynasty. She is identified as the daughter of Ahab in v. 18. The reference to Athaliah as the daughter of Omri in 8:26 may represent the use of daughter in the general sense of granddaughter or descendant. One would assume that through this marriage the influence of Baalism pervaded the court of Jerusalem and that it is for this reason that both Jehoram and Ahaziah are condemned by the editor. Additionally, the Chronicler suggests that when Jehoram ascended the throne "he slew all his brothers with the sword, and also some of the princes of Judah" (2 Chron. 21:4).

The revolts of Edom and Libnah are offered as concrete evidence of the judgmental effects of such infidelity as was associated with Jehoram (v. 18). The only reason that Judah was not absolutely destroyed, according to the Deuteronomic editor, was the faithfulness of Yahweh to the Davidic covenant: *for the sake of David his servant, since he promised to give a lamp to him and to his sons for ever* (cf. 2 Sam. 7:8–17). The Davidic covenant stands alongside the Mosaic covenant in its theological importance for Judah, and was the means whereby Israelite theologians translated the patriarchal covenant promises of a land and people into terms more specifically suited to monarchial conditions.

(2) The Reign of Ahaziah (8:25–29)

25 In the twelfth year of Joram the son of Ahab, king of Israel, Ahaziah the son of Jehoram, king of Judah, began to reign. 26 Ahaziah was twenty-two years old when he began to reign, and he reigned one year in Jerusalem. His mother's name was Athaliah; she was a granddaughter of Omri king of Israel. 27 He also walked in the way of the house of Ahab, and did what was evil in the sight of the LORD, as the house of Ahab had done, for he was son-in-law to the house of Ahab.
28 He went with Joram the son of Ahab to make war against Hazael king of Syria at Ramoth-gilead, where the Syrians wounded Joram. 29 And King Joram returned to be healed in Jezreel of the wounds which the Syrians had given him at Ramah, when he fought against Hazael king of Syria. And Ahaziah the son of Jehoram king of Judah went down to see Joram the son of Ahab in Jezreel, because he was sick.

Ahaziah is condemned by the Deuteronomic editor of Kings for following the ways of Ahab, presumably in his religious commitment. Because of his association with Jehoram of Israel he was eventually killed (9:27 ff.).

2. Elisha Instigates the Rebellion of Jehu (9:1-13)

The political involvements of Elisha are again elucidated in the narrative on the rebellion of Jehu which eventuated in the death of Joram of Israel, Ahaziah of Judah, and Jezebel (9:21-37); plus Israelite and Judaean princes, the men of Samaria, and other worshipers of Baal (10:1-27). Although the rebellion was fomented by Elisha, his action was but the match that fired the pent up emotions and frustrations of both religious and socio-economic character which had already built up during the Omride dynasty (John Bright, pp. 231 ff.).

(1) Elisha Commissions a Prophet to Anoint Jehu King (9:1-3)

¹ Then Elisha the prophet called one of the sons of the prophets and said to him, "Gird up your loins, and take this flask of oil in your hand, and go to Ramoth-gilead. ² And when you arrive, look there for Jehu the son of Jehoshaphat, son of Nimshi; and go in and bid him rise from among his fellows, and lead him to an inner chamber. ³ Then take the flask of oil, and pour it on his head, and say, 'Thus says the LORD, I anoint you king over Israel.' Then open the door and flee; do not tarry."

Anointing was the traditional act by which either persons or objects were dedicated to God. Sacred sites could be anointed, but especially anointing was the means of setting persons apart for a consecrated role in the service of God. Elisha anticipated immediate and serious repercussions from the act of anointing Jehu (v. 3). Yet, this did not deter him from fulfilling his prophetic role. He was far more concerned with implementing the will of God than with maintaining the status quo.

Jehu's father, *Jehoshaphat, son of Nimshi,* is not to be confused with Jehoshaphat, king of Judah, who was son of Asa (cf. 1 Kings 22:41).

(2) The Prophetic Act of Anointing Jehu (9:4-10)

⁴ So the young man, the prophet, went to Ramothgilead. ⁵ And when he came, behold, the commanders of the army were in council; and he said, "I have an errand to you, O commander." And Jehu said, "To which of us all?" And he said, "To you, O commander." ⁶ So he arose, and went into the house; and the young man poured the oil on his head, saying to him, "Thus says the LORD the God of Israel, I anoint you king over the people of the LORD, over Israel. ⁷ And you shall strike down the house of Ahab your master, that I may avenge on Jezebel the blood of my servants the prophets, and the blood of all the servants of the LORD. ⁸ For the whole house of Ahab shall perish; and I will cut off from Ahab every male, bond or free, in Israel. ⁹ And I will make the house of Ahab like the house of Jeroboam the son of Nebat, and like the house of Baasha the son of Ahijah. ¹⁰ And the dogs shall eat Jezebel in the territory of Jezreel, and none shall bury her." Then he opened the door, and fled.

Ramothgilead (i.e., probably Ramah of Gilead) was apparently the site at which the army was gathered while Jehoram recovered from wounds received in the battle with Hazael, king of Aram (cf. 8:28 ff.). Jehu was probably among the generals if not the commander in chief of the army. He was mature and prominent enough to have ridden alongside King Ahab earlier (cf. 9:25).

Jezebel is a specific object of concern for the prophetic school(s), and at one juncture in the commission the natural word order of the sentence is altered so as to emphasize her fate: "and *Jezebel* the dogs shall eat" (cf. v. 10; 1 Kings 21:23).

(3) Proclamation of Jehu's Kingship (9:11-13)

¹¹ When Jehu came out to the servants of his master, they said to him, "Is all well? Why did this mad fellow come to you?" And he said to them, "You know the fellow and his talk." ¹² And they said, "That is not true; tell us now." And he said, "Thus and so he spoke to me, saying, 'Thus says the LORD, I anoint you king over Israel.'" ¹³ Then in haste every man of them took his garment, and put it under him on the bare steps, and they blew the trumpet, and proclaimed, "Jehu is king."

Reference to the prophet as a *mad fellow* is not quite so derogatory as the modern mind might conclude. Holy men of many cultures have been interpreted as mad men, and madness may at times have been no mark of possession. The word (*shagaʻ*) occurs seven times in the Old Testament and is specifically used of prophets, as in "every madman who prophesies" (Jer. 29:26) and "The prophet is a fool, and the man of the spirit is mad" (Hos. 9:7).

That the prophet who anointed Jehu was apparently well known in Israel is suggested in Jehu's response to his fellow commanders, *You know the fellow and his talk* (*shiach*). *Shiach* most often is used for complaint (Job 7:13; Prov. 23:29), musing (1 Kings 18:27; Psalm 104:34), or anxiety or trouble (1 Sam. 1:16), but only in 2 Kings 9:11 for talk.

The blowing of the trumpet was probably a cultic act in which the king was initiated into what was not only a political but also a sacral office. The trumpet (*shophar*) was used in worship, as passages such as Psalms 47:5; 81:3; 98:6; 150:3; and 2 Chronicles 15:14 suggest. It was, of course, used mainly in war (cf. Judg. 7:8,16; 1 Sam. 13:3; Amos 3:6). The consummation of the anointing is achieved in the coronation shout: *malak yehuʼ, Jehu is king.*

3. The Assassinations That Purged Israel of Baalism (9:14—10:27)

Although the blood purge of Jehu originated in a genuine prophetic concern for the interests of Yahwism, both the motivation for the rebellion and the eventual attitude toward it are far more complicated than would initially appear. For despite the genuine desire to purge the land from an apostate religion, there were doubtless strong socio-economic factors, military ambition, and general discontent which were equally involved in the precipitation of the revolt.

(1) The Assassination of Jehoram (9:14–26)

14 Thus Jehu the son of Jehoshaphat the son of Nimshi conspired against Joram. (Now Joram with all Israel had been on guard at Ramoth-gilead against Hazael king of Syria; **15** but King Joram had returned to be healed in Jezreel of the wounds which the Syrians had given him, when he fought with Hazael king of Syria.) So Jehu said, "If this is your mind, then let no one slip out of the city to go and tell the news in Jezreel." **16** Then Jehu mounted his chariot, and went to Jezreel, for Joram lay there. And Ahaziah king of Judah had come down to visit Joram.

17 Now the watchman was standing on the tower in Jezreel, and he spied the company of Jehu as he came, and said, "I see a company." And Joram said, "Take a horseman, and send to meet them, and let him say, 'Is it peace?'" **18** So a man on horseback went to meet him, and said, "Thus says the king, 'Is it peace?'" And Jehu said, "What have you to do with peace? Turn around and ride behind me." And the watchman reported, saying, "The messenger reached them, but he is not coming back." **19** Then he sent out a second horseman, who came to them, and said, "Thus the king has said, 'Is it peace?'" And Jehu answered, "What have you to do with peace? Turn round and ride behind me." **20** Again the watchman reported, "He reached them, but he is not coming back. And the driving is like the driving of Jehu the son of Nimshi; for he drives furiously."

21 Joram said, "Make ready." And they made ready his chariot. Then Joram king of Israel and Ahaziah king of Judah set out, each in his chariot, and went to meet Jehu, and met him at the property of Naboth the Jezreelite. **22** And when Joram saw Jehu, he said, "Is it peace, Jehu?" He answered, "What peace can there be, so long as the harlotries and the sorceries of your mother Jezebel are so many?" **23** Then Joram reined about and fled, saying to Ahaziah, "Treachery, O Ahaziah!" **24** And Jehu drew his bow with his full strength, and shot Joram between the shoulders, so that the arrow pierced his heart, and he sank in his chariot. **25** Jehu said to Bidkar his aide, "Take him up, and cast him on the plot of ground belonging to Naboth the Jezreelite; for remember, when you and I rode side by side behind Ahab his father, how the Lord uttered this oracle against him: **26** 'As surely as I saw yesterday the blood of Naboth and the blood of his sons —says the Lord—I will requite you on this plot of ground.' Now therefore take him up and cast him on the plot of ground, in accordance with the word of the Lord."

Counseling absolute secrecy, Jehu rushed to Jezreel where Jehoram was recuperating from wounds received in the battle with Hazael at Ramothgilead. Jezreel the town should be distinguished from the Valley of Jezreel. Ramah (8:29) is apparently synonymous with Ramothgilead. *Furiously* uses the same root as that for a mad man (cf. 9:11). *Shigga'on,* madly, is used as a hyperbole in v. 20 (*furiously*), "he drives madly," i.e., he drives like a madman.

Baalism was essentially a fertility cult which featured cultic prostitution. Beginning with Hosea, Israel's infidelity in worshiping Baal was characterized as harlotry (cf. Hos. 2). Of the 38 usages of harlotry and harlotries cited in the RSV concordance 80 percent, or a total of 30 usages, occur in Hosea and Ezekiel, with Hosea as the creator of the analogy (cf. also Rev. 17:1,15,16; 19:2).

In accord with the oracle of judgment passed upon Ahab for having procured the vineyard of Naboth (1 Kings 21:1 ff.), Jehoram's body was thrown on the same plot of ground. Thus was fulfilled the word of judgment to Ahab: *I will requite you on this plot of ground* (cf. 1 Kings 21:17 ff.). Behind such action rests the Deuteronomic conviction that the deeds of the fathers are visited upon the children, and that within history sin finds its own judgment and righteousness its own reward.

(2) *The Assassination of Ahaziah (9:27–29)*

27 When Ahaziah the king of Judah saw this, he fled in the direction of Bethhaggan. And Jehu pursued him, and said, "Shoot him also"; and they shot him in the chariot at the ascent of Gur, which is by Ibleam. And he fled to Megiddo, and died there. 28 His servants carried him in a chariot to Jerusalem, and buried him in his tomb with his fathers in the city of David.
29 In the eleventh year of Joram the son of Ahab, Ahaziah began to reign over Judah.

The death of Ahaziah is to be understood as far more than a mere accident occasioned by visiting Jehoram at the time Jehu slew the king of Israel. Rather, Ahaziah was slain because he was a blood relative of Ahab's family (being the daughter of Athaliah, Ahab's daughter). The purge of Ahab is designed to eradicate every vestige of Ahab's lineage: "For the whole house of Ahab shall perish" (9:8). This vendetta extended not only to those who lived in Israel, as specifically stated in 9:8, but to those in Judah, as the death of Ahaziah and of the 42 Judahite princes reveals.

(3) *The Assassination of Jezebel (9:30–37)*

30 When Jehu came to Jezreel, Jezebel heard of it; and she painted her eyes, and adorned her head, and looked out of the window. 31 And as Jehu entered the gate, she said, "Is it peace, you Zimri, murderer of your master?" 32 And he lifted up his face to the window, and said, "Who is on my side? Who?" Two or three eunuchs looked out at him. 33 He said, "Throw her down." So they threw her down; and some of her blood spattered on the wall and on the horses, and they trampled on her. 34 Then he went in and ate and drank; and he said, "See now to this cursed woman, and bury her; for she is a king's daughter." 35 But when they went to bury her, they found no more of her than the skull and the feet and the palms of her hands. 36 When they came back and told him, he said, "This is the word of the LORD, which he spoke by his servant Elijah the Tishbite, 'In the territory of Jezreel the dogs shall eat the flesh of Jezebel; 37 and the corpse of Jezebel shall be as dung upon the face of the field in the territory of Jezreel, so that no one can say, This is Jezebel.'"

Prior to the account of Jezebel's assassination there appears a chronological note on the reign of Ahaziah that has obviously been either misplaced or inserted at an inopportune point (9:29). This is one of the earliest efforts to rectify the chronology of the book, for in 8:25 the eleventh year of Joram (841 B.C.) is given as the accession date for Ahaziah. The present text corrects that calculation. One may well consult the Introduction for a brief statement on the problems of chronology in the books of Kings.

The Hebrew text suggests that Jezebel "set her eyes in antimony" (*puk,* antimony; Lat. *stibium*), a black mineral powder (there are suggestions that in antiquity it had varying colors) for increasing brilliance of eyes by darkening edges of the lids (cf. Jer. 4:30; Ezek. 23:40). Jezebel's attention to her physical appearance was more than a show of vanity, for the condition of the body at the time of death was believed to characterize the nature of existence following death.

Although Jehu does eventually show consideration for Jezebel, on the ground that she was of royal blood, he did not do so until the dogs had all but devoured her body. His action seems to be deliberately cruel—stopping to eat and drink before sending servants to see to her burial. Some suggest, however, that more than callousness was involved: that the meal was a communal ceremony binding the town's leadership to Jehu and his purge.

Again, the editor reminds the reader that the assassination and total dismemberment were a partial fulfillment of the earlier condemnation which arose out of the Naboth experience (cf. 1 Kings 21:23).

(4) The Assassination of Ahab's Progeny and Supporters (10:1–11)

¹ Now Ahab had seventy sons in Samaria. So Jehu wrote letters, and sent them to Samaria, to the rulers of the city, to the elders, and to the guardians of the sons of Ahab, saying, ² "Now then, as soon as this letter comes to you, seeing your master's sons are with you, and there are with you chariots and horses, fortified cities also, and weapons, ³ select the best and fittest of your master's sons and set him on his father's throne, and fight for your master's house." ⁴ But they were exceedingly afraid, and said, "Behold, the two kings could not stand before him; how then can we stand?" ⁵ So he who was over the palace, and he who was over the city, together with the elders and the guardians, sent to Jehu, saying, "We are your servants, and we will do all that you bid us. We will not make any one king; do whatever is good in your eyes." ⁶ Then he wrote to them a second letter, saying, "If you are on my side, and if you are ready to obey me, take the heads of your master's sons, and come to me at Jezreel tomorrow at this time." Now the king's sons, seventy persons, were with the great men of the city, who were bringing them up. ⁷ And when the letter came to them, they took the king's sons, and slew them, seventy persons, and put their heads in baskets, and sent them to him at Jezreel. ⁸ When the messenger came and told him, "They have brought the heads of the king's sons," he said, "Lay them in two heaps at the entrance of the gate until the morning." ⁹ Then in the morning, when he went out, he stood, and said to all the people, "You are innocent. It was I who conspired against my master, and slew him; but who struck down all these? ¹⁰ Know then that there shall fall to the earth nothing of the word of the LORD, which the LORD spoke concerning the house of Ahab; for the LORD has done what he said by his servant Elijah" ¹¹ So Jehu slew all that remained of the house of Ahab in Jezreel, all his great men, and his familiar friends, and his priests, until he left him none remaining.

The assassination of the 70 "sons," a round number suggesting all male descendents (cf. 70 sons of Gideon, Judg. 8:30; 70 who came into Egypt, Gen. 46:27), revolves around two letters. In the first Jehu suggests that guardians of the sons of Ahab equip them and prepare to do battle. Their response is natural. If two kings, possessing unique power because of their sacral and political office, could not prevail against Jehu, but were slain in a single day, how could they stand? Thus, they agree to *do whatever is good in your eyes.* The second letter commands that the guardians behead the sons of Ahab and place the heads in two stacks at the city gate, the traditional seat of judgment.

Jehu absolves the community of any ritual guilt for the death of Jehoram and others in or near the city (cf. Deut. 21:1 ff. for the law on communal responsibility for a dead body in the vicinity of towns and villages). He assumes full responsibility for the death of Jehoram, but concludes by raising the question, *But who struck down all these?* The most common interpretation is that Jehu answers his own question with the suggestion that all of this has happened to fulfill the word of Elijah.

Another option is more probable, although less flattering to Jehu (but even the editor later stresses Jehu's "cunning," 10:19). Jehu tricked the supporters of Ahab, consisting of politically and militarily powerful persons, into killing the descendants of Ahab. He assumes responsibility for the death of Jehoram (v. 9a), but his question, *But who struck down all these?* is designed to place the blame for the death of Ahab's sons on the guardians. Then, vv.

10 and 11 should be read consecutively. Because of Elijah's word of judgment, *Jehu slew all that remained of the house of Ahab in Jezreel, all his great men, and his familiar friends, and his priests, until he left him none remaining.* Jehu gains everything and looses little: (1) he tricks the guardians into killing the descendants of Ahab, thus pleasing large numbers of the people; (2) he places responsibility for this crime on the shoulders of the guardians; (3) he executes the guardians, thus pleasing both friends of Ahab who opposed the guardians' betrayal of the sons and those who had long opposed the dynasty of Omri.

(5) Assassination of the Judahite Princes (10:12–14)

¹² Then he set out and went to Samaria. On the way, when he was at Betheked of the Shepherds, ¹³ Jehu met the kinsmen of Ahaziah king of Judah, and he said, "Who are you?" And they answered, "We are the kinsmen of Ahaziah, and we came down to visit the royal princes and the sons of the queen mother." ¹⁴ He said, "Take them alive." And they took them alive, and slew them at the pit of Betheked, forty-two persons, and he spared none of them.

The addition of two to the round number 40 may be to create a sense of precision within the narrative. Hence 42 may itself be, in effect, a round number.

(6) Assassination of Ahab's Descendants in Samaria (10:15–17)

¹⁵ And when he departed from there, he met Jehonadab the son of Rechab coming to meet him; and he greeted him, and said to him, "Is your heart true to my heart as mine is to yours?" And Jehonadab answered, "It is." Jehu said, "If it is, give me your hand." So he gave him his hand. And Jehu took him up with him into the chariot. ¹⁶ And he said, "Come with me, and see my zeal for the Lord." So he had him ride in his chariot. ¹⁷ And when he came to Samaria, he slew all that remained to Ahab in Samaria, till he had wiped them out, according to the word of the Lord which he spoke to Elijah.

Jehonadab was evidently looked upon as the founder of the Rechabites (cf. Jer. 35:19), and Rechab was probably a more distant ancestor of Jehonadab. All direct information about this strange group comes from Jeremiah (cf. 35:1 ff.). They were apparently of desert origin, of Kenite relationship (cf. 1 Chron. 2:55), and sought to live according to primitive customs. They rejected settled life altogether, lived in tents; refused to build houses, sow seed, or tend vineyards. Apparently faithful in the extreme to the desert traditions, such a group would have been totally sympathetic to Jehu's blood purge.

Rechabite support would have strengthened Jehu's position, and Jehonadab's chariot ride is for the purpose of favorably influencing more conservatively oriented Israelites toward Jehu. This is more than a casual meeting. The pledge and the handshake signified a formal coalition between Jehu and the Rechabites.

(7) Assassination of the Devotees of Baal (10:18–27)

¹⁸ Then Jehu assembled all the people, and said to them, "Ahab served Baal a little; but Jehu will serve him much. ¹⁹ Now therefore call to me all the prophets of Baal, all his worshipers and all his priests; let none be missing, for I have a great sacrifice to offer to Baal; whoever is missing shall not live." But Jehu did it with cunning in order to destroy the worshipers of Baal. ²⁰ And Jehu ordered, "Sanctify a solemn assembly for Baal." So they proclaimed it. ²¹ And Jehu sent throughout all Israel; and all the worshipers of Baal came, so that there was not a man left who did not come. And they entered the house of Baal, and the house of Baal was filled from one end to the other. ²² He said to him who was in charge of the wardrobe, "Bring out the vestments for all the worshipers of Baal." So he brought out the vestments for them. ²³ Then Jehu went into the house of Baal with Jehonadab the son of Rechab; and he said to the worshipers of Baal, "Search, and see that there is no servant of the Lord here among you, but only the worshipers of Baal." ²⁴ Then he went in to offer sacrifices and burnt offerings.

The deception of Jehu (vv. 18–24a). At this juncture the editor not only admits the cunning of Jehu, but magnifies it. Although such deception may be offensive to the modern reader, one should recognize that the ancient world gloried in accounts of ancestral heroes who were able to outwit their opponents. Jehu's final orders to search the building to insure that no servants of Yahweh are present hints at the calamity which is to come. Jehonadab, quite significantly, is party to the massacre.

The statement that *Jehu did it with cunning* suggests deception (*'aqbah*). The present verse is the only use of the word; "insidiousness" appears to be the meaning (BDB). The adjective *'aqob* means insidious or deceitful (Jer. 17:9, where it is used of man's heart).

Reference to *all the worshipers of Baal* is best understood in a relative sense. The statement may be later hyperbole, or those invited to such a stately convocation may have been a limited number of more prominent and influential devotees of Baal. The extension to all Israel may be a later expansion and originally the victims may all have been residents of Jezreel. All in all, however, it is better to treat the statement as hyperbole. It is the writer's way of insisting that Baalism was totally purged from the land. That this was not actually the case is graphically reflected in the amazing strength of the movement during the following century (cf. Hos. 1 ff.).

Now Jehu had stationed eighty men outside, and said, "The man who allows any of those whom I give into your hands to escape shall forfeit his life." 25 So as soon as he had made an end of offering the burnt offering, Jehu said to the guard and to the officers, "Go in and slay them; let not a man escape." So when they put them to the sword, the guard and the officers cast them out and went into the inner room of the house of Baal 26 and they brought out the pillar that was in the house of Baal, and burned it. 27 And they demolished the pillar of Baal, and demolished the house of Baal, and made it a latrine to this day.

The destruction of the worshipers (vv. 24b–27). That 80 men were sufficient as a guard for the massacre confirms the previous suggestion that the number of worshipers was less than "all" those in Israel or suggests that they were residents of Jezreel.

Whether land from so large a temple area actually became a latrine (*mach°ra'ah* occurs only in the plural, and only in v. 27; BDB suggests "cesspool") is open to question. But there is no reason to question that at least part of it was so used. Such action was not only an effort to degrade Baalism by insult, but also rendered the site ritually unclean. Or, at least there is evidence for this assumption on the basis of an Old Testament attitude toward human excrement (cf. Deut. 23:12–14).

4. An Appraisal of Jehu's Reign (10:28–36)

(1) The Deuteronomic Evaluation of Jehu (10:28–31)

28 Thus Jehu wiped out Baal from Israel. 29 But Jehu did not turn aside from the sins of Jeroboam the son of Nebat, which he made Israel to sin, the golden calves that were in Bethel, and in Dan. 30 And the LORD said to Jehu, "Because you have done well in carrying out what is right in my eyes, and have done to the house of Ahab according to all that was in my heart, your sons of the fourth generation shall sit on the throne of Israel." 31 But Jehu was not careful to walk in the law of the LORD the God of Israel with all his heart; he did not turn from the sins of Jeroboam, which he made Israel to sin.

In view of Jehu's zeal for Yahweh, it is surprising that the Deuteronomic editor limits his summary of Jehu's reign to seven words (v. 28). This is in keeping, however, with the consistent practice of that editor, for he never gives wholehearted approval to any ruler of the Northern Kingdom. The stereotyped evaluation of Israelite kings is applied to Jehu; he continued the religious practices of Jeroboam I.

An additional commendatory note appears in v. 30, which speaks well of and rewards Jehu. Yet the editor does not allow this to stand long without the reminder that Jehu did not repudiate the action of Jeroboam I. The truth of the matter is, however, that, despite the attitude of literary editors and theologians from Judah, the system of worship inaugurated by Jeroboam was not meant to be altogether apostate, however much it may have violated certain normative stipulations. Israel continued to worship Yahweh, not some other god. Her literary traditions and laws paralleled those in the South, and the golden calves as cult objects were the visible symbols above which Yahweh was enthroned. They paralleled the symbols of the ark in the Jerusalem Temple. Despite their questionable origin and possibly undue popular veneration, they were not "idols" in the strictest sense.

We are not to fail to see in full perspective, however, the genuinely theological implications of the worship practices inaugurated by Jereboam. They tended toward the corruption of worship, initiated concepts that turned the people more and more toward idolatry, invoked the displeasure of the Lord, and ultimately involved the doom of God's judgment.

(2) An Excerpt from the Chronicles of the Kings of Israel (10:32-36)

³² In those days the LORD began to cut off parts of Israel. Hazael defeated them throughout the territory of Israel: ³³ from the Jordan eastward, all the land of Gilead, the Gadites, and the Reubenites, and the Manassites, from Aroer, which is by the valley of the Arnon, that is, Gilead and Bashan. ³⁴ Now the rest of the acts of Jehu, and all that he did, and all his might, are they not written in the Book of the Chronicles of the Kings of Israel? ³⁵ So Jehu slept with his fathers, and they buried him in Samaria. And Jehoahaz his son reigned in his stead. ³⁶ The time that Jehu reigned over Israel in Samaria was twenty-eight years.

During this period Aram dominated Israel, and the whole of the Transjordan territory was lost. It was not restored until the conquests of Jeroboam II in the mid-eighth century. Hazael's attack on Israel was probably precipitated by her refusal to join in a coalition with Aram against the Assyrians.

It was also during the reign of Jehu that Israel was subjected to Assyrian domination, and one of the better known archaeological discoveries of this era, the black obelisk of Shalmaneser III, in which Jehu is depicted kneeling before the Assyrian king, gives the only pictorial representation of a Hebrew king ever discovered. The text reads: "The tribute of Jehu (*Ia-u-a*), son of Omri (*Hu-um-ri*); I received from him silver, gold, a golden *saplu*-bowl, a golden vase with pointed bottom, golden tumblers, golden buckets, tin, a staff for a king (and) wooden *puruhtu* [meaning unknown]" (ANET, p. 281).

VI. Reformation in Judah Under Joash (11:1—12:21)

The primary motif of the prophetic revolution (1 Kings 17 to 2 Kings 13) is the triumph of Yahwism over Baalism. Thus, the reformation in Judah under Jehoiada-Joash is a fitting motif to be included within the prophetic revolution; despite the sad fate of Joash.

1. The Usurpation of Athaliah and Joash's Coronation (11:1-21)

(1) Athaliah's Seizure of the Throne (11:1-3)

¹ Now when Athaliah the mother of Ahaziah saw that her son was dead, she arose and destroyed all the royal family. ² But Jehosheba, the daughter of King Joram, sister of Ahaziah, took Joash the son of Ahaziah, and stole him away from among the king's sons who were about to be slain, and she put him and his nurse in a bedchamber. Thus she hid him from Athaliah, so that he was not slain; ³ and he remained with her six years, hid in the house of the LORD, while Athaliah reigned over the land.

Athaliah's name may mean "Yahweh is exalted," suggesting a certain loyalty on the part of Ahab her father, despite her mother Jezebel's actions in furthering Baalism. The only woman to reign on the throne of either Judah or Israel, Athaliah seized the throne following the death of her son Ahaziah. Her action in slaying the royal household is akin to Jehoram's murder of his brothers (cf. 2 Chron. 21:4) and suggests that there had long been opposition within Judah to both the political influences and pagan religious practices which had been imported from the North. The fact that the Deuteronomic editor makes no appraisal of her reign, as he consistently does with each of the kings,

2 KINGS 11

suggests that he considered Athaliah a usurper to the throne who never achieved regnal status.

(2) The Coronation of Joash (11:4–12)

⁴ But in the seventh year Jehoiada sent and brought the captains of the Carites and of the guards, and had them come to him in the house of the LORD; and he made a covenant with them and put them under oath in the house of the LORD, and he showed them the king's son. ⁵ And he commanded them, "This is the thing that you shall do: one third of you, those who come off duty on the sabbath and guard the king's house ⁶ (another third being at the gate Sur and a third at the gate behind the guards), shall guard the palace; ⁷ and the two divisions of you, which come on duty in force on the sabbath and guard the house of the LORD, ⁸ shall surround the king, each with his weapons in his hand; and whoever approaches the ranks is to be slain. Be with the king when he goes out and when he comes in."

⁹ The captains did according to all that Jehoiada the priest commanded, and each brought his men who were to go off duty on the sabbath, with those who were to come on duty on the sabbath, and came to Jehoiada the priest. ¹⁰ And the priest delivered to the captains the spears and shields that had been King David's, which were in the house of the LORD; ¹¹ and the guards stood, every man with his weapons in his hand, from the south side of the house to the north side of the house, around the altar and the house. ¹² Then he brought out the king's son, and put the crown upon him, and gave him the testimony; and they proclaimed him king, and anointed him; and they clapped their hands, and said, "Long live the king!"

Jehoiada is the crucial figure in the Joash narrative. This significance is recognized by the Chronicler, who qualifies his commendation of Joash with the observation that "Joash did what was right in the eyes of the Lord all the days of Jehoiada the priest" (2 Chron. 24:2), as though with the death of Jehoiada the life of Joash changed (cf. 2 Chron. 24:17 ff. for confirmation of this presupposition).

The use of "covenant" in the context of the agreement is a good illustration of the nontheological usage of covenant in the Old Testament (cf. also 2 Sam. 5:3; Jer. 34:8 ff.; 1 Sam. 18:3; Mal. 2:14). Such usage is illustrative of the connotation of the theologically oriented covenant.

Jehoiada apparently selected the time of the changing of the guard for the sabbath watch for the coronation. He retained the division previously on duty, and to it the two coming on duty for the sabbath. Thus he arranged for all three divisions to be present without causing any alarm.

The symbols of coronation were the *crown* (*nezer*) and the *testimony* (*'eduth*). Another significant element was the public shout of acclamation which can be identified in successive coronation narratives (cf. 1 Sam. 10:24; 2 Sam. 15:10; 1 Kings 1:39; 2 Kings 9:13. Notice that the sounding of the trumpet often preceeds the shout of acclamation). The *nezer* is closely related to the vocabulary of the Nazarite and means a symbol of dedication (the same meaning as Nazarite). *Nezer* is a word reserved for the royal and priestly crown (cf. 2 Sam. 1:10; Zech. 9:16; Ex. 29:6), whereas the *"tarah* designated the general, poetic term (cf. 2 Sam. 12:30; Job 19:9). John Gray says of the testimony as a feature of the coronation ritual that it was "specifically associated with the covenant of Yahweh with the Davidic King . . . it seems obvious that *'edut* or *'edot* signified specifically the king's obligations in the covenant."

The necessity for troops in support of Jehoiada's action is indicative of the strong division which must have characterized the southern kingdom at this time. It would seem from the response of the people, however, that whatever opposition to the coronation Jehoiada expected probably was associated with the elements of the guard loyal to Athaliah. Yet, even so, at the time of her execution there is no demonstration of power in opposition.

(3) Athaliah's Execution (11:13–16)

¹³ When Athaliah heard the noise of the guard and of the people, she went into the house of the LORD to the people; ¹⁴ and when she looked, there was the king standing by the pillar, according to the custom, and the captains and the trumpeters beside the king, and

all the people of the land **rejoicing and blowing trumpets.** And Athaliah rent her clothes, and cried, "Treason! Treason!" 15 Then Jehoiada the priest commanded the captains who were set over the army, "Bring her out between the ranks; and slay with the sword any one who follows her." For the priest said, "Let her not be slain in the house of the LORD." 16 So they laid hands on her; and she went through the horses' entrance to the king's house, and there she was slain.

The **horses' entrance** was a gate outside the Temple area, leading to the Kidron. It was toward the southeast of the Temple area in the vicinity of the palace (cf. IDB). Beyond its dissociation with the Temple it has no particular significance for this narrative (cf. 1 Kings 14:27 f.; Jer. 31:38; Neh. 3:28).

(4) The Renewal of the Covenant (11:17-21)

17 And Jehoiada made a covenant between the LORD and the king and people, that they should be the LORD's people; and also between the king and the people. 18 Then all the people of the land went to the house of Baal, and tore it down; his altars and his images they broke in pieces, and they slew Mattan the priest of Baal before the altars. And the priest posted watchmen over the house of the LORD. 19 And he took the captains, the Carites, the guards, and all the people of the land; and they brought the king down from the house of the LORD, marching through the gate of the guards to the king's house. And he took his seat on the throne of the kings. 20 So all the people of the land rejoiced; and the city was quiet after Athaliah had been slain with the sword at the king's house.
21 Jehoash was seven years old when he began to reign.

The **covenant renewal** ceremony was an important aspect of religious commitment in the Old Testament. The covenant was not merely an agreement made in years past with one's ancestors, but an experience into which one continually reentered as one shared in the cultic observances of the worshiping community.

Against the background of religious enthusiasm, new political and social freedom, and the general ferment characteristic of reform movements, the people destroyed every vestige of Baalism: sanctuary, altar, and images, even slaying the high priest.

To this account of the establishment of Joash as king over Judah there has been appended a chronological note underscoring the age of Joash at the time of his accession to kingship (v. 21). This should be understood in the context of 12:1.

2. The Repair of the Temple: an Independent Tradition (12:1-16)

Chapter 12 is composed of several sources: a special Temple stratum from state records which was concerned with the building, furnishing, and contents of that structure (vv. 4-16); the Book of the Chronicles of the Kings of Judah (vv. 19-21); a special source from state records (vv. 17-18); and the characteristic Deuteronomic evaluation (vv. 1-3). This source consistently uses Jehoash rather than Joash (cf. 11:1 ff.; 2 Chron. 24:1 ff.).

(1) An Evaluation of Joash (12:1-3)

1 In the seventh year of Jehu Jehoash began to reign, and he reigned forty years in Jerusalem. His mother's name was Zibiah of Beersheba. 2 And Jehoash did what was right in the eyes of the LORD all his days, because Jehoiada the priest instructed him. 3 Nevertheless the high places were not taken away; the people continued to sacrifice and burn incense on the high places.

The editor of Deuteronomy, as did the Chronicler, directly related the good record of Joash to the influence of Jehoiada the priest (cf. 2 Chron. 24:2,17 ff.). The hesitancy of the writer fully to commend Joash is reflected in the judgment of the **high places,** local sanctuaries which were in violation of the Deuteronomic principle of the single sanctuary. It is by no means certain that this refers to Baalism, as some suggest, although, quite obviously, Baalism did persist for a century or more after the death of Athaliah.

(2) The Repair of the Temple (12:4-16)

4 Jehoash said to the priests, "All the money of the holy things which is brought into the house of the LORD, the money for which each man is assessed—the money from the assessment of persons—and the money which a

man's heart prompts him to bring into the house of the Lord, ⁵ let the priests take, each from his acquaintance; and let them repair the house wherever any need of repairs is discovered." ⁶ But by the twenty-third year of King Jehoash the priests had made no repairs on the house. ⁷ Therefore King Jehoash summoned Jehoiada the priest and the other priests and said to them, "Why are you not repairing the house? Now therefore take no more money from your acquaintances, but hand it over for the repair of the house." ⁸ So the priests agreed that they should take no more money from the people, and that they should not repair the house.

⁹ Then Jehoiada the priest took a chest, and bored a hole in the lid of it, and set it beside the altar on the right side as one entered the house of the Lord; and the priests who guarded the threshold put in it all the money that was brought into the house of the Lord. ¹⁰ And whenever they saw that there was much money in the chest, the king's secretary and the high priest came up and they counted and tied up in bags the money that was found in the house of the Lord. ¹¹ Then they would give the money that was weighed out into the hands of the workmen who had the oversight of the house of the Lord; and they paid it out to the carpenters and the builders who worked upon the house of the Lord, ¹² and to the masons and the stonecutters, as well as to buy timber and quarried stone for making repairs on the house of the Lord, and for any outlay upon the repairs of the house. ¹³ But there were not made for the house of the Lord basins of silver, snuffers, bowls, trumpets, or any vessels of gold, or of silver, from the money that was brought into the house of the Lord ¹⁴ for that was given to the workmen who were repairing the house of the Lord with it. ¹⁵ And they did not ask an accounting from the men into whose hand they delivered the money to pay out to the workmen, for they dealt honestly. ¹⁶ The money from the guilt offerings and the money from the sin offerings was not brought into the house of the Lord; it belonged to the priests.

Holy things suggest the full gamut of money or goods in kind brought into the Temple, including the assessed poll tax (cf. Ex. 30:12–30), vows that were made and fulfilled (Lev. 27:2–8), fines (cf. Amos 2:8), the free-will offerings. All of this was to be designated for the Temple.

The word *acquaintance* is difficult. Does it mean that the money is to come from personal acquaintances of individual priests? Or does it mean that the money is to come from those to whom the priest ministers (and thus is an "acquaintance")? Generally stated, the *makar* (acquaintance) was a person with whom the priest came in contact during the course of his professional duties, and from whom money was received for services rendered or obligations due.

In v. 4 the priests are instructed to give all *holy* money for the Temple, reserving that which comes to them on a more personal basis (v. 5) for their own livelihood. Because over two decades passed without repairing the Temple, Joash then prohibits the priest from keeping even personal money, and demands that it also be used in the repair of the Temple.

The problem concerning the negligence of the priests was not solved until Joash took two specific actions. *First*, he refused to permit the priests to handle the money. One should not confuse money with coins. Coins were not introduced until the post-exilic era, although there are records of regular weights of metal stamped with the name of a trader as early as the ninth century (Gray). At this stage money would have been precious metal.

Second, the work was put into the hands of competent craftsmen rather than the priests, a rebuff to the priests and their improprieties. The whole of the narrative is suggestive concerning the break that came between Joash and the ways of Jehoiada.

3. The Fate of Joash (12:17–21)

Joash's nobility and commendable virtues seem to have lasted only shortly, if at all (cf. 2 Chron. 24:17 ff.), after the death of Jehoiada. The fate of the king is reflected in two narratives, drawn from separate sources.

(1) The Conflict of Hazael and Joash (12:17–18)

¹⁷ At that time Hazael king of Syria went up and fought against Gath, and took it. But when Hazael set his face to go up against Jerusalem, ¹⁸ Jehoash king of Judah took all the votive gifts that Jehoshaphat and Jehoram and Aha-

ziah, his fathers, the kings of Judah, had dedicated, and his own votive gifts, and all the gold that was found in the treasuries of the house of the Lord and of the king's house, and sent these to Hazael king of Syria. Then Hazael went away from Jerusalem.

The writer seeks in the closing lines to highlight the failure of Joash. It is as though the editor is concerned to suggest that following the death of Jehoiada Joash followed a course of action which brought him lower and lower, until finally he was destroyed.

(2) *The Assassination of Joash (12:19-21)*

¹⁹ Now the rest of the acts of Joash, and all that he did, are they not written in the Book of the Chronicles of the Kings of Judah? ²⁰ His servants arose and made a conspiracy, and slew Joash in the house of Millo, on the way that goes down to Silla. ²¹ It was Jozacar the son of Shimeath and Jehozabad the son of Shomer, his servants, who struck him down, so that he died. And they buried him with his fathers in the city of David, and Amaziah his son reigned in his stead.

Joash, whose public life began in the throes of an insurrection in which the queen mother was executed, himself died as the victim of assassins. Perhaps the appraisal is too severe, but someone has suggested that by the time Joash reached the end of life he was no better than Athaliah (cf. 2 Chron. 24:17 ff.). Although placed in the hands of religious leaders who sought to mold his life from infancy, Joash never became in fact what Jehoiada and others had anticipated. In the final analysis the individual, under God's leadership, must make his own decisions, create his own integrity, and achieve his own destiny.

VII. The Trials of Israel and the Death of Elisha (13:1-25)

1. *Aramean Advances Under Hazael (13:1-13)*

One factor in the ability of the Arameans to stand against nations so strong as Assyria was their adroitness in creating alliances among numerous smaller groups. Continuing pressure to join such coalitions was one cause of friction between Israel and Aram. Israel was involved in this coalition, and it was probably out of that experience that Ahab and Jehoshaphat moved to take Ramothgilead (1 Kings 22:29).

Hazael was constantly involved with successive kings of both Israel and Judah—seriously wounding Joram of Israel (8:28 f.), stripping Israel of territory in the time of Jehu (10:32 f.) and constantly harassing Joash of Judah (12:17 f.; 2 Chron. 24:23), as well as Jehoahaz of Israel (13:1 ff.; cf. R. A. Bowman, "Hazael," IDB). It is against this king's advances, in all probability, that the narratives of 2 Kings 6:8 ff. are set, as well as the narrative on Jehoahaz.

(1) *Jehoahaz of Israel (13:1-9)*

¹ In the twenty-third year of Joash the son of Ahaziah, king of Judah, Jehoahaz the son of Jehu began to reign over Israel in Samaria, and he reigned seventeen years. ² He did what was evil in the sight of the Lord, and followed the sins of Jeroboam the son of Nebat, which he made Israel to sin; he did not depart from them. ³ And the anger of the Lord was kindled against Israel, and he gave them continually into the hand of Hazael king of Syria and into the hand of Benhadad the son of Hazael. ⁴ Then Jehoahaz besought the Lord, and the Lord hearkened to him; for he saw the oppression of Israel, how the king of Syria oppressed them. ⁵ (Therefore the Lord gave Israel a savior, so that they escaped from the hand of the Syrians; and the people of Israel dwelt in their homes as formerly. ⁶ Nevertheless they did not depart from the sins of the house of Jeroboam, which he made Israel to sin, but walked in them; and the Asherah also remained in Samaria.) ⁷ For there was not left to Jehoahaz an army of more than fifty horsemen and ten chariots and ten thousand footmen; for the king of Syria had destroyed them and made them like the dust at threshing. ⁸ Now the rest of the acts of Jehoahaz and all that he did, and his might, are they not written in the Book of the Chronicles of the Kings of Israel? ⁹ So Jehoahaz slept with his fathers, and they buried him in Samaria; and Joash his son reigned in his stead.

Jehoahaz ("Yahweh has grasped") is introduced by the customary formula used to disclaim kings of Israel. The inroads of Hazael are directly related to the action of Yahweh in response to his infidelity. This oppression by Hazael may be the background of the oracle by Amos (cf. Amos 1:3 ff.).

Reference to a *savior* is strangely like the motif of the book of Judges, and its framework of sin, judgment, repentance, and deliverance (through a deliverer or savior). The *savior* was probably an Assyrian king whose approach drew the attention of Hazael away from Israel—likely Adadnirari III (810–793 B.C.).

Asherah is frequently mentioned in the Old Testament, and especially associated with Baalism. Asherah might indicate a goddess (who is mentioned in the Ras Shamra literature and passages such as 1 Kings 15:13; 18:19; 2 Kings 21:7; 23:4 ff. in the Old Testament), or as a cult object as in the present verse (cf. also Deut. 16:21; Judg. 6:25; 1 Kings 16:33), although the word appears most often in the plural form (*asherim* and *asherot*, "groves" in KJV). The form of the cult object is not discussed in the Old Testament. Consequently, scholars variously identify it as "a plain pole, a carved pole, a staff, a triangle on a staff, a cross, a double axe, a tree, a tree stump, a headdress for priests, and a wooden image" (cf. W. L. Reed, "Asherah," IDB).

The limited military resources left to Israel following Hazael's ravages stand in marked contrast to the equipment available to Ahab almost a half century earlier. Of Ahab's military contribution to the coalition which fought against Shalmaneser at Qarqar in 853 B.C., an Assyrian record cites the following: ". . . 2,000 chariots, 10,000 foot soldiers of Ahab, the Israelite" (according to the Bull Inscription from the bull statues found in Calah; cf. ANET).

(2) *Jehoash of Israel* (13:10–13)

¹⁰ In the thirty-seventh year of Joash king of Judah Jehoash the son of Jehoahaz began to reign over Israel in Samaria, and he reigned sixteen years. ¹¹ He also did what was evil in the sight of the LORD; he did not depart from all the sins of Jeroboam the son of Nebat, which he made Israel to sin, but he walked in them. ¹² Now the rest of the acts of Joash, and all that he did, and the might with which he fought against Amaziah king of Judah, are they not written in the Book of the Chronicles of the Kings of Israel? ¹³ So Joash slept with his fathers, and Jeroboam sat upon his throne; and Joash was buried in Samaria with the kings of Israel.

Jehoash of Israel should not be confused with Jehoash of Judah (837–800 B.C.).

2. *Elisha's Prophetic Action and the Reversal of Hazael* (13:14–25)

The last narrative on the life of Elisha to appear in the book of Kings recounts the prophet's use of symbolic action (vv. 14–19); and the account of his death, which includes a popular story on the miraculous power of Elisha's bones (vv. 20–24).

(1) *Hebrew Prophetic Action* (13:14–19)

¹⁴ Now when Elisha had fallen sick with the illness of which he was to die, Joash king of Israel went down to him, and wept before him, crying, "My father, my father! The chariots of Israel and its horsemen!" ¹⁵ And Elisha said to him, "Take a bow and arrows"; so he took a bow and arrows. ¹⁶ Then he said to the king of Israel, "Draw the bow"; and he drew it. And Elisha laid his hands upon the king's hands. ¹⁷ And he said, "Open the window eastward"; and he opened it. Then Elisha said, "Shoot"; and he shot. And he said, "The LORD's arrow of victory, the arrow of victory over Syria! For you shall fight the Syrians in Aphek until you have made an end of them." ¹⁸ And he said, "Take the arrows"; and he took them. And he said to the king of Israel, "Strike the ground with them"; and he struck three times, and stopped. ¹⁹ Then the man of God was angry with him, and said, "You should have struck five or six times; then you would have struck down Syria until you had made an end of it, but now you will strike down Syria only three times."

Prophets often acted in strange ways in proclaiming their message (cf. 1. Sam. 15: 27 f.; Isa. 20:2; Jer. 13:1 ff.; Ezek. 4:1 ff., 5:1 ff., 37:15 ff.). Yet this reflected far more than an object lesson as a teaching medium. Prophetic symbolic action is closely akin to the magical conception that specific action(s) can be precipitated within history in response to the mimetic actions of holy men.

Hebrew prophetic symbolical action is the key to understanding the strange directions of Elisha to the king of Israel that he shoot an arrow out the window toward the east; also that he strike the ground with other of the remaining arrows. Such action was thought actually to have set in motion the forces that would bring defeat to the king of Aram or Syria.

My father, my father! reflects the veneration of the king for Elisha, and probably also refers to the anticipated powers available to deliver Israel, and for which the king is in effect beseeching Elisha.

Shooting the arrow eastward directs the forces of Yahweh against the Syrians (cf. Joshua's spear outstretched toward Ai, Josh. 8:18). The king strikes the arrows to the ground but thrice, thus angering Elisha who suggests that only the king's limited faith precluded a more significant victory.

(2) *The Death and Veneration of Elisha (13:20-21)*

²⁰ So Elisha died, and they buried him. Now bands of Moabites used to invade the land in the spring of the year. ²¹ And as a man was being buried, lo, a marauding band was seen and the man was cast into the grave of Elisha; and as soon as the man touched the bones of Elisha, he revived, and stood on his feet.

The account of the return to life of the man whose body was thrown in upon the bones of Elisha when the burial party was frightened by a band of Moabite raiders illustrates the veneration and awe with which Elisha was held within the schools of the prophets, and elsewhere, in later years.

The more immediate purpose of the inclusion of this popular story at this juncture is the demonstration of power associated with Elisha. This is confirmatory evidence for the symbolic action in the preceding verses; insuring that through such prophetic power as characterized Elisha the act would come to pass, as indeed it did come to pass (cf. 13:22 f.).

(3) *Fulfillment of the Prophetic Symbolic Act (13:22-25)*

²² Now Hazael king of Syria oppressed Israel all the days of Jehoahaz. ²³ But the LORD was gracious to them and had compassion on them, and he turned toward them, because of his covenant with Abraham, Isaac, and Jacob, and would not destroy them; nor has he cast them from his presence until now. ²⁴ When Hazael king of Syria died, Benhadad his son became king in his stead. ²⁵ Then Jehoash the son of Jehoahaz took again from Benhadad the son of Hazael the cities which he had taken from Jehoahaz his father in war. Three times Joash defeated him and recovered the cities of Israel.

Within the broader context of 2 Kings 13:14 ff. the redactor has used historical information from the national archives to validate the symbolic act of Elisha, and to show that prophetic words are fulfilled. Thus, interest in historical events between Israel and Aram is intermingled with the continuing prophetic concern on the part of the Deuteronomic redactor to stress the significant contribution of Elisha and the prophetic office.

Part Two
Decades of Bitterness and Defeat in Judah and Israel (14:1—17:41)

This larger section begins with the bitterness expressed in the conflict between Judah at the instigation of Amaziah (14:8 ff.) and concludes with the defeat of the Northern Kingdom (17:1 ff.). Theologically, the passage reflects the conviction that national apostasy and infidelity can only lead to national fragmentation and defeat. Kings of this era in both the North and the South, are negatively evaluated by the editor(s) of Kings.

I. *Sectional Warfare Between Judah and Israel (14:1-22).*

Throughout the era of the divided kingdoms sectional warfare was interrupted only by periods of Israelite ascendancy over Judah. To understand this hostility better, one might consider the historical evidence which suggests that the two were never one in spirit and that their period of union was not only brief but that it was forged primarily because of the unique power of David.

1. The Occasion for the War (14:1–10)

¹ In the second year of Joash the son of Joahaz, king of Israel, Amaziah the son of Joash, king of Judah, began to reign. ² He was twenty-five years old when he began to reign, and he reigned twenty-nine years in Jerusalem. His mother's name was Jehoaddin of Jerusalem. ³ And he did what was right in the eyes of the Lord, yet not like David his father; he did in all things as Joash his father had done. ⁴ But the high places were not removed; the people still sacrificed and burned incense on the high places. ⁵ And as soon as the royal power was firmly in his hand he killed his servants who had slain the king his father. ⁶ But he did not put to death the children of the murderers; according to what is written in the book of the law of Moses, where the Lord commanded, "The fathers shall not be put to death for the children, or the children be put to death for the fathers; but every man shall die for his own sin."
⁷ He killed ten thousand Edomites in the Valley of Salt and took Sela by storm, and called it Joktheel, which is its name to this day.
⁸ Then Amaziah sent messengers to Jehoash the son of Jehoahaz, son of Jehu, king of Israel, saying, "Come, let us look one another in the face." ⁹ And Jehoash king of Israel sent word to Amaziah king of Judah, "A thistle on Lebanon sent to a cedar on Lebanon, saying, 'Give your daughter to my son for a wife'; and a wild beast of Lebanon passed by and trampled down the thistle. ¹⁰ You have indeed smitten Edom, and your heart has lifted you up. Be content with your glory, and stay at home; for why should you provoke trouble so that you fall, you and Judah with you?"

The firm hand of Amaziah (800–783 B.C.) is reflected in the 29-year length of his reign, the manner in which he avenged his father's death, and his victory over the Edomites (cf. 2. Chron. 25:5 ff., which suggests that initially an Israelite contingent was to have participated in the Edomite campaign).

The writer emphasizes that although Amaziah put to death those who murdered his father, the children of Joash's murderers were not put to death (v. 6)—a point which reflects the Deuteronomic conception of individualism (Deut. 24:16). Blood revenge was an accepted Israelite custom, and earlier conceptions of corporate solidarity led to the punishment of one generation for the sins of another (cf. Ex. 20:5 f.; Josh. 7:22 ff.). Fuller comprehension of the will of God led Israel to understand that each man is responsible for his own life, not that of his predecessors (cf. Jer. 31:29 f.; Ezek. 18:1 ff.). The Old Testament thus ultimately repudiated inherited guilt.

Elated by his demonstration of strength over the Edomites, or perhaps reflecting a border dispute with Israel, Amaziah challenged Jehoash, king of Israel. The fable by which Jehoash answers Amaziah is but one of several used in the Old Testament, often with the common purpose of demonstrating the ridiculous weakness of a challenger or pretender to power (cf. Judg. 9:7 ff.; Ezek. 17:3 ff.). Verses 8–10 are probably from a northern source.

2. Judah's Defeat by Israel (14:11–14)

¹¹ But Amaziah would not listen. So Jehoash king of Israel went up, and he and Amaziah king of Judah faced one another in battle at Bethshemesh, which belongs to Judah. ¹² And Judah was defeated by Israel, and every man fled to his home. ¹³ And Jehoash king of Israel captured Amaziah king of Judah, the son of Jehoash, son of Ahaziah, at Bethshemesh, and came to Jerusalem, and broke down the wall of Jerusalem for four hundred cubits, from the Ephraim Gate to the Corner Gate. ¹⁴ And he seized all the gold and silver, and all the vessels that were found in the house of the Lord and in the treasuries of the king's house, also hostages, and he returned to Samaria.

Later theological reflection led to the conviction that Judah's defeat reflected the Lord's judgment upon her for having worshiped Edomite gods (cf. 2 Chron. 25:20 ff.). Amaziah's defeat and the attendant destruction of Jerusalem's walls, plus the plundering of the Temple, may well have led to the later question about his reign (14:3) as well as the conspiracy against him (14:19 f.).

3. A Summary of Amaziah's Reign (14:15–22)

¹⁵ Now the rest of the acts of Jehoash which he did, and his might, and how he fought with Amaziah king of Judah, are they not written in the Book of the Chronicles of the Kings of

Israel? ¹⁶ And Jehoash slept with his fathers, and was buried in Samaria with the kings of Israel; and Jeroboam his son reigned in his stead.

¹⁷ Amaziah the son of Joash, king of Judah, lived fifteen years after the death of Jehoash son of Jehoahaz, king of Israel. ¹⁸ Now the rest of the deeds of Amaziah, are they not written in the Book of the Chronicles of the Kings of Judah? ¹⁹ And they made a conspiracy against him in Jerusalem, and he fled to Lachish. But they sent after him to Lachish, and slew him there. ²⁰ And they brought him upon horses; and he was buried in Jerusalem with his fathers in the city of David. ²¹ And all the people of Judah took Azariah, who was sixteen years old, and made him king instead of his father Amaziah. ²² He built Elath and restored it to Judah, after the king slept with his fathers.

The Deuteronomic appraisal of Amaziah is either favorable (14:2 ff.) or noncommittal (vv. 15 ff.). The favorable interpretation of his reign is considerably increased if the phrase "yet not like David his father" (14:3) is treated as a later gloss; a view suggested by Montgomery and Gehman (p. 439), and which should probably be followed.

The cause of the conspiracy raised against Amaziah is indeterminate: whether the old hostility within the circle of those who assassinated his father (12:20 f.) or those sympathetic with the men whom Amaziah had earlier put to death (14:5), the antagonism of the priests and their supporters for Amaziah's plundering the Temple (whether by the force of Jehoash when he came to Jerusalem, 14:13, or an act whereby Amaziah used Temple funds to buy off Jehoash), or the general disenchantment of those disappointed by his debacle with Israel.

II. A Succession of Evil Kings (14:23—17:6)

1. Jeroboam II of Israel (14:23–29)

²³ In the fifteenth year of Amaziah the son of Joash, king of Judah, Jeroboam the son of Joash, king of Israel, began to reign in Samaria, and he reigned forty-one years. ²⁴ And he did what was evil in the sight of the Lord; he did not depart from all the sins of Jeroboam the son of Nebat, which he made Israel to sin. ²⁵ He restored the border of Israel from the entrance of Hamath as far as the Sea of the Arabah, according to the word of the Lord, the God of Israel, which he spoke by his servant Jonah the son of Amittai, the prophet, who was from Gathhepher. ²⁶ For the Lord saw that the affliction of Israel was very bitter, for there was none left, bond or free, and there was none to help Israel. ²⁷ But the Lord had not said that he would blot out the name of Israel from under heaven, so he saved them by the hand of Jeroboam the son of Joash.

²⁸ Now the rest of the acts of Jeroboam, and all that he did, and his might, how he fought, and how he recovered for Israel Damascus and Hamath, which had belonged to Judah, are they not written in the Book of the Chronicles of the Kings of Israel? ²⁹ And Jeroboam slept with his fathers, the kings of Israel, and Zechariah his son reigned in his stead.

Not since the era of Solomon had Israel known the prosperity and grandeur associated with Jeroboam II. Rivaled only by the Omride dynasty in the significance which he brought to Israel, Jeroboam is quite strangely and almost totally ignored by the Deuteronomic editor. The political stability of his 41-year reign, however, stands in marked contrast to the turmoil which followed (cf. 15:8 ff.).

In keeping with the theological position of the editor, Jeroboam's success was attributed to the Lord, who *had not said that he would blot out the name of Israel from under heaven.* The prophetic works of Amos and Hosea, however, are fitting commentaries upon the actual moral and religious plight of Israel at this time, and the prosperity and national grandeur which attended Jeroboam's leadership were misdirected to say the least.

2. Azariah (Uzziah) of Judah (15:1–7)

¹ In the twenty-seventh year of Jeroboam king of Israel Azariah the son of Amaziah, king of Judah, began to reign. ² He was sixteen years old when he began to reign, and he reigned fifty-two years in Jerusalem. His mother's name was Jecoliah of Jerusalem. ³ And he did what was right in the eyes of the Lord, according to all that his father Amaziah had done. ⁴ Nevertheless the high places were not taken away; the people still sacrificed and burned incense on the high places. ⁵ And the Lord smote the king, so that he was a leper to the day of his death, and he dwelt in a sepa-

rate house. And Jotham the king's son was over the household, governing the people of the land. ⁶ Now the rest of the acts of Azariah, and all that he did, are they not written in the Book of the Chronicles of the Kings of Judah? ⁷ And Azariah slept with his fathers, and they buried him with his fathers in the city of David, and Jotham his son reigned in his stead.

Azariah's long reign of 52 years was marred by his leprosy, which apparently caused his removal from public service (cf. the *separate house*) and the coregency of his son Jotham. The names Azariah and Uzziah are synonymous. Azariah ("Yahweh has helped") is common to Kings, and Uzziah to Isaiah and Chronicles (cf. Isa. 6:1; 2 Chron. 26:1 ff.).

Separate house has been variously understood as a dwelling (cf. ASV), as a state, "unmolested" (Moffatt), or "released from obligation" (John Gray's translation in his commentary). The question revolves around whether "free" (*chaphshi*, free; from *chaphash*, to be free; cf. Lev. 19:20) is a description of the kind of dwelling in which the king lived or the king's responsibilities. Second Chronicles 26:21 and ten manuscripts on 2 Kings 15:5 read *chaphshith*, separated; hence separate. The use of *chaphshi* in 1 Samuel 17:25 in the sense of free from taxes, obligations, etc., suggests that here in v. 5 the writer may have in mind Uzziah's duties. Uzziah was free of certain regnal responsibilities which were assumed by his son Jotham.

The nature of the *leprosy* would help determine whether Uzziah (1) dwelt in a separate building, (2) had separate quarters in the palace, or (3) relinquished some regnal duties. But as suggested previously it is impossible to determine from the word leper (*meṣora'*) the precise nature of the ailment, whether a superficial skin ailment or the more serious form of leprosy. From the Chroniclers' statement on Uzziah's death it may be inferred that he was buried apart from others (cf. 2 Chron. 26:23).

3. Political Turmoil in Israel (15:8–31)

Israel's period of political upheaval was directly related to a double problem: that of succession to the Israelite throne and the Assyrian resurgence under the leadership of Tiglathpileser III. First, possible disenchantment with the Jehu dynasty which was reflected in the assassination of his successor Zechariah (v. 8 ff.), led to a period of revolt under Shallum (v. 16 ff.). followed by a longer period of stability under Menahem (v. 17 ff.). His successor Pekahiah (v. 23 ff.), however, was soon assassinated by Pekah (v. 26) whose relatively short reign of approximately 5 years (v. 27 ff.) was terminated by assassination at the hands of Hoshea (17:1 ff.).

Second, the fate of Israel in the last two decades of her existence was largely determined by the Assyrian domination of the Near East. Eventually even Judah came within the determinative influence of Assyria. Tiglathpileser III, who assumed the name "Pul" as a Babylonian throne name upon ascending that throne in 729 B.C., was a primary key to Israelite fortunes of this era. Although his historical records (745–727 B.C.) are incomplete, one can reconstruct the basic skeleton of events affecting Israel. In 743 he began a series of campaigns during which he received tribute from Rezin of Damascus and neighboring rulers. During a further campaign which ended in victory in 739 he received tribute from Menahem of Israel. In 734 Tiglathpileser III moved down the coast through Phoenicia and Philistia, probably in response to an appeal from Ahaz of Judah, who, according to both biblical and Assyrian recores, paid tribute to him. By 732 Damascus had been defeated and territory in the north of Israel absorbed. Cf. D. J. Wiseman, in D. Winton Thomas, p. 53.

(1) Zechariah (15:8–12)

⁸ In the thirty-eighth year of Azariah king of Judah Zechariah the son of Jeroboam reigned over Israel in Samaria six months. ⁹ And he did what was evil in the sight of the LORD, as his fathers had done. He did not depart from the sins of Jeroboam the son of Nebat, which he made Israel to sin. ¹⁰ Shallum the son of Jabesh conspired against him, and struck him down at

Ibleam, and killed him, and reigned in his stead. ¹¹ Now the rest of the deeds of Zechariah, behold, they are written in the Book of the Chronicles of the Kings of Israel. ¹² (This was the promise of the LORD which he gave to Jehu, "Your sons shall sit upon the throne of Israel to the fourth generation." And so it came to pass.)

Zechariah ("Yahweh remembered"), son of Jeroboam II, reigned but 2 months. Other than the stereotyped appraisal of kingship used by the Deuteronomic editor, little is known of his tenure. He was the victim of a conspiracy, apparently under the leadership of Shallum, who murdered him at Ibleam.

(2) Shallum (15:13–16)

¹³ Shallum the son of Jabesh began to reign in the thirty-ninth year of Uzziah king of Judah, and he reigned one month in Samaria. ¹⁴ Then Menahem the son of Gadi came up from Tirzah and came to Samaria, and he struck down Shallum the son of Jabesh in Samaria and slew him, and reigned in his stead. ¹⁵ Now the rest of the deeds of Shallum, and the conspiracy which he made, behold, they are written in the Book of the Chronicles of the Kings of Israel. ¹⁶ At that time Menahem sacked Tappuah and all who were in it and its territory from Tirzah on; because they did not open it to him, therefore he sacked it, and he ripped up all the women in it who were with child.

The assassination of Zechariah by Shallum reflects continued tension concerning dynastic succession, some preferring to choose another king than the descendant of Jehu. Hosea was probably active during this era, and may have dealt with such dynastic instability (cf. Hos. 13:10 f.).

Menahem's harsh treatment of the town of Tappuah reflects the loyalty of its citizens to Shallum. Such action toward an Israelite town is without precedent during the sectional warfare between Judah and Israel: *he ripped up all the women in it.* The atrocity of putting pregnant women ("with child") to the sword is paralleled only by the severe cruelty of invading armies such as the Arameans (8:12) or raiding parties such as the Ammonites (Amos 1:13).

(3) Menahem (15:17–22)

¹⁷ In the thirty-ninth year of Azariah king of Judah Menahem the son of Gadi began to reign over Israel, and he reigned ten years in Samaria. ¹⁸ And he did what was evil in the sight of the LORD; he did not depart all his days from all the sins of Jeroboam the son of Nebat, which he made Israel to sin. ¹⁹ Pul the king of Assyria came against the land; and Menahem gave Pul a thousand talents of silver, that he might help him to confirm his hold of the royal power. ²⁰ Menahem exacted the money from Israel, that is, from all the wealthy men, fifty shekels of silver from every man, to give to the king of Assyria. So the king of Assyria turned back, and did not stay there in the land. ²¹ Now the rest of the deeds of Menahem, and all that he did, are they not written in the Book of the Chronicles of the Kings of Israel? ²² And Menahem slept with his fathers, and Pekahiah his son reigned in his stead.

Menahem ("comforting") came to the throne following the period of severe civil disturbances (cf. 15:14), and may have required some months actually to ascend the throne. When contrasted with the brief reigns of Zechariah and Shallum, the length of his tenure provided an interim of stability. This should obscure, however, neither his negative evaluation by the writer nor his obvious subjection by Assyria. The tribute which Menahem collected from the wealthy men of Israel is indirectly mentioned in the annals of Tiglathpileser III's campaigns against Syria and Palestine which refer to Menahem:

. . . As for Menahem I over whelmed him like a snowstorm and he . . . fled like a bird, along, and bowed to my feet? I returned him to his place and imposed tribute upon him, to wit: gold, silver, linen garments with multicolored trimmings, . . . great . . . I received from him (Rawlinson, in ANET, pp. 281 f.).

(4) Pekahiah (15:23–26)

²³ In the fiftieth year of Azariah king of Judah Pekahiah the son of Menahem began to reign over Israel in Samaria, and he reigned two years. ²⁴ And he did what was evil in the sight of the LORD; he did not turn away from the sins of Jeroboam the son of Nebat, which he made Israel to sin. ²⁵ And Pekah the son of Remaliah, his captain, conspired against him

with fifty men of the Gileadites, and slew him in Samaria, in the citadel of the king's house; he slew him, and reigned in his stead. 26 Now the rest of the deeds of Pekahiah, and all that he did, behold, they are written in the Book of the Chronicles of the Kings of Israel.

Pekahiah ("Yahweh has opened") according to the biblical chronology came to the throne two years following his father's death (cf. 15:23 and 15:17). This interval may reflect the time necessary for Assyria to approve Pekahiah's enthronement. The assassination of Pekahiah may have been stimulated by the tribute which his father Menahem paid to the Assyrians.

(5) Pekah (15:27-31)

27 In the fifty-second year of Azariah king of Judah Pekah the son of Remaliah began to reign over Israel in Samaria, and reigned twenty years. 28 And he did what was evil in the sight of the LORD; he did not depart from the sins of Jeroboam the son of Nebat, which he made Israel to sin.
29 In the days of Pekah king of Israel Tiglathpileser king of Assyria came and captured Ijon, Abelbethmaacah, Janoah, Kedesh, Hazor, Gilead, and Galilee, all the land of Naphtali; and he carried the people captive to Assyria. 30 Then Hoshea the son of Elah made a conspiracy against Pekah the son of Remaliah, and struck him down, and slew him, and reigned in his stead, in the twentieth year of Jotham the son of Uzziah. 31 Now the rest of the acts of Pekah, and all that he did, behold, they are written in the Book of the Chronicles of the Kings of Israel.

When Pekahiah's officer, the son of Remaliah, usurped the throne he may well have taken the throne name Pekah (Bright, p. 254). Ascription of *twenty years* to the reign of Pekah is the first of several notable chronological problems associated with the eighth century, and some scholars substitute five years while others suggest two years for the reign of Pekah.[4]

Prior to the invasion of Tiglathpileser, Pekah and Rezin of Damascus sought to form an anti-Assyrian coalition with Judah,

and when this failed they attacked Judah (cf. 15:37). This crisis forms the background of the "Immanuel" passage of Isaiah 7:1 ff.

The fact that the Assyrians, according to the annals of Tiglathpileser III, "placed Hoshea as king over them" suggests that the conspiracy against Pekah was probably part of a pro-Assyrian revolt by Hoshea.

4. Two Judean Kings (15:32—16:20)

Against the background of intrigue and revolution which characterized Israel during the middle and latter eighth century, the stability of Judah stands in marked contrast.

(1) Jotham (15:32-38)

32 In the second year of Pekah the son of Remaliah, king of Israel, Jotham the son of Uzziah, king of Judah, began to reign. 33 He was twenty-five years old when he began to reign, and he reigned sixteen years in Jerusalem. His mother's name was Jerusha the daughter of Zadok. 34 And he did what was right in the eyes of the LORD, according to all that his father Uzziah had done. 35 Nevertheless the high places were not removed; the people still sacrificed and burned incense on the high places. He built the upper gate of the house of the LORD. 36 Now the rest of the acts of Jotham, and all that he did, are they not written in the Book of the Chronicles of the Kings of Judah? 37 In those days the LORD began to send Rezin the king of Syria and Pekah the son of Remaliah against Judah. 38 Jotham slept with his fathers, and was buried with his fathers in the city of David his father; and Ahaz his son reigned in his stead.

The suggestion that Jotham ("Yahweh is complete," i.e., "perfect") reigned 16 years should be counterbalanced by the realization that he was co-regent with his father Azariah, or Uzziah (15:5), a period extending from about 750–742 B.C. Except for references to building operations (cf. Jer. 20:2; Ezek. 8:3; 9:2), little of Jotham's biography is recorded in Kings.

(2) Ahaz (16:1-20)

Concern for the reign of Ahaz revolves principally around his involvements with Tiglathpileser III, his imitation of Assyrian

---

[4] A full consideration of this problem cannot be entered upon here, and those concerned about the reconciliation of chronological problems related to this and other texts might well consult Edwin R. Thiele, *The Mysterious Numbers of the Hebrew Kings* (Chicago: University of Chicago Press, 1951).

cultic objects, and the pillaging of Temple environs.

¹ In the seventeenth year of Pekah the son of Remaliah, Ahaz the son of Jotham, king of Judah, began to reign. ² Ahaz was twenty years old when he began to reign, and he reigned sixteen years in Jerusalem. And he did not do what was right in the eyes of the LORD his God, as his father David had done, ³ but he walked in the way of the kings of Israel. He even burned his son as an offering, according to the abominable practices of the nations whom the LORD drove out before the people of Israel. ⁴ And he sacrificed and burned incense on the high places, and on the hills, and under every green tree.

The evaluation of Ahaz (vv. 1–4). *He walked in the way of the kings of Israel* is a reference to the nature cults of Canaan, especially those associated with the baalim (cf. 2 Chron. 28:2 ff.). Ahaz's most heinous crime, however, was the reintroduction of the ancient practice of child sacrifice (cf., 2 Chron. 28:3). Probably the desperation of his situation, analogous to that of Mesha of Moab (3:27), precipitated this action.

⁵ Then Rezin king of Syria and Pekah the son of Remaliah, king of Israel, came up to wage war on Jerusalem, and they besieged Ahaz but could not conquer him. ⁶ At that time the king of Edom recovered Elath for Edom, and drove the men of Judah from Elath; and the Edomites came to Elath, where they dwell to this day. ⁷ So Ahaz sent messengers to Tiglathpileser king of Assyria, saying, "I am your servant and your son. Come up, and rescue me from the hand of the king of Syria and from the hand of the king of Israel, who are attacking me." ⁸ Ahaz also took the silver and gold that was found in the house of the LORD and in the treasures of the king's house, and sent a present to the king of Assyria. ⁹ And the king of Assyria hearkened to him; the king of Assyria marched up against Damascus, and took it, carrying its people captive to Kir, and he killed Rezin.

Capitulation to Assyria (vv. 5–9). Anticipating the impending advance of Assyria, Pekah and Rezin sought an anti-Assyrian coalition with Judah (although this is not stated precisely it is clearly implied). Judah's refusal led to the Syro-Ephraimitic war of 734–733 B.C. (cf. 2 Chron. 28:8–15; Isa. 7:1 ff.) and the temptation to appeal to Assyria for help. Although Isaiah strongly counseled dependence upon the Lord (cf. Isa. 7:3 ff.), Ahaz sought aid from Tiglathpileser III and stripped the Temple in order to finance that overture (v. 8 f.).

¹⁰ When King Ahaz went to Damascus to meet Tiglathpileser king of Assyria, he saw the altar that was at Damascus. And King Ahaz sent to Uriah the priest a model of the altar, and its pattern, exact in all its details. ¹¹ And Uriah the priest built the altar; in accordance with all that King Ahaz had sent from Damascus, so Uriah the priest made it, before King Ahaz arrived from Damascus. ¹² And when the king came from Damascus, the king viewed the altar. Then the king drew near to the altar, and went up on it, ¹³ and burned his burnt offering and his cereal offering, and poured his drink offering, and threw the blood of his peace offerings upon the altar. ¹⁴ And the bronze altar which was before the LORD he removed from the front of the house, from the place between his altar and the house of the LORD, and put it on the north side of his altar. ¹⁵ And King Ahaz commanded Uriah the priest, saying, "Upon the great altar burn the morning burnt offering, and the evening cereal offering, and the king's burnt offering, and his cereal offering, with the burnt offering of all the people of the land, and their cereal offering, and their drink offering; and throw upon it all the blood of the burnt offering, and all the blood of the sacrifice; but the bronze altar shall be for me to inquire by." ¹⁶ Uriah the priest did all this, as King Ahaz commanded.

Removal of the alter (vv. 10–16). The substitution of an Assyrian altar which Ahaz had seen in Damascus for the traditional bronze altar which stood before the Temple was a symbol of allegiance to Assyria, not merely the reflection of an architectural fancy by Ahaz.

¹⁷ And King Ahaz cut off the frames of the stands, and removed the laver from them, and he took down the sea from off the bronze oxen that were under it, and put it upon a pediment of stone. ¹⁸ And the covered way for the sabbath which had been built inside the palace, and the outer entrance for the king he removed from the house of the LORD, because of the king of Assyria. ¹⁹ Now the rest of the acts of Ahaz which he did, are they not written in the Book of the Chronicles of the Kings of Judah? ²⁰ And Ahaz slept with his fathers, and was buried with his fathers in the city of David; and Hezekiah his son reigned in his stead.

Pillaging the Temple (vv. 17–20). *Frames of the stands* refers to the wheeled stands (cf. 1 Kings 7:27 ff.) which were ornately carved and probably of great value, as were the basins within them, and the bronze oxen on which the laver stood (1 Kings 7:25). All these were removed from the Temple environs, probably as tribute for the Assyrian alliance.

The *covered way* is a difficult phrase. It is variously translated as "dais for the throne" (*The Jerusalem Bible*) and *covered way for the sabbath* (RSV, ASV). The key to the translation is the Hebrew *myysak*, which is an unknown word. Hence, some follow the Septuagint (*themelion tēs kathedras*) and read "foundation of the seat."

It seems preferable to follow this Septuagint translation. The "foundation of the seat" may have been constructed of valuable metal which was removed as tribute for the king of Assyria (which is consonant in view of the concern of preceding verses for tribute). More likely, however, is the possibility that the foundation constituted a special position of significance and honor for the Judean king which would have been an offence to the Assyrian king (cf. "the dais for the throne," in *The Jerusalem Bible*). This conclusion is supported by the fact that the king did stand at a designated spot when assuming the crown (cf. 11:14) or when making official decrees (cf. Josiah in 23:3).

5. Hoshea, Last King of Israel (17:1-6)

¹ In the twelfth year of Ahaz king of Judah Hoshea the son of Elah began to reign in Samaria over Israel, and he reigned nine years. ² And he did what was evil in the sight of the LORD, yet not as the kings of Israel who were before him. ³ Against him came up Shalmaneser king of Assyria; and Hoshea became his vassal, and paid him tribute. ⁴ But the king of Assyria found treachery in Hoshea; for he had sent messengers to So, king of Egypt, and offered no tribute to the king of Assyria, as he had done year by year; therefore the king of Assyria shut him up, and bound him in prison. ⁵ Then the king of Assyria invaded all the land and came to Samaria, and for three years he besieged it. ⁶ In the ninth year of Hoshea the king of Assyria captured Samaria, and he carried the Israelites away to Assyria, and placed them in Halah, and on the Habor, the river of Gozan, and in the cities of the Medes.

Hoshea ("Yahweh saves") came to the throne through his assassination of Pekah (15:30). Assyrians records, however, specifically state that Tiglathpileser III placed him on the throne: "Pekah their king they deposed and Hoshea I set [as king] over them" (Nimrud Tablet, in Thomas, p. 55). This suggests that the Hoshea revolt was related to a pro-Assyrian party which would have supported the Menahem dynasty and concurrently would have opposed the usurpation of Pekahiah by Pekah (cf. 15:25 ff.).

Shalmaneser is Shalmaneser V (727–722 B.C.), son of Tiglathpileser III. He besieged Samaria as a consequence of the Israelite overture toward Egypt. The siege may have lasted for three years, but Shalmaneser V most likely died during the course of the siege. He was succeeded by his brother Sargon II (722–705 B.C.). From the Assyrian Eponym List, the three years which he besieged Samaria for failing to pay tribute to Assyria would have been 725–723 B.C. (cf. Wiseman, p. 58).

Reference to *the king of Assyria* may be taken as ascribing the fall of Samaria to Shalmaneser V. Sargon II (722–705 B.C.), however, claims to have conquered Samaria in his accession year. His annal gives a vivid picture of the event.

At the beginning [of my rule . . . the city of the Sa]marians I [besieged and conquered . . .] who let me achieve victory . . . carried off prisoner [27,290 of the people who dwelt in it; from among them I equipped 50 chariots for my royal army units . . . the city of Samaria] I restored and made it more habitable than before. [I brought into it] people of the countries conquered by my own hands. [My official I set over them as district-governor and] imposed upon them tribute as on an Assyrian (city) . . . I made to mix with each other; the market price . . . (cf. Annals, 10–18; in Thomas, p. 59. Lacunae, marked by brackets, can be supplied from other sources such as the "Display Inscription" or the "Nimrud Prism," IV, 25–41).

Sargon's victory could have involved joint participation in the capture of the city or, as Gray presupposes, could mean that Sargon, brother of Shalmaneser, captured Samaria prior to ascending to the throne as his brother's successor.

III. The Fall and Subsequent Resettlement of Israel: a Later Appraisal (17:7–41)

The thesis that the books of Kings reached their present form essentially under the hands of two Deuteronomic editors, one living during the seventh century and the other in the mid-sixth century (cf. Weiser, pp. 170 ff., but especially p. 179; Georg Fohrer, pp. 227 ff.) is clearly reflected in the structure and character of vv. 7–41.

1. A Deuteronomic Appraisal of the Disintegration of the Northern Kingdom (17:7–23)

From the perspective of the Deuteronomic theology with its insistence upon the divine control of history, but especially the principle of sin and retribution within the framework of historical events, the fall of Samaria was interpreted as the result of divine judgment upon Israel for a succession of sins as old as the Exodus-Conquest era and as recent as the action of Sargon II.

(1) A Theological Interpretation of Israel's Salvation History (17:7–18)

⁷ And this was so, because the people of Israel had sinned against the LORD their God, who had brought them up out of the land of Egypt from under the hand of Pharaoh king of Egypt, and had feared other gods ⁸ and walked in the customs of the nations whom the LORD drove out before the people of Israel, and in the customs which the kings of Israel had introduced. ⁹ And the people of Israel did secretly against the LORD their God things that were not right. They built for themselves high places at all their towns, from watch tower to fortified city; ¹⁰ they set up for themselves pillars and Asherim on every high hill and under every green tree; ¹¹ and there they burned incense on all the high places, as the nations did whom the LORD carried away before them. And they did wicked things, provoking the LORD to anger, ¹² and they served idols, of which the LORD had said to them, "You shall not do this." ¹³ Yet the LORD warned Israel and Judah by every prophet and every seer, saying, "Turn from your evil ways and keep my commandments and my statutes, in accordance with all the law which I commanded your fathers, and which I sent to you by my servants the prophets." ¹⁴ But they would not listen, but were stubborn, as their fathers had been, who did not believe in the LORD their God. ¹⁵ They despised his statutes, and his covenant that he made with their fathers, and the warnings which he gave them. They went after false idols, and became false, and they followed the nations that were round about them, concerning whom the LORD had commanded them that they should not do like them. ¹⁶ And they forsook all the commandments of the LORD their God, and made for themselves molten images of two calves; and they made an Asherah, and worshiped all the host of heaven, and served Baal. ¹⁷ And they burned their sons and their daughters as offerings, and used divination and sorcery, and sold themselves to do evil in the sight of the LORD, provoking him to anger. ¹⁸ Therefore the LORD was very angry with Israel, and removed them out of his sight; none was left but the tribe of Judah only.

In a recital of Yahweh's action which is closely related in spirit to the creedal affirmations (Deut. 26:5 ff.), the prefatory appeal in the commandments (Ex. 20:1), or the recapitulative narratives on Yahweh's leadership of Israel (Josh. 24:1 ff.; Neh. 9:1 ff.), the writer appeals to Israel's salvation history (v. 7) and illustrates the irresponsible attitude of Israel toward that redemptive experience.

The "fear" of the Lord is the nearest synonym for religion in the Old Testament, yet here fear is given to other gods (a violation of the First Commandment). The conception of religion as fear arises out of the feeling of dread, awfulness, or otherness, fascination which arises in the presence of the holy.

Customs (*chuq*) is the same word translated *statutes* in v. 15. It is variously used within the remainder of the Old Testament as an enactment, decree, or ordinance of either God or man (cf. Ex. 12:24; 15:25; Isa. 24:5) or civil enactments prescribed by God (Ex. 18:16). The contrast between the statutes of Yahweh and the customs of the people is the measure of Israel's apostasy (later *chuq* is used of Israel's customs, after which Israel walked, cf. 17:19).

Despite such conduct by the people, however, the Lord was faithful to the covenant and sent prophets who sought to call men to the covenant life. Yet, *"they would not listen"* is a phrase which is reminiscent of the stubbornness of Israel in the wilderness.

(2) *The Subsequent Disintegration of Judah (17:19-20)*

19 Judah also did not keep the commandments of the LORD their God, but walked in the customs which Israel had introduced. 20 And the LORD rejected all the descendants of Israel, and afflicted them, and gave them into the hand of spoilers, until he had cast them out of his sight.

An editor living after the fall of Jerusalem, probably of the Deuteronomic school, has evaluated Judah's experience in the light of Israel's debacle. His brief insertion into the narrative underscores the continuing validity of the Deuteronomic theology: National sin inevitably brings national retribution.

(3) *The Continued Rejection of Jeroboam I (17:21-23)*

21 When he had torn Israel from the house of David they made Jeroboam the son of Nebat king. And Jeroboam drove Israel from following the LORD and made them commit great sin. 22 The people of Israel walked in all the sins which Jeroboam did; they did not depart from them, 23 until the LORD removed Israel out of his sight, as he had spoken by all his servants the prophets. So Israel was exiled from their own land to Assyria until this day.

In words which echo the stereotyped condemnation of successive Israelite kings, *He did not depart from all the sins of Jeroboam the son of Nebat* (15:18, *et al.*), the Deuteronomic editor returns to the fall of Samaria. This occurred, he insists, because the people did not repudiate the ways of Jeroboam: a fitting conclusion to the editor's treatment of the fall of Samaria.

2. *A Priestly View of the Resettlement (17:24-41)*

Although the final shaping of this passage came from the Deuteronomic school following the Exile, the narrative(s) gives every evidence of priestly characteristics. For example, this is present in the role of the priest in vv. 24-28, the continuing concern for worship, the altars, and those who serve as priests (vv. 29-34*a*, although the Deuteronomists were equally concerned with the site of worship). Reflected throughout the narrative is the post-exilic problem of the Samaritans, the descendants of those who were resettled in Israel (cf. 17:6).

(1) *The Contribution of Priestly Leadership: Teaching the Law of God (17:24-28)*

24 And the king of Assyria brought people from Babylon, Cuthah, Avva, Hamath, and Sepharvaim, and placed them in the cities of Samaria instead of the people of Israel; and they took possession of Samaria, and dwelt in its cities. 25 And at the beginning of their dwelling there, they did not fear the LORD; therefore the LORD sent lions among them, which killed some of them. 26 So the king of Assyria was told, "The nations which you have carried away and placed in the cities of Samaria do not know the law of the god of the land; therefore he has sent lions among them, and behold, they are killing them, because they do not know the law of the god of the land." 27 Then the king of Assyria commanded, "Send there one of the priests whom you carried away thence; and let him go and dwell there, and teach them the law of the god of the land." 28 So one of the priests whom they had carried away from Samaria came and dwelt in Bethel, and taught them how they should fear the LORD.

The physical crisis which befell the settlers of Israel was interpreted according to the ancient belief that each land had its own god. Consequently, if the settlers are to live peaceably in the land they must have knowledge of Yahweh. To this end a priest of Israel is dispatched to Samaria in order to *teach them the law of the god of the land*. Although this narrative reflects the early view which directly associates

Yahweh with the land and ascribes all action to the Lord (cf. Amos 4:6 ff.; Ex. 21:12-14), it positively emphasizes the Israelite conviction that Yahweh of Israel must be feared (worshiped) before all others (cf. Ex. 20:3). Also of primary concern is the positive function of the teaching priest. This concern for the priest marks this passage as priestly in ultimate origin.

(2) The Necessity for Purity of Worship (17:29-34a)

29 But every nation still made gods of its own, and put them in the shrines of the high places which the Samaritans had made, every nation in the cities in which they dwelt; 30 the men of Babylon made Succothbenoth, the men of Cuth made Nergal, the men of Hamath made Ashima, 31 and the Avvites made Nibhaz and Tartak; and the Sepharvites burned their children in the fire to Adrammelech and Anammelech, the gods of Sepharvaim. 32 They also feared the LORD, and appointed from among themselves all sorts of people as priests of the high places, who sacrificed for them in the shrines of the high places. 33 So they feared the LORD but also served their own gods, after the manner of the nations from among whom they had been carried away. 34 To this day they do according to the former manner.

Samaritans does not necessarily mark this passage as postexilic in origin, although it probably is, for Assyrian records consistently speak of Samaria during this period of time.[5]

The editor continues to stress the corrupt nature of religion among the Samaritans by his attention to the fact that they *feared* Yahweh while serving their own gods (vv. 32-33). Other specific breaches are culminated by the observation *to this day they do according to the former manner.* Although dating the narrative on the basis of v. 34 is impossible, the general tenor does suggest a period of time considerably removed from the events; and one is probably correct in positing a date when the Samaritan problem of the postexilic era had emerged (although v. 24 could well be a late editorial insertion).

[5] Cf. "Nimrud Prism," Display Inscription *Annals*, 23-57.

(3) Failure to Respond to the Lord's Instruction (17:34b-40)

They do not fear the LORD, and they do not follow the statutes or the ordinances or the law or the commandment which the LORD commanded the children of Jacob, whom he named Israel. 35 The LORD made a covenant with them, and commanded them, "You shall not fear other gods or bow yourselves to them or serve them or sacrifice to them; 36 but you shall fear the LORD, who brought you out of the land of Egypt with great power and with an outstretched arm; you shall bow yourselves to him, and to him you shall sacrifice. 37 And the statutes and the ordinances and the law and the commandment which he wrote for you, you shall always be careful to do. You shall not fear other gods, 38 and you shall not forget the covenant that I have made with you. You shall not fear other gods, 39 but you shall fear the LORD your God, and he will deliver you out of the hand of all your enemies." 40 However they would not listen, but they did according to their former manner.

At this juncture the writer returns to the manner in which Israel repudiated divine revelation, and the contents of vv. 34b-40 are hardly appropriate to the Samaritan settlers. The Lord made no covenant with the settlers, nor are they descendants of Jacob; the Lord did not write the law and commandments for them, nor did he bring them out of Egypt. The passage should clearly be read in connection with vv. 7-18. Verses 34b-40 make no essential advance upon the thought within the earlier passage, and are doubtless a parallel account which developed independently from vv. 7-18. The passage is appropriately included within a different literary stratum, having come from the second Deuteronomic editor who wrote in the mid-sixth century.

(4) Samaritan Amalgamation of Yahweh and Other Gods (17:41)

41 So these nations feared the LORD, and also served their graven images; their children likewise, and their children's children—as their fathers did, so they do to this day.

Accustomed to the worship of many gods, the settlers sought to adapt the worship of Yahweh to their own pantheon. The phrase, *as their fathers did, so they do to this day,* is indicative of a late date of composition for the editorial notation.

Part Three
Decades of Renewal and Eventual Destruction: The Kingdom of Judah Alone (18:1—25:30)

Alternating decades of renewal and apostasy marked the path that Judah eventually followed to destruction. The commendable reformations of Hezekiah and Josiah soon gave way to the erosive actions of kings such as Manasseh, Amon, or Jehoiakim. Although the prophets preached a message grounded in the assumption that repentance and renewal could bring restoration, even they finally came to see the inevitability of national destruction. Jeremiah, for example, believed that Judah would not change (Jer. 13:23 ff.), and in view of her obstinacy advised men no longer to pray for her (cf. Jer. 14:11; 15:1).

Not only did spiritual apostasy and moral irresponsibility contribute to national destruction, but the circumstances of international politics as well. Viewed from the perspective of later centuries, the rise of Assyria and Babylon and their continued advances into Syria-Palestine made national stability short-lived and annihilation all but inevitable.

I. Prophetic Renewal: Hezekiah and the Assyrian Crisis (18:1—20:21)

The lengthy space occupied by the narratives associated with the reign of Hezekiah is comparable to that of the Ahab narratives. In both instances the length of the material is shaped by an editorial concern for prophetic figures, and interests which marked the Deuteronomic school.

So much was Isaiah related to the Assyrian crisis that 18:13—19:37 (with minor exception) reappears at the conclusion of proto-Isaiah (cf. Isa. 37). As in the case of the Elijah-Elisha narratives, it is the purpose of the writer to trace prophetic influence upon national affairs. Additionally, the editor is also concerned with the prophetic emphasis upon the inviolability of Zion, the belief that Jerusalem would not fall in the face of enemy attack (1 Kings 19:6 f.), a belief destined to become a doctrine, and a blessing destined to be perverted into a false presumption upon the grace of God (cf. Jer. 7:1 ff.). Also, the editor is concerned to trace the Deuteronomic theology of history as reflected in Judean affairs of state. He is further concerned to illustrate the continued theological relationship between apostasy and adversity, faithfulness and prosperity.

1. Hezekiah's Reformation and Independence (18:1-12)

¹ In the third year of Hoshea son of Elah, king of Israel, Hezekiah the son of Ahaz, king of Judah, began to reign. ² He was twenty-five years old when he began to reign, and he reigned twenty-nine years in Jerusalem. His mother's name was Abi the daughter of Zechariah. ³ And he did what was right in the eyes of the LORD, according to all that David his father had done. ⁴ He removed the high places, and broke the pillars, and cut down the Asherah. And he broke in pieces the bronze serpent that Moses had made, for until those days the people of Israel had burned incense to it; it was called Nehushtan. ⁵ He trusted in the LORD the God of Israel; so that there was none like him among all the kings of Judah after him, nor among those who were before him. ⁶ For he held fast to the LORD; he did not depart from following him, but kept the commandments which the LORD commanded Moses. ⁷ And the LORD was with him; wherever he went forth, he prospered. He rebelled against the king of Assyria, and would not serve him. ⁸ He smote the Philistines as far as Gaza and its territory, from watchtower to fortified city.

⁹ In the fourth year of King Hezekiah, which was the seventh year of Hoshea son of Elah, king of Israel, Shalmaneser king of Assyria came up against Samaria and besieged it ¹⁰ and at the end of three years he took it. In the sixth year of Hezekiah, which was the ninth year of Hoshea king of Israel, Samaria was taken. ¹¹ The king of Assyria carried the Israelites away to Assyria, and put them in Halah, and on the Habor, the river of Gozan, and in the cities of the Medes, ¹² because they did not obey the voice of the LORD their God but transgressed his covenant, even all that Moses the servant of the LORD commanded; they neither listened nor obeyed.

Placing Hezekiah's accession in the **third year of Hoshea** reflects a most difficult problem associated with the synchronistic dating used in Kings. Thiele's statement of one facet of the problem is suggestive for the complexity and confusion characteristic of the entire issue of the synchronistic chronology in Kings. Ahaz came to the throne at twenty years of age (16:2; 2 Chron. 28:1), in the seventeenth year of Pekah (16:1). Thus, Ahaz was 20 years of age in Pekah's seventeenth year. Pekah was on the throne 20 years (15:27), which would make Ahaz 23 at the time Pekah terminated his reign. Pekah was slain and succeeded by Hoshea (15:30). According to the present passage Hezekiah began to reign in the third year of Hoshea (18:1). By that time Ahaz would have been 26. Hezekiah was 25 when he began to reign (18:2; 2 Chron. 29:1). As Thiele concludes, in what is an understatement, "Obviously something is here seriously wrong, for certainly a child of one year could not be a father" (Thiele, p. 104). He resolves this by moving the reigns of Pekah and Hoshea earlier in relation to the reign of Hezekiah than is called for in v. 1—a problem into which we cannot enter here (cf. Thiele, pp. 105 ff.; 136 ff.).

The name **Nehushtan** suggests the word serpent (*nachash*) but is more directly related to *n^echushah*, bronze. The similarity is doubtless a deliberate play on words. That the figure was a violation of the Second Commandment is both obvious and adequate grounds for purging it from cultic life.

Trust is the common word (*batach*) for reliance upon God (cf. 19:10; Psalm 9:10; 21:7; 22:5–6; Isa. 26:3–4), but is also used of human relationships (Judg. 9:26; Psalm 41:9; Jer. 17:5; Micah 7:5), and of reliance upon things, which is often condemned (cf. Amos 6:1; Hos. 10: 13; Ezek. 16:15).

That Hezekiah **held fast** (*dabaq*) to the Lord meant for him to cleave or keep close (*dabaq*) to the Lord in loyalty; he also **kept the commandments** of the Lord with fidelity.

The statement that Hezekiah **rebelled** accurately describes both the political situation and the religious reform. The unrest occasioned by the death of Sargon II and the early years of Sennacherib led to a general rebellion, and the religious reformation was directly related thereto. Religious and political commitments were closely intertwined, and conquered nations were required to make concessions if not to adopt the religion of the conquering power.

Reference to having smitten the Philistines (v. 8) is confirmed in Sennacherib's statement, "I caused Padi, their king [i.e. of Ekron], to come out of Jerusalem and sat him on the throne." [6]

2. The Isaiah Tradition (18:13—20:19)

Much like the Elijah-Elisha episodes in the narratives concerned with the Omride dynasty, the present narratives focus in the prophetic activity of a unique and creative person, the prophet Isaiah. Except for the historical summary of vv. 14–16, the larger collection is composed primarily of those prophetic traditions which gathered around the Assyrian crisis and the role that Isaiah played in it.

(1) The Sennacherib Crisis (18:13—19:37)

One of the most vexing problems of the book of 2 Kings, indeed, of the whole fabric of Old Testament history, emerges in the Sennacherib crisis and the interrelationships of the several narratives now interwoven in 18:13—19:37 (cf. Isa. 36—37; 2 Chron. 32). The fundamental question concerns whether there was a single or a double invasion by Sennacherib.

Although a majority of scholars maintain the option of a double invasion, a scholar so competent and thorough as H. H. Rowley argues strongly for the single invasion. In a more recent publication than Rowley's, E. W. Heaton concludes that on the

---

[6] "Taylor Prism," British Museum No. 91032.

basis of present knowledge it is difficult to decide, but that the divergence of the double invasion theory from both Assyrian annals and authentic records of Isaiah argue strongly for the validity of the view that 18:13–16 is a bare and factual summary of the invasion, and that 18:17—19:8 must be placed prior to the payment of tribute. The single invasion is accepted as a working hypothesis for this study.

a. Hezekiah's Capitulation to Sennacherib (18:13–18)

13 In the fourteenth year of King Hezekiah Sennacherib king of Assyria came up against all the fortified cities of Judah and took them. 14 And Hezekiah king of Judah sent to the king of Assyria at Lachish, saying, "I have done wrong; withdraw from me; whatever you impose on me I will bear." And the king of Assyria required of Hezekiah king of Judah three hundred talents of silver and thirty talents of gold. 15 And Hezekiah gave him all the silver that was found in the house of the LORD, and in the treasuries of the king's house. 16 At that time Hezekiah stripped the gold from the doors of the temple of the LORD, and from the doorposts which Hezekiah king of Judah had overlaid and gave it to the king of Assyria. 17 And the king of Assyria sent the Tartan, the Rabsaris, and the Rabshakeh with a great army from Lachish to King Hezekiah at Jerusalem. And they went up and came to Jerusalem. When they arrived, they came and stood by the conduit of the upper pool, which is on the highway to the Fuller's Field. 18 And when they called for the king, there came out to them Eliakim the son of Hilkiah, who was over the household, and Shebnah the secretary, and Joah the son of Asaph, the recorder.

Verses 14b–16—which strictly relate to this capitulation—are drawn from an annalistic source describing the capitulation of Hezekiah and his attendant effort to appease Sennacherib through the payment of tribute. This narrative is generally accepted as the condensed version of the 701 B.C. crisis.

The presence of Sennacherib at *Lachish* is graphically confirmed by a wall relief on his royal palace at Nineveh in which he is portrayed sitting on the throne in his camp outside Lachish. Above the bas-relief of the king is the inscription, "Sennacherib, king of all, king of Assyria, sitting on his *nimedu*-throne while the spoil of the city of Lachish passed before him" (Wiseman, in Thomas, referring to British Museum Relief No. 124911).

Tartan (*tarten*) is a loan word meaning field marshal or commander in chief (cf. Isa. 20:1) and is used for the Assyrian general in command. *Rabsaris* (*rab-saris*, i.e., chief eunuch, may mean "he who stands by [the king]"). *Rabshakeh* (*rab-shaqeh*) designated the chief cupbearer, who was a court official of high rank (cf. Nehemiah), and often in charge of administrative affairs (cf. IDB).

b. A Unique Confidence in the Face of Adversity (18:19—19:37)

It is widely agreed that 2 Kings 18:17—19:37 contains two parallel accounts of the same event, the Sennacherib crisis, whether a single crisis of 701 B.C. or a double crisis of that year, and an additional invasion 15 or 20 years later. The interrelationship of the two narratives is graphically depicted by the following analysis drawn from Fohrer.

Sennacherib demands capitulation	18:13, 17–37	....19:9b–13
Hezekiah's reaction	19:1–5	....19:14–19
Isaiah's promise	19:6,7	....19:20–34
Retreat of the Assyrians	19:8–9a, 36–37	....19:34

This analysis of the text, more than the sequence of the RSV, should be kept in mind as a better basis of understanding the complications of this entire section.

19 And the Rabshakeh said to them, "Say to Hezekiah, 'Thus says the great king, the king of Assyria: On what do you rest this confidence of yours? 20 Do you think that mere words are strategy and power for war? On whom do you now rely, that you have rebelled against me? 21 Behold, you are relying now on Egypt, that broken reed of a staff, which will pierce the hand of any man who leans on it. Such is Pharaoh king of Egypt to all who rely on him. 22 But if you say to me, "We rely on the LORD

our God," is it not he whose high places and altars Hezekiah has removed, saying to Judah and to Jerusalem, "You shall worship before this altar in Jerusalem"? 23 Come now, make a wager with my master the king of Assyria: I will give you two thousand horses, if you are able on your part to set riders upon them. 24 How then can you repulse a single captain among the least of my master's servants, when you rely on Egypt for chariots and for horsemen? 25 Moreover, is it without the LORD that I have come up against this place to destroy it? The LORD said to me, Go up against this land, and destroy it.' "

26 Then Eliakim the son of Hilkiah, and Shebnah, and Joah, said to the Rabshakeh, "Pray, speak to your servants in the Aramaic language, for we understand it; do not speak to us in the language of Judah within the hearing of the people who are on the wall." 27 But the Rabshakeh said to them, "Has my master sent me to speak these words to your master and to you, and not to the men sitting on the wall, who are doomed with you to eat their own dung and to drink their own urine?"

28 Then the Rabshakeh stood and called out in a loud voice in the language of Judah: "Hear the word of the great king, the king of Assyria! 29 Thus says the king: 'Do not let Hezekiah deceive you, for he will not be able to deliver you out of my hand. 30 Do not let Hezekiah make you to rely on the LORD by saying, The LORD will surely deliver us, and this city will not be given into the hand of the king of Assyria.' 31 Do not listen to Hezekiah; for thus says the king of Assyria: 'Make your peace with me and come out to me; then every one of you will eat of his own vine, and every one of his own fig tree, and every one of you will drink the water of his own cistern; 32 until I come and take you away to a land like your own land, a land of grain and wine, a land of bread and vineyards, a land of olive trees and honey, that you may live, and not die. And do not listen to Hezekiah when he misleads you by saying, The LORD will deliver us. 33 Has any of the gods of the nations ever delivered his land out of the hand of the king of Assyria? 34 Where are the gods of Hamath and Arpad? Where are the gods of Sepharvaim, Hena, and Ivvah? Have they delivered Samaria out of my hand? 35 Who among all the gods of the countries have delivered their countries out of my hand, that the LORD should deliver Jerusalem out of my hand?' "

36 But the people were silent and answered him not a word, for the king's command was, "Do not answer him." 37 Then Eliakim the son of Hilkiah, who was over the household, and Shebna the secretary, and Joah the son of Asaph, the recorder, came to Hezekiah with their clothes rent, and told him the words of the Rabshakeh.

Demand for capitulation (18:19–37). The futility of resistance (vv. 19-25) is declared by Sennacherib's representative: (1) Egypt is unable to deliver and will prove to be like a broken reed, suggesting the inevitable fate of those who depend upon such an alliance. (2) The removal of the high places has separated the people from the availability of divine power. (3) The inherent weakness of Judah, epitomized in her inability to provide chariots (or even cavalrymen) even should Assyria provide her with horses, meant that Judah could not repulse a single contingent of Assyrian chariotry or cavalry. The king of Assyria's claim that Yahweh had also spoken to him arose from the practice of consulting the gods of new lands once one entered the land of the god.

Political expedience (vv. 26–27) was the basis of a further appeal for capitulation, an effort to break the morale of the people.

Sennacherib's statement is clarified by the following inscription: "But as for Hezekiah, the Jew, who did not bow in submission . . . He himself I shut up like a caged bird within Jerusalem, his royal city. I put watchposts strictly around it and turned back to his disaster any one who went out of its city gate." [7] For all practical purposes, Jerusalem was under siege. The Assyrian (vv. 28–35) warned—really persuaded by threats—against believing that Hezekiah could deliver them or that the Lord could help them, against overlooking the power of the Assyrian to help them, and against believing that the Lord would deliver them. Cities so recently captured by Sennacherib found that their gods could not deliver them. The dependability of God is the crux of the entire appeal for capitulation. Can man trust God?

Although no vocal response to the Assyrian proposal is indicated, it clearly was the editor's purpose to suggest (vv. 36–37)

[7] "Taylor Prism," British Museum No. 91032.

that the silence which met those proposals was, in effect, a distinct repudiation.

¹ When King Hezekiah heard it, he rent his clothes, and covered himself with sackcloth, and went into the house of the Lord. ² And he sent Eliakim, who was over the household, and Shebna the secretary, and the senior priests, covered with sackcloth, to the prophet Isaiah the son of Amoz. ³ They said to him, "Thus says Hezekiah, This day is a day of distress, of rebuke, and of disgrace; children have come to the birth, and there is no strength to bring them forth. ⁴ It may be that the Lord your God heard all the words of the Rabshakeh, whom his master the king of Assyria has sent to mock the living God, and will rebuke the words which the Lord your God has heard; therefore lift up your prayer for the remnant that is left." ⁵ When the servants of King Hezekiah came to Isaiah,

Hezekiah's reaction (19:1-5). Having presented himself to the Lord, however, the king immediately sent a delegation to Isaiah; apparently for a prophetic oracle. Hezekiah's message concerned (1) the nature of the day: one of distress, rebuke, disgrace, and weakness, (2) a suggestion, which is an actual request, that the Lord might both hear and rebuke the words of scorn addressed to him, and (3) the entreaty that Isaiah pray for the remnant.

⁶ Isaiah said to them, "Say to your master, 'Thus says the Lord: Do not be afraid because of the words that you have heard, with which the servants of the king of Assyria have reviled me. ⁷ Behold, I will put a spirit in him, so that he shall hear a rumor and return to his own land; and I will cause him to fall by the sword in his own land.' "

Isaiah's promise (19:6-7). Because the words were addressed against the Lord (*words . . . with which the servants of the king of Assyria have reviled me,*), the Lord has already set in motion the king's judgment. This takes the form of two historical events: (1) a *rumor* which will cause Sennacherib to return to his own land, and (2) he will be killed by violence in his own country. The use of *spirit* is an illustration of the manner in which the purposes of Yahweh were thought to have been fulfilled by a spirit other than God's Spirit (cf. the "evil spirit from the Lord" used to express Saul's strange action, 1 Sam. 16:14). Inexplicable actions were often ascribed to one's possession by a spirit, whether good or evil.

⁸ The Rabshakeh returned, and found the king of Assyria fighting against Libnah; for he heard that the king had left Lachish. ⁹ And when the king heard concerning Tirhakah king of Ethiopia, "Behold, he has set out to fight against you,"

Retreat of the Assyrian (19:8-9a). The view taken here is that vv. 36-37 are to be properly considered as a sequence to vv. 8-9a. The withdrawal of the Assyrians, according to this summary (cf. vv. 8,37), took place solely because of the word (which was probably true) of an insurrection at home; probably an internal palace revolt. The insurrection itself ultimately led to Sennacherib's death (v. 36), a fact borne out by the Babylonian Chronicle: "Sennacherib king of Assyria departed, and went and returned, and dwelt at Nineveh. And it came to pass, as he was worshipping in the house of Nisroch his god, that Adrammelech and Sharezer *his sons* smote him with the sword: and they escaped into the land of Ararat. And Esarhaddon his son reigned in his stead" (Wiseman, p. 70).

he sent messengers again to Hezekiah, saying, ¹⁰ "Thus shall you speak to Hezekiah king of Judah: 'Do not let your God on whom you rely deceive you by promising that Jerusalem will not be given into the hand of the king of Assyria. ¹¹ Behold, you have heard what the kings of Assyria have done to all lands, destroying them utterly. And shall you be delivered? ¹² Have the gods of the nations delivered them, the nations which my fathers destroyed, Gozan, Haran, Rezeph, and the people of Eden who were in Telassar? ¹³ Where is the king of Hamath, the king of Arpad, the king of the city of Sepharvaim, the king of Hena, or the king of Ivvah?'"
¹⁴ Hezekiah received the letter from the hand of the messengers, and read it; and Hezekiah went up to the house of the Lord, and spread it before the Lord. ¹⁵ And Hezekiah prayed before the Lord, and said: "O Lord the God of Israel, who art enthroned above the cherubim, thou art the God, thou alone, of all the kingdoms of the earth; thou hast made heaven and earth. ¹⁶ Incline thy ear, O Lord, and hear; open thy eyes, O Lord, and see; and hear the words of Sennacherib, which he has

sent to mock the living God. 17 Of a truth, O LORD, the kings of Assyria have laid waste the nations and their lands, 18 and have cast their gods into the fire; for they were no gods, but the work of men's hands, wood and stone; therefore they were destroyed. 19 So now, O LORD our God, save us, I beseech thee, from his hand, that all the kingdoms of the earth may know that thou, O LORD, art God alone."

20 Then Isaiah the son of Amoz sent to Hezekiah, saying, "Thus says the LORD, the God of Israel: Your prayer to me about Sennacherib king of Assyria I have heard. 21 This is the word that the LORD has spoken concerning him:

"She despises you, she scorns you—
   the virgin daughter of Zion;
she wags her head behind you—
   the daughter of Jerusalem.

22 "Whom have you mocked and reviled?
   Against whom have you raised your voice
and haughtily lifted your eyes?
   Against the Holy One of Israel!
23 By your messengers you have mocked the Lord,
   and you have said, 'With my many chariots
I have gone up the heights of the mountains,
   to the far recesses of Lebanon;
I felled its tallest cedars,
   its choicest cypresses;
I entered its farthest retreat,
   its densest forest.
24 I dug wells
   and drank foreign waters,
and I dried up with the sole of my foot
   all the streams of Egypt.'

25 "Have you not heard
   that I determined it long ago?
I planned from days of old
   what now I bring to pass,
that you should turn fortified cities
   into heaps of ruins,
26 while their inhabitants, shorn of strength,
   are dismayed and confounded,
and have become like plants of the field,
   and like tender grass,
like grass on the housetops;
   blighted before it is grown?

27 "But I know your sitting down
   and your going out and coming in,
   and your raging against me.
28 Because you have raged against me
   and your arrogance has come into my ears,
I will put my hook in your nose
   and my bit in your mouth,
and I will turn you back on the way
   by which you came.

29 "And this shall be the sign for you: this year you shall eat what grows of itself, and in the second year what springs of the same; then in the third year sow, and reap, and plant vineyards, and eat their fruit. 30 And the surviving remnant of the house of Judah shall again take root downward, and bear fruit upward; 31 for out of Jerusalem shall go forth a remnant, and out of Mount Zion a band of survivors. The zeal of the LORD will do this.

32 "Therefore thus says the LORD concerning the king of Assyria, He shall not come into this city or shoot an arrow there, or come before it with a shield or cast up a siege mound against it. 33 By the way that he came, by the same he shall return, and he shall not come into this city, says the LORD. 34 For I will defend this city to save it, for my own sake and for the sake of my servant David."

35 And that night the angel of the LORD went forth, and slew a hundred and eighty-five thousand in the camp of the Assyrians, and when men arose early in the morning, behold, these were all dead bodies. 36 Then Sennacherib king of Assyria departed, and went home, and dwelt at Nineveh. 37 And as he was worshiping in the house of Nisroch his god, Adrammelech and Sharezer, his sons, slew him with the sword, and escaped into the land of Ararat. And Esarhaddon his son reigned in his stead.

Still later reflections on the Sennacherib crisis (19:9b–37). The present summary is chronologically later than the fixation of the tradition of the crisis of 701 B.C. which appears in 18:13,17—19:9a. Whether this latter evaluation came from priestly circles, as suggested by Gray, is debatable; but that it is a parallel to the account immediately preceding is widely accepted.

As the narrative now stands, the *demand for capitulation* (vv. 9b–13) is a continuation of the previous narrative. The king's rationale for capitulation differs significantly at one point from that of his messenger's: people should not let God *deceive* them by believing that Jerusalem will escape. God is a deceiver, or so Sennacherib suggested. Judah cannot expect to fare better than other nations under their gods.

The *reaction of Hezekiah* in this instance (vv. 14–19) in contrast with the description in 19:1–5 is much more theologically oriented. Here there is no appeal to Isaiah; prayer to the Lord is the sole focus of the king's reaction.

The appeal of Hezekiah is theologically significant, involving the conception of God as: divine king, *enthroned,* sole God of all kingdoms, and creator of heaven and earth. Hezekiah beseeches God that he might open both his eyes and his ears that he might see and *hear the words of Sennacherib,* suggesting the concrete nature of "word." *Dabar* means both word and thing, and the word is often described as so concrete as to be seen.

The *reply of Isaiah* in this section (vv. 20–34) is distinguished from the previous promise (19:6–7) by both length (14 *vs.* 2 verses) and content.

This taunt song on Sennacherib or Assyria's fate (vv. 21–28) seems clearly related to Isaiah's lamentation on Assyria (Isa. 10:5–29), and probably originated within the circle of Isaiah's disciples. Even a cursory examination reveals the parallels between (1) the mission entrusted to Assyria and her past successes in Isaiah 10:5–11 and the self-confident pride in international successes in 2 Kings 19:21–24, and (2) the fate of Assyria as Yahweh turns upon her in Isaiah 10:12–19 and Yahweh's vindictive action, planned so long beforehand, in 2 Kings 19:25–28. The poetic form of vv. 21–28 stands in marked contrast to the prose of 2 Kings and suggests that this lament is an intrusion, either prepared for the occasion or utilized from another source. For the continuation of Isaiah's prophetic word one might well turn from verse 21*a* directly to verses 29 ff.

Reference to the timber of Lebanon (v. 23) is consonant with the Assyrian value placed upon such resources. Not having timbered land of its own, a prime spoil of war was the timber of Lebanon. Esarhaddon, Sennacherib's successor, records the following concerning the spoils of his own victories: "I sent all of these to drag with pain and difficulty to Nineveh, the city of my dominion, as supplies needed for my palace, big beams, long posts and trimmed planks of cedar and cypress wood, products of the Sirara and Lebanon mountains, where for long they had grown tall and thick . . ." (cf. the Assyrian letter, found at Nineveh; British Museum Tablet K. 1295; Wiseman, in Thomas).

Yahweh is now to bring Sennacherib's *raging against me* to an end (vv. 27–28). Emphasis upon the manner in which history reveals the hidden purposes of God is characteristic of the thought of Isaiah of the Exile (cf. 41:21 f., 25 ff.). Yahweh's use of Sennacherib is illustrated by the Isaianic reference to Assyria as a rod or staff in the hand of God (Isa. 10:5 ff.). The same idea is further exhibited in the reference to Cyrus the Persian as "my anointed" (Isa. 45:1), plus the further indication that Yahweh brought about the rise of Cyrus (cf. Isa. 41:2 ff.; 45:1 ff.; 44:28). There is a consistent emphasis from within the Isaianic school of thought upon the Yahwistic use of history, a theological interpretation clearly parallel to the Deuteronomic view of history, and graphically brought together in the combined Isaianic-Deuteronomic theology of 2 Kings 19.

Verses 29–31 declare Isaiah's grounds for a renewal of hope. His specific response to the anxiety of Hezekiah is the assurance concerning the crops in vv. 29–31. Yet this is more than merely a statement on food supply. It is a promise concerning both the termination of the invasion under Sennacherib, and the future possibilities of the people of God. The termination of the invasion is graphically suggested in the statement that although (1) the people must eat *what grows of itself* the first year, no crops being harvested during the invasion, and (2) they must eat the same kind of food the second year, for no crops could be planted during the latter part of the year of the invasion, (3) normal ploughing and sowing could take place during the summer following the crisis, with the result that food gathered from agricultural pursuits could be eaten in the third year.

The doctrine of the inviolability of Jerusalem (vv. 32–34) is also a part of Isaiah's encouragement. The inviolability of Jerusalem is uniquely associated with the prophetic ministry of Isaiah. Since Jerusalem was the city of Yahweh, it was inconceivable that he should allow its destruction. The Isaianic conception began as early as Isaiah's conversations with Ahaz in the Syro-Ephraimitic crisis of *ca.* 734 B.C., and emerges again in the Sennacherib crisis of 701.

By the time of Jeremiah, however, the concept had been perverted into the presumptive and superficial belief that God would protect Jerusalem, whatever happened. Jeremiah clearly emphasized that ethical conduct was not unrelated to the inviolability of Zion (cf. Jer. 7:1 ff.). As with most heresies, which so often originate in the undue emphasis of one facet of truth, the inviolability of Zion began as a doctrine of grace and comfort, but concluded as a perverted and cheapened presumption upon the grace of God—a "cheap grace."

The retreat of the Assyrians (vv. 35–37) closes the account of the Sennacherib crisis.

The sudden death which smote the Assyrian was probably a plague of outrageous proportions. To suggest a plague as the causative factor in v. 35 is but to emphasize that God works through history and the natural order, and not apart from it.

Summary of the interrelationship of 18:14b–16; 18:13,17—19:9a; 19:36–37; and 19:9b–35. The interrelationship of the three passages under consideration is complex, but the following reconstruction appears reasonable. (1) The annalistic record of the Sennacherib crisis stands behind 18:14b–16, and one stands nearer a historical reconstruction of the events here than at any other point. The essential historicity of this passage is clear. (2) At a time subsequent to the historical context of the Sennacherib crisis the historical annal was expanded during the course of its transmission. In the process it developed along the lines of the historical saga associated with Elijah and Elisha. (3) Still later reflection upon the Sennacherib crisis from the perspective of yet another circle of religionists in Judah precipitated the narrative now in 19:9b–35. This narrative developed along the literary lines of the saga-legend associated with the Elisha narratives which appear in the context of the Aramean crises.

The distinct theological emphasis which marks the final reflection on the crisis sets it apart from the earlier consideration of the same event.

First, the Assyrian demand for capitulation (18:13 ff.) stresses Judah's false confidence in Egypt, although both the powerlessness of the gods to oppose Assyria and the previous Assyrian victories are also part of the rationale offered. The later reflection (19:9b ff.) is much more oriented toward God, and the Assyrian messengers accuse God himself of deceiving the people (formerly Hezekiah is so accused).

Second, the former narrative suggests that Hezekiah goes into the house of the Lord, but immediately sends a delegation to call on Isaiah. The later reflection on the crisis makes no mention of sending for Isaiah, and the whole of Hezekiah's action is summarized in a relatively long and theologically significant prayer.

Third, Isaiah's promise is quite brief in the earlier source, consisting of but two verses which promise that Sennacherib will hear the rumor of insurrection and return to his home where he will be killed. The theological concern of the latter account is revealed in the extensive taunt song on Sennacherib (vv. 21–28), and the role of the remnant (vv. 29–31). Deliverance is promised through Yahweh's direct intervention.

Fourth, the retreat of the Assyrians is related to the activity of Tirhakah and the rumor of insurrection, a rumor which leads to Sennacherib's withdrawal (vv. 35 f.) and eventual assassination. But the later reflection represented in 19:9b ff. places much more emphasis upon the miraculous. Deliverance according to this narrative takes place not through insurrection, but through the coming of the angel of the Lord; an action which was probably intended and interpreted quite literally in the biblical era.

The first reflection (18:13,17 ff.) has the marks of saga akin to the Elijah school, while the second reflection (19:9b) is much more characteristic of the Elisha stories.

(2) Hezekiah's Sickness and Recovery (20:1–11)

Closely related to the stories of healing associated with Elijah and Elisha is the account of Hezekiah's sickness and recovery (vv. 1–7). Especially is the wonder deed of vv. 8–11 closely parallel to the deeds of Elisha. The tradition of Hezekiah's healing is distinct from that of the shadow.

¹ In those days Hezekiah became sick and was at the point of death. And Isaiah the prophet the son of Amoz came to him, and said to him, "Thus says the LORD, 'Set your house in order; for you shall die, you shall not recover.'" ² Then Hezekiah turned his face to the wall, and prayed to the LORD, saying, ³ "Remember now, O LORD, I beseech thee, how I have walked before thee in faithfulness and with a whole heart, and have done what is good in thy sight." And Hezekiah wept bitterly. ⁴ And before Isaiah had gone out of the middle court, the word of the LORD came to him: ⁵ "Turn back, and say to Hezekiah the prince of my people, Thus says the LORD, the God of David your father: I have heard your prayer, I have seen your tears; behold, I will heal you; on the third day you shall go up to the house of the LORD. ⁶ And I will add fifteen years to your life. I will deliver you and this city out of the hand of the king of Assyria, and I will defend this city for my own sake and for my servant David's sake." ⁷ And Isaiah said, "Bring a cake of figs. And let them take and lay it on the boil, that he may recover."

Healing and added life (vv. 1–7). Although *in those days* is not specific enough to date this narrative, the later assurance of deliverance presupposes the Assyrian crisis (cf. v. 6). Following Isaiah's oracle of death, the king seeks divine aid in a prayer grounded in four characteristics of Hezekiah. He had *walked* in the presence of God (lit., "before thy face"), a phrase often used of the godly and righteous life of men such as Enoch (Gen. 5:21), Noah (Gen. 6:9), Abraham and Isaac (Gen. 48:15), and David (1 Kings 3:6). *Faithfulness* (*'emeth*) could also be translated "truth," and means reliability, stability (Isa. 39:8), or reliableness (as of men cf. Neh. 7:2). It clarifies the manner in which Hezekiah walked before God. The king's conduct before God had also been that of a *whole heart* (*leb shalem*). Hezekiah's personality was single or complete, lacking in duplicity. Additionally, Hezekiah suggests that he had done *good* before God.

"Hear" (*shama'*) is more than aural in the Old Testament and suggests action. For example, on occasion *shama'* is translated "obey" or "obedient" when used of man (cf. Isa. 1:19). When used of Yahweh it usually suggests to hear with favor.

The reference to 15 years may be a general figure to suggest that Hezekiah's life will be of normal length. If he was about 35 at the time of the illness (assuming that his illness coincided with the coronation of his son Manasseh at the age of 12), this would mean a life span of about 50 years for Hezekiah.

The *cake of figs* was a poultice which was used to draw ulcers, according to Pliny (Hist. Nat. XXII,7), and two veterinary texts from Ras Shamra dating to the second millennium B.C. prescribe raisins and bean-flour (cf. Gray). Isaiah's medication was probably common to the day. The prescription, it should be noted, obscures the continuity between vv. 6 and 8.

⁸ And Hezekiah said to Isaiah, "What shall be the sign that the LORD will heal me, and that I shall go up to the house of the LORD on the third day?" ⁹ And Isaiah said, "This is the sign to you from the LORD, that the LORD will do the thing that he has promised: shall the shadow go forward ten steps, or go back ten steps?" ¹⁰ And Hezekiah answered, "It is an easy thing for the shadow to lengthen ten steps; rather let the shadow go back ten steps." ¹¹ And Isaiah the prophet cried to the LORD; and he brought the shadow back ten steps, by which the sun had declined on the dial of Ahaz.

A confirmatory sign (vv. 8–11). Signs often accompanied prophetic messages as well as other media of revelation within the Old Testament. *Sign* (*'oth*) was a physical event with a meaning that pointed beyond itself, most often an ordinary event with an extraordinary meaning implied (cf. Josh. 2:17; Ex. 12:13; Psalm 86:17). The withdrawal of the sun's shadow was a sign of God's presence in the prophetic statement concerning Hezekiah's healing.

Declaratory words were viewed as quasi-physical, semi-independent entities, which could not be recalled (cf. the blessings and the cursings, Deut. 28). They carried within themselves the power of their own fulfillment. This is suggested by the inability of Isaac to retract the blessing he gave to the wrong son (cf. Gen. 27:7 ff.), as well as the more positive illustration of Yahweh's word which does not return without fulfilling the purpose for which it is sent (Isa. 55:10–11). In the case at hand, Isaiah had just issued a *word* from Yahweh (cf. 20:1 ff.), a word that could not be recalled. Thus, Isaiah's suggested revocation (cf. 20:4,6) accounts for Hezekiah's request for a sign. The request reflected Hezekiah's perplexity concerning how the illness could be retracted once the word had gone forth. The turning back of the shadow upon the steps is a forceful declaration that with God such a retraction of the word is possible. As the shadow was turned back, so can the oracle of doom and the certainty of death be turned back.

Some historical phenomenon such as an eclipse of the sun which occurred on January 11, 689 B.C. (cf. Gray), may well have been the historical nucleus around which the present popular narrative developed. It should be noted, however, that this was not a total eclipse, for F. R. Stephenson of the Department of Geophysics, The University, Newcastle upon Tyne, suggests that "between B.C. 1130 and B.C. 310 only two eclipses of the sun could cause the sun to be 'turned to darkness' in Judah. The dates of these are B.C. 357 February 29 and B.C. 336 July 4." [8]

[8] F. R. Stephenson, "The Dating of the Book of Joel," *Vetus Testamentum*, XIX, April 1969, pp. 224 ff., 229.

The inherent danger in rational explanations of this and other wonder stories or miracles is the failure to realize that the theology expressed by the redactor uses the story *as it was understood within its cultural context*. The writer lived in an environment in which people believed that God did act in this precise, literal fashion implied in the turning back (cf. *shub*) of the shadow on the steps. As the story is now constructed it is impossible to conclude other than that it was the purpose of the writer directly to link the event to Yahweh's action. Whatever the secondary media, Yahweh caused the shadow to turn back. Rational explanations fail to do justice to the author's ultimate purpose and theological intent.

The *dial* should not be taken as a traditional sun dial, and one should retain the more literal *steps* (*ma°lah*, step, stair; cf. Ezra 7:9; 1 Chron. 17:17; Ezek. 40:6). One could estimate the time of day from the position of the shadow on the steps.

Whatever the historical nucleus of the story, it is closely akin to the popular stories associated with Elisha. Its purpose is to guarantee that as the sun has withdrawn, so shall the oracle of death be withdrawn. Thus, although possibly originating in a different circle of tradition than 20:1 ff., vv. 8 ff. are integrally linked in ultimate purpose with the narrative of Hezekiah's illness and restoration.

(3) *Babylonian Overture to Judah* (*20:12–19*)

Chronologically this narrative belongs to the range of events falling *ca.* 710 B.C. Thematically it concerns the Babylonian intrigue directed against Assyria, and the effort to elicit the support of Judah. More specifically, it concerns the friendly welcome accorded the Babylonian embassy and Isaiah's criticism of Hezekiah's naïveté in disclosing the material condition of Judah as expressed in the treasury and armory to the Babylonians.

12 At that time Merodachbaladan the son of Baladan, king of Babylon, sent envoys with

letters and a present to Hezekiah; for he heard that Hezekiah had been sick. 13 And Hezekiah welcomed them, and he showed them all his treasure house, the silver, the gold, the spices, the precious oil, his armory, all that was found in his storehouses; there was nothing in his house or in all his realm that Hezekiah did not show them. 14 Then Isaiah the prophet came to King Hezekiah, and said to him, "What did these men say? And whence did they come to you?" And Hezekiah said, "They have come from a far country, from Babylon." 15 He said, "What have they seen in your house?" And Hezekiah answered, "They have seen all that is in my house; there is nothing in my storehouses that I did not show them."

Hezekiah's naïveté (vv. 12-15). The historical context of the Babylonian visit is the period of rebellion by Merodachbaladan, who ruled Babylon between 721 and 710 B.C. He was displaced by Sargon in 710 and took refuge in the salt marshes from which he emerged to foment rebellion against the Assyrians at the time of Sargon's death in 704 B.C. (cf. IDB, Gray, Snaith).

*Treasure house (beyth n*kothoh)* is probably an Assyrian loan word, and one can but speculate on the actual building which fits this description. Perhaps the Forest of Lebanon (cf. 1 Kings 7:2-5) was an armory (a common assumption); it may have contained not only portions of Judah's arsenal but have served as a treasury as well (cf. the contents mentioned in v. 13).

16 Then Isaiah said to Hezekiah, "Hear the word of the LORD: 17 Behold, the days are coming, when all that is in your house, and that which your fathers have stored up till this day, shall be carried to Babylon; nothing shall be left, says the LORD. 18 And some of your own sons, who are born to you, shall be taken away; and they shall be eunuchs in the palace of the king of Babylon." 19 Then said Hezekiah to Isaiah, "The word of the LORD which you have spoken is good." For he thought, "Why not, if there will be peace and security in my days?"

A prophetic judgment on naïve statesmanship (vv. 16-19). Always opposed to foreign alliances, which can so often substitute human ingenuity and strength for divine direction and support, Isaiah severely reprimanded Hezekiah. Wisdom should have dictated a more responsible, and reserved, course of action.

The suggestion that Isaiah's word is "good" (v. 19) does not mean that Hezekiah felt that captivity was good. Rather, it is indicative of that indomitable spirit which sees the Lord's action as ultimately good: much in the spirit of Job who can lose everything, yet say, "Blessed be the name of the Lord" (Job 1:21).

Hezekiah's closing phrase is difficult (v. 19b). As it now stands in the RSV it suggests an almost irresponsible self-interest, implying that so long as there is peace and security for Hezekiah's day, why not barter the future in exchange for the present?

Comparison of the Isaianic parallel reveals significant differences (cf. Isa. 39:8). For Isaiah 39:8 could well be translated, "And he spoke (in this fashion) because there were peace and security in his days."

Thus, far from self-interest at the expense of the future, the verse suggests that Hezekiah could interpret the prophetic message (even of doom) as *good* because it was the Lord's message (cf. Job 1:21) —the Lord who had postponed calamity because of merit's sake (cf. 22:18 ff.) and had blessed Hezekiah's generation with peace and security.

3. The Deuteronomic Appraisal of Hezekiah (20:20-21)

20 The rest of the deeds of Hezekiah, and all his might, and how he made the pool and the conduit and brought water into the city, are they not written in the Book of the Chronicles of the Kings of Judah? 21 And Hezekiah slept with his fathers; and Manasseh his son reigned in his stead.

The appraisal of Hezekiah's reign should properly be read following 18:1-12. The Isaianic traditions related to the Assyrian crisis have been interwoven into the historical annals in such manner as to break the continuity of what was probably at one time 18:1-12; 20:20-21.

Through the construction of a *conduit* tunneled through the mountain Hezekiah brought waters through the Temple mount into the pool of Siloam (cf. 2 Chron. 32:30;

Snaith). The tunnel may still be examined in Jerusalem, and its construction was an engineering feat of considerable proportions for that day. Beginning at opposite ends, workmen dug a tunnel measuring over 1,700 feet through solid rock, and met toward the center. The Siloam Inscription is carved inside the tunnel and records some details of construction which are listed here:

> /. . . when/ (the tunnel) was driven through. And this is the way in which it was cut through: —While /. . ./ (were) still (. . .) axe(s), each man toward his fellow, and while there were still three cubits to be cut through, /there was heard/ the voice of a man calling to his fellow, for there was *an overlap* in the rock on the right (and on the left). And when the tunnel was driven through, the quarrymen hewed (the rock), each man toward his fellow, axe against axe; and the water flowed from the spring toward the reservoir for 1,200 cubits, and the height of the rock above the head(s) of the quarrymen was 100 cubits (Wright, p. 170).

II. Decades of Faithlessness and Apostasy (21:1–26)

The era of greatest infidelity and apostasy in the history of Judah emerged in the reign of Manasseh and continued in the days of his son Amon. Although not unrelated to Assyrian domination, Manasseh's apostasy is without specific explanation. His marked departure from the reformation marks his apostasy among the inexplicable actions of those generations who repudiate the ways of their parents.

1. Manasseh (21:1–18)

The *fifty-five years* of Manasseh's reign must either be reduced by ten years, or assume, as does Gray, that Manasseh was co-regent with Hezekiah. Of this verse Gray says, "The reference is to the designation of Manasseh as co-regent or heir-apparent at the age of 12. . . ."

(1) The Apostasy of Manasseh (21:1–9)

¹ Manasseh was twelve years old when he began to reign, and he reigned fifty-five years in Jerusalem. His mother's name was Hephzibah. ² And he did what was evil in the sight of the Lord, according to the abominable practices of the nations whom the Lord drove out before the people of Israel. ³ For he rebuilt the high places which Hezekiah his father had destroyed; and he erected altars for Baal, and made an Asherah, as Ahab king of Israel had done, and worshiped all the host of heaven, and served them. ⁴ And he built altars in the house of the Lord, of which the Lord had said, "In Jerusalem will I put my name." ⁵ And he built altars for all the host of heaven in the two courts of the house of the Lord. ⁶ And he burned his son as an offering, and practiced soothsaying and augury, and dealt with mediums and with wizards. He did much evil in the sight of the Lord, provoking him to anger. ⁷ And the graven image of Asherah that he had made he set in the house of which the Lord said to David and to Solomon his son, "In this house, and in Jerusalem, which I have chosen out of all the tribes of Israel, I will put my name for ever; ⁸ and I will not cause the feet of Israel to wander any more out of the land which I gave to their fathers, if only they will be careful to do according to all that I have commanded them, and according to all the law that my servant Moses commanded them." ⁹ But they did not listen, and Manasseh seduced them to do more evil than the nations had done whom the Lord destroyed before the people of Israel.

The multiplied apostasies of Manasseh reflect such wide diversity and such marked contrast to the reformation of Hezekiah as to suggest a deliberate repudiation of his father's reform. The inclusion of some aspects of non-Israelite religious practices was necessitated by the totally subservient role of Judah to Assyria. Yet, this does not explain the inclusion of non-Assyrian religious motifs. One suspects, therefore, that within Judah there was a deliberate repudiation of Hezekiah's reform movement, and that the apostasy of Manasseh had at least three bases: (1) an imposed indication of national subservience to Assyria; (2) the activity of group(s) in Judah opposed to the stringent actions of Hezekiah's reform (This possibility is greatly increased if Manasseh actually assumed the throne at the age of 12, for he would likely have been controlled or strongly influenced by an adult(s).); (3) Manasseh's personal apostasy and infidelity.

(2) The Effects of Manasseh's Apostasy (21:10–15)

10 And the LORD said by his servants the prophets, 11 "Because Manasseh king of Judah has committed these abominations, and has done things more wicked than all that the Amorites did, who were before him, and has made Judah also to sin with his idols; 12 therefore thus says the LORD, the God of Israel, Behold, I am bringing upon Jerusalem and Judah such evil that the ears of every one who hears of it will tingle. 13 And I will stretch over Jerusalem the measuring line of Samaria, and the plummet of the house of Ahab; and I will wipe Jerusalem as one wipes a dish, wiping it and turning it upside down. 14 And I will cast off the remnant of my heritage, and give them into the hand of their enemies, and they shall become a prey and a spoil to all their enemies, 15 because they have done what is evil in my sight and have provoked me to anger, since the day their fathers came out of Egypt, even to this day."

The Deuteronomic editor places full responsibility for the fall of Jerusalem on Manasseh. Even so, the editor assumes that such apostasy had its roots in the rebellions of the wilderness and traces the antecedents of the current period of apostasy and inevitable destruction to *the day their fathers came out of Egypt*.

(3) The Persecutions of Manasseh (21:16)

16 Moreover Manasseh shed very much innocent blood, till he had filled Jerusalem from one end to another, besides the sin which he made Judah to sin so that they did what was evil in the sight of the LORD.

The tradition which associates Manasseh with the persecution of the prophets, and especially with Isaiah, originated in noncanonical writings and culminated in the general reference to the persecutions of the prophets in Hebrews 11:32 ff. The pseudepigraphical book entitled *The Martyrdom of Isaiah* suggests that a false prophet named Belchira of Bethlehem accused Isaiah before king Manasseh:

And he [Belchira] brought many accusations against Isaiah and the prophets before Manasseh. But Beliar [angel of lawlessness and ruler of this world] dwelt in the heart of Manasseh . . . and he sent and seized Isaiah. And he sawed him asunder with a wood-saw . . . But Isaiah was (absorbed) in a vision of the Lord, and though his eyes were open, he saw them (not).[9]

(4) Deuteronomic Summary (21:17–18)

17 Now the rest of the acts of Manasseh, and all that he did, and the sin that he committed, are they not written in the Book of the Chronicles of the Kings of Judah? 18 And Manasseh slept with his fathers, and was buried in the garden of his house, in the garden of Uzza; and Amon his son reigned in his stead.

The location of Manasseh's burial site *in the garden of his house, in the garden of Uzza* is open to several interpretations. First, one might conclude that his apostasy precluded burial with the kings of Judah (cf. "Ahaz . . . was buried with his fathers in the city of David," 16:20, a location common for the kings). But in view of the strong views of his son and the entrenched power of Assyria, as well as that of his own dynasty, this is questionable. Second, it was said of Hezekiah that he was buried "in the ascent of the tombs of the sons of David" (2 Chron. 32:33), which probably means that the burial plot used for the kings was filled. Third, John Gray suggests that the enclosure of Uzza was a precinct of the cult of that deity, and that this was located in the king's garden.[10] This is an attractive and likely proposal. Only Manasseh and Amon are said to have been buried in the "garden of Uzza" (cf. 21:18,26).

2. Amon (21:19–26)

19 Amon was twenty-two years old when he began to reign, and he reigned two years in Jerusalem. His mother's name was Meshullemeth the daughter of Haruz of Jotbah. 20 And he did what was evil in the sight of the LORD, as Manasseh his father had done. 21 He walked in all the way in which his father walked, and

---
[9] *The Martyrdom of Isaiah* 3:10–5:14, in *The Pseudepigrapha*, R. H. Charles ed., cf. 4:10–5:8.
[10] *Op. cit.*, p. 646; cf. "The Desert God 'Attar in the Literature and Religion of Canaan," JNES, VIII, 1949, p. 80.

served the idols that his father served, and worshiped them; 22 he forsook the Lord, the God of his fathers, and did not walk in the way of the Lord. 23 And the servants of Amon conspired against him, and killed the king in his house. 24 But the people of the land slew all those who had conspired against King Amon, and the people of the land made Josiah his son king in his stead. 25 Now the rest of the acts of Amon which he did, are they not written in the Book of the Chronicles of the Kings of Judah? 26 And he was buried in his tomb in the garden of Uzza; and Josiah his son reigned in his stead.

Amon continued the apostasies of his father Manasseh, but died in a palace revolt two years after ascending the throne. No reason is given for his assassination, but at least two parties appear to have been involved in the turmoil (cf. vv. 23 f.). The pro-Assyrian commitments of Manasseh (and, assumedly, Amon) lend credence to the thesis that Amon was slain by a pro-Egyptian party. Opposing those who slew Amon, the *people of the land* (an independent group, unrelated to the royal structure) slew those who conspired against Amon and then established Josiah on the throne.

III. Josiah and the Religious Reformation (22:1—23:30)

The reform of Josiah was but the outcropping of a much more fundamental and far-reaching theological movement which ranked among the primary watersheds of Israel's religious pilgrimage. Fundamental to the theological ferment responsible for the Josianic reformation were the theocentric nature of history, the centrality of Jerusalem as the focus of worship, the principle of moral retribution on both the individual and corporate levels, and the positive emphases upon the prophetic interpretation of life. These characteristics mark this theological movement as a unique and determinative influence for the religion and theology of Israel.

The effects of this theology were to be measured not only in the specific reform of Josiah and the implementation of Deuteronomic principles within national life, but also in contemporary religious activity such as that which characterized the era of Jeremiah. Additionally, the theology of the Deuteronomic school marked such books as Joshua, Judges, 1 and 2 Samuel, and 1 and 2 Kings, each of which was compiled from the perspective of the Deuteronomic school as a determinative influence.

1. Josiah (22:1–2)

¹ Josiah was eight years old when he began to reign, and he reigned thirty-one years in Jerusalem. His mother's name was Jedidah the daughter of Adaiah of Bozkath. ² And he did what was right in the eyes of the Lord, and walked in all the way of David his father, and he did not turn aside to the right hand or to the left.

The early age of Josiah at the time of his accession to the throne parallels that of Jehoash (cf. 11:21), and suggests the possibility that the party which brought about his accession was quite influential during Josiah's early years (cf. the role of Jehoiada in Jehoash's early reign).

2. The Inception of the Reformation (22:3–20)

The theological and religious interests of the Deuteronomic editor are clearly revealed in his minimal concern for historical events unrelated to the reform movement. Except for 23:1–2 and 23:28–30, the whole of his treatment of Josiah focuses in the reformation. That the discovery of "the book of the law" was not the sole impetus for Josiah's reformation, however, is confirmed both by the Chronicler's statement that the reform had been underway for at least six years prior to the discovery of the law (cf. 2 Chron. 34:3 ff.) and the fact that the book was found in the course of a renovation program probably related to the reform.

(1) Repair of the Temple (22:3–7)

³ In the eighteenth year of King Josiah, the king sent Shaphan the son of Azaliah, son of Meshullam, the secretary, to the house of the Lord, saying, ⁴ "Go up to Hilkiah the high priest, that he may reckon the amount of the money which has been brought into the house of the Lord, which the keepers of the thresh-

old have collected from the people; 5 and let it be given into the hand of the workmen who have the oversight of the house of the LORD; and let them give it to the workmen who are at the house of the LORD, repairing the house, 6 that is, to the carpenters, and to the builders, and to the masons, as well as for buying timber and quarried stone to repair the house. 7 But no accounting shall be asked from them for the money which is delivered into their hand, for they deal honestly."

Both the Temple repairs and the subsequent reformation were related to the diminishing power of Assyria, whose capital fell to a coalition of Babylonians, Medes, and Scythians in 612 B.C. The reform was not only a genuine movement of spiritual renewal but an equally genuine avowal of national independence.

The family of *Shaphan* ("rock badger") was a strong supporter of the reformation, and both Shaphan himself and his sons Ahikam and Elasah were of considerable assistance to Jeremiah (cf. 20:12; Jer. 26:24; 29:3).

(2) *Discovery and Reading of the Book* (22:8–10)

8 And Hilkiah the high priest said to Shaphan the secretary, "I have found the book of the law in the house of the LORD." And Hilkiah gave the book to Shaphan, and he read it. 9 And Shaphan the secretary came to the king, and reported to the king, "Your servants have emptied out the money that was found in the house, and have delivered it into the hand of the workmen who have the oversight of the house of the LORD." 10 Then Shaphan the secretary told the king, "Hilkiah the priest has given me a book." And Shaphan read it before the king.

Since as early as Jerome, "the book of the law" discovered during the repair of the Temple in 622 B.C. has been identified as the book of Deuteronomy. That this book was not the entire book of Deuteronomy has been often argued, especially on the ground that it was read through in its entirety twice in a single day (cf. v. 10; 23:2). In addition, the actual reform of Josiah inaugurated only limited stipulations of the book of Deuteronomy.

(3) *Response to the Book* (22:11–13)

11 And when the king heard the words of the book of the law, he rent his clothes. 12 And the king commanded Hilkiah the priest, and Ahikam the son of Shaphan, and Achbor the son of Micaiah, and Shaphan the secretary, and Asaiah the king's servant, saying, 13 "Go, inquire of the LORD for me, and for the people, and for all Judah, concerning the words of this book that has been found; for great is the wrath of the LORD that is kindled against us, because our fathers have not obeyed the words of this book, to do according to all that is written concerning us."

The most significant response of Josiah to the reading of the book of the law was the delegation of messengers to seek a prophetic oracle concerning the welfare of himself, the people, and the whole of Judah. Thus, from its inception the reform is directly related to prophetic foundations. Such prophetic emphasis is altogether consonant with the continuing exaltation of the prophetic office throughout the books of Kings.

(4) *Prophetic Impetus to the Reform* (22:14–20)

14 So Hilkiah the priest, and Ahikam, and Achbor, and Shaphan, and Asaiah went to Huldah the prophetess, the wife of Shallum the son of Tikvah, son of Harhas, keeper of the wardrobe (now she dwelt in Jerusalem in the Second Quarter); and they talked with her. 15 And she said to them, "Thus says the LORD, the God of Israel: 'Tell the man who sent you to me, 16 Thus says the LORD, Behold, I will bring evil upon this place and upon its inhabitants, all the words of the book which the king of Judah has read. 17 Because they have forsaken me and have burned incense to other gods, that they might provoke me to anger with all the work of their hands, therefore my wrath will be kindled against this place, and it will not be quenched. 18 But as to the king of Judah, who sent you to inquire of the LORD, thus shall you say to him, Thus says the LORD, the God of Israel: Regarding the words which you have heard, 19 because your heart was penitent, and you humbled yourself before the LORD, when you heard how I spoke against this place, and against its inhabitants, that they should become a desolation and a curse, and you have rent your clothes and wept before me, I also have heard you, says the LORD. 20 Therefore, behold, I will gather you to your fathers, and you shall be gathered to your grave in

peace, and your eyes shall not see all the evil which I will bring upon this place.'" And they brought back word to the king.

Prophetess appears but six times in the Old Testament: Miram, Deborah, Huldah, and Noadiah being the only women to function as prophetesses (cf. Ex. 15:20; Judg. 4:4; 2 Kings 22:14; 2 Chron. 34:22; Neh. 6:14). The term being once applied to Isaiah's wife, but hardly in the functional sense (cf. Isa. 8:3).

Huldah's oracle reveals that (1) the nation is to suffer a wrath that *will not be quenched,* a reference to the fall of Jerusalem; but (2) the king, because of his humility and response to Yahweh will not live to see the destruction which Huldah envisions for the nation. This double emphasis probably reflects the editorial activity of a postexilic editor who has incorporated the memory of Jerusalem's fall into the Huldah oracle. During the course of the oracle Huldah uses the traditional *Thus says the Lord* (*ko amar Yahweh*) to introduce three authoritative commands or revelations.

That Josiah was himself gathered to his grave *in peace* is highly questionable, for he died violently at the hands of Pharaoh Neco at Megiddo (cf. 23:29). The original Huldah prophecy may have been written prior to Megiddo, and thus have been unaware of the king's fate. It is preferable, however, to understand *in peace* to refer to the state as still intact. The Huldah oracle is often interpreted as a conflation of two oracles (vv. 15 ff. and vv. 18 ff.) later edited by someone acquainted with the destruction of Jerusalem. This is consonant with editorial activity within the Old Testament, although there is nothing inherently impossible in the assumption that Huldah saw with gifted sagacity the inevitable destruction of Judah, an event which came to pass in less than 40 years.

3. Implementing the Reform (23:1–25)

The reform probably moved through a series of distinguishable phases: (1) renovation of the Temple, (2) cultic purge of non-Israelite influences, and (3) the effort to include people of the former Northern Kingdom. The effect of the reform movement was to give visible presence and political authority to the stipulations of the book of the law. As such the reform was both religious and political.

(1) Public Reading of the Book (23:1–3)

¹ Then the king sent, and all the elders of Judah and Jerusalem were gathered to him. ² And the king went up to the house of the LORD, and with him all the men of Judah and all the inhabitants of Jerusalem, and the priests and the prophets, all the people, both small and great; and he read in their hearing all the words of the book of the covenant which had been found in the house of the LORD. ³ And the king stood by the pillar and made a covenant before the LORD, to walk after the LORD and to keep his commandments and his testimonies and his statutes, with all his heart and all his soul, to perform the words of this covenant that were written in this book; and all the people joined in the covenant.

Public proclamation of covenant stipulations within the Old Testament is as old as Sinai (cf. Ex. 20:1 ff.; Deut. 5:4 ff.) and as late as Ezra's public reading of the law following the Exile (cf. Neh. 8:1). Public recitation of the covenant stipulations seems to have been related to a covenant renewal ceremony, most likely celebrated in conjunction with the Feast of Tabernacles in the fall of the year. In the present context the purpose of the public reading was to give official political sanction to the stipulations of the covenant, especially those related to the purification of the cult.

Reference to the king standing *by the pillar* suggests an authoritative location from which the king acted. Joash at the time of his coronation was "standing by the pillar, according to the custom" (11:14), and of the same event the Chronicler says that the king was standing "by his pillar" (2 Chron. 23:13; cf. Neh. 8:4). Such an interpretation undergirds the interpretation of 16:18 as a royal foundation which was removed from the Temple as a sign of Ahaz's subservience to the Assyrian king.

(2) Political Implementation of Covenant Stipulations (23:4-14)

⁴ And the king commanded Hilkiah, the high priest, and the priests of the second order, and the keepers of the threshold, to bring out of the temple of the LORD all the vessels made for Baal, for Asherah, and for all the host of heaven; he burned them outside Jerusalem in the fields of the Kidron, and carried their ashes to Bethel. ⁵ And he deposed the idolatrous priests whom the kings of Judah had ordained to burn incense in the high places at the cities of Judah and round about Jerusalem; those also who burned incense to Baal, to the sun, and the moon, and the constellations, and all the host of the heavens. ⁶ And he brought out the Asherah from the house of the LORD, outside Jerusalem, to the brook Kidron, and burned it at the brook Kidron, and beat it to dust and cast the dust of it upon the graves of the common people. ⁷ And he broke down the houses of the male cult prostitutes which were in the house of the LORD, where the women wove hangings for the Asherah. ⁸ And he brought all the priests out of the cities of Judah, and defiled the high places where the priests had burned incense, from Geba to Beer-sheba; and he broke down the high places of the gates that were at the entrance of the gate of Joshua the governor of the city, which were on one's left at the gate of the city. ⁹ However, the priests of the high places did not come up to the altar of the LORD in Jerusalem, but they ate unleavened bread among their brethren. ¹⁰ And he defiled Topheth, which is in the valley of the sons of Hinnom, that no one might burn his son or his daughter as an offering to Molech. ¹¹ And he removed the horses that the kings of Judah had dedicated to the sun, at the entrance to the house of the LORD, by the chamber of Nathanmelech the chamberlain, which was in the precincts; and he burned the chariots of the sun with fire. ¹² And the altars on the roof of the upper chamber of Ahaz, which the kings of Judah had made, and the altars which Manasseh had made in the two courts of the house of the LORD, he pulled down and broke in pieces, and cast the dust of them into the brook Kidron. ¹³ And the king defiled the high places that were east of Jerusalem, to the south of the mount of corruption, which Solomon the king of Israel had built for Ashtoreth the abomination of the Sidonians, and for Chemosh the abomination of Moab, and for Milcom the abomination of the Ammonites. ¹⁴ And he broke in pieces the pillars, and cut down the Asherim, and filled their places with the bones of men.

The purification of cultic life was related to an assertion of national autonomy by Josiah (just as the reverse was true under Ahaz and Manasseh). The limitation of the reformation to cultic life is one basis for the assumption that the "book of the law" did not constitute the total book of Deuteronomy, but only a portion dealing with the purity of cultic life (i.e., especially Deut. 12—26). E. W. Nicholson helpfully summarizes parallels between Deuteronomy and Kings:

2 Kings xxiii	Deuteronomy
Abolition of the Asherim vv. 4,6,7,14	vii. 5; xii. 3; xvi. 21
The host of heaven vv. 4,5	xvii. 3
Destruction of the pillars v. 14	vii. 5; xii. 3; etc.
Heathen high places v. 13	vii. 5; xii. 2 f.; etc.
Sun and moon worship vv. 5,11	xvii. 3
Sacred prostitution v. 7	xxiii. 18 (EVV 17).
Molech cult v. 10	xii. 31; xviii. 10.
Foreign gods, etc. v. 13	xii; xiii.
Necromancy v. 24	xviii. 11.
Passover celebrated in Jerusalem, i.e., centralized Passover vv. 21-23	xvi. 1-8.[11]

According to the order of the present chapter (probably drawn from the annals of Judah), the reform consisted in the following actions: (1) the burning of all vessels related to Baal, Asherah, and the host of heaven and the removal of the ashes to Bethel, thus purging the last vestige of their influence from Judah, while at the same time casting rebuke upon a temple shrine of the Northern Kingdom; (2) removal of all idolatrous priests; (3) the removal of a particular idol related to Asherah, and the complete extermination of it through burning; (4) the removal of female cult prostitutes, women dedicated to Canaanite fertility rites associated with Baalism which assumed that ritual sexual union precipitated the union of cosmic pro-

---

11 E. W. Nicholson, *Deuteronomy and Tradition* (Philadelphia: Fortress Press, 1967), p. 3. Nicholson cites L. B. Paton for a more complete list: "The Case for the Post-exilic Dating of Deuteronomy," JBL 47 (1928), pp. 325 ff.

creative power with the earth mother, thereby increasing the productivity of family, flock, and field; (5) the removal of local places of worship dedicated to Yahweh, thus emphasizing the central role of Jerusalem; (6) the desecration of the site near Jerusalem where child sacrifice was practiced; (7) removal of horses related to sun worship, an infrequent but apparently valid reference to the role of the horse as a cultic symbol; (8) altars, probably related to astral worship, which had been erected by Ahaz and Manasseh, doubtless in imitation of Assyrian practices; (9) the defilement of those places of idolatrous worship associated with the innovations precipitated by Solomon's marital commitments.

(3) *Extension of the Purge to the North* (23:15–20)

15 Moreover the altar at Bethel, the high place erected by Jeroboam the son of Nebat, who made Israel to sin, that altar with the high place he pulled down and he broke in pieces its stones, crushing them to dust; also he burned the Asherah. 16 And as Josiah turned, he saw the tombs there on the mount; and he sent and took the bones out of the tombs, and burned them upon the altar, and defiled it, according to the word of the LORD which the man of God proclaimed, who had predicted these things. 17 Then he said, "What is yonder monument that I see?" And the men of the city told him, "It is the tomb of the man of God who came from Judah and predicted these things which you have done against the altar at Bethel." 18 And he said, "Let him be; let no man move his bones." So they let his bones alone, with the bones of the prophet who came out of Samaria. 19 And all the shrines also of the high places that were in the cities of Samaria, which kings of Israel had made, provoking the LORD to anger, Josiah removed; he did to them according to all that he had done at Bethel. 20 And he slew all the priests of the high places who were there, upon the altars, and burned the bones of men upon them. Then he returned to Jerusalem.

Although questions have often arisen concerning whether or not Josiah actually sought to include the Northern Kingdom in the reform movement, such an attempt is in keeping with the Chronicler's belief (cf. 2 Chron. 34:6–7) and is consistent with the disintegration of Assyrian control over Palestine of this specific era. Reclamation of the Northern Kingdom apparently characterized Josiah's reform and may have been one facet of his ultimate difficulty with Egypt and his subsequent death at Megiddo (cf. 23:29–30).

Within the larger format of the narrative there is a double emphasis upon (1) purging Bethel of the altar associated with the golden calf episode in the time of Jeroboam I (a sin which the Deuteronomist never forgot, and one for which he held every successive king of Israel responsible); and (2) veneration of the prophet who warned Jeroboam I (cf. 1 Kings 13:1 ff.)

Defilement through burning bones on the altar reflects the common attitude toward "clean" and "unclean." The unclean nature of a dead body was a clear means to the defilement of the altar (cf. Lev. 21:10 ff.; 22:4). The desecration of Bethel and the further purge of Israelite sanctuaries are directly related to the Levitical warning; "And I will destroy your high places, and cut down your incense altars, and cast your dead bodies upon the dead bodies of your idols; and my soul will abhor you" (Lev. 26:30).

(4) *Public Celebration of the Passover* (23:21–23)

21 And the king commanded all the people, "Keep the passover to the LORD your God, as it is written in this book of the covenant." 22 For no such passover had been kept since the days of the judges who judged Israel, or during all the days of the kings of Israel or of the kings of Judah; 23 but in the eighteenth year of King Josiah this passover was kept to the LORD in Jerusalem.

The account of Josiah's centralized, public celebration of the Passover in Jerusalem, as opposed to the home-centered nature of the festival, is used by the editor at this juncture in the chapter as a means of confirming Jerusalem as *the* place of worship. That *no such passover had been kept since the days of the Judges* probably refers to the celebration of Joshua 5:10 ff.

(cf. "Joshua," BBC, Vol. 2) and subsequent observances related to the cultic center, Gilgal. Josiah's action elevated the Passover to the status of a pilgrimage festival of national significance, with both religious and political overtones.

(5) Summary of the Reformation (23:24-25)

24 Moreover Josiah put away the mediums and the wizards and the teraphim and the idols and all the abominations that were seen in the land of Judah and in Jerusalem, that he might establish the words of the law which were written in the book that Hilkiah the priest found in the house of the Lord. 25 Before him there was no king like him, who turned to the Lord with all his heart and with all his soul and with all his might, according to all the law of Moses; nor did any like him arise after him.

Mediums (*'oboth*) suggests necromancy, the art of alleged communication with the dead. This was, to judge from the condemnatory passages, a common problem in Israel (cf. Lev. 19:31; 20:27; Deut. 18:11). Saul consulted a woman supposedly able to contact the dead (cf. 1 Sam. 28:7), and the practice was especially related to the evils of Manasseh's reign (21:6). The word *wizards* (*yidd^eoni*, "familiar spirit," from *yada'*, to know) properly means knowing or wise in the sense of acquaintance with the unseen world (cf. Deut. 18:11; 1 Sam. 28:3,9; Isa. 8:19; 19:3). According to Isaiah 2:6 the "art" was introduced from Philistia. *Teraphim* were household gods or idols (cf. Gen. 31:19; Judg. 17:5; 1 Sam. 19:13).

4. The Failure of the Reformation and the Last Act of Josiah (23:26-30)

26 Still the Lord did not turn from the fierceness of his great wrath, by which his anger was kindled against Judah, because of all the provocations with which Manasseh had provoked him. 27 And the Lord said, "I will remove Judah also out of my sight, as I have removed Israel, and I will cast off this city which I have chosen, Jerusalem, and the house of which I said, My name shall be there." 28 Now the rest of the acts of Josiah, and all that he did, are they not written in the Book of the Chronicles of the Kings of Judah? 29 In his days Pharaoh Neco king of Egypt went up to the king of Assyria to the river Euphrates. King Josiah went to meet him; and Pharaoh Neco slew him at Megiddo, when he saw him. 30 And his servants carried him dead in a chariot from Megiddo, and brought him to Jerusalem, and buried him in his own tomb. And the people of the land took Jehoahaz the son of Josiah, and anointed him, and made him king in his father's stead.

Having lived through the fall of Jerusalem, the second Deuteronomic editor inserts a note of warning concerning the irrevocable nature of Yahweh's wrath. Not even a figure so noble and faithful as Josiah could avert the calamity. The inevitability of destruction was related to the severity of Manassseh's apostasy (cf. 21:10 ff.). The editor properly notes that there is a point beyond which national disintegration cannot be averted; religious, moral, and political forces of retribution having already been set in motion by the nation's religio-political character.

The minor attention given to the catastrophic and tragic death of Josiah at Megiddo underscores the primary concern of the editor for religious and theological renewal as opposed to a history of Judah.

On what basis Josiah went to meet Neco, whether to oppose him (as is likely) or in response to a demand by Neco, or voluntarily to parley with him, we are not told. The death of Josiah at Megiddo, *ca.* 609 b.c. for all practical purposes, brought the reformation to an end. His death was itself a refutation of the Deuteronomic thesis that faithfulness was always rewarded in history.

IV. The Destruction of Jerusalem and the Fall of Judah (23:31—25:30)

The destruction of Jerusalem and especially the Temple form the climax toward which the book of 2 Kings consistently moves. It is the editor's purpose to illustrate from historical evidences the principle that religious infidelity (which is seldom distinct from moral irresponsibility in the Old Testament) brought about the end of the nation. This primary thesis is clearly revealed in the relatively minor attention given to historical events related to traditional concerns of government as compared with the extensive attention given to the religious characteristics of successive kings. The writer's point is clear and the reigns of kings following Josiah demonstrate the Deuteronomic principle of retribution within the framework of history.

1. Jehoahaz (23:31–35)

31 Jehoahaz was twenty-three years old when he began to reign, and he reigned three months in Jerusalem. His mother's name was Hamutal the daughter of Jeremiah of Libnah. 32 And he did what was evil in the sight of the Lord, according to all that his fathers had done. 33 And Pharaoh Neco put him in bonds at Riblah in the land of Hamath, that he might not reign in Jerusalem, and laid upon the land a tribute of a hundred talents of silver and a talent of gold. 34 And Pharaoh Neco made Eliakim the son of Josiah king in the place of Josiah his father, and changed his name to Jehoiakim. But he took Jehoahaz away, and he came to Egypt, and died there. 35 And Jehoiakim gave the silver and the gold to Pharaoh, but he taxed the land to give the money according to the command of Pharaoh. He exacted the silver and the gold of the people of the land, from every one according to his assessment, to give it to Pharaoh Neco.

Jehoahaz ("Yahweh has grasped") ruled but three months before being deposed and taken to Egypt by Pharaoh Neco. His deposition may have been related to circumstances surrounding his selection as king. Although younger than Jehoiakim (cf. 23; 36), he was selected by *the people of the land* (23:30) and anointed as king. Although both Jehoiakim and Jehoahaz were sons of Josiah, they had different mothers (vv. 31,36), suggesting the possibility of a different background and attitude by Jehoahaz/Zedekiah and Jehoiakim/Jehoiachin. Pharaoh Neco apparently never recognized Jehoahaz's succession, as indicated by the statement that when Neco made Jehoiakim (Eliakim) king he caused him to reign, not in place of Jehoahaz but *in the place of Josiah*. One suspects that the people of the land were anti-Egyptian, while Jehoiakim (Eliakim) was more conciliatory.

2. Jehoiakim (23:36—24:7)

36 Jehoiakim was twenty-five years old when he began to reign, and he reigned eleven years in Jerusalem. His mother's name was Zebidah the daughter of Pedaiah of Rumah. 37 And he did what was evil in the sight of the Lord, according to all that his fathers had done.
1 In his days Nebuchadnezzar king of Babylon came up, and Jehoiakim became his servant three years; then he turned and rebelled against him. 2 And the Lord sent against him bands of the Chaldeans, and bands of the Syrians, and bands of the Moabites, and bands of the Ammonites, and sent them against Judah to destroy it, according to the word of the Lord which he spoke by his servants the prophets. 3 Surely this came upon Judah at the command of the Lord, to remove them out of his sight, for the sins of Manasseh, according to all that he had done, 4 and also for the innocent blood that he had shed; for he filled Jerusalem with innocent blood, and the Lord would not pardon. 5 Now the rest of the deeds of Jehoiakim, and all that he did, are they not written in the Book of the Chronicles of the Kings of Judah? 6 So Jehoiakim slept with his fathers, and Jehoiachin his son reigned in his stead. 7 And the king of Egypt did not come again out of his land, for the king of Babylon had taken all that belonged to the king of Egypt from the Brook of Egypt to the river Euphrates.

Jehoiakim ("Yahweh raises up"), whose name was changed by Pharaoh from *Eliakim* ("God raises up") in order both to appease Judah (according to H. B. MacLean, IDB) and to underscore Neco's power, was an older brother of King Jehoahaz, whom the Pharaoh placed on the throne of Jehoahaz (23:34 f.). Jeremiah is especially caustic in his condemnation of the kings of Judah who reigned during this period of time, and his remarks concerning Jehoiakim clearly underscore the moral and social insensitivity of the king (cf. Jer. 22:13 ff.).

With the fall of Nineveh at the hands of Babylonians, Scythians, and Medes in 612 B.C., the Assyrian empire came to an end. The emergence of Nebuchadnezzar to the throne of Babylon in 605 B.C. ushered that empire into an era of international power which lasted throughout the 43 years of his reign (605–562 B.C.).

Nebuchadnezzar (cf. 25:1; 2 Chron. 36:6; Dan. 1:1) appears elsewhere in the Old Testament as "Nebuchadrezzar" (which is used only by Jeremiah and Ezekiel; cf. Jer. 21:2; 32:1 ff.; Ezek. 26:7; 30:10). Nebuchadrezzar is closer to the Akkadian spelling *Nabu-kudurri-usur*, but Nebuchadnezzar is the more popular form in the Old Testament (58 *vs.* 33 occurrences). An immediate contemporary such as Jeremiah prefers Nebuchadrezzar (33 Nebuchadrezzar *vs.* 8 Nebuchadnezzar), and this spelling is generally preferable. Of 58 occurrences of Nebuchadnezzar, 32 occur in the book of Daniel. Notice the preference of a contemporary, Jeremiah, for Nebuchadrezzar, and the preference of late sources such as Daniel for Nebuchadnezzar. We follow in this commentary, however, the spelling of the related biblical text.

There is no basis within 2 Kings for dating the occasion when Jehoiakim, after a three-year period of faithfulness, *rebelled* against Nebuchadnezzar. A brief reconstruction of Nebuchadnezzar's activities may help to positionize Jehoiakim's action.

The Babylonian Chronicle reveals that Nebuchadnezzar, then crown-prince, was in command of the Babylonian forces that defeated Egypt at Carchemish in 605 B.C., and then swept through Syria and parts of Palestine. Upon the death of his father Nabopolassar (August 16, 605 B.C.), Nebuchadrezzar returned home to assume the throne. But he was on the border of Egypt in 604 B.C., and captured Ashkelon in the month of Kislev (November–December). Of this expedition the Babylonian Chronicle specifically states that "All the kings of the Hatti-land came before him and he received their heavy tribute" (*British Museum Tablet* No. 21946; cf. Wiseman). Among these would have been Jehoiakim (although Gray feels that Jehoiakim was left alone at this time, and tribute was not imposed until the 601 B.C. expedition).

After the submission of Palestine and Syria, Nebuchadrezzar made annual marches to collect tribute. But in 601 B.C. he moved to attack Neco II of Egypt, who so severely defeated him that for a year and a half the Babylonians remained in Babylon reequipping their forces (Wiseman, p. 80). In 599/98 B.C. Nebuchadnezzar defeated the Arab tribes in preparation for an advance against Judah (cf. Jer. 49:28–33).

The Babylonian army was mustered for the attack on Jerusalem on November 29, 598, and the city fell on March 16, 597 (Wiseman, pp. 80–81). The Babylonian Chronicle contains this record: ". . . and, having marched to the land of Hatti, besieged the city of Judah, and on the second day of the month of Adar took the city and captured the king. He appointed therein a king of his own choice, received its heavy tribute and sent (them) to Babylon" (*British Museum Tablet* No. 21946 rev. 11–13, Plate 5, cited in Wiseman).

This historical background and the narrative of 2 Kings suggest that Jehoiakim began paying tribute to Nebuchadnezzar (v. 1) in 604 B.C. and continued until 601 B.C. when, because of the Babylonian defeat by Neco II, he ceased to pay tribute (Jeremiah strongly condemned dependence upon Egypt, cf. Jer. 37:1 ff.). Further, the forays by scattered tribes described in v. 2 probably occurred in the interval between *ca.* 599–598 B.C., and were used by Nebuchadnezzar to occupy Judah's attention until Nebuchadnezzar could move the Babylonian army once again into Palestine. This attack by border nations was interpreted by the editor as an expression of Yahweh's judgment upon Judah for the sins of Manasseh, who came to occupy much the same role in the South as Jeroboam I did in the North (v. 3).

Jehoiakim's death may be dated quite accurately on the basis of the Babylonian Chronicle as having occurred on December 7, 598 B.C., "three months and ten days before the capture of Jerusalem" (Wiseman, p. 81; cf. also 2 Chron. 36:9 *vs.* 2 Kings 24:6).

3. *Jehoiachin (24:8–17)*

8 Jehoiachin was eighteen years old when he became king, and he reigned three months in

Jerusalem. His mother's name was Nehushta the daughter of Elnathan of Jerusalem. ⁹ And he did what was evil in the sight of the LORD, according to all that his father had done.

¹⁰ At that time the servants of Nebuchadnezzar king of Babylon came up to Jerusalem, and the city was besieged. ¹¹ And Nebuchadnezzar king of Babylon came to the city, while his servants were besieging it; ¹² and Jehoiachin the king of Judah gave himself up to the king of Babylon, himself, and his mother, and his servants, and his princes, and his palace officials. The king of Babylon took him prisoner in the eighth year of his reign, ¹³ and carried off all the treasures of the house of the LORD, and the treasures of the king's house, and cut in pieces all the vessels of gold in the temple of the LORD, which Solomon king of Israel had made, as the LORD had foretold. ¹⁴ He carried away all Jerusalem, and all the princes, and all the mighty men of valor, ten thousand captives, and all the craftsmen and the smiths; none remained, except the poorest people of the land. ¹⁵ And he carried away Jehoiachin to Babylon; the king's mother, the king's wives, his officials, and the chief men of the land, he took into captivity from Jerusalem to Babylon. ¹⁶ And the king of Babylon brought captive to Babylon all the men of valor, seven thousand, and the craftsmen and the smiths, one thousand, all of them strong and fit for war. ¹⁷ And the king of Babylon made Mattaniah, Jehoiachin's uncle, king in his stead, and changed his name to Zedekiah.

Jehoiachin ("Yahweh establishes"), also known as "Jeconiah" (1 Chron. 3:16–17; Jer. 24:1) and by the contraction Coniah (Jer. 22:24,28; 37:1), followed his father to the throne for a brief reign of three months. The statement that *he did what was evil* may suggest political involvement with Egypt rather than spiritual or moral faithlessness. This is the editor's way of explaining the fall of Jerusalem and its attendant tragedies.

Although the Temple treasures were plundered, and leading persons deported, Jerusalem was not at this time depopulated, nor was the Temple itself ravaged. Jehoiachin and his family were taken captive to Babylon, where they were apparently well treated (cf. 25:27 ff.), probably living under house arrest and drawing supplies from the kings quartermaster (cf. 27:30, plus confirmation in the Babylonian records known as "The Jehoiachin Tablets").

The variation between the date for the fall of Jerusalem in 24:12 (the *eighth year* of Nebuchadnezzar) and Jeremiah 52:28 (the "seventh year") reflects a different system of reckoning dates. In Judah the accession year was not counted as the first year; hence, Jeremiah is one year short of the total given in Kings. The number of deportees (10,000, v. 14) should be compared with the figure of 3,023 (cf. Jer. 52:28). Kings may use a round number, and may also include members of the families while Jeremiah may refer only to the men. Reference to *all Jerusalem* is general and vv. 13–14 are probably anachronistic. They suggest the hand of a postexilic editor who has telescoped the catastrophes of 597 and 586 B.C.

4. Zedekiah (24:18—25:21)

(1) An Evaluation of Zedekiah (24:18–20)

¹⁸ Zedekiah was twenty-one years old when he became king, and he reigned eleven years in Jerusalem. His mother's name was Hamutal the daughter of Jeremiah of Libnah. ¹⁹ And he did what was evil in the sight of the LORD, according to all that Jehoiakim had done. ²⁰ For because of the anger of the LORD it came to the point in Jerusalem and Judah that he cast them out from his presence.

And Zedekiah rebelled against the king of Babylon.

Mattaniah ("Gift of Yahweh") was Jehoiachin's uncle (24:17) and the full brother of Jehoahaz, Hamutal, the daughter of Jeremiah of Libnah, being mother of both Jehoahaz and Mattaniah (cf. 23:31; 24:18). Jehoiakim was also a son of Josiah, but a half-brother to Jehoahaz and Mattaniah, his mother being Zebidah the daughter of Pedaiah of Rumah (23:36). Contrasting ideological characteristics within the family circles of Jehoahaz-Mattaniah and Jehoikim-Zedekiah may help to explain (1) why Neco turned to Eliakim (Jehoiakim) when he had so recently deposed his brother Jehoahaz and (2) why Nebuchadrezzar should have turned to

Mattaniah, Jehoiachin's uncle, when he had so recently deposed Jehoiachin.

(2) The Rebellion and Fate of Zedekiah (25:1–7)

¹ And in the ninth year of his reign, in the tenth month, on the tenth day of the month, Nebuchadnezzar king of Babylon came with all his army against Jerusalem, and laid siege to it; and they built siegeworks against it round about. ² So the city was besieged till the eleventh year of King Zedekiah. ³ On the ninth day of the fourth month the famine was so severe in the city that there was no food for the people of the land. ⁴ Then a breach was made in the city; the king with all the men of war fled by night by the way of the gate between the two walls, by the king's garden, though the Chaldeans were around the city. And they went in the direction of the Arabah. ⁵ But the army of the Chaldeans pursued the king, and overtook him in the plains of Jericho; and all his army was scattered from him. ⁶ Then they captured the king, and brought him up to the king of Babylon at Riblah, who passed sentence upon him. ⁷ They slew the sons of Zedekiah before his eyes, and put out the eyes of Zedekiah, and bound him in fetters, and took him to Babylon.

The editor is concerned primarily with the sad plight of his own people and offers no suggestion concerning the international crisis which may have precipitated the rebellion under Zedekiah. It was quite likely related, however, to a resurgence of Egypt in 588 B.C. Jeremiah specifically refers to Egyptian activity during this period of time (cf. Jeremiah for parallel accounts of the fall of Jerusalem, 34:1 ff.; 39:1 ff.; 40:7—41; 52).

The *ninth year of his reign, in the tenth month* would have begun in December/January (the month Tebet) of 588 B.C. The 19-month seige does not reflect the power of Judah and Jerusalem so much as it does the Egyptian diversionary attack mentioned by Jeremiah (Jer. 37:5).

The first sign of defeat was the flight of the king and the *men of war* on the *ninth day of the fourth month,* or the ninth of June/July, 586 B.C. In Old Testament literature the *Arabah* may signify (1) the Jordan Valley, (2) the region of the Dead Sea, and (3) the territory from the Dead Sea to the Gulf of Aqabah. In this instance it probably refers to the Jordan Valley. Zedekiah was apparently attempting to cross the ford near Jericho, for he was overtaken *in the plains of Jericho.*

Riblah, to judge by frequent references to Assyrian, Egyptian, and Babylonian locations there, was a prominent military fortress. It stood at the juncture of the military highways to Egypt and Mesopotamia, near Kadesh. Babylonian military headquarters was apparently there, and it was there that Zedekiah was sentenced.

(3) The Fall of Jerusalem (25:8–21)

⁸ In the fifth month, on the seventh day of the month—which was the nineteenth year of King Nebuchadnezzar, king of Babylon—Nebuzaradan, the captain of the bodyguard, a servant of the king of Babylon, came to Jerusalem. ⁹ And he burned the house of the LORD, and the king's house and all the houses of Jerusalem; every great house he burned down. ¹⁰ And all the army of the Chaldeans, who were with the captain of the guard, broke down the walls around Jerusalem. ¹¹ And the rest of the people who were left in the city and the deserters who had deserted to the king of Babylon, together with the rest of the multitude, Nebuzaradan the captain of the guard carried into exile. ¹² But the captain of the guard left some of the poorest of the land to be vinedressers and plowmen.
¹³ And the pillars of bronze that were in the house of the LORD, and the stands and the bronze sea that were in the house of the LORD, the Chaldeans broke in pieces, and carried the bronze to Babylon. ¹⁴ And they took away the pots, and the shovels, and the snuffers, and the dishes for incense and all the vessels of bronze used in the temple service, ¹⁵ the firepans also, and the bowls. What was of gold the captain of the guard took away as gold, and what was of silver, as silver. ¹⁶ As for the two pillars, the one sea, and the stands, which Solomon had made for the house of the LORD, the bronze of all these vessels was beyond weight. ¹⁷ The height of the one pillar was eighteen cubits, and upon it was a capital of bronze; the height of the capital was three cubits; a network and pomegranates, all of bronze, were upon the capital round about. And the second pillar had the like, with the network.
¹⁸ And the captain of the guard took Seraiah the chief priest, and Zephaniah the second priest, and the three keepers of the threshold; ¹⁹ and from the city he took an officer who had

been in command of the men of war, and five men of the king's council who were found in the city; and the secretary of the commander of the army who mustered the people of the land; and sixty men of the people of the land who were found in the city. ²⁰ And Nebuzaradan the captain of the guard took them, and brought them to the king of Babylon at Riblah. ²¹ And the king of Babylon smote them, and put them to death at Riblah in the land of Hamath. So Judah was taken into exile out of its land.

Destruction of the city (vv. 8–12). Following the abandonment of Jerusalem by Zedekiah, the city fell the following month: the *fifth month, on the seventh day of the month,* or the fifth of July/August, 586 B.C. Jeremiah 52:29 dates the fall of Jerusalem in the eighteenth year of Nebuchadnezzar, while Kings dates it in the nineteenth year. Nebuchadnezzar came to the throne of Babylon in 605 B.C. In Judah the accession year was not reckoned with the regnal years of the king. The writer apparently assumed that 605 B.C. was Nebuchadnezzar's accession year and 604 B.C. his regnal year. Consequently he dated the fall of Jerusalem in the eighteenth year (i.e., 604 less 18, or 586 B.C., as in Kings).

Burning the Temple and other buildings destroyed wooden components, but only in case of extreme heat would the stones have been ruined. The disparaging way in which the Samaritans later derided the attempt to build the wall under Nehemiah does suggest, however, that stones of the city wall were ruined for building purposes (cf. Neh. 4:2).

Plundering the Temple (vv. 13–17). A more specific account of the plundering of the Temple occurs in Jeremiah 52:17–23. In both instances, however, the writers are concerned with the valuable metals, especially bronze, but also gold and silver, which were taken from the Temple (cf. 1 Kings 7:13–51 for a description of the equipment for the Temple).

Execution of Judean leaders (vv. 18–21). In what was probably intended as an example to the captives, the captain of the guard took leading persons of the priesthood and Temple servants, a military officer, five members of the king's cabinet, and an official related to the conscription of troops, plus 60 men at large who were likely prominent leaders, and executed them at the Babylonian military headquarters at Riblah. The closing phrase, *So Judah was taken into exile out of its land,* is the close of the redactor's work, and constitutes the actual conclusion to Kings. The verses which follow are appendices on the Mizpah event and a final reference to Jehoiachin's good treatment and release by the Babylonians.

5. The Aftermath of Jerusalem's Fall: Two Appendices (25:22–30)

(1) Gedaliah's Governorship at Mizpah (25:22–26)

²² And over the people who remained in the land of Judah, whom Nebuchadnezzar king of Babylon had left, he appointed Gedaliah the son of Ahikam, son of Shaphan, governor. ²³ Now when all the captains of the forces in the open country and their men heard that the king of Babylon had appointed Gedaliah governor, they came with their men to Gedaliah at Mizpah, namely, Ishmael the son of Nethaniah, and Johanan the son of Kareah, and Seraiah the son of Tanhumeth the Netophathite, and Jaazaniah the son of the Maacathite. ²⁴ And Gedaliah swore to them and their men, saying, "Do not be afraid because of the Chaldean officials; dwell in the land, and serve the king of Babylon, and it shall be well with you." ²⁵ But in the seventh month, Ishmael the son of Nethaniah, son of Elishama, of the royal family, came with ten men, and attacked and killed Gedaliah and the Jews and the Chaldeans who were with him at Mizpah. ²⁶ Then all the people, both small and great, and the captains of the forces arose, and went to Egypt; for they were afraid of the Chaldeans.

Gedaliah ("Yahweh is great") was a grandson of Shaphan, head of a prominent family in Judah and active in the Josianic reformation (22:3,8). Ahikam, son of Shaphan and Gedaliah's father, was also active in the reform of Josiah (22:12) and supported Jeremiah at a time when the prophet's life was at stake (cf. Jer. 26:24). Jeremiah himself was escorted home by Gedaliah following the fall of the city (Jer.

39:14). Such a family background was not only a likely reason for Nebuchadnezzar's choice of Gedaliah as governor, but in part helps to explain the conciliatory attitude of Gedaliah (cf. vv. 24 f.). A much more detailed account of Gedaliah's governorship at Mizpah, and a source more directly related to the historical events, is present in Jeremiah 40:7 ff.

Nebuchadnezzar adopted a conciliatory attitude toward those left in the land, as evidenced by his appointment of a member of so prominent family as Gedaliah's to the office of governor.

The men who came to Gedaliah at Mizpah constituted portions of those military forces which were scattered during and immediately following the seige of Jerusalem. Gedaliah advised much the same course of action which Jeremiah offered the exiles (Jer. 29:11); be patient, accept Babylonian life, wait for the time of release. That his counsel was repudiated is clearly reflected in Gedaliah's assassination at the hands of Ishmael.

Jews is a terminological reference to the Judeans characteristic of the Exile and following. Technically the word (*y^ehudi*) is an adjective often used as a noun to describe Judeans. The word Judah (*y^ehudah*) is inextricably interrelated with Jew (*y^ehudi*). One could as well translate *y^ehudi* as Judean as Jew. Technically, one should limit "Hebrew" to the preconquest period, "Israel" to the era of the conquest and the monarchy, and "Jew" to the postexilic era.

Chaldean (kasdim) is used in the Old Testament to designate both a people and a land. The term comes from the earlier Babylonian *Kaldu*, prior to the time that *s* replaced *l* (cf. BDB). The region was located in the southern area of the Tigris and Euphrates rivers. Historically the Chaldeans lived a loosely knit tribal existence, opposed to city life as epitomized in Babylon. They opposed both Assyrian advances and the tendency of Babylon (the city) to develop into a culturally and politically dominant power. Out of this struggle (cf. Merodach-baladan) the Chaldeans became undisputed rulers of the Babylonian Empire and the term Chaldean came to be applied to the last dynasty of Babylon (626–539 B.C.; cf. IDB). An examination of the usage in the Old Testament suggests a preference for Chaldean (81) as opposed to Babylonian (12), with the usage predominant in Jeremiah (43). Babylon (276) is more popular in the Old Testament than Chaldea (9), but the preponderant usage remains in Jeremiah. Chaldean and Babylonian are synonymous in 25:25.

Egypt was a common source of safety in times of international crisis. From as early as Abraham to as late as Jesus it gave protection to Semitic fugitives. Exiles had fled to Egypt during crises associated with the Northern Kingdom, and those plus later Judeans constituted the Israelite nucleus for a Jewish center in Egypt which was extremely significant not only for Judaism, but especially for Christianity.

(2) *The Care and Freedom of Jehoiachin* (*25:27–30*)

27 And in the thirty-seventh year of the exile of Jehoiachin king of Judah, in the twelfth month, on the twenty-seventh day of the month, Evilmerodach king of Babylon, in the year that he began to reign, graciously freed Jehoiachin king of Judah from prison; 28 and he spoke kindly to him, and gave him a seat above the seats of the kings who were with him in Babylon. 29 So Jehoiachin put off his prison garments. And every day of his life he dined regularly at the king's table; 30 and for his allowance, a regular allowance was given him by the king, every day a portion, as long as he lived.

Perhaps because of the desire to conclude the book on an auspicious note rather than with the somber account of Jerusalem's destruction, the details of Jehoiachin's care and eventual freedom form a concluding appendix to 2 Kings. *Evilmerodach* (cf. the Akkadian, *Amel-marduk*, man of Marduk), king of Babylon from 562–560 B.C., began his reign with a conciliatory gesture strangely akin to that of Cyrus, who later gave freedom to all exiles.

Amel-marduk freed Jehoiachin, likely, as Gray suggests, because of the ancient belief that one's reign would be like the initiatory actions. Hence, beneficient actions at the time of accession were designed to precipitate a prosperous reign.

Reference to Jehoiachin's *allowance* has been confirmed by archaeological discoveries related to Nebuchadrezzar's palace. There are now available texts which date to the period 595–570 B.C. and refer to the monthly rations for Jehoiachin (cf. W. J. Martin in Thomas, pp. 84 ff.). "The Jehoiachin Tablets" clarify this passage; "To Ya'u-kinu (of the land of Yaudu). ½ (PI) [a PI was about 6½ gallons] for Ya'u kinu, king of the land of Ya (hu-du) 2½ sila [a sila was slightly less than 1½ pints] for the fi(ve) sons of the king of the land of Yahudu 4 sila for eight men, Judeans (each) ½ (sila)." The tablets continue to list supplies for Jehoiachin, his sons, and other Judeans, and appear to be either receipts or inventory lists used by someone in charge of dispensing supplies in the palace of Nebuchadrezzar.

1-2 Chronicles

CLYDE T. FRANCISCO

Introduction

I. Title

The two books of Chronicles contain an account of the dealings of God with man from Adam to Cyrus the Great. They parallel Genesis through 2 Kings, although the material until the Davidic era is composed primarily of genealogies, themselves primarily derived from the earlier biblical materials. Originally 1 and 2 Chronicles were one book; but when the Septuagint translation was made, it was necessary to divide them into two books, the Greek requiring twice as much space as the Hebrew, which had no written vowels.

The Hebrew title for the books reads "things of the days," meaning "things that have happened in the past," that is, history. The Septuagint title means "omitted things," referring to the fact that Chronicles includes material not found in 1 and 2 Kings, which are its principal parallel. Although the Vulgate preserved this title, its translator Jerome suggested that a better one would be "Chronicle of the Whole of Sacred History"; and this is responsible for the present name of the books.

II. Chronicles in the Canon

Although the same author can be discovered in the books of Chronicles and in Ezra-Nehemiah, which deals with Israel's history subsequent to that treated in Chronicles, their order is reversed in the Hebrew canon: the Chronicles are the last books in that canon. This position implies considerable discussion concerning their inclusion. We do not have records, however, that reveal the nature of the causes of hesitation on the part of those responsible for recognizing canonicity.

Debates concerning the admission of Chronicles into the canon must have centered upon whether these books were necessary to the understanding of Israel's history. The rabbis finally admitted this indispensability, a fact which pays tribute to their understanding and discernment. The most skeptical readers must admit that even if the Chronicler has read his own times and viewpoint back into Israel's early history, he has surely at the same time revealed valuable knowledge about his own day, which provides a solid contribution to our understanding of the period of history which he clearly represents. While discussing the past, he revealed the present (cf. Myers, I, xv-xvi).

III. Authorship and Date

It is generally conceded that the same author composed the Chronicles and Ezra-Nehemiah (cf. Bright, pp. 378–383). The same viewpoint is evident everywhere. Some, supported by the Talmud, Baba Bathra 15a, have assumed that Ezra himself is the author. C. C. Torrey (p. 243) sees a remarkable similarity between Ezra and the Chronicler and asserts that "we know that he was a man precisely like the Chronicler himself; interested very noticeably in the Levites, and especially the class of singers; deeply concerned at all times with the details of the cult and with ecclesiastical organization in Jerusalem; armed with lists of names giving the genealogy and official standing of those who constituted the true church; with his heart set on teaching and enforcing the neglected law of Moses. . . . There is not a garment in all Ezra's wardrobe that does not fit the Chronicler exactly."

Torrey asserts that the remarkable similarity is due to the fact that the Chronicler has freely invented an imaginary Ezra in his own image in order to demonstrate the primacy of the returned exiles. From the same evidence, W. F. Albright (XL, 104-124) however, does not see why one cannot identify with the Talmudic tradition that Ezra himself is indeed the author of the accounts. Yet there are remarkable differences between the portrayal of the Chronicler and Ezra. In the first place, the Chronicler was more flexible in his attitude toward the strict keeping of the law. He believed that the Levites should perform priestly functions beyond the menial tasks that the law of Moses prescribed (1 Chron. 23:32; 2 Chron. 5:11; 30:16 f.). He approved of Hezekiah's relaxing the ceremonial laws at the Passover (2 Chron. 30:18-20). Also the extant addresses reveal the Chronicler as speaking in more graphic language than the clerically stylized Ezra. In none of Ezra's memoirs do we find such remarkable phrasing as characterizes the Chronicler. Certainly the Chronicler was related to Ezra, for he was greatly influenced by him. This is probably the origin of the tradition assigning his work to Ezra.

Fleming James [1] believes that the author was a Levite and a Temple singer, for no other section of Scripture is so concerned with sacred music as is the Chronicles. However, this does not necessarily mean that he was a professional musician. He was more than a musician for he clearly performed a prophetic role in the interpretation of Israel's history. He was aware of music's importance in worship and may have been an accomplished musician, but we cannot be certain. That he was an able declarer of the word of God for his day is clearly demonstrated.

His identification seems to be with the Levites more than with the priests (2 Chron. 29:34). His work combines priestly concepts with those of the Deuteronomic school, which produced 1 and 2 Samuel and 1 and 2 Kings. He is the only historian to combine them creatively. To try to understand the history of Israel without comparing Chronicles with Samuel and Kings would be comparable to studying the life of Christ by reading only one Gospel.

He shows no enmity or jealousy toward priests. If he was a Levitical preacher, more of a lay preacher than a cleric, this would explain his somewhat limited views of the course of history. One would expect in such a work a lack of sophistication.

The Chronicler, however, is no narrow churchman. He is an able lay preacher, faithfully using the tools available to him, declaring to the people of his day what they need in order to remain true to their purpose. Rather than establishing a "David-religion," he was trying to show that worship was more important in Israel than the political state, even in David's mind. His concern with Jerusalem worship did not reflect his lack of concern for people everywhere. In 2 Chronicles 16:9 he makes one of the strongest statements concerning the universal concern of God in the entire Old Testament. Only the Chronicler has a foreign king utter a valid prophetic word. (2 Chron. 35:22). Absorbed in his tasks in the Jerusalem cultic community, he did not have time for other concerns with which he must have had many sympathies. No one who used Jeremiah, "the rebel prophet," as the Chronicler did could be a narrow churchman (cf. 2. Chron. 36:21-22 and 15:2-4 with Jer. 29:10-14).

The date of the Chronicler is difficult to determine. The fact that Chronicles ends with the decree of Cyrus, and Ezra begins

---

[1] *Personalities of the Old Testament* (New York: Charles Scribner's Sons, 1946), pp. 483-499.

with that same decree, indicates the exact point where the original work was divided. Certainly the author of Chronicles lived at the earliest in the time of Ezra, the late fifth or the early fourth century. He cannot be later than 180 B.C., for Ecclesiasticus 47:8–10, which echoes 1 Chronicles 23—29, was written at that time. The genealogy in 1 Chronicles 3:19-24 is apparently brought down to the sixth generation after Zerubbabel, who lived about 537–516 B.C., which would place the author no earlier than 350. The list of priests in Nehemiah 12:10–23 extends to Jaddua, who according to Josephus (*Antiq.*, XI.7.8) was high priest in the time of Alexander the Great. Such genealogies, of course, might have been added by editors working later than the original author.[2] Until recent years the tendency has been to place the books of Chronicles during the Greek period (after 333 B.C.). However, there has arisen an increasing conviction that W. F. Albright (pp. 104–124) was correct in his analysis in 1921, although there is little inclination to agree that he has proven Ezra the author. Certainly his evidence points to an earlier date than 333 B.C., as follows: (1) The Elephantine Papyri show conclusively that the Aramaic of Ezra is from the Persian Period. (2) The style of the Chronicler also shows evidence that Hebrew was still a living language, not yet replaced by Aramaic. (3) Also, there are many Persian words, especially in Ezra, that ceased to be common after the Greeks assumed control. (4) The latest Persian king to be mentioned is Darius II (423–402 B.C.). All this evidence points toward a date closer to 400 B.C. than 300. This indicates that the principal author lived just after the time of Ezra, although some materials were added later.[3]

IV. Contents

Chronicles begins with genealogical lists that treat the period from Adam to Saul (1 Chron. 1:1—9:44). Then the united monarchy is treated with great detail, particular emphasis being given to David (1 Chron. 10:1—2 Chron. 9:31). The Chronicler is especially interested in showing that the Levitical and priestly functions of his day were authenticated in that era. His treatment of Solomon is concerned primarily with his building and dedicating the Temple.

Following the division of the united kingdom, the Chronicler discussed only the kings of Judah. In this lengthy section (2 Chron. 10:1—36:21) he gives particular stress to the kings who favored the true worship of God as the Chronicler saw it: Asa, Jehoshaphat, Hezekiah, and Josiah.

Second Chronicles concludes with the decree of Cyrus to rebuild Jerusalem. All has not been lost (2 Chron. 36:22–23).

V. Sources Used by the Chronicler

1. Canonical

About half of Chronicles is either quotations of or clear references to other canonical accounts. These parallels are listed in detail by Curtis and Madsen (XI, 17–19).

It is quite apparent, as one notes the use that the Chronicler makes of these canonical sources, that he is faithful in handling them, copying them into his text with little change. In fact in places where formerly it was believed that he arbitrarily made changes, we now have reason to conclude that he was following a text older than the Masoretic Text and similar to the fragments discovered at Qumran (Myers, I, lxxxix-xc).

2. Noncanonical

As for the other material used by the Chronicler, he states that he is basing many of his remarks upon original sources of information. These are of two basic sorts, annals of the kings of Judah and Israel and excerpts from prophetical works. Although these are referred to under various titles, it is probable that most of this non-canonical source material was from one work which the Chronicler notes under

---
[2] Otto Eissfeldt, *The Old Testament*. (New York: Harper and Row, 1965), p. 540.
[3] Cf. Eissfeldt, *loc. cit.*

various descriptive phrases, a composition that is commonly called the "Commentary of the Book of Kings" (2 Chron. 24:27). This might even have contained most of the prophetic materials mentioned by the Chronicler, though some of these could have been independent sources. Some authorities doubt the existence of the sources mentioned by the Chronicler. They claim that these references are purely literary imitations of the methodology of the canonical books of Kings (Noth, Torrey). Eissfeldt is confident the Chronicler used his sources with integrity.[4] His care in handling the canonical passages indicates he did not deal carelessly with his sources.

It is possible that these sources used by the Chronicler contained the troublesome elements discussed in the following section. These traditional materials had been expanded since the original events. He simply used what he had received (cf. von Rad, p. 350, especially fn. 7).

VI. *The Problem of Historicity*

This is a major concern. Since we do not possess materials in any form except those preserved by the Chronicler, it is most difficult to tell where he is quoting and where he is making his own observations. However, his basic style is obvious when compared with that of the books of Kings. It is marked by a twofold stress: an emphasis in history upon divine intervention in response to prayer and song, and a remarkable interest in cultic activities, particularly those of the Levites. In this respect, he does not so much contradict the books of Kings as he supplements them. Did such events actually occur? Was the developed cult already a part of preexilic Israel? R. H. Pfeiffer says that to "regard Chronicles as genuine history, as orthodox Jews and Christians have done, is to misunderstand the works. . . . [The Chronicler never] allows facts to limit in the least the realm of faith."[5]

[4] Cf. Eissfeldt, *op. cit.*, pp. 532–534.
[5] "Chronicles," IDB (Nashville: Abingdon, 1962), I, 577.

There are two types of passages that raise the question of literal credibility. One is exorbitant claims concerning amounts of money (1 Chron. 22:14) or size of armies. David is said to have saved 100,000 talents of gold and 1,000,000 talents of silver, which would certainly have amounted to billions of dollars. Jehoshaphat is accorded an army of more than a million men. Yet later he is said to be hopelessly outnumbered by the peoples around him.

Actually, we do not know the value of a talent of silver or gold, but the amount attributed to David appears to be too high. The Chronicler may be using "thousand" in a figurative sense. As for the size of Jehoshaphat's army, obviously it was not a million. The word translated "thousand" may mean company, with the number of soldiers in any one company undetermined. There were so many "companies" in Jehoshaphat's army rather than thousands (cf. G. E. Mendenhall, pp. 52–66). It is hardly likely that the Chronicler would claim in chapter 17 that Jehoshaphat had a million in his army and then in chapter 20 picture him as being hopelessly outnumbered. Either the Chronicler was naive, which he could not have been and written such a remarkable book, or we need to look further at the figures in chapter 17 and similar passages. They must surely be understood as less than usual translations indicate.

The other basis for skepticism is the Chronicler's tendency to emphasize the direct intervention of God in history irrespective of the military action of men and other aspects of the human situation. It is quite possible that the Chronicler has embellished the account with details of his own cultic pattern, for what other way would he express himself in his day? This does not have to do with the fact of the basic event, but with the embellishment of the event by a gifted narrator. Yet, even here, we do not know enough about the actual practices ourselves. To pass final judgment upon what he says about such matters as Levitical activities in David's day is presumptuous. With the present developments in the study of the Psalms, which see more and more early preexilic characteristics in the Psalms, we are forced to envision a more highly developed cult in early Israel than was formerly believed.

Recently, the negative criticism of the Chronicler has been tempered by more sober realism. Jacob M. Myers (I, lxiii) remarks: "Furthermore, within the limits of its purpose, the Chronicler's story is accurate wherever it can be checked, though the method of presentation is homiletical."

VII. *Purposes*

It is the Chronicler's clear purpose to give a priestly (or Levitical) interpretation of Israel's history in order to meet the needs of the Hebrew people of the fourth century B.C. He is first of all a theologian, not a historian (cf. Dentan, VII, 12). It would surely be most unfair, therefore, to approach these books with the same expectations that one would bring to a modern historical study. Each form of literature must be understood in light of its own principles of interpretation. We do not dare ask of a historian today that he write concerning everything that has happened, but "a record of what has mattered" (Elmslie). We should not demand more of the Chronicler. What were the issues of the fourth century B.C. that mattered to the writer of this book?

1. *Union with North Israel*

After the fall of Samaria in 721 B.C., the Assyrians forbade the worship of Yahweh in North Israel except in one shrine at Bethel. Even here idolatrous practices had come in. True Yahweh worshipers were inclined to move into Judah or occasionally to attend the Temple worship there. Many northern Levites had ceased to function as priests. When Jerusalem fell in 587 B.C., most of the people were left in the land; but the Temple was destroyed and the Zadokite priests (proper sons of Aaron) were carried into captivity. The lower classes of Levites, north and south, were left to officiate at the ruins of the sanctuary.

Out of this situation the Samaritan crisis began to develop. The returning exiles (primarily from Judah) had rejected as irregular most of the people who were in Palestine when they returned. These gradually found coherence in a Samaritan party, claiming only the Pentateuch as their authority and rejecting the Prophets and the Writings.

The Chronicler was clearly trying to show that although Judah was indeed the chosen nation of God, all those North Israelites who desired to identify with them in true faith and practice should be received with open arms. This had happened during Rehoboam's day (2 Chron. 11:13 ff.) and in the reigns of Hezekiah (2 Chron. 30:1 ff.) and Josiah (2 Chron. 35:18). Obviously the Chronicler longed for it to happen again; he was laying the ground work for it in his writings. He was especially interested in the acceptance of the Levites from whatever region they came.

2. *The Nation Becoming a Congregation*

"The writer is concerned above everything else with the life of Israel centered in the worship at the Temple in Jerusalem" (Curtis and Madsen, p. 7). He discusses David's removal of the ark at great length, and is concerned primarily about his preparation for the Temple construction and Solomon's carrying out those plans. When he describes the reign of later kings, he inserts frequent references to Levitical and priestly activities where other sources are silent. This causes some expositors to feel that he is reading the conditions of his own day, or what ought to be, back into the earlier periods. We cannot tell, however, whether these are anachronisms or if they have been copied from his sources. David is seen as the prime organizer of Levitical orders and choral ministers; all later developments truly originated with him. From his first programs, later forms had their natural development. Believing that David began this worship movement, the Chronicler naturally sees him at the head of all its complexities.

David is of immeasurable significance to the Chronicler (2 Chron. 21:7). Although Judah has ceased to exist as a political power and the Davidic kingship seems farther away than ever, the writer sees in the proper cultic observance in Jerusalem the essentials of the Davidic kingdom (cf. von Rad, pp. 347-354). In his mind the Temple was the principal concern of David; the Temple and its Davidic cult they still possessed. The political entity had become a congregation. In the postexilic observances of the worshiping Israelite congregation the essentials of David's concern were being realized. This substantial fulfillment of promise was God's guarantee of the ultimate achievement of the final victory of the kingdom of God (1 Chron. 29:11-12). As Israel meets the challenge of its call to worship and service, it expresses faithfulness to God. All is not lost if the cult remains. In fact, the most essential aspects of the kingdom of God are preserved—a holy people acting under God. As in a glass darkly the Chronicler has seen the clear outline of what must yet be because of what remained. Admittedly, he emphasizes strict worship in the one sacred spot, yet his emphasis was what was needed in a time when broadmindedness would have resulted in the loss of all uniqueness for Israel (Curtis and Madsen, pp. 16-17).

3. A Call to Repentance

Although the Chronicler is primarily interested in cultic personnel and practices, he nevertheless is vitally concerned with the prophetic word. The words of Jehoshaphat express his own conviction: "Believe in the Lord your God, and you will be established; believe in his prophets, and you will succeed" (2 Chron. 20:20). In every crisis in Judah's history a prophet appears. In fact, the Chronicler produces prophets where they do not occur in other accounts. This causes some to conjecture that he creates the prophet for the occasion (Elmslie, Torrey); the occasion cries out for a prophet. A more likely fact is that he had found these prophets in his sources because he was looking for them.

It is the purpose of the Chronicler, therefore, to show that when the people of Israel heeded the prophetic word, they prospered; when they neglected it, they met disaster (1 Chron. 10:13; 2 Chron. 14:5-6). Even though they have sinned, if they will repent they will find forgiveness from a merciful God (2 Chron. 7:14; 33:11 ff.). The reconciled people will express their faith in God in the prescribed way he has ordained, in proper cultic forms. However, sincerity is more important than religious regularity. In emergencies, the Levites may assume priestly functions (2 Chron. 29:34), and the layman who has not been properly cleansed ceremonially may observe the Passover (2 Chron. 30:18 ff.) The Chronicler respects the law of God but is not a legalist.

4. Learning from History

The Chronicler accepts the Deuteronomic philosophy of history—that there is an automatic connection between evil and disaster, good and prosperity; and he seems to have the mechanical view of this doctrine that is denied by the book of Job. Yet this is not an accurate assessment of his views. He does not necessarily view every act as automatically assuming immediate reward or punishment. Rather, he has selected from the history of Israel only those events that illustrate this. He is well acquainted with David's sin with Bathsheba, for he starts copying the very chapter that contains the story in 2 Samuel. He knows that his readers are also familiar with this story. He is concerned, however, only with David's virtues and their rewards. Likewise, he says nothing about Solomon's sins, for he must show how Solomon's building the Temple is rewarded. He and his readers are aware of the other aspect, but he does not want to stress it now.

Again, the Chronicler has discerned virtues in Rehoboam that no other writer has seen. These were rewarded. This writer is not blind to reality but is simply relating material to prove his point. Only in this way will his readers be warned. If his readers had been left in ignorance, it would be a fault in the author. Since they knew the other facts well, he felt free to dwell upon events that were essential to his purpose. Even with this selectivity, the Chronicler's entire work (Chronicles-Nehemiah) comprises one-tenth of all the Old Testament!

5. *A Reinterpretation of History*

The writer also sought to explain certain difficulties that the former accounts had raised in the minds of the people of his day. Second Samuel 21:19 had said that Elhanan had killed Goliath. This raised doubts that David had performed the act. The Chronicler asserts that Elhanan killed "Lahmi the brother of Goliath" (1 Chron. 20:5). The best known emendation of the Chronicler is found in 1 Chronicles 21:1 which is to be seen over against 2 Samuel 24:1. The passage in Samuel says that God influenced David to take a census and then became angry with him when he took it. The Chronicler, faced with such a dilemma, says that it was Satan who tempted David rather than God. Thus he claims that one must make a distinction between what God permits and what he actively causes. He is involved in all things but not in the same way. First Chronicles 21:1 alone justifies the work of the Chronicler. It reveals the necessity in every generation for a fresh look at history in light of the new revelation that God is always giving of himself.

6. *The Means of Achieving Israel's Purpose*

Essential to the Chronicler's view is his belief that peace is better than war, that the presence of God is more important than armies. David is forbidden to build the Temple because he is a man of war (1 Chron. 22:8). God gives peace when a nation is true to him, so his people do not need to fight (2 Chron. 14:6). If attacked, God protects them (2 Chron. 20:1 ff.). Although the writer's sources contain many bloodthirsty references, which he sometimes repeats without comment (cf. 2 Chron. 13:13 ff.), not a single time in his writings is Israel sent on a typical holy war by God. Most of Judah's battles are defensive. It is the Chronicler's clear conviction that the ideal for a people is peace. Wars are necessary evils when men will not set their hearts upon God. When the nations turn to God, then the age of peace will come in. Therefore, when God's people lift their prayers and praise to God, they are closer to the kingdom of God than when warriors count their slain. When North Israelites and Judeans worship at the common shrine in Jerusalem, they are realizing their true destiny more than when their armies are trying to dominate or use one another.

Outline

I. The family tree (1 Chron. 1:1—9:44)
  1. The patriarchal period (1:1–54)
  2. The tribe of Judah (2:1–55)
  3. The line of David (3:1–24)
  4. Southern tribal lists (4:1–43)
  5. The tribes of Transjordan (5:1–26)
  6. The family of Levi (6:1–81)
  7. North Israelite genealogies (7:1–40)
  8. Benjamite tribal lists (8:1–40)
  9. Metropolitan Jerusalem (9:1–44)
II. Davidic cultic contributions (10:1—29:30)
  1. The tragedy of Saul (10:1–14)
  2. David's rise to power (11:1—12:40)
    (1) God directs his career (11:1–9)
    (2) Davidic heroes (11:10–47)
    (3) His early followers (12:1–22)
    (4) Made king of all Israel (12:23–40)
  3. Moving the ark (13:1—16:43)
    (1) The first abortive effort (13:1–14)
    (2) Heeding prophetic warning (14:1–17)
    (3) Levites bring the ark (15:1—16:3)
    (4) Levitical duties (16:4–43)
  4. The Davidic line established (17:1—20:8)
    (1) The divine covenant (17:1–27)
    (2) David's victories (18:1—20:8)
  5. Temple preparations (21:1—29:25)
    (1) Choice of a building site (21:1—22:1)

(2) Charge to Solomon (22:2–19)
(3) The cultic leaders (23:1—25:31)
(4) Peripheral officials (26:1–32)
(5) Standing army (27:1–15)
(6) Tribal rulers (27:16–24)
(7) The king's officers (27:25–34)
(8) The final charge to Solomon and Israel (28:1—29:25)
6. Summary of the reign (29:26–30)
III. Solomon and the Temple (2 Chron. 1:1—9:31)
1. Prosperity of Solomon (1:1–17)
2. Building of the Temple (2:1—7:22)
   (1) Final arrangements (2:1–18)
   (2) Temple furnishings (3:1—4:22)
   (3) Sanctuary dedicated (5:1—7:22)
3. The later reign of Solomon (8:1—9:31)
   (1) Admirable domestic policies (8:1–18)
   (2) International fame (9:1–12)
   (3) Economic wealth (9:13–28)
   (4) Summary of Solomon's reign (9:29–31)
IV. Embattled Judah (10:1—20:37)
1. The reign of Rehoboam (10:1—12:46)
   (1) Judah alone left (10:1–19)
   (2) Conflicts with Israel (11:1–12)
   (3) Loyal North Israelites (11:13–17)
   (4) The apostasy of Rehoboam (11:18—12:1)
   (5) Shishak of Egypt (12:2–12)
   (6) Summary of the reign (12:13–16)
2. Abijah and Jeroboam (13:1–22)
   (1) A sermon on a mount (13:1–12)
   (2) The battle with Jeroboam (13:13–22)
3. The rule of Asa (14:1—16:14)
   (1) Loyalty to God (14:1—16:14)
   (2) His reward (14:6–15)
   (3) Renewed religious fervor (15:1–19)
   (4) The apostasy of Asa (16:1–10)
   (5) Summary of Asa's rule (16:11–14)
4. The Jehoshaphat era (17:1—20:37)
   (1) His faithfulness (17:1–19)
   (2) The alliance with Ahab (18:1—19:3)
   (3) Religious reform (19:4–11)
   (4) Moabite-Ammonite attack (20:1–30)
   (5) Significance of Jehoshaphat's reign (20:31–37)
V. The struggle with Baalism (21:1—24:27)
1. The house of Ahab (21:1—22:9)
   (1) Jehoram and Athaliah (21:1–20)
   (2) Ahaziah's folly (22:1–9)
2. Athaliah assumes the throne (22:10–12)
3. Jehoiada and Joash (23:1–21)
   (1) Joash proclaimed king (23:1–11)
   (2) The death of Athaliah (23:12–21)
4. The restoration of the Temple (24:1–14)
5. The apostasy of Joash (24:15–27)
VI. In the midst of the years (25:1—32:33)
1. Vacillations of Amaziah (25:1–28)
   (1) An unprecedented act of mercy (25:1–4)
   (2) North Israelite mercenaries (25:5–13)
   (3) Edomite gods worshiped (25:14–16)
   (4) Israel challenged (25:17–24)
   (5) Summary of Amaziah's reign (25:25–28)
2. Uzziah's prosperity and pride (26:1–23)
   (1) Domestic interests (26:1–15)
   (2) Conflict with priests (26:16–23)
3. Godly father, wicked son (27:1—28:27)
   (1) Jotham, loyal to God (27:1–9)
   (2) Ahaz, the idolator (28:1–27)
4. Revival under Hezekiah (29:1—32:33)
   (1) Hezekiah's reformation (29:1–36)
   (2) Passover for all Israel (30:1–27)
   (3) High places destroyed (31:1)
   (4) Providing for clergy (31:2–21)
   (5) The Sennacherib invasion (32:1–23)
   (6) Summary of his reign (32:24–33)
VII. The final years (33:1—36:21)
1. The Manasseh debacle (33:1–25)
   (1) His evil influence (33:1–9)
   (2) His repentance (33:10–17)
   (3) Consequences of his reign (33:18–25)
2. The reform of Josiah (34:1—35:27)
   (1) Destruction of idolatry (34:1–7)
   (2) Renovation of the Temple (34:8–13)
   (3) Discovery of the law (34:14–33)
   (4) The great Passover (35:1–19)
   (5) Josiah's fatal rebellion (35:20–27)
3. The last hours (36:1–21)
   (1) Inept kings (36:1–14)
   (2) The wrath of God (36:15–21)
Postscript: A new era begins (36:22–23)

Selected Bibliography

ALBRIGHT, W. F. "The Date and Personality of the Chronicler," *Journal of Biblical Literature*, XL (1921).
BRIGHT, JOHN. *A History of Israel*. Philadelphia: Westminster Press, 1959.
CURTIS, E. L. and MADSEN, A. A. *A Critical and Exegetical Commentary on the Books Chronicles*. ("The International Critical Commentary.") New York: Scribners, 1910.

DENTAN, ROBERT C. *Kings, Chronicles.* ("The Layman's Bible Commentary.") Richmond: John Knox, 1964.

ELMSLIE, W. A. L. *The First and Second Books of Chronicles.* ("The Interpreter's Bible.") New York and Nashville: Abingdon Press, 1954.

FREEDMAN, D. N. "The Chronicler's Purpose," *Catholic Bible Quarterly,* XXIII (1961).

MENDENHALL, G. E. "The Census Lists of Numbers 1 and 26," *Journal of Biblical Literature,* LXXVII (1958).

MYERS, JACOB M. *I–II Chronicles.* ("The Anchor Bible.") New York: Doubleday and Company, 1965. 2 vols.

NOTH, MARTIN. *The History of Israel.* New York: Harper and Brothers, 1958.

RICHARDSON, H. N. "The Historical Reliability of Chronicles," *Journal of Bible and Religion,* XXVI (1958).

RUDOLPH, W. "Problems of the Books of Chronicles," *Vetus Testamentum,* IV (1954).

RUDOLPH, W. *Chronikbucher* (Handbuch zum Alten Testament) Tübingen: Mohr, 1955.

SLOTKI, I. W. *Chronicles* ("Soncino Books of the Bible.") London: The Soncino Press, 1952.

TORREY, C. C. *Ezra Studies.* University of Chicago Press, 1910.

VON RAD, GERHARD. *Old Testament Theology,* Vol. I. New York: Harper & Row, 1962.

WELCH, A. C. *The Work of the Chronicler.* London: The British Academy, 1939.

Commentary on the Text

1. The Family Tree (1:1—9:44)

Just as modern historians begin their accounts with a discussion of the ethnic backgrounds of a people, the Chronicler prefaces his work with material relating to the origins of Israel. Whether these genealogical lists were prefixed by the Chronicler himself is a matter of debate. Myers is inclined toward attributing the basic lists to the Chronicler while Elmslie denies their original presence in this work. Obviously there have been additions to the original material as new information was discovered or the need arose for bringing the lists up to date. It is impossible to settle the problem of original authorship upon the meager evidence available, since genealogical lists borrowed from various sources hardly present clear identification of the editors. It is sufficient to note that in the last analysis it was thought that no history of Israel was satisfactory that started with the united kingdom in the midst of time. The story of Israel must be viewed in light of the history of man.

The concern with genealogies, therefore, is not the mark of a lack of imagination in a meticulous statistician, but rather evidence of an ecumenical concern. The national history of Israel was the culmination of the history of the race, the building of the Temple where God would dwell becoming the pivotal point in world events. Each generation is the heir of what has gone before, the tides of each age flowing from antiquity. Man's understanding of his own existence as a part of the entire adventure of mankind is essential to his view of life's meaning.

It is important to note that the Chronicler has drawn his earlier material from the book of Genesis, which itself begins with a genealogy of the heaven and the earth (Gen. 2:4). Likewise the New Testament begins with a list that traces Jesus back to Abraham (Matt. 1:1–17), setting his life and work in the context of all that has gone before, seeing his advent as the climax of history until that point.

There were practical uses made of these lists, of course. Not only did they serve as useful tools as reference lists, noting when a king or high priest functioned, but they were important in maintaining the pure Israelite community after the Exile. Here the Levitical families found authentication for their function in Israelite worship, and other clans proved their right to count themselves as sons of Abraham, heirs of the promise. There is no denying that this also produced inordinate pride in some who regarded their pedigree as marking them as better than their neighbors. On the other hand, it safeguarded a national solidarity that individualism could not have preserved. During the days of national oblivion Israel's genealogical heritage was the bond that held them together. Even today the ground of Israelite unity is more their common ancestry than their common faith.

1. The Patriarchal Period (1:1-54)

These lists are drawn entirely from the book of Genesis. The editor assumes that his readers are familiar with the material there and uses only what will contribute to his purposes, although most of the Genesis genealogies are included. Conspicuous for its absence is that of the life of Cain, which the Chronicler considers to lead to a dead end.

(1) The Antediluvian Patriarchs (1:1-3)

¹ Adam, Seth, Enosh; ² Kenan, Mahalalel, Jared; ³ Enoch, Methuselah, Lamech;

Here appears the bare list of the ten men who carried the human race until the flood. There is no attempt to embellish the accounts, even with material from the book of Genesis. No one is mentioned except those in the direct line of the Hebrews. Why does the Chronicler go back to Adam rather than beginning with Abraham? In a time of exclusiveness it might be expected that the Jews would only be interested in their own little segment of humanity. However, even in such a time they could never forget that they were an integral part of a world community, and that all men essentially belonged to one family.

(2) The Family of Noah (1:4-27)

⁴ Noah, Shem, Ham, and Japheth. ⁵ The sons of Japheth: Gomer, Magog, Madai, Javan, Tubal, Meshech, and Tiras. ⁶ The sons of Gomer: Ashkenaz, Diphath, and Togarmah. ⁷ The sons of Javan: Elishah, Tarshish, Kittim, and Rodanim.

⁸ The sons of Ham: Cush, Egypt, Put, and Canaan. ⁹ The sons of Cush: Seba, Havilah, Sabta, Raama, and Sabteca. The sons of Raamah: Sheba and Dedan. ¹⁰ Cush was the father of Nimrod; he began to be a mighty one in the earth.

¹¹ Egypt was the father of Ludim, Anamim, Lehabim, Naphtuhim, ¹² Pathrusim, Casluhim (whence came the Philistines), and Caphtorim.

¹³ Canaan was the father of Sidon his first-born, and Heth, ¹⁴ and the Jebusites, the Amorites, the Girgashites, ¹⁵ the Hivites, the Arkites, the Sinites, ¹⁶ the Arvadites, the Zemarites, and the Hamathites.

¹⁷ The sons of Shem: Elam, Asshur, Arpachshad, Lud, Aram, Uz, Hul, Gether, and Meshech. ¹⁸ Arpachshad was the father of Shelah; and Shelah was the father of Eber. ¹⁹ To Eber were born two sons: the name of the one was Peleg (for in his days the earth was divided), and the name of his brother Joktan. ²⁰ Joktan was the father of Almodad, Sheleph, Hazarmaveth, Jerah, ²¹ Hadoram, Uzal, Diklah, ²² Ebal, Abimael, Sheba, ²³ Ophir, Havilah, and Jobab; all these were the sons of Joktan.

²⁴ Shem, Arpachshad, Shelah; ²⁵ Eber, Peleg, Reu; ²⁶ Serug, Nahor, Terah; ²⁷ Abram, that is, Abraham.

As in the book of Genesis, these lists describe a common geographical and cultural lineage rather than biological. The Japhites were located chiefly in Asia Minor and Europe, the Hamites primarily in Africa and Arabia, and the Shemites in Mesopotamia and Palestine.

The Japhite list is quite abbreviated, probably because they were not so closely involved in Israelite affairs. Fourteen names appear in their list. For Ham, there are 30 (omitting Nimrod), and for Shem, 26, making 70 in all. These represent the 70 nations of the earth which played a conspicuous part in later Jewish thought. Note also the occurrence of 70 in Numbers 11:16, Luke 10:1 ff. The translators of the Septuagint were 70, the title meaning just that.

(3) The Descendants of Abraham (1:28-33)

²⁸ The sons of Abraham: Isaac and Ishmael. ²⁹ These are their genealogies: the first-born of Ishmael, Nebaioth; and Kedar, Adbeel, Mibsam, ³⁰ Mishma, Dumah, Massa, Hadad, Tema, ³¹ Jetur, Naphish, and Kedemah. These are the sons of Ishmael. ³² The sons of Keturah, Abra-

ham's concubine: she bore Zimran, Jokshan, Medan, Midian, Ishbak, and Shuah. The sons of Jokshan: Sheba and Dedan. 33 The sons of Midian: Ephah, Epher, Hanoch, Abida, and Eldaah. All these were the descendants of Keturah.

Isaac is mentioned before Ishmael although he was the younger. This is a change of the order in Genesis, stressing Isaac as the heir. The sons of Ishmael precede those of Keturah, which is also a reversal of the Genesis arrangement.

(4) The Edomites (1:34-37)

34 Abraham was the father of Isaac. The sons of Isaac: Esau and Israel. 35 The sons of Esau: Eliphaz, Reuel, Jeush, Jalam, and Korah. 36 The sons of Eliphaz: Teman, Omar, Zephi, Gatam, Kenaz, Timna, and Amalek. 37 The sons of Reuel: Nahath, Zerah, Shammah, and Mizzah.

The Chronicler copied all the material available from Genesis applying to the Edomites. On the analogy of his omission of the line of Cain completely and his cursory treatment of Ishmael, it is quite significant that he deals with Edom so extensively in this passage and through the rest of the chapter. Apparently the Edomites were still a significant group at the time of writing of this account. By the fourth century B.C. (about the time of the Chronicler) the Edomites had been driven out of their ancestral territory around Petra and had been replaced there by the Nabateans (cf. Obadiah). Some of them remained subject to the new conqueror, while others migrated into southern Judah, and became inhabitants of Idumea. This influx must have had considerable influence on the interest in this people by the Chronicler.

In fact, although there was considerable hostility between Edom and Judah, there is some evidence of a softening of their attitudes in this period. The writer of the book of Job (ca. 550-450 B.C.) has his hero living in Edom being counseled by an Edomite (Eliphaz) who utters traditional Hebrew theology. Herod was an Idumean. Indeed during the last struggle against Rome (A.D. 66-73), these descendants of Esau were the most fanatical defenders of Judah and Jerusalem, certainly justifying the Chronicler's inclusion of their ancestral line in his list.

(5) Sons of Seir (1:38-42)

38 The sons of Seir: Lotan, Shobal, Zibeon, Anah, Dishon, Ezer, and Dishan. 39 The sons of Lotan: Hori and Homam; and Lotan's sister was Timna. 40 The sons of Shobal: Alian, Manahath, Ebal, Shephi, and Onam. The sons of Zibeon: Aiah and Anah. 41 The sons of Anah: Dishon. The sons of Dishon: Hamran, Eshban, Ithran, and Cheran. 42 The sons of Ezer: Bilhan, Zaavan, and Jaakan. The sons of Dishan: Uz and Aran.

This is a list of the earlier inhabitants of the area before the Edomites settled there. Genesis 36:20 calls them Horites (cave-dwellers). They are the sons of the country of Seir, rather than of Esau. This list is apparently included to explain the origin of certain Edomite personal and place names. Uz is mentioned, which is the locale for the book of Job.

The word Seir means "hairy" or "covered with brushwood." The area is mostly high pleateau land, some elevations reaching 5600 feet. The complete denuding of these hills was consummated during World War I.

(6) The Rulers of Edom (1:43-54)

43 These are the kings who reigned in the land of Edom before any king reigned over the Israelites: Bela the son of Beor, the name of whose city was Dinhabah. 44 When Bela died, Jobab the son of Zerah of Bozrah reigned in his stead. 45 When Jobab died, Husham of the land of the Temanites reigned in his stead. 46 When Husham died, Hadad the son of Bedad, who defeated Midian in the country of Moab, reigned in his stead; and the name of his city was Avith. 47 When Hadad died, Samlah of Masrekah reigned in his stead. 48 When Samlah died, Shaul of Rehoboth on the Euphrates reigned in his stead. 49 When Shaul died, Baalhanan, the son of Achbor, reigned in his stead. 50 When Baalhanan died, Hadad reigned in his stead; and the name of his city was Pai, and his wife's name Mehetabel the daughter of Matred, the daughter of Mezahab. 51 And Hadad died.

The chiefs of Edom were: chiefs Timna, Aliah, Jetheth, 52 Oholibamah, Elah, Pinon,

⁵³ Kenaz, Teman, Mibzar, ⁵⁴ Magdiel, and Iram; these are the chiefs of Edom.

Since no king in this list is the son of his predecessors, and each resides in a different place, it appears that a situation existed that was similar to that of the judges in early Israel and to the constant change of dynasties in Northern Israel. The phrase *before any king reigned over the Israelites* literally reads, "before there reigned a king of the children of Israel" and could mean "before a king of Israel reigned over Edom"; that is, before the conquest of Edom by David (2 Sam. 8:14).

Bela, the son of Beor could possibly be the same as Balaam the son of Beor in Numbers 22—24. Thus this early prophet of the true God who turned traitor could have been an Edomite chieftain as well as an oracle. Political motives could have influenced him as well as Balak's bribes.

2. The Tribe of Judah (2:1–55)

Here begins a list of tribal personalities that continues through the chapter. All the descendants of Israel (Jacob) that were of interest to the Chronicler are included. The historian never calls the patriarch by the name Jacob. He is always Israel, the inheritor of the covenant promises, never Jacob.

The most significant impression of this chapter is the variety of peoples assimilated within Judah. Although Judah himself may be seen as a direct descendant of Israel, many of the later members of the tribe of Judah were of a different background. Yet they also considered Judah to be their father, since they were now members of that tribe.

(1) The Sons of Judah (2:1–4)

¹ These are the sons of Israel: Reuben, Simeon, Levi, Judah, Issachar, Zebulun, ² Dan, Joseph, Benjamin, Naphtali, Gad, and Asher. ³ The sons of Judah: Er, Onan, and Shelah; these three Bathshua the Canaanitess bore to him. Now Er, Judah's first-born, was wicked in the sight of the Lord, and he slew him. ⁴ His daughter-in-law Tamar also bore him Perez and Zerah. Judah had five sons in all.

Verse 1 lists all the sons of Israel, placing Judah in his proper relation to the others. Although he is mentioned fourth, he is immediately pointed out in v. 2 as the center of the concern of the Chronicler. The most unusual aspect of the list is the mention of Dan, the son of Rachel's handmaid, before the Rachel tribes. In lists in other books he always follows Benjamin. The tribal roll in Revelation 7 omits Dan altogether. The tribes, however, are seldom enumerated uniformly.

(2) The Descendants of Tamar (2:5–8)

⁵ The sons of Perez: Hezron and Hamul. ⁶ The sons of Zerah: Zimri, Ethan, Heman, Calcol, and Dara, five in all. ⁷ The sons of Carmi: Achar, the troubler of Israel, who transgressed in the matter of the devoted thing; ⁸ and Ethan's son was Azariah.

The sons of Perez are mentioned first, but the Chronicler quickly goes on to present the line of Zerah. Then he feels free to come back to Perez with more detail. Achar is the same as Achan in Joshua 7. There we learn (v.1) that Carmi was a grandson of Perez, Zabdi being listed there as his father (which is a variation of the Zimri in v. 6). The Chronicler makes a play on the word Achar. The participle "troubler" has the same consonants as his name. The final "r" in the name rather than "n" is either the result of association with the place of the sin (Valley of Achor) or a mistake in copying.

(3) The Ancestry of David (2:9–17)

⁹ The sons of Hezron, that were born to him: Jerahmeel, Ram, and Chelubai. ¹⁰ Ram was the father of Amminadab, and Amminadab was the father of Nahshon, prince of the sons of Judah. ¹¹ Nahshon was the father of Salma, Salma of Boaz, ¹² Boaz of Obed, Obed of Jesse. ¹³ Jesse was the father of Eliab his first-born, Abinadab the second, Shimea the third, ¹⁴ Nethanel the fourth, Raddai the fifth, ¹⁵ Ozem the sixth, David the seventh; ¹⁶ and their sisters were Zeruiah and Abigail. The sons of Zeruiah: Abishai, Joab, and Asahel, three. ¹⁷ Abigail bore Amasa, and the father of Amasa was Jether the Ishmaelite.

Hezron was a son of Perez. His name means "enclosure" and his people probably lived in villages rather than being nomads. Ram is traced first, for this leads to David (cf. Ruth 4:18–22). Here we discover that Jesse had seven sons, including David. First Samuel 16:6–11 says that there were eight. The Rabbis suggested that perhaps one died childless so was not mentioned by the Chronicler. The Syriac version adds Elihu, who is mentioned as a brother of David (1 Chron. 27:18). However, this may be a variant of Eliab. The name Eliab means "God is father" and is the earliest attestation to that concept in the Old Testament. It should be noted that the designated parent of the famous "sons of Zeruiah" was a woman, not a man. The other sister, Abigail, married an Ishmaelite, further mixing the blood lines of Judah.

(4) The Ancestry of Bezalel (2:18-24)

18 Caleb the son of Hezron had children by his wife Azubah, and by Jerioth; and these were her sons: Jesher, Shobab, and Ardon. 19 When Azubah died, Caleb married Ephrath, who bore him Hur. 20 Hur was the father of Uri, and Uri was the father of Bezalel. 21 Afterward Hezron went in to the daughter of Machir the father of Gilead, whom he married when he was sixty years old; and she bore him Segub; 22 and Segub was the father of Jair, who had twenty-three cities in the land of Gilead. 23 But Geshur and Aram took from them Havvoth-jair, Kenath and its villages, sixty towns. All these were descendants of Machir, the father of Gilead. 24 After the death of Hezron, Caleb went in to Ephrathah, the wife of Hezron his father, and she bore him Ashhur, the father of Tekoa.

This genealogy is given in order to explain the background of the famous artisan Bezalel, who perfected the furnishings of the tabernacle (cf. Ex. 31, 35–38; 2 Chron. 1:5). He was a descendant of Caleb by his second wife. Also he was the grandson of Hur, who bore the same name as that of Aaron's associate (Ex. 17:10–12; 24:14).

The most important contribution of this passage is the association of the tribe of Judah with the North Israelite inhabitants of Gilead. Their intermarriage illustrates the fact that tribal lines were not always strictly observed within Israel. There was a good deal of settling by small groups in one another's territory.

(5) David's Country Cousins (2:25-41)

25 The sons of Jerahmeel, the first-born of Hezron: Ram, his first-born, Bunah, Oren, Ozem, and Ahijah. 26 Jerahmeel also had another wife, whose name was Atarah; she was the mother of Onam. 27 The sons of Ram, the first-born of Jerahmeel: Maaz, Jamin, and Eker. 28 The sons of Onam: Shammai and Jada. The sons of Shammai: Nadab and Abishur. 29 The name of Abishur's wife was Abihail, and she bore him Ahban and Molid. 30 The sons of Nadab: Seled and Appaim; and Seled died childless. 31 The sons of Appaim: Ishi. The sons of Ishi: Sheshan. The sons of Sheshan: Ahlai. 32 The sons of Jada, Shammai's brother: Jether and Jonathan; and Jether died childless. 33 The sons of Jonathan: Peleth and Zaza. These were the descendants of Jerahmeel. 34 Now Sheshan had no sons, only daughters; but Sheshan had an Egyptian slave, whose name was Jarha. 35 So Sheshan gave his daughter in marriage to Jarha his slave; and she bore him Attai. 36 Attai was the father of Nathan and Nathan of Zabad. 37 Zabad was the father of Ephlal, and Ephlal of Obed. 38 Obed was the father of Jehu, and Jehu of Azariah. 39 Azariah was the father of Helez, and Helez of Eleasah. 40 Eleasah was the father of Sismai, and Sismai of Shallum. 41 Shallum was the father of Jekamiah, and Jekamiah of Elishama.

This preexilic list is the only genealogy of the Jerahmeelites found in the Old Testament. They are mentioned as living in the rural sections of Judah in 1 Samuel 27:10 and 1 Samuel 30:29. Beyond this nothing is known of them. They appear to be originally non-Israelite families that later were absorbed into Judah.

The passage concerning Sheshan (vv. 34–41) is not in the Samuel source. Ahlai could have been a daughter. The story attests to further intermarriage between Jews and Egyptians, in this case an Egyptian male slave (v. 34). The Nathan of this list (v. 36) could well be the same as the prophet of David's day.

(6) The Family of Caleb (2:42-50a)

42 The sons of Caleb the brother of Jerahmeel: Mareshah his first-born, who was the father of Ziph. The sons of Mareshah: Hebron. 43 The sons of Hebron: Korah, Tappuah, Rekem, and Shema. 44 Shema was the father of

Raham, the father of Jorkeam; and Rekem was the father of Shammai. ⁴⁵ The son of Shammai: Maon; and Maon was the father of Bethzur. ⁴⁶ Ephah also, Caleb's concubine, bore Haran, Moza, and Gazez, and Haran was the father of Gazez. ⁴⁷ The sons of Jahdai: Regem, Jotham, Geshan, Pelet, Ephah, and Shaaph. ⁴⁸ Maacah, Caleb's concubine, bore Sheber and Tirhanah. ⁴⁹ She also bore Shaaph the father of Madmannah, Sheva the father of Machbenah and the father of Gibea; and the daughter of Caleb was Achsah. ⁵⁰ These were the descendants of Caleb.

This further delineation of Caleb's descendants is remarkable in its revelation of the composite nature of that clan. There is little doubt that the Caleb of this chapter is the same as Caleb, the son of Jephunneh of the time of the Exodus (Num. 13—14). In each instance Achsah is said to be the daughter (1 Chron. 2:49; Josh. 15:16). Caleb is said to be a Kenizzite (Num. 32:12; Josh. 14:6). Kenaz was a descendant of Esau (1 Chron. 1:36). Thus it is likely that the Calebites were of Edomite origin, but later became a part of Judah. Korah was an Edomite name (1:35), as were Shammah (1:37) and Ephah (1:33).

(7) Kenite Origins (2:50b–55)

The sons of Hur the first-born of Ephrathah: Shobal the father of Kiriath-jearim, ⁵¹ Salma, the father of Bethlehem, and Hareph the father of Beth-gader. ⁵² Shobal the father of Kiriath-jearim had other sons: Haroeh, half of the Menuhoth. ⁵³ And the families of Kiriath-jearim: the Ithrites, the Puthites, the Shumathites, and the Mishraites; from these came the Zorathites and the Eshtaolites. ⁵⁴ The sons of Salma: Bethlehem, the Netophathites, Atroth-beth-joab, and half of the Manahathites, the Zorites. ⁵⁵ The families also of the scribes that dwelt at Jabez: the Tirathites, the Shimeathites, and the Sucathites. These are the Kenites who came from Hammath, the father of the house of Rechab.

The word Kenite means "smith" and describes the itinerant metal workers that had a significant part in early Israelite history. Jethro (Hobab), the father-in-law of Moses came from this background (Judg. 4:11), and the Rechabites of the time of Jeremiah continued some of their old ways (Jer. 35).

Verse 55 presents many difficulties. Most translations regard the people mentioned as inhabitants of unknown towns: Tirathites, Shimeathites, and Sucathites. Jerome discovered here three different types of religious functionaries. Wellhausen also believed that they were something of this sort. It could be that there were three classes of scribes, either in the earlier period, or in the time of the Chronicler, or in both. The root meaning of Tirathite is "mouth," of Shimeathite, "hearing," and of Sucathite, "fence." These terms may well describe the three classes of scribes: those who read aloud for those copying, those who listened or copied, and those who checked the final copies ("fenced them in," protected and preserved them).

3. The Line of David (3:1–24)

One might have expected this material to follow immediately upon the Davidic genealogy in 2:9–17. However, in characteristic fashion the Chronicler dealt with the rest of the family of Hezron before discussing David at greater length. In this chapter the royal line is traced until at least 400 B.C., perhaps until 350, depending upon one's method of counting the total years of a generation. The Septuagint lists the royal line until ca. 250. It cannot be certain that the Chronicler himself completed the records in this chapter. They could have been brought up to date by late compilers. Thus the passage gives no certain clue to the Chronicler's date unless one assumes that he is the final editor, an assumption the evidence would not establish.

(1) The Sons of David (3:1–9)

¹ These are the sons of David that were born to him in Hebron: the first-born Amnon, by Ahinoam the Jezreelitess; the second Daniel, by Abigail the Carmelitess, ² the third Absalom, whose mother was Maacah, the daughter of Talmai, king of Geshur; the fourth Adonijah, whose mother was Haggith; ³ the fifth Shephatiah, by Abital; the sixth Ithream, by his wife Eglah; ⁴ six were born to him in Hebron, where he reigned for seven years and six months. And he reigned thirty-three years in

Jerusalem. ⁵ These were born to him in Jerusalem: Shimea, Shobab, Nathan, and Solomon, four by Bathshua, the daughter of Ammiel; ⁶ then Ibhar, Elishama, Eliphelet, ⁷ Nogah, Nepheg, Japhia, ⁸ Elishama, Eliada, and Eliphelet, nine. ⁹ All these were David's sons, besides the sons of the concubines; and Tamar was their sister.

Here is found the most complete list of David's offspring in the Bible. There are some differences between this list and the names in 2 Samuel 3:2–5; 5:14–16; and 1 Chronicles 14:3–7. The second son of David is Daniel here in v. 1, while he is called Chileab in 2 Samuel 3:3. Eliphelet occurs twice in the present list (vv. 6,8), as Elpelet and Eliphelet in 1 Chronicles 14:5,7, but appears only once in 2 Samuel 5:14–16. Other names are spelled differently in different places. Bathshua is a variant of Bathsheba (v. 5). Her father is said to be Eliam in 2 Samuel 11:3. Ammiel (v. 5) is produced by reversing the two basic syllables of Eliam. These variations emphasize both the difficulty of copying names accurately and the independence of the transmission of the material used by the Chronicler.

(2) *The Descendants of Solomon (3:10–24)*

¹⁰ The descendants of Solomon: Rehoboam, Abijah his son, Asa his son, Jehoshaphat his son, ¹¹ Joram his son, Ahaziah his son, Joash his son, ¹² Amaziah his son, Azariah his son, Jotham his son, ¹³ Ahaz his son, Hezekiah his son, Manasseh his son, ¹⁴ Amon his son, Josiah his son. ¹⁵ The sons of Josiah: Johanan the first-born, the second Jehoiakim, the third Zedekiah, the fourth Shallum. ¹⁶ The descendants of Jehoiakim: Jeconiah his son, Zedekiah his son; ¹⁷ and the sons of Jeconiah, the captive: Shealtiel his son, ¹⁸ Malchiram, Pedaiah, Shenazzar, Jekamiah, Hoshama, and Nedabiah; ¹⁹ and the sons of Pedaiah: Zerubbabel and Shimei; and the sons of Zerubbabel: Meshullam and Hananiah, and Shelomith was their sister; ²⁰ and Hashubah, Ohel, Berechiah, Hasadiah, and Jushabhesed, five. ²¹ The sons of Hananiah: Pelatiah and Jeshaiah, his son Rephaiah, his son Arnan, his son Obadiah, his son Shecaniah. ²² The sons of Shecaniah: Shemaiah. And the sons of Shemaiah: Hattush, Igal, Bariah, Neariah, and Shaphat, six. ²³ The sons of Neariah: Elioenai, Hizkiah, and Azrikam, three. ²⁴ The sons of Elioenai: Hodaviah, Eliashib, Pelaiah, Akkub, Johanan, Delaiah, and Anani, seven.

This material corresponds to the books of Kings until it reaches Josiah (v. 15). Johanan is mentioned as his firstborn, a name found nowhere else. By analogy with 2 Kings 23:30, this should be Jehoahaz, whom Jeremiah calls Shallum (Jer. 22:11). Yet Shallum is listed by the Chronicler as the fourth son of Josiah (v. 15). Apparantly Johanan died at an early age, and Shallum was put on the throne by the people who preferred him to Jehoiakim, who was older.

Another problem is that Zerubbabel is mentioned as the son of Pedaiah, whereas in Ezra 3:2 and elsewhere he is referred to as the "son of Shealtiel." The usual explanation is that Zerubbabel was the actual son of Pedaiah but that Shealtiel had no sons and died early, Pedaiah taking his place as the head of the family. Zerubbabel was considered by Jewish law to be the son of Shealtiel.

It is also of considerable interest that the list past Zerubbabel does not correspond to the genealogy of Jesus in Matthew 1 or Luke 3. These appear to be quite independent of the Chronicler. There are eight generations listed between Jehoiachin and Anani (the last name).

4. *Southern Tribal Lists (4:1–43)*

Assembled in this chapter is additional information about Judah and a summary of the genealogies of Simeon. Much of the material is preexilic and reinforces the Chronicler's claim to historicity. He mentions that some of the lists are quite ancient (v. 22). "To this day" (vv. 41,43) refers not to the Chronicler's day but to the time of the original source. The Chronicler has copied the material verbatim.

(1) *The Tribe of Judah (4:1–23)*

¹ The sons of Judah: Perez, Hezron, Carmi, Hur, and Shobal. ² Reaiah the son of Shobal was the father of Jahath, and Jahath was the father of Ahumai and Lahad. These were the families of the Zorathites. ³ These were the

sons of Etam: Jezreel, Ishma, and Idbash; and the name of their sister was Hazzelelponi, ⁴ and Penuel was the father of Gedor, and Ezer the father of Hushah. These were the sons of Hur, the firstborn of Ephrathah the father of Bethlehem. ⁵ Ashhur, the father of Tekoa, had two wives, Helah and Naarah; ⁶ Naarah bore him Ahuzzam, Hepher, Temeni, and Haahashtari. These were the sons of Naarah. ⁷ The sons of Helah: Zereth, Izhar, and Ethnan. ⁸ Koz was the father of Anub, Zobebah, and the families of Aharhel the son of Harum. ⁹ Jabez was more honorable than his brothers; and his mother called his name Jabez, saying, "Because I bore him in pain." ¹⁰ Jabez called on the God of Israel, saying, "Oh that thou wouldst bless me and enlarge my border, and that thy hand might be with me, and that thou wouldst keep me from harm so that it might not hurt me!" And God granted what he asked. ¹¹ Chelub, the brother of Shuhah, was the father of Mehir, who was the father of Eshton. ¹² Eshton was the father of Bethrapha, Paseah, and Tehinnah the father of Irnahash. These are the men of Recah. ¹³ The sons of Kenaz: Othniel and Seraiah; and the sons of Othniel: Hathath and Meonothai. ¹⁴ Meonothai was the father of Ophrah; and Seraiah was the father of Joab the father of Geharashim, so-called because they were craftsmen. ¹⁵ The sons of Caleb the son of Jephunneh: Iru, Elah, and Naam; and the sons of Elah: Kenaz. ¹⁶ The sons of Jehallelel: Ziph, Ziphah, Tiria, and Asarel. ¹⁷ The sons of Ezrah: Jether, Mered, Epher, and Jalon. These are the sons of Bithiah, the daughter of Pharaoh, whom Mered married; and she conceived and bore Miriam, Shammai, and Ishbah, the father of Eshtemoa. ¹⁸ And his Jewish wife bore Jered the father of Gedor, Heber the father of Soco, and Jekuthiel the father of Zanoah. ¹⁹ The sons of the wife of Hodiah, the sister of Naham, were the fathers of Keilah the Garmite and Eshtemoa the Maacathite. ²⁰ The sons of Shimon: Amnon, Rinnah, Benhanan, and Tilon. The sons of Ishi: Zoheth and Benzoheth. ²¹ The sons of Shelah the son of Judah: Er the father of Lecah, Laadah the father of Mareshah, and the families of the house of linen workers at Beth-ashbea; ²² and Jokim, and the men of Cozeba, and Joash, and Saraph, who ruled in Moab and returned to Lehem (now the records are ancient). ²³ These were the potters and inhabitants of Netaim and Gederah; they dwelt there with the king for his work.

This list contains names that were not included in earlier materials, although some of the names are the same. Of paramount importance is the Jabez episode (vv. 9–10). Because of her pain (*jozeb*) in childbirth, his mother names him Jabez (reversing the last two consonants).

In an age when the curse of a name could, in popular views, only be offset by the magical application of another name (cf. Gen. 35:18), the Chronicler shows that sincere prayer could be even more effective. Admittedly the prayer was an immature one, for Jabez asked to be spared pain at the expense of the suffering of people whom he would replace.

An additional emphasis of this new material is the fact that the Judah families were gifted craftsmen (v. 14), linen workers, (v. 21) and potters (v. 23). The latter were so able that they were retained by the king. This list might have been used to certify the guild members of later times.

(2) *The Tribe of Simeon* (4:24–43)

²⁴ The sons of Simeon: Nemuel, Jamin, Jarib, Zerah, Shaul; ²⁵ Shallum was his son, Mibsam his son, Mishma his son. ²⁶ The sons of Mishma: Hammuel his son, Zaccur his son, Shimei his son. ²⁷ Shimei had sixteen sons and six daughters; but his brothers had not many children, nor did all their family multiply like the men of Judah. ²⁸ They dwelt in Beersheba, Moladah, Hazarshual, ²⁹ Bilhah, Ezem, Tolad, ³⁰ Bethuel, Hormah, Ziklag, ³¹ Beth-marcaboth, Hazarsusim, Bethbiri, and Shaaraim. These were their cities until David reigned. ³² And their villages were Etam, Ain, Rimmon, Tochen, and Ashan, five cities, ³³ along with all their villages which were round about these cities as far as Baal. These were their settlements, and they kept a genealogical record.

³⁴ Meshobab, Jamlech, Joshah the son of Amaziah, ³⁵ Joel, Jehu the son of Joshibiah, son of Seraiah, son of Asiel, ³⁶ Elioenai, Jaakobah, Jeshohaiah, Asaiah, Adiel, Jesimiel, Benaiah, ³⁷ Ziza the son of Shiphi, son of Allon, son of Jedaiah, son of Shimri, son of Shemaiah— ³⁸ these mentioned by name were princes in their families, and their fathers' houses increased greatly. ³⁹ They journeyed to the entrance of Gedor, to the east side of the valley, to seek pasture for their flocks, ⁴⁰ where they found rich, good pasture, and the land was very broad, quiet, and peaceful; for the former inhabitants there belonged to Ham. ⁴¹ These, registered by name, came in the days of Hezekiah, king of Judah, and destroyed their tents and the Meunim who were found there, and exterminated them to this day, and settled in their place, because there was pasture there for their flocks. ⁴² And some of them, five hundred

men of the Simeonites, went to Mount Seir, having as their leaders Pelatiah, Neariah, Rephaiah, and Uzziel, the sons of Ishi; ⁴³ and they destroyed the remnant of the Amalekites that had escaped, and they have dwelt there to this day.

The genealogy of Simeon is found in three other places in the Old Testament: Genesis 46:10; Exodus 6:15; Numbers 26:12–13. As they are compared, there are the usual differences in spelling and omission of names. In the main, however, there is close affinity. Simeon settled within the territory allotted to Judah (Josh. 19:1–9) and, as the Chronicler notes, was far less numerous than that tribe (v. 27). Simeon began to lose its identity early in Israel's history. It is absent from the Blessing of Moses (Deut. 33) and is not among the list of places to which David sent booty (1 Sam. 30:27–31). However, the Chronicler was interested in all Israel. There were probably still Jews in his time that were aware of their individual lineage from Simeon, although the tribe no longer had a conspicuous role to play (cf. Ezek. 48:24).

The list of towns occupied by Simeon should be compared with those in Joshua 19:2–7 and 15:26–32,42. The Chronicler's account appears to be the best preserved of the three, the names being more accurately copied.⁶ Yet the other two sources are earlier. This further illustrates the meticulous care the Chronicler used in the transmission of his material. As he stated, he used an official register (v. 33).

It should be observed that an elderly man who bore the name of the warring tribe was the first one to see that the promised Messiah would be the Suffering Servant rather than a mighty warrior (see Luke 2:25–35). Simeon had come of age!

5. The Tribes of Transjordan (5:1–26)

Although the Chronicler has dealt first with Judah and its component, Simeon, he was nevertheless concerned with all twelve tribes, even those who were no longer sig-

⁶ Cf. Yohanan Aharoni, *Israel Exploration Journal*, VIII, 26–38, 1958.

nificant elements in Israel's life. Here he treats Reuben, Gad, and part of Manasseh, who lost tribal identity during the Assyrian age. Why was he concerned with them? Surely some members of those tribes were still known to him, else the genealogies would be of little value. It is possible, however, that he preserved these old documents simply for the sake of understanding and perpetuating the Hebrew heritage.

(1) The Reuben Clan (5:1–10)

¹ The sons of Reuben the first-born of Israel (for he was the first-born; but because he polluted his father's couch, his birthright was given to the sons of Joseph the son of Israel, so that he is not enrolled in the genealogy according to the birthright; ² though Judah became strong among his brothers and a prince was from him, yet the birthright belonged to Joseph), ³ the sons of Reuben, the first-born of Israel: Hanoch, Pallu, Hezron, and Carmi. ⁴ The sons of Joel: Shemaiah his son, Gog his son, Shimei his son, ⁵ Micah his son, Reaiah his son, Baal his son, ⁶ Beerah his son, whom Tilgath-pilneser king of Assyria carried away into exile; he was a chieftain of the Reubenites. ⁷ And his kinsmen by their families, when the genealogy of their generations was reckoned: the chief, Jeiel, and Zechariah, ⁸ and Bela the son of Azaz, son of Shema, son of Joel, who dwelt in Aroer, as far as Nebo and Baalmeon. ⁹ He also dwelt to the east as far as the entrance of the desert this side of the Euphrates, because their cattle had multiplied in the land of Gilead. ¹⁰ And in the days of Saul they made war on the Hagrites, who fell by their hand; and they dwelt in their tents throughout all the region east of Gilead.

It is necessary for the Chronicler to explain why the birthright did not stay with Reuben, Israel's firstborn; in fact he starts his explanation in the middle of his statement and has to repeat his beginning (vv. 1,3). Reuben's sin is described in Genesis 35:22; 49:4b. Although he is partial to Judah, the Chronicler dutifully admits that Joseph received the birthright. Because of his birthright Joseph was given two portions—that is, two tribal allotments, Ephraim and Manasseh.

Although Joseph received the birthright, Judah became the most powerful tribe through its *prince* (*nagid*, "leader"). This same word is used of David in 2 Samuel 7:8 ff. It is David who is referred to in v. 2 (cf. Psalm 78:67-68).

The name *Baal* is a mark of an early date for this source, for the name was suppressed after the united kingdom. Names compounded with "baal" were changed by scribes to *bosheth*, which means shame (cf. Eshbaal, 1 Chron. 8:33 with Ishbosheth, 2 Sam. 2:8). Some elements of this list must precede 850 B.C. Baalmeon, Aroer, and Nebo fell into Moabite hands after that time. The Hagrites were Arab tribes living in this area. Some derive the name from Hagar, but this derivation is not certain. The Hagrites are also mentioned by the Greek geographers Strabo and Ptolemy, and by Pliny, the Roman.

(2) The Sons of Gad (5:11-17)

11 The sons of Gad dwelt over against them in the land of Bashan as far as Salecah: 12 Joel the chief, Shapham the second, Janai, and Shaphat in Bashan. 13 And their kinsmen according to their fathers' houses: Michael, Meshullam, Sheba, Jorai, Jacan, Zia, and Eber, seven. 14 These were the sons of Abihail the son of Huri, son of Jaroah, son of Gilead, son of Michael, son of Jeshishai, son of Jahdo, son of Buz; 15 Ahi the son of Abdiel, son of Guni, was chief in their fathers' houses; 16 and they dwelt in Gilead, in Bashan and in its towns, and in all the pasture lands of Sharon to their limits. 17 All of these were enrolled by genealogies in the days of Jotham king of Judah, and in the days of Jeroboam king of Israel.

This list is drawn from material unknown to us. There is no relation between this and the one in Genesis 46:16 or Numbers 26:15-18. Sharon is not the plain near Carmel but an area to the east of Transjordan. The mention of Jotham and Jeroboam II dates the source being used by the Chronicler (*ca.* 750-745 B.C).

(3) War with the Hagrites (5:18-22)

18 The Reubenites, the Gadites, and the half-tribe of Manasseh had valiant men, who carried shield and sword, and drew the bow, expert in war, forty-four thousand seven hundred and sixty, ready for service. 19 They made war upon the Hagrites, Jetur, Naphish, and Nodab; 20 and when they received help against them, the Hagrites and all who were with them were given into their hands, for they cried to God in the battle, and he granted their entreaty because they trusted in him. 21 They carried off their livestock: fifty thousand of their camels, two hundred and fifty thousand sheep, two thousand asses, and a hundred thousand men alive. 22 For many fell slain, because the war was of God. And they dwelt in their place until the exile.

This does not appear to be a typical "holy war" in the sense that the eastern tribes were sent into battle on a divine mission. It appears that they went into battle first and then in the midst of it cried to God for help, finding that aid available. It was after the fighting was over that they saw that God was behind it all. The *exile* is the Assyrian one.

The war was of God. How should we understand this statement? Obviously it expressed how the North Israelites and the Chronicler thought about it. They were convinced that God was behind both the battle and the victory. Valuable insight into this soul-searching problem is furnished by G. E. Wright: "Wars exist because of human sin; yet even in war man can hope for salvation because God is actively and righteously at work in it." [7]

The number of fighting men in East Jordan is excessive, although not nearly as high as the census in Numbers 1 and 26. Some exaggeration is possible in the account of the booty taken.

(4) The Half-Tribe of Manasseh (5:23-26)

23 The members of the half-tribe of Manasseh dwelt in the land; they were very numerous from Bashan to Baal-hermon, Senir, and Mount Hermon. 24 These were the heads of their fathers' houses: Epher, Ishi, Eliel, Azriel, Jeremiah, Hodaviah, and Jahdiel, mighty warriors, famous men, heads of their fathers' houses. 25 But they transgressed against the God of their fathers, and played the harlot after the gods of the peoples of the land, whom God had destroyed before them. 26 So the God of Israel stirred up the spirit of Pul king of Assyria, the spirit of Tilgath-pilneser king of Assyria, and he carried them away, namely, the Reubenites, the Gadites, and the half-tribe of

---

[7] "Deuteronomy," IB (New York and Nashville: Abingdon, 1953), II, 391.

Manasseh, and brought them to Halah, Habor, Hara, and the river Gozan, to this day.

Manasseh will be treated further in 7:14–19. Here the eastern tribal elements are mentioned because they shared the common fate of Reuben and Gad, being depopulated by Tiglathpileser in 734 B.C. The passage draws upon 2 Kings 15:19,29; 17:6; 18:11 for its historical material.

So the God of Israel stirred up the spirit of Pul king of Assyria, the spirit of Tilgathpilneser king of Assyria. This verse could be translated by inserting "and" after "king of Assyria." This would assume that the Chronicler confused Pul and Tiglathpileser, thinking that two different kings were meant in 2 Kings 15:19,29 (cf. Curtis and Madsen). However, it is better to understand the terms as synonymous: "the spirit of Pul king of Assyria, even the spirit of Tilgathpilneser." This sort of parallelism is commonly expressed by *waw* (and) in Hebrew (cf. Myers, I, 34).

The theology of the Chronicler is apparent in vv. 25–26. It is the *God of Israel* who stirs up the King of Assyria. Israel's God is supreme over the world. He moves a heathen king to do his will. The campaign of Tiglathpileser was an expression of the wrath of God against the Transjordan tribes. They had foolishly worshiped the gods of the people whom they had displaced. Yahweh had proven his supremacy over these gods when the Hebrews first possessed their land. Now he displayed his power by using heathen people to judge Israel.

6. The Family of Levi (6:1–81)

There are a number of lists in this chapter, all dealing with the priests and the Levites. A clear distinction is made between the functions of the Levites (v. 48) who ministered at the tabernacle and the sons of Aaron who made the sacrifices (v. 49 ff.). The Chronicler implies that this has been true since the days of Aaron. Since Wellhausen, some scholars have challenged the common priestly view in the Old Testament, insisting that before 587 B.C. such limitations were not made. At present the debate continues.[8]

(1) The Chief Priests (6:1–15)

¹ The sons of Levi: Gershom, Kohath, and Merari. ² The sons of Kohath: Amram, Izhar, Hebron, and Uzziel. ³ The children of Amram: Aaron, Moses, and Miriam. The sons of Aaron: Nadab, Abihu, Eleazar, and Ithamar. ⁴ Eleazar was the father of Phinehas, Phinehas of Abishua, ⁵ Abishua of Bukki, Bukki of Uzzi, ⁶ Uzzi of Zerahiah, Zerahiah of Meraioth, ⁷ Meraioth of Amariah, Amariah of Ahitub, ⁸ Ahitub of Zadok, Zadok of Ahimaaz, ⁹ Ahimaaz of Azariah, Azariah of Johanan, ¹⁰ and Johanan of Azariah (it was he who served as priest in the house that Solomon built in Jerusalem). ¹¹ Azariah was the father of Amariah, Amariah of Ahitub, ¹² Ahitub of Zadok, Zadok of Shallum, ¹³ Shallum of Hilkiah, Hilkiah of Azariah, ¹⁴ Azariah of Seraiah, Seraiah of Jehozadak; ¹⁵ and Jehozadak went into exile when the LORD sent Judah and Jerusalem into exile by the hand of Nebuchadnezzar.

Verses 1–3 present the sons of Aaron. Verses 4–15 trace the descendants of Eleazar down to the Babylonian exile, omitting the family of Ithamar. The continuation of a postexilic list is found in Nehemiah 12:10. Elsewhere in the Old Testament the line of Aaron is traced only through Phinehas, his grandson. Omitted from the genealogy are two prominent chief priests, Jehoiada (2 Kings 11—12) and Uriah (2 Kings 16:10 ff.), so the account is not an exhaustive one. It is simply an attempt to show the general line of descent.

When the Lord sent Judah and Jerusalem into exile by the hand of Nebuchadnezzar. This is a clear example of the Chronicler's view of history. The God of Israel, even as he used Assyrian kings, employed Babylon for his purposes of judgment.

(2) The Levites (6:16–30)

¹⁶ The sons of Levi: Gershom, Kohath, and Merari. ¹⁷ And these are the names of the sons of Gershom: Libni and Shimei. ¹⁸ The sons of Kohath: Amram, Izhar, Hebron, and Uzziel.

---

[8] For two different views concerning this most difficult matter see Elmslie, (pp. 364–365), denying early distinctions, and R. Abba, ("Priests and Levites," IDB, III, pp. 876–889), questioning the Wellhausen position.

19 The sons of Merari: Mahli and Mushi. These are the families of the Levites according to their fathers. 20 Of Gershom: Libni his son, Jahath his son, Zimmah his son, 21 Joah his son, Iddo his son, Zerah his son, Jeatherai his son. 22 The sons of Kohath: Amminadab his son, Korah his son, Assir his son, 23 Elkanah his son, Ebiasaph his son, Assir his son, 24 Tahath his son, Uriel his son, Uzziah his son, and Shaul his son. 25 The sons of Elkanah: Amasai and Ahimoth, 26 Elkanah his son, Zophai his son, Nahath his son, 27 Eliab his son, Jeroham his son, Elkanah his son. 28 The sons of Samuel: Joel his first-born, the second Abijah. 29 The sons of Merari: Mahli, Libini his son, Shimei his son, Uzzah his son, 30 Shimea his son, Haggiah his son, and Asaiah his son.

This account follows closely the one in Numbers 3:17 ff. The most noticeable aspect is the inclusion of Samuel in the Levitical line. We read in 1 Samuel 1:1 that Elkanah, the father of Samuel, was an Ephraimite. Of course he could have been a Levite who lived in Ephraim, yet there is no indication of this in the books of Samuel. Apparently a person who was not a Levite by birth could be adopted into the tribe.

(3) *The Levitical Choirs (6:31-48)*

31 These are the men whom David put in charge of the service of song in the house of the LORD, after the ark rested there. 32 They ministered with song before the tabernacle of the tent of meeting, until Solomon had built the house of the LORD in Jerusalem; and they performed their service in due order. 33 These are the men who served and their sons. Of the sons of the Kohathites: Heman the singer the son of Joel, son of Samuel, 34 son of Elkanah, son of Jeroham, son of Eliel, son of Toah, 35 son of Zuph, son of Elkanah, son of Mahath, son of Amasai, 36 son of Elkanah, son of Joel, son of Azariah, son of Zephaniah, 37 son of Tahath, son of Assir, son of Ebiasaph, son of Korah, 38 son of Izhar, son of Kohath, son of Levi, son of Israel; 39 and his brother Asaph, who stood on his right hand, namely, Asaph the son of Berechiah, son of Shimea, 40 son of Michael, son of Baaseiah, son of Malchijah, 41 son of Ethni, son of Zerah, son of Adaiah, 42 son of Ethan, son of Zimmah, son of Shimei, 43 son of Jahath, son of Gershom, son of Levi. 44 On the left hand were their brethren the sons of Merari: Ethan the son of Kishi, son of Abdi, son of Malluch, 45 son of Hashabiah, son of Amaziah, son of Hilkiah, 46 son of Amzi, son of Bani, son of Shemer, 47 son of Mahli, son of Mushi, son of Merari, son of Levi; 48 and their brethren the Levites were appointed for all the service of the tabernacle of the house of God.

Each of the three main families of the Levitical order furnished representatives who conducted the worship in music: Heman, the descendant of Kohath, Asaph, of the line of Gershom; and Ethan, of the family of Merari. It is claimed by the Chronicler that David was the organizer of these musical guilds and first appointed the three leaders listed above. Not only does the historian assert this here but also in many other passages (15:16,27; 25:1 ff.; 2 Chron. 29:26 ff.; Neh. 12:46 ff.). Traditions about David claimed that he was an accomplished musician (1 Sam. 16:14 ff.; 2 Sam. 1:17 ff.), and the association of his name with the Psalms certainly has some basis in fact, although all Psalms attributed to him were not composed by him. Such early musical guilds, influenced by Canaanite culture, very likely existed.[9]

(4) *The Zadokite Priests (6:49-53)*

49 But Aaron and his sons made offerings upon the altar of burnt offering and upon the altar of incense for all the work of the most holy place, and to make atonement for Israel, according to all that Moses the servant of God had commanded. 50 These are the sons of Aaron: Eleazar his son, Phinehas his son, Abishua his son, 51 Bukki his son, Uzzi his son, Zerahiah his son, 52 Meraioth his son, Amariah his son, Ahitub his son, 53 Zadok his son, Ahimaaz his son.

The purpose of this section seems to be to provide a link between Aaron and Zadok, and to stress the distinctive role of the Zadokite priests. They were the ones designated to conduct the sacrifice and incense offerings, to go into the holy place, and to effect atonement for Israel.

Zadok is almost as mysterious a person as his predecessor Melchizedek (Gen. 14), whose name is compounded with his own. He suddenly appears during the reign of David. Although he has a father (Ahitub, 2 Sam. 8:17) and sons (Ahimaaz, 2 Sam.

---

[9] Cf. W. F. Albright, *Archaeology and the Religion of Israel* (5th ed.; Baltimore: Johns Hopkins University Press, 1956), p. 126.

15:36; 18:19; Azariah, 1 Kings 4:2), nothing else is known about his ancestry from contemporary sources or any other until the work of the Chronicler. There are some who insist that he was in the succession of Jebusite priests related to Melchizedek, and that he was serving in this capacity when David captured Jerusalem. His appointment as priest alongside the Aaronic Abiathar was an attempt to bring the Jebusite and Israelite factions together.[10] Others conjecture that he was the one in charge of the ark while it was still at Kiriathjearim, and David retained him in his service.[11] Von Rad (pp. 248–249) is skeptical of a satisfactory conclusion to the problem. Zadok's own generation regarded him as a legitimate priest; and if it was necessary for him to be adopted into the Aaronic family for later generations to accept this, the process is understandable.

(5) *Levitical Land Allotments* (6:54–81)

These statistics are similar to the ones in Joshua 21. The list here combines cities of refuge with cities in which Levites were living. This does not mean that only Levites were living in the particular cities listed but rather that they had a portion there. There is every indication that the basic list came from the time of David. Such Canaanite cities as Gezer (v. 67) and Bileam (v. 70) did not become a part of Israelite territory until then. Gezer was destroyed by Shishak of Egypt (*ca.* 900 B.C.), and Golan (v. 71) probably came under Syrian control after the time of Benhadad (1 Kings 15:20). The distribution of the Levitical cities by tribes rather than administrative districts reveals a time before Solomon.

a. *The Cities of the Priests* (6:54–65)

54 These are their dwelling places according to their settlements within their borders: to the sons of Aaron of the families of Kohathites, for theirs was the lot, 55 to them they gave Hebron

[10] Cf. H. H. Rowley, "Zadok and Nehushtan," JBL, LVIII (1939), 113–41.
[11] Cf. R. W. Corney, IDB, IV, p. 928.

in the land of Judah and its surrounding pasture lands, 56 but the fields of the city and its villages they gave to Caleb the son of Jephunneh. 57 To the sons of Aaron they gave the cities of refuge: Hebron, Libnah with its pasture lands, Jattir, Eshtemoa with its pasture lands, 58 Hilen with its pasture lands, Debir with its pasture lands, 59 Ashan with its pasture lands, and Beth-shemesh with its pasture lands; 60 and from the tribe of Benjamin, Geba with its pasture lands, Alemeth, with its pasture lands, and Anathoth with its pasture lands. All their cities throughout their families were thirteen.
61 To the rest of the Kohathites were given by lot out of the family of the tribe, out of the half-tribe, the half of Manasseh, ten cities. 62 To the Gershomites according to their families were allotted thirteen cities out of the tribes of Issachar, Asher, Naphtali, and Manasseh in Bashan. 63 To the Merarites according to their families were allotted twelve cities out of the tribes of Reuben, Gad, and Zebulun. 64 So the people of Israel gave the Levites the cities with their pasture lands. 65 They also gave them by lot out of the tribes of Judah, Simeon, and Benjamin these cities which are mentioned by name.

The Aaronic priests were given cities in Judah and Benjamin, near their place of service in Jerusalem. An adjustment had to be made in respect to the Caleb family, who had conquered the territory of Hebron and who owned it by right of conquest. To avoid conflict a compromise was worked out. The priests would be allotted the city of Hebron and its nearby pastures, but the Calebites kept possession of the villages and farm land of the area. The descendants of Caleb probably were more rural than urban, and the Jerusalem priests were the opposite.

This arrangement will be treated at greater length in the treatment of 6:66–81 when the nonsacrificing priests' territory is mentioned. The Kohathites were given cities in the western territory of Manasseh; the Gershomites cities in Issachar, Asher, Naphtali, and East-Manasseh; the Merarites cities in Reuben, Gad, and Zebulun. The Israelites voluntarily consigned these living areas within their territories. Such provisions would inevitably mean that local worship services would be developed.

b. Levitical Cities in Ephraim and West-Manasseh (6:66–70)

⁶⁶ And some of the families of the sons of Kohath had cities of their territory out of the tribe of Ephraim. ⁶⁷ They were given the cities of refuge: Shechem with its pasture lands in the hill country of Ephraim, Gezer with its pasture lands, ⁶⁸ Jokmeam with its pasture lands, Bethhoron with its pasture lands, ⁶⁹ Aijalon with its pasture lands, Gathrimmon with its pasture lands, ⁷⁰ and out of the half-tribe of Manasseh, Aner with its pasture lands, and Bileam with its pasture lands, for the rest of the families of the Kohathites.

Corresponding to the apportionment of cities in Judah to the Aaronic priests, other descendants of Kohath, the grandfather of Aaron, had assignments in Ephraim and West-Manasseh, close by Jerusalem. These were given dwellings farther away from Jerusalem. This might have been both by choice and governmental design.

c. Gershomite and Merarite Territory (6:71–81)

⁷¹ To the Gershomites were given out of the half-tribe of Manasseh: Golan in Bashan with its pasture lands and Ashtaroth with its pasture lands; ⁷² and out of the tribe of Issachar: Kedesh with its pasture lands, Daberath with its pasture lands, ⁷³ Ramoth with its pasture lands, and Anem with its pasture lands; ⁷⁴ out of the tribe of Asher: Mashal with its pasture lands, Abdon with its pasture lands, ⁷⁵ Hukok with its pasture lands, and Rehob with its pasture lands; ⁷⁶ and out of the tribe of Naphtali: Kedesh in Galilee with its pasture lands, Hammon with its pasture lands, and Kiriathaim with its pasture lands. ⁷⁷ To the rest of the Merarites were allotted out of the tribe of Zebulun: Rimmono with its pasture lands, Tabor with its pasture lands, ⁷⁸ and beyond the Jordan at Jericho, on the east side of the Jordan, out of the tribe of Reuben: Bezer in the steppe with its pasture lands, Jahzah with its pasture lands, ⁷⁹ Kedemoth with its pasture lands, and Mephaath with its pasture lands; ⁸⁰ and out of the tribe of Gad: Ramoth in Gilead with its pasture lands, Mahanaim with its pasture lands, ⁸¹ Heshbon with its pasture lands, and Jazer with its pasture lands.

The Kohath (Aaronic) family now being disposed of, the Chronicler first lists the allotment of Gershom, the firstborn of Levi, and Merari, his youngest. Gershom was assigned towns in East-Manasseh, Asher, Issachar, and Naphtali, primarily in Galilee. The Merari group was settled in Reuben, Zebulun, and Gad—the Transjordan area and a pocket (Zebulun) in north-central Israel. The Golan heights above the Sea of Galilee control the entire area. This is why Benhadad moved so quickly to acquire that area. When the Levites possessed it in ancient Israel, they owned the best land in the region.

7. North Israelite Genealogies (7:1–40)

With this chapter the Chronicler begins a new emphasis, stressing the number of warriors among the northern tribes. Since he has no particular concern with military prowess, but more with priestly cult and ritual, this is quite strange, for he continues this theme through chapter 8. This has not been his emphasis before with the exception of the account of another North Israelite situation (5:18–22). Could he be teaching that Judah's strength was in an area other than the military and that military prowess did not guarantee the future of a people? However, his account may simply illustrate the thrust of the sources he was using. They were military census lists, while he had access in the South to other types of family records.

(1) The Sons of Issachar (7:1–5)

¹ The sons of Issachar: Tola, Puah, Jashub, and Shimron, four. ² The sons of Tola: Uzzi, Rephaiah, Jeriel, Jahmai, Ibsam, and Shemuel, heads of their fathers' houses, namely of Tola, mighty warriors of their generations, their number in the days of David being twenty-two thousand six hundred. ³ The sons of Uzzi: Izrahiah. And the sons of Izrahiah: Michael, Obadiah, Joel, and Isshiah, five, all of them chief men; ⁴ and along with them, by their generations, according to their fathers' houses, were units of the army for war, thirty-six thousand, for they had many wives and sons. ⁵ Their kinsmen belonging to all the families of Issachar were in all eighty-seven thousand mighty warriors, enrolled by genealogy.

This list parallels Genesis 46:13 and Numbers 26:23–25. The most interesting variation is the mention of Jashub in v. 1 where Genesis 46 has Iob (Job). In the census lists of Numbers 1 and 26 the totals for Issachar are 54,400 and 64,300 respectively. Here it is 87,000. Where the Chronicler is getting his statistics we do not know. There is even uncertainty about the meaning of "thousand." It may mean a military unit whose normal complement of men is a thousand but whose quota is not always filled (cf. C. F. Mendenhall, pp. 52–66; also discussion in Introduction).

(2) *The Sons of Zebulun and Dan (7:6–12)*

6 The sons of Benjamin: Bela, Becher, and Jediael, three. 7 The sons of Bela: Ezbon, Uzzi, Uzziel, Jerimoth, and Iri, five, heads of fathers' houses, mighty warriors; and their enrollment by genealogies was twenty-two thousand and thirty-four. 8 The sons of Becher: Zemirah, Joash, Eliezer, Elioenai, Omri, Jeremoth, Abijah, Anathoth, and Alemeth. 9 All these were the sons of Becher; and their enrollment by genealogies, according to their generations, as heads of their fathers' houses, mighty warriors, was twenty thousand two hundred. 10 The sons of Jediael: Bilhan. And the sons of Bilhan: Jeush, Benjamin, Ehud, Chenaanah, Zethan, Tarshish, and Ahishahar. 11 All these were the sons of Jediael according to the heads of their fathers' houses, mighty warriors, seventeen thousand and two hundred, ready for service in war. 12 And Shuppim and Huppim were the sons of Ir, Hushim the sons of Aher.

There have apparently been scribal errors in connection with this section. Chapter 8 contains the genealogy of Benjamin, and there is no Zebulun list unless it is here (vv. 6–12). The totals 59,434 compare with 57,400 and 60,500 of the Numbers lists for Zebulun, whereas for Benjamin, these lists total 35,400 and 45,600. The account here begins strangely: *Benjamin*, where one would expect the usual expression "sons of" preceding the name of the tribe. This record also is in the place in the tribal lists where Zebulun usually occurs.

Most of the names in the list are not those usually assigned to Benjamin. Others are recognizable Zebulun personages. When one compares the Hebrew of Genesis 46:14 with that of 1 Chronicles 7:6 it is easy to see how later scribes read *bene zebulun* (sons of Zebulun) for Benjamin, since there were no vowels written in the words, and *j* and *z* were written very much alike (for an exhaustive study of this problem see Curtis and Madsen, pp. 145–150).

Verse 12 probably is a reference to Dan, although the name of the tribe has dropped out in transmission. In Genesis 46:23 Dan only has one son, Hushim, as indicated here. *Hushim the sons of Aher* should read, "Hushim, one son."

(3) *The Sons of Naphtali and Manasseh (7:13–19)*

13 The sons of Naphtali: Jahziel, Guni, Jezer, and Shallum, the offspring of Bilhah.
14 The sons of Manasseh: Asriel, whom his Aramaean concubine bore; she bore Machir the father of Gilead. 15 And Machir took a wife for Huppim and for Shuppim. The name of his sister was Maacah. And the name of the second was Zelophehad; and Zelophehad had daughters. 16 And Maacah the wife of Machir bore a son, and she called his name Peresh; and the name of his brother was Sheresh; and his sons were Ulam and Rakem. 17 The sons of Ulam: Bedan. These were the sons of Gilead the son of Machir, son of Manasseh. 18 And his sister Hammolecheth bore Ishhod, Abiezer, and Mahlah. 19 The sons of Shemida were Ahian, Shechem, Likhi, and Aniam.

The Naphtali list is derived from Genesis 46:24 and is identical with it. Evidently that account and Numbers 26:48 were the only records available to the Chronicler. This was not true of most of the other tribal lists. It could have been that this tribe suffered more destruction in the Assyrian conquests, the tribal records being lost.

The Manasseh account deals both with Transjordan and West-Manasseh. As usual the name Machir (v. 14) is the most prominent. Also the daughters of Zelophehad appear (cf. Num. 26:33). The Chronicler gives more place to women in his genealogies than is common in the Old Testament. The mention of the Aramaean concubine of East-Manasseh and Syria acknowledges the close interrelationship existing between them. This eventually led to Syrian domination of Manasseh, the Hebrew women becoming the concubines of

(4) The Sons of Ephraim (7:20-29)

²⁰ The sons of Ephraim: Shuthelah, and Bered his son, Tahath his son, Eleadah his son, Tahath his son, ²¹ Zabad his son, Shuthelah his son, and Ezer and Elead, whom the men of Gath who were born in the land slew, because they came down to raid their cattle. ²² And Ephraim their father mourned many days, and his brothers came to comfort him. ²³ And Ephraim went in to his wife, and she conceived and bore a son; and he called his name Beriah, because evil had befallen his house. ²⁴ His daughter was Sheerah, who built both Lower and Upper Bethhoron, and Uzzensheerah. ²⁵ Rephah was his son, Resheph his son, Telah his son, Tahan his son, ²⁶ Ladan his son, Ammihud his son, Elishama his son, ²⁷ Nun his son, Joshua his son. ²⁸ Their possessions and settlements were Bethel and its towns, and eastward Naaran, and westward Gezer and its towns, Shechem and its towns, and Ayyah and its towns; ²⁹ also along the borders of the Manassites, Bethshean and its towns, Taanach and its towns, Megiddo and its towns, Dor and its towns. In these dwelt the sons of Joseph the son of Israel.

The most illustrious person in this account is Joshua, the son of Nun (v. 27).

The reference to the slaying of Ephraim's sons by the men of Gath points to an early date for this account for it reveals the sort of situation that must have prevailed when the tribes first lived in Palestine. They had conducted a cattle raid, like the forays of Western outlaws in the early days of the United States.

Ephraim's daughter Sheerah is said to have built two cities. Curtis and Madsen (p. 154) doubt the authenticity of the statement "since elsewhere in the OT the founders of cities are men." This is exactly the point of the account. Here is a woman doing something that only men had done before.

(5) The Sons of Asher (7:30-40)

³⁰ The sons of Asher: Imnah, Ishvah, Ishvi, Beriah, and their sister Serah. ³¹ The sons of Beriah: Heber and Malchiel, who was the father of Birzaith. ³² Heber was the father of Japhlet, Shomer, Hotham, and their sister Shua. ³³ The sons of Japhlet: Pasach, Bimhal, and Ashvath. These are the sons of Japhlet. ³⁴ The sons of Shemer his brother: Rohgah, Jehubbah, and Aram. ³⁵ The sons of Helem his brother: Zophah, Imna, Shelesh, and Amal. ³⁶ The sons of Zophah: Suah, Harnepher, Shual, Beri, Imrah, ³⁷ Bezer, Hod, Shamma, Shilshah, Ithran, and Beera. ³⁸ The sons of Jether: Jephunneh, Pispa, and Ara. ³⁹ The sons of Ulla: Arah, Hanniel, and Rizia. ⁴⁰ All of these were men of Asher, heads of fathers' houses, approved, mighty warriors, chief of the princes. Their number enrolled by genealogies, for service in war, was twenty-six thousand men.

One third of the names in this list are found only here, and appear to be quite ancient (cf. Curtis and Madsen). The fullness of this account is quite unusual in light of the fact that Asher was one of the lesser Zilpah (Leah's handmaid) tribes. An ancient record must have been used by the Chronicler. The total number of warriors for the tribe is listed as 26,000. This is considerably less than the 41,500 and 53,400 of Numbers 1 and 26. Some contend that this is the total of one of the families, but that is not the claim of the Chronicler. With his tendency to exaggerate numbers, why does he not do so here? This statistic is solid evidence that he copied down his figures as he found them. His exorbitant figures in other places must have been derived from later sources. Where his sources are realistic, so is he.

8. Benjamite Tribal Lists (8:1-40)
(1) The Benjamite Families (8:1-28)

¹ Benjamin was the father of Bela his firstborn, Ashbel the second, Aharah the third, ² Nohah the fourth, and Rapha the fifth. ³ And Bela had sons: Addar, Gera, Abihud, ⁴ Abishua, Naaman, Ahoah, ⁵ Gera, Shephuphan, and Huram. ⁶ These are the sons of Ehud (they were heads of fathers' houses of the inhabitants of Geba, and they were carried into exile to Manahath): ⁷ Naaman, Ahijah, and Gera, that is, Heglam, who was the father of Uzza and Ahihud. ⁸ And Shaharaim had sons in the country of Moab after he had sent away Hushim and Baara his wives. ⁹ He had sons by Hodesh his wife: Jobab, Zibia, Mesha, Malcam, ¹⁰ Jeuz, Sachia, and Mirmah. These were his sons, heads of fathers' houses. ¹¹ He also had sons by Hushim: Abitub and Elpaal. ¹² The sons of Elpaal: Eber, Misham, and

Shemed, who built Ono and Lod with its towns, 13 and Beriah and Shema (they were heads of fathers' houses of the inhabitants of Aijalon, who put to flight the inhabitants of Gath); 14 and Ahio, Shashak, and Jeremoth. 15 Zebadiah, Arad, Eder, 16 Michael, Ishpah, and Joha were sons of Beriah. 17 Zebadiah, Meshullam, Hizki, Heber, 18 Ishmerai, Izliah, and Jobab were the sons of Elpaal. 19 Jakim, Zichri, Zabdi, 20 Elienai, Zillethai, Eliel, 21 Adaiah, Beraiah, and Shimrath were the sons of Shimei. 22 Ishpan, Eber, Eliel, 23 Abdon, Zichri, Hanan, 24 Hananiah, Elam, Anthothijah, 25 Iphdeiah, and Penuel were the sons of Shashak. 26 Shamsherai, Shehariah, Athaliah, 27 Jaareshiah, Elijah, and Zichri were the sons of Jeroham. 28 These were the heads of fathers' houses, according to their generations, chief men. These dwelt in Jerusalem.

When this list is compared with the accounts in Genesis 46:21 and Numbers 26:38–40, it has affinities and differences with each of them. The Chronicler must have supplemented both these sources with independent material. This passage is fraught with distressing difficulties. There is no section in these genealogies with more insuperable problems. Most of them result from apparent textual corruption. Perhaps after copying all the preceding statistics in Chronicles, the scribes were utterly exhausted!

Nothing is known about the exile to Manahath (v. 6). In v. 7 *that is, Heglam* literally reads in the Hebrew, "he exiled them." We do not know who exiled whom in this statement. Did Ehud exile Naaman, Ahijah, and Gera and go into voluntary exile? Or is Gera the one who did the exiling? We know nothing elsewhere of Shaharaim (v. 8). Did he divorce two of his wives, even one who had borne him children (v. 11)? This would be the only example of such double divorce in the Old Testament. This could have happened, of course; but the name Hushim, that of the supposed first wife, in other places is always a man's name. Yet women sometimes are given masculine names.

Satisfactory resolutions of these and similar problems await further discoveries. There are many conjectural restorations of the text, but such guesses are precarious.

(2) *The Family of Saul (8:29–40)*

29 Jeiel the father of Gibeon dwelt in Gibeon, and the name of his wife was Maacah. 30 His first-born son: Abdon, then Zur, Kish, Baal, Nadab, 31 Gedor, Ahio, Zecher, 32 and Mikloth (he was the father of Shimeah). Now these also dwelt opposite their kinsmen in Jerusalem, with their kinsmen. 33 Ner was the father of Kish, Kish of Saul, Saul of Jonathan, Malchishua, Abinadab, and Eshbaal; 34 and the son of Jonathan was Meribbaal; and Meribbaal was the father of Micah. 35 The sons of Micah: Pithon, Melech, Tarea, and Ahaz. 36 Ahaz was the father of Jehoaddah; and Jehoaddah was the father of Alemeth, Azmaveth, and Zimri; Zimri was the father of Moza. 37 Moza was the father of Binea; Raphah was his son, Eleasah his son, Azel his son. 38 Azel had six sons, and these are their names: Azrikam, Bocheru, Ishmael, Sheariah, Obadiah, and Hanan. All these were the sons of Azel. 39 The sons of Eshek his brother: Ulam his first-born, Jeush the second, and Eliphelet the third. 40 The sons of Ulam were men who were mighty warriors, bowmen, having many sons and grandsons, one hundred and fifty. All these were Benjaminites.

It is obvious that the purpose of this passage is to present the ancestors and kinsmen of Saul. Yet this is not done in unbroken line. After presenting Jeiel (whose name is not actually present in this list but is gleaned from 9:35) and his sons, the genealogy moves to Saul's immediate kin. However these are not connected with Jeiel. In fact Kish is said to be the son of Ner. Elsewhere Abner, the commander of the armies of Saul, is said to be the son of Ner and the cousin of Saul (1 Sam. 14:50). Abner's grandfather was Abiel (1 Sam. 14:51). Thus it would appear that Abiel was also the grandfather of Kish. First Samuel 9:1 says Kish was the son of Abiel, but this could also mean grandson. Again a scribal mistake has possibly been made. Verse 33 might have read, "Ner was the father of Abner, Kish of Saul." In the copying, Abner's name was overlooked and Kish written twice. However, it is also possible that Ner was the father of Kish as well as of Abner and that Abner was the uncle of Saul rather than his cousin. This would authenticate the present text.

The presence of Baal among the names in this passage (vv. 30,33–34), which happens in many of the Chronicler's accounts, reveals again his faithfulness to his records. Later generations suppressed such names, often substituting *bosheth* (shame) for Baal. In 2 Samuel, Eshbaal (8:33) becomes Ishbosheth (2 Sam. 2:8), and Meribaal (8:34) becomes Mephibosheth (2 Sam. 9:6). Why is this substitution made in Samuel, the earlier account, and not in Chronicles? The passages in Samuel were regularly read aloud in the later synagogue and Chronicles was not.

9. Metropolitan Jerusalem (9:1–44)

There is a close relationship between this chapter and Nehemiah 11. They correspond most closely in the priestly and Levitical names. However, the Hebrew text of Nehemiah 11 has about 81 names to 1 Chronicles' 71, yet only about 35 closely resemble one another. There are also many differences in the lists. Possibly what has happened is that an earlier preexilic list is brought up to date by the Chronicler with the help of Nehemiah's statistics. The basic setting for the chapter is similar to the situation after the return from Babylonian exile pictured in Nehemiah.

(1) The First Returnees (9:1–9)

¹ **So all Israel was enrolled by genealogies; and these are written in the Book of the Kings of Israel. And Judah was taken into exile in Babylon because of their unfaithfulness.** ² **Now the first to dwell again in their possessions in their cities were Israel, the priests, the Levites, and the temple servants.** ³ **And some of the people of Judah, Benjamin, Ephraim, and Manasseh dwelt in Jerusalem:** ⁴ **Uthai the son of Ammihud, son of Omri, son of Imri, son of Bani, from the sons of Perez the son of Judah.** ⁵ **And of the Shilonites: Asaiah the first-born, and his sons.** ⁶ **Of the sons of Zerah: Jeuel and their kinsmen, six hundred and ninety.** ⁷ **Of the Benjaminites: Sallu the son of Meshullam, son of Hodaviah, son of Hassenuah,** ⁸ **Ibneiah the son of Jeroham, Elah the son of Uzzi, son of Michri, and Meshullam the son of Shephatiah, son of Reuel, son of Ibnijah;** ⁹ **and their kinsmen according to their generations, nine hundred and fifty-six. All these were heads of fathers' houses according to their fathers' houses.**

So all Israel was enrolled refers back to chapters 1—8. "All Israel" includes all twelve tribes. *The Book of the Kings of Israel* is not the canonical books, but one of the primary sources used by the Chronicler.

The temple servants (*Nethinim*, "the given ones"). Originally there seem to have been foreign slaves assigned to labor in the house of God, such as the Gibeonites (Josh. 9:23). The Chronicler includes them among the Levites (9:26–32). It seems that they were eventually adopted into Levitical families. The Chronicler contributed to this, for he is the first to list them among the Levites. Nehemiah mentions a rank below the *Nethinim*, "the descendants of Solomon's servants" (11:3). Apparently the Chronicler found it too difficult even with his generous spirit to assign Levitical rank to them.

(2) The Priestly Families (9:10–13)

¹⁰ **Of the priests: Jedaiah, Jehoiarib, Jachin,** ¹¹ **and Azariah the son of Hilkiah, son of Meshullam, son of Zadok, son of Meraioth, son of Ahitub, the chief officer of the house of God;** ¹² **and Adaiah the son of Jeroham, son of Pashhur, son of Malchijah, and Maasai the son of Adiel, son of Jahzerah, son of Meshullam, son of Meshillemith, son of Immer;** ¹³ **besides their kinsmen, heads of their fathers' houses, one thousand seven hundred and sixty, very able men for the work of the service of the house of God.**

Jehoiarib was the forefather of the famous Maccabees.

Very able men (*gibbor*, strong men of power). This is usually a term applied to great warriors (cf. to Gideon, by anticipation, Judg. 6:12). It is used in this sense by the Chronicler in 7:5 ("mighty warriors"). Here the term is applied to the priests as they serve in the Temple. This vividly illustrates the Chronicler's conviction that the priest's spiritual warfare is as significant as the prowess of the soldier. Strength appears in many forms, not the least of them in the man of God.

(3) The Levites (9:14–34)

a. The Sacred Singers (9:14–16)

¹⁴ **Of the Levites: Shemaiah the son of Hasshub, son of Azrikam, son of Hashabiah, of the**

sons of Merari; 15 and Bakbakkar, Heresh, Galal, and Mattaniah the son of Mica, son of Zichri, son of Asaph; 16 and Obadiah the son of Shemaiah, son of Galal, son of Jeduthun, and Berechiah the son of Asa, son of Elkanah, who dwelt in the villages of the Netophathites.

The persons listed simply as *Levites* appear to be singers. The Netophathites (inhabitants of Netophah, near Jerusalem) are said to be musicians in Nehemiah 12:28. Asaph and Jeduthun (vv. 15,16) were musical guild leaders (6:39; 16:41). Elkanah represents Heran the singer (6:33–34). For the Chronicler the singers were the most important Levites, so he lists them first. They are indeed the Levites.

b. *The Gatekeepers* (9:17–27)

17 The gatekeepers were: Shallum, Akkub, Talmon, Ahiman, and their kinsmen (Shallum being the chief), 18 stationed hitherto in the king's gate on the east side. These were the gatekeepers of the camp of the Levites. 19 Shallum the son of Kore, son of Ebiasaph, son of Korah, and his kinsmen of his fathers' house, the Korahites, were in charge of the work of the service, keepers of the thresholds of the tent, as their fathers had been in charge of the camp of the Lord, keepers of the entrance. 20 And Phinehas the son of Eleazar was the ruler over them in time past; the Lord was with him. 21 Zechariah the son of Meshelemiah was gatekeeper at the entrance of the tent of meeting. 22 All these, who were chosen as gatekeepers at the thresholds, were two hundred and twelve. They were enrolled by genealogies in their villages. David and Samuel the seer established them in their office of trust. 23 So they and their sons were in charge of the gates of the house of the Lord, that is, the house of the tent, as guards. 24 The gatekeepers were on the four sides, east, west, north, and south; 25 and their kinsmen who were in their villages were obliged to come in every seven days, from time to time, to be with these; 26 for the four chief gatekeepers, who were Levites, were in charge of the chambers and the treasures of the house of God. 27 And they lodged round about the house of God; for upon them lay the duty of watching, and they had charge of opening it every morning.

There are only two names given in Nehemiah 11:19; here there are four, one for each gate. The principal gatekeeper was Shallum, who kept the last gate, for it was the one that the king usually entered, and it faced the sanctuary. The Chronicler traces the work of the gatekeepers back to Phinehas (v. 20) and attributes their Temple responsibilities to the assignments of David and Samuel the seer (v. 22). The mention of Samuel in this role is quite unusual. The title, seer, which was his original one (1 Sam. 9:9), may mean that he began the reorganization soon after the death of Eli. Although few would insist that Samuel and David organized the Levites as completely as the Chronicler implies, there is no reason to deny that the worship at the time of Samuel and David was organized. From the rudimentary structure of their day the later system developed.

The *gatekeepers, who were Levites,* as were their helpers (23:24), had the responsibility of guarding the treasures of the Temple. The doors were opened at dawn (*boker*, v. 27). Thus they both made available and protected the holy things of the sanctuary. This is in the background of Matthew 16:19, "I will give you the keys of the kingdom." Not only Simon Peter but the church itself must both guard and make available the kingdom of heaven to those who seek it. The point of the Chronicler is that only those qualified for this task performed it. Self-appointed guardians of orthodoxy are certainly not in his tradition.

c. *Routine Services* (9:28–32)

28 Some of them had charge of the utensils of service, for they were required to count them when they were brought in and taken out. 29 Others of them were appointed over the furniture, and over all the holy utensils, also over the fine flour, the wine, the oil, the incense, and the spices. 30 Others, of the sons of the priests, prepared the mixing of the spices, 31 and Mattithiah, one of the Levites, the firstborn of Shallum the Korahite, was in charge of making the flat cakes. 32 Also some of their kinsmen of the Kohathites had charge of the showbread, to prepare it every sabbath.

The routine services of the house of God were carried out by Levites except for one function, the making of the perfumed oil

d. The Duties of the Singers (9:33-34)

³³ Now these are the singers, the heads of fathers' houses of the Levites, dwelling in the chambers of the temple free from other service, for they were on duty day and night. ³⁴ These were heads of fathers' houses of the Levites, according to their generations, leaders, who lived in Jerusalem.

The singers as well as the gatekeepers were on duty day and night (cf. Psalm 134; Isa. 30:29). They would begin and close the day of worship, so they needed to live in the Temple area. Because of their musical responsibilities, they were freed of any other duties.

Now these are the singers. A list of singers should either precede or follow this statement. Either the list has been lost or 9:17-32, concerning the gatekeeper and routine workers, has been inserted between the list of singers in 9:14-16 and this summary. The latter is possible. Sources friendly to the gatekeepers might have inserted their own lists into the chapter.

(4) The Family of Saul (9:35-44)

³⁵ In Gibeon dwelt the father of Gibeon, Jeiel, and the name of his wife was Maacah, ³⁶ and his first-born son Abdon, then Zur, Kish, Baal, Ner, Nadab, ³⁷ Gedor, Ahio, Zechariah, and Mikloth; ³⁸ and Mikloth was the father of Shimeam; and these also dwelt opposite their kinsmen in Jerusalem, with their kinsmen. ³⁹ Ner was the father of Kish, Kish of Saul, Saul of Jonathan, Malchishua, Abinadab, and Eshbaal; ⁴⁰ and the son of Jonathan was Meribbaal; and Meribbaal was the father of Micah. ⁴¹ The sons of Micah: Pithon, Melech, Tahrea, and Ahaz; ⁴² and Ahaz was the father of Jarah, and Jarah of Alemeth, Azmaveth, and Zimri; and Zimri was the father of Moza. ⁴³ Moza was the father of Binea; and Rephaiah was his son, Eleasah his son, Azel his son. ⁴⁴ Azel had six sons and these are their names: Azrikam, Bocheru, Ishmael, Sheariah, Obadiah, and Hanan; these were the sons of Azel.

This account is essentially the same as 8:29-38. Yet there are differences that can hardly be explained by copyist errors. Ner is found among the sons of Jeiel (v. 36), and several names are spelled differently. If the list in chapter 8 is a copy of this, the scribe has also intentionally made some changes based upon his own information. If this list is the Chronicler's introduction to the story of Saul, why does it not end with Saul's sons (v. 39)? Instead it continues on for many more generations, possibly until the Babylonian exile. We must remember that the Chronicler is not writing for the twentieth century A.D. In the genealogy of Saul he includes all he knows about his family. His descendants needed these facts for their own records. He does not neatly lead up to Saul, as we would. Since he will not come back to him after reaching David, he puts him in historical perspective.

II. Davidic Cultic Contributions (10:1—29:30)

It is significant that the Chronicler begins his actual history with the death of Saul, for it reveals that he was not concerned with reinterpreting Israel's history before the time of David. This was probably due to the fact that the viewpoint of the exilic and postexilic cultic leaders was already expressed in the priestly traditions of the Pentateuch, Joshua, and Judges. There was still a need for a similar interpretation of the Hebrew kingdom. The priestly source had dealt with the cultic contributions of Moses. The Chronicler would supplement that work with a treatment of the influence of David upon Israel's worship. This would provide a badly needed perspective that was not furnished by the Deuteronomic historians. They were concerned primarily with the kings and prophets. Although the Chronicler had other interests, he was primarily concerned with the role of the priests and other religious leaders in that same period. It was not his purpose to replace the books of Samuel and Kings, but to supplement them.

1. The Tragedy of Saul (10:1-14)

¹ Now the Philistines fought against Israel; and the men of Israel fled before the Philis-

tines, and fell slain on Mount Gilboa. ² And the Philistines overtook Saul and his sons; and the Philistines slew Jonathan and Abinadab and Malchishua, the sons of Saul. ³ The battle pressed hard upon Saul, and the archers found him; and he was wounded by the archers. ⁴ Then Saul said to his armor-bearer, "Draw your sword, and thrust me through with it, lest these uncircumcised come and make sport of me." But his armor-bearer would not; for he feared greatly. Therefore Saul took his own sword, and fell upon it. ⁵ And when his armor-bearer saw that Saul was dead, he also fell upon his sword, and died. ⁶ Thus Saul died; he and his three sons and all his house died together. ⁷ And when all the men of Israel who were in the valley saw that the army had fled and that Saul and his sons were dead, they forsook their cities and fled; and the Philistines came and dwelt in them.

⁸ On the morrow, when the Philistines came to strip the slain, they found Saul and his sons fallen on Mount Gilboa. ⁹ And they stripped him and took his head and his armor, and sent messengers throughout the land of the Philistines, to carry the good news to their idols and to the people. ¹⁰ And they put his armor in the temple of their gods, and fastened his head in the temple of Dagon. ¹¹ But when all Jabesh-gilead heard all that the Philistines had done to Saul, ¹² all the valiant men arose, and took away the body of Saul and the bodies of his sons, and brought them to Jabesh. And they buried their bones under the oak in Jabesh, and fasted seven days.

¹³ So Saul died for his unfaithfulness; he was unfaithful to the Lord in that he did not keep the command of the Lord, and also consulted a medium, seeking guidance, ¹⁴ and did not seek guidance from the Lord. Therefore the Lord slew him, and turned the kingdom over to David the son of Jesse.

This beginning is not abrupt unless it is viewed separately from the genealogies that have gone before. If the work of the original Chronicler is found only in 1 Chronicles 10:1—2 Chronicles 36, (cf. Elmslie, IB; Freedman, pp. 436-42) this beginning presents a serious problem. It could be that an original beginning has been replaced by the present genealogies. However, we possess no such evidence. It is more logical to take the position that the Chronicler prefixed genealogies to his history as an introduction to it, although later additions might have been made in some lists from time to time. The Chronicler is not interested in portraying the life of Saul. He is presented simply as a backdrop for the arrival of David. For the Chronicler, it is David's shadow that covered the later history of Israel. His grand work was contrasted with Saul's dismal failure.

All his house died together. First Samuel 31:6 says "his armor bearer, and all his men, on the same day together." The Chronicler's account seems to imply that all of Saul's descendants perished. Later he does not mention any other sons of Saul as found in the book of Samuel. Is he trying to give the impression that David had no difficulties assuming the throne? This could be claimed only if the genealogies are not by the Chronicler. Other descendants of Saul are listed there (9:39-40). *All his house* means all his relatives who were there with him in battle and his own personal bodyguard. Some of his bodyguard were probably also his kin.

Did not seek guidance from the Lord. Yet Saul is said to have sought such guidance (1 Sam. 28:6). Is the Chronicler being unfair to him? Probably he is saying that Saul should have continued to seek a word from God rather than turning to the medium. God could have been testing him. Further inquiry might have brought better results.

The Lord slew him. Literally, "The Lord caused him to die." God did not strike him dead, but rather he used the circumstances of the battle as the means of exercising his wrath. Saul killed himself. If God slew him, then the death was not suicide. Saul was responsible for what he did. His last act was the ultimate decision of a life at odds with its maker.

2. *David's Rise to Power* (11:1—12:40)

(1) *God Directs His Career* (11:1-9)

¹ Then all Israel gathered together to David at Hebron, and said, "Behold, we are your bone and flesh. ² In times past, even when Saul was king, it was you that led out and brought in Israel; and the Lord your God said to you, 'You shall be shepherd of my people Israel, and you shall be prince over my people Israel.'" ³ So all the elders of Israel came to

the king at Hebron; and David made a covenant with them at Hebron before the Lord, and they anointed David king over Israel, according to the word of the Lord by Samuel.

⁴ And David and all Israel went to Jerusalem, that is Jebus, where the Jebusites were, the inhabitants of the land. ⁵ The inhabitants of Jebus said to David, "You will not come in here." Nevertheless David took the stronghold of Zion, that is, the city of David. ⁶ David said, "Whoever shall smite the Jebusites first shall be chief and commander." And Joab the son of Zeruiah went up first, so he became chief. ⁷ And David dwelt in the stronghold; therefore it was called the city of David. ⁸ And he built the city round about from the Millo in complete circuit; and Joab repaired the rest of the city. ⁹ And David became greater and greater, for the Lord of hosts was with him.

Both paragraphs of this section end with the notation that David's glory was due to the favor of God upon him. He became king according to the word of the Lord by Samuel and went on to other success because of God's presence with him.

Verses 1–3 are parallel to 2 Samuel 5:1–3; vv. 4–9 to 2 Samuel 5:6–10. Although most of the material corresponds exactly, the differences are significant. Where 2 Samuel 5:1 says "all the tribes of Israel," Chronicles mentions *all Israel*. The former source is referring to the northern tribes who came to Hebron to add their allegiance to Judah's, where David had already been ruling. The Chronicler never mentions David's earlier rule at Hebron unless he implies it by saying that David was already king when all Israel came there (v. 3). He pictures all twelve tribes gathering at Hebron, which they probably did, but speaks of no division between Judah and North Israel. Anxious to emphasize the unity of the nation of Israel, he saw no need to point out their divisions.

In the story of the conquest of Jerusalem, the Samuel source says that "the king and his men" went against it. The Chronicler mentions "David and all Israel." He wants to make it clear that Jerusalem was not David's private holding but was the property of the whole nation. It was called "the city of David," not because he owned it but because he made it his capital.

Only the Chronicler mentions the way Joab became David's commander. Second Samuel 2:13 claims that he was a leader already, but perhaps without official title. Only the Chronicler mentions Joab's place in the rebuilding of Jerusalem. In fact he never mentions anything negative about Joab, not even David's last curse upon him (1 Kings 2:5). In Chronicles he is always the loyal servant of David. This is not an inaccurate appraisal, however. Although Joab infuriated David, what he did was out of his loyalty to him, and not just from personal ambition.

(2) *Davidic Heroes (11:10–47)*

Not only did David win the favor of God; he was loved and respected by a loyal following of men. These accounts are similar to those found in Samuel with an occasional omission and some additions. The major difference, however, is that they appear in Samuel in an appendix at the close of the life of David (2 Sam. 23), whereas here they are given at the beginning of his reign. Obviously some of the names may belong to the successful years of his reign. There is no way to settle this question, however. The Chronicler thereby asserts that the loyalty of David's men was a significant factor in his rise to fame. The historian had no way of telling which followers were early and which ones appeared later. So he inserts the list where it will give witness to his purpose.

a. *The Three Mighty Men (11:10–14)*

¹⁰ Now these are the chiefs of David's mighty men, who gave him strong support in his kingdom, together with all Israel, to make him king, according to the word of the Lord concerning Israel. ¹¹ This is an account of David's mighty men: Jashobeam, a Hachmonite, was chief of the three; he wielded his spear against three hundred whom he slew at one time.

¹² And next to him among the three mighty men was Eleazar the son of Dodo, the Ahohite. ¹³ He was with David at Pasdammim when the Philistines were gathered there for battle. There was a plot of ground full of barley, and the men fled from the Philistines. ¹⁴ But he took his stand in the midst of the plot, and

1 CHRONICLES 11

defended it, and slew the Philistines; and the LORD saved them by a great victory.

Only two of the three men are mentioned here, probably a result of textual corruption. From 2 Samuel 23:11 we learn that the third name was Shammah.

b. Water from the Well (11:15-19)

15 Three of the thirty chief men went down to the rock to David at the cave of Adullam, when the army of Philistines was encamped in the valley of Rephaim. 16 David was then in the stronghold; and the garrison of the Philistines was then at Bethlehem. 17 And David said longingly, "O that some one would give me water to drink from the well of Bethlehem which is by the gate!" 18 Then the three mighty men broke through the camp of the Philistines, and drew water out of the well of Bethlehem which was by the gate, and took and brought it to David. But David would not drink of it; he poured it out to the LORD, 19 and said, "Far be it from me before my God that I should do this. Shall I drink the lifeblood of these men? For at the risk of their lives they brought it." Therefore he would not drink it. These things did the three mighty men.

This story gives the reason why David was so beloved by his men. Not only was he a remarkable person, endowed with charisma, but he was sincerely concerned about his followers. When the accounts of this event in Samuel and Chronicles are compared they are more closely identical than any that have been examined thus far in Chronicles. The only significant variation is David's saying *before my God* where Samuel reports that he addressed God as "O Lord" (2 Sam. 23:17). This is a mark of the Chronicler's assessment of David's relationship to his God (cf. 11:2). The accounts are identical because the original event was impressed indelibly upon the memory of Israel. Almost anyone could tell that story word for word.

c. The Mighty Men of David (11:20-47)

20 Now Abishai, the brother of Joab, was chief of the thirty. And he wielded his spear against three hundred men and slew them, and won a name beside the three. 21 He was the most renowned of the thirty, and became their commander; but he did not attain to the three. 22 And Benaiah the son of Jehoiada was a valiant man of Kabzeel, a doer of great deeds; he smote two ariels of Moab. He also went down and slew a lion in a pit on a day when snow had fallen. 23 And he slew an Egyptian, a man of great stature, five cubits tall. The Egyptian had in his hand a spear like a weaver's beam; but Benaiah went down to him with a staff, and snatched the spear out of the Egyptian's hand, and slew him with his own spear. 24 These things did Benaiah the son of Jehoiada, and won a name beside the three mighty men. 25 He was renowned among the thirty, but he did not attain to the three. And David set him over his bodyguard.

26 The mighty men of the armies were Asahel the brother of Joab, Elhanan the son of Dodo of Bethlehem, 27 Shammoth of Harod, Helez the Pelonite, 28 Ira the son of Ikkesh of Tekoa, Abiezer of Anathoth, 29 Sibbecai the Hushathite, Ilai the Ahohite, 30 Maharai of Netophah, Heled the son of Baanah of Netophah, 31 Ithai the son of Ribai of Gibeah of the Benjaminites, Benaiah of Pirathon, 32 Hurai of the brooks of Gaash, Abiel the Arbathite, 33 Azmaveth of Baharum, Eliahba of Shaalbon, 34 Hashem the Gizonite, Jonathan the son of Shagee the Hararite, 35 Ahiam the son of Sachar the Hararite, Eliphal the son of Ur, 36 Hepher the Mecherathite, Ahijah the Pelonite, 37 Hezro of Carmel, Naarai the son of Ezbai, 38 Joel the brother of Nathan, Mibhar the son of Hagri, 39 Zelek the Ammonite, Naharai of Beeroth, the armor-bearer of Joab the son of Zeruiah, 40 Ira the Ithrite, Gareb the Ithrite, 41 Uriah the Hittite, Zabad the son of Ahlai, 42 Adina the son of Shiza the Reubenite, a leader of the Reubenites, and thirty with him, 43 Hanan the son of Maacah, and Joshaphat the Mithnite, 44 Uzzia the Ashterathite, Shama and Jeiel the sons of Hotham the Aroerite, 45 Jediael the son of Shimri, and Joha his brother, the Tizite, 46 Eliel the Mahavite, and Jeribai, and Joshaviah, the sons of Elnaam, and Ithmah the Moabite, 47 Eliel, and Obed, and Jaasiel the Mezobaite.

This list is essentially the same as the one in 2 Samuel 23, which ends with Uriah the Hittite. In Chronicles the names following Uriah (vv. 41-47) are the Chronicler's additions to the company. Almost all of these names are connected with Transjordan. Perhaps they belonged to the latter reign of David, when he fled into that area. The Chronicler indeed is the only biblical writer to memorialize them. He might have used a list prepared in the Transjordan area.

The most conspicuous name missing from the Chronicler's list is that of Eliam, the son of Ahithophel (2 Sam. 23:34), the father of Bathsheba. Since he did not choose to mention David's sin with Bathsheba, it may follow that he does not want Eliam and Uriah the Hittite in close company. However, the omission may be due simply to a textual problem.

He smote two ariels of Moab. An *ariel* is an altar hearth. Perhaps Benaiah destroyed the sacred altars of the Moabites. However, the verb "to smite" should apply to animate beings. Therefore, many scholars translate "two heroes" (lion-like men) since the Hebrew word for lion (v. 22*b*) is similar to ariel.

David set him over his bodyguard. The word "bodyguard" is literally "obedience." These were his obedient ones, those who would carry out any command he issued. They were not just to protect him, but also to serve him. It is such obedience that God requires of those who are his intimates. Most men are more anxious to defend their God than to do his will.

(3) His Early Followers (12:1-22)

There is no parallel to this section in the Old Testament. The Chronicler had access to old records that form the background for the passage. However, in its present form this material and the rest of the chapter present serious problems. Benjamin is said to have sent a sizable delegation to David at Ziklag, yet 2 Samuel 2:9,15,25 indicates that Benjamin was solidly behind Saul and Ishbosheth, his son. The outlaw followers of David during his wilderness wanderings are said to be as numerous as "an army of God" (v. 22) compared with the 400 or 600 of 1 Samuel 22:2; 27:2. Assembling at Hebron are said to be nearly 400,000 Israelites, while 2 Samuel 5:3 simply says "all the elders of Israel came." Such statements lead Curtis and Madsen (p. 194) to say, "Our chapter then has no real historical worth." In the same vein Elmslie (p. 389) remarks, "It piles the incredible on the unhistorical."

However, these observations need to be read with some reservation. Although the tribe of Benjamin did support Saul, some of its members were certainly disappointed in him. The Chronicler lists only a small group of them (v. 23). Even if the expression *great army, like an army of God* is hyperbole, it does not make the rest of the passage unhistorical. The terms hundred (*meah*) and thousand (*'elep*) in v. 14 appear to apply to military units that might not always have had their full complement of men, as Mendenhall (pp. 52–66) has shown. Even if the large numbers are actually intended by the Chronicler, there is little reason to doubt the other data in the chapter. The basic material (vv. 2,8,15,17–19) shows evidence of authentic popular tradition. The poem in v. 18 has the ring of the earlier poetry of Israel.

a. Men from Benjamin (12:1-7)

¹ Now these are the men who came to David at Ziklag, while he could not move about freely because of Saul the son of Kish; and they were among the mighty men who helped him in war. ² They were bowmen, and could shoot arrows and sling stones with either the right or the left hand; they were Benjaminites, Saul's kinsmen. ³ The chief was Ahiezer, then Joash, both sons of Shemaah of Gibeah; also Jeziel and Pelet the sons of Azmaveth; Beracah, Jehu of Anathoth, ⁴ Ishmaiah of Gibeon, a mighty man among the thirty and a leader over the thirty; Jeremiah, Jahaziel, Johanan, Jozabad of Gederah, ⁵ Eluzai, Jerimoth, Bealiah, Shemariah, Shephatiah the Haruphite; ⁶ Elkanah, Isshiah, Azarel, Joezer, and Jashobeam, the Korahites; ⁷ and Joelah and Zebadiah, the sons of Jeroham of Gedor.

The men from Benjamin are listed first because of the special honor they brought to David by defecting from Saul! These mighty men from Benjamin are said to be skillful with the sling or bow with either the left or right hand. In earlier days (Judg. 20:16) they were noted for the remarkable accuracy of their left-handed marksmen. Evidently the succeeding years had been ample time for them to develop the use of their right hands also. It is noteworthy that in the process of becoming more conventional in these skills, they did not lose their former efficiency.

A mighty man among the thirty. Ishmaiah is not mentioned in the list of thirty in 2 Samuel 23 or in 1 Chronicles 11. This "thirty" may be a group of famous Benjamites, or perhaps Saul had his "thirty." Some take this to be figurative: Ishmaiah is compared with the thirty heroes of David, even being superior to them, although never making the official list. There is little doubt that this was true of many warriors in David's day. Genuine worth is not always publicly recognized. Some of the greatest sermons will never be published in the best sermons of the year.

b. The Remarkable Gadites (12:8–15)

8 From the Gadites there went over to David at the stronghold in the wilderness mighty and experienced warriors, expert with shield and spear, whose faces were like the faces of lions, and who were swift as gazelles upon the mountains: 9 Ezer the chief, Obadiah second, Eliab third, 10 Mishmannah fourth, Jeremiah fifth, 11 Attai sixth, Eliel seventh, 12 Johanan eighth, Elzabad ninth, 13 Jeremiah tenth, Machbannai eleventh. 14 These Gadites were officers of the army, the lesser over a hundred and the greater over a thousand. 15 These are the men who crossed the Jordan in the first month, when it was overflowing all its banks, and put to flight all those in the valleys, to the east and to the west.

The Gadites must have come to David when he was in the hills around Engedi (1 Sam. 24:1). They were experts in hand-to-hand combat (*shield and spear*), fierce as lions, and swift as deer. In addition they were remarkable swimmers, crossing the Jordan at floodstage in the spring when the distant snows were melting. When Saul's followers tried to stop their defection, they routed the loyalists on both banks of the Jordan! The scene is a vivid one. They forced their way to the Jordan, swam its raging waters, and fought their way to David.

c. The Warrior Prophet (12:16–18)

16 And some of the men of Benjamin and Judah came to the stronghold to David. 17 David went out to meet them and said to them, "If you have come to me in friendship to help me, my heart will be knit to you; but if to betray me to my adversaries, although there is no wrong in my hands, then may the God of our fathers see and rebuke you." 18 Then the Spirit came upon Amasai, chief of the thirty, and he said,

"We are yours, O David;
    and with you, O son of Jesse!
Peace, peace to you,
    and peace to your helpers!
For your God helps you."

Then David received them, and made them officers of his troops.

This passage contains a rhythmic poem that gives evidence of belonging to antiquity. Even more remarkable is the statement that *the Spirit came upon Amasai* (lit., "clothed himself with Amasai," as a man puts on a garment). This expression is used also in Judges 6:34 and 2 Chronicles 24:20. In Judges it describes how the Spirit enabled Gideon to fight victoriously. In 2 Chronicles it speaks of the empowering of Zechariah the priest to speak prophetically. Here a more remarkable event than ever is mentioned. A man of war speaks a prophetic word, being invaded by the divine Spirit, who uses his mouth to declare God's favor on David. This graphic concept "may be a forerunner of the idea of incarnation." (Myers, p. 97).

Who is the Amasai mentioned here? Some say he is Abishai, who was the chief of the thirty (11:20). Others equate him with Amasa, (2 Sam. 17:25; 19:13; 20:10).

d. The Manasseh Contingent (12:19–22)

19 Some of the men of Manasseh deserted to David when he came with the Philistines for the battle against Saul. (Yet he did not help them, for the rulers of the Philistines took counsel and sent him away, saying, "At peril to our heads he will desert to his master Saul.") 20 As he went to Ziklag these men of Manasseh deserted to him: Adnah, Jozabad, Jediael, Michael, Jozabad, Elihu, and Zillethai, chiefs of thousands in Manasseh. 21 They helped David against the band of raiders; for they were all mighty men of valor and were commanders in the army. 22 For from day to day men kept coming to David to help him, until there was a great army, like an army of God.

For from day to day men kept coming to David. This explains more realistically than anything in the Samuel sources why Saul lost the battle with the Philistines. Many of his best soldiers had defected to David. The forces of the son of Jesse contained more than an assortment of renegades.

A great army, like an army of God. The word army is literally "a camp." It is the word used in Genesis 32:2 when Jacob saw the angels of God. He named the place Mahanaim, "two camps." What are the two? His own and God's? This appears to be the best meaning of the word. What does this have to say about the size of such an army? Jacob's group was not excessively large. A "great army" would most naturally be a multitude, but the term could describe a powerful army. The expression could mean an invincible army and not necessarily a force composed of huge numbers. In fact the number of men mentioned by the Chronicler in 12:1–21 does not indicate a tremendous multitude. One may well understand the army of David to be great in its battle potential rather than in its size.

(4) Made King of All Israel (12:23–40)

23 These are the numbers of the divisions of the armed troops, who came to David in Hebron, to turn the kingdom of Saul over to him, according to the word of the Lord. 24 The men of Judah bearing shield and spear were six thousand eight hundred armed troops. 25 Of the Simeonites, mighty men of valor for war, seven thousand one hundred. 26 Of the Levites four thousand six hundred. 27 The prince Jehoiada, of the house of Aaron, and with him three thousand seven hundred. 28 Zadok, a young man mighty in valor, and twenty-two commanders from his own father's house. 29 Of the Benjaminites, the kinsmen of Saul, three thousand, of whom the majority had hitherto kept their allegiance to the house of Saul. 30 Of the Ephraimites twenty thousand eight hundred, mighty men of valor, famous men in their fathers' houses. 31 Of the half-tribe of Manasseh eighteen thousand, who were expressly named to come and make David king. 32 Of Issachar men who had understanding of the times, to know what Israel ought to do, two hundred chiefs, and all their kinsmen under their command. 33 Of Zebulun fifty thousand seasoned troops, equipped for battle with all the weapons of war, to help David with singleness of purpose. 34 Of Naphtali a thousand commanders with whom were thirty-seven thousand men armed with shield and spear. 35 Of the Danites twenty-eight thousand six hundred men equipped for battle. 36 Of Asher forty thousand seasoned troops ready for battle. 37 Of the Reubenites and Gadites and the half-tribe of Manasseh from beyond the Jordan, one hundred and twenty thousand men armed with all the weapons of war.

38 All these, men of war, arrayed in battle order, came to Hebron with full intent to make David king over all Israel; likewise all the rest of Israel were of a single mind to make David king. 39 And they were there with David for three days, eating and drinking, for their brethren had made preparation for them. 40 And also their neighbors, from as far as Issachar and Zebulun and Naphtali, came bringing food on asses and on camels and on mules and on oxen, abundant provisions of meal, cakes of figs, clusters of raisins, and wine and oil, oxen and sheep, for there was joy in Israel.

One of the most interesting facets of this account is the small number of men from Judah compared with those from North Israel. This may be the Chronicler's way of declaring that northern tribes were more identified with David than was commonly thought. On the other hand, warriors from Judah might already have been with David in Hebron before the new arrivals mentioned by the Chronicler.

Also of note is the inclusion of the priests along with the warriors, especially Zadok, with his 22 commanders, who represented the priests (cf. 24:7 ff.). Their prowess was probably not military but religious (cf. 9:13). They are mentioned here in accordance with the Chronicler's purpose, for he considered their role just as important as the military one in the establishment of the kingdom.

With singleness of purpose. Literally, "without heart and heart," without two wills; that is, not with one will to serve their king and another to serve themselves, but with an undivided will to serve.

2. Moving the Ark (13:1—16:43)

(1) The First Abortive Effort (13:1–14)

1 David consulted with the commanders of thousands and of hundreds, with every leader. 2 And David said to all the assembly of Israel, "If it seems good to you, and if it is the will of

the LORD our God, let us send abroad to our brethren who remain in all the land of Israel, and with them to the priests and Levites in the cities that have pasture lands, that they may come together to us. ³ Then let us bring again the ark of our God to us; for we neglected it in the days of Saul." ⁴ All the assembly agreed to do so, for the thing was right in the eyes of all the people.

⁵ So David assembled all Israel from the Shihor of Egypt to the entrance of Hamath, to bring the ark of God from Kiriath-jearim. ⁶ And David and all Israel went up to Baalah, that is, to Kiriath-jearim which belongs to Judah, to bring up from there the ark of God, which is called by the name of the LORD who sits enthroned above the cherubim. ⁷ And they carried the ark of God upon a new cart, from the house of Abinadab, and Uzzah and Ahio were driving the cart. ⁸ And David and all Israel were making merry before God with all their might, with song and lyres and harps and tambourines and cymbals and trumpets.

⁹ And when they came to the threshing floor of Chidon, Uzzah put out his hand to hold the ark, for the oxen stumbled. ¹⁰ And the anger of the LORD was kindled against Uzzah; and he smote him because he put forth his hand to the ark; and he died there before God. ¹¹ And David was angry because the LORD had broken forth upon Uzzah; and that place is called Perezuzza to this day. ¹² And David was afraid of God that day; and he said, "How can I bring the ark of God home to me?" ¹³ So David did not take the ark home into the city of David, but took it aside to the house of Obededom the Gittite. ¹⁴ And the ark of God remained with the household of Obededom in his house three months; and the LORD blessed the household of Obededom and all that he had.

The Samuel passage (2 Sam. 5:11-25) relates how David first built his own house and then battled with the Philistines before his throne was secure. The Chronicler postpones that part of the story because he is anxious to extol the glory of David and to tell of David's plan to bring the ark to Jerusalem. The religious theme is his principal concern.

Verses 1-4 have no parallel in Samuel. Here we learn that David consulted with the great assembly who were to crown him at Hebron before they had left for their homes. Even during his coronation week he was concerned about the ark.

If it seems good to you, and if it is the will of . . . God. Whatever David desired was what the people wanted (cf. 2 Sam. 3:36). David had no difficulty getting the people to agree with his desires. He was still on his political honeymoon. However, discerning the will of God was quite another matter. David seems to assume that if he desires this move and the people agree, God's approval will surely coincide. There is no indication in the passage that he actually sought the will of God.

So David assembled all Israel. The Samuel source says that David "gathered all the chosen men of Israel, thirty thousand," (2 Sam. 6:1). Although the Chronicler's totals are higher, the statements are similar. It was a movement participated in by a large host of people from all the land. Such a procession following the new king was a significant tribute to his leadership. How disconcerting the unexpected death of Uzzah! The great procession stopped.

(2) *Heeding Prophetic Warnings* (14:1-17)

¹ And Hiram king of Tyre sent messengers to David, and cedar trees, also masons and carpenters to build a house for him. ² And David perceived that the LORD had established him king over Israel, and that his kingdom was highly exalted for the sake of his people Israel.

³ And David took more wives in Jerusalem, and David begot more sons and daughters. ⁴ These are the names of the children whom he had in Jerusalem: Shammua, Shobab, Nathan, Solomon, ⁵ Ibhar, Elishua, Elpelet, ⁶ Nogah, Nepheg, Japhia, Elishama, Beeliada, and Eliphelet.

⁸ When the Philistines heard that David had been anointed king over all Israel, all the Philistines went up in search of David; and David heard of it and went out against them. ⁹ Now the Philistines had come and made a raid in the valley of Rephaim. ¹⁰ And David inquired of God, "Shall I go up against the Philistines? Wilt thou give them into my hand?" And the LORD said to him, "Go up, and I will give them into your hand." ¹¹ And he went up to Baalperazim, and David defeated them there; and David said, "God has broken through my enemies by my hand, like a bursting flood." Therefore the name of that place is called Baalperazim. ¹² And they left their gods there, and David gave command, and they were burned.

¹³ And the Philistines yet again made a raid

in the valley. ¹⁴ And when David again inquired of God, God said to him, "You shall not go up after them; go around and come upon them opposite the balsam trees. ¹⁵ And when you hear the sound of marching in the tops of the balsam trees, then go out to battle; for God has gone out before you to smite the army of the Philistines." ¹⁶ And David did as God commanded him, and they smote the Philistine army from Gibeon to Gezer. ¹⁷ And the fame of David went out into all lands, and the Lord brought the fear of him upon all nations.

This chapter is closely related to 2 Samuel 5:11–25, but in the former passage these events are mentioned before the first attempt to move the ark. Here they are placed between the first and second efforts. In fact they could well have happened in this sequence, for the frustration that caused David to use the expression "Perezuzzah" (breaking forth upon Uzzah, 13:11) was relieved when God broke through likewise upon David's enemies and their gods (14:11–12), perhaps encouraging him to try again to transfer the symbol of God's presence.

It is the clear purpose of the Chronicler in this chapter to show that David was the opposite of Saul. He regularly inquired of Yahweh and heeded whatever replies that came. The oracles of God were unpredictable and often of contrasting import. David would go into battle or refrain according to the divine instructions. The reward for such conscientiousness was unqualified success and increasing fame. First Chronicles 14:17 is the Chronicler's summation: David was recognized and respected by all the surrounding nations.

And David took more wives. This is one of the few times that the Chronicler mentions anything that might reflect upon the character of David. It should be noted that he does soften the unpleasantness of this matter by omitting the reference to concubines that 2 Samuel 5:13 includes. Since the Chronicler does not refer to David's sin with Bathsheba, the inclusion of this material may be his way of alluding to it in the least offensive way since Solomon, their son, is listed. The warning of Deuteronomy 17:17, that polygamous practices would lead to straying from God, hangs heavily over this passage.

God has broken through my enemies by my hand. Second Samuel 5:20 states that "the Lord has broken through my enemies before me." At first glance it appears that the later historian has arbitrarily declared that David was more directly involved in the victory by substituting *by my hand* for "before me." Yet it is his inclination to emphasize the activity of God more than that of man, even when speaking of David. The intriguing appearance of "God" (*Elohim*) in Chronicles rather than "the Lord" (*Yahweh*) in the Samuel passage, may suggest that different sources are being used by the two history writers. This phenomenon continues into the following passage. The presence of different sources is even more plausible when it is noticed that when the Chronicler is telling the story, he uses the title *Elohim* for God, but when he makes his own observation, he employs the term Yahweh (v. 17). Plainly he is copying from traditional material that differed from that used by the Samuel sources.

(3) *Levites Bring the Ark (15:1–16:3)*

a. *Levitical Assignments (15:1–24)*

¹ David built houses for himself in the city of David; and he prepared a place for the ark of God, and pitched a tent for it. ² Then David said, "No one but the Levites may carry the ark of God, for the Lord chose them to carry the ark of the Lord and to minister to him for ever." ³ And David assembled all Israel at Jerusalem, to bring up the ark of the Lord to its place, which he had prepared for it. ⁴ And David gathered together the sons of Aaron and the Levites: ⁵ of the sons of Kohath, Uriel the chief, with a hundred and twenty of his brethren; ⁶ of the sons of Merari, Asaiah the chief, with two hundred and twenty of his brethren; ⁷ of the sons of Gershom, Joel the chief, with a hundred and thirty of his brethren; ⁸ of the sons of Elizaphan, Shemaiah the chief, with two hundred of his brethren; ⁹ of the sons of Hebron, Eliel the chief, with eighty of his brethren; ¹⁰ of the sons of Uzziel, Amminadab the chief, with a hundred and twelve of his brethren. ¹¹ Then David summoned the priests Zadok and Abiathar, and the Levites Uriel, Asaiah, Joel, Shemaiah, Eliel, and Amminadab, ¹² and said to them, "You are the heads of the

fathers' houses of the Levites; sanctify yourselves, you and your brethren, so that you may bring up the ark of the Lord, the God of Israel, to the place that I have prepared for it. 13 Because you did not carry it the first time, the Lord our God broke forth upon us, because we did not care for it in the way that is ordained." 14 So the priests and the Levites sanctified themselves to bring up the ark of the Lord, the God of Israel. 15 And the Levites carried the ark of God upon their shoulders with the poles, as Moses had commanded according to the word of the Lord.

16 David also commanded the chiefs of the Levites to appoint their brethren as the singers who should play loudly on musical instruments, on harps and lyres and cymbals, to raise sounds of joy. 17 So the Levites appointed Heman the son of Joel; and of his brethren Asaph the son of Berechiah; and of the sons of Merari, their brethren, Ethan the son of Kushaiah; 18 and with them their brethren of the second order, Zechariah, Jaaziel, Shemiramoth, Jehiel, Unni, Eliab, Benaiah, Maaseiah, Mattithiah, Eliphelehu, and Mikneiah, and the gatekeepers Obededom and Jeiel. 19 The singers, Heman, Asaph, and Ethan, were to sound bronze cymbals; 20 Zechariah, Aziel, Shemiramoth, Jehiel, Unni, Eliab, Maaseiah, and Benaiah were to play harps according to Alamoth; 21 but Mattithiah, Eliphelehu, Mikneiah, Obededom, Jeiel, and Azaziah were to lead with lyres according to the Sheminith. 22 Chenaniah, leader of the Levites in music, should direct the music, for he understood it. 23 Berechiah and Elkanah were to be gatekeepers for the ark. 24 Shebaniah, Joshaphat, Nethanel, Amasai, Zechariah, Benaiah, and Eliezer, the priests, should blow the trumpets before the ark of God. Obededom and Jehiah also were to be gatekeepers for the ark.

This section is entirely the contribution of the Chronicler. Whereas the book of Samuel attributes David's renewed determination to move the ark to the news that God had blessed the household of Obededom (2 Sam. 6:12), we are told here that the king concluded that the trouble was due to the fact that it was not properly handled according to Mosaic law (v. 2). Rather than using a cart the Levites should have carried it on poles (vv. 13–15). The opinion given here probably represents not only the Chronicler's attitude toward the cause of the trouble but was also the diagnosis of the difficulty common to the priestly party.

The organization of the Levites described here may be more involved than the simple arrangements of the Davidic era, but there is every reason to accept the tradition that David instituted some such guilds (cf. Myers, I, 111–112). The question of whether the early musicians were also Levites is another matter, which cannot be settled with finality.

He prepared a place for the ark of God. Not only did David have a tent ready for the ark, but some sort of permanent enclosure was provided. It is significant that when Jesus said he would "prepare a place" for his disciples that he used this same expression (cf. John 14:2 with LXX here). Just as David prepared a place for God's indwelling, Jesus makes ready a place for his followers.

Play loudly on musical instruments . . . raise sounds of joy. A church in Cornwall, England, has inscribed above its choir stalls the observation, "Amor, non clamor, ascendit in aures Dei" ("Love, not noise, rises to the ears of God"). However, the two are not necessarily in conflict. The sort of worship pleasing to God is rooted in love and expressed with feeling.

Harps, . . . lyres, and cymbals. This is the usual combination in ancient Hebrew worship, a contrast of percussion and stringed instruments. The harps and lyres were similar, but the former tended to have more strings. The lyre was the more common instrument for solo playing and was the one played by David. There were normally more lyres in an orchestra than harps.

According to Alamoth . . . according to Sheminith. Alamoth is the plural of the Hebrew word *almah* (young woman; cf. Isa. 7:14). Since women did not sing in the Levitical choirs this is a difficult term to understand. It may refer to the soprano notes or a high key. Likewise Sheminith means "upon the eighth," perhaps an octave below. In other words, the harps might have stressed the higher notes and the lyres the lower ones.

Leader of the Levites in music. The

word translated "music" literally means burden. When a person lifts up his voice, shouting or singing, he is making positive use of his burden. Even today we speak of "carrying a tune." As the Hebrews looked at it, a burden could be either simply a heavy load to be borne or an opportunity to express one's praise of God. The connection with singers (15:27) favors the translation "music" in this context. Those who disclaim this regard the phrase "of the singers" (v. 27) as a scribal gloss due to a later misunderstanding of the text.

It is also noteworthy that Obededom and Jehiah were both musicians and gatekeepers (cf. v. 21 with v. 24). Some take this to be either a confusion of two traditions, or the Chronicler's attempt to give Levitical standing to Obededom, who had housed the ark. However, in the earlier days of the kingdom it was very likely that men performed dual functions. Although the singers were not required to perform any other tasks (9:33), they were free to volunteer. Since both singers and gatekeepers lived at the sanctuary, this dual activity was quite possible.

b. The Procession to Jerusalem (15:25—16:3)

25 So David and the elders of Israel, and the commanders of thousands, went to bring up the ark of the covenant of the LORD from the house of Obededom with rejoicing. 26 And because God helped the Levites who were carrying the ark of the covenant of the LORD, they sacrificed seven bulls and seven rams. 27 David was clothed with a robe of fine linen, as also were all the Levites who were carrying the ark, and the singers, and Chenaniah the leader of the music of the singers; and David wore a linen ephod. 28 So all Israel brought up the ark of the covenant of the LORD with shouting, to the sound of the horn, trumpets, and cymbals, and made loud music on harps and lyres.

29 And as the ark of the covenant of the LORD came to the city of David, Michal the daughter of Saul looked out of the window, and saw King David dancing and making merry; and she despised him in her heart.

¹ And they brought in the ark of God, and set it inside the tent which David had pitched for it; and they offered burnt offerings and peace offerings before God. ² And when David had finished offering the burnt offerings and the peace offerings, he blessed the people in the name of the LORD, ³ and distributed to all Israel, both men and women, to each a loaf of bread, a portion of meat, and a cake of raisins.

In the 2 Samuel 6:12–19 account David is pictured as wearing only a linen ephod, which was a short skirt, such as a priest would wear under his robe. The Chronicler has him dressed properly in a robe as well as the ephod, the robes perhaps flying open in his ecstatic dancing. As the Chronicler paints the picture, Michal's displeasure at David's behavior occurs because of his devotion to the ark, a loyalty lacking in Saul. In Samuel the point at issue is his exposing himself in his frenzied dancing (2 Sam. 6:20). Again there is a difference in perspective between the two sources that does not feature opposing views but supplementary ones. Although in Samuel, Michal voices the thoughts disturbing her conscious mind, her unconscious lack of reverence toward the ark also affected her attitude toward David's ecstatic devotion to it.

Although the Chronicler agrees with Samuel that the *shophar* (ram's horn) was used in the procession (cf. 15:28 with 2 Sam. 6:15), he adds the trumpet, a straight metal instrument, usually about two feet in length, which was a favorite in Levitical orchestras. The *shophar* is mentioned far more frequently than is any other musical instrument in the Bible. Yet it is referred to only twice in Chronicles, here and in 2 Chronicles 15:14. This could be due to the fact that although it was used for signalling of every sort, its principal function was related to war (cf. Amos 3:6). The Chronicler's reluctance to use it in his account is probably due to his ambivalent attitude toward the military. After the destruction of the Temple in A.D. 70 the *shophar*, which lost its military role, was preserved in the ritual of the synagogues.

And when David had finished offering the burnt offerings. The Chronicler now mentions for the first time that David was in charge of the sacrifices. However, he has by now made it clear that the sacrifices were presented by the whole community with the Levitical priests performing their proper functions. David is now seen, not as a priest, but as the king who supervised the proper activities of worship. It was he who blessed the people, however, and not the priests.

(4) Levitical Duties (16:4–43)

a. The Choral Work (16:4–36)

⁴ Moreover he appointed certain of the Levites as ministers before the ark of the Lord, to invoke, to thank, and to praise the Lord, the God of Israel. ⁵ Asaph was the chief, and second to him were Zechariah, Jeiel, Shemiramoth, Jehiel, Mattithiah, Eliab, Benaiah, Obededom, and Jeiel, who were to play harps and lyres; Asaph was to sound the cymbals, ⁶ and Benaiah and Jahaziel the priests were to blow trumpets continually, before the ark of the covenant of God.

⁷ Then on that day David first appointed that thanksgiving be sung to the Lord by Asaph and his brethren.

⁸ O give thanks to the Lord, call on his name,
    make known his deeds among the peoples!
⁹ Sing to him, sing praises to him,
    tell of all his wonderful works!
¹⁰ Glory in his holy name;
    let the hearts of those who seek the Lord rejoice!
¹¹ Seek the Lord and his strength,
    seek his presence continually!
¹² Remember the wonderful works that he has done,
    the wonders he wrought, the judgments he uttered,
¹³ O offspring of Abraham his servant,
    sons of Jacob, his chosen ones!

¹⁴ He is the Lord our God;
    his judgments are in all the earth.
¹⁵ He is mindful of his covenant for ever,
    of the word that he commanded, for a thousand generations,
¹⁶ the covenant which he made with Abraham,
    his sworn promise to Isaac,
¹⁷ which he confirmed as a statute to Jacob,
    as an everlasting covenant to Israel,
¹⁸ saying, "To you I will give the land of Canaan,
    as your portion for an inheritance."

¹⁹ When they were few in number,
    and of little account, and sojourners in it,
²⁰ wandering from nation to nation,
    from one kingdom to another people,
²¹ he allowed no one to oppress them;
    he rebuked kings on their account,
²² saying, "Touch not my anointed ones,
    do my prophets no harm!"

²³ Sing to the Lord, all the earth!
    Tell of his salvation from day to day.
²⁴ Declare his glory among the nations,
    his marvelous works among all the peoples!
²⁵ For great is the Lord, and greatly to be praised,
    and he is to be held in awe above all gods.
²⁶ For all the gods of the peoples are idols;
    but the Lord made the heavens.
²⁷ Honor and majesty are before him;
    strength and joy are in his place.

²⁸ Ascribe to the Lord, O families of the peoples,
    ascribe to the Lord glory and strength!
²⁹ Ascribe to the Lord the glory due his name;
    bring an offering, and come before him!
Worship the Lord in holy array;
³⁰   tremble before him, all the earth;
    yea, the world stands firm, never to be moved.
³¹ Let the heavens be glad, and let the earth rejoice,
    and let them say among the nations, "The Lord reigns!"
³² Let the sea roar, and all that fills it,
    let the field exult, and everything in it!
³³ Then shall the trees of the wood sing for joy
    before the Lord, for he comes to judge the earth.
³⁴ O give thanks to the Lord, for he is good;
    for his steadfast love endures for ever!

³⁵ Say also:
"Deliver us, O God of our salvation,
    and gather and save us from among the nations,
that we may give thanks to thy holy name,
    and glory in thy praise.
³⁶ Blessed be the Lord, the God of Israel,
    from everlasting to everlasting!"

Then all the people said "Amen!" and praised the Lord.

First Chronicles 16:4–42 has no parallel in 2 Samuel. Therefore, we find here a distinctive contribution of the Chronicler and his followers. The appointments made in 15:16 ff. were only for moving the ark to Jerusalem. Now David makes the permanent appointments, which involve fewer persons. There appear to be only two duties to be performed before the ark, music and protection. This first section deals with the music, for which Asaph was put in charge.

The word translated *to invoke* is difficult to understand. Literally, it means "to call to mind," and then "to commemorate." The problem centers around which of the two meanings applies here. The RSV favors the former, *The Jerusalem Bible* the latter. The titles for Psalms 38 and 70 contain this same word, which the RSV renders "memorial offering." It is more likely that these Psalms were used to invoke the attention of God to the sufferer rather than to accompany a memorial offering, since both picture a man in desperate straits, needing immediate attention.

It appears, then, that the three emphases of the singers were upon (1) calling God's attention to the worshiper's needs, (2) thanking him for what he had previously done, and (3) praising him for what he was.

The psalm found in 16:8-36 contains elements of other psalms in the Psalter. Verses 8-22 correspond to Psalm 105:1-15. Verses 23-33 are also found in Psalm 96:1-113. Verse 34 and Psalm 106:1 are the same, as are vv. 35-36. and Psalm 106:47-48. The differences are minor and of little significance. It is generally agreed that Chronicles is borrowing from the Psalms and not vice versa (cf. Myers, I, 121). The music of the second Temple is used to illustrate how Asaph must have sung. Surely the later music was rooted in him, although it became more refined.

Verse 36 is actually the doxology that closes the fourth book of the Psalter, which did not reach its final form until after the Chronicler's day. Obviously this verse, and possibly the entire psalm is later than the Chronicler. First Chronicles 16:37 follows easily after either vv. 6 or 7, suggesting the possibility that the psalm has been inserted after the Chronicler's day.

When the psalm is read in its present form it is obvious that the Jews of the postexilic period saw in the return of the ark to Jerusalem a reason for believing that God would also one day bring his dispersed people back home from their wandering. The emphases of the psalm are upon God's rule of the whole earth, his care of his people when they were in alien lands, and the eventual recognition of Yahweh's lordship by all people. The climactic verse calls upon God *to gather and 'save us'* [the Chronicler's addition] *from among the nations.* Indeed, the hope of the faithful being gathered to the city of God, so eloquently expressed here, is continued in the new Jerusalem of the book of Revelation.

b. The Ark and the Sanctuary (16:37-43)

37 So David left Asaph and his brethren there before the ark of the covenant of the LORD to minister continually before the ark as each day required, 38 and also Obededom and his sixty-eight brethren; while Obededom, the son of Jeduthun, and Hosah were to be gatekeepers. 39 And he left Zadok the priest and his brethren the priests before the tabernacle of the LORD in the high place that was at Gibeon, 40 to offer burnt offerings to the LORD upon the altar of burnt offering continually morning and evening, according to all that is written in the law of the LORD which he commanded Israel. 41 With them were Heman and Jeduthun, and the rest of those chosen and expressly named to give thanks to the LORD, for his steadfast love endures for ever. 42 Heman and Jeduthun had trumpets and cymbals for the music and instruments for sacred song. The sons of Jeduthun were appointed to the gate.

43 Then all the people departed each to his house, and David went home to bless his household.

In this passage the Chronicler makes clear what he implied before. The services before the ark were only musical. No sacrifices were performed there after the procession to Jerusalem ended. In no way was that special occasion to be considered a threat to the sacrificing priests who remained with the tabernacle of the Lord at Gibeon (cf. 1 Kings 3:4 ff.).

The most significant contribution of the Chronicler in this passage is his stress upon the importance of worship without sacrifice (cf. Myers, I, 121-122). In Jerusalem Asaph's company worshiped before the ark without the aid of sacrifice. This he believed to be a unique contribution of

David. The name of Moses occurs only 31 times in Chronicles–Nehemiah, whereas David is mentioned more than 250 times. It was Moses who planned the tabernacle services, but David originated the liturgy before the ark. Israel now had two sanctuaries. The Chronicler was not actually saying that music was better than sacrifice, but he was saying that there could be meaningful worship without sacrifice, and this was a bold stand indeed for his day. He gave precedent for other ceremonies, apart from sacrifices, that reflected either tendencies of his times or actually encouraged new ones, both in the Temple and synagogue.

Instruments for sacred song (lit., "for the song of God," cf. Psalm 137:4; 2 Chron. 29:27, where the expression "song of the Lord" parallels this). Note how the Chronicler, like the priestly source in the Pentateuch, often prefers *Elohim* (God) to *Yahweh* (the Lord). This expression can be translated "God's song," the one ordained by him, or "sacred song," the one dedicated to him.

First Chronicles 16:43 (cf. 2 Sam. 6:19–20) jars the reader back to the realization that the entire passage 16:4–42 has been inserted into the traditional story of the ark's removal. Elmslie believes that most of vv. 37–42 were added to the work of the Chronicler as a misguided attempt to explain how Solomon could sacrifice at the high place in Gibeon after David established a sanctuary in Jerusalem. However, it seems best to assume with Myers that the insertion is the Chronicler's own. It must be regarded as his unless it can be proven otherwise.

4. The Davidic Line Established (17:1—20:8)

This section is characterized by the Chronicler's close adherence to traditional materials. He achieves his purpose by omitting all that material which is irrelevant to his scheme and by presenting an occasional reinterpretation of the events to be described.

(1) The Divine Covenant (17:1–27)

a. The Oracles of Nathan (17:1–15)

¹ Now when David dwelt in his house, David said to Nathan the prophet, "Behold, I dwell in a house of cedar, but the ark of the covenant of the Lord is under a tent." ² And Nathan said to David, "Do all that is in your heart, for God is with you."

³ But that same night the word of the Lord came to Nathan, ⁴ "Go and tell my servant David, 'Thus says the Lord: You shall not build me a house to dwell in. ⁵ For I have not dwelt in a house since the day I led up Israel to this day, but I have gone from tent to tent and from dwelling to dwelling. ⁶ In all places where I have moved with all Israel, did I speak a word with any of the judges of Israel, whom I commanded to shepherd my people, saying, "Why have you not built me a house of cedar?"' ⁷ Now therefore thus shall you say to my servant David, 'Thus says the Lord of hosts, I took you from the pasture, from following the sheep, that you should be prince over my people Israel; ⁸ and I have been with you wherever you went, and have cut off all your enemies from before you; and I will make for you a name, like the name of the great ones of the earth. ⁹ And I will appoint a place for my people Israel, and will plant them, that they may dwell in their own place, and be disturbed no more; and violent men shall waste them no more, as formerly, ¹⁰ from the time that I appointed judges over my people Israel; and I will subdue all your enemies. Moreover I declare to you that the Lord will build you a house. ¹¹ When your days are fulfilled to go to be with your fathers, I will raise up your offspring after you, one of your own sons, and I will establish his kingdom. ¹² He shall build a house for me, and I will establish his throne for ever. ¹³ I will be his father, and he shall be my son; I will not take my steadfast love from him, as I took it from him who was before you, ¹⁴ but I will confirm him in my house and in my kingdom for ever and his throne shall be established for ever.'" ¹⁵ In accordance with all these words, and in accordance with all this vision, Nathan spoke to David.

This passage is dependent upon 2 Samuel 7, but the Chronicler looks at its thrust from his own perspective. Second Samuel 7:1 records that when David held his audience with Nathan, God "had given him rest from all his enemies round about." Yet in the next chapter there is a list of subsequent conquests achieved by David. Also, this expression implies that considerable time elapsed between David's taking the ark to Jerusalem and his expression of a desire to provide a proper temple to house it. The Chronicler resolves both these tensions by omitting the statement.

One of the most significant variations is the substitution of *go to be with your fathers* for the traditional "lie down with your fathers" of 2 Samuel 7:12. This is an unusual phrase and may imply a conviction that the afterlife may involve more than mere sleep. Second Samuel 7:14 mentions the possibility of iniquity on the part of David's son, but the Chronicler does not. Again, although Samuel mentions the rejected Saul by name, the later passage speaks of him only in general terms. Very remarkable indeed is the change from "your house and your kingdom" (2 Sam. 7:16) to "in my house and in my kingdom" (v. 14). The Hebrew kingdom is here viewed as a theocracy (cf. 1 Chron. 28:5; 29:11; 29:23). *House* in this context is parallel to *kingdom* and refers to the people of Israel, not the Temple. They are the house of God in whom he truly dwells.

b. The Prayer of David (17:16-27)

16 Then King David went in and sat before the Lord, and said, "Who am I, O Lord God, and what is my house, that thou hast brought me thus far? 17 And this was a small thing in thy eyes, O God; thou hast also spoken of thy servant's house for a great while to come, and hast shown me future generations, O Lord God! 18 And what more can David say to thee for honoring thy servant? For thou knowest thy servant. 19 For thy servant's sake, O Lord, and according to thy own heart, thou hast wrought all this greatness, in making known all these great things. 20 There is none like thee, O Lord, and there is no God besides thee, according to all that we have heard with our ears. 21 What other nation on earth is like thy people Israel, whom God went to redeem to be his people, making for thyself a name for great and terrible things, in driving out nations before thy people whom thou didst redeem from Egypt? 22 And thou didst make thy people Israel to be thy people for ever; and thou, O Lord, didst become their God. 23 And now, O Lord, let the word which thou hast spoken concerning thy servant and concerning his house be established for ever, and do as thou hast spoken; 24 and thy name will be established and magnified for ever, saying, 'The Lord of hosts, the God of Israel, is Israel's God,' and the house of thy servant David will be established before thee. 25 For thou, my God, hast revealed to thy servant that thou wilt build a house for him; therefore thy servant has found courage to pray before thee. 26 And now, O Lord, thou art God, and thou hast promised this good thing to thy servant; 27 now therefore may it please thee to bless the house of thy servant, that it may continue for ever before thee; for what thou, O Lord, hast blessed is blessed for ever."

This is the only mention in the Old Testament of anyone sitting down to pray, and it is repeated in both Samuel and Chronicles. David is not prostrate before God, but is sitting with bowed head. Regardless of the meaning of the common statement, a new dignity is given to both David and Israel in the Chronicler's version. Second Samuel says that the covenant was made because of God's promise or word (7:21), whereas the Chronicles version asserts that it was for his servant David's sake (v. 19). God rules over Israel in 2 Samuel 7:26, but in Chronicles he is Israel's God and acts as God *toward* them, in person-to-person relationships. In 2 Samuel, God is referred to as "thou, O Lord of hosts, the God of Israel." In Chronicles the more personal "thou, my God" occurs.

One needs to be careful, however, in asserting that the Chronicler has arbitrarily altered his sources. In some cases he has simply reinterpreted their spirit. In others he may be using a source that contained the variations he uses in his accounts. In the passages above, it appears that the variations are reinterpretations rather than textual variants, since they all tend to elucidate the book's basic themes. One other statement, however, is quite debatable. In 2 Samuel 7:23 the literal Hebrew ambiguously says "whom gods went to redeem" (where the plural *elohim* occurs without the article and governs a plural verb). The Chronicler's text presents no problems, for the article appears with *elohim,* which now governs a singular verb, which is the usual way of speaking of Israel's God: "whom (the) God went to redeem" (v. 21).

(2) David's Victories (18:1—20:8)

This section corresponds closely with the material in 2 Samuel (cf. 1 Chron. 18:1–17 and 2 Sam. 8:1–18; 1 Chron. 19:1—20:3 and 2 Sam. 10:1—11:1; 12:26-31; 1 Chron. 20:4–8 and 2 Sam. 21:18–22). The Chronicler has arranged his material in the same order as the earlier sources, omitting the passages dealing with domestic matters. The reason he gives for denying to David the privilege of building the Temple is that he is a warrior (22:8; 28:3). Therefore, immediately after Nathan informs David that he will not be permitted to do this, the Chronicler arranges a cluster of references to David's wars. His inclusion of these military exploits, therefore, does not necessarily imply his endorsement of them. On the other hand it would not be accurate to assert that he considered military activities sinful. However, he does imply that such pursuits interfered with the more intimate activities of cultic worship. Whether the taint was merely ritualistic it is difficult to determine.[12] The important fact is that the Chronicler is the first biblical writer to focus on the problem. This is particularly remarkable in light of his reluctance to say anything that might present David in an unfavorable light.

In at least two places the text of the Chronicler is superior to the one in Samuel (1 Chron. 18:1,12). The mysterious "Methegammah" of 2 Samuel 8:1 in 1 Chronicles 18:1 becomes the likely "Gath and its villages." Certainly the "Edomites" (18:12) is the correct term rather than the "Syrians" (Heb. text) of 2 Samuel 8:13. This probably indicates that the Chronicler was using a different text from the Masoretes. The Hebrew text of the Old Testament was not standardized until several centuries after the Chronicler did his work.

a. Wars of Conquest (18:1–13)

¹ After this David defeated the Philistines and subdued them, and he took Gath and its villages out of the hand of the Philistines. ² And he defeated Moab, and the Moabites became servants to David and brought tribute. ³ David also defeated Hadadezer king of Zobah, toward Hamath, as he went to set up his monument at the river Euphrates. ⁴ And David took from him a thousand chariots, seven thousand horsemen, and twenty thousand foot soldiers, and David hamstrung all the chariot horses, but left enough for a hundred chariots. ⁵ And when the Syrians of Damascus came to help Hadadezer king of Zobah, David slew twenty-two thousand men of the Syrians. ⁶ Then David put garrisons in Syria of Damascus; and the Syrians became servants to David, and brought tribute. And the LORD gave victory to David wherever he went. ⁷ And David took the shields of gold which were carried by the servants of Hadadezer, and brought them to Jerusalem. ⁸ And from Tibhath and from Cun, cities of Hadadezer, David took very much bronze; with it Solomon made the bronze sea and the pillars and the vessels of bronze. ⁹ When Tou king of Hamath heard that David had defeated the whole army of Hadadezer, king of Zobah, ¹⁰ he sent his son Hadoram to King David, to greet him, and to congratulate him because he had fought against Hadadezer and defeated him; for Hadadezer had often been at war with Tou. And he sent all sorts of articles of gold, of silver, and of bronze; ¹¹ these also King David dedicated to the LORD, together with the silver and gold which he had carried off from all the nations, from Edom, Moab, the Ammonites, the Philistines, and Amalek.

¹² And Abishai, the son of Zeruiah, slew eighteen thousand Edomites in the Valley of Salt. ¹³ And he put garrisons in Edom; and all the Edomites became David's servants. And the LORD gave victory to David wherever he went.

It is significant that the Chronicler omits David's cruel treatment of the Moabites. It is obvious that he considers this a reflection upon his hero's image. However, he does mention his hamstringing of the horses of the Aramaeans of Zobah, and does not appear to see enough fault in this to warrant its omission. This was a logical practice when a victorious army could not make use of such animals. Solomon, however, was wiser and less wasteful. He had a lucrative business selling such horses (1 Kings 10:28–29) to other nations!

A thousand chariots, seven thousand horsemen, and twenty thousand footmen. Second Samuel 8:4 mentions "a thousand and seven hundred horsemen" and 20,000

---

[12] Goettsberger, J., *Die Bucher der Chronik oder Paralipomenon* (Bonn: Peter Hanstein, 1939), p. 163.

footmen. The number of chariots is not listed there. Although the Chronicler's numbers are often larger than the earlier source, here we have an increase in one item, and the same figure for another. There may be a textual problem here, since the first "thousand" of Samuel might have been taken to apply to chariots and the same number substituted for the "hundred" in reference to the horsemen. Obviously 700 horsemen would not be adequate for an army with a thousand chariots.

David slew twenty-two thousand. This number is exactly the same as in 2 Samuel 8:5. Again the Chronicler is faithful to his source and does not arbitrarily increase the number.

With it Solomon made the bronze sea. Verse 8 is an addition to the Samuel account. Although the Chronicler sensed the taint associated with war that denied to David the building of the Temple, he shows no consciousness of the moral problem involved in using the booty of war for making holy vessels.

And Abishai . . . slew eighteen thousand Edomites. Second Samuel 8:13 attributes this feat to David and says the enemies were Syrians. The Chronicler is using a more reliable text, for it was not likely that Syrians would be fighting in the Valley of Salt. With the Chronicler's tendency to exalt David, it is significant that the Samuel account gave David the credit as the commander, while the later writer did not. If the text he was using had attributed the victory to David, it is difficult to see how the Chronicler would have failed to perpetuate that claim. Apparently his source did not contain that tribute.

b. David's Cabinet (18:14–17)

14 So David reigned over all Israel; and he administered justice and equity to all his people. 15 And Joab the son of Zeruiah was over the army; and Jehoshaphat the son of Ahilud was recorder; 16 and Zadok the son of Ahitub and Ahimelech the son of Abiathar were priests; and Shavsha was secretary; 17 and Benaiah the son of Jehoiada was over the Cherethites and the Pelethites; and David's sons were the chief officials in the service of the king.

The administrative organization of David's kingdom was apparently modeled after Egypt. From sources there we learn a good deal more about the various duties. Joab's duties are obvious. The responsibilities of the recorder (*mazkir*) were more complicated, for he made all the official arrangements for the king; he was chief of protocol. The secretary not only kept the state papers, but he also protected the king. Benaiah's duty was to command the king's professional bodyguard. The nature of the task of the sons of David is the most controversial one. Second Samuel says they held the office of priest (*cohen*). The Chronicler, however, says they were *chief officials in the service of the king*. Since *cohen* usually applies to the office of sacrificing priest, many interpreters feel that the Chronicler has redefined the office because of his artificial view that no one but a descendant of Aaron could act as a priest. However, it is possible that *cohen* might have had a less restrictive meaning in David's day, a fact that the Chronicler was aware of. There are two other passages that present a similar problem. In 2 Samuel 20:26 it is said that Ira, the Jairite, was a priest to David, and in 1 Kings 4:5 Zabud, the son of Nathan, was a priest and the king's friend.

In early religious cults this term was applied to various activities in the sanctuary, particularly divining. Among the Hebrews it might have had this more general use. Later the title was confined to one office, that of the sacrificing priest. In David's day it might have described "a domestic chaplain" (cf. IDB, III, 882). The fact that Zadok and Abiathar, the sacrificing priests, were also in David's cabinet (2 Sam. 20:25) would indicate that the office of his sons was a different one from theirs, but the exact nature of the function is not known. They might have served as a liaison between the official cult and the crown in this time of transition, when tensions were probably severe.

c. The Ammonite-Syrian Campaign (19:1–19)

¹ Now after this Nahash the king of the Ammonites died, and his son reigned in his stead. ² And David said, "I will deal loyally with Hanun the son of Nahash, for his father dealt loyally with me." So David sent messengers to console him concerning his father. And David's servants came to Hanun in the land of the Ammonites, to console him. ³ But the princes of the Ammonites said to Hanun, "Do you think, because David has sent comforters to you, that he is honoring your father? Have not his servants come to you to search and to overthrow and to spy out the land?" ⁴ So Hanun took David's servants, and shaved them, and cut off their garments in the middle, at their hips, and sent them away; ⁵ and they departed. When David was told concerning the men, he sent to meet them, for the men were greatly ashamed. And the king said, "Remain at Jericho until your beards have grown, and then return."

⁶ When the Ammonites saw that they had made themselves odious to David, Hanun and the Ammonites sent a thousand talents of silver to hire chariots and horsemen from Mesopotamia, from Arammaacah, and from Zobah. ⁷ They hired thirty-two thousand chariots and the king of Maacah with his army, who came and encamped before Medeba. And the Ammonites were mustered from their cities and came to battle. ⁸ When David heard of it, he sent Joab and all the army of the mighty men. ⁹ And the Ammonites came out and drew up in battle array at the entrance of the city, and the kings who had come were by themselves in the open country.

¹⁰ When Joab saw that the battle was set against him both in front and in the rear, he chose some of the picked men of Israel, and arrayed them against the Syrians; ¹¹ the rest of his men he put in the charge of Abishai his brother, and they were arrayed against the Ammonites. ¹² And he said, "If the Syrians are too strong for me, then you shall help me; but if the Ammonites are too strong for you, then I will help you. ¹³ Be of good courage, and let us play the man for our people, and for the cities of our God; and may the Lord do what seems good to him." ¹⁴ So Joab and the people who were with him drew near before the Syrians for battle; and they fled before him. ¹⁵ And when the Ammonites saw that the Syrians fled, they likewise fled before Abishai, Joab's brother, and entered the city. Then Joab came to Jerusalem.

¹⁶ But when the Syrians saw that they had been defeated by Israel, they sent messengers and brought out the Syrians who were beyond the Euphrates, with Shophach the commander of the army of Hadadezer at their head. ¹⁷ And when it was told David, he gathered all Israel together, and crossed the Jordan, and came to them, and drew up his forces against them. And when David set the battle in array against the Syrians, they fought with him. ¹⁸ And the Syrians fled before Israel; and David slew of the Syrians the men of seven thousand chariots, and forty thousand foot soldiers, and killed also Shophach the commander of their army. ¹⁹ And when the servants of Hadadezer saw that they had been defeated by Israel, they made peace with David, and became subject to him. So the Syrians were not willing to help the Ammonites any more.

The Chronicler omits from his account the story of David's care for Mephibosheth (2 Sam. 9), which he must have been tempted to include, for it portrays David in a favorable light. However, because of his reluctance to mention anything related to the house of Saul, he passes it by. The Nahash story as told by the late writer differs very little from the Samuel account. One noticeable variation is the Chronicler's obvious effort to avoid an objectionable word in the description of the disgraceful exposure of David's envoys by Hanum. The Samuel account says their robes were cut off in the middle, even to their buttocks (Heb., seats). The Chronicler, apparently more delicate-minded, used a euphemism ("at their hips"), literally, "to the step," "to the place where the body divides toward the feet." In his translation Myers uses a euphemism of his own: "just at the point they were intended to cover!"

In this passage we find examples both of exaggerated and conservative estimates. Second Samuel 10:6 lists 20,000, 1,000, and 12,000 men fighting against David, or a total of 33,000. Chronicles has 32,000 chariots alone and states that Hanum hired them for 1,000 talents of silver, which would weigh about 37½ tons. Second Chronicles 25:6 says that Amaziah hired 100,000 men from Israel for just 100 talents of silver. Obviously 1,000 talents is too high a figure. It is quite possible that we have here an example of someone recording the story from memory, confusing the list of men with the numbers concerning money and chariots. The original 1,000 referred to the men of Maacah (2 Sam. 10:6). Now it is applied to monetary items. That left 32,000 men who are listed in the Chronicler's source as 32,000 chariots.

In v. 18 there is an increase from the 700 chariots in Samuel to 7,000 in Chronicles. Again, this is probably the result of the tendencies of the midrash that the Chronicler is using. Yet at the same time the 40,000 horsemen of the Samuel passages has become 40,000 footmen, a far more conservative count. If the Chronicler was bent on exaggerating, why did he increase one figure and lessen the number of the other? Normally, he would have indeed expanded all his materials. His inconsistent figures surely reflect the varied sources he was employing.

d. The Siege of Rabbah (20:1–3)

¹ In the spring of the year, the time when kings go forth to battle, Joab led out the army, and ravaged the country of the Ammonites, and came and besieged Rabbah. But David remained at Jerusalem. And Joab smote Rabbah, and overthrew it. ² And David took the crown of their king from his head; he found that it weighed a talent of gold, and in it was a precious stone; and it was placed on David's head. And he brought forth the spoil of the city, a very great amount. ³ And he brought forth the people who were in it, and set them to labor with saws and iron picks and axes; and thus David did to all the cities of the Ammonites. Then David and all the people returned to Jerusalem.

Here is an obvious example of the Chronicler's editorial practices. He begins his account like that of 2 Samuel 11:1, but follows it for only a few phrases, leaving out the entire story of David's sin with Bathsheba that continues into 2 Samuel 12. That he had the whole passage before him is apparent, for in 20:2 he mentions that David had arrived at the scene of the battle without telling how he got there, which 2 Samuel is careful to do. Then the account closely parallels Samuel again. The crown of gold must have been on the head of Milcom, their god (*malcam,* king). It was too heavy for a man to wear (ca. 75½ pounds). The precious stone in it was set upon David's head, either in his own crown or in one made especially for the jewel.

The fate of the conquered people is not at all clear. Second Samuel 12:31 says that they were put under saws; that is, they were forced into slave labor. However, the Chronicles passage apparently says that David cut the people with saws, although the meaning of the verb is debated. G. C. O'Ceallaigh, noting obvious textual corruption, contends that the restored text should read, "He made them desecrate (or demolish) the Molechs." [13] Since the Chronicler omitted the treatment of the Moabites as unsuitable to mention, why would he include this statement if it pictures David as even more cruel? It should be noted that the present Hebrew of Chronicles says that David brought forth the people "and cut with saws and iron picks and axes." It is not claimed that he cut the people with the instruments.

e. Philistine Engagements (20:4–8)

⁴ And after this there arose war with the Philistines at Gezer; then Sibbecai the Hushathite slew Sippai, who was one of the descendants of the giants; and the Philistines were subdued. ⁵ And there was again war with the Philistines; and Elhanan the son of Jair slew Lahmi the brother of Goliath the Gittite, the shaft of whose spear was like a weaver's beam. ⁶ And there was again war at Gath, where there was a man of great stature, who had six fingers on each hand, and six toes on each foot, twenty-four in number; and he also was descended from the giants. ⁷ And when he taunted Israel, Jonathan the son of Shimea, David's brother, slew him. ⁸ These were descended from the giants in Gath; and they fell by the hand of David and by the hand of his servants.

Interest in this passage centers around its relationship to David's slaying of Goliath. Second Samuel 21:19 says that Elhanan slew Goliath. This is in apparent conflict with the familiar account in 1 Samuel 17. Could it be that David did not kill Goliath after all, but one of his men performed the act? It was common for a king

[13] *Vetus Testamentum,* 12 (1962), pp. 179–189.

to get credit for all the exploits of his soldiers. In the passage before us, the Chronicler mentions several mighty deeds by David's men, yet he gives David the credit also.

The Chronicler resolves the problem by suggesting that Elhanan slew Lahmi, the brother of Goliath, rather than Goliath himself. Yet the descriptive phrase, *whose spear was like a weaver's beam* is the very one used to describe Goliath's weapon in 1 Samuel 17:7. Again Lahmi may simply be a name derived from the fragmented *lehem* (from Bethlehem) of 2 Samuel 21:19. Slotki believes that Elhanan was a title for David, like Pharaoh or Sultan. It is possible that Elhanan was his boyhood name and David a throne-name acquired when he became king. Yet here we have no evidence.

Another possible solution is that the personal name Goliath did not occur in the story of David's exploit in 1 Samuel 17 but that it was inserted later by someone more familiar with the text in Chronicles than in 2 Samuel. Certainly we should not easily discount the story that has meant so much to generations of believers.

5. Temple Preparations (21:1—29:25)

Except for 21:1—22:1, which retells and interprets the story recorded in 2 Samuel 24:1 ff. and 2 Chronicles 22:2–19 which summarizes David's preparations for the Temple, this section is entirely the work of the Chronicler and has no parallels in the Old Testament. Accordingly, it is the longest passage of this sort in the books of Chronicles. Although some would contend that the material throws little light upon the Davidic period, and instead reflects the conditions of the times of the Chronicler, it is more realistic to view this work as a compilation and reediting of materials received from various sources, some quite ancient and others of more recent origin. Each must be examined in the light of its own tendencies. The Chronicler was limited both by his sources and his own incomplete knowledge of the earlier period. In spite of this, he has provided us with information both about the earlier cultic organization and his own. Without his contributions our knowledge of priestly and Levitical life from David to Ezra would be sorely lacking.

(1) Choice of a Building Site (2:11—22:1)

This passage resembles 2 Samuel 24:1–25 and appears to be an expansion either of that passage or a similar text. With this section the Chronicler completed his treatment of material from the books of Samuel. The last chapter of 2 Samuel appears to be part of an appendix (chs. 22—24) to that book, containing a psalm attributed to David (ch. 22) and his last words (23:1–7). In Samuel it is a floating fragment and is not connected with any particular time in David's reign. The Chronicler finds a home for it, seeing in this story the basis of the authority for moving the sanctuary from Gibeon to Jerusalem. Although the account portrays David in a rather dubious light, the Chronicler was willing to use the tradition because of its importance in establishing the Temple in Jerusalem. Here it is evident that although the Chronicler was a devoted admirer of David, his first love was the Temple itself. If David's decrease meant the Temple's increase, then the Chronicler had no qualms about proceeding to tell the story.

a. The Census (21:1–6)

¹ Satan stood up against Israel, and incited David to number Israel. ² So David said to Joab and the commanders of the army, "Go, number Israel, from Beersheba to Dan, and bring me a report, that I may know their number." ³ But Joab said, "May the LORD add to his people a hundred times as many as they are! Are they not, my lord the king, all of them my lord's servants? Why then should my lord require this? Why should he bring guilt upon Israel?" ⁴ But the king's word prevailed against Joab. So Joab departed and went throughout all Israel, and came back to Jerusalem. ⁵ And Joab gave the sum of the numbering of the people to David. In all Israel there were one million one hundred thousand men who drew

the sword, and in Judah four hundred and seventy thousand who drew the sword. 6 But he did not include Levi and Benjamin in the numbering, for the king's command was abhorrent to Joab.

Here is one of the most significant reinterpretations the Chronicler made. Whereas the earlier story had attributed David's sinful act to the influence of God, and then pictured God as getting angry when David sinned, the later historian saw the moral problem involved in such behavior. Surely David could not be rightly blamed for something God moved him to do. The earlier source, rightly seeing God's involvement in all events, had no problem with this apparent conflict. God did what he pleased, and no one questioned his acts of sovereignty. The Chronicler, however, was more perceptive. He too believed in God's total involvement, not always in actively determining men's behavior but rather in permitting what he did not cause. Therefore, he attributed the influence upon David to Satan rather than to God. Elsewhere in the Old Testament, Satan (the adversary) always appears as a servant of God, an angel who acts only as God assigns or permits him (cf. Job 1:6; 2:1; Zech. 3:1–2). Only in this passage does the word appear without the article, therefore indicating that it has now become a personal name. His function is also different. For the first time he does more than accuse men before God or carry out God's orders. Here he is pictured as tempting David to sin. Yet even here he is acting only as God will permit. God has not lost control of the situation.

Why should he bring guilt upon Israel? Here is a strange situation. The tough warrior, Joab, is more sensitive than David to the implication of this act. In fact Joab's question, *Are they not, my Lord the king, all of them my Lord's servants?* implies that the census was taken in order to regulate more completely the people's responsibilities to the crown. Joab was afraid that the populace would realize this and be moved toward open rebellion, such as did occur when Solomon died.

The total number of men counted in the census was listed as 1,300,000 in 2 Samuel, but only 1,100,000 in Chronicles. The number in Judah is 30,000 less than the number ascribed to Judah in Samuel. The Chronicler mentions, however, that Levi and Benjamin were not counted in his list. Perhaps the Samuel account included them, thus explaining the discrepancy. Whatever the reason, the Chronicler is here adhering closely to his sources, and there is no attempt to exaggerate on his part.

Levi was not included because they were exempted from military service (cf. Num. 1:49). Why Benjamin was not counted is not clear. There are three possibilities: (1) Joab did not finish the census. (2) Benjamin had become so small that they were spared military service. (3) The Gibeon sanctuary was in Benjamin territory and this made the whole tribe exempt.

b. *David's repentance (21:7–13)*

7 But God was displeased with this thing, and he smote Israel. 8 And David said to God, "I have sinned greatly in that I have done this thing. But now, I pray thee, take away the iniquity of thy servant; for I have done very foolishly." 9 And the Lord spoke to Gad, David's seer, saying, 10 "Go and say to David, 'Thus says the Lord, Three things I offer you; choose one of them, that I may do it to you.'" 11 So Gad came to David and said to him, "Thus says the Lord, 'Take which you will: 12 either three years of famine; or three months of devastation by your foes, while the sword of your enemies overtakes you; or else three days of the sword of the Lord, pestilence upon the land, and the angel of the Lord destroying throughout all the territory of Israel.' Now decide what answer I shall return to him who sent me." 13 Then David said to Gad, "I am in great distress; let me fall into the hand of the Lord, for his mercy is very great; but let me not fall into the hand of man."

Omitting the particulars concerning the taking of the census, the Chronicler immediately observes that as Joab anticipated, David had incurred serious guilt. He seems to imply that David's awareness of his people's suffering awakened his conscience. Second Samuel 24:10–14, however, clearly states that David was conscience stricken before disaster ever struck. Here we have the unusual circumstance of David's being pictured in a better light in the earlier source than in the later. Upon close scrutiny, it appears that the Chronicler means the same thing as Samuel. If the pestilence had already occurred, why was David given his choice? Apparently v. 7 anticipates David's choice, the Chronicler being anxious to show the displeasure of God in this matter. In doing so, however, he inadvertently presents David in a less favorable light than does Samuel.

The sword of the Lord, pestilence upon the land. David's people whom he had proudly counted, would be decimated by pestilence, referred to as "the sword of the Lord."

Let me fall into the hand of the Lord. Second Samuel says, "Let us fall." Here David does not ask that God's wrath fall upon the people because of his sin; he only refers to himself. David is aware of the fact that God is more likely to show him mercy than will his enemies. Indeed this is one of the most significant teachings of the Bible. God is more inclined to be gracious than men.

c. *David's Change of Mind (21:14–17)*

14 So the LORD sent a pestilence upon Israel; and there fell seventy thousand men of Israel. 15 And God sent the angel to Jerusalem to destroy it; but when he was about to destroy it, the LORD saw, and he repented of the evil; and he said to the destroying angel, "It is enough; now stay your hand." And the angel of the LORD was standing by the threshing floor of Ornan the Jebusite. 16 And David lifted his eyes and saw the angel of the LORD standing between earth and heaven, and in his hand a drawn sword stretched out over Jerusalem. Then David and the elders, clothed in sackcloth, fell upon their faces. 17 And David said to God, "Was it not I who gave command to number the people? It is I who have sinned and done very wickedly. But these sheep, what have they done? Let thy hand, I pray thee, O LORD my God, be against me and against my father's house; but let not the plague be upon thy people."

The Chronicler gives the same number of slain Israelites as does the Samuel account. His description of the sparing of Jerusalem is far more vivid, however, and may be closer to the original in some of its details than 2 Samuel. The mention of the angel there is abrupt and presupposes a previous mention of him in the source. In fact 2 Samuel 24 itself is not one of the earliest sources in Samuel. Clear additions of the Chronicler, however, can be seen in the phrase *the Lord saw* and the awesome picture of the angel standing between earth and heaven, which is a mark of late theology. In earlier Israel, angels always appeared as men and could not be distinguished from them in appearance.

d. *A Site for the Temple (21:18—22:1)*

18 Then the angel of the LORD commanded Gad to say to David that David should go up and rear an altar to the LORD on the threshing floor of Ornan the Jebusite. 19 So David went up at Gad's word, which he had spoken in the name of the LORD. 20 Now Ornan was threshing wheat; he turned and saw the angel, and his four sons who were with him hid themselves. 21 As David came to Ornan, Ornan looked and saw David and went forth from the threshing floor, and did obeisance to David with his face to the ground. 22 And David said to Ornan, "Give me the site of the threshing floor that I may build on it an altar to the LORD—give it to me at its full price—that the plague may be averted from the people." 23 Then Ornan said to David, "Take it; and let my lord the king do what seems good to him; see, I give the oxen for burnt offerings, and the threshing sledges for the wood, and the wheat for a cereal offering. I give it all." 24 But King David said to Ornan, "No, but I will buy it for the full price; I will not take for the LORD what is yours, nor offer burnt offerings which cost me nothing." 25 So David paid Ornan six hundred shekels of gold by weight for the site. 26 And David built there an altar to the LORD and presented burnt offerings and peace offerings, and called upon the LORD, and he answered him with fire from heaven upon the altar of burnt offering. 27 Then the LORD commanded the angel; and he put his sword back into its sheath.

28 At that time, when David saw that the LORD had answered him at the threshing floor of Ornan the Jebusite, he made his sacrifices there. 29 For the tabernacle of the LORD, which Moses had made in the wilderness, and the altar of burnt offering were at that time in the high place at Gibeon; 30 but David could not go before it to inquire of God, for he was afraid of the sword of the angel of the LORD.

1 Then David said, "Here shall be the house

of the LORD God and here the altar of burnt offering for Israel."

In this passage the Chronicler reveals the reason for including this account in his history. Second Samuel 24:18 ff. did not state what significance the story had in the history of Israel but leaves it as a picture of another meaningful facet of David's character. The Chronicler sees in this event the authentication of a new site for the sanctuary.

He turned and saw the angel. Second Samuel does not mention the fact that Ornan (Araunah) saw the angel, but rather he saw the king. The Hebrew word for angel is *mala'k,* and for king is *melek,* and it is obvious that the two terms could be confused. The Chronicler alone mentions the sons of Ornan. This is not necessarily an addition by him, for it could have been present in his source.

In Chronicles the amount of money that David paid for the property is 12 times that mentioned in 2 Samuel. There are several explanations given: (1) Some would take this as another example of the Chronicler's exaggeration. Everything for the Temple should be in gold rather than silver; it should be more than Abraham paid for the field of Machpelah (Gen. 23:15). (2) An ancient Jewish explanation is that 2 Samuel mentions only the amount assigned to each tribe as its assessment in the acquiring of the Temple property. Chronicles gives the total amount, which would be 600 shekels of gold, twelve times as much as 50 shekels of silver. (3) It is more likely that the larger amount is due to the fact that 2 Samuel refers only to the cost of the threshing floor and sacrificial animals while Chronicles mentions the total cost of the entire Temple site (cf. v. 22).

He answered him with fire from heaven. This is not in 2 Samuel. Here God is pictured as authenticating the site (cf. Lev. 9:24). In a similar way God approved the acceptance of Gentiles in the church by the sending of the Holy Spirit (Acts 10:44).

For the tabernacle of the Lord. Verses 29–30 are a parenthetical explanation of the reason why David was permitted to sacrifice here rather than in the official center at Gibeon. Verse 28 should be read as the beginning of a clause that is completed in 22:1: "At that time, when David saw . . . then David said, 'Here shall be the house.'"

In 2 Chronicles 3:1 we are told that this site was the same as Mount Moriah, where Abraham had taken Isaac for the sacrifice, and upon this spot Solomon's Temple was built. It is now occupied by the Dome of the Rock Mosque.

(2) *Charge to Solomon (22:2–19)*

a. *Provisions for the Building (22:2–5)*

² David commanded to gather together the aliens who were in the land of Israel, and he set stonecutters to prepare dressed stones for building the house of God. ³ David also provided great stores of iron for nails for the doors of the gates and for clamps, as well as bronze in quantities beyond weighing, ⁴ and cedar timbers without number; for the Sidonians and Tyrians brought great quantities of cedar to David. ⁵ For David said, "Solomon my son is young and inexperienced, and the house that is to be built for the LORD must be exceedingly magnificent, of fame and glory throughout all lands; I will therefore make preparation for it." So David provided materials in great quantity before his death.

Although the account in Kings mentions that Solomon used both Israelite and alien forced labor (1 Kings 5:13; 9:15; 11:28), the Chronicler only mentions the latter (cf. 2 Chron. 8:7). Second Samuel 20:24 indicates that David used forced labor, but it does not say who composed the labor gangs. It is quite possible that David did not extend the requirements to Israelites also, a move which became necessary under Solomon with his more extensive operations. If David did use Israelite forced labor, the Chronicler probably would have been silent on the subject, even as he was in reference to Solomon, for it would not contribute favorably to his portrait of David.

The aliens who were in the land. The

Hebrew word is *gerim* (sing. *ger*). This word is sometimes translated "sojourners." It described the foreigners living in Israel. They were personally free but without political rights. Therefore, they could easily be exploited, and the Hebrews were often warned not to oppress them (Ex. 22:21; 23:9; Lev. 19:33; Deut. 24:14; Jer. 7:6; Zech. 7:10). Here David is pictured as assembling them to work out their responsibilities to the crown rather than forcing them into slavery. The Chronicler does not identify the national backgrounds of these aliens. Those who served Solomon are described as the remnants of the Canaanites (1 Kings 9:15 f.). Second Chronicles 30:25 refers to the *gerim* as proselytes (sojourners, RSV), which was their position in the post-exilic community (cf. Ex. 12:49; Lev. 24:22; Num. 9:14; 15:15). It is possible that the Chronicler regards them as voluntary proselyte labor in this passage. It is significant that the book of Isaiah anticipates that foreigners will participate in the building of the second Temple (Isa. 60:10), just as they did in the work of the first.

Must be exceedingly magnificent, of fame and glory. This is, literally, "must be beyond being great, for a name and for an ornament." Since God's house will be the outward evidence of his magnificence and greatness, it should be beyond anything known before that his fame might be known in all the world. Although David was aware of the impossibility of the task, he knew the nature of the challenge.

b. The Word to Solomon (22:6–16)

6 Then he called for Solomon his son, and charged him to build a house for the LORD, the God of Israel. 7 David said to Solomon, "My son, I had it in my heart to build a house to the name of the LORD my God. 8 But the word of the LORD came to me, saying, 'You have shed much blood and have waged great wars; you shall not build a house to my name, because you have shed so much blood before me upon the earth. 9 Behold, a son shall be born to you; he shall be a man of peace. I will give him peace from all his enemies round about; for his name shall be Solomon, and I will give peace and quiet to Israel in his days. 10 He shall build a house for my name. He shall be my son, and I will be his father, and I will establish his royal throne in Israel for ever.' 11 Now, my son, the LORD be with you, so that you may succeed in building the house of the LORD your God, as he has spoken concerning you. 12 Only, may the LORD grant you discretion and understanding, that when he gives you charge over Israel you may keep the law of the LORD your God. 13 Then you will prosper if you are careful to observe the statutes and the ordinances which the LORD commanded Moses for Israel. Be strong, and of good courage. Fear not; be not dismayed. 14 With great pains I have provided for the house of the LORD a hundred thousand talents of gold, a million talents of silver, and bronze and iron beyond weighing, for there is so much of it; timber and stone too I have provided. To these you must add. 15 You have an abundance of workmen: stonecutters, masons, carpenters, and all kinds of craftsmen without number, skilled in working 16 gold, silver, bronze, and iron. Arise and be doing! The LORD be with you!"

David said to Solomon. First Kings 8:17–18 mentions Solomon's report on this charge. Some expositors feel that the Chronicler possessed only the account in Kings and put the speech of Solomon back into David's mouth. However, it is also possible that the later writer was using an earlier source.

You have shed much blood. It is only in this passage and in 28:3 that such a reason is given for God's refusal to let David build the Temple. The Chronicler is the first writer to perceive that there is something innately wrong with war, even if it is a just one. Most of David's fighting was forced upon him, first in self-defense and later for national security. Yet he was disqualified from doing what he longed for more than anything, building the house of God. David is not blamed for his military activities since someone had to do this bloody work. But a man of peace must build the Temple, for it was the purpose of God to eliminate war one day; to this his house was dedicated (cf. Isa. 2:2–4).

For his name shall be Solomon. The root of the name is *shalom,* peace. In 2 Samuel 12:24 f. he is named Jedidiah, "beloved of the Lord." The name Solomon might have been a throne-name given him when he assumed the kingship. It pictured the purpose to which he would give himself, in contrast to the career of his father. The giving of a second name favors the possibility that the name "David" or "beloved" was also a throne-name, his original name being Elhanan (2 Sam. 21:19).

Peace and quiet to Israel in his days. David did well to urge Solomon to be true to the law of God, for when Solomon departed from it, wars broke out in his kingdom (cf. 1 Kings 11:14,23,26).

Now, my son, the Lord be with you. The passage that follows (vv. 11–16) draws heavily upon 1 Kings 2:1–9. As in that passage, David speaks to Solomon with the same words Moses addressed to Joshua. David is viewed as a sort of second Moses even in the Deuteronomic account in Kings, so the Chronicler has historical precedent for his view of David. As Joshua followed Moses to fulfill the dream denied to the great lawgiver, even so Solomon would complete the aim of David.

However, it is significant that whereas in the book of Kings David's last words have to do with revenge on his enemies, here he speaks of his thoughts concerning the Temple and his dream of peace. The book of Kings says nothing about the Temple in David's last words to Solomon. Here the house of God is the principal matter on his mind in these last hours, and he says nothing about his enemies.

With great pains I have provided . . . To these you must add. The word pains means affliction. David accumulated this wealth in the midst of his wars and personal troubles. Solomon in a peaceful reign should do far more.

A hundred thousand talents of gold, a million talents of silver, and bronze and iron beyond weighing . . . craftsmen without number. One hundred thousand talents of gold would amount to 3,775 tons. A million talents of silver would be 37,750 tons. The equivalent in dollars would be high in the billions (cf. Myers, I, 152). Such amounts are out of the realm of possibility, for it is said that Solomon's later annual income was only 666 talents of gold (1 Kings 10:14). The Chronicler is obviously using hyperbole. He specifically says that the bronze and iron were beyond weighing and the workmen beyond numbering, and he surely intended to say that the amount of gold and silver was beyond counting.

Elmslie (p. 420) is correct when he says, "Neither the Jewish Chronicler nor his Jewish readers could have imagined that there could ever be anyone so prosaic as to take the golden words literally."

c. The Charge to the Leaders (22:17–19)

¹⁷ David also commanded all the leaders of Israel to help Solomon his son, saying, ¹⁸ "Is not the Lord your God with you? And has he not given you peace on every side? For he has delivered the inhabitants of the land into my hand; and the land is subdued before the Lord and his people. ¹⁹ Now set your mind and heart to seek the Lord your God. Arise and build the sanctuary of the Lord God, so that the ark of the covenant of the Lord and the holy vessels of God may be brought into a house built for the name of the Lord."

Here David exhorts the leaders to stand by Solomon in his building operations. He calls upon them to *seek the Lord your God* by arising and building him a house. By doing so they will be inviting him to come and make a proper dwelling with them. For the Chronicler, true religion was not simply a pious reflection upon the deity, but it involved active participation in the institutional life that celebrated his living presence among his people.

That the ark . . . may be brought into a house. A settled people needed a permanent house for God. His abode should not be inferior to theirs. This principle still has validity.

(3) The Cultic Leaders (23:1—25:31)

a. The Levites (23:1–32)

¹ When David was old and full of days, he made Solomon his son king over Israel. ² David assembled all the leaders of Israel and the priests and the Levites. ³ The Levites, thirty years old and upward, were numbered, and the total was thirty-eight thousand men. ⁴ "Twenty-four thousand of these," David said,

"shall have charge of the work in the house of the Lord, six thousand shall be officers and judges, ⁵ four thousand gatekeepers, and four thousand shall offer praises to the Lord with the instruments which I have made for praise." ⁶ And David organized them in divisions corresponding to the sons of Levi: Gershom, Kohath, and Merari.

⁷ The sons of Gershom were Ladan and Shimei. ⁸ The sons of Ladan: Jehiel the chief, and Zetham, and Joel, three. ⁹ The sons of Shimei: Shelomoth, Haziel, and Haran, three. These were the heads of the fathers' houses of Ladan. ¹⁰ And the sons of Shimei: Jahath, Zina, and Jeush, and Beriah. These four were the sons of Shimei. ¹¹ Jahath was the chief, and Zizah the second; but Jeush and Beriah had not many sons, therefore they became a father's house in one reckoning.

¹² The sons of Kohath: Amram, Izhar, Hebron, and Uzziel, four. ¹³ The sons of Amram: Aaron and Moses. Aaron was set apart to consecrate the most holy things, that he and his sons for ever should burn incense before the Lord, and minister to him and pronounce blessings in his name for ever. ¹⁴ But the sons of Moses the man of God were named among the tribe of Levi. ¹⁵ The sons of Moses: Gershom and Eliezer. ¹⁶ The sons of Gershom: Shebuel the chief. ¹⁷ The sons of Eliezer: Rehabiah the chief; Eliezer had no other sons, but the sons of Rehabiah were very many. ¹⁸ The sons of Izhar: Shelomith the chief. ¹⁹ The sons of Hebron: Jeriah the chief, Amariah the second, Jahaziel the third, and Jekameam the fourth. ²⁰ The sons of Uzziel: Micah the chief and Isshiah the second.

²¹ The sons of Merari: Mahli and Mushi. The sons of Mahli: Eleazar and Kish. ²² Eleazar died having no sons, but only daughters; their kinsmen, the sons of Kish, married them. ²³ The sons of Mushi: Mahli, Eder, and Jeremoth, three.

²⁴ These were the sons of Levi by their fathers' houses, the heads of fathers' houses as they were registered according to the number of the names of the individuals from twenty years old and upward who were to do the work for the service of the house of the Lord. ²⁵ For David said, "The Lord, the God of Israel, has given peace to his people; and he dwells in Jerusalem for ever. ²⁶ And so the Levites no longer need to carry the tabernacle or any of the things for its service"—²⁷ for by the last words of David these were the number of the Levites from twenty years old and upward— ²⁸ "but their duty shall be to assist the sons of Aaron for the service of the house of the Lord, having the care of the courts and the chambers, the cleansing of all that is holy, and any work for the service of the house of God; ²⁹ to assist also with the showbread, the flour for the cereal offering, the wafers of unleavened bread, the baked offering, the offering mixed with oil, and all measures of quantity or size. ³⁰ And they shall stand every morning, thanking and praising the Lord, and likewise at evening, ³¹ and whenever burnt offerings are offered to the Lord on sabbaths, new moons, and feast days, according to the number required of them, continually before the Lord. ³² Thus they shall keep charge of the tent of meeting and the sanctuary, and shall attend the sons of Aaron, their brethren, for the service of the house of the Lord."

This chapter deals first with the census takers of the Levitical families (vv. 1–23), who had not been included in the troublesome venture recorded in 21:1—22:1. This passage should be viewed over against the former one as a sequel and a contrast. This census did not evoke the wrath of God such as the other had, for it was not a military census designed to further the personal ambitions of David. Rather its purpose was the organizing of the cultic army of God to perform the services of the worshiping congregation. Such a move in the Chronicler's view surely enjoyed the favor of God.

The count dealt with those Levites who were 30 years of age or older. Yet those 20 years old and above were to carry on the permanent work of the new Temple according to the last instructions of David (23:27). This discrepancy is difficult to explain. Verse 3 might have originally read "twenty" instead of "thirty." On the other hand some interpreters feel that v. 27 is the contribution of a later revision of Chronicles when the Levites were less numerous and therefore the age limit needed to be lowered. Others insist that v. 27 reflects the conditions prevailing when the Zadokite priests succeeded in establishing themselves in authority, causing many Levites to leave the Temple service, thus decimating their ranks. It is more likely that the Chronicler is simply saying that the census was taken just as Moses prescribed it in Numbers 4:3 ff., which dealt only with those 30 years of age and above. He was convinced that the 20-year limit was established by David himself and had continued ever since (cf. 2 Chron. 31:17; Ezra 3:8). David himself made the adjustment for the permanent services of the new sanctuary. Building the Temple required the services of the more mature Levites. The regular services would call for the systematic training of the younger ones as well.

The description of the work of the Levites (vv. 24-32) leaves no doubt that their position is subservient to that of the priests. They were to be the servants of the priests as well as Temple musicians, the latter duty somewhat improving their status. Yet v. 32 reminds us again that as musicians they were still answerable to the priests and were not a group independent of Aaronic authority. This section, although it corresponds to the regulations in Numbers 3, so circumscribes the role of the Levite, while the Chronicler tends to exalt it, that some feel that this section is a late addition to his work, placed there in a time when the distinctions were more rigid. However, this view seems to be that of the Chronicler throughout his work. Although he does exalt the Levites, he refuses to do so at the expense of the importance of the priests. Whenever he treats one group in relation to the other, the priests always have the superior role (cf. 6:48-49; 16:39-40).

The number of the Levites recorded in the census has occasioned considerable debate. Thirty-eight thousand men above 30 years of age were counted. This compares with 8,580 in the time of Moses (Num. 4:36 ff.). Some interpreters take this to be another example of the Chronicler's tendency to exaggerate, for the number appears to be too high for David's time. Yet if there were over 8,000 in the Mosaic period, five times that amount should not be too many for the time of David. The essential question is the meaning of the word "thousand" (Heb., *'elep*). If it is taken to be a unit of indeterminate number (cf. Myers, I, 159), then the description is more realistic. The census revealed that there were 38 units in David's reign over against eight units during the time of Moses. There were 580 Levites in the earlier period, the exact number not being listed in the later one. In such an analysis the number following *'elep* (thousand) would be the actual count. Another explanation may be that the Chronicler's source, the Levitical midrash, had made an estimate of what the numbers must have been in David's time. The Chronicler is following his source in this matter.

b. Priests and Levites (24:1-31)

¹ The divisions of the sons of Aaron were these. The sons of Aaron: Nadab, Abihu, Eleazar, and Ithamar. ² But Nadab and Abihu died before their father, and had no children, so Eleazar and Ithamar became the priests. ³ With the help of Zadok of the sons of Eleazar, and Ahimelech of the sons of Ithamar, David organized them according to the appointed duties in their service. ⁴ Since more chief men were found among the sons of Eleazar than among the sons of Ithamar, they organized them under sixteen heads of fathers' houses of the sons of Eleazar, and eight of the sons of Ithamar. ⁵ They organized them by lot, all alike, for there were officers of the sanctuary and officers of God among both the sons of Eleazar and the sons of Ithamar. ⁶ And the scribe Shemaiah the son of Nethanel, a Levite, recorded them in the presence of the king, and the princes, and Zadok the priest, and Ahimelech the son of Abiathar, and the heads of the fathers' houses of the priests and of the Levites; one father's house being chosen for Eleazar and one chosen for Ithamar.

⁷ The first lot fell to Jehoiarib, the second to Jedaiah, ⁸ the third to Harim, the fourth to Seorim, ⁹ the fifth to Malchijah, the sixth to Mijamin, ¹⁰ the seventh to Hakkoz, the eighth to Abijah, ¹¹ the ninth to Jeshua, the tenth to Shecaniah, ¹² the eleventh to Eliashib, the twelfth to Jakim, ¹³ the thirteenth to Huppah, the fourteenth to Jeshebeab, ¹⁴ the fifteenth to Bilgah, the sixteenth to Immer, ¹⁵ the seventeenth to Hezir, the eighteenth to Happizzez, ¹⁶ the nineteenth to Pethahiah, the twentieth to Jehezkel, ¹⁷ the twenty-first to Jachin, the twenty-second to Gamul, ¹⁸ the twenty-third to Delaiah, the twenty-fourth to Maaziah. ¹⁹ These had as their appointed duty in their service to come into the house of the LORD according to the procedure established for them by Aaron their father, as the LORD God of Israel had commanded him.

²⁰ And of the rest of the sons of Levi: of the sons of Amram, Shubael; of the sons of Shu-

bael, Jehdeiah. ²¹ Of Rehabiah: of the sons of Rehabiah, Isshiah the chief. ²² Of the Izharites, Shelomoth; of the sons of Shelomoth, Jahath. ²³ The sons of Hebron: Jeriah the chief, Amariah the second, Jahaziel the third, Jekameam the fourth. ²⁴ The sons of Uzziel, Micah; of the sons of Micah, Shamir. ²⁵ The brother of Micah, Isshiah; of the sons of Isshiah, Zechariah. ²⁶ The sons of Merari: Mahli and Mushi. The sons of Jaaziah: Beno. ²⁷ The sons of Merari: of Jaaziah, Beno, Shoham, Zaccur, and Ibri. ²⁸ Of Mahli: Eleazar, who had no sons. ²⁹ Of Kish, the sons of Kish: Jerahmeel. ³⁰ The sons of Mushi: Mahli, Eder, and Jerimoth. These were the sons of the Levites according to their fathers' houses. ³¹ These also, the head of each father's house and his younger brother alike, cast lots, just as their brethren the sons of Aaron, in the presence of King David, Zadok, Ahimelech, and the heads of fathers' houses of the priests and of the Levites.

In this passage the Chronicler first of all deals with the principal priestly families and then presents another Levitical list (vv. 20–31) that raises the most serious problems in the chapter. It is not at all clear why it has been added as a supplement to the account in 23:7–23. Ten names occur in the list that are not in Chapter 23, most of them representing an additional generation beyond that list. The family of Gershon is not mentioned at all, probably because there were no new families involved in this case. Either the Chronicler used an older list in Chapter 23 and in this passage brings it up-to-date, or the former chapter refers to the families in the Chronicler's day and the present passage was appended after his time. Some expositors feel that this list, with its additional names, is an attempt to raise the number of Levitical families to 24, the same as that of the priests (v. 18) and the singers (25:31). All attempts to identify the 24, however, have required drastic revision of the text without adequate objective evidence.

The mention of Ahimelech as serving alongside Zadok is a disconcerting statement. Elsewhere it is Abiathar (2 Sam. 15:35; 17:15; 1 Chron. 15:11; 1 Kings 4:4) except in 2 Samuel 8:17. Ahimelech is the name of both the father of Abiathar and his son (1 Sam. 22:20; 2 Sam. 8:17). Apparently either a textual corruption has occurred here or the reference represents a confusion of traditions in the Chronicler's sources, the latter being more likely. A reversed transposing of the names of Ahimelech and Abiathar occurs in Mark 2:26 where Abiathar is mentioned as the priest when David ate the holy bread, whereas the Samuel account clearly says it was Ahimelech (1 Sam. 21:1).

The tensions existing between the two rival houses of Ithamar and Eleazar, finally resolved in favor of Eleazar (the Zadokite priests), are relaxed in the Chronicler's account by a compromise agreeable to all parties. There would be equality of rank, but more courses were allotted to the Eleazar descendants, since they were more numerous. By weight of majority numbers the Zadok branch would have the most to say about Temple offices, and would control the high priesthood, as it had done since Solomon's day (cf. 1 Kings 4:2; 2 Chron. 31:10; 1 Chron. 6:4 ff.). The Chronicler mentions one of the sons of Ithamar who came back with Ezra, and it can be assumed that he would serve as a priest (Ezra 8:2) but certainly would not be eligible for the high priesthood. Strangely, Ezekiel did not specifically mention the status of Ithamar's line but referred only to Levites and Zadokites. Perhaps he knew of no survivors in the Exile (Ezek. 44:15 ff.).

c. The Singers (25:1–31)

¹ David and the chiefs of the service also set apart for the service certain of the sons of Asaph, and of Heman, and of Jeduthun, who should prophesy with lyres, with harps, and with cymbals. The list of those who did the work and of their duties was: ² Of the sons of Asaph: Zaccur, Joseph, Nethaniah, and Asharelah, sons of Asaph, under the direction of Asaph, who prophesied under the direction of the king. ³ Of Jeduthun, the sons of Jeduthun: Gedaliah, Zeri, Jeshaiah, Shimei, Hashabiah, and Mattithiah, six, under the direction of their father Jeduthun, who prophesied with the lyre in thanksgiving and praise to the LORD. ⁴ Of Heman, the sons of Heman: Bukkiah, Mattaniah, Uzziel, Shebuel, and Jerimoth, Hananiah, Hanani, Eliathah, Giddalti, and Romamtiezer, Joshbekashah, Mallothi, Hothir, Mahazioth. ⁵ All these were the sons of Heman the king's

seer, according to the promise of God to exalt him; for God had given Heman fourteen sons and three daughters. ⁶ They were all under the direction of their father in the music in the house of the Lord with cymbals, harps, and lyres for the service of the house of God. Asaph, Jeduthun, and Heman were under the order of the king. ⁷ The number of them along with their brethren, who were trained in singing to the Lord, all who were skilful, was two hundred and eighty-eight. ⁸ And they cast lots for their duties, small and great, teacher and pupil alike.

⁹ The first lot fell for Asaph to Joseph; the second to Gedaliah, to him and his brethren and his sons, twelve; ¹⁰ the third to Zaccur, his sons and his brethren, twelve; ¹¹ the fourth to Izri, his sons and his brethren, twelve; ¹² the fifth to Nethaniah, his sons and his brethren, twelve; ¹³ the sixth to Bukkiah, his sons and his brethren, twelve; ¹⁴ the seventh to Jesharelah, his sons and his brethren, twelve; ¹⁵ the eighth to Jeshaiah, his sons and his brethren, twelve; ¹⁶ the ninth to Mattaniah, his sons and his brethren, twelve; ¹⁷ the tenth to Shimei, his sons and his brethren, twelve; ¹⁸ the eleventh to Azarel, his sons and his brethren, twelve; ¹⁹ the twelfth to Hashabiah, his sons and his brethren, twelve; ²⁰ to the thirteenth, Shubael, his sons and his brethren, twelve; ²¹ to the fourteenth, Mattithiah, his sons and his brethren, twelve; ²² to the fifteenth, to Jeremoth, his sons and his brethren, twelve; ²³ to the sixteenth, to Hananiah, his sons and his brethren, twelve; ²⁴ to the seventeenth, to Joshbekashah, his sons and his brethren, twelve; ²⁵ to the eighteenth, to Hanani, his sons and his brethren, twelve; ²⁶ to the nineteenth, to Mallothi, his sons and his brethren, twelve; ²⁷ to the twentieth, to Eliathah, his sons and his brethren, twelve; ²⁸ to the twenty-first, to Hothir, his sons and his brethren, twelve; ²⁹ to the twenty-second, to Giddalti, his sons and his brethren, twelve; ³⁰ to the twenty-third, to Mahazioth, his sons and his brethren, twelve; ³¹ to the twenty-fourth, to Romamtiezer, his sons and his brethren, twelve.

This chapter is an attempt to extol the office of the Levitical singers. Their organization is traced back to David, and they were responsible for 24 courses, just as the priests. There is no reason to doubt that the persistent tradition of David's interest in music was historical (cf. 1 Sam. 16:23; 18:10; 19:9; 2 Sam. 1:77 ff.; 6:5,14). Music was highly developed among the Canaanites and was advanced enough in the time of Hezekiah for Sennacherib to accept both male and female singers from him as tribute. Obviously, however, the women were not cultic performers (cf. 1 Sam. 18:6 ff.).

The chiefs of the service. Literally, "the captains (princes) of the host." This term elsewhere applies to military commanders (cf. 2 Sam. 2:8; 1 Chron. 19:16; 27:3,34). There was no reason why military commanders should appoint Levitical singers. Here is another example of the Chronicler's application of military terminology to cultic officials. They were the true defense of Israel. The Deuteronomic editors earlier preserved a similar feeling about Elijah (2 Kings 2:12). What the tradition said about Elijah, the Chronicler applied to the leaders in public worship.

Who should prophesy with lyres. Here the function of the Levitical singers is connected with prophecy. The connection between music and prophecy was an ancient one (cf. 1 Sam. 10:5). In the earlier period prophecy seems to be related to an ecstatic experience, probably influenced by music (cf. 2 Kings 3:15). Here the singer apparently played his own accompaniment, like the traditional David. The prophets of the Old Testament had a more intimate contact with the cult than was formerly recognized. However, during the classical period (eighth and seventh century B.C.) their part seemed to be a speaking role rather than a singing one. Certainly few of them were Levites. By the Chronicler's day they had become absorbed into the Levitical system (cf. 2 Chron. 20:13–17). Although this merging of prophecy and worship tended to suppress individuality and featured more *thanksgiving and praise* than censure for sin, it did stress the possibility of music as a proper mode of communicating the divine word. In the Levitical choirs it was likely that more of God's people could be prophets, fulfilling the wish of Moses (Num. 11:29), than in the day of the great prophetic personalities when lone individuals preached the word. Yet it was easier in this medium for prophecy to become institutionalized. There is the possibility that the Chronicler himself was one of these prophetic singers (cf. his interest in this area, 1 Chron. 15:16–22; 16:4–42; 2 Chron. 5:12–13; 29:27–30; Ezra 3:10; Neh. 12:27), such a prophetic vocation preparing him for his role as historian. In Hebrew tradition the books Joshua–2 Kings were called the Former Prophets. Surely the Chronicler, then, in that sense is one of the latter ones.

Under the direction of the king. The singers were not directly responsible to the high priest, but to the king himself, who was a sacral and not just a political leader. *Heman, . . . Mahazioth.* This list of names might originally have been a prayer. How the redaction could have taken place, no one knows. For a possible reconstruction, cf. Myers, I, 172 f.

According to the promise of God to exalt him.—literally, "according to the words of God to lift up his horn." The idiom "to lift up the horn" elsewhere means to heighten one's power (cf. 1 Sam. 2:10; Psalms 89:18; 92:10; 148:14; Lam. 2:17). Here it probably refers to the exaltation that came to Heman because of his many children.

And they cast lots for their duties. Asaph was assigned the first duty, and thus his family alternated first with Jeduthun and then with Heman. The latter's family manned courses 15–24, since it was so numerous. It is interesting to note that teacher and pupils shared alike in the practical duties. The word translated "teacher" literally means "one who causes to discern." Their method therefore certainly was not one of rote memory or slavish imitation. Nor was it pure theory, for the teacher himself was assigned practical tasks.

(4) *Peripheral Officials (26:1–32)*

a. *Gate Keepers (26:1–19)*

¹ As for the divisions of the gatekeepers: of the Korahites, Meshelemiah the son of Kore, of the sons of Asaph. ² And Meshelemiah had sons: Zechariah the first-born, Jediael the second, Zebadiah the third, Jathniel the fourth, ³ Elam the fifth, Jehohanan the sixth, Elie- hoenai the seventh. ⁴ And Obededom had sons: Shemaiah the first-born, Jehozabad the second, Joah the third, Sachar the fourth, Nethanel the fifth, ⁵ Ammiel the sixth, Issachar the seventh, Peullethai the eighth; for God blessed him. ⁶ Also to his son Shemaiah were sons born, who were rulers in their fathers' houses, for they were men of great ability. ⁷ The sons of Shemaiah: Othni, Rephael, Obed, and Elzabad, whose brethren were able men, Elihu and Semachiah. ⁸ All these were of the sons of Obededom with their sons and brethren, able men qualified for the service; sixty-two of Obededom. ⁹ And Meshelemiah had sons and brethren, able men, eighteen. ¹⁰ And Hosah, of the sons of Merari, had sons: Shimri the chief (for though he was not the first-born, his father made him chief), ¹¹ Hilkiah the second, Tebaliah the third, Zechariah the fourth: all the sons and brethren of Hosah were thirteen.

¹² These divisions of the gatekeepers, corresponding to their chief men, had duties, just as their brethren did, ministering in the house of the LORD; ¹³ and they cast lots by fathers' houses, small and great alike, for their gates. ¹⁴ The lot for the east fell to Shelemiah. They cast lots also for his son Zechariah, a shrewd counselor, and his lot came out for the north. ¹⁵ Obededom's came out for the south, and to his sons was allotted the storehouse. ¹⁶ For Shuppim and Hosah it came out for the west, at the gate of Shallecheth on the road that goes up. Watch corresponded to watch. ¹⁷ On the east there were six each day, on the north four each day, on the south four each day, as well as two and two at the storehouse; ¹⁸ and for the parbar on the west there were four at the road and two at the parbar. ¹⁹ These were the divisions of the gatekeepers among the Korahites and the sons of Merari.

This is an outstanding example of the Chronicler's inclination to upgrade the lesser ranks of Temple servants. Their Levitical status is not clear in Ezra 2:42,70; 7:24; 10:24; Neh. 10:28; 11:19. Here it is evident.

Came out for the south. The Temple of Solomon had no south gate, for the palace was there. Some expositors therefore see this as an anachronism, the Chronicler arbitrarily making assignments according to the arrangement in the second Temple (cf. Ezek. 40:24,28). However, this verse could be taken to mean that Obededom's family was given the storehouse rather than the south gate. In addition, although the palace was situated to the south, a private entrance was also there and needed to be guarded lest some unauthorized person enter the palace from the Temple area. In some cases unqualified persons might try to enter the Temple compound from the palace, such as warriors from a palace coup, or someone ceremonially unclean.

The gate of Shallecheth. This is not mentioned elsewhere in the Bible, but the reference to the "ascending road" marks its position opposite the Tyropoeon Valley, on the principal approach from the lower city and the western hill.

Watch corresponded to watch. Either they performed their duties alternately or had stations facing one another.

The parbar. This mysterious Hebrew word is related to the *parwarim* (precincts) of 2 Kings 23:11. It seems to come from a Persian root meaning "possessing light." The opinion of older scholars that there was some sort of open pavilion adjacent to the Temple has been confirmed by a Lydian inscription from Sardis.

b. Treasurers (26:20-28)

20 And of the Levites, Ahijah had charge of the treasuries of the house of God and the treasuries of the dedicated gifts. 21 The sons of Ladan, the sons of the Gershonites belonging to Ladan, the heads of the fathers' houses belonging to Ladan the Gershonite: Jehieli. 22 The sons of Jehieli, Zetham and Joel his brother, were in charge of the treasuries of the house of the LORD. 23 Of the Amramites, the Izharites, the Hebronites, and the Uzzielites— 24 and Shebuel the son of Gershom, son of Moses, was chief officer in charge of the treasuries. 25 His brethren: from Eliezer were his son Rehabiah, and his son Jeshaiah, and his son Joram, and his son Zichri, and his son Shelomoth. 26 This Shelomoth and his brethren were in charge of all the treasuries of the dedicated gifts which David the king, and the heads of the fathers' houses, and the officers of the thousands and the hundreds, and the commanders of the army, had dedicated. 27 From spoil won in battles they dedicated gifts for the maintenance of the house of the LORD. 28 Also all that Samuel the seer, and Saul the son of Kish, and Abner the son of Ner, and Joab the son of Zeruiah had dedicated—all dedicated gifts were in the care of Shelomoth and his brethren.

Treasuries of the house of God . . . treasuries of the dedicated gifts. The former resulted from the regular contributions by the people; the latter were the special gifts of the prizes of war.

All that Samuel . . . Saul . . . Abner . . . Joab . . . had dedicated. The Chronicler, who is reluctant to mention Saul, does so here. Apparently it was a regular rite for a returning military chieftain or king to donate part of his booty to his God as a token of his gratitude for the victory. Abraham paid his tithe from the spoils of war to Melchizedek (Gen. 14:20). Rather than a lack of spiritual perception (Elmslie, p. 430), it was a mark of sincere devotion to deity in that time.

c. Civil Authorities (26:29-32)

29 Of the Izharites, Chenaniah and his sons were appointed to outside duties for Israel, as officers and judges. 30 Of the Hebronites, Hashabiah and his brethren, one thousand seven hundred men of ability, had the oversight of Israel westward of the Jordan for all the work of the LORD and for the service of the king. 31 Of the Hebronites, Jerijah was chief of the Hebronites of whatever genealogy or fathers' houses. (In the fortieth year of David's reign search was made and men of great ability among them were found at Jazer in Gilead.) 32 King David appointed him and his brethren, two thousand seven hundred men of ability, heads of fathers' houses, to have the oversight of the Reubenites, the Gadites, and the half-tribe of the Manassites for everything pertaining to God and for the affairs of the king.

Outside duties for Israel, as officers and judges. These Levites had responsibilities outside the Temple itself among the general populace. There is no evidence that David had any system of taxation, so their duties apparently concerned the collection of materials for the construction of the Temple. In disputed cases they were also to be judges. According to 2 Chronicles 19:4-11, Levites were appointed to judicial posts in Jehoshaphat's reign. Josephus confirms this early practice (*Antiq.* IV.8,14). Whatever their actual duties were, here was an example of Levites' being given authority over civilians outside the regular cultus.

Everything pertaining to God and for the affairs of the king.—literally, "for every matter (word) of God and every matter (word) of the king." This appears to be a very ambiguous assignment. How were secular matters to be distinguished from sacred? It is not likely that the ancient Hebrew made any such distinction. How was an order of God to be viewed as distinct from that of the king? For many Israelites there was no difference here either. It is no wonder they needed judges in this area, but the Levites must have had difficulty being objective. The problem is still with us. Jesus certainly viewed every area of life as being lived under God's authority; there can be no separation of the secular from the sacred (Luke 16:10–13). However, he did not relax the tension between loyalty to Caesar (the state) and one's primary duties to God (Matt. 22:17 ff.).

(5) Standing Army (27:1–15)

¹ This is the list of the people of Israel, the heads of fathers' houses, the commanders of thousands and hundreds, and their officers who served the king in all matters concerning the divisions that came and went, month after month throughout the year, each division numbering twenty-four thousand: ² Jashobeam the son of Zabdiel was in charge of the first division in the first month; in his division were twenty-four thousand. ³ He was a descendant of Perez, and was chief of all the commanders of the army for the first month. ⁴ Dodai the Ahohite was in charge of the division of the second month; in his division were twenty-four thousand. ⁵ The third commander, for the third month, was Benaiah, the son of Jehoiada the priest, as chief; in his division were twenty-four thousand. ⁶ This is the Benaiah who was a mighty man of the thirty and in command of the thirty; Ammizabad his son was in charge of his division. ⁷ Asahel the brother of Joab was fourth, for the fourth month, and his son Zebadiah after him; in his division were twenty-four thousand. ⁸ The fifth commander, for the fifth month, was Shamhuth, the Izrahite; in his division were twenty-four thousand. ⁹ Sixth, for the sixth month, was Ira, the son of Ikkesh the Tekoite; in his division were twenty-four thousand. ¹⁰ Seventh, for the seventh month, was Helez the Pelonite, of the sons of Ephraim; in his division were twenty-four thousand. ¹¹ Eighth, for the eighth month, was Sibbecai the Hushathite, of the Zerahites; in his division were twenty-four thousand. ¹² Ninth, for the ninth month, was Abiezer of Anathoth, a Benjaminite; in his division were twenty-four thousand. ¹³ Tenth, for the tenth month, was Maharai of Netophah, of the Zerahites; in his division were twenty-four thousand. ¹⁴ Eleventh, for the eleventh month, was Benaiah of Pirathon, of the sons of Ephraim; in his division were twenty-four thousand. ¹⁵ Twelfth, for the twelfth month, was Heldai the Netophathite, of Othniel; in his division were twenty-four thousand.

This passage closely resembles the list of David's military heroes recorded in 2 Samuel 23:8–39 and 1 Chronicles 11:11–47, but it is not simply derived from them. It represents an independent source that, in its original form, was probably somewhat later than the other two, for, instead of Benaiah and Asahel, their sons are in charge of their divisions. The arrangement into regular rotating tours of duty may be an invention either of the Levitical midrash used by the Chronicler or of the Chronicler himself. It might even have originated with David but surely not on any grand scale. If each division was composed of 24,000 men, this would be far more than David's simple court required. If the term *'elep* (thousand) is taken to be a unit whose exact compliment of men is not always the same, averaging closer to 100 than 1000, then the arrangement was quite possible. Then about 3,000 men would be on duty during each tour of service.

The commanders of thousands and hundreds. These appear to be definite terms for military units rather than exact numbers. The larger unit was called an *'elep* (thousand), the smaller a *me'ah* (hundred). The names do not indicate the exact number in the unit, but only the upper limits. The *'elep* never numbered more than 1,000 but could be much less. Just so the *me'ah* was never more than 100 but was usually less. Any unit past 100 was an *'elep*. When exact numbers were indicated, they would follow the name of the unit. The "one thousand seven hundred" (26:30) who had oversight of Israel west of the Jordan were "one unit with seven hundred men." Likewise the "two thousand seven hundred" (26:32) who oversaw east Jordan were "two units totaling seven hundred men."

(6) Tribal Rulers (27:16–24)

16 Over the tribes of Israel, for the Reubenites Eliezer the son of Zichri was chief officer; for the Simeonites, Shephatiah the son of Maacah; 17 for Levi, Hashabiah the son of Kemuel; for Aaron, Zadok; 18 for Judah, Elihu, one of David's brothers; for Issachar, Omri the son of Michael; 19 for Zebulun, Ishmaiah the son of Obadiah; for Naphtali, Jeremoth the son of Azriel; 20 for the Ephraimites, Hoshea the son of Azaziah; for the half tribe of Manasseh, Joel the son of Pedaiah; 21 for the half tribe of Manasseh in Gilead, Iddo the son of Zechariah; for Benjamin, Jaasiel the son of Abner; 22 for Dan, Azarel the son of Jeroham. These were the leaders of the tribes of Israel. 23 David did not number those below twenty years of age, for the LORD had promised to make Israel as many as the stars of heaven. 24 Joab the son of Zeruiah began to number, but did not finish; yet wrath came upon Israel for this, and the number was not entered in the chronicles of King David.

Only five persons out of the 25 in this list are mentioned elsewhere in the Old Testament, although most of the names are common ones. There is no reference to the leaders of the tribes of Gad and Asher. Because the tribal rolls always contain twelve tribes and since in this list there were already twelve before the Chronicler came to Gad and Asher, these tribes had to be omitted. Note that in 1 Chronicles 2:2 they are last in the order.

Joab . . . began to number, but did not finish. This refers to 1 Chronicles 21:6, where it said that he did not number Levi and Benjamin.

The number was not entered in the chronicles of King David. Yet we have the census figures in 1 Chronicles 21:5. This statement may mean that David would not permit the results of the census to be on the public record. The Chronicler and the writer of Samuel might have secured their figures from unofficial statistics. This may be one reason why they differed (cf. comments on 1 Chron. 21:1–6).

(7) The King's Officers (27:25–34)

25 Over the king's treasuries was Azmaveth the son of Adiel; and over the treasuries in the country, in the cities, in the villages and in the towers, was Jonathan the son of Uzziah; 26 and over those who did the work of the field for tilling the soil was Ezri the son of Chelub; 27 and over the vineyards was Shimei the Ramathite; and over the produce of the vineyards for the wine cellars was Zabdi the Shiphmite. 28 Over the olive and sycamore trees in the Shephelah was Baalhanan the Gederite; and over the stores of oil was Joash. 29 Over the herds that pastured in Sharon was Shitrai the Sharonite; over the herds in the valleys was Shaphat the son of Adlai. 30 Over the camels was Obil the Ishmaelite; and over the she-asses was Jehdeiah the Meronothite. Over the flocks was Jaziz the Hagrite. 31 All these were stewards of King David's property.

32 Jonathan, David's uncle, was a counselor, being a man of understanding and a scribe; he and Jehiel the son of Hachmoni attended the king's sons. 33 Ahithophel was the king's counselor, and Hushai the Archite was the king's friend. 34 Ahithophel was succeeded by Jehoiada the son of Benaiah, and Abiathar. Joab was commander of the king's army.

The Chronicler presents a list (vv. 25–31) of the officers who supervised the king's crown property. Because David apparently had no direct taxation, he had acquired considerable personal property from which he derived the income that supported the life of his court. This included everything from farming to camel caravans. If crown properties had become so extensive during this one reign, one can imagine how later kings added to their possessions as time went by. This is one reason why Ezekiel recommended that the prince be given an allotted portion which he could not enlarge (Ezek. 46:16–18).

David's cabinet (vv. 32–34) differs from that in the other similar records (cf. 2 Sam. 8:15–18; 20:23–26; 1 Chron. 18:15–17). Jonathan, the *dod* (uncle, friend of the family) of David is mentioned nowhere else. David had a nephew by this name (1 Chron. 20:7), but he would hardly have welcomed counsel from his nephew. The word *dod* also means beloved (Isa. 5:1 and throughout the Song of Solomon). Curtis and Madsen were convinced that the reference is to Jonathan the son of Saul, David's intimate friend during his early wanderings.

(8) The Final Charge to Solomon and Israel (28:1—29:25)

A great assembly was called by David for all Israel to commit the people to the building of the Temple and to anoint Solomon as the new king. It is strange that in the list of those invited to the gathering the priests and Levites are not mentioned. That they were there is obvious (cf. 28:21; 29:21), but the Chronicler must have used real restraint in not mentioning the specific role they were playing. Perhaps the priests and Levites were not referred to because they were already at work or had already arrived for their organization (23:2—26:32).

a. The Charge to Solomon (28:1–21)

¹ David assembled at Jerusalem all the officials of Israel, the officials of the tribes, the officers of the divisions that served the king, the commanders of thousands, the commanders of hundreds, the stewards of all the property and cattle of the king and his sons, together with the palace officials, the mighty men, and all the seasoned warriors. ² Then King David rose to his feet and said: "Hear me, my brethren and my people. I had it in my heart to build a house of rest for the ark of the covenant of the Lord, and for the footstool of our God; and I made preparations for building. ³ But God said to me, 'You may not build a house for my name, for you are a warrior and have shed blood.' ⁴ Yet the Lord God of Israel chose me from all my father's house to be king over Israel for ever; for he chose Judah as leader, and in the house of Judah my father's house, and among my father's sons he took pleasure in me to make me king over all Israel. ⁵ And of all my sons (for the Lord has given me many sons) he has chosen Solomon my son to sit upon the throne of the kingdom of the Lord over Israel. ⁶ He said to me, 'It is Solomon your son who shall build my house and my courts, for I have chosen him to be my son, and I will be his father. ⁷ I will establish his kingdom for ever if he continues resolute in keeping my commandments and my ordinances, as he is today.' ⁸ Now therefore in the sight of all Israel, the assembly of the Lord, and in the hearing of our God, observe and seek out all the commandments of the Lord your God; that you may possess this good land, and leave it for an inheritance to your children after you for ever.
⁹ "And you, Solomon my son, know the God of your father, and serve him with a whole heart and with a willing mind; for the Lord searches all hearts, and understands every plan and thought. If you seek him, he will be found by you; but if you forsake him, he will cast you off for ever. ¹⁰ Take heed now, for the Lord has chosen you to build a house for the sanctuary; be strong, and do it."
¹¹ Then David gave Solomon his son the plan of the vestibule of the temple, and of its houses, its treasuries, its upper rooms, and its inner chambers, and of the room for the mercy seat; ¹² and the plan of all that he had in mind for the courts of the house of the Lord, all the surrounding chambers, the treasuries of the house of God, and the treasuries for dedicated gifts; ¹³ for the divisions of the priests and of the Levites, and all the work of the service in the house of the Lord; for all the vessels for the service in the house of the Lord, ¹⁴ the weight of gold for all golden vessels for each service, the weight of silver vessels for each service, ¹⁵ the weight of the golden lampstands and their lamps, the weight of gold for each lampstand and its lamps, the weight of silver for a lampstand and its lamps, according to the use of each lampstand in the service, ¹⁶ the weight of gold for each table for the showbread, the silver for the silver tables, ¹⁷ and pure gold for the forks, the basins, and the cups; for the golden bowls and the weight of each; for the silver bowls and the weight of each; ¹⁸ for the altar of incense made of refined gold, and its weight; also his plan for the golden chariot of the cherubim that spread their wings and covered the ark of the covenant of the Lord. ¹⁹ All this he made clear by the writing from the hand of the Lord concerning it, all the work to be done according to the plan.
²⁰ Then David said to Solomon his son, "Be strong and of good courage, and do it. Fear not, be not dismayed; for the Lord God, even my God, is with you. He will not fail you or forsake you, until all the work for the service of the house of the Lord is finished. ²¹ And behold the divisions of the priests and the Levites for all the service of the house of God; and with you in all the work will be every willing man who has skill for any kind of service; also the officers and all the people will be wholly at your command."

Already David had privately charged Solomon with the task of building the sanctuary (22:6 ff.). Now he did it publicly.

My brethren and my people. David skillfully described his relationship to them. They were both his own kin and his subjects.

You are a warrior and have shed blood. This may be better understood in the light of 22:8.

I have chosen him to be my son, and I will be his father. Psalm 2:7 was probably used at the coronation of each new king, as this adoption by God was acted out liturgically. It might also have been an annual ceremony when this was reenacted.

In the sight of all Israel, . . . and in the hearing of our God. Israel is witness to the charge to Solomon, and God is the judge before whom it is given. This divine court situation is probably the reason why David arose to speak (v. 2) rather than addressing the assembly from his throne, as his age and rank might suggest.

Observe and seek out all the commandments of the Lord. Not only was Solomon to follow the commands with which he was acquainted, but he was constantly to search to be sure he knew all that God required. Most men are satisfied with trying to live by what little they know about God's word. Why know more of its requirements when one falls short of what he already knows?

Know the God of your father. This means, experience in your own life the God whom your father knows. Here is a masterful suggestion concerning how the generation gap was to be bridged: Let the religious traditions that have come down to you lead you to a fresh experience of your own.

David gave Solomon his son the plan. Written specifications were handed to Solomon in the public ceremony. The Chronicler says that just as Moses, instructed by God, handed down the plans for the tabernacle (Ex. 25:9), even so David, similarly inspired (v. 19), laid his plans before Solomon.

The golden chariot of the cherubim. It is not clear whether there was an actual chariot portrayed there, as in the vision of Ezekiel (ch. 1), or whether the cherubim themselves were the chariot (cf. Psalm 18:10).

Be strong and of good courage, . . . He will not fail you. The words of Moses to Joshua are repeated here (Deut. 31:8); David, the new Moses, speaks to Solomon the new Joshua, who must now accomplish the dream denied his father.

b. The Challenge to the Assembly (29:1–9)

¹ And David the king said to all the assembly, "Solomon my son, whom alone God has chosen, is young and inexperienced, and the work is great; for the palace will not be for man but for the LORD God. ² So I have provided for the house of my God, so far as I was able, the gold for the things of gold, the silver for the things of silver, and the bronze for the things of bronze, the iron for the things of iron, and wood for the things of wood, besides great quantities of onyx and stones for setting, antimony, colored stones, all sorts of precious stones, and marble. ³ Moreover, in addition to all that I have provided for the holy house, I have a treasure of my own of gold and silver, and because of my devotion to the house of my God I give it to the house of my God: ⁴ three thousand talents of gold, of the gold of Ophir, and seven thousand talents of refined silver, for overlaying the walls of the house, ⁵ and for all the work to be done by craftsmen, gold for the things of gold and silver for the things of silver. Who then will offer willingly, consecrating himself today to the LORD?"
⁶ Then the heads of fathers' houses made their freewill offerings, as did also the leaders of the tribes, the commanders of thousands and of hundreds, and the officers over the king's work. ⁷ They gave for the service of the house of God five thousand talents and ten thousand darics of gold, ten thousand talents of silver, eighteen thousand talents of bronze, and a hundred thousand talents of iron. ⁸ And whoever had precious stones gave them to the treasury of the house of the LORD, in the care of Jehiel the Gershonite. ⁹ Then the people rejoiced because these had given willingly, for with a whole heart they had offered freely to the LORD; David the king also rejoiced greatly.

David called upon the assembly to offer freely for the building of the Temple. This passage draws heavily upon the challenge of Moses addressed to Israel when the tabernacle was first built (Ex. 35:4 ff.). The basic difference was that Moses had little to contribute in material wealth, whereas David led the way with gifts from his personal fortune that amounted to more than $60,000,000. This amount is much more than one would expect to be available in those early days of the kingdom. Either the amount has been exaggerated in the Levitical tradition, or the Chronicler was sincerely listing what he thought was a proper amount for the occasion. Certainly, he was not purposefully fabricating history. His concept of God revealed in 1 Chronicles 28—29 would not permit him to teach what he knew was not true. His God, even as David's, "searches all hearts, and understands every plan and thought" (28:9); he has "pleasure in uprightness."

The palace will not be for man but for the Lord God. The word palace is a Persian word describing the dwelling of a king. Only the Chronicler applies it to the sanctuary itself.

Consecrating himself today—literally, "filling his hand today," accepting his responsibilities. This same expression is used when the sons of Levi came to Moses' side when Israel made the golden calf (Ex. 32:29). It is used of the ordination of priests on other occasions. Here laymen are asked to consecrate themselves even as the priestly family did. "They who contribute wholeheartedly to the erection of the Temple are comparable to the priests who minister in it" (Slotki, p. 154). To the generous Chronicler, gatekeepers become Levites and laymen act as priests.

Ten thousand darics of gold. These were Persian coins worth about $56,000. Why was such a small amount listed among the other millions? Perhaps here the actual amounts are preserved in terms of the monitary exchange of the Chronicler's day, while the other figures were based upon systems that the historian himself did not understand. Then there is always the possibility that we do not know what the Chronicler means by the terms he uses.

c. The Prayer of David (29:10–19)

10 Therefore David blessed the Lord in the presence of all the assembly; and David said: "Blessed art thou, O Lord, the God of Israel our father, for ever and ever. 11 Thine, O Lord, is the greatness, and the power, and the glory, and the victory, and the majesty; for all that is in the heavens and in the earth is thine; thine is the kingdom, O Lord, and thou art exalted as head above all. 12 Both riches and honor come from thee, and thou rulest over all. In thy hand are power and might; and in thy hand it is to make great and to give strength to all. 13 And now we thank thee, our God, and praise thy glorious name.

14 "But who am I, and what is my people, that we should be able thus to offer willingly? For all things come from thee, and of thy own have we given thee. 15 For we are strangers before thee, and sojourners, as all our fathers were; our days on the earth are like a shadow, and there is no abiding. 16 O Lord our God, all this abundance that we have provided for building thee a house for thy holy name comes from thy hand and is all thy own. 17 I know, my God, that thou triest the heart, and hast pleasure in uprightness; in the uprightness of my heart I have freely offered all these things, and now I have seen thy people, who are present here, offering freely and joyously to thee. 18 O Lord, the God of Abraham, Isaac, and Israel, our fathers, keep for ever such purposes and thoughts in the hearts of thy people, and direct their hearts toward thee. 19 Grant to Solomon my son that with a whole heart he may keep thy commandments, thy testimonies, and thy statutes, performing all, and that he may build the palace for which I have made provision."

This is one of the most beautiful prayers in the Bible. It speaks for itself. Here is the Chronicler at his best. No man who could write such a magnificent prayer could be a narrow propagandist. He reveals himself as a mature theologian and a consecrated believer. As David speaks, the Chronicler is also breathing the prayer. "The whole composition is an excellent illustration of the Chronicler's high conception of God, and of man's proper relationship to him, and it exhibits a sensitive appreciation of the art of public prayer" (Dentan, VII, pp. 139–140). The morning liturgy of the Jewish service of worship includes vv. 10–13. Christian responses often feature v. 14.

David blessed the Lord. How can a man bless God? It seems that it should be the other way around. The word originally meant "to bend the knee." David probably is no longer standing, and he is expressing his adoration of God, not just by genuflection, but in the glorious words that follow. *To bless God,* therefore, is to give appropriate worship and praise by act and word.

There is no abiding. Literally, "there is no hope," that is, there is no hope in life lived without God.

d. The Response of the People (29:20-25)

20 Then David said to all the assembly, "Bless the Lord your God." And all the assembly blessed the Lord, the God of their fathers, and bowed their heads, and worshiped the Lord, and did obeisance to the king. 21 And they performed sacrifices to the Lord, and on the next day offered burnt offerings to the Lord, a thousand bulls, a thousand rams, and a thousand lambs, with their drink offerings, and sacrifices in abundance for all Israel, 22 and they ate and drank before the Lord on that day with great gladness.

And they made Solomon the son of David king the second time, and they anointed him as prince for the Lord, and Zadok as priest. 23 Then Solomon sat on the throne of the Lord as king instead of David his father; and he prospered, and all Israel obeyed him. 24 All the leaders and the mighty men, and also all the sons of King David, pledged their allegiance to King Solomon. 25 And the Lord gave Solomon great repute in the sight of all Israel, and bestowed upon him such royal majesty as had not been on any king before him in Israel.

The congregation worshiped God, honored their king, made their sacrifices, and sat down to a glorious feast. Joy and gladness prevailed. The most momentous act of the day was the crowning of Solomon as David had desired.

The second time. This may refer to 23:1, but hardly so. It probably pertains to 1 Kings 1:6 and 2:12. The Chronicler did not mention the first installation but was aware of it (cf. Myers, I, 197-198).

Sat on the throne of the Lord. The king occupied God's throne, not his own. The royal office did not belong to the incumbent but to God who put him there and who could remove him.

6. Summary of the Reign (29:26-30)

26 Thus David the son of Jesse reigned over all Israel. 27 The time that he reigned over Israel was forty years; he reigned seven years in Hebron, and thirty-three years in Jerusalem. 28 Then he died in a good old age, full of days, riches, and honor; and Solomon his son reigned in his stead. 29 Now the acts of King David, from first to last, are written in the Chronicles of Samuel the seer, and in the Chronicles of Nathan the prophet, and in the Chronicles of Gad the seer, 30 with accounts of all his rule and his might and of the circumstances that came upon him and upon Israel, and upon all the kingdoms of the countries.

This is the only time that the Chronicler mentions David's seven-year reign in Hebron, but even then it was over *Israel.* Some think that these verses were added to the Chronicler's work. The references of the Chronicler to Samuel, Nathan, and Gad are variously interpreted. Since the Chronicler, when he mentions these three, only used materials found in the books of Samuel, many scholars insist that these references do not imply the existence of independent sources. These sources, however, might not have given the Chronicler any more personal information about the men than we already possess. Yet such books could have furnished the Chronicler with much of his material. Books bearing these names, the result of long years of Hebrew tradition, might have belonged to a later date than the men themselves. It is certain that the Chronicler used many traditions, both early and late, else his parallel name-lists would not have contained so many variants. Fabricated work would have fitted more neatly. The differences reveal the independence of the traditions. Recent archaeological finds further authenticate this.

The circumstances that came upon him —literally, "that came over him," as waves run to the shore. Here is a valuable clue to the Chronicler's view of history. It consists of great waves over which one has little control but which one must face heroically and in which one must learn to navigate. The times cried out for the new Temple, but wars kept coming upon David. "With great pains" (22:14) he kept his head above water and charted the course of the future. Solomon would have to build while the sea was calm.

III. Solomon and the Temple (2 Chron. 1:1—9:31)

The book of 2 Chronicles was originally a continuation of the history now recorded in 1 Chronicles 1—29 and did not comprise a second book. It was divided for practical reasons. Some scholars feel that further editorial work was done when the division was made. Elmslie (p. 442) is convinced that 2 Chronicles 1:1-13 was added later, especially 1:1-6. In his opinion 1 Chronicles 29:26, 23-25 formed the original introduction to the present 2 Chronicles 1:14 ff., following 1 Chronicles 29:28-30. Such opinions are difficult to prove and it is more realistic to accept the material as coming from the Chronicler unless the evidence is conclusive against his authorship. However, it is possible that some editing accompanied the division of the original material into two books.

In 2 Chronicles the writer does not insert as much of his own material as he did in 1 Chronicles. His unique contribution results primarily from his perspective on Israel's history. He is able to present a viewpoint that is not found elsewhere in the Old Testament. Other historical writings contain the priestly orientation alongside the Deuteronomic, such as in Joshua-Samuel. At his later moment in history, the Chronicler had absorbed the Deuteronomic outlook into his priestly viewpoint. One has been assimilated into the other, two contrasting facets of Israel's life being combined. At no place is this more obvious than in his treatment of the Deuteronomic materials concerning Solomon's Temple.

It is not the Chronicler's intention to replace the Deuteronomic histories found in 1 and 2 Kings but rather to reinterpret them. He accepted these traditions, but felt a need to reassess them. In his opinion not enough attention had been given to Levitical and priestly activities in Israel's sacred history. To him this was the area in which Israel's destiny was bound up, the realm where she unquestionably excelled, the worship of her God. The collapse of the state and attempts at military conquest had made apparent to the Chronicler that Israel's future would be realized in the uniqueness of her religion.

1. The Prosperity of Solomon (1:1-17)

¹ Solomon the son of David established himself in his kingdom, and the LORD his God was with him and made him exceedingly great.
² Solomon spoke to all Israel, to the commanders of thousands and of hundreds, to the judges, and to all the leaders in all Israel, the heads of fathers' houses. ³ And Solomon, and all the assembly with him, went to the high place that was at Gibeon; for the tent of meeting of God, which Moses the servant of the LORD had made in the wilderness, was there. ⁴ (But David had brought up the ark of God from Kiriathjearim to the place that David had prepared for it, for he had pitched a tent for it in Jerusalem.) ⁵ Moreover the bronze altar that Bezalel the son of Uri, son of Hur, had made, was there before the tabernacle of the LORD. And Solomon and the assembly sought the LORD. ⁶ And Solomon went up there to the bronze altar before the LORD, which was at the tent of meeting, and offered a thousand burnt offerings upon it.
⁷ In that night God appeared to Solomon, and said to him, "Ask what I shall give you." ⁸ And Solomon said to God, "Thou hast shown great and steadfast love to David my father, and hast made me king in his stead. ⁹ O LORD God, let thy promise to David my father be now fulfilled, for thou hast made me king over a people as many as the dust of the earth. ¹⁰ Give me now wisdom and knowledge to go out and come in before this people, for who can rule this thy people, that is so great?" ¹¹ God answered Solomon, "Because this was in your heart, and you have not asked possessions, wealth, honor, or the life of those who hate you, and have not even asked long life, but have asked wisdom and knowledge for yourself that you may rule my people over whom I have made you king, ¹² wisdom and knowledge are granted to you. I will also give you riches, possessions, and honor, such as none of the kings had who were before you, and none after you shall have the like." ¹³ So Solomon came from the high place at Gibeon, from before the tent of meeting, to Jerusalem. And he reigned over Israel.
¹⁴ Solomon gathered together chariots and horsemen; he had fourteen hundred chariots and twelve thousand horsemen, whom he stationed in the chariot cities and with the king in Jerusalem. ¹⁵ And the king made silver and gold as common in Jerusalem as stone, and he made cedar as plentiful as the sycamore of the Shephelah. ¹⁶ And Solomon's import of horses

was from Egypt and Kue, and the king's traders received them from Kue for a price. ¹⁷ They imported a chariot from Egypt for six hundred shekels of silver, and a horse for a hundred and fifty; likewise through them these were exported to all the kings of the Hittites and the kings of Syria.

Solomon . . . established himself in his kingdom. Although the Chronicler does not specifically treat the internal struggles for the throne recorded in 1 Kings 1—2, he appears to refer to them here in summary. All of vv. 1–6 are clearly his addition to the material recorded in Kings. Where Kings refers to the "great high place" at Gibeon, he has reduced it simply to the *high place,* a term that he was reluctant to use at all. He felt it necessary to explain again why the high place was used by Solomon at all. The Mosaic tabernacle was there. Only he says that the bronze altar made by Bezalel was still in existence (cf. Ex. 31:1 ff.; 38:1 ff.), giving legitimacy to the sanctuary at Gibeon.

Solomon and the assembly sought the Lord. Literally, the people "sought it" or "sought him." This could mean that they sought the altar (because of the ancient significance), but more likely it refers to the Lord in the preceding phrase *tabernacle of the Lord,* since this verb *(darash)* is frequently used for inquiring of God (cf. Gen. 25:22; 2 Kings 22:13).

In that night God appeared. In Kings this appearance is in the form of a dream. Here no dream is mentioned; it is a vision. The Chronicler's account is more concise, which is quite unusual, since he was inclined to elaborate.

Wisdom and knowledge to go out and come in before this people. This is a military term used of a warrior (cf. 1 Sam. 18:13,16; 1 Chron. 11:2). In 1 Kings 3:7 Solomon confesses that he is not old enough to be a warrior king and march at the head of his armies. To compensate for this he asks for wisdom. Here the Chronicler shows his own unique insight. Wisdom and knowledge are not viewed as an addition to or substitution for warlike qualities; they are the virtues by which a king truly rules his people rather than as a warrior. Solomon wished *to go out and come in* (fight the wars of God) with the weapons of justice and wisdom. He had no ambition for military conquests; his purpose went beyond such materialistic aims.

Solomon gathered together chariots and horsemen. The passage found in vv. 14–17 comes at the close of the account of Solomon's reign in 1 Kings (10:26–29). The Chronicler has put it at the beginning to show that God kept his pledge to Solomon. Solomon could not be more disposed to be faithful to God than the Lord was to him.

Made silver and gold as common in Jerusalem as stone. The account in 1 Kings says "made silver as common." The addition of "gold" is a typical example of popular Levitical preaching, which favored the use of hyperbole. Whether the Chronicler was borrowing from an oral or written midrash or whether he was proceeding on his own is impossible to discern. However, his tendency was to follow the direction of his sources.

2. Building of the Temple (2:1—7:22)

(1) Final Arrangements (2:1–18)

¹ Now Solomon purposed to build a temple for the name of the LORD, and a royal palace for himself. ² And Solomon assigned seventy thousand men to bear burdens and eighty thousand to quarry in the hill country, and three thousand six hundred to oversee them. ³ And Solomon sent word to Huram the king of Tyre: "As you dealt with David my father and sent him cedar to build himself a house to dwell in, so deal with me. ⁴ Behold, I am about to build a house for the name of the LORD my God and dedicate it to him for the burning of incense of sweet spices before him, and for the continual offering of the showbread, and for burnt offerings morning and evening, on the sabbaths and the new moons and the appointed feasts of the LORD our God, as ordained for ever for Israel. ⁵ The house which I am to build will be great, for our God is greater than all gods. ⁶ But who is able to build him a house, since heaven, even highest heaven, cannot contain him? Who am I to build a house for him, except as a place to burn incense before him? ⁷ So now send me a man skilled to work in gold, silver, bronze, and iron, and in purple, crimson, and

blue fabrics, trained also in engraving, to be with the skilled workers who are with me in Judah and Jerusalem, whom David my father provided. 8 Send me also cedar, cypress, and algum timber from Lebanon, for I know that your servants know how to cut timber in Lebanon. And my servants will be with your servants, 9 to prepare timber for me in abundance, for the house I am to build will be great and wonderful. 10 I will give for your servants, the hewers who cut timber, twenty thousand cors of crushed wheat, twenty thousand cors of barley, twenty thousand baths of wine, and twenty thousand baths of oil."

11 Then Huram the king of Tyre answered in a letter which he sent to Solomon, "Because the LORD loves his people he has made you king over them." 12 Huram also said, "Blessed be the LORD God of Israel, who made heaven and earth, who has given King David a wise son, endued with discretion and understanding, who will build a temple for the LORD, and a royal palace for himself.

13 "Now I have sent a skilled man, endued with understanding, Huramabi, 14 the son of a woman of the daughters of Dan, and his father was a man of Tyre. He is trained to work in gold, silver, bronze, iron, stone, and wood, and in purple, blue, and crimson fabrics and fine linen, and to do all sorts of engraving and execute any design that may be assigned him, with your craftsmen, the craftsmen of my lord, David your father. 15 Now therefore the wheat and barley, oil and wine, of which my lord has spoken, let him send to his servants; 16 and we will cut whatever timber you need from Lebanon, and bring it to you in rafts by sea to Joppa, so that you may take it up to Jerusalem."

17 Then Solomon took a census of all the aliens who were in the land of Israel, after the census of them which David his father had taken; and there were found a hundred and fifty-three thousand six hundred. 18 Seventy thousand of them he assigned to bear burdens, eighty thousand to quarry in the hill country, and three thousand six hundred as overseers to make the people work.

A royal palace for himself—literally, "for his kingdom." It was not simply his royal residence, but the center of all state activities.

And Solomon assigned seventy thousand men . . . eighty thousand . . . three thousand six hundred. The Chronicler omits from his account the drafting of forced Israelite labor (30,000) found in the parallel in 1 Kings 5:13-18. Otherwise the passages are identical, except that Kings has 3,300 overseers and Chronicles has 3,600. The difference is not due to exaggeration but is probably a more accurate count than in Kings (cf. Curtis and Madsen, p. 323). The 600 may be the total number in each 'elep.

And Solomon sent word to Huram. In Kings the name is Hiram (1 Kings 5:1), which is the same name with an alternate spelling. Obviously the Chronicler's text had this spelling.

The Chronicler says that Solomon sent word to Huram, implying that he initiated the proceedings. First Kings says that first of all Hiram sent goodwill ambassadors to Solomon. It was then that Solomon made his request.

For our God is greater than all gods. This is a rare occurrence; a Hebrew king gives his witness to a heathen king concerning the greatness of his God in formal state correspondence. In fact the Chronicler gives the impression that Huram is helpful because he believes in Yahweh himself. The king of Tyre uses the name Yahweh and confesses that it is he who made heaven and earth (rather than the gods of Tyre). Cyrus makes a similar statement in a later passage (2 Chron. 36:22 ff.). Perhaps Huram was being diplomatic, as Cyrus was surely doing. He even calls Solomon his *lord.* The Kings passage says that Hiram was interested because of his affection for David and says nothing about his religious attitudes (1 Kings 5:1). Some interpreters feel that the Chronicler is putting his own belief in the universal power of Yahweh into the mouth of Huram. Who could say it more appropriately than the king of Tyre?

Twenty thousand cors of barley, . . . wine. The Chronicler adds these to the King's list of supplies. The oil is multiplied a hundred-fold!

A skilled man, . . . Huramabi—literally, "a skilled man, . . . Huram, my father." First Kings 7:13 ff. says his name was Hiram, and that he was the son of a widow from Naphtali and of a man of Tyre. This passage says his mother was of the tribe of Dan. The difference in the two tribal traditions is probably due to the association of Bezalel (who performed a similar function for the Mosaic tabernacle), with a worker from the tribe of Dan (cf. Ex. 31:6).

In Chronicles, Huram's responsibilities are greatly expanded. In Kings, he is only skilled in metal work. Here he also fashions wood and cloth. Again the influence of the Bezalel traditions may be noticeable in this description for he, too, possessed all of these abilities.

By sea to Joppa. The Kings account does not mention the name of the port. This was the principal port of Israel until modern Tel-Aviv was built. Jonah departed from this town for his intended visit to Tarshish.

A census of all the aliens. First Kings 5:13 ff. says that Solomon raised a levy of 30,000 Israelites for forced labor. It also lists more than 153,000 other workers, but it does not identify them. The Chronicler is notably silent about the 30,000 Israelites but claims that the 153,000 were aliens. This was very likely, for their work was more menial.

(2) Temple Furnishings (3:1—4:22)

a. Building Specifications (3:1-17)

¹ Then Solomon began to build the house of the Lord in Jerusalem on Mount Moriah, where the Lord had appeared to David his father, at the place that David had appointed, on the threshing floor of Ornan the Jebusite. ² He began to build in the second month of the fourth year of his reign. ³ These are Solomon's measurements for building the house of God: the length, in cubits of the old standard, was sixty cubits, and the breadth twenty cubits. ⁴ The vestibule in front of the nave of the house was twenty cubits long, equal to the width of the house; and its height was a hundred and twenty cubits. He overlaid it on the inside with pure gold. ⁵ The nave he lined with cypress, and covered it with fine gold, and made palms and chains on it. ⁶ He adorned the house with settings of precious stones. The gold was gold of Parvaim. ⁷ So he lined the house with gold—its beams, its thresholds, its walls, and its doors; and he carved cherubim on the walls.

⁸ And he made the most holy place; its length, corresponding to the breadth of the house, was twenty cubits, and its breadth was twenty cubits; he overlaid it with six hundred talents of fine gold. ⁹ The weight of the nails was one shekel to fifty shekels of gold. And he overlaid the upper chambers with gold.

¹⁰ In the most holy place he made two cherubim of wood and overlaid them with gold. ¹¹ The wings of the cherubim together extended twenty cubits: one wing of the one, of five cubits, touched the wall of the house, and its other wing, of five cubits, touched the wing of the other cherub; ¹² and of this cherub, one wing, of five cubits, touched the wall of the house, and the other wing, also of five cubits, was joined to the wing of the first cherub. ¹³ The wings of these cherubim extended twenty cubits; the cherubim stood on their feet, facing the nave. ¹⁴ And he made the veil of blue and purple and crimson fabrics and fine linen, and worked cherubim on it.

¹⁵ In front of the house he made two pillars thirty-five cubits high, with a capital of five cubits on the top of each. ¹⁶ He made chains like a necklace and put them on the tops of the pillars; and he made a hundred pomegranates, and put them on the chains. ¹⁷ He set up the pillars in front of the temple, one on the south, the other on the north; that on the south he called Jachin, and that on the north Boaz.

In Jerusalem on Mount Moriah. This is the only time in the Old Testament that the Temple mountain is called by this name. It associates the spot with the place of Abraham's sacrifice of Isaac (Gen. 22:2).

In cubits of the old standard. The old standard was about three inches longer than the new one (*ca.* 21 inches compared to *ca.* 18 inches). The change might have been due to merchants who through the years were inclined to give less length for the money. By the old standard the sanctuary then was *ca.* 105 feet by 35 feet, quite small by our standards. But as the Chronicler will show, what it lacked in size was compensated for in quality.

Its height was a hundred and twenty cubits. This would make the height of the vestibule more than 200 feet. First Kings 6:2 says that the height of the main sanctuary was only 30 cubits (*ca.* 52 ft.). There is some textual evidence that 20 cubits was the height of the vestibule. Herod's Temple porch was 100 cubits in height, and knowledge of this might have led a later scribe to insert the 100 cubits. On the other hand the porch of Solomon might have been of such a height. First Kings does not give a suggestion at all. The Septuagint of Chronicles also has 120 cubits. (Cf. comment on 2 Chron. 7:21.)

He adorned the house. The statements concerning the use of precious stones and the gold of Parvaim only occur here. Parvaim was probably in Yemen.

He overlaid it with 600 talents of fine gold. This would weigh more than 22½ tons. This is not out of line with the claim of 1 Chronicles 29:4, but that passage appears to be hyperbole. The Chronicler is ecstatic about the glory of the Temple. Although 1 Kings elaborates on the amount of gold used, the Chronicler speaks glowingly of the gold used in the sanctuary. In vv. 3–10 he mentions gold overlaying nine times. He is silent concerning many details referred to in 1 Kings, especially 6:4–8 (the windows, side chambers, and stairs). They were not overlaid with gold! In fact, concerning actual details of the building, "There appears to be a greater concern for the cultus than for the building itself" (Myers, II, 16). It was not a museum but a place to worship God!

The weight of the nails was one shekel to fifty shekels of gold. Literally, "the weight of the nails was fifty shekels of gold." By some measurements this would make each nail weigh about two pounds! Others suggest that the fifty-shekel weight for each nail was one and one-fourth pounds (cf. Myers). If the total weight of all the nails is taken to be 50 shekels, then less than two pounds of gold nails were supposed to hold up 52 tons of gold sheeting. The RSV suggests that the text should be slightly emended to read that one shekel of nail weight was to be used for every fifty shekels of gold sheeting (cf. marg.).

He overlaid the upper chambers. Only the Chronicler refers to these rooms (cf. 1 Chron. 28:11). No one is certain concerning their use or location. Slotki suggests that they were storage rooms situated between the walls, but such rooms were not likely to be overlaid with gold.

The cherubim stood on their feet, facing the nave, thus guarding against anyone approaching the holy of holies unlawfully from the holy place (nave).

And he made the veil. First Kings does not mention a veil in Solomon's Temple. There was one in the Mosaic tabernacle (Ex. 26:31 ff.).

Two pillars thirty-five cubits high—literally, "thirty-five cubits long." First Kings 7:15 says that each one was 18 cubits high. The discrepancy is explained by the possibility that originally there was one length of bronze that was cut into two equal pillars of 17½ cubits. Then half-cubit capitals were added later to each. However it is also likely that there was some confusion in the traditions used by the two biblical accounts.

He made chains like a necklace. Literally, "he made chains in the inner sanctuary" (*debir*). He would hardly have made chains in the sanctuary and then *put them on the tops of the pillars.* The word *debir* is often used for the holy of holies. It means either the hidden place or the place of the oracle, depending upon how one traces the history of the word. By a slight change in the Hebrew word the RSV reads "necklace," which is very probable here.

b. Temple Furniture (4:1–22)

¹ He made an altar of bronze, twenty cubits long, and twenty cubits wide, and ten cubits high. ² Then he made the molten sea; it was round, ten cubits from brim to brim, and five cubits high, and a line of thirty cubits measured its circumference. ³ Under it were figures of gourds, for thirty cubits, compassing the sea round about; the gourds were in two rows, cast with it when it was cast. ⁴ It stood upon twelve oxen, three facing north, three facing west, three facing south, and three facing east; the sea was set upon them, and all their hinder parts were inward. ⁵ Its thickness was a handbreadth; and its brim was made like the brim of a cup, like the flower of a lily; it held over three thousand baths. ⁶ He also made ten lavers in which to wash, and set five on the south side, and five on the north side. In these they

were to rinse off what was used for the burnt offering, and the sea was for the priests to wash in.

⁷ And he made ten golden lampstands as prescribed, and set them in the temple, five on the south side and five on the north. ⁸ He also made ten tables, and placed them in the temple, five on the south side and five on the north. And he made a hundred basins of gold. ⁹ He made the court of the priests, and the great court, and doors for the court, and overlaid their doors with bronze; ¹⁰ and he set the sea at the southeast corner of the house.

¹¹ Huram also made the pots, the shovels, and the basins. So Huram finished the work that he did for King Solomon on the house of God: ¹² the two pillars, the bowls, and the two capitals on the top of the pillars; and the two networks to cover the two bowls of the capitals that were on the top of the pillars; ¹³ and the four hundred pomegranates for the two networks, two rows of pomegranates for each network, to cover the two bowls of the capitals that were upon the pillars. ¹⁴ He made the stands also, and the lavers upon the stands, ¹⁵ and the one sea, and the twelve oxen underneath it. ¹⁶ The pots, the shovels, the forks, and all the equipment for these Huramabi made of burnished bronze for King Solomon for the house of the LORD. ¹⁷ In the plain of the Jordan the king cast them, in the clay ground between Succoth and Zeredah. ¹⁸ Solomon made all these things in great quantities, so that the weight of the bronze was not ascertained.

¹⁹ So Solomon made all the things that were in the house of God: the golden altar, the tables for the bread of the Presence, ²⁰ the lampstands and their lamps of pure gold to burn before the inner sanctuary, as prescribed; ²¹ the flowers, the lamps, and the tongs, of purest gold; ²² the snuffers, basins, dishes for incense, and firepans, of pure gold; and the sockets of the temple, for the inner doors to the most holy place and for the doors of the nave of the temple were of gold.

He made an altar of bronze. This altar is not described in the list of the specially made furnishings as in 1 Kings 7. However, one is mentioned in 2 Kings 16:14 when Ahaz changed its location. This silence could mean that the editor of Kings assumed that the altar built by Bezalel for Moses had been transferred to Jerusalem from Gibeon. It would have been strange indeed if this ancient altar had been allowed to stay at Gibeon. Obviously the Chronicler's altar of bronze was not the same, however, for it was much larger. In Exodus 27:1 we are told that the old altar was 5 cubits by 5 cubits and 3 cubits high. Here it is 20 by 20 cubits, and 10 cubits high. This compares with Ezekiel's altar (Ezek. 43:13 f.) Perhaps the Chronicler believed that Huram enlarged the Bezalel altar due to the increased sacrifices in the Jerusalem cult.

Then he made the molten sea. The Chronicler says that this huge tank, about 17 feet in diameter and holding about 10,000 gallons, was used for priestly washings. The rabbis believed that the priests completely immersed themselves (Slotki). It is quite possible that the *molten sea* originally symbolized the triumph of Yahweh over the primeval chaos.

Figures of gourds (Heb., "likenesses of oxen"). The RSV has connected the text with the expression found in 1 Kings 7:24. However the Chronicles passage is probably closer to the original. The problem was the mention of oxen and their association with the bulls worshiped by Israel in the wilderness and in North Israel. Gourds may have been substituted for oxen in the Kings account and the expression watered down here into "something like" oxen.

For thirty cubits—Hebrew, either "ten cubits" or literally, "ten in a cubit," ten ornaments to every ten cubits, totalling 300. Because this number seems exorbitant, the RSV has made the correction to *thirty,* the circumference of the tank. The Chronicler says that it held over 3000 baths. In 1 Kings it is 2000 baths. A bath was approximately 6 gallons, but by the Chronicler's time it might have contained less (cf. the reduction of the cubit).

Ten golden lampstands . . . ten tables. Only the Chronicler has this many. Usually the Old Testament writers speak only of one candlestick and one table of shewbread (cf. Ex. 25:23). Kings mentions the ten lampstands, but the passage may be of late origin (1 Kings 7:49). The ten golden lampstands probably were placed on the ten tables.

The court of the priests, and the great court. The second word for court is different from the first. It is used only in Chronicles and Ezekiel. Solomon's Temple had an inner public court, but the outer area contained the grounds for public buildings and the palace. In 1 Kings 7:12 the same word is used for the two courts, one describing the great Solomonic court and the other the Temple court. In the time of the Chronicler the inner court was entered only by the priests, due to the influence of Ezekiel, and the outer court was for the use of the people. This was called the *azarah,* the term used by the Chronicler. He was employing a term familiar to him to describe the earlier area, although the word was probably not used in the Solomonic era.

Basins of gold—for dashing the blood against the altar. The pots were used for boiling the flesh of sacrifices, and the shovels for disposing of the ashes. The forks were used for handling the flesh.

The king cast them. He ordered it done, not that he performed the work himself. Likewise this meaning may apply to the king making a sacrifice; it is under his supervision (cf. 1 Chron. 16:2).

In the clay ground between Succoth and Zeredah. Nelson Glueck [14] contends that these were earthen foundries. First Kings locates this activity near Zarethan rather than Zeredah and is probably the more accurate text.

The golden altar, the tables. The altar was for incense burning (cf. Ex. 30:1). Only the Chronicler has the plural tables for the showbread. This corresponds with 1 Chronicles 28:16 but is probably to be identified with the tables in v. 8. All the tables did not contain showbread, probably only one. They held lampstands connected with the area dominated by the showbread, so were known by that name.

Pure gold. This may be red gold (cf. Myers, II, 21).

The doors . . . were of gold. First Kings says they were overlaid with gold (6:32). This may be what the Chronicler means.

[14] BASOR 90 (April, 1943) pp. 13 ff.

(3) *Sanctuary Dedicated* (5:1—7:22)

a. *Moving to the Temple* (5:1-14)

¹ Thus all the work that Solomon did for the house of the LORD was finished. And Solomon brought in the things which David his father had dedicated, and stored the silver, the gold, and all the vessels in the treasuries of the house of God. ² Then Solomon assembled the elders of Israel and all the heads of the tribes, the leaders of the fathers' houses of the people of Israel, in Jerusalem, to bring up the ark of the covenant of the LORD out of the city of David, which is Zion. ³ And all the men of Israel assembled before the king at the feast which is in the seventh month. ⁴ And all the elders of Israel came, and the Levites took up the ark. ⁵ And they brought up the ark, the tent of meeting, and all the holy vessels that were in the tent; the priests and the Levites brought them up. ⁶ And King Solomon and all the congregation of Israel, who had assembled before him, were before the ark, sacrificing so many sheep and oxen that they could not be counted or numbered. ⁷ So the priests brought the ark of the covenant of the LORD to its place, in the inner sanctuary of the house, in the most holy place, underneath the wings of the cherubim. ⁸ For the cherubim spread out their wings over the place of the ark, so that the cherubim made a covering above the ark and its poles. ⁹ And the poles were so long that the ends of the poles were seen from the holy place before the inner sanctuary; but they could not be seen from outside; and they are there to this day. ¹⁰ There was nothing in the ark except the two tables which Moses put there at Horeb, where the LORD made a covenant with the people of Israel, when they came out of Egypt. ¹¹ Now when the priests came out of the holy place (for all the priests who were present had sanctified themselves, without regard to their divisions; ¹² and all the Levitical singers, Asaph, Heman, and Jeduthun, their sons and kinsmen, arrayed in fine linen, with cymbals, harps, and lyres, stood east of the altar with a hundred and twenty priests who were trumpeters; ¹³ and it was the duty of the trumpeters and singers to make themselves heard in unison in praise and thanksgiving to the LORD), and when the song was raised, with trumpets and cymbals and other musical instruments, in praise to the LORD,

"For he is good,
for his steadfast love endures for ever,"

the house, the house of the LORD, was filled with a cloud, ¹⁴ so that the priests could not stand to minister because of the cloud; for the glory of the Lord filled the house of God.

First, all the treasures stored up by David were transferred to the new Temple. Then, the ark and the tabernacle were brought there. The latter move required a great ceremonial procession.

Which is in the seventh month. First Kings 8:2 identifies this month as Ethanim, a Canaanite word. The Chronicler omits this reminder of the old days. The Hebrew name for the month was Tishri (our mid-September—mid-October). First Kings 6:38 says the Temple was not completed until the eighth month. Was the ceremony held before the completion? This would parallel many modern situations, where the occasion will no longer wait on the work. Some have suggested the dedication was not observed until the following year.

The Levites took up the ark. First Kings 8:3 says the priests did this. Scholars of another generation pointed out that this is an illustration of the fact that the sharp distinction in function between Levites and priests was not made until after the Babylonian exile. In earlier Israel a Levite could carry out priestly functions. The Chronicler carefully noted the difference in duties. However 2 Chronicles 5:5 does not make a sharp distinction for it mentions *the priests and the Levites* (the Levitical priests). The Hebrew does not have the conjunction "and" between the two terms. Here, too, the Levites are regarded as priests, but not as sacrificing priests. Only the latter could carry the ark to its resting place in the holy of holies.

They are there to this day. Here is an example of the Chronicler's faithfulness in copying his source. Obviously this did not apply to his day, for the Temple of Solomon had been destroyed and the ark lost. The source said this, however, and he copied it down the way it read. The earlier source might have meant the impression of the poles on the veil could be seen from outside the holy of holies rather than the poles themselves being visible.

Verses 11-13 appear as an addition by the Chronicler, describing the activities of the Levitical choirs in the ceremonies. It is possible that this was the actual situation preserved in the traditions of the Levites but not of interest to the editors of Kings. The Kings account says that the glory cloud appeared as the priests were leaving the holy place after depositing the ark. The Chronicler, in characteristic fashion, relates it to the song of praise of the Levites. The inspired music brought the realization of the divine presence. Even if the Chronicler was not historically precise concerning what happened on that occasion, he well knew how often such events had occurred and sought to stress their continued importance.

b. *The Words of Solomon (6:1–42)*

(a) *The Solomonic Blessing (6:1–11)*

¹ Then Solomon said,
"The Lord has said that he would dwell in thick darkness.

² I have built thee an exalted house,
 a place for thee to dwell in for ever."

³ Then the king faced about, and blessed all the assembly of Israel, while all the assembly of Israel stood. ⁴ And he said, "Blessed be the Lord, the God of Israel, who with his hand has fulfilled what he promised with his mouth to David my father, saying, ⁵ 'Since the day that I brought my people out of the land of Egypt, I chose no city in all the tribes of Israel in which to build a house, that my name might be there, and I chose no man as prince over my people Israel; ⁶ but I have chosen Jerusalem that my name may be there and I have chosen David to be over my people Israel.' ⁷ Now it was in the heart of David my father to build a house for the name of the Lord, the God of Israel. ⁸ But the Lord said to David my father, 'Whereas it was in your heart to build a house for my name, you did well that it was in your heart; ⁹ nevertheless you shall not build the house, but your son who shall be born to you shall build the house for my name.' ¹⁰ Now the Lord has fulfilled his promise which he made; for I have risen in the place of David my father, and sit on the throne of Israel, as the Lord promised, and I have built the house for the name of the Lord, the God of Israel. ¹¹ And there I have set the ark, in which is the covenant of the Lord which he made with the people of Israel."

2 CHRONICLES 6

This passage is identical with 1 Kings 8:12–21, with two exceptions. The divine covenant is said to be made *with the people of Israel* (v. 11) rather than "with our fathers" (1 Kings 8:21). First Kings lacks the statements in 2 Chronicles 6:5b–6a, which are elaborations. The Septuagint has a first line as an initial remark of Solomon (v. 1) that is also missing from Kings. It probably was originally in the text but was dropped because of the theological implications of sun worship. The RSV in 1 Kings 8:12 has restored the passage correctly:

"The Lord has set the sun in the heaven but has said that he would dwell in thick darkness."

(b) *The General Prayers of Solomon (6:12–21)*

12 Then Solomon stood before the altar of the Lord in the presence of all the assembly of Israel, and spread forth his hands. 13 Solomon had made a bronze platform five cubits long, five cubits wide, and three cubits high, and had set it in the court; and he stood upon it. Then he knelt upon his knees in the presence of all the assembly of Israel, and spread forth his hands toward heaven; 14 and said, "O Lord, God of Israel, there is no God like thee, in heaven or on earth, keeping covenant and showing steadfast love to thy servants who walk before thee with all their heart; 15 who hast kept with thy servant David my father what thou didst declare to him; yea, thou didst speak with thy mouth, and with thy hand hast fulfilled it this day. 16 Now therefore, O Lord, God of Israel, keep with thy servant David my father what thou hast promised him, saying, 'There shall never fail you a man before me to sit upon the throne of Israel, if only your sons take heed to their way, to walk in my law as you have walked before me.' 17 Now therefore, O Lord, God of Israel, let thy word be confirmed, which thou hast spoken to thy servant David.

18 "But will God dwell indeed with man on the earth? Behold, heaven and the highest heaven cannot contain thee; how much less this house which I have built! 19 Yet have regard to the prayer of thy servant and to his supplication, O Lord my God, hearkening to the cry and to the prayer which thy servant prays before thee; 20 that thy eyes may be open day and night toward this house, the place where thou hast promised to set thy name, that thou mayest hearken to the prayer which thy servant offers toward this place. 21 And hearken thou to the supplications of thy servant and of thy people Israel, when they pray toward this place; yea, hear thou from heaven thy dwelling place; and when thou hearest, forgive.

Again the Chronicler closely follows Kings, but with one major addition. He mentions a raised platform constructed for the occasion. The Hebrew word is the one translated "lavers" in 4:6. It was a sort of "super bowl!" The top was squared, but it might have had an oval base. Some expositors think that the Chronicler has invented the platform in order to avoid the impression given by the Kings account that Solomon is standing before the altar functioning like a priest. However, the platform was probably recorded in the Chronicler's source and was quite necessary for the occasion if Solomon was to be seen and heard by the great crowd.

There are three other minor variations from the Kings account that are significant. Where Kings says "to walk before me" (1 Kings 8:25), this passage says *to walk in my law* (v. 16). Verse 18 has added *with man* to the question concerning where God dwells. The common "night and day" of Kings has become *day and night* (v. 20).

(c) *Sample Petitions (6:22–39)*

22 "If a man sins against his neighbor and is made to take an oath, and comes and swears his oath before thy altar in this house, 23 then hear thou from heaven, and act, and judge thy servants, requiting the guilty by bringing his conduct upon his own head, and vindicating the righteous by rewarding him according to his righteousness.

24 "If thy people Israel are defeated before the enemy because they have sinned against thee, when they turn again and acknowledge thy name, and pray and make supplication to thee in this house, 25 then hear thou from heaven, and forgive the sin of thy people Israel, and bring them again to the land which thou gavest to them and to their fathers.

26 "When heaven is shut up and there is no rain because they have sinned against thee, if they pray toward this place, and acknowledge thy name, and turn from their sin, when thou dost afflict them, 27 then hear thou in heaven, and forgive the sin of thy servants, thy people Israel, when thou dost teach them the good

way in which they should walk; and grant rain upon thy land, which thou hast given to thy people as an inheritance. ²⁸ "If there is famine in the land, if there is pestilence or blight or mildew or locust or caterpillar; if their enemies besiege them in any of their cities; whatever plague, whatever sickness there is; ²⁹ whatever prayer, whatever supplication is made by any man or by all thy people Israel, each knowing his own affliction, and his own sorrow and stretching out his hands toward this house; ³⁰ then hear thou from heaven thy dwelling place, and forgive, and render to each whose heart thou knowest, according to all his ways (for thou, thou only, knowest the hearts of the children of men); ³¹ that they may fear thee and walk in thy ways all the days that they live in the land which thou gavest to our fathers.

³² "Likewise when a foreigner, who is not of thy people Israel, comes from a far country for the sake of thy great name, and thy mighty hand, and thy outstretched arm, when he comes and prays toward this house, ³³ hear thou from heaven thy dwelling place, and do according to all for which the foreigner calls to thee; in order that all the peoples of the earth may know thy name and fear thee, as do thy people Israel, and that they may know that this house which I have built is called by thy name.

³⁴ "If thy people go out to battle against their enemies, by whatever way thou shalt send them, and they pray to thee toward this city which thou hast chosen and the house which I have built for thy name, ³⁵ then hear thou from heaven their prayer and their supplication, and maintain their cause.

³⁶ "If they sin against thee—for there is no man who does not sin—and thou art angry with them, and dost give them to an enemy, so that they are carried away captive to a land far or near; ³⁷ yet if they lay it to heart in the land to which they have been carried captive, and repent, and make supplication to thee in the land of their captivity, saying, 'We have sinned, and have acted perversely and wickedly'; ³⁸ if they repent with all their mind and with all their heart in the land of their captivity, to which they were carried captive, and pray toward their land, which thou gavest to their fathers, the city which thou hast chosen, and the house which I have built for thy name, ³⁹ then hear thou from heaven thy dwelling place their prayer and their supplications, and maintain their cause and forgive thy people who have sinned against thee. ⁴⁰ Now, O

This section corresponds closely with Kings. In fact there are no significant differences. How is this unusual correspondence to be explained? It is quite likely that these prayers were actually used in Temple services and were preserved in the liturgy. In these petitions there is a remarkable balance between concerns for war with their enemies and the interests of foreigners identified with Israel. The universality of sin is another significant assertion (v. 36).

(d) Conclusion to the Prayer (6:40–42)

my God, let thy eyes be open and thy ears attentive to a prayer of this place.

⁴¹ "And now arise, O Lord God, and go to thy resting place,
thou and the ark of thy might.
Let thy priests, O Lord God, be clothed with salvation,
and let thy saints rejoice in thy goodness.
⁴² O Lord God, do not turn away the face of thy anointed one!
Remember thy steadfast love for David thy servant."

Here the Chronicler has replaced the prosaic ending of the Solomonic prayer in 1 Kings (8:50b–53) with a more impressive one. He has combined Psalm 132:8 with Isaiah 55:3 in a remarkable way. Psalm 132 is closely associated with royal enthronement ceremonies (cf. Myers, II, 37). It may well represent (especially 6:41–42a) the actual words spoken when the ark was deposited in Solomon's day and repeated in the annual covenant renewal ritual of succeeding generations. On the other hand, later ceremonies might have influenced the portrayal of the situation here. Either way, the true spirit of the occasion has been preserved. The Chronicler is associating, as did Israel, the presence of the ark with the security of the throne. It is significant that the ark and the Davidic reign were lost simultaneously with the fall of Jerusalem.

c. The Dedication Ceremonies (7:1–10)

¹ When Solomon had ended his prayer, fire came down from heaven and consumed the burnt offering and the sacrifices, and the glory of the Lord filled the temple. ² And the priests could not enter the house of the Lord, because the glory of the Lord filled the Lord's house.

3 When all the children of Israel saw the fire come down and the glory of the LORD upon the temple, they bowed down with their faces to the earth on the pavement, and worshiped and gave thanks to the LORD, saying,

"For he is good,
for his steadfast love endures for ever."

4 Then the king and all the people offered sacrifice before the LORD. 5 King Solomon offered as a sacrifice twenty-two thousand oxen and a hundred and twenty thousand sheep. So the king and all the people dedicated the house of God. 6 The priests stood at their posts; the Levites also, with the instruments for music to the LORD which King David had made for giving thanks to the LORD—for his steadfast love endures for ever—whenever David offered praises by their ministry; opposite them the priests sounded trumpets; and all Israel stood.
7 And Solomon consecrated the middle of the court that was before the house of the LORD; for there he offered the burnt offering and the fat of the peace offerings, because the bronze altar Solomon had made could not hold the burnt offering and the cereal offering and the fat.
8 At that time Solomon held the feast for seven days, and all Israel with him, a very great congregation, from the entrance of Hamath to the Brook of Egypt. 9 And on the eighth day they held a solemn assembly; for they had kept the dedication of the altar seven days and the feast seven days. 10 On the twenty-third day of the seventh month he sent the people away to their homes, joyful and glad of heart for the goodness that the LORD had shown to David and to Solomon and to Israel his people.

Now something is mentioned that was not recorded in Kings. Fire is said to have come down from heaven and consumed the offerings. It had happened when David presented offerings on the threshing floor of Ornan (1 Chron. 21:26), and when Aaron was consecrated (Lev. 9:24). Both these occasions featured the authentication of God in reference to the offering of sacrifice. Here it was in response to prayer. It is the Chronicler's way of saying that Solomon's prayer was an offering more acceptable to God than animal sacrifices, which are an anticlimax in his account. He does not exaggerate the number of animals offered but dutifully follows the report in Kings.

David offered praises by their ministry. This is a remarkable statement. It means: because he provided them with these instruments and opportunity to minister, their ministry was his own. Thus the monarch served through the ministers he assisted.

On the eighth day they held a solemn assembly. Many problems arise in comparing the account in Kings with this one. In 1 Kings 8:65–66 it is stated that this was a feast for seven days, and on the eighth day the people were sent home. However, the Hebrew says "seven days and seven days, fourteen days." This is still the more probable meaning. The eighth day, that is of the second week, they were sent away at the close of the day. They were there two weeks, two seven-day periods, but actually 15 days, if one counts the day they left, which the Hebrew text of Kings does.

The Chronicler clarifies this difficult text. They had the dedication feast for seven days, starting on the eighth day of the seventh month. On the fourteenth they began the sacred feast (Tabernacles), with the eighth day of that feast the climax (the 22nd). On the twenty-third day they went home. According to the King's account, however, they were sent away on the eighth day of the feast (the 22nd). Here there seems to be a minor difference in the tradition. Did they leave on the eighth day or after it? The very independence of the traditions at this point validates the basic event.

A more significant problem is the fact that the Day of Atonement came on the tenth day of the month, while the Feast of Dedication was going on, and no mention is made of its observance (cf. Num. 29:7). Some scholars insist that this shows that the Chronicler was ignorant of such a day and that it was inaugurated after his time. Others say it might have been observed and is not mentioned. Still another explanation is that the unusual occasion permitted the deviation (Slotki).

d. The Divine Response (7:11-22)

11 Thus Solomon finished the house of the Lord and the king's house; all that Solomon had planned to do in the house of the Lord and in his own house he successfully accomplished. 12 Then the Lord appeared to Solomon in the night and said to him: "I have heard your prayer, and have chosen this place for myself as a house of sacrifice. 13 When I shut up the heavens so that there is no rain, or command the locust to devour the land, or send pestilence among my people, 14 if my people who are called by my name humble themselves, and pray and seek my face, and turn from their wicked ways, then I will hear from heaven, and will forgive their sin and heal their land. 15 Now my eyes will be open and my ears attentive to the prayer that is made in this place. 16 For now I have chosen and consecrated this house that my name may be there for ever; my eyes and my heart will be there for all time. 17 And as for you, if you walk before me, as David your father walked, doing according to all that I have commanded you and keeping my statutes and my ordinances, 18 then I will establish your royal throne, as I covenanted with David your father, saying, 'There shall not fail you a man to rule Israel.'

19 "But if you turn aside and forsake my statutes and my commandments which I have set before you, and go and serve other gods and worship them, 20 then I will pluck you up from the land which I have given you; and this house, which I have consecrated for my name, I will cast out of my sight, and will make it a proverb and a byword among all peoples. 21 And at this house, which is exalted, everyone passing by will be astonished, and say, 'Why has the Lord done thus to this land and to this house?' 22 Then they will say, 'Because they forsook the Lord the God of their fathers who brought them out of the land of Egypt, and laid hold on other gods, and worshiped them and served them; therefore he has brought all this evil upon them.'"

This passage parallels 1 Kings 9:1-9, with the addition in vv. 12b-14. On the one hand it refers to the Temple as *house of sacrifice* rather than the more advanced "house of prayer." Such an expression reveals more of a traditional priestly concept than the Chronicler's own spiritualized outlook (cf. comment on 1 Chron. 7:1 ff.).

Immediately, however, he was transported from institutionalized language into one of his most inspired statements, an utterance that has appealed to more people than any other passage in Chronicles.

If my people who are called by my name—or literally, "If my people will humble themselves, they upon whom my name has been called." Two concepts are basic here: (1) Israel belonged to God; his name had been called upon then; (2) they must acknowledge this and submit to his authority.

James 2:7 is based upon this concept. The name of Christ has been "called upon" the believer in baptism.

And pray and seek my face. Not only are they to pray to God, but they are not to settle for less than being admitted into his presence. They must see him.

Turn from their wicked ways. God will not hear prayers unaccompanied by true repentance.

Hear . . . forgive . . . heal. When once the ear of God is reached, he will not only remove the guilt but will restore to health and usefulness.

Which is exalted, or "which was high." The text in Kings has apparently been corrupted. This statement favors the literal interpretation of 2 Chronicles 3:4, which says that the height of the vestibule of the Temple was 200 feet (cf. comment on 2 Chron. 3:4). If no part of the Temple was more than 30 cubits (*ca.* 52 ft.), it could hardly have been said to be high. The RSV takes the statement to be figurative (*exalted*), which is possible.

3. The Later Reign of Solomon (8:1—9:31)

(1) Admirable Domestic Policies (8:1-18)

1 At the end of twenty years, in which Solomon had built the house of the Lord and his own house, 2 Solomon rebuilt the cities which Huram had given to him, and settled the people of Israel in them.

3 And Solomon went to Hamathzobah, and took it. 4 He built Tadmor in the wilderness and all the store-cities which he built in Hamath. 5 He also built Upper Beth-horon and Lower Beth-horon, fortified cities with walls, gates, and bars, 6 and Baalath, and all the store-cities that Solomon had, and all the cities

for his chariots, and the cities for his horsemen, and whatever Solomon desired to build in Jerusalem, in Lebanon, and in all the land of his dominion. 7 All the people who were left of the Hittites, the Amorites, the Perizzites, the Hivites, and the Jebusites, who were not of Israel, 8 from their descendants who were left after them in the land, whom the people of Israel had not destroyed—these Solomon made a forced levy and so they are to this day. 9 But of the people of Israel Solomon made no slaves for his work; they were soldiers, and his officers, the commanders of his chariots, and his horsemen. 10 And these were the chief officers of King Solomon, two hundred and fifty, who exercised authority over the people.

11 Solomon brought Pharaoh's daughter up from the city of David to the house which he had built for her, for he said, "My wife shall not live in the house of David king of Israel, for the places to which the ark of the LORD has come are holy."

12 Then Solomon offered up burnt offerings to the LORD upon the altar of the LORD which he had built before the vestibule, 13 as the duty of each day required, offering according to the commandment of Moses for the sabbaths, the new moons, and the three annual feasts—the feast of unleavened bread, the feast of weeks, and the feast of tabernacles. 14 According to the ordinance of David his father, he appointed the divisions of the priests for their service, and the Levites for their offices of praise and ministry before the priests as the duty of each day required, and the gatekeepers in their divisions for the several gates; for so David the man of God had commanded. 15 And they did not turn aside from what the king had commanded the priests and Levites concerning any matter and concerning the treasuries.

16 Thus was accomplished all the work of Solomon from the day the foundation of the house of the LORD was laid until it was finished. So the house of the LORD was completed.

17 Then Solomon went to Eziongeber and Eloth on the shore of the sea, in the land of Edom. 18 And Huram sent him by his servants ships and servants familiar with the sea, and they went to Ophir together with the servants of Solomon, and fetched from there four hundred and fifty talents of gold and brought it to King Solomon.

The activities mentioned in vv. 1–10 were previously for the purposes of national defense and security, not for expansion. Yet they were extensive. In the Chronicler's account these moves went far beyond the situation described in 1 Kings 9. The seizure of Hamathzobah is not claimed there. Activities in Zobah were natural, for David himself had trouble there (cf. 2 Sam. 8:9; 10:8; 1 Chron. 19:6). But Hamath was far to the north. Some think that this Hamath was close to Zobah, but otherwise unknown. Tadmor (1 Kings 9:18 says Tamar, a town in Southern Judah) was later named Palmyra, and was situated about 50 miles northeast of Damascus. Is this a case of the Chronicler's exaggeration of Solomon's outreach, or does the Chronicler have information not familiar to the editor of Kings? Again, there is nothing conclusive. The placing of Tadmor in connection with Hamath favors this name as the correct reading in Chronicles, so the problem cannot be resolved by resorting to textual corruption from an original mention of Tamar.

But of the people of Israel Solomon made no slaves. This statement parallels 1 Kings 9:22 and does not contradict 1 Kings 5:13, which mentions the use of Israelites as forced labor. Thus the Israelites were drafted only on brief shifts; the aliens were assigned to permanent servitude. The use of Israelites was comparable to our military draft. The Chronicler follows a text very close to 1 Kings here. It is significant that Solomon was doing the very thing that Pharaoh did to Israel in Egypt. The aliens were forced to build store cities. The same words are used for these cities and this labor in the first chapter of Exodus. Perhaps the Hebrew historian perceived the inconsistency of Solomon. Did not God also hear the cry of these exploited people?

My wife shall not live in the house of David. The event is described in Kings, but only the Chronicler gives an explanation. The RSV translation *my wife* assumes that the statement is limited to the daughter of Pharaoh and that she was not allowed to live in the palace because she was a foreigner. However, the phrase can be translated, "No wife of mine shall live," meaning that the holy area would be contaminated if any woman lived in the palace. An emphasis upon the ceremonial uncleanness of women led the builders of the second Temple to provide for a court of the women outside the one for the men. Myers thinks this idea is found here, but the Chronicler's enlightened attitude toward women in other places hardly favors it (cf. comment on 1 Chron. 7:24). Besides, it is inconceivable that Solomon kept no women at all in the palace area.

The places to which the ark of the Lord has come are holy. This is, literally, "Holy are they to which the ark of the Lord has come." The Chronicler's concept of holiness includes the palace area as well as the Temple. The king's quarters and the priestly ones are alike sacred. To him Israel was no secular state. The king's throne was God's throne (9:8, but cf. 1 Kings 10:9 which says "throne of Israel").

Then Solomon offered up burnt offerings. First Kings 9:25 also includes peace offerings and incense burning. This presented problems to the Chronicler's priestly circle. It seemed to this group that Solomon was performing priestly functions, particularly the burning of incense before the holy of holies. Here his activities are confined to the altar outside the holy place. In both cases, however, he is directing the activities, not necessarily involved, personally, in the priestly action (cf. comment in 2 Chron. 4:17). Verses 13–16a are a further expansion of the Chronicler, where detailed Temple activities are added to the three special weeks of 1 Kings. Here he may present a priestly tradition not used by the editor of Kings.

David the man of God. This description also occurs in Nehemiah 12:24,36. This emphasizes a prophetic function in David's career as he revealed in his kingly activities the ways of God to his people. Thus to the Chronicler the king was a man of God as well as a prophet (cf. 1 Kings 13:1 ff.; 2 Chron. 11:2).

And Huram sent him by his servants ships. First Kings 9:27 claims only that he sent him sailors. How could Huram sail his ships from Tyre to the Gulf of Aqabah? There was no Suez Canal. The only way would be to sail around the southern tip of Africa! This was hardly likely in those days. Perhaps Huram already owned ships in the Persian Sea area and sent them to Solomon; or more likely, he sent them on the overland route, along with the sailors, in sections to be assembled later into finished ships.

(2) *International Fame (9:1–12)*

¹ Now when the queen of Sheba heard of the fame of Solomon she came to Jerusalem to test him with hard questions, having a very great retinue and camels bearing spices and very much gold and precious stones. When she came to Solomon, she told him all that was on her mind. ² And Solomon answered all her questions; there was nothing hidden from Solomon which he could not explain to her. ³ And when the queen of Sheba had seen the wisdom of Solomon, the house that he had built, ⁴ the food of his table, the seating of his officials, and the attendance of his servants, and their clothing, his cupbearers, and their clothing, and his burnt offerings which he offered at the house of the Lord, there was no more spirit in her.
⁵ And she said to the king, "The report was true which I heard in my own land of your affairs and of your wisdom, ⁶ but I did not believe the reports until I came and my own eyes had seen it; and behold, half the greatness of your wisdom was not told me; you surpass the report which I heard. ⁷ Happy are your wives! Happy are these your servants, who continually stand before you and hear your wisdom! ⁸ Blessed be the Lord your God, who has delighted in you and set you on his throne as king for the Lord your God! Because your God loved Israel and would establish them for ever, he has made you king over them, that you may execute justice and righteousness." ⁹ Then she gave the king a hundred and twenty talents of gold, and a very great quantity of spices, and precious stones: there were no spices such as those which the queen of Sheba gave to King Solomon.
¹⁰ Moreover the servants of Huram and the servants of Solomon, who brought gold from Ophir, brought algum wood and precious stones. ¹¹ And the king made of the algum wood steps for the house of the Lord and for the king's house, lyres also and harps for the singers; there never was seen the like of them before in the land of Judah.
¹² And King Solomon gave to the queen of Sheba all that she desired, whatever she asked

besides what she had brought to the king. So she turned and went back to her own land, with her servants.

The account of the notoriety of Solomon that led to the visit of the Queen of Sheba from South Arabia is almost identical with the story in 1 Kings 10:1-13. It must have been a very familiar one whose form was so well established that little change was possible. The primary variation is the change of *whatever she asked* besides *what she had brought to the king*. The original story might have included both aspects of this arrangement. What is meant is that she brought gifts that were matched by presents from Solomon. Then she was given gifts above that official interchange.

Lyres also and harps for the singers. Since this occurs also in Kings, it is apparent that earlier tradition also preserved memories of organized musical guilds. If these instruments were so exquisite, surely the performance upon them must have matched them.

(3) *Economic Wealth* (9:13-28)

13 Now the weight of gold that came to Solomon in one year was six hundred and sixty-six talents of gold, 14 besides that which the traders and merchants brought; and all the kings of Arabia and the governors of the land brought gold and silver to Solomon. 15 King Solomon made two hundred large shields of beaten gold; six hundred shekels of beaten gold went into each shield. 16 And he made three hundred shields of beaten gold; three hundred shekels of gold went into each shield; and the king put them in the House of the Forest of Lebanon. 17 The king also made a great ivory throne, and overlaid it with pure gold. 18 The throne had six steps and a footstool of gold, which were attached to the throne, and on each side of the seat were arm rests and two lions standing beside the arm rests, 19 while twelve lions stood there, one on each end of a step on the six steps. The like of it was never made in any kingdom. 20 All King Solomon's drinking vessels were of gold, and all the vessels of the House of the Forest of Lebanon were of pure gold; silver was not considered as anything in the days of Solomon. 21 For the king's ships went to Tarshish with the servants of Huram; once every three years the ships of Tarshish used to come bringing gold, silver, ivory, apes, and peacocks.

22 Thus King Solomon excelled all the kings of the earth in riches and in wisdom. 23 And all the kings of the earth sought the presence of Solomon to hear his wisdom, which God had put into his mind. 24 Every one of them brought his present, articles of silver and of gold, garments, myrrh, spices, horses, and mules, so much year by year. 25 And Solomon had four thousand stalls for horses and chariots, and twelve thousand horsemen, whom he stationed in the chariot cities and with the king in Jerusalem. 26 And he ruled over all the kings from the Euphrates to the land of the Philistines, and to the border of Egypt. 27 And the king made silver as common in Jerusalem as stone, and cedar as plentiful as the sycamore of the Shephelah. 28 And horses were imported for Solomon from Egypt and from all lands.

Six hundred and sixty-six talents of gold. Worth more than $20,000,000. The same amount appears in Kings. This is the number of the beast in the book of Revelation (Rev. 13:18), which may be coincidence.

And a footstool of gold. First Kings 10:19 lacks this phrase but says that the back of the throne was a calf's head (possibly "a round head"). Evidently the Chronicler's school found the possible application to the abhorred calf of Northern Israel objectionable enough to cause the omission of that reference.

For the King's ships went to Tarshish. First Kings simply refers to the "ships of Tarshish," a possible idiomatic expression for ships going to distant ports. Tarshish was probably in southern Spain. From the Gulf of Aqabah they would have to go around Africa and into the Atlantic to get to Spain. The goods they brought back indicate trade in the Indian Ocean. The present text of Chronicles probably represents an earlier misunderstanding of the original source. The Chronicler preserved it as he found it (cf. 2 Chron. 8:18).

With the servants of Huram. Kings also records the presence of the fleet of Huram. The Chronicler stresses the Solomonic forces.

And Solomon had four thousand stalls for horses and chariots. First Kings 10:26 says he had 1,400 chariots but 1 Kings 4:26 mentions 40,000 stalls for horses. The

Chronicler's estimate appears quite realistic and is not exaggerated.

(4) Summary of Solomon's Reign (9:29-31)

²⁹ Now the rest of the acts of Solomon, from first to last, are they not written in the history of Nathan the prophet, and in the prophecy of Ahijah the Shilonite, and in the visions of Iddo the seer concerning Jeroboam the son of Nebat? ³⁰ Solomon reigned in Jerusalem over all Israel forty years. ³¹ And Solomon slept with his fathers, and was buried in the city of David his father; and Rehoboam his son reigned in his stead.

This is the same as in Kings with the addition of the mention of sources that the Chronicler had been using. These may simply be references to material in our present book of Kings, or they more likely refer to a Levitical midrash on Judah's history containing independent prophetic collections, both early and late. It is becoming more obvious today that the Chronicler was using sources otherwise not familiar to us. Before giving this summary, he left out the description of Solomon's apostasy found in 1 Kings 11. He wanted the last thoughts about Solomon to be good ones.

Iddo the seer—actually spelled *Jedo* in this text. The more familiar "Iddo" form occurs in 2 Chronicles 12:15; 13:22.

IV. Embattled Judah (10:1—20:37)

1. The Reign of Rehoboam (10:1—12:46)

(1) Judah Alone Left (10:1-19)

¹ Rehoboam went to Shechem, for all Israel had come to Shechem to make him king. ² And when Jeroboam the son of Nebat heard of it (for he was in Egypt, whither he had fled from King Solomon), then Jeroboam returned from Egypt. ³ And they sent and called him; and Jeroboam and all Israel came and said to Rehoboam, ⁴ "Your father made our yoke heavy. Now therefore lighten the hard service of your father and his heavy yoke upon us, and we will serve you." ⁵ He said to them, "Come to me again in three days." So the people went away.

⁶ Then King Rehoboam took counsel with the old men, who had stood before Soloman his father while he was yet alive, saying, "How do you advise me to answer this people?" ⁷ And they said to him, "If you will be kind to this people and please them, and speak good words to them, then they will be your servants for ever." ⁸ But he forsook the counsel which the old men gave him, and took counsel with the young men who had grown up with him and stood before him. ⁹ And he said to them, "What do you advise that we answer this people who have said to me, 'Lighten the yoke that your father put upon us'?" ¹⁰ And the young men who had grown up with him said to him, "Thus shall you speak to the people who said to you, 'Your father made our yoke heavy, but do you lighten it for us'; thus shall you say to them, 'My little finger is thicker than my father's loins. ¹¹ And now, whereas my father laid upon you a heavy yoke, I will add to your yoke. My father chastised you with whips, but I will chastise you with scorpions.'"

¹² So Jeroboam and all the people came to Rehoboam the third day, as the king said, "Come to me again the third day." ¹³ And the king answered them harshly, and forsaking the counsel of the old men, ¹⁴ King Rehoboam spoke to them according to the counsel of the young men, saying, "My father made your yoke heavy, but I will add to it; my father chastised you with whips, but I will chastise you with scorpions." ¹⁵ So the king did not hearken to the people; for it was a turn of affairs brought about by God that the LORD might fulfil his word, which he spoke by Ahijah the Shilonite to Jeroboam the son of Nebat.

¹⁶ And when all Israel saw that the king did not hearken to them, the people answered the king,

"What portion have we in David?
  We have no inheritance in the son of Jesse.
Each of you to your tents, O Israel!
  Look now to your own house, David."

So all Israel departed to their tents. ¹⁷ But Rehoboam reigned over the people of Israel who dwelt in the cities of Judah. ¹⁸ Then King Rehoboam sent Hadoram, who was taskmaster over the forced labor, and the people of Israel stoned him to death with stones. And King Rehoboam made haste to mount his chariot, to flee to Jerusalem. ¹⁹ So Israel has been in rebellion against the house of David to this day.

To the Chronicler, North Israel moved out of the main thrust of the kingdom of God when the northern tribes rejected the house of David. True Israel was to be found in the South (cf. 10:17; 11:3; 13:4 ff.). Therefore he did not treat the history of the Northern Kingdom as such, but concentrated upon the affairs of Judah.

Only as the history of North Israel intimately involved Judah did he mention it. Much of the material that he did include is almost identical with the accounts in Kings. In this treatment we will not duplicate the discussion of the history treated in the exposition of 1 and 2 Kings. Rather we will concentrate upon the underlying philosophy that led the Chronicler to omit material or add to it. It is assumed that the reader is familiar with the history of Israel that is presented in the books of Kings.

This chapter adheres closely to the text of 1 Kings 12:1–19. There are only a few variations, but they reveal the Chronicler plainly. His recording of the passage reveals that while he had no desire to hide Solomon's sins, he disliked to talk about them.

If you will be kind to their people and please them. First Kings 12:7 says, "If you will be a servant to this people today and serve them!" It suggests that the advice of the old men might have been deceitful. They might have been suggesting that he promise anything the people wanted that day, then when he became king, he could do what he pleased. "Be their slave *today* and they will be your slaves forever!" Rehoboam, having the attitude of a young man, would have despised this deceitful position of those familiar with court intrigue, preferring the honest approach of youth. He would frankly tell them what he intended to do; thus he divided the kingdom.

The Chronicler, on the other hand, removed the possibility of such an interpretation from the passage. "Today" is not in the statement to be contrasted with "forever." The old men do not suggest that the son of David pose as a slave of the people, but that he be considerate and conciliatory. Such a position would earn their respect and obedience. In other words, the advice of the old men was without reproach. One wonders in light of this if the Chronicler were not an old man himself!

And when all Israel saw . . . So all Israel departed. On the one hand, the rebellious northern tribes are referred to as "all Israel." On the other, the faithful in Judah and Benjamin are called "all Israel." The Chronicler found it difficult to use the term Israel without prefixing it with "all." For him the people of God were one.

Each of you to your tents. First Kings 12:16 lacks "each of you." Thus the Chronicler's account is more vivid.

Then king Rehoboam sent Hadoram. In 1 Kings 12:18 it is Adoram. The later historian is using a different text from that followed by the editors of Kings. Both texts are probably copies of an original older than either one.

(2) Conflicts with Israel (11:1–12)

¹ When Rehoboam came to Jerusalem, he assembled the house of Judah, and Benjamin, a hundred and eighty thousand chosen warriors, to fight against Israel, to restore the kingdom to Rehoboam. ² But the word of the LORD came to Shemaiah the man of God: ³ "Say to Rehoboam the son of Solomon king of Judah, and to all Israel in Judah and Benjamin, ⁴ 'Thus says the LORD, You shall not go up or fight against your brethren. Return every man to his home, for this thing is from me.'" So they hearkened to the word of the LORD, and returned and did not go against Jeroboam.
⁵ Rehoboam dwelt in Jerusalem, and he built cities for defense in Judah. ⁶ He built Bethlehem, Etam, Tekoa, ⁷ Bethzur, Soco, Adullam, ⁸ Gath, Mareshah, Ziph, ⁹ Adoraim, Lachish, Azekah, ¹⁰ Zorah, Aijalon, and Hebron, fortified cities which are in Judah and in Benjamin. ¹¹ He made the fortresses strong, and put commanders in them, and stores of food, oil, and wine. ¹² And he put shields and spears in all the cities, and made them very strong. So he held Judah and Benjamin.

He built cities for defense in Judah. From this list it appears that his territory was already less extensive in the South than Solomon's (cf. 1 Kings 9:15b,17,18). All of these cities are on the Egyptian frontier; none of them face North Israel. As the invasion of Shishak indicates (12:1 ff.), Rehoboam did well to be concerned about this danger. This list of cities is not in Kings but comes from an independent source. Archaeology has authenticated its integrity, which tends to add weight to the historicity of other independent sources used by the Chronicler (cf. Myers, II, 69–70).

So he held Judah and Benjamin. This statement is taken by some to mean that he used the fortifications to reinforce his control of his own kingdom. However, it probably refers to his ability to withstand Egyptian presence on his southern border.

(3) Loyal North Israelites (11:13–17)

13 And the priests and the Levites that were in all Israel resorted to him from all places where they lived. 14 For the Levites left their common lands and their holdings and came to Judah and Jerusalem, because Jeroboam and his sons cast them out from serving as priests of the LORD, 15 and he appointed his own priests for the high places, and for the satyrs, and for the calves which he had made. 16 And those who had set their hearts to seek the LORD God of Israel came after them from all the tribes of Israel to Jerusalem to sacrifice to the LORD, the God of their fathers. 17 They strengthened the kingdom of Judah, and for three years they made Rehoboam the son of Solomon secure, for they walked for three years in the way of David and Solomon.

This passage is the work of the Chronicler. First Kings 12:31–32; 13:33 says that Jeroboam appointed non-Levites to the priesthood, but it does not claim that he denied the priesthood to Levites. The Chronicler says that he removed the Levites and replaced them with his own choices. This probably occurred when the legitimate priests refused to join his new cult. Those who were deposed could still have kept their lands, but they relinquished them to settle in Judah where they could carry on their calling. They were accompanied by laymen who shared their disillusionment.

And for the satyrs. Kings does not mention these. They are referred to in Leviticus 17:7. Some suppose them to be hairy, animal-like demons. The word may simply mean "he-goats."

For three years they made Rehoboam . . . secure. After three years they lost the battle to the general apostasy (cf. 12:2, "the fifth year"). This was tragic. They left their homes and property only to be caught up in another type of degeneracy. Verse 17b implies that even these loyalists succumbed to the new temptation.

In the way of David and Solomon. These two are not usually so joined. In 1 Kings 11:4 they are contrasted. Here they are both endorsed for their common virtues.

(4) The Apostasy of Rehoboam (11:18—12:1)

18 Rehoboam took as wife Mahalath the daughter of Jerimoth the son of David, and of Abihail the daughter of Eliab the son of Jesse; 19 and she bore him sons, Jeush, Shemariah, and Zaham. 20 After her he took Maacah the daughter of Absalom, who bore him Abijah, Attai, Ziza, and Shelomith. 21 Rehoboam loved Maacah the daughter of Absalom above all his wives and concubines (he took eighteen wives and sixty concubines, and had twenty-eight sons and sixty daughters); 22 and Rehoboam appointed Abijah the son of Maacah as chief prince among his brothers, for he intended to make him king. 23 And he dealt wisely, and distributed some of his sons through all the districts of Judah and Benjamin, in all the fortified cities; and he gave them abundant provisions, and procured wives for them. 1 When the rule of Rehoboam was established and was strong, he forsook the law of the LORD, and all Israel with him. 2 In the fifth

Here we are told that Rehoboam was blessed by God with many wives and children and was endowed with wisdom like unto his father Solomon, only to throw it all away by forsaking the law of God. We are not told what his sin was. Perhaps the Chronicler himself did not know. The successful invasion of Shishak of Egypt demonstrated to the Chronicler that some sin surely had been committed. It is more likely, however, that he did know what it was, but lacked the space to describe it.

Maacah the daughter of Absalom. Second Samuel 12:27 says Absalom only had one daughter, Tamar. Second Chronicles 13:2 says Maacah was the daughter of Uriel. Therefore she was probably the granddaughter of Absalom.

And procured wives for them. Literally, "He sought a multitude of wives." Some think that this originally described his sin. He turned to the gods of his wives, even as

Solomon had done. The statement would mean that he sought to please his many wives by joining them in their heathen worship.

He forsook the law of the Lord, and all Israel with him. How easily the people followed their leader into sin. To lead them in the right paths was far more difficult.

(5) Shishak of Egypt (12:2–12)

year of King Rehoboam, because they had been unfaithful to the Lord, Shishak king of Egypt came up against Jerusalem ³ with twelve hundred chariots and sixty thousand horsemen. And the people were without number who came with him from Egypt—Libyans, Sukkiim, and Ethiopians. ⁴ And he took the fortified cities of Judah and came as far as Jerusalem. ⁵ Then Shemaiah the prophet came to Rehoboam and to the princes of Judah, who had gathered at Jerusalem because of Shishak, and said to them, "Thus says the Lord, 'You abandoned me, so I have abandoned you to the hand of Shishak.' " ⁶ Then the princes of Israel and the king humbled themselves and said, "The Lord is righteous." ⁷ When the Lord saw that they humbled themselves, the word of the Lord came to Shemaiah: "They have humbled themselves; I will not destroy them, but I will grant them some deliverance, and my wrath shall not be poured out upon Jerusalem by the hand of Shishak. ⁸ Nevertheless they shall be servants to him, that they may know my service and the service of the kingdoms of the countries."

⁹ So Shishak king of Egypt came up against Jerusalem; he took away the treasures of the house of the Lord and the treasures of the king's house; he took away everything. He also took away the shields of gold which Solomon had made; ¹⁰ and King Rehoboam made in their stead shields of bronze, and committed them to the hands of the officers of the guard, who kept the door of the king's house. ¹¹ And as often as the king went into the house of the Lord, the guard came and bore them, and brought them back to the guardroom. ¹² And when he humbled himself the wrath of the Lord turned from him, so as not to make a complete destruction; moreover, conditions were good in Judah.

This invasion is also recorded in 1 Kings 14:25–28, but that account does not mention the number of the men involved or the composition of the Egyptian forces. The prophecy of Shemaiah is also the Chronicler's contribution. The historian's view is that God never favored war between the two Hebrew nations. Shemaiah's speech affirmed this, and Rehoboam heeded the warning.

Twelve hundred chariots and sixty thousand horsemen. The 60,000 were 60 military units of unknown size. Twelve hundred chariots were possible, for this was a major campaign. Its results are recorded on the wall of the temple at Karnak in Egypt. First Kings only gives two verses to this episode. The Chronicler was aware of its major importance. Again he shows himself to be historically reliable when he adds to the older accounts.

The *Sukkiim* were Egyptian mercenaries.[15]

That they may know my service and the service of the kingdom of the countries. This means, that Israel might learn the difference between serving under a foreign king and serving under God.

Conditions were good in Judah. Literally, "And also in Judah there were good things." Now the Chronicler modified the sweeping generalization he had made in v. 1. There were some who remained faithful during all of this apostasy. In quiet places people still took their stand for the truth.

(6) Summary of the Reign (12:13–16)

¹³ So King Rehoboam established himself in Jerusalem and reigned. Rehoboam was forty-one years old when he began to reign, and he reigned seventeen years in Jerusalem, the city which the Lord had chosen out of all the tribes of Israel to put his name there. His mother's name was Naamah the Ammonitess. ¹⁴ And he did evil, for he did not set his heart to seek the Lord.

¹⁵ Now the acts of Rehoboam, from first to last, are they not written in the chronicles of Shemaiah the prophet and of Iddo the seer? There were continual wars between Rehoboam and Jeroboam. ¹⁶ And Rehoboam slept with his fathers, and was buried in the city of David; and Abijah his son reigned in his stead.

This parallels the account in 1 Kings 14, with the addition of the notation concern-

---

[15] Cf. W. F. Albright in *The Old Testament and Modern Study*, ed. H. H. Rowley (London: Oxford, 1951), p. 18.

ing Shemaiah and Iddo. A puzzling matter is the occurrence in the Hebrew text after *Iddo the seer* of the phrase "to enroll oneself," or "for a genealogical table" (cf. RSV marg. note). The word may be used either as a verb or a noun. It could be a marginal scribal error, perhaps referring to the scribe's own enrollment in his work. It may possibly refer to the name of the source being used (its first word). Or it could assert that a genealogy could be found in the prophetic work cited.

2. *Abijah and Jeroboam (13:1-22)*

(1) *A Sermon on a Mount (13:1-12)*

¹ In the eighteenth year of King Jeroboam Abijah began to reign over Judah. ² He reigned for three years in Jerusalem. His mother's name was Micaiah the daughter of Uriel of Gibeah.

Now there was war between Abijah and Jeroboam. ³ Abijah went out to battle having an army of valiant men of war, four hundred thousand picked men; and Jeroboam drew up his line of battle against him with eight hundred thousand picked mighty warriors. ⁴ Then Abijah stood up on Mount Zemaraim which is in the hill country of Ephraim, and said, "Hear me, O Jeroboam and all Israel! ⁵ Ought you not to know that the LORD God of Israel gave the kingship over Israel for ever to David and his sons by a covenant of salt? ⁶ Yet Jeroboam the son of Nebat, a servant of Solomon the son of David, rose up and rebelled against his lord; ⁷ and certain worthless scoundrels gathered about him and defied Rehoboam the son of Solomon, when Rehoboam was young and irresolute and could not withstand them.

⁸ "And now you think to withstand the kingdom of the LORD in the hand of the sons of David, because you are a great multitude and have with you the golden calves which Jeroboam made you for gods. ⁹ Have you not driven out the priests of the LORD, the sons of Aaron, and the Levites, and made priests for yourselves like the peoples of other lands? Whoever comes to consecrate himself with a young bull or seven rams becomes a priest of what are no gods. ¹⁰ But as for us, the LORD is our God, and we have not forsaken him. We have priests ministering to the LORD who are sons of Aaron, and Levites for their service. ¹¹ They offer to the LORD every morning and every evening burnt offerings and incense of sweet spices, set out the showbread on the table of pure gold, and care for the golden lampstand that its lamps may burn every evening; for we keep the charge of the LORD our God, but you have forsaken him. ¹² Behold, God is with us at our head, and his priests with their battle trumpets to sound the call to battle against you. O sons of Israel, do not fight against the LORD, the God of your fathers; for you cannot succeed."

The Chronicler has a way of seeing excellence in Judah's kings that other writers did not. Only he had a good word to say about Rehoboam, and now he does the same for Abijah (who is called Abijam in 1 Kings 14—15, probably to distinguish him from Abijah the son of Jeroboam, whom the Chronicler does not mention). Some expositors think that these good qualities that the later historian describes exist only in his fertile imagination, but it is quite likely that kings possessed virtues overlooked by the earlier editors who assessed their reigns by other standards.

His mother's name was Micaiah. In 11:22 her name is Maacah, and also in 1 Kings 15:2. Yet the mother of Asa is also Maacah (2 Chron. 15:16). Elsewhere Micaiah is always a man's name, so a scribal error is apparent in v. 2. Maacah, who is said to be the daughter of both Absalom and Uriel, must have been the granddaughter of Absalom and the grandmother rather than mother of Asa.

Abijah went out to battle. No account of this engagement occurs in Kings. The Chronicler suggests that his source is the *midrash* of Iddo (v. 22). The Hebrew word *midrash* is from a root meaning to seek, to inquire, and describes a didactic exposition or interpretation. The extant examples of such Jewish works, all of which are later, are sometimes quite fanciful. The Chronicler makes use of midrashic materials in his work. He is not creating a midrash but copying one. The number of men in the engagement agrees with the figures given for David's time, except Judah has 100,000 less (cf. 2 Sam. 24:9). The thousands (*'elepim*) were probably units, the exact number of men not indicated.

Then Abijah stood up on Mount Zemaraim. This was on the border between

Judah and Israel. In his inspired address, preserved only by the Chronicler, he claimed that Judah alone had the true God, the true kingdom and the true cult.

A covenant of salt (cf. Lev. 2:13; Num. 18:19). Even among Arabs today salt is used in making a lasting covenant. Since salt preserves, it symbolizes a permanent agreement.

And certain worthless scoundrels—or sons of Belial (worthlessness). The picture of the callous rebellion against Rehoboam given here is quite different from the earlier account in Chapter 11 and 1 Kings 12. This may be the Chronicler's composition, but it presents a different viewpoint from the one he presented earlier, when he blamed Rehoboam for the rupture. Here he may simply be presenting Abijah's perspective on those events.

(2) *The Battle with Jeroboam (13:13-22)*

13 Jeroboam had sent an ambush around to come on them from behind; thus his troops were in front of Judah, and the ambush was behind them. 14 And when Judah looked, behold, the battle was before and behind them; and they cried to the Lord, and the priests blew the trumpets. 15 Then the men of Judah raised the battle shout. And when the men of Judah shouted, God defeated Jeroboam and all Israel before Abijah and Judah. 16 The men of Israel fled before Judah, and God gave them into their hand. 17 Abijah and his people slew them with a great slaughter; so there fell slain of Israel five hundred thousand picked men. 18 Thus the men of Israel were subdued at that time, and the men of Judah prevailed, because they relied upon the Lord, the God of their fathers. 19 And Abijah pursued Jeroboam, and took cities from him, Bethel with its villages and Jeshanah with its villages and Ephron with its villages. 20 Jeroboam did not recover his power in the days of Abijah; and the Lord smote him, and he died. 21 But Abijah grew mighty. And he took fourteen wives, and had twenty-two sons and sixteen daughters. 22 The rest of the acts of Abijah, his ways and his sayings, are written in the story of the prophet Iddo.

Outnumbered and outmaneuvered, it seemed that Abijah was doomed. But then the priests blew the trumpets, signifying Yahweh's entrance into the battle, and the men gave the battle shout (cf. Josh. 6:16 where the same word occurs). When the victory was given to Judah by God, 500 military units were destroyed.

The presence of the priests with the army was quite probable, for Deuteronomy mentions this custom (Deut. 20:2). The statements in v. 19 are certainly authentic for this same territory is listed as Judah's possession in Joshua 18:21 ff. in a list that probably comes from the time of Jehoshaphat.[16]

And the Lord smote him. This expression is used of Nabal (1 Sam. 25:38), who died suddenly, but an act of God can take many forms. This blow is not mentioned in Kings, but the account of the death of Jeroboam's son does occur. The Chronicler may be referring to this (1 Kings 14:1 ff.).

3. *The Rule of Asa (14:1—16:14)*

(1) *Loyalty to God (14:1-5)*

1 So Abijah slept with his fathers, and they buried him in the city of David; and Asa his son reigned in his stead. In his days the land had rest for ten years. 2 And Asa did what was good and right in the eyes of the Lord his God. 3 He took away the foreign altars and the high places, and broke down the pillars and hewed down the Asherim, 4 and commanded Judah to seek the Lord, the God of their fathers, and to keep the law and the commandment. 5 He also took out of all the cities of Judah the high places and the incense altars. And the kingdom had rest under him.

He took away the foreign altars and the high places. First Kings 15:14 says that the high places were not taken away. However, so does the Chronicler later (15:17, where "Israel" is applied to Judah). What is meant is that he ordered the high places destroyed, but it was easier said than done for he probably met considerable resistance in remote areas. Although Kings mentions that he removed the male prostitutes and the idols of his fathers (Rehoboam and Abijah?), the Chronicler, who writes to present their good traits, is silent about this.

The incense altars. Formerly interpreters

---

16 Cf. Cross and Wright, JBL 75 (1956) pp. 222 f.

thought these were sun images. Now the opinion has changed.[17] This reform was thoroughgoing for it went beyond destroying sacrificial altars.

(2) *Asa's Reward* (14:6-15)

⁶ He built fortified cities in Judah, for the land had rest. He had no war in those years, for the LORD gave him peace. ⁷ And he said to Judah, "Let us build these cities, and surround them with walls and towers, gates and bars; the land is still ours, because we have sought the LORD our God; we have sought him, and he has given us peace on every side." So they built and prospered. ⁸ And Asa had an army of three hundred thousand from Judah, armed with bucklers and spears, and two hundred and eighty thousand men from Benjamin, that carried shields and drew bows; all these were mighty men of valor. ⁹ Zerah the Ethiopian came out against them with an army of a million men and three hundred chariots, and came as far as Mareshah. ¹⁰ And Asa went out to meet him, and they drew up their lines of battle in the valley of Zephathah at Mareshah. ¹¹ And Asa cried to the LORD his God, "O LORD, there is none like thee to help, between the mighty and the weak. Help us, O LORD our God, for we rely on thee, and in thy name we have come against this multitude. O LORD, thou art our God; let not man prevail against thee." ¹² So the LORD defeated the Ethiopians before Asa and before Judah, and the Ethiopians fled. ¹³ Asa and the people that were with him pursued them as far as Gerar, and the Ethiopians fell until none remained alive; for they were broken before the LORD and his army. The men of Judah carried away very much booty. ¹⁴ And they smote all the cities round about Gerar, for the fear of the LORD was upon them. They plundered all the cities, for there was much plunder in them. ¹⁵ And they smote the tents of those who had cattle, and carried away sheep in abundance and camels. Then they returned to Jerusalem.

Asa's faithfulness was rewarded by a peaceful reign and by a notable victory over a mighty invading army.

The land is still ours. Although God had given Asa peace, he did not become careless. He prepared for war.

Zerah the Ethiopian (Heb., Zerah the Cushite). Thus he could have been either an Ethiopian or an Arabian. The nature of the booty indicates the possibility of an invasion from Arabia, but the direction from which the attack came (southwest) and the mention of Lybians (16:8) favor Ethiopia. The term *million* (thousand thousand) is figurative. It means "impossible to number" (cf. comment on 1 Chron. 22:14). The *three hundred chariots* are a better indication of the actual size of the invading force. We have no records of this war except for those in Chronicles. However, it is rooted in history, for the place names mentioned are prominent. The army might have consisted of mercenaries settled by Egypt as a buffer between that country and Palestine. It is possible that the size of the army had been exaggerated in the tradition before the Chronicler received the story.

There is none like thee to help, between the mighty and the weak. In other words, God makes no distinction between the mighty and the weak. He can help either one he pleases. He was called upon to help the weak on that occasion, but this verse says that he is not automatically with any side, weak or strong.

Let not man prevail against thee—Hebrew, "Let not a man restrain with thee." Do not let a man hinder you or "box you in."

And the Ethiopians fell until none remained alive. This is literally, "And there fell from the Ethiopians so that there was not to them from life," which does not mean that all of them died but that some of them did. "Not to them from life" could mean they lost their will to live, that is, to fight.

They smote the tents of those who had cattle—Hebrew, "They smote the tents of cattle." Did they keep cattle in tents? This was not likely. These were the tents associated with cattle, where their owners lived. This is the assumption of the RSV translation.

(3) *Renewed Religious Fervor* (15:1-19)

¹ The Spirit of God came upon Azariah the son of Oded, ² and he went out to meet Asa, and said to him, "Hear me, Asa, and all Judah

---

[17] Cf. W. F. Albright, *Archaeology and the Religion of Israel*, p. 215, fn. 58.

and Benjamin: The LORD is with you, while you are with him. If you seek him, he will be found by you, but if you forsake him, he will forsake you. ³ For a long time Israel was without the true God, and without a teaching priest, and without law; ⁴ but when in their distress they turned to the LORD, the God of Israel, and sought him, he was found by them. ⁵ In those times there was no peace to him who went out or to him who came in, for great disturbances afflicted all the inhabitants of the lands. ⁶ They were broken in pieces, nation against nation and city against city, for God troubled them with every sort of distress. ⁷ But you, take courage! Do not let your hands be weak, for your work shall be rewarded."

⁸ When Asa heard these words, the prophecy of Azariah the son of Oded, he took courage, and put away the abominable idols from all the land of Judah and Benjamin and from the cities which he had taken in the hill country of Ephraim, and he repaired the altar of the LORD that was in front of the vestibule of the house of the LORD. ⁹ And he gathered all Judah and Benjamin, and those from Ephraim, Manasseh, and Simeon who were sojourning with them, for great numbers had deserted to him from Israel when they saw that the LORD his God was with him. ¹⁰ They were gathered at Jerusalem in the third month of the fifteenth year of the reign of Asa. ¹¹ They sacrificed to the LORD on that day, from the spoil which they had brought, seven hundred oxen and seven thousand sheep. ¹² And they entered into a covenant to seek the LORD, the God of their fathers, with all their heart and with all their soul; ¹³ and that whoever would not seek the LORD, the God of Israel, should be put to death, whether young or old, man or woman. ¹⁴ They took oath to the LORD with a loud voice, and with shouting, and with trumpets, and with horns. ¹⁵ And all Judah rejoiced over the oath; for they had sworn with all their heart, and had sought him with their whole desire, and he was found by them, and the LORD gave them rest round about.

¹⁶ Even Maacah, his mother, King Asa removed from being queen mother because she had made an abominable image for Asherah. Asa cut down her image, crushed it, and burned it at the brook Kidron. ¹⁷ But the high places were not taken out of Israel. Nevertheless the heart of Asa was blameless all his days. ¹⁸ And he brought into the house of God the votive gifts of his father and his own votive gifts, silver, and gold, and vessels. ¹⁹ And there was no more war until the thirty-fifth year of the reign of Asa.

Azariah appears only in Chronicles. His address is an excellent example of Levitical preaching with its three emphases: (1) God's presence with Israel as long as she trusts him (v. 2); (2) illustration from sacred history, the period of the judges (vv. 3–6); (3) exhortation and promise (v. 7). In fact, the Chronicler in this section seems to have the cycle of the time of the judges in mind. A king seeks God, prospers, and then falls into apostasy to be followed by a new king who restores the kingdom; then the downward process is initiated all over again. Azariah warns Asa to learn from history; but he learned only the first part of the lesson: those who trust God prosper. After he was successful, he thought he could neglect God and retain his position.

Without the true God, and without a teaching priest, and without law. These were the conditions during the period of the judges. It was not that Israel did not have instruction; Israel would not receive it.

The prophecy of Azariah the son of Oded—Hebrew, "the prophecy, Oded the prophet." Obviously a scribal error has omitted the name Azariah and the RSV has rightly restored it.

He repaired the altar, or renewed the altar. No mention is made of its destruction. Probably unclean offerings had been made upon it, and there had to be a ceremonial cleansing and rededication.

And Simeon. In spite of the fact that Simeon was south of Judah after the division, it must have stubbornly kept its identity. Some of its citizens now moved to Jerusalem. Vital religious faith transcended the strongest national prejudice.

The third month of the fifteenth year of Asa. The feast came at the time of Pentecost, which celebrated the giving of the law. It is not certain that the people observed this feast, but it would have been appropriate. *The fifteenth year* is puzzling. This event appears to follow the Zerah battle immediately, for they offer spoil from it to God (v. 11). If ten years of peace preceded the engagement (14:1), the time should have been in the eleventh year. Did the war last four years? The problem will be dealt with more fully in comments on 2 Chronicles 16:1 ff.

They entered into a covenant. This was covenant-renewal at its best, for the people took the oath enthusiastically. Royal persuasion also lay behind it, with the death penalty of Deuteronomy 17:2 ff. hanging over nonconformers.

Maacah, his mother. More likely she was his grandmother, who still dominated the scene. He was probably glad to be rid of her. Her abominable image (image of horror) is not identified. Some versions indicate that not only did he cut it down but crushed it to powder, as in the case of the golden calf of Aaron.

The votive gifts. Why were they not in the Temple already? Could they have been offered at some other sanctuary? Perhaps they were kept in the palace under more strict security.

(4) The Apostasy of Asa (16:1-10)

¹ In the thirty-sixth year of the reign of Asa, Baasha king of Israel went up against Judah, and built Ramah, that he might permit no one to go out or come in to Asa king of Judah. ² Then Asa took silver and gold from the treasures of the house of the LORD and the king's house, and sent them to Benhadad king of Syria, who dwelt in Damascus, saying, ³ "Let there be a league between me and you, as between my father and your father; behold, I am sending to you silver and gold; go, break your league with Baasha king of Israel, that he may withdraw from me." ⁴ And Benhadad hearkened to King Asa, and sent the commanders of his armies against the cities of Israel, and they conquered Ijon, Dan, Abelmaim, and all the store-cities of Naphtali. ⁵ And when Baasha heard of it, he stopped building Ramah, and let his work cease. ⁶ Then King Asa took all Judah, and they carried away the stones of Ramah and its timber, with which Baasha had been building, and with them he built Geba and Mizpah.

⁷ At that time Hanani the seer came to Asa king of Judah, and said to him, "Because you relied on the king of Syria, and did not rely on the LORD your God, the army of the king of Syria has escaped you. ⁸ Were not the Ethiopians and the Libyans a huge army with exceedingly many chariots and horsemen? Yet because you relied on the LORD, he gave them into your hand. ⁹ For the eyes of the LORD run to and fro throughout the whole earth, to show his might in behalf of those whose heart is blameless toward him. You have done foolishly in this; for from now on you will have wars." ¹⁰ Then Asa was angry with the seer, and put him in the stocks, in prison, for he was in a rage with him because of this. And Asa inflicted cruelties upon some of the people at the same time.

The principal problem in this section is the date of the war with Baasha. The famous stele of Benhadad authenticates the basic historicity of the event, as does 1 Kings 15, but there is a most difficult problem. The passage says that the war began in the thirty-sixth year of Asa. However, 1 Kings 16:8 says that Elah the son of Baasha began to rule during the twenty-sixth year of Asa. How could Baasha wage a war ten years after his death? 1 Kings 15:16 says "there was war between Asa and Baasha king of Israel all their days." How, then, could Asa have the ten years of peace referred to in Chronicles, since Baasha began to rule during the third year of Asa (1 Kings 15:33)?

One solution is to consider 2 Chronicles 15:19 and 16:1 as scribal mistakes and read instead of "thirty-fifth" and "thirty-sixth" the more likely "twenty-fifth" and "twenty-sixth." The ten years of peace, then, would come between the fifteenth year and the twenty-fifth. Baasha died just after the war ended disastrously for him, probably from the frustration of it. The Zerah invasion would have occurred during the fourteenth year. The statement of Kings that there was continuous war could be interpreted to mean that a cold war existed that finally erupted in the twenty-sixth year of Asa. Even the Chronicler declares that during the time of peace Asa was preparing for war, probably with Baasha (14:6 ff.). It is quite possible, too, that the Chronicler had an entirely different chronological scheme from the book of Kings. Some say that thirty-fifth and thirty-sixth refer to the time that had elapsed since the kingdom divided. This would coincide with the chronology in Kings.

Hanani the seer. He is referred to as the

father of the prophet Jehu in 1 Kings 16:1,7. This particular section (vv. 7–10) is the work of the Chronicler. The Kings account simply tells the story of Asa's maneuver with Benhadad. The Chronicler shows what was wrong with it.

The army of the king of Syria has escaped you. Should this read "king of Israel"? (Cf. Myers.) As it stands, it says that Asa could even have conquered Syria if he had trusted God; he could possibly have united the divided kingdom!

For the eyes of the Lord run to and fro throughout the whole earth (cf. Zech. 4:10). God is eagerly watching for the opportunity to help those who trust him. He was far more available than another king, and he could give far more effective aid! How foolish to run to Benhadad. We have no record of the wars that were threatened except the trouble Asa had with his own people.

He was in a rage. The appeal to Syria was good, practical politics. "What was the matter with this crazed fanatic?" Asa must have thought thus. Then he proceeded to have him silenced by imprisoning him. Yet the prophet still speaks through the work of the Chronicler.

(5) Summary of Asa's Rule (16:11–14)

¹¹ The acts of Asa, from first to last, are written in the Book of the Kings of Judah and Israel. ¹² In the thirty-ninth year of his reign Asa was diseased in his feet, and his disease became severe; yet even in his disease he did not seek the Lord, but sought help from physicians. ¹³ And Asa slept with his fathers, dying in the forty-first year of his reign. ¹⁴ They buried him in the tomb which he had hewn out for himself in the city of David. They laid him on a bier which had been filled with various kinds of spices prepared by the perfumer's art; and they made a very great fire in his honor.

The Chronicler does not say that the disease was punishment for his sin but, rather, that wars were. So this could well have come 13 years after the Baasha episode. Neither does he blame him for consulting physicians, but for seeking them rather than God. Medicine and religion are not seen in opposition to one another, but faith was primary. Medicine in that day was not like that of the twentieth century A.D. These physicians might have used magic. In fact physicians are seldom mentioned in the Old Testament (Gen. 50:2; Job 13:4; Jer. 8:22). Ben Sirach has a famous observation on physicians in Ecclesiasticus 38:9–15. Prophets, however, were frequently gifted in healing (cf. Isa. 28:31).

Even in his disease he did not seek the Lord. This amazed the Chronicler. This great king was so hardened that nothing would turn him to God. If Hanani had been more tactful, could this hardening have been prevented? Asa felt that he had been unjustly condemned.

The tomb which he had hewn out for himself—under his direction, of course, not with his own hands. If he had prepared for the future of his people as carefully as for the resting place of his body, the immortality of his name would have been more assured.

A very great fire. This was not a cremation ceremony but the burning of spices (cf. Jer. 34:5).

4. The Jehoshaphat Era (17:1—20:37)

(1) His Faithfulness (17:1–19)

¹ Jehoshaphat his son reigned in his stead, and strengthened himself against Israel. ² He placed forces in all the fortified cities of Judah, and set garrisons in the land of Judah, and in the cities of Ephraim which Asa his father had taken. ³ The Lord was with Jehoshaphat, because he walked in the earlier ways of his father; he did not seek the Baals, ⁴ but sought the God of his father and walked in his commandments, and not according to the ways of Israel. ⁵ Therefore the Lord established the kingdom in his hand; and all Judah brought tribute to Jehoshaphat; and he had great riches and honor. ⁶ His heart was courageous in the ways of the Lord; and furthermore he took the high places and the Asherim out of Judah.

⁷ In the third year of his reign he sent his princes, Benhail, Obadiah, Zechariah, Nethanel, and Micaiah, to teach in the cities of Judah; ⁸ and with them the Levites, Shemaiah, Nethaniah, Zebadiah, Asahel, Shemiramoth, Jehonathan, Adonijah, Tobijah, and Tobadonijah; and with these Levites, the priests Elishama and Jehoram. ⁹ And they taught in Judah,

having the book of the law of the LORD with them; they went about through all the cities of Judah and taught among the people. 10 And the fear of the LORD fell upon all the kingdoms of the lands that were round about Judah, and they made no war against Jehoshaphat. 11 Some of the Philistines brought Jehoshaphat presents, and silver for tribute; and the Arabs also brought him seven thousand seven hundred rams and seven thousand seven hundred he-goats. 12 And Jehoshaphat grew steadily greater. He built in Judah fortresses and store-cities, 13 and he had great stores in the cities of Judah. He had soldiers, mighty men of valor, in Jerusalem. 14 This was the muster of them by fathers' houses: Of Judah, the commanders of thousands: Adnah the commander, with three hundred thousand mighty men of valor, 15 and next to him Jehohanan the commander, with two hundred and eighty thousand, 16 and next to him Amasiah the son of Zichri, a volunteer for the service of the LORD, with two hundred thousand mighty men of valor. 17 Of Benjamin: Eliada, a mighty man of valor, with two hundred thousand men armed with bow and shield, 18 and next to him Jehozabad with a hundred and eighty thousand armed for war. 19 These were in the service of the king, besides those whom the king had placed in the fortified cities throughout all Judah.

This entire chapter is the contribution of the Chronicler. His sources are not used by any other Old Testament writer.

He walked in the earlier ways of his father—Hebrew, "in the earlier ways of his father David." The RSV has read the text as applying to Asa because in no other place does the Chronicler refer to the sins of David's old age. Here, however, in the Hebrew text he does imply David's later transgression. The fact that he had left out the Bathsheba episode did not mean that he was intentionally misrepresenting David. Here by implication he sets the record straight.

His heart was courageous, was lifted up. Elsewhere this verb is always used in a negative sense (cf. 26:16; 32:25; Ezek. 28:2,5,17; Psalm 131:1; Prov. 18:12). Here he takes pride *in the ways of the Lord* rather than in himself. Pride is not always a sin.

He took the high places . . . out of Judah. Yet 1 Kings 22:43 says that he did not. Second Chronicles 20:33 agrees with Kings. The Chronicler obviously means that Jehoshaphat by royal decree abolished the high places but that the people resisted the implementation. The problem was in the enforcement of the law.

He sent his princes. Laymen as well as priests and Levites were sent out to teach. If they also did the teaching, this story is certainly from the earlier period, for by the time of Hosea in the eighth century B.C. the priests were the teachers of the law (Hosea 4:6 ff.). It is more likely that the princes were sent along to make certain that the people assembled to hear the teaching of the priests and Levites. They had a captive audience.

The book of the law of the Lord. Some take this to be a royal law, but the Chronicler and his sources regarded it as the law of Moses. Although not in its final form, this was the traditional law as it existed in Jehoshaphat's day.

This was the muster of them. Although the problem of numbers occurs in vv. 14–18 (1,160,000 or 1160 units of unknown consistency), the names and organization are authentic records of the time. It is not likely that there were over a million men in Jehoshaphat's standing army. They were hopelessly outnumbered by the invading forces from Ammon, Moab, and Mount Seir! (20:12).

A volunteer for the service of the Lord. This is the same expression used by Deborah to describe the commanders who volunteered to fight against Sisera. Does this mean that all the other commanders of Jehoshaphat had to be drafted into service? If so, this statement throws considerable light upon the nature of the military in ancient Israel.

(2) The Alliance with Ahab (18:1—19:3)

a. The Ramoth-gilead Crisis (18:1–34)

¹ Now Jehoshaphat had great riches and honor; and he made a marriage alliance with Ahab. ² After some years he went down to Ahab in Samaria. And Ahab killed an abun-

dance of sheep and oxen for him and for the people who were with him, and induced him to go up against Ramoth-gilead. 3 Ahab king of Israel said to Jehoshaphat king of Judah, "Will you go with me to Ramoth-gilead?" He answered him, "I am as you are, my people as your people. We will be with you in the war."

4 And Jehoshaphat said to the king of Israel, "Inquire first for the word of the Lord." 5 Then the king of Israel gathered the prophets together, four hundred men, and said to them, "Shall we go to battle against Ramoth-gilead, or shall I forbear?" And they said, "Go up; for God will give it into the hand of the king." 6 But Jehoshaphat said, "Is there not here another prophet of the Lord of whom we may inquire?" 7 And the king of Israel said to Jehoshaphat, "There is yet one man by whom we may inquire of the Lord, Micaiah the son of Imlah; but I hate him, for he never prophesies good concerning me, but always evil." And Jehoshaphat said, "Let not the king say so." 8 Then the king of Israel summoned an officer and said, "Bring quickly Micaiah the son of Imlah." 9 Now the king of Israel and Jehoshaphat the king of Judah were sitting on their thrones, arrayed in their robes; and they were sitting at the threshing floor at the entrance of the gate of Samaria; and all the prophets were prophesying before them. 10 And Zedekiah the son of Chenaanah made for himself horns of iron, and said, "Thus says the Lord, 'With these you shall push the Syrians until they are destroyed.'" 11 And all the prophets prophesied so, and said, "Go up to Ramoth-gilead and triumph; the Lord will give it into the hand of the king."

12 And the messenger who went to summon Micaiah said to him, "Behold, the words of the prophets with one accord are favorable to the king; let your word be like the word of one of them, and speak favorably." 13 But Micaiah said, "As the Lord lives, what my God says, that I will speak." 14 And when he had come to the king, the king said to him, "Micaiah, shall we go to Ramoth-gilead to battle, or shall I forbear?" And he answered, "Go up and triumph; they will be given into your hand." 15 But the king said to him, "How many times shall I adjure you that you speak to me nothing but the truth in the name of the Lord?" 16 And he said, "I saw all Israel scattered upon the mountains, as sheep that have no shepherd; and the Lord said, 'These have no master; let each return to his home in peace.'" 17 And the king of Israel said to Jehoshaphat, "Did I not tell you that he would not prophesy good concerning me, but evil?" 18 And Micaiah said, "Therefore hear the word of the Lord: I saw the Lord sitting on his throne, and all the host of heaven standing on his right hand and on his left; 19 and the Lord said, 'Who will entice Ahab the king of Israel, that he may go up and fall at Ramoth-gilead?' And one said one thing, and another said another. 20 Then a spirit came forward and stood before the Lord, saying, 'I will entice him.' And the Lord said to him, 'By what means?' 21 And he said, 'I will go forth, and will be a lying spirit in the mouth of all his prophets.' And he said, 'You are to entice him, and you shall succeed; go forth and do so.' 22 Now therefore behold, the Lord has put a lying spirit in the mouth of these your prophets; the Lord has spoken evil concerning you."

23 Then Zedekiah the son of Chenaanah came near and struck Micaiah on the cheek, and said, "Which way did the Spirit of the Lord go from me to speak to you?" 24 And Micaiah said, "Behold, you shall see on that day when you go into an inner chamber to hide yourself." 25 And the king of Israel said, "Seize Micaiah, and take him back to Amon the governor of the city and to Joash the king's son; 26 and say, 'Thus says the king, Put this fellow in prison, and feed him with scant fare of bread and water, until I return in peace.'" 27 And Micaiah said, "If you return in peace, the Lord has not spoken by me." And he said, "Hear, all you peoples!"

28 So the king of Israel and Jehoshaphat the king of Judah went up to Ramoth-gilead. 29 And the king of Israel said to Jehoshaphat, "I will disguise myself and go into battle, but you wear your robes." And the king of Israel disguised himself; and they went into battle. 30 Now the king of Syria had commanded the captains of his chariots, "Fight with neither small nor great, but only with the king of Israel." 31 And when the captains of the chariots saw Jehoshaphat, they said, "It is the king of Israel." So they turned to fight against him; and Jehoshaphat cried out, and the Lord helped him. God drew them away from him, 32 for when the captains of the chariots saw that it was not the king of Israel, they turned back from pursuing him. 33 But a certain man drew his bow at a venture, and struck the king of Israel between the scale armor and the breastplate; therefore he said to the driver of his chariot, "Turn about, and carry me out of the battle, for I am wounded." 34 And the battle grew hot that day, and the king of Israel propped himself up in his chariot facing the Syrians until evening; then at sunset he died.

After a summary statement (vv. 1–2) the account is identical with 1 Kings 22. This is the only time in his entire work that the Chronicler includes annals from North

Israel. In light of the fact that he leaves out all the extensive material on Elijah and Elisha, why does he include this passage? It might have been that these independent traditions were not in his text of Kings. Yet there still must be a reason why he selects and follows so closely this story which does not reveal his hero Jehoshaphat in a good light. His interest in cultic prophecy (cf. vv. 9 ff.) surely had something to do with it. All of the cultic prophets he mentions from Judah are true ones. Here we get a look at the false ones in North Israel. Also he could show us the courageous Micaiah whom he certainly admired.

The king said to him, Micaiah. The Hebrew text in Chronicles (but not in Kings) says Micah. This helps us to see how v. 27b (1 Kings 22:28b) came to be added to this passage. Some scribes mistakenly thought Micaiah and Micah (whose prophecies begin with "Hear all you peoples") were the same prophet.

And the Lord helped him. God drew them away. The only addition of the Chronicler to the story.

Then at sunset he died. The Chronicler now omits the rest of the account. He is not writing the story of the life of Ahab but of Jehoshaphat.

b. The Encounter with Jehu (19:1-3)

¹ Jehoshaphat the king of Judah returned in safety to his house in Jerusalem. ² But Jehu the son of Hanani the seer went out to meet him, and said to King Jehoshaphat, "Should you help the wicked and love those who hate the Lord? Because of this, wrath has gone out against you from the Lord. ³ Nevertheless some good is found in you, for you destroyed the Asherahs out of the land, and have set your heart to seek God."

First Kings says nothing about this, but the Chronicler feels that Jehoshaphat's involvement with Ahab needs further clarification. He did not invent this encounter but discovered it in his sources and used it for his purposes.

Those who hate the Lord. This is strong language to apply to Ahab, who appears to be a worshiper of Yahweh, although an inconsistent one. His children bore names compounded from Yahweh (Athaliah, Ahaziah, Jehoram). The zealous prophet overstated his case, but he was guided by Ahab's actions rather than his attitude. It is fortunate that hostile factions within religious communities are not the ultimate judge of personal destiny.

Nevertheless some good is found in you —literally, "good things are found with you." Just as redeeming features were found in sinful Israel (12:12), so they are seen in Jehoshaphat. It is unfortunate that Jehu could not see some good in Ahab also. But he lived across the border. The good in people offers more hope than the evil in them gives reason for despair.

(3) Religious Reform (19:4-11)

⁴ Jehoshaphat dwelt at Jerusalem; and he went out again among the people, from Beersheba to the hill country of Ephraim, and brought them back to the Lord, the God of their fathers. ⁵ He appointed judges in the land in all the fortified cities of Judah, city by city, ⁶ and said to the judges, "Consider what you do, for you judge not for man but for the Lord; he is with you in giving judgment. ⁷ Now then, let the fear of the Lord be upon you; take heed what you do, for there is no perversion of justice with the Lord our God, or partiality, or taking bribes."

⁸ Moreover in Jerusalem Jehoshaphat appointed certain Levites and priests and heads of families of Israel, to give judgment for the Lord and to decide disputed cases. They had their seat at Jerusalem. ⁹ And he charged them: "Thus you shall do in the fear of the Lord, in faithfulness, and with your whole heart: ¹⁰ whenever a case comes to you from your brethren who live in their cities, concerning bloodshed, law or commandment, statutes or ordinances, then you shall instruct them, that they may not incur guilt before the Lord and wrath may not come upon you and your brethren. Thus you shall do, and you will not incur guilt. ¹¹ And behold, Amariah the chief priest is over you in all matters of the Lord; and Zebadiah the son of Ishmael, the governor of the house of Judah, in all the king's matters; and the Levites will serve you as officers. Deal courageously, and may the Lord be with the upright!"

This material is from the Chronicler's pen. Since the days of Julius Wellhausen scholars have beem tempted to be suspicious of its historicity. He suggested that the Chronicler looked at the name Jehoshaphat (Yahweh judges) and fabricated a story to agree with the name. On the other hand Myers (II, 108) expresses the tendencies of present scholarship to emphasize the general historicity of this material. The reform was aimed primarily at a reorganization of the judiciary after the pattern of Deuteronomic law (cf. Deut. 16:18–20; 17:8 ff.).

Jehoshaphat himself went out into the kingdom to encourage this reform, which underscores the difficulties of achieving it. The legal decisions were not just civil but were always under God, although some were more concerned with religious matters than others.

They had their seat at Jerusalem—Hebrew, "They returned (to) Jerusalem." This difficult phrase may be out of place. If it followed v. 7, it would describe the return of Jehoshaphat to Jerusalem. A slight change in vowels brings the RSV reading.

Amariah, the chief priest. The Hebrew expression is *kohen har'osh*, rather than *kohen hagadol* (great priest). Only once does the Chronicler use the latter expression (34:9). It is possible that the expression *kohen har'osh* is the earlier of the two terms.[18]

(4) *Moabite-Ammonite Attack (20:1–30)*

There is no parallel to this passage except 2 Kings 3:4–27. But in that account Jehoshaphat and Jehoram of Israel, along with the king of Edom, go on the offensive against Moab. A miracle from God saves the Hebrew armies from disaster, and they put the Moabites to flight, devastating their land. If the two stories are related, long centuries of retelling have left them far apart. It is more likely that they refer to entirely different occasions.

It appears that the Chronicler has derived his account from "the chronicles of Jehu the son of Hanani" (20:34), which he

---

[18] Cf. J. Morgenstern, "A Chapter in the History of the High Priesthood," AJSL 55 (1938), pp. 1–24, 183–97, 360–77.

says had been recorded (Heb., inserted) in the major work he had been using, the "Book of the Kings of Israel," which was probably a Levitical midrash itself (cf. 2 Chron. 24:27). Elmslie doubts that such a source ever existed, for he observes that the style of this story is that of the Chronicler. However, the situation could have been the reverse. The popular Levitical style in the midrash used by the Chronicler could also be the style of the Levitical circles to which the Chronicler belonged. Therefore to tell on stylistic grounds the difference between one and the other is impossible.

a. The Historical Setting (20:1–4)

¹ After this the Moabites and Ammonites, and with them some of the Meunites, came against Jehoshaphat for battle. ² Some men came and told Jehoshaphat, "A great multitude is coming against you from Edom, from beyond the sea; and, behold, they are in Hazazontamar" (that is, Engedi). ³ Then Jehoshaphat feared, and set himself to seek the LORD, and proclaimed a fast throughout all Judah. ⁴ And Judah assembled to seek help from the LORD; from all the cities of Judah they came to seek the LORD.

Some of the Meunites (Heb., Ammonites)—from 20:10; 26:7. Likewise "Edom" (v. 2) is correct rather than Syria (Heb.).

To seek the Lord. Three times this verb occurs in vv. 3–4. This was different from the reaction of Asa to misfortune (16:12).

b. The Prayer of Jehoshaphat (20:5–12)

⁵ And Jehoshaphat stood in the assembly of Judah and Jerusalem, in the house of the LORD, before the new court, ⁶ and said, "O LORD, God of our fathers, art thou not God in heaven? Dost thou not rule over all the kingdoms of the nations? In thy hand are power and might, so that none is able to withstand thee. ⁷ Didst thou not, O our God, drive out the inhabitants of this land before thy people Israel, and give it for ever to the descendants of Abraham thy friend? ⁸ And they have dwelt in it, and have built thee in it a sanctuary for thy name, saying, ⁹ 'If evil comes upon us, the sword, judgment, or pestilence, or famine, we will stand before this house, and before thee, for thy name is in this house, and cry to thee in

our affliction, and thou wilt hear and save.' ¹⁰ And now behold, the men of Ammon and Moab and Mount Seir, whom thou wouldest not let Israel invade when they came from the land of Egypt, and whom they avoided and did not destroy—¹¹ behold, they reward us by coming to drive us out of thy possession, which thou hast given us to inherit. ¹² O our God, wilt thou not execute judgment upon them? For we are powerless against this great multitude that is coming against us. We do not know what to do, but our eyes are upon thee."

We must not let historical perplexities blind us to the greatness of this prayer and the prophetic oracle that follows. Regardless of its original setting, it expresses man's cry of need and the responses of God that have characterized man's authentic history. The faith expressed here has encouraged others in their helplessness to cast themselves on the mercy of God and to have their faith confirmed. Those who have had this experience do not find it difficult to believe that a miracle happened here.

Before the new court. The Chronicler was using a term applied in his day to the outer or great court, with its new arrangement in the second Temple (cf. 2 Chron. 4:9).

Abraham, thy friend. The Chronicler was familiar with Isaiah 41:8 (cf. James 2:23).

A sanctuary for thy name. His appeal is a masterful description of the situation: (1) God is able to help them. (2) It is God's own house to which they come for help. (3) It was God who forbade the extermination of the people now troubling them. (4) These people were attempting to do to Israel what the Hebrews were forbidden to do to them. (5) Their enemies should be judged by God. (6) The only hope of the people of God is in him, and they are looking to him for help.

c. *The Word from God (20:13–17)*

¹³ Meanwhile all the men of Judah stood before the Lord, with their little ones, their wives, and their children. ¹⁴ And the Spirit of the Lord came upon Jahaziel the son of Zechariah, son of Benaiah, son of Jeiel, son of Mattaniah, a Levite of the sons of Asaph, in the midst of the assembly. ¹⁵ And he said, "Hearken, all Judah and inhabitants of Jerusalem, and King Jehoshaphat: Thus says the Lord to you, 'Fear not, and be not dismayed at this great multitude; for the battle is not yours but God's. ¹⁶ Tomorrow go down against them; behold, they will come up by the ascent of Ziz; you will find them at the end of the valley, east of the wilderness of Jeruel. ¹⁷ You will not need to fight in this battle; take your position, stand still, and see the victory of the Lord on your behalf, O Judah and Jerusalem.' Fear not, and be not dismayed; tomorrow go out against them, and the Lord will be with you."

A Levitical prophet of the family of Asaph receives and utters the response of God: (1) The battle will be won by God. (2) They need only confront the enemy; there will be no battle; God will do it all. (3) They are to stand still and watch God act (cf. Ex. 14:13; Psalm 46).

Some expositors are dismayed by this counsel. Does man have nothing to do? "Yes," said the Chronicler, "he must have faith in God and follow his word." In the face of an overwhelming enemy, it would take more faith to stand still than to fight.

The Chronicler did not mean that all battles were to be won that way. This was the word of God for that occasion. He himself described wars that required more active participation.

d. *Fulfilling the Prophetic Word (20:18–30)*

¹⁸ Then Jehoshaphat bowed his head with his face to the ground, and all Judah and the inhabitants of Jerusalem fell down before the Lord, worshiping the Lord. ¹⁹ And the Levites, of the Kohathites and the Korahites, stood up to praise the Lord, the God of Israel, with a very loud voice.

²⁰ And they rose early in the morning and went out into the wilderness of Tekoa; and as they went out, Jehoshaphat stood and said, "Hear me, Judah and inhabitants of Jerusalem! Believe in the Lord your God, and you will be established; believe his prophets, and you will succeed." ²¹ And when he had taken counsel with the people, he appointed those who were to sing to the Lord and praise him in holy array, as they went before the army, and say,

"Give thanks to the Lord,
for his steadfast love endures for ever."

22 And when they began to sing and praise, the Lord set an ambush against the men of Ammon, Moab, and Mount Seir, who had come against Judah, so that they were routed. 23 For the men of Ammon and Moab rose against the inhabitants of Mount Seir, destroying them utterly, and when they had made an end of the inhabitants of Seir, they all helped to destroy one another.
24 When Judah came to the watchtower of the wilderness, they looked toward the multitude; and behold, they were dead bodies lying on the ground; none had escaped. 25 When Jehoshaphat and his people came to take the spoil from them, they found cattle in great numbers, goods, clothing, and precious things, which they took for themselves until they could carry no more. They were three days in taking the spoil, it was so much. 26 On the fourth day they assembled in the Valley of Beracah, for there they blessed the Lord; therefore the name of that place has been called the Valley of Beracah to this day. 27 Then they returned, every man of Judah and Jerusalem, and Jehoshaphat at their head, returning to Jerusalem with joy, for the Lord had made them rejoice over their enemies. 28 They came to Jerusalem, with harps and lyres and trumpets, to the house of the Lord. 29 And the fear of God came on all the kingdoms of the countries when they heard that the Lord had fought against the enemies of Israel. 30 So the realm of Jehoshaphat was quiet, for his God gave him rest round about.

Early the next morning, the Chronicler says, they set out for the wilderness of Tekoa (about 14 miles). Then Jehoshaphat organized a holy procession, the priests and Levites marching ahead of the army toward the enemy. Could it really have happened that way? Who can say? Perhaps the writer or his source was reading later conditions back into the earlier period. However, it is commonly accepted today that cultic processions marked the worship of early Israel on both special holy days and before battle.[19] It is not unreasonable to suppose that on an unusual occasion the priests assembled at the scene of battle, especially if they had been instructed by a divine oracle to do so. Something like this occurred under Hophni and Phinehas (1 Sam. 4:1 ff.), although then they were not marching under divine orders.

Believe in the Lord . . . believe his prophets. This is why they marched in holy array toward the enemy. God's prophet had said they must. Now the outcome would be assured. Note that they are to believe *in* the Lord, but *believe* his prophets. They are to place their trust in God, not in the prophets.

The Lord set an ambush. This was not necessarily an angelic surprise attack. It could have been other enemies of the Edomites, probably not Israelites, since they were instructed not to fight. (The instruction in v. 17, "Tomorrow go out against them," applied to the cultic confrontation, not military battle, for the warriors marched behind the priests.) However, some of those who had not gone to Jerusalem might have acted ignorantly on their own and were used of God.

They found . . . clothing—Hebrew, "dead bodies," which they stripped. A slight textual change is given in the RSV reading.

The Valley of Beracah. The word means blessing. The modern Wadi Berekut, between Tekoa and Engedi preserves the name.

(5) *Significance of Jehoshaphat's Reign (20:31–37)*

31 Thus Jehoshaphat reigned over Judah. He was thirty-five years old when he began to reign, and he reigned twenty-five years in Jerusalem. His mother's name was Azubah the daughter of Shilhi. 32 He walked in the way of Asa his father and did not turn aside from it; he did what was right in the sight of the Lord. 33 The high places, however, were not taken away; the people had not yet set their hearts upon the God of their fathers.
34 Now the rest of the acts of Jehoshaphat, from first to last, are written in the chronicles of Jehu the son of Hanani, which are recorded in the Book of the Kings of Israel.
35 After this Jehoshaphat king of Judah joined with Ahaziah king of Israel, who did wickedly. 36 He joined him in building ships to go to Tarshish, and they built the ships in

---

[19] Cf. F. M. Cross, "The Divine Warrior in Israel's Early Cult," *Biblical Motifs Studies and Texts*, ed. Alexander Altmann (Cambridge: Harvard University Press, 1966), III, 11–30.

Eziongeber. ³⁷ Then Eliezer the son of Dodavahu of Mareshah prophesied against Jehoshaphat, saying, "Because you have joined with Ahaziah, the LORD will destroy what you have made." And the ships were wrecked and were not able to go to Tarshish.

The Chronicler follows the summary in 1 Kings 22, except that he has a different approach to the Ahaziah alliance. The Kings passage says that after a naval disaster Jehoshaphat rejected an offer of Ahaziah for an alliance. The later historian says he was aligned with him in building ships, and that as a consequence of a prophetic condemnation of that relationship, his ships were wrecked. Some interpreters reconcile the two accounts by saying that Ahaziah worked with Jehoshaphat in building the ships (v. 36) but was not permitted to provide for the sailings (1 Kings 22:49). For the reading *to Tarshish* see comment on 2 Chronicles 9:21.

V. The Struggle with Baalism (21:1—24:27)

1. The House of Ahab (21:1—22:9)

The Chronicler was not concerned with the North Israelite Kingdom as such, but it had such a marked influence upon the corruption of Judah during this period that he felt compelled to describe the interrelationship in more detail than was his custom. The marriage of Jehoram, the son of Jehoshaphat, and Athaliah, the daughter of Ahab, was the catalyst.

(1) Jehoram and Athaliah (21:1-20)

a. Summary of Their Reign (21:1-7)

¹ Jehoshaphat slept with his fathers, and was buried with his fathers in the city of David; and Jehoram his son reigned in his stead. ² He had brothers, the sons of Jehoshaphat: Azariah, Jehiel, Zechariah, Azariah, Michael, and Shephatiah; all these were the sons of Jehoshaphat king of Judah. ³ Their father gave them great gifts, of silver, gold, and valuable possessions, together with fortified cities in Judah; but he gave the kingdom to Jehoram, because he was the first-born. ⁴ When Jehoram had ascended the throne of his father and was established, he slew all his brothers with the sword, and also some of the princes of Israel. ⁵ Jehoram was thirty-two years old when he became king, and he reigned eight years in Jerusalem. ⁶ And he walked in the way of the kings of Israel, as the house of Ahab had done; for the daughter of Ahab was his wife. And he did what was evil in the sight of the LORD. ⁷ Yet the LORD would not destroy the house of David, because of the covenant which he had made with David, and since he had promised to give a lamp to him and to his sons for ever.

A negative opinion is given concerning the nature of their regnancy. The evil that transpired is traced to the influence of Athaliah upon Jehoram. Perhaps she influenced him to kill all his brothers and other rivals, for this procedure was quite similar to what she did later after his death. The account of the murders is found only here, but there is no reason to doubt the reliability of the report.

Some of the princes of Israel. Officials from Israel might well have been in Judah during this period of close political ties. Some of these might have been friendly toward Jehoshaphat's reforms and now were in disfavor.

Would not destroy the house of David. Second Kings 8:19 says "would not destroy Judah." The Chronicler has also substituted *because of the covenant which he had made with David* for the simple "for the sake of David his servant." This is further evidence of his interest in the Davidic promises.

b. Rebellion of Edom (21:8-10)

⁸ In his days Edom revolted from the rule of Judah, and set up a king of their own. ⁹ Then Jehoram passed over with his commanders and all his chariots, and he rose by night and smote the Edomites who had surrounded him and his chariot commanders. ¹⁰ So Edom revolted from the rule of Judah to this day. At that time Libnah also revolted from his rule, because he had forsaken the LORD, the God of his fathers.

This account is also found in 2 Kings 8:20-22, where it is clear that the Israelite army was surrounded but managed to break out and flee home in disarray. The Chronicler's report leaves out the reference to the flight home and makes the defeat less noticeable. Yet he mentions that Edom and Libnah (in western Judah) remained independent of Judah, which implies that the campaign of Jehoram was a failure. Only the Chronicler explains that this loss of territory was due to Jehoram's neglect of Yahweh.

c. The Letter from Elijah (21:11-15)

11 Moreover he made high places in the hill country of Judah, and led the inhabitants of Jerusalem into unfaithfulness, and made Judah go astray. 12 And a letter came to him from Elijah the prophet, saying, "Thus says the LORD, the God of David your father, 'Because you have not walked in the ways of Jehoshaphat your father, or in the ways of Asa king of Judah, 13 but have walked in the way of the kings of Israel, and have led Judah and the inhabitants of Jerusalem into unfaithfulness, as the house of Ahab led Israel into unfaithfulness, and also you have killed your brothers, of your father's house, who were better than yourself; 14 behold, the LORD will bring a great plague on your people, your children, your wives, and all your possessions, 15 and you yourself will have a severe sickness with a disease of your bowels, until your bowels come out because of the disease, day by day.'"

This is a most intriguing episode and has caused considerable discussion. Second Kings 3:11 ff. implies that Elijah had died before the death of Jehoshaphat, for only Elisha was available for the crisis. Was there a letter prepared by Elijah before his death, prophetically anticipating the apostasy of Jehoram? Or did he, as some of the rabbis suggested, speak to some unnamed prophet after his death and dictate a letter to him? In fact this passage might have influenced the Hebrews to anticipate the return of Elijah in the last days (Mal. 4:5). He had already returned once!

However, Elijah might still have been alive during the first part of Jehoram's reign, but he would have been notoriously difficult to find. Jehoshaphat went to Elisha because he was more readily available. Second Kings 1:1 ff. says that Ahaziah of Israel died in accordance with an oracle from Elijah and was succeeded by Jehoram "in the second year of Jehoram the son of Jehoshaphat" (2 Kings 1:17). So Elijah could have been at work, at least until the second year of Jehoram. Although the passage does not say how long it took for Ahaziah to die, it implies a brief time. Elijah wrote the letter because he did not make personal appearances in Judah.

It is also possible the name Elisha appeared in the original, although there is no textual evidence of this, or that some later prophet took words that Elijah addressed to Ahab and reapplied them to Jehoram in a letter to him. Still another suggestion is that an unknown prophet wrote the letter and later tradition associated it with Elijah. Perhaps the best approach is to acknowledge the uncertain nature of the historical evidence and to recognize that regardless of the actual event (prophets seldom wrote their oracles; they confronted their audiences personally), the detailed prediction of the wrath of God upon the king was certainly in the Elijah tradition. The spirit of Elijah inspired this oracle, so it was truly Elijah still at work.

d. The Invasion of Judah (21:16-17)

16 And the LORD stirred up against Jehoram the anger of the Philistines and of the Arabs who are near the Ethiopians; 17 and they came up against Judah, and invaded it, and carried away all the possessions they found that belonged to the king's house, and also his sons and his wives, so that no son was left to him except Jehoahaz, his youngest son.

This story is from the Chronicler's sources. It is not necessary to suppose that Jerusalem was captured. The *king's house* was probably a reference to the king's family who were visiting outside Jerusalem. The attack was a border raid that nevertheless was disastrous for the royal family. The name Jehoahaz means "the Lord has taken," and his other name Ahaziah has the same meaning.

e. The Unmourned Death (21:18-20)

18 And after all this the LORD smote him in his bowels with an incurable disease. 19 In course of time, at the end of two years, his bowels came out because of the disease, and he died in great agony. His people made no fire in his honor, like the fires made for his fathers. 20 He was thirty-two years old when he began to reign, and he reigned eight years in Jerusalem; and he departed with no one's regret.

They buried him in the city of David, but not in the tombs of the kings.

The disease was probably chronic diarrhea. It happened as the prophet had declared. The notation that he was not buried with the other kings is the Chronicler's.

With no one's regret (lit., without desire). This could mean either that no one desired him to live on (had regret for his passing) or that he had lost all desire to live.

(2) Ahaziah's Folly (22:1-9)

¹ And the inhabitants of Jerusalem made Ahaziah his youngest son king in his stead; for the band of men that came with the Arabs to the camp had slain all the older sons. So Ahaziah the son of Jehoram king of Judah reigned. ² Ahaziah was forty-two years old when he began to reign, and he reigned one year in Jerusalem. His mother's name was Athaliah, the granddaughter of Omri. ³ He also walked in the ways of the house of Ahab, for his mother was his counselor in doing wickedly. ⁴ He did what was evil in the sight of the LORD, as the house of Ahab had done; for after the death of his father they were his counselors, to his undoing. ⁵ He even followed their counsel, and went with Jehoram the son of Ahab king of Israel to make war against Hazael king of Syria at Ramoth-gilead. And the Syrians wounded Joram, ⁶ and he returned to be healed in Jezreel of the wounds which he had received at Ramah, when he fought against Hazael king of Syria. And Ahaziah the son of Jehoram king of Judah went down to see Joram the son of Ahab in Jezreel, because he was sick.

⁷ But it was ordained by God that the downfall of Ahaziah should come about through his going to visit Joram. For when he came there he went out with Jehoram to meet Jehu the son of Nimshi, whom the LORD had anointed to destroy the house of Ahab. ⁸ And when Jehu was executing judgment upon the house of Ahab, he met the princes of Judah and the sons of Ahaziah's brothers, who attended Ahaziah, and he killed them. ⁹ He searched for Ahaziah, and he was captured while hiding in Samaria, and he was brought to Jehu and put to death. They buried him, for they said, "He is the grandson of Jehoshaphat, who sought the LORD with all his heart." And the house of Ahaziah had no one able to rule the kingdom.

The disastrous reign of Ahaziah is traced to the influence of his mother, Athaliah, and to his relatives in the royal house of Ahab. The Chronicler's story varies from that in Kings in some particulars and is considerably abbreviated. Apparently he is dependent upon a different source, for he does not usually abbreviate when he chooses to retell a story; rather, he expands it.

And the inhabitants of Jerusalem made Ahaziah . . . king. This was not the usual custom, but unsettled conditions in Judah must have demanded it. This was probably not well received in the outlying areas, where people were more faithful to the tradition of the Hebrews than to the family of Ahab.

Ahaziah was forty-two years old. If this was true, he would have been born two years before his father's birth! Jehoram was only 40 years old when he died (2 Chron. 21:20). Second Kings 8:26 says Ahaziah was 22 years old; the Septuagint says he was 20. Perhaps these two traditions were conflated by adding them together! (Myers). Some suggest that the figures represent the length of the reign of the house of Omri at this time. The Hebrew says he was "the son of forty-two years" which is the usual way of giving a man's age, but could possibly have another meaning here.

The granddaughter of Omri (lit., the daughter of Omri). From this statement some interpreters have tried to prove that she was the sister of Ahab rather than his daughter. However, the term can carry the meaning of granddaughter, and it surely does here if other statements are considered (cf. 2 Chron. 21:6).

And Ahaziah . . . went down. The Masoretic Text says "Azariah." Unless this is a throne name for Ahaziah (cf. Jehoahaz, 21:17), a scribal error has occurred.

But it was ordained by God. In the Hebrew the Chronicler's statement was not this strong: "It was from God." That is, it was the working out of his providence.

The sons of Ahaziah's brother. He had no brothers left after the Philistine raid. These were his kinsmen.

He searched for Ahaziah. Second Kings 9:21-28 says that Ahaziah and Joram went out together and that after Jehu's attack Ahaziah fled. Here we have two accounts supplementing one another. The Chronicler was using a different tradition from the editors of Kings.

2. *Athaliah Assumes the Throne* (22:10–12)

10 Now when Athaliah the mother of Ahaziah saw that her son was dead, she arose and destroyed all the royal family of the house of Judah. 11 But Jehoshabeath, the daughter of the king, took Joash the son of Ahaziah, and stole him away from among the king's sons who were about to be slain, and she put him and his nurse in a bedchamber. Thus Jehoshabeath, the daughter of King Jehoram and wife of Jehoiada the priest, because she was a sister of Ahaziah, hid him from Athaliah, so that she did not slay him; 12 and he remained with them six years, hid in the house of God, while Athaliah reigned over the land.

With two exceptions this section corresponds to 2 Kings 11:1–3. Jehosheba becomes Jehoshabeath, which is a simple variant of the name. Where Kings says Athaliah "destroyed" all the royal family, the Chronicler uses the intensive form of the verb "to speak." Some Hebrew and Greek manuscripts have "destroyed" in Chronicles, as in the RSV, but this may be an attempt to reconcile Kings with the later history. Both accounts may mean that she did not destroy them personally, but gave orders to that effect. Here the Chronicler is apparently even sensitive to the motherly feelings of wicked Athaliah. He makes it clear that what she would not bring herself to do, she ordered to be done.

3. *Jehoiada and Joash* (23:1–21)

This passage is parallel to 2 Kings 11:4–20 throughout, except that the Levites take the part of the military guard in the insurrection. Is this due to the fact that the Chronicler does not believe that the foreign guard operated in the Temple area, and consequently put Levites there as more appropriate? Or is he using a source that recalls the activity of the Levites in the affair, a matter of little concern to the writers of Kings? In other words, does the Chronicler's story supplement from old sources the Kings account or is he rewriting that account as he thinks it should have happened? It is more likely either that he was rewriting the story in the light of Levitical records and the Kings account or that the Levitical midrash that he was using preserved the story in the form he recorded. Certainly the Chronicler was using actual records from which he copied the names of the leaders involved (23:1).

The twofold emphasis in the story upon the sanctity of the Temple and the covenant with David favors the fact that he has rewritten the old Levitical tradition from his own perspective rather than having copied verbatim from the midrash. Jehoiada proclaims: "Let him reign, as the Lord spoke concerning the sons of David" (v. 3). In Kings there is only care for the safety of the young king; in Chronicles that anxiety is coupled with a concern lest the Temple be profaned in the excitement of the occasion (vv. 6–7). The simple narration in 2 Kings delineating the priests' command not to desecrate the Temple with Athaliah's murder, is replaced by an imperative, "Do not slay her in the house of the Lord" (v. 14).

(1) *Joash Proclaimed King* (23:1–11)

1 But in the seventh year Jehoiada took courage, and entered into a compact with the commanders of hundreds, Azariah the son of Jeroham, Ishmael the son of Jehohanan, Azariah the son of Obed, Maaseiah the son of Adaiah, and Elishaphat the son of Zichri. 2 And they went about through Judah and gathered the Levites from all the cities of Judah, and the heads of fathers' houses of Israel, and they came to Jerusalem. 3 And all the assembly made a covenant with the king in the house of God. And Jehoiada said to them, "Behold, the king's son! Let him reign, as the LORD spoke concerning the sons of David. 4 This is the thing that you shall do: of you priests and Levites who come off duty on the sabbath, one third shall be gatekeepers, 5 and one third shall be at the king's house and one third at the Gate of the Foundation; and all the people shall be in the courts of the house of the LORD. 6 Let no one enter the house of the LORD

except the priests and ministering Levites; they may enter, for they are holy, but all the people shall keep the charge of the Lord. ⁷ The Levites shall surround the king, each with his weapons in his hand, and whoever enters the house shall be slain. Be with the king when he comes in, and when he goes out."

⁸ The Levites and all Judah did according to all that Jehoiada the priest commanded. They each brought his men, who were to go off duty on the sabbath, with those who were to come on duty on the sabbath; for Jehoiada the priest did not dismiss the divisions. ⁹ And Jehoiada the priest delivered to the captains the spears and the large and small shields that had been King David's, which were in the house of God; ¹⁰ and he set all the people as a guard for the king, every man with his weapon in his hand, from the south side of the house to the north side of the house, around the altar and the house. ¹¹ Then he brought out the king's son, and put the crown upon him, and gave him the testimony; and they proclaimed him king, and Jehoiada and his sons anointed him, and they said, "Long live the king."

The Gate of the Foundation. This is another name for "the gate Sur" of 2 Kings 11:6.

Shall keep the charge of the Lord. That is, they shall obey the injunction to stay in the outer court and not enter the sacred Temple. How close to the altar the people could go in the first Temple is not known. It is apparent here that rewriting of the Kings source has occurred. The expression "keep the charge of the house of God" is formed in 2 Kings 11:7 as "guard the house of the Lord" and is applied to the guards rather than the people. They are to protect the king rather than the Temple.

The Levites . . . each with his weapons. Here is the opposite of the Chronicler's usual tendency to apply military terms to spiritual functions. Here Levites take up arms, but dedicated weapons (cf. v. 7 with v. 9). This was an exceptional occasion; for the Levites apparently did not have weapons of their own.

Gave him the testimony. Testimony comes from the root to repeat, to give witness. The noun means witness or precept, something reaffirmed. This is the word used in the phrase "ark of the testimony." We do not know the exact nature of this testimony. It probably contained something like the charge to the king recorded in Deuteronomy 17:14 ff. and 1 Samuel 10:25. Part of the law was incorporated in it (Deut. 17:18). This incident may well have led to the custom of presenting the monarch of England with a copy of the Bible at the coronation.

Jehoiada and his sons anointed him. This is from the Chronicler.

(2) The Death of Athaliah (23:12-21)

¹² When Athaliah heard the noise of the people running and praising the king, she went into the house of the Lord to the people; ¹³ and when she looked, there was the king standing by his pillar at the entrance, and the captains and the trumpeters beside the king, and all the people of the land rejoicing and blowing trumpets, and the singers with their musical instruments leading in the celebration. And Athaliah rent her clothes, and cried, "Treason! Treason!" ¹⁴ Then Jehoiada the priest brought out the captains who were set over the army, saying to them, "Bring her out between the ranks; any one who follows her is to be slain with the sword." For the priest said, "Do not slay her in the house of the Lord." ¹⁵ So they laid hands on her; and she went into the entrance of the horse gate of the king's house, and they slew her there.

¹⁶ And Jehoiada made a covenant between himself and all the people and the king that they should be the Lord's people. ¹⁷ Then all the people went to the house of Baal, and tore it down; his altars and his images they broke in pieces, and they slew Mattan the priest of Baal before the altars. ¹⁸ And Jehoiada posted watchmen for the house of the Lord under the direction of the Levitical priests and the Levites whom David had organized to be in charge of the house of the Lord, to offer burnt offerings to the Lord, as it is written in the law of Moses, with rejoicing and with singing, according to the order of David. ¹⁹ He stationed the gatekeepers at the gates of the house of the Lord so that no one should enter who was in any way unclean. ²⁰ And he took the captains, the nobles, the governors of the people, and all the people of the land; and they brought the king down from the house of the Lord, marching through the upper gate to the king's house. And they set the king upon the royal throne. ²¹ So all the people of the land rejoiced; and the city was quiet, after Athaliah had been slain with the sword.

The account now closely follows 2 Kings 11:13–20. The Chronicler's additions are the references to Athaliah's hearing the *people running and praising the king,* (v. 12) rather than hearing the guards and the people; the placing of Levitical guards (vv. 18–19); and the picture of the royal procession (v. 20). In this passage the Chronicler continued to reinterpret the King's account in light of his Levitical traditions and personal interest. Certainly he adds vividness to the scene.

4. *The Restoration of the Temple (24:1–14)*

¹ Joash was seven years old when he began to reign, and he reigned forty years in Jerusalem; his mother's name was Zibiah of Beersheba. ² And Joash did what was right in the eyes of the LORD all the days of Jehoiada the priest. ³ Jehoiada got for him two wives, and he had sons and daughters.
⁴ After this Joash decided to restore the house of the LORD. ⁵ And he gathered the priests and the Levites, and said to them, "Go out to the cities of Judah, and gather from all Israel money to repair the house of your God from year to year; and see that you hasten the matter." But the Levites did not hasten it. ⁶ So the king summoned Jehoiada the chief, and said to him, "Why have you not required the Levites to bring in from Judah and Jerusalem the tax levied by Moses, the servant of the LORD, on the congregation of Israel for the tent of testimony?" ⁷ For the sons of Athaliah, that wicked woman, had broken into the house of God; and had also used all the dedicated things of the house of the LORD for the Baals.
⁸ So the king commanded, and they made a chest, and set it outside the gate of the house of the LORD. ⁹ And proclamation was made throughout Judah and Jerusalem, to bring in for the LORD the tax that Moses the servant of God laid upon Israel in the wilderness. ¹⁰ And all the princes and all the people rejoiced and brought their tax and dropped it into the chest until they had finished. ¹¹ And whenever the chest was brought to the king's officers by the Levites, when they saw that there was much money in it, the king's secretary and the officer of the chief priest would come and empty the chest and take it and return it to its place. Thus they did day after day, and collected money in abundance. ¹² And the king and Jehoiada gave it to those who had charge of the work of the house of the LORD, and they hired masons and carpenters to restore the house of the LORD, and also workers in iron and bronze to repair the house of the LORD. ¹³ So those who were engaged in the work labored, and the repairing went forward in their hands, and they restored the house of God to its proper condition and strengthened it. ¹⁴ And when they had finished, they brought the rest of the money before the king and Jehoiada, and with it were made utensils for the house of the LORD, both for the service and for the burnt offerings, and dishes for incense, and vessels of gold and silver. And they offered burnt offerings in the house of the LORD continually all the days of Jehoiada.

In the parallel passage in 2 Kings 12:1 ff. it appears that Joash asked the priests to give part of the regular offerings presented to them for the purpose of repairing the Temple. The priests passively resisted this invasion of their priestly prerogatives. Joash soon realized that he needed to make a different approach. In Chronicles the priests and Levites are told to go out and raise a special offering for this purpose rather than taking it from personal revenues. However, this also meets with passive resistance on the part of the Levites. Joash calls the chief priest to task for this negligence, asking him why this has been permitted. He gets no reply to his question. Apparently the Levites have reacted in a similar way to the priests. It was not a part of their duties to become moneyraisers. If this story supplements the one in Kings, as it probably does, it reveals real insight into the Levitical concept of their task.

And he had sons and daughters. This is a phrase that runs throughout Genesis, chapter 5 (cf. vv. 4,6,10,13,16,22,26,30). This raises the problem of the Chronicler's relationship to the priestly traditions of the Pentateuch.

To repair the house of your God from year to year. They were to raise enough money so that the Temple could be kept under constant repair, rather than letting it depreciate for years and then making a mighty effort to put it back in proper condition.

The tax levied by Moses (cf. Ex. 30:12 ff.).

For the sons of Athaliah, that wicked woman—literally, "For Athaliah, that wicked woman, her sons." They were following her bad example.

Set it outside the gate. Second Kings 12:9 says it was placed beside the altar. Either the Chronicler was using another source which located the box in a different place, or there were two boxes.

And with it were made utensils. Second Kings 12:13 says the money was not used for such things. However, that account may refer to the regular amounts coming in every day. The Chronicler suggests that when a surplus remained after the repairs were made, they were able to provide the vessels after all.

5. The Apostasy of Joash (24:15–27)

15 But Jehoiada grew old and full of days, and died; he was a hundred and thirty years old at his death. 16 And they buried him in the city of David among the kings, because he had done good in Israel, and toward God and his house.
17 Now after the death of Jehoiada the princes of Judah came and did obeisance to the king; then the king hearkened to them. 18 And they forsook the house of the LORD, the God of their fathers, and served the Asherim and the idols. And wrath came upon Judah and Jerusalem for this their guilt. 19 Yet he sent prophets among them to bring them back to the LORD; these testified against them, but they would not give heed.
20 Then the Spirit of God took possession of Zechariah the son of Jehoiada the priest; and he stood above the people, and said to them, "Thus says God, 'Why do you transgress the commandments of the LORD, so that you cannot prosper? Because you have forsaken the LORD, he has forsaken you.'" 21 But they conspired against him, and by command of the king they stoned him with stones in the court of the house of the LORD. 22 Thus Joash the king did not remember the kindness which Jehoiada, Zechariah's father, had shown him, but killed his son. And when he was dying, he said, "May the LORD see and avenge!"
23 At the end of the year the army of the Syrians came up against Joash. They came to Judah and Jerusalem, and destroyed all the princes of the people from among the people, and sent all their spoil to the king of Damascus. 24 Though the army of the Syrians had come with few men, the LORD delivered into their hand a very great army, because they had forsaken the LORD, the God of their fathers. Thus they executed judgment on Joash.

25 When they had departed from him, leaving him severely wounded, his servants conspired against him because of the blood of the son of Jehoiada the priest, and slew him on his bed. So he died; and they buried him in the city of David, but they did not bury him in the tombs of the kings. 26 Those who conspired against him were Zabad the son of Shimeath the Ammonitess, and Jehozabad the son of Shimrith the Moabitess. 27 Accounts of his sons, and of the many oracles against him, and of the rebuilding of the house of God are written in the Commentary on the Book of the Kings. And Amaziah his son reigned in his stead.

The perversity of Joash reveals the depths to which a decent man can sink. Perhaps Jehoiada had so dominated him while he was young that he tried to assert his own individuality after the great man's death, only to become subject to other men whose counsel was the opposite. In a struggle for identity he had exchanged a good master for evil ones. The Chronicler states it like this: "Now after the death of Jehoiada the princes of Judah came and did obeisance to the king; then the king hearkened to them."

And they buried him in the city of David among the kings. Only the Chronicler lets us know about this signal honor for a priest. His age at death, exceeding that of Moses or Aaron, has been attributed to a desire of later traditionalists to honor him even further. This matter, however, cannot be settled with any certainty. If he died at 130, he was in his nineties when Joash became king.

Zechariah the son of Jehoiada. The incident about Zechariah, found only in the Chronicles, made a profound influence on later generations. Jesus refers to it in such a way as to indicate that his canon of the Old Testament was the same as ours. The Jews had killed their prophets from Abel to Zechariah (Matt. 23:35). This meant that from Genesis to Chronicles the martyrdom of the prophets had been going on, for Chronicles was the last book in the final Hebrew canon.

May the Lord see and avenge! How different this cry from that of Stephen in a similar situation: "Lord, do not hold this sin against them" (Acts 7:60).

The army of the Syrians came up. Second Kings 12:17 ff. says that Hazael of Syria approached Jerusalem and was bought off by Joash. The Chronicler depicts a much more serious encounter, Hazael capturing much booty and leaving Joash seriously wounded. His sources are apparently more explicit about the first engagement. He does not claim that Jerusalem was captured. After the defeat Joash probably paid Hazael to come no farther. The writers of Kings do not record the first battle, only the consequence of it.

The Ammonites . . . the Moabites. Only the Chronicler mentions the nationality of the mothers of the assassins of Joash. Does he imply by this his objections to marriage of Jews and foreign wives?

The many oracles against him. This is confirmed by 24:19.

The Commentary on the Book of Kings. This was the *midrash* (Heb.) that was the principal source of the Chronicler's material. He refers to it under several other titles. (See the Introduction.)

VI. In the Midst of the Years (25:1—32:33)

1. Vacillations of Amaziah (25:1-28)

The life of Amaziah is a portrait of man "unstable in all his ways" (James 1:8), as Elmslie has pointed out. He made a noble beginning when he spared the families of his enemies. Then he thought he had done a sensible thing when he hired mercenaries from North Israel for a reasonable price for his army was much smaller than that of Asa (14:7) or Jehoshaphat (17:14). When a prophet condemned him for it, he released the hired soldiers, much to their disgust, for they also were due a share of the booty after the battle. Having won a great victory over Edom, he senselessly worshiped their gods, and this time rejected prophetic warnings. So charged with ego after such a glorious victory, he thought himself to be invincible and challenged Jehoash of North Israel to battle. He was ignominiously defeated by Jehoash, who captured Jerusalem, broke down part of the wall, and took all the wealth of the city. The last we see of Amaziah is a flight from would-be assassins who catch him in Lachish and kill him there.

(1) An Unprecedented Act of Mercy (25:1-4)

¹ Amaziah was twenty-five years old when he began to reign, and he reigned twenty-nine years in Jerusalem. His mother's name was Jehoaddan of Jerusalem. ² And he did what was right in the eyes of the Lord, yet not with a blameless heart. ³ And as soon as the royal power was firmly in his hand he killed his servants who had slain the king his father. ⁴ But he did not put their children to death, according to what is written in the law, in the book of Moses, where the Lord commanded, "The fathers shall not be put to death for the children, or the children be put to death for the fathers; but every man shall die for his own sin."

Amaziah recognized the difference between corporate and individual responsibility for crime. When Achan sinned against God, his whole family was stoned (Josh. 7:14-25). Amaziah's judicial landmark is mentioned in both Kings and Chronicles. They quote from Deuteronomy 24:16. Does this mean that this passage was known to be in the law of Moses at this time? The passage does not exactly say so; it only claims that it is in the law of Moses at the time of the writing down of Israel's history—in the case of 2 Kings, just after 587 B.C. Did Amaziah contribute to the formulation of that law, or did he obey it? One's critical presupposition concerning the date of Deuteronomy enters at this point. Regardless of one's conclusion on this vexing problem, it must be admitted that Amaziah was indeed off to a favorable start.

(2) North Israelite Mercenaries (25:5-13)

⁵ Then Amaziah assembled the men of Judah, and set them by fathers' houses under commanders of thousands and of hundreds for all Judah and Benjamin. He mustered those twenty years old and upward, and found that they were three hundred thousand picked men,

fit for war, able to handle spear and shield. ⁶ He hired also a hundred thousand mighty men of valor from Israel for a hundred talents of silver. ⁷ But a man of God came to him and said, "O king, do not let the army of Israel go with you, for the LORD is not with Israel, with all these Ephraimites. ⁸ But if you suppose that in this way you will be strong for war, God will cast you down before the enemy; for God has power to help or to cast down." ⁹ And Amaziah said to the man of God, "But what shall we do about the hundred talents which I have given to the army of Israel?" The man of God answered, "The LORD is able to give you much more than this." ¹⁰ Then Amaziah discharged the army that had come to him from Ephraim, to go home again. And they became very angry with Judah, and returned home in fierce anger. ¹¹ But Amaziah took courage, and led out his people, and went to the Valley of Salt and smote ten thousand men of Seir. ¹² The men of Judah captured another ten thousand alive, and took them to the top of a rock and threw them down from the top of the rock; and they were all dashed to pieces. ¹³ But the men of the army whom Amaziah sent back, without letting go with him to battle, fell upon the cities of Judah, from Samaria to Bethhoron, and killed three thousand people in them, and took much spoil.

Affairs were going well for Amaziah until he collided with a prophet. Having hired North Israelite mercenaries, and on the eve of departure into battle, he was confronted by the *man of God* who told him the whole affair was misconceived and destiny-doomed. Amaziah never recovered from the shock to his self-confidence. Perhaps he could have been helped sooner, with more tender care. But such was not the way of prophets.

The Lord is not with Israel. They were a rejected nation after the division or separation from Judah.

You will be strong for war. The Hebrew is far more vivid. It may be paraphrased: "If you are determined to fight, put up a good one, for God is against you!" This is a classic example of prophetic irony.

But what shall we do about the hundred talents? Amaziah would lose all his investment. The reply was a simple declaration of faith: "The Lord is able to give you much more than this" (cf. Matt. 6:33).

Smote ten thousand men of Seir. This success is also reported in 2 Kings 14:7. Only the Chronicler speaks of the 10,000 others dashed to the rocks. Surely Amaziah had already forgotten his earlier views on corporate responsibility. Or did the rights of individuals apply only to Jews?

Took much spoil. The mercenaries collected their booty anyway, from the people of Judah! Sometimes repentance comes too late to spare men the consequences of their sin.

(3) *Edomite Gods Worshiped (25:14-16)*

¹⁴ After Amaziah came from the slaughter of the Edomites, he brought the gods of the men of Seir, and set them up as his gods, and worshiped them, making offerings to them. ¹⁵ Therefore the LORD was angry with Amaziah and sent to him a prophet, who said to him, "Why have you resorted to the gods of a people, which did not deliver their own people from your hand?" ¹⁶ But as he was speaking the king said to him, "Have we made you a royal counselor? Stop! Why should you be put to death?" So the prophet stopped, but said, "I know that God has determined to destroy you, because you have done this and have not listened to my counsel."

This is the only time in the Old Testament that a Hebrew king worshiped the gods captured in war. None of the others were that foolish. How could the gods defeated by Yahweh be of any help to an Israelite? The prophet reminded Amaziah of this. No king likes to be called stupid in public. So he ordered the prophet to stop. He stopped the oracle (what was he going to say?), but not the personal witness. Note the distinction made between the divine oracle and personal observation on the part of the prophet.

(4) *Israel Challenged (25:17-24)*

¹⁷ Then Amaziah king of Judah took counsel and sent to Joash the son of Jehoahaz, son of Jehu, king of Israel, saying, "Come, let us look one another in the face." ¹⁸ And Joash the king of Israel sent word to Amaziah king of Judah, "A thistle on Lebanon sent to a cedar on Lebanon, saying, 'Give your daughter to my son for a wife'; and a wild beast of Lebanon passed by and trampled down the thistle. ¹⁹ You say, 'See, I have smitten Edom,' and your heart has lifted you up in boastfulness.

But now stay at home; why should you provoke trouble so that you fall, you and Judah with you?"
²⁰ But Amaziah would not listen; for it was of God, in order that he might give them into the hand of their enemies, because they had sought the gods of Edom. ²¹ So Joash king of Israel went up; and he and Amaziah king of Judah faced one another in battle at Bethshemesh, which belongs to Judah. ²² And Judah was defeated by Israel, and every man fled to his home. ²³ And Joash king of Israel captured Amaziah king of Judah, the son of Joash, son of Ahaziah, at Bethshemesh, and brought him to Jerusalem, and broke down the wall of Jerusalem for four hundred cubits, from the Ephraim Gate to the Corner Gate. ²⁴ And he seized all the gold and silver, and all the vessels that were found in the house of God, and Obededom with them; he seized also the treasuries of the king's house, and hostages, and he returned to Samaria.

This story also appears in 2 Kings 14:8 ff. The Chronicler has a different introduction. He notes that Amaziah *took counsel* of his court advisors in contrast to his refusal to listen to the prophet's counsel (cf. v. 17 with v. 16). He also observes that events were being influenced by the working out of the wrath of God upon Amaziah. The prophetic word could not be ignored without dire consequences.

(5) *Summary of Amaziah's Reign (25: 25-28)*

²⁵ Amaziah the son of Joash king of Judah lived fifteen years after the death of Joash the son of Jehoahaz, king of Israel. ²⁶ Now the rest of the deeds of Amaziah, from first to last, are they not written in the Book of the Kings of Judah and Israel? ²⁷ From the time when he turned away from the LORD they made a conspiracy against him in Jerusalem, and he fled to Lachish. But they sent after him to Lachish, and slew him there. ²⁸ And they brought him upon horses; and he was buried with his fathers in the city of David.

The text for Chronicles was similar to that of 2 Kings 14:17-20. The Chronicler only adds that the conspiracy against Amaziah had been going on since his first defection. The Hebrew text says that he was buried in the "city of Judah" (RSV, also 2 Kings 14:20, "city of David"). It is interesting to note that Esarhaddon, king of Assyria, described Manasseh as "king of the city of Judah." The Chronicler did not likely prefer "city of Judah" to "city of David." We may have a textual variation here, as the Chronicler may be faithfully following an authentic old reading.

2. *Uzziah's Prosperity and Pride (26:1-23)*

The name Uzziah is familiar because of its appearance in Isaiah 6:1. Except for this chapter in Chronicles, Isaiah 6:1, and Zechariah 14:5, the name is always Azariah. This is true in Kings and even in 1 Chronicles 3:12. In Hebrew the two names are very similar and may simply be variations of the same word. The Chronicler prefers Uzziah in order to distinguish the king from the chief priest Azariah (v. 17), who is only mentioned by him. Isaiah's use of the name possibly indicated that Uzziah was the way he originally spelled his name, whereas the official way, presented in Kings, was Azariah.

(1) *Domestic Interests (26:1-15)*

¹ And all the people of Judah took Uzziah, who was sixteen years old, and made him king instead of his father Amaziah. ² He built Eloth and restored it to Judah, after the king slept with his fathers. ³ Uzziah was sixteen years old when he began to reign, and he reigned fifty-two years in Jerusalem. His mother's name was Jecoliah of Jerusalem. ⁴ And he did what was right in the eyes of the LORD, according to all that his father Amaziah had done. ⁵ He set himself to seek God in the days of Zechariah, who instructed him in the fear of God; and as long as he sought the LORD, God made him prosper.
⁶ He went out and made war against the Philistines, and broke down the wall of Gath and the wall of Jabneh and the wall of Ashdod; and he built cities in the territory of Ashdod and elsewhere among the Philistines. ⁷ God helped him against the Philistines, and against the Arabs that dwelt in Gurbaal, and against the Meunites. ⁸ The Ammonites paid tribute to Uzziah, and his fame spread even to the border of Egypt, for he became very strong. ⁹ Moreover Uzziah built towers in Jerusalem at the Corner Gate and at the Valley Gate and at the Angle, and fortified them. ¹⁰ And he built towers in the wilderness, and hewed out many cisterns, for he had large herds, both in the Shephelah and in the plain, and he had farmers and vinedressers in the hills and in the fertile lands, for he loved the

soil. ¹¹ Moreover Uzziah had an army of soldiers, fit for war, in divisions according to the numbers in the muster made by Jeiel the secretary and Maaseiah the officer, under the direction of Hananiah, one of the king's commanders. ¹² The whole number of the heads of fathers' houses of mighty men of valor was two thousand six hundred. ¹³ Under their command was an army of three hundred and seven thousand five hundred, who could make war with mighty power, to help the king against the enemy. ¹⁴ And Uzziah prepared for all the army shields, spears, helmets, coats of mail, bows, and stones for slinging. ¹⁵ In Jerusalem he made engines, invented by skilful men, to be on the towers and the corners, to shoot arrows and great stones. And his fame spread far, for he was marvelously helped, till he was strong.

Kings has a very short summary of Uzziah's reign, but Chronicles has included far more material. The account of Uzziah's building and agricultural activities has been remarkably confirmed by archaeology (cf. Myers, II, 152–153). Here the Chronicler has preserved a record for us that otherwise would have been completely lost. His comments have been an invaluable aid to archaeologists as they have sought to interpret the meaning of what they have found.

And all the people of Judah took Uzziah. It was an unusual move for the people to rise up to crown a king. Apparently it was a reaction against Amaziah's rule. Note the contrast with the accession of Ahaziah (22:1) when only the people of Jerusalem prevailed.

In the days of Zechariah. We do not know his identity. Although Uzziah is referred to in Zechariah 14:5, this does not mean that the passage was written by that particular Zechariah. In fact Zechariah 9—14 might have been added to Zechariah 1—8, with which it has few affinities, because of a later notion connecting these prophecies with the Zechariah mentioned in this Chronicles passage. They were joined to the passages known to be by a Zechariah, although he was not the same one, for he preached after the Babylonian exile.

The wall of Jabneh. This town, located between Joppa and Ashdod, is the same as the Jabneel of Joshua 15:11 and later became the Jamnia (1 Macc. 4:15) of the early Christian period. It was the seat of the Great Sanhedrin after the destruction of the Temple in A.D. 70. It was here that the Jewish canon of the Old Testament was debated and agreed upon.

Mighty men of valor . . . two thousand six hundred . . . an army of three hundred and seven thousand five hundred. By the unit principle, this would be 2 units totaling 600 for the leaders, and 300 units of warriors with a total of 7500.

He made engines, invented by skillful men. This is the only mention in the Old Testament of such war machines. Uzziah had the latest military equipment.

(2) Conflict with the Priests (26:16–23)

¹⁶ But when he was strong he grew proud, to his destruction. For he was false to the Lord his God, and entered the temple of the Lord to burn incense on the altar of incense. ¹⁷ But Azariah the priest went in after him, with eighty priests of the Lord who were men of valor; ¹⁸ and they withstood King Uzziah, and said to him, "It is not for you, Uzziah, to burn incense to the Lord, but for the priests the sons of Aaron, who are consecrated to burn incense. Go out of the sanctuary; for you have done wrong, and it will bring you no honor from the Lord God." ¹⁹ Then Uzziah was angry. Now he had a censer in his hand to burn incense, and when he became angry with the priests leprosy broke out on his forehead, in the presence of the priests in the house of the Lord, by the altar of incense. ²⁰ And Azariah the chief priest, and all the priests, looked at him, and behold, he was leprous in his forehead! And they thrust him out quickly, and he himself hastened to go out, because the Lord had smitten him. ²¹ And King Uzziah was a leper to the day of his death, and being a leper dwelt in a separate house, for he was excluded from the house of the Lord. And Jotham his son was over the king's household, governing the people of the land.

²² Now the rest of the acts of Uzziah, from first to last, Isaiah the prophet the son of Amoz wrote. ²³ And Uzziah slept with his fathers, and they buried him with his fathers in the burial field which belonged to the kings, for they said, "He is a leper." And Jotham his son reigned in his stead.

The account is from the pen of the Chronicler, although he must have found it in his sources. Second Kings 15:5 mentions that Uzziah's leprosy was due to an act of God but it does not give specifics. Some expositors question the historicity of the Chronicler's account in its present form, but it is certainly based upon an actual event. The fact that the story was traditionally told among the priests and Levites may explain its present characteristics.

It is not for you, Uzziah. Note how the chief priest did not address him with the usual flattering terms applied to kings. He stripped him of all his royal titles.

Leprosy broke out on his forehead. There were many kinds of leprosy. Naaman was allowed to go about his duties although a leper (2 Kings 5:1 ff.). Uzziah's disease was of the sort that deprived him of public life. The probable meaning of its appearance on his forehead is that it was judgment for his pride.

He himself hastened to go out. It was no problem to get him to leave now. He was quite cooperative.

He was excluded from the house of the Lord. We are told today by medical authorities that leprosy now is one of the least contagious diseases. It is not known how it is communicated. Modern leprosy, however, should not automatically be identified with that of the Old Testament (cf. Lev. 13—14). That disease was often communicated by touch.

They buried him with his fathers in the burial field. This does not mean the same tombs but in the field adjacent to the royal cemetery. The stigma of the disease was left upon him even after his death.

3. Godly Father, Wicked Son (27:1—28:27)

Far too often it happened that a good king was succeeded by a wicked one. However, the reverse was also true; a wicked king was sometimes followed by a good one. Generations often tend to react radically to one another. The son, in an attempt to be different from his godly father, abandons his father's best traits and picks up his worst. Or seeing the faults of a wicked father, he determines to be a better man. It would hardly be claimed that the wicked father was responsible for his son's goodness. Our knowledge of the tragic course of Ahaz should not prevent a generous appraisal of his father, Jotham.

(1) Jotham, Loyal to God (27:1–9)

¹ Jotham was twenty-five years old when he began to reign, and he reigned sixteen years in Jerusalem. His mother's name was Jerushah the daughter of Zadok. ² And he did what was right in the eyes of the Lord according to all that his father Uzziah had done—only he did not invade the temple of the Lord. But the people still followed corrupt practices. ³ He built the upper gate of the house of the Lord, and did much building on the wall of Ophel. ⁴ Moreover he built cities in the hill country of Judah, and forts and towers on the wooded hills. ⁵ He fought with the king of the Ammonites and prevailed against them. And the Ammonites gave him that year a hundred talents of silver, and ten thousand cors of wheat and ten thousand of barley. The Ammonites paid him the same amount in the second and the third years. ⁶ So Jotham became mighty, because he ordered his ways before the Lord his God. ⁷ Now the rest of the acts of Jotham, and all his wars, and his ways, behold, they are written in the Book of the Kings of Israel and Judah. ⁸ He was twenty-five years old when he began to reign, and he reigned sixteen years in Jerusalem. ⁹ And Jotham slept with his fathers, and they buried him in the city of David; and Ahaz his son reigned in his stead.

The reign of Jotham must have presented real problems to Jewish historians, as both the authors of Kings and Chronicles illustrate. So far as they could tell he was a good king during all his life. His only failure was the inability to get all the people to follow his leadership, particularly in regard to worship in the high places. Yet all the good kings before him failed to solve that problem. If God prospered a good king, as they believed, why did Jotham not get more done, and why did he die so young? It remained for Jesus to show that the rewards of God are not always material. To the ancient Hebrews this was an insoluble puzzle (cf. the book of Job). Neither Kings nor Chronicles sees any fault in this man, yet they have little to say about his successes. There is a tendency to move on to the next king lest embarrassing questions be asked. Indeed the Chronicler includes a few short notes about Jotham's exploits, but they hardly compare with the deeds of Asa, Jehoshaphat, or Uzziah. Second Kings 15:32–38 says nothing explicit at all and seems to blame his abbreviated reign upon his failure to remove the high places. No wonder 2 Chronicles chapter 27 contains only a few verses. The Chronicler is strangely at a loss to know what to say.

Only he did not invade the temple of the Lord. Jotham imitated his father in all his virtues but not his faults. He did not try to usurp the functions of the priests.

And the Ammonites gave him that year. The money amounted to about $180,000 a year, and the grain was about 120,000 bushels of each variety, according to this tradition.

He ordered his ways before the Lord. This is in sharp contrast to Amaziah, who was swayed by every wind that blew. Jotham set his course and stayed on it. We could wish that we knew more about this man.

(2) *Ahaz, the Idolater* (28:1–27)

a. *The Syro-Ephraimitic War* (28:1–15)

¹ Ahaz was twenty years old when he began to reign, and he reigned sixteen years in Jerusalem. And he did not do what was right in the eyes of the Lord, like his father David, ² but walked in the ways of the kings of Israel. He even made molten images for the Baals; ³ and he burned incense in the valley of the son of Hinnom, and burned his sons as an offering, according to the abominable practices of the nations whom the Lord drove out before the people of Israel. ⁴ And he sacrificed and burned incense on the high places, and on the hills, and under every green tree.

⁵ Therefore the Lord his God gave him into the hand of the king of Syria, who defeated him and took captive a great number of his people and brought them to Damascus. He was also given into the hand of the king of Israel, who defeated him with great slaughter. ⁶ For Pekah the son of Remaliah slew a hundred and twenty thousand in Judah in one day, all of them men of valor, because they had forsaken the Lord, the God of their fathers. ⁷ And Zichri, a mighty man of Ephraim, slew Maaseiah the king's son and Azrikam the commander of the palace and Elkanah the next in authority to the king.

⁸ The men of Israel took captive two hundred thousand of their kinsfolk, women, sons, and daughters; they also took much spoil from them and brought the spoil to Samaria. ⁹ But a prophet of the Lord was there, whose name was Oded; and he went out to meet the army that came to Samaria, and said to them, "Behold, because the Lord, the God of your fathers, was angry with Judah, he gave them into your hand, but you have slain them in a rage which has reached up to heaven. ¹⁰ And now you intend to subjugate the people of Judah and Jerusalem, male and female, as your slaves. Have you not sins of your own against the Lord your God? ¹¹ Now hear me, and send back the captives from your kinsfolk whom you have taken, for the fierce wrath of the Lord is upon you." ¹² Certain chiefs also of the men of Ephraim, Azariah the son of Johanan, Berechiah the son of Meshillemoth, Jehizkiah the son of Shallum, and Amasa the son of Hadlai, stood up against those who were coming from the war, ¹³ and said to them, "You shall not bring the captives in here, for you propose to bring upon us guilt against the Lord in addition to our present sins and guilt. For our guilt is already great, and there is fierce wrath against Israel." ¹⁴ So the armed men left the captives and the spoil before the princes and all the assembly. ¹⁵ And the men who have been mentioned by name rose and took the captives, and with the spoil they clothed all that were naked among them; they clothed them, gave them sandals, provided them with food and drink, and anointed them; and carrying all the feeble among them on asses, they brought them to their kinsfolk at Jericho, the city of palm trees. Then they returned to Samaria.

But walked in the ways of the kings of Israel. This was the worst epithet that the historian could apply to him. He follows 2 Kings 16:1 ff. here and continues through v. 4, with the additional note that Ahaz "made molten images for Baal." Many of these types of idols have been found in Palestine.

Therefore the Lord . . . gave him into the hand of the king of Syria. Second Kings 16:5 says that the kings of Syria and Israel "could not conquer" Ahaz. Isaiah 7:1 ff. reinforces that statement. Is this an example of the Chronicler's fabrication of history? Did he think that wicked Ahaz deserved such a fate, and invent it for him? The inclusion of important names from the casualty lists in 28:7 gives an atmosphere of authenticity to the account. Chronicles and Kings can be reconciled, for the Chronicler did not claim that Jerusalem was captured. However, the later historian depicts the trouble that came to the forces of Ahaz in Judah before the siege of Jerusalem. The Chronicler apparently was using the Levitical midrash for the account, which explains the apparent exaggeration in numbers.

The next in authority to the king. This expression is not used elsewhere in the Old Testament except in Esther 10:3. It probably applies here to a cabinet member, possibly the recorder.

He went out to meet. The prophets did not always wait for people to come to them. They confronted them in public places where they could be resisted but not ignored. The Chronicler is fond of using pictures of such confrontations (cf. 2 Chron. 16:7; 19:2; 25:7), although he also spoke of the faithful oracle during regular public worship (cf. 2 Chron. 20:14; 24:20).

In a rage which has reached up to heaven. There may be a circumlocution here, an intentional avoiding of the name of God, but it is probably a vivid way of picturing the rise of their guilt, like smoke ascending into the sky.

Have you not sins of your own. This brings to mind the words of Jesus, "Let him who is without sin among you be the first to throw a stone" (John 8:7, RSV marg.).

Send back the captives from your kinsfolk (lit., from your brothers). Here is the view of the Chronicler, also. Although its king is apostate and, as a nation, North Israel is doomed, the individuals were still part of the people of God and could, upon presenting themselves in Jerusalem, be accepted back into the commonwealth of Israel. The Chronicler at every point taught that no attempt on the part of North or South to harm or subjugate the other could be successful. It was in the plan of God that all the people of God should unite in the cultic worship at Jerusalem. The Temple was the authentic fountainhead of Israel's destiny.

Certain chiefs also of the men of Ephraim. These names reveal that the Chronicler was using actual records for his account, although the original event was reported in the form of an old tradition.

For our guilt is already great—in forsaking the Davidic cult and king. Some North Israelites realized their guilt but did not have the courage to break free.

They clothed all that were naked . . . provided them with food and drink . . . carrying all the feeble . . . to their kinsfolk (Heb., brethren). This passage may be related to Matthew 25:35–40: "For I was hungry and you gave me food . . . thirsty . . . a stranger . . . naked . . . as you did it unto one of the least of these my brethren."

This is one of the few times that a prophet was successful in his appeal. Was it because he appealed to love, consideration, and kinship rather than delivering a harangue? Was it because he called upon the nobility of men rather than reminding them of their hostility? Yet he did this while reminding them of their sinfulness. His preaching of love was no superficial sentimentality.

b. The Faithlessness of Ahaz (28:16–27)

16 At that time King Ahaz sent to the king of Assyria for help. 17 For the Edomites had again invaded and defeated Judah, and carried away captives. 18 And the Philistines had made raids on the cities in the Shephelah and the Negeb of Judah, and had taken Bethshemesh, Aijalon, Gederoth, Soco with its villages, Timnah with its villages, and Gimzo with its villages; and they settled there. 19 For the LORD brought Judah low because of Ahaz king of Israel, for he had dealt wantonly in Judah and had been faithless to the LORD. 20 So Tilgath-pilneser king of Assyria came against him, and afflicted him instead of strengthening him. 21 For Ahaz took from the house of the LORD and the house of the king and of the princes, and gave tribute to the king of Assyria; but it did not help him. 22 In the time of his distress he became yet

more faithless to the LORD—this same King Ahaz. 23 For he sacrificed to the gods of Damascus which had defeated him, and said, "Because the gods of the kings of Syria helped them, I will sacrifice to them that they may help me." But they were the ruin of him, and of all Israel. 24 And Ahaz gathered together the vessels of the house of God and cut in pieces the vessels of the house of God, and he shut up the doors of the house of the LORD; and he made himself altars in every corner of Jerusalem. 25 In every city of Judah he made high places to burn incense to other gods, provoking to anger the LORD, the God of his fathers. 26 Now the rest of his acts and all his ways, from first to last, behold, they are written in the Book of the Kings of Judah and Israel. 27 And Ahaz slept with his fathers, and they buried him in the city, in Jerusalem, for they did not bring him into the tombs of the kings of Israel. And Hezekiah his son reigned in his stead.

It now appears that Ahaz sent to Tiglathpileser of Assyria not so much because of Syria and Ephraim as because of the Edomite peril. In fact he was beset on every side. Second Kings 16:10 appears to be saying that Ahaz and the king of Assyria were on friendly terms as allies, but the Chronicler says "he afflicted him instead of strengthening him." There probably was a temporary treaty which Tiglathpileser ignored as soon as it was to his advantage. Ahaz was mentioned in Assyrian records as a tributary along with other conquered peoples. The troubles of Ahaz, says the Chronicler, were all due to his neglect of Yahweh, not to the inexorable working out of the world's political forces. Ahaz could have written the history of his time differently if he had been faithful.

This same King Ahaz. Thus he is classified with Athaliah "that wicked woman" (24:7).

Because the gods of the kings of Syria helped them, I will sacrifice to them. Some expositors have difficulty with this statement for the gods of Syria had not helped Syria against Assyria. This, however, is the point the Chronicler is making. A man who worshiped idols could not be expected to be sensible. He had already forfeited his good sense. Ahaz only thought about how Syria defeated him; he did not consider Syria's relation to Assyria. He was a typical senseless idolater!

He shut up the doors of the house of the Lord. Second Kings 16:10 ff. does not seem to say this. Rather, regular worship still seemed to go on while Ahaz had his own private altar. Kings speaks of the chief priest's cooperation with the apostasy of Ahaz. The Chronicler does not give the priest the honor of perpetuating his infamous memory. It is possible that Ahaz did not order regular worship to be stopped, but that the presence of his rival altar eventually led to a general lack of concern for worship on the part of the people. There are many ways to close down a religious institution. The least effective is to order it closed. The most likely way is through neglect.

The tombs of the kings of Israel. "Israel" is used because these were not originally intended for the kings of Judah. David and Solomon were kings of Israel. Thus the royal tombs were for the true kings of Israel, David's sons. Ahaz was not buried there, however. The statement in 2 Kings 16:20 that he was "buried with his fathers" does not necessarily mean that he was placed in the royal cemetery. The Chronicler had the more specific information; 2 Kings only made a general statement.

4. Revival Under Hezekiah (29:1—32:33)

To the Chronicler, Hezekiah (whose name he spells *Yechizqiyyahu* rather than the *Chizqiyyahu* of Kings, a shortened form) was a second David, just as David was another Moses. In contrast to the editors of Kings, who portray the Sennacherib invasion in remarkable detail, the Chronicler devoted only a portion of one chapter (32) to this event and characteristically concentrated upon the cultic reforms of Hezekiah.

(1) *Hezekiah's Reformation (29:1–36)*

Hezekiah probably came to the throne in 715 B.C. and reigned until 687.[20] Samaria

[20] Cf. Albright, BASOR 100 (Dec. 1945), 22; H. H. Rowley, BJRL 44 (1961–62), 409 ff.

had already fallen, and Judah was in desperate straits. It is quite reasonable, therefore, that Hezekiah would call for a return to the faith of their fathers as the only way to recovery. His success at this surely inspired Josiah to similar procedures. Myers (II, 177) suggests that Deuteronomy was completed in connection with Hezekiah's reform and discarded during Manasseh's defection, only to be rediscovered by Josiah.

a. The Appeal of Hezekiah (29:1–11)

¹ Hezekiah began to reign when he was twenty-five years old, and he reigned twenty-nine years in Jerusalem. His mother's name was Abijah the daughter of Zechariah. ² And he did what was right in the eyes of the Lord, according to all that David his father had done. ³ In the first year of his reign, in the first month, he opened the doors of the house of the Lord, and repaired them. ⁴ He brought in the priests and the Levites, and assembled them in the square on the east, ⁵ and said to them, "Hear me, Levites! Now sanctify yourselves, and sanctify the house of the Lord, the God of your fathers, and carry out the filth from the holy place. ⁶ For our fathers have been unfaithful and have done what was evil in the sight of the Lord our God; they have forsaken him, and have turned away their faces from the habitation of the Lord, and turned their backs. ⁷ They also shut the doors of the vestibule and put out the lamps, and have not burned incense or offered burnt offerings in the holy place to the God of Israel. ⁸ Therefore the wrath of the Lord came on Judah and Jerusalem, and he has made them an object of horror, of astonishment, and of hissing, as you see with your own eyes. ⁹ For lo, our fathers have fallen by the sword and our sons and our daughters and our wives are in captivity for this. ¹⁰ Now it is in my heart to make a covenant with the Lord, the God of Israel, that his fierce anger may turn away from us. ¹¹ My sons, do not now be negligent, for the Lord has chosen you to stand in his presence, to minister to him, and to be his ministers and burn incense to him."

When he was twenty-five years old, and he reigned twenty-nine years. The same is said about Amaziah (25:1). The reference to the former king's reign might have been confused with that of Hezekiah for it appears to be too long a reign for him.[21]

Hear me, Levites. This is a most unusual statement. Hezekiah addresses both priests and Levites as "Levites." Here we can see the dignity that the Chronicler gives to that title. In v. 11 Hezekiah refers to them as "my sons."

Carry out the filth. This word in Hebrew is often used in reference to menstruation (cf. Lev. 15:24,25,33, "impurity"). Here it probably describes the pollution of the sacred place, not just a collection of trash. It would hardly have taken them two weeks to remove the debris from the Temple area. They were also cleansing ceremonially as they proceeded.

Therefore the wrath of the Lord came on Judah. This refers to the disaster of the Syro-Ephraimitic war and the aftermath when Assyria must have also added Judah to its subjects (2 Chron. 28:20).

b. The Cleansing of the Temple (29:12–19)

¹² Then the Levites arose, Mahath the son of Amasai, and Joel the son of Azariah, of the sons of the Kohathites; and of the sons of Merari, Kish the son of Abdi, and Azariah the son of Jehallelel; and of the Gershonites, Joah the son of Zimmah, and Eden the son of Joah; ¹³ and the sons of Elizaphan, Shimri and Jeuel; and of the sons of Asaph, Zechariah and Mattaniah; ¹⁴ and of the sons of Heman, Jehuel and Shimei; and of the sons of Jeduthun, Shemaiah and Uzziel. ¹⁵ They gathered their brethren, and sanctified themselves, and went in as the king had commanded, by the words of the Lord, to cleanse the house of the Lord. ¹⁶ The priests went into the inner part of the house of the Lord to cleanse it, and they brought out all the uncleanness that they found in the temple of the Lord into the court of the house of the Lord; and the Levites took it and carried it out to the brook Kidron. ¹⁷ They began to sanctify on the first day of the first month, and on the eighth day of the month they came to the vestibule of the Lord; then for eight days they sanctified the house of the Lord, and on the sixteenth day of the first month they finished. ¹⁸ Then they went in to Hezekiah the king and said, "We have cleansed all the house of the Lord, the altar of burnt offering and all its utensils, and the table for the showbread and all its utensils. ¹⁹ All the utensils which King

---

[21] Cf. Albright, *op. cit.*

Ahaz discarded in his reign when he was faithless, we have made ready and sanctified; and behold, they are before the altar of the LORD."

The priests went into the inner part. Although the Chronicler gave the term "Levite" a new dignity by applying it to all the priestly tribe, he was still convinced of a distinction between sacrificing and non-sacrificing priests. In his opinion the former could go into the inner sanctuary. To the Chronicler, the Levitical role was the same as the common priestly view of his times, but it had gained in respectability. It is quite likely that the term Levites is also used in v. 12 of both priests and Levites. The three families of Levi are presented, including the Aaronic priests among the sons of Kohath and then the Levitical singers.

Carried it out to the brook Kidron. This was the stream east of the city formerly used for a similar purpose (2 Chron. 15:16). It is not likely that the trash was abundant or it would have clogged the stream. This cleansing must have been primarily ritualistic.

c. The Sin Offering (29:20-24)

20 Then Hezekiah the king rose early and gathered the officials of the city, and went up to the house of the LORD. 21 And they brought seven bulls, seven rams, seven lambs, and seven he-goats for a sin offering for the kingdom and for the sanctuary and for Judah. And he commanded the priests the sons of Aaron to offer them on the altar of the LORD. 22 So they killed the bulls, and the priests received the blood and threw it against the altar; and they killed the rams and their blood was thrown against the altar; and they killed the lambs and their blood was thrown against the altar. 23 Then the he-goats for the sin offering were brought to the king and the assembly, and they laid their hands upon them, 24 and the priests killed them and made a sin offering with their blood on the altar, to make atonement for all Israel. For the king commanded that the burnt offering and the sin offering should be made for all Israel.

Seven he-goats for a sin offering. The other animals were probably for the burnt offering. However, they might have been for a sin offering, also, for it was customary for a sin offering to precede the burnt offering on such an occasion (cf. Lev. 8:1 ff.). The burnt offering is mentioned in v. 27 again. Perhaps the Chronicler has introduced the burnt offering in this section, but he discusses it more fully in the next section in its proper chronological order.

For the kingdom and for the sanctuary and for Judah. The sin offering was made for the rebellious royal house, the polluted Temple and its personnel, and the straying people.

To make atonement for all Israel. Hezekiah was already including North Israel in the area of his concern.

d. The Worship Service (29:25-36)

25 And he stationed the Levites in the house of the LORD with cymbals, harps, and lyres, according to the commandment of David and of Gad the king's seer and of Nathan the prophet; for the commandment was from the LORD through his prophets. 26 The Levites stood with the instruments of David, and the priests with the trumpets. 27 Then Hezekiah commanded that the burnt offering be offered on the altar. And when the burnt offering began, the song to the LORD began also, and the trumpets, accompanied by the instruments of David king of Israel. 28 The whole assembly worshiped, and the singers sang, and the trumpeters sounded; all this continued until the burnt offering was finished. 29 When the offering was finished, the king and all who were present with him bowed themselves and worshiped. 30 And Hezekiah the king and the princes commanded the Levites to sing praises to the LORD with the words of David and of Asaph the seer. And they sang praises with gladness, and they bowed down and worshiped. 31 Then Hezekiah said, "You have now consecrated yourselves to the LORD; come near, bring sacrifices and thank offerings to the house of the LORD." And the assembly brought sacrifices and thank offerings; and all who were of a willing heart brought burnt offerings. 32 The number of the burnt offerings which the assembly brought was seventy bulls, a hundred rams, and two hundred lambs; all these were for a burnt offering to the LORD. 33 And the consecrated offerings were six hundred bulls and three thousand sheep. 34 But the priests were too few and could not flay all the burnt offerings, so until other priests had sanctified themselves their brethren the Levites helped

them, until the work was finished—for the Levites were more upright in heart than the priests in sanctifying themselves. 35 Besides the great number of burnt offerings there was the fat of the peace offerings, and there were the libations for the burnt offerings. Thus the service of the house of the LORD was restored. 36 And Hezekiah and all the people rejoiced because of what God had done for the people; for the thing came about suddenly.

The service began with the assembly prostrate before God. As the burnt offering began, the Levitical choir lifted their instruments and voices in praise, continuing throughout the offering. When Hezekiah and the priests requested an encore, the Levites gladly responded. Then the assembly was called upon to respond in freewill offerings, and they did so with such abundance that the priests were not prepared to process them. The service ended with joyful praise for the goodness of God.

From the Lord through his prophets. Nowhere else are Gad and Nathan pictured as being concerned with cultic music. Perhaps they were, however.

And when the burnt offering began, the song of the Lord began also. In the case of the burnt offering all the sacrifice was consumed. No part of it was kept by the priests or worshipers. It has been noted that when a man's whole will is laid upon God's altar, *the song of the Lord* always rises in his heart.

The words of David and of Asaph the seer. This indicates that there was already a collection of Davidic and Asaphic Psalms in the Chronicler's day and perhaps even in Hezekiah's time.

Could not flay all the burnt offerings. In Leviticus 1:6 we are told that the layman flayed his own offering. Probably by the time of the Chronicler, if not by Hezekiah's day, the professional clergy had assumed the original role of the layman.

For the Levites were more upright in heart than the priests. This may reveal the Chronicler's bias, but it is quite likely that the priests were more closely identified with the court of Ahaz, and therefore more reluctant to cooperate with Hezekiah.

(2) *Passover for All Israel (30:1–27)*

a. *The Proclamation (30:1–12)*

¹ Hezekiah sent to all Israel and Judah, and wrote letters also to Ephraim and Manasseh, that they should come to the house of the LORD at Jerusalem, to keep the passover to the LORD the God of Israel. ² For the king and his princes and all the assembly in Jerusalem had taken counsel to keep the passover in the second month—³ for they could not keep it in its time because the priests had not sanctified themselves in sufficient number, nor had the people assembled in Jerusalem—⁴ and the plan seemed right to the king and all the assembly. ⁵ So they decreed to make a proclamation throughout all Israel, from Beersheba to Dan, that the people should come and keep the passover to the LORD the God of Israel, at Jerusalem; for they had not kept it in great numbers as prescribed. ⁶ So couriers went throughout all Israel and Judah with letters from the king and his princes, as the king had commanded, saying, "O people of Israel, return to the LORD, the God of Abraham, Isaac, and Israel, that he may turn again to the remnant of you who have escaped from the hand of the kings of Assyria. ⁷ Do not be like your fathers and your brethren, who were faithless to the LORD God of their fathers, so that he made them a desolation, as you see. ⁸ Do not now be stiff-necked as your fathers were, but yield yourselves to the LORD, and come to his sanctuary, which he has sanctified for ever, and serve the LORD your God, that his fierce anger may turn away from you. ⁹ For if you return to the LORD, your brethren and your children will find compassion with their captors, and return to this land. For the LORD your God is gracious and merciful, and will not turn away his face from you, if you return to him."

¹⁰ So the couriers went from city to city through the country of Ephraim and Manasseh, and as far as Zebulun; but they laughed them to scorn, and mocked them. ¹¹ Only a few men of Asher, of Manasseh, and of Zebulun humbled themselves and came to Jerusalem. ¹² The hand of God was also upon Judah to give them one heart to do what the king and the princes commanded by the word of the LORD.

The news of this attempt to rally all Israel would not be received with favor by Assyria. However, Sargon was involved in affairs at home. A general revolt was brewing in Palestine of which Hezekiah's maneuver was only a part. This would eventually lead to his return to that region to quiet the situation.

The second month. The regular time for the Passover was the first month. The law suggested that if this were not possible, the second month could be used (Num. 9:11).

So couriers went throughout all Israel and Judah. This word (lit., runner) is also used of the king's guards (2 Kings 11:4). They were to go or stay at the king's command.

Only a few men. A small remnant of North Israel responded, except that there apparently were none from Ephraim. The closer the proximity to Judah, the more the hostility was manifested.

b. The Observance (30:13-27)

13 And many people came together in Jerusalem to keep the feast of unleavened bread in the second month, a very great assembly. 14 They set to work and removed the altars that were in Jerusalem, and all the altars for burning incense they took away and threw into the Kidron valley. 15 And they killed the passover lamb on the fourteenth day of the second month. And the priests and the Levites were put to shame, so that they sanctified themselves, and brought burnt offerings into the house of the Lord. 16 They took their accustomed posts according to the law of Moses the man of God; the priests sprinkled the blood which they received from the hand of the Levites. 17 For there were many in the assembly who had not sanctified themselves; therefore the Levites had to kill the passover lamb for every one who was not clean, to make it holy to the Lord. 18 For a multitude of the people, many of them from Ephraim, Manasseh, Issachar, and Zebulun, had not cleansed themselves, yet they ate the passover otherwise than as prescribed. For Hezekiah had prayed for them, saying, "The good Lord pardon every one 19 who sets his heart to seek God, the Lord the God of his fathers, even though not according to the sanctuary's rules of cleanness." 20 And the Lord heard Hezekiah, and healed the people. 21 And the people of Israel that were present at Jerusalem kept the feast of unleavened bread seven days with great gladness; and the Levites and the priests praised the Lord day by day, singing with all their might to the Lord. 22 And Hezekiah spoke encouragingly to all the Levites who showed good skill in the service of the Lord. So the people ate the food of the festival for seven days, sacrificing peace offerings and giving thanks to the Lord the God of their fathers.

23 Then the whole assembly agreed together to keep the feast for another seven days; so they kept it for another seven days with gladness. 24 For Hezekiah king of Judah gave the assembly a thousand bulls and seven thousand sheep for offerings, and the princes gave the assembly a thousand bulls and ten thousand sheep. And the priests sanctified themselves in great numbers. 25 The whole assembly of Judah, and the priests and the Levites, and the whole assembly that came out of Israel, and the sojourners who came out of the land of Israel, and the sojourners who dwelt in Judah, rejoiced. 26 So there was great joy in Jerusalem, for since the time of Solomon the son of David king of Israel there had been nothing like this in Jerusalem. 27 Then the priests and the Levites arose and blessed the people, and their voice was heard, and their prayer came to his holy habitation in heaven.

Also observed in connection with the Passover was the Feast of Unleavened Bread (Heb., *Mazzoth*), which immediately followed. The people had such a great time that they decided to have an extra week.

And the priests and Levites were put to shame. The laymen were more responsive to the Passover than either the priests or Levites. The professional clergy, occupied with perpetuating the institution, had become insensitive to its reason for existence.

The Levites had to kill the passover lamb. It was the responsibility of the laymen to kill this lamb, not of the priests (Ex. 12:6). Apparently the people were regarded as unclean due to their apostasy and, therefore, unfit to kill the lamb.

They ate the passover otherwise than prescribed. This is a remarkable passage. Here we see that the Chronicler was not a legalist in spite of his cultic interests.

The good Lord. Only here is this expression found in the Old Testament. It has now become proverbial.

And the Lord heard Hezekiah. Here the Chronicler stresses his belief in the efficacy of prayer (cf. James 5:16).

Hezekiah spoke encouragingly to all the Levites. The Chronicler would know how much this helped them, if he were one himself.

And their voice was heard. This implies

that such acceptance was not always true. The benediction of the clergy was not guaranteed by God.

His holy habitation in heaven. To the Chronicler, as sacred as the Temple was, it was not God's true palace but rather bore his name on the earth, just as a king's embassy in a foreign land.

(3) *High Places Destroyed* (31:1)

¹ Now when all this was finished, all Israel who were present went out to the cities of Judah and broke in pieces the pillars and hewed down the Asherim and broke down the high places and the altars throughout all Judah and Benjamin, and in Ephraim and Manasseh, until they had destroyed them all. Then all the people of Israel returned to their cities, every man to his possession.

At last a king had arisen who would lead Israel to do what none had done before. In the zeal of their spirit the assembly left their feasting to conduct a holy war on idolatry throughout all Judah and North Israel. The symbols of idolatry were broken over the whole land, as far as the limited resources of Hezekiah allowed. He was particularly handicapped in North Israel, for those who came from those regions were few (30:11).

(4) *Providing for the Clergy* (31:2–21)

² And Hezekiah appointed the divisions of the priests and of the Levites, division by division, each according to his service, the priests and the Levites, for burnt offerings and peace offerings, to minister in the gates of the camp of the LORD and to give thanks and praise. ³ The contribution of the king from his own possessions was for the burnt offerings: the burnt offerings of morning and evening, and the burnt offerings for the sabbaths, the new moons, and the appointed feasts, as it is written in the law of the LORD. ⁴ And he commanded the people who lived in Jerusalem to give the portion due to the priests and the Levites, that they might give themselves to the law of the LORD. ⁵ As soon as the command was spread abroad, the people of Israel gave in abundance the first fruits of grain, wine, oil, honey, and of all the produce of the field; and they brought in abundantly the tithe of everything. ⁶ And the people of Israel and Judah who lived in the cities of Judah also brought in the tithe of cattle and sheep, and the dedicated things which had been consecrated to the LORD their God, and laid them in heaps. ⁷ In the third month they began to pile up the heaps, and finished them in the seventh month. ⁸ When Hezekiah and the princes came and saw the heaps, they blessed the LORD and his people Israel. ⁹ And Hezekiah questioned the priests and the Levites about the heaps. ¹⁰ Azariah the chief priest, who was of the house of Zadok, answered him, "Since they began to bring the contributions into the house of the LORD we have eaten and had enough and have plenty left; for the LORD has blessed his people, so that we have this great store left."

¹¹ Then Hezekiah commanded them to prepare chambers in the house of the LORD; and they prepared them. ¹² And they faithfully brought in the contributions, the tithes and the dedicated things. The chief officer in charge of them was Conaniah the Levite, with Shimei his brother as second; ¹³ while Jehiel, Azaziah, Nahath, Asaahel, Jerimoth, Jozabad, Eliel, Ismachiah, Mahath, and Benaiah were overseers assisting Conaniah and Shimei his brother, by the appointment of Hezekiah the king and Azariah the chief officer of the house of God. ¹⁴ And Kore the son of Imnah the Levite, keeper of the east gate, was over the freewill offerings to God, to apportion the contribution reserved for the LORD and the most holy offerings. ¹⁵ Eden, Miniamin, Jeshua, Shemaiah, Amariah, and Shecaniah were faithfully assisting him in the cities of the priests, to distribute the portions to their brethren, old and young alike, by divisions, ¹⁶ except those enrolled by genealogy, males from three years old and upwards, all who entered the house of the LORD as the duty of each day required, for their service according to their offices, by their divisions. ¹⁷ The enrollment of the priests was according to their fathers' houses; that of the Levites from twenty years old and upwards was according to their offices, by their divisions. ¹⁸ The priests were enrolled with all their little children, their wives, their sons, and their daughters, the whole multitude; for they were faithful in keeping themselves holy. ¹⁹ And for the sons of Aaron, the priests, who were in the fields of common land belonging to their cities, there were men in the several cities who were designated by name to distribute portions to every male among the priests and to every one among the Levites who was enrolled.

²⁰ Thus Hezekiah did throughout all Judah; and he did what was good and right and faithful before the LORD his God. ²¹ And every work that he undertook in the service of the house of God and in accordance with the law and the commandments, seeking his God, he did with all his heart, and prospered.

The problem of the proper support for the priestly and Levitical families now began to concern Hezekiah. We can be certain that this was a serious matter in the Chronicler's day as well. The response was beyond anything that Hezekiah or the priests expected. When the offerings surpassed the available storage space, the priests provided rooms for them. Then all the priestly and Levitical families were organized to give the proper distribution to the bounty.

To minister in the gates of the camp of the Lord. This was an expression brought over from the old days of the tabernacle. Yet for many generations the priests and Levites had been living in permanent housing. Especially in religious circles words persist that have been removed from their original setting.

The contribution of the king. Hezekiah led the way, providing the animals for the stated sacrifices.

The people of Israel gave in abundance. Included in the list are two items not mentioned in the tithing laws, *honey* and *dedicated things.* These were given beyond the tithe. In fact, it seemed to surprise the priests that so many people tithed, for it had not been a regular practice.

We have eaten and had enough and have plenty left. These are not only the words of the priests but also the Chronicler's word to his generation. If the people would be faithful in their tithes and offerings, the clergy would never have to make special demands or suffer hardship (cf. 1 Cor. 16:2).

Except those enrolled by genealogy, males from three years old and upwards. These were those on duty at the Temple. They were excepted because they were supported by the regular gifts brought each day and did not need to draw from the reserves. This statement implies that the boys began to do some sort of service from the age of three (cf. 1 Sam. 1:21-28). Although child labor laws have become necessary, we are likely to underestimate the contribution that children can make to society in their own way.

And every work . . . seeking his God. Hezekiah sought God in what he was doing. He expected to find God as he worked in his name (cf. Matt. 25:40).

(5) *The Sennacherib Invasion* (32:1-23)

¹ After these things and these acts of faithfulness Sennacherib king of Assyria came and invaded Judah and encamped against the fortified cities, thinking to win them for himself. ² And when Hezekiah saw that Sennacherib had come and intended to fight against Jerusalem, ³ he planned with his officers and his mighty men to stop the water of the springs that were outside the city; and they helped him. ⁴ A great many people were gathered, and they stopped all the springs and the brook that flowed through the land, saying, "Why should the kings of Assyria come and find much water?" ⁵ He set to work resolutely and built up all the wall that was broken down, and raised towers upon it, and outside it he built another wall; and he strengthened the Millo in the city of David. He also made weapons and shields in abundance. ⁶ And he set combat commanders over the people, and gathered them together to him in the square at the gate of the city and spoke encouragingly to them, saying, ⁷ "Be strong and of good courage. Do not be afraid or dismayed before the king of Assyria and all the horde that is with him; for there is one greater with us than with him. ⁸ With him is an arm of flesh; but with us is the LORD our God, to help us and to fight our battles." And the people took confidence from the words of Hezekiah king of Judah.
⁹ After this Sennacherib king of Assyria, who was besieging Lachish with all his forces, sent his servants to Jerusalem to Hezekiah king of Judah and to all the people of Judah that were in Jerusalem, saying, ¹⁰ "Thus says Sennacherib king of Assyria, 'On what are you relying, that you stand siege in Jerusalem? ¹¹ Is not Hezekiah misleading you, that he may give you over to die by famine and by thirst, when he tells you, "The LORD our God will deliver us from the hand of the king of Assyria"? ¹² Has not this same Hezekiah taken away his high places and his altars and commanded Judah and Jerusalem, "Before one altar you shall worship, and upon it you shall burn your sacrifices"? ¹³ Do you not know what I and my fathers have done to all the peoples of other lands? Were the gods of the nations of those lands at all able to deliver their lands out of my hand? ¹⁴ Who among all the gods of those nations which my fathers utterly destroyed was able to deliver his people from my hand, that your God should be

able to deliver you from my hand? 15 Now therefore do not let Hezekiah deceive you or mislead you in this fashion, and do not believe him, for no god of any nation or kingdom has been able to deliver his people from my hand or from the hand of my fathers. How much less will your God deliver you out of my hand!' "

16 And his servants said still more against the Lord God and against his servant Hezekiah. 17 And he wrote letters to cast contempt on the Lord God of Israel and to speak against him, saying, "Like the gods of the nations of the lands who have not delivered their people from my hands, so the God of Hezekiah will not deliver his people from my hand." 18 And they shouted it with a loud voice in the language of Judah to the people of Jerusalem who were upon the wall, to frighten and terrify them, in order that they might take the city. 19 And they spoke of the God of Jerusalem as they spoke of the gods of the peoples of the earth, which are the work of men's hands.

20 Then Hezekiah the king and Isaiah the prophet, the son of Amoz, prayed because of this and cried to heaven. 21 And the Lord sent an angel, who cut off all the mighty warriors and commanders and officers in the camp of the king of Assyria. So he returned with shame of face to his own land. And when he came into the house of his god, some of his own sons struck him down there with the sword. 22 So the Lord saved Hezekiah and the inhabitants of Jerusalem from the hand of Sennacherib king of Assyria and from the hand of all his enemies; and he gave them rest on every side. 23 And many brought gifts to the Lord to Jerusalem and precious things to Hezekiah king of Judah, so that he was exalted in the sight of all nations from that time onward.

The Chronicler is following the account recorded in 2 Kings 18:13—19:37, but he makes additions and reinterpretations in places. On the whole he gives far less attention to this episode than the book of Kings. In fact, it appears to present real problems to his theology. When Hezekiah was faithful to God, he prospered (31:20-21). Then why was Sennacherib permitted to come against him?

After these things and these acts of faithfulness Sennacherib . . . invaded Judah. Here the Chronicler honestly puts his troubled faith into words. Perhaps it was a test of Hezekiah's faith. He responded nobly to the crisis. Only the Chronicler mentions Hezekiah's attempts to thwart the Assyrians by stopping up the springs near the city. He says nothing of Hezekiah's vacillation recorded in 2 Kings.

With us is the Lord our God. This is reminiscent of Isaiah 7:14. The Hebrew reads *Immanu* (with us)—*Yahweh* (the Lord)—*Elohenu* (our God). The first and last words are a lengthened form of "Immanuel." Yahweh has been inserted between the two component parts of the name. This may possibly mean that a later generation associated the Immanuel prophecies with Hezekiah.

Verses 9-18 follow Kings except that the Chronicler omits the offensive allusion of Rabshakeh to the people's eating their own dung and drinking their own urine (2 Kings 18:27) and his ridicule of Hezekiah's army.

And they spoke of the God of Jerusalem as they spoke of the gods of the peoples of the earth. The Chronicler was amazed at their blasphemous references to the one God of all men.

He gave them rest. Thus Hezekiah passed the test of his faith and received the reward that should have been his. (Cf. Psalm 23:2 where the same word for rest occurs.) It is noteworthy that the Chronicler does not record the total of 185,000 dead among Sennacherib's host (2 Kings 19:35). It was possibly not in his text. Or perhaps he was being conservative.

(6) Summary of His Reign (32:24–33)

24 In those days Hezekiah became sick and was at the point of death, and he prayed to the Lord; and he answered him and gave him a sign. 25 But Hezekiah did not make return according to the benefit done to him, for his heart was proud. Therefore wrath came upon him and Judah and Jerusalem. 26 But Hezekiah humbled himself for the pride of his heart, both he and the inhabitants of Jerusalem, so that the wrath of the Lord did not come upon them in the days of Hezekiah.

27 And Hezekiah had very great riches and honor; and he made for himself treasuries for silver, for gold, for precious stones, for spices, for shields, and for all kinds of costly vessels; 28 storehouses also for the yield of grain, wine, and oil; and stalls for all kinds of cattle, and sheepfolds. 29 He likewise provided cities for himself, and flocks and herds in abundance;

for God had given him very great possessions. ³⁰ This same Hezekiah closed the upper outlet of the waters of Gihon and directed them down to the west side of the city of David. And Hezekiah prospered in all his works. ³¹ And so in the matter of the envoys of the princes of Babylon, who had been sent to him to inquire about the sign that had been done in the land, God left him to himself, in order to try him and to know all that was in his heart.

³² Now the rest of the acts of Hezekiah, and his good deeds, behold, they are written in the vision of Isaiah the prophet the son of Amoz, in the Book of the Kings of Judah and Israel. ³³ And Hezekiah slept with his fathers, and they buried him in the ascent of the tombs of the sons of David; and all Judah and the inhabitants of Jerusalem did him honor at his death. And Manasseh his son reigned in his stead.

Like the great kings before him, Hezekiah, who had been loyal to God in his youth, yielded to pride when he became old. The temptations peculiar to advanced years were more deceptive than those of youth. The Chronicler seems to assume that his readers knew the details about the visit of the embassy of Merodachbaladan (2 Kings 20:12 ff.), but he infers that Hezekiah's behavior at that time was evidence of the pride of his heart. Although Kings says that these ambassadors came to inquire concerning Hezekiah's health, the Chronicler suggests that they were curious about the miracle of the sundial of Ahaz. Both factors were involved of course, but also a third. The king of Babylon was using the occasion to encourage rebellion against Assyria.

God left him to himself. In Genesis 22:1 ff. and Job 1—2 we have instances where man meets the test of God by his own strength of character. It is the teaching of the New Testament that with the presence of God in the heart, Christians do not have to face such tests alone (1 Cor. 10:13).

The vision of Isaiah . . . in the Book of Kings. These appear to be prophecies attributed to Isaiah and unknown to us. One cannot help but mourn the loss to posterity of such passages.

VII. The Final Years (33:1—36:21)

1. The Manasseh Debacle (33:1-25)

Manasseh was besieged by problems similar to those that confronted Ahaz, and reacted in a similar way. Assyria was dominant on the world scene, and Manasseh felt that he must be cooperative. This involved religious as well as political concessions. Evidently he was a willing victim, and he found a sympathetic following in his nation. Apparently Hezekiah's iconoclastic policies had not been too popular in some quarters, for worship in the high places had enjoyed a long tradition. In addition the new cultic innovations in Jerusalem attracted the avant-garde elements in the capital. Many in the prophetic party took a dim view of this, however. They were convinced that unswerving loyalty to God witnessed to by the old traditions of Israel would guarantee divine favor. Manasseh did not give this position a chance to prove itself, so its practical wisdom remained a debatable issue. Certainly Josiah's reforms did not assure stability, but the prophetic group insisted that by that time it was too late.

(1) His Evil Influence (33:1-9)

¹ Manasseh was twelve years old when he began to reign, and he reigned fifty-five years in Jerusalem. ² He did what was evil in the sight of the Lord, according to the abominable practices of the nations whom the Lord drove out before the people of Israel. ³ For he rebuilt the high places which his father Hezekiah had broken down, and erected altars to the Baals, and made Asherahs, and worshiped all the host of heaven, and served them. ⁴ And he built altars in the house of the Lord, of which the Lord had said, "In Jerusalem shall my name be for ever." ⁵ And he built altars for all the host of heaven in the two courts of the house of the Lord. ⁶ And he burned his sons as an offering in the valley of the son of Hinnom, and practiced soothsaying and augury and sorcery, and dealt with mediums and with wizards. He did much evil in the sight of the Lord, provoking him to anger. ⁷ And the image of the idol which he had made he set in the house of God, of which God said to David and to Solomon his son, "In this house, and in Jerusalem, which I have chosen out of all the

tribes of Israel, I will put my name for ever; ⁸ and I will no more remove the foot of Israel from the land which I appointed for your fathers, if only they will be careful to do all that I have commanded them, all the law, the statutes, and the ordinances given through Moses." ⁹ Manasseh seduced Judah and the inhabitants of Jerusalem, so that they did more evil than the nations whom the LORD destroyed before the people of Israel.

The Chronicler here stays close to the text that agrees with 2 Kings 21:1–10. The only significant variations are the absence of the comparison with Ahab (the historian not caring to mention him again) and the lack of a notation about the mother of Manasseh. Until now the Chronicler has failed to mention the queen mother only in the cases of Joram and Ahaz whom he rated very poorly. After Manasseh he fails to mention the mother of any other kings, even omitting the mother of Josiah. Evidently he did not think it a compliment to have mothered these last kings of Judah, although it is strange that Josiah's mother is not memorialized. Perhaps either he was unhappy with that king's rejection of prophecy (35:22) or he saw that Josiah's reform was more political than religious.

(2) *His Repentance* (33:10–17)

¹⁰ The LORD spoke to Manasseh and to his people, but they gave no heed. ¹¹ Therefore the LORD brought upon them the commanders of the army of the king of Assyria, who took Manasseh with hooks and bound him with fetters of bronze and brought him to Babylon. ¹² And when he was in distress he entreated the favor of the LORD his God and humbled himself greatly before the God of his fathers. ¹³ He prayed to him, and God received his entreaty and heard his supplication and brought him again to Jerusalem into his kingdom. Then Manasseh knew that the LORD was God.

¹⁴ Afterwards he built an outer wall for the city of David west of Gihon, in the valley, and for the entrance into the Fish Gate, and carried it round Ophel, and raised it to a very great height; he also put commanders of the army in all the fortified cities in Judah. ¹⁵ And he took away the foreign gods and the idol from the house of the LORD, and all the altars that he had built on the mountain of the house of the LORD and in Jerusalem, and he threw them outside of the city. ¹⁶ He also restored the altar of the LORD and offered upon it sacrifices of peace offerings and of thanksgiving; and he commanded Judah to serve the LORD the God of Israel. ¹⁷ Nevertheless the people still sacrificed at the high places, but only to the LORD their God.

Questions have been raised about the authenticity of this passage. It is quite probable that Manasseh was summoned before the king of Assyria, which only the Chronicler mentions, but that he reformed afterward is very dubious. The book of Kings is silent about this, and Jeremiah has unqualified condemnation for the consequences of his reign (Jer. 15:4). Some scholars suggest that the Chronicler has invented the story because he was convinced that no king could have ruled as long as wicked Manasseh unless he repented in later life. However, it still is possible that he personally reformed but was unable to change the tide that he had unleashed.

(3) *Consequences of His Reign* (33:18–25)

¹⁸ Now the rest of the acts of Manasseh, and his prayer to his God, and the words of the seers who spoke to him in the name of the LORD the God of Israel, behold, they are in the Chronicles of the Kings of Israel. ¹⁹ And his prayer, and how God received his entreaty, and all his sin and his faithlessness, and the sites on which he built high places and set up the Asherim and the images, before he humbled himself, behold, they are written in the Chronicles of the Seers. ²⁰ So Manasseh slept with his fathers, and they buried him in his house; and Amon his son reigned in his stead.

²¹ Amon was twenty-two years old when he began to reign, and he reigned two years in Jerusalem. ²² He did what was evil in the sight of the LORD, as Manasseh his father had done. Amon sacrificed to all the images that Manasseh his father had made, and served them. ²³ And he did not humble himself before the LORD, as Manasseh his father had humbled himself, but this Amon incurred guilt more and more. ²⁴ And his servants conspired against him and killed him in his house. ²⁵ But the people of the land slew all those who had conspired against King Amon; and the people of the land made Josiah his son king in his stead.

Whether Manasseh repented or not, the evil that he did lived on after him. His son Amon followed his pattern of apostasy and perpetuated it. This led to his assassination and to the execution of his assassins in a last minute move to save the honor of the crown.

And his prayer to his God. The mention of this literature led to the later creation of the apocryphal *Prayer of Manasseh* which attempted to recreate his mood at that time.

Written in the Chronicles of the Seers (lit., in the Chronicles of Hozai). This could be a proper name, but we know nothing of such a prophet. It is from this source that the Chronicler has secured his material about Manasseh's repentance. This reference militates against his free creation of the account. The literary nature of that source, however, is not known.

2. The Reform of Josiah (34:1—35:27)

The Chronicler adheres to the story as told in 2 Kings 22:1—23:30, for the book of Kings in these passages presented the sort of cultic material that the Chronicler was fond of preserving. His principal additions are an account of the reform before the book of the law was discovered (whereas Kings stresses the results of the find), a characteristic emphasis upon the work of priests and Levites in the activities, and a more detailed discussion of the death of Josiah.

(1) Destruction of Idolatry (34:1–7)

¹ Josiah was eight years old when he began to reign, and he reigned thirty-one years in Jerusalem. ² He did what was right in the eyes of the Lord, and walked in the ways of David his father; and he did not turn aside to the right or to the left. ³ For in the eighth year of his reign, while he was yet a boy, he began to seek the God of David his father; and in the twelfth year he began to purge Judah and Jerusalem of the high places, the Asherim, and the graven and the molten images. ⁴ And they broke down the altars of the Baals in his presence; and he hewed down the incense altars which stood above them; and he broke in pieces the Asherim and the graven and the molten images, and he made dust of them and strewed it over the graves of those who had sacrificed to them. ⁵ He also burned the bones of the priests on their altars, and purged Judah and Jerusalem. ⁶ And in the cities of Manasseh, Ephraim, and Simeon, and as far as Naphtali, in their ruins round about, ⁷ he broke down the altars, and beat the Asherim and the images into powder, and hewed down all the incense altars throughout all the land of Israel. Then he returned to Jerusalem.

This passage is seriously questioned by many interpreters for it has no parallel elsewhere. It may be automatically following a pattern recorded in the account of the reigns of Asa (15:8–15) and Hezekiah (ch. 29). However, it would be natural that there would be early influences upon Josiah to reverse the policies of Manasseh and Amon, and it is a known fact that the Assyrian control over Palestine was declining. Both Myers and Elmslie are convinced of the authenticity of this early movement. After the discovery of the book of the law, the reform became more complete. It is quite reasonable that some years elapsed from the time that the reform began and a "Unity Passover" could be observed, for there must have been opposition to the wholesale destruction of tradition-honored sites of worship.

Thus it seems clear in the work of the Chronicler that the discovery of the book of Deuteronomy did not inspire the reform, but rather that the book was found during the reformation. The ideals of the law were already present in Israel and were confirmed by that discovery.

(2) Renovation of the Temple (34:8–13)

⁸ Now in the eighteenth year of his reign, when he had purged the land and the house, he sent Shaphan the son of Azaliah, and Maaseiah the governor of the city, and Joah the son of Joahaz, the recorder, to repair the house of the Lord his God. ⁹ They came to Hilkiah the high priest and delivered the money that had been brought into the house of God, which the Levites, the keepers of the threshold, had collected from Manasseh and Ephraim and from all the remnant of Israel and from all Judah and Benjamin and from the inhabitants of Jerusalem. ¹⁰ They delivered it to the workmen who had the oversight of the house of the Lord; and the workmen who were working in the house of the Lord gave it for repairing and restoring the house. ¹¹ They gave it to the carpenters and the builders to buy quarried

stone, and timber for binders and beams for the buildings which the kings of Judah had let go to ruin. 12 And the men did the work faithfully. Over them were set Jahath and Obadiah the Levites, of the sons of Merari, and Zechariah and Meshullam, of the sons of the Kohathites, to have oversight. The Levites, all who were skilful with instruments of music, 13 were over the burden bearers and directed all who did work in every kind of service; and some of the Levites were scribes, and officials, and gatekeepers.

The distinctive contribution of the Chronicler in this section is his mention that it was the Levites who collected the money for the renovation; and although they were primarily musicians, they directed all the details of the repair work. When Herod rebuilt the Temple, this idea of assigning everything connected with the building to the clergy was carried even further. The priests were trained to do the carpentry and masonry (cf. Josephus, *Antiq.* XV.11,2).

(3) *Discovery of the Law* (34:14–33)

14 While they were bringing out the money that had been brought into the house of the Lord, Hilkiah the priest found the book of the law of the Lord given through Moses. 15 Then Hilkiah said to Shaphan the secretary, "I have found the book of the law in the house of the Lord"; and Hilkiah gave the book to Shaphan. 16 Shaphan brought the book to the king, and further reported to the king, "All that was committed to your servants they are doing. 17 They have emptied out the money that was found in the house of the Lord and have delivered it into the hand of the overseers and the workmen." 18 Then Shaphan the secretary told the king, "Hilkiah the priest has given me a book." And Shaphan read it before the king.
19 When the king heard the words of the law he rent his clothes. 20 And the king commanded Hilkiah, Ahikam the son of Shaphan, Abdon the son of Micah, Shaphan the secretary, and Asaiah the king's servant, saying, 21 "Go, inquire of the Lord for me and for those who are left in Israel and in Judah, concerning the words of the book that has been found; for great is the wrath of the Lord that is poured out on us, because our fathers have not kept the word of the Lord, to do according to all that is written in this book."
22 So Hilkiah and those whom the king had sent went to Huldah the prophetess, the wife of Shallum the son of Tokhath son of Hasrah, keeper of the wardrobe (now she dwelt in Jerusalem in the Second Quarter) and spoke to her to that effect. 23 And she said to them, "Thus says the Lord, the God of Israel: 'Tell the man who sent you to me, 24 Thus says the Lord, Behold, I will bring evil upon this place and upon its inhabitants, all the curses that are written in the book which was read before the king of Judah. 25 Because they have forsaken me and have burned incense to other gods, that they might provoke me to anger with all the works of their hands, therefore my wrath will be poured out upon this place and will not be quenched. 26 But to the king of Judah, who sent you to inquire of the Lord, thus shall you say to him, Thus says the Lord, the God of Israel: Regarding the words which you have heard, 27 because your heart was penitent and you humbled yourself before God when you heard his words against this place and its inhabitants, and you have humbled yourself before me, and have rent your clothes and wept before me, I also have heard you, says the Lord. 28 Behold, I will gather you to your fathers, and you shall be gathered to your grave in peace, and your eyes shall not see all the evil which I will bring upon this place and its inhabitants.'" And they brought back word to the king.
29 Then the king sent and gathered together all the elders of Judah and Jerusalem. 30 And the king went up to the house of the Lord, with all the men of Judah and the inhabitants of Jerusalem and the priests and the Levites, all the people both great and small; and he read in their hearing all the words of the book of the covenant which had been found in the house of the Lord. 31 And the king stood in his place and made a covenant before the Lord, to walk after the Lord and to keep his commandments and his testimonies and his statutes, with all his heart and all his soul, to perform the words of the covenant that were written in this book. 32 Then he made all who were present in Jerusalem and in Benjamin stand to it. And the inhabitants of Jerusalem did according to the covenant of God, the God of their fathers. 33 And Josiah took away all the abominations from all the territory that belonged to the people of Israel, and made all who were in Israel serve the Lord their God. All his days they did not turn away from following the Lord the God of their fathers.

The Chronicler parallels 2 Kings 22:8–20 exactly here, even in the Huldah prophecy in v. 28, *you shall be gathered to your grave in peace,* which was hardly fulfilled literally by the violent death of Josiah. The later historian could easily have deleted this troublesome statement from his story. Apparently he felt it was essentially fulfilled, for Josiah did not live to see the total disaster that fell upon Judah.

The priests and the Levites. This is a characteristic emendation of the Chronicler. Second Kings 23:2 reads "the priests and the prophets." For the later writer, the cultic prophets were also Levites. It is possible that the Levitical midrash used by the Chronicler read this way.

(4) The Great Passover (35:1–19)

¹ Josiah kept a passover to the LORD in Jerusalem; and they killed the passover lamb on the fourteenth day of the first month. ² He appointed the priests to their offices and encouraged them in the service of the house of the LORD. ³ And he said to the Levites who taught all Israel and who were holy to the LORD, "Put the holy ark in the house which Solomon the son of David, king of Israel, built; you need no longer carry it upon your shoulders. Now serve the LORD your God and his people Israel. ⁴ Prepare yourselves according to your fathers' houses by your divisions, following the directions of David king of Israel and the directions of Solomon his son. ⁵ And stand in the holy place according to the groupings of the fathers' houses of your brethren the lay people, and let there be for each a part of a father's house of the Levites. ⁶ And kill the passover lamb, and sanctify yourselves, and prepare for your brethren, to do according to the word of the LORD by Moses."

⁷ Then Josiah contributed to the lay people, as passover offerings for all that were present, lambs and kids from the flock to the number of thirty thousand, and three thousand bulls; these were from the king's possessions. ⁸ And his princes contributed willingly to the people, to the priests, and to the Levites. Hilkiah, Zechariah, and Jehiel, the chief officers of the house of God, gave to the priests for the passover offerings two thousand six hundred lambs and kids and three hundred bulls. ⁹ Conaniah also, and Shemaiah and Nethanel his brothers, and Hashabiah and Jeiel and Jozabad, the chiefs of the Levites, gave to the Levites for the passover offerings five thousand lambs and kids and five hundred bulls.

¹⁰ When the service had been prepared for, the priests stood in their place, and the Levites in their divisions according to the king's command. ¹¹ And they killed the passover lamb, and the priests sprinkled the blood which they received from them while the Levites flayed the victims. ¹² And they set aside the burnt offerings that they might distribute them according to the groupings of the fathers' houses of the lay people, to offer to the LORD, as it is written in the book of Moses. And so they did with the bulls. ¹³ And they roasted the passover lamb with fire according to the ordinance; and they boiled the holy offerings in pots, in caldrons, and in pans, and carried them quickly to all the lay people. ¹⁴ And afterward they prepared for themselves and for the priests, because the priests the sons of Aaron were busied in offering the burnt offerings and the fat parts until night; so the Levites prepared for themselves and for the priests the sons of Aaron. ¹⁵ The singers, the sons of Asaph, were in their place according to the command of David, and Asaph, and Heman, and Jeduthun the king's seer; and the gatekeepers were at each gate; they did not need to depart from their service, for their brethren the Levites prepared for them.

¹⁶ So all the service of the LORD was prepared that day, to keep the passover and to offer burnt offerings on the altar of the LORD, according to the command of King Josiah. ¹⁷ And the people of Israel who were present kept the passover at that time, and the feast of unleavened bread seven days. ¹⁸ No passover like it had been kept in Israel since the days of Samuel the prophet; none of the kings of Israel had kept such a passover as was kept by Josiah, and the priests and the Levites, and all Judah and Israel who were present, and the inhabitants of Jerusalem. ¹⁹ In the eighteenth year of the reign of Josiah this passover was kept.

Second Kings 23:21–23 mentions the "Unity Passover" of Josiah, but the Chronicler describes it in great detail. This time, in contrast to that of Hezekiah, it was observed during the correct month. His description of the feast reveals that measures taken as an exceptional procedure at that time had now become normative. The Passover lambs were to be slain by the Levites and not by the laymen, as had been the custom before. However, by New Testament times the laymen had recovered this role again.

Encouraged them in the service. The priests needed the urging of the king to perform their duty. They did not take the initiative. His zeal initiated the observance.

Put the holy ark in the house. Where had it been? Some suppose that Manasseh had removed it, or Josiah while he was making repairs. The statement recalls David's words before his death, "and so the Levites no longer need to carry the tabernacle or any of the things for its service" (1 Chron. 23:26). Since Israel continued to carry the ark in procession during covenant renewal ceremonies, these references may possibly indicate not only a return to the Davidic ideal of the ark permanently at rest but a renunciation of the old covenant renewal ceremonies.

The chief officers of the house of God. Here we have three of them (v. 8), whereas it was customary to have only one chief priest (cf. 1 Chron. 9:11).

And they set aside the burnt offerings. Only the Chronicler associates the burnt offerings with the Passover observance.

Since the days of Samuel the prophet. Second Kings 23:22 says "since the days of the judges who judged Israel." The Chronicler wanted to make it clear that Samuel was to be included among those judges. Joshua 5:10 mentions an observance of the Passover in the earlier period.

(5) Josiah's Fatal Rebellion (35:20-27)

20 After all this, when Josiah had prepared the temple, Neco king of Egypt went up to fight at Carchemish on the Euphrates and Josiah went out against him. 21 But he sent envoys to him, saying, "What have we to do with each other, king of Judah? I am not coming against you this day, but against the house with which I am at war; and God has commanded me to make haste. Cease opposing God, who is with me, lest he destroy you." 22 Nevertheless Josiah would not turn away from him, but disguised himself in order to fight with him. He did not listen to the words of Neco from the mouth of God, but joined battle in the plain of Megiddo. 23 And the archers shot King Josiah; and the king said to his servants, "Take me away, for I am badly wounded." 24 So his servants took him out of the chariot and carried him in his second chariot and brought him to Jerusalem. And he died, and was buried in the tombs of his fathers. All Judah and Jerusalem mourned for Josiah. 25 Jeremiah also uttered a lament for Josiah; and all the singing men and singing women have spoken of Josiah in their laments to this day. They made these an ordinance in Israel; behold, they are written in the Laments. 26 Now the rest of the acts of Josiah, and his good deeds according to what is written in the law of the LORD, 27 and his acts, first and last, behold, they are written in the Book of the Kings of Israel and Judah.

This is a much fuller description of the events leading to the death of Josiah. Pharaoh Neco goes to fight *at Carchemish* rather than "to the king of Assyria" (2 Kings 23:29), a very ambiguous phrase that at one time was thought to mean that Neco fought "against" the king of Assyria (KJV). It is now known that Neco was allied with Assyria, and Josiah with Babylon. The Chronicler or his source must have known the nature of the problem.

The words of Neco from the mouth of God. This is an amazing observation. The Chronicler believed that God was speaking to Josiah through the heathen king, and that if the Jewish monarch had been sensitive to the voice of God he would have taken the warning. This is his explanation of why the reforming king was cut down so prematurely. He rejected a divine prophecy. The fact that it came from an unexpected source made no difference. He warns his readers that they should be prepared for prophetic voices from unorthodox sources, not just from the cultic rituals of the Temple. His God was greater than the Temple, and his rule universal.

But disguised himself. Note the similarity to the death of Ahab (2 Chron. 18:29 ff.).

Jeremiah also uttered a lament. Jeremiah is strangely missing from the book of Kings. The Chronicler mentions him twice. (cf. 36:21 ff.).

Written in the Laments. These are not the same as our book of Lamentations, which relates to the fall of Jerusalem and not to the death of Josiah.

3. The Last Hour (36:1-21)

(1) Inept Kings (36:1-14)

1 The people of the land took Jehoahaz the son of Josiah and made him king in his father's

stead in Jerusalem. ² Jehoahaz was twenty-three years old when he began to reign; and he reigned three months in Jerusalem. ³ Then the king of Egypt deposed him in Jerusalem and laid upon the land a tribute of a hundred talents of silver and a talent of gold. ⁴ And the king of Egypt made Eliakim his brother king over Judah and Jerusalem, and changed his name to Jehoiakim; but Neco took Jehoahaz his brother and carried him to Egypt.

⁵ Jehoiakim was twenty-five years old when he began to reign, and he reigned eleven years in Jerusalem. He did what was evil in the sight of the LORD his God. ⁶ Against him came up Nebuchadnezzar king of Babylon, and bound him in fetters to take him to Babylon. ⁷ Nebuchadnezzar also carried part of the vessels of the house of the LORD to Babylon and put them in his palace in Babylon. ⁸ Now the rest of the acts of Jehoiakim, and the abominations which he did, and what was found against him, behold, they are written in the Book of the Kings of Israel and Judah; and Jehoiachin his son reigned in his stead.

⁹ Jehoiachin was eight years old when he began to reign, and he reigned three months and ten days in Jerusalem. He did what was evil in the sight of the LORD. ¹⁰ In the spring of the year King Nebuchadnezzar sent and brought him to Babylon, with the precious vessels of the house of the LORD, and made his brother Zedekiah king over Judah and Jerusalem.

¹¹ Zedekiah was twenty-one years old when he began to reign, and he reigned eleven years in Jerusalem. ¹² He did what was evil in the sight of the LORD his God. He did not humble himself before Jeremiah the prophet, who spoke from the mouth of the LORD. ¹³ He also rebelled against King Nebuchadnezzar, who had made him swear by God; he stiffened his neck and hardened his heart against turning to the LORD, the God of Israel. ¹⁴ All the leading priests and the people likewise were exceedingly unfaithful, following all the abominations of the nations; and they polluted the house of the LORD which he had hallowed in Jerusalem.

Quickly the Chronicler disposed of the dying hours of the kingdom. He considerably abbreviated the account in 2 Kings 23:31—25:21. However he did take time to state that Jehoiakim was taken in fetters to Babylon after Nebuchadnezzar had come against him. Daniel 1:1 is another allusion to this episode, which cannot be identified with the 597 B.C. invasion, since Jehoiakim was already dead at that time. It is quite possible that Nebuchadnezzar visited Judah after the battle of Carchemish, before his return to Babylon. Or this may simply refer to Nebuchadnezzar's summoning Jehoiakim and other leaders to him while he was still at Carchemish.

Jehoiachin was eight years old. Second Kings 24:8 and the Septuagint probably preserved the correct text in saying "eighteen." By 592 B.C. Jehoiachin seems to have had five sons; he became king in 597 (cf. Myers, II, 218).

(2) *The Wrath of God (36:15-21)*

¹⁵ The LORD, the God of their fathers, sent persistently to them by his messengers, because he had compassion on his people and on his dwelling place; ¹⁶ but they kept mocking the messengers of God, despising his words, and scoffing at his prophets, till the wrath of the LORD rose against his people, till there was no remedy.

¹⁷ Therefore he brought up against them the king of the Chaldeans, who slew their young men with the sword in the house of their sanctuary, and had no compassion on young man or virgin, old man or aged; he gave them all into his hand. ¹⁸ And all the vessels of the house of God, great and small, and the treasures of the house of the LORD, and the treasures of the king and of his princes, all these he brought to Babylon. ¹⁹ And they burned the house of God, and broke down the wall of Jerusalem, and burned all its palaces with fire, and destroyed all its precious vessels. ²⁰ He took into exile in Babylon those who had escaped from the sword, and they became servants to him and to his sons until the establishment of the kingdom of Persia, ²¹ to fulfil the word of the LORD by the mouth of Jeremiah, until the land had enjoyed its sabbaths. All the days that it lay desolate it kept sabbath, to fulfil seventy years.

The Chronicler contends that God did all he could to save Israel. He only abandoned his people when nothing else could be done. Their fatal sin was their failure to heed the prophetic warnings. Their original transgression could have been pardoned if they had repented.

To fulfil the word of the Lord by the mouth of Jeremiah (cf. Jer. 25:12; 587–516 B.C. = 70 years).

It kept sabbath, to fulfil seventy years. Some believe this refers to 70 × 7 years or the approximately 490 years of rebellion in Israel from Solomon to Zedekiah, including 70 sabbatic years. It is more natural to assume that the Chronicler is saying that at last the land kept its long neglected sabbatic rest to fulfill Jeremiah's 70-year prophecy, rather than to fulfill seventy sabbatic years.

Postscript: A New Era Begins (36:22–23)

22 Now in the first year of Cyrus king of Persia, that the word of the LORD by the mouth of Jeremiah might be accomplished, the LORD stirred up the spirit of Cyrus king of Persia so that he made a proclamation throughout all his kingdom and also put it in writing: 23 "Thus says Cyrus king of Persia, 'The LORD, the God of heaven, has given me all the kingdoms of the earth, and he has charged me to build him a house at Jerusalem, which is in Judah. Whoever is among you of all his people, may the LORD his God be with him. Let him go up.'"

It is strange that the decree of Cyrus, which so obviously refers to Isaiah 44:28, should be mentioned as a fulfillment of the prophecy of Jeremiah rather than that of Isaiah. Possibly the Chronicler was aware of the fact that the author of this section of Isaiah was a contemporary of Cyrus rather than Isaiah of the eighth century prophesying 150 years beforehand. Otherwise Jeremiah's 70 years would seem small in comparison.

This passage also occurs as the opening verses of the book of Ezra, which originally was probably an unbroken continuation of the Chronicler's history. When Ezra-Nehemiah were accepted into the Hebrew canon, these books were separated from Chronicles, which was not acknowledged as canonical until later, and placed as the last entry in the canon (cf. The Introduction). When Chronicles was accepted, the opening verses of Ezra were added to it in order not only to have it end in a word of hope but to remind the reader that the story was continued in Ezra-Nehemiah. In our English canon the repetition is quite superfluous, since Chronicles-Ezra-Nehemiah are arranged in their original order.

Ezra-Nehemiah

EMMETT WILLARD HAMRICK

Introduction

I. Authorship and Composition

The books of Ezra and Nehemiah are treated as a unit in this Commentary because they were once a single book known as Ezra. It was not until the time of Origen in the third Christian century that one finds the first mention of Ezra as two books, and it was apparently Jerome around A.D. 400 who first applied the name Nehemiah to the second part of the narrative.

In the Jewish tradition the two books were treated as a single unit throughout the Middle Ages. The Masoretes calculated that the middle of the unit was found at Nehemiah 3:32, and provided only one set of statistics and comments for the entire work (cf. Bowman, pp. 551-52). This tradition that the two books were a single work may have contributed to the fact that part of the Ezra narrative (Neh. 7:73b—9:37) has found its way into the Nehemiah story and to the apparently false conclusion that Ezra and Nehemiah were contemporaries.

In addition to the evidence that the two books were originally one, there is reason to believe that they were once part of the books now known as 1 and 2 Chronicles. The story of the edict of Cyrus, which is interrupted abruptly at the end of 2 Chronicles 36:23, is repeated in part and completed in Ezra 1:1-4. In the apocryphal book of 1 Esdras (which preserves in Greek a very ancient and valuable recension of a portion of the Chronicler's text) the ending of the story found in 2 Chronicles makes a smooth unbroken transition to that found in Ezra 1.

Even without the foregoing evidence, Chronicles, Ezra, and Nehemiah can be seen as primarily the compilation of a single writer in that they share substantially the same style, vocabulary, and major emphases.

The unknown author-compiler of Chronicles-Ezra-Nehemiah is commonly referred to as the Chronicler. It is necessary to use this term throughout the treatment of these books to distinguish the principal author from the writers of the sources which he incorporates and from subsequent editors who made minor changes in his composition.

Most contemporary scholars have accepted the view of Albright ("The Date and Personality of the Chronicler," pp. 104-124), that the Chronicler's work was composed shortly after 400 B.C. This date would fall soon after the mission of Ezra, which appears to be the latest major event recorded by the Chronicler. It would also accord with Nehemiah 12:23, which notes that the Chronicler's list of Levites terminated with the high priesthood of Johanan (Jehohanan). The latter, who was presumably a near contemporary of the Chronicler, occupied that office in 408 B.C. (according to the Elephantine Papyri, a collection of Jewish documents from fifth century B.C. Egypt). Recent research has shown that the genealogy of Jeconiah (Jehoiachin) in 1 Chronicles 3:17-24 and the witness of the Jewish historian Josephus (*Antiq.* XI.8.4) do not necessitate a substantially later date.

II. Sequence of Events

There is a general consensus among scholars that the events related in Ezra-Nehemiah are not now in strict chronological order. There is less agreement as to whether this disorder was the work of the Chronicler himself or of some post-Chronicler redactor. Ancient Jewish writers were not primarily concerned with history for its own sake and felt little compulsion to relate historical data in exact chronological sequence. Nevertheless, the modern reader is concerned about the original order of the events.

1. Ezra 1—6

The first major block of material is found in chapters 1—6 of the book of Ezra. It relates the story of the postexilic restoration of Judah from the edict of Cyrus through the rebuilding and rededication of the Temple.

There are two major problems of chronological sequence in this narrative. The first concerns the relationship between Sheshbazzar and Zerubbabel. The relation between the two men is extremely vague, and the transition between the two is completely lost. The Chronicler had a tradition that Sheshbazzar led the first return from the Exile, reestablished the cult in Jerusalem, and laid the foundations for a new Temple (cf. Ezra 1:5–11; 5:14–16). One may assume that this tradition was accurate and that the work of Sheshbazzar has been telescoped with that of his successor (and nephew?) Zerubbabel. Since Haggai mentions no previous attempt on the part of Zerubbabel to rebuild the Temple, one may presume that his building activity did not begin until the reign of Darius I (522–486 B.C.). Therefore references to Zerubbabel in Ezra 3 and 4 would be premature, and one would assume that he became governor of Judah in the interim between Sheshbazzar's failure to finish the Temple about 536 B.C. and the preaching of Haggai in 520 B.C.

The second major chronological problem in this narrative is created by the correspondence described in Ezra 4:6–23. The Temple was rebuilt during the reign of Darius I, yet in the midst of the narrative a writer has inserted correspondence relating to a much later period. Reference is made in 4:6 to a letter written against the Jews during the reign of Ahasuerus (Xerxes, 486–465 B.C.). And two letters, the second of which is quoted, are dated to the reign of Artaxerxes (almost certainly Artaxerxes I, 465–424 B.C.). Moreover, the correspondence between Rehum and Shimshai and Artaxerxes has to do with the refortification of the city and makes no reference to the Temple.

Ezra 4:6–23 was most likely inserted into the story of the rebuilding of the Temple to illustrate the type of friction which caused the cessation of building for about 16 years between Cyrus and Darius I. The exchange of letters between Rehum and Shimshai and Artaxerxes belongs to the period just before Nehemiah 1 and provides the immediate background for Nehemiah's sorrow and concern.[1]

2. Ezra 7—10; Nehemiah 1—13

There are three major problems of chronological sequence in the remaining portions of Ezra-Nehemiah. They are the chronological order of Ezra and Nehemiah, the sequence of events in the career of Nehemiah, and the sequence of events in the ministry of Ezra.

The present narrative leaves the impression that Ezra came first in the seventh year of a king named Artaxerxes (Ezra 7:7). He led back a group of exiles laden with treasures for the Temple (Ezra 7—8), then assisted in the mixed marriage reforms (Ezra 9—10). At this point, without any transition, Nehemiah is introduced. He arrived in Jerusalem in the twentieth

---

[1] Cf. Alben van Hoonacker, "Néhémie et Esdras. Une Nouvelle Hypothèse sur la Chronologie de la Restauration," *Le Muséon*, 1890, pp. 159–174).

year of a king named Artaxerxes (Neh. 2:1). He succeeded in rebuilding the walls (Neh. 1—6) and began measures for the repopulation of the city (7:1—73a). At this juncture, Ezra is introduced again, and he leads the people to renew their allegiance to God and to his law (Neh. 7:73b—9:37). The narrative which follows (9:38—10:37) presents a list of men who signed a covenant and the vows which they made, but the passage seems unrelated to what immediately precedes or follows. In Nehemiah 11, the story returns to the account of the population reforms which was interrupted in chapter 7. In chapter 12, after a series of miscellaneous lists (vv. 1–26), the account of the rededication of the walls is presented (vv. 27–43). Finally, following the Chronicler's introduction to the passage (12:44—13:3), we have the story of the reforms made by Nehemiah at the time of his second visit.

The final editors of the book obviously believed that Ezra preceded Nehemiah and that the two leaders were contemporary. This view has been increasingly challenged, however, since the careful research of Alben van Hoonacker [2] nearly a century ago. We take the position in this treatment of Ezra-Nehemiah that the two men were not contemporaries, but that Nehemiah came first in the twentieth year of Artaxerxes I (445 B.C.) and was followed by Ezra in the seventh year of Artaxerxes II (398 B.C.). Typical evidence for this view may be summarized briefly:

1. The two men apparently ignore each other and do not actually collaborate in their work. The story of Ezra's revival, although in the book of Nehemiah (7:73b—9:37), interrupts the account of Nehemiah's population reforms and is obviously out of place. Moreover, the single reference to Nehemiah in the Ezra narrative (Neh. 8:9) does not occur in the corresponding passage in 1 Esdras and is almost certainly a late gloss. The reference to Ezra in Nehemiah 12:33, on the other hand, does not identify him as the scribe and is in conflict with the role assigned to him in Nehemiah 12:36. In the latter passage, the statement "and Ezra the scribe went before them" must be a later interpolation because the leadership of the first company of marchers had already been assigned to Hoshaiah (v. 32), and Ezra's presence spoils the symmetry of the two companies. It is most unlikely that the original Ezra story mentioned Nehemiah or vice versa.

2. Eliashib was high priest during the missions of Nehemiah (Neh. 3:1; 13:4–9, 28); but Jehohanan (Jonathan, Johanan) Eliashib's grandson (Neh. 12:10–11,22), appears to have been high priest at the time of Ezra (Ezra 10:6). Moreover, the Elephantine Papyri show that Jehohanan was high priest in 408 B.C., at least a generation after the time of Nehemiah.[3]

3. Nehemiah was a contemporary of Sanballat (Neh. 4:1; 6:1), yet the Elephantine Papyri show that Sanballat's sons were the authority in Samaria at the time of Ezra's contemporary, Jehohanan (*ibid.*).

4. Nehemiah's silence with regard to Ezra in Nehemiah 1—2 is incredible if Ezra's mission had begun 13 years earlier and was still in progress.

5. Nehemiah's action toward mixed marriages involved only a promise that no more would be contracted (Neh. 13:25; cf. 10:30). Ezra's dissolution of the prohibited marriages must have followed the less severe measures taken by Nehemiah.

6. Nehemiah found Jerusalem ruined and almost unpopulated (2:17; 7:4). Ezra found the city alive with activity (Ezra 9:4; 10:1; he is not listed among the wall-builders in Neh. 3).

7. The board of Treasurers established by Nehemiah (13:13) was apparently still functioning, but with new personnel, when Ezra arrived (Ezra 8:33).

Efforts to solve the problem of the relationship between Ezra and Nehemiah by

---

[2] *Op. cit.*, pp. 151–184; 317–351; 389–401.

[3] A. Cowley, *Aramaic Papyri of the Fifth Century B.C.* (Oxford: Clarendon Press, 1923), pp. 108–119.

emending the text of Ezra 7:7–8 to read the "twenty-seventh" or "thirty-seventh" year of Artaxerxes are unsupported by textual evidence and do not solve such basic problems as why Ezra and Nehemiah were so oblivious to the work of one another.

The sequence of events during the career of Nehemiah has given rise to only a few minor problems. From the rededication of the Temple in 515 B.C. (Ezra 6), the Chronicler's story skips chronologically to the beginning of the Nehemiah story (Neh. 1). Ezra 4:6–23 belongs to this silent period and, together with the book of Malachi and perhaps parts of Isaiah 56—66, forms background material for an understanding of Nehemiah's work.

With minor exceptions, the first seven chapters of Nehemiah reflect a logical historical sequence. Chapter 5 does indeed interrupt the story of the rebuilding of the wall; however, the chapter occupies a logical position since it was the rigorous requirements of the wall building that brought long-standing social and economic abuses to a crisis.

The census list (Neh. 7:6–73a) is complicated and of uncertain origin, but it was associated with the population reforms begun in 7:1–5. This story was concluded in Nehemiah 11, and the intervening material interrupts the narrative. Chapters 7:73b—9:37 have already been identified with the Ezra story, but Nehemiah 9:38—10:39 presents a special problem. It is best understood as an anonymous account of the making of a covenant designed to implement the reforms undertaken by Nehemiah in 13:4–31 (cf. Batten, pp. 372–373) and, therefore, belongs to the period of his second administration. The story of the dedication of the wall (12:27–43) surely belongs soon after the completion of the wall but it is not necessary to assume that the population reforms could not have preceded the ceremony. This leaves Nehemiah 13 and 10 (in that order) as the only evidence available concerning Nehemiah's second administration.

The Ezra story is composed of three major episodes: (1) the Artaxerxes Rescript and the journey to Jerusalem (Ezra 7—8), (2) the mixed marriage crisis (Ezra 9—10), and (3) the reading of the law (Neh. 7:73b—9:37). The narrative is not in its original order, because the reading of the law intervened between the arrival in Jerusalem and the marriage reforms. Ezra arrived in Jerusalem in the fifth month of the year 398 B.C. (Ezra 7:7). He read the law and led the people in their religious reforms in the seventh month (Neh. 7:73b). This revival led to renewed concern about mixed marriages (cf. Neh. 9:2), and these reforms were begun in the ninth month (Ezra 10:9).

In summary, the material in Ezra-Nehemiah begins with the edict of Cyrus about 539 B.C. and continues through the rededication of the Temple about 515 B.C. (Ezra 1—6). Then follows an interval of about 70 years illuminated only by the few data from Ezra 4:6–23. The story of Nehemiah begins in 445 B.C. His first term as governor may have lasted 12 years (Neh. 5:14). The final part of his second term is unknown, but it began shortly after 432 B.C. (Neh. 13:6–8). From the reforms of Nehemiah's second term the narrative is silent until the mission of Ezra about 398 B.C. All of the events of his mission are dated within about one year, and the Chronicler offers no further information.

III. The Sources

A comparison of Chronicles with Samuel-Kings shows that the Chronicler often interpreted his sources in the light of his own religious convictions. Nevertheless, the Chronicler was not primarily an inventor of history. He used valuable source documents, many of which can be isolated and identified. Although his purpose was religious and cultic, his account in Ezra-Nehemiah, at least, appears to be substantially historical. Only the more important source documents used in this narrative will be mentioned.

1. The Cyrus Edict and the Aramaic Sources

The Chronicler has preserved two edicts relating to permission for the Jews to return to Jerusalem to rebuild their Temple. The first edict is in Hebrew (Ezra 1:2–4) and the other in the cognate Semitic language of ancient Syria, Aramaic (Ezra 6:3–5). This commentary reflects the contemporary opinion that the two decrees are independent pronouncements and that both decrees can be assumed to be substantially accurate (cf. Bickerman, pp. 249–275).

The Aramaic edict is part of a larger collection of documents written in this language (Ezra 4:8—6:18; 7:12–26), which deals mostly with official communications between Persian kings and their subordinates. The fact that Aramaic is known to have been the usual language of diplomacy in the Persian Empire lends credibility to these narratives. The Chronicler, who had this document at his disposal, incorporated substantial parts of it with little if any refining. The Jewishness of certain passages (e.g., 6:3–5; 7:12–26) need not be attributed to the Chronicler nor to a previous Jewish editor who had compiled the Aramaic source. Persian kings were in consultation with Jewish leaders, and the language of their edicts naturally reflected even the specific cultic details of the Jewish requests.

2. The Nehemiah Memoirs

The least controversial of all the sources used in Ezra-Nehemiah is the Nehemiah document. The Chronicler used large sections of material from a journal, memoir, or memorial inscription written by Nehemiah. The first person passages (Neh. 1:1—2:20; 4:1—7:5; 12:27–43; 13:4–31), while reflecting some occasional touches by the Chronicler, were taken from this document with a minimum of editorial change. Moreover, other parts of the book, especially 11:1–2, may derive from the Nehemiah memoirs even though the first person is not used.

3. The Ezra Memoirs

The most controversial of all the sources attributed to the Chronicler are the Ezra memoirs. There is no consensus on the extent of the memoirs, their reliability as a historical source, or even on their actual existence. The vocabulary and style of the entire Ezra narrative is essentially that of the Chronicler, and not even the first person passages (Ezra 7:27—8:34; 9:1–15) can be identified as verbatim extracts from the work of Ezra. Contemporary scholars generally maintain that the Chronicler did use a memoir or report from Ezra himself and that the Ezra narrative is substantially historical. It must remain uncertain whether the Chronicler thoroughly rewrote the Ezra memoirs in his own style, or whether the style of the two men is simply indistinguishable. There are positive indications, however, that the Chronicler used sources in composing the Ezra story (and was therefore not Ezra himself) and that one of these documents was from the pen of Ezra. Only typical evidence will be suggested.

(1) The Chronicler alternates between the first and third persons. If he had been trying to invent a memoir for Ezra, as Torrey (pp. 238–248) thought, it is unthinkable that he would have begun by composing 7:1–11 in the third person. It is more likely that he simply neglected to maintain uniformity of person as he edited the Ezra memoirs.

(2) The Ezra narrative includes material which is uncomplimentary to the Chronicler's favorites, the Levites. He must have been unusually faithful to a source document to admit that the Levites were reluctant to accompany Ezra to Jerusalem (8:15) or that they were guilty of unlawful marriages (10:23).

(3) Ezra 7:6–10, composed in the third person, is an anticipatory summary of 7:27—8:34, which is written in the first person. Such a duplication of material suggests that the author began the story in his own words and then turned to follow more closely the details of the Ezra memoirs.

4. The Lists

The Chronicler, in Ezra-Nehemiah as in Chronicles, has made abundant use of lists. Since each list is treated in its proper place in the commentary, only a few observations need be made at this time. In the first place, the origin of most of the lists cannot be determined. Since they deal primarily with the cultic community they may have been found in the Temple archives. The best evidence that the Chronicler did not himself originate the lists is to be seen in his frequent confusion about the significance of them. For example, he interprets the long list in Ezra 2:1–70 (Neh. 7:6–73a) as a registry of Jews who returned during the reign of Cyrus. Actually, it appears to be a heterogeneous collection of census data which accumulated over a period of nearly a century (note also the different interpretations of a single source document in Neh. 11:3–24 and 1 Chron. 9:2–34).

It is not possible to generalize about the authenticity of all of the lists in Ezra-Nehemiah. Some of the lists may be essentially accurate and in their original context. This might be true, for example, of the list of those who returned with Ezra (8:1–20), those who were guilty of mixed marriages (10:18–43), those who rebuilt the wall (Neh. 3), those who assisted at the reading of the law (Neh. 8:4–8), those who signed Nehemiah's covenant (Neh. 10:1–27), and those who participated in the dedication of the wall (Neh. 12:27–43). On the other hand, the list of Ezra's ancestors (Ezra 7:1–5) is manifestly defective, and the miscellaneous clerical registers in Nehemiah 12:1–26 are obviously out of context and of unknown significance.

5. Other Sources

Nehemiah 3 deserves further mention because it contains a valuable account of the rebuilding of the walls which is independent of the Nehemiah memoirs (cf. Batten, pp. 206–207). Likewise, Nehemiah 9:38—10:39 appears to preserve a source independent of these memoirs, which tells the story of a covenant designed to guarantee the observance of the reforms of Nehemiah described in 13:4–31.

The prayers present a special problem. Most of the prayers of Nehemiah are terse and clearly authentic. The prayer in 1:5–11a, however, is composed mostly of quotations from Deuteronomy and reflects the style of the Chronicler. The long prayer in Nehemiah 9:6–37 may have been attributed to Ezra (as in the LXX, but not in the MT), but it is actually a psalm which does not fit its context and may have been borrowed from a book of Temple liturgies. The prayer of Ezra in Ezra 9:6–15 is an indispensable part of the total scene and doubtless reflects the content of Ezra's actual supplication on the occasion of the marriage crisis.

IV. Appraisal of the Three Leaders

1. Zerubbabel, the hero of Ezra 1—6, played the leading role in the rebuilding of the Temple during the reign of Darius I. He was a cautious man and might never have risked rearousing the ire of the local nonexilic population, had it not been for the prodding of the prophets Haggai and Zechariah (Ezra 5:1–2; 6:14; cf. Haggai 1—2). Once he and the high priest Jeshua had begun the project, however, there was no reluctance or hesitation, even in the face of the investigation described in 5:3–17. Zechariah praises his work in enthusiastic terms (Zech. 4:1–14).

Zerubbabel was a royal prince and a linear descendant of king Jehoiachin (Jeconiah; cf. 1 Chron. 3:16–20). As such, many believed that he would be the long-awaited Messiah. This hope was encouraged by Haggai (2:20–23) and Zechariah (3:6–10; 4:4–14; 6:9–14). There is no evidence that Zerubbabel planned an insurrection against Persia or that he had royal ambitions. The fervent nationalism which accompanied his work, however, may have alarmed the Persians because Zerubbabel was apparently removed from his position before the completion of the Temple (cf. Ezra 6:14–15).

2. Nehemiah is the brightest star of the restoration period. He came to Jerusalem in 445 B.C., about 70 years after the rededication of the Temple. The collapse of the nationalistic hopes, so evident in Ezra 1—0, Haggai, and Zechariah, had left the community depressed and defeated, with resulting moral, spiritual and cultic neglect (cf. Mal.; Isa. 57:1–21; 58:3–14; 59:1–15). Moreover, Jerusalem was still largely in ruins, because the efforts to rebuild it had been violently frustrated by Rehum and Shimshai (Ezra 4:8–23).

Nehemiah arrived in Judah fully authorized by Artaxerxes I to rebuild the walls of Jerusalem and to serve as governor of the Judean community. He did rebuild and rededicate the walls (1:1—6:16; 12:27–43); he restored and repopulated the city (7:1–5; 11:1–2). Moreover, he vigorously attacked all moral and cultic abuses during both his first (ch. 5) and second administrations (13:4–31). He was dedicated to God and an efficient governor. If anyone deserves to be thought of as the father of Judaism, it is surely Nehemiah.

Yet certain questions must be raised about the man. One wonders, for example, why Nehemiah did not try a more conciliatory approach toward Sanballat and his other local adversaries. He was encroaching upon territory which they considered to be under their jurisdiction, but at no time did he inform them of his credentials from Artaxerxes I. Instead, he categorically condemned them and rejected all overtures for a conference.

Other questions are raised by his prayers. On two different occasions he prayed for God's judgment upon his enemies (Neh. 4:4–5; 13:29). To be sure, this reflects an understandable human response to harassment (cf. Jer. 12:3; 20:12), yet it reflects an imperfect understanding of God's love (cf. Luke 23:34; Acts 7:60).

In most of his other prayers, Nehemiah prayed that God would grant him special remembrance and credit for his work as governor (5:19; 13:14,22,31). Many writers attribute this undue concern about his own personal future to the fact that he was a eunuch (see comment on Neh. 1:11b—2:8; 5:14–19) and had no hope of leaving a family to perpetuate his memory. He obviously wanted his work to be a lasting memorial to his name, and this may have been the motivation for the writing of his memoirs.

3. Any appraisal of Ezra is complicated by the fact that one cannot distinguish clearly between the Ezra memoirs and the Chronicler's application of them. However, since the Chronicler composed his work soon after the mission of Ezra, one may assume that his account of Ezra's work is substantially reliable.

The story of Ezra reveals that he played a role in postexilic Judaism which was of lasting importance, but perhaps relatively minor when compared with the contributions of Nehemiah. He was commissioned by Artaxerxes II to go to Judah about 398 B.C., to lead back a caravan of Jews laden with gifts for the Temple, and to establish Jewish Torah as the legitimate law of the Judean community (Ezra 7—8). Soon after his arrival in Jerusalem he led the people to a new devotion to God's law (Neh. 7:73b—9:37), and shortly thereafter assisted in the dissolving of the mixed marriages (Ezra 9—10), which had previously been condemned by Nehemiah (13:25–28). All of his activities in Judah appear to have required less than one year.

There is no evidence that Ezra wrote or promulgated a new law code or that he deserves to be referred to as the founder of Judaism. These ideas arose in later Jewish circles (cf. the apocalypse known as 4 Ezra, the Mishnah, and the Talmud) and have unfortunately influenced many modern appraisals of Ezra's work.

The work of Nehemiah and Ezra was still seen in proper perspective as late as the second century B.C. In Ben Sirach's passage in praise of the fathers (Ecclesiasticus 44–50) Nehemiah is praised (49:13), but Ezra is ignored (cf. 2 Macc. 1, where

Nehemiah is given great credit without any mention of Ezra).

Later tradition made Ezra the central figure of the restoration instead of Nehemiah, however, and doubtless influenced some unknown scribe to transpose the stories of the two men. It was easy for a later editor to justify such a transposition in view of the fact that the seventh year of Artaxerxes (Ezra 7:7) ought logically to precede the twentieth year of Artaxerxes (Neh. 2:1).

V. *The Religious Emphases*

Historical and literary inquiries into the writings of the Chronicler are worthy undertakings. They sometimes result in unfair appraisals of the author's work, however, because his primary purposes and emphases were religious.

The religious messages and presuppositions found in Ezra-Nehemiah cannot be separated from those of Chronicles, and the reader should familiarize himself with this prior part of the Chronicler's work.[4] Throughout his entire work, the Chronicler was primarily concerned with religious insights which he considered relevant to his own day. He used the history of his people all the way back to Adam to dramatize these messages. Only typical emphases which have particular relevance for Ezra-Nehemiah will be presented.

1. The Chronicler believed that there was one legitimate community of God and that its very survival depended on its purity from pagan contamination. Therefore he agreed that the returned exiles dared not accept the local peoples of Palestine although they worshiped the same God (Ezra 4:1-3). Nehemiah and Ezra could not tolerate mixed marriages because they contaminated the holy people. Registries and genealogies were used to legitimate the holy seed, and anyone who could not prove his ancestry was set apart from the rest of the community (cf. Ezra 2:59-60). Such particularistic ideas do not belong in the Christian church, but for the Chronicler they were matters of survival or destruction.

2. He likewise believed that there was one legitimate cult. Its organization and functions, which were traced back to David (cf. Ezra 3:10; Neh. 12:36), must be authentic and without deviation. Maintenance of a pure cult was essential to the welfare of the community, and even priests who could not establish their sacral genealogies were "defrocked" (Ezra 2:61-63).

3. He believed in immediate and proportionate retribution for all offenses against God. This is the explanation offered for the Babylonian exile (Ezra 5:12) and for all the sufferings which the Jews endured thereafter (cf. Ezra 9:7; Neh. 1:8-9; 9:26-37).

4. The Chronicler was not without a doctrine of grace, however. Ezra admits the guilt of his people and the justice of God's punishment and yet dares to cast the community on the mercy of God without a defense (Ezra 9:10-15). The same theme permeates the prayer-psalm of Nehemiah 9:6-37.

5. The Chronicler stresses the sovereignty of God in history and the role of divine grace in the achieving of his eternal purposes. Israel had often been spared when it deserved to be destroyed (Neh. 9:16-31). The nation was saved from the Exile because God "stirred up the spirit of Cyrus" (Ezra 1:1). It was God who moved Artaxerxes I to send Nehemiah (Neh. 2:8), who prompted Artaxerxes II to commission Ezra (Ezra 7:6), and by whose gracious assistance the restoration was carried through (Ezra 6:22; 8:22-23; Neh. 6:16).

6. For the Chronicler religion was a privilege and a source of endless joy. Even the cultic minutiae were considered a joyful way of making a positive response to

---

[4] See the Introduction to Chronicles in this volume, in *The Interpreter's Bible*, Vol. III, and in *The Anchor Bible*, Vols. XII, XIII. See also W. F. Stinespring, "Eschatology in Chronicles," *Journal of Biblical Literature* Sept., 1961, pp. 209-219 (subsequently abbreviated *JBL*); Robert North, "Theology of the Chronicler," *JBL*, Dec., 1963, pp. 369-381.

God. There was singing, shouting, and thanksgiving on every possible occasion (Ezra 3:10–11; Neh. 8:12,17; 12:43). The people felt an intimate relationship with God and responded to his goodness with music and singing.

7. The Chronicler was torn between a sense of realized eschatology and an eager anticipation of the future. On the one hand, the Temple had been rebuilt, the walls erected, the cult restored, and the community purified from paganism. Yet one senses throughout the entire work that the final fulfillment was yet to come. Zerubbabel had not been the Messiah, and the eschatological David was still a future hope. The people of God were still under the yoke of Persia, and so the writer must include such statements as "We are bondmen" (Ezra 9:9) and "We are in great distress" (Neh. 9:37). He was enthusiastic about what God had accomplished in the Judah of his day (cf. Neh. 12:44—13:3), yet he longed for a more complete fulfillment of God's purposes in the future.

Outline of Ezra

I. First return from the Exile (1:1–11)
  1. The Cyrus edict (1:1–4)
  2. The return (1:5–11)
II. The census list (2:1–70)
  1. Introduction (2:1–2a)
  2. Lay families (2:2b–35)
  3. Temple personnel (2:36–58)
  4. Uncertified families (2:59–63)
  5. Summary totals (2:64–67)
  6. Gifts to the Temple (2:68–69)
  7. The land resettled (2:70)
III. Restoration of the cult (3:1–13)
  1. The rebuilding of the altar (3:1–2)
  2. The reinstitution of the rituals (3:3–6)
  3. The first attempt to rebuild the Temple (3:7–13)
IV. Building of the Temple interrupted (4:1–24)
  1. Encounter with adversaries (4:1–5)
  2. Later conflicts (4:6–23)
  3. Work on the Temple abandoned (4:24)
V. The second attempt to rebuild the Temple (5:1—6:22)
  1. The beginning of the work (5:1–2)
  2. The Tattenai episode (5:3—6:13)
  3. The completion of the work (6:14–18)
  4. Observance of the Passover (6:19–22)
VI. Ezra's journey to Jerusalem (7:1—8:36)
  1. Introduction (7:1–10)
  2. The Artaxerxes rescript (7:11–26)
  3. The first person acount of the return (7:27—8:34)
  4. Epilogue (8:35–36)
VII. Crisis concerning mixed marriages (9:1—10:44)
  1. The complaint to Ezra (9:1–2)
  2. Ezra's reaction to the mixed marriages (9:3–15)
  3. The response of the Jews (10:1–4)
  4. Ezra's leadership in the marriage reforms (10:5–17)
  5. List of marriage offenders (10:18–44)

Outline of Nehemiah

I. Nehemiah at the court of Artaxerxes (1:1—2:8)
  1. News from Judah (1:1–4)
  2. Nehemiah's prayer (1:5–11a)
  3. Artaxerxes' grant to Nehemiah (1.11b—2:8)
II. Nehemiah assumes the governorship (2:9–20)
  1. Arrival in the west (2:9–10)
  2. Inspection of Jerusalem (2:11–16)
  3. Challenge to the local officials (2:17–18)
  4. Reaction of neighboring authorities (2:19–20)
III. Organization of the wall builders (3:1–32)
  1. Rebuilding the north and west walls (3:1–15)
  2. Building the new east wall (3:16–32)
IV. Building under pressure (4:1–23; Heb. 3:33–4:17) [5]
  1. Further reaction from neighboring authorities (4:1–3; Heb. 3:33–35)
  2. Nehemiah's prayer (4:4–5; Heb. 3:36–37)
  3. Progress amid threats (4:6–12; Heb. 3:38—4:6)
  4. Nehemiah's defense measures (4:13–23, Heb. 4:7–17)
V. Economic exploitation of the builders (5:1–19)
  1. Complaint of the workers (5:1–5)
  2. Nehemiah's confrontation with the profiteers (5:6–13)
  3. Nehemiah's example as governor (5:14–19)
VI. Further harassment of Nehemiah (6:1–19)
  1. Invitation to a conference (6:1–4)
  2. Charge of treason (6:5–9)
  3. Schemes of false prophets (6:10–14)

[5] The divisions in the Hebrew text, which differ from the divisions in the RSV text, are indicated.

4. Completion of the wall (6:15–16)
5. Tobiah's allies in Judah (6:17–19)
VII. Restoration of Jerusalem (7:1–73a; Heb. 7:1–72a)
   1. Organization of defenses (7:1–3)
   2. Need for repopulation (7:4–5)
   3. The census list (7:6–73a; Heb. 7:6–72a)
VIII. Ezra's revival (7:73b—9:37; Heb. 7:72b—9:37)
   1. Reading of the law (7:73b—8:8; Heb. 7:72b—8:8)
   2. Response of the people (8:9–12)
   3. Observance of the feast of booths (8:13–18)
   4. Fasting and confession (9:1–5)
   5. Prayer of repentance (9:6–37)
IX. A written covenant (9:38—10:39; Heb. 10:1–40)
   1. The document and the witnesses (9:38—10:27; Heb. 10:1–28)
   2. Summary of the pledges (10:28–39; Heb. 10:29–40)
X. Distribution of population (11:1–36)
   1. Resettlement of Jerusalem (11:1–2)
   2. Leaders residing in the city (11:3–24)
   3. Towns inhabited by Jews (11:25–36)
XI. Clerical registers (12:1–26)
   1. Priests and Levites who came with Zerubbabel (12:1–9)
   2. Postexilic high priests (12:10–11)
   3. Priests and Levites from time of Joiakim (12:12–26)
XII. Dedication of the wall (12:27–43)
   1. Preparations (12:27–30)
   2. Ceremonies of dedication (12:31–43)
XIII. The cultic norm (12:44—13:3)
   1. The Temple services (12:44–47)
   2. The exclusion of foreigners (13:1–3)
XIV. Nehemiah's cultic reforms (13:4–31)
   1. Tobiah expelled from the Temple (13:4–9)
   2. Temple finances put in order (13:10–14)
   3. Sabbath observance regulated (13:15–22)
   4. Mixed marriages prohibited (13:23–29)
   5. Conclusion (13:30–31)

Selected Bibliography

ACKROYD, PETER R. *Exile and Restoration.* Philadelphia: Westminster Press, 1968.

ALBRIGHT, W. F. *The Biblical Period from Abraham to Ezra.* (Harper Torchbooks) New York: Harper and Row, 1963.

ALBRIGHT, W. F. "The Date and Personality of the Chronicler," *Journal of Biblical Literature*, XL (1921).

BATTEN, LORING W. *The Books of Ezra and Nehemiah,* ("International Critical Commentary.") New York: Charles Scribner's Sons, 1913.

BICKERMAN, E. L. "The Edict of Cyrus in Ezra 1," *Journal of Biblical Literature*, LXV (1946).

BOWMAN, RAYMOND A. "Ezra and Nehemiah," *The Interpreter's Bible*, III. Nashville: Abingdon Press, 1954.

BRIGHT, JOHN. *A History of Israel.* Philadelphia: Westminster Press, 1959.

BROCKINGTON, L. H. *Ezra, Nehemiah, and Esther* ("The Century Bible, New Series.") ed. H. H. Rowley and Matthew Black. London: Thomas Nelson and Sons, 1969.

COOK, S. A. "The Age of Zerubbabel," *Studies in Old Testament Prophecy*, ed. H. H. ROWLEY. Edinburgh: T. and T. Clark, 1950.

KAPELRUD, A. S. *The Question of Authorship in the Ezra-Narrative.* Oslo: Dybwad, 1944.

MYERS, JACOB M. *Ezra-Nehemiah* ("Anchor Bible" 14.) Garden City: Doubleday and Co., 1965.

OLMSTEAD, A. T. *History of the Persian Empire.* Chicago: University of Chicago Press, 1948.

PRITCHARD, J. B. ed. *Ancient Near Eastern Texts Relating to the Old Testament.* Princeton: Princeton University Press, 1950.

ROWLEY, H. H. "Nehemiah's Mission and Its Background," *Bulletin of the John Rylands Library*, XXXVII (1954–55), 528–566.

ROWLEY, H. H. *The Servant of the Lord and Other Essays on the Old Testament.* London: Lutterworth Press, 1952, 131–159.

RUDOLPH, WILHELM. *Esra und Nehemia* (Handbuch zum Alten Testament.) Tübingen: J. C. B. Mohr, 1949.

TORREY, C. C. *Ezra Studies.* Chicago: University of Chicago Press, 1910.

WRIGHT, J. S. *The Date of Ezra's Coming to Jerusalem.* London: Tyndale Press, 1958.

Commentary on Ezra

I. First Return from the Exile (1:1–11)

1. The Cyrus Edict (1:1–4)

(1) Introduction (1:1)

¹ In the first year of Cyrus king of Persia, that the word of the LORD by the mouth of Jeremiah might be accomplished, the LORD stirred up the spirit of Cyrus king of Persia so that he made a proclamation throughout all his kingdom and also put it in writing:

The sovereignty of God in history is a keynote in Ezra-Nehemiah and indeed throughout the entire Bible. God not only moved Jeremiah to predict a return from the Babylonian exile (Jer. 29:10; 50:18–19), but he *stirred up the spirit of Cyrus* to make such a return possible. The Chronicler sees in the work of Cyrus the fulfillment of God's word in much the same way that the writers of the Gospels saw in Jesus the fulfillment of Old Testament predictions.

The first year of Cyrus was not 559 B.C. when he became king of Anshan, nor 550 B.C. when he defeated Astyages and became head of the Median Empire. The year in question is rather 538 B.C., which was his first full year after conquering the Chaldean Empire. It was during this year that Cyrus released the Jews from their exile, and it is understandable that the Chronicler should regard this as his *first year*.

The edict which follows was presented both as an oral *proclamation* and *in writing*. Bickerman (p. 274) has shown that such double promulgation of a decree was regular in ancient Rome. It was presumably common in the Near East also, and apparently was used by Hezekiah on the occasion of his Passover announcement (2 Chron. 30:1). The phrase *made a proclamation* can be translated more literally as "caused a voice to pass through." It refers to the well-known practice of dispatching heralds to deliver messages orally (cf. 10:7; Neh. 8:15). The word rendered *writing* is a rather rare technical term which designates some kind of poster or placard on which the message was reproduced for the public eye. Thus Cyrus' edict was announced orally by heralds and in writing through publicly displayed bulletins.

(2) The Decree (1:2–4)

² "Thus says Cyrus king of Persia: The LORD, the God of heaven, has given me all the kingdoms of the earth, and he has charged me to build him a house at Jerusalem, which is in Judah. ³ Whoever is among you of all his people, may his God be with him, and let him go up to Jerusalem, which is in Judah, and rebuild the house of the LORD, the God of Israel—he is the God who is in Jerusalem; ⁴ and let each survivor, in whatever place he sojourns, be assisted by the men of his place with silver and gold, with goods and with beasts, besides freewill offerings for the house of God which is in Jerusalem."

Cyrus' edict relating to the Jews has been preserved by the Chronicler in two forms. In addition to the Hebrew edict in this passage, there is a somewhat different Aramaic edict in 6:3–5. Scholars who have accepted the authenticity of the edict in principle have felt compelled to choose between the Hebrew and Aramaic passages.[6] Several recent scholars, including Myers (p. 5), have accepted the view of Bickerman (pp. 250–253) that such a choice is not necessary. The Hebrew passage is best understood as the oral announcement made by the royal heralds, while the Aramaic passage appears to be

---

[6] Martin Noth, for example, considers the Hebrew to be the Chronicler's paraphrase of the original Aramaic decree (*The History of Israel*, trans. S. Godman [London: Adam and Charles Black, 1958], p. 307).

an official memorandum to the royal treasury concerning the rebuilding of the Temple.

It is no longer considered surprising that a Persian king should have concerned himself with the welfare of the Jewish people and of their cult. An impressive amount of archaeological evidence is available to demonstrate that the Persian government did, in fact, show specific concern for subject peoples and for their religions. The Cyrus Cylinder is typical of the imposing number of ancient documents which illustrate the policies reflected in the book of Ezra. Cyrus says:

I returned to these sacred cities on the other side of the Tigris, the sanctuaries of which have been ruins for a long time, the images which (used) to live therein and established for them permanent sanctuaries. I (also) gathered all their (former) inhabitants and returned (to them) their habitations.[7]

The most common argument against the authenticity of the edict is its Jewishness. This quality, although discernible in both forms of the decree, is decidedly noticeable in the Hebrew passage. It is, in fact, unthinkable that the specific content of this document originated entirely on the initiative of a Persian. Further, we need not conclude that the document was phrased by a Jewish secretary or drawn up by some kind of department of Jewish affairs in the Persian bureaucracy. It is necessary to assume, however, that the Persians were in consultation with Jewish leaders about the return to Judah and the restoration of the Jewish cult in Jerusalem. It is possible, of course, that the Chronicler may have retouched the document. The phrase *all his people* in v. 3, for example, is designed to include northern Israelites, whom the Chronicler viewed as living in preexilic Judah (cf. 2 Chron. 30:21; 31:6).

Thus says Cyrus, while reminiscent of the familiar "thus says the Lord," was an official Persian formula (cf. Bowman, p.

[7] J. B. Pritchard, ed., *Ancient Near Eastern Texts Relating to the Old Testament* p. 316 (subsequently abbreviated ANET).

571). *King of Persia* does not occur in royal Persian inscriptions. The words *of Persia* are best understood as having been supplied by the Chronicler in keeping with terminology which was current in the western part of the empire (cf. Bickerman, pp. 255–256). The phrase *God of heaven* is not found in early Hebrew literature but is common in both biblical and nonbiblical Jewish sources during the Persian period. It is a well-documented fact that the Persians referred to the gods of subject peoples by the titles which the latter themselves preferred (cf. Bickerman, pp. 256–257). When Cyrus says that the God of the Jews *has given me all the kingdoms of the earth,* he is using the same kind of terminology that he customarily used with respect to other non-Persian gods. In the Cyrus Cylinder, for example, he says that it was Marduk, the god of Babylon, who had given him sovereignty over the world. Such recognition of the gods of subject peoples was politically astute, but it was doubtless more than that. Cyrus almost certainly believed that his political authority derived from the several gods who were worshipped within his empire. Bickerman (p. 258) assumes that *may his God be with him* is no more than a typical Oriental expression of good wishes. It is better understood, however, in a different light. According to the Cyrus Cylinder, each displaced people was allowed to take its god back to the homeland. The Jews are allowed that privilege too; although, of course, they have no image of their God to carry back physically with them (cf. Bowman, p. 572).

The Hebrew of vv. 3–4 is complex and has resulted in a somewhat ambiguous translation. The meaning, however, is clear. Permission is given that any Jew who wishes may return to Judah. He is to be assisted financially by those who decide to remain in Babylonia. There is no reason to assume that *the men of his place* included non-Jews, since the exiles were allowed to have their own local Jewish communities in Babylonia.

2. The Return (1:5-11)

(1) Response of the Leaders (1:5)

⁵ Then rose up the heads of the fathers' houses of Judah and Benjamin, and the priests and the Levites, every one whose spirit God had stirred to go up to rebuild the house of the LORD which is in Jerusalem;

One of the often repeated themes in the Bible is that God reveals himself and man responds to the revelation. God on his own initiative stirred up the spirit of Cyrus to release the Jews from their exile. The Jews in turn, whose spirit also had been stirred by God, made a positive response to God's revelation by beginning preparations for the return to Judah.

The heads of the fathers' houses are the clan chieftains. Jewish society remained substantially patriarchal throughout the biblical period and major decisions were made by the heads of family groups.

Although the edict may have applied to "all his people" (1:3), including presumably northern Israelites, the Chronicler is being realistic in noting that the response to the edict came from *Judah and Benjamin*. These two tribes had constituted the southern kingdom of Judah (cf. 1 Kings 12:21) after the death of Solomon, and were recognized by the Chronicler to constitute the postexilic community in Judah (cf. Neh. 11:4).

By the time of the Chronicler the Jewish clergy was rigidly divided into two major groups—a first class priesthood called *the priests* and a second class priesthood called *the Levites*. Although later writers sought to trace this division back to the Mosaic period (cf. Num. 3:9-10), the total biblical evidence indicates that it did not take place until the late preexilic or early exilic era.[8]

(2) Assistance from Fellow Jews (1:6)

⁶ and all who were about them aided them with vessels of silver, with gold, with goods,

---

[8] For a discussion of the Levites, see Roland de Vaux, *Ancient Israel: Its Life and Institutions* trans. John McHugh (New York: McGraw-Hill, 1961), pp. 358-397.

with beasts, and with costly wares, besides all that was freely offered.

According to the edict, each returning exile was to receive aid from "the men of his place" (1:4), but the Chronicler says that *all who were about them aided them.* The latter statement is usually held to include Babylonians. Whether or not the Babylonians did make contributions is a moot question. It is not unlikely, however, that this was in the mind of the Chronicler. Second Isaiah had clearly intimated that the return from Babylonia would be comparable to the exodus from Egypt (cf. Isa. 41:17-18; 43:16-17; 48:21). The Chronicler, interpreting the Cyrus edict in the light of the Exodus narrative (Ex. 3:21-22; 11:2-3; 12:35-36), believes that the Babylonians, as the Egyptians earlier, had rendered financial assistance to the departing Hebrews (cf. Myers, pp. 8-9).

Two minor scribal errors can be detected in the Masoretic Text. 1 Esdras 2:9 shows that the phrase *with vessels* was originally a Hebrew phrase meaning "with everything." The Hebrew phrase rendered *besides* is otherwise unknown. Bowman (p. 573) argues convincingly that it read originally "in abundance, in addition to." Thus the RSV should be corrected to read, "aided them with everything, with silver . . . , and with costly wares in abundance, in addition to all that was freely offered."

The last part of the verse is ambiguous. It appears to draw a constrast between what the Jews were required to give and what they gave willingly. Such a contrast is apparently not intended. *All that was freely offered* should be understood as referring to the "freewill offerings" of 1:4. The latter is a technical term designating a special category of cultic offerings.

(3) Return of the Temple Vessels (1:7-11)

⁷ Cyrus the king also brought out the vessels of the house of the LORD which Nebuchadnezzar had carried away from Jerusalem and

placed in the house of his gods. ⁸ Cyrus king of Persia brought these out in charge of Mithredath the treasurer, who counted them out to Shesh-bazzar the prince of Judah. ⁹ And this was the number of them: a thousand basins of gold, a thousand basins of silver, twenty-nine censers, ¹⁰ thirty bowls of gold, two thousand four hundred and ten bowls of silver, and a thousand other vessels; ¹¹ all the vessels of gold and of silver were five thousand four hundred and sixty-nine. All these did Shesh-bazzar bring up, when the exiles were brought up from Babylonia to Jerusalem.

In 597 and 587 B.C. Nebuchadrezzar had looted the sacred *vessels* (including a variety of cult objects) from Solomon's Temple (cf. 2 Kings 24:13; 25:13–14; Jer. 52:17–19), and had carried them as trophies to his gods in Babylon. Cyrus, in keeping with his benevolent attitude toward the several religions of his empire, permitted the Jews to return these vessels to Jerusalem. *Mithredath,* who acts for Cyrus in this transaction, has a typically Persian name and is designated *treasurer,* which is a Persian loan word. The Jew to whom the objects were delivered is called *Sheshbazzar the prince of Judah.* It was he, according to v. 11, who led the first return back to Judah.

The identity of Sheshbazzar is uncertain. The problem is aggravated by the Chronicler's failure to distinguish clearly between the work of Sheshbazzar and that of his successor Zerubbabel. Most contemporary scholars accept the view of Albright ("The Date and Personality of the Chronicler," pp. 108–110) that Sheshbazzar is to be identified with the Shenazzar of 1 Chronicles 3:18. The latter was the fourth son of the exiled king Jehoiachin and uncle of the subsequent governor Zerubbabel.

The word translated *vessels* is a word used for implements and utensils in general. The specific character of the objects enumerated is not well known. The figures mentioned in the inventory are confused. In the Masoretic Text the total is given as 5,400, which is quite different from the sum of the numbers listed for each item. The RSV dealt with the problem by adopting the reading found in 1 Esdras 2:13–14, but it is not at all certain that this is the correct solution.

II. The Census List (2:1–70)

1. Introduction (2:1–2a)

¹ Now these were the people of the province who came up out of the captivity of those exiles whom Nebuchadnezzar the king of Babylon had carried captive to Babylonia; they returned to Jerusalem and Judah, each to his own town. ² They came with Zerubbabel, Jeshua, Nehemiah, Seraiah, Reelaiah, Mordecai, Bilshan, Mispar, Bigvai, Rehum, and Baanah.

The origin of the list in this chapter (repeated with minor variations in Neh. 7:6–73a) has been a matter for considerable debate. It purports to be a list of the exiles who returned from Babylonia to Judea under Zerubbabel. It was so understood by the Chronicler, who clearly intended it as an enumeration of the returning exiles referred to in 1:11. That the Chronicler could associate a list headed by *Zerubbabel* with a return led by Sheshbazzar illustrates his confusion about the two men. In fact, it would suggest that he intended to identify them.

The list in its present form should not be interpreted as a simple register of those who returned with either Sheshbazzar or Zerubbabel. It has earmarks of a later period and probably contains material as late as the time of Nehemiah, with whom it is associated in Nehemiah 7. It is believed to be an authentic census list of the postexilic Judean community and may have been begun as early as the time of Zerubbabel. In its present form, however, it appears to have been corrected and revised over a considerable period of time and to include both returned exiles and those who had not been in Babylonia (cf. Albright, *The Biblical Period from Abraham to Ezra,* p. 92 and fn. 180, pp. 110–111).

The RSV interprets v. 2a as a list of postexilic leaders from several different periods. The presence of *Nehemiah* (445 B.C.) along with *Zerubbabel* and *Jeshua* (520 B.C.) would indicate that this interpretation is correct. The version of the list given in Nehemiah 7:7 has 12 names, which was undoubtedly the original number. This number is reminiscent of the 12 tribes of Israel who left Egypt and may be another reflection of the popular idea that the return from Babylonia was a second exodus.

2. Lay Families (2:2b–35)

(1) By Ancestor (2:2b–20)

The number of the men of the people of Israel: 3 the sons of Parosh, two thousand one hundred and seventy-two. 4 The sons of Shephatiah, three hundred and seventy-two. 5 The sons of Arah, seven hundred and seventy-five. 6 The sons of Pahathmoab, namely the sons of Jeshua and Joab, two thousand eight hundred and twelve. 7 The sons of Elam, one thousand two hundred and fifty-four. 8 The sons of Zattu, nine hundred and forty-five. 9 The sons of Zaccai, seven hundred and sixty. 10 The sons of Bani, six hundred and forty-two. 11 The sons of Bebai, six hundred and twenty-three. 12 The sons of Azgad, one thousand two hundred and twenty-two. 13 The sons of Adonikam, six hundred and sixty-six. 14 The sons of Bigvai, two thousand and fifty-six. 15 The sons of Adin, four hundred and fifty-four. 16 The sons of Ater, namely of Hezekiah, ninety-eight. 17 The sons of Bezai, three hundred and twenty-three. 18 The sons of Jorah, one hundred and twelve. 19 The sons of Hashum, two hundred and twenty-three. 20 The sons of Gibbar, ninety-five.

The first part of the list (through v. 20) identifies each family group by the remote ancestor who is thought of as its founder. The phrase *sons of* means, of course, descendants of, as is often the case in the Old Testament.

There are numerous differences in names and figures between the lists in Ezra 2 and those in Nehemiah 7. Many of them can be explained as simple scribal errors. H. L. Allrik [9] has traced most of variations in numbers, however, to mistakes made in copying a pre-Masoretic numeral notation system in which the numbers were not spelled out in words, as they are in the Masoretic Text.

Many of the ancestral names in the list

---

[9] "The Lists of Zerubbabel (Nehemiah 7 and Ezra 2) and the Hebrew Numeral Notation," *Bulletin of the American Schools of Oriental Research*, Dec., 1954, pp. 21–27.

are used by the Chronicler in other genealogical lists, but few of them can be identified with personalities known elsewhere in the Old Testament.

(2) By Town (2:21–35)

21 The sons of Bethlehem, one hundred and twenty-three. 22 The men of Netophah, fifty-six. 23 The men of Anathoth, one hundred and twenty-eight. 24 The sons of Azmaveth, forty-two. 25 The sons of Kiriatharim, Chephirah, and Beeroth, seven hundred and forty-three. 26 The sons of Ramah and Geba, six hundred and twenty-one. 27 The men of Michmas, one hundred and twenty-two. 28 The men of Bethel and Ai, two hundred and twenty-three. 29 The sons of Nebo, fifty-two. 30 The sons of Magbish, one hundred and fifty-six. 31 The sons of the other Elam, one thousand two hundred and fifty-four. 32 The sons of Harim, three hundred and twenty. 33 The sons of Lod, Hadid, and Ono, seven hundred and twenty-five. 34 The sons of Jericho, three hundred and forty-five. 35 The sons of Senaah, three thousand six hundred and thirty.

Without any warning or transition, the list ceases to identify families by ancestor and begins to identify them by hometown. This abrupt change in the list is an argument against its unity. Although the Chronicler may have assumed that these families were exiles returning to their preexilic hometowns, the list probably derives from a census taken after the land had been substantially resettled. The phrasing alternates between "men of" and "sons of." Although this creates ambiguity, it may be assumed that both phrases mean "inhabitants of." Lack of uniformity in this formula may be further evidence of the multiple origins of the list.

The location of the towns is believed to be a clue to the extent of the Jewish community in the fifth century B.C. That Nehemiah 3 mentions towns such as Tekoa, Bethzur, and Keilah, which are not mentioned in this list, may indicate that the list antedates Nehemiah. The towns range from Bethlehem and Netophah in the south to Bethel and Ai in the north, and from Senaah and Jericho in the east to Lod and Ono in the west. It is noteworthy that there is no reference to towns in the Judean Negeb. This may indicate that this area, which was plundered and detached from Judah in 597 B.C. (Jer. 13:19), was not inhabited by Jews at the time this census was taken.

3. Temple Personnel (2:36–58)

(1) The Priests (2:36–39)

36 The priests: the sons of Jedaiah, of the house of Jeshua, nine hundred and seventy-three. 37 The sons of Immer, one thousand and fifty-two. 38 The sons of Pashhur, one thousand two hundred and forty-seven. 39 The sons of Harim, one thousand and seventeen.

After enumerating the lay families, the list concerns itself with the various groups of cult officials. They are arranged by class and are identified by ancestors as in 2:2b–20.

The *priests* comprise by far the largest group of Temple personnel. Although only four clans are mentioned, they constitute nearly a tenth of all the people listed in the document. The various returns from Babylonia undoubtedly did include large numbers of priests. This would be expected, not only because many priests had been included among the original exiles, but also because the priests could never really be at home in Babylonia. The Deuteronomic reforms had restricted the practice of the cult to Jerusalem. Consequently, Jerusalem was the only place in the world where a Jewish priest could function legally as a priest.

The priests included in the list are all descendants of David's priest Zadok (1 Chron. 24).[10] However, in the postexilic period the genealogical criteria for defining the priesthood were changing.

Although the lines were not strictly drawn at first (cf. David's sons as priests, 2 Sam. 8:18), the tribe of Levi had emerged as the priestly tribe by the time of the Monarchy (cf. the Blessing of Moses, Deut. 33). As late as the seventh century B.C., members of this tribe without distinction constituted the priesthood (Deut.

---

[10] Cf. DeVaux, *op. cit.*, p. 388, and Bowman, pp. 582–583.

10:6–9; 18:1–7). After the Deuteronomic reforms of 621 B.C., however, the Zadokite priesthood at Solomon's Temple achieved preeminence. In spite of an abortive movement to restrict the priesthood to the Zadokites (Ezek. 44:9–16), during and after the Exile a priest came to be defined as any descendant of Aaron (cf. Lev. 21:1; Ex. 29:1–9; 1 Chron. 24; Neh. 10:38). The Zadokites were not excluded, but were provided with an Aaronic genealogy (1 Chron. 24:3).

(2) The Levites (2:40)

40 The Levites: the sons of Jeshua and Kadmiel, of the sons of Hodaviah, seventy-four.

Members of the tribe of Levi who were excluded from the priesthood as a result of Josiah's reforms came to be called *Levites*. They constituted a kind of second-class priesthood charged with the service of the priests and the congregation (Num. 3:5–10). Very few Levites are listed among those returning from Babylonia. In this list there are only 74, in contrast with 4,289 priests; and Ezra had to make a special effort to find any Levites who were willing to return (8:15–19). One may assume that because of their lower status, fewer Levites were exiled by Nebuchadrezzar. Of those in Babylonia many doubtless preferred the secular opportunities there to the menial tasks which awaited them in Jerusalem.

(3) Other Ministrants (2:41–58)

41 The singers: the sons of Asaph, one hundred and twenty-eight. 42 The sons of the gatekeepers: the sons of Shallum, the sons of Ater, the sons of Talmon, the sons of Akkub, the sons of Hatita, and the sons of Shobai, in all one hundred and thirty-nine.

43 The temple servants: the sons of Ziha, the sons of Hasupha, the sons of Tabbaoth, 44 the sons of Keros, the sons of Siaha, the sons of Padon, 45 the sons of Lebanah, the sons of Hagabah, the sons of Akkub, 46 the sons of Hagab, the sons of Shamlai, the sons of Hanan, 47 the sons of Giddel, the sons of Gahar, the sons of Reaiah, 48 the sons of Rezin, the sons of Nekoda, the sons of Gazzam, 49 the sons of Uzza, the sons of Paseah, the sons of Besai, 50 the sons of Asnah, the sons of Meunim, the

sons of Nephisim, ⁵¹ the sons of Bakbuk, the sons of Hakupha, the sons of Harhur, ⁵² the sons of Bazluth, the sons of Mehida, the sons of Harsha, ⁵³ the sons of Barkos, the sons of Sisera, the sons of Temah, ⁵⁴ the sons of Neziah, and the sons of Hatipha.

⁵⁵ The sons of Solomon's servants: the sons of Sotai, the sons of Hassophereth, the sons of Peruda, ⁵⁶ the sons of Jaalah, the sons of Darkon, the sons of Giddel, ⁵⁷ the sons of Shephatiah, the sons of Hattil, the sons of Pochereth-hazzebaim, and the sons of Ami.

⁵⁸ All the temple servants and the sons of Solomon's servants were three hundred and ninety-two.

The 128 *singers* mentioned in the list belonged to the clan of Asaph. They are listed separately from the Levites in this document, as they are in 7:7,24; 10:23–24; and in Nehemiah 13:5. By the Chronicler's time, however, they appear to have been included among the Levites (1 Chron. 16:4–7,41–42). The Chronicler attributes the organization of the Temple singers to David (1 Chron. 25). The story of David in Samuel-Kings does not give him such credit. Moreover, since Temple singers as a guild are not mentioned in preexilic literature, one may assume that the institution familiar to the Chronicler was of postexilic origin. On the other hand, as de Vaux [11] points out, there were probably singers in the preexilic Temple. Cultic singing clearly antedates the Exile. This is indicated by the reference to it in Amos 5:23, by the fact that many early psalms were written to be sung, and by the presence of singers among those returning from Babylonia (7:7,24).

The 139 *gatekeepers* belonged to six small clans. Like the singers, they are listed separately from the Levites (cf. 7:7,24), but the Chronicler apparently regarded them as a division of the Levites (1 Chron. 9:26; 23:2–5). The gatekeepers were primarily attendants who guarded the doors of the Temple. There were doubtless such gatekeepers in the preexilic Temple, although it is not certain that the three "keepers of the threshold" (2 Kings 23:4; 25:8) were the type of menial servants indicated by the postexilic office. At any rate, the elaborate organization of the gatekeepers as a guild (1 Chron. 26:1–19), attributed by the Chronicler to David (1 Chron. 9:22), appears to be postexilic. In the Chronicler's own day, at least, the keepers of the gate performed not only simple guard duty at the Temple doors, but also general custodial duties associated with the Temple (1 Chron. 9:23–29). The psalmist obviously considered the office to be one of the least prestigious held by any of the Temple personnel (Psalm 84:10).

The temple servants (nethinim) and *the sons of Solomon's servants* are obscure. The two groups are counted together (v. 58; cf. Neh. 10:28, where only a single group is mentioned) and must have been closely related. The noun *nethinim* has the connotation of "given ones," i.e., those given for and dedicated to the service of the Temple. They were subordinate to the Levites (1 Chron. 9:2),[12] and were assistants to them (8:20). Although B. A. Levine [13] has argued that they originated as a guild of royal merchants, their origin is actually unknown. Since the names of the *nethinim* are mostly foreign (cf. Bowman, p. 584), some of them may have originated as slaves or prisoners of war. The Chronicler characteristically associates the institution with David (8:20), and such servants doubtless were among the attendants of the preexilic Temple. De Vaux [14] may be correct in assuming that the *nethinim* were the descendants of those who attended the preexilic clergy, that the *sons of Solomon's servants* were the descendants of the secular attendants of the royal palace, and that after the fall of the state in 587 B.C. the two groups merged as special assistants to the Levites.

4. Uncertified Families (2:59–63)

⁵⁹ The following were those who came up from Telmelah, Telharsha, Cherub, Addan,

---

[11] *Op. cit.*, p. 382.

[12] Cf. E. A. Speiser, "Unrecognized Dedication," *Israel Exporation Journal*, 1963, pp. 69–73.
[13] "The Nethinim," *JBL*, June, 1963, pp. 207–212.
[14] *Op. cit.*, pp. 89–90.

and Immer, though they could not prove their fathers' houses or their descent, whether they belonged to Israel: ⁶⁰ the sons of Delaiah, the sons of Tobiah, and the sons of Nekoda, six hundred and fifty-two. ⁶¹ Also, of the sons of the priests: the sons of Habaiah, the sons of Hakkoz, and the sons of Barzillai (who had taken a wife from the daughters of Barzillai the Gileadite, and was called by their name). ⁶² These sought their registration among those enrolled in the genealogies, but they were not found there, and so they were excluded from the priesthood as unclean; ⁶³ the governor told them that they were not to partake of the most holy food, until there should be a priest to consult Urim and Thummim.

The first appendix to the principal list relates that there were three lay families and three priestly families who could not prove their ancestry. Because their genealogies could not be certified from the carefully preserved registers, they were temporarily denied full status in the community. In the absence of the conventional proof of origin they were identified by the five Babylonian towns from which they had come.

This passage is a valuable clue to the significance of the preceding list. It was manifestly an instrument of legitimation.[15] After the fall of the nation there was a decided increase in emphasis upon ethnic and cultic purity. A special effort was made to maintain "pure blood" and to guard against the twin dangers of assimilation and contamination.

The person who added this appendix has combined two entirely different cases. The lay families were under suspicion because they could not prove that they were authentic Israelites. In the case of the priestly families, however, the issue was whether or not they belonged to the legitimate priesthood. Because of the belief that uncertified priests could contaminate the cult and thereby greatly endanger the community, they were barred from the priesthood until the matter could be settled by proper authority. The identity of *the governor* who took the initiative in the matter is not known.

[15] Cf. Kurt Galling, "The 'Gola-List' according to Ezra 2/Nehemiah 7," *JBL*, June, 1951, pp. 149–158; North, *op. cit.*, p. 372.

The uncertified priests were excluded from the duties and privileges of the priesthood, including the eating of *the most holy food.* The food so designated was doubtless that which was expressly reserved for the priesthood. It consisted of the breast and right thigh of sacrificial animals and the flour which was left over from the cereal offering (Lev. 2:3; 7:31–33).

A permanent solution to the problem was postponed *until there should be a priest to consult Urim and Thummim.* The latter were the sacred lots which were used to determine the will of God in a given situation. Whether they were specially shaped pebbles or small sticks or some other kind of small object is not known. It is clear, however, that their use was somewhat analogous to the toss of a coin (cf. 1 Sam. 14:36–42). Why the Urim and Thummim could not be consulted by the certified priests of the community is not clear. The Blessing of Moses implies that any member of the tribe of Levi might use them (Deut. 33:8). The postexilic priestly legislation apparently reserved the use of these lots to the high priest (cf. Lev. 8:8); several ancient versions read "high priest" in this passage. If this verse implies that no high priest had yet been consecrated, the appendix would appear to be quite early since Jeshua (or Joshua) was already high priest in 520 B.C. (Hag. 1:1; Zech. 3:1).

5. *Summary Totals (2:64–67)*

⁶⁴ The whole assembly together was forty-two thousand three hundred and sixty, ⁶⁵ besides their menservants and maidservants, of whom there were seven thousand three hundred and thirty-seven; and they had two hundred male and female singers. ⁶⁶ Their horses were seven hundred and thirty-six, their mules were two hundred and forty-five, ⁶⁷ their camels were four hundred and thirty-five, and their asses were six thousand seven hundred and twenty.

The total given for *the whole assembly* does not tally with the figures given in the list itself. The discrepancy may result from copyist errors, or it may result from the heterogeneous origins of the document. The figures given in the summary are believed to reflect the population of Judah in the late fifth century B.C. and may represent a corrected total based on figures later than those in the list.

Most of the theories which have been offered to account for the inclusion of slaves [16] and livestock in the list are unconvincing. One need not look beyond the simple fact that the ancient Jew thought of his property as part of his total personality. The writer of Jonah, for example, notes that when the Ninevites repented, the livestock was included in the fast and covered with sackcloth and ashes (Jonah 3:7-8;).[17] The compiler of this second appendix to the list thinks of the Judean community as comprising the assembly with its slaves and domestic animals.

6. *Gifts to the Temple* (2:68–69)

⁶⁸ Some of the heads of families, when they came to the house of the LORD which is in Jerusalem, made freewill offerings for the house of God, to erect it on its site; ⁶⁹ according to their ability they gave to the treasury of the work sixty-one thousand darics of gold, five thousand minas of silver, and one hundred priests' garments.

The corresponding passage in Nehemiah 7:70–72 shows that this appendix has been edited more severely than any other part of the list. The Chronicler used the list in two entirely different contexts and in each case he had to make certain adjustments. In this version the Chronicler anticipates the story that begins in the following chapter and says that the gifts were made for the building of the Temple. The version in Nehemiah interprets the gifts as being made for the work of the cult. The latter

---

[16] Not only were the *menservants and maidservants* slaves, but also the *male and female singers*. The latter are not to be confused with the Temple singers of 2:41. They are rather slaves maintained for the entertainment of the rich (cf. Eccl. 2:8; 2 Chron. 35:25), and should be compared with those which Hezekiah gave as tribute to Sennacherib (ANET, p. 288).

[17] Cf. A. R. Johnson, *The One and the Many in the Israelite Conception of God* [Cardiff: University of Wales Press, 1961], pp. 6–7.

seems to be the original version, inasmuch as *one hundred priests' garments* would scarcely be an appropriate gift for the construction of the Temple.

The *darics of gold* are Persian coins, which weighed 8.424 grams each. The *minas of silver* refer not to coins but to weight. The standard was not uniform throughout the ancient world; but in Palestinean usage the mina appears to have been about 1.26 pounds. Batten (p. 99) estimates the total value of the gifts to be about half a million dollars. There may have been such wealth in the Judean community by the late fifth century, but Haggai makes it clear that its resources were considerably less abundant at the time of the rebuilding of the Temple (cf. Hag. 2:3).

The contributors gave *according to their ability*. The tithes, firstfruits, and most of the other offerings expected of the ancient Jew reflect this principle of giving. Paul gives it classic expression in 1 Corinthians 16:2.

7. *The Land Resettled* (2:70)

⁷⁰ The priests, the Levites, and some of the people lived in Jerusalem and its vicinity; and the singers, the gatekeepers, and the temple servants lived in their towns, and all Israel in their towns.

The Masoretic Text omits the words *in Jerusalem and its vicinity*. The RSV has recovered this missing phrase from 1 Esdras 5:40. This verse presupposes a time long after Sheshbazzar when Jerusalem and the other towns of Judah have been rebuilt and repopulated. It also reflects once again the idea that the return from Babylonia was a second exodus. The second conquest has now been completed, and the people are settled comfortably in their towns (cf. Josh. 11:23).

III. *Restoration of the Cult* (3:1–13)

1. *The Rebuilding of the Altar* (3:1–2)

¹ When the seventh month came, and the sons of Israel were in the towns, the people gathered as one man to Jerusalem. ² Then

arose Jeshua the son of Jozadak, with his fellow priests, and Zerubbabel the son of Sheal iel with his kinsmen, and they built the altar of the God of Israel, to offer burnt offerings upon it, as it is written in the law of Moses the man of God.

According to the Chronicler, the first thing that the newly returned exiles did was to rebuild the altar and reestablish the prescribed routine of cultic functions. That he is substantially correct need not be doubted since the prime motive for returning to Jerusalem was to restore the cult. Nevertheless, the narrative is fraught with obscurity and ambiguity.

The first verse is almost identical to the introduction to the reading of the law (Neh. 7:73b, 8:1a; cf. 1 Esdras 9:37b–38a), which follows the census list in the book of Nehemiah. The close verbal agreement between the two passages has led some scholars to believe that most of the statement (except for the place of the gathering) stood originally in the concluding portion of the census document (e.g., Bowman, p. 588). It is more likely, however, that the Chronicler began two different stories with an almost identical formula (cf. Myers, p. 26). It was probably the coincidence that both the events of Ezra 3 and of Nehemiah 8 took place in *the seventh month* (September–October) which caused the Chronicler to begin the two passages with the same words. The seventh month referred to in Nehemiah 7:73b is probably that of the year in which Ezra came to Jerusalem (398 B.C.). In this passage, however, the Chronicler may still be alluding to the first year of Cyrus (cf. 1:1).

The Chronicler has inadvertently telescoped the careers of Sheshbazzar and Zerubbabel (see Introduction). It was Sheshbazzar who first undertook the restoration of the cult in Jerusalem (1:8–11; 5:14–16). Chapters 3 and 4 must reflect primarily his work, which was undertaken during the reign of Cyrus. If these two chapters preserve authentic data about Zerubbabel (as well they may), these data belong chronologically after 5:1. Haggai and Zechariah date the beginning of the building activity of Zerubbabel and Jeshua to the second year of Darius I (520 B.C.).

The altar was built according to the prescriptions of *the law of Moses,* which means that it was constructed of unhewn field stones (Ex. 20:25; Deut. 27:6). It was apparently completed and put into use on the same day (cf. 3:6). It is strange that the altar should have been built on the first day of the seventh month (3:1–6), since both the Holiness Code (Lev. 23:23–25) and the priestly legislation (Num. 29:1) forbid work on that day. If the Chronicler's date is correct, one would assume that the building of the altar antedates this specific regulation.

2. *The Reinstitution of the Rituals* (3:3–6)

3 They set the altar in its place, for fear was upon them because of the peoples of the lands, and they offered burnt offerings upon it to the Lord, burnt offerings morning and evening. 4 And they kept the feast of booths, as it is written, and offered the daily burnt offerings by number according to the ordinance, as each day required, 5 and after that the continual burnt offerings, the offerings at the new moon and at all the appointed feasts of the Lord, and the offerings of every one who made a freewill offering to the Lord. 6 From the first day of the seventh month they began to offer burnt offerings to the Lord. But the foundation of the temple of the Lord was not yet laid.

The Chronicler attributes the community's haste in restoring the cult to the fact that *fear was upon them because of the peoples of the lands.* This statement is to be understood in the light of the troubles described in chapters 4–6. By *the peoples of the lands* the Chronicler probably intended all of the varied inhabitants of the Palestinian area except the returned exiles and the few kindred spirits who had been allowed to join them (cf. 6:21). He singles out the Samaritans, however, as the chief troublemakers. They were the Yahweh worshiping descendants of the north Israelites who had been mixed with Mesopotamians brought into Israel by Sargon II (2 Kings 17:24), Esarhaddon (Ezra 4:2), and Osnapper (i.e., Ashurbanipal, Ezra 4:9–

10). The returned exiles had reason to expect interference from the Samaritans. A large part of northern Judah, including Jerusalem, had been under Samaritan control since shortly after the fall of Judah (cf. Bright, p. 324). The returning exiles were uninvited immigrants in a land which was no longer their own. The fear which they felt for their neighbors was soon to prove justified.

The Chronicler's catalogue of cultic observances doubtless reflects the practices of his own day. Nevertheless, it calls attention to some of the basic features of the cult which date back to the time of Sheshbazzar and even into the preexilic period.

The *continual burnt offerings* were those offered twice daily, *morning and evening*. On each occasion a lamb was offered whole on the altar, accompanied by a mixture of olive oil and flour and a libation of wine (Ex. 29:38–42; Num. 28:1–8). The number of burnt offerings was increased for special occasions. For example, four were offered on the sabbath (Num. 28:9) and seven (together with two bulls and a ram) were offered on each of the seven days following the Passover (Num. 28:16–24). During the *feast of booths* the requirement for *each day* was different, ranging from 32 animals on the first day of the feast to 12 on the eighth day (Num. 29:12–38).

The *feast of booths* (KJV: tabernacles), was observed beginning on the fifteenth day of the seventh month, two weeks after the altar was built. It was originally a feast of joy to celebrate the harvest of grain and grapes (Deut. 16:13–15). The word booths (Heb. *sukkoth*) referred to the huts made of tree branches and erected in the fields to serve as guardhouses during the harvest (cf. Isa. 1:8). By the postexilic period the feast was primarily a commemoration of the wilderness experience, and the booths were associated with the temporary dwellings used by the Israelites after the Exodus (Lev. 23:39–43). The Chronicler considered it particularly appropriate that this feast should be observed on the heels of the new exodus and the new settlement of the land.

Additional sacrifices were prescribed for the occasion of *the new moon* (Num. 28:11–15). On this day trumpets were blown (Num. 10.10), work ceased (Amos 8:5), and special meals were prepared (1 Sam. 20:5).

All the appointed feasts of the Lord included the *feast of booths* as well as the other cultic festivals which recurred annually at fixed times. The three feasts which received special attention in the preexilic period were the ancient pilgrimage festivals: Passover and the Feast of Unleavened Bread, the Feast of Weeks, and the Feast of Booths (Ex. 34:18,22,23; Deut. 16:1–16). The new year festival and the Day of Atonement received equal attention in the postexilic calendar (Lev. 23:4–44), and special sacrifices were ordained for each of the five occasions (Num. 28:16—29:39).

Most of the sacrifices and offerings of the postexilic era were regulated by explicit legislation. A partial exception was the *freewill offering*. This was an offering not prompted by any law or vow, but made entirely at the pleasure of the worshiper. While it was to be made according to a specific formula (Num. 15:1–10), it was so free of restrictions that it might include even a blemished animal (Lev. 22:23).

3. The First Attempt to Rebuild the Temple (3:7–13)

(1) Donations for Labor and Supplies (3:7)

⁷ So they gave money to the masons and the carpenters, and food, drink, and oil to the Sidonians and the Tyrians to bring cedar trees from Lebanon to the sea, to Joppa, according to the grant which they had from Cyrus king of Persia.

After the cult had been reestablished, the returned exiles turned their attention to the urgent matter of rebuilding the cultic center, the Temple. The narrative is strongly reminiscent of the story of the building of Solomon's Temple (1 Kings 5; 1 Chron. 22; 2 Chron. 2), but Wilhelm

Rudolph (p. 31) observes correctly that this is no argument against the essential historicity of the account.

Masons were employed to quarry and shape the stones and *carpenters* to engrave the stone, wood, and metal (cf. Bowman, p. 592). Cedars of Lebanon were cut and brought to the Phoenician ports of Sidon and Tyre, where they were made into rafts and floated to Joppa (cf. 1 Kings 5:9). Payment was made partly in silver (*money*) and partly by barter (cf. 1 Kings 5:11). (That no mention is made of the vast quantity of gold and silver cited in 2:68–69 is evidence that the census list does not belong wholly to the time of the first return.) *The grant which they had from Cyrus king of Persia* authorized that the expenses be paid from the royal treasury (6:4). It is not clear, however, that all of the payment came from the Persian coffers.

(2) *Organization of the Work (3:8–9)*

⁸ Now in the second year of their coming to the house of God at Jerusalem, in the second month, Zerubbabel the son of Shealtiel and Jeshua the son of Jozadak made a beginning, together with the rest of their brethren, the priests and the Levites and all who had come to Jerusalem from the captivity. They appointed the Levites, from twenty years old and upward, to have the oversight of the work of the house of the Lord. ⁹ And Jeshua with his sons and his kinsmen, and Kadmiel and his sons, the sons of Judah, together took the oversight of the workmen in the house of God, along with the sons of Henadad and the Levites, their sons and kinsmen.

The Chronicler credits Zerubbabel and Jeshua with laying the foundation of the Temple, just as he had given them credit for building the altar (3:2). The explicit statement in 5:16 that Sheshbazzar had laid the foundation of the Temple shows that the Chronicler confused the abortive efforts of Sheshbazzar (during the reign of Cyrus) with the successful undertaking of Zerubbabel several years later (5:1—6:15). The organization of the workmen, which centers around Zerubbabel and Jeshua, is probably to be associated with the second attempt to rebuild the Temple. Specific details about Sheshbazzar's work, likely unavailable to the Chronicler, seem to have been replaced with details drawn from the later episode.

The laymen, priests, and Levites cooperated in the laying of the foundation of the Temple. Special responsibility was given to the Levites, who regularly served as assistants to the priests. The minimum age for Levites serving in this capacity was 20, although in other contexts the minimum age for service was 25 (Num. 8:24) and 30 (Num. 4:3). *Kadmiel* and *Henadad* are common levitical names in the postexilic period, but the individuals mentioned here are not otherwise known. Two other levitical names have apparently been lost in the Masoretic Text. The Greek texts suggest that *his sons* should be read "Binnui," and *Judah* should be read "Hodevah" (cf. Bowman, p. 593).

(3) *Laying of the Foundation (3:10–11)*

¹⁰ And when the builders laid the foundation of the temple of the Lord, the priests in their vestments came forward with trumpets, and the Levites, the sons of Asaph, with cymbals, to praise the Lord, according to the directions of David king of Israel; ¹¹ and they sang responsively, praising and giving thanks to the Lord,

"For he is good,
for his steadfast love endures for ever toward Israel."

And all the people shouted with a great shout, when they praised the Lord, because the foundation of the house of the Lord was laid.

It was appropriate that the laying of *the foundation of the temple* should be accompanied by a service of praise and thanksgiving. Since 587 b.c. the Temple site had been a mass of ruins. The cult had been interrupted, the nation destroyed, and the people scattered. Now through the divine initiative Cyrus has permitted a new beginning. The laying of the foundation signaled the dawn of a new day. It had been possible only because the Lord *is good* and because *his steadfast love endures forever.*

Three groups participated in the ceremony. *The priests* blew the long slender trumpets assigned to them (Num. 10:8). *The Levites* were represented by a group of musicians called *the sons of Asaph* (cf. 2:41). The latter, whose organization is traced back to *David* (cf. 1 Chron. 25:1–6; 2 Chron. 29:25), played the *cymbals* and sang a hymn (quoted from Psalm 106:1; 136:1; cf. 1 Chron. 16:34; 2 Chron. 5:13; 7:3). *The people* responded in turn *with a great shout.* The shout was probably more than a mere spontaneous outburst of joy. It appears to be an integral part of the ceremony. Liturgical shouting was common in ancient Israel (cf. Josh. 6:5–20; 1 Sam. 4:5–6; 2 Sam. 6:15; 2 Chron. 13:15; 15:14) and was often accompanied by music.

(4) Reaction of the Community (3:12–13)

12 But many of the priests and Levites and heads of fathers' houses, old men who had seen the first house, wept with a loud voice when they saw the foundation of this house being laid, though many shouted aloud for joy; 13 so that the people could not distinguish the sound of the joyful shout from the sound of the people's weeping, for the people shouted with a great shout, and the sound was heard afar.

The beginning of the new Temple was a glad occasion, and the air was filled with happy sounds. But *the old men who had seen the first house* mingled their tears with the joyous shouts. These were tears of sadness that the new Temple could never equal the one that had stood on the same site half a century before (cf. Hag. 2:3; Zech. 4:10).

IV. Building of the Temple Interrupted (4:1–24)

1. Encounter with Adversaries (4:1–5)

(1) The Offer to Zerubbabel (4:1–2)

1 Now when the adversaries of Judah and Benjamin heard that the returned exiles were building a temple to the Lord, the God of Israel, 2 they approached Zerubbabel and the heads of fathers' houses and said to them, "Let us build with you; for we worship your God as you do, and we have been sacrificing to him ever since the days of Esarhaddon king of Assyria who brought us here."

The work on the Temple attracted the attention of the nonexilic peoples of the land (cf. 6:6). A group of them approached Zerubbabel [18] and asked to be allowed to assist in the project. They identified themselves as the descendants of immigrants brought into the land during the reign of Esarhaddon.

It was the policy of the Assyrians to transplant populations of conquered countries. Aliens had been settled in the northern part of Palestine since the conquest of Israel by Sargon II in 722 B.C. (2 Kings 14:24; cf. ANET, p. 284). Esarhaddon (681–669 B.C.) conquered Tyre and Sidon (ANET, p. 290), and it may have been in this connection that he brought new immigrants into Israel. These non-Israelite newcomers mixed with the native Israelites (cf. ANET, pp. 284–285) and came to be designated as Samaritans.

There is no reason to assume that the initial approach of this group was in the spirit of *adversaries.* They did indeed worship the same God and had been *sacrificing to him* for many generations (cf. 2 Kings 17:26–28, 32; 2 Chron. 30:11; 34:9; 35:18; Jer. 41:5). Even Sanballat, the contemporary of Nehemiah, named his sons after Yahweh.[19] It is not too much to assume that the Samaritans were acting in good faith when they came to *Judah and Benjamin* (cf. 1:5) and offered their assistance for the building of the Temple.

(2) Zerubbabel's Rejection of Assistance (4:3)

3 But Zerubbabel, Jeshua, and the rest of the heads of fathers' houses in Israel said to them, "You have nothing to do with us in building a house to our God; but we alone will build to the Lord, the God of Israel, as King Cyrus the king of Persia has commanded us."

---

[18] It must remain uncertain whether this episode is to be associated with Sheshbazzar or Zerubbabel. The Chronicler understood the event to belong to the time of Cyrus and to lead to the interruption of the building of the Temple (cf. 4:24).
[19] Cowley, *op. cit.*, p. 114.

Zerubbabel rejected with bluntness and finality the offer of the Samaritans to help rebuild the Temple. From his point of view, this was the only decision that he could make. As long as the Hebrews had their own Temple and their own state, they could afford a certain tolerance toward outsiders. But after 587 B.C. there was an increasing demand for the rigid exclusion of all things foreign (cf. Ezek. 44:4–31). The danger that the Jews would be assimilated by their neighbors and that their religion would be contaminated by outside influences brought a new demand for ethnic and religious purity.

Zerubbabel considered the Samaritans particularly ineligible to join his group of returned exiles. (While the final schism between Jews and Samaritans may not have occurred until the time of Nehemiah or later, there was clearly no period of harmonious relationships between the two groups.) In the first place, they were ethnically mixed. They had been brought from remote corners of Babylonia and Assyria (cf. 2 Kings 17:24; Ezra 4:9) and had surely intermarried with the Israelites whom Sargon had left in the land. In the second place, their religion was syncretistic. They worshiped Yahweh, to be sure, but they had also to some extent clung to the religions of their previous homelands (2 Kings 17:29–34). In the third place, they had violated the Deuteronomic prohibition of sacrifice outside of Jerusalem. Although they had worshiped in Jerusalem from time to time, most of their sacrifices had clearly occurred at the shrines in the north. Acceptance of such a group would threaten the "racial" and religious purity of Jews and recreate the very conditions which were believed to have caused the destruction of the nation in the first place (cf. 2 Kings 17:7–23; 2 Chron. 36:14). It was unthinkable that these people should be permitted to touch the holy stones of Yahweh's Temple.

It is also possible that Zerubbabel was influenced in his decision by more mundane motives. His reference to the Cyrus edict may indicate a jealous attempt to guard his prerogatives. Any gesture of cooperation with the Samaritans might have compromised the already ambiguous political status of Judah.[20]

Our understanding of Zerubbabel's motives does not make his arrogant attitude toward the Samaritans any more attractive. The Jews, who had been so sinned against, were now slamming the door in the face of those who wished to share in their community and join them in the worship of their God. Seeds of racism were being sown which were to bear bitter fruit in the days ahead and for centuries into the future. Instead of heeding the Second Isaiah's missionary appeal to spread the faith, Zerubbabel sought to keep it pure by building a wall around it. Paradoxically, it may have been this wall of racism and particularism that did protect the faith in this period from the inroads of compromise and dilution. It is the biblical conviction that if God's purposes cannot be achieved through man's wisdom, they will nevertheless be achieved through his folly.

(3) *The Builders Harassed* (4:4–5)

4 Then the people of the land discouraged the people of Judah, and made them afraid to build, 5 and hired counselors against them to frustrate their purpose, all the days of Cyrus king of Persia, even until the reign of Darius king of Persia.

Zerubbabel's uncivil rejection of the Samaritans caused an unfavorable reaction among them and among the other *people of the land.* Hostility toward the builders was the inevitable result, so that nothing could be accomplished *until the reign of Darius* (cf. v. 24). The Chronicler does not identify the *hired counselors* nor does he specify how they undertook *to frustrate* the builders. He does say, however, that *the people of the land discouraged the people of Judah* (i.e., the returned exiles). The Hebrew phrase translated *discouraged*

---

20 Cf. A. Alt, "Die Rolle Samarias bei der Entstehung des Judentums," *Kleine Schriften zur Geschichte des Volkes Israel* [München: C. H. Beck'sche Verlagsbuchhandlung, 1953], II, 327–329.

means literally "weakened the hands of." This is a common Hebrew idiom which means to incapacitate by causing despair (cf. 2 Sam. 4:1; Isa. 13:7; Jer. 6:24; and the Lachish letters [ANET, p. 322]).

2. Later Conflicts (4:6-23)

The Chronicler had at his disposal some valuable source documents written in Aramaic (see Introduction). One of these documents related the story of the difficulties encountered by the Jews in rebuilding the Temple and the city of Jerusalem. The Chronicler used this document as the basis for the narrative in 4:6—6:18. He copied freely from his source with only minor editorial changes. The Aramaic language has been preserved in 4:8—6:18.

The Chronicler has inserted into his narrative about the rebuilding of the Temple some material which is out of place chronologically. Verses 5 and 24 relate that the building of the Temple was delayed from the reign of Cyrus until the second year of Darius I (520 B.C.). Chapters 5 and 6 relate the story of the successful attempt to rebuild the Temple under the latter king. Yet vv. 6-23 deal with events associated with the reigns of Xerxes (486-465) and Artaxerxes I (465-424). These verses, which are concerned with the rebuilding of the walls of the city (4:12), are out of context and originally had nothing to do with the rebuilding of the Temple.

One may surmise that the original Aramaic source related the story of the rebuilding of the Temple under Darius, and then continued with the story of similar frustrations in connection with attempts to rebuild the city under Xerxes and Artaxerxes. The Chronicler, however, was preoccupied with the problem of rebuilding the Temple. Specifically, he needed data to illustrate the kind of friction which caused the postponement of the rebuilding of the Temple until the reign of Darius. He lacked such data and in lieu of them he substituted the stories about events in the time of Xerxes and Artaxerxes. These stories, which he found in the latter part of his source document, illustrated friction, but in their new context greatly confused the chronological picture.

(1) Accusation to Xerxes (4:6)

⁶ And in the reign of Ahasuerus, in the beginning of his reign, they wrote an accusation against the inhabitants of Judah and Jerusalem.

If Ahasuerus (cf. Esther 10:1; Dan. 9:1) is to be identified with Xerxes (486-465 B.C.), this verse alludes to an episode which took place about three decades after the building of the Temple had been completed. Consequently, the *accusation against the inhabitants of Judah and Jerusalem* is unrelated to that event. If the Aramaic source gave the details of this accusation, the Chronicler did not choose to use them.

(2) Letters to Artaxerxes (4:7-16)

⁷ And in the days of Artaxerxes, Bishlam and Mithredath and Tabeel and the rest of their associates wrote to Artaxerxes king of Persia; the letter was written in Aramaic and translated. ⁸ Rehum the commander and Shimshai the scribe wrote a letter against Jerusalem to Artaxerxes the king as follows—⁹ then wrote Rehum the commander, Shimshai the scribe, and the rest of their associates, the judges, the governors, the officials, the Persians, the men of Erech, the Babylonians, the men of Susa, that is, the Elamites, ¹⁰ and the rest of the nations whom the great and noble Osnappar deported and settled in the cities of Samaria and in the rest of the province Beyond the River, and now ¹¹ this is a copy of the letter that they sent— "To Artaxerxes the king: Your servants, the men of the province Beyond the River, send greeting. And now ¹² be it known to the king that the Jews who came up from you to us have gone to Jerusalem. They are rebuilding that rebellious and wicked city; they are finishing the walls and repairing the foundations. ¹³ Now be it known to the king that, if this city is rebuilt and the walls finished, they will not pay tribute, custom, or toll, and the royal revenue will be impaired. ¹⁴ Now because we eat the salt of the palace and it is not fitting for us to witness the king's dishonor, therefore we send and inform the king, ¹⁵ in order that search may be made in the book of the records of your fathers. You will find in the book of the records and learn that this city is a rebellious city, hurtful to kings and provinces, and that

sedition was stirred up in it from of old. That was why this city was laid waste. 16 We make known to the king that, if this city is rebuilt and its walls finished, you will then have no possession in the province Beyond the River."

Although there were three Persian kings named Artaxerxes, it was Artaxerxes I (465–424 B.C.) who followed Xerxes and who is surely intended in this passage. Since he began to reign about 50 years after the Temple had been completed, the events related in this narrative are again unrelated to the Temple. They have to do rather with an abortive attempt to refortify Jerusalem during the two decades immediately preceding Nehemiah.

The Aramaic source contained the account of two different letters written from Palestine to Artaxerxes I. The Chronicler gave only a brief notice about the first one in a short Hebrew statement (v. 7). He relates that it was written by a man with the Persian name *Mithredath* and another with the Aramaic name *Tabeel* (cf. the Hebrew name Tobiah). We can only surmise that the former was a representative of the Persian king and the latter a local chieftain, perhaps in Samaria.

Bishlam is not a proper name, but an Aramaic word which means "in peace." Rudolph (p. 34) is doubtless correct that the original read "against Jerusalem." Thus we are told only that two officials *and the rest of their associates wrote* "against Jerusalem." The substance of the charge is not given.

The letter was written in Aramaic, the principal language of diplomacy and commerce used throughout the western part of the empire. It was presumably either *translated* into Hebrew for the benefit of the local Jews or into Persian for the benefit of the king. The words "in Aramaic" found in the Hebrew at the end of v. 7 (and in the margin of the RSV) indicate simply that what follows beginning in v. 8 is in the Aramaic language.

The story of the second letter to Artaxerxes is presented in full and contains the text of the letter to the king and his reply. The correspondence is not dated, but it is generally agreed that it belongs to the period shortly before the mission of Nehemiah.

The letter to Artaxerxes is attributed to *Rehum the commander* and *Shimshai the scribe*. Both men have Babylonian names and are assumed to be representatives of the Persian government. The word translated *commander* does not refer to a military officer, but to a high-ranking commissioner charged with royal affairs. Likewise, Shimshai's title *scribe* denotes an official capacity of considerably more importance than that of a mere amanuensis. Both men are probably official government investigators sent by the crown to check on the royal interests in the west (cf. Bowman, pp. 599, 600). They *eat the salt of the palace* (v. 14), which means that their allegiance is to the king. The Jews understood the idiom because they had a sacred bond with God which they called a covenant of salt (Lev. 2:13; Num. 18:19; 2 Chron. 13:5).

Rehum and Shimshai are joined in their complaint by a variety of *associates*. *The judges, the governors, the officials* and *the Persians* are all doubtless members of the political hierarchy in Palestine and its vicinity. The other groups are the descendants of immigrants settled in the west during the period of the Assyrian Empire, some of whom have come to be known as Samaritans. These are the people whom the Chronicler refers to as "the adversaries" (4:1) and "the people of the land" (4:4). Ashurbanipal (669–633 B.C.) is the king referred to as *Osnappar*. He is known to have followed the regular Assyrian policy of deporting and resettling conquered peoples.

The accusation made to Artaxerxes is that the Jews are rebuilding the city of Jerusalem and restoring its fortified walls. In the absence of any Persian authorization to turn Jerusalem into a fortified bastion, Rehum and Shimshai interpret this activity as treason and as a threat to the entire *province Beyond the River* (the official name for the Persian satrapy that lay between the Euphrates and the Mediterranean). The Persians allowed a maximum of local autonomy throughout the empire, but never tolerated any sign of insubordination. In all probability, the Jews were building defenses against hostile neighbors, and not against Persia. Nevertheless, Jerusalem did have a well-earned reputation as *a rebellious city, hurtful to kings and provinces* (cf. 2 Kings 18:13—19:37; 24:1-16; 24:20—25:21). It was all recorded *in the book of the records* of the predecessors (*fathers*) of the Persian kings. Rehum and Shimshai could not let the unauthorized refortification of Jerusalem go unreported. The people of the land were glad to add their endorsement because the Jews had for decades posed a threat to their political and economic status in the region.

(3) *Artaxerxes' Reply (4:17-23)*

¹⁷ The king sent an answer: "To Rehum the commander and Shimshai the scribe and the rest of their associates who live in Samaria and in the rest of the province Beyond the River, greeting. And now ¹⁸ the letter which you sent to us has been plainly read before me. ¹⁹ And I made a decree, and search has been made, and it has been found that this city from of old has risen against kings, and that rebellion and sedition have been made in it. ²⁰ And mighty kings have been over Jerusalem, who ruled over the whole province Beyond the River, to whom tribute, custom, and toll were paid. ²¹ Therefore make a decree that these men be made to cease, and that this city be not rebuilt, until a decree is made by me. ²² And take care not to be slack in this matter; why should damage grow to the hurt of the king?"
²³ Then, when the copy of King Artaxerxes' letter was read before Rehum and Shimshai the scribe and their associates, they went in haste to the Jews at Jerusalem and by force and power made them cease.

Artaxerxes' assistants searched the royal archives and confirmed the charge that Jerusalem *from of old has risen against kings.* Such evidence would have been readily available in the Chaldean records which had fallen to Cyrus in 539 B.C. Artaxerxes was probably misinformed that any king in Jerusalem had ever *ruled over the whole province Beyond the River.* However, under David and Solomon, Jerusalem was the major focus of power between the Euphrates and the Nile.

At any rate, Artaxerxes could not tolerate the unauthorized building of military fortifications within the boundaries of his empire. Rehum and Shimshai were ordered to put an immediate end to the Jewish activity. *Until a decree is made by me* is understood as an editorial touch by someone; this same king did in fact later authorize Nehemiah to refortify the city.

Rehum and Shimshai *by force and power* brought the rebuilding of the walls of Jerusalem to a sudden halt. This must have been a violent clash which resulted in the defeat of the Jews and the destruction of their work. It was ostensibly this catastrophe which took Hanani to Susa to report to Nehemiah that "the wall of Jerusalem is broken down, and its gates are destroyed by fire" (Neh. 1:3).

3. *Work on the Temple Abandoned (4:24)*

²⁴ Then the work on the house of God which is in Jerusalem stopped; and it ceased until the second year of the reign of Darius king of Persia.

This verse was composed by the Chronicler to resume the story of the rebuilding of the Temple. *Then* cannot mean that the work on the Temple stopped after the preceding episode from the reign of Artaxerxes I. If *then* is temporal, it must refer back to the interruption described in vv. 1–5. It is unthinkable that the Chronicler intended to imply that the reigns of Xerxes and Artaxerxes intervened between those of Cyrus and Darius.

V. *The Second Attempt to Rebuild the Temple (5:1—6:22)*

1. *The Beginning of the Work (5:1-2)*

¹ Now the prophets, Haggai and Zechariah the son of Iddo, prophesied to the Jews who were in Judah and Jerusalem, in the name of the God of Israel who was over them. ² Then

Zerubbabel the son of Shealtiel and Jeshua the son of Jozadak arose and began to rebuild the house of God which is in Jerusalem; and with them were the prophets of God, helping them.

After an interval of some sixteen years, the prophets Haggai and Zechariah persuaded Zerubbabel and Jeshua to make a fresh attempt to rebuild the Temple. The Aramaic source, unlike the Chronicler, does not confuse Sheshbazzar and Zerubbabel. It notes clearly that Sheshbazzar laid the foundations of the Temple during the reign of Cyrus, but that he never finished the work (5:13–16). It agrees with Haggai and Zechariah that Zerubbabel's building efforts took place during the reign of Darius. Therefore it appears that the narrative in 3:1—4:5 reflects the work of Sheshbazzar, although perhaps supplemented with details drawn from the later career of Zerubbabel.

The prophet Haggai preached in Jerusalem during the second year of Darius I, which was 520 B.C. In his first sermon he urged Zerubbabel and Jeshua (Joshua) to rebuild the Temple (Hag. 1:3–11). The passage which follows indicates that they responded to his preaching and set to work on the building within a month (Hag. 1:12–15). Haggai does not mention any previous attempt to rebuild the Temple by Sheshbazzar or by anyone else. This probably means no more than that Sheshbazzar's beginnings had been so meager that the project had to be started anew.

About two months after Haggai began to preach he was joined by Zechariah, whose ministry is dated from 520 to 518 B.C. (Zech. 1:1; 7:1). By the time Zechariah began to preach, work on the Temple was already underway. He hails the work of Zerubbabel and predicts that he will be successful in finishing the task (Zech. 4:6–10*a*).

Zerubbabel was *the son of Shealtiel,* who was the eldest son of king Johoiachin (Jeconiah; cf. 1 Chron. 3:17). The latter, rather than Zedekiah, was generally considered the last legitimate king of Judah. Thus Zerubbabel was looked upon as the head of the Davidic house. We are not told whether he accompanied his uncle Sheshbazzar (Shenazzar; cf. 1 Chron. 3:18) to Jerusalem or whether he came at some subsequent time. Haggai leaves the impression that Zerubbabel and Jeshua had been in Judah for some period of time before 520 B.C.

2. The Tattenai Episode (5:3—6:13)

(1) The Investigation (5:3–5)

³ At the same time Tattenai the governor of the province Beyond the River and Shetharbozenai and their associates came to them and spoke to them thus, "Who gave you a decree to build this house and to finish this structure?" ⁴ They also asked them this, "What are the names of the men who are building this building?" ⁵ But the eye of their God was upon the elders of the Jews, and they did not stop them till a report should reach Darius and then answer be returned by letter concerning it.

The new attempt to rebuild the Temple attracted the attention of two Persian officials, *Tattenai the governor of the province Beyond the River and Shetharbozenai.* They inquired about the authorization of the Jews to build the Temple and demanded the names of the builders. They allowed the building to continue, however, pending an exchange of letters with Darius I. The 18 years which had passed since Cyrus had authorized the building of the Temple had brought a major change in the Persian government. It is not surprising that Tattenai, a member of the new regime of Darius I, should be unfamiliar with the edict.

It is extraordinary, however, that a Persian governor should have been so suspicious of the construction of a cultic shrine. The benevolence of the Persian government toward the religions of subject peoples is well attested in all periods.

Haggai and Zechariah reveal the circumstances which may have caused Tattenai to view the building project with suspicion. The building of the Temple was accompanied by, and perhaps motivated by, a seething nationalistic movement. The Persian Empire had been gripped with turmoil and confusion as a result of the rebellion of Bardiya and the suicide of Cambyses in 522 B.C. These events were understood in Judah as a sign that God was intervening to release the Jews from foreign domination. Haggai had predicted the violent overthrow of the Persian Empire (2:21–22) and had promised the Jews that its treasures would be theirs (2:6–9). Zechariah, in similar terms, had announced divine intervention "to cast down the horns of the nations" (1:21) and to give them as "plunder for those who served them" (2:9). Both prophets had more than hinted that the rule of Zerubbabel would replace the rule of Persia. Haggai referred to him as God's "signet ring" (2:23). And Zechariah, in bolder and more explicit terms, announced that he would "bear royal honor" and "sit and rule upon his throne" (6:13). It is small wonder that Tattenai felt obliged to check the credentials of these Jews.

That Tattenai did not put an immediate stop to the building is attributed to the providence of God. God, who sent his punishment through Nebuchadrezzar and his release through Cyrus, is still sovereign. His benevolent watchfulness is seen in the patience of the Persian governor.

(2) *The Letter to Darius* (5:6–17)

⁶ The copy of the letter which Tattenai the governor of the province Beyond the River and Shetharbozenai and his associates the governors who were in the province Beyond the River sent to Darius the king; ⁷ they sent him a report, in which was written as follows: "To Darius the king, all peace. ⁸ Be it known to the king that we went to the province of Judah, to the house of the great God. It is being built with huge stones, and timber is laid in the walls; this work goes on diligently and prospers in their hands. ⁹ Then we asked those elders and spoke to them thus, 'Who gave you a decree to build this house and to finish this structure?' ¹⁰ We also asked them their names, for your information, that we might write down the names of the men at their head. ¹¹ And this was their reply to us: 'We are the servants of the God of heaven and earth, and we are rebuilding the house that was built many years ago, which a great king of Israel built and finished. ¹² But because our fathers had angered the God of heaven, he gave them into the hand of Nebuchadnezzar king of Babylon, the Chaldean, who destroyed this house and carried away the people to Babylonia. ¹³ However in the first year of Cyrus king of Babylon, Cyrus the king made a decree that this house of God should be rebuilt. ¹⁴ And the gold and silver vessels of the house of God, which Nebuchadnezzar had taken out of the temple that was in Jerusalem and brought into the temple of Babylon, these Cyrus the king took out of the temple of Babylon, and they were delivered to one whose name was Sheshbazzar, whom he had made governor; ¹⁵ and he said to him, "Take these vessels, go and put them in the temple which is in Jerusalem, and let the house of God be rebuilt on its site." ¹⁶ Then this Sheshbazzar came and laid the foundations of the house of God which is in Jerusalem; and from that time until now it has been in building, and it is not yet finished.' ¹⁷ Therefore, if it seem good to the king, let search be made in the royal archives there in Babylon, to see whether a decree was issued by Cyrus the king for the rebuilding of this house of God in Jerusalem. And let the king send us his pleasure in this matter."

Tattenai sent a letter to Darius reporting the building activity of the Jews. In the letter he recounted the conversation which he had had with the Jewish elders, and requested instructions from Darius. He was joined in sending the letter not only by his Persian colleague Shetharbozenai, but also by *his associates the governors*. The latter were Persian authorities, often held to be royal investigators. The word translated "governors" is not the title applied to Tattenai or to Zerubbabel (Hag. 1:1). The incorrect translation in the RSV is based on 1 Esdras 6:7. The word might be rendered "authorities" or "officials" since the exact status and duties are unknown.

Tattenai, a Persian, did not refer to the Jewish Temple as *the house of the great God* (v. 8). The recension in 1 Esdras 6:9 shows that *great* modifies *house*, instead of *God*. Thus he was referring to the size of the building. On the other hand, although he was impressed with the size of the structure, the word translated *huge* in the following sentence does not refer to the size of the *stones*. It is a little known word which appears to designate a type of stone (cf. Bowman, p. 610).

In v. 10, as in v. 4, we are told that the Persians requested the names of the builders. No names are mentioned, however, not even that of Zerubbabel.

In reply to Tattenai's inquiry, the Jewish elders gave a lengthy rehearsal of their history since the time of Solomon (vv. 11–16). Such historical reviews are common in the Old Testament (cf. Deut. 1:5—3:29; Amos 2:9–12; Neh. 9:6–37), for the Israelite people had always understood themselves in terms of their past. The elders' explanation for why they were rebuilding the Temple logically began with Solomon, who had built the Temple there in the first place.

The elders attributed the destruction of Judah and the loss of the first Temple to the anger of their God (v. 12). It was the conviction of the biblical writers that God used foreign invaders to punish his people for their sins (cf. Amos 3:11; Judg. 2:13–15; 2 Chron. 36:15–17). They never intended to imply, however, that God approved of the evil invader or that his sins would go unpunished (cf. Isa. 10:5–19).

Tattenai requested Darius to search the royal archives in Babylon to determine whether or not Cyrus had issued the decree claimed by the elders (v. 17). That Babylon was indeed an appropriate place to seek the early records of Cyrus is indicated by the discovery there of the famous Cyrus Cylinder, which tells of Cyrus' conquest of the Chaldean Empire and of his initial acts for the restoration of the cults of subject peoples.

(3) *The Cyrus Decree (6:1–5)*

¹ Then Darius the king made a decree, and search was made in Babylonia, in the house of the archives where the documents were stored. ² And in Ecbatana, the capital which is in the province of Media, a scroll was found on which this was written: "A record. ³ In the first year of Cyrus the king, Cyrus the king issued a decree: Concerning the house of God at Jerusalem, let the house be rebuilt, the place where sacrifices are offered and burnt offerings are brought; its height shall be sixty cubits and its breadth sixty cubits, ⁴ with three courses of great stones and one course of timber; let the cost be paid from the royal treasury. ⁵ And also let the gold and silver vessels of the house of God, which Nebuchadnezzar took out of the temple that is in Jerusalem and brought to Babylon, be restored and brought back to the temple which is in Jerusalem, each to its place; you shall put them in the house of God."

After an unsuccessful *search was made in Babylonia,* a copy of the Cyrus edict was found in *Ecbatana.* Ecbatana was the former *capital* of Media and one of the capitals of the Persian empire, but the word translated "capital" here means a "fortress." Cyrus went from Babylon to this fortress city within months after his conquest of the Chaldean Empire (Olmstead, p. 57) and from there issued the edict. The document was then filed away "in the house of the rolls, where the treasures were laid up" (KJV).[21]

The wording of the decree in vv. 3–5 resembles what the elders had told Tattenai in 5:13–15. The similarity between the two passages need not mean that either one was fabricated by the author. It is more likely that the builders were thoroughly familiar with the wording of the edict and had committed parts of it to memory.

The differences between this Aramaic document and the Hebrew edict in 1:2–4 have received much attention. Bickerman argues convincingly that they are not to be understood as two versions of the same pronouncement (see comment on 1:2–4). The latter was an oral proclamation made to the Jews by heralds. The Aramaic edict, however, was a written "memorandum" (*record*), filed in the treasury because it involved the expenditure of royal funds.

The instructions for building the new Temple (which reflect consultation with Jewish subjects) are designed to restore the Temple which the Chaldeans had destroyed. Therefore it is clear that the impossible *sixty cubits* by *sixty cubits* (v. 3)

---

[21] The RSV makes an unwarranted change in the MT. Archaeological research has shown that it was the Persian practice to include document rooms in the royal treasury (cf. Bowman, p. 614).

represents a garbled version of the dimensions found in 1 Kings 6:2. The restored Temple, like the Temple of Solomon, was to be "sixty cubits long, twenty cubits wide, and thirty cubits high." [22]

The Temple is correctly described as *the place where sacrifices are offered*, but the words *and burnt offerings are brought* have been incorrectly translated. The Aramaic says literally "and its foundations brought." The latter phrase belongs with *let the house be rebuilt*, and apparently refers to the bringing of materials for foundations.

The type of construction indicated by courses of stone alternating with courses of timber is not clear. *Great stones* is the same phrase as that incorrectly translated "huge stones" in 5:8. This method was apparently used in the construction of Solomon's Temple (1 Kings 7:12), and Tattenai observed that the Jews were employing it at the time of his visit (5:8). It is believed to be an architectural technique designed to protect against earthquakes.[23]

(4) The Reply to Tattenai (6:6-13)

6 "Now therefore, Tattenai, governor of the province Beyond the River, Shetharbozenai, and your associates the governors who are in the province Beyond the River, keep away; 7 let the work on this house of God alone; let the governor of the Jews and the elders of the Jews rebuild this house of God on its site. 8 Moreover I make a decree regarding what you shall do for the elders of the Jews for the rebuilding of this house of God; the cost is to be paid to these men in full and without delay from the royal revenue, the tribute of the province from Beyond the River. 9 And whatever is needed—young bulls, rams, or sheep for burnt offerings to the God of heaven, wheat, salt, wine, or oil, as the priests at Jerusalem require—let that be given to them day by day without fail, 10 that they may offer pleasing sacrifices to the God of heaven, and pray for the life of the king and his sons. 11 Also I make a decree that if anyone alters this edict, a beam shall be pulled out of his house, and he shall be impaled upon it, and his house shall be made a dunghill. 12 May the God who has caused his name to dwell there overthrow any king or people that shall put forth a hand to alter this, or to destroy this house of God which is in Jerusalem. I Darius make a decree; let it be done with all diligence."

13 Then, according to the word sent by Darius the king, Tattenai, the governor of the province Beyond the River, Shetharbozenai, and their associates did with all diligence what Darius the king had ordered.

As soon as Darius saw the Cyrus memorandum, he sent a sharp reply to Tattenai, Shetharbozenai, and their fellow investigators. The Jews were not only to be allowed to continue the building, but they were to be subsidized generously from *the royal revenue*. Threats were added to assure that there would be no further interference with the Jewish cult.

The customary epistolary introduction is missing from the letter. The compiler utilizing the Aramaic source was intent upon the edict. He proceeded directly from the story of its discovery into the quotation of its contents. The latter was part of the reply to Tattenai, but the beginning of the letter was inadvertently omitted.

Darius shared the concern of the other Persian kings for the religions of subject peoples. On another occasion Darius intervened also to protect a non-Persian cult from government interference.[24]

The motivation of Darius in protecting the religious rights of the Jews was, in part at least, that they should *pray for the life of the king and his sons*. He may have had political motives, too, for Egypt had rebelled in 522 B.C. and was not recovered by Darius until 518 (Olmstead, pp. 113, 142). The friendship of the Jews, who were so close to the border of Egypt, was surely a concern of Darius.

---

[22] The cubit was the length of the forearm, once standardized as 17.6 inches. The cubit mentioned here may be the "long cubit" (Ezek. 41:8), however, which was 20.57 inches (cf. Bowman, p. 615).

[23] For the use of timber in walls of stone and brick, see H. C. Thomson, "A Row of Cedar Beams," *Palestine Exploration Quarterly*, January-June, 1960, pp. 57–63. Cf. Nelson Glueck, "Ezion-geber," *Biblical Archaeologist*, Sept., 1965, pp. 73–74.

[24] For his intervention in the Gadatas affair, see G. W. Botsford and E. G. Sihler, *Hellenic Civilization* (New York: Columbia University Press, 1920), p. 162.

The general content of Darius' instruction to Tattenai is historically credible. The cultic language of v. 9, however, could not have originated with Darius. It might be explained as the result of consultation with Jewish leaders, or as wording supplied by a Jewish scribe at the Persian court (cf. Rudolph, pp. 57–58). However, in this case, there are unmistakable earmarks of the Chronicler's language and style. The list of offerings and the phrase *day by day* are best understood as amplification supplied by the Chronicler when he adapted the Aramaic source to his narrative.

In addition to animals for sacrifice the cult required other products. *Wheat* was used for cereal offerings, which usually required also the use of olive *oil* and *salt* (cf. Lev. 2:1–16). *Wine* was regularly used as a libation or drink offering to accompany public sacrifices (Ex. 29:40–42). The extent to which the Persians actually furnished all these things from the royal revenue is not known. We are told that Tattenai and his associates *did with all diligence what Darius the king had ordered.* However, the silence of Haggai and Zechariah about any kind of grants suggests that the help, if any, was only token. It is well-known that the royal will was not always fully implemented in the remote provinces.

Darius decreed the most severe punishment for anyone who dared to alter his edict. His home was to be pulled down and to *be made a dunghill,* i.e., turned into a public latrine (cf. 2 Kings 10:27). Moreover, the guilty man was to be taken from his homeless family and executed by being impaled on a sharpened beam which had been torn from his own house. This type of execution is particularly well-attested in the Assyrian records, and Herodotus (*History*, III.159) confirms that it was a Persian practice, also.

Darius expected that God himself would stand ready also to punish anyone who altered the edict or otherwise interfered with his Temple. The phrase *the God who has caused his name*[25] *to dwell there* is distinctly Deuteronomic (e.g., Deut. 12:11; 14:33). If it is original in the decree it must be attributed to one of Darius' Jewish consultants.

3. *The Completion of the Work (6:14–18)*

14 And the elders of the Jews built and prospered, through the prophesying of Haggai the prophet and Zechariah the son of Iddo. They finished their building by command of the God of Israel and by decree of Cyrus and Darius and Artaxerxes king of Persia; 15 and this house was finished on the third day of the month of Adar, in the sixth year of the reign of Darius the king.
16 And the people of Israel, the priests and the Levites, and the rest of the returned exiles, celebrated the dedication of this house of God with joy. 17 They offered at the dedication of this house of God one hundred bulls, two hundred rams, four hundred lambs, and as a sin offering for all Israel twelve he-goats, according to the number of the tribes of Israel. 18 And they set the priests in their divisions and the Levites in their courses, for the service of God at Jerusalem, as it is written in the book of Moses.

The letter of Darius cleared the way for the speedy completion of the Temple. When the work was finished, the building was dedicated, and the priests and Levites were organized for their official cultic functions.

Haggai and Zechariah are associated with the final stages of the work. Indeed, they may have remained active in Jerusalem for many years. Yet the books attributed to the two prophets do not reflect any knowledge of the completion of the Temple. All the messages in Haggai are dated in the year 520 B.C., and the latest date in Zechariah is in the year 518 B.C. (Zech. 7:1). Though Haggai and Zechariah may have been still present in Jerusalem when the Temple was completed in 515 B.C., it is reasonably certain that Zerubbabel was not. The work was com-

---

25 The divine name shared in, and was almost identified with, the very being of God. In the postexilic period "the name" actually becomes a surrogate for "God" (cf. Lev. 24:11–16).

pleted by *the elders of the Jews,* and nothing further is said about Zerubbabel. It is surmised that the Persians heard about the nationalistic excitement in Judah and recalled him.

The decrees of *Cyrus and Darius* were instrumental in making it possible for the Temple to be rebuilt. Mention of Artaxerxes creates a problem, however, since this king did not begin to reign until 50 years after the Temple had been completed. The phrase *and Artaxerxes king of Persia* is possibly an addition by someone who misunderstood the significance of 4:7–23.

The Temple was completed *in the sixth year of the reign of Darius.* The Masoretic Text says *on the third day of the month of Adar* (the Babylonian name for February–March, the twelfth month of the year). According to 1 Esdras 7:5, however, the work was completed on the twenty-third day of Adar. The latter date is preferred since the third day was apparently a sabbath, on which no work would be done (cf. Bowman, p. 619). Thus the building of the Temple came to a successful conclusion in the early spring of the year 515 B.C.

The story of the dedication of the new Temple indicates that there was a conscious attempt to imitate the ceremony associated with the dedication of Solomon's Temple (1 Kings 8; 2 Chron. 5—7). This is what one would expect. The general reliability of the account is indicated by the relatively modest number of animals sacrificed. The postexilic community could not afford the large number of animals sacrificed at the dedication of the first Temple.

Verses 16–18 do not appear to be homogeneous with the rest of the Aramaic source. In the first part of the narrative the people of Jerusalem are "the Jews," but here they are *the people of Israel,* who offer a sacrifice *for all Israel . . . according to the number of the tribes of Israel.* This portrayal of the Judean community as the original 12 tribes of Israel undoubtedly reflects a change of authorship. The second author is not the Chronicler, however, for the latter characteristically attributes the organization of the priests and Levites to David (1 Chron. 23—26). The unknown author of this short appendix to the Aramaic source attributes it to *the book of Moses.*

4. Observance of the Passover (6:19–22)

19 On the fourteenth day of the first month the returned exiles kept the passover. 20 For the priests and the Levites had purified themselves together; all of them were clean. So they killed the passover lamb for all the returned exiles, for their fellow priests, and for themselves; 21 it was eaten by the people of Israel who had returned from exile, and also by every one who had joined them and separated himself from the pollutions of the peoples of the land to worship the LORD, the God of Israel. 22 And they kept the feast of unleavened bread seven days with joy; for the LORD had made them joyful, and had turned the heart of the king of Assyria to them, so that he aided them in the work of the house of God, the God of Israel.

About three weeks after the dedication of the Temple, the Jews celebrated another joyous occasion—the Passover and the Feast of Unleavened Bread. The celebration of these feasts was also associated with the rededication of the Temple under Hezekiah (2 Chron. 30:13–22) and under Josiah (2 Kings 23:21–23; 2 Chron. 35:1–19).

The Chronicler in presenting this story abandoned the Aramaic language and resumed the Hebrew in which he had composed 1:1—4:7.

The origin of the Passover may be traced to an early pastoral festival and that of the Feast of Unleavened Bread to an agricultural celebration. Yet the Israelites combined the two feasts and used them to commemorate the exodus from Egypt (Ex. 12:1–27; 2 Chron. 35:1–19). The Passover was celebrated *on the fourteenth day of the first month* (Nisan or Abib), and the Feast of Unleavened Bread on the seven succeeding days.

Although the Masoretic Text is ambiguous, it was apparently the Levites who *had purified themselves* and who *killed the* passover lamb for all the returned exiles, for their fellow priests, and for themselves. The purification was a ritual cleansing with water (Ex. 29:4; Num. 8:7) designed to remove any contamination which might render them unfit to participate in the sacrifice.

The feast was observed *by the people of Israel who had returned from the exile.* The Chronicler characteristically looks upon these as constituting the heart and core of the postexilic community. He notes, however, that the returned exiles were joined by certain individuals who had purified themselves *from the pollutions of the peoples of the land.* In the light of 4:1-3, the identity of those who were allowed to join the returned exiles in the celebration of the Passover must remain uncertain. They may have been nonexilic Jews who had agreed to accept the rigid orthodoxy of those who had come from Babylonia. On the other hand, even circumcised aliens were eligible to join in the feast (Num. 9:14; Ex. 12:48).

The celebration of the feasts was accompanied by great joy. *The Lord had made them joyful* because he had given them favor in the eyes of the king and had thus made it possible for them to complete their Temple. *The king of Assyria* is, of course, Darius whose letter to Tattenai had paved the way for the completion of the work. He was really king of Persia, but both titles may have been applied to him since Persia included all of what had once been the Assyrian Empire.

VI. Ezra's Journey to Jerusalem (7:1—8:36)

1. Introduction (7:1-10)

(1) Ezra's Genealogy (7:1-5)

¹ Now after this, in the reign of Artaxerxes king of Persia, Ezra the son of Seraiah, son of Azariah, son of Hilkiah, ² son of Shallum, son of Zadok, son of Ahitub, ³ son of Amariah, son of Azariah, son of Meraioth, ⁴ son of Zerahiah, son of Uzzi, son of Bukki, ⁵ son of Abishua, son of Phinehas, son of Eleazar, son of Aaron the chief priests—

After completing the story of the rebuilding of the Temple the present text proceeds directly into the Ezra narrative. There is a major chronological gap between 6:22 and 7:1. By any interpretation of the data, Ezra's career must be dated many decades after 515 B.C. Such gaps in the time sequence were of minor concern to the ancient Jew. His primary purpose was to disclose "the saving acts of the Lord" (Mic. 6:5) and not to present a complete unbroken history.

The work of Ezra is dated *in the reign of Artaxerxes king of Persia.* There were three Persian kings who bore the name Artaxerxes. Although the Chronicler does not specify which one is intended, tradition has assumed that it was Artaxerxes I (465-424 B.C.). There are compelling reasons, however, to identify the king as Artaxerxes II (404-358 B.C.; see Introduction). His seventh year (7:7) was 398 B.C., and thus apparently the year in which Ezra came to Jerusalem.

If the narrative is now in its original order, *now after this* would refer back approximately 117 years to the dedication of the second Temple. There is reason to believe, however, that the story of Nehemiah once stood in correct chronological sequence between chapters 1—6 and 7—10 (see Introduction). In this event the phrase could refer to the work of Nehemiah, which was completed only about three decades before the mission of Ezra.

Ezra's credentials as a priest are presented in the form of a genealogy. He is shown to be a descendant of Aaron, which was the usual criterion of legitimation in the postexilic period. But he is presented also as a descendant of Zadok. This datum rendered him acceptable to any who still maintained that the priesthood should be strictly Zadokite (cf. Ezek. 40—48).

Ezra's genealogy is based on 1 Chronicles 6:3-15, but it has apparently suffered from transmission. Six names (which appear in 1 Chron. 6:7-11) are missing between Azariah and Meraioth of v. 3. These names were probably omitted unintentionally by a scribe who was confused by the double appearance of the name Amariah in his list (1 Chron. 6:7,11; cf. Bowman, p. 623).

The same type of error could have resulted in the omission of four or five names between Ezra and Seraiah. Ezra's father may have had the name Seraiah, but *Seraiah, son of Azariah* was not the father of Ezra. He was the high priest killed by the Chaldeans at the time of the fall of Jerusalem in 587 B.C. (2 Kings 25:18-21). The Chronicler could have intended only that Ezra was a descendant (another meaning for *son*) of the high priest Seraiah. It is equally possible, however, that the eye of a scribe passed from Seraiah father of Ezra to Seraiah the high priest, accidentally omitting the intervening generations.

(2) *Anticipatory Summary of Ezra's Work* (7:6-10)

⁶ this Ezra went up from Babylonia. He was a scribe skilled in the law of Moses which the LORD the God of Israel had given; and the king granted him all that he asked, for the hand of the LORD his God was upon him.
⁷ And there went up also to Jerusalem, in the seventh year of Artaxerxes the king, some of the people of Israel, and some of the priests and Levites, the singers and gatekeepers, and the temple servants. ⁸ And he came to Jerusalem in the fifth month, which was in the seventh year of the king; ⁹ for on the first day of the first month he began to go up from Babylonia, and on the first day of the fifth month he came to Jerusalem, for the good hand of his God was upon him. ¹⁰ For Ezra had set his heart to study the law of the LORD, and to do it, and to teach his statutes and ordinances in Israel.

After presenting Ezra's priestly credentials, the Chronicler offers a brief summary of Ezra's work, composed in the third person. This summary anticipates specifically the first person passage in 7:27—8:34 and looks forward more generally to the rest of Ezra's career.

Ezra is referred to as *a scribe.* Originally a scribe (*sopher*) was one who possessed the skill to cipher (*saphar*). Gradually the term came to be applied to anyone who cultivated the art of numbers and writing. Since this skill was indispensable in government, scribes were always found among the officers of a king. Note the role of scribes in the government of David (2 Sam. 8:17; 20:25); Solomon (1 Kings 4:3); Hezekiah (Isa. 36:1-22); Josiah (2 Kings 22:3-20); and Jehoiakim (Jer. 36:20,21).

The scribal skill was nurtured also for religious purposes, with the result that the term scribe came to designate one who specialized in the interpretation of the Torah. This technical use of the word however is not encountered until late in the postexilic period (cf. 1 Chron. 2:55; 2 Chron. 34:13; Sirach 38:24—39:11; Matt. 2:4; 13:52). Both the political and religious connotations of the word may be relevant to some extent in the case of Ezra.

It has long been held that Ezra was an officer in the Persian bureaucracy and that he came to Judah in his official capacity. His title may have been that conveyed by his position, for it is known that there were scribes in the service of the Persian government (4:8-9; cf. Esther 3:12; 8:9). That he held any office before his commission to go to Judah must remain a matter of conjecture. The commission itself, however, gave him official standing.

Although Ezra's title may have derived originally from a political role, the Chronicler understood it differently. For him Ezra was a scribe because he was *skilled in the law of Moses.* The legitimacy of the Chronicler's use of the title cannot be denied. Ezra was, if anything, a student and teacher of the law, and the Chronicler was too nearly a contemporary of Ezra (see Introduction) for his use of the title to be an anachronism. If Ezra held the political office of scribe, he held it because he was in fact an expert in Jewish law.

The Chronicler has not preserved the story of Ezra's interview with Artaxerxes II. He tells us simply that *the king granted him all that he asked.* It is implied that Ezra took the initiative in making a specific request to the king and that the king responded by granting him the rescript found in vv. 12–26.

Ezra's trip to Jerusalem required about four months. The journey was begun in *the first month* (Nisan: March–April) and completed in *the fifth month* (Ab: July–August). *The first day of the first month* may have been the day on which the first lap of the journey was begun, or it may have been the day on which a firm decision about the journey was made. (A minor change in the Masoretic vowel points will permit the latter interpretation; cf. Bowman, p. 625.) The final departure from the river Ahava did not take place until the twelfth day, however (8:31).

Ezra was accompanied on his return by a group of laymen and cultic personnel. The corresponding list in chapter 8 does not specify *singers and gatekeepers.* This phrase may have been inserted by a later editor who did not realize that the Chronicler characteristically included these groups among the *Levites,* and who therefore concluded that they had been overlooked.

The Chronicler had a profound awareness of the sovereignty and benevolence of God in the affairs of his people. Ezra's mission was made possible through a generous grant from the king, but Ezra received the grant only because *the hand of the Lord his God was upon him.* Likewise, the long dangerous journey from Babylonia to Judea was safe and successful because *the good hand of his God was upon him.* It was the Chronicler's faith that God was working out his purpose in history and that he had chosen Ezra as an instrument of that purpose.

Ezra is described as a man completely dedicated to the task which God had set for him. He *had set his heart to study the law of the Lord* and to learn its meaning for his own life and for that of his people. But he would not only learn the law, he would *do it,* and he would conform himself to it. For only then would he be able effectively *to teach his statutes and ordinances in Israel.*

2. The Artaxerxes Rescript (7:11–26)

(1) The Chronicler's Introduction (7:11)

11 This is a copy of the letter which King Artaxerxes gave to Ezra the priest, the scribe, learned in matters of the commandments of the Lord and his statutes for Israel:

The Chronicler offers the Aramaic document in vv. 12–26 as *a copy of the letter which King Artaxerxes gave to Ezra.* Although a majority of scholars defend the essential authenticity of the document, many remain uncertain whether or not it is a verbatim copy free of editorial supplement.

Even the most conservative critics admit that a Jew has had some kind of role in the composition of the decree. This is indicated by the fact that the document reflects a familiarity with the minutiae of the Jewish religion which a Persian would not possess. It need not follow, however, that the edict has been revised or supplemented by a later Jewish editor. It is possible that the grant simply reflects specific requests made to the king by Ezra (cf. v. 6). In any event, Artaxerxes did not dictate the decree without prior consultation with Jews.[26]

More perplexing than the Jewish character of the rescript is the fact that it grants Ezra vast powers which he apparently never used. There is a marked contrast between the authority granted Ezra in the decree and that which he actually exercised during his mission. The easiest solution to the problem is to propose that the original edict has been supplemented and expanded by an overzealous admirer of Ezra. While this possibility cannot be ruled out entirely, neither can it be proved. The discrepancy could be accounted for in other ways. The edict reflects the ambitious hopes and plans of Jews who have

---

[26] In 419 B.C. a Jew named Yedoniah wrote a letter to the Jews at Elephantine in Egypt. He included in this letter a decree of Darius II setting forth specific instructions for the observance of the Passover and the Feast of Unleavened Bread (ANET, p. 491). One need not doubt the authenticity of this decree, yet both the granting of the decree and the nature of its contents must be attributed to Jewish initiative.

never been to Judea and who live hundreds of miles away in Babylonia. It would not be surprising if the actual implementation of Ezra's commission were substantially different from the idealistic hopes projected before the journey began.

(2) Authorization for the Trip (7:12-14)

¹² "Artaxerxes, king of kings, to Ezra the priest, the scribe of the law of the God of heaven. And now ¹³ I make a decree that any one of the people of Israel or their priests or Levites in my kingdom, who freely offers to go to Jerusalem, may go with you. ¹⁴ For you are sent by the king and his seven counselors to make inquiries about Judah and Jerusalem according to the law of your God, which is in your hand,

The letter of Artaxerxes to Ezra is in the Aramaic language. This in itself is an argument for its genuineness. Aramaic was the regular language of diplomacy in the western part of the Persian Empire (cf. 4:8—22; 5:7—6:12), as is so clearly attested by the Elephantine Papyri, for example. The orthography of the Aramaic in Ezra is in some respects less archaic than that of the fifth-century Elephantine Papyri. This is not to be considered as evidence against the authenticity of the former, however. It is well known that the orthography of biblical books has been modernized by copyists (cf. Albright, "The Date and Personality of the Chronicler," p. 118).

Ezra is referred to as *the scribe of the law of the God of heaven.* The fact that the word for *law* is Persian, instead of Hebrew or Aramaic, lends support to the view that Ezra may have held some kind of official position in the Persian government. Although this theory must remain tentative for lack of clear evidence, it would throw light on the origin of Ezra's mission and on the Jewishness of Artaxerxes' decree.

Artaxerxes' permission that any Jew who wished might *go to Jerusalem* was simply a reaffirmation of the well-established policy of his predecessors (cf. 1:3). The language of the grant, however, is of Jewish origin. The division of the people into *people of Israel, . . . priests* and *Levites* did not originate with a Persian. Moreover, the phrase *any one . . . who freely offers* is a stereotyped Jewish expression which originated with the request of Ezra or with the king's Jewish consultants.

Ezra was commissioned *by the king and his seven counselors* (cf. Esther 1:14; Xenophon, *Anabasis* I.6.4–5) to investigate the extent to which Jewish law was being observed in *Judah and Jerusalem.* The investigation was, of course, associated with his commission to promulgate Jewish law among all of the Jews who lived west of the Euphrates (vv. 25–26). It was the Persian policy to encourage such local autonomy among all of the loyal, peaceful peoples of the empire.[27] That Jewish law rather than Persian law was used in Judea during the Persian period is evident from the memoirs of Nehemiah (cf. Neh. 5, 13). Moreover, if the Torah had been proscribed by the Persians, it would have left an indelible mark on the literature of the era.

The law of your God, which is in your hand does not refer to some specific scroll which Ezra was carrying. This is made clear in v. 25 where we have the synonymous phrase "the wisdom of God which is in your hand." Ezra was authorized to regulate the affairs of the Judean community by Jewish law in general. It has often been held that Ezra was commissioned to introduce some previously unknown code in Judea. That this was not the case is seen by the fact that the law which he taught there was already known to most of the Jews (v. 25). They even wept when they heard the reading of the familiar words (Neh. 8:9). It was clearly the role of Ezra to call the Jews back to the Torah, with which they were already acquainted.

It is impossible to determine exactly what form the Torah had taken by the time of Ezra. There was a scroll called "the book of the law of Moses" (Neh. 8:1), but evidence is insufficient to identify it with

---

[27] cf. R. W. Rogers, *A History of Ancient Persia* (New York: Charles Scribner's Sons, 1929), pp. 188, 189).

any specific document such as Deuteronomy or the completed Pentateuch.

(3) Gifts from Babylonia (7:15-20)

15 and also to convey the silver and gold which the king and his counselors have freely offered to the God of Israel, whose dwelling is in Jerusalem, 16 with all the silver and gold which you shall find in the whole province of Babylonia, and with the freewill offerings of the people and the priests, vowed willingly for the house of their God which is in Jerusalem. 17 With this money, then, you shall with all diligence buy bulls, rams, and lambs, with their cereal offerings and their drink offerings, and you shall offer them upon the altar of the house of your God which is in Jerusalem. 18 Whatever seems good to you and your brethren to do with the rest of the silver and gold, you may do, according to the will of your God. 19 The vessels that have been given you for service of the house of your God, you shall deliver before the God of Jerusalem. 20 And whatever else is required for the house of your God, which you have occasion to provide, you may provide it out of the king's treasury.

The rescript anticipated that Ezra would be liberally supplied with gifts for the Temple and cult before he left for Judah. It is entirely credible that *the king and his counselors* would join *the people and the priests* in providing generous support for the worship of *the God of Jerusalem.* It was necessary, however, that Ezra have royal permission to transport this wealth across several hundreds of miles to Judah and to put it to the use for which it was intended. Such permission was specifically granted. That Ezra was authorized *to convey . . . all the silver and gold which* he should *find in the whole province of Babylonia* has often been misunderstood. Obviously, it does not mean that he is being given indiscriminate access to all the wealth of Babylonia. It simply means that he is being granted an export permit for all the funds which he can raise.

Again in this passage one observes Jewish influence. References to *freewill offerings, cereal offerings,* and *drink offerings,* for example, show that the rescript has been shaped to meet the specific and technical needs of the Jewish cult.

Permission to draw supplies from *the king's treasury* for the use of the Jewish cult creates no problem of credibility. Cyrus, Cambyses, and both Darius I and Darius II are noted for their generosity to non-Persian cults in various parts of the empire.

(4) Instructions to Officials in the West (7:21-24)

21 "And I, Artaxerxes the king, make a decree to all the treasurers in the province Beyond the River: Whatever Ezra the priest, the scribe of the law of the God of heaven, requires of you, be it done with all diligence, 22 up to a hundred talents of silver, a hundred cors of wheat, a hundred baths of wine, a hundred baths of oil, and salt without prescribing how much. 23 Whatever is commanded by the God of heaven, let it be done in full for the house of the God of heaven, lest his wrath be against the realm of the king and his sons. 24 We also notify you that it shall not be lawful to impose tribute, custom, or toll upon any one of the priests, the Levites, the singers, the doorkeepers, the temple servants, or other servants of this house of God.

Ezra's authorization to use royal supplies could not be implemented without the cooperation of *the treasurers in the province Beyond the River.* Consequently, Artaxerxes included a paragraph of instructions to these officials.

Very generous limits are placed on the amount of *silver, wheat, wine,* and *oil* which Ezra could requisition from the royal treasuries. The very fact that limits are prescribed, however, may be evidence for the general authenticity of this part of the decree. There is no evidence that Ezra ever requested or received such large quantities of supplies.

Artaxerxes' motive for subsidizing the Jewish cult was to secure the goodwill of the *God of heaven* for *the realm of the king and his sons.* This is the same motive expressed by Cyrus for his benevolent acts toward non-Persian gods (ANET, p. 316). There were doubtless more mundane considerations also. It was clearly in the interests of Persia to cultivate goodwill among vassal people. It was particularly important for Artaxerxes II to have the friendship of Judah at this time. Only a few years earlier Egypt had rebelled and had temporarily pulled itself out of the empire (cf. Olmstead, pp. 373-374) A friendly Judah would be important for the anticipated reconquest of Egypt.

The authorities in the west were notified that no *tribute, custom,* or *toll* were to be imposed upon any of the clerical personnel associated with *this house of God.* The listing of *the priests, the Levites, the singers, the doorkeepers,* and *the temple servants* can be attributed to Jewish origins. The policy of exempting cultic personnel from the payment of taxes, however, was genuinely Persian. Darius I reprimanded Gadatas for imposing such burdens upon cultic personnel at an Apollo shrine in Magnesia.[28]

(5) *Ezra's Political Prerogatives (7:25–26)*

25 "And you, Ezra, according to the wisdom of your God which is in your hand, appoint magistrates and judges who may judge all the people in the province Beyond the River, all such as know the laws of your God; and those who do not know them, you shall teach. 26 Whoever will not obey the law of your God and the law of the king, let judgment be strictly executed upon him, whether for death or for banishment or for confiscation of his goods or for imprisonment."

The closing paragraph of the edict appears to give Ezra a great deal of political power. He was commissioned to set up the political machinery (*appoint magistrates and judges*) necessary for the implementation of Torah as the officially recognized law for the Jews. His authority extended to apostate Jews (who were to be taught the law), but certainly not to *all the people in the province Beyond the River.* His jurisdiction was confined to *such as know the laws of your God,* who were of course the Jews of Judah.

It is not surprising that the power to punish was included with the power to implement Torah. The Torah provided for punishment, even execution. True local autonomy for the Jews of Judah necessarily included the power to impose punishments prescribed by the Torah. *The law of your God and the law of the king* are not to be understood as two different laws. The phrase means simply that Jewish law had royal sanction and therefore the backing of the Persian government.

E. The First Person Account of the Return (7:27—8:34)

(1) *Ezra's Doxology (7:27–28)*

27 Blessed be the LORD, the God of our fathers, who put such a thing as this into the heart of the king, to beautify the house of the LORD which is in Jerusalem, 28 and who extended to me his steadfast love before the king and his counselors, and before all the king's mighty officers. I took courage, for the hand of the LORD my God was upon me, and I gathered leading men from Israel to go up with me.

Following the Artaxerxes rescript, which is written in Aramaic, the narrative is resumed in the Hebrew language. These verses comprise a short doxology in which Ezra praises God as the one who has made his mission possible. To this man of faith, it was not his own initiative or even the ulterior motives of Artaxerxes II but rather the sovereign purpose of God which had *put such a thing as this into the heart of the king.*

The doxology introduces a substantial passage composed in the first person. Such passages in which Ezra is the speaker may not be verbatim excerpts from an Ezra memoir. They are, however, important evidence that the Chronicler employed a journal of Ezra in the preparation of the Ezra narrative (see Introduction).

(2) *Genealogy of Those Returning with Ezra (8:1–14)*

1 These are the heads of their fathers' houses, and this is the genealogy of those who went up with me from Babylonia, in the reign of Artaxerxes the king: 2 Of the sons of Phinehas, Gershom. Of the sons of Ithamar, Daniel. Of the sons of David, Hattush, 3 of the sons of Shecaniah. Of the sons of Parosh, Zechariah, with whom were registered one hundred and

---

[28] Botsford and Sihler, *op. cit.,* p. 162.

fifty men. 4 Of the sons of Pahathmoab, Eliehoenai the son of Zerahiah, and with him two hundred men. 5 Of the sons of Zattu, Shecaniah the son of Jahaziel, and with him three hundred men. 6 Of the sons of Adin, Ebed the son of Jonathan, and with him fifty men. 7 Of the sons of Elam, Jeshaiah the son of Athaliah, and with him seventy men. 8 Of the sons of Shephatiah, Zebadiah the son of Michael, and with him eighty men. 9 Of the sons of Joab, Obadiah the son of Jehiel, and with him two hundred and eighteen men. 10 Of the sons of Bani, Shelomith the son of Josiphiah, and with him a hundred and sixty men. 11 Of the sons of Bebai, Zechariah, the son of Bebai, and with him twenty-eight men. 12 Of the sons of Azgad, Johanan the son of Hakkatan, and with him a hundred and ten men. 13 Of the sons of Adonikam, those who came later, their names being Eliphelet, Jeuel, and Shemaiah, and with them sixty men. 14 Of the sons of Bigvai, Uthai and Zaccur, and with them seventy men.

At the end of the preceding passage Ezra says that he "gathered leading men from Israel" (7:28) to accompany him to Jerusalem. Before telling the story of the actual journey he provides brief genealogical legitimation for those who are to go with him.

The first two names are those of priests. *Gershom* is a descendant of Aaron through his grandson *Phinehas* (cf. Ex. 6:25). *Daniel* is descended from Aaron through his son *Ithamar* (cf. Num. 3:2). By the time of Ezra, the legitimate priesthood was comprised of the descendants of Aaron. One should not get the impression that there were only two priests in Ezra's company. Twelve additional priests are referred to in v. 24, and there were probably many more. *Gershom* and *Daniel* are family heads, but the number of priests who accompanied them is not given.

The third person mentioned is *Hattush, of the sons of Shecaniah*. Unlike most of the other men listed in the genealogy, Hattush was not the head of a family group. He is listed separately because he was a royal prince of the house of David and a descendant of king Jehoiachin.

Twelve lay families are enumerated in vv. 3–14. The formula included the name of the remote ancestor who founded the family, the name of the representative (with his father's name) who accompanied Ezra, and the number of males who returned with him. The formula is incomplete in v. 3 where the name of the father of *Zechariah* is lacking. The names *Zattu* and *Bani* have been lost from the Masoretic Text, but recovered with the aid of 1 Esdras. The latter recension shows also that *Uthai* was the son of *Zaccur,* and that the text should read "with him seventy men" (1 Esd. 8:40). Verse 13 is as obscure in the Masoretic Text as it is in the RSV, but the Greek recensions of the text suggest that the phrase translated *those who came later* means that *Eliphelet, Jeuel, and Shemaiah* were the final members of the family of *Adonikam* to return from the Babylonian exile.

All of the founding fathers mentioned in vv. 3–14 are also listed in 2:3–15 (cf. Neh. 7:8–20). This does not mean that either list was fabricated from the other (cf. Rudolph, p. 79). It is not surprising that the same prominent families of exilic Jews should be mentioned in more than one context. Moreover, the two lists are significantly different.

(3) Recruitment of Levites (8:15–20)

15 I gathered them to the river that runs to Ahava, and there we encamped three days. As I reviewed the people and the priests, I found there none of the sons of Levi. 16 Then I sent for Eliezer, Ariel, Shemaiah, Elnathan, Jarib, Elnathan, Nathan, Zechariah, and Meshullam, leading men, and for Joiarib and Elnathan, who were men of insight, 17 and sent them to Iddo, the leading man at the place Casiphia, telling them what to say to Iddo and his brethren the temple servants at the place Casiphia, namely, to send us ministers for the house of our God. 18 And by the good hand of our God upon us, they brought us a man of discretion, of the sons of Mahli the son of Levi, son of Israel, namely Sherebiah with his sons and kinsmen, eighteen; 19 also Hashabiah and with him Jeshaiah of the sons of Merari, with his kinsmen and their sons, twenty; 20 besides two hundred and twenty of the temple servants, whom David and his officials had set apart to attend the Levites. These were all mentioned by name.

Ezra assembled his large caravan [29] in the open countryside in order to make necessary preparations for the long, dangerous journey. Positive identification for *the river that runs to Ahava* is lacking, but it was doubtless a small stream or canal in the Euphrates Valley.

While organizing and reviewing the caravan, Ezra discovered that there were no *sons of Levi* among the group. The encampment was extended from *three days* to 12 (v. 31), so that this situation could be remedied. A delegation was dispatched *to Iddo, the leading man at the place Casiphia* (both otherwise unidentified) to seek *ministers* (cultic servants) for the Temple. As a result, three leading Levites and 38 of their colleagues, along with 220 of the temple servants, were induced to join the caravan.

The word translated "for" in v. 16 is also used in Hebrew as the sign of the direct object, so that one should translate v. 16, "I sent Eliezer, Ariel, . . ." The names of the delegates have been somewhat confused in transmission. First Esdras 8:44 shows that *and for Joiarib and Elnathan* is an accidental repetition of the *Jarib, Elnathan* above and should be omitted. *Men of insight* would then correctly apply to the entire group.

(4) Fasting and Prayer (8:21–23)

21 Then I proclaimed a fast there, at the river Ahava, that we might humble ourselves before our God, to seek from him a straight way for ourselves, our children, and all our goods. 22 For I was ashamed to ask the king for a band of soldiers and horsemen to protect us against the enemy on our way; since we had told the king, "The hand of our God is for good upon all that seek him, and the power of his wrath is against all that forsake him." 23 So we fasted and besought our God for this, and he listened to our entreaty.

In spite of the general efficiency of the Persian government the road from Babylonia to Judah was not secure (cf. v. 31). A

---

[29] The total number of males listed in the genealogy amounts to about 1,500. In addition, allowance should be made for the women, children, and the unspecified number of priests who accompanied Gershom and Daniel.

---

large caravan with women and children and rich treasures (vv. 25–27) would be vulnerable to every band of robbers along the way. Nehemiah, who was no less a man of faith than Ezra, had accepted the sensible precaution of a military escort (Neh. 2:9). Ezra, however, *was ashamed to ask the king for a band of soldiers and horsemen*, lest he create the impression that he doubted the providence of God. Instead, he took the responsibility for the security of the caravan himself, and held a special prayer service to seek from God *a straight way* (American Translation: "a safe journey"). The phrase *to protect us against the enemy* is in the Masoretic Text "to help us against the enemy" (KJV). This implies that Ezra was willing for the members of his caravan to use every means at their disposal to protect themselves. His prayer therefore is not a substitute for security measures but a plea that God will render them successful.

Ezra's season of prayer was accompanied by fasting. Fasting was a means by which the supplicant expressed his humility and earnestness before God. The right kind of fast was believed to be effective in making one's "voice to be heard on high" (Isa. 58:4).

(5) Securing the Treasures (8:24–30)

24 Then I set apart twelve of the leading priests: Sherebiah, Hashabiah, and ten of their kinsmen with them. 25 And I weighed out to them the silver and the gold and the vessels, the offering for the house of our God which the king and his counselors and his lords and all Israel there present had offered; 26 I weighed out into their hand six hundred and fifty talents of silver, and silver vessels worth a hundred talents, and a hundred talents of gold, 27 twenty bowls of gold worth a thousand darics, and two vessels of fine bright bronze as precious as gold. 28 And I said to them, "You are holy to the Lord, and the vessels are holy; and the silver and the gold are a freewill offering to the Lord, the God of your fathers. 29 Guard them and keep them until you weigh them before the chief priests and the Levites and the heads of fathers' houses in Israel at Jerusalem, within the chambers of the house of the Lord." 30 So the priests and the Levites

took over the weight of the silver and the gold and the vessels, to bring them to Jerusalem, to the house of our God.

After praying that God would grant his caravan a safe journey, Ezra took special precautions for the safety of the treasures. He delegated this important responsibility to *twelve of the leading priests* and to twelve Levites, including *Sherebiah* and *Hashabiah*, who had recently joined the group (cf. 8:18–19).[30] The priests probably had the major responsibility for the offerings, while the Levites were in charge of the actual transportation (cf. Num. 3:8,31; 4:1–15). It was customary for the consecrated cultic officials to have the oversight of objects which had been dedicated to the service of God.

The quantity of the treasure is staggering. The Chronicler was sometimes overly enthusiastic in reporting numbers (contrast 2 Sam. 24:24 with 1 Chron. 21:25), and it is possible that the numbers here have been inflated. On the other hand, one would expect the amount of the treasure to be substantial. It had been donated in part by *the king and his counselors and his lords*, who were concerned to have the goodwill of the Jews and the blessings of their God. It also represented the donations of *all Israel* who remained in Babylonia.

(6) *Journey and Arrival (8:31–34)*

31 Then we departed from the river Ahava on the twelfth day of the first month, to go to Jerusalem; the hand of our God was upon us, and he delivered us from the hand of the enemy and from ambushes by the way. 32 We came to Jerusalem, and there we remained three days. 33 On the fourth day, within the house of our God, the silver and the gold and the vessels were weighed into the hands of Meremoth the priest, son of Uriah, and with him was Eleazar the son of Phinehas, and with them were the Levites, Jozabad the son of Jeshua and Noadiah the son of Binnui. 34 The whole was counted and weighed, and the weight of everything was recorded.

---

30 The corresponding passage in 1 Esd. 8:54 shows that there should be a conjunction before *Sherebiah*. *Sherebiah* and *Hashabiah* were Levites (8:18–19), as were, of course, the *ten of their kinsmen*.

Ezra's caravan *departed from the river Ahava on the twelfth day of the first month* (March–April) and arrived in Jerusalem on the first day of the fifth month (July–August; cf. 7:9). The journey was long and perilous but it was completed without serious incident. Credit for the safe arrival was given to God, who had delivered them *from the hand of the enemy and from ambushes by the way.*

The first *three days* in Jerusalem were doubtless occupied with unpacking and with the usual social amenities (cf. Neh. 2:11). *On the fourth day*, the treasure was deposited with the proper authorities at the Temple. Everything *was counted and weighed, and the weight of everything was recorded.* Such an inventory was judicious for many reasons, but was absolutely necessary to exonerate the priests and Levites to whom the treasure had been committed during the trip. Ezra had weighed everything into their hands at Ahava (8:25–27), and they were legally responsible for the trust.

One of the priests who received the treasure at the Temple was *Meremoth*. He was the *son of Uriah* of the family of Hakkoz, one of the priestly families which at first could not prove its credentials (2:61–63). He was a prominent builder of the wall at the time of Nehemiah (Neh. 3:4,21), but was not at that time referred to as a priest. It is conjectured that his priestly status was clarified between the time of the building of the wall (445 B.C.) and the arrival of Ezra (398 B.C.). The data concerning Meremoth are often used as evidence that Nehemiah preceded Ezra.

4. *Epilogue (8:35–36)*

35 At that time those who had come from captivity, the returned exiles, offered burnt offerings to the God of Israel, twelve bulls for all Israel, ninety-six rams, seventy-seven lambs, and as a sin offering twelve he-goats; all this was a burnt offering to the Lord. 36 They also delivered the king's commissions to the king's satraps and to the governors of the province Beyond the River; and they aided the people and the house of God.

After depositing the treasure in the Temple, Ezra and his group made appropriate sacrifices to God and delivered the royal documents to the local officials. These data may be regarded as essentially historical, although in this passage the Chronicler is apparently no longer following his first-person source.

The precise nature and purpose of the ceremony held on this occasion is not clear. The sacrifice of *bulls, rams, lambs,* and *he-goats,* however, is reminiscent of ceremonies characteristically associated with the dedication or rededication of cultic shrines (cf. Moses' dedication of the altar, Num. 7:84–88; Hezekiah's rededication of the Temple, 2 Chron. 29:1–35; and the dedication of the second Temple, Ezra 6:17).

The king's commissions (lit., "laws") which Ezra delivered to the royal officials may have been the instructions to the royal treasurers (7:21–24), or they may have been independent documents (cf. Neh. 2:7–9). They were delivered to the *satraps,* who were the powerful provincial *governors*[31] of the Persian Empire. Although the Masoretic Text is ambiguous, Josephus (*Antiq.* XI.5.2) is doubtless correct that the satraps rather than Ezra and his colleagues were the ones who *aided the people and the house of God.*

VII. Crisis Concerning Mixed Marriages (9:1—10:44)

1. The Complaint of Ezra (9:1–2)

¹ After these things had been done, the officials approached me and said, "The people of Israel and the priests and the Levites have not separated themselves from the peoples of the lands with their abominations, from the Canaanites, the Hittites, the Perizzites, the Jebusites, the Ammonites, the Moabites, the Egyptians, and the Amorites. ² For they have taken some of their daughters to be wives for themselves and for their sons; so that the holy race has mixed itself with the peoples of the lands. And in this faithlessness the hand of the officials and chief men has been foremost."

---

[31] It is unlikely that the commissions were delivered to two different groups of officials. The phrase *"and to the governors"* probably began as an explanation for the less familiar term "satraps" (cf. Batten, p. 329).

After these things seems to imply that the controversy over mixed marriages followed immediately upon Ezra's arrival in Jerusalem. Actually, although Ezra arrived on the first day of the fifth month (7:9), the action against mixed marriages did not begin until about the twentieth day of the ninth month (10:9). The present order of the narratives appears to leave the first four months of Ezra's mission in Jerusalem unaccounted for.

It is usually recognized that the story of the reading of the law and its aftermath (Neh. 7:73b—9:37) stood originally between chapters 8 and 9 of the book of Ezra. Since the events of this narrative are dated in the seventh month (Neh. 7:73b), the phrase *after these things* would refer to them. Thus after arriving in the fifth month, Ezra conducted his spiritual revival in the seventh month and met the marriage crisis in the ninth.

The story of the reading of the law is clearly out of context in the book of Nehemiah, but it fits perfectly after Ezra 8. Ezra was, if anything, an expert in the law, and he had come to Jerusalem expressly to teach it and apply it. One would expect that public instruction in the law would be among his first official acts. It is unthinkable that this should have been postponed until the seventh month of his second year or later. Moreover, rededication to the law is exactly the type of stimulus which would have moved the community leaders to press action against illicit marriages.

Ezra was not the vigorous aggressive type of leader that Nehemiah had been. Just as he had waited to read the law until invited to do so (Neh. 8:1), he took action on mixed marriages only on the initiative of the community leaders. The *officials* who approached him are not identified by name or office, but the term employed is that used by Nehemiah to refer to district leaders (Neh. 3:9; 12:31–32).

The charge made to Ezra was that the Jews had *not separated themselves from the peoples of the lands,* but had been intermarrying with them. The *peoples of the lands* are here identified as the local non-Jewish population. Although *Canaanites, Hittites, Perizzites,* and *Jebusites* had long ago ceased to be identifiable minorities in the land, their names are still used in typical Deuteronomic fashion (cf. Deut. 7:1; 20:17) to designate the non-Jewish inhabitants. *Ammonites, Moabites,* and *Egyptians* were no doubt still to be found among the local population. *Amorites* is probably a scribal error for Edomites (cf. 1 Esd. 8:69).

The Israelites did not originally condemn intermarriage. Joseph was married to an Egyptian (Gen. 41:45), Moses to a Cushite (Num. 12:1), David to a Geshurite (2 Sam. 3:3); and the harems of all kings from the reign of Solomon were filled with foreign women. Because of the dangers of idolatry the Deuteronomists severely restricted intermarriage (Deut. 7:1–4), but did not condemn it in principle (Deut. 21:10–14). In the postexilic period, however, all intermarriage was ultimately banned. The Jewish people sought to maintain their identity as *the holy race* [32] through strict attention to circumcision, sabbath observance, and marriage within the group.

2. Ezra's Reaction to the Mixed Marriages (9:3–15)

(1) Mourning and Self-Abasement (9:3–5)

³ When I heard this, I rent my garments and my mantle, and pulled hair from my head and beard, and sat appalled. ⁴ Then all who trembled at the words of the God of Israel, because of the faithlessness of the returned exiles, gathered round me while I sat appalled until the evening sacrifice. ⁵ And at the evening sacrifice I rose from my fasting, with my garments and my mantle rent, and fell upon my knees and spread out my hands to the LORD my God,

Ezra's excessive reaction to the report about the mixed marriages could imply that, although he had been in Jerusalem over four months, this was the first that he had heard about the marriage abuses.

---

[32] Lit., "the holy seed" (cf. Isa. 6:13). The reference is to the seed ("descendants") of Abraham (Gen. 15:5,18; 2 Chron. 20:7).

There are strong indications, however, that this was not the case. Shecaniah refers to advice given by Ezra and some of the Jews concerning mixed marriages (10:2–3), which apparently antedates the principal crisis. This advice is doubtless to be associated with the instruction which accompanied the reading of the law (Neh. 8:7–8). During the assembly which concluded those ceremonies of the seventh month, the people led Ezra to believe that they were in fact separating themselves from all foreigners (Neh. 9:2). It was the news that the people had not kept their solemn commitment and had "not separated themselves from the peoples of the lands" (v. 1) which left Ezra *appalled*. He felt that his mission was in grave danger of failure because the offenders were the very men who had *trembled at the words of the God of Israel* only a few weeks earlier.

Ezra expressed his grief and dismay by the conventional gestures of tearing his clothes and pulling hair from his head and beard. Ezra's mourning was genuine and sincere, but Josephus (*Antiq.* XI.5.3) notes correctly that it was also a skillful means of moulding public opinion for the measures which lay ahead. As Ezra sat with his garments torn and his hair in disarray, a crowd naturally *gathered round* him. Then at the time of the *evening sacrifice* (about 3:00 P.M.), he rose from his *fasting* to assume the leadership of the assembled crowd. He led them through prayer, confession, and weeping to propose the very measure which he wished to enact (10:1–3).

The Hebrew word translated "fasting" in this passage is more literally "self-abasement" (American Translation). Not enough time had elapsed for fasting to have become meaningful.

(2) Ezra's Prayer (9:6–15)

⁶ saying:
"O my God, I am ashamed and blush to lift my face to thee, my God, for our iniquities have risen higher than our heads, and our guilt has mounted up to the heavens. ⁷ From the days of our fathers to this day we have been in

great guilt; and for our iniquities we, our kings, and our priests have been given into the hand of the kings of the lands, to the sword, to captivity, to plundering, and to utter shame, as at this day. ⁸ But now for a brief moment favor has been shown by the Lord our God, to leave us a remnant, and to give us a secure hold within his holy place, that our God may brighten our eyes and grant us a little reviving in our bondage. ⁹ For we are bondmen; yet our God has not forsaken us in our bondage, but has extended to us his steadfast love before the kings of Persia, to grant us some reviving to set up the house of our God, to repair its ruins, and to give us protection in Judea and Jerusalem.

¹⁰ "And now, O our God, what shall we say after this? For we have forsaken thy commandments, ¹¹ which thou didst command by thy servants the prophets, saying, 'The land which you are entering, to take possession of it, is a land unclean with the pollutions of the peoples of the lands, with their abominations which have filled it from end to end with their uncleanness. ¹² Therefore give not your daughters to their sons, neither take their daughters for your sons, and never seek their peace or prosperity, that you may be strong, and eat the good of the land, and leave it for an inheritance to your children for ever.' ¹³ And after all that has come upon us for our evil deeds and for our great guilt, seeing that thou, our God, hast punished us less than our iniquities deserved and hast given us such a remnant as this, ¹⁴ shall we break thy commandments again and intermarry with the peoples who practice these abominations? Wouldst thou not be angry with us till thou wouldst consume us, so that there should be no remnant, nor any to escape? ¹⁵ O Lord the God of Israel, thou art just, for we are left a remnant that has escaped, as at this day. Behold, we are before thee in our guilt, for none can stand before thee because of this."

Because this prayer shares certain features of the Chronicler's vocabulary and style, some scholars have declined to attribute it to Ezra. The content and function of the prayer, however, reveal that it fits perfectly into its present context. Not only are the transitions preceding and following it convincing, but the prayer itself is a subtle and indispensable part of the total scene. The Chronicler may have taken it without much change from the Ezra memoirs.

The prayer begins with a confession of guilt. The prayer has been classified as a "doxology of judgment" because it is both a confession of guilt and praise to God for the justness of his punishment.[33] In the first clause Ezra uses the first person singular but switches immediately to the first person plural. In this way he identifies himself with the corporate community and speaks in its behalf. Although he himself has not engaged in a mixed marriage, he must speak of *our guilt* because he cannot disassociate himself from the corporate body.

The guilt which he confesses is not only the guilt of his contemporary generation, but that of the entire period *from the days of our fathers to this day*. The corporate community includes and transcends the generations, so that Ezra must speak of the sins of his forefathers as *our iniquities* (cf. Deut. 5:3). It was for *our iniquities*, he says, that *we, our kings, and our priests have been given into the hand of the kings of the lands*.

In vv. 8 and 9, the mood of the prayer changes dramatically. Although the punishment of the exile had been just and even merciful, God's grace had ushered in a new day. *For a brief moment* (since the edict of Cyrus in 538 b.c.) God had shown undeserved *favor* to his people. The *remnant*, predicted by the preexilic prophets, had been allowed to return and had been granted a *secure hold* (the hold of a tent nail) *within his holy place*. They were not an independent nation, to be sure, but God had shown his *steadfast love* through the benevolent acts of the *kings of Persia*. Through these kings, he had returned the sparkle to their eyes, rebuilt their Temple, and given them *protection*[34] in the land.

Reference is made apparently to

---

[33] Gerhard von Rad, *Old Testament Theology*, trans. D. M. G. Stalker (New York: Harper and Bros., 1962), I, 358.

[34] The word rendered protection (KJV: "wall") has caused considerable controversy. It obviously refers to some kind of wall. If it refers to a city wall, this passage could be used as evidence that Nehemiah's wall-building preceded the ministry of Ezra. Inscribed jar handles from the recent excavation at Gibeon, however, add significantly to the evidence that a city wall is not intended (J. B. Pritchard, *Hebrew Inscriptions and Stamps from Gibeon* [Philadelphia: The University Museum, 1959], pp. 9–10).

smaller, less pretentious walls used most commonly to enclose vineyards (cf. Isa. 5:5; Num. 22:24–25). The use of the word in Ezra then would be metaphorical, referring to the wall of *protection* which God had erected around his restored vineyard in Judah.

But Judah had made an inappropriate response to the *steadfast love* which God had revealed through the Persian kings. There was no excuse, and nothing which could be said, except *we have forsaken thy commandments.*

The *commandments* which the Jews had violated through their mixed marriages are articulated in vv. 11–12. The quotation attributed to *thy servants the prophets* is not a word-for-word quotation from any single scriptural passage. Much of it is found in Deuteronomy 7:1–3 and 23:3–6, but it is a patchwork of phrases and ideas from several different sources (cf. Myers, p. 79).

The prayer ends in a manner doubtless calculated to move the people to immediate confession and drastic action. The sins of the past had brought the Exile, but God had cut it short and had preserved a *remnant.* But now the remnant had sinned and no further mercy could be expected. God is *just*, and his justice would be served through the total annihilation of the rebellious community. Ezra offers no word of hope. He can only confess that *we are before thee in our guilt.*

For none can stand before thee because of this probably means that because of the marriage abuses no one can be vindicated or acquitted before God.

3. *The Response of the Jews (10:1–4)*

¹ While Ezra prayed and made confession, weeping and casting himself down before the house of God, a very great assembly of men, women, and children, gathered to him out of Israel; for the people wept bitterly. ² And Shecaniah the son of Jehiel, of the sons of Elam, addressed Ezra: "We have broken faith with our God and have married foreign women from the peoples of the land, but even now there is hope for Israel in spite of this. ³ Therefore let us make a covenant with our God to put away all these wives and their children, according to the counsel of my lord and of those who tremble at the commandment of our God; and let it be done according to the law. ⁴ Arise, for it is your task, and we are with you; be strong and do it."

Ezra's prayer together with his *weeping and casting himself down* attracted *a very great assembly of men, women, and children* to the Temple precincts where he was praying. They too *wept bitterly.* Ezra had skillfully led the Jews to initiate voluntarily the reforms which he presumably had the power to impose on them by force (cf. 7:25–26).

Shecaniah, whose father *Jehiel* was one of the offenders (10:26), spoke in behalf of the weeping crowd. He found *hope for Israel* in the traditional affirmation that repentance and restitution will move God to show mercy to his people (cf. 1 Kings 8:33–34; 2 Chron. 7:14; Psalm 106). But tears alone were not enough. Shecaniah proposed that the foreign wives with their children be separated from the husbands and fathers. Since this was clearly what Ezra and his advisors had already counseled, Ezra needed no persuasion to accept Shecaniah's invitation to effect the reforms.

4. *Ezra's Leadership in the Marriage Reforms (10:5–17)*

(1) *Preparation for Public Assembly (10:5–8)*

⁵ Then Ezra arose and made the leading priests and Levites and all Israel take oath that they would do as had been said. So they took the oath.

⁶ Then Ezra withdrew from before the house of God, and went to the chamber of Jehohanan the son of Eliashib, where he spent the night, neither eating bread nor drinking water; for he was mourning over the faithlessness of the exiles. ⁷ And a proclamation was made throughout Judah and Jerusalem to all the returned exiles that they should assemble at Jerusalem, ⁸ and that if any one did not come within three days, by order of the officials and the elders all his property should be forfeited, and he himself banned from the congregation of the exiles.

The active support of the community was vital to the success of Ezra's plan to dissolve the offensive marriages. Now that he had been assured of this support, he acted vigorously to implement the proposal which Shecaniah had made. Even before leaving the place of prayer he exacted an *oath* from the leaders of those gathered around that they would support him in his efforts.

After administering the oath, Ezra withdrew for the night *to the chamber of Jehohanan*. There he not only *spent the night* fasting and *mourning*, but apparently conducted some very important business. Since Jehohanan was almost certainly the high priest at this time, it would have been judicious for Ezra to plan his strategy in consultation with him.

Couriers were sent *throughout Judah* with the *proclamation* that *within three days* the entire Jewish community (*all the returned exiles*) should assemble at Jerusalem. The penalty for failure to comply was severe but was well within the authority which had been granted to Ezra by the Artaxerxes rescript (7:26). The administration of the order was delegated to *the officials and the elders*.

The reference to *Jehohanan the son of Eliashib* is important for the dating of Ezra's mission. According to the lists of high priests in Nehemiah 12:10–11,22, Jehohanan (Jonathan and Johanan are clearly alternate readings for Jehohanan), was the grandson of Eliashib and the second high priest after him. Papyrus no. 30 from Elephantine supplies the further evidence that Jehohanan was high priest in Jerusalem in 411 and 408 B.C.[35] Jehohanan's grandfather Eliashib, on the other hand, was a contemporary of Nehemiah, both at the time of his first mission (Neh. 3:1) and at the time of his second (Neh. 13:4,7,28). Thus the priority of Nehemiah seems to be firmly established.

(2) The Jerusalem Assembly and Its Commission (10:9–17)

⁹ Then all the men of Judah and Benjamin assembled at Jerusalem within the three days; it was the ninth month, on the twentieth day of the month. And all the people sat in the open square before the house of God, trembling because of this matter and because of the heavy rain. ¹⁰ And Ezra the priest stood up and said to them, "You have trespassed and married foreign women, and so increased the guilt of Israel. ¹¹ Now then make confession to the LORD the God of your fathers, and do his will; separate yourselves from the peoples of the land and from the foreign wives." ¹² Then all the assembly answered with a loud voice, "It is so; we must do as you have said. ¹³ But the people are many, and it is a time of heavy rain; we cannot stand in the open. Nor is this a work for one day or for two; for we have greatly transgressed in this matter. ¹⁴ Let our officials stand for the whole assembly; let all in our cities who have taken foreign wives come at appointed times, and with them the elders and judges of every city, till the fierce wrath of our God over this matter be averted from us." ¹⁵ Only Jonathan the son of Asahel and Jahzeiah the son of Tikvah opposed this, and Meshullam and Shabbethai the Levite supported them.

¹⁶ Then the returned exiles did so. Ezra the priest selected men, heads of fathers' houses, according to their fathers' houses, each of them designated by name. On the first day of the tenth month they sat down to examine the matter; ¹⁷ and by the first day of the first month they had come to the end of all the men who had married foreign women.

Within the three days allowed, *all the men of Judah and Benjamin* (cf. 4:1) *assembled at Jerusalem*. It was *the twentieth day* of the *ninth month* (Nov.–Dec.), and a cold winter rain drenched the crowd which stood unprotected *in the open square* in front of the Temple. They were *trembling* with fear and shivering from the cold rain as Ezra addressed them.

Ezra's speech was mercifully short and to the point. The people had *trespassed* and had *increased the guilt of Israel*. Now they must *make confession* and exclude from their midst *the peoples of the land* and *the foreign wives*.

The crowd readily agreed, but the implementation of the decision was far too complex to be worked out while they stood there soaked by the rain. It was proposed that a commission be appointed to handle the matter in an orderly and expeditious

---

[35] Cf. Cowley, *op. cit.*, pp. 108–119.

manner.

Ezra appointed to the commission the *heads of fathers' houses* (clan leaders), and for three months they sat in session in Jerusalem. *The elders and judges of every city* brought cases from all over the land, but the nature of the legal proceedings is not explained. Since the decision to dissolve the marriages had already been settled by popular assent, the litigation was not concerned with that. In all probability the commission dealt with complex property settlements, including the inheritance rights of the disowned children and the return of doweries to the rejected wives.

The principal motive for marriage to foreign women was almost certainly economic. The Jews returning from Babylonia found most, if not all, of the land in Judah owned by foreign families. The quickest and easiest way to get possession of some of the land was to divorce Jewish wives and take the daughters of wealthy aliens (cf. Mal. 2:10–16), or to arrange such marriages for one's sons (cf. Myers, p. 77). Because the wives who were being divorced were from prominent and powerful non-Jewish families the matter of property settlements would have been extremely delicate.

5. List of Marriage Offenders (10:18–44)

(1) Cultic Personnel (10:18–24)

18 Of the sons of the priests who had married foreign women were found Maaseiah, Eliezer, Jarib, and Gedaliah, of the sons of Jeshua the son of Jozadak and his brethren. 19 They pledged themselves to put away their wives, and their guilt offering was a ram of the flock for their guilt. 20 Of the sons of Immer: Hanani and Zebadiah. 21 Of the sons of Harim: Maaseiah, Elijah, Shemaiah, Jehiel, and Uzziah. 22 Of the sons of Pashhur: Elioenai, Maaseiah, Ishmael, Nethanel, Jozabad, and Elasah.
23 Of the Levites: Jozabad, Shimei, Kelaiah (that is, Kelita), Pethahiah, Judah, and Eliezer. 24 Of the singers: Eliashib. Of the gatekeepers: Shallum, Telem, and Uri.

The list of marriage offenders was presumably drawn up by the Jerusalem commission. It is in a rather bad state of preservation, and is surprisingly short in view of the three months that the commission sat. It may be only a fragment of the original list (cf. Bowman, pp. 87–88).

Guilty members of the high priestly family of *Jeshua* are listed first, followed by the names of offenders from the other three major Zadokite priestly families (cf. 2:36–39). A shorter list of *Levites, singers,* and *gatekeepers* completes the roster of the offending clergy.

Each member of the high priestly family offered *a ram of the flock* as his *guilt offering* (cf. Lev. 5:14–16). The guilt offerings of the other offenders are not specified, but the type of offering required depended on the status of the guilty one (cf. Lev. 4).

(2) Israelite Laymen (10:25–44)

25 And of Israel: of the sons of Parosh: Ramiah, Izziah, Malchijah, Mijamin, Eleazar, Hashabiah, and Benaiah. 26 Of the sons of Elam: Mattaniah, Zechariah, Jehiel, Abdi, Jeremoth, and Elijah. 27 Of the sons of Zattu: Elioenai, Eliashib, Mattaniah, Jeremoth, Zabad, and Aziza. 28 Of the sons of Bebai were Jehohanan, Hananiah, Zabbai, and Athlai. 29 Of the sons of Bani were Meshullam, Malluch, Adaiah, Jashub, Sheal, and Jeremoth. 30 Of the sons of Pahathmoab: Adna, Chelal, Benaiah, Maaseiah, Mattaniah, Bezalel, Binnui, and Manasseh. 31 Of the sons of Harim: Eliezer, Isshijah, Malchijah, Shemaiah, Shimeon, 32 Benjamin, Malluch, and Shemariah. 33 Of the sons of Hashum: Mattenai, Mattattah, Zabad, Eliphelet, Jeremai, Manasseh, and Shimei. 34 Of the sons of Bani: Maadai, Amram, Uel, 35 Benaiah, Bedeiah, Cheluhi, 36 Vaniah, Meremoth, Eliashib, 37 Mattaniah, Mattenai, Jaasu. 38 Of the sons of Binnui: Shimei, 39 Shelemiah, Nathan, Adaiah, 40 Machnadebai, Shashai, Sharai, 41 Azarel, Shelemiah, Shemariah, 42 Shallum, Amariah, and Joseph. 43 Of the sons of Nebo: Jeiel, Mattithiah, Zabad, Zebina, Jaddai, Joel, and Benaiah. 44 All these had married foreign women, and they put them away with their children.

The list of laymen is, as would be expected, longer than that of the clergy. The names are presented according to families and each family is identified by the traditional ancestral name. Most of the families represented are also represented in the census list in chapter 2.

Verse 44 is particularly obscure in the MT (cf. KJV). The RSV translation, which is based on 1 Esdras 9:36, appears to preserve the original ending of the story, however. There is little doubt that the reforms were completed and that the foreign wives with their half-Israelite children were expelled from their homes.

A compelling fear of religious and ethnic contamination led Ezra and the other leaders of Judah to these drastic and unprecedented measures. With utter disregard for human feelings and human rights they broke the homes asunder, sent away the innocent wives, and disowned the helpless children. While one may understand the motives which prompted this action, he may not agree that such brutality was necessary to the preservation of the faith.

This passage probably marks the end of the Ezra narrative. Nehemiah 9 is sometimes considered to be the sequel to Ezra 10, but it is best understood in connection with the reading of the law.

Commentary on Nehemiah

I. Nehemiah at the Court of Artaxerxes (1:1—2:8)

1. News from Judah (1:1-4)

¹ The words of Nehemiah the son of Hacaliah.
Now it happened in the month of Chislev, in the twentieth year, as I was in Susa the capital, ² that Hanani, one of my brethren, came with certain men out of Judah; and I asked them concerning the Jews that survived, who had escaped exile, and concerning Jerusalem. ³ And they said to me, "The survivors there in the province who escaped exile are in great trouble and shame; the wall of Jerusalem is broken down, and its gates are destroyed by fire."
⁴ When I heard these words I sat down and wept, and mourned for days; and I continued fasting and praying before the God of heaven.

The story of Nehemiah, like that of Zerubbabel and of Ezra, has been compiled and edited by the Chronicler. The latter had at his disposal several important source documents, including a journal or memoir of Nehemiah himself. He quotes extensively from this valuable source, and frequently with little or no alteration.

The words of Nehemiah the son of Hacaliah (the title of the book) appears to be a post-Chronicler contribution. Similar editorial titles can be noted at the beginning of many other books (cf. Jer. 1:1; Amos 1:1).

Nehemiah's mission began nearly a century after Cyrus had removed the stigma of the Exile by permitting the Jews to return to Judah. Nehemiah was a descendant of one of the numerous Jewish families who had chosen to remain in the East. His sympathies, however, were with the little group who were struggling to build a new life in the homeland. He was, therefore, greatly distressed when he received news that all was not well in Judah.

The date of Nehemiah's mission is firmly established. The Artaxerxes in whose "twentieth year" (2:1) he came to Jerusalem was Artaxerxes I (465–424 B.C.). This is indicated clearly by Papyrus 30 from Elephantine (Cowley, *op. cit.*, pp. 108–119). This document, dated in 408 B.C., establishes that at that time Jehohanan (Johanan) was high priest in Jerusalem and that the sons of Sanballat were the authorities in Samaria. Since Nehemiah was a contemporary both of Sanballat (4:1) and of Jehohanan's grandfather Eliashib (3:1; cf. 12:22), his mission must be dated before 408 B.C. Thus Nehemiah could not have served under Artaxerxes II (404–358 B.C.). His mission began in the twentieth year of Artaxerxes I, 445 B.C.

Nehemiah is said to have received the news from Judah **in the month of Chislev,** *in the twentieth year.* His interview with Artaxerxes is dated "in the month of Nisan, in the twentieth year" (2:1). Since Chislev was the ninth month of the Babylonian calendar and Nisan was the first, it is difficult to reconcile the two dates. Most scholars assume that Nehemiah received the news in the nineteenth year of the king. It is possible, however, that Nehemiah was using the Syrian calendar, according to which the year began in the autumn.[36] In that event, Chislev would have been the third month and Nisan the seventh, and both dates could belong to the twentieth year.

Nehemiah was at his royal post in *Susa the capital* when *Hanani* (usually believed to be the blood brother of Nehemiah who was later put in charge of Jerusalem, 7:2) and *certain men out of Judah* brought distressing news about the community in the homeland. Nehemiah was told that *the wall of Jerusalem is broken down, and its gates are destroyed by fire.* His reaction to the report shows clearly that this catastrophe could not have been that perpetrated by Nebuchadrezzar over one hundred and forty years earlier. Nehemiah would scarcely have *mourned for days* over a situation which had been known to him all of his life. The destruction of Jerusalem related by Hanani was almost certainly a recent event. It is usually identified as the work of Rehum and Shimshai, whom Artaxerxes had previously instructed to halt the rebuilding and refortification of the city (Ezra 4:8–23). The Jews of Judah are called by Nehemiah those *who had escaped exile.* This is in contrast with the terminology used by the Chronicler, who usually refers to them as "the returned exiles" (cf. Ezra 4:1; 10:16). The Judean community was doubtless composed of both.

2. Nehemiah's Prayer (1:5–11a)

5 And I said, "O LORD God of heaven, the great and terrible God who keeps covenant and steadfast love with those who love him and keep his commandments; 6 let thy ear be attentive, and thy eyes open, to hear the prayer of thy servant which I now pray before thee day and night for the people of Israel thy servants, confessing the sins of the people of Israel, which we have sinned against thee. Yea, I and my father's house have sinned. 7 We have acted very corruptly against thee, and have not kept the commandments, the statutes, and the ordinances which thou didst command thy servant Moses. 8 Remember the word which thou didst command thy servant Moses, saying, 'If you are unfaithful, I will scatter you among the peoples; 9 but if you return to me and keep my commandments and do them, though your dispersed be under the farthest skies, I will gather them thence and bring them to the place which I have chosen, to make my name dwell there.' 10 They are thy servants and thy people, whom thou hast redeemed by thy great power and by thy strong hand. 11 O LORD, let thy ear be attentive to the prayer of thy servant, and to the prayer of thy servants who delight to fear thy name; and give success to thy servant today, and grant him mercy in the sight of this man."

Nehemiah was a man of prayer (2:4; 4:4–5; 5:19; 6:14; 13:14,22,29,31). It was in his nature to turn to God in moments of distress or victory. He surely prayed when he heard Hanani's report (cf. v. 4), and doubtless recorded the prayer in his memoirs. Yet the prayer in this passage is probably not a verbatim quotation from the pen of Nehemiah.

The Chronicler, in keeping with the well-known literary custom of ancient writers, sometimes composed prayers or speeches to express the sentiments of his heroes. Because this prayer is so different from the other prayers of Nehemiah (cf. 4:4–5; 5:19; 6:14), one may suspect that it has been supplemented by the Chronicler's hand.

Reference to Artaxerxes as *this man* before he has been referred to by name has led Bowman (pp. 666–670) to conclude that this is an expanded version of a prayer that once stood in 2:4. He suggests that the short prayer in Josephus (*Antiq.* XI, 5.6) may preserve the substance of the prayer which Nehemiah uttered after hearing the words of Hanani.

---
[36] Cf. Julius Wellhausen, *Israelitische und Jüdische Geschichte.* Dritte Ausgabe. (Berlin: G. Reimer, 1897), p. 169.

Whatever its authorship, this prayer is particularly valuable for the insight that it gives us into the character of postexilic prayer in general. Certain features of the prayer are especially noteworthy. (1) Like the prayers in 9:6-37 and in Daniel 9:4-19, it is composed mostly of stereotyped Deuteronomic phrases (cf. Deut. 7:9,21; 9:29; 21:15; 30:1-5). This seems to have been the typical language of formal prayer during this period. (2) The suppliant, although presumably innocent, identifies himself with the guilty people (cf. Ezra 9:6-15; Dan. 9:4-19; Neh. 9:32-37). (3) The dispersion is attributed to the sins of the corporate community (vv. 7-8; cf. Ezra 9:7; Neh. 9:29-30; Dan. 9:7-8). (4) A gracious remnant is acknowledged (v. 10; cf. Ezra 9:8,15; Neh. 9:31; Dan. 9:15). (5) The covenant is reaffirmed (v. 5; cf. Neh. 9:32; Dan. 9:4). (6) Hope for the community is sought in confession and repentance (vv. 6-9; cf. Ezra 9:15; Neh. 9:32-37; Dan. 9:15-19).

3. Artaxerxes' Grant to Nehemiah (1:11b—2:8)

Now I was cupbearer to the king.
¹ In the month of Nisan, in the twentieth year of King Artaxerxes, when wine was before him, I took up the wine and gave it to the king. Now I had not been sad in his presence. ² And the king said to me, "Why is your face sad, seeing you are not sick? This is nothing else but sadness of the heart." Then I was very much afraid. ³ I said to the king, "Let the king live for ever! Why should not my face be sad, when the city, the place of my fathers' sepulchres, lies waste, and its gates have been destroyed by fire?" ⁴ Then the king said to me, "For what do you make request?" So I prayed to the God of heaven. ⁵ And I said to the king, "If it pleases the king, and if your servant has found favor in your sight, that you send me to Judah, to the city of my fathers' sepulchres, that I may rebuild it." ⁶ And the king said to me (the queen sitting beside him), "How long will you be gone, and when will you return?" So it pleased the king to send me; and I set him a time. ⁷ And I said to the king. "If it pleases the king, let letters be given me to the governors of the province Beyond the River, that they may let me pass through until I come to Judah; ⁸ and a letter to Asaph, the keeper of the king's forest, that he may give me timber to make beams for the gates of the fortress of the temple, and for the wall of the city, and for the house which I shall occupy." And the king granted me what I asked, for the good hand of my God was upon me.

Nehemiah was *cupbearer* to Artaxerxes I, king of Persia. He was much more than a menial servant, however. Throughout the ancient Near East the office was one of signal influence and honor. Persian art portrays the cupbearer as next to the crown prince in attendance upon the king.

The cupbearer was associated intimately with the king's inner household (cf. v. 6) and was apparently always a eunuch. Traditionally, a eunuch was excluded from the "assembly of the Lord" (Deut. 23:1), but by the time of Nehemiah this restriction had been relaxed (Isa. 56:3-5). It is not impossible, however, that Nehemiah may have had to fight vestiges of this prejudice during his governorship in Judah.

Nehemiah was normally in good spirits when he served the king. The news which Hanani had brought from Jerusalem, however, had left him anxious and depressed. The king noted correctly that he was suffering from *sadness of the heart,* and his sadness was genuine. Although he himself enjoyed a good position in Persia and apparently had never thought of emigrating to Judah, he felt a deep sense of kinship with the Jewish community there, and their problems became his own.

More than three months elapsed between the time that Nehemiah received the news from Hanani in the month of Chislev (Nov.–Dec.) and the conference with Artaxerxes *in the month of Nisan* (Mar.–Apr.). It is often suggested that Artaxerxes was absent from Susa during this season of winter storms. It is also possible that the delay was occasioned by Nehemiah's reluctance to broach the subject to the king and that he had hidden his true feelings until he felt that he could postpone the matter no longer. In either case, it does appear that Nehemiah had serious misgivings about approaching Artaxerxes concerning the fate of Jerusalem. Nehemiah's fear and hesitation are not surprising in view of the fact that Artaxerxes had so recently commissioned Rehum and Shimshai to bring to a stop the rebuilding and refortification of Jerusalem (Ezra 4:8–23).

Nehemiah received permission to rebuild Jerusalem and its walls in spite of the fact that Artaxerxes had recently forbidden it. The Jews whose building activity was stopped by Rehum and Shimshai had been building surreptitiously and had created an understandable suspicion of treason. Nehemiah, on the other hand, was a trusted aide of the king and gave the king no reason to suspect his motives. Moreover, he referred to Jerusalem as *the city of my fathers' sepulchres,* thus making his appeal personal and sentimental, and cautiously nonpolitical.

Detailed arrangements were made for Nehemiah's mission. An understanding was reached concerning when Nehemiah would leave and when he would return. (According to 5:14 Nehemiah's first term as governor of Judah lasted 12 years.) Letters were prepared instructing *the governors of the province Beyond the River* to grant Nehemiah safe passage through their districts. A special letter was addressed to *Asaph, the keeper of the king's forest,* authorizing him to grant Nehemiah timber (probably the famous cedars of Lebanon) for his building needs. And finally a military escort was provided (v. 9).

Nehemiah was keenly conscious of God's gracious presence with him throughout these delicate negotiations with the king. There was a prayer on his lips as he opened the question of Judah's future, and there was thanksgiving in his heart as the arrangements were completed.

II. Nehemiah Assumes the Governorship (2:9–20)

1. Arrival in the West (2:9–10)

⁹ Then I came to the governors of the province Beyond the River, and gave them the king's letters. Now the king had sent with me officers of the army and horsemen. ¹⁰ But when Sanballat the Horonite and Tobiah the servant, the Ammonite, heard this, it displeased them greatly that someone had come to seek the welfare of the children of Israel.

Nehemiah's arrival in *the province Beyond the River* with a military escort and with official letters from Artaxerxes I alarmed the local governors in the area. *Sanballat,* the representative of the Persian government in Samaria, had special reason to be concerned. Northern Judah, including Jerusalem, was under his jurisdiction. Whether or not it was actually the intention of Artaxerxes to detach this area from Samaritan control is not clear. But Sanballat sensed that this was the intention of Nehemiah and reacted in a predictably hostile manner.

Sanballat was joined in his opposition to Nehemiah by *Tobiah,* who is called *the servant, the Ammonite.* The term servant does not imply that he was a servant of Sanballat. Like Sanballat he was a servant of the crown and a deputy governor under the satrap of the province. *Ammonite* is used here in a political rather than an ethnic sense. Tobiah, whose name means "Yahweh is good," was a member of a famous Jewish family in Ammon. Since Judah bordered the district of Ammon, Nehemiah's arrival posed a threat to the power and influence of Tobiah.

2. Inspection of Jerusalem (2:11–16)

¹¹ So I came to Jerusalem and was there three days. ¹² Then I arose in the night, I and a few men with me; and I told no one what my God had put into my heart to do for Jerusalem. There was no beast with me but the beast on which I rode. ¹³ I went out by night by the Valley Gate to the Jackal's Well and to the Dung Gate, and I inspected the walls of Jerusalem which were broken down and its gates which had been destroyed by fire. ¹⁴ Then I went on to the Fountain Gate and to the King's Pool; but there was no place for the beast that was under me to pass. ¹⁵ Then I went up in the night by the valley and inspected the wall; and I turned back and entered by the Valley Gate, and so returned. ¹⁶ And the officials did not know where I had gone or what I was doing; and I had not yet told the Jews, the priests, the nobles, the officials, and the rest that were to do the work.

After the customary three days (cf. Ezra 8:32), presumably devoted to typically Oriental social amenities, Nehemiah began to formulate specific plans for the rebuilding of Jerusalem's wall.

Nehemiah, always a shrewd and practical administrator, did not wish to involve the local authorities in his plans until he himself had a clear idea about how he ought to proceed. Therefore, he inspected the city walls secretly by moonlight, accompanied only by a few personal servants.

Kathleen Kenyon's [37] recent excavations in Jerusalem have made it necessary to revise all previous interpretations of the topographical references in this passage. Apparently the ruins of the preexilic wall which Nehemiah inspected encircled only the eastern hill. It is certain that the southern part of the western hill, at least, was not included in the city until the later postexilic period. Although the actual remains of the west wall of the preexilic city have not been found, it is clear that this wall followed the western crest of the eastern hill overlooking what was later to be called the Tyropoeon Valley. The *Valley Gate* through which Nehemiah left the city must have been located near the northern limits of the west wall of the city of David. Proceeding southward, Nehemiah followed the slopes of the valley past the unidentified *Jackal's Well, Dung Gate,* and *Fountain Gate* until he came to the *King's Pool.* The latter is identified by Miss Kenyon as the Pool of Siloam or the nearby Birket el Hamra near which the wall curved sharply to the north to follow the lower slopes of the Kidron Valley. As Nehemiah tried to follow the east wall toward the north, he found that there was nowhere for his mount to walk, so he had to inspect the east wall from lower in the Kidron Valley. Then Nehemiah retraced his steps back to the Valley Gate.

Miss Kenyon's excavation has revealed dramatically why Nehemiah's mount could not pass along the eastern wall of the preexilic city. The steep slopes of Ophel had been built up with gigantic stone terraces. When Nebuchadrezzar destroyed the city, these terraces with the buildings constructed on them began to collapse down into the valley below. By the time of Nehemiah the entire area along the east wall was an incredible mass of fallen stones. Nehemiah abandoned the preexilic line of the east wall altogether and constructed a new line along the eastern crest of the hill.

3. Challenge to the local officials (2:17–18)

17 Then I said to them, "You see the trouble we are in, how Jerusalem lies in ruins with its gates burned. Come, let us build the wall of Jerusalem, that we may no longer suffer disgrace." 18 And I told them of the hand of my God which had been upon me for good, and also of the words which the king had spoken to me. And they said, "Let us rise up and build." So they strengthened their hands for the good work.

When he had arrived at a firm plan of operation, Nehemiah disclosed for the first time his intention to rebuild the wall. The *trouble* to which he called the attention of the people was of more than one kind. There was to be sure the physical distress created by the inability of the Jews to defend themselves against hostile neighbors. But there was also the lingering shame and *disgrace* associated with the humiliation suffered at the hands of Nebuchadrezzar and more recently at the hands of Rehum and Shimshai. The people responded with predictable enthusiasm when Nehemiah told them how God had intervened to remove their frustrations and to make possible the restoration of the city. They volunteered to support the building operation and began immediately to make preparations *for the good work.*

4. Reaction of Neighboring Authorities (2:19–20)

19 But when Sanballat the Horonite and Tobiah the servant, the Ammonite, and Geshem the Arab heard of it, they derided us and despised

---

[37] *Jerusalem: Excavating 3000 Years of History* (New York: McGraw-Hill, 1967), pp. 107–111.

us and said, "What is this thing that you are doing? Are you rebelling against the king?" 20 Then I replied to them, "The God of heaven will make us prosper, and we his servants will arise and build; but you have no portion or right or memorial in Jerusalem."

Since chapter 3 must be regarded as an independent version of the wall-building inserted into the Nehemiah memoirs by the Chronicler, the relationship between these two verses and 4:1–3 is left obscure. This passage may be understood as the reaction of Nehemiah's neighbors to his initial preparations for building, while 4:1–3 may reflect a subsequent reaction after the construction was under way. The Chronicler, however, has not preserved the transition between the two passages.

Sanballat and Tobiah had been displeased when Nehemiah arrived in Judah (v. 10), but the news that he planned to rebuild the walls of Jerusalem intensified their hostility. The refortification of Jerusalem would be a clear indication that Nehemiah intended to detach Judah from Samaritan administration. If Nehemiah had any document from Artaxerxes specifically authorizing him to rebuild the city walls, he did not disclose it. In the absence of such written authority it is not surprising that the local governors suggested that Nehemiah might be *rebelling against the king*. It is surprising, however, that Artaxerxes had not been more explicit about Nehemiah's authority in his letters to his subordinates in the west.

Sanballat and Tobiah were joined in their hostility by *Geshem the Arab*. Unlike Sanballat and Tobiah, Geshem was more than a local governor ruling in behalf of the Persian crown. He was an ally of the Persian king and possibly a vassal, but he ruled a vast area stretching from north Arabia to Egypt and including what had once been Moab and Edom. He controlled areas which had previously been part of Judah, so that any resurgence of Jewish nationalism would be a threat to him.

One might expect that Nehemiah's response to his neighbors would have been a straightforward explanation of the authority which the king had granted him. He remained silent about his authority, however, either because he could not document it or because he did not wish to have any kind of intercourse with the other officials in the area. The latter is indicated by his curt exclusion of them from any *portion or right or memorial in Jerusalem*. This was not only a declaration of independence from Samaritan administration but a kind of personal excommunication of Sanballat and Tobiah from the Jewish religious community.[38]

III. Organization of the Wall-Builders (3:1–32)

1. Rebuilding the North and West Walls (3:1–15)

1 Then Eliashib the high priest rose up with his brethren the priests and they built the Sheep Gate. They consecrated it and set its doors; they consecrated it as far as the Tower of the Hundred, as far as the Tower of Hananel. 2 And next to him the men of Jericho built. And next to them Zaccur the son of Imri built.

3 And the sons of Hassenaah built the Fish Gate; they laid its beams and set its doors, its bolts, and its bars. 4 And next to them Meremoth the son of Uriah, son of Hakkoz repaired. And next to them Meshullam the son of Berechiah, son of Meshezabel repaired. And next to them Zadok the son of Baana repaired. 5 And next to them the Tekoites repaired; but their nobles did not put their necks to the work of their Lord.

6 And Joiada the son of Paseah and Meshullam the son of Besodeiah repaired the Old Gate; they laid its beams and set its doors, its bolts, and its bars. 7 And next to them repaired Melatiah the Gibeonite and Jadon the Meronothite, the men of Gibeon and of Mizpah, who were under the jurisdiction of the governor of the province Beyond the River. 8 Next to them Uzziel the son of Harhaiah, goldsmiths, repaired. Next to him Hananiah, one of the perfumers, repaired; and they restored Jerusalem as far as the Broad Wall. 9 Next to them Rephaiah the son of Hur, ruler of half the district of Jerusalem, repaired. 10 Next to them

---

[38] Although Sanballat has a Babylonian name his worship of Yahweh is indicated by the Yahwistic names Delaiah and Shelemiah, which he gave to his sons (Cowley, *op. cit.*, p. 110). Tobiah has a yahwistic name and is husband and father-in-law to Jewish women (6:18).

Jedaiah the son of Harumaph repaired opposite his house; and next to him Hattush the son of Hashabneiah repaired. ¹¹ Malchijah the son of Harim and Hasshub the son of Pahathmoab repaired another section and the Tower of the Ovens. ¹² Next to him Shallum the son of Hallohesh, ruler of half the district of Jerusalem, repaired, he and his daughters.

¹³ Hanun and the inhabitants of Zanoah repaired the Valley Gate; they rebuilt it and set its doors, its bolts, and its bars, and repaired a thousand cubits of the wall, as far as the Dung Gate.

¹⁴ Malchijah the son of Rechab, ruler of the district of Bethhaccherem, repaired the Dung Gate; he rebuilt it and set its doors, its bolts, and its bars.

¹⁵ And Shallum the son of Colhozeh, ruler of the district of Mizpah, repaired the Fountain Gate; he rebuilt it and covered it and set its doors, its bolts, and its bars; and he built the wall of the Pool of Shelah of the king's garden, as far as the stairs that go down from the City of David.

Chapter 3 is an account of the rebuilding of the wall which is parallel to, but independent of, Nehemiah's own story in chapters 4—6. The former narrative, which probably came from the Temple archives (cf. Myers, p. 112), interrupts Nehemiah's memoirs and nowhere refers to Nehemiah. It is intent upon underscoring the role of the clergy in the rebuilding of the wall.

The narrative delineates approximately 40 sections of unequal length and proportions. They are listed in counterclockwise order beginning and ending with the *Sheep Gate*. Each crew of builders was assigned the responsibility for building one or more of the sections.

The work on the northern and western walls was probably limited entirely to repairing and rebuilding the line of the preexilic wall. The gates and towers that stood in the earlier wall were restored, and it is unlikely that the line of the wall deviated in any respect from that of the late monarchic period.

No segment of the northern and western walls belonging to the time of Nehemiah has been identified with certainty. Therefore it is impossible to make any exact correlation of the landmarks mentioned in the passage with the contemporary topography of the city. The *Sheep Gate* was clearly in the north wall and doubtless a major entrance into the vicinity of the Temple precincts. The name is believed to be associated with a nearby market where sheep were sold for sacrifices at the Temple. *The Tower of the Hundred* and *the Tower of Hananel* were likely associated with "the fortress of the temple" (2:8) which reinforced the vulnerable northern defense line of the city. The *Fish Gate* was named for the merchants who brought their fish into the city through this entrance (cf. 13:16). Its location, however, is uncertain because it is not known whether the northern part of the western hill was part of the city as early as the time of Nehemiah. The same uncertainty surrounds the location of the *Old Gate*, the *Broad Wall*, and the *Tower of the Ovens*, although they were all associated with the northwestern part of the city.

The *Valley Gate*, used by Nehemiah on the night of his inspection of the walls (2:13,15), overlooked the Tyropoeon Valley. It was located in the west wall of the City of David just below its juncture with the extension which Solomon had made to include the Temple area. The long line of wall from the Valley Gate to the *Dung Gate* ran along the western crest of the eastern hill. Although later quarrying has destroyed the actual remains of the wall, Miss Kenyon's [39] excavations have determined its approximate line. The *Fountain Gate*, the *Pool of Shelah*, and *the stairs* are associated with the extreme southern tip of the *City of David* (the *Pool of Shelah* may be identified with the Birket el Hamra). It was approximately at this point that Nehemiah ceased to follow the line of the preexilic wall and began a new east wall.

This list of workmen throws valuable light on the geographical distribution of Jews in the postexilic community. The list may be incomplete, however, for it is noteworthy that Bethlehem is not mentioned. Some towns may simply have declined to cooperate. The nobles of Tekoa *did not put*

[39] *Op. cit.*, pp. 106–110.

their necks to the work (Heb., "to the work of their lords"), possibly because they were loyal to their neighbor Geshem (cf. 6:1–9).

The translation of v. 7 is misleading. The clause, *who were under the jurisdiction of the governor of the province Beyond the River,* seems useless, since all of the Jews were under this jurisdiction. This clause is in apposition with *Mizpah* and should read "the seat of the governor of the province Beyond the River" (Bowman, p. 686). The translation *ruler of half the district of Jerusalem* (v. 9; cf. vv. 12,14) is incorrect also. The margin in the RSV gives the correct reading: "foreman of half the portion assigned to Jerusalem."

2. Building the New East Wall (3:16–32)

16 After him Nehemiah the son of Azbuk, ruler of half the district of Bethzur, repaired to a point opposite the sepulchres of David, to the artificial pool, and to the house of the mighty men. 17 After him the Levites repaired: Rehum the son of Bani; next to him Hashabiah, ruler of half the district of Keilah, repaired for his district. 18 After him their brethren repaired: Bavvai the son of Henadad, ruler of half the district of Keilah; 19 next to him Ezer the son of Jeshua, ruler of Mizpah, repaired another section opposite the ascent to the armory at the Angle. 20 After him Baruch the son of Zabbai repaired another section from the Angle to the door of the house of Eliashib the high priest. 21 After him Meremoth the son of Uriah, son of Hakkoz repaired another section from the door of the house of Eliashib to the end of the house of Eliashib. 22 After him the priests, the men of the Plain, repaired. 23 After them Benjamin and Hasshub repaired opposite their house. After them Azariah the son of Maaseiah, son of Ananiah repaired beside his own house. 24 After him Binnui the son of Henadad repaired another section, from the house of Azariah to the Angle 25 and to the corner. Palal the son of Uzai repaired opposite the Angle and the tower projecting from the upper house of the king at the court of the guard. After him Pedaiah the son of Parosh 26 and the temple servants living on Ophel repaired to a point opposite the Water Gate on the east and the projecting tower. 27 After him the Tekoites repaired another section opposite the great projecting tower as far as the wall of Ophel.

28 Above the Horse Gate the priests repaired, each one opposite his own house. 29 After them Zadok the son of Immer repaired opposite his own house. After him Shemaiah the son of Shecaniah, the keeper of the East Gate, repaired. 30 After him Hananiah the son of Shelemiah and Hanun the sixth son of Zalaph repaired another section. After him Meshullam the son of Berechiah repaired opposite his chamber. 31 After him Malchijah, one of the goldsmiths, repaired as far as the house of the temple servants and of the merchants, opposite the Muster Gate, and to the upper chamber of the corner. 32 And between the upper chamber of the corner and the Sheep Gate the goldsmiths and the merchants repaired.

The eastern slopes of the eastern hill were covered with masses of stones fallen from the terraces and buildings above.[40] It was not practicable to restore the eastern line of the wall, and the greatly reduced size of the Jewish community after the Exile made it possible for Nehemiah to decrease the area enclosed by the wall. Miss Kenyon's excavation reveals that he built a new line of wall along the crest of the hill leaving outside the walls the steep, terraced slopes of the previous city.

The landmarks referred to in connection with the building of the east wall suggest that a new line of wall has been undertaken, rather than a rebuilding of the old one. One section is built *from the door of the house of Eliashib to the end of the house of Eliashib.* One crew built *opposite their house,* and the priests built *each* opposite his own *house.* When the gates of the previous east wall are mentioned, they are not said to have been rebuilt. The building was done *opposite the Water Gate, above the Horse Gate,* and *opposite the Muster Gate.* Even north of the hill of Ophel the line of wall established in the eighth century B.C. on the lower slopes of the Kidron was abandoned and moved back to the crest where it had been at the time of Solomon.[41] Although the line of Nehemiah's east wall has been located and partially excavated, most of the landmarks referred to in the passage are unidentifiable. It may be surmised, however, that vv.

---
[40] Cf. Kenyon, *op. cit.,* pp. 106–111.
[41] Kenyon, *op. cit.,* pp. 111–200.

16–27 describe the line of the wall from its southern limits to the beginning of Solomon's northern extension, and that vv. 18–32 trace the wall around the area of the palace and the Temple.

IV. Building Under Pressure (4:1–23)

1. Further Reaction from Neighboring Authorities (4:1–3)

¹ Now when Sanballat heard that we were building the wall, he was angry and greatly enraged, and he ridiculed the Jews. ² And he said in the presence of his brethren and of the army of Samaria, "What are these feeble Jews doing? Will they restore things? Will they sacrifice? Will they finish up in a day? Will they revive the stones out of the heaps of rubbish, and burned ones at that?" ³ Tobiah the Ammonite was by him, and he said, "Yes, what they are building—if a fox goes up on it he will break down their stone wall!"

When Sanballat heard that the wall of Jerusalem had actually been begun, he held a conference of his fellow officials, his allies, and his army officers. The text of v. 2 is not well preserved, but it is clear that Sanballat was trying to appraise the motives of Nehemiah and his builders. This is indicated by the question, *Will they sacrifice?* The Jews had had official Persian permission to sacrifice in Jerusalem since the time of Cyrus. Sanballat's question implies that the refortification of Jerusalem is a political and not a cultic act, and therefore is not covered by the permission to sacrifice. Sanballat's reaction is understandable if he has still had no notification of Artaxerxes' change of policy with respect to Judah.

Reference to *the army of Samaria* need not cause surprise. Sanballat as the local representative of Persian authority had troops under his command. Nehemiah clearly expected armed intervention (cf. 4:13–23).

It was Tobiah who injected a note of ridicule into the conference. He predicted that Nehemiah's wall would be so flimsy that even a fox (or jackal) could burrow through it. This was wishful thinking. Miss Kenyon's [42] excavation reveals that Nehemiah's wall was 2.75 meters (about nine feet) thick.

2. Nehemiah's Prayer (4:4–5)

⁴ Hear, O our God, for we are despised; turn back their taunt upon their own heads, and give them up to be plundered in a land where they are captives. ⁵ Do not cover their guilt, and let not their sin be blotted from thy sight; for they have provoked thee to anger before the builders.

News of Sanballat's conference goaded Nehemiah into an unfortunate loss of composure. He prayed that his enemies would suffer the same fate that the Jews had suffered, and that God would not forgive them for their sins. Such an emotional outburst is an understandable response to the provocation, particularly in view of the fact that Nehemiah believed that God himself had been offended.

3. Progress Amid Threats (4:6–12)

⁶ So we built the wall; and all the wall was joined together to half its height. For the people had a mind to work.
⁷ But when Sanballat and Tobiah and the Arabs and the Ammonites and the Ashdodites heard that the repairing of the walls of Jerusalem was going forward and that the breaches were beginning to be closed, they were very angry; ⁸ and they all plotted together to come and fight against Jerusalem and to cause confusion in it. ⁹ And we prayed to our God, and set a guard as a protection against them day and night.
¹⁰ But Judah said, "The strength of the burden-bearers is failing, and there is much rubbish; we are not able to work on the wall." ¹¹ And our enemies said, "They will not know or see till we come into the midst of them and kill them and stop the work." ¹² When the Jews who lived by them came they said to us ten times, "From all the places where they live they will come up against us."

In spite of ridicule and threats the construction of the wall progressed steadily. *The people had a mind to work,* and they continued against all odds. Yet the work was difficult and the pace was exhausting. It was inevitable that there would be problems of morale. Verse 10 is a poetic frag-

[42] *Op. cit.,* p. 111.

ment of a lament, perhaps chanted by the workmen in moments of discouragement.

The RSV of v. 6 interprets the Hebrew to mean that *all the wall was joined together to half its height*. The Masoretic Text is not so explicit, however, and may indicate only that the total task was half completed. At this point, the enemies of the Jews intensified their hostility and circulated rumors that they planned physical violence. The threats were ominous because the Jews were surrounded by unfriendly neighbours. *Sanballat* of Samaria threatened Judah from the north. *Tobiah,* governor of *the Ammonites,* was on the east. Geshem and *the Arabs* controlled all of the area to the south. The *Ashdodites,* who are identified as enemies of Nehemiah for the first time, were the Philistines to the west.

Nehemiah's response to the threats of violence was to pray and *set a guard.* Nehemiah was a man of prayer and a man of great faith. But he was also a practical administrator. He did not believe that prayer was a substitute for a maximum effort on his own part.

The rumors of impending violence were circulated by the Jews who lived in the outlying areas near the enemies. These informers may have been loyal to Nehemiah, or they may have been collaborators (cf. 6:17–18) engaged in a war of nerves against the builders (cf. Myers, p. 126). Nehemiah's displeasure with the rumormongers is indicated when he accuses them of reporting *ten times.* This expression characteristically conveys exasperation and disapproval (cf. Gen. 31:7; Num. 14:22; Job 19:3).

4. Nehemiah's Defense Measures (4:13–23)

13 So in the lowest parts of the space behind the wall, in open places, I stationed the people according to their families, with their swords, their spears, and their bows. 14 And I looked, and arose, and said to the nobles and to the officials and to the rest of the people, "Do not be afraid of them. Remember the Lord, who is great and terrible, and fight for your brethren, your sons, your daughters, your wives, and your homes."

15 When our enemies heard that it was known to us and that God had frustrated their plan, we all returned to the wall, each to his work. 16 From that day on, half of my servants worked on construction, and half held the spears, shields, bows, and coats of mail; and the leader stood behind all the house of Judah, 17 who were building on the wall. Those who carried burdens were laden in such a way that each with one hand labored on the work and with the other held his weapon. 18 And each of the builders had his sword girded at his side while he built. The man who sounded the trumpet was beside me. 19 And I said to the nobles and to the officials and to the rest of the people, "The work is great and widely spread, and we are separated on the wall, far from one another. 20 In the place where you hear the sound of the trumpet, rally to us there. Our God will fight for us."

21 So we labored at the work, and half of them held the spears from the break of dawn till the stars came out. 22 I also said to the people at that time, "Let every man and his servant pass the night within Jerusalem, that they may be a guard for us by night and may labor by day." 23 So neither I nor my brethren nor my servants nor the men of the guard who followed me, none of us took off our clothes; each kept his weapon in his hand.

It is unlikely that Sanballat and his allies would actually have attacked Nehemiah without authorization from Artaxerxes (cf. 6:7; Ezra 4:6–8,23; 5:5), but Nehemiah could not take the chance. Besides, his people were in a state of panic and had abandoned the work on the wall (v. 15). Nehemiah had no choice but to set up a strict security system for the workmen.

Nehemiah's first move was to arm the people and station them *behind the wall* so that this structure, though incomplete, could serve as cover in case of attack. He sought further to bolster their faith by reminding them of God's presence with them and of their duty to God and to their families. When Sanballat and his allies saw that the Jews were determined to offer armed resistance, they decreased their harassment, and the work on the wall was resumed.

In order to anticipate future trouble and to allay the fears of the builders, Nehemiah established a defense system which would serve for the duration of the project.

Half of his military retainers (*servants*), heavily armed and in complete readiness to fight, were stationed around the wall. Each of *those who carried burdens* and *each of the builders* (masons) was armed also, so that he could fight if necessary without any delay. Buglers were stationed around the city to sound the alarm. The Septuagint and the Peshitta support the view of Josephus (*Antiq.* XI.5.8) that there were many buglers stationed beside the builders around the city. Everyone was instructed to converge upon any point where the trumpet was sounded. To strengthen still further the security of the city all workmen were ordered to be on hand 24 hours a day so that there would be an adequate fighting force in case of a night attack. Nehemiah and his own circle of associates and retainers slept in their clothes in order to be ready for any emergency.

It is not clear what is meant by *the leaders stood behind all the house of Judah, who were building on the wall,* unless it means that they served as a second security force inside the line of the wall.

V. Economic Exploitation of the Builders (5:1–19)

1. Complaint of the Workers (5:1–5)

¹ Now there arose a great outcry of the people and of their wives against their Jewish brethren. ² For there were those who said, "With our sons and our daughters, we are many; let us get grain, that we may eat and keep alive." ³ There were also those who said, "We are mortgaging our fields, our vineyards, and our houses to get grain because of the famine." ⁴ And there were those who said, "We have borrowed money for the king's tax upon our fields and our vineyards. ⁵ Now our flesh is as the flesh of our brethren, our children are as their children; yet we are forcing our sons and our daughters to be slaves, and some of our daughters have already been enslaved; but it is not in our power to help it, for other men have our fields and our vineyards."

The building of the wall was interrupted not only by trouble from outside the Jewish community but also by discord from within. The poor financial condition of most of the builders had been aggravated by famine and by the rigorous demands of the construction work. Unscrupulous loan sharks preyed upon the workers and made an already bad situation intolerable. *There arose a great outcry* from the oppressed which demanded the immediate attention of Nehemiah.

The economic abuses of which the people complained could scarcely have originated during the 52 days of the wall-building. Nevertheless, it was the emergency precipitated by the wall-building and by the recent crop failures which caused the situation to reach crisis proportions.

There were two principal complaints. The creditors were demanding exorbitant collateral for their loans, and they were enslaving the sons and daughters of debtors who had no property. Unfortunately, both practices were technically legal.

If a creditor chose to do so, he was entitled to demand and receive a pledge as security for a loan to a fellow Hebrew (Ex. 22:26; Deut. 24:10–13). He was permitted to take possession of the pledge and to use it until the debt was repaid (cf. v. 5c). Brotherly concern demanded that the pledge be reasonable; and the truly righteous man is described as one who exacts no pledge at all (Ezek. 18:16). Yet the profiteers of Nehemiah's time were taking *fields, vineyards,* and *houses* and thus were reducing the poor to abject poverty and starvation. In order to get food to eat and money to pay the *king's tax* (not that referred to in 5:15 but rather the imperial tax which had to be paid in metal [cf. Ezra 6:8]) the poor were being required to surrender their sources of livelihood. The restoration of a single Hebrew letter in v. 2 makes it possible to translate: "We are giving our sons and our daughters in pledge to secure grain that we may eat and live" (American Translation).

A poor man who had no collateral or who could not meet his financial obligations was allowed to pledge his son or his daughter, and the creditor was entitled to claim the services of such a person for a period not to exceed six years (Ex. 21:1-6; Deut. 15:12-18). The profiteers may not have been violating the letter of the Torah, unless some had overstepped the limits of the Torah by violating the girl slaves. The RSV translates v. 5 *some of our daughters have already been enslaved,* but the passage probably means "some of our daughters have already been violated" (cf. Esther 7:8).

Even if they were not exceeding the letter of the law, however, they were surely violating its spirit by requiring such outrageous pledges that the poor were reduced to the necessity of giving their children as security or payment for debt. The oppressed were understandably incensed that members of their own *flesh* and community would apply the law in such a brutal and unfeeling manner.

2. Nehemiah's Confrontation with the Profiteers (5:6-13)

⁶ I was very angry when I heard their outcry and these words, ⁷ I took counsel with myself, and I brought charges against the nobles and the officials. I said to them, "You are exacting interest, each from his brother." And I held a great assembly against them, ⁸ and said to them "We, as far as we are able, have bought back our Jewish brethren who have been sold to the nations; but you even sell your brethren that they may be sold to us!" They were silent, and could not find a word to say. ⁹ So I said, "The thing that you are doing is not good. Ought you not to walk in the fear of our God to prevent the taunts of the nations our enemies? ¹⁰ Moreover I and my brethren and my servants are lending them money and grain. Let us leave off this interest. ¹¹ Return to them this very day their fields, their vineyards, their olive orchards, and their houses, and the hundredth of money, grain, wine, and oil which you have been exacting of them." ¹² Then they said, "We will restore these and require nothing from them. We will do as you say." And I called the priests, and took an oath of them to do as they had promised. ¹³ I also shook out my lap and said, "So may God shake out every man from his house and from his labor who does not perform this promise. So may he be shaken out and emptied." And all the assembly said "Amen" and praised the LORD. And the people did as they had promised.

When the plight of the poor was brought to the attention of Nehemiah, he became *very angry* (cf. 13:8,25) and confronted the guilty *nobles* and *officials* with charges of exploitation. In order to reinforce his demands for reform he *held a great assembly* against the offenders.

According to the RSV, the principal charge which Nehemiah made against the accused was that of *exacting interest.* This translation is undoubtedly incorrect. The outcry of the poor had not included such a complaint. Moreover, it was an explicit violation of the Torah for a Jew to exact interest from another Jew (Ex. 22:25; Deut. 23:20), yet Nehemiah did not accuse anyone of violating the letter of the law. The actual offense for which the creditors were called to account was lending on pledge (cf. the American Jewish Translation). *Let us leave off this interest* means "let us stop requiring collateral for loans" (cf. Wilhelm Rudolph, p. 130). This practice, although legal, was reprehensible because it was causing severe hardships among the poor.

Nehemiah sought to shame the offenders into giving up their abusive practices. He reminded them that he and his associates had been buying back Jews who had become the slaves of Gentiles (v. 8). This was normal procedure (Lev. 25:47-49), but it was an outrage to have to redeem Jewish slaves from fellow Jews. Nehemiah is pleading for a humanitarian emancipation of all of the slaves.

The profiteers were not only making life miserable for their less affluent brethren, but they were endangering the security of the community. They were giving aid and comfort to the enemy in the midst of a dangerous military emergency. By weakening the community from within, they were encouraging *the taunts of the nations* and undermining Nehemiah's efforts to rebuild the wall. Nehemiah suggests that enlightened self-interest, if nothing else, ought to motivate them *to walk in the fear of our God,* which includes the idea of maintaining a right relationship with one's fellow-men.

Many scholars believe that Nehemiah implicated himself in the economic abuses. It is true that he said he and his associates had been *lending them money and grain.* Verses 14–19, however, suggest that he is contrasting his behavior with that of the greedy nobles. The statement *let us leave off this* lending on pledge need not imply that he himself had been taking pledges. (Ezra identified himself with the marriage offenders [Ezra 9:6] although he had not contracted an illicit marriage.) The community was a corporate whole, and it was believed that the sin of any group within the community (the corporate whole) would bring guilt upon all.

Nehemiah demanded that the creditors return to the debtors the *fields, . . . vineyards, . . . olive orchards and . . . houses* which they had possessed as pledges.

The reference to *the hundredth of money,* etc., is obscure. The Hebrew word translated *hundredth* does not have that meaning in any other context and is apparently an ancient scribal error.[43] The original word must have had reference to pledges. The context suggests that Nehemiah was demanding the return of all collateral which had been exacted for loans of *money, grain, wine, and oil.* Because of the famine and tax squeeze, the money and food must be understood as loans from the rich and not as pledges offered by the poor.

The offenders promised to restore the pledges and not to exact any more in the future. But Nehemiah was not satisfied with a simple affirmation. He *called the priests* to administer an oath that the abuses would not be repeated. Then Nehemiah shook out the fold of his garment (*lap*) in which he kept his personal belongings to dramatize what would happen to the man who broke the oath. He would be emptied of his house and livelihood as one shakes the contents out of a pocket.

[43] Cf. E. Neufeld, "The Rate of Interest and the Text of Nehemiah 5:11," *Jewish Quarterly Review,* Jan., 1954, pp. 199–200.

3. Nehemiah's Example as Governor (5:14–19)

14 Moreover from the time that I was appointed to be their governor in the land of Judah, from the twentieth year to the thirty-second year of Artaxerxes the king, twelve years, neither I nor my brethren ate the food allowance of the governor. 15 The former governors who were before me laid heavy burdens upon the people, and took from them food and wine, besides forty shekels of silver. Even their servants lorded it over the people. But I did not do so, because of the fear of God. 16 I also held to the work on this wall, and acquired no land; and all my servants were gathered there for the work. 17 Moreover there were at my table a hundred and fifty men, Jews and officials, besides those who came to us from the nations which were about us. 18 Now that which was prepared for one day was one ox and six choice sheep; fowls likewise were prepared for me, and every ten days skins of wine in abundance; yet with all this I did not demand the food allowance of the governor, because the servitude was heavy upon this people. 19 Remember for my good, O my God, all that I have done for this people.

Not only did Nehemiah not exploit the poor through greedy economic practices, but he did not even accept the customary *food allowance of the governor.* Instead he himself bore the expense of feeding the administrative officials and foreign guests who were entitled to eat at the governor's table. He saw that *the servitude was heavy upon this people,* and he was unwilling to add to their burden in any way. He did not acquire land (which was in short supply), and the governor's mansion which he had anticipated building (2:8) was apparently never built.

The identity of *the former governors* is not disclosed. Since it was not until the time of Nehemiah that Judah was detached from Samaria as a separate administrative district, the governors referred to were probably Samaritan governors. These governors *laid heavy burdens upon the people,* but the Hebrew cannot mean that the *food and wine* were in addition to *forty shekels of silver.* The reading in the Vulgate suggests that the governors levied a tax of forty shekels per day to provide food and wine for the governor's table (cf. Bowman, p. 712).

Nehemiah did not deliver this defense of his governorship on the occasion of the great assembly. It was composed sometime after the close of his first term as governor (v. 14). The purpose of the apology was religious (cf. v. 19). Nehemiah, in keeping with orthodox Deuteronomic teaching, believed that his reward from God would be in proportion to his loyalty to Torah. This explicit record of his good deeds was designed to demonstrate that he was a God-fearing man, worthy of God's remembrance.[44]

Nehemiah had more than the usual concern about the future (cf. 13:14,22,31), because he was a eunuch. His reward would not include the perpetuation of his name in his offspring (cf. 2 Sam. 18:18). His prayer to God was that he would be remembered for his good deeds. This was indeed the promise of an earlier postexilic writer in Isaiah 56:4-5.

VI. Further Harassment of Nehemiah (6:1-19)

1. Invitations to a Conference (6:1-4)

¹ Now when it was reported to Sanballat and Tobiah and to Geshem the Arab and to the rest of our enemies that I had built the wall and that there was no breach left in it (although up to that time I had not set up the doors in the gates), ² Sanballat and Geshem sent to me, saying, "Come and let us meet together in one of the villages in the plain of Ono." But they intended to do me harm. ³ And I sent messengers to them, saying, "I am doing a great work and I cannot come down. Why should the work stop while I leave it and come down to you?" ⁴ And they sent to me four times in this way and I answered them in the same manner.

The narrative about the economic abuses (ch. 5) interrupts the story of the rebuilding of the wall but serves to indicate continuing progress with the construction. In 4:6 the wall is only half completed, but when the narrative resumes everything is finished except the setting of the wooden doors into the gate openings.

When Nehemiah's enemies found that they were getting nowhere with threats of military interference, they resorted to more subtle and devious attempts to frustrate Nehemiah's work. They sent four different invitations urging him to meet them for a conference *in the plain of Ono*. Nehemiah was convinced that they were trying to entice him away from the security of Jerusalem, and so refused to go. He did not give them a categorical rejection, however, but used the work on the wall as a reason for not meeting them. He was apparently stalling for time so that he could finish the work before risking a showdown.

Nehemiah had doubtless appraised the motives of his enemies correctly. Friendly gestures were frequently used to lure a man into a death trap (2 Sam. 13:23-29; Jer. 41:1-3), and Nehemiah could not take the chance. However, if Nehemiah had documents from Artaxerxes authorizing the work in which he was engaged, one wonders why he did not propose a conference on his own terms so that the matter could be clarified.

The plain of Ono was part of the plain of Sharon, about 20 miles northwest of Jerusalem. This site may have been considered neutral territory (cf. Bowman, pp. 715–716), although Jews lived there during the postexilic period (7:37; cf. Ezra 2:33).

2. Charge of Treason (6:5-9)

⁵ In the same way Sanballat for the fifth time sent his servant to me with an open letter in his hand. ⁶ In it was written, "It is reported among the nations, and Geshem also says it, that you and the Jews intend to rebel; that is why you are building the wall; and you wish to become their king, according to this report. ⁷ And you have also set up prophets to proclaim concerning you in Jerusalem, 'There is a king in Judah.' And now it will be reported to the king according to these words. So now come, and let us take counsel together." ⁸ Then I sent to him, saying, "No such things as you say have been done, for you are inventing them out of your own mind." ⁹ For they all wanted to frighten us, thinking, "Their hands will drop from the work, and it will not be done." But now, O God, strengthen thou my hands.

---

[44] Cf. Walther Eichrodt, *Theology of the Old Testament* (Philadelphia: Westminster, 1961), II, 346-47.

The fifth letter (*open letter* probably refers to the commonly used ostracon, cf. Bowman, p. 716) from Sanballat repeated the demand for a conference, but this time it included an ultimatum. Nehemiah was told that unless he agreed to meet with his enemies a report would be sent to the Persian king and that this letter would be accusing him of treason.

If Nehemiah had in fact been fortifying Jerusalem without Persian authorization, as Sanballat apparently believed, it could have been interpreted as treason. Such an act on the part of an earlier group had prompted Rehum and Shimshai to lodge a complaint with Artaxerxes I (Ezra 4:8–16).

Nehemiah had assuredly not *set up prophets* to proclaim himself king,[45] but it is not unthinkable that Sanballat had heard such rumors. Just as Haggai (2:23) and Zechariah (3:8; 6:10–14) had voiced political hopes for Zerubbabel, so unnamed prophets a century later may have been whispering such plans for Nehemiah. In the light of vv. 10–14, it is possible that unscrupulous prophets had circulated false rumors about Nehemiah's ambitions for the purpose of creating trouble for him.

Nehemiah flatly denied any plans for rebellion against Persia and accused Sanballat of inventing the charges. He refused to be frightened or to be deterred from the work. Instead, he took courage and renewed his efforts. The last sentence in v. 9 is not a prayer. In the Masoretic Text the verb is in the imperative, but the words "*O God*" were added by the translators. The Greek and Latin versions show that Nehemiah strengthened his own hands, which means that he bolstered his courage and increased his determination. Bowman (p. 718) prefers the rendering of the Vulgate, "I strengthened my hands all the more."

---

[45] Even if Nehemiah had been disloyal to Artaxerxes, he could scarcely have aspired to the throne. He was apparently not a member of the Davidic line. Moreover, as a eunuch he would doubtless have been ineligible (cf. Deut. 23:1).

3. Schemes of False Prophets (6:10–14)

10 Now when I went into the house of Shemaiah the son of Delaiah, son of Mehetabel, who was shut up, he said, "Let us meet together in the house of God, within the temple, and let us close the doors of the temple; for they are coming to kill you, at night they are coming to kill you." 11 But I said, "Should such a man as I flee? And what man such as I could go into the temple and live? I will not go in." 12 And I understood, and saw that God had not sent him, but he had pronounced the prophecy against me because Tobiah and Sanballat had hired him. 13 For this purpose he was hired, that I should be afraid and act in this way and sin, and so they could give me an evil name, in order to taunt me. 14 Remember Tobiah and Sanballat, O my God, according to these things that they did, and also the prophetess Noadiah and the rest of the prophets who wanted to make me afraid.

Nehemiah did not have the unanimous support of all the Jews of Judah. There were some prophets and at least one prophetess who were sympathetic with Nehemiah's enemies. *Tobiah and Sanballat* exploited this internal disunity in a further effort to undermine Nehemiah's work.

A man named *Shemaiah,* presumably a local Jewish prophet, was employed to try to panic Nehemiah into committing acts of cowardice and sacrilege. He told Nehemiah that he was about to be assassinated and should take refuge immediately inside the Temple sanctuary. The phrase *who was shut up* has not been satisfactorily explained.

Nehemiah refused to heed the advice of Shemaiah, even before he perceived that the latter was in the pay of his enemies. To have locked himself inside the Temple would have cost him the confidence of the people and would have demoralized those who were working on the wall. Moreover, it would have been a serious cultic offense for Nehemiah to have entered the Temple building. Laymen were allowed in the Temple courts but not in the building itself (cf. Num. 18:7). It would doubtless have been doubly offensive for a eunuch to enter the Temple (cf. Lev. 21:17–24; Deut. 23:1).

Nehemiah faced the alleged danger bravely and refused to tarnish his reputation by any act of indiscretion. When he discovered that the report was simply a further ruse to ensnare him, he prayed again that God's judgment would fall upon his enemies (cf. 4:4–5).

4. Completion of the Wall (6:15–16)

15 So the wall was finished on the twenty-fifth day of the month Elul, in fifty-two days. 16 And when all our enemies heard of it, all the nations round about us were afraid and fell greatly in their own esteem; for they perceived that this work had been accomplished with the help of our God.

There is no convincing reason for one to reject the biblical datum that the wall was completed *in fifty-two days*. The entire account of the construction reflects a great sense of urgency and haste. The task was completed with such phenomenal speed that the surrounding peoples were amazed and attributed the accomplishment to the help of God (v. 16).

One may surmise that, except for the east wall, Nehemiah simply repaired and restored the preexilic wall. Miss Kenyon's [46] excavations show that Nehemiah did, in fact, build an entirely new east wall, but by doing so he greatly reduced the size of the city and thus reduced the task of refortifying it. It is not historically improbable that Nehemiah completed the wall *on the twenty-fifth day of the month Elul* (August–September) in the same year in which he received permission from Artaxerxes (cf. 2:1). The journey from Susa and the rebuilding of the wall could well have been accomplished in six months.

Verse 16 contains some problems of translation and interpretation. In the first place the Masoretic Text reads "saw" (cf. RSV marg.) instead of *were afraid*. The enemies in Samaria and in other distant places *heard* that the wall had been finished, while the peoples living nearby

[46] *Op. cit.*, p. 110.

"saw" for themselves. In the second place, *fell greatly in their own esteem* is a very doubtful translation of the Hebrew text. The correction of only one Hebrew letter gives the reading "and it was exceedingly marvelous in their eyes" (cf. Bowman, p. 722). This translation fits the context perfectly in the light of the concluding statement that *they perceived that this work had been accomplished with the help of our God*.

5. Tobiah's Allies in Judah (6:17–19)

17 Moreover in those days, the nobles of Judah sent many letters to Tobiah, and Tobiah's letters came to them. 18 For many in Judah were bound by oath to him, because he was the son-in-law of Shecaniah the son of Arah: and his son Jehohanan had taken the daughter of Meshullam the son of Berechiah as his wife. 19 Also they spoke of his good deeds in my presence, and reported my words to him. And Tobiah sent letters to make me afraid.

In this appendix to the story of the rebuilding of the wall, Nehemiah explains why *Tobiah* was a particularly dangerous enemy to him. Many of the nobles of Judah were friends and relatives of Tobiah and did not share Nehemiah's antipathy toward him. Both Tobiah himself and his son *Jehohanan* were related by marriage to the families of prominent wall-builders (cf. 3:4,29–30). It is possible that Tobiah's friends in Judah tried sincerely to mediate between him and Nehemiah, but Nehemiah considered them to be informers.

VII. Restoration of Jerusalem (7:1–73a)

1. Organization of Defenses (7:1–3)

1 Now when the wall had been built and I had set up the doors, and the gatekeepers, the singers, and the Levites had been appointed, 2 I gave my brother Hanani and Hananiah the governor of the castle charge over Jerusalem, for he was a more faithful and God-fearing man than many. 3 And I said to them, "Let not the gates of Jerusalem be opened until the sun is hot; and while they are still standing guard let them shut and bar the doors. Appoint guards from among the inhabitants of Jerusalem, each to his station and each opposite his own house."

The completion of the wall did not eliminate all danger to Jerusalem. There were still foes in the surrounding provinces and potential traitors within the community. Measures had to be taken immediately for the security of the city. *Gatekeepers* were appointed to control access to the city. The gatekeepers of 7:45 were the guards at the entrances to the Temple. Confusion between the two groups resulted in the addition of the words *the singers, and the Levites* to v. 1, where they obviously do not belong. *Guards from among the inhabitants of Jerusalem* were posted in the vicinity of their homes as an added precaution. Except in broad daylight all entrances to the city were shut and barred.

Possibly in anticipation of his return to Susa, Nehemiah placed his brother Hanani (cf. 1:2) in charge of the city. The position carried with it a heavy responsibility and demanded a *faithful and God-fearing man.* Hanani's title *governor of the castle* may imply that he was commander of the fortress of the Temple (cf. 2:8) before he was placed over the entire city.

Hanani and *Hananiah* are variant forms of the same name and undoubtedly refer to the same man. The conjunction *and* frequently serves as an explicative in Hebrew and should be translated here as "that is" or "namely" (cf. Bowman, p. 724).

2. *Need for Repopulation (7:4-5)*

⁴ The city was wide and large, but the people within it were few and no houses had been built.
⁵ Then God put it into my mind to assemble the nobles and the officials and the people to be enrolled by genealogy. And I found the book of the genealogy of those who came up at the first, and I found written in it:

The new wall around Jerusalem could be truly effective only when the city had been fully restored and repopulated. Nehemiah summoned *the nobles and the officials and the people* for the purpose of working out such a plan. The plan itself, which is not described until 11:1-2, required ten percent of the local population to move inside the city.

The city of Jerusalem was sparsely populated at the time the wall was built, but a few people did live there (7:3; cf. 3:21,23,28-29; 11:1). Perhaps the statement that *no houses had been built* means that no new houses had been constructed during or after the rebuilding of the wall.

It is possible that Nehemiah conducted a genealogical enrollment of some kind in connection with his program for the restoration of Jerusalem. If the results of such an enrollment were found in the Nehemiah memoirs, however, the Chronicler did not choose to use them. Instead, he presented a genealogical list which was understood to contain the names of *those who came up at the first* (presumably at the time of the first return, during the reign of Cyrus).

3. *The Census List (7:6-73a)*

⁶ These were the people of the province who came up out of the captivity of those exiles whom Nebuchadnezzar the king of Babylon had carried into exile; they returned to Jerusalem and Judah, each to his town. ⁷ They came with Zerubbabel, Jeshua, Nehemiah, Azariah, Raamiah, Nahamani, Mordecai, Bilshan, Mispereth, Bigvai, Nehum, Baanah.
The number of the men of the people of Israel: ⁸ the sons of Parosh, two thousand a hundred and seventy-two. ⁹ The sons of Shephatiah, three hundred and seventy-two. ¹⁰ The sons of Arah, six hundred and fifty-two. ¹¹ The sons of Pahathmoab, namely the sons of Jeshua and Joab, two thousand eight hundred and eighteen. ¹² The sons of Elam, a thousand two hundred and fifty-four. ¹³ The sons of Zattu, eight hundred and forty-five. ¹⁴ The sons of Zaccai, seven hundred and sixty. ¹⁵ The sons of Binnui, six hundred and forty-eight. ¹⁶ The sons of Bebai, six hundred and twenty-eight. ¹⁷ The sons of Azgad, two thousand three hundred and twenty-two. ¹⁸ The sons of Adonikam, six hundred and sixty-seven. ¹⁹ The sons of Bigvai, two thousand and sixty-seven. ²⁰ The sons of Adin, six hundred and fifty-five. ²¹ The sons of Ater, namely of Hezekiah, ninety-eight. ²² The sons of Hashum, three hundred and twenty-eight. ²³ The sons of Bezai, three hundred and twenty-four. ²⁴ The sons of Hariph, a hundred and twelve. ²⁵ The sons of Gibeon, ninety-five. ²⁶ The men of Bethlehem and Netophah, a hundred and eighty-eight. ²⁷ The men of Anathoth, a hundred and twenty-eight. ²⁸ The men of Bethazmaveth, forty-two. ²⁹ The men of Kiri-

athjearim, Chephirah, and Beeroth, seven hundred and forty-three. ³⁰ The men of Ramah and Geba, six hundred and twenty-one. ³¹ The men of Michmas, a hundred and twenty-two. ³² The men of Bethel and Ai, a hundred and twenty-three. ³³ The men of the other Nebo, fifty-two. ³⁴ The sons of the other Elam, a thousand two hundred and fifty-four. ³⁵ The sons of Harim, three hundred and twenty. ³⁶ The sons of Jericho, three hundred and forty-five. ³⁷ The sons of Lod, Hadid, and Ono, seven hundred and twenty-one. ³⁸ The sons of Senaah, three thousand nine hundred and thirty.

³⁹ The priests: the sons of Jedaiah, namely the house of Jeshua, nine hundred and seventy-three. ⁴⁰ The sons of Immer, a thousand and fifty-two. ⁴¹ The sons of Pashhur, a thousand two hundred and forty-seven. ⁴² The sons of Harim, a thousand and seventeen.

⁴³ The Levites: the sons of Jeshua, namely of Kadmiel of the sons of Hodevah, seventy-four. ⁴⁴ The singers: the sons of Asaph, a hundred and forty-eight. ⁴⁵ The gatekeepers: the sons of Shallum, the sons of Ater, the sons of Talmon, the sons of Akkub, the sons of Hatita, the sons of Shobai, a hundred and thirty-eight.

⁴⁶ The temple servants: the sons of Ziha, the sons of Hasupha, the sons of Tabbaoth, ⁴⁷ the sons of Keros, the sons of Sia, the sons of Padon, ⁴⁸ the sons of Lebana, the sons of Hagaba, the sons of Shalmai, ⁴⁹ the sons of Hanan, the sons of Giddel, the sons of Gahar, ⁵⁰ the sons of Reaiah, the sons of Rezin, the sons of Nekoda, ⁵¹ the sons of Gazzam, the sons of Uzza, the sons of Paseah, ⁵² the sons of Besai, the sons of Meunim, the sons of Nephushesim, ⁵³ the sons of Bakbuk, the sons of Hakupha, the sons of Harhur, ⁵⁴ the sons of Bazlith, the sons of Mehida, the sons of Harsha, ⁵⁵ the sons of Barkos, the sons of Sisera, the sons of Temah, ⁵⁶ the sons of Neziah, the sons of Hatipha.

⁵⁷ The sons of Solomon's servants: the sons of Sotai, the sons of Sophereth, the sons of Perida, ⁵⁸ the sons of Jaala, the sons of Darkon, the sons of Giddel, ⁵⁹ the sons of Shephatiah, the sons of Hattil, the sons of Pochereth-hazzebaim, the sons of Amon.

⁶⁰ All the temple servants and the sons of Solomon's servants were three hundred and ninety-two.

⁶¹ The following were those who came up from Telmelah, Telharsha, Cherub, Addon, and Immer, but they could not prove their fathers' houses nor their descent, whether they belonged to Israel: ⁶² the sons of Delaiah, the sons of Tobiah, the sons of Nekoda, six hundred and forty-two. ⁶³ Also, of the priests: the sons of Hobaiah, the sons of Hakkoz, the sons of Barzillai (who had taken a wife of the daughters of Barzillai the Gileadite and was called by their name). ⁶⁴ These sought their registration among those enrolled in the genealogies, but it was not found there, so they were excluded from the priesthood as unclean; ⁶⁵ the governor told them that they were not to partake of the most holy food, until a priest with Urim and Thummim should arise.

⁶⁶ The whole assembly together was forty-two thousand three hundred and sixty, ⁶⁷ besides their menservants and maidservants, of whom there were seven thousand three hundred and thirty-seven; and they had two hundred and forty-five singers, male and female. ⁶⁸ Their horses were seven hundred and thirty-six, their mules two hundred and forty-five, ⁶⁹ their camels four hundred and thirty-five, and their asses six thousand seven hundred and twenty.

⁷⁰ Now some of the heads of fathers' houses gave to the work. The governor gave to the treasury a thousand darics of gold, fifty basins, five hundred and thirty priests' garments. ⁷¹ And some of the heads of fathers' houses gave into the treasury of the work twenty thousand darics of gold and two thousand two hundred minas of silver. ⁷² And what the rest of the people gave was twenty thousand darics of gold, two thousand minas of silver, and sixty-seven priests' garments.

⁷³ So the priests, the Levites, the gatekeepers, the singers, some of the people, the temple servants, and all Israel, lived in their towns.

This list is found almost word for word in the narrative of the restoration of the cult (see the discussion of Ezra 2:1-70).

A list such as this might have been of value to Nehemiah in arranging for the repopulation of Jerusalem, and he might conceivably have had access to it. It was the Chronicler, however, who was responsible for including the list in this narrative. If Nehemiah had inserted the document in his memoirs, he would scarcely have used the irrelevant material in vv. 64-73. Moreover, he would surely have alluded to the list in connection with the actual population reform, described in 11:1-2. The absence of any reference to a census list in 11:1-2 suggests that Nehemiah did not use such a document. Ths second part of 7:5, beginning with the words "to be enrolled by genealogy," is often understood as the Chronicler's own introduction to the list. Nehemiah's reason for summoning the leaders and the people to Jerusalem may have been to have them cast lots (11:1–2) rather than to have them "enrolled by genealogy."

VIII. Ezra's Revival (7:73b—9:37)

1. Reading of the Law (7:73b–8:8)

And when the seventh month had come, the children of Israel were in their towns.
¹ And all the people gathered as one man into the square before the Water Gate; and they told Ezra the scribe to bring the book of the law of Moses which the LORD had given to Israel. ² And Ezra the priest brought the law before the assembly, both men and women and all who could hear with understanding, on the first day of the seventh month. ³ And he read from it facing the square before the Water Gate from early morning until midday, in the presence of the men and the women and those who could understand; and the ears of all the people were attentive to the book of the law. ⁴ And Ezra the scribe stood on a wooden pulpit which they had made for the purpose; and beside him stood Mattithiah, Shema, Anaiah, Uriah, Hilkiah, and Maaseiah on his right hand; and Pedaiah, Mishael, Malchijah, Hashum, Hashbaddanah, Zechariah, and Meshullam on his left hand. ⁵ And Ezra opened the book in the sight of all the people, for he was above all the people; and when he opened it all the people stood. ⁶ And Ezra blessed the LORD, the great God; and all the people answered, "Amen, Amen," lifting up their hands; and they bowed their heads and worshiped the LORD with their faces to the ground. ⁷ Also Jeshua, Bani, Sherebiah, Jamin, Akkub, Shabbethai, Hodiah, Maaseiah, Kelita, Azariah, Jozabad, Hanan, Pelaiah, the Levites, helped the people to understand the law, while the people remained in their places. ⁸ And they read from the book, from the law of God, clearly; and they gave the sense, so that the people understood the reading.

The story of the reading of the law and of the ceremonies associated with it is part of the Ezra narrative and is out of place chronologically in its present context. The events related in this passage are best understood as having taken place soon after those of Ezra 7—8 and shortly before those of Ezra 9—10. It is indeed likely that the narrative itself stood orignally in that location.

How the Ezra narrative came to be disarranged is uncertain. It may be significant, however, that the story of the reading of the law begins with the statement, *And when the seventh month had come, the children of Israel were in their towns.* The fact that this is almost exactly the same statement found in Ezra 3:1 immediately following the census list (Ezra 2:1–70) may have influenced a scribe to insert the account of the reading of the law immediately after the census list in Nehemiah 7:6–73a. The witness of 1 Esdras is that the error was discovered later and that an attempt was made to restore the passage to the Ezra narrative. By that time, however, it was no longer known where within the Ezra story the reading of the law belonged. Therefore, the latter account (and inadvertently, a portion of the conclusion to the census list) was attached to the end of Ezra 7—10, where it stands in that recension.

The recovery of the original sequence of events reveals the work of Ezra in its proper historical perspective. He arrived in Jerusalem on the first day of the fifth month (Ezra 7:9) and used the first few weeks to learn the people and their needs. During *the seventh month* (7:73b) he led the people in renewing their devotion to Torah and in observing the Feast of Booths. The religious revival prepared the community to accept the marriage reforms, which followed in the ninth month (Ezra 10:9).

The first day of the seventh month became a holy day in postexilic Judah (cf. Lev. 23:24–25; Num. 29:1–6), but the assembly *before the Water Gate* does not appear to have been a routine assembly. Special preparations had been made including the construction of *a wooden pulpit,* and even the women and older children had been assembled for what was clearly an extraordinary occasion.

Ezra, the teacher of Torah who had recently arrived from Babylonia, was invited to read from *the book of the law of Moses.* He, assisted by the Levites (cf. v. 8), read *from early morning until midday.*

As the service began, Ezra *opened the*

book (unrolled the scroll) *of the law of Moses* and *all the people stood* in reverent respect for the holy book. They remained standing while Ezra offered a prayer of praise, then raised their hands and said *Amen, Amen* (a liturgical response by which the worshipers express their wholehearted participation in the prayer). Finally they prostrated themselves *with their faces to the ground.* This ritual to introduce the reading of the law was already thoroughly familiar to the people.

The narrative does not indicate on whose initiative the assembly was called, but the community leaders took an important part in the service. Ezra read at the invitation of some spokesman for the people (v. 1), and prominent community leaders accompanied him on the platform. *The Levites helped the people to understand the law* by translating it from the Hebrew into the Aramaic vernacular of the people.

No attempt to identify the specific content of the scroll from which Ezra read has been convincing. It is clear, however, that Ezra did not introduce a new or previously unknown code. The scroll from which he read was already known and accepted by the community as *the law of Moses which the Lord had given to Israel.* The people stood up as an expression of their respect for it and wept when they heard its familiar words (8:9; see comment on Ezra 7:12–14). Ezra must have read from a portion of the Torah which was already considered authoritative and canonical by the community.

2. *Response of the People* (8:9–12)

9 And Nehemiah, who was the governor, and Ezra the priest and scribe, and the Levites who taught the people said to all the people, "This day is holy to the Lord your God; do not mourn or weep." For all the people wept when they heard the words of the law. 10 Then he said to them, "Go your way, eat the fat and drink sweet wine and send portions to him for whom nothing is prepared; for this day is holy to our Lord; and do not be grieved, for the joy of the Lord is your strength." 11 So the Levites stilled all the people, saying, "Be quiet, for this day is holy; do not be grieved." 12 And all the people went their way to eat and drink and to send portions and to make great rejoicing, because they had understood the words that were declared to them.

The generation which had passed since the time of Nehemiah's effective religious leadership had brought laxness and neglect in the observance of Torah. The reading of the law made the people keenly aware of their failure and guilt and caused them to weep and mourn.

But the reading of the law was not an occasion for grief and sadness in ancient Israel. It was an occasion for joy and thanksgiving (cf. Psalm 19:7–10; Deut. 12:12). Ezra comforted the people and proclaimed a feast to celebrate the renewal of their commitment to God. The religion proclaimed by the Bible is never a burden to be borne, but an opportunity for genuine joy and spiritual fulfillment. When the writer said *the joy of the Lord is your strength* he was expressing a profound truth for all generations.

The *great rejoicing,* however, was not to be expressed through unbridled revelry. God's presence can be an occasion for joy and even for shouting, but it can also be an occasion for silence. When the Levites said to the people, *Be quiet, for this day is holy* (v. 11), they were expressing the rare insight that reverent silence itself can be a positive response to the presence and greatness of God (cf. Zech. 2:13; Hab. 2:20; Zeph. 1:7).

Nehemiah's name in v. 9 is almost certainly intrusive. Apart from the strong evidence that Ezra and Nehemiah were not contemporaries (see Introduction), there are reasons to believe that his name is not original in this context. In the first place, the parallel passage in 1 Esdras 9:49 omits the name Nehemiah and simply reads "the governor." In the second place, the word used for *governor* (*tirshatha*) in v. 9 was apparently not the correct title for Nehemiah (the LXX omits the title in 10:1). The latter referred to his office as *pehah* (a different word for governor; cf. 5:18). Finally, the verb *said* in v. 9 is singular. While this is not grammatically impossible with a plural subject, it is likely that only one person did the speaking (cf. v. 10), and that that person was Ezra. One may assume that Nehemiah's name found its way into this passage as a result of the transposition of the passage into the midst of the Nehemiah narrative.

3. Observance of the Feast of Booths (8:13–18)

¹³ On the second day the heads of fathers' houses of all the people, with the priests and the Levites, came together to Ezra the scribe in order to study the words of the law. ¹⁴ And they found it written in the law that the LORD had commanded by Moses that the people of Israel should dwell in booths during the feast of the seventh month, ¹⁵ and that they should publish and proclaim in all their towns and in Jerusalem, "Go out to the hills and bring branches of olive, wild olive, myrtle, palm, and other leafy trees to make booths, as it is written." ¹⁶ So the people went out and brought them and made booths for themselves, each on his roof, and in their courts and in the courts of the house of God, and in the square at the Water Gate and in the square at the Gate of Ephraim. ¹⁷ And all the assembly of those who had returned from the captivity made booths and dwelt in the booths; for from the days of Jeshua the son of Nun to that day the people of Israel had not done so. And there was very great rejoicing. ¹⁸ And day by day, from the first day to the last day, he read from the book of the law of God. They kept the feast seven days; and on the eighth day there was a solemn assembly, according to the ordinance.

Formal study of the law did not cease after the great assembly on the first day of the seventh month. A smaller group of community leaders reassembled *on the second day* to continue the study. On this occasion Ezra directed their attention to a passage which contained instructions for the observance of the Feast of Booths (see comment on Ezra 3:3–6). Since the prescribed time for the celebration of this feast was near, plans were made, and the festival itself followed shortly.

Preparations began immediately, but the actual celebration probably did not begin until the fifteenth day (cf. Lev. 23:34,39). The last day of the feast would have fallen on the twenty-first, with the *solemn assembly* on the twenty-second. The next convocation occurred two days later on the twenty-fourth (9:1).

The observance of the feast followed closely the specifications found in the Holiness Code (Lev. 23:33–36,39–43), which presumably superseded the less exact instructions of Deuteronomy 16:13–15. It is not clear, therefore, what there was about the feast that caused the Chronicler to suggest that there had not been such a celebration *from the days of Jeshua the son of Nun to that day.* It is unlikely that Ezra restored any feature of the feast which had been abandoned since the time of Joshua. Perhaps we have here a conventional literary formula which merely expresses the superlative quality of the occasion (cf. 2 Kings 23:22; 2 Chron. 30:26; 35:18; Isa. 7:17; Matt. 24:21).

4. Fasting and Confession (9:1–5)

¹ Now on the twenty-fourth day of this month the people of Israel were assembled with fasting and in sackcloth, and with earth upon their heads. ² And the Israelites separated themselves from all foreigners, and stood and confessed their sins and the iniquities of their fathers. ³ And they stood up in their place and read from the book of the law of the LORD their God for a fourth of the day; for another fourth of it they made confession and worshiped the LORD their God. ⁴ Upon the stairs of the Levites stood Jeshua, Bani, Kadmiel, Shebaniah, Bunni, Sherebiah, Bani, and Chenani; and they cried with a loud voice to the LORD their God. ⁵ Then the Levites, Jeshua, Kadmiel, Bani, Hashabneiah, Sherebiah, Hodiah, Shebaniah, and Pethahiah, said, "Stand up and bless the LORD your God from everlasting to everlasting. Blessed be thy glorious name which is exalted above all blessing and praise."

The transition from rejoicing in chapter 8 to fasting in chapter 9 is abrupt. This has led to the suggestion that chapter 9 stood originally after Ezra 10 and described the response of the people to the marriage reforms rather than to the study of the law. Such a solution to the problem must be rejected, however. It does not explain how 23 days could have elapsed between the end of the work of the mixed marriage commission (Ezra 10:17) and the implementation of its decisions (cf. v. 1). Moreover, it fails to take note of the fact that vv. 1–5 do not mention the sending away of wives and children at all, but refer to a much more general separation from foreigners.

The fasting and confession of this passage must be interpreted as part of Ezra's revival and as a sequel to the events of chapter 8. The solemn assembly following the Feast of Booths took place on the twenty-second of the month (8:18), and the fast followed directly *on the twenty-fourth.*

Such a fast need not be unexpected. Although the people were urged to rejoice rather than to weep when the law was read at first (8:9–12), the ultimate aim of the revival was surely repentance and rededication. A ceremony of confession and renewal was a fitting climax to three weeks of joyful study of the law.

The separation from foreigners was a step preliminary to the marriage reform of Ezra 9—10 rather than its consequence. The aliens mentioned in v. 2 obviously do not include wives and children. The reading of the law made the Jews freshly conscious that their relations with non-Jews were illicit. The exclusion of foreigners near the end of the seventh month was the beginning of a process which culminated in the separation from wives and children in the ninth (Ezra 9—10).

The Levites played a leading role in the ceremonies of the twenty-fourth day as they had in the ceremonies of the first day (8:7–12). The text of vv. 4–5 had been poorly preserved, however, and it is impossible to discover the relationship between the two groups of Levites.

5. Prayer of Repentance (9:6–37)

(1) God's Mighty Acts and Israel's Response (9:6–31)

6 And Ezra said: "Thou art the LORD, thou alone; thou hast made heaven, the heaven of heavens, with all their host, the earth and all that is on it, the seas and all that is in them; and thou preservest all of them; and the host of heaven worships thee. 7 Thou art the LORD, the God who didst choose Abram and bring him forth out of Ur of the Chaldeans and give him the name Abraham; 8 and thou didst find his heart faithful before thee, and didst make with him the covenant to give to his descendants the land of the Canaanite, the Hittite, the Amorite, the Perizzite, the Jebusite, and the Girgashite; and thou hast fulfilled thy promise, for thou art righteous.

9 "And thou didst see the affliction of our fathers in Egypt and hear their cry at the Red Sea, 10 and didst perform signs and wonders against Pharaoh and all his servants and all the people of his land, for thou knewest that they acted insolently against our fathers; and thou didst get thee a name, as it is to this day. 11 And thou didst divide the sea before them, so that they went through the midst of the sea on dry land; and thou didst cast their pursuers into the depths, as a stone into mighty waters. 12 By a pillar of cloud thou didst lead them in the day, and by a pillar of fire in the night to light for them the way in which they should go. 13 Thou didst come down upon Mount Sinai, and speak with them from heaven and give them right ordinances and true laws, good statutes and commandments, 14 and thou didst make known to them thy holy sabbath and command them commandments and statutes and a law by Moses thy servant. 15 Thou didst give them bread from heaven for their hunger and bring forth water for them from the rock for their thirst, and thou didst tell them to go in to possess the land which thou hadst sworn to give them.

16 "But they and our fathers acted presumptuously and stiffened their neck and did not obey thy commandments; 17 they refused to obey, and were not mindful of the wonders which thou didst perform among them; but they stiffened their neck and appointed a leader to return to their bondage in Egypt. But thou art a God ready to forgive, gracious and merciful, slow to anger and abounding in steadfast love, and didst not forsake them. 18 Even when they had made for themselves a molten calf and said, 'This is your God who brought you up out of Egypt,' and had committed great blasphemies, 19 thou in thy great mercies didst not forsake them in the wilderness; the pillar of cloud which led them in the way did not depart from them by day, nor the pillar of fire by night which lighted for them the way by which they should go. 20 Thou gavest thy good Spirit to instruct them, and didst not withhold thy manna from their mouth, and gavest them water for their thirst. 21 Forty years didst thou sustain them in the wilderness, and they lacked nothing; their

clothes did not wear out and their feet did not swell. 22 And thou didst give them kingdoms and peoples, and didst allot to them every corner; so they took possession of the land of Sihon king of Heshbon and the land of Og king of Bashan. 23 Thou didst multiply their descendants as the stars of heaven, and thou didst bring them into the land which thou hadst told their fathers to enter and possess. 24 So the descendants went in and possessed the land, and thou didst subdue before them the inhabitants of the land, the Canaanites, and didst give them into their hands, with their kings and the peoples of the land, that they might do with them as they would. 25 And they captured fortified cities and a rich land, and took possession of houses full of all goods things, cisterns hewn out, vineyards, olive orchards and fruit trees in abundance; so they ate, and were filled and became fat, and delighted themselves in thy great goodness.

26 "Nevertheless they were disobedient and rebelled against thee and cast thy law behind their back and killed thy prophets, who had warned them in order to turn them back to thee, and they committed great blasphemies. 27 Therefore thou didst give them into the hand of their enemies, who made them suffer; and in the time of their suffering they cried to thee and thou didst hear them from heaven; and according to thy great mercies thou didst give them saviors who saved them from the hand of their enemies. 28 But after they had rest they did evil again before thee, and thou didst abandon them to the hand of their enemies, so that they had dominion over them; yet when they turned and cried to thee thou didst hear from heaven, and many times thou didst deliver them according to thy mercies. 29 And thou didst warn them in order to turn them back to thy law. Yet they acted presumptuously and did not obey thy commandments, but sinned against thy ordinances, by the observance of which a man shall live, and turned a stubborn shoulder and stiffened their neck and would not obey. 30 Many years thou didst bear with them, and didst warn them by thy Spirit through thy prophets; yet they would not give ear. Therefore thou didst give them into the hand of the peoples of the lands. 31 Nevertheless in thy great mercies thou didst not make an end of them or forsake them; for thou art a gracious and merciful God.

This long prayer, which is appended to the story of the rededication ceremony, is attributed to Ezra in the LXX but not in the Masoretic Text. Many scholars maintain that it was originally attributed to the Levites and that it is a continuation of the doxology of v. 5b. It is more likely, however, that the words *And Ezra said* have been lost from the Masoretic Text. Eight Levites could have said the liturgical statement in v. 5b in unison, but the lengthy prayer must have been attributed originally to only one man.

The origin of the prayer is unknown. It was composed at a time when the Jews were in great distress and were being brutally exploited by foreign kings (vv. 36–37). This excludes the time of Nehemiah and Ezra, both of whom were friendly toward the Persian government and grateful for its benefits to the Jews (cf. 2:6–8; Ezra 7:27–28). The prayer was used in its present context because it expresses the spirit of repentance and renewal which was appropriate to the rededication ceremony.

The primary theme of the prayer is God's gracious self-revelation of himself in history and Israel's miserable response to his revelation. This is, in fact, one of the most common themes in the Old Testament from the earliest to the latest literature (cf. Amos 2:9–12; Mic. 6:1–8; Deut. 1–5; Dan. 9:3–16). The author of this passage is restating the oft-repeated confession that God's benevolent initiative has been characteristically met by man's defiance and self-will.

The suppliant confesses that God's mighty acts in behalf of Israel began with the creation of the heavens and the earth. The phrase *heaven of heavens* is idiomatic for "the highest heaven" and reflects the common idea that there were several heavens (cf. Deut. 10:14; Eph. 4:10). *The host of heaven* refers to the angelic beings created by God to attend his heavenly throne (cf. 1 Kings 22:19);[47] God's gracious initiative continued in the election of Abraham and the making of a covenant with him. The bondage in Egypt did not frustrate God's plan, for he intervened to bring the people out of slavery and to lead them safely through the wilderness. At Sinai he

[47] For an excellent treatement of the phrase, see A. R. Johnson, *op. cit.*

gave them his law and his holy sabbath and provided for all of their needs.

But in defiant response to God's wonderful deeds and his benevolent care Israel *acted presumptuously* and *refused to obey*. Nevertheless God was patient and forgiving, even when they *made for themselves a molten calf*. He sustained them for forty years in the wilderness, then gave them victory over Sihon and Og, and led them in to possess the riches of Canaan.

Again Israel responded with disobedience and rebellion and killed the prophets whom God had sent to warn them. God chastised them repeatedly in a patient attempt to bring them back to him, but to no avail. Finally, he allowed the Chaldeans to destroy their land. But even in the Exile he did *not make an end of them or forsake them*. God's acts had been consistently gracious and loving in spite of Israel's unworthy response.

(2) *Appeal for Mercy* (9:32–37)

32 "Now therefore, our God, the great and mighty and terrible God, who keepest covenant and steadfast love, let not all the hardship seem little to thee that has come upon us, upon our kings, our princes, our priests, our prophets, our fathers, and all thy people, since the time of the kings of Assyria until this day. 33 Yet thou hast been just in all that has come upon us, for thou hast dealt faithfully and we have acted wickedly; 34 our kings, our princes, our priests, and our fathers have not kept thy law or heeded thy commandments and thy warnings which thou didst give them. 35 They did not serve thee in their kingdom, and in thy great goodness which thou gavest them, and in the large and rich land which thou didst set before them; and they did not turn from their wicked works. 36 Behold, we are slaves this day; in the land that thou gavest to our fathers to enjoy its fruit and its good gifts, behold, we are slaves. 37 And its rich yield goes to the kings whom thou hast set over us because of our sins; they have power also over our bodies and over our cattle at their pleasure, and we are in great distress.

In the concluding portion of the prayer, the suppliant appeals to God for mercy upon himself and upon his people. Terrible misfortunes have overtaken the covenant people since the *kings of Assyria* destroyed Israel (722 B.C.) and devastated Judah (701 B.C.). The punishment has been deserved; and through it all, God has been *just* and has *dealt faithfully* with his wicked people (see comments on Ezra 9:6–15). No attempt is made in the prayer to excuse the Jews or to minimize their guilt. But throughout history God has revealed himself to be merciful and forgiving. It is because of this divinely revealed grace that the petitioner can look for pity and relief from his *hardship* and *distress*.

IX. *A Written Covenant* (9:38—10:39)

1. *The Document and the Witnesses* (9:38—10:27)

38 Because of all this we make a firm covenant and write it, and our princes, our Levites, and our priests set their seal to it.
1 Those who set their seal are Nehemiah the governor, the son of Hacaliah, Zedekiah, 2 Seraiah, Azariah, Jeremiah, 3 Pashhur, Amariah, Malchijah, 4 Hattush, Shebaniah, Malluch, 5 Harim, Meremoth, Obadiah, 6 Daniel, Ginnethon, Baruch, 7 Meshullam, Abijah, Mijamin, 8 Maaziah, Bilgai, Shemaiah; these are the priests. 9 And the Levites: Jeshua the son of Azaniah, Binnui of the sons of Henadad, Kadmiel; 10 and their brethren, Shebaniah, Hodiah, Kelita, Pelaiah, Hanan, 11 Mica, Rehob, Hashabiah, 12 Zaccur, Sherebiah, Shebaniah, 13 Hodiah, Bani, Beninu. 14 The chiefs of the people: Parosh, Pahathmoab, Elam, Zattu, Bani, 15 Bunni, Azgad, Bebai, 16 Adonijah, Bigvai, Adin, 17 Ater, Hezekiah, Azzur, 18 Hodiah, Hashum, Bezai, 19 Hariph, Anathoth, Nebai, 20 Magpiash, Meshullam, Hezir, 21 Meshezabel, Zadok, Jaddua, 22 Pelatiah, Hanan, Anaiah, 23 Hoshea, Hananiah, Hasshub, 24 Hallohesh, Pilha, Shobek, 25 Rehum, Hashabnah, Maaseiah, 26 Ahiah, Hanan, Anan, 27 Malluch, Harim, Baanah.

This narrative presents the account of a *firm covenant* in which the people of Judah pledge themselves to obey certain specific ordinances relating to marriage, the sabbath, and Temple offerings. In its present context, the passage appears to describe events associated with the conclusion of Ezra's revival. Ezra's name, however, is conspicuously missing from the narrative. Moreover, it is difficult to understand how the renewal ceremonies of chapters 8 and 9 could be the antecedents for the specific oaths embodied in the covenant of chapter 10. On the other hand, the presence of Nehemiah's name suggests that the passage relates to his mission rather than to that of Ezra. Furthermore, the abuses with which Nehemiah dealt during his second mission (ch. 13) are indeed those which the covenant seeks to correct. The events of chapter 10 are best understood as following directly upon the events of chapter 13.

Chapter 10 cannot be attributed to the Nehemiah memoirs or to the Chronicler. It appears to be an independent source document possibly preserved in the Temple archives. It may have been incorrectly associated with Ezra's revival because of the reference to the separation "from the peoples of the lands to the law of God" (10:28; cf. 9:1–3).

Eighty-four names are listed as signatories to the covenant. If the list has been preserved in its original form, this use of a multiple of 12 may be a further attempt to symbolize the whole people of Israel.

Nehemiah's name heads the list. The title *governor* appears awkwardly after his name in the Masoretic Text, but is not found in the Septuagint. The name *Zedekiah*, which follows that of Nehemiah, may be that of the scribe (possibly called by the variant form "Zadok" in 13:13) who drew up the document (cf. Myers, p. 176).

The document was signed also by groups of *priests* (vv. 2–8), *Levites* (vv. 9–13), and *chiefs of the people* (vv. 14–27). The sequence of these groups in the list is different from that of the introductory statement (9:38). This may be a clue to the composite character of the narrative.

Many of those who signed the document are identified only by the names of their remote ancestors. The use of the name of the founding father to identify the contemporary representative of the family was a convenient way to express the legitimacy of his genealogy.

2. Summary of the Pledges (10:28–39)

(1) Introduction (10:28–29)

²⁸ The rest of the people, the priests, the Levites, the gatekeepers, the singers, the temple servants, and all who have separated themselves from the peoples of the lands to the law of God, their wives, their sons, their daughters, all who have knowledge and understanding, ²⁹ join with their brethren, their nobles, and enter into a curse and an oath to walk in God's law which was given by Moses the servant of God, and to observe and do all the commandments of the LORD our Lord and his ordinances and his statutes.

The text of the "firm covenant" (9:38) anticipated at the beginning of the narrative is not given. Instead, the author presents an account of the making of the vows and supplies a summary of the commitments.

The entire community joined in making solemn vows to live by *God's law*. The leaders affixed their signatures to the document, and *the rest of the people*, lay and clerical, parents and older children, accepted the commitments as their own. Even nonexilic Jews who had *separated themselves from the peoples of the lands* (cf. Ezra 6:21) were accepted as parties to the covenant.

The people entered *into a curse and an oath to walk in God's law*. This means that they vowed to live by the law and agreed to accept the penalties (cf. Deut. 29:20–21) if they broke the vow. The regular Hebrew oath formula invites God's curse upon anyone who fails to keep his solemn vow.

(2) Marriage and Sabbath Reforms (10:30–31)

³⁰ We will not give our daughters to the peoples of the land or take their daughters for our sons; ³¹ and if the peoples of the land bring in wares or any grain on the sabbath day to sell, we will not buy from them on the sabbath or on a holy day; and we will forego the crops of the seventh year and the exaction of every debt.

Following the brief anticipatory summary of the making of the covenant (vv. 28–29), the author enumerates the specific pledges to which the people committed themselves. The first vow was not to arrange any more marriages between Judeans and *the peoples of the land.* The vow was the formal written counterpart of the oath which Nehemiah had already extracted from the offenders (13:26).

The second vow was not to buy wares from non-Jews on the sabbath day. Nehemiah noted widespread abuse of the sabbath in Judah (13:15–22), but the most serious problem was created by non-Jewish merchants who brought in fish and other kinds of merchandise to sell in Jerusalem on the sabbath day. The written oath was designed to cope with the most troublesome breach of the sabbath ordinance. It was doubtless taken for granted that other infractions would cease also.

The vow was extended to include any *holy day* on which commercial transactions were prohibited. Buying and selling were forbidden on the day of the new moon festival (Amos 8:5), and probably on the various days of holy convocation (cf. Ex. 12:16; Num. 28:18,25–26; 29:1).

Although the sabbatical year is not mentioned in chapter 13, memory of the abuses described in chapter 5 probably caused it to be included in the covenant. During this year, the land was to lie fallow; and the produce of uncultivated fields and unpruned vineyards was to be for the poor (Ex. 23:11; Lev. 25:2–7). At the end of the seventh year, debts were to be cancelled and pledges returned (cf. Deut. 15:1–4). Regular observance of the sabbatical year with its relief for the poor would help to ensure that the kind of emergency reflected in chapter 5 would not occur again.

(3) *Commitment for Support of the Temple (10:32–39)*

32 We also lay upon ourselves the obligation to charge ourselves yearly with the third part of a shekel for the service of the house of our God: 33 for the showbread, the continual cereal offering, the continual burnt offering, the sabbaths, the new moons, the appointed feasts, the holy things, and the sin offerings to make atonement for Israel, and for all the work of the house of our God. 34 We have likewise cast lots, the priests, the Levites, and the people, for the wood offering, to bring it into the house of our God, according to our fathers' houses, at times appointed, year by year, to burn upon the altar of the LORD our God, as it is written in the law. 35 We obligate ourselves to bring the first fruits of our ground and the first fruits of all fruit of every tree, year by year, to the house of the LORD; 36 also to bring to the house of our God, to the priests who minister in the house of our God, the first-born of our sons and of our cattle, as it is written in the law, and the firstlings of our herds and of our flocks; 37 and to bring the first of our coarse meal, and our contributions, the fruit of every tree, the wine and the oil, to the priests, to the chambers of the house of our God; and to bring to the Levites the tithes from our ground, for it is the Levites who collect the tithes in all our rural towns. 38 And the priest, the son of Aaron, shall be with the Levites when the Levites receive the tithes; and the Levites shall bring up the tithe of the tithes to the house of our God, to the chambers, to the storehouse. 39 For the people of Israel and the sons of Levi shall bring the contribution of grain, wine, and oil to the chambers, where are the vessels of the sanctuary, and the priests that minister, and the gatekeepers and the singers. We will not neglect the house of our God.

The final section of the covenant includes a series of vows for the support of the Temple and its clergy. At the time of his second administration, Nehemiah had found such support woefully inadequate (Neh. 13:10–13,31). Convinced that neglect of the cult threatened the very existence of the community, he undertook thoroughgoing reforms. The people responded by pledging to assume specific financial obligations.

They vowed to pay annually a *third part of a shekel.* Although such a tax may have been collected earlier (cf. Ex. 30:13),[48] it was particularly important in the postexilic period. The subsidy from the Davidic dynasty was no longer available, and the occasional support from Persia (cf. Ezra 6:4; 7:20–23) was inadequate to meet continuing expenses.

---

[48] According to Ex. 30:13 (cf. Matt. 17:24–27) the tax was one-half shekel. The difference is doubtless to be explained by different standards of weight.

The Temple tax was to be used to provide a variety of cultic offerings. The *showbread*, or "bread of the Presence" (Ex. 25:30) consisted of a dozen cakes displayed on a table in the Temple as an offering to God (Lev. 24:5–9). *The continual cereal offering* and *the continual burnt offering* were those made regularly twice each day, and these were supplemented with special offerings on *sabbaths, new moons,* and *appointed feasts* (see comment on Ezra 3:3–6). The phrase *the holy things* is obscure, but probably refers to the supplies which are essential to the various offerings. *Sin offerings* were special expiatory sacrifices *to make atonement for Israel* for sins committed unwittingly or inadvertently (Num. 15:22–31; Lev. 4:1—5:13). *All the work of the house of our God* may refer to the physical upkeep of the sanctuary, since this is not otherwise provided for in the covenant.

A second obligation which the people assumed for the support of the cult was the provision of firewood for the great altar of sacrifice (cf. 13:31). Since the fire was supposed to burn perpetually (Lev. 6:12–13), a regular supply of wood was needed. *The priests, the Levites, and the people* cast lots to determine the order in which the respective *father's houses* (family groups) would be responsible for supplying the wood.

In vowing *to bring the first fruits . . . to the house of the Lord* the people were recognizing an ancient obligation (cf. Ex. 23:19; 34:26; Deut. 26:1–11). This duty was particularly important to Nehemiah (cf. 13:31), because the firstfruits were for the use of the clergy (Num. 18:13), who were being inadequately supported during his second administration (cf. 13:10–13).

The firstfruits of the ground were the first of the harvest brought to the Temple in grateful recognition of God as the owner of the land and the giver of its increase. Until the firstfruits had been brought no one was allowed to eat anything from the new crop (Lev. 23:14).

In like manner the firstborn of livestock and men were dedicated to God (Ex. 13:2). Animals that were ritually clean were sacrificed, and their flesh was eaten by the priesthood (Num. 18:17–18). The firstborn of men and of unclean animals were redeemed with cash (Num. 18:15–16).

Closely associated with the firstfruits was the offering of *the first* (i.e., the prime or choicest) of certain types of products (Num. 18:12; Deut. 18:4). Although a different Hebrew word is used for *the first*, the distinction between the two types of offerings is not always made clear. In Deuteronomy 26:1–11, for example, *the first* is apparently used to refer to the firstfruits. It is generally believed, however, that the two constituted separate categories of gifts. Apparently, the firstfruits were legally obligatory while the first products were freewill contributions (cf. Bowman, p. 767). The *coarse meal* was dough (KJV) made from the finest flour and presented to the priests as an offering to God (cf. Num. 15:20–21; Ezek. 44:30).

The final pledge recorded in the covenant was *to bring to the Levites the tithes of our ground.* Failure to do this had been the principal cause for the crisis described in 13:10–13. During the preexilic period the tithe was shared with the Levites (Deut. 14:22–29), but during the postexilic era it was the primary source of their livelihood (Num. 18:21–32).

The Chronicler's editorial touch is noted throughout the covenant, but nowhere more clearly than in the section on the tithe. In a short supplement (vv. 37b–39a), he explains how the tithes were collected in his own day. Instead of the tithes being brought to the Levites, as they were at the time of Nehemiah (v. 37a), the Levites went out into the countryside to collect them. *Rural towns* does not translate the meaning of the Hebrew, which says literally "cities of our work." This refers to the towns of Palestine where the Jewish cult was practiced (Bowman, p. 768). This qualification was relevant because during the postexilic period Jewish and non-Jewish towns were often located in close proximity to one another. They were accompanied by representatives of the Aaronite priesthood (see comment on Ezra 2:36-39), presumably as a check on the accuracy of the work.

The pledges for the support of the Temple are appropriately concluded with the words: *We will not neglect the house of our God.* This summary vow may be understood as a specific response to Nehemiah's question "Why is the house of God forsaken?" (13:11).

X. Distribution of Population (11:1-36)

1. Resettlement of Jerusalem (11:1-2)

¹ Now the leaders of the people lived in Jerusalem; and the rest of the people cast lots to bring one out of ten to live in Jerusalem the holy city, while nine tenths remained in the other towns. ² And the people blessed all the men who willingly offered to live in Jerusalem.

This chapter is a continuation of the story begun in 7:1-5, although the actual transition from the first part of the narrative to the second is not clear. The previous passage noted the need for people to move inside the new walls of Jerusalem and told how Nehemiah had convened an assembly, presumably for the purpose of meeting this need. This concluding passage may be understood to describe the principal activity of that assembly. The Jews who lived in the surrounding towns *cast lots to bring one out of ten to live in Jerusalem the holy city.*

Although *the leaders of the people* already resided inside the city, "the people within it were few" (7:4). The effectiveness of the new walls depended on a thorough repopulation and rebuilding of the entire site. Therefore, Nehemiah led the people to select 10 percent of their number to join their leaders inside the walls. The choice was made impartially by lot and doubtless according to family groups. Volunteers *who willingly offered to live in Jerusalem* were given special praise, because it was a major sacrifice to abandon already established homes to build new ones.

2. Leaders Residing in the City (11:3-24)

³ These are the chiefs of the province who lived in Jerusalem; but in the towns of Judah every one lived on his property in their towns: Israel, the priests, the Levites, the temple servants, and the descendants of Solomon's servants. ⁴ And in Jerusalem lived certain of the sons of Judah and of the sons of Benjamin. Of the sons of Judah: Athaiah the son of Uzziah, son of Zechariah, son of Amariah, son of Shephatiah, son of Mahalalel, of the sons of Perez; ⁵ and Maaseiah the son of Baruch, son of Colhozeh, son of Hazaiah, son of Adaiah, son of Joiarib, son of Zechariah, son of the Shilonite. ⁶ All the sons of Perez who lived in Jerusalem were four hundred and sixty-eight valiant men.

⁷ And these are the sons of Benjamin: Sallu the son of Meshullam, son of Joed, son of Pedaiah, son of Kolaiah, son of Maaseiah, son of Ithiel, son of Jeshaiah. ⁸ And after him Gabbai, Sallai, nine hundred and twenty-eight. ⁹ Joel the son of Zichri was their overseer; and Judah the son of Hassenuah was second over the city.

¹⁰ Of the priests: Jedaiah the son of Joiarib, Jachin, ¹¹ Seraiah the son of Hilkiah, son of Meshullam, son of Zadok, son of Meraioth, son of Ahitub, ruler of the house of God, ¹² and their brethren who did the work of the house, eight hundred and twenty-two; and Adaiah the son of Jeroham, son of Pelaliah, son of Amzi, son of Zechariah, son of Pashhur, son of Malchijah, ¹³ and his brethren, heads of fathers' houses, two hundred and forty-two; and Amashsai, the son of Azarel, son of Ahzai, son of Meshillemoth, son of Immer, ¹⁴ and their brethren, mighty men of valor, a hundred and twenty-eight; their overseer was Zabdiel the son of Haggedolim.

¹⁵ And of the Levites: Shemaiah the son of Hasshub, son of Azrikam, son of Hashabiah, son of Bunni; ¹⁶ and Shabbethai and Jozabad, of the chiefs of the Levites, who were over the outside work of the house of God; ¹⁷ and Mattaniah the son of Mica, son of Zabdi, son of Asaph, who was the leader to begin the thanksgiving in prayer, and Bakbukiah, the second among his brethren; and Abda the son of Shammua, son of Galal, son of Jeduthun. ¹⁸ All the Levites in the holy city were two hundred and eighty-four.

¹⁹ The gatekeepers, Akkub, Talmon and their brethren, who kept watch at the gates, were a hundred and seventy-two. ²⁰ And the rest of Israel, and of the priests and the Levites, were in all the towns of Judah, every one in his inheritance. ²¹ But the temple servants lived on

Ophel; and Ziha and Gishpa were over the temple servants.

22 The overseer of the Levites in Jerusalem was Uzzi the son of Bani, son of Hashabiah, son of Mattaniah, son of Mica, of the sons of Asaph, the singers, over the work of the house of God. 23 For there was a command from the king concerning them, and a settled provision for the singers, as every day required. 24 And Pethahiah the son of Meshezabel, of the sons of Zerah the son of Judah, was at the king's hand in all matters concerning the people.

Two lists have been appended to the story of the repopulation of Jerusalem. The first is identified as a list of *the chiefs* or leaders who already had their homes inside the city (cf. 11:1). The second purports to be a catalogue of the towns in the surrounding area where the rest of the Jews lived (11:25–36). Both lists seem to be out of context, and are of doubtful value for the time of Nehemiah.

The date and original purpose of the list of the leaders who resided in Jerusalem must remain uncertain for several reasons. In the first place, this list is closely related to the list found in 1 Chronicles 9:2–34. Since nearly half the names in the two lists are either identical or almost so one must conclude that they derive from a common source document. Yet the list in 1 Chronicles 9 is identified as that of the first residents of Jerusalem after the return from Babylonia, while this list in Nehemiah 11 claims to be that of the leaders who lived in Jerusalem after the wall was completed, nearly one hundred years later. In the second place, "Zaccur the son of Imri" (3:2), who helped rebuild the wall, appears to be the grandfather of *Athaiah* (11:4) who heads the Judahites in this list. Zaccur is a short form of *Zechariah* and Imri is a short form of *Amariah* [cf. Bowman, p. 773]. This would suggest that the list was compiled many years after the rebuilding of the wall. The same kind of evidence may be seen in the names *Shabbethai* and *Jozabad*, who were contemporaries of Ezra (8:7; Ezra 8:33; 10:15) rather than of Nehemiah. Finally, there is evidence that the list was supplemented long after it was orig-

inally compiled. *Uzzi,* who is called *the overseer of the Levites* (v. 22), was the great grandson of *Mattaniah,* who was a Levitical leader when the list was first drawn up (v. 17).

Although this document cannot be attributed to the Nehemiah memoirs or even to a contemporary of Nehemiah, it may offer some valuable information about the situation in Jerusalem during the following century. For example, each major group of the population is said to have had an *overseer* (vv. 9,14,22). While nothing else is said about these officers, it must be surmised that they functioned as part of the municipal government. Another important datum revealed by the passage is that the Judean community had a representation at the Persian court (v. 24). Such an envoy would have played a crucial role in advising the king about the specific needs and desires of the community.

Several allusions in the document are obscure. We do not know, for example, whether the *command from the king* concerning *the singers* (v. 23) refers to the Davidic instructions in Chronicles, or whether it refers to some edict from the Persian king negotiated perhaps by the Jewish envoy.

3. Towns Inhabited by Jews (11:25–36)

25 And as for the villages, with their fields, some of the people of Judah lived in Kiriatharba and its villages, and in Dibon and its villages, and in Jekabzeel and its villages, 26 and in Jeshua and in Moladah and Bethpelet, 27 in Hazarshual, in Beersheba and its villages, 28 in Ziklag, in Meconah and its villages, 29 in Enrimmon, in Zorah, in Jarmuth, 30 Zanoah, Adullam, and their villages, Lachish and its fields, and Azekah and its villages. So they encamped from Beersheba to the valley of Hinnom. 31 The people of Benjamin also lived from Geba onward, at Michmash, Aija, Bethel and its villages, 32 Anathoth, Nob, Ananiah, 33 Hazor, Ramah, Gittaim, 34 Hadid, Zeboim, Neballat, 35 Lod, and Ono, the valley of craftsmen. 36 And certain divisions of the Levites in Judah were joined to Benjamin.

This list is offered as a guide to the towns and villages outside of Jerusalem where about nine-tenths of the Jewish population of Palestine resided (cf. v. 1). The origin of the list is unknown, but it does not appear to have been drawn up during the administration of Nehemiah. This is indicated by the fact that the geographical distribution of Jews according to this list is entirely different from that reflected in chapter 3. The two lists have only the town of *Zanoah* (3:13) in common.

XI. Clerical Registers (12:1–26)

1. Priests and Levites Who Came with Zerubbabel (12:1–9)

¹ These are the priests and the Levites who came up with Zerubbabel the son of Shealtiel, and Jeshua: Seraiah, Jeremiah, Ezra, ² Amariah, Malluch, Hattush, ³ Shecaniah, Rehum, Meremoth, ⁴ Iddo, Ginnethoi, Abijah, ⁵ Mijamin, Maadiah, Bilgah, ⁶ Shemaiah, Joiarib, Jedaiah, ⁷ Sallu, Amok, Hilkiah, Jedaiah. These were the chiefs of the priests and of their brethren in the days of Jeshua.
⁸ And the Levites: Jeshua, Binnui, Kadmiel, Sherebiah, Judah, and Mattaniah, who with his brethren was in charge of the songs of thanksgiving. ⁹ And Bakbukiah and Unno their brethren stood opposite them in the service.

Postexilic Jews believed that the security of the community depended upon the legitimacy of the clergy (cf. 7:61–65; Ezra 2:59–63). The compiler of Ezra-Nehemiah searched his sources, therefore, to find every genealogical list which might help to establish the authenticity of the Temple personnel. Several such lists have been grouped together at the beginning of this chapter.

The first list (vv. 1–7) purports to name the priests who returned to Judah with *Zerubbabel* and *Jeshua*. This claim cannot be substantiated, however, because a different list is attributed to the time of Zerubbabel in 7:39–42 (Ezra 2:36–39). The origin of the list is unknown, but it doubtless derives from the fifth century rather than from the sixth.

The list is probably composite. The Masoretic Text has the conjunction "and" before *Joiarib* (cf. KJV). His name is also preceded by the conjunction in 12:19; and the list in 10:2–8 concludes with the preceding name *Shemaiah*. The six names Joiarib through Jedaiah may be considered a later supplement.

The second list (vv. 8–9) offers the names of the Levites who were supposed to have returned with Zerubbabel. The list appears to be at least as late as the time of Ezra, however, because *Mattaniah* and *Bakbukiah* are associated with contemporaries of Ezra (Shabbethai and Jozabad) in 11:16–17.

Most of the names can be identified as ancestral Levitical names because they occur in lists from several postexilic contexts (cf. 7:43; 8:7; 10:9).

2. Postexilic High Priests (12:10–11)

¹⁰ And Jeshua was the father of Joiakim, Joiakim the father of Eliashib, Eliashib the father of Joiada, ¹¹ Joiada the father of Jonathan, and Jonathan the father of Jaddua.

Without any transition from the previous list, the compiler inserts the genealogy of the first six high priests who held office during the postexilic era. Since the list spans considerably more than a century it is possible that some names do not appear. Moreover, *Jaddua* may have been added by a subsequent editor. Verse 22 (ch. 12) reads "and Johanan, and Jaddua" (cf. KJV), as though the latter name had been inserted by a later hand. *Jeshua* (Joshua) was the first postexilic high priest and was associated with Zerubbabel (Ezra 3:2), Haggai (Hag. 1:1), and Zechariah (Zech. 3:1). *Joiakim* held office during the long and little known period between the rebuilding of the Temple and the governorship of Nehemiah. The lists in 12:12–21,24–25 are attributed to the period of his tenure in office. *Eliashib* was high priest during both of the administrations of Nehemiah (3:1; 13:28). *Joiada* (Jehoiada) apparently held the office briefly between Nehemiah and Ezra (cf. 13:28), but Johanan (Jehohanan; "Jonathan" is clearly an error for Johanan, cf. 12:22) occupied the position during the ministry of Ezra (Ezra 10:6). *Jaddua* may have been the son of Johanan, but if he was, Josephus (*Antiq.* XI.8.2) must have been mistaken about his being in office at the time of Alexander the Great.

9. Priests and Levites from Time of Joiakim (12:12-26)

12 And in the days of Joiakim were priests, heads of fathers' houses: of Seraiah, Meraiah; of Jeremiah, Hananiah; 13 of Ezra, Meshullam; of Amariah, Jehohanan; 14 of Malluchi, Jonathan; of Shebaniah, Joseph; 15 of Harim, Adna; of Meraioth, Helkai; 16 of Iddo, Zechariah; of Ginnethon, Meshullam; 17 of Abijah, Zichri; of Miniamin, of Moadiah, Piltai; 18 of Bilgah, Shammua; of Shemaiah, Jehonathan; 19 of Joiarib, Mattenai; of Jedaiah, Uzzi; 20 of Sallai, Kallai; of Amok, Eber; 21 of Hilkiah, Hashabiah; of Jedaiah, Nethanel.
22 As for the Levites, in the days of Eliashib, Joiada, Johanan, and Jaddua, there were recorded the heads of fathers' houses; also the priests until the reign of Darius the Persian. 23 The sons of Levi, heads of fathers' houses, were written in the Book of the Chronicles until the days of Johanan the son of Eliashib. 24 And the chiefs of the Levites: Hashabiah, Sherebiah, and Jeshua the son of Kadmiel, with their brethren over against them, to praise and to give thanks, according to the commandment of David the man of God, watch corresponding to watch. 25 Mattaniah, Bakbukiah, Obadiah, Meshullam, Talmon, and Akkub were gatekeepers standing guard at the storehouses of the gates. 26 These were in the days of Joiakim the son of Jeshua son of Jozadak, and in the days of Nehemiah the governor and of Ezra the priest the scribe.

The priests listed in vv. 12–21 are identified as those who officiated *in the days of Joiakim* (between the time of Zerubbabel and Nehemiah). The list gives the ancestral name and also the name of the contemporary representative of the family. For example, *Meraiah* was the priest who, during the time of Joiakim, was the head of the family which had been founded by *Seraiah* (cf. 2 Kings 25:18). The ancestral or family names are essentially the same as those in 12:1–7.

After completing the list of priests, the compiler turns his attention to the corresponding list of *Levites*. Before he presents the names of the Levites (vv. 24–26), however, he inserts a note about the recording of genealogies in the postexilic era (vv. 22–23). Verse 22 may be interpreted to mean that the registration included both *the heads of fathers' houses* (the ancestral names) and the names of the individual *priests* who represented these families.

The phrase translated *until the reign of Darius the Persian* is obscure in the Masoretic Text. If Darius I (522–486 B.C.) is indicated, it must mean that the registration began during his reign. If the reference is to Darius II (423–404 B.C.), it could mean that the registration continued until that time, or that the names were recorded during his reign. At any rate, the names were recorded only until the tenure of Johanan which was during the reign of Darius II. *Jaddua* must be a secondary interpolation, as in 12:11.

The names of the Levites were recorded until the same period (presumably the time in which the compiler himself lived). *The Book of the Chronicles,* in which the names were preserved, cannot refer to the canonical books by that name. It was apparently an official Temple record book (cf. the similar preexilic book: 1 Kings 14:29; 15:23).

The chiefs of the Levites during the time of Joiakim included five ancestral names. *Jeshua* was not *the son of Kadmiel;* the two names represented separate families. The word translated *the son of* should be read as the graphically similar Binnui (12:8), or possibly as Bani (9:4). The division of the Levites into courses, or watches, for praise and thanksgiving is characteristically attributed to *David the man of God* (cf. 1 Chron. 25; 2 Chron. 8:14).

Six names identified in the Masoretic Text as *gatekeepers* are included in the Levitical register. *Meshullam* (alternate form of Shallum), *Talmon,* and *Akkub* are ancestral names of gatekeepers (7:45; 11:19; 1 Chron. 9:17). *Mattaniah, Bakbukiah,* and *Obadiah,* on the other hand, were doubtless identified as musicians originally (cf. 11:17, where Obadiah is written as Abda), but the designation has been lost.

The list of the Levites, like that of the

priests, is assigned to *the days of Joiakim.* The addition of the names of *Nehemiah* and *Ezra,* however, is misleading. The three men belonged to successive generations. Nehemiah was associated with Joiakim's son Eliashib (3:1), and Ezra with Eliashib's grandson Johanan (Jehohanan; Ezra 10:6). The names of Nehemiah and Ezra were probably inserted in anticipation of the narrative which follows.

XII. Dedication of the Wall (12:27–43)

1. Preparations (12:27–30)

27 And at the dedication of the wall of Jerusalem they sought the Levites in all their places, to bring them to Jerusalem to celebrate the dedication with gladness, with thanksgivings and with singing, with cymbals, harps, and lyres. 28 And the sons of the singers gathered together from the circuit round Jerusalem and from the villages of the Netophathites; 29 also from Bethgilgal and from the region of Geba and Azmaveth; for the singers had built for themselves villages around Jerusalem. 30 And the priests and the Levites purified themselves; and they purified the people and the gates and the wall.

The account of the dedication of the wall (mostly from the Nehemiah memoirs) is removed from the story of the building (chs. 2—6) by several chapters. The two events, however, were probably not separated by any significant period of time. In the Nehemiah memoirs the dedicatory ceremonies were doubtless related either immediately after the completion of the wall (6:15) or after the population reforms (11:1–2).

It is not surprising that Nehemiah should plan a formal ceremony for the dedication of the city wall. He did not think of the affairs of his administration as divided into sacred and secular. All of his work was in the service of God, and the building of the wall in particular was viewed as a religious exercise (cf. 2:12; 4:4–5; 6:16). Through the dedication ceremony the wall was formally committed to the service of God for which it had been constructed.

Since the ceremonies involved music and singing, the Levitical musicians were assigned an important role. Some of them presumably lived in Jerusalem (cf. 11:15–18), but the others had to be summoned from outlying villages. They sang the hymns of thanksgiving to the accompaniment of *cymbals, harps, and lyres.* Harps and lyres were played only on occasions of great joy (cf. Isa. 5:12; 24:8; Gen. 31:27; Psalm 137:2). They were both stringed instruments which could be played in processions. The harp was strummed with the fingers, while the lyre was played with a plectrum (Bowman, p. 793).

Before the ceremony of dedication could begin, the clergy *purified themselves* and then *purified the people and the gates and the wall.* The ritual of cleansing is not described here, probably because it was so well known that it could be taken for granted. The purification of persons sometimes involved sexual abstinence, bathing, sprinkling with water or blood, the shaving of the body, the washing of the garments, and special sacrifices (cf. Ex. 19:10–15; Lev. 14:1–9; Num. 8:5–8; 19:17–19). The purification of the wall may have included some of the ceremonies prescribed for the purification of a house (Lev. 14:48–53).

2. Ceremonies of Dedication (12:31–43)

31 Then I brought up the princes of Judah upon the wall, and appointed two great companies which gave thanks and went in procession. One went to the right upon the wall to the Dung Gate; 32 and after them went Hoshaiah and half of the princes of Judah, 33 and Azariah, Ezra, Meshullam, 34 Judah, Benjamin, Shemaiah, and Jeremiah, 35 and certain of the priests' sons with trumpets: Zechariah the son of Jonathan, son of Shemaiah, son of Mattaniah, son of Micaiah, son of Zaccur, son of Asaph; 36 and his kinsmen, Shemaiah, Azarel, Milalai, Gilalai, Maai, Nethanel, Judah, and Hanani, with the musical instruments of David the man of God; and Ezra the scribe went before them. 37 At the Fountain Gate they went up straight before them by the stairs of the city of David, at the ascent of the wall, above the house of David, to the Water Gate on the east.

38 The other company of those who gave thanks went to the left, and I followed them with half of the people, upon the wall, above the Tower of the Ovens, to the Broad Wall, 39 and above the Gate of Ephraim, and by the

Old Gate, and by the Fish Gate and the Tower of Hananel and the Tower of the Hundred, to the Sheep Gate; and they came to a halt at the Gate of the Guard. ⁴⁰ So both companies of those who gave thanks stood in the house of God, and I and half of the officials with me; ⁴¹ and the priests Eliakim, Maaseiah, Miniamin, Micaiah, Elioenai, Zechariah, and Hananiah, with trumpets; ⁴² and Maaseiah, Shemaiah, Eleazar, Uzzi, Jehohanan, Malchijah, Elam, and Ezer. And the singers sang with Jezrahiah as their leader. ⁴³ And they offered great sacrifices that day and rejoiced, for God had made them rejoice with great joy; the women and children also rejoiced. And the joy of Jerusalem was heard afar off.

The dedicatory services began with a ritual procession along the top of the newly completed city wall.⁴⁹ The participants were organized into two large companies which assembled in the southwestern part of the city. The first company marched *to the right* (southward) in a counterclockwise fashion. The other company proceeded clockwise in the opposite direction. They met in the Temple courts in the northeast sector of the city, where a great celebration took place. Several landmarks are mentioned in connection with the routes of the processions, but evidence is not available to permit exact identification of them in terms of the modern topographical features of the city.

Although the present text is not entirely clear, it appears that both companies were constituted in exactly the same way. At the head of each procession there was a choir which sang hymns of praise. Then followed the secular officials with their leader, and after them, the priests and the Levites.

Following the choir in the first company was an important lay leader named *Hoshaiah* who was accompanied by *half of the princes of Judah*. Then followed seven priests (vv. 33–34) with their trumpets (cf. Ezra 3:10), and a Levite named *Zechariah* together with eight of *his kinsmen* bearing their *musical instruments*. The

---

⁴⁹ The recently excavated segment of Nehemiah's fall is about nine feet wide (Kenyon, *op. cit.*, p. 111). Thus there was ample room for a procession to move along the top of it.

priests' sons (v. 35) is an idiomatic expression which refers to the group of priests just named (cf. 12:28) and not to the Levitical names that follow.

In the second company Nehemiah took the role comparable to that of Hoshaiah (v. 32) as leader of *half of the officials* (v. 40). Again, there were the seven priests with trumpets (v. 41) and a Levite named *Jezrahiah* with his eight colleagues (v. 42).

The words *and Ezra the scribe went before them* must be understood as a late interpolation into the Chronicler's narrative. The presence of Ezra's name spoils the symmetry of the two companies; but more important, there is convincing evidence that Nehemiah and Ezra were not contemporaries (see Introduction).

When the two companies met at the Temple, *they offered great sacrifices* and *rejoiced*. With God's help, they had completed their task. It was a joyful experience to respond to his benevolence and sovereignty by dedicating the wall to his service.

The joy of Jerusalem was heard afar off. The sounds of praise and thanksgiving rang throughout the countryside. But beyond the environs of the city the joy was heard in Samaria and Ammon and Philistia, declaring the mighty works which God was doing for his people (cf. Jer. 31:1–14).

XIII. The Cultic Norm (12:44—13:3)

1. The Temple Services (12:44-47)

⁴⁴ On that day men were appointed over the chambers for the stores, the contributions, the first fruits, and the tithes, to gather into them the portions required by the law for the priests and for the Levites according to the fields of the towns; for Judah rejoiced over the priests and the Levites who ministered. ⁴⁵ And they performed the service of their God and the service of purification, as did the singers and the gatekeepers, according to the command of David and his son Solomon. ⁴⁶ For in the days of David and Asaph of old there was a chief of the singers, and there were songs of praise and thanksgiving to God. ⁴⁷ And all Israel in the days of Zerubbabel and in the days of Nehemiah gave the daily portions for the singers

and the gatekeepers; and they set apart that which was for the Levites; and the Levites set apart that which was for the sons of Aaron.

The compiler of the Nehemiah narrative was concerned that Nehemiah's memoirs had so much to say about cultic abuses and infractions (especially 13:4-31). In order that the reader not get the impression that such deviations were commonplace during the postexilic period, he composed this passage to show that the cult usually functioned smoothly and effectively. (The reference to Nehemiah, v. 47, shows that the passage is independent of the Nehemiah memoirs.) In two paragraphs the writer sketched first, the normal procedure in the Temple cultus (12:44-47), and second, the normal exclusive stance toward Gentiles (13:1-3). *On that day* (also 13:1) does not refer to any one occasion but to the general period from *Zerubbabel* to *Nehemiah.*

The writer asserts, in the first place, that the people were usually faithful to their financial responsibilities to the clergy (contrast 13:10-13; Mal. 3:6-12). The people *rejoiced over the priests and the Levites* and gladly *gave the daily portions* for their upkeep. Treasurers at the Temple gathered into the storage *chambers* the *contributions, first fruits,* and *tithes* which the people of every town offered from their surrounding *fields.*

The writer affirms further that the clergy normally conducted themselves blamelessly *according to the command of David* (cf. 1 Chron. 23—26) *and his son Solomon* (cf. 2 Chron. 8:14). Verse 46 explains that the organization of the Temple music dates back to the time of *David and Asaph* (cf. 1 Chron. 6:31-48). The Levites performed their duties, including that of *purification* (v. 45; cf. 12:30), and paid their tithes to the priestly *sons of Aaron* (v. 47; cf. 10:38). *The singers and the gatekeepers* were loyal to their respective responsibilities. Thus the reader is assured that the episode referred to in 13:10 is unusual and extraordinary (note however clerical negligence in Mal. 1:6—2:9).

2. The Exclusion of Foreigners (13:1-3)

¹ On that day they read from the book of Moses in the hearing of the people; and in it was found written that no Ammonite or Moabite should ever enter the assembly of God; ² for they did not meet the children of Israel with bread and water, but hired Balaam against them to curse them—yet our God turned the curse into a blessing. ³ When the people heard the law, they separated from Israel all those of foreign descent.

The writer continues his defense of the cult by seeking to show that the norm during the postexilic period was separation from *all those of foreign descent.* This principle may indeed have been well established by the time of the Chronicler, but the problem of mixing with Gentiles recurred repeatedly in the earlier postexilic period. The abuse is clearly attested in Malachi 2:10-12, throughout both administrations of Nehemiah (6:17-19; 13:4-9,23-30), and during the ministry of Ezra (Neh. 9:1-2; Ezra 9—10).

The writer cities Deuteronomy 23:3-5 as the legal basis for excluding Gentiles from *the assembly of God.* This passage refers only to Ammonites and Moabites who are to be excluded because of their unfriendliness toward Israel preceding the conquest of Canaan (Num. 22—24). The Chronicler, however, considers this passage to be sufficient grounds for the exclusion of all foreigners from the Jewish cultic community. By asserting that the separation was effected, he prepares the reader to see the episodes of chapter 13 (vv. 4-9,23-30) as unusual deviations from the ideal standard of behavior.

XIV. Nehemiah's Reforms (13:4-31)

1. Tobiah Expelled from the Temple (13:4-9)

⁴ Now before this, Eliashib the priest, who was appointed over the chambers of the house of our God, and who was connected with Tobiah, ⁵ prepared for Tobiah a large chamber where they had previously put the cereal offering, the frankincense, the vessels, and the tithes of grain, wine, and oil, which were given by commandment to the Levites, singers, and gatekeepers, and the contributions for the priests.

⁶ While this was taking place I was not in Jerusalem, for in the thirty-second year of Artaxerxes king of Babylon I went to the king. And after some time I asked leave of the king ⁷ and came to Jerusalem, and I then discovered the evil that Eliashib had done for Tobiah, preparing for him a chamber in the courts of the house of God. ⁸ And I was very angry, and I threw all the household furniture of Tobiah out of the chamber. ⁹ Then I gave orders and they cleansed the chambers; and I brought back thither the vessels of the house of God, with the cereal offering and the frankincense.

After spending about 12 years in Judah (cf. 5:14), Nehemiah returned to Persia, presumably to resume his duties at the court of Artaxerxes I. *After some time,* however, he requested that Artaxerxes allow him to go back to Judah. Neither the date nor the length of the second mission can be ascertained. Presumably, he stayed in Persia long enough for the situation in Judah to deteriorate seriously, and it may have been news of such developments which prompted Nehemiah to request a second term as governor. This part of chapter 13 is understood as an account of reforms undertaken by Nehemiah when he arrived in Judah the second time.

While Nehemiah was in Persia a priest named *Eliashib* (possibly the high priest; cf. v. 28; 3:1) assigned to *Tobiah a large chamber* within the precincts of the Temple. Tobiah had some kind of close relationship with Eliashib, as he did with other Judean leaders (6:17–19), but he was among the arch enemies of Nehemiah. Tobiah, although doubtless a Jew himself, was governor of Ammon; and Nehemiah probably used this as a pretext (cf. Deut. 23:3) to have him expelled from the chamber and to have his furnishings thrown out.

2. Temple Finances Put in Order (13:10–14)

¹⁰ I also found out that the portions of the Levites had not been given to them; so that the Levites and the singers, who did the work, had fled each to his field. ¹¹ So I remonstrated with the officials and said, "Why is the house of God forsaken?" And I gathered them together and set them in their stations. ¹² Then all Judah brought the tithe of the grain, wine, and oil into the storehouses. ¹³ And I appointed as treasurers over the storehouses Shelemiah the priest, Zadok the scribe, and Pedaiah of the Levites, and as their assistant Hanan the son of Zaccur, son of Mattaniah, for they were counted faithful; and their duty was to distribute to their brethren. ¹⁴ Remember me, O my God, concerning this, and wipe not out my good deeds that I have done for the house of my God and for his service.

When Nehemiah returned from Persia, he found *the house of God forsaken.* The Levites who played a prominent role in most cultic ceremonies had left the Temple and *had fled each to his field.* The people of Judah, lacking dedicated leadership, had stopped paying the tithes (cf. Mal. 3:8–10). The Levites, thus deprived of their livelihood, left *their stations* in the Temple and went home where they could earn a living.

Nehemiah reprimanded *the officials* for allowing such a situation to develop. He brought the Levites back to their positions in the Temple, and the people responded by resuming the payment of the tithe. Since the clergy as a group was not always *faithful* and trushworthy (cf. Mal. 1:6—2:9), he set up a board of four *treasurers* to make a proper allocation of Temple income.

Nehemiah's prayer in v. 14 reflects again his anxiety over his own personal future. Lacking offspring to perpetuate his name and having an imperfect understanding of God's grace, Nehemiah wants his good deeds to become a memorial for him. He pleads with God not to erase them from the divine record book (cf. Ex. 32:32; Dan. 12:1).

3. Sabbath Observance Regulated (13:15–22)

¹⁵ In those days I saw in Judah men treading wine presses on the sabbath, and bringing in heaps of grain and loading them on asses; and also wine, grapes, figs, and all kinds of burdens, which they brought into Jerusalem on the sabbath day; and I warned them on the day when they sold food. ¹⁶ Men of Tyre also, who lived in the city, brought in fish and all kinds of wares and sold them on the sabbath to the

people of Judah, and in Jerusalem. 17 Then I remonstrated with the nobles of Judah and said to them, "What is this evil thing which you are doing, profaning the sabbath day? 18 Did not your fathers act in this way, and did not our God bring all this evil on us and on this city? Yet you bring more wrath upon Israel by profaning the sabbath."

19 When it began to be dark at the gates of Jerusalem before the sabbath, I commanded that the doors should be shut and gave orders that they should not be opened until after the sabbath. And I set some of my servants over the gates, that no burden might be brought in on the sabbath day. 20 Then the merchants and sellers of all kinds of wares lodged outside Jerusalem once or twice. 21 But I warned them and said to them, "Why do you lodge before the wall? If you do so again I will lay hands on you." From that time on they did not come on the sabbath. 22 And I commanded the Levites that they should purify themselves and come and guard the gates, to keep the sabbath day holy. Remember this also in my favor, O my God, and spare me according to the greatness of thy steadfast love.

Although early Israelite literature often stressed humanitarian motives for keeping the sabbath (cf. Ex. 23:12; Deut. 5:12–15), later literature emphasized the importance of sabbath observance as a special sign of the covenant people (cf. Ex. 31:12,16–17; Ezek. 20:12). To disregard or defile the sabbath was to break the covenant and to invite the wrath of God upon the community (cf. Jer. 17:19–27; Ezek. 20:13; 23:38). The keeping of the sabbath distinguished the Jew from the non-Jew, and this was particularly crucial after the collapse of the state when the dangers of assimilation were so great.

Nehemiah was therefore particularly disturbed when it came to his attention that the Judeans were ignoring the holy day. In his characteristic way he reprimanded the *nobles of Judah,* not only because they were guilty themselves but because they were setting a bad example for the people. Then in his usual forthright manner, he took practical measures to enforce the observance of the day. He ordered the gates of the city to be closed when the sabbath began at sundown and not to be opened until sundown the following day. Merchants who expressed their impatience (cf. Amos 8:5) by camping outside the wall of the city were threatened with physical action if they persisted in the offense. Nehemiah used members of his own staff to guard the gates at first, but later replaced them with Levites since the enforcement of the sabbath was a cultic undertaking.

In his attempt to use his secular authority to compel compliance with sabbath regulations, Nehemiah encountered a special problem. Some of the offenders were *men of Tyre . . . who brought in fish and all kinds of wares.* These foreigners were outsiders in the Judean community and yet were required to observe a Jewish cultic regulation. Those who make blue laws today are faced with a similar dilemma with respect to Jews, Seventh Day Adventists, and nonbelievers, who do not choose to observe Sunday as a holy day.

This passage, like many others, concludes with a short prayer. This prayer, however, is different from most of the others. Nehemiah not only includes a request that God remember his good deeds, but he acknowledges that his salvation is dependent upon the *greatness* of God's *steadfast love* and not upon the multiplicity of his good works. The doctrine of grace in the Old Testament is often tragically overlooked.

4. Mixed Marriages Prohibited (13:23–29)

23 In those days also I saw the Jews who had married women of Ashdod, Ammon, and Moab; 24 and half of their children spoke the language of Ashdod, and they could not speak the language of Judah, but the language of each people. 25 And I contended with them and cursed them and beat some of them and pulled out their hair; and I made them take oath in the name of God, saying, "You shall not give your daughters to their sons, or take their daughters for your sons or for yourselves. 26 Did not Solomon king of Israel sin on account of such women? Among the many nations there was no king like him, and he was beloved by his God, and God made him king over all Israel; nevertheless foreign women made even him to sin. 27 Shall we then listen to you and do all this great evil and act treacher-

ously against our God by marrying foreign women?" ²⁸ And one of the sons of Jehoiada, the son of Eliashib the high priest, was the son-in-law of Sanballat the Horonite; therefore I chased him from me. ²⁹ Remember them, O my God, because they have defiled the priesthood and the covenant of the priesthood and the Levites.

Marriages between Jews and non-Jews had been common throughout most of the preexilic period, and apparently no attempt had been made to prohibit them until the Deuteronomic writings (Deut. 7:3; cf. Exodus 34:16). Nehemiah, during his first administration, had presumably tolerated marriages which he considered to be dangerous to the community (cf. 6:17–19). During the postexilic era, however, there was an increasing conviction that such marriages threatened physical and spiritual purity and the safety of the community (cf. Mal. 2:10–12).

Nehemiah was particularly concerned that the children of mixed marriages could not speak the holy language in which the Torah was written. He took direct and violent action against the offenders and forced them to take an oath that no further mixed marriages would be contracted. He did not, however, attempt to dissolve the marriages that already existed, as Ezra was to do in the following generation (cf. Ezra 9—10).

Nehemiah's lecture on this occasion included a reminder that even the incomparable Solomon had been led into sin by foreign wives (cf. 1 Kings 11:1–11). With such an example before them it was unthinkable that the community should continue to offend God by arranging such marital ties.

The writer relates one notorious example of a marriage between a grandson of the high priest and a daughter of Sanballat. Because of Nehemiah's antipathy toward Sanballat, this marriage was particularly offensive to him and the offender was expelled from the community.⁵⁰

This passage concludes with a prayer in which Nehemiah calls for God's judgment upon those who have defiled their glorious vocations by participating in marriages with non-Jews.

5. Conclusion (13:30–31)

³⁰ Thus I cleansed them from everything foreign, and I established the duties of the priests and Levites, each in his work; ³¹ and I provided for the wood offering, at appointed times, and for the first fruits. Remember me, O my God, for good.

In the two final verses of the book Nehemiah summarizes the work which he has done. The purpose of the summary is indicated by the last sentence: *Remember me, O my God, for good.* In his final prayer, Nehemiah pleads that God will give him appropriate credit for what he has done. A eunuch, without hope of offspring to carry on the family name, he expresses an almost desperate anxiety that he may live on in the work which he has done. The writer of Isaiah 56:4–5 promised that God would give "a monument and a name better than sons and daughters" to eunuchs who are faithful to his will.

Although the *wood offering* and *first fruits* had not been previously mentioned in chapter 13, the account of the assembly which followed these reforms shows that provision for these had been made during Nehemiah's second term as governor of Judah (10:34–37).

⁵⁰ Josephus (*Antiq.* XI.7.2) relates the same episode but confuses the chronology because he failed to recognize that there were several Samaritan rulers named Sanballat. See Frank M. Cross, "The Discovery of the Samaria Papyri," *The Biblical Archaeologist*, Dec., 1963, p. 121.